ALSO BY HEATHER CLARK

The Grief of Influence: Sylvia Plath and Ted Hughes

The Ulster Renaissance: Poetry in Belfast 1962–1972

Red Comet

Red Comet

The Short Life and
Blazing Art of Sylvia Plath

HEATHER CLARK

ALFRED A. KNOPF New York
2020

THIS IS A BORZOI BOOK
PUBLISHED BY ALFRED A. KNOPF

Copyright © 2020 by Heather Clark

All rights reserved. Published in the United States by Alfred A. Knopf,
a division of Penguin Random House LLC, New York, and distributed
in Canada by Penguin Random House Canada Limited, Toronto.

www.aaknopf.com

Knopf, Borzoi Books, and the colophon are registered
trademarks of Penguin Random House LLC.

Library of Congress Cataloging-in-Publication Data
Names: Clark, Heather L., author.
Title: Red comet : the short life and blazing art of Sylvia Plath / Heather Clark.
Description: First edition. | New York : Alfred A. Knopf, 2020. |
Identifiers: LCCN 2019041635 (print) | LCCN 2019041636 (ebook) |
ISBN 9780307961167 (hardcover) | ISBN 9780307961174 (ebook)
Subjects: LCSH: Plath, Sylvia. | Poets, American—20th century—Biography.
Classification: LCC PS3566.L27 Z616 2020 (print) |
LCC PS3566.L27 (ebook) | DDC 811/.54—dc23
LC record available at https://lccn.loc.gov/2019041635
LC ebook record available at https://lccn.loc.gov/2019041636

Front-of-jacket photograph by Ramsey and Muspratt, Cambridge, UK
Courtesy Lilly Library, Indiana University, Bloomington, Indiana, USA
Spine-of-jacket photograph: Sylvia Plath, Paris, 1956, by Gordon Lameyer

Jacket design by John Gall

Manufactured in the United States of America
First Edition

For Nathan, Isabel, and Liam

and

In Memory of Jon Stallworthy

. . . everyday, one has to earn the name of "writer" over again, with much wrestling.

—*Sylvia Plath to Aurelia Plath, October 2, 1956*

They thought death was worth it, but I
Have a self to recover, a queen.
Is she dead, is she sleeping?
Where has she been,
With her lion-red body, her wings of glass?

Now she is flying
More terrible than she ever was, red
Scar in the sky, red comet
Over the engine that killed her—
The mausoleum, the wax house.

—*Sylvia Plath*, "Stings"

Contents

Prologue

In December 1962, Sylvia Plath moved into William Butler Yeats's old house. Yeats was one of Plath's greatest literary heroes, and she had been thrilled to discover the vacant townhouse in London's Primrose Hill after the breakdown of her marriage. She was starting over, and she felt the move to Yeats's house was propitious. "My work should be blessed," she wrote her mother.[1] She offered a year's rent to secure the two-story maisonette—nearly all the money she had. Three months before, she and her husband, Ted Hughes, had traveled from their home in Devon to the west coast of Ireland, where they had collected apples from Yeats's garden at Thoor Ballylee and climbed the famous winding staircase to his tower's roof. Plath threw coins in the stream below for luck. The couple hoped that the trip to Ireland and the pilgrimage to Yeats's sacred tower would rekindle their marriage. But Plath returned to Devon alone. There, and in Yeats's house, she would write some of the finest poems of the twentieth century.

One of Sylvia Plath's favorite short stories was Henry James's "The Beast in the Jungle." The story concerns a man, John Marcher, who spends his life waiting for an extreme experience—"*the* thing"—which he likens to a beast crouching in the jungle. It will be, he says, "natural" and "unmistakable." It may be "violent," a "catastrophe." Only too late does Marcher realize he has lived a passionless existence awaiting *the* thing. He has instead become the man to "whom nothing on earth was to have happened." The story ends as he flings himself at the tomb of the woman he should have loved. "When the possibilities themselves had accordingly turned stale, when the secret of the gods had grown faint, had perhaps even quite evaporated, that, and that only, was failure," James wrote. "It wouldn't have been failure to be bankrupt, dishonoured, pilloried, hanged; it was failure not to be anything."[2]

Sylvia Plath dreaded the prospect of such failure. In 1955, before setting off for England and Cambridge University, she wrote to her boyfriend

Gordon Lameyer, "the horror, to be jamesian [*sic*], is to find there are plenty of beasts in the jungle but somehow to have missed all the potshots at them. I am always afraid of letting 'life' slip by unobtrusively and waking up some 'fine morning' to wail windgrieved around my tombstone."[3] Modernist visions of human paralysis terrified her. T. S. Eliot's "The Waste Land" and James Joyce's "The Dead" became personal admonitions. "NEUTRALITY, BOREDOM become worse sins than murder, worse than illicit love affairs," she told her Smith College students in 1958. "BE RIGHT OR WRONG, don't be indifferent, don't be NOTHING."[4] Plath's appetite for food was legendary—she once emptied a host's refrigerator before a dinner party— but she was equally hungry for experience. She was determined to live as fully as possible—to write, to travel, to cook, to draw, to love as much and as often as she could. She was, in the words of a close friend, "operatic" in her desires, a "Renaissance woman" molded as much by Romantic sublimity as New England stoicism.[5] She was as fluent in Nietzsche as she was in Emerson; as much in thrall to Yeats's gongs and gyres as Frost's silences and snow.

Sylvia Plath took herself and her desires seriously in a world that often refused to do so. She published her first poem at age eight and later vowed to become "The Poetess of America."[6] In the years that followed, Plath pursued her literary vocation with a fierce, tireless determination. She hoped to be a writer, wife, and mother, but she was raised in a culture that openly derided female artistic ambition. Such derision is clear in the speech Democratic presidential candidate Adlai Stevenson gave at Plath's 1955 Smith commencement, titled, "A Purpose for Modern Woman." The best way these brilliant graduates could contribute to their nation, Stevenson said, was to embrace "the humble role of housewife, which, statistically, is what most of you are going to be whether you like the idea or not just now—and you'll like it!" Stevenson, the liberal darling of his day, went on:

> This assignment for you, as wives and mothers, has great advantages. In the first place, it is home work—you can do it in the living room with a baby in your lap, or in the kitchen with a can opener in your hands. If you're really clever, maybe you can even practice your saving arts on that unsuspecting man while he's watching television.

Stevenson acknowledged "the sense of contraction, the lost horizons" these women would feel in their new domestic roles. "Once they wrote poetry," he mused. "Now it's the laundry list. . . . They had hoped to play their part in the crisis of the age. But what they do is wash diapers." He hoped this view was not "too depressing" but concluded that "women 'never had it so good' as you do."[7]

Plath was determined to play her part, but, as Stevenson's speech suggests, the odds were against her. She lived in a shamelessly discriminatory age when it was almost impossible for a woman to get a mortgage, loan, or credit card; when newspapers divided their employment ads between men and women ("Attractive Please!"); the word "pregnant" was banned from network television; and popular magazines encouraged wives to remain quiet because, as one advice columnist put it, "his topics of conversation are more important than yours."[8] Government, finance, law, media, academia, medicine, technology, science—nearly all the professions were controlled by men. Some women made inroads, but the costs were high. As one of Plath's Cambridge contemporaries wrote, women in the 1950s had "internalized from a lifetime of messages that achievement and autonomy were simply incompatible with love and family," and that "independence equaled loneliness."[9] Still, Plath thought a different fate from the one Stevenson had predicted for her might be possible. Like her Joycean hero Stephen Dedalus, she was filled with "Icarian lust": she would seek out her destiny abroad, collect experience for her art, and stay in motion.[10] Anything to evade the life not lived, the poem not written, the love not realized. Plath spread her wings, over and over, at a time when women were not supposed to fly.

The Oxford professor Hermione Lee, Virginia Woolf's biographer, has written, "Women writers whose lives involved abuse, mental-illness, self-harm, suicide, have often been treated, biographically, as victims or psychological case-histories first and as professional writers second."[11] This is especially true of Sylvia Plath, who has become cultural shorthand for female hysteria. When we see a female character reading *The Bell Jar* in a movie, we know she will make trouble. As the critic Maggie Nelson reminds us, "to be called the Sylvia Plath of anything is *a bad thing*."[12] Nelson reminds us, too, that a woman who explores depression in her art isn't perceived as "a shamanistic voyager to the dark side, but a 'madwoman in the attic,' an abject spectacle."[13] Perhaps this is why Woody Allen teased Diane Keaton for reading Plath's seminal collection *Ariel* in *Annie Hall*. In the 1980s, a prominent reviewer noted that a Plath "backlash" had resulted in some "grisly" jokes in college newspapers. " 'Why did SP cross the road?' 'To be struck by an oncoming vehicle.' "[14] Male writers who kill themselves are rarely subject to such black humor: there are no dinner-party jokes about David Foster Wallace. In a 2017 article that went viral, Claire Dederer argued that Plath had become the culture's ultimate "female monster" for committing suicide and "abandoning" her children.[15] As the critic Carolyn Heilbrun noted, "If you admire Auden, that's good taste. If you admire Sylvia Plath, it's a cult. . . . It is the usual no-win situation: either a woman author isn't studied, or studying her is reduced to an act of misplaced religious fanaticism."[16]

Since her suicide in 1963, Sylvia Plath has become a paradoxical symbol of female power and helplessness whose life has been subsumed by her afterlife. Caught in the limbo between icon and cliché, she has been mythologized and pathologized in movies, television, and biographies as a high priestess of poetry, obsessed with death. These distortions gained momentum in the 1960s when *Ariel* was published. Most reviewers didn't know what to make of the burning, pulsating metaphors in poems like "Lady Lazarus" or the chilly imagery of "Edge." *Time* called the book a "jet of flame from a literary dragon who in the last months of her life breathed a burning river of bale across the literary landscape."[17] *The Washington Post* dubbed Plath a "snake lady of misery" in an article entitled "The Cult of Plath."[18] Robert Lowell, in his introduction to *Ariel*, characterized Plath as Medea, hurtling toward her own destruction. Even Plath's closest reader, her husband Ted Hughes, often portrayed her as a passive vessel through which a dangerous muse spoke.

Recent scholarship has deepened our understanding of Plath as a master of performance and irony.[19] Yet the critical work done on Plath has not sufficiently altered her popular, clichéd image as the Marilyn Monroe of the literati. Melodramatic portraits of Plath as a crazed poetic priestess are still with us. A recent biographer called her "a sorceress who had the power to attract men with a flash of her intense eyes, a tortured soul whose only destiny was death by her own hand." He wrote that she "aspired to transform herself into a psychotic deity."[20] These caricatures have calcified over time into the popular, reductive version of Sylvia Plath we all know: the suicidal writer of *The Bell Jar* whose cultish devotees are black-clad young women. ("Sylvia Plath: The Muse of Teen Angst," reads the title of a 2003 article in *Psychology Today*.)[21] Plath thought herself a different kind of "sorceress": "I am a damn good high priestess of the intellect," she wrote her friend Mel Woody in July 1954.[22]

Many of Plath's friends have grown impatient with these distorted versions of her. Plath's close friend Phil McCurdy does not recognize the "literary psycho" he encounters in biographies that fail to capture her ebullient, brainy essence. "We were crazy, but it was crazy about Kafka," he said.[23] Plath's Smith confidante Ellie Friedman Klein is tired of her brilliant friend being chained to "the death machine," her suicide sensationalized.[24] That Plath is now identified with the clichés she examined ironically in her work is part of her tragedy.

Elizabeth Hardwick once wrote of Sylvia Plath, "when the curtain goes down, it is her own dead body there on the stage, sacrificed to her own plot."[25] Yet to suggest that Plath's suicide was some sort of grand finale only perpetuates the Plath myth that simplifies our understanding of her work and her life. Previous biographies have focused on the trajectory of Plath's suicide, as if her every act, from childhood on, was predetermined to bring her closer to a fate she deserved for flying too close to the sun. This book will trace Plath's literary and intellectual development rather than her undoing.

This is the first full biography of Sylvia Plath to incorporate all of her surviving letters—including fourteen newly discovered letters she sent to her psychiatrist in 1960–63 and several important unpublished letters—and to draw extensively on Plath's unpublished diaries, calendars, and creative work in addition to her published writings. Because the Plath and Hughes estates allowed me to scan Plath's and Hughes's published and unpublished papers throughout this project, I have been able to quote directly from sources rather than hastily scribbled archival notes. This is also the first Plath biography to delve deeply into Plath's family history, including her father's FBI investigation and her grandmother's institutionalization; to feature a surviving portion of Plath's lost novel, *Falcon Yard*, which I discovered misfiled in an archive; to make use of previously unexamined police, court, and hospital records; to offer new interpretations and insights into Plath's life based on the testimony and archival holdings of more than fifty contemporaries; to put forward new information that changes our understanding of Plath's last week; and to draw on the entirety of Ted Hughes's archives at Emory University and the British Library, which hold many unpublished poems and journal entries by Hughes about Plath. Lastly, this is the first biography of Plath to incorporate material from the Harriet Rosenstein archive at Emory University, which opened in 2020. Rosenstein interviewed scores of Plath's contemporaries in the early 1970s while she was working on a Plath biography, which she never finished. These spectral voices from the past shed new light on Plath's relationships, her medical treatment, and her writing.

This book is by no means the last word on Sylvia Plath. Over time, new material will surface and new questions will emerge. But it is, I hope, a richer, more accurate, and less pathological portrait of Sylvia Plath's life than what now exists. By sifting through Plath's poems, prose, sketches, journals, and letters, as well as the transatlantic archives of her husband and contemporaries—and listening to the testimony of dozens of friends, many on record for the first time—I have tried to recover what Plath gave to us rather than what she gave up. I hope to free Plath from the cultural baggage of the past fifty years and reposition her as one of the most important American writers of the twentieth century. Plath's best poetry is as aesthetically accomplished, groundbreaking, and reflective of its historical moment as the poetry of her idols, W. B. Yeats and T. S. Eliot. She ought to be remembered for her transcendent, trailblazing poems, not for gassing herself in her kitchen.

Of course, what makes Sylvia Plath's life compelling to so many readers is its tragedy. Her life, her fame, and her art will always be tied to her
suicide—there is no changing that. But the most famous woman poet of the
twentieth century was neither fragile ingénue nor femme fatale. She was
no Medea, no Eurydice, no Electra. Rather, she was a highly disciplined
craftswoman whose singular voice helped transform American and British
literature, and whose innovative work gave new energy to the burgeoning
literary and cultural revolutions of her time. The goal, then, is to recover
Sylvia Plath from cliché—to offer an alternative narrative to the Plath myth,
to debunk the sensational and melodramatic rhetoric that surrounds her,
and, finally, to examine her life through her commitment not to death, but
to art.

Sylvia Plath was one of the most highly educated women of her generation, an
academic superstar and perennial prizewinner. Even after a suicide attempt
and several months at McLean Hospital, she still managed to graduate from
Smith College summa cum laude. She was accepted to graduate programs in
English at Columbia, Oxford, and Radcliffe and won a Fulbright Fellowship
to Cambridge, where she graduated with high honors. She was so brilliant
that Smith asked her to return to teach in their English department without
a PhD. Her mastery of English literature's past and present intimidated her
students and even her fellow poets. In Robert Lowell's 1959 creative writing
seminar, Plath's peers remembered how easily she picked up on obscure literary allusions. "'It reminds me of Empson,' Sylvia would say. . . . 'It reminds
me of Herbert.' 'Perhaps the early Marianne Moore?'"[26] Later, Plath made
small talk with T. S. Eliot and Stephen Spender at London cocktail parties,
where she was the model of wit and decorum.

Very few friends realized that she struggled with depression, which
revealed itself episodically. In college, she aced her exams, drank in moderation, dressed sharply, and dated men from Yale and Amherst. She struck most
as the proverbial golden girl. But when severe depression struck, she saw no
way out. In 1953, a depressive episode led to botched electroshock therapy
sessions at a notorious asylum. Plath told her friend Ellie Friedman that
she had been led to the shock room and "electrocuted." "She told me that it
was like being murdered, it was the most horrific thing in the world for her.
She said, 'If this should ever happen to me again, I *will* kill myself.'"[27] Plath
attempted suicide rather than endure further tortures.

In 1963, the stressors were different. A looming divorce, single motherhood, loneliness, illness, and a brutally cold winter fueled the final depression
that would take her life. Plath had been a victim of psychiatric misman-

agement and negligence at age twenty, and she was terrified of depression's "cures," as she wrote in her last letter to her psychiatrist—shock treatment, insulin injections, institutionalization, "a mental hospital, lobotomies."[28] It is no accident that Plath killed herself on the day she was supposed to enter a British psychiatric ward.

Sylvia Plath did not think of herself as a depressive. She considered herself strong, passionate, intelligent, determined, and brave, like a character in a D. H. Lawrence novel. She was tough-minded and filled her journal with exhortations to work harder—evidence, others have said, of her pathological, neurotic perfectionism. Another interpretation is that she was—like many male writers—simply ambitious, eager to make her mark on the world. She knew that depression was her greatest adversary, the one thing that could hold her back. She distrusted psychiatry—especially male psychiatrists—and tried to understand her own depression intellectually through the work of Fyodor Dostoevsky, Sigmund Freud, Carl Jung, Virginia Woolf, Thomas Mann, Erich Fromm, and others. Self-medication, for Plath, meant analyzing the idea of a schizoid self in her honors thesis on *The Brothers Karamazov*.

Bitter experience taught her how to accommodate depression—exploit it, even—in her art. "There is an increasing market for mental-hospital stuff. I am a fool if I don't relive, or recreate it," she wrote in her journal.[29] The remark sounds trite, but her writing on depression was profound. Her own immigrant family background and experience at McLean Hospital gave her insight into the lives of the outcast. Elizabeth Hardwick's claim that Plath had "nothing of the social revolutionary in her" is simply not true.[30] Plath would fill her late work, sometimes controversially, with the disenfranchised—women, the mentally ill, refugees, political dissidents, Jews, prisoners, divorcées, mothers. As she matured, she became more determined to speak out on their behalf. In *The Bell Jar*, one of the greatest protest novels of the twentieth century, she probed the link between insanity and repression. Plath set *The Bell Jar* in 1953, but she wrote it in 1961, when she was moving in left-wing circles in London and becoming interested in the anti-psychiatry movement of R. D. Laing. *The Bell Jar*, like Allen Ginsberg's *Howl*, exposed a repressive Cold War America that could drive even the "best minds" of a generation crazy. Are you really sick, Plath asks, or has your society made you so? She never romanticized depression and death; she did not swoon into darkness. Rather, she delineated the cold, blank atmospherics of depression, without flinching. Plath's ability to resurface after her depressive episodes gave her courage to explore, as Ted Hughes put it, "psychological depth, very lucidly focused and lit."[31] The themes of rebirth and renewal are as central to her poems as depression, rage, and destruction.

"What happens to a dream deferred?" Langston Hughes asked in his poem "Harlem." Did it "crust and sugar over— / like a syrupy sweet?"[32] For most women of Plath's generation, it did. But Plath was determined to follow her literary vocation. She dreaded the condescending label of "lady poet," and she had no intention of remaining unmarried and childless like Marianne Moore and Elizabeth Bishop. She wanted to be a wife, mother, and poet—a "triple-threat woman," as she put it to a friend.[33] These spheres hardly ever overlapped in the sexist era in which she was trapped, but for a time, she achieved all three goals.

Then, in the autumn of 1962, her marriage ended. The edifice fell, but the poetry came fast and strong. Alone with her two young children in a cold thatched manor home in rural England, she began writing the poems that would, as she predicted, make her name. While her early, formally intricate poems helped her achieve modest success, these *Ariel* poems—with their speed, daring, and bravado, and their rage against personal and historical oppressions—sounded a new note in postwar poetry. Plath died just eight days before Betty Friedan's *The Feminine Mystique* was published, but her work broke through a literary glass ceiling. Poems like "Lady Lazarus" and "Daddy" seethe at the sexist prescriptions of Plath's society, while "Edge" concedes with a cool, horrific irony that only a dead woman is "perfected." She seemed to have scored the emerging women's liberation movement to poetry.

More than fifty years later, Plath's poems now seem locked in a fixed context: "confessional," "feminist." Yet she wrote her poems before these terms entered the cultural imagination. While she learned much from Robert Lowell and Anne Sexton, whom she met in the late fifties, her aesthetic impulse was more surrealist than confessional. Indeed, she treated the "confessional" impulse ironically in poems like "Lady Lazarus," where the heroine performs a striptease for the "peanut-crunching crowd" that has come to watch her bare all and attempt another suicide. (The poem practically predicts reality television.) And while Plath looked to female writers like Virginia Woolf, Marianne Moore, Elizabeth Bishop, Sara Teasdale, Edna St. Vincent Millay, Edith Sitwell, and Anne Sexton for models, her education was grounded in male modernism. The psychological and anthropological writings of Carl Jung, Robert Graves, and James Frazer, as well as the poetry and prose of W. B. Yeats, Dylan Thomas, Wallace Stevens, James Joyce, T. S. Eliot, W. H. Auden, Robert Lowell, and Ted Hughes himself, were the bedrock on which she built her scaffolding. The psychoanalytic approaches that have dominated previous Plath biographies ignore this "impersonal" literary tradition in which she was steeped and out of which her work grew. Jane Baltzell Kopp, who knew Plath and Hughes well at Cambridge, spoke of "the old, High Culture" that permeated their student existence: "that tradition had everything to do with the way we in those days all saw ourselves, each other, and our lives." Anyone seriously interested in understanding Sylvia Plath's poetry, Kopp suggested, would learn more by studying her English Tripos exam at Cambridge than her relationship with her dead father. "The amount—and range—of reading implied by those questions tells the tale."[34]

Plath mastered this body of work, from Chaucer to Eliot. Her literary expertise may not be immediately apparent in a poem like "Daddy," with its stuttering lines and nursery rhyme cadences. But the poem is the product of a long apprenticeship; it is Picasso on the verge of Cubism. Plath had to master her tradition in order to create something new. Her *Ariel* poems explore family trauma, marital problems, and sexual jealousy, yes, but they also interrogate history, war, totalitarianism, and a male literary tradition that had shut women out. The allusions in "Daddy" to T. S. Eliot's "The Waste Land" are easy to miss amid the poem's many controversies. Likewise, "Edge" responds to W. B. Yeats, Robert Graves, and Shakespeare. *The Bell Jar* uses James Joyce's *Portrait of the Artist as a Young Man* as a template, while "Ariel" argues with Ted Hughes's "The Thought-Fox" about the sources of creative inspiration. Plath redefined the elegy in "The Colossus" and "Daddy," making space for anger as well as love and pathos. She pioneered the poetry of motherhood and challenged the male Romantic notion that the moorland outside her door was more sublime than her baby's nursery. She is one of the first poets in English to write about miscarriage, abortion, and postpartum anxiety. Her poems about depression's ravages—"Tulips," "Elm," "The Moon and the Yew Tree," "Sheep in Fog," "Edge"—are some of the finest in the language. They, and Plath herself, deserve a dispassionate reappraisal.

As does her marriage to Ted Hughes. The sensational nature of their first meeting—Plath famously bit Hughes's cheek when he kissed her at a raucous party—has obscured the literary context that brought them together. Their relationship was, from its first theatrical moments, soldered on the work of Lawrence, Yeats, and Thomas.[35] On the night they met in 1956, both were searching for a new idiom, eager to smash false poetic idols. For all their outward differences, they were, as a BBC commentator perceptively suggested, "two of a kind."[36] Their best poetry would be incantatory and unflinching; original, yet rooted in tradition; composed as much for the ear as for the eye. During the happy years of their marriage, Plath and Hughes dedicated themselves to writing a new kind of poetry, something "unliterary," as Plath put it, which would break from the "Elegant Academicians."[37] "Such unbelievable making of words do physical things—the words seem to *be* the things," the artist Barrie Cooke said of Hughes's poems in 1962.[38] The same is true of *Ariel*.

Plath and Hughes were not only husband and wife, they were also aesthetic collaborators: "If SP and I managed to get through it all, it was because for crucial years we defended each other, we were a sufficient world to each other: our poetic folie à deux saved us from being isolated, surrounded and eliminated," Hughes said.[39] "I see now that when we met, my writing, like hers, left its old path and started to circle and search."[40] Though the marriage did not last, its legacy reverberates still in the cadences of postwar fiction and poetry: *The Colossus, The Bell Jar, Ariel, The Hawk in the Rain,* and *Lupercal,* five of the most important works of the postwar period, were all largely written during the years of Plath and Hughes's marriage. Plath's confidence in their future had been prescient. As she wrote to Hughes in October 1956, "Darling, be scrupulous and date your letters. When we are old and spent, they will come asking for our letters; and we will have them dove-tailable."[41]

Hughes has been vilified for his behavior toward Plath, whom he left for Assia Wevill in 1962. At the height of the women's movement, protesters disrupted his American readings; Plath fans still vandalize the name "Hughes" on Plath's gravestone in Yorkshire. An American poet, Robin Morgan, accused Hughes in a poem of murdering Plath. "He was being haunted and tormented in the name of feminism," the American poet Ruth Fainlight, who was close to Plath and Hughes in the early 1960s, remembered.[42] Hughes's mishandling of Plath's papers and his rearrangement of her original *Ariel* manuscript did little to reassure Plath's readers that he was a responsible steward; he claimed that he destroyed her last 1963 journal, and, under his watch, her 1960–62 journals and 1962–63 unpublished novel disappeared.[43] Still, the venom baffled him. To him, Plath was "'Laurentian,' not 'women's lib'"—that is, a disciple of D. H. Lawrence's sexually liberated, creative philosophy, not a campaigner for women's rights.[44] Hughes thought she would have resented the feminist label, as his friend Doris Lessing did, for Plath had often expressed contempt for "career women" who disdained homemaking and child-rearing. (Plath's psychiatrist, Dr. Ruth Beuscher, also felt that "Sylvia was not a feminist.")[45] Hughes did not recognize that Lawrence's novels offered Plath a template for equality and autonomy before the advent of second-wave feminism. Hughes retreated, and he let his sister Olwyn handle the Plath estate. But the two women, who met only six times, were bitter enemies; Olwyn once called Sylvia, in a published interview, "a complete bitch."[46] Olwyn portrayed Plath as selfish and unhinged in *Bitter Fame,* the controversial 1989 biography she coauthored with Anne Stevenson, and over the years she denied many feminist critics permission to quote Plath's work. As Edward Lucie-Smith said, Olwyn "made no bones about the fact that she detested Sylvia."[47]

The end of Plath and Hughes's marriage was indeed terrible and destructive. There was violence in the relationship—Hughes admitted to sometimes slapping Plath when she was in a rage, while Plath once wrote in her journal of bloody scratches, sprained thumbs, and broken crockery. After the couple separated, Plath told Dr. Beuscher that Hughes had hit her in February 1961 when he returned home from an appointment and found her tearing up his manuscripts. Plath told Dr. Beuscher it was an "aberration," and there is evidence that Hughes deeply regretted this act for the rest of his life.[48] Violence was itself part of Plath and Hughes's shared mythology, something they explored in the bedroom and on the page. They felt British poetry was at a low point, full of a destructive gentility, and they were determined to shock it out of submission. Writing forcefully about the horrors of humanity and nature became part of their joint project—one that gave both much happiness before, as Plath wrote in an early poem, "the play turned tragic."[49]

Despite its bitter end, Plath and Hughes's experimental, creative marriage was progressive for its time. In the mid-fifties, most women abandoned professional aspirations when they married. Yet Hughes prodded Plath, sometimes to exhaustion, to become a better poet. He created exercises for her, made elaborate charts, hypnotized her, exhorted her to concentrate—all to access the inner depths of consciousness where he thought the raw poetic material was buried. Plath, too, constantly prodded Hughes to be more productive. He published very little at Cambridge University before he met Plath; after graduation he drifted, worked odd jobs, and hardly qualified as a minor poet. Plath changed that. She acted as his agent, sending out his manuscripts and entering contests for him. Within a year of their meeting, he was on his way to becoming the most famous young poet in England. He later acknowledged that he owed his literary career to her. She would have gone on writing and publishing if they had never met; he might not have. Without Plath's ambition at his back, as he wrote in a late poem, "I'd be fishing off a rock / In Western Australia."[50]

Plath and Hughes were eager to support each other's writing and ambitions during the early years of their marriage, but both eventually came to regret the time they spent tending to the other. Plath was furious about the precious, wasted hours she had spent advancing Hughes's career—typing his manuscripts, sending out his poetry, keeping track of his rejections and acceptances, pasting his reviews in scrapbooks, and managing his finances. Hughes complained that he had spent too long attending to what he called Plath's "helplessness" and "impending thunderstorm" moods.[51] He wrote to his close friend Luke Myers in 1987, "Poor old Sylvia! If only I hadn't humoured her, & nursed her like a patient, & coddled her like a child—if only I'd had the guts to carry on just as I was, instead of wrapping my life up in a cupboard, while I tended her. Then maybe she'd have emerged in better shape. And me too."[52] But still he felt that the marriage had been productive, despite what the public wanted to hear. When Myers sent him a draft of a memoir about their early years at Cambridge in which he discussed the couple's poetic dialogue, Hughes asked him to remove the entire section:

> No doubt Sylvia & I plundered each other merrily—but if you say it, in my words—God, what new theses of accusation, what Job-loads of righteous wrath! If you say that, our generous readers will multiply it by ten. Your balancing statement, that she profited a little from me, will be reduced to one tenth. That's the biological 1st law of human malice in action. It's no good for me to say I designed prototypes, which she put into full Germanic production—though there's truth in it. I would never be believed. But to say I stole from her—that would be an instant religion of verification, & my wretched undated efforts would reveal the new gospel, under compulsion.[53]

To suggest that Plath borrowed from Hughes or that Hughes borrowed from Plath does not diminish their individual achievements; on the contrary, reading these poets side by side (indeed, they often wrote literally back to back) reveals how deeply each influenced the other. But the strains of mutual ambition would become hard for both to bear. As the couple's friend Al Alvarez wrote,

> it was a question not of differences but of intolerable similarities. When two genuinely original, ambitious, full-time poets join in one marriage, and both are productive, every poem one writes probably feels to the other as though it had been dug out of his, or her, own skull. At a certain pitch of creative intensity it must be more unbearable for the Muse to be unfaithful to you with your partner than for him, or her, to betray you with a whole army of seducers.[54]

This is the first biography of Sylvia Plath to examine those "intolerable similarities" in depth, and to take Plath and Hughes's literary dialogue—and rivalry—seriously.

Hughes's coaching would eventually upset Plath; in 1959, three years after they met, she vowed to stop showing him her work. But he could hardly help himself, for he never doubted her genius. When the prestigious *Poetry* magazine accepted six of Plath's poems in 1956, Hughes wrote to her, "Joy, Joy as the hyena cried. Now you are set. I never read six poems of anyone all together in Poetry. It means the wonderful thing. It will spellbind every Editor in America. It will also be a standing bottomless battery to charge what you write from now on, because you are almost certain to sell nearly everything you write now. . . . Joy, Joy."[55] They split their days: he watched their children for five hours every morning while Plath wrote; she cared for them during the afternoons. This was an unusual arrangement in the early 1960s. Although Plath bore the brunt of the domestic load in general, Plath's London friend Suzette Macedo was "amazed at his [Hughes's] readiness to help with cooking and other household chores, including nappy changing. . . . Astonishing at that period."[56]

Hughes took Plath's talent as seriously as she did and encouraged her to move beyond the sometimes stilted, thesaurus-heavy verse of her apprentice years; she, in turn, helped introduce him to contemporary American poetry that then left its mark on his own work. In 1962, when a Devon neighbor came round for tea and asked, "Does Sylvia write poetry, too?" Hughes responded, "No, she *is* a poet."[57] He had dared her to choose the artistic life she truly wanted over the comfortable bourgeois life her mother had carefully planned. Plath, always eager to show she had "guts," took the gamble. Together, Plath thought, they would fly close to the sun: "no precocious hushed literary circles for us: we write, read, talk plain and straight and produce from the fiber of our hearts and bones."[58] She knew she was breaking new ground in her own creative marriage as writer rather than muse. In her journal she wrote, "there are no rules for this kind of wifeliness—I must make them up as I go along & will do so."[59] But those rules would be harder to make up than she realized.

Plath's desire for reinvention was American, but her transformation could not occur in the United States. In late 1959, she left America for England with Hughes, never to return. Her flight was cloaked in respectability. By then Hughes was on his way to becoming the most famous young poet in England. In London, they could support themselves doing freelance work for the BBC, while British editors seemed more impressed than her own countrymen with Plath's dark wit. She became a prodigal daughter, brazenly forgoing a comfortable life as a doctor's wife for a peripatetic, jobless poet. Even Hughes would wonder if he had led Plath astray, far from her shining Cape Cod beaches into a world of gloom and fog. He once called Plath a "pioneer / In the wrong direction."[60] But England offered her a freer intellectual life; as an expatriate, she could make up her own rules. Ruth Fainlight felt that by moving to England, Plath "was defending her poetic self." Fainlight thought the distance from home was as liberating for Plath as it was for her. "It's a great advantage being a foreigner . . . you're not expected to know what you should be conforming to."[61] In England, with her mid-Atlantic accent, Plath escaped the class snobbery she had experienced in Massachusetts. English friends simply assumed that she was a rich American. Plath delighted in English eccentricity; in America, she told friends, peculiarity was suspect.

She would write her best works, *The Bell Jar* and *Ariel*, in England, far from the homilies of her mother and the *Ladies' Home Journal*. Yet autonomy came at a cost. As she was separated from her husband and cut off from her family and close friends, a brutal loneliness would descend on her. In the months before her February 11, 1963, suicide, she asked her American psychiatrist if she should come home. Dr. Beuscher told her to stay.

It was on a less notorious early February day that I prefer to think of Sylvia Plath as I have come to know her during the eight years I spent writing this book. On February 10, 1960—three years to the day before she died—she signed her first book contract, for *The Colossus*, in a London pub. She was dressed in a black wool maternity suit, a cashmere coat, and fine Parisian calfskin gloves. She was seven months pregnant with her first child, newly installed in sunny Chalcot Square with her cherished husband, and free, finally, from the watchful eyes of the benefactors who had always paid her way. She had just signed with D. H. Lawrence's publishers; it was the high-water mark of her professional life. She exulted in her triumph; in a letter to her mother she called herself "resplendent."[62] She rarely complimented herself, for she was relentlessly self-critical. No sooner had she scaled one "Annapurna," as she called her literary goals, than she mounted another expedition. But not that day. That afternoon, in the waning winter light, she celebrated. Ted Hughes brought champagne and the *Complete Poems of D. H. Lawrence* to mark the occasion.

Sylvia Plath would not see major literary success in her lifetime. *The Colossus* would barely make an impact on the Anglo-American poetry world. But after years of tirelessly pursuing her vocation in a profession hostile to women, she had cracked the door open—and not just for herself, but for the scores of women poets who came after her. Plath's second collection, *Ariel*, became a best seller, as did her 1963 novel *The Bell Jar*, which would go on to sell more than four million copies. She would win a posthumous Pulitzer Prize in 1982 for her *Collected Poems* and is now widely considered one of the most innovative, accomplished, and influential poets of the twentieth century. Sipping champagne with Ted Hughes in 1960, she may not have foreseen how famous she would become, but she knew she was taking flight.

Her life was about to become more difficult—two babies, a miscarriage, enmities, infidelities. Certainties would start to crumble like the masonry in Thoor Ballylee. She herself would become closed in, the key turned. But writing, even then, was her salvation; it was not her undoing. Ensconced in Yeats's childhood home at the end of her life, this beekeeper's daughter would have understood Yeats's famous entreaty to reconstruct in the halls of ruin:

> The bees build in the crevices
> Of loosening masonry, and there
> The mother birds bring grubs and flies.
> My wall is loosening; honey-bees,
> Come build in the empty house of the stare.[63]

In fact, she had built. There on her desk when she died was "*the* thing," the carefully calibrated counterweight to destruction: her new book of poems, the manuscript neatly bound, awaiting its revelation.

Part I

1
———

The Beekeeper's Daughter

Prussia, Austria, America, 1850–1932

Like Sylvia Plath herself, Plath's parents, Otto and Aurelia, have had
to bear a difficult posthumous burden. Plath used her parents, like so
many others in her life, as material for her writing. They existed as
real people whose praise she craved and, at the same time, a deep fictional
resource. They were of her, but not her—a looking glass that reflected the
possibility of what might or might not be, and she could not resist plumbing
their depths as she sought to understand her own. She came to feel that in
her parents lay the root of her anxieties, and, encouraged by her psychiatrist
in the late fifties, she began to lash out at them in her journals and, later, her
poems. Plath would express rage toward her parents—at her father for abandoning her, at her mother for hovering too close. They remain distorted caricatures, stuck in amber. In Plath's most famous poem, "Daddy," Otto—who
died when she was eight—is a patriarchal tyrant, a Nazi "bastard." Aurelia,
skewered in *The Bell Jar*, is a menacing martyr who demands perfection from
her daughter. But if Plath inherited anxiety and depression from her parents,
she also inherited intelligence, discipline, and ambition. They stand Janus-
faced, curse and blessing, at the beginning and end of Sylvia Plath's story.

In Otto Plath's case, myth has overshadowed truth in the popular imagination. For many readers of Sylvia Plath, Otto Plath *is* "Daddy": Aryan, fascist, Nazi. In fact, Otto Plath was a committed pacifist who renounced his
German citizenship in 1926 and watched Hitler's rise with trepidation. He
held himself to rigid moral standards and expected others to do the same.
In a photograph taken when he was a college student in Wisconsin, around
1910, he gives the impression of a man who does not suffer fools gladly. He
sits unsmiling in the front row surrounded by drunken peers, laughing and
holding steins. This is the serious, driven young man who would not com-

promise his ideals, even if that meant severing ties with his family—a decision that would have a profound impact on his daughter.

At least three generations of the Plath family lived in Posen Province, West Prussia, before coming to America. Today Posen (Poznan) is part of Poland, in the area known as the "Polish Corridor" when it was transferred from the German empire to Poland after the Treaty of Versailles in 1919. Like the Alsace-Lorraine region, it became a disputed territory, where tensions between ethnic Poles and Germans ran high. Despite the fact that the majority of those living in this area were Poles, Hitler attempted to annex it in 1939—one of the early acts of aggression that spurred France, Britain, and other Commonwealth nations to declare war on Germany. Though Otto Plath left Posen in 1900, well before both world wars, his daughter would eventually portray him as an embodiment of German imperialist aggression in "Daddy."

Posen, whose population comprised Germans, Poles, and Jews who lived in separate ethnic enclaves, was perhaps the poorest region in Prussia.[1] By the late 1800s, ethnic Germans, lured by the booming industrial economy in the Rhine and Ruhr regions, as well as free land in America, began leaving the region en masse in the *Ostflucht*, or "flight from the east." More than two million had left by the early 1900s, including Sylvia Plath's paternal great-grandparents, grandparents, uncles, aunts, and father. Her great-grandfather, Johann Plath, was an illiterate farmer, but his grandson Otto would eventually become a Harvard-educated professor, and his great-granddaughter a trailblazing poet and novelist. Sylvia's "perfectionism," often derided as neurotic or pathological, needs to be understood within the historical and sociological context of the American immigrant experience, which framed her life. Her desire to excel on all fronts has its roots in the Germanic aspirational work ethic that was her inheritance.

Otto Plath's German provenance was important to his daughter. Sylvia wrote that she felt her "German background very strongly," and talked up her German-Austrian roots to her German pen pal, Hans-Joachim Neupert, in high school.[2] "I feel a strong kinship for anything German," she told him in 1949. "I think that it is the most beautiful language in the world, and whenever I meet anyone with a German name or German traits, I have a sudden secret warmth."[3] She felt "patriotic pride" when she read German authors such as Thomas Mann and spoke lovingly of her grandmother's hearty Austrian cooking.[4] She was well aware of the dazzling artistic and intellectual achievements of German musicians, writers, and philosophers; she listened to Bach and Beethoven, and read Nietzsche and Goethe with her mother. But hers was a dual inheritance, for she had also heard how her mother's family was harassed during the First World War by Irish and

Italian neighbors in Winthrop, Massachusetts. Sylvia may have been picked on for similar reasons during the Second World War and possibly nervous that members of her family would be sent to a domestic detention camp for German Americans. (Her father was, in fact, detained by the FBI for alleged pro-German sympathies in 1918.) In December 1958, she described a short-story plot in her journal—which eventually became "The Shadow"—about a young German American girl who is treated suspiciously by her neighbors during the Second World War:

> My present theme seems to be the awareness of a complicated guilt sys-tem whereby Germans in a Jewish and Catholic community are made to feel, in a scapegoat fashion, the pain, psychically, the Jews are made to feel in Germany by Germans without religion. The child can't understand the larger framework. How does her father come into this? How is she guilty for her father's deportation to a detention camp? As this is how I think the story must end?[5]

These questions suggest that Sylvia understood from a young age that the German identity she shared with her father was somehow dangerous—a secret source of shame.

Plath's journals are full of frustration about her inability to master the German language. In January 1953 she regrets not having taken more German in college; in February 1956 she wants to "revive German again," declaring, "I haven't really <u>worked</u> at learning it"; she vows to spend the summer of 1957 studying the language; in 1958 she berates herself for "wast-ing my German hours" and writes, "to learn that would be a great triumph for me."[6] In 1960, exhausted and homesick in London, she was comforted by her German-speaking friend Helga Huws, whose German cooking made her weep. As late as 1962, she listened to German linguaphone records and tuned into a BBC German radio program.[7] She hired a German-speaking au pair shortly before her death in 1963.

Sylvia was the daughter of a German immigrant and a first-generation Austrian who had studied German language and literature and knew Middle High German. Her mother's parents, the Schobers, with whom she lived in Wellesley, spoke German at home.[8] Despite her exposure to the language—and the fact that she excelled at every other academic subject—German did not come easily to her. In her 1962 poem "Daddy," the German language itself becomes the "barb wire snare" and "the language obscene," "An engine, an engine / Chuffing me off like a Jew" to the death camps. Plath's notorious metaphorical appropriation of Jewishness may not have been a fantasy of victimization, but rather a fantasy of purgation and purity: only by aligning her speaker with the enemy of the Germans could she reject her own Germanness, which, in the wake of the Holocaust, seemed like a curse.

Previous biographers have stated that the Plath name was originally "Platt," and that it was anglicized on entry to America. According to a family member, the family name in Germany was von Plath.[9] Sylvia's paternal great-grandparents, John (Johann) von Plath and Caroline (Katrina) Katzsezmadek, were born in the Posen region in 1829 and 1826, respectively. John was German and Lutheran, Caroline Polish and Catholic, but the couple overcame the religious divide to marry in the 1850s. They raised their children as Lutherans, though there was religious tension within the marriage.[10] Both spoke Polish and German; in later years, Otto would list both languages as his mother tongue.[11] The couple settled in the small town of Budsin, now Budzyn, in Posen Province.[12] They had eight children, of whom Otto's father, Theodore (b. 1850), was the eldest.[13] The six children who survived into adulthood—Emil, Augusta, Mathilde, Mary, Emilie, and Theodore—all immigrated to America between 1882 and 1901 and settled across the West and Midwest in North Dakota, Illinois, Wisconsin, and Oregon.

The fact that all of John and Caroline's children emigrated suggests that the family did not prosper in Posen. In America they became blacksmiths and seamstresses, their spouses railroad laborers and meat cutters. Mary Plath endured a particularly dark fate. According to a family story, she fell in love with a young man from Cando, a neighboring town in North Dakota, while she was visiting her relatives in Maza. She became pregnant by him, but he left her for another woman in Cando. Jilted and alone, she ran away to a boardinghouse in St. Paul, Minnesota, where she died in childbirth. Mary's lonely death speaks to the cost of veering from traditional Lutheran codes of behavior. (Later, one of Mary's nieces expressed guilt over her aunt's sad fate.)[14] Otto, too, would be cast out after his peregrinations from the faith.

In their fifties and sixties, John and Caroline decided to follow their children across the Atlantic, and they immigrated to the Lincoln–Fall Creek area of Wisconsin, where they had Posen connections, in the 1880s.[15] Immigration officials struck the "von" from the Plath surname when John landed in New York. When he protested that the prefix was a matter of "family pride," the immigration official replied, "there is no aristocracy in America!"[16]

John and Caroline were uneducated: neither could read, write, nor speak fluent English even after living in America for two decades.[17] "They were poor people when they came to Fall Creek," a resident said.[18] Yet by farming and taking in boarders such as the local public school teacher, they were able to buy a house and eventually help their grandson Otto come to America. Caroline, who had "deep-set intense eyes," died in Fall Creek in November 1913.[19] John died two years later, in June 1915, the year his grandson Otto turned thirty. They were hearty people who lived into their eighties at a time when life expectancy was much shorter. An undated photograph shows John and Caroline seated on stools outdoors, probably in their yard, while a young Otto and his aunt Emilie stand stiffly behind. Otto, with his jacket, vest, tie, and neatly combed hair, embodies the grandson made good. John, however, wears a dark, rumpled suit, while Caroline and Emilie are in plain, faded housedresses. The grandparents' stern, weathered faces look straight out of *American Gothic.*

John and Caroline's eldest child, Theodore Friedrich Plath, married Ernestine Kottke (b. 1853) in a Protestant church in Posen Province in 1882. He was thirty-two, and she was twenty-nine—a rather late marriage for the time.[20] Ernestine was Otto's mother and Sylvia Plath's grandmother. Otto remembered his mother as "a rather melancholy person . . . weighed down with the care of six children and an ulcer on her leg that never wholly healed." He described Theodore, however, as "energetic, jovial, inventive."[21] Ernestine and Theodore had six children: Otto, Paul, Max Theodore, Hugo, Martha, and Frieda, all born between 1885 and 1896.[22] Another child, born when Ernestine was just nineteen and possibly out of wedlock, died. Ernestine raised the children on her own for long stretches of time while her husband sold equipment for the McCormick company in Germany, Poland, France, and Russia. Theodore picked up several languages during his travels and was able to converse easily with his clients; his son Otto would inherit his linguistic talents.

Theodore's job in Germany was steady and well paid, but around the turn of the century McCormick was restructured, and family members later speculated that Theodore had been laid off or was unhappy with the changes in the company.[23] Theodore left Hamburg on March 3, 1901, on the *Batavia* and arrived in New York sixteen days later. He listed his occupation in the ship's log as "master blacksmith." At fifty, he was the last of the Plath siblings to emigrate. He arrived with $125, no contract of employment, and plans to stay with his sister Mathilde and her husband in Chicago. Ernestine sailed from Liverpool to St. John, Canada, on the RMS *Lake Ontario* in December 1901 with five of her six young children.[24] She moved first to Maza, North Dakota, where Theodore's brother Emil worked as a blacksmith, and where at some point she reunited with her husband. They lived in Maza until 1906 or 1907.[25] By 1907, the couple was living in Harney, Oregon, and by 1912, Oregon City. Theodore worked as a blacksmith and farmer.

From this time on Ernestine vanishes both from the general record and from family anecdote. Sylvia's mother Aurelia said that after Sylvia's suicide attempt in 1953, Otto's sister Frieda wrote to her confiding that their mother Ernestine had been hospitalized for depression, and that a sister and niece had also suffered from the illness. According to Frieda, they had "all made some sort of recovery."[26] Yet this was not quite true. Ernestine Plath died in September 1919 at the Oregon Hospital for the Insane.

Theodore had committed her to the Salem asylum in October 1916. She was sixty-three. According to the admission form he filled out, her physical and mental health had been "normal" until 1905, when she suffered her first episode of "insanity" in North Dakota. The symptoms then had consisted of "head-ache, sleep and appetite loss, and anxious as persecution [sic]." Theodore stated that Ernestine had received treatment for this condition in Jamestown, North Dakota, in 1905, but that the same symptoms had recently reappeared. His wife had no previous history of suicidal thoughts or attempts, he wrote—no seizures or fits, no history of alcohol or drug abuse, and no hint of violent temperament. Her general disposition was, according to court records, "Good when well."

The admitting doctor found Ernestine reluctant to speak with him, and "much depressed & fearful. . . . Appears to be hallucinated but will not converse." The admitting nurse further noted that she was "well nourished, clean but helpless." She was also, the nurse thought, depressed. Another set of hospital admission notes observed that the brown-haired, blue-eyed, five-foot-five-inch, 130-pound woman "Gets out of bed at unreasonable periods . . . Thinks someone might kill her, begs to stay with us. Worrys [sic] for fear we will send her away." The admitting doctor's provisional diagnosis was "senile dementia."

Ernestine Plath's fear may have been pathological. Or it could have been a terrified reaction to an involuntary commitment to a mental hospital whose decrepit wards were later used as the film set for *One Flew Over the Cuckoo's Nest.* By January 1918, fourteen months after her admission, her notes read that she was "old, very quiet, causes no trouble, has to be cared for, physical health good, appetite fair, sleeps well." Another doctor wrote that month that she was "depressed. Refuses to converse tho she comprehends fairly well what was said." By September 1919, after steady weight loss, she was down to eighty-six pounds. She died of tuberculosis on September 28.

After Sylvia's suicide in 1963, her mother told a friend, "Sylvia's tendency to depression was experienced by members of her father's family, stretching to three generations."[27] Indeed, in 1988 Otto's great-niece Anita Helle confirmed that "Plath was not the only woman in her family to have undergone shock treatments, institutionalization, or prolonged and apparent bouts of depression."[28] Aurelia never told her daughter that depression ran in Otto's family, because Sylvia "so revered her father's memory."[29] But the medical records suggest that Ernestine probably suffered from age-related dementia rather than severe, debilitating depression. She was not a threat to herself or others, and was, apart from some memory loss, coherent, "tidy," quiet, and—after her initial admission—cooperative. She did not enter the asylum—or remain there—in a state of raving lunacy. A doctor reiterated her initial diagnosis in October 1918: "This old lady a case of senile dementia."[30] Theodore may just not have had the means or the will to take care of her.

Ernestine Plath was cremated at the asylum in 1919, and her ashes were stored on a dark basement shelf in a copper canister for nearly a century. None of her six children ever retrieved her remains. Otto's great-niece claimed that Ernestine had emotionally abandoned her family long before she ended up in an Oregon psychiatric hospital. She had "reluctantly followed her husband westward . . . her reaction was long-term silence, the communication to her children of exactly nothing in the last thirty years of her life." Otto's "hard-bitten anguish" over his mother's neglect remained "well hidden," Helle wrote, from his wife and children.[31] Silence would also mark Ernestine's afterlife. Sylvia Plath, one of the twentieth century's greatest chroniclers of mental illness, never knew that her grandmother died forgotten and abandoned in an insane asylum.

BORN IN GRABOWO, Posen Province, Germany, on April 13, 1885, Otto Emil Plath was the oldest of Ernestine and Theodore Plath's children. Otto later moved with his family to Budsin. From an early age, Otto exhibited a rarefied intelligence. He earned extremely high grades in school and was an amateur entomologist, studying the habits of local honeybees. When Otto's grandparents in Wisconsin heard of his academic success, they offered to pay his tuition at both the Northwestern Preparatory School and Northwestern College, the latter a small Wisconsin college that prepared Lutheran ministers. Before he immigrated to the United States, his parish held a going-away party for him; the members of his community agreed that he was likely to go far in America.[32] They were not wrong: he would eventually earn a doctorate at Harvard and become a full professor at Boston University.

In 1900, at age fifteen, Otto arrived in Manhattan, where he worked in a relation's shop and learned English by auditing local classes. In just one year, he progressed through eight grade levels, mastering the language.[33] After joining his Plath grandparents in Wisconsin, he spent 1903–1906 at the Northwestern Preparatory School and then entered Northwestern College in Watertown in late August 1906. There, one friend remembered him as a "clean-cut, neat, well-dressed young man" who played tennis, played clarinet in the school band, and took piano lessons.[34]

Many of the professors during Otto's time had earned their PhDs in Germany. Some had worked formerly as missionaries, and, indeed, the college prepared German American farm boys for the Wisconsin Synod with missionary zeal. Northwestern offered reduced tuition to those who intended to join the Lutheran clergy or teach in a religious school. These special terms allowed John and Caroline to send their bright grandson to college—an unlikely prospect in Posen. The college's civic and religious mission was to give its students "moral stamina and nobleness of character and prepare them for the higher and better ideals of life."[35] Though Otto would never enter the ministry, he would remain committed to the idea of "moral stamina"—a vow that may have cost him his life.

Northwestern's curriculum was conservative, with an emphasis on Latin, Greek, religion, and history rather than math and science.[36] Instruction was modeled on the German *Gymnasium* system and delivered in both German and English. Otto would have read the standard canon in his English classes: Chaucer, Spenser, Shakespeare, Milton, Bacon, Wordsworth, Dickens, Macaulay, and Burke. American literature was given short shrift, however. Only a "brief outline" was offered at the end of senior year: Hawthorne's *House of the Seven Gables*, *The Scarlet Letter*, and *The Blithedale Romance*.[37] Hawthorne, with his intense interest in sin, probably seemed a safe choice, though an observant reader would also find a dark reflection of the puritanism Northwestern avowed. It was a message perhaps not lost on Otto Plath, who began to doubt the religious path laid out for him midway through his college years. He later told Aurelia that in 1907 he wrestled for six months with questions about his own faith, "miserable months of agonizing doubt and self-evaluation."[38] He graduated with an honors BA in classical languages in 1910 and reluctantly began his studies at the Wisconsin Lutheran Seminary in Milwaukee that fall.

Otto had always shown an interest in science, particularly entomology; as a young boy in Germany he had spent much of his free time observing the habits of bumblebees. At Northwestern, he read Darwin, whose work increased his passion for biology. Darwin became his "hero" in college, and he was upset to find that the biologist's work had been banned at the seminary.[39] He eventually came to the conclusion that he did not have a calling and left the seminary shortly before Christmas in 1910, "without the consent of the faculty," as the registrar noted.[40] He would preach not the gospel of Luther, but of secular humanism. He would become a college professor—a profession he felt was nearly as respectable as the ministry. His grandparents, however, were crushed, and threatened to disown him. In the end, he did not bow to pressure from his family, teachers, or his small, midwestern, German Lutheran community. He would follow his vocation, whatever the cost. His daughter would do the same. Otto enrolled in a master of arts program in German at the University of Washington, and his grandparents struck his name from the family Bible.

John and Caroline's actions shocked Otto, but he remained resolved. "He was on his own for the rest of his life," Aurelia later wrote.[41] His father died at the age of sixty-eight in November 1918 from an abscess on the lung; Ernestine died eleven months later at the asylum. Otto visited infrequently with his parents and siblings after they had settled in America, and by the time he married Aurelia in 1932 he seems to have severed most family connections—though Aurelia would later become friendly with his sister Frieda Plath Heinrichs in California, and Otto's niece (Martha Plath Johnson's daughter), June Helle. He would cut all ties with the Lutheran Church, too. In *The Bell Jar*, Esther Greenwood described her father, based on Otto: "My father had been a Lutheran in Wisconsin, but they were out of style in New England, so he had become a lapsed Lutheran and then, my mother said, a bitter atheist."[42] Otto eventually became a member of the Society for Ethical Culture in Boston.[43]

One of Otto's closest friends at Northwestern was Hans Gaebler, the only other student in Otto's year who did not become a Lutheran minister.[44] This friendship may have played a key role in Otto's decision to pursue academia rather than the ministry, for after graduation Gaebler decamped to the University of Washington in Seattle, where Otto followed. There he served as an assistant instructor while studying German literature, in which he earned an MA in 1912. He was active in the German Club and performed in at least one play, the eighteenth-century comedy *Minna von Barnhelm*, put on by the group in April 1911.[45] He wrote his thesis in German on the influence of Washington Irving (author of "The Legend of Sleepy Hollow" and "Rip Van Winkle") on Wilhelm Hauff, a nineteenth-century southern German poet and novelist.[46] Hauff, who died at twenty-five, was a contemporary of Goethe's and part of the German Romantic movement. Otto was drawn, like his daughter, to dark Romanticism.

On August 7, 1912, in Spokane, Washington, Otto married Lydia Clara Bartz, a second-generation German American born in Fall Creek in 1889 and the sister of Otto's Wisconsin friend Rupert Bartz. The marriage was short-lived; the childless couple separated after two years and never saw each other again.[47] They finally divorced on January 4, 1932, in Ormsby County, Nevada, on the grounds that they had not cohabitated in more than five years. Lydia, represented by an attorney, was not present. Lydia never remarried, and she worked as a nurse at various midwestern hospitals until her retirement. She died in Fall Creek on February 22, 1988. Aurelia describes this mysterious first wife as nothing more than a footnote in Otto's young life. But she was part of the fabric of his close-knit German American community.

After graduating from the University of Washington, Otto taught German at the nearby University Heights School in Seattle before moving to Berkeley, California. There, he worked as a research assistant for a professor in UC Berkeley's German department, Dr. Schilling, and was a teaching fellow and PhD candidate in German from 1912 to 1914.[48] Lydia lived with him during these years and was registered as a "special student" at Berkeley's College of Social Sciences from 1913 to 1914. The marriage deteriorated—Otto lost a large sum of his wife's money in land speculation, and she refused to allow his ill brother to live with them in Berkeley. By this time, Otto's professional reputation was such that when he visited relatives in Reno, Nevada, in September 1914, his presence was reported in the "Comings and Goings" section of the local newspaper.[49] But when the First World War began, he was passed over for a permanent instructorship at Berkeley—on account of his German background, he suspected.[50] In August 1914, the *Oakland Tribune* reported that many German professors at the university would be forced to return to Germany; Otto was mentioned as one of the instructors whose status was in doubt.[51] While some German professors did decide to return to Germany to fight, many, including Otto, wanted to stay in America. The university later passed an edict barring German citizens from the faculty during the war.

Otto headed east, telling Lydia he would send for her when she finished her degree at Berkeley. An angry Lydia instead moved back to Fall Creek; Otto never sent for her. A Fall Creek resident remembered older people in town telling her that Otto had thought Lydia, though "very pretty," was "not good enough" for him because she was uneducated.[52] In 1914–15 he spent a year as the Carl Schurz Fellow at Columbia University, where he began, but abandoned, a PhD in German Language and Literature; he then taught modern languages at MIT from 1915 to 1918 before considering changing his field of studies altogether.

When the United States entered the war in 1917, teaching German was no longer a practical or even safe way to make a living. By the fall semester of 1918, Otto was back at UC Berkeley, now taking biology classes. He lived in a boarding house, worked part-time at a local market during the day, and ran an elevator at night.[53] His German citizenship barred him from the lectern, and he did not receive any financial help from his father, who died that year in an Oregon City hospital. Cemetery records reveal there was no money for a headstone for Theodore Plath, who was buried in a pauper's lot.[54] At least two of Otto's siblings had also fallen on hard times by 1917: draft records show that Max Theodore was an unemployed auto mechanic in Oregon City, while Paul worked as a mechanic in San Francisco. He eventually returned to Oregon and died relatively young, at age forty-six. Otto had been lucky to receive a college education.

More challenges lay ahead. Otto was reported to the FBI by one Mr. McCay, who stated in his initial FBI report that Otto "seems to have assumed a rather pro-German attitude towards the War on account of losing his positions."[55] McCay also claimed that Otto had told him he would return to Germany when the war was over. The investigator, Armin Nix, questioned the young academic. When Nix showed up at Otto's listed address, his suspicions were roused, for Otto no longer lived at that address and had not reported the change to the police as required by all enemy aliens. Nix stopped by Otto's employer, Sills Grocery Store, and was told that Otto had been fired for "refusing to buy Liberty Bonds."[56]

Otto got word that the FBI wanted a meeting, and he called at the FBI office on the morning of October 22, 1918. He gave Nix a short summary of his life to date, including his various residences and degrees. When Nix questioned him about his opinion regarding Germany's involvement in the war, he noted that Otto "assumed a rather indifferent attitude."[57] But Otto denied that he had ever told McCay he wanted to return to Germany. In fact, he told Nix, he "would never dream of going back to Germany," though he had considered going to South America. He also explained that he had not been fired from Sills Grocery, and that he had not bought Liberty Bonds because he was "$1400 in debt on which he was paying 5 and 6% interest, and that he was attempting to earn a living and do work at the University at the same time and did not feel that he could afford to do so." He denied having corresponded with anyone in Germany since he had left in 1900.

Otto said that his parents left Germany for a better life in America because "some things are rotten in Germany, but not all; that the German people and their character is not altogether rotten, but that they are misled." He told Nix that he hadn't read a single newspaper between 1903 and 1910—the years he was a student at Northwestern Prep and College—and had no idea that he was required to report his change of address to the police. He had signed a Loyalty Pledge when he registered at Berkeley, but admitted to Nix that "he took several weeks to think it over to make absolutely sure, as he believes that Roosevelt's saying that a man cannot be 50-50 now— must either be 100% American or not American at all, and this he believes is true." This was a dangerous but honest admission. Otto also told Nix that he had lost his chance at an instructorship in biology at Berkeley because of his enemy alien status, and that "he is being persecuted without just cause."

Nix then interviewed Otto's references at the university, one of whom, Dr. Cort, told him Otto was an excellent scientist but a poor teacher—"very nervous and not being able to interest students." Cort admitted, however, that the university had passed a rule forbidding the employment of Germans on the faculty, and that this rule was partly to blame for Otto's failure to land the instructorship. Dr. Schilling, a professor in the German department who had worked with Otto before the war, told Nix that Otto felt "slighted" when he was passed over for a permanent position. He believed that Otto was loyal but that "his main trouble is not being a good sport and being able to take hard luck the way a man should take it." At this point Otto knew all about hard luck: though he had taught in university classrooms since 1911, he now found himself working menial jobs stacking groceries and operating elevators for twenty cents an hour because he was German.

The next day Otto reported his change of address to the Berkeley police, which seemed to satisfy Nix. He closed the case, and ended his eight-page report on Otto:

> I could not find any further evidence against this man, and as he seemed to be a man who makes no friends, and with whom no one is really well acquainted, was not able to locate any one knowing him intimately....
> The indiscreet remarks he has probably made at times, and the indifference he seems to have towards the War, are due in my opinion to his being interested in a very narrow field, and to his very nervous and morbid disposition.

Otto filed naturalization papers in 1921.[58] He renounced Germany and Poland, and became an American citizen in 1926, a move that may have protected him from similar suspicion in the late 1930s.[59]

Otto was one of thousands of German aliens who were questioned—and in some cases arrested and sent to detention camps in Utah and Georgia—during the First World War. In June 1917, during his Flag Day speech, President Woodrow Wilson emboldened Americans to root out "vicious spies and conspirators" in "unsuspecting communities"; the following year, a German coal miner, Robert Prager, was lynched by a mob of two hundred.[60] Otto's German background would have made him a target of constant harassment, and he shrank from socializing. Already someone had reported him to the FBI on false pretenses. Under normal circumstances, Otto could be personable and warm. George Fulton, a former graduate student of Otto's who eventually became the chair of the Boston University biology department, remembered him as a "friendly and very talkative person." He described Otto as a "kind" mentor to him and his other graduate students, whom he treated to convivial faculty lunches.[61] In 1966, after an article on Sylvia Plath appeared in *Time*, another of Otto's former students, Thomas Clohesy, wrote to Aurelia to express his frustration with how Otto had been portrayed by both his daughter and the media:

> Otto was not the fearful Teuton which Sylvia apparently thought him to be. I remember Otto Plath with great fondness, having first met him in 1939 when I became a student of German at Boston University. Another friend and I thought him a very unusual man, and we respected his political opinions even though they did not prevail at that time. Much of what he has predicted has since come to pass, and I have often felt that his analysis of Germany's position in the world was a correct one. Were he with us today, I am sure he would feel vindicated in many of his beliefs. He was certainly not the "ogre" that the poem thinks he was. I shall never forget his kindness to me when he suggested that I might tutor a student of his who was having difficulties in German. At that time jobs were extremely scarce, and his kindness will never be forgotten.[62]

Far from being a Nazi sympathizer, it seems Otto saw through Hitler's rhetoric and surmised the horror that awaited Europe at a time when Neville Chamberlain was still proclaiming he had secured "Peace for Our Time." Aurelia, too, thought "Daddy" a betrayal, and would later write to the poetry critic Helen Vendler (whose mother Aurelia had befriended in the 1930s) that Sylvia's "barbed writing" was a way of finding "catharsis" by "lashing out in poetic form," often using "exaggerations" to make her point: "Her father never had any affiliation with the Nazi party and was utterly revolted by any departure from 'reverence for life.'"[63] Sylvia's childhood friend Ruth Freeman Geissler, who knew Otto, claimed that the Nazi figure in "Daddy" was "very much a fantasy."[64] Aurelia told a close friend that Otto would never have let Sylvia join the Girl Scouts, had he lived, because he so abhorred militaristic uniforms.[65]

After his FBI interrogation, Otto again left the West Coast. He took up an assistant in zoology post at Johns Hopkins; then, in 1921, he began his studies in biology at Harvard, where he earned a master of science in 1925 and a doctorate of science in 1928.

Otto was forty when he began working on his Harvard doctorate, but he seemed even older to the eleven young graduate students he lived with at Harvard's Bussey Mansion, near the Bussey Institution.[66] One thought of him as a "permanent Bussey fixture."[67] Acquaintances from the Harvard years remembered Otto as a "sentimental" dreamer fascinated by what he called the "wonders of nature."[68] George Salt, who lived with Otto at the Bussey Mansion for four years, recalled, somewhat condescendingly, "He was a German teacher with biology interests. He cared not for Science but for bumblebees, rather like a clergyman with a butterfly collection."[69] While Prof. W. M. Wheeler's students discussed the exciting new field of genetics, Otto seemed to care only about his bees. His "blinkers" became a running joke in the biology department, though his cohorts remember that he applied himself rigorously to his work.[70] The only other passion Otto's Bussey housemates recognized was his love for the German language. One night a housemate was having trouble translating a German word and asked Otto, who still spoke with a slight German accent, for help. Otto became a different person before his eyes: "he rolled the idiom off his tongue as though relishing it and read the German words with intense and longing pleasure."[71] Another housemate remembered that Otto was "very meticulous, even fussy, in his use of words. I recall that one evening he came to my room and debated for a long time the question of whether he should entitle a forthcoming research paper 'The Bee-eating Propensities of the Skunk' or 'The Bee-eating Proclivities of the Skunk.'"[72]

Some of the "Bussey Boys," as they called themselves, thought Otto "awkward," a "timid outsider," as he tried to join their conversations in the sitting room each evening. Most of them never really got to know the "slight, thin, gentle man who smiled at the edges of their dinnertime conversation."[73] When Germany's role in the First World War came up at these communal meals, Otto vacillated between defending Germany and criticizing it.[74] His lack of conviction was unusual for a Harvard scientist. But being questioned by the FBI and losing his position at Berkeley likely made Otto wary of speaking his mind and forming close friendships. It was better to agree than to raise suspicions; better to keep a distance than to share intimacy. It is perhaps no accident that both of Otto's wives spoke German, or that once he had children he sought to keep them, Aurelia remembered, "absolutely isolated"—he did not want them even to attend dance classes.[75]

Bussey contemporaries remembered that he always seemed to have a cold (a predisposition Sylvia inherited) and had little luck with women. His experience with Lydia left him bitter about marriage: one housemate said that Otto was "consumed with hate for his ex-wife, whose faults . . . he extended to the entire sex."[76] He spoke of himself as "a romantic" and said his first wife was "cold."[77] Being older than the other graduate students, he fancied himself an expert on sex and would sometimes tell "salacious" stories on the subject.[78] Others remembered his special diets and food fads, his neat clothes, his honesty, his frugal nature, and his passion for his work. A house-mate recalled that, like his daughter, "He frequently worked to the point of extreme fatigue."[79]

Otto's closest friend at the Bussey Mansion, Philip Darlington, felt that there were a few students who were disliked, "but Otto was not one of these. He was a bit obtuse and a bit too literal; we teased him a little but not too much; and we accepted him and liked him. . . . he was neither domineering nor high-handed with us."[80] Some of the Bussey Boys remembered his speaking angrily about religion and the years he had wasted in the seminary, but they generally found him "gentle by nature," "serious, but with a sense of humor," "over-sensitive," "not an aggressive person," and certainly not violent.[81]

Otto was "seldom jovial," but one friend remembered him "relaxed and happy" while making "home brew" in the Bussey Mansion basement. Otto claimed to have a specialist's knowledge of beer brewing and took pride in his batch's high alcohol content. The Bussey Boys spent a sunny day outside at the Arboretum drinking Otto's beer. "I had never seen Plath so sociable nor such amity between him and the others," one recalled.[82] Ralph Singleton, who "knew Otto rather well and liked him very much," said he was generous—Otto frequently lent him money to tide him over.[83] Clyde Keeler, the illustrator of Otto's groundbreaking book, *Bumblebees and Their Ways*, recalled his close friend's compassion: one rainy night, Otto welcomed a stray cat, crying pitifully outside, into the mansion. He even constructed a box with a cushion for her. This same friend remembered Otto's insecurity—he put off his oral doctorate exam for years on account of nerves. Keeler finally convinced him to go through with it. "Otto went to the exam with his knees shaking. When he returned there was a grin on his face. 'It was easy,' said Otto."[84] A Bussey housemate who went on to become the president of the University of Hawaii stated, "To many he seemed cold, distant, and arrogant, but in reality he was a warm-hearted rather shy person."[85] They found it hard to reconcile the quiet, gentle man they knew with the Nazi father in Plath's poem "Daddy."

After the 1934 publication of Otto's monograph, *Bumblebees and Their Ways*, based on his Harvard doctoral thesis, he became a highly respected entomologist. He was appointed a full professor at Boston University, where he taught from 1922 until his death in 1940, and published in journals such as *The American Naturalist*, the *Biological Bulletin of the American Naturalist*, the *Annals of the Entomological Society of America*, and the *Handbook of Social Psychology*, among others. Some of his findings even made their way into the popular press, where he was cited as an authority on bee stings and insect behavior.[86] A former graduate student described him as being "ahead of his time" in his research and suggested that he would now be called an expert in behavioral biology.[87]

At Boston University, Otto seems to have been a conscientious and thorough teacher, though, as one former student remembered him, somewhat inflexible.[88] Another student remembered him as a "good teacher . . . very considerate to students," who had "a sense of humor." (Otto liked to tell students about the time the Bussey Boys, experimenting with concepts of taste, ate rat stew for dinner—a sight which made Otto vomit.)[89] Seniors at BU wrote of him warmly in their yearbooks, referring to him as the *Bienen-König*—the bee king. In the 1929 BU yearbook he was described as a professor who "makes subjects interesting. If you don't believe it, watch the crowds which flock into his classes in Ornithology, Entomology, and even German! If you want to spend an interesting half-hour just get him to talking about birds and insects. You'll not consider it time wasted, we assure you."

In the introduction to *Bumblebees and Their Ways*, Otto discusses the origins of his interest in bees and beekeeping. Part of this passage is worth quoting at length, for it offers a rare chance to hear Sylvia Plath's father discoursing passionately in his own words. After discussing how he transferred several bee colonies to his backyard while a young boy in Germany, he writes,

My interest in bumblebees constantly grew, and when I found that even my teacher in natural history knew very little about the complex life of these fascinating Social Hymenoptera, I decided to write a short treatise on their life-history and habits. This youthful ambition was interrupted rather suddenly, however, when I was sent to live with some relatives in New York City, and it was not until the summer of 1920, that—due to the accidental discovery of two bumblebee colonies at Berkeley, California—my former interest was again awakened. On June 15 of the following year, I began to make detailed observations on the New England species at the Bussey Institution. The facilities which this school of research and the adjoining Arnold Arboretum offer for the study of bumblebees are probably not surpassed anywhere in the world. On the approximately three hundred acres belonging to these two departments of Harvard University, I have taken thirteen of the seventeen bumblebee species recorded from the New England States. During the past thirteen years there were also discovered more than 250 bumblebee colonies on, or near, the grounds of these two institutions. Of this large number of colonies . . . about 200 were transferred to nest-boxes for further study.

In addition, I have made extensive observations on the activities of these industrious insects out in the fields. This work has resulted in the disclosure of many new and significant facts.[90]

The missionary impulse has been applied to science rather than religion; the book is as close as Otto would ever come to spiritual autobiography.

Bumblebees and Their Ways was Otto's life work and was all that remained of the man after his death. Sylvia, who was only eight when he died, would eventually write a celebrated series of poems about bumblebees. She often discussed her father's bee studies in letters to others, and in 1962 she raised bees herself in Devon. While Aurelia Plath is often blamed for pressuring her daughter to scale increasingly perilous heights of achievement, the legacy of Otto, the Harvard-educated professor, may have exerted its own pressure. Indeed, Sylvia later told her psychiatrist, Dr. Ruth Beuscher, that Otto was "a brilliant professor who would have expected them to be outstanding."[91] *Bumblebees and Their Ways* was evidence that her father was a "great man" whose insights had moved his scientific field forward, but it also laid the groundwork for the portrait of Otto in "Daddy"—a pedant who looms "at the blackboard" with his "Aryan eye," always ready to correct or punish. It is not just Otto's German heritage that connects him to Nazism in "Daddy," but his role as a professor and scientist. These were occupations Sylvia respected when she was young, but, as her resentment toward her father and her husband grew in the early sixties, they appeared more sinister. By then, her father's occupation had become an embodiment of patriarchal authority. *Bumblebees and Their Ways* unwittingly laid the groundwork not only for Plath's bee poems, but also for "Daddy" and "Lady Lazarus." The respected entomologist who kept, as he wrote, "more than fifty colonies under observation . . . on boards on the shady side of a partly covered, abandoned cellar," would become the model for Plath's "Herr Doktor," who tortures defenseless creatures.[92]

Bees were always connected to the memory of the father Sylvia loved—she would suggest as much in her poem "The Beekeeper's Daughter"—but who she felt had abandoned her. In the uplifting "Wintering," which was supposed to be the last poem in *Ariel*, Plath chose her father's totem as a talisman of recovery and resilience during her own bleak winter:

> Will the hive survive, will the gladiolas
> Succeed in banking their fires
> To enter another year?
> What will they taste of, the Christmas roses?
> The bees are flying. They taste the spring.

This literary evolution suggests that near the end of her life Sylvia had perhaps begun reconciling with her father's ghost. Although Ted Hughes changed the order of the *Ariel* poems after her death, Plath was adamant that her book end on a note of hope and renewal with the word "spring." And, indeed, we are far from the red-hot anger of "Daddy" in "Wintering." We cannot know for sure whether Plath's original order in *Ariel* was meant to suggest a narrative of recovery from anger, depression, and self-punishment. But her placement of "Wintering" at the collection's end hints that she believed she was becoming more resilient, and that she may have begun, before her own death, to forgive her father for dying.

IN THE POPULAR IMAGINATION it is Otto, the absent father, who haunts and torments his daughter. The roots of this phenomenon go back to the first sentence of the first biography of Sylvia Plath, Edward Butscher's 1976 *Sylvia Plath: Method and Madness:* "For Sylvia Plath, as even the most casual reading of her poetry demonstrates, the central obsession from the beginning to the end of her life and career was her father, Professor Otto Emile [*sic*] Plath." Butscher suggested that Plath would not have become a poet had her father not died. "A situation was needed," he wrote, "a plot ripe with secret tension and geared towards a climax of destruction, betrayal, a re-enactment of an ancient tragedy to forge the tragic poet."[93] Plath's poem "Daddy"—and Ted Hughes's 1998 collection, *Birthday Letters*—have strengthened the common assumption that Otto's ghost lay at the source of Sylvia's genius and her "madness," and that her suicidal drive was in part an effort, as she writes in "Daddy," to "get back, back, back" to him.

Yet it was Sylvia's mother, Aurelia, who had the more lasting and significant impact on her daughter. Sylvia and her mother had a close, complicated, and often difficult relationship, especially after Otto's death. Sylvia shared a bedroom with her for most of her late childhood and adolescence. Aurelia recognized the relationship's mixed blessings, noting, "Between Sylvia and me there existed—as between my own mother and me—a sort of psychic osmosis which, at times, was very wonderful and comforting; at other times, an unwelcome invasion of privacy."[94]

Aurelia was her daughter's confidante, sounding board, model of womanhood, and moral guide. She also embodied the demure, submissive self that blocked access to the deeper, subversive poet-self. Aurelia stood for a particular aesthetic that, from the late fifties on, seemed to Sylvia a vestige of her own early, meticulously crafted, safe verse. Both Plath and Hughes wanted to infuse a more Lawrentian aesthetic into contemporary Anglo-

American poetry. Their joint project meant exploring an alternative moral structure—self-expansion rather than self-sacrifice—of which Aurelia would have disapproved. Where Plath sought originality, her mother valued conformity. When Sylvia famously told Dr. Beuscher, in 1958, that she hated her mother, she was also expressing her disgust with the self that had sought her mother's approval for so many years, and the self that had written the kind of poetry that would appeal to her mother's parochial taste. When Marianne Moore criticized the sexual imagery in Hughes's *The Hawk in the Rain*, Plath saw a mirror of her mother's attitude. Moore's grumbles strengthened Plath's determination to write a bolder, less decorous poetry.

Aurelia has been portrayed in biographies, movies, the media, criticism, and Plath's own writing as a meddler—someone who was wary of Ted Hughes; whose visits to her daughter's British household provoked anxiety; and whose epistolary platitudes Sylvia grimly endured in an endless stream of letters. She is the devil whispering in Sylvia's ear that she is not sufficiently demure, popular, modest, or wealthy. Aurelia, the story goes, put so much pressure on her daughter to excel that Sylvia felt the only way to win her mother's love was to outperform herself again and again; because she could not sustain this cycle, she had no choice but to give up. The main source of this narrative is Plath's own novel, *The Bell Jar*, in which Esther Greenwood's icy, critical mother seems partly to blame for her daughter's breakdown and suicide attempt. The novel was a source of unending grievance to Aurelia.

Whether or not Aurelia's high expectations damaged her daughter will always be a matter of debate. Sylvia's childhood and college friends defend Aurelia fiercely. Sylvia's closest Wellesley confidante, Betsy Powley Wallingford, said, "Aurelia certainly was aware of all her daughter's gifts and made darn sure those gifts were properly used and encouraged, which can be seen as being pushy." But she insisted this was not the case, and was upset that many thought Sylvia had a "nasty relationship with her mother.... Whatever Aurelia did was for Sylvia's benefit. She sacrificed her whole self for her children." Betsy felt that Aurelia had become a "scapegoat" who was unfairly vilified in order to give others "a reason" for Plath's suicide and "a feeling of power over the story."[95] Sylvia's Wellesley friend Phil McCurdy called Aurelia a kind, "hardworking widow," while other friends like Janet Salter Rosenberg and Ellie Friedman Klein also described her as quiet and generous, formal but warm.[96] Perry Norton, another close Wellesley friend, remembered Aurelia as "somewhat shy," a "very sweet, decent, hardworking person. Domineering does not apply." Perry's father was a history professor at Boston University, and the two families had gotten to know each other through faculty social events when Otto was still alive. Perry felt that both his and Sylvia's parents expected their children to succeed, but that these kinds of expectations were typical in their professorial milieu. Academic success, rather than material wealth, was the currency such families valued: they were "decent people who had done their best and tried their hardest" to pass on their humanistic, intellectual values to their children.[97] Sylvia's brother, Warren, did not believe that his mother pushed his sister to excel. In 1975 he told a biographer, "Sylvia didn't need any pushing."[98]

As with Sylvia herself, there seems to be only one version of Aurelia in the popular imagination. Yet Aurelia's own letters and writings present a more complicated portrait of a woman whose intellectual and creative aspirations were thwarted by a culture that derided female ambition. Like Otto, Aurelia inherited an intense work ethic, which she passed down to her daughter. Aurelia's father, Francis, or Frank, Schober (b. 1881), was one of thirteen children, born in Bad Aussee, Austria. His mother, who came from a wealthy family, died when he was only ten, leaving him, her favorite child, a fortune that his father quickly spent on a Viennese showgirl. The family's finances became so precarious that Frank was forced to leave home at fourteen.

After brief stints in Italy and Paris, Frank found his way to England; by the time he was twenty, he spoke four languages and worked as a servant in Westgate-on-Sea, Kent.[99] He arrived in Boston on June 1, 1902, at the age of twenty-one, to join a friend he had made in England, Josef Grünwald.[100] Frank helped Josef run a boarding house he had opened in South Boston. Josef brought over his two sisters, Aurelia (senior) and Annie, from Vienna, their hometown, in April 1904.[101] Frank welcomed the anxious teenagers inside the boarding house—Aurelia, Sylvia's future grandmother, was just sixteen—and reassured them that all would be well in America. He married Aurelia a little over a year later and became an American citizen in 1909.[102] Two more Grünwald siblings, Ernst and Otto, came to America in 1905. Ernst, who lived to be 101, settled in Jamaica Plain, where Sylvia visited him as a child.

All the Grünwalds changed their surnames to Greenwood upon arriving in America. (Plath would eventually choose this surname for Esther, the protagonist of *The Bell Jar*.) While anglicizing foreign names was not unusual, the family may have wanted to distinguish themselves from the many Jewish Grünwalds pouring into America from Austria and Hungary at this time. As for Plath's identifying herself with Jewish Holocaust victims ("I may be a bit of a Jew"), the Grünwald name and the speed at which it was abandoned may have caused her to wonder whether there had in fact been a Jewish relative in her maternal line.[103] In her brief introduction of "Daddy" for a 1962 BBC program, she wrote that the poem's speaker's mother was "very possibly part Jewish."[104] Indeed, Aurelia said that her maternal Viennese grandmother, Barbara Meyer, was an orphan, and possibly Jewish.[105]

Frank Schober married Aurelia Greenwood in July 1905, a week after her eighteenth birthday. A daughter, Aurelia Frances, was born on April 26, 1906. In the decades that followed, Aurelia Sr. ran the home while Frank worked as a waiter and, later, as an accountant for the Dorothy Muriel Company. By 1920, he had earned enough to move his young family from the Boston suburb of Jamaica Plain into a three-bedroom, two-thousand-square-foot rented house at 892 Shirley Street, on Point Shirley in Winthrop. The house, built in 1900, provided plenty of space for three children—Aurelia Frances, Dorothy, and Frank Jr. Uncle Ernst, his American wife Pauline, and their two sons lived nearby in Jamaica Plain.

Winthrop, a coastal suburb north of Boston, was then populated by working- and middle-class Catholics of mainly Irish and Italian descent, with smaller pockets of Protestants and Jews. While many of its homes faced the Atlantic, the lots were small and the neighbors close. Flanked by Boston's main airport to the west and Deer Island Prison to the south, Winthrop would never develop into an affluent town like nearby Marblehead. But it was safe, clean, and unpretentious. The Schober house, perched between the beach and Boston Harbor, had a spectacular view of the sea that would leave an indelible impression on the young Aurelia Schober and, eventually, her daughter. Before Logan Airport became a busy international hub, Winthrop was quiet and the seawater clean enough for swimming. On Point Shirley, Sylvia lived with her grandparents during Otto's illness and began her love affair with the sea.

Aurelia writes in her memoir that she grew up in a "peaceful, loving home," but her childhood was marked by moments of crisis. She entered school as a native German speaker with no English, and recalled "how isolated I felt at recess as I stood by myself in a corner of the schoolyard." From this time on, the family spoke English at home, but the family's Austrian heritage meant that neighbors regarded them suspiciously during the First World War. Despite the fact that the Schobers were American citizens, Aurelia said she was "ostracized by the neighborhood 'gang,' called 'spy-face,' and . . . pushed off the school bus steps and dumped on the ground, while the busdriver, keeping his eyes straight ahead, drove off." (Plath would later draw on this story when writing "The Shadow" and "Superman and Paula Brown's New Snowsuit.") More than sixty years later, these incidents still upset Aurelia: "I felt this prejudice was completely unjust for my parents' sake as well as my own, for they were ardent converts to American democracy."[106] Aurelia was eight when the First World War began and twelve when it ended—formative years to come of age as an "other" who was unfairly bullied. This dislocating experience helps explain her reluctance to cause trouble later in life, or to question the dominant certainties of her age. Aurelia's embrace of mainstream American values and her frequent suppression of anger—habits that would grate mightily on her daughter—grew partly out of her experience as an ostracized Austrian American girl during the First World War.

On account of disastrous investments in the stock market, Frank Schober brought the family close to financial ruin during the 1920s. When he was laid off from his accounting job in the late 1930s, Aurelia's mother demanded control of the family's finances—a move that broke Frank's spirit.[107] He had to scramble for work and was lucky to find a position as the maître d'hôtel at the elite Brookline Country Club in 1940. Aurelia remembered that she and her two younger siblings "grew up in a matriarchy"—just as Sylvia would after her father's death. Aurelia, the good girl and peacemaker, took pride in her high marks and the pleasure they brought her parents, who made her education a top priority: "Support at home compensated for outside unpleasantness, as well as did success in the classroom." She was allowed to skip the second grade, "a great boon for me."[108] The same cycle—praise from parents and teachers making up for "outside unpleasantness"—would again play itself out between Aurelia and her daughter years later.

Aurelia forged her identity around her intellect from an early age. When she was not playing with her siblings, going to museums, or visiting her uncle's family in Jamaica Plain, she spent most of her free time reading Horatio Alger, Harold Bell Wright, and Gene Stratton-Porter. Her favorite book was, notably, Louisa May Alcott's *Little Women*. She preferred novels in which "the poor and the virtuous always ultimately triumphed," perhaps because of her own battles with the neighborhood gang some years before. Later, she devoured "all the romantic historical novels I could find in the public library." She took pains, in her memoir, to portray herself as a reader:

> Emily Dickinson's poetry became my new bible; the novels of Scott, Dickens, Thackeray, Eliot, the Brontës, Jane Austen, Thomas Hardy, Galsworthy, Cooper, Hawthorne, Melville, and Henry James—in fact, the world of American and English prose and poetry burst upon me, filling me with the urgency to read, read. I lived in a dream world, a book tucked under every mattress of the beds it was my chore to make up daily; a book in the bathroom hamper, and the family's stock answer to "What's RiRi [my nickname] doing?" was "Oh, she's reading *again*."[109]

Aurelia suggests in this memoir that Sylvia inherited her literary precociousness, and perhaps even her literary talent, from her. Indeed, when Aurelia later gave Sylvia books by Friedrich Nietzsche and James Frazer at Christmas, she reaffirmed the sense that they shared an intellectual bond. But Sylvia was the voyager; Aurelia could only wave from the shore with a mix of envy and pride. Aurelia once told an interviewer, "I had hoped to become a writer once, but I didn't feel that I could expose my children to the uncertainty of a writer's success or failure."[110]

Aurelia graduated salutatorian of her 1924 high school class. She wanted to study at Wellesley College, but the cost was prohibitive.[111] She later regretted not applying for a scholarship and made sure her daughter did not repeat the same mistake. She settled on a liberal arts degree from Boston University to prepare for a career teaching English. Her father, however, had other plans for her. "I was to be a 'business woman.'"[112] In the end, they compromised: after Aurelia finished the two-year vocational course, she completed two more years at the university studying the humanities. There, she served as the president of the German Club and participated in student government, the English Club, and the Writers' Club.[113] She graduated valedictorian of her college class in 1928.

Aurelia then pursued a master's degree in English and German at Boston University, where her "most memorable" class was "The Philosophy of Faust," taught by Marshall Perrin.[114] She met Otto, the professor of her Middle High German class, in 1929. She thought him "a very fine-looking gentleman . . . with extraordinarily vivid blue eyes, and a fair, ruddy complexion." On the last day of class, as Aurelia said good-bye to him, he shyly invited her to a picnic at a friend's farm the next weekend. "It was a bolt out of the blue," Aurelia wrote. That weekend, she learned that Otto "could be spontaneous, jolly, and certainly was confiding." He told her he admired her thesis on the Renaissance physician and alchemist Paracelsus, which he had read and which, he said, "proved we had much in common." He "astounded" her by revealing that he had a wife from whom he had been separated for thirteen years, but that he would get a divorce were he "to form a serious relationship with a young woman now."[115] This was perhaps the real "bolt out of the blue": Otto was already thinking about marrying Aurelia on their first date.

The couple separated for the summer while Aurelia worked as an office manager at a camp in Pine Bush, New York. The two corresponded throughout July and August, then began dating in earnest in the fall of 1930. Aurelia's recollection of their courtship recalls the early promise of the marriage:

> From the fall of 1930 on, our friendship developed and deepened. Weekends found us hiking through the Blue Hills, the Arnold Arboretum, or the Fells Reservation. The worlds of ornithology and entomology were opening for me, and we dreamed of projects, jointly shared, involving nature study, travel, and writing. "The Evolution of Parental Care in the Animal Kingdom" was our most ambitious vision, planned to be

embarked upon after we had achieved some lesser goals and had established our family of at least two children. I succeeded in interesting Otto at that time in the fine productions then given at the Boston Repertory Theatre—Ibsen, Shaw, and modern plays of that era—as well as sharing my enthusiasm for literature.[116]

In 1932 they traveled to Nevada so that Otto could obtain a formal divorce from his first wife. Divorces were difficult to obtain, and the whole affair contained a whiff of scandal. Otto and Aurelia married on the same day the divorce was granted, January 4, in a rushed civil ceremony that probably disappointed the bride, who had a deeply sentimental side. (Both of Aurelia's siblings eventually married in festive, family-centered ceremonies.)

After the wedding, Otto asked Aurelia to give up a promising career as a teacher of English and German at Brookline High School, one of the state's best public schools, to become, as she put it, "a full-time homemaker."[117] Otto's request reflected the mores of the time: before the Second World War, twenty-six states had laws prohibiting married women from working.[118] Otto respected Aurelia's intellect enough to ask her to ghostwrite sections of his scientific work, but, as a college professor, he saw no need for her to remain in the workforce. Indeed, a "working wife" in the 1930s carried a stigma.

Aurelia claimed that the first year of her marriage was almost exclusively devoted to "THE BOOK"—*Bumblebees and Their Ways*. "After Sylvia was born," she wrote, "it was 'THE CHAPTER.'"[119] This was a chapter on "Insect Societies" that Otto was preparing for *The Handbook of Social Psychology*. Aurelia said she wrote the entire first draft of this chapter from Otto's notes. In this respect, Otto and Aurelia's marriage bears some resemblance to Sylvia's marriage to Ted Hughes. Both marriages began in academic settings, and both women were initially content to put their own ambitions aside to help their foreign husbands. The two highly educated couples embarked on their relationships in a collaborative spirit: Ted and Sylvia sought to become the most important poets of their generation, while Otto and Aurelia also saw themselves as partners in a joint intellectual and scientific endeavor. Sylvia's friend Ruth Freeman Geissler picked up on this connection: "Sylvia helped Ted many times . . . the same as Aurelia had helped Otto a generation before."[120]

Aurelia's transition from professional to housewife was bittersweet. She may have thought life with Otto would be like the evenings she had once spent with a bachelor professor at MIT for whom she did German-English translation work during her junior year at Boston University. The two often dined together, and, she wrote, "It was during these meals that I listened, fascinated, to his accounts of travel and colorful adventures, fully realizing that I was in the presence of a true genius in both the arts and sciences. I came away with my notebook filled with reading lists that led me to Greek drama, Russian literature, the works of Herman Hesse, the poems of Rainer Maria Rilke, as well as the writings of great world philosophers."[121] She later confided to Sylvia's daughter, Frieda, that this man had made her feel "transfigured, beautiful . . . I felt I spilled joy from every pore." But in 1927 he left her to work abroad, and she never saw him again. Crushed, she felt her world diminish and her possibilities narrow. She told Frieda, "I don't want to recall the hurt that remained in lessening degrees until your mother was born."[122] Otto courted her while she was nursing her broken heart.

Marriage, Aurelia soon learned, was not the endless dinner party she had once imagined. Indeed, Otto's earlier life as an immigrant bachelor was poor preparation for the negotiations and compromises of married life. Aurelia explained:

> Despite the fact that he was only sixteen when he arrived in the United States, the Germanic theory that the man should be *der Herr des Hauses* (head of the house) persisted, contrary to Otto's earlier claims that the then modern aim of "fifty-fifty" appealed to him. . . . The age difference between us (twenty-one years), Otto's superior education, his long years of living in college dormitories or rooming by himself, our former student-teacher relationship, all made this sudden change to home and family difficult for him, and led to an attitude of "rightful" dominance on his part. . . . At the end of my first year of marriage, I realized that if I wanted a peaceful home—and I did—I would simply have to become more submissive, although it was not in my nature to do so.[123]

After "Daddy," Aurelia challenged the public perception of Otto Plath as a tyrannical husband. Yet she chafed under his patriarchal assumptions and could not quite bring herself to absolve him. She resented the fact that he commandeered the dining room table as his desk for a year while he was writing "Insect Societies," not allowing anyone to move a single book or paper. On the rare evenings when he went out to teach an evening class at Harvard, Aurelia invited friends over for dinner. She drew a diagram of his papers' arrangement and carefully placed everything back in its original position before he returned.[124] Aurelia later told Dr. Beuscher she was "not happily married," especially as Otto grew more ill and "emotionally unbalanced."[125] A Boston University colleague who met Aurelia a few times recalled a frostiness between husband and wife, though it was quite clear Otto "had deep affection for his little daughter."[126]

Like her mother, Sylvia, as wife to a "genius" husband, masked what was smoldering inside with perfect deportment. She would embrace the role of housewife to her friends and correspondents, and then seethe in her journal about the injustices of that role. Her mother had paid the high price of personal autonomy to keep a "peaceful" household; even after Otto's death, she remained faithful, promising Sylvia she would never marry again. But Sylvia had no wish to become a martyr. To her, alone with her children in those dark winter days of 1963, it seemed that for all her achievements she had simply become her mother.[127] Plath's 1948 poem "Recognition" nearly predicts this circular domestic fate. The speaker, trying to outrun her memories, moves into a new home—only to realize it is all too "familiar":

> And when I realized that the paint
> Had camouflaged an ancient door,
> And that beneath the smooth shellac
> There lay a trampled hardwood floor,
> I looked about through angry tears.
>
> For that remodeled house was all
> That I could ever own. And while
> I gazed around the shadowed hall
> My mouth curved in a bitter smile:
> I knew I had lived there before.[128]

2

Do Not Mourn

Winthrop, 1932–1940

Nineteen thirty-two was hardly an auspicious year for a new baby. America was three years into the Great Depression, and a mood of pessimism had settled over the country. National unemployment had skyrocketed to an unprecedented 25 percent. Waves of migrants began their hopeless journeys from farm to city, where they found not jobs but squalid shantytowns. Hungry citizens sold apples from urban sidewalks and mobs began to loot supermarkets. That summer, J. P. Morgan decided to keep his yacht, the *Corsair*, in dry dock on the grounds that it was "wiser and kinder not to flaunt such luxuriant amusement."[1] The Ku Klux Klan enjoyed a resurgence, and ranchers from Oklahoma threatened revolution.[2] President Hoover still insisted that Americans would pull themselves up by their bootstraps as they always had. Yet the nation was teetering on the brink of collapse. Apocalyptic scenes became common. One woman knew that everything had changed in 1931 the day she saw fifty men, all "American citizens," fighting "like animals" for garbage scraps behind a restaurant.[3] The New Deal and its modest measures of relief were still years away, but the need was desperate. An unemployed man expressed the situation succinctly when he wrote to the president, "Can you not find a quicker way of Executing us than to starve us to death."[4]

Otto and Aurelia's marriage was a gesture of optimism in the face of national calamity, but there were practical reasons to wed. Otto, at forty-seven, had a secure teaching position at a time when school enrollments were contracting and departments downsizing. Given the unemployment rate, Aurelia would have considered him a very eligible bachelor. And both, perhaps, found solace in their mutual Germanic heritage at a time when anti-

German sentiment was on the rise. They knew that the American Dream could suddenly collapse around them as it had for so many others.

They conceived within a month of their wedding day on January 4, 1932. The couple had a progressive approach to child-rearing, and read works by Friedrich Fröbel and Maria Montessori. Otto had unpleasant recollections of his own mother's rigid parenting and, Aurelia claimed, "believed in the natural unfolding of an infant's development."[5] Both thought their baby should be fed on demand and picked up when crying—methods then frowned upon by pediatricians, who expected new mothers to follow strict feeding schedules. But Aurelia was reluctant to expose herself as a nonconformist: "I would never confess to it in front of my contemporaries."[6]

Sylvia Plath was born on October 27, three weeks early, at 2:10 p.m. at Robinson Memorial Hospital in Boston's South End. She weighed eight pounds, eleven ounces and was twenty-two inches long. The birth of a healthy baby girl, announced on a prim, pink-ribbon-trimmed card, brought Otto and Aurelia closer to their idyllic vision of bourgeois family life.[7] Aurelia later said she and Otto chose the name Sylvia for its connotations of "the herb salvia and the poetic adjective sylvan."[8] The name married Otto and Aurelia's interests—botany and poetry—and bestowed a beneficent blessing on their daughter.[9]

They brought their baby home to the ground-floor apartment at 24 Prince Street in Jamaica Plain, a large arts-and-crafts-style house with an elegant front porch and an upstairs balcony. The new house was a step up from the shabby student dwellings of Otto's past. Though the yard was tiny, their proximity to Harvard's Arnold Arboretum and Jamaica Pond allowed the small family to spend much of their time outdoors in the warmer months. A photograph shows a happy outing at the arboretum in July 1933. The family poses in relaxed contentment: Aurelia, in pearls and a fur stole, holds her blond infant while Otto, shirtsleeves rolled up, reclines in the grass next to his daughter. Another early photograph of Sylvia, in March 1933, at five months old, shows her sitting happily on Aurelia's lap. Mother holds daughter tenderly and smiles while Sylvia, dressed in a matching crocheted dress and cap, returns her gaze. Yet another photograph shows Sylvia at nine months smiling brightly in the August sun. (In the margin, Aurelia wrote, "Sylvia is always merry!") Aurelia would later become friendly with another young mother in the neighborhood named Helen Hennessy, whose infant daughter, the future Helen Hennessy Vendler, would eventually become the most influential poetry critic in America. As a toddler, Sylvia used to "dance around" the two mothers as they walked. Little did she know the baby in the carriage would become a renowned Harvard professor who would one day champion her poetry.[10]

Aurelia loved her daughter, but she resented giving up a professional career in teaching and education administration, itself a downsized ambition from her true goal of writing fiction. She was caught between two conflicting sets of ambitions—career and motherhood—which in 1932 were still poles apart. She had thought combining both might be possible when she married Otto, who had claimed to believe in equal parenting. Yet his progressive attitude dissolved when their first child was born. Aurelia, a college valedictorian with a master's degree, had little choice but to sacrifice her own intellectual aspirations for the sake of domestic harmony. She poured her intelligence and ambition into the only outlet she could: her child.

At fifteen, Sylvia told Aurelia, "'When I am a mother I want to bring up my children just as you have us.'"[11] Aurelia later wrote that this was the remark she "treasured most" from her daughter. She was determined that Sylvia would have the scholarly and literary opportunities she did not; yet she wanted Sylvia, the daughter and granddaughter of Germanic immigrants on the eve of another war with Germany, to be a good American. This meant abiding by the sexist mores of the time and behaving like a lady. Aurelia's own mother reaffirmed such values when, on the eve of Sylvia's departure for Cambridge University in 1955, she said, "I don't mind her understanding artists; I don't mind her working like an artist, just so long as she doesn't live like one!"[12] Yet in her daughter, Aurelia saw a reflection of her own artistic ambition. Sylvia understood, and even sympathized. Later in life she encouraged Aurelia to write stories for women's magazines, and offered to be her editor. But Sylvia, her mother's double in so many ways, would long to separate herself from this hovering shadow of dreams deferred.

Aurelia sensed this desire for separation, and was sometimes embittered by it. Her memory of Sylvia's disdain for her wardrobe suggests a charged mother-daughter dynamic:

> In the eyes of my Smith girl my hair was not properly "styled"; my suits (bought at cooperative sales, some good Davidow suits, but, of course, not new) were too conservative, and my inevitable white blouses "did nothing for me." I had expected it; I was amused, and refrained from uttering my thought, "I dress this way the better to provide for you, my dear."[13]

Aurelia also remembered that when she revealed to her daughter that she had been asked to model in the spring of 1928 for the Boston Home Beautiful Exposition, Sylvia responded, "Standards must have been very different in your day."[14]

When Aurelia was offered a position as dean of women at Northeastern University in 1947, Sylvia, age fifteen, yelled, "For your self-agrandizement [*sic*] you would make us complete orphans!" Aurelia turned down the position. "Later she reproached me for my negative decision, saying, 'You didn't have the guts to make the break!' An element of truth was there, I suppose, or I wouldn't have remembered it verbatim."[15] These stories, in the draft of Aurelia's memoir, were eventually omitted from the published version. The public would not be privy to mother-daughter score settling. The roots of the painful, competitive relationship that would propel and repel Sylvia all her life might be traced back to the day Aurelia turned her back on her professional ambitions and embraced, instead, her newborn daughter.

AURELIA RECORDED every detail of her infant's progress in her baby book.[16] This remarkable square pink album provides a glimpse of her parenting style, which, depending on one's perspective, was either hands-on or hovering. Aurelia was a playful and engaged mother in an era when well-behaved children were still generally seen and not heard. But her precise recordings betray an anxiety about whether her daughter's growth and development conformed to normal patterns. A typical entry regarding Sylvia's teething activity in 1933, for example, reads: "July 10, upper left central incisor—small appetite; Oct. 5, upper left lateral incisor (restless at night); Dec. 11—upper right molar (No lower left teeth to match right side!)." Aurelia was concerned throughout Sylvia's infancy that she was a "small eater." From June 1933 on, she wrote down her daughter's weekly weight. Her anxieties help explain Sylvia's detailed reports about food in her letters from summer camps, which are filled with reassurances that she is gaining weight.

Sylvia's baby gifts—silver spoons, silk bonnets, a gold locket—suggest a solidly middle-class social circle comprising university families. None of Otto's relatives appears to have sent a gift; there was little communication between the two families apart from Aurelia's correspondence with Otto's sister, Frieda Plath Heinrichs, who lived in California. Sylvia would always remain intensely curious, in the manner of an orphan, about her lost Plath relatives. She would eventually name her daughter after her paternal aunt Frieda, whom she barely knew. Otto himself did not feature in Aurelia's description of Sylvia's first Christmas. She rarely mentions him at all in the baby book apart from a short note about Christmas 1933, when he gave Sylvia her favorite gift—a stuffed Pekinese dog that she "loved to death."[17]

Sylvia was verbally precocious and spoke her first words at eight months.

Aurelia's list of her speech milestones provide an intimate glimpse of family life in the Plath and Schober homes during the early 1930s:

Eight months: Mama, dad, bye-bye, tick-tick ("bye bye" was spoken consciously, but the other words were accidents)

Sept. 1 Ragman passed calling "Rags" and Sylvia called "Ags!"

Oct. 1 "Ow gaw" (all gone!—means bottle is empty)

Oct. 20 "Birdie!"

Nov. 1 "I tee" (I see!) and "haw" (for hot), ba for bath and baw for ball

Dec. 19 Daddy! (said specially when someone shakes the furnace!)
Sounds are made for the dog, the duck, the cow, horse, wind, sheep; she says "car" whenever she hears an auto pass. She has been making replies to such queries as: What does the sheep say? "Ba," etc. for 2 months. She imitates grandpa's puffing on his pipe to the query "What does grandpa do?"[18]

When Aurelia told Sylvia they were going to the arboretum, she would jump up and down, "squealing with glee. It's a treat to take her out now, for she notices everything: birds, squirrels, chipmunks, horses, automobiles—and, best of all to her little mind, other babies. She wants to touch other babies, and stretches out her arms to them, shouting with excitement." Even as a toddler, Sylvia was deeply stirred by her senses. "She gets excited about plants and flowers and wants to smell them immediately," Aurelia wrote in February 1934. From about mid-May of 1933, Aurelia gave Sylvia sunbaths for an hour each morning and afternoon, which she felt was important for her baby's health. Sunbathing would become Sylvia's lifelong habit.

On September 14, 1933, Aurelia's baby girl took her first steps, into Otto's arms. By December she was walking unaided. Her first birthday was a small but "bright and festive" affair. Aurelia expressed disbelief that her infant was already a year old: "It is hard to imagine that my baby is emerging from her state of precious babyhood! She looks so grown-up in the knitted suit and beret which I recently bought her! . . . Well her daddy and I agree that the whole world doesn't hold another one-year old so wonderful—and so sweet!—at least it doesn't for us!" When it came time to blow out the candle on the sponge cake Grammy Schober had made, Aurelia wrote, "We wanted Sylvia to 'poof' out her candle but she eagerly reached toward the flame, becoming vocally indignant when not allowed to grasp it!"

Aurelia soon taught Sylvia to hold out her hand in greeting and say, "How do you do?" But at fifteen months, Sylvia was testing her limits: "If Sylvia wants attention, she announces, 'ga-ga' (which means 'nasty' and 'forbidden'). She may then go determinedly to the fireplace and lick the bricks with her tongue or pop some microscopic speck of thread or dust into her mouth. It is done in good humor, and the rush for the 'ga-ga' on the part of either parent is met by giggles from Sylvia. Her end is then achieved!"

Sylvia's baby book suggests that Aurelia was a woman who cared about precision and control even as she extolled the virtues of freedom and play. Although she was sometimes critical of the status quo, she rarely veered from it; when she did, she kept her small rebellions to herself. Conformist values kept her moored in a world veering wildly off course, where families lost their homes and fortunes every day. The Plaths never went without food, clothing, or shelter during the Depression. Not all immigrant families were so lucky.

————

DURING THE FIRST YEAR of Sylvia's life, Aurelia collaborated with Otto on "Insect Societies" while her parents helped mind the new baby. Aurelia's parents lived with the young family in Jamaica Plain during the summers, when they rented out their Winthrop house for extra money. The living quarters were tight, but Aurelia appreciated her parents' support, writing that their "humor, love, and laughter" lightened "what would otherwise have been too academic an atmosphere."[19] During this period Frank Schober would often take his granddaughter for walks to the arboretum while Aurelia and Otto worked. Over time, an especially tight bond formed between Sylvia and her grandfather. He swam with her in the summer and amused her with games indoors. Plath remembered, in her 1963 Winthrop memoir "Ocean 1212-W," how one day, after a spanking, "grandfather extracted me from the domestic furies for a long beachcoming [sic] stroll over mountains of rattling and cranking purple stones." When Aurelia was in the hospital giving birth to Warren, her grandfather's "lyrical whistle beckoned me to adventure and forgetting." Sylvia's uncle Frank also distracted the children by taking them out on the water to fish for mackerel and cod in his new sailboat, which he built himself. He rigged up a beach swing that propelled them into the water at high tide. In the evenings the family feasted on Grammy Schober's home-made seafood chowder, steamers, and lobster gathered from the Schobers' own lobster pots. Sylvia always shielded her eyes when her grandmother threw the live lobsters into the boiling pot: "I felt the awful scald of the water too keenly on my skin."[20]

Sylvia's younger brother, Warren, was born on April 27, 1935, two and a half years to the day after her birth. Afflicted throughout toddlerhood with asthma and bronchial pneumonia, Warren required near constant attention from Aurelia. Sylvia was often sent to her grandparents' home in Winthrop while her mother tended to her sickly infant son; when she was home, Sylvia sought out Otto's attention in an attempt to become his "pet," just as she believed Warren was Aurelia's.

While Aurelia was nursing Warren, Sylvia occupied herself by finding capital letters in newspapers and reciting them to her mother. She read her first word (a Stop sign, which she read as "pots") at three and displayed artistic talent early. Otto was excited when one day he found her quietly outlining the Taj Mahal on a bath mat with small mosaic tiles—"to us a definite sign of visual memory developing at an early age."[21] Aurelia remembered, "My husband wouldn't let me vacuum clean. He had that down for weeks."[22] Otto took special pleasure in teaching and observing his daughter, who could recite on command the Latin names of the insects he was studying. "Bombiculanus!" she would exclaim when she saw a bee. Aurelia recounted that one night, while gazing down at his sleeping children, Otto said, "All parents *think* their children are wonderful. We *know!*"[23] A family friend said that Otto spoke to Sylvia as if she were his intellectual peer; she was, for him, "the recipient, the chosen one."[24] Otto may have been a loving father, but he was not playful. He seemed most interested in Sylvia when she excelled. Aurelia recalled, "She never played with Daddy, she never went out with Daddy, never went on the beach with Daddy except in the evenings she would play piano. And then when he was ill she dressed up in a nurse's uniform and brought him drinks and so forth."[25]

Aurelia and the children spent most of the hot summer of 1936 with the Schobers in Winthrop while Otto taught summer school at Boston University. She commuted back to Jamaica Plain weekly to do housekeeping and spend time with Otto, who had begun to complain about increasingly alarming symptoms: "constantly tired; develops chronic cough; sleeps poorly," Aurelia recorded.[26] She worried that what at first seemed like fatigue from a long commute by railway, boat, and subway into Boston was something more serious. But Otto stubbornly refused to see a doctor. In fact, wrote Aurelia, he had "no personal physician and boasted that he had never been to a doctor in his life."[27] Otto had seen a friend die from lung cancer after several operations, and he was determined to avoid the same fate. "I know what my ailment is, and I'm not going to submit to any butchering," he told Aurelia.[28] He decided he was terminally ill. Otto's self-diagnosis and deeply pessimistic refusal to seek medical help, as well as his reclusive domestic habits, suggest that he may have been suffering from depression. "Why me?" he would ask despondently.[29]

That fall, Aurelia kept the children in Winthrop with her parents while she nursed Otto in Jamaica Plain. The Plaths soon moved to their own seven-room stucco house in Winthrop at 92 Johnson Avenue, only two miles from the Schober house on Point Shirley. Aurelia called it "spacious."[30] Sylvia would have felt the bracing wind of the sea from her earliest days: only one house stood between the new Plath home and the ocean. She would have seen light change as it refracted off the ocean over the course of an afternoon, "full of red sun and sea lights," as she later wrote.[31] She would have heard the sound of gulls constantly. It was here that she chose to sanctify her earliest memories, here that she began an infatuation with the sea that would become a touchstone throughout her life.

She learned to swim three months before her fifth birthday; photographs from this time show her at the beach, wading in the water or standing against a sea wall looking happy and tan.[32] She beams for the camera as she stands in her swimsuit on the bow of Uncle Frank's sailboat, holding a six-and-a-half-pound cod. Aurelia remembered her "roaming over the 'flats' at low tide, gathering shells or digging in the coarse sand," exploring "shallow pools teeming with miniature sea life," and climbing rocks.[33] Later, in her 1940s scrapbook, Sylvia described her relationship with the ocean:

> I gradually developed a love for the stormy, turbulent ocean that few people can understand. I enjoyed lying for hours in the bright, white sand, gazing at the sparkling blue-green waves bounding in on the west beach, and the silvery seagulls dipping for fish on the crest of a frothy white-cap before it broke and washed among the pebbles. I speak so much of the ocean, because it was an important part of my heritage and environment, and my love for it is hard to explain.[34]

Parts of her early short story "The Green Rock," written in 1949 when she was sixteen or seventeen, seem to come straight out of her scrapbook:

> Something within her soared at the sight of the cloudless sky and the waves washing on the shore with a scalloped fringe of foam. . . . As she stared out at the ocean, she wondered if she could ever explain to anyone how she felt about the sea. It was part of her, and she wanted to reach out, out, until she encompassed the horizon within the circle of her arms.[35]

In her memoir "Ocean 1212-W," Plath wrote, "I sometimes think my vision of the sea is the clearest thing I own." "Ocean 1212-W" was Plath's attempt to write her own creation myth. When Aurelia first set her down on the beach, Sylvia "crawled straight for the coming wave and was just through the wall of green when she caught my heels." Later, she claimed she taught herself to swim: "I should, according to mother, have sunk like a stone, but

I didn't." The sea protected her, and brought her a "sign of election and specialness" when Aurelia was in the hospital giving birth to Warren: "I was not forever to be cast out."[36] Sylvia's childhood friend Ruth Freeman Geissler remembered that Otto, too, loved the sea—he "sat in the sun at the beach every day" in the summer. When Ruth's father saw Otto at the beach, Otto would say, in his German accent, "I'm storing up health vor the vinter."[37]

Plath described with particular relish the "sulphurous afternoon" when the deadly hurricane of '38 struck, "the sea molten, steely-slick, heaving at its leash like a broody animal." She and Warren watched the destruction that night out their window: "Nothing could be seen. The only sound was a howl, jazzed up by the bangs, slams, groans and splinterings of objects tossed like crockery in a giant's quarrel." (Aurelia remembered that her young daughter always found storms "exciting and dramatic.")[38] The morning after the hurricane, Sylvia remembered seeing upended telephone poles and fallen trees, even small cottages floating out at sea. It was, she wrote, "all one could wish." Her grandmother's Winthrop house survived the storm intact, despite nature's best attempt to send it out to sea: "My grandfather's seawall had saved it, neighbors said. . . . a dead shark filled what had been the geranium bed, but my grandmother had her broom out, it would soon be right."[39] Plath identified equally with the raging sea and the Germanic stoicism that held its destructions at bay.

At night Aurelia read to the children in the brightly decorated upstairs playroom equipped with an art easel, paint, clay, and a record player on which she played classical and children's music. She put money toward a "book fund" and built up a "respectable" library for the children, augmented by Otto's two thousand scientific books and her own collection of German, English, and American literature.[40] She read the children Robert Louis Stevenson, Eugene Field, A. A. Milne, Dr. Seuss, and J. R. R. Tolkien. *Alice's Adventures in Wonderland* and *The Wind in the Willows* were favorites. She also made up stories about a teddy bear named Mixie Blackshort and read the children poems from an anthology called *Sung Under the Silver Umbrella*. They, in turn, composed their own poems. Aurelia read poetry to both children from the time they were born, for she "believed that even babies responded to the cadence of poetry." In addition to children's verse, she recited "John Donne, Browning, Yeats, Tennyson, Coleridge, Rupert Brooke, Edna St. Vincent Millay, Sara Teasdale, T. S. Eliot and many others."[41] Sylvia's toddlerhood was intensely literary.

Aurelia referred to the work of Emily Dickinson as her "bible," but Plath remembered that her first literary frisson was Matthew Arnold's "The Forsaken Merman."[42] She loved the rhyme and cadences:

> Sand-strewn caverns, cool and deep,
> Where the winds are all asleep;
> Where the spent lights quiver and gleam;
> Where the salt weed sways in the stream;
> Where the sea beasts rang'd all round
> Feed in the ooze of their pasture-ground; . . .

The poem tells of a human wife who abandons her merman husband and children to pray at the village church on Easter Sunday. Despite the family's pleas, she never returns to the sea. "Children's voices should be dear / (Call once more) to a mother's ear; / Children's voices, wild with pain. / Surely she will come again." But she does not come—she remains on land, committed to God. "Come away, children, call no more," says the merman.

Sylvia, a young child, felt "gooseflesh" on her skin after Aurelia read her the poem. "I did not know what made it. I was not cold. Had a ghost passed over? No, it was the poetry. A spark flew off Arnold and shook me, like a chill. I wanted to cry; I felt very odd. I had fallen into a new way of being happy."[43] Plath would later use ocean imagery to explore the themes of parental abandonment and childhood grief in her 1958 poem "Full Fathom Five," in which the landlocked daughter is forsaken by her sea-dwelling, changeling father: "I walk dry on your kingdom's border / Exiled to no good. // Your shelled bed I remember. / Father, this thick air is murderous. / I would breathe water." The poem owes an obvious debt to Shakespeare's *The Tempest*, but its dramatic trajectory also suggests Arnold's "The Forsaken Merman."

Aurelia's ambitious reading program quickly yielded dividends. In 1937, at only five years old, Sylvia was reading and writing. She wrote her first poem, the two-lined "Thoughts," in December 1937: "When Christmas comes, smiles creep into my heart. / I'm always happiest when I'm singing a song or skipping along."[44] Inspired by the progressive ideas of Montessori and Fröbel, who eschewed rote learning, Aurelia enrolled Sylvia at a local progressive preschool, the Sunshine School. There, Sylvia made a lifelong friend in Ruth Freeman. Marion Freeman, Ruth's mother, became Aurelia's closest friend at this time; Sylvia later wrote that she became "a sort of 'second mother' to me."[45] Aurelia remembered that the "children practically lived together in one home or the other" and called the "relaxed, cheerful" Freeman home "a refuge in inclement weather when Otto was at home." (Ruth would eventually live with the Plaths for some months when Marion was hospitalized for a nervous breakdown.) Sylvia also became friendly with Ruth's brother David, who inspired the character of Ben in her short story "The Day Mr. Prescott Died." David, Ruth, and Sylvia spent hours playing at the beach, where Sylvia made up "romantic tales of far-fetched adventure."

Otto seemed to David "a stern, severe person" who preferred Sylvia to Warren. (Otto would purr "Seeel-vya" and bark "Wrn!") Another neighborhood playmate, William Sterling, remembered long afternoons sitting on the shore with Sylvia, half-watching the construction of Logan Airport as they hunted for horseshoe crabs and searched for shells. He remembered that at age eight or nine, he, along with Sylvia and a few other children, sneaked into the Reynolds Funeral Home, near their church, after choir practice. Inside, they saw a cadaver, which terrified them.[46] Most of the neighborhood kids, William said, were rough. Sylvia did not make any close friends besides himself and the Freemans—all bookish types.

Another regular visitor to the Plath household was Max Gaebler, the son of Otto's old friend Hans Gaebler. When Max entered college in Boston in 1937, Otto took him under his wing: he treated Max to lunch and joined him for walks around Faneuil Hall, initiating him "into the mysteries of academic life." Otto offered Max a "standing invitation" to come to Winthrop, and the Plath home became his refuge in the late 1930s and early '40s. The family seemed warm and loving to Max; he never forgot the sumptuous Thanksgiving feasts Aurelia and her mother prepared. He remembered Sylvia as "bright and sunny and eager" and was impressed by her vivid imagination and skillful drawings. During the hurricane of '38, he slept, slightly terrified, on the Plaths' sun porch, which faced the ocean. The next morning he walked around the neighborhood with Sylvia, Warren, Aurelia, Uncle Frank, Marion Freeman, and her children to take stock of the destruction. He photographed a delighted Sylvia climbing and playing on the fallen trees.

Otto frequently complained to Max about his health. In 1937–38, he "attributed it to age," but closer to 1940 "he decided he had cancer."[47] The rambunctious young children were not allowed to play in the house while Otto was working. Aurelia's short record of the 1938–39 year suggests tension: "Warren developed many allergies to foods, pollens, dust, etc. . . . he suffered two serious bouts with bronchial pneumonia and began having asthmatic attacks. Otto was steadily losing weight; his health continued to deteriorate. . . . I seldom knew an unbroken night's sleep."[48]

By 1938, Aurelia realized that her husband was seriously ill. Day after day, Otto came home from work so exhausted he could barely walk; he corrected papers and planned his classes while reclined on the den sofa, where he also ate when he was too weak to sit at the dinner table. Aurelia's attempts to persuade him to seek a doctor's opinion "brought on explosive outbursts of anger." Undeterred, she consulted a doctor in Winthrop about Otto's worsening condition, but the doctor refused to see him, saying it would be "both unwise and unethical" to do so without her husband's consent.[49] Aurelia did not have much choice but to watch helplessly as the tragedy unfolded. A call from a husband about a stubborn sick wife would have yielded a completely different outcome, of course. Otto's despondent arrogance and Germanic stoicism may have inspired Plath's Nazi comparison in "Daddy."

Aurelia shepherded the children out of the house when Otto was home and allowed them only a few minutes each night with their father before bedtime. She called theirs an "upstairs-downstairs" household—by separating the children from Otto she ensured that they would not bother him with "noisy play and squabbling."[50] Nor would his painful moans, caused by leg cramps, frighten them. The children ate apart from their mother and father at their own table upstairs in the playroom, for Otto found it "more restful" to eat without them. After dinner, the children came downstairs to perform for their father. This half hour, Aurelia recalled, was "the one time of the day we were together as a family for the last four years of my husband's life."[51] Sylvia, then, had no real spontaneous interaction with her father for four years. She would play the piano, draw, and recite poems she had memorized or written herself. Sometimes she would leave poems under his napkin at dinner. Her dying father was her first audience.

Aurelia endured the daily torment of watching her husband grow closer—as they now both assumed—to death. Meanwhile, she had to care for her young asthmatic son. In the age before the mass production of penicillin, the pneumonia he suffered from was one of the leading causes of death in children. Aurelia, possibly on the brink of losing both her husband and her son, tried to keep up appearances for her young daughter's sake. When the strain became too great, she would send Sylvia to the Schobers' house at Point Shirley. There, she mailed her six-year-old daughter letters praising her for good behavior and high marks, while trying to convey the gravity of the situation: "You are a lucky girl to be with grandmother. She takes better care of you than I could now. You see, Warren is still in bed and needs me all the time."[52] Aurelia's letters give the impression that she was writing from a great distance rather than two miles away. There are vague promises of reunion: "When he [Warren] is well, we shall all be together again. Then what happy times we shall have. When the weather gets warm, we shall play on the beach together"; "I love you, sweetheart, and I am looking forward to Easter Sunday. Probably we shall all be well together on that happy day."[53] The equivocal "probably" must have disappointed Sylvia. But caring for Warren and Otto took a heavy physical and emotional toll on Aurelia. She was treated for an ulcer not long after Otto's death.

Aurelia sent Sylvia poems and illustrated stories to cheer her up. One poem, about a doll named Rebecca, attempted to make Sylvia understand the demands and sacrifices of mothering:

I have a doll, Rebecca,
She's quite a little care
I have to press her ribbons
And comb her fluffy hair.

I keep her clothes all mended,
And wash her hands and face,
And make her frocks and aprons,
All trimmed in frills and lace.

I have to cook her breakfast,
And pet her when she's ill;
And telephone the doctor
When Rebecca has a chill.

Rebecca doesn't like that,
And says she's well and strong;
And says she'll try—oh! Very hard,
To be good all day long.

But when night comes, she's nodding;
So into bed we creep
And snuggle up together
And soon are fast asleep.

I have no other dolly,
For you can plainly see,
In caring for Rebecca,
I'm busy as can be![54]

When Sylvia herself became a mother, she would try to emulate this vision of "the angel in the house." But she would rail against it as an artist.

An April 1939 letter shows Aurelia straddling the fine line between pressure and encouragement. She congratulated Sylvia for receiving all A's on her report card, something that made her "a proud and happy mother." She explained the concept of clay modeling and asked if Sylvia could find curves in pictures at her grandmother's house: "In grandmother's living room is the black and white picture of an old lady sitting in a chair. She is the mother of the man who made the picture. He made such wonderful pictures that he was called an <u>artist</u>. He loved his mother so much, that he made this picture of

her."[55] Aurelia had unwittingly defined the concept of art as parental homage, an idea Plath later mocked in poems such as "The Disquieting Muses,"
"Medusa," "The Colossus," and "Daddy." Aurelia encouraged her daughter's artistic leanings, but she could be prescriptive. Though she often wrote
poems and drew pictures for Sylvia to color, sometimes her letters contained specific directives: "I am so proud of the fine coloring you are doing.
Try to write as nicely as you color. Try to write words instead of printing
them."[56]

Sylvia's own early letters from this time display a precocious ability with
words and spelling; at age seven, she was writing in cursive and using correct
grammar. Though her sentences are short, they possess a pleasing cadence
that suggests an ear already tuned to lyricism. In late February 1940, she
tried to make her father laugh, writing to him about a seagull that sat on an
ice-cake: "Isn't that funny (Ha Ha)." She reassured him that she was coming home soon, and asked, "Are you glad as I am?" But the bulk of this letter
is about writing itself. She told her father that she got ink on her fingers
that "never comes of! [sic]."[57] Already she described the medium of writing
as something that was *of* her, something permanent, but also a stain. A few
months later, she sent Otto a Father's Day card—his last—whose cover read,
"My Heart Belongs to Daddy." Inside, Sylvia wrote, "Happy Father's Day"
and "Raining Happiness" in neat cursive next to her drawing of an umbrella
in the rain.[58] The card was mailed from the Schobers' house; Sylvia was away
from home yet again.

A few early poems from this period survive. "My Mother and I," "Snow,"
"Pearls of Dew," and probably "A-a-choo" and "Dover" date from 1940.
Plath copied them, along with their dates of composition, into an illustrated
notebook now held at the Morgan Library.[59] She likely wrote them before
her father's death. At only seven and eight, she already understood the basic
techniques of rhyme and iambic meter. "Dover," for example, shows an
assured use of the limerick form:

> There was a young lady from Dover
> Who happened to sit on some clover
> The clover said, "Ow!"
> She made it a bow, this queer young lady of Dover.

"A-a-choo" also draws on the limerick form. The poem is intriguing for its
use of the phrase "achoo," which would provide a baseline rhyme in "Daddy"
many years later ("Barely daring to breathe or Achoo"). Critics have discussed the nursery rhyme cadences of "Daddy," but Plath may have drawn
on this earlier, half-remembered rhyme:

> I saw a lady with a muff.
> Her face was red as a powder puff.
> She carried a big, big box of snuff.
> That was made of every kind of stuff.
> A-a-choo

Though these early poems are nonsensical, they show the young Sylvia delighting in formal rhyme and meter—and "queer" women.

Other poems from 1940 in the same notebook show similar experiments with rhyme and meter. In "My Mother and I," Plath writes, "I love my mother / My mother loves me / And that is the way / That happy we be." In the second stanza the poet claims that she would prefer "A hug or kiss" from her mother, rather than candy, as a reward for her good behavior. The poem consists of two quatrains with an *a-b-c-b* rhyme, and shows Plath discovering iambic and dactylic meter. "Pearls of Dew (Chant)," in its variations and assured use of caesurae, achieves a relative sophistication that Plath's other 1940 poems lack:

> In the early morning
> When the dawn is breaking,
> Lacy cobweb scarves lie
> Strewn amongst the grass,
> Jeweled with pearly dew;
> Fairies must have used them
> Dancing 'neath the moon.

The influence of children's fairy tales is obvious here, but the voice of William Butler Yeats, whom Aurelia had read to Sylvia as a toddler, is also present. "Pearls of Dew" and other juvenilia show that Plath had begun assimilating Yeats's influence very early.

Another of the 1940 notebook poems is simply titled "Snow." Three different versions of this poem exist in early notebooks, suggesting that at an extremely young age Plath was beginning to experiment with revision. The first stanza of the earliest version reads:

> Snow, Snow sifting down
> Sifting quietly 'round the town
> Sending it a blanket of cold white
> To keep it warm every night.
> Snow, Snow
> Sifting down
> Sifting quietly 'round the town.

"Snow" is sentimental in the manner of a Currier and Ives print, yet its evocation of a town muffled within cold white depths is not strictly childlike; it suggests a familiar mournful element present in Plath's later works that depict white, frozen imagery. As in the famous ending of James Joyce's "The Dead," the snow both protects and entombs. The precocious young poet likely delighted in her paradoxical imagery—the blanket of cold snow keeping the town warm—as well as her use of repetition to achieve perfect trochaic tetrameter in the first stanza's last line. She had not yet learned formal metric terms and rules, but they came to her naturally.

Biographers have used the trope of addiction to describe Plath's literary ambition, writing that she was "addicted to achievement in the same way an alcoholic is hooked on booze." Or that her "competitive drive" was "pathological" and stemmed from "interior hollowness."[60] Such rhetoric trivializes Plath's commitment to her academic success and her literary vocation. (Male ambition is rarely described in this way.) These very early poems, and perhaps many others that have not survived, suggest that the origins of her art were not rooted in trauma or supplication, but in confidence, pleasure, and self-satisfaction. Writing was not something Sylvia did to please others, but to please herself—as necessary as breathing, as she would later remark in a 1962 interview.

———

ON A SUMMER MORNING in 1940, Otto stubbed his toe on his dresser while getting ready to teach. By the time he arrived home late that afternoon, it had turned black. Aurelia invited a doctor into the house on the pretext of examining the children.[61] The doctor surreptitiously examined Otto's urine, which revealed he did not have lung cancer but diabetes—a condition that could have been managed with insulin treatments had it been caught in time. But it had not been caught in time, and Otto Plath died less than three months later.

Plath has written about feeling "sealed off" from her childhood when her family left Winthrop for Wellesley, but she was also sealed off, at her grandparents' house, from her father's illness and her mother's struggles. Sylvia sensed the severity of the crisis during the late summer of 1940, when she asked to remain at home to help care for her father alongside the visiting nurse. As Aurelia recalled, "the friendly nurse cut down an old uniform for her and called Sylvia her 'assistant,' who could bring Daddy fruit or cool drinks now and then, along with the drawings she made for him, which gave him some cheer."[62] A photograph from this time shows Sylvia outside in her nurse's uniform, complete with apron and hat, smiling as she tends a baby doll. She later pasted this photo in her scrapbook. In her 1959 poem "The Colossus," a lonely, exiled daughter—half nun, half nurse—remains a caretaker to her father's monumental corpus statue.

Plath rendered this time in her autobiographical story "Among the Bumblebees," written during the fall of 1954. The protagonist, Alice Denway, describes her entomologist father as "proud and arrogant," a Nietzschean demi-god. Alice's mother, based on Aurelia, is "tender and soft like the Madonna pictures in Sunday school." Alice does not want to be tender and soft; she wants to be "strong and superior" like her father, who "did not like anyone to cry." Unlike her little brother, Warren (Plath used her brother's real name in the story), who is asthmatic and coddled, Alice is full of vitality and strength, able to withstand the full brunt of the sun that burns Warren's skin. Alice and her father make up the strong team, her mother and brother the weak one.

> Alice learned to sing the thunder song with her father: "Thor is angry. Thor is angry. Boom, boom, boom! Boom, boom, boom! We don't care. We don't care. Boom, boom, boom!" And above the resonant resounding baritone of her father's voice, the thunder rumbled harmless as a tame lion. . . . The swollen purple and black clouds broke open with blinding flashes of light, and the thunderclaps made the house shudder to the root of its foundations. But with her father's strong arms around her and the steady reassuring beat of his heart in her ears, Alice believed that he was somehow connected with the miracle of fury beyond the windows, and that through him, she could face the doomsday of the world in perfect safety.[63]

In truth, it was Aurelia who sang the "thunder song" to the children and soothed them during the hurricane of '38.[64] Yet in the story, it is the ghostly father who protects, who would always embody the Gothic sublimity of raging storms.

As Otto's health deteriorated, he became too weak to teach effectively. Aurelia hired someone to help with household chores during the day, then spent her evenings reading through Otto's biology and entomology books, "abstracting material to update his lectures, correcting German quizzes, and attending to his correspondence."[65] The Germanic values of order, stoicism, obedience, and hard work had morphed, in extremity, into a coping mechanism akin to denial; self-pity was a weakness not to be tolerated. Plath's later fetishization of health, strength, and vigor were likely rooted in her parents' conspiratorial denial of illness, which she witnessed as a girl.

But the time came when the truth could no longer be ignored. Soon after receiving his diabetes diagnosis, Otto contracted pneumonia and spent two weeks in the hospital. He returned home with a full-time nurse, an expense that added to the growing pile of medical bills (he had no health insurance). On the nurse's first day off, he suggested that Aurelia take the children to the beach for the afternoon. She did so, reluctantly, and returned to find her husband collapsed on the stairs. He was, according to Aurelia, "a fanatical gardener" and had mustered all his strength to plant bulbs in his yard.[66] Another doctor was summoned, Dr. Loder, who declared Otto's foot gangrened; the whole leg would have to be amputated. As the doctor left, he muttered, "How could such a brilliant man be so stupid."[67]

The amputation was performed on October 12, 1940, about two weeks before Sylvia's eighth birthday. The Boston University community rallied to lift Otto's spirits: colleagues covered his classes, former students donated blood, and the university president wrote, "We'd rather have you back at your desk with one leg than any other man with two."[68] But Otto fell into a depression after the surgery and refused to discuss learning to walk with a prosthesis. At 9:35 p.m. on November 5, 1940, shortly after Aurelia returned home from the hospital, he died of an embolism in the lung. The official cause of death was listed as diabetes mellitus and bronchial pneumonia, due to gangrene in the left foot.[69] During his last few hours alive, Otto said to Aurelia, "I don't mind the thought of death at all, but I would like to see how the children grow up."[70]

In *Letters Home*, Aurelia's story of Otto's illness is determinedly straightforward; duty and sacrifice animate the memoir rather than unseemly feelings of anger, guilt, or grief. Only once does Aurelia hint at her agony:

> In the middle of the night he called me and I found him feverish, shaking from head to foot with chills, his bed clothes soaked with perspiration. All the rest of that night I kept changing sheets, sponging his face, and holding his trembling hands. At one point he caught my hands, and holding on, said hoarsely, "God knows, why I have been so cussed!" As tears streamed down my face, I could only think, "All this needn't have happened; it needn't have happened."[71]

If Aurelia had disobeyed her husband and found a doctor willing to treat the reluctant patient, Otto might have lived. Later, Sylvia would secretly blame Aurelia for standing by while Otto committed what she saw as his slow suicide. Otto became, as Sylvia's college boyfriend Richard Sassoon remembered, "a highly charged legend for her."[72]

AURELIA WAITED UNTIL the morning to tell the children that Otto had died. She found Sylvia already awake and reading in her bed. "She looked at me sternly for a moment, then said woodenly, 'I'll never speak to God again!' I told her that she did not need to attend school that day if she'd rather stay at home. From under the blanket she had pulled over her head came her muffled voice, 'I *want* to go to school.'"[73] Sylvia's reaction demonstrated equal measures of rebellion and conformity—the very traits that continued to drive her behavior throughout the rest of her life. In the young girl's rejection of God, there is an echo of the bold, assertive *Ariel* voice that would later mock patriarchal ideologies and symbols of power. That voice dates to this moment of rupture. Yet, in a pivot that would become increasingly habitual, she composed herself for her schoolfellows, perhaps seeking solace and connection in the ordinary. But it was a difficult day for Sylvia, who came home from school crying and upset. There were playground taunts about the prospect of a stepfather. That afternoon Sylvia made Aurelia sign a note promising she would never remarry, which for years she kept folded in the back of her diary. Aurelia kept her promise, though she later assured her daughter the decision had nothing to do with her vow.

On the afternoon of November 9, Otto was buried on Azalea Path in Winthrop's town cemetery. Aurelia and her family, as well as friends and colleagues from Boston University, attended his funeral at Winthrop's United Methodist Church. Aurelia kept the children home. A brief obituary ran in the *Winthrop Review* and *The Boston Globe*. Otto's colleagues at Boston University published a moving tribute to him in the university magazine, citing the international impact of *Bumblebees and Their Ways* and recalling his "loyalty to the highest ideals of science, his genuine frankness in discussion of any subject, and the sincerity of his beliefs. . . . His generous, sincere, and energetic nature won him a lasting place in the affection and regard of those privileged to work with him." The university had lost "a worthy teacher and a great scholar."[74] Otto's gravestone, number 1123, was a modest slab laid flat on the ground. Years later, when Sylvia finally visited the grave, she would have difficulty locating it. The small stone angered her, but Aurelia insisted that Otto would have wanted something unassuming. Besides, he did not have a pension, and most of his small life insurance policy of $5,000 went to medical bills and funeral costs. There was no money for a larger memorial.

Aurelia's stoicism in the face of Otto's death implied that personal tragedy was not something to be indulged. One had to move on; one could not yield. In *The Bell Jar*, Plath wrote of Esther Greenwood,

Then I remembered I had never cried for my father's death.

My mother hadn't cried either. She had just smiled and said what

a merciful thing it was for him he had died, because if he had lived he
would have been crippled and an invalid for life, and he couldn't have
stood that, he would rather have died than had that happen.[75]

Aurelia claimed that concern for her children's fragile emotional state caused
her to hide her grief, and keep them away from their father's funeral.

> What I intended as an exercise in courage for the sake of my children
> was interpreted years later by my daughter as indifference. "My mother
> never had time to mourn my father's death." I had vividly remembered a
> time when I was a little child, seeing my mother weep in my presence and
> feeling that my whole personal world was collapsing. *Mother*, the tower
> of strength, my one refuge, *crying*! It was this recollection that compelled
> me to withhold my tears until I was alone in bed at night.[76]

As a Wellesley neighbor and family friend remembered, "There was no
dwelling upon its effects. . . . If the going was difficult at home, there was no
complaining."[77]

Aurelia was the sole breadwinner now. "Here I was, a widow with two
young children to support. I had a man's responsibilities, but I was making a single woman's salary."[78] She began substitute teaching for $25 a week
at Braintree High School, where she taught three German classes and two
Spanish classes each day; her commute necessitated a predawn departure.
Aurelia's parents moved in to help with child care. Resolutely pragmatic,
Aurelia tried to make the best of a tragedy. Her parents were "healthy,
optimistic, strong in their faith, and loved the children dearly. My young
brother, only thirteen years Sylvia's senior, and my sister would be close to
us—the children would have a sense of family and be surrounded with care
and love."[79] But Otto's death was financially and emotionally devastating for
the small family. Sylvia later told Dr. Beuscher that from then on Aurelia
was a "beaten down woman constantly emphasizing poverty and sacrifice for
intellect."[80]

Plath's unpublished journals from the 1940s do not contain a single mention of Otto. She later wrote that after he died, "those first nine years of
my life sealed themselves off like a ship in a bottle—beautiful, inaccessible,
obsolete, a fine, white flying myth."[81] She never discussed her father with
her best friend, Betsy Powley, with whom she shared everything throughout the 1940s.[82] Betsy eventually asked how Otto had died and received a
vague response about how he had lost a leg to tuberculosis. She never asked
again, and Sylvia never offered more details.[83] One of Sylvia's Smith College
friends remembered her saying only that she had loved Otto, that he had

been a "wonderful father," and that he had died.[84] But Plath wrote about him, many times, starting with "Dirge," later retitled "Lament," when she was a student at Smith. It is the first surviving elegy she wrote for her father:

> The sting of bees took away my father
> who walked in a swarming shroud of wings
> and scorned the tick of the falling weather.
> . . . .
> He counted the guns of god a bother,
> laughed at the ambush of angels' tongues,
> and scorned the tick of the falling weather.
>
> O ransack the four winds and find another
> man who can mangle the grin of kings:
> the sting of bees took away my father
> who scorned the tick of the falling weather.[85]

In this villanelle, Plath attempts to bring technical order to chaotic loss. The speaker mythologizes her father as all-powerful, arrogant, and proud—yet he is "taken away" by a bee sting. The image is emasculating; the father's arrogance is punished, just as Otto Plath's was in real life. Sylvia may have been justified in thinking that it was not diabetes that killed her father, but arrogance—his false belief that his own self-diagnosis was more accurate than a doctor's. The tender, elegiac music of "Lament" contains a subtext of anger. "The Colossus" and "Daddy," too, would contain competing voices, one lacerating and scornful, the other grief-stricken.

Otto's death did not set Sylvia on poetry's path, but it may have exacerbated her chances of suicide. The most significant recent study on the effect of parental death on children, which followed nearly 200,000 bereaved Scandinavian children for forty years, found that "Parental death in childhood is, irrespective of cause, associated with an increased long-term risk of suicide."[86] Bereaved children's vulnerability to suicide remained high for twenty-five years after the parent's death.[87] Ted Hughes's intuitive sense that Otto's ghost lay behind his wife's depression and eventual suicide may have been partly correct. In another study on the subject, the authors found that the more severe repercussions of sudden parental loss could be mitigated by therapy and counseling during a "critical window of intervention" that occurred shortly after the parent's death.[88] When Max Gaebler joined the family for Thanksgiving just a few weeks after Otto's death, he found the family "muted," yet the feast proceeded as usual.[89] Aurelia's strategy of protecting her children from grief and mourning may have been counterproductive.

Sylvia's English friend Elizabeth Compton Sigmund, whose father left her family when she was a small child, speculated that she and Sylvia both "felt a burden of responsibility for our mother's well-being."[90] The young Sylvia wanted to assuage her mother's grief by being a good daughter. Academic success came easily to her, and winning prizes and publishing poetry was a sure way to win approval. But Plath was at heart an iconoclast who longed for personal and political freedom. The debt she owed her mother clashed with her instinct for self-individuation. Sylvia would struggle all her life to reconcile these dueling instincts, which sometimes made her feel, as she put it, schizophrenic.

By 1961, when Plath wrote *The Bell Jar*, with its merciless portrait of Aurelia, the mother-daughter dynamic had morphed into something more destructive. Letters of mutual reassurance across the Atlantic took on the character of an arms race. A Smith friend recalled that Aurelia seemed like a "stage mother" who pushed her daughter to fulfill her own unrealized creative longings.[91] Another friend who knew Sylvia in London at the end of her life, Suzette Macedo, said that Sylvia always referred extravagantly to Aurelia as her "demon mother."[92] Suzette was astonished and disturbed by the deference Sylvia showed Aurelia in her letters, when they were published. She could not understand how the same person who had railed against her mother so bitterly could have written those sweet, cheerful notes. Ted Hughes thought he understood. In an unpublished poem about *The Bell Jar*, he suggested that his wife's emotional conflicts were forged in the crucible of grief:

> Her mother said: what is past—is past.
> Her mother said: do not mourn: onward.
> Life is for living, Earth is beautiful.
> Do not be unhappy. For you
> There is only happiness: look:
> I will show you happiness because
> I cannot bear you to be unhappy
> Because I love you so much.
>
> . . . .
>
> And the I stood, the pale girl stood there
> And could not bear to see her mother unhappy
> She loved her so much. So she obeyed.
> When her mother laughed, she too laughed.
> When her mother said "work," she worked so hard

Her schoolmates were alarmed.
When her mother said: This is the perfect
Way to be, she was so perfect that—
All exclaimed: this girl is exceptional.
This is how she kept her mother happy.

And she said to her brother: we must never
Let Mummy be unhappy: unhappiness
Is the feeling none of us must feel
Because it is the abyss, where Daddy lies.
Let us do everything to keep her happy
And never speak of Daddy & never be sad.[93]

3

The Shadow

Wellesley, 1940–1945

Sylvia Plath came of age during a harrowing decade marked by the twin apocalyptic horrors of world war and genocide. When she was twelve, a six-page spread of Nazi atrocities appeared in the May 7, 1945, issue of *Life* magazine; three months later, she learned with all the world that nuclear bombs had been dropped on Hiroshima and Nagasaki. Although she filled her diaries with schoolgirl descriptions of middle-class comforts, the decade's horror left its mark on her strongest work: her *Ariel* poems are seared with the imagery of the Holocaust and the bomb.

Plath's childhood friend William Sterling remembered that coastal Winthrop "was like an armed camp" in 1940. There were three forts, and the shoreline was blacked out at night. He and Sylvia used to sit on a sea-wall at Point Shirley and watch the Navy convoys form in the afternoon. There were air-raid drills and military target practices. Sometimes house windows shattered from the great guns' reverberations. The atmosphere was one of danger and anticipation.[1]

Aurelia wrote that the period after the United States entered the Second World War was a "tense time" for the family because of their Germanic heritage.[2] Only one generation removed from the hardships of old-world poverty and new-world discrimination, the shadow of persecution was never far behind Plath. Two of her short stories, set in Winthrop at the beginning of the Second World War—"The Shadow" (1959) and "Superman and Paula Brown's New Snowsuit" (1955)—capture the mood of fear and apprehension within the Plath-Schober household in the early 1940s. "The threat of war was seeping in everywhere," Plath wrote. "There was no escape. It invaded our radio programs and our games."[3] It invaded school, too: in "Superman and Paula Brown's New Snowsuit," crying children are herded into a dark basement of "cold black stone" during air raid drills, where they are told to put pencils between their teeth "so the bombs wouldn't make us bite our tongues by mistake."[4] In both stories, neighborhood children bully young female narrators on account of their Germanic backgrounds. Meanwhile, torture scenes from a newsreel about Japanese prison camps replay over and over in the girls' nightmares. They begin to fear that they or members of their family will be sent away to a prison camp. What happened to Japanese Americans during the war is well known, but more than eleven thousand Germans and German Americans—including American citizens—were also detained during World War II. As U-boat activity increased along the Atlantic corridor, those living on the East Coast were most vulnerable. A detention center in East Boston, which bordered Winthrop, was eventually filled beyond capacity with German detainees.

Sadie, the young protagonist of "The Shadow," struggles to comprehend such xenophobia in language that evokes the plight of Jews in Germany in the 1930s and '40s, as well as the McCarthy witch hunts that were in full swing when Plath wrote the story in 1959:

> I had an ingrained sense of the powers of good protecting me: my parents, the police, the F. B. I., the President, the American Armed Forces, even those symbolic champions of Good from a cloudier hinterland—the Shadow, Superman, and the rest. Not to mention God himself. Surely, with these ranked around me, circle after concentric circle, reaching to infinity, I had nothing to fear. Yet I was afraid. Clearly, in spite of my assiduous study of the world, there was something I had not been told; some piece of the puzzle I did not have in hand.[5]

The "mystery" is solved by a neighborhood child who blurts out, "it's because your father's German." Soon after, Sadie's German father prepares to depart for a detention camp "out West."[6] Plath's fantasy of Jewishness in "Daddy" may be partly based on her family's experiences of being singled out, questioned, scapegoated, and shunned in wartime America. As she wrote in her 1958 notes for "The Shadow," "Look up German concentration, I mean American detention camps."[7]

Aurelia worried about her children's welfare in working-class Winthrop amid rising anti-German sentiment. David Freeman remembered that there were not many families of German or Austrian descent in Winthrop; the only such family he knew had a swastika flag raised on their flagpole by "neighborhood kids."[8] Aurelia was also concerned that Winthrop's damp climate was exacerbating Warren's bronchial ailments. Determined to improve her family's prospects, she devoted herself to finding more stable employment that would fund a move. After teaching Spanish and German as a substitute at Braintree High School, in 1941 she finally earned a full-time position at Winthrop Junior High School. There she taught ninth-grade English and managed most of the school's finances. Although she now had a $1,600 yearly salary and a coveted state pension, she was exhausted by her teaching and administrative duties—when she left, her job had to be shared by three men. Her ulcer worsened.

Aurelia's luck changed in the summer of 1942, when she accepted an instructorship at the Boston University College of Practical Arts and Letters, her alma mater, teaching medical secretarial procedures. Betsy Powley Wallingford, who knew Aurelia then, felt that she "could have had a better job . . . she was capable of more than that."[9] Yet at the time Aurelia thought the offer was "providential." Though the new job did not then include a pension, it was a step up in money and prestige. She vowed to make the course "fascinating" and took biology classes at the Harvard Extension School to strengthen her credentials. Her salary allowed her to buy a foothold in a more affluent suburb.[10]

Aurelia chose Wellesley. The Nortons, another Boston University family, already lived there and would provide a warm welcome, while Aurelia's sister Dot lived in neighboring Weston. With its top-rated public schools, bucolic parks, easy proximity to Boston, and town-funded scholarships to Wellesley College, it was an obvious—if ambitious—choice. Above all, Wellesley held the promise of civility. There, Aurelia hoped, her children would not be called "spy-face" and pushed off the school bus.

By merging households, Aurelia and her parents soon realized they could save money and provide a more stable life for the children. Grammy Schober would handle child care, housekeeping, cooking, and driving, while Grampy supplemented Aurelia's income by waiting tables at the Brookline Country Club, where he boarded during the week. Aurelia sold the Winthrop house at a loss in the fall of 1942 and bought a six-room colonial at 26 Elmwood Road, a "modest" section of Wellesley just a short distance from the town center.[11] The street was lined with small, well-kept colonials, a Baptist church, and acres of woods. The Plaths' white clapboard house had black shutters, a garage, a breezeway, and a quarter-acre yard. It was smaller than the Winthrop house, but its corner lot gave the setting a more expansive feel.[12] On the first floor there was a living room, dining room, kitchen, screened-in porch, and a bedroom for Warren; upstairs, a bathroom, a bedroom for the Schobers, and another bedroom that Sylvia shared with her mother. Sylvia would spend many afternoons reading high in the backyard's apple tree, the next best thing to a room of her own. She called the new house "cosy" and "felt mingled regrets and anticipation as we bade good-by to the Freeman's [*sic*]."[13] They left Winthrop on October 26, one day before her tenth birthday. Later, Plath spoke of the move with sadness, saying that it sealed her off from her father and the sea. But it also provided a fresh start, and welcome respite from schoolyard whispers about a dead parent.

Although Sylvia had been enrolled in the sixth grade in Winthrop, Aurelia decided to keep her back a year when they moved. Wellesley's school system was more rigorous, and Aurelia felt that her daughter would be challenged by the new curriculum. During her first day of school, Sylvia sat across the aisle from a girl with thick braids, just like hers. Her name was Betsy Powley, and from that day through high school, the two were inseparable. Sylvia also made new friends through Girl Scouts, and still saw Ruth Freeman regularly. If she missed her old life, she sensed the privileges of the new: supportive teachers, hardworking peers, a well-stocked town library, top-notch recreation programs, and the possibility of a scholarship to Wellesley College. Sylvia was hungry for all that the town of Wellesley had to offer; but, through the years, she would feel increasingly constricted by its culture of gentility.

BY THE TIME the family moved, Sylvia had been writing poems for about five years. She began sending out her work for publication at age eight, an act that has struck some as an early sign of a "pathological" obsession with achievement.[14] Yet the Brontë sisters and Virginia Woolf, among others, began "publishing" their work as children in homemade newspapers. Plath simply sent her work to the children's page of an actual newspaper. Later, she would try to sell her writing and artwork in order to avoid the cleaning and babysitting jobs she relied on for spending money. When she wrote in her 1944 diary of her attempt to win an art contest sponsored by the *Boston Herald*, she noted that the $2 prize was twenty times her weekly allowance of ten cents.

Sylvia did not have to wait long for public recognition. On August 10, 1941, nine months after her father's death, she published her first poem (titled, simply, "Poem") on the "Good Sport" page of the Sunday *Boston Herald*. Plath began her submission with a note to the editor, which was published with the poem: "Dear Editor, I have written a short poem about what I see and hear on hot summer nights":

> Hear the crickets chirping
> In the dewy grass
> Bright little fireflies
> Twinkle as they pass.[15]

Not yet nine, Sylvia was already able to write in near-perfect trochaic trimeter. She was proud of her achievement and later pasted the newspaper clipping in her high school scrapbook. That year, she expanded "Poem" into a longer verse, which she titled "My House." The stanza she added at the beginning shows dexterity with iambic meter: "I have a little house / Between two trees / And there the birdies always sing / Among the whispering leaves."[16] The Yeatsian image of "whispering leaves" seems a purposeful, slightly unsettling counterweight to the cheerful singing birds. Her ear was already tuned to the darker cadences of Romanticism.[17]

In March 1943, Aurelia left her family for a short stay in the hospital on account of her increasingly troublesome ulcer. Sylvia sent her mother highly graded schoolwork and several short poems—many about fairies. Fairies played an important role in Sylvia's young imagination. In the mid-1940s she began working on a fairy story that was supposed to be her first novel. She planned the book out in chapters and frequently returned to it over the years as the project, which had several different titles, grew in scope. (By 1946 it comprised nine chapters and twenty-six typed pages.) In the first chapter of the first version of the novel, which Plath subsequently titled *Stardust*, the heroine, Nancy, is a Messiah figure chosen by fairies:

> "I am Star," she began. "Once, in every generation, my Queen chooses one child on earth who has the strongest belief in fairy magic, and then selects one out of her band of fairies to show this child that magic, good magic, still exists in the world today. I am the fairy who has been given the power to take you on many travels to places that most humans are sure do not exist. But first I must clear away the invisible film over your eyes that prevents you from seeing the fairy miracles that happen each day!" Thereupon the fairy passed her tiny gold wand across Nancy's forehead. Before Nancy could utter a word, Star gave her a smiling nod, and faded away in the air.[18]

The fairy's act recalls Plato's Allegory of the Cave, which the young Sylvia might have known. She was discovering her talent, learning that her ability to create art gave her imaginative access to other worlds.

In a 1943 letter to Aurelia, Sylvia described a book she had recently read, *A Fairy to Stay* (1929), by Margaret Beatrice Lodge. The book is about a motherless young girl raised by her two strict aunts while her father is away in East Africa. In Plath's synopsis, she calls it "the nicest book I have ever read" and displays an emerging fascination with the themes of exile, revenge, rebellion, purity, and the supernatural. Her description is worth quoting, as it is the earliest surviving example of Plath's literary criticism. She describes the plot of a girl who gets into trouble when her strict aunts find her reading a book about fairies. She cuts off her braids in protest:

> When the aunts came in her room and found out they were horrified and told her to look in the mirror. Her hair was all straight and long on one side and short on the other for punishment she would have to go like that for one week. Sending her out in the garden they decided that disipline [*sic*] was the best thing they could do. Out side the little girl rubbed her eyes and looked about what did she see but a fairy! The fairy asked her what was the matter, Pamela (for that was her name) poured out her story. The fairy told her to shut her eyes and she would dry clean her, she touched Pamelas [*sic*] hair, it began to curl, she touched her dirty tear-stained face it grew pink and clean she touched her wrinkled dress, it grew clean and white. . . . The whole book is about the fairy and the little girl trying (comicly [*sic*]) to disipline [*sic*] the aunts.[19]

The young heroine of *A Fairy to Stay*, like Sylvia, has lost a parent and is being raised by extended family members. Sylvia suggests that the book is a comic tale, yet her summary focuses on Pamela's loneliness, her rebellious reading, and her shocking decision to chop off her hair in an effort to subvert her aunts' authority. Embedded within this seemingly innocent children's story is a blueprint for feminist rebellion that resonated with Plath.

Plath's 1943 poem "Angelic Girls," written when she was ten or eleven, also uses the image of disheveled hair to emphasize girls' rebellious nature:

> O we're two little girls
> We never comb our tangled curls,
> We disobey our mothers
> And tease our younger brothers,
> O we're angelic little girls.[20]

This is perhaps the earliest poetic example of Plath's "other" voice: the seething, private, caustic voice—so at odds with idealized feminine decorousness—that would eventually draw millions of readers to *The Bell Jar* and the *Ariel* poems. In her real life, however, Sylvia was a dutiful and diligent daughter. In a January 1943 letter to Aurelia, written during one of her hospital stays, Sylvia reported that she had been "very good" with "no mishaps": "In music I did the fingering just like you told me to. And I kept saying to myself, 'This is what mother would want me to do' so I got along very well."[21]

In July 1943, Aurelia was again in the hospital because of another gastric hemorrhage. Though Sylvia was just ten, her mother felt she was ready for sleep-away camp, which would give Grammy Schober a break from full-time child care and distract Sylvia from her mother's illness. Before Sylvia left for camp, she stayed with her aunt Dot and uncle Joe in nearby Weston for a few days. While there, she found thirty cents and bought herself paper doll books of Rita Hayworth and Hedy Lamarr, though she vowed to spend the rest "on a defense stamp."[22] She then traveled by train to Moultonville, New Hampshire, where she began the last leg to Camp Weetamoe on Lake Ossipee.

Camp Weetamoe was founded in 1934 as a Girl Scout camp that catered to middle- and upper-class girls from Cambridge and Boston.[23] It operated in typical Girl Scout fashion—there were bugle calls in the morning, swimming, arts and crafts, hayrides, blueberry picking, hikes, and campfires after dinner. Sylvia was put into the "Oehda" unit, and was pleased to have a view of both Lake Ossipee and the mountains from her tent. Though she told her mother she was having fun, she did not quite understand what was happening: "Am I going to camp for a month?" she wrote home.[24]

In her letters, she stressed her happiness, and her appetite. "For breakfast I had 1 orange, a bowl of rice krispies, a cup of milk, and a cup of cocoa. . . . For lunch I had two helpings of corn, ham and beans a glass of water and the biggest helping of raspberry jello. . . . For supper I had 2 pieces of bread with chopped beef, salad, prunes and milk."[25] Sylvia's long, descriptive menus, sent from summer camp from 1943 through 1946, suggest that she was trying hard to gain weight and to reassure an anxious mother in the midst of wartime rationing. (Betsy Powley Wallingford said Sylvia simply had an enormous appetite and "a fabulous metabolism.")[26] After the hardships of the 1930s and 1940s, curves were in. To look thin was to look like one of the "refugees" in Europe Sylvia sometimes spoke of in her diary; she longed to "fill out." Five months into her seventh-grade year, for example, she made herself an apron at school with a wide girth and long belt. She showed it to her teacher, who said, "My dear! You'll never grow that fat." Sylvia drew a plump picture of herself on the page with the caption "How I'd love to be able to wear it."[27]

Most of the girls at Camp Weetamoe came from more affluent families. Sylvia, whose grandfather waited tables at a country club, would have felt her own class difference keenly. In one postcard, she reported that the girls in her tent were, despite their relative privilege, "not well brought up. . . . The new girls say 'ain't' 'youse' kids, 'guys' 'horsebackin.' It just hurts my ears. I long for my familys [sic] soft, sweet talk."[28] Her snobbish remarks about her tentmates may have been her way of preempting whispers about her own background. She felt that Camp Weetamoe had matured her, as she told her mother: "When I come home you will see a great difference in my caracter [sic]."[29]

Sylvia began her sixth-grade year in September 1943. Her homeroom teacher, Miss Norris, recognized her intelligence early on; when Sylvia did not raise her hand to answer a difficult question, Miss Norris would gently chide her, for she knew she was "smart."[30] She read the *Odyssey* to the class and introduced them to the opera *Aida*. (This was not the only opera Sylvia heard that year: she received an introduction to Wagner when her mother gave her *Der Ring des Nibelungen* as an early birthday gift, and she also spent time listening to *Carmen*.)[31] When Sylvia asked for more work, her teacher cheerfully obliged: "After arithmetic I went up to Miss Norris and said, 'I'm going to make you give me a book report right this minute.' So she did."[32]

That Christmas, Sylvia's uncle Frank, who was in the Army, came all the way from Spokane, Washington, with his wife Louise and his Army buddy Gibby Wyer. Sylvia found Wyer's stories fascinating and wrote about them in her only diary entry from the week after Christmas 1943:

> He was in the Medical Corp in Algeria and has traveled through Egypt, he was in Tripoli when it fell and was in the campaign to chase Rommel out of Africa. He was with Montgomery's 8th army. They went from El-Almein to Tunis. He also brought many things that he found there such as a German bayonet, a German pistol, a German camera, a German belt, a German helmet, some German binoculars.[33]

Sylvia had an uncle in the forces and relatives in Germany and Poland. For her, the war was not a distant distraction. Sometimes, it landed on her doorstep.

Sylvia began 1944 with a "special resolution to be nice to everyone and make people think I am not stuck up."[34] Yet there is only one diary entry that year that hints at ostracization. In October 1944 at Sunday school, she reported, "The girls were an ordeal they were so rude but mother took care of them and put them in their place. After she went home I rode around on my bike and gave my knee a hard bang. I have had a hard day—tired."[35] In general, though, Sylvia's diary does not give the impression of someone who suffered, as her biographer Anne Stevenson has written, from "social isolation" as a girl.[36] Quite the opposite: in the mid-1940s she had a solid set of girlfriends—Betsy Powley, Marcia Egan, Prissy Steele, and Barbara McKay—with whom she spent almost every afternoon.

Sylvia also became close to Perry Norton, who lived in nearby Wellesley Hills and has said that he and Sylvia "were like siblings without attendant rivalry."[37] He and his brother Dick would play formative roles in Sylvia's life and art. There were three Norton boys in all: Perry, who was Sylvia's age; Dick, two years older; and David, born in 1944.[38] Sylvia attended several dances with Perry in junior high and high school, but she nearly married Dick, who inspired the character of Buddy Willard in *The Bell Jar*. Their mother, Mildred, had been a student in Otto's German class before she graduated with a BA from Boston University in 1925. In 1927 she married William Norton, who completed a PhD in history at Yale while she finished her MA in English at Radcliffe. When William joined Boston University's history department, Mildred and Aurelia got to know each other through the Faculty Wives' Club; William recalled meeting Sylvia when she was two or three at a faculty Christmas party. The two families shared similar values centered on intellectual achievement and service to others rather than material wealth.[39] William Norton called his an "incorrigibly 'egghead' and 'square' family" and said that his three boys were raised to "study hard and earn their way through college by scholarships and term-time and summer jobs, then go after some kind of graduate or professional degree."[40] (All three Norton boys obliged—Perry and Dick received MDs and David a PhD.) Both families attended the Unitarian church in Wellesley Hills, where Aurelia and William taught Sunday school. After Otto's death, when Aurelia decided to relocate to Wellesley, it was partly because the Nortons lived there; she could depend on Mildred Norton—like her, an educated woman with a master's degree in English—for support and friendship.

Mildred, who did not believe women should work outside the home, took charge of the domestic front.[41] She could be more confrontational than her husband, who was quiet and reserved.[42] Plath ridiculed Mrs. Norton's conservatism in *The Bell Jar*, but in the 1940s she enjoyed spending time with her after school as she waited for Perry, who later speculated that Sylvia may have been attracted to the stability of his home because there was a mother present, which was not the case at 26 Elmwood Road.[43] Over time, the Nortons and the Plaths grew so close that the children began to think of themselves as "cousins," and they addressed each other's mothers as "aunt." Though Mildred Norton encouraged Sylvia to date Perry, she instead fell in love with Dick, a move that would have great consequences both for her art and for the Norton family.[44]

Perry, who eventually became a doctor and a practicing Quaker, was bright and intellectually curious. He remembered the first time he met Sylvia at her home in Wellesley, where they played a board game together and she complimented him on his winning strategy. "Right off the bat it cemented a mutual fondness," he said. Sylvia attended dancing lessons with him and often stopped by his house after school to talk. "I was a little bit overawed by her," he remembered, "so I didn't fancy ever being somebody who would be her suitor." He feigned "disgust" when others played kissing games at parties they attended, and Sylvia admired his haughty remove.[45] In February 1946 he took her to a dance at the Unitarian church, where they deflected emotion with talk of "comets and planets."[46]

Betsy Powley was Sylvia's closest friend during most of her adolescence. "She lived half the time at my house and I lived half the time at her house," said Betsy. "We built tree huts in the woods and wrote poetry together."[47] Betsy, who lived just a short walk from Elmwood Road, came from a more affluent family; her father worked for an oil company, and they vacationed at a country farmhouse in East Colrain, Massachusetts, near the Vermont border. But Sylvia never felt judged by the Powleys. Her extraordinary intelligence might have made her a target of envious teasing in the schoolyard, but her friendship with Betsy was free from competition; together they enjoyed all the regular adolescent rites—movies, snowball fights, Girl Scout camp, dances, Spin the Bottle, Truth or Dare. Sylvia was happiest with Betsy on winter days when they spent hours making snow forts and sledding. "Coasting" was pure exhilaration: "The hill rose shining, white and vacant. We flew down and the stinging wind brought tears to our eyes. It was glorious!!"[48] She taught herself to ski at Betsy's farm, where she often spent her February vacations. Skiing, with its possibilities of flight and fall, became an important metaphor in *The Bell Jar*, in which Esther feels "saintly and thin and essential as the blade of a knife" while she barrels down a ski slope before breaking her leg.[49] Betsy helped make this feeling of transcendence possible, for she was connected to Sylvia's love of nature, physical activity, humor, and mischief.

Betsy also encouraged Sylvia to indulge her innate but suppressed cynicism. (As Sylvia wrote one day after Girl Scouts, "I tried <u>so</u> hard to be serene, quiet, etc but, as usual, didn't succeed.")[50] The two shared "convulsions of laughter" in church as they quietly mocked their pastor, and "laughed silently" behind their art teacher's back.[51] Sylvia was already developing the skepticism of institutional authority that later marked her work; she and Betsy read poems to each other "overexpressively and overgegesturingly" [*sic*] and decided that their favorite word was "fuzzbuttons."[52] (Nearly twenty years later, Plath described falling into fits of laughter with a female friend after reading her poem "Daddy" aloud.)

Sylvia thrived in one-on-one relationships with girls who appreciated, as her friend Pat O'Neil Pratson later put it, her "tremendous hunger and love for life" and her desire "to expand in everything."[53] Later, at Smith, Plath's intense studying habits and competitive nature made it harder for her to cultivate close friendships, and she often put up a protective front. Her sense of inhabiting two selves—one interior, one exterior—would deepen there. Her old Wellesley friend Frank Irish recalled feeling disoriented on a date with Sylvia while she was at Smith: "she had become an urbane sophisticate that she was not when she was in high school."[54] Sylvia needed female confidantes like Betsy and Ruth who could bring her out of herself and, at the same time, allow her to *be* herself, insecurities and all. Without such a connection, her mental health would suffer. As she wrote to a Smith friend who transferred to a new college in January 1951, "I need so to love a person—be it girl or boy, friend or enemy. And without being able to, I sort of dry up."[55]

Sylvia would at times feel pressure to neutralize her passionate personality to avoid alienating potential friends and dates. At Smith she was ridiculed for studying on Saturday nights, while at Cambridge she suspected that other girls gossiped about her academic intensity. Years later, in her radio play *Three Women*, she wrote in the voice of a mother speaking to her newborn: "I do not will him to be exceptional. / It is the exception that interests the devil." Plath's spectacular intelligence may have felt like a burden at times, especially for a young woman who wanted to fit in during an age that prized conformity. As America moved into the McCarthy era, the words "artist" and "communist" were not infrequently linked. By the mid-fifties, when Sylvia graduated from Smith, there was even less tolerance for subversive artistic expression—especially from women. The opening lines of *The Bell Jar*, which conjure up the specter of the Rosenbergs' electrocution during the summer of 1953, leave little doubt as to Plath's view of this suffocating time. Her search for artistic freedom would finally take her away from America altogether, to England, where she found a husband who was deeply contemptuous of American materialism and "normality."

SYLVIA'S FORMULAIC DIARY ENTRIES for 1944, her sixth-grade year, bear almost no resemblance to the vivid, literary entries of her 1950s journals. She thrived on her routines and was unhappy when she was sick and had to stay home from school.[56] (On her first day back at school after the Christmas holiday she admitted, "I really like it more than vacation sometimes.")[57] She often recounted her after-school activities, usually Girl Scouts or outdoor play with her friends: "In the afternoon I went over to Marcia's with Betsy to cut out cartoons for our red cross badge in Scouts."[58]

"Playing Army" was a frequent pastime, as snowballs could serve as grenades. When it was too cold to play outside, she read in bed or played cards and dolls with her girlfriends. In the warmer weather she rode her bike, walked through the woods, and swam at Morses Pond and Winthrop beaches. There were large family dinners, shopping trips with her mother and aunts, outings to the Arnold Arboretum, the Museum of Natural History, and the movies. But what dominates Sylvia's 1944 diary is her record of academic achievement. A student at Boston University's School of Education administered the Stanford-Binet IQ test to students at Plath's school during her sixth-grade year and remembered that Sylvia received a score of "about 160," which she classified as "genius" range.[59]

Sylvia enjoyed taking the test, and she probably learned of her high IQ. She was eager to earn the small black-and-white certificates awarded by the Massachusetts Department of Education for reading five books at a time; her goal was to earn the coveted Honor Certificate given only to those who had read twenty-four books in a year—a goal she achieved easily.[60] She read, on average, three books a week, most of them from the Wellesley Public Library. Reading for pleasure in her bedroom, on her porch, or up in the apple tree was a form of meditation akin to her languorous afternoons in the sun. In her 1944 poem "Enchantment," written in the language of biblical redemption, books provide a gateway to a rarefied life:

> No wall will bar this land of joy;
> No sign will keep the poor away.
> A book may lead each girl and boy
> From darkest night to brilliant day.[61]

Though she felt she could not afford to buy books at the Hathaway bookshop in Wellesley Square, she managed to amass an impressive book collection for an eleven-year-old: in April she received her one hundredth book and wrote, "I am in a reverie of happiness for I love books."[62]

On March 10, 1944, *The Wellesley Townsman* published Plath's first story: "Troop 5 Valentine Party." She wrote in her diary that she felt "very proud."[63] She continued writing poems and prose steadily, sometimes stumbling on a theme that would resurface years later. "In the Corner of My Garden" (also titled "The Home of Straying Blossoms") is a two-stanza poem about the relationship between the domestic and the wild:

> In the corner of my garden
> There is a favorite spot,
> Which sun and rain tend faithfully
> And which I planted not.
>
> Here is the haven of wild flowers,
> The kingdom of birds and bees;
> Here in the silvery moonlight
> Sprites dance 'neath singing trees.[64]

Plath's budding Romantic sensibilities are on full display—the area free from human cultivation is a Yeatsian "haven" inhabited by wildflowers and sprites dancing in moonlight. She is already a poet of the moor rather than the country garden.

At night she listened to *Silver Theatre*, *The Jack Benny Program*, *The Great Gildersleeve*, *Superman*, *Quiz Kids*, *Jerry and the Pirates*, and *The Lone Ranger* on the radio. She was supposed to go to bed at eight p.m., but she frequently stayed up late reading and writing in her diary, "unknown to mummy."[65] She saw several movies with friends: *The Scarlet Pimpernel*, *Love Crazy*, *Madame Curie* ("sad but beautiful"), *Jane Eyre*, *Greenwich Village*, *Holiday Inn*, *Night of Adventure*, *Riding High*, and *What a Woman!*, as well as the war films *Up in Arms*, *Passport to Destiny*, and *Destination Tokyo*.[66] Some of these films were a little mature for Sylvia, who brought her dolls to the movies and wrote that she was shocked when she heard "swears" on-screen.[67] But the sultry glamour of Hollywood starlets spoke to her; she enjoyed playing with her Rita Hayworth paper dolls and pasting magazine photographs of movie stars in her scrapbook. She was thrilled to get Bette Davis's autograph from a Girl Scout friend who was Davis's niece. Around this time she began reading magazines such as *Ladies' Home Journal*, *The American Girl*, and *Calling All Girls*, which she read "cover to cover" when it arrived.[68] The magazines imprinted on her notions of femininity that both attracted and troubled her, and inspired her to satire later on.

There was occasional talk of boys. She listed four in the back of her 1944 diary under the heading "Boys I like": William Moore (the future president of her high school class), Betsy's brother Mark, Jack Duffin, Sanford Frazier. But her interest in boys was mostly competitive. She was excited when she beat them on tests, especially in math.[69] In April, after getting 100 on a social studies test, she wrote, "I am even with Donald Cheney!!!"[70] She frequently wrote about being chased and taunted by groups of boys. By early 1944, she began to fight back. In February she "gave the boys a good lecture and now they won't take my hat," while a month later she noted that she and another girlfriend formed a "2 girl army" to "attack" the boys, one of whom, William Moore, she nicknamed "Hercules."[71] She had already formed the habit of giving larger-than-life characteristics and nicknames to her crushes, as in her 1945 poem "King of the Ice":

> A streak of red, a flash of silver.
> My heroe [*sic*] on skates speeds by!
> As an arrow fleet
> With wings on his feet
> He races the wind on high.

The onlookers cry, "A goal! A goal!"
My heroe [*sic*] would win at any price,
'Twould be a feat
In hockey to beat
A star like my King of the Ice.[72]

Here, Plath transforms a schoolgirl crush into a "hero," "king," "arrow," and "star." She compares him to the Greek god Hermes. Dick Norton would be a blond god, Mallory Wober Hercules, Ted Hughes Adam. Even as a young girl, she was inspired by the male muses around her.

After another stint at Camp Weetamoe in July 1944, Sylvia spent the rest of her summer in Wellesley, sitting by the brook, picking dandelions, and trying to catch dragonflies with her cat, Mowgli. She swam, played with friends, and enjoyed long, leisurely dinners with her family. Aurelia was proud that Sylvia managed to save up $15 to buy herself a bike at the end of August. Her summer respite ended when she began her seventh-grade year at the Alice L. Phillips Junior High School in September.[73] She shuffled dutifully through math, gym, chorus, English, lunch, utility, orchestra, social studies, music, and health. She looked forward to slumber parties at Betsy's house, where the girls told each other ghost stories late into the night.

Girl Scouts was Sylvia's most time-consuming after-school activity that year. Founded in 1912 by Juliette Gordon Low and modeled on the British Girl Guides, Girl Scouts had one million members by 1944. Girl Scouts embodied a nonthreatening, almost Victorian ideal of womanhood that emphasized virtue, charity, and service. But it also taught girls strength and self-reliance. Unlike most female civic activities in American life, Girl Scout camps gave young women the freedom to leave the confines of domesticity, if only for a few weeks, and behave like boys. At camp, they too wore uniforms, woke up to bugle calls, made fires, rowed boats, hiked, swam, and learned archery.

Sylvia spent parts of six summers, 1943–1948, at Girl Scout–affiliated camps. She enjoyed the physical and outdoor camp activities more than her weekly after-school sessions, which revolved around earning badges and community service drives. In May 1944 at her local Girl Scouts award ceremony, she received an attendance star and ten badges—Birdfinder, World Knowledge, Group Music, Childcare, Readers, Scribe, Campcraft, Foot Traveler, Boating, and Weaving. Amassing these badges was not always pleasant. "Good riddance to that," she wrote after she finished working on her "Scribe" badge that March.[74]

Girl Scouts required its young charges to adopt military standards of precision and neatness. When hands were inspected for cleanliness at afternoon meetings, Sylvia was proud that hers were "the neatest."[75] She was equally cheered after winning weekly tent inspections at summer camp. But she also sensed a darker side to such inspections. In her eighth-grade year, she wrote that during her school physical she "stood shivering (stripped to the waist) in a room with open windows and cold drafts" waiting for a doctor—"an old codger, shaking all over"—to examine her.[76] Her language suggests that she was already attuned to the situation's disturbing power dynamics; the scene evokes "Herr Doktor" of "Daddy." Another teacher that year advised her to walk with perfect posture if she ever hoped to command authority.[77] At the time, slovenliness in women was often equated with madness; appearance and mental health were linked in a way that did not allow for the relaxation of what Sylvia, at age twelve, called "gruesome" beauty practices.[78] Plath later came to understand how obsession with cleanliness and purity could lead, in extremis, to genocide. In her late poems, she ruthlessly mocked the idea of "purity" with "gruesome" heroines. Lady Lazarus reeks of ash and sour breath; the speaker of "Cut" enjoys being a "Dirty girl"; the heroine of "Fever 103°" asks defiantly, "Pure? What does it mean?" before transcending her "old whore petticoats" to a paradise free of repression. Male doctors, especially in *The Bell Jar*, are agents of torture rather than healing. Plath occasionally foreshadows such moments in her adolescent diary, as in her 1944 school physical entry, and, later, in an entry about a school nurse who "almost asphyxiated" her while swabbing alcohol on her rash.[79]

Sylvia celebrated her twelfth birthday in October 1944 over dinner with girlfriends, including Ruth Freeman, who slept over. She noted somewhat forlornly that she was now "too old" to go trick-or-treating for Halloween. Instead she wrote "Halloween," a catchy ditty that displayed her ability to alternate smoothly between iambic tetrameter and trimeter:

> A little wind is whistling by,
> Bright leaves are whirling 'round,
> The harvest moon is hanging low
> O'er corn shocks dry and browned.
> The witches are about tonight,
> Above the ground they fly,
> On magic broomsticks with their cats
> They sail across the sky.[80]

Though she was leaving girlhood behind, she was gaining confidence in her burgeoning adolescent identity. In October she was asked to write for the school newspaper, the *Phillipian*, an early ratification of her calling. The invitation probably came through her seventh-grade English teacher, Miss

Raguse, who often praised Sylvia's work and who told her, "'You have a gift in that and should build it up.'"[81] By late November, Sylvia was so anxious to please Miss Raguse that she wrote ten book reports in three days. She sensed that her teacher was a kindred spirit and, in at least one instance, was impressed by her resistance to jingoism and propaganda. When Sylvia risked reading a Japanese poem aloud in English class in April 1945, she wrote that Miss Raguse "gave me an understanding sort of wink as if to say, 'It's beautiful, Japanese or not!'"[82]

On November 7, 1944, Franklin D. Roosevelt was reelected president. In her diary Sylvia wrote "Dewey" all over the page—likely a reflection of her family's politics—though the next day she happily reported, "Roosevelt's president!" The family celebrated a traditional Christmas Eve that year with caroling and a "hearty supper," after which Sylvia and Warren "went out and sat in the apple tree and listened and looked up at the moon, covered now and then by passing clouds."[83] Sylvia received another new journal (in which Aurelia wrote, "Rule: Not to be written in after 8 pm"), clothes, books—including an etiquette book—art supplies, mittens, candy, and pencils. Three days after Christmas, Sylvia wrote about a sledding excursion in language that looks forward to the flight and fall of "Ariel": "I traveled around quite a bit before I found the perfect hill. I was alone in an ice glittering world. Down the steep slopes I flew! The wind whistled through me. It was better than a mountain in fairyland. I was brought to earth by sunset."[84]

————

ON NEW YEAR'S DAY, 1945, Sylvia awoke early and balanced her budget, pleased to end the year with $2.55. Even at age twelve, she had a strong aversion to debt. Her eagerness to set her accounts right at the start of the new year points to an often overlooked aspect of Plath's young life: class.

Sylvia never complained to friends like Betsy or Pat about sharing a room with Aurelia in the merged Plath-Schober household, and many contemporaries remembered Sylvia's affectionate relationship with Grammy Schober. Nevertheless, Sylvia resented being raised in a matriarchy. While Aurelia was grateful for her parents' help, the situation had the potential to become infantilizing, and there were probably unspoken tensions in the home over authority. Plath wrote to Dr. Beuscher in 1962, "She was always a child while my grandmother was alive—cooked for, fed, her babies minded while she had a job. I hated this."[85] There would be no reprieve for Frank Schober, either, who lived and worked at the Brookline Country Club during the week—and often through the weekends—to help support the family. Those who came to know the Plath-Schobers in Wellesley, like Sylvia's friend Pat

O'Neil, described a warm, close-knit unit. But Pat saw Aurelia as "a bridge" between the conservative, old-world sensibilities of her Austrian parents and the modern ambitions of her American children. "It was very lonely for her," Pat said.[86]

Sylvia's Smith roommate Marcia Brown characterized Aurelia as "someone struggling every minute of every day of every year to pay the bills and to keep herself together—just holding on for dear life."[87] Friends like Ruth Freeman Geissler, Perry Norton, and Phil McCurdy went so far as to use the word "poor" to describe the Plath family.[88] The label seems an exaggeration given all that Aurelia was able to provide for her children. Indeed, several college friends later noted that while Sylvia was not wealthy by Smith standards, she appeared much better off than most of the other scholarship students in her year. Yet in affluent, "insular" Wellesley, Sylvia felt her class difference, describing her household as "middle-middle class."[89] Phil McCurdy, Sylvia's Wellesley friend, was also raised by a single mother in precarious financial circumstances. "Aurelia and Sylvia lived in the Fells. It was nearing Natick, which was poverty level. . . . I think both of us picked up easily that we were not second-class citizens, but we were a different cut from the average Wellesley crew. . . . We were poor people, relatively, in Wellesley, and worried a lot about money." They knew from a young age that they would have to earn scholarships to attend college—Sylvia to Smith, Phil to Harvard. He always felt that money was the "clue" to understanding *The Bell Jar*. "It's a big part of it. You can't romanticize it away."[90] Louise Giesey White, who knew Sylvia throughout her Wellesley and Smith years, said, "I did not think of her as 'poor.' But her mother worked. None of our mothers worked. . . . She was probably more vulnerable than people knew. Vulnerable about class, and those distinctions."[91] As Betsy put it, "It was just very evident that Aurelia either worked or starved."[92]

Some of Sylvia's friends lived in mansions with servants; she was particularly impressed after a visit to Nancy Wiggins's "gigantic and beautiful house," where she was "served a delicious luncheon by a 'Ritzy' maid."[93] Her own house was small and low-ceilinged, and the Plath-Schobers rarely had household help. Aurelia once said she had released Sylvia from her chores so she could focus on her reading, writing, painting, and music. "Sylvia required the most consideration, the most time, the most money. . . . We all adored her and catered to our 'prima donna,' as we teasingly called her."[94] But in her diary Plath wrote about doing housework: "What a job-beds-dishes-dusting-steps-I am worn out."[95] She shoveled the driveway when it snowed, which gave her backaches, and she babysat often. When Mildred Norton was ill, Sylvia helped her with household chores. In a thank-you note to Aurelia,

Mildred demurred that her sons were too "busy" to clean the kitchen, which was a "struggle" for them. Sylvia had performed her role, Mildred noted, with ladylike "cheerfulness of spirit."[96]

When Sylvia began seventh grade, she got a job dusting the school offices. She was unsure of her status—student or custodial staff?—and hesitant to dust when the offices were in use: "I rushed through my two dusting jobs and just got back to my homeroom before the last bell. In my first English study period I was called to the office and Miss Bahnor said 'You didn't dust the counter on the principal's desk this morning. Please do it now!' I could have cried and I <u>did</u> apologize about five times. (I never had dared to do the Principal's desk while he was sitting at it!)"[97] Word got around that she was available for housecleaning. At least one neighborhood woman took advantage of her:

> Mrs. Chapman called me up and asked if I would go to her house for a few hours and help her. I could not refuse so—first she had me shake and sweep by broom all of the rugs in the house.... She handed me a basin of soapy water and a cloth.... I set to work scrubbing the floors of her lengthy and wide drawing rooms, livingroom, sunporch, and kitchen (backboards too!) ... and waxed all the floors by hand (on my knees too) and polished them.... I received a dollar for my work which I felt (or rather my body felt) was not too much for all that work![98]

Sylvia was not greedy—that winter she refused a dollar from a neighbor after she helped shovel her driveway—but she knew when she was being exploited. She probably also knew that Mrs. Chapman would not have summoned her school friend Nancy Wiggins, who lived in a mansion, or Arden Tapley, whose father was a violinist in the Boston Symphony Orchestra, to do her cleaning. The day after Sylvia cleaned for Mrs. Chapman, Aurelia took her daughter into Boston, where they spent the afternoon at the Isabella Stewart Gardner Museum viewing John Singer Sargent's *The Dancer* and listening to the Gordon String Quartet. Sylvia, deeply moved, summed up the experience in her diary with a single word: "Magnificent!" This day of high culture made up for the previous day of hard labor. Plath's entry, full of exclamation points, is among the happiest in her 1945 diary.

Sylvia became adept at moving between classes—donning her red velvet dress, "real pearls," and white gloves for an elegant wedding after an unpleasant morning spent babysitting two toddlers.[99] It was a skill that would serve her well as a Smith scholarship student. A 1944 drawing suggests that Sylvia, already attuned to the soft undertones of hypocrisy, saw beyond Wellesley's gentility to something darker. Her sketch shows two well-dressed matrons conversing in front of a grand house with a white picket fence. In the background, one boy is beating another with a baseball bat as blood spurts from his head. "Oh, Junior has always been a poor loser," says his mother.[100] A story from the mid-1940s, "Mary Jane's Passport," also explores class issues in its portrayal of an unlikely friendship between an affluent but sickly teenage girl, Mary Jane, and a poor orphan, Judy, from the wrong side of town. Plath reverses the usual class hierarchy so that it is the rich girl who yearns to enter the poor one's world. Mary Jane eventually takes on a babysitting job— her "passport" into the working class—in hopes that she will meet Judy, also a babysitter, in the park.[101] Both characters have attributes of Sylvia herself— Mary Jane has an overprotective mother, while Judy lives with a widow who must work to support her family.

Sylvia understood that summer camp, in particular, was a luxury. In a handmade birthday card to her mother in April 1946, she enfolded $7 to help defray camp costs. She attempted to mitigate the complicated implications of her gift, which seemed to embarrass both mother and daughter. On the card's front flap she wrote, "I'll give my money to you / (That was supposed to be for your present) / For you to send in for my joy. / (Doesn't seem very pleasant.)" She drew a picture of herself at camp, with the caption, "Your present, your money." Inside the card she wrote, "But, 'Your joy is my joy,' to me you say / So it's joy for you in the end—When your daughter comes home healthy / Plumper (no taller) and tanned!" On the back of the card, she drew a daffodil and wrote, as if apologizing, "love, I love you, and Love, not money."[102] Sylvia had to keep up the façade that money did not matter, yet she understood quite well that it did.

———

IN EARLY 1945, Sylvia began to complain of fatigue. There were more instances of highs and lows in her diary than in the previous year. ("I have an iron-tong feeling of excitement coming on! As though ice cold iron tongs are thrust in me to make me tense, and, when everything's over, taken out fast!")[103] She was overscheduled (piano, viola) but fiercely disciplined. As she wrote in early January, "I came home to my homework . . . with a right good will."[104] After Betsy "dragged" her to see *Thirty Seconds Over Tokyo*, a patriotic war film, she "rushed home on the 5:20 bus, remorseful on how I wasted the afternoon but I got all my piano, viola and homework done and got to bed early for once."[105] Her home and school were always chilly, and she came down with several colds that winter. She longed for spring and wrote a poem called "Dreams" in which the poet fantasizes about "blossoming boughs": "Softly will the petals go, / Drifting earthward as now—the snow."[106] But there was little rest for the weary: her mother brought home Sunday school tests for her to do while she convalesced in bed.[107]

That January, she saw her first play in Boston—Shakespeare's *The Tempest*—and sat next to a handsome sailor on the train ride home. She marked the occasion as a rite of passage:

> Today is the biggest day of my life. I had a dreamless sleep and woke as fresh as dew on spring buttercups. All day I was in another world, far better than this. I took the bus to Boston with mother and Warrie to see Shakespeare's "The Tempest" at the Colonial Theatre. It was too perfect for words. I am keeping the program for a souvenir. We took the train to Wellesley and there were only separate seats. I sat next to a young sensitive boy from the navy. He had blond wavy hair and blue eyes. In all my life I have never loved anyone as I did him. Our talk was of travel, life, of Shakespeare.[108]

She drew scenes from the play in this diary entry and wrote, in capital letters, "THE TEMPEST MY IDEAL." Her hyperbole sounds like trivial schoolgirl sentiment, but she is nonetheless describing a creative epiphany. This *was* one of the "biggest days" of her life as an artist. *The Tempest* was a major influence on Plath's poetry, providing her with metaphors and imagery she would associate with her own lost father in "The Colossus" and "Full Fathom Five"; it also supplied the title for her final book of poetry, *Ariel*. The play unlocked something within her, and her experience colored her encounter with the handsome Navy sailor. Sexual longing and creative exuberance already existed in Lawrentian tandem.

Boys, in fact, were an increasing distraction, as were sports. Unlike other entries about music lessons and oral reports, which are filled with anxiety and self-doubt—"I <u>almost</u> fainted when I saw that I got all As and S's (in effort) on my report card"—Sylvia's descriptions of basketball, gymnastics, sledding, and biking are always spirited and confident.[109] That spring, she wrote frequently about gardening, which, like exercise, prompted meditation rather than anxiety:

> I got up before anybody else and went out in the dewy, early morning and transplanted violets and lilies-of-the-valley into my garden.... [After lunch] I went outside and examined every bud of the forsythia and apple tree, begging them to open. I worked on my Spring Booklet and illus-

trated many of my poems. . . . I watered my plants and now my garden looks lovely as it is full of sprouting green leaves and sweet smelling, fresh, overturned earth.[110]

As spring progressed, she enjoyed walking in the woods picking "loads and loads" of violets and identifying trilliums, bellwort, fringed milkwort, violets, anemones, ladyslippers, and marsh marigolds.[111] It was warm enough in mid-April for her to sunbathe with Betsy in the afternoon before going on after-school "missions" to find flowers to press, an activity that soon became an "obsession" for the two girls.[112] The theme of triumphant rebirth after wintering already exerted a powerful influence on her young imagination, and Sylvia finally achieved her goal of publishing three spring poems in the *Phillipian* in April and June: "The Spring Parade" ("Bud and leaf have now uncurled, / Daffodils their gold unfurled"), "Rain," and "March," the least sentimental of the three.[113] With its violent imagery of predators and wind, "March" brings to mind later Plath poems such as "Pursuit" and "The Snowman on the Moor," and suggests an early affinity for the types of wild, natural scenes that later captivated her poet-husband Ted Hughes:

> The wind-wolves are prowling about today,
> They're chasing the cloud lambs that carelessly stray
> While majestic skies loom vast and gray
> The powerful Mastero [*sic*] of March holds sway.
> . . . .
> And as over earth the planets swing
> I hear at last the Song of Spring![114]

Spring arrived, but the war lagged on. It had become a part of daily life, both in school and at home. In gym class, Sylvia performed so many drilling marches that she felt she could march in her sleep. When Uncle Frank and his wife Louise came for a February visit, they talked for hours after dinner about Frank's experiences in the Army as Sylvia listened, "enthralled."[115] A soldier spoke in a school assembly a week later about his sixty-four missions while Sylvia again listened intently. For someone longing for "experience," stories about war and Army life provided a vicarious thrill. Despite her earlier enthusiasm for Dewey, she grieved Roosevelt's death, on April 12, writing "ROOSEVELT DIES" in her diary next to a picture of herself crying and praying with eyes closed. She drew a casket surrounded by flowers and an American flag. The European war's end finally came on May 8. At school, she listened to President Truman proclaim VE Day. She wrote in her diary, "We had an assembly program that was very fitting and then went back to our regular classes for, as Truman said this morning, 'To show the appreciation of our victory in Europe we must do work, work, work and more work and still remember that there is a war to be won in the East.' "

Despite the gee-whiz tone of her 1940s diaries, there were occasional glimpses of a more subversive spirit. In April, she wrote about a happy afternoon swinging from her apple tree: "Soon I may grow wings (not angels)."[116] In May, she cut her finger with a knife while fiddling with a roll of tape, and wrote that it "bled until it filled a bandage, hankie and sink."[117] She drew a close-up of her bleeding finger next to another of herself with a knife. She finished off the tableau with a dark circle she captioned "my blood." The drawings recall the poem "Cut," with its fascinated description of a nearly severed thumb. In June, she read the "thrilling" novel *She* by H. Rider Haggard, whose queen Ayesha, an African femme fatale, may have been an early model for Lady Lazarus—at the novel's end, Ayesha declares, "I die not. I will come again."

As spring turned to summer, Sylvia read *Treasure Island* and *Anne of Green Gables* up in her apple tree. She was relieved that the school year was nearing its end. The *Phillipian* had invited her to join its staff the next year, a triumph that earned her a hug from Miss Raguse, who said, "Be sure to tell your mother."[118] She won the Wellesley Award for the highest academic achievement in the seventh grade and a unique award for "excellence in English Expression." The next day in class Miss Raguse presented her with two more "commendation cards." One was for scholarly excellence; the other for "unusual creative work," an award that pleased Sylvia greatly.[119] She also received an award for her efforts selling war stamps. Miss Raguse, one in a long line of supportive English teachers, had given Sylvia reason to take her writing seriously; her teacher's congratulations, she said, "really meant more than anyone else's."[120] She ended the school year on a high note with seven A's on her report card, marred only by a B in music. She was "swamped with requests for autographs."[121] Sylvia was learning that achievement brought admiration, not just from her teacher and mother, but from her peers as well.

In early July, the Powleys drove Sylvia and Betsy to Camp Helen Storrow, a Girl Scout camp in the coastal town of Plymouth, Massachusetts. The girls were both housed in the same cabin in the "Ridge" unit for two "joyous weeks."[122] Sylvia filled her letters home with the usual details about starchy menus and third helpings. In her diary, however, there is not a single mention of food. One night, she and other girls performed in blackface in a minstrel show—such was the casual racism of the era.[123]

She advanced in swimming, built an outdoor kitchen, and wrote of the landscape in her diary. She described how she watched the "tawny-red ball of sun sink slowly out of sight in the west" and wrote repeatedly of the ocean, how "The pure white sand gleamed through its crystal, pale, blue-green depths."[124] The highlight of the summer was a five-mile hike to Fisherman's Cove, where there was a long sandbar, sand dunes, and sea cliffs inhabited by kingfishers. Privately she wrote that the hike exhausted her, but she showed more bravado in a letter to her grandparents: "I had to laugh at some of the girls because I was the only one who dared to go in first for the waves were strong and cold until you ducked."[125] As in "Ocean 1212-W," she cast herself as the sea's elect.

Back in Wellesley, she played the piano, drew Rhine maidens and German castles, and held hands with Betsy as they jumped off the raft at Morses Pond. Her book collection became so large that Aurelia had to clear out a bigger bookcase for her.

In late July, the family journeyed by train and bus to Welchville, Maine, near Lewiston, where they stayed with Aurelia's friends the Loungways until August 8. The Loungways' property, named Innisfree, consisted of a "big house" and a smaller cabin, where Sylvia, Aurelia, and Warren slept. Sylvia was amazed by the clarity of the night sky in Maine; she saw her first shooting star and called the Milky Way "a gossamer scarf flung across the sky."[126] During thunderstorms, the children stayed inside and played Murder in the darkened living room, a game Sylvia found "terribly exciting."[127] She became fast friends with thirteen-year-old Margot Loungway, with whom she took long walks and attended Bible school. Like Sylvia, Margot was creative and cerebral; she eventually earned a doctorate in history at Harvard and founded the Social Thought and Institutions program at Stanford. Sylvia was competitive with Margot, and they sometimes quarreled. Sylvia dealt with her own anger through writing: she simply "went off alone in back of the house and made up a seventeen line poem titled 'the Wind.'"[128] But they spent most days in easy camaraderie, fishing, sketching, sunbathing, and writing in their "secret place"—a bed of pine needles in a field surrounded by trees.

Margot, a precocious young writer, was the first of Sylvia's "doppelgängers"—girls who shared her interests and talent but who often became targets in her fiction and journal. The two would remain close in the coming years. Instead of playing outside in the woods, as Sylvia did with Betsy, they stayed indoors and wrote when they were together. "Somehow, at her home I feel I could write my best stories," Sylvia wrote in her diary in 1947.[129] When Sylvia slept over, they "tortured each other by reading aloud our stories." During one weekend with Margot in May 1946, Sylvia wrote two new stories: "The Mummy's Tomb," which she called a "frightful murder-mystery"; and "On the Penthouse Roof," "a smuggler's story."[130] In "The Mummy's Tomb," a young woman working on a history project decides to spend the night in the Egyptian section of a museum after she smells decaying flesh in one of the mummy's coffins. She awakens to find the museum janitor about to torture a young kidnapped girl by scooping out her eyes and pushing spikes into her body. He sees the narrator and lurches toward her: "'Ha!' he leered. 'You got away yesterday, but you won't now. I'll muffle your screams of anguish and let you die from loss of blood and in terrible pain.'"[131] The academic heroine, however, knocks him unconscious with her umbrella and frees the kidnapped girl. Though the plot is ridiculous, the story is more vivid and well paced than Plath's other prose pieces from this period.[132]

The only other surviving story from 1946 that approaches the success of "The Mummy's Tomb" is "Victory," which describes the attempted murder of a young woman, Judith, on a dark country road during a storm: "The girl stood paralyzed with fright as she heard the labored breathing of her pursuer. He loomed tall beside her. The next moment she felt his fingers close about her neck, choking the cry of terror that had risen to her throat."[133] At the story's end, however, Plath reveals that Judith is an actress who has successfully completed her first movie scene. In both stories, Plath indulges the darker, Gothic side of her imagination with considerable skill. She would return to the theme of torture—of women by crazed men—in several poems during the 1960s.

————

SYLVIA'S SUMMER IDYLL ENDED on August 8 when the Plaths left Innisfree and emerged into a dark new age:

> At Portland we had a few minutes between trains and so we bought a newspaper. We learned that the United States dropped the first atomic bomb on Japan and that it destroyed 60% of Hiroshima! This bomb, it is said by President Truman, can be used for constructive as well as destructive purposes. For instance, the same power may be used to cultivate and save food so that there will be no worry of the loss of crops or of starvation. Also, Russia has at last declared war on Japan (the latter nation may capitulate within a few months many people hope).[134]

A few days later she recorded Japan's surrender in similar newsreel cadences: "The news today is: Japs Offer to Quit!"[135] When Truman declared peace on August 14, Plath's neighborhood erupted in shouts and firecrackers. She had difficulty writing about war in her own voice, but not peace: "The sky put on its rainbow colors as thanks for peace. Pale pink cloud streamers hung across the azure sky. The west was a golden red-yellow glow and hazy white clouds floated here and there, but, best of all, there was a bright <u>blue</u> crescent moon in the heavens."[136]

Sylvia spent the rest of the summer making a book of her poems from 1937 to the present, copying them out in her apple tree. She painted her bicycle "geranium red," a color that would have special resonance in her later work.[137] When Betsy returned home from a trip to New York, the two quickly fell into their old patterns of building forts in the woods and playing with their handmade paper dolls, for which Sylvia designed her own stunning dresses. In late August, however, she grimly submitted to the hairdresser's scissors: her hair was cut, and she sported a shoulder-length bob. Though Betsy had already cut her long hair earlier in the summer, Sylvia was upset. "I miss my braids," she wrote in her diary.[138]

Her initiation into this new feminine world was unpleasant. She spent a sleepless night on her hair curlers and noted that the task of washing and setting her hair, performed by her mother, was "gruesome." After her curlers were removed, she thought she looked like Medusa.[139] Braids lent themselves to days spent swinging upside down in trees and biking down hills, but her new hairstyle required maintenance and deportment. Sylvia seemed to sense, as in *A Fairy to Stay*, that the haircut was "discipline" of a sort. "To My Sylvia," a poetic homily Aurelia wrote for her daughter on her thirteenth birthday, reinforced the message that the playful whimsy of girlhood must now give way to the responsibilities of womanhood:

Oh, dear, my head's awhirl!
Today, my darling,
You're my <u>teen</u>-age girl!

Your life's been happy?
You wish no change?
Why, my sweetheart,
<u>That</u> isn't strange.

But now Life opens
So many doors
To friends and knowledge—
All <u>can</u> be yours.

To keep on growing
In mind and soul,
To serve and learn
Must be your goal.[140]

"To serve and learn" were not necessarily the goals Sylvia had in mind as she began to plot an ambitious literary career. But it was what American culture expected of well-behaved young ladies.

In eighth grade, Sylvia was elected president of her homeroom and secretary of her English class. She kept herself busy with the *Phillipian*, Girl Scouts, viola, piano, and dancing lessons, the Art Club, the Recreational Club, orchestra, and the Stamp Club. (In Maine, Margot Loungway had introduced her to stamp collecting, and it had become a minor obsession.) She still dusted the school offices for money; her supervisor was so impressed with her work that she told Sylvia she would someday "make a good wife."[141] When she did something for pleasure, such as reading "a trashy Nancy Drew mystery," she chastised herself for wasting time. When she slept late on weekends, she immediately wrote to-do lists and began working. But she still found time to play cards with Betsy, debate philosophical issues with Perry, and read several books by Caroline Snedeker. She took long walks with her family during fall afternoons, which she described in luxurious language: "The sun was hanging low in the west and shining through the graceful milkweed parachutes still clinging to the stalk, in a silver glow."[142]

The war had been over for almost two months, but meat and butter lines still formed before the grocery shops opened in Wellesley; a local newspaper captured a photograph of Sylvia and her grandmother waiting in one such line. Sylvia sat through endless school assemblies "with a multitude of speakers on war,"[143] on one occasion debating the merits of the draft, which she was firmly against.[144] She did not mention the horror of the Holocaust in her adolescent diary, but there were oblique references to the misery in Europe. With her friends, she played Refugee, a game that involved dressing in rags and going from door to door to beg for food ("fortunately . . . no one was home).[145] She wrote of a captivating social studies class about the atomic bomb, and a lecture on Jewishness in her Unitarian Sunday school from a Wellesley College student: "She spoke to us about the Jewish customs, beliefs and ways. It was very interesting. She promised to take us to a Jewish Synagogue in the future. I had a beautiful time listening to her."[146] Miss Wyneberg kept her word and hosted the group at her temple in Boston early the next year. Sylvia recorded the visit in detail; it was likely her first real introduction to Judaism. That fall she published another poem in the *Phillipian*—"My Garden"—which she called "no good."[147] Her grandfather's praise—and his gift of a dollar—provided incentive to keep publishing, but the drive to make art came from inside. She published regularly in the *Phillipian* until she left junior high, thirteen poems in all, as well as four articles and four prose pieces.

December 1945 brought an eclipse of the moon—"a gray shadow spreading over it till only a pale ball of faint light hung in the sky," she wrote in her diary.[148] Sylvia found the December blizzards, with their "driving" winds and "howling" snow, exhilarating. The family spent their "big Christmas" at Aunt Dot's house. (Grampy was working at the Brookline Country Club.) Sylvia faithfully recorded her gifts as usual: mittens, a nightgown, money, slippers, clothes, jewelry, a pocketbook, stamps (she now had more than 8,500), and a new diary. Writing in her diary was becoming essential to her well-being: "Dear Diary You're one of the 'musts' for peace of mind."[149] All her friends were away, and her obligations were on hold, and the lull seems to have unnerved her. Unusual physical symptoms appeared; a few days after Christmas she vomited and fainted, hitting her head on a table as she fell. She stayed in bed and did not dress for three straight days. She channeled her unease into Gothic iambs:

> The night is crouched in wait outside
> Stealthy, catlike, dark and wide,
> The night wind moans and plays a game
> Of rattling every window frame—
> My tiny, flick'ring lamp shines bright—
> Small proof against the fearful night.
> The hordes of darkness start their dance—
> Retreat, advance; retreat, advance.
> The night it lurks in wait outside
> Hollow, hungry, dark and wide.
> It waits to pounce into my room
> And swallow it within the gloom.[150]

On New Year's Eve, still in bed, she felt "very funny (peculiar) and lonely."[151] She had turned thirteen only two months before and seemed aware of an impending, nebulous shadow on the horizon. Like her mother, she tried to banish the bad with the good and end the year on a high note. She was "sort of optimistic" about the New Year and hoped that she would "succeed in my viola and piano and dancing and school and sports."[152] The war was over, just as she had hoped in her 1944 poem "Wish Upon A Star": "I wish that all the wars would end; / Their homeward way the soldiers wend."[153] Her own struggles with depression were just beginning, however. In the coming years, she would fight an increasingly sinister opponent as she matured into a world that seemed to reflect the dark paranoia of her worst sleepless nights. Both Plath and the nation were moving toward a different kind of war, one in which the enemy was hidden, out of reach, but armed with an arsenal of annihilation.

4

My Thoughts to Shining Fame Aspire

Wellesley, 1946–1947

In January 1946, Sylvia received a fountain pen from her grandfather with her name inscribed in gold. She treasured the gift the way other teenage girls treasured silk dresses and pearl necklaces. When the pen was stolen five months later, she wrote that it was among the worst days of her life: "I felt ill all day and know now how much I loved it. . . . My whole world has turned gray and black."[1] Aurelia replaced it two months later with "an exact duplicate," which pleased Sylvia enormously.[2] This unusual extravagance suggests that Aurelia understood how much her daughter had come to see the gleaming, monogrammed pen as an embodiment of her calling.

Plath put her pen to good use in 1946. Although most of her poems from this time are sentimental, they provide a glimpse of her developing thematic interests. Almost every poem Plath wrote during junior high school described a natural landscape. In "The Lake," which dates from 16 July 1946, the water "is really / the earth's clear eye, / Where are mirrored the moods / Of the wind and the sky."[3] Plath's titles reflect her preoccupations: "Awake," "Rain," "The Spring Parade," "March," "The Lake," "The Wind," "Mornings of Mist," "A Winter Sunset," "Steely-Blue Crags," "May," "October." These nature poems conveyed emotional truth within safe, impersonal parameters.

Plath began to explore darker images in early 1946. "A Winter Sunset," written in her diary on January 16 and sent to her grandfather, reads:

> Over the earth's dark rim
> The daylight softly fades,
> The sky from orange to gold
> And then to copen shades.

> The moon hangs, a globe of iridescent light,
> In a frosty winter sky,
> While against the western glow one sees
> The bare, black skeleton of the trees.
>
> The stars come out and one by one
> Survey the world with lofty stare;
> But, from the last turn in the road
> A cosy home beckons to me there.[4]

The first sound of Plath's mature poetic voice is audible here. The middle stanza, suffused with the language of dark Romanticism, is the emotional heart of the poem. It contains several tropes that would reappear in Plath's later work: a cold moon, liminal evening light, winter frost, and black, menacing trees. The stark vision nearly overwhelms the thirteen-year-old poet, who retreats to home and safety as if frightened of her own descriptive powers. Sylvia soon realized that the sentimental image of the "cosy home" weakened an otherwise powerful Gothic portrait; notably, she omitted the final stanza when she published the poem in the *Phillipian* in February 1946. This sound aesthetic decision suggests a shift away from sentimentality toward sublimity.

The same voice sounds again in other poems from 1946. Sylvia dedicated "To Miss Cox," published in the *Phillipian* in November 1946, to a beloved schoolteacher who had passed away. It was Plath's first public elegy. The somber poem considers the fleeting nature of life and hints at the consoling promise of an afterlife. The final stanza is the most powerful, though Plath again tempers her dark imagery with a cheerful ending:

> The winter skies are leaden,
> The flying snowflakes sting;
> But behind the cold white stillness
> There's the promise of a spring.[5]

Leaden skies and "cold white stillness" are familiar elements of Plath's mature poetic universe, while "the promise of a spring" would remain a resilient theme in her work. She never abandoned the idea of resurrection.

———

WHILE SYLVIA'S FRIENDSHIPS with Ruth Freeman, Margot Loungway, Perry Norton, Betsy Powley, Prissy Steele, and others[6] flourished throughout her eighth-grade year, school was beginning to feel more like a "prison."[7] Missing school had once made Sylvia upset; now she cherished the "luxury" of lying in bed on weekends and lamented how quickly Monday came. She continued to earn straight A's on her report cards, and was pleased when her English teacher, Mrs. Warren, told her that she was writing at near-college level and should apply for a college scholarship.[8] But she counted down the days until her next vacation. That spring, her grandmother had to drive her to school because she was lugging ten pounds' worth of books.[9] She was stressed and overwhelmed, and admitted as much when she finally quit piano lessons in March.

She began to fall ill more frequently as her anxiety levels rose. Some of these illnesses may have been psychosomatic, as sickness seemed the only acceptable way to give herself a break. Days in bed gave her time to read and write for pleasure. In April 1946, for example, she was "itching" to read two books by Adele DeLeeuw but complained that she wouldn't have time with all her schoolwork. Two days later she was conveniently home sick and "devoured" both books.[10] Illness became her only respite from the pressures of schoolwork and extracurricular activities, and Aurelia was surprisingly lenient about letting her stay home. This was a pattern that would continue throughout Sylvia's life. (It is possible that Plath's breakdown in August 1953, which was partly brought on by the prospect of writing her senior thesis on James Joyce's *Ulysses*, was an extreme version of the illness patterns that had developed in girlhood.)

Sometimes even a day off could not quell her anxiety. "I went to bed with a spinning brain," she wrote in March 1946 after a day sick at home.[11] When she returned to school, she complained of her "eyes spinning and the black and white flashes grew worse in my study periods so that I couldn't even read or work."[12] After resting in the nurse's office for an hour she felt better, though the mysterious condition went undiagnosed. In May, after a hard day at school and a wet walk home in the rain, she was "angry with the world"; the following day, too, was "very raw and discouraging."[13] She began to have "gruesome" nightmares and did not sleep well.[14] In a notebook dating from junior high, she described one of these nightmares in language reminiscent of Poe:

All there was overhead, below and on either hand was damp, suffocating, slimy, clinging blackness. Things padded silently, stealthily close by, but even though their presence could be sensed they were unknown things. They were made all the more terrifying by being unseen and yet <u>there</u>, because the imagination has the power to create monstrosities out of the vague unknown more horrible than the creations of nature itself. There was no feeling or seeing—only consciousness. Suddenly a spot of light appeared. It shaped itself deftly into a woman's head. Beautiful and yet frightening. The skin was blue-white as marble. The nose finely modeled, the mouth vividly red, and the eyebrows were thin black arches. Her hair, black also, dissolved into the living darkness. But where her eyes should have been there were two gaping holes from which issued licking red tongues of fire. The face began to glow and, little by little, the blackness was forced back.[15]

Sylvia was excited by gruesome scenes elsewhere, as when she narrated a performance of "Horatius at the Bridge" in English class: "I reveled in those bloody lines." After reading *The Scarlet Pimpernel*, a book about the French Revolution that she called "thrilling" and "rather bloody," she drew a blood-stained guillotine surrounded by decapitated heads in her diary.[16] She was again excited by blood—this time her own—when she scraped her knee during a basketball game that May: "To my delight it bled all over the bus and drew pitying attention and sighs."[17] When a fire struck a neighbor's garage that spring, she wrote, "thrill, thrill" as she watched the "screaming engines" rush to put it out.[18] Her Romantic mind seized on violence as it did hurricanes and winter storms—as a sublime force that brought her closer to an unveiling, an edge. When she heard Sibelius's *Finlandia* in Boston's Symphony Hall that May, she praised its stormy rhythms: "marvelous! It sounded like waves pounding on the wet beach, tossing up mists of spray with the theme of lightning and thunder rising through the powerful melody."[19] *Finlandia* inspired her to write a poem, "Sea Symphony," in which she described "The boom of the breakers on sharp, black rocks, / The scream of the gulls as they dip and soar" and the "pale green light / Of stormy, blustering afternoons."[20] The Gothic romance and moorland setting of *Jane Eyre*—which made her "estatically happy" [*sic*]—moved her more than the drawing room dramas of *Pride and Prejudice*, which she read in June: "I enjoy it greatly. Of course the artificial speeches they made in those days are rather boring."[21]

In mid-June she won the school spelling bee and a special Wellesley pennant for her academic achievement, but she longed for the final weeks of school, when the workload lightened. She was the only eighth grader to receive a fourth "letter" for academic success, and when school let out she was up in her apple tree voraciously reading Adele DeLeeuw books "about girls beginning their life work": "she writes about many different careers in very professional language."[22] Sylvia also resumed work on her novella *Stardust*, based on the Nancy-Star sequence she had begun in the mid-1940s. She was pleased to see that after typing out her longhand, her second chapter took up seven pages.[23]

At June's end the Powleys drove Sylvia up to Camp Helen Storrow for her second summer. She was again in the same tent with Betsy; Ruth Freeman soon joined them. (Sylvia was pleased that Ruth entered the cabin as she was washing the windows: "What a good impression that must have made.")[24] Back in Wellesley later in the summer, she studied Eleanor Gates's play *The Poor Little Rich Girl* for ideas about plot and structure that she could use in her own stories.[25] She also became more serious about painting. Aurelia bought her a set of oil paints and four canvasses that July, which gave her a "thrill."[26] She painted birch trees and zinnias and began typing lessons in August. She loved the speed tests and looked forward to the day when she could type her own stories quickly.[27]

Betsy and Ruth often came for weekends, and they enjoyed convivial family suppers with Sylvia's grandparents, aunts, uncles, and young cousins. The three friends played cards, often with Betsy's parents, and swam. Sylvia mastered the diving board at the Morses Pond bathing beach. "It is such fun to cut the water like a knife," she wrote. "I am just bursting glad that I'm learning how to dive!"[28] She still noted days that summer when she felt "queer" and "off," "yawny, miserable" days when she retreated to bed.[29] Yet it was in bed that she often did some of her best creative work. In late August she wrote four poems while she recuperated from a sore throat, writing, "I picked these thoughts out of the air when they came flying by on winds."[30] Lounging in bed also gave her time to catch up on current events through the radio. Sometimes the implications were disturbing: "I listened to the news—about the troubles with Palestine, Jugoslavia [*sic*], and Russia. Boy! If only there isn't another war in this world! I do so want peace."[31] She wished that she "could run things for a while."[32]

Sylvia spent the last two weeks of August lounging on the sun porch, where she drew "bathing beauties" in sultry poses, and read *Wuthering Heights*. She found the book "rather dark and morbid" but enjoyed it.[33] Aurelia, meanwhile, gave her *Triumph Clear*, a book about a young girl crippled by polio. After the high drama of *Wuthering Heights*, the novel's moral message was a letdown: "The books [*sic*] lesson is, I guess, that we never know how much we appreciate something until we loose [*sic*] it."[34] In Sylvia's diary, Aurelia stands in the background of all this activity as a source of comfort. One night Sylvia left Betsy's house late, and feared riding home in the dark. "As I started on the dark bike ride home, I saw a familiar figure ahead. Mother had come to meet me. Was relieved and happy."[35]

Sylvia started the ninth grade, her last year of junior high, in September 1946. She added Latin, Ancient History, and Algebra to her usual roster of subjects. She was in an honors-level English class taught by Helen Lawson, who remembered that, though Plath was at the top of the class, she had "the complete respect of her fellow pupils—not that of a 'grind.'"[36] Sylvia began Dickens's *A Tale of Two Cities* the first week of September and called it "the most wonderful, magnificent book I've ever read!"[37] She soon began *David Copperfield* and *Oliver Twist*, and declared her love for Dickens in her diary.[38]

She loved, too, the clear blue skies, tawny leaves, and bracing winds of autumn. It was now too cold to read in the apple tree, so she camped out in her grandmother's room, which was sun filled and "airy," reading *The Count of Monte Cristo* and letters from her Belgian pen pal Claudine Dufrane, which her grandfather helped translate from French.[39] After drawing pictures of starlets in her diary that month, she wrote, "Some old nagging thing inside me prompts me to waste such nice paper. . . . From now on I won't let the weak side of my character hold sway."[40]

She attended her first school dance with Perry Norton that October in a yellow evening dress with velvet black bows; she happily recorded that she danced with seven boys. Her fourteenth birthday soon followed (her favorite present was an avocado from her grandfather), but she did not greet it with the usual enthusiasm. She felt she was growing old, and seemed despondent about the passage of time.

She discovered Sara Teasdale's poetry in November and copied several of Teasdale's nature poems into her diary, writing, "What I wouldn't give to be able to write like this!"[41] The poems she copied—"Late October," "Full Moon," "The Fountain," "Autumn Dusk," "Mountain Water," "There Will Be Stars," and "Beautiful, Proud Sea"—are similar in tone to the kind of lyric nature poetry she was then writing. In "Late October," for example, Teasdale writes:

> Listen, the damp leaves on the walks are blowing
> With a ghost of sound;
> Is it fog or is it rain dripping
> From the low trees to the ground?[42]

Sylvia transcribed these lines in her diary and wrote, "they express my thoughts beautifully."[43] The Teasdale poem that seems to have had the most influence on her was "The Crystal Gazer," whose first four lines she transcribed in her diary that November:

> I shall gather myself into myself again,
> I shall take my scattered selves and make them one
> Fusing them into a polished crystal ball
> Where I can see the moon and flashing sun.[44]

The lines bring to mind the tropes of dissolution and rebirth in Plath's "The Stones," "Ariel," and "Lady Lazarus." After her first suicide attempt, Plath would work hard in therapy to recover her "scattered selves," but in her poems and novel she regarded this retrieval process with more cynicism.

Teasdale was an important early female literary role model. Shortly after the Teasdale diary entries, Sylvia described roaming about her house "storing descriptions and thoughts in my mind to be taken out at random some day in the future. I feel a poem coming on soon, too."[45] Later, though, Teasdale would serve a darker mentorship as one of the "brilliant women— neurotic" who committed suicide, about whom Plath wrote in her journal.[46] (Plath eventually wrote her own poem titled "Crystal Gazer" in 1956, after she married Ted Hughes, transforming Teasdale's self-satisfied sibyl into a dark reflection of horror: "Each love blazing blind to its gutted end— / And, fixed in the crystal center, grinning fierce: / Earth's ever-green death's head.")

In late November Sylvia began art lessons with a respected local teacher, Miss Hazelton, in addition to her regular art class in school. Sylvia never felt her drawings were good enough, but Aurelia praised them. Indeed, Sylvia had real talent. That spring she would learn that two of her watercolors won a spot at the Massachusetts Regional Art Exhibit in Boston. One even went on to earn a place at the National High School Art Exhibition at the Carnegie Institute in Pittsburgh and was ranked eighth in the nation. Her school principal, Mr. Thistle, delivered this "bombshell" in person, along with the news that a poem of hers won honorable mention in the National Poetry Contest.[47]

Though Sylvia admired and respected her art teacher—she would visit Miss Hazelton at Newton-Wellesley Hospital in 1953 and feed her as she lay dying[48]—she couldn't resist a few barbs in her diary, calling her "a tiny, wizened old lady" with skin "like wrinkled yellow parchment."[49] That same month she delighted in berating a teacher who had offended her, describing her "sardonic, implacable smile." She referred to another teacher as "old Dope."[50] A story she wrote for English class that December, "From the Memoirs of a Babysitter," objected to the common feminine description of little children as "angelic" and instead described them as "bothersome" and "a nuisance."[51] She later called a boy at a dance a "fat old puff."[52] Plath was beginning to develop the blasphemous voice that would propel some of her most memorable writing.

As 1946 drew to a close, however, glimpses of this "other" Sylvia were still rare. The writer who would cast a harsh light on Cold War America was still moved by jingoistic patriotism and scientific propaganda. When she saw a movie called *America the Beautiful* during a school assembly, she nearly wept with pride. "How wonderful it is just to live in AMERICA!"[53] She was fascinated by a "thrilling" school lecture on the atomic bomb that May. The audience was breathless as the presenting scientist, Dr. White,

> turned on a sounding machine and said, "Now listen to the voice of God." When he said this, we all heard a series of little sharp clicks. These were cosmic bullets. He put various stones over the Geiger counter and each one either increased the count or remained the same. He told us that if the count ran together and the clicks got up to 235, the whole school would blow up![54]

Plath's poems connecting patriarchy, fascism, and science were far in the future. She remained an obedient daughter who received certificates for book reports and perfect attendance at Sunday school. She continued to send her work to contests and frequently won. No contest was too obscure— she received $5 worth of music recordings that fall from a local shop for an essay about Daniel Boone.

Margot Loungway came for a visit two days after Christmas 1946. They attended a party at the Nortons' house, where Sylvia trusted Perry to play "nice, clean games—pencil and paper games, guessing games, and puzzles etc."[55] But someone else at the party inspired less innocent feelings: Perry's brother Dick. "(Pant! Pant!)"[56]

She and Margot enjoyed walking through the woods during a blizzard: "It was a dry, hushed cold, and all we could hear was the ceaseless sifting of the snow through the tree branches. We thought that we might get frozen to death like some famous explorers, but—no such luck." The purity of winter landscapes always mesmerized Sylvia.

> Today was fit for a poem. The world was etched in frosty lace. The trees were soft, powdery skirts, and the air was like a crystal breath—I mean extraordinarily clear. Over all was a fragile blue sky, and a far-off sun set the icicles to twinkling like myriads of stars or sparklers. I tracked about in the snow, heedless of anything else except the beauty of this glorious world.[57]

Plath's poetic inclinations still gestured toward dramatic natural land-scapes. Years later, "Ariel" would feature an early-morning gallop over the moors through "blue / Pour of tor and distances." The poem echoes the pure, unadulterated joy Sylvia experienced coasting down the snowy hills of

Wellesley: "We sped on fleet silver wings over snow and ice. We felt as if we were birds soaring in the blue, blue sky for one brief morning."[58]

———

SYLVIA LOST THE ELECTION for school secretary in January 1947, but she had better luck in the school spelling bee that year; she came in second, after losing on "apparel" to a ninth-grade boy. She pasted the *Wellesley Townsman* clipping about the spelling bee in her scrapbook with the caption, "I was glad that Bill got first prize because I always like having a <u>boy</u> ahead of me!"[59] She repeated the sentiment in her diary: "I had hoped he would win, for its [*sic*] always nice to have a boy ahead."[60] When Plath reread her diary as a young woman, she would place an asterisk above this sentence, as she often did above naive or well-mannered entries that seemed absurd to her in hindsight. She often wrote "Ha!" in pencil above her polite entries about the Norton boys.

Sylvia still preferred the company of books to that of boys; in early 1947, she was particularly impressed by Thackeray's *Vanity Fair*. A day after a school dance, she wrote "Fireside Reveries," a manifesto of her own literary ambition, which concluded:

> I'm dreaming dreams by the fireside,
> A book of poems in my lap;
> . . . .
> While through the living screen of fire
> I see gold castles in the air,
> My thoughts to shining fame aspire
> For there is much to do and dare.
>
> Just as I reach the summit's height,
> And gaze down far below,
> The vision fades into the night,
> But still the embers flow.[61]

Here, writing poetry is construed as a risky act, a "dare" akin to playing with fire. The public expression of this desire—Plath published "Fireside Reveries" in the *Phillipian*—was remarkable at a time when modesty was considered an essential female virtue. "Didn't you know I'm going to be the greatest, most entertaining author and artist in the world?" she wrote in her diary that March.[62] Aurelia had recently given her books about female artists such as Edna St. Vincent Millay, Wanda Hazel Gág, and Anna Pavlova, and Sylvia and her mother developed a close rapport that winter. There were long walks through the Wellesley woods, afternoons making molasses candy and hot chocolate, and evenings typing up poems together. Sylvia brainstormed with her "angel-of-a-mother" when she suffered from writer's block: "mother planted some ideas after long minutes of thought, and accordingly I began to write a story."[63] (The story was "Mary Jane's Passport," for which Aurelia also provided the title.)

Yet Sylvia was beginning to move, ever so slowly, out of Aurelia's shadow. In early February 1947 she revised her fairy story, *Stardust*, in a way that would not have pleased her mother, who was fond of morally uplifting narratives: "I've decided not to make it all goody-ish, preachy, or moraly [*sic*]."[64] Indeed, an event that March caused Sylvia to question her mother's moral judgment for the first time. Her old Winthrop friend, William Sterling, who took Sylvia to a school dance that March, read her diary during a sleepover party and saw that she had called him "shallow." Aurelia told Sylvia that he had been "terribly hurt" by the revelation and implied that she should have had better manners. Sylvia, miserable and embarrassed, felt that Aurelia's criticism was unfair. "Heaven knows I write things in here that I don't mean two minutes later—but!"[65] William eventually apologized for reading her diary, but Sylvia was learning that Aurelia would not tolerate her sharp, critical voice, and she sensed a double standard. Why was it all right for the boys to read through her private diary but not for her to write honestly about her feelings? A few days later she practically dared William—and Aurelia—to admonish her: "I think he is nauseating, and if he ever reads this again and sees what I think it will serve him right for being so conceited and nosy! . . . Mother says I have to be nice to him! Phooey!@*!!"[66] The same pattern would play out to disastrous effect during Sylvia's relationship with Dick Norton, a "nice" boy whom Aurelia wanted her daughter to marry. The personal attacks in *The Bell Jar* were a kind of "writing back" to those who had upset her during the years she had dated Dick.

By 1947, Plath's diary was becoming more of a working writer's notebook than a daily record of events. She longed for drama but found it hard to invent such scenarios when she had so little "experience." Because the only dramatic events that ever seemed to happen in Wellesley revolved around the weather, her lyrical descriptions of snow and storms and sunsets were often more impressive than her fictional vignettes, which were still derivative. Before she turned to plot and character, she learned to write by describing landscapes. These descriptions also—perhaps in a subconscious or coded way—describe her mood, a practice that would intensify as she matured. In a summer entry, whose atmospherics bring her masterful late poem "Sheep in Fog" to mind, she writes, "Today had quite an eerie, though tiring atmosphere. A uniform gray sky hung low and oppressing overhead, deadly quiet. Occasional wraith-like mists drifted here and there."[67]

If Sylvia lacked experience she found it in unexpected places, for she simply *had* to write. "Once I write it is so hard to stop. There are so many things that I feel deeply about and want to get written down in here before it is to [sic] late and they have slipped away."[68] And again, a few days later, "I feel so much like writing tonight that I have to stopper my feelings up tight so that they won't leak out because I haven't enough time to use them."[69] She was beginning to see dramatic potential in mundane situations, like taking the subway to Ruth's house: "The air was foul with the smell of smoke and wetness, and the subway seemed to be full of evil-looking men who gazed at innocent me from out of shifty, bloodshot eyes."[70] She began having "wonderful technicolor dreams" in which she played the heroine—rescuing her "friends from drowning on a huge ice flow in Antarctica," or a "detective-ess who solved the ghostly murder of a young man."[71] She identified closely with the hot-tempered Scarlett O'Hara that year when she saw *Gone with the Wind* ("I was Scarlett"), and she envied Rudyard Kipling's experience living in India.[72] She loved the "throbbing rhythm" of his "Mandalay": "I'm all in the mood for thundery poetry now. I wish I had the experience to write about it. It's so sad to ache to write wonderful poems and not have things to do with it!"[73] The "coarse language" of "Gunga Din," her favorite Kipling poem, thrilled her, and she quoted him in her diary: "'E'll be squattin' on the coals / Givin' drink to pore [sic] damned souls, / An' I'll get a swig in hell from Gunga Din!"[74] Kipling was a refreshing change from Teasdale. By late July, she was writing stories that were "quite passionate and rather lustful," though she admitted this only in her secret "Obbish" diary code.[75]

Sylvia raced through her assignments in order to lounge in bed with *David Copperfield, The Mysterious Island, The Man with the Iron Mask, Ivanhoe,* or her diary. In May 1947, she created a scrapbook of her poems—an activity she would repeat each year as her collection grew. She was proud of the twenty-four poems that made the cut, which she called "very good," unlike her "silly little jingles!"[76] That spring, she was "in the poetry mood" and wrote five new poems.[77] The best was the Gothic "Steely-Blue Crags," with its Hughesian description of cliffs, "Eerie and strange," full of "rough-hewn crags."[78]

In April, Sylvia wrote a poem, "I thought that I could not be hurt," about a pastel drawing her grandmother had accidentally smudged. For months Sylvia had struggled to earn Miss Hazleton's praise in art class; as time passed her teacher became "stricter than ever about every little speck of color going in the right place."[79] Finally, in the spring of 1947, Miss Hazleton began to compliment her efforts. A drawing of a Tiffany glass vase, for example, "pleased because I really got the feeling of the luminosity of the gleaming glass!"[80] In May, Miss Hazleton told Sylvia that a still life of a Chinese jug was her "best pastel yet."[81] Unequivocal praise from a teacher with such exacting standards thrilled her.

> I took it home proudly, and immediately showed it to mum, who was very pleased. However, someone accidentally rubbed a cloth against it and destroyed part of the clear coloring. I was heart broken. I patched it up again, but, you know, nothing like that is as good as new. However, I wrote a poem about it (my best one yet) in a very new, modern style.[82]

Plath turned pain into art and proved to herself that nothing is truly lost as she produced this substitute "best" composition:

> I thought that I could not be hurt;
> I thought that I must surely be
> impervious to suffering—
> immune to mental pain
> or agony.

The poem goes on to describe how the speaker's "world turned gray" when "careless hands" destroyed her "silver web of happiness." But the poem contains a surprisingly astute moment of self-reflection about the fragility of human emotion:

> (How frail the human heart must be—
> a throbbing pulse, a trembling thing—
> a fragile, shining instrument
> of crystal, which can either weep,
> or sing.)[83]

Previous biographers have presented "I thought that I could not be hurt" as a piece of verse that foreshadows Plath's future neuroses.[84] Anne Stevenson began her famously negative biography of Plath with a discussion of this poem, which she noted was occasioned by a "minor mishap."[85] Without any knowledge of Plath's struggles to earn Miss Hazelton's praise, or an understanding of the pleasure she derived from using "experience" to create poems, "I Thought That I Could Not Be Hurt" does seem melodramatic. But placed back in its original context and read through the lens of Sylvia's own diary description, it stands out as a creative experiment and an artistic turning point. "I Thought That I Could Not Be Hurt" represents a courageous turn, for it is the first poem in which Plath dares to write in the first person about "mental pain" and "agony"—risky terrain for a daughter raised in a household that had tried to banish the specter of tragedy. Sylvia recognized that the poem was "new, modern"—an exciting departure from the emotionally safe landscape poetry of her juvenilia. For the first time, her poem's speaker refuses to keep quiet about anger and disappointment. Plath has left Plato's shadow cave to emerge into the bright glare of a world in which suffering occurs, and is deeply felt. The poem sounds, at times, like elegy; in mourning the loss of her perfect art, she hints obliquely at a deeper, unspoken grief. This poem, far from being neurotic, was a healthy way to redeem and transform her disappointment into art.

———

IN JUNE, Sylvia graduated from junior high school and won the much-coveted Wellesley Award, for which she received Cleanth Brooks's and Robert Penn Warren's *Understanding Poetry*, a foundational New Critical text. She was also, as she had hoped, the first student to ever receive a sixth "letter" award for academic achievement. Yet she described the ceremony as a "nightmare of continually going up on the stage to get awards and certificates."[86] She was nervous that so much academic publicity would ruin her chances of joining the popular crowd, but her fears were unwarranted—she received more than seventy-five signatures in her yearbook. As usual, she was greeted by "an enthusiastically appreciative family" after the ceremony.[87] Now that her days were free, she turned to writing. She was composing a radio play she called *The White Mantle Murders*. Sylvia noted Aurelia's aversion to the genre ("Mum hates murder stories!"), though she *was* reading Edgar Allan Poe that summer.[88] Sylvia spent many hours working on the plot; as she flirted with her crush Tommy Duggin on the bus, she "deliberated silently who I should murder in my new story."[89]

In late June she traveled by train and ferry to Martha's Vineyard, where she spent two weeks at a Girl Scout–affiliated sailing camp in Oak Bluffs. The camp was nestled in the woods on the shores of a calm lagoon where the girls sailed each day. She reveled in the drama of sailing, "coming about and hard-a-leeing . . . skimming over the green waves and cutting through the lagoon with a dash of spray."[90] She loved her long bike rides to East and West Chop and Chappaquiddick, and languorous afternoons lying on the beach, where she could meditate in silence.

She began experimenting with different looks. She donned a new hairstyle, parted on the side and braided, and even took on a new name. "Everybody calls me 'Sherry' and I feel like a different person without any old restrictions," she wrote Aurelia. "If someone says something mean about me (which no one does, thank goodness) I can just go back home and start being 'sylvia' [sic] again."[91] Years before her Smith College thesis on "the double," she was already interested in dualities.

Sylvia made a few new friends, such as Ann Bowker and June Smith, and felt that she had conquered the popular camp clique; she was so well liked, she proudly reported, that her friends threw her a going-away party before her departure. In her high school scrapbook she later wrote that this time was "the beginning of my new found self."[92] But to Aurelia she wrote that her new friends fell short—"I inwardly find fault with a lot of them"—and complained that there was no one like Betsy or Ruth to share her confidences. Though she chastised herself for being critical about other campers, she acknowledged that writing down her feelings served a practical purpose: "at least when I write it down in here I can get it off my chest and act alot [sic] nicer that way!"[93] She was beginning to realize that her diary could serve as both a sounding board for her writing and a private channel for letting off steam. It may have been the only place she could do so. On Visiting Day, she and the other girls were "very quiet and demure, and resting on our beds and reading etc. to show the visitors that we were really quite ladylike."[94] The girls and their parents seemed to prefer the illusion of passive femininity to the reality of shin-bruising dinghy sails and twenty-mile bike rides.

Sylvia had a strong reaction to the movie *Cynthia*, which she saw with Aurelia during her first weekend home that July. She made a cryptic yet important remark about *Cynthia* in her diary: it "solved many of my own problems, and I loved every minute of it."[95] The movie, which starred a fifteen-year-old Elizabeth Taylor, begins as Cynthia's ambitious, career-minded parents fall in love. The couple wants to leave the United States for Vienna, where Cynthia's mother aspires to become a concert pianist and her father hopes to work in medicine. But when their daughter is born frail and sickly, they abandon their dreams and move to a small town where Cynthia's uncle, a doctor, can monitor her health. Cynthia's mother becomes a housewife while her father takes a demeaning job in a shop. Over the years, Cynthia's parents shadow her every move and prevent her from experiencing a normal life for fear that any strain will exhaust her. Everyone is unhappy—Cynthia's parents are bitter about their fate while Cynthia resents their hovering. By the movie's end, Cynthia finally breaks free of their overprotective ways and finds love through the use of her musical talent.

Sylvia may have begun to feel that her own mother was sheltering her from "real living" in order to shield her from more tragedy. She may also have begun to suspect that Aurelia was, as she would later claim in her journal, living vicariously through her achievements. The movie "solved her problem" by presenting art as a path to autonomy. However, she was grateful that Aurelia took her to an elegant French restaurant in Boston after the movie. "Mother knew just what I wanted, or rather needed . . . in the quiet, antiquated atmosphere we could almost fancy ourselves to be dining in a foreign courtyard."[96] The deep symbiotic nature of Sylvia's relationship with her mother is clear in her *Cynthia* diary entry. She longs to break free of Aurelia's influence (her "problem"), yet she reveals her dependency (Aurelia knows just what she needs). Later that summer she complained that Aurelia wouldn't let her see *Gone with the Wind* in Boston alone—"I guess she thinks that something would crawl out of the sewer and 'get me' "—but then admitted that she was "really glad" Aurelia accompanied her "after all."[97]

Aurelia frequently indulged her daughter by taking her out to plays, movies, museums, department stores, and restaurants. But such outings sometimes led to frayed nerves for both. Shortly after seeing *Cynthia*, while shopping for a new dress in Filene's, Sylvia lashed out at Aurelia in her "Obbish" code language when her mother refused to buy her an expensive green and black plaid dress. "She was the one who picked it out, but when she saw how I looked in it she wouldn't let me get it—the horrid stinker! How I hate her! I won't be happy until I get it. I hate her I hate her she's a damn cuss'd old thing." This was the angriest language Sylvia had ever used against her mother, and she immediately apologized. "I really don't mean all that—really, but I feel better to have gotten it out of my system."[98] Years later Aurelia would explain the outbursts of anger in Plath's fiction in similar terms at a public lecture in Wellesley: only by writing down her negative feelings could her daughter exorcise them.[99]

Sylvia admitted that the dress had to be specially washed and wasn't "much of a bargain"—perhaps the real reason Aurelia changed her mind.[100] The incident speaks as much to Plath's frustration over her family's financial circumstances as it does to anger toward her mother. Though Sylvia and her grandmother enjoyed Sunday dinner at the Brookline Country Club the following weekend—waited on by Grampy Schober—she was mature enough to realize that the "airy" table, the "crisp white cloth," views of the "rolling green golf course," and sumptuous four-course meal were illusions of affluence.[101] The Powleys had an Irish maid, but Sylvia's grandfather *was* the help.

During Sylvia's fourteenth summer, men began to take notice of her. She was elated, she wrote, when truck drivers or men in passing cars whistled at her, which now happened frequently. Sometimes these encounters were fraught with danger: twice when she was riding her bicycle along a deserted country road, men driving in the opposite direction turned around to pursue her. In both cases, she pulled up to a house or store and laughed off the incident as the men passed slowly by. On the bus ride back to Wellesley after seeing *Cynthia*, a boy pulled her hair out the window and called her "Blondie," a gesture that provoked not anger but excitement from both mother and daughter. Sylvia was happy that a boy had paid attention to her, while Aurelia remarked, "She has bloomed into beauty."[102] So sexist was the society in which they lived that male harassment was met with pride.

Sylvia fell in love, briefly, with the son of a family friend named Redmond, who tried to grope her during outings to the Boston Common. She claimed that she was eager for the attention. She became more confident about her appearance and declared that her hair was her "crowning glory" with its "gleaming blonde and copper lights."[103] She even tried smoking once with her friend Ruth Geisel—only "pretending to inhale"—in order to impress a group of boys, but felt "very cheap and ashamed" afterward. Despite the recurring motifs of violence, madness, and risk taking in her later poetry, Sylvia was not a particularly rebellious teenager, and she judged others for bowing to peer pressure. After the smoking incident, for example, Ruth was forever tainted. "I said that of course it didn't make any difference, but way deep down inside of course it did!"[104]

In September 1947, Plath entered Wellesley's Gamaliel Bradford Senior High School as a sophomore. She decided not to run for student council again because she did not want to open herself up to "malicious attacks" that might threaten her popularity. But the decision was not an easy one for the ambitious teenager; she called the day a "queer" one for her "spirit." Still, she felt it was the right choice given her stressful schedule the year before: "It was good to sit on the sidelines for once."[105] Within a month, however, she had joined the features staff of the school newspaper, *The Bradford*.

Sylvia, now almost fifteen, reflected in her scrapbook that she had lost her junior high bid for secretary because it was "popularity that counted" rather than "good marks": "Perhaps I was doomed always to be on the outside."[106] She may have felt that her ambiguous class position, or perhaps her studious nature, prevented her from climbing to the top of the social ladder. Sylvia's closest friends from this time do not remember her this way; Betsy spoke of her as "not a loner at all," as someone full of energy and enthusiasm "with a zest for life."[107] Her self-identification as an "outsider" did not ring true to Perry, either, who said "she didn't seem to suffer any disapproval because of her grades . . . everybody seemed to like her." This was quite a feat since even in honors classes, Perry remembered, students tended not to "shine too much because you had to fit in with the crowd." He called Sylvia "statuesque" and "very wholesome" in an all-American way.

He saw no hint during high school of her future battles with depression: "Just a very normal kid, very brilliant, very popular."[108] Betsy agreed; she described Sylvia as "happy, wholesome, and healthy," though she remembered Aurelia once told Mrs. Powley that Sylvia wished she were as popular as Betsy.[109]

Plath's diary entries from this period do not suggest that she suffered from "strangeness" or "strange behavior," as at least two biographers have suggested.[110] Aurelia, however, noted that Sylvia did not menstruate until she was sixteen; she "worried about being different from other girls" and was "teased about this by her playmates."[111] Yet Sylvia was never at a loss for male and female friends with whom to spend weekends at football games and rec room parties (the "light, breezy" Arden Tapley was again part of her close circle).[112] When she was not out riding her bike, she was "roaring" around in cars with boys: "How we got to Arden's house in one piece, I don't know, but we did."[113] She looked down on those, like Margot Loungway, who shunned school social events and football games—true loners who did not show enough "school spirit." She grew more confident of her beauty, calling herself "resplendent" in her burgundy coat and black velvet skirt that November, and "really glamorous" after dressing up for a Christmas dance.[114]

Sylvia was maturing, but she still relied heavily on Aurelia despite her efforts to become more independent. While Aurelia was in the hospital in September, Sylvia sent her a poem titled "Missing Mother" and told her, "I must have someone understanding to talk to."[115] But not everything could be shared with Aurelia. Sylvia spent afternoons in her girlfriends' rooms recounting the minutiae of school dances and flirtations, and reading "spicy parts" of "nasty books" out loud.[116] Sylvia was somewhat embarrassed by her new "sad" preoccupation, as she called it, and admitted that she became bored reading over past diary entries about boys she no longer liked. Her crushes changed every few weeks, but Tommy Duggin ("handsome, magnificent, drooly, superb, wonderful"), John Hall (a "handsome athlete"), Perry Norton, and John Stenberg shuffled through the top of her list.[117] Around this time she started lying to Aurelia about her after-school whereabouts and continued joyriding with Arden and boys who drove too fast. One afternoon they all crashed into a snowbank as the driver played a harmonica. None of it bothered Sylvia, who enjoyed watching the scenery speed by and listening to the boys' "nasty" comments from the back seat.[118]

Despite the brief, glancing attentions of several boys in her class, it was Perry Norton, the safe choice, to whom she was most attached. Running into him one night unexpectedly during the spring of 1948, she reflected on the value of their friendship:

He is so pure and wonderful. It just seems unnecessary to talk when we're together because our thoughts run along the same lines. I feel so natural and perfect when I'm with him. . . . I can be happy as long as Perry is alive, I guess, because I know there's one person in the world [in] whom I can confide and be sure of confidence in return.[119]

Perry would continue to play this role as they grew older. He remembered Sylvia's "proprietary" suspicion when he brought his future wife, Shirley, to meet her when she was home from Smith. Shirley told him later, "I had the feeling that I was being observed and critiqued, like she felt possessive of you and that she wanted to make sure that I was the right person for you." Shirley passed the test, and, Perry remembered, "They got along fine."[120] Although the two lost touch after Sylvia left for England, he would remain her ideal example of a pure male-female friendship, the first of several "psychic brothers."

Aurelia said that she had been forthright with her children about sex from the time they were young. When Sylvia was eleven, Aurelia gave her the book *Growing Up* by Karl De Schweinitz. "She knew the full facts about sexual intercourse by fifteen, when she began to date." Plath asked her mother many questions about sex and homosexuality, which Aurelia, somewhat embarrassed, did her best to answer. Aurelia explained that, regretfully, a double standard existed when it came to men's and women's sexuality, and that Sylvia "should not be shocked on hearing boys of her acquaintance having had experience." Like most mothers in the 1950s, Aurelia advised her teenage daughter to abstain from sex until marriage.[121]

As Sylvia began to date other boys, she became increasingly aware of those double standards. On a bus ride that October she gushed over a handsome young stranger who smiled at her as he exited. "Sometimes things like that make me wonder why couldn't I have just said to him 'I like you' and let him know? I know he wanted to meet me, but of course it wouldn't be 'proper' to pick up a 'chance acquaintance' like that, no matter how nice it would seem to be—convention or something."[122] That same month she again expressed doubt in the prevailing conventions as she began to feel estranged from all that was familiar to her:

I don't know what it is, but my thoughts seem to be very hazy. I can usually be comfortable in building up my little life with natural hopes and fears of what goes on about me, but lately I have acquired the discomforting habit of questioning those truths which my life has been based upon—such as religion, human nature, and other laws.[123]

Otto Plath as a young man

Otto Plath upon his graduation from
Northwestern College, Wisconsin, 1910

Otto Plath, 1924

Otto Plath in the 1930s

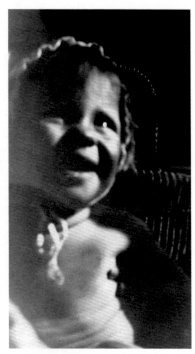

Aurelia Plath with her daughter, Sylvia, April 1933

Sylvia Plath, 1935. In the margin of this photo, Aurelia Plath wrote, "Sylvia is always merry!"

Aurelia, Otto, and Sylvia Plath at the Arnold Arboretum, Jamaica Plain, Massachusetts, July 1933

Sylvia Plath, posed with a book, 1934

Sylvia Plath, Winthrop, Massachusetts, c. July 1936

Aurelia Plath (left) with her sister, Dorothy Schober, and Sylvia Plath, Point Shirley, Winthrop, Massachusetts, c. 1936

Aurelia and Sylvia Plath, August 1937

spring
Here are Warren and I in our back yard in Winthrop. The flowers are in bloom, and you can see all the lovely petunias. Warren holds his beloved teddy, Trixie, and I have my own Nancy-doll in my arms.

winter

winter in winthrop ③
This is quite a change from the opposite picture. It is February, 1939, now, and Warren and I are "coasting" together on our small sled. Mother later got us a much larger one which we still have now. This is down on the beach by the bayside. The snow is melting, and the Humsteins house is the big one on the right.

1938

Fall
This is Warren in our back yard towards fall. It is quite bare, because flowers do not soften the angular fence with their leaves and blooms any more, the Wood's house is shown over the fence, and you can even see Mrs. Wood's closing the window upstairs.

Summer

This was taken by the white sand dunes on the shores of the Ipswich waters. We were driven down there by Grammy to spend a day and have a picnic. I will never forget the clear blue ripply water and the tiny shells along the beach.

Here I am just when I started to grow braids?

This is the best picture taken of Warren and me together. I am wearing my favorite sunsuit, and Warren holds the huge fish that Frankie caught. We are standing on Frankie's sailboat that he made, and it is drawn up on the shores of the sea that I love so much. The big footprint in the sand is not mine, but Frankie's.

WINTHROP

Warren and I are admiring the cat. This is not Mowgli, but his mother, Mitzi. We are in front of our house in Winthrop. Mitzi is willingly posing in my dollies bonnet, her paws patting my chin. This picture was taken the summer after I had my crucial sinus attack, so I don't look too healthy. The picture is in here to show off Mitzi, anyway. [t]

a picture of Ruthie a man as a little g[irl] still bears quite [a] semblance to Th[e] you can see in th[e pict]ure on the opposite [page] taken when she was 12 years old.

A page from Sylvia Plath's scrapbook with photos from her childhood in Winthrop, Massachusetts

Sylvia Plath doing tricks on her bicycle,
c. 1942–43. Sylvia pasted this photo in her
scrapbook with the caption "The acrobat
on her new bike!"

Sylvia Plath in her Girl Scout uniform,
August 1946

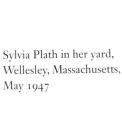

26 Elmwood Road, Wellesley, Massachusetts, 1948

Sylvia Plath in her yard,
Wellesley, Massachusetts,
May 1947

Sylvia Plath's drawing of her mother, August 1948

Sylvia, Warren, and Aurelia Plath, September 1949

Sylvia Plath, dressed up for a dance, 1949

The Norton boys. From left, Perry, David, and Dick. Sylvia pasted this photo in her scrapbook.

Sylvia Plath and friends at the King Philip dance club, Wrentham, Massachusetts, summer 1949. Her date is second from left.

Sylvia Plath's high school graduation portrait, 1950

Sylvia Plath, marked by her mother with a star above her head, at the Star Island Unitarian retreat, New Hampshire, June 1949

Sylvia Plath, the day of her high school graduation, June 1950. Above this photo she wrote in her scrapbook, "You knew that if you just let time go by, you would very soon be old."

Paradise Pond, Smith College, Northampton,
Massachusetts

Olive Higgins Prouty at her sixtieth
Smith College reunion, 1964

Sylvia Plath and Marcia Brown,
Francestown, New Hampshire,
February 1951

Sylvia Plath (bottom
row, third from
left) at a party for
first-year students,
Haven House, Smith
College, May 1951

For the first time in her life—as for many teens—the specter of doubt had begun to infiltrate her thinking. But doubt was not compatible with the person she was expected to become, so she silenced herself. The repression of doubt could sometimes morph into the desire for self-sabotage: "Part of me is urging on ahead to better grades, and another shabby little part (that knows it's in the wrong) wants to hold me back and make me get only mediocre 'B' marks," she wrote in her diary that fall.[124]

Mother and daughter celebrated Sylvia's fifteenth birthday with an afternoon of shopping in Boston, where Sylvia found "THE DRESS" in Chandler's department store. A circle of salesladies cooed over her as she tried it on. "What a dear child!" one remarked. Sylvia scoffed at the label now that she was fifteen and hoped instead that "some tall dark MAN" might find her attractive in the dress.[125] Later that afternoon, she flirted with the elevator boy near the shoe department, and even Aurelia got in on the fun. "Don't tell me you're getting signals," she whispered to her daughter. Sylvia took the elevator down before her mother had time to pay for the shoes, so she could be alone with the boy. It was a bold move, and she was embarrassed when the elevator opened and she rushed out the wrong door. Aurelia found the episode amusing and joked with her daughter about it over chowder later that afternoon.

Sylvia went on her "first <u>real</u> date" that December with John Pollard, a tall and wealthy classmate. They joined another couple at a local dance hall; "what luxury—what class," she exclaimed. But John tried to grope her on the dance floor, and by the end of the night she found him "nauseating." In order to avoid "parking," she told him she needed to be home before midnight. Still, she regarded the date as a minor success, for it allowed her to meet other boys and let "everyone know how fun I am."[126] Being asked out by a boy—any boy—was a mark of popularity. But her lack of power to change or control the situation made her miserable. "There are so few people that I don't like at all! I would have one of them ask me out! Oh, well! He'll probably never ask me again; and tell all the boys that I'm prissy and unresponsive—He'll never realize it's just with him. I'm probably the dope, but I don't care—too much."[127] She dramatized her predicament in notes for a short story, "Party Girl," from this time. At a co-ed party, a teenage girl "suddenly realizes how horrible and nightmarish the whole thing is. . . . Cries upstairs in the bathroom, but her hostess comforts her—telling her that the only thing to do is play the role—flirt with other boys. She'll get used to it—They all do."[128]

In this way, Sylvia's early dates were another rude encounter with "convention," a concept she would question in the years ahead. A visit to a Boston jail with a Unitarian minister that December made a deeper impression than her dates with John. There, she saw petty thieves and "Negro" prostitutes who regarded her disdainfully. She felt a sexual charge as she passed "the handsomest tall boy in a white sweatshirt (jailed for [a] holdup with a car and a gun) looking at me," and described the arms of a burglar as "admirably tattooed."[129] This was her first real encounter with sin and vice. But fascination quickly turned to fright when the warden "playfully" shut her up in solitary confinement. "It was awful! Pitch black—no windows no benches, just floor, and a slot to put bread and water through. The warden told us proudly that a certain gang was planning to knock out the guards . . . and stage a break, but each had been locked up in 'solitary' and had come out a day later—meek and submissive—promising to be 'good boys.' "[130] Plath suspected that the warden had simplified a more disturbing truth—one she would attempt to reveal in her own work after she, too, veered from the prescribed course.

5

The Voice Within

Wellesley, 1947–1948

B y the start of her tenth-grade year in 1947, Sylvia had begun to aim a more skeptical eye at jingoistic nationalism. Her interest in politics— particularly the politics of pacifism—was growing. Despite Americans' deep desire to avoid another world war, pacifism was an unpopular ideology in the late 1940s. In 1948, the Soviets had installed a communist government in Czechoslovakia and begun annexing East Berlin. In 1949 they would detonate their first atomic bomb, and Mao Tse-tung's communist government would take over China. The Truman Doctrine, which stated that the United States would "support free peoples who are resisting attempted subjugation by armed minorities," took effect in 1947. This was the same year Truman issued Executive Order 9835, which sought to protect "the United States against infiltration of disloyal persons into the ranks of its employees." The Red Hunt was on, and between 1947 and 1952 more than six million people would be investigated.

It was during this time that the rhetoric of "soft" and "hard" transformed American political discourse, and even American society: to be "soft" on communism—as Joseph McCarthy accused Truman—was as good as committing treason. The progressive liberalism of the New Deal and left-wing intellectualism were casualties of this rhetoric. By McCarthy's heyday in the 1950s, 78 percent of Americans polled in a national survey supported reporting friends and neighbors with suspected communist sympathies to the FBI. Liberalism, along with the entire Democratic Party, was vilified by Republicans and many Republican-backed newspapers. Dwight D. Eisenhower sailed to victory in the 1952 presidential race, ending twenty years of Democratic control. Dissent and difference were to be repressed at all costs. By 1956, Robert Lindner, the prominent psychiatrist and author of *Rebel*

Without a Cause: The Story of a Criminal Psychopath—the book on which the James Dean film was based—could declare that communism was "a haven for neurosis and a refuge for neurotics."[1]

For politicians and the media, taking a hard line against communism meant trumpeting nuclear armament as the only strong course for America. Though John Hersey's *Hiroshima* had exposed the horrors of the bomb as early as 1946, "horror had its hypnotic appeal."[2] Ethical questions about the bomb were generally dismissed in the early 1950s, in favor of a narrative of optimism that portrayed nuclear superiority as a virtual guarantee of global manifest destiny. The bomb even had sex appeal: "atomic" became a cute colloquialism that teenagers—including Sylvia—used to describe their crushes. The Las Vegas Chamber of Commerce even crowned a Miss Atomic Blast.[3]

In this environment, pacifism was linked to other suspect "isms": atheism, liberalism, and Marxism. In 1951, an antinuclear, pacifist group called the Stockholm Appeal, co-organized by W. E. B. Du Bois, was denounced by the *Los Angeles Times*. The paper urged its readers to report pacifist petitioners—who, it claimed, were "straight from Moscow"—to the FBI.[4] Du Bois and four of his co-organizers were later indicted by the United States government "for failure to register as agents of a 'foreign principal.'"[5] They were acquitted, but the trial underscores just how risky it was to practice pacifism during the Cold War, when "peace" itself became a suspect ideology. Quakers were harassed, as were prominent peace activists such as A. J. Muste, who advocated for civil disobedience in the style of Gandhi. Against this backdrop, Plath's burgeoning pacifism—influenced by Unitarian Church principles, her own parents' pacifism, and friends like Perry Norton (who eventually became a Quaker)—appears less quaint.

In 1946, Sylvia grew more aware of the West's past and future horrors. In March she produced a social studies report titled "The United States and the World," in which she assembled newspaper clippings about the buildup to the Cold War ("Russia Tightens Grip on Balkans") and the fledgling attempts of the new United Nations to avoid "atomic diplomacy." She included a political cartoon, with satirical undertones, of Uncle Sam lecturing representatives from other nations as Cuba leaves with a diploma and titled one section "Can the UNO Prevent Another World War?"[6] Her report suggests a left-leaning attitude toward the expanding international crisis: she declared that the United States and Great Britain should do everything they could to placate Russia, and argued that the United States should cede its wartime acquisitions in the Pacific if it expected Russia to back away from Turkey, Iran, and eastern Europe. She seemed to understand that the end of one war had ushered in the start of another, and that the threat of nuclear annihilation was real. This was the beginning of her education in

Cold War politics, a subject to which she would return throughout her life and work.

In February 1946, Sylvia wrote a thirty-eight-page school report about World War I, called, ironically, "A War to End All Wars," revealing a mind disturbed by war's violence. Her accompanying illustration of a wounded man with a bloody, bandaged head stands as a sobering counterpoint to her original ditty that instructed soldiers to "pack up" their troubles in their kit bag and "smile, smile, smile." In another drawing, a neatly dressed schoolgirl reads a book about the war, a tear rolling down her cheek as she imagines a scene of carnage that includes cannons, smoke, barbed wire, and dead bodies. The landscape of war stands in obscene contrast to her homey room; the schoolgirl will never be the same.[7]

Plath deplored war on a moral level, yet, like her hero W. B. Yeats, the artist in her was fascinated by apocalypse. In April 1947, she began writing to a new pen pal in Grebenhain, Germany, Hans-Joachim Neupert.[8] She was eager to correspond with a German; she told him, proudly, that her own father had been a professor from Germany, and that her grandmother was an Austrian who served hearty European meals.[9] But she was interested in the relationship for more dramatic reasons. Her World War I report had given her a more accurate understanding of what Europe's beleaguered citizens had suffered, and she was ready to hear from the front lines. Part of what drew her to Hans was his firsthand knowledge of mass destruction. "Is it true that many bodies are still buried under the crumbled rubble of the large buildings?" she asked him in October 1949. "We saw some colored slides of the ruins in large German towns."[10] When Hans pointed out that Americans could not understand what the war had been like in Europe, she agreed. "How right you are when you say one can not fully understand the seriousness of life when one lives in good conditions!" she wrote him in 1948. "Take the last war, for instance. To me, it was as unreal as a fairytale. . . . I would like to plunge into the vital world, if I could."[11] As if offering consolation for the ruin of his nation, she tried to convince Hans that Americans were not "frivolous" and "spoiled," and she emphasized that she herself was "far from rich." She expounded on her pacifist views: "We want so much to have peace—we students. . . . Do you not feel as I do—that war is futile in the end?"[12]

Sylvia later pasted a photo of Hans in her scrapbook, and wrote, "the youth all over the world has the same ideals and emotions—a universal bond. Yet as we grow up, we are unfortunately nationalized and carefully taught to hate those who challenge our complacent mode of living."[13] This seemingly innocuous statement was in fact quite radical; the idea that young Americans were "unfortunately nationalized" would have sounded almost treasonous in the context of late-1940s political paranoia.

She repeated her antiwar stance to Hans in several letters throughout 1948–50. In August 1950, she called dropping the bomb on Hiroshima a "sin" and quoted an antiwar poem by Thomas Hardy. She felt that American children did not take war seriously because they had "never seen the effects"—a "dangerous" predicament.[14]

> Of course there are dances and parties on weekends, but this war-scare bothers me so much that I can never completely forget myself in artificial gaiety. Always in the background there is the fear that I will never be able to live in peace. . . . Surely democracy and freedom would mean little in a world of rubble and radioactive rays. . . . I think of us as of the Roman Empire and feel that this is the fall, perhaps, of our new and bright civilization.[15]

The Korean War, which began in 1950, made her "ill." "There is nothing brave or heroic about this war. What are we fighting for?" she asked Hans. "For nothing. Against communism. That word, communism, is blinding. No one knows exactly what it means, and yet they hate everything associated with it. One thing I am convinced of: you can't kill an idea."[16] She felt the anti-communist war hawks were "fools."[17]

These ideas could have earned Plath a place on an FBI blacklist. Sylvia and her family had been targeted during the previous world wars on account of their German heritage, and the experience had left its mark on her psyche. She had little sympathy for intolerance of "others," even communists. Yet her leftist tolerance did not include those with disabilities. At times, her obsession with health and vitality—perhaps rooted in the childhood trauma of her father's early death—could lead her perilously close to eugenic thinking. "It is entirely against reason to kill the best and the healthiest—why not the aged cripples, if we must kill . . . ?" she asked Hans in 1949.[18] Yet elsewhere she showed liberal sympathies antithetical to such disturbing comments. In a tenth-grade paper about witchcraft in America, for example, she seized on the connection between the colonial witch-hunts and present-day Jim Crow. "There may come a time," she warned, "when our descendants laugh at our cruel, thoughtless prosecution of different racial groups. Yes, we may wonder how intelligent people could murder 'witches,' but how similar are the race riots and skirmishes of today!"[19]

Hans, a German who lived an ocean away, was an early, safe sounding board for the subversive political ideas Plath would later express in her creative work. In the March 1950 *Christian Science Monitor*, she coauthored an article with Perry titled "Youth's Plea for World Peace," in which they publicly rejected the apocalyptic logic of the arms race between America and the Soviet Union.

Youth programs that fostered international cooperation and exchange would be far more valuable, they argued, than a bomb that could annihilate humanity. Though they took pains to support the United States' mission to spread democracy and capitalism, writing that American society was "ideal," many of their points could have been read, given the paranoia of the time, as subversive. "Is it any wonder, then, that some of us young people feel rebellious when we watch the futile armaments race beginning again?" they wrote. They called nationalism a "dilemma" and advocated instead an embrace of "the basic brotherhood of all human beings." Their final thoughts rejected the patriotic, pro-bomb rhetoric of the time: "For those of us who deplore the systematic slaughter legalized by war, the hydrogen bomb alone is not the answer."[20] Perry remembered that he and Sylvia "felt very passionately about the need for avoiding international conflict right after the Second World War." The two of them were acutely aware, he said, not only of the war's "horrors," "but particularly of the Holocaust." Their pacifism colored their politics. "She and I were on a liberal track," Perry said. "She would have been a liberal Democrat."[21]

But even as Sylvia decried the use of the bomb in a mainstream newspaper and in her letters to Hans, she was taking stock of its metaphoric potential. Her 1948 poem "Youth's Appeal for Peace" shows her already rendering the apocalypse in her poetry: the four horsemen come "Thundering, thundering over the hill. . . . / And out of the cloud-blank from whence they came / The whine of shrill bombs and a burst of flame." Though the poem is an appeal for peace, Plath reveled in the violent, trochaic rhythms of the hoofbeats' portending doom:

> Desert breezes sighing, sobbing;
> Drums of thunder thudding, throbbing;
> Lightning cymbals clash and then—
> The tortured screams of a million men.[22]

This was an early rendition of the "strong" voice Ted Hughes would later encourage Plath to cultivate in her poetry. She would spend years writing elaborate, well-wrought, New Critical poetry before she broke out of "the glass caul" of formalism and embraced a bolder voice.[23] In "Ariel" she would pare down the four horsemen of the apocalypse to one horse and one woman, flying into the burning sun on a journey of rebirth and renewal.

In 1948, Sylvia and her mother were reading Ralph Waldo Emerson's benevolent philosophy together, but Sylvia's marginalia—considerably more skeptical than Aurelia's—suggests that she was ready for something bolder. Where Aurelia frequently annotated Emerson's prose with phrases like "good!" "lovely!" and "universal quality of beauty!" Sylvia wrote comments

like "Why?" "Does it?" "Meaning what?" "Perhaps," and "Please explain."
When Emerson extolled humility and moderation, Plath wrote, "Is this the
best way?" in the margin.[24] She could not contain her dry cynicism when
she read Emerson's dictum, "But one day all men will be lovers; and every
calamity will be dissolved in the universal sunshine." "Always the optimist
[sic]," she wrote pithily.[25]

Though Sylvia would come to associate what she saw as Emerson's naive
optimism with her mother, it was Aurelia who presented her with a much
more provocative philosophy: Nietzsche's *Thus Spake Zarathustra*, which
she gave Sylvia for Christmas in 1949. During the postwar years, Nietzsche
was associated with Nazism and atheism, and would have been considered a
potentially dangerous moral guide for a young middle-class woman.[26] Yet his
ideas regarding autonomy and his dramatic, headstrong prose inspired Plath.
Her copy of *Thus Spake Zarathustra* is heavily annotated. She called it "our
bible of individualism at present" in a 1954 college paper.[27] Her Yale boyfriend Mel Woody, who eventually became a philosophy professor, remembered discussing Nietzsche with her while she was at Smith. "She responded
to it. She loved Nietzsche's aphorisms."[28] In 1955, Plath called Nietzsche
her "favorite philosopher (the wit and poetry and shock of his epigrams
makes my soul 'sneeze' itself awake, to use a Nietzschean verb!)"[29] She was
later drawn to the work of D. H. Lawrence—and Ted Hughes—for similar
reasons. But her interest in Nietzsche and the aesthetics of violence would
always remain in tension with her commitment to pacifist ideals.

OF ALL SYLVIA'S ADOLESCENT TEACHERS, it was her high school English
teacher, Wilbury Crockett, who had the most profound influence on her
liberal and intellectual education. In his college-level honors seminar, which
lasted for three years of high school, Sylvia and her fellow "Crocketteers"
read between forty and fifty works of literature each year by major American
authors, as well as modern British and Irish authors such as Hardy, Conrad,
Joyce, Woolf, Yeats, Lawrence, Auden, and Dylan Thomas. The class was
small—about fifteen students. As Sylvia's friend Phil McCurdy remembered,
"The Crocketteers really were a different class of people in the high school.
Was it precious? Was it literary? Gilded? Yes. On the other hand, we were a
bunch of kids who loved school, who loved Crockett, who came to love literature and poetry. . . . When you spoke he listened. When he commented, it
was to the point and personal. The work was very hard, but he balanced that
by saying we're not going to do any silly testing. . . . We talked about books

literature and writing like the kids talk about records today. . . . He made you feel at times that you had produced gold."[30]

Crockett also taught Greek drama and philosophy, Shakespeare, Donne, Milton, Blake, and a few European writers such as Mann, Flaubert, Chekhov, Dostoevsky, and Tolstoy—though Phil could not remember reading a single woman writer over the three years. Three of Sylvia's friends from her class all mentioned that they had read *War and Peace* with Crockett; looking back, they were astonished that he thought them capable of the task.[31] They also remembered presenting four five-thousand-word papers over the course of the year, far beyond the typical high school workload. Phil felt everyone wanted to be there. "The forty-two minutes went by like forty-two seconds. You looked forward to it."[32]

Crockett supplemented class readings with theater trips to Boston, where his students saw *The Glass Menagerie*, *A Doll's House*, and *Death of a Salesman*. "In other classrooms we learned to memorize," recalled Perry Norton. "In his classroom we learned to think."[33] Sylvia's friend Frank Irish similarly recalled that the emphasis was on "understanding and appreciating literature" rather than test taking, and that there was "a lot of class discussion."[34] Louise Giesey White, who took Crockett's class with Sylvia, remembered that he was "dignified" and would address his students by their last names: Miss Plath, Miss Giesey. She recalled, too, one memorable essay topic: "Poetry is frozen music."[35] Pat O'Neil Pratson, who sat next to Sylvia in class, remembered another, which Crockett wrote on the board on the very first day of class: "What is the good life?" She and Sylvia "realized suddenly that this was going to be the opening of ourselves."[36]

Crockett was not only a respected teacher, but a compassionate listener, always ready to hear about "the depths of our adolescent angst."[37] He took his students seriously. One year when the class president died suddenly of pneumonia, none of the hastily arranged school assemblies comforted—but Crockett did. That day, Crockett came into class, paused, and read "To an Athlete Dying Young" by A. E. Housman. When he finished, he simply got up and left. For Crockett's grieving students, poetry had adequately expressed what the formal rituals of mourning could not.[38]

In early September 1947 Sylvia wrote excitedly to Aurelia, who was in the hospital recovering from stomach surgery, about her new honors class, English 21. "I could sit and listen to Mr. Crockett all day. . . . My English Class has so stimulated me that I'm chock-full of ideas for new poems. I can't wait to get time to write them down. I can't let Shakespeare get too far ahead of me, you know."[39] That afternoon, she went straight to the bookstore in Wellesley Square and bought a copy of Robert Frost's poems. (Frost was a favorite of Crockett's.) A month later, she decided it was time to show Crockett her own poetry. "Trembling inwardly," she presented him with several poems, four of which he read aloud in class. In her diary she wrote, "He liked 'Alone and Alone' and 'I Thought That I Could Not Be Hurt' above the rest, and encouraged me greatly by remarking that I had a lyric gift beyond the ordinary. I was overjoyed, and although I am doubtfully doubtful about poetry's affect [sic] on the little strategy of 'popularity' that I have been slowly building up, I am confident of admiration from Mr. C!"[40]

Admiration from "Mr. C" would become one of the driving forces behind Plath's creative life during high school. Aurelia said Sylvia had been offered a scholarship to Dana Hall, a prestigious private girls' boarding school, but that she chose to stay in Wellesley so that she could continue her studies with Crockett.[41] He was her first true literary mentor; he nurtured her ambition and urged her to take her literary goals seriously. He was, Pat remembered, "truly a spiritual father for her."[42] Crockett encouraged his students to write creatively and to read their work to the class. Louise remembered, "Several times he'd have Sylvia read her poetry aloud. We were all just astonished. I remember one poem, 'Five Smooth Stones,' and it was beautiful."[43] Plath's desire to become a great writer solidified in Crockett's class.

Crockett's literary approach dovetailed with the New Criticism then sweeping across high school and college English departments. New Criticism focused on a work's symbols, patterns, and metaphors rather than the life and times of its author. In Crockett's class, there were no lectures about authors' lives, a work's cultural context, or anything resembling literary history. Yet he held an abiding belief that literature could teach compassion and morality, and he encouraged his students to consider the relationship between literature and politics. Harold Kolb, who went on to become an English professor at the University of Virginia, remembered discussions about "the Korean war, the United Nations, the use of the atomic bomb, civil rights, post–World War II refugees, the Cold War, communism, the establishment of Israel, world religions, and world peace."[44] At one point Crockett even asked his students to send $1 a month to CARE. For him, morality was nearly as important as aesthetics; he was no Dadaist. Perry Norton remembered the day Crockett dismissed modern art as "a bunch of garbage." Several students, including Sylvia, "brought in a canvas and some paints and challenged him to create something modernistic." Crockett, to everyone's amusement, "failed miserably."[45] For someone as passionate about social justice as Crockett, splashes on a canvas were the epitome of amoral art.

Crockett was a Democrat, and his liberal sympathies made him a target in conservative, Republican Wellesley. "He believed," recalled Kolb, "that American society, in its tail-finned post-war boom of success, was in danger of getting it all wrong. His strictures—on materialism, television, spectator sports, celebrities, conspicuous consumption, Miss America contests, fraternities and sororities, political platitudes, journalistic distortion, and deceptive advertising—were brought home intact by youngsters eager to twit to their parents and caused many an uproar around Wellesley dinner tables."[46] Crockett's attitude toward America's hollow pleasures was closer to that of the Beat poets than to that of his students' parents. "Wellesley was highly Republican," Louise said. "He would talk about moral issues or ethical issues, consumption, and it was probably the only place we were getting it." He thought, she said, that they "were much too preoccupied with *things*."[47] Crockett made them see, Pat recalled, "that nobody in this town had been really and truly shaken and that we were to come forth and we were to shake!"[48] During the McCarthy era, rumors swirled that he was a communist, and in 1952 he was asked to go before the Wellesley town board to discuss his political beliefs. Crockett stated that he was not a communist but a pacifist, which evidently satisfied the board. Phil McCurdy thought the investigation "ridiculous."[49]

When he was later asked about his years teaching Plath, Crockett refused to fan the flames of melodrama. "I've received letters from all over the world," he said in 1981, "asking if I saw any instability in her; did anything about her suggest tragedy? I did not see any of this at all, no indication whatsoever. She was a happy, brilliant girl."[50] He was "astounded" by her gifts, her "almost frightening" talent, her "mercurial brilliance," and her "fine shining wit."[51] Indeed, Crockett's intimate, demanding seminar suited Plath's intellectual and creative needs perfectly. "She had a feeling of vocation," he said. "She would never be swayed from it."[52] Plath called him "an extraordinary man. I like him so—he does not try to indoctrinate us with ideas whatsoever, but is continually striving to get us to speak for ourselves and think also for ourselves."[53] She relished Crockett's poised, formal diction and donnish sense of humor.

Unlike most high school English teachers, Crockett encouraged his students to write and send their work to national magazines. Rejection slips were to be regarded as "battle scars that precede the victory of publication."[54] Sylvia took his advice to heart: she sent out more than fifty stories before her first *Seventeen* acceptance in 1950.[55] Aurelia remembered that during their first parent-teacher conference, Crockett told her that Sylvia would "be able to make writing her profession."[56] Here was someone who recognized her daughter's enormous potential. When Plath published her first poetry collection, *The Colossus*, in 1960, she sent her former mentor an inscribed copy that read, "To Mr. Crockett, in whose classroom and wisdom these poems have root." To her, he was "the teacher of a lifetime."[57]

Plath's skepticism toward the stifling norms of the 1950s also took root in Crockett's class. As she wrote in one assignment,

> In our era of cellophane-wrapped food, of deep freezes and television sets, we may not only buy things, but we may also purchase ideas and ideals, neatly packaged and labeled according to their contents. "Ladies and gentlemen, you see before you a selection of political opinions. Choose what you will, and fight for your possession. Socialism, Communism, Capitalism, Facism [sic]. Names, names, names."
>
> Truly there are "masked words" abroad, and masked words have a strange, hypnotic power over us. Instead of asking oneself, "What does this term mean; what are the laws, the real ideals behind it?" we lazily accept the word and use it thoughtlessly in our own speech. . . . We are skeptical about the value of our own thought.[58]

Crockett's pacifism strengthened Plath's own. Pacifist ideas began to appear in her creative and academic work in the late 1940s. In April 1948, she published a front-page article in *The Bradford* titled "The Atomic Threat."[59] A year later, in March 1949, she wrote an antiwar poem, "Seek No More the Young," modeled on the World War I verse of Wilfred Owen and Siegfried Sassoon:

> They came, the iron men; their rifles whined,
> And some fell limp upon the spattered stone –
> The light extinguished and their eyes glazed blind.
> But oh! the eyes of those alive—alone!
> The tortured panic of the world was there.
> Ah! seek no more the young with golden hair.[60]

Veiled diatribes against war found their way into a 1948–49 English paper on *Romeo and Juliet*, which quickly turned into a meditation on "the theme of all wars: two groups being in a deadly battle of extermination for a trumped-up reason." In the margin, Crockett challenged Plath, writing, "always?" For her, the feud between the Montagues and the Capulets symbolized Cold War aggression: "No one pauses to investigate the absurd little cause of the struggle. The aim is to devastate the opposing side, and that aim is all important. . . . That is the sadness of all wars."[61]

In other papers for Crockett, she was drawn to taboo subjects like adultery, madness, and suicide. During her tenth-grade year, she wrote about several novels and short stories by Nathaniel Hawthorne, whose Gothic explorations of Puritan sin fascinated her. She found Hester Prynne, from

The Scarlet Letter, a "regal, full-blooded" woman, though Dimmesdale "moved me not to pity, but rather to scorn.... I feel a strong contempt for his weakness."[62] Hawthorne's short story "Rappaccini's Daughter" may have inspired her later portrait of "Lady Lazarus": Plath wrote that she was "caught in the spell" of "the idea of a woman so nourished by poison, that her very breath or touch was fatal to other human beings," though she was "disappointed to find the typical Hawthorne climax—a moral."[63] In her later letters and journals, Plath would frequently refer to Rappaccini's daughter. "The Minister's Black Veil" also intrigued her: "Every one of us has a veil. Sometimes we succeed in covering our inner selves so thoroughly that it is difficult for us to pierce our own veil."[64]

During her sophomore year with Crockett, she read Virginia Woolf's *Mrs. Dalloway*. It was her "first encounter" with stream-of-consciousness narrative, and the effect was "electrifying." "At first you thought, 'What a jumbled conglomeration of vague shapes and shadows!' But as the faint light rose and increased, strange tints were revealed, and a glossy depth was apparent in the furnishings."[65] Her favorite character in the novel was not Mrs. Dalloway but Septimus Smith, the shell-shocked Great War veteran who commits suicide. His understanding of evil's hidden but pervasive presence in "civilized" society spoke to her. She also wrote a short report on the 1948 film *The Snake Pit* (based on the novel by Mary Jane Ward) about a schizophrenic writer's experiences in a mental hospital. Sylvia felt the film took an admirable moral stand in its depiction of the mentally ill. "There was no suggestion of embarrassed laughter at the sight of 'crazy people,' " she wrote, "but rather a feeling of compassion." This novel and movie eventually influenced her decision to write about her own experiences at McLean Hospital in *The Bell Jar*. "Must get out SNAKE PIT," she wrote in her journal in July 1959. "There is an increasing market for mental-hospital stuff. I am a fool if I don't relive, recreate it."[66] Indeed, *The Snake Pit*'s message, as Plath wrote in her high school report, was very similar to that of *The Bell Jar*: "In this woman's fight for her sanity, we see the struggle of the individual against the institution."[67]

———

UNDER WILBURY CROCKETT'S TUTELAGE, Plath began serving her literary apprenticeship in earnest. She wrote papers that dug deep into the technicalities of dactylic and anapestic meter, masculine and feminine rhyme schemes, liquid and sibilant consonants, villanelles, sonnets, rime royal, ottava rima, and rondeau. She explored how poets used particular meters and rhymes to achieve a desired aural effect. At times, she almost seemed to be writing about her own future work; when she writes of Walter de la Mare's "The Listener," for example—"The rhythm suggests the sound of distant hoofbeats: now soft, now loud, it fits in perfectly with the mood of the poem"—we are reminded of what has often been said about her technique in "Ariel."[68]

She created her own twenty-one-page "Anthology of American Poetry" for Crockett, which featured poems by H.D., Emily Dickinson, Robert Frost, T. S. Eliot, Edna St. Vincent Millay, Edgar Allan Poe, Ezra Pound, Walt Whitman, Carl Sandburg, Sara Teasdale (who had the most entries with five poems), and others.[69] Some of the poems she chose sound like precursors of "Ariel," in which the speaker flies with her mare into the sun, the "cauldron of morning": Amy Lowell's "Night Clouds" tells of a white mare with "golden hoofs" who flies into the heavens. ("Fly, mares!" Lowell writes. "Or the tiger sun will leap upon you and destroy you.") In "The Sea Gypsy" Richard Hovey writes of flying, by sail, into the sunset on a "trail of rapture." "Who Am I?" by Carl Sandburg looks forward to the austere, authoritative poetic voice in poems like Plath's "Elm":

> I have been to hell and back many times.
> I know all about heaven, for I have talked with God.
> I dabble in the blood and guts of the terrible.

She included two poems about depression—Edwin Arlington Robinson's "Richard Cory," in which a wealthy man who is the envy of the town shoots himself, and Robert Frost's "Desert Places," in which an "absent-spirited" speaker traveling through a snowy field describes his numbingly white surroundings:

> They cannot scare me with their empty spaces
> Between stars—on stars where no human race is.
> I have it in me so much nearer home
> To scare myself with my own desert places.

Plath's 1963 "Sheep in Fog," with its bleak imagery of whiteness, absence, and stars, would evoke a similar mood.

The introspective, sorrowful lilt of her high school poems was probably due to the heady influence of the Romantic and early modernist literature she was reading with Crockett; first-person speakers rarely made appearances in Plath's work before 1946, but after she began taking Crockett's class, they crowd her poems. She also made a pointed metaphorical shift from spring to autumn, which she found a more appropriate season to illuminate her speakers' Romantic despondency. Excited by her new theme, she circled back repeatedly to imagery of dead, dry leaves, gray dawns, fog, and cold rain. In "Reverie," the "autumn wind laughed through the bare trees / with a hollow sound"; in "Let the Rain Fall Gently," she writes, "Let the rain fall with a whisper / On the leaves and on the ground"; in "Wild Geese," "The only sound is the rattle and scrape / Of withered leaves down the windswept street"; and in "Bereft," "the thin rains fall, / And autumn is lonely and bitter brown."[70]

"Sorrow," which dates from 1947, is a good example of how she was learning to use nature as an objective correlative for her speaker's moods:

> Oh, no one in the world was kin
> To me or my sorrow.
> "Just wait," they said complacently,
> "Your sun will shine tomorrow."
>
> But all last night the rain came down,
> Monotonous and musical,
> Till, in the timid grey of dawn,
> I heard its murmuring grow still.
>
> Alas, tomorrow has arrived;
> My lonely heart still grieves,
> But I have found my solace in
> The restless sound of rain-soaked leaves.

Luxurious Keatsian despondency, touched by Teasdale, is on full display here as the poet tries her hand at Romantic self-fashioning.

Her tenth-grade poem titles suggest that she mined her sorrows for dramatic effect: "Bereft," "Alone and Alone in the Woods Was I," "Persecuted," and "Wallflower." Sometimes the speakers of these poems suffer from unrequited love, as in "Have You Forgotten?" (dedicated to Perry Norton). "Earthbound," from 1948, also looks inward, mixing existentialism and Romanticism. "I am too oppressed by earthly things," the speaker begins; she then complains of the "chairs and tables," "books and pencils," and "surface talk of friends and foes" that "crowd upon my sight." Her final stanza summons the ghost of Young Werther, Goethe's dark Romantic hero:

> Would that I were clear of mortal dust—
> Freed at last from these confining bars
> To drift forever through the endless sky,
> Illumined only by the thin, cold gleam of stars!

"In Passing" and "Lonely Song," which Plath wrote in 1949 under the pseudonym Sandra Peters, likewise revel in Romantic rhetoric.

Under Crockett, Plath also read T. S. Eliot and began experimenting with modernist poetic language. During her eleventh-grade year, she wrote a long paper for him in which she analyzed sections of "The Waste Land," "Ash Wednesday," "Mr. Apollinax," "The Hollow Men," "La Figlia Che Piange," and "The Love Song of J. Alfred Prufrock."[71] The paper, for which she received an A–, is not critically enlightening, but it is a deeply personal reflection on Eliot's work that suggests the extent of his future influence. Though Plath bemoaned her "lack of insight" and "ignorance" concerning the origins of Eliot's allusions, she admitted that she had found "little oases" of "revelation and beauty" within his work, and defended him as a lyric master. One did not need to understand all of Eliot's erudite allusions to enjoy his poetry, she argued. She liked the Cockney slang of "A Game of Chess," writing, "all this one hears daily on busses, trams and street cars. The hollow jargon of our country."

Plath valued Eliot's "striking irony"—his ability to render deep pathos through absurdity, as in Prufrock's "I have measured out my life with coffee spoons." She lauded his technical ability as well, noting that he was "a master for making the rhythm of his lines conform to his needs." Critics would eventually point out her own ability to master poetic momentum through rhythm. Indeed, her depiction of death in Eliot's "Ash Wednesday" almost reads like a critical description of her own poem "Edge": "Eliot transcends the terror and has a 'mystical vision of the serenity that will follow upon release from the body; even the very agents of dissolution themselves no longer seem terrifying, but are merged into the radiance of death become life.'"

She ended her paper with a meditation on Eliot's "Preludes," the one work by Eliot that she included in her anthology for Crockett. "Preludes" follows a young, disaffected poet-speaker as he navigates his way through "grimy scraps" and "newspapers from vacant lots" in Boston's slums, bearing witness to "the burnt-out ends of smoky days." Eliot's poem, itself heavily influenced by the French symbolism of Jules Laforgue, struck a modern note when it was published in 1920 for the way it married a Romantic quest with the urban imagery of squalor: "broken blinds," "dingy shades," "smells of beer," "muddy feet"—"The thousand sordid images / Of which your soul was constituted." She was struck by this unlikely marriage, and ended her paper by aligning Eliot's "realism" with D. H. Lawrence's. In Eliot, Plath found someone who reveled in the juxtaposition of high and low, placing the sordid and the lyrical side by side in fragile tandem, just as she would in her poems. Here was a new model—a poet who could seamlessly allude to Shakespearean tragedy and a slavey's abortion in the same poem.

Plath's "City Streets," written for Crockett in November 1947, explores the metaphoric potential of urban debris in imagistic free verse:

> A yellow fog slinks low along the ground
> And clings to the dingy brick walls of the tenements
> that crowd by the gutter.
> A damp newspaper somersaults along with the wind
> And then succumbs on the flat pavement, lonely, left behind.
>
> Blue spirals of smoke curl out of the sooty factory chimneys.
> A lean gray cat sulks around a rubbish heap,
> Seeking food, yet finding none.
>
> These are the wan, gray shreds of the tattered day.[72]

"City Streets" was utterly unlike anything Plath had written before. She dispenses with formal rhyme and writes free verse reminiscent of Eliot and Ezra Pound, and turns away from her usual landscape settings to explore, instead, an urban streetscape. She would return to urban imagery in other high school poems.

Plath was self-conscious and self-reflective about her literary vocation in early poems like 1948's "I Reach Out," "Obsession" (about writing), and "Neither Moonlight Nor Starlight," in which she defends her vocation to herself and to a society skeptical of women writers:

> Why do I stay at my inkstained desk
> From the dim gray dawn to the dusk of day?
> Why do I linger in the loneliness of this bleak place
> When I could be bathing in moonlight, stardust
> Or the spilling gold of the sun?
> (Neither moonlight nor starlight are for me.)
>
> You ask me why I spend my life writing?
> Do I find entertainment?
> Is it worthwhile?
> Above all, does it pay?
> If not, then, is there a reason?
> (Ah, I would like to give you an answer
> To satisfy you completely, but that is impossible.)
> Listen awhile, and believe in me,
> There is a reason for my writing, yes.

I write only because
There is a voice within me
That will not be still.

The last stanza of this poem was eventually printed on a plaque dedicated
to Plath outside the Wilbury Crockett Library at Wellesley High School—a
fitting tribute to the young woman remembered by her classmates not as
a suicide but as an exemplar of high literary ambition.

Other unpublished Plath poems from this period strike a modern, self-
questioning note. The free verse "I put my fingers in my ears . . ." tells of a
speaker in the throes of an existential crisis.

In wonder
I listen.
This is I.
This is my life I hear
Beating like a muffled airplane engine,
Pulsing loud.
Over what barren wastes of rock
And tattered cloud
Is that plane winging?
And why am I struck chill by
Its strange high singing?

In "Spring Again," the speaker rejoices in the arrival of the new season
but realizes that something inside her is off-kilter: "Yet minutes are dragging, / hours are long— / can it be I who am act- / ing wrong?" "Portrait"
explores a bleaker moment of self-reflection:

I start to speak:
each word, alas,
is but an echo,
meaningless . . .

By reflections on the water
I am caught;
I revolve in narrow rings
of surface thought . . .

Among the shadow throngs
I pass,

An idle whisper
through the grass.

"Portrait" rehearses now-familiar Plathian language: echoes, reflections, shadows, grass, catching, and revolving resurface in later poems. But the poem from 1947–1948 that most looks forward to Plath's future work is the surreal "Tulips at Dawn," which merges landscape and mindscape. It begins:

Thin blue shadows spatter the lawn;
The tulips are calm in the light of dawn.
The sunlight through their sharp green leaves
Is metallic and chill.

Plath then takes an imaginative leap—"I plummeted downward / Into a well of gold"—as the language of *Ariel* tentatively emerges:

Into the depths of austere whiteness
I go.
Gray shade
And white flashes of cold
Lance my wings.
I am a captive
Of white worlds.
Snow on snow
And steel-gray skies.

"Tulips at Dawn" challenges the idea that Plath discovered her *Ariel* voice in the 1960s. "Into the depths of austere whiteness I go" looks forward to "the substanceless blue / Pour of tor and distances" that begins "Ariel"— another dawn poem—fourteen years later. As in "Ariel," the short lines here give momentum to the speaker's metaphorical flight, while the language of martyrdom and captivity will reemerge in the bee poems, "Lady Lazarus," "Fever 103°," and "Purdah."

Other poems from this period also suggest future work. "Bereft," an elegiac poem about a speaker who says goodbye to a loved one at the edge of the sea, already exhibits that particular Plathian combination of anger and tenderness toward the lost that will resurface in "Daddy," "Full Fathom Five," and "The Colossus":

So glad to be rid of a part of me
That long after you were gone

I stood on the beach and exultantly
Watched the rising tide come on.

I saw the tide cover the gaunt black rocks
And the water smooth the sand,
And when all your footprints were washed away—
Then I started back to land.

"I Have Found the Perfect World" (1948), which draws on Plath's interest in the Gothic, anticipates the murderous heroines of *Ariel*. In the poem,
the speaker confronts a rival, and admits,

I used to feel the primitive desire to kill you.
I wanted to claw at your face until the blood ran down in wet red
    drops.
I wanted to tear your hair out in rough handfuls.
I wanted to beat your head against the ground until your skull
    was smashed to fragments.
I wanted to do all this and more, while I laughed a mad vicious
    laughter.

Poems like "Tulips at Dawn" and "I Have Found the Perfect World" make
clear that the *Ariel* voice was always within Plath, though it would become
silenced, over the years, under layers of New Critical shellac. Ted Hughes
would help her recognize the superiority of this starker, less rarefied voice, so
antithetical to the formal, thesaurus-heavy verse she spent her college years
honing to perfection. Indeed, sections of "I Have Found the Perfect World"
sound straight out of Hughes's oeuvre.

Yeats was another important early model for Plath. She was particularly
drawn to his late poem "The Cold Heaven," which would influence several
of her own poems from this period:

Suddenly I saw the cold and rook-delighting heaven
That seemed as though ice burned and was but the more ice,
And thereupon imagination and heart were driven
So wild that every casual thought of that and this
Vanished, and left but memories, that should be out of season
With the hot blood of youth, of love crossed long ago;
And I took all the blame out of all sense and reason,
Until I cried and trembled and rocked to and fro,
Riddled with light. . . .[73]

The metaphorical possibilities embodied in Yeats's dueling, paradoxical visions of heat and cold, blood and ice, appealed to the young poet searching for new ways to voice competing senses of ecstasy and despair. Plath's "Alone and Alone in the Woods Was I"—the first poem she wrote for Crockett, with its imagery of ice and heat, exultation and birdsong—is clearly indebted to "The Cold Heaven":

> The tones poured about me where I stood
> And crashed on the crystal of the wood.
> I broke the icy bond that bound me
> And tore the frost-film from my eyes.
> In ecstasy I gazed around me
> At the early morning skies.
> . . . .
> And where my soul had sent its cry—
> There curved the blue dome of the sky.

"Joy" (1948) depicts a speaker whose "very soul" "is drenched / With shining melody," while "Summer Street," also written that year, uses similar Yeatsian language:

> Languidly I was drawn
> Up—heavenward.
>
> Chill blue waves washed over me,
> and iceberg clouds
> were needled through with sharp white rays.
> Sunlight wavered in the depths,
> devoid of heat,
> while frigid water lapped against
> glittering silver fields
> of ice and snow.
>
> Numbed by giddy, shifting lights
> and caught amidst
> a whirl of ice, my soul became
> part of heaven's boundless sea:
> a frosty spear
> of shining steel; and just as ice
> cracks a thin glass, the spear
> began to grow,

shattering the fragile shell
of numbness that
encompassed me. I gasped for breath,
struggled up through death-cold blue—
and I was free!

The biographical value of these early poems lies not in what they reveal about Sylvia Plath's psyche, but in what they show us about her literary predilections. Though "City Streets," "Alone and Alone," and "Summer Street" are derivative, their Eliotic and Yeatsian models suggest Plath's artistic direction. The imagery of fire and frost, and their corresponding color tones of blue and red, would become symbolic touchstones for Plath just as they had for Yeats, Eliot, Lawrence, and Dylan Thomas. Like Yeats, Eliot, and her future husband, Ted Hughes, she, too, would fuse elements of Romanticism and modernism in her poetry to striking effect.

6

Summer Will Not Come Again

Wellesley, 1948–1950

Sylvia ended her tenth-grade year with straight A's and set off for Martha's Vineyard in July. At sailing camp that summer, she, Ruth, and Betsy all lived in a tent for counselors in training. She again called herself "Sherry" and was noticeably shorter with Aurelia. "Don't expect more than a post card each day," she wrote curtly in early July 1948.[1] She did not have enough money to join the other girls, the majority of whom went on outings to Nantucket or day trips around the island, and she could barely afford to take the camp's pottery class. But she loved biking and sailing, and felt "a thrill" at the tiller.[2] Aurelia received mixed messages— Sylvia worried about feeling "left out," but told her mother not to send more money. "I'll manage," she wrote despondently.[3] The food was subpar this time around, and she came down with a phlegmy cough that bothered the other girls, who thought she had tuberculosis. Even her close friends began to annoy her; she called Ruth "a pain in the neck." "At times like this I long for my very own mummy. . . . but I'll cheer up."[4] Aurelia's visit on July 11 soothed her. The day she left, Sylvia wrote, "I feel like I've had an emotional purge—all my pent up feelings let go when I cried, and I feel so much better."[5] She kept Aurelia abreast of her "emotional thermometer," which by July 17 was "stationed permanently at the 'Highly Happy' mark."[6]

Sylvia was aware that her moods were slipping perilously from her control. She seemed to improve for a few days—she wrote about the beauty of the clear night skies and a pleasant picnic on Indian Hill, the island's highest point—but by July 20 she was again beset by unhappiness. In the first of four letters she wrote to Aurelia that day, she described her frustration:

Honestly, this is one of those rare moments when I just could cry! Both Bets and Ruth have gone sailing in the harbor race, and I haven't yet. I'm glad I can be alone in my tent for a few minutes so I won't have to go through the torture of gay talk while I feel so sad inside. . . . Well, my first wave of sadness has left me—If only I wasn't so easily hurt and so darn sensitive![7]

By her third week at camp, Sylvia was writing to Aurelia three times a day, saying she had "to blow off steam to someone."[8] The day after she wrote Aurelia about her "sadness," she was all exuberance: "I am so happy it bubbles over! My 'thermometer' is back to it's [sic] high normal again. Nothing special has happened except that I have, in the midst of my petty jealousies, found myself. I am filled with complete serenity and love for you and your cheery little cards which have arrived so faithfully!"[9] The manic component of her depression had begun its deadly onset.

After camp ended, Sylvia spent a calming week in Falmouth, on the Cape, at her friend Ann Bowker's summer home, and she returned to Wellesley "very brown and healthy."[10] For the rest of the summer, between 10:00 and 11:00 each morning, Aurelia taught her to type; by the end of August, Sylvia could type 80 words per minute.[11] She began her junior year at "High," as she called it, and continued to dominate her classes, especially Crockett's. She played guard on the junior varsity basketball team and became close to two teammates, Pat O'Neil and Jeanne Woods. Athletic competition appealed to her: she found traveling to other towns exciting, and enjoyed the half-time huddles, water breaks, and orange slices between quarters. Physical exertion eased her academic and social anxiety.

In early October 1948, she was thrilled to receive a handwritten invitation on expensive white stationery from Barbara Botsford, the secretary of the Sub-Deb sorority. Barbara asked Sylvia to join the club and attend a tea. Plath pasted the card in her scrapbook, calling it a "passport to acceptance in the social world." During initiation week, she was assigned a "big sister" who made her embarrass herself in public and come to school with unkempt hair and no makeup. Sylvia called the week "gruelling" and said she barely "squeaked through." But she obediently endured public humiliation for the sake of acceptance. "It's amazing but true. After such a long time of getting ignored it's hard to believe I'm a Sub-Deb."[12]

A few years later, in July 1952, Plath would transform this experience in her short story "Initiation," which she sold for $200 to *Seventeen*. The protagonist, Millicent, decides *not* to join the sorority after surviving initiation week. She realizes she has nothing to gain by proving herself to a shallow, conformist group of girls and decides, heroically, to remain an outsider. It is hard not to read "Initiation" in the context of early 1950s McCarthyism. Though Millicent is initially delighted by the invitation to join the sorority, she is troubled when she learns that her best friend Tracy is blackballed for being "a bit <u>too</u> different." Millicent cannot bring herself to become her big sister Bev's "gopher": "It was a denial of individuality. Rebellion flooded through her." But she still participates in initiation week, kneeling at the sorority altar as her sister breaks an egg over her head, and then sitting for hours in a dark cellar and playing mute in school.

After an inspiring encounter with a stranger, Millicent decides to take the "harder" route to "victory"—alone—rather than experience "coronation as a princess . . . as one of the select flock." Plath's larger metaphor is political: her heroine stands up not only for herself, but for those who refuse to conform. An image of heather birds in the story symbolizes her acceptance of strangeness, which she romanticizes: "Swooping carefree over the moors, they would go singing and crying out across the great spaces of air, dipping and darting, strong and proud in their freedom and their sometime loneliness."[13]

Louise Giesey White remembered that she, Pat O'Neil, and Sylvia—girls who cried when they got B's—joined the Sub-Debs with high hopes of popularity, despite the fact that Crockett thought the sorority absurd and mocked it during class. "I was willing to go along with the others, sell my soul," Louise said. But they all soon dropped out. The club did little more than meet every two weeks at a member's house, where the girls' mothers were expected to put on an elaborate tea. "Really the mothers had to perform," Louise recalled.[14] Plath may have had misgivings about staying in the sorority for the reasons she laid out in "Initiation." But Pat recalled that Sylvia dropped out because Aurelia "did not feel that she could have people over to the house."

Aurelia loved having Pat over, however. After school, Pat and Sylvia would "bomb into the Plath house . . . laughing our heads off . . . all girlish passion and enthusiasm. And Mrs. Plath enjoying it all." Pat remembered that Sylvia decorated her bedroom with her own artwork, as well as prints of post-war German abstract expressionists. Sylvia was "impressed" with their depictions of "the break-up of order, reality," especially the work of Max Beckmann. She admired Picasso, too: "She made her own copy of *Guernica* that she put up over her dresser."[15] Pat remembered that Sylvia was particularly affected by works of "social realism" they saw at a spring art festival on the Boston Common. Pat felt all of this artwork had influenced Sylvia's own work. As did her bedroom itself: Sylvia told Pat she watched the moon through her two bedroom windows on nights when she had trouble sleeping.

———

PLATH'S SHORT STORIES FROM HIGH SCHOOL already display a left-leaning sympathy for those on the margins of society, especially women. The squalor, poverty, and loneliness that afflict her protagonists lend her late-1940s stories a subversive and at times anti-capitalist edge very likely influenced by Crockett. Populated by single, friendless, unfulfilled women living in lonely boarding houses and working menial jobs, these stories were works of both social protest and high literary experimentation—equal parts James Joyce and Charles Dickens. They were utterly unlike the short fiction that Plath would eventually publish in women's magazines and were, predictably, turned down by *Seventeen* and *Mademoiselle*. These modernist stories almost seem to have been written by another author—one with literary aspirations and political concerns very different from the author of teen melodramas such as "And Summer Will Not Come Again," which Plath published in *Seventeen* in 1950.

Plath's stories about forgotten women were destined themselves to remain forgotten—like her early poetry, they have received virtually no attention from scholars or biographers. Yet these early stories are among the most interesting in Plath's juvenilia, for they reveal her intense interest in lonely women living on the periphery of society. After numerous rejections, she would abandon this subject matter in favor of less literary, more formulaic stories designed to appeal to a mass audience that, in the early 1950s, had little taste for what Thoreau called "lives of quiet desperation." Yet she thought that these rejected stories were "better, less trite, less syrupy" than those she would eventually publish, which she called "the usual 'Seventeen' drivel."[16] She would return to the image of the disenfranchised woman in both *The Bell Jar* and *Ariel*, in which her female characters deliver scathing critiques of the patriarchal, conformist society that had relegated them to the margins.

Eight of the nineteen stories Plath wrote during high school (1948–1950) are about working-class women full of dreams and paralyzed by their meager circumstances. If James Joyce's *Dubliners* was a literary model, Aurelia was a personal one. In nearly all of these stories, Plath pits freedom and escape against a small life of drudgery and solitude. Madness and suicide threaten.

In "Heat" (1948), Judith Anders trudges home from her boring office job to her boarding house. As she waits for the bus in unbearable heat, a voice inside her head berates her for succumbing to a life of "The same work, day in, day out. . . . Filing letters, pounding typewriters. So dull, so dull." The voice within exhorts her to "get away" and "Break the pattern"—"Find yourself." Judith answers back that she likes to draw and write; the voice tells her it's not too late to pursue a different, less bleak life. When she reaches her boarding house, she goes to her room and immediately falls asleep. When she hears the phone ringing for her, she is too tired to answer. The voice in her mind says the person calling is about to give her a "chance to open the door" to another life. But Judith keeps sleeping. "There was no escape," Plath ends.

Similarly, in "East Wind" (1949), the spinster Miss Minton suddenly realizes, on her way home from her dull job, that she must "escape" from her "monotonous" life. Her resolve to escape weakens as she nears her dismal apartment building, and she contemplates drowning herself in the nearby river. But at the last minute she pulls back and returns to her lodgings, haunted by the "thin, lonely weeping" of an orphan child outside. Miss Minton would reappear, in richer form, in Plath's award-winning short story "Sunday at the Mintons," which would win first prize in the 1952 *Mademoiselle* college fiction contest.

Like "East Wind," "Gramercy Park" (1948), "Sarah" (1948), and "The Island" (1949) all feature older women living alone and longing for company.[17] In "The Island"—a "radio play" Plath cowrote with her Crockett classmate Mary Ventura—the drowning cry of Helen, a lonely widow ("I'm sinking down . . . down") recalls the last line of Plath's poem "Lorelei": "Stone, stone, ferry me down there." In "The Dark River" (1949), a single woman cannot feel love on account of "the mysterious black river" of her childhood; the girl she once was is "doomed forever to wander through the lonely hallways of my mind." The source of the "black river" is never revealed, but the protagonist's hints of childhood trauma suggest a dramatic, perhaps paternal, loss.

"The Brink" (1948), which was rejected by *Seventeen*, is the psychologically distressing story of a single woman, Janet, who loses her grip on reality while riding a city bus on her way home from a dead-end job. The following passage looks forward to the sinister train ride, dark tunnels, and mocking wheels in Plath's 1952 short story "Mary Ventura and the Ninth Kingdom":

When had she started her journey? She had been on the bus for ages, but she remembered nothing before that. There had been houses, people, and cars, but no beginning—nothing before her bus ride. Her memories suddenly trailed down into darkness. The motion of the bus was ironic now. The turning wheels mocked her. They gulped up the miles and mocked her for not remembering. Darkness, she recalled. A dark tunnel! That was it! She had come out of a dark tunnel on the bus. Still, there was something, something more.

The story's title suggests that she has come close to an unveiling, and looks forward to Plath's late poem "Edge." Is Janet mad, or has she simply come out of the "darkness" to finally understand the true, hollow nature of existence? Is it this realization that drives her to "the brink" of insanity? Plath will posit similar questions in *The Bell Jar* regarding Esther Greenwood's breakdown, which may, she hints, be a "sane" response to the oppressive society in which she lives.

The nameless young woman searching for a cheap room in 1948's "The Attic View" suffers a darker fate. She rents an attic garret with a view of the sea in a boarding house near the harbor, despite its lack of heat and electricity; the view is her only solace in a tedious existence. One day, she hears about a "secretarial night-course for working-girls. This sudden possibility of a future—of advancement—was like a glittering rainbow in her dismal world." She enrolls in the course, but falls ill after walking home in a blizzard. No one except a fellow boarder, "a shy young artist," notices that she has not appeared for meals. The landlady eventually finds her dead, and complains to her cronies "how she had been done out of a month's rent." Only the young artist cares about the woman's death—a significant detail in a story that pits uncaring and "impersonal" humanity against the sensitive individual. The story ends as another young woman moves in, similarly seduced by the "romantic vistas of ocean, land and sky from her attic window."

"The Attic View" is melodramatic, but it contains a pointed, politically subversive message: the heroine, who dares to hope for more, dies when she tries to escape oppression. For the editors of women's magazines in the late 1940s and early '50s, these stories' messages were perhaps too close to the kind of leftist ideology that was increasingly linked to communism. Plath, whose family lived on the edge of financial hardship, sympathized with characters trapped in poverty by economic and social forces beyond their control. By her third year with Crockett, she was writing working-class dramas in the tradition of the Irish socialist playwright Seán O'Casey, such as her short, grim 1950 play, *Room in the World*, about a poor tenement family facing desperate times. Plath was a keen observer of the American political landscape and the double standards that defined her socioeconomic place within it.

Another group of high school stories provides a clue about what would come to be one of the central concerns of Plath's writing life: power. These stories, written between 1948 and 1950, are all set in a comfortable, suburban, middle-class world, yet they too explore the politics of gender and circle back to women's powerlessness.

"The Visitor" (1948) weighs the merits of marriage against those of a career. The narrator, Margot, recounts a visit from her mother's old art school friend, Esther Holbrook, who has now become a famous fashion designer.

Margot's mother, by contrast, married a minister and had four children after graduation. The story explores the two women's choices in simplistic terms. Margot thinks, initially, that Esther is the more secure: "Esther would describe an experience in Paris or an amusing incident that occurred in London, always managing to suggest the slight superiority of the career woman over the woman who had forfeited ambition and settled down in marriage." Yet by the story's end, Esther reveals her "envy" of Margot's mother: "I never realized how empty my life has been without a family." The married mother would achieve a similar victory over the "career woman" years later in Plath's 1960 short story "Day of Success" (published posthumously in 1975).

Plath probably wrote "The Visitor" with an eye toward publication in a conservative women's magazine like *Ladies' Home Journal*. Her own feelings about a career versus marriage and motherhood were much more complicated. Her mother's experience as a college instructor, with both its intellectual rewards and familial sacrifices, provided a vivid example of this conflict in her own home. After the war, there was tremendous pressure on women to vacate the workforce for returning soldiers; to remain employed was considered an abdication of feminine duty. Aurelia's experience assured Plath that it was possible to join a profession and raise a family, yet the stigma of a working mother was very real in white, middle-class, mid-century America. Plath's constant negotiation between domesticity and a literary career would become one of the central dramas of her life.

Other "suburban" stories from this period are narrated by high school girls and based on events in Plath's adolescence. They examine "the game" played between girls and boys in sexually charged situations. In "A Day in June," two girlfriends trick a pair of boys into paying for their canoe during an outing. "Why not prove your power? Why not?" asks the female narrator, who attempts to appear "coquettish." "It takes a while to persuade the boys that you have no money, but you conceal your wallets in your pockets and play the game." Later, the girls feel "ashamed," and they eventually repay the boys, who walk away, disgusted. The narrator is overcome by self-hatred: "The afternoon shatters around you into a million glassy fragments. Malicious, dancing slivers of green and blue and yellow light rise and whirl about you . . . suffocating, smothering flakes of color." Plath suggests that the narrator's misery is the result of larger societal forces beyond her control. The girls have been taught to "prove" their "power" through passive coquetry, but they sense that they have demeaned their self-worth in the process.

"First Date" is an interior monologue in which a teenage girl feels paralyzed as she waits to be picked up by the proverbial "boy in a yellow convertible." She longs to run from the scene, to tell her date that she is sick, but she knows her mother will not allow this. At the same time, she fears the boy will *not* come. "I think I am going to be sick. This time I really am," the girl says, gliding demurely down the staircase to her waiting date, who has no idea how much anxiety he has caused. But the reader knows. Plath suggests that there is something wrong with a ritual in which a woman waits while a man acts. Her protagonist longs to be subject rather than object. The girl's repeated claim of sickness becomes a metaphor for all that is wrong between the sexes.

The lonely, single women in Plath's boarding house stories are casualties of romantic failure; without a marriage and family, they are doomed to lives of monotony and wage slavery. They are obvious examples of what happens when women opt out of "the game." But stories like "A Day in June" and "First Date," with their portraits of unhappy young women trapped within a game whose rules they have not created, also hint at the roots of female powerlessness. The fate of Plath's single women suggests the high price of not playing.

AS COLLEGE APPLICATION SEASON DREW NEAR, Sylvia, now a junior, was increasingly aware of the financial gulf that separated her from friends who regarded European graduation trips and fully paid college tuition as their birthright. Earning top grades was no longer just for fun. She had to win a scholarship if she hoped to attend Smith College. Aurelia was distressed by the way Sylvia would work at her typewriter for eight consecutive hours, forgetting to eat: "She drove herself furiously."[18] Yet Pat remembered that Aurelia would often say, "She's just got to get this scholarship," and that Sylvia knew "the pressure was on."[19]

In January 1949, she began studying hard for her midyear exams in English, Latin, French, and math. Despite her hours in the library, she still found time for weekend dates. In her diary she listed twelve boys she had "gone out with" during the 1948–1949 academic year. Many of these dates took place at school dances or the Totem Pole club, but one stood out: the Phillips Andover spring prom with Mike Sides, the brother of a Wellesley friend. Andover was the most elite prep school in the nation, and Sylvia could not help but marvel at the invitation. She spent the balmy May evening dancing amid Japanese lanterns and belle époque decorations, "falling in love" with her dance partners. The posh weekend was the "most outstanding" of her junior year—yet another tantalizing reminder of the privileged world that awaited her if she worked hard enough.[20] This was also the month Mr. Crockett famously rounded up his charges to watch the sun rise over

Babson Park and recite poetry. Sylvia wrote, "The early hour was so that everyone could hear 'dawn take her first breath' and thereby reach a higher 'kinship with infinity.' "[21] At year's end, she and her old crush Frank Irish were named coeditors of *The Bradford*. Her "exceptional ability as a writer," her "keen critical eye," and her "noteworthy reputation of sticking to a task until it is done" were all noted in the *Bradford* article that announced her editorship.[22]

In June, Sylvia began playing tennis at the Wellesley College and town courts. She often played with Mary Ventura, a fellow Crocketteer and talented writer to whom she had grown close. (She would later write a short story about Mary and use her name in some of her fiction, though their paths diverged after high school.) She called the tennis courts, where she met several dates, her "stage" that summer. Under the informal instruction of various athletic young men, she made progress, though her high school friends remembered that she did not play very well.[23] Still, by the end of the summer she was confident enough to compete in local tournaments. "I must talk firmly to myself and be convinced that it is not a matter of life and death or lifelong disgrace if I lose!" she wrote Hans in August 1949.[24]

On the tennis courts she met John Hodges, a Wellesley boy and rising Denison University sophomore. They started playing regularly, and soda dates to Howard Johnson's and drives around the countryside followed. John began teaching her how to drive, letting her steer as he put his arm around her. She called the lessons a "nervous strain."[25] The two exchanged photos during the last week of June before she left for a Unitarian youth conference on Star Island in New Hampshire.

Star Island, part of the Isles of Shoals off the New Hampshire coast, had been a Unitarian retreat destination since 1915. Visitors stayed at the Oceanic Hotel, a grand white Victorian structure with a long, expansive porch that overlooked Gosport Harbor. The co-ed youth retreat, officially dubbed the "High School Week at Star Island," attracted about 160 Unitarian high school students from well-off Massachusetts suburbs. There were two-hour-long morning workshops on "religion, world affairs, human relations, and personal and racial problems" and afternoon sessions devoted to developing Unitarian youth groups at home.[26] Sylvia chose to attend the "Personal Problems" workshop, held outdoors each morning. "What a place!" she wrote to Hans in early July. "I came away even more determined that there is a magnificent power above us all—call it nature, or call it God— which is responsible for the vast beauty of heaven and earth. . . . I cannot help but be awed by the huge glory of the painted sunsets, or the first rosy light of dawn across the ocean."[27] Each night, the retreat members (or "Shoalers") carried candlelight lanterns up the steep hill into the Gosport Chapel, a stark, stone meetinghouse built on the island's highest point, where they hung them on brackets in the wall. The ritual's simple beauty astonished Plath. In her diary, she wrote, "Chapel is lovely. . . . There is something here I have never experienced before—complete peace and love for all the clean-cut, scrubbed young faces around me, with promise and talent latent in them."[28]

Sylvia had no shortage of dates when she returned to Wellesley on July 3, just in time to attend the Independence Day fireworks in the town park. When she and John Pollard went on a double date with Betsy and Jack Hoag in early July, Jack pulled up in a "flashy convertible," but Sylvia claimed to be unimpressed, especially when he began bragging about his position as a junior manager at his father's advertising firm. "Betsy and I nearly burst out laughing as he explained how he wears a 'coat & tie' to work, and he's eventually going to take over his 'father's place as president.' So he's enterprising . . . so money's important—(so I think of John sweating it out in Denison's [sic] factory in Framingham)."[29]

She normally came home from dates at one or two in the morning after a long but frustrating necking session. One date, Bruce Ellwell, took her to the stock car races in Westboro, which, to her surprise, she enjoyed: "the roar of the motors is quite intoxicating and there are enough minor accidents to make things exciting—wheels coming off, skids into fences, collisions, etc." Later, though, she was horrified by a bad accident she witnessed, and disgusted by her own attraction to the violence: "I was shocked & sick that life seemed such a paltry thing—that people could enjoy the rest of the races—the speeding cars, courting death & destruction. But I was too much one of the crowd—the spirit was intoxicating. . . . Am I heartless like the rest of that bloodthirsty mob?"[30]

She was troubled by her desire to go parking with Bruce after the accident; there was something perverse about sexual desire after the "death & destruction" of the races. But she was "only human," she mused in her diary, not "bad." She worried, as usual, about appearing "fast," and upset that she had to play a "prim part." But she did not want to attract the "wrong kind of boy."

Why is everyone so embarrassed and secretive about physical differences & intercourse, etc? Maybe if we could talk without such inhibitions, sex problems would be easier to solve. Mine is = how far can I go & still have a guy respect me? Naturally I would never have intercourse & I know enough now to control any guy I meet. Also I don't go in for heavy petting even though it might prove satisfying. But just kissing & hugging or necking . . . it's fun and what's wrong with that?

She felt that she had been naive about her previous romantic encounters and had developed a reputation as "cheap & easy-to-get." But she vowed that things would be "different" her senior year. She had learned her lesson. "I'm pretty," she declared, "and someday, if I'm ready, I'll create the right one in my mind & he'll come."[31]

By mid-July, she was tired. She had been on a date every day since she had returned from Star Island and needed time to herself. "Today I recuperated—rested from boys."[32] She had her first drink at a party that July. "No, lightening [*sic*] didn't blast me on the spot, and I didn't turn purple! It tastes good, sort of, but it burns like fire inside."[33] Bruce wanted to go steady with her, but she decided she was not ready. It was still John Hodges, her tennis fling, who occupied most of her thoughts. He treated her too casually; sometimes he showered her with attention, while other times he ignored her. His behavior made her "weepy" and "boy-crazy."[34] One day after he saw her at the tennis courts with another boy, he called and asked her out on a canoe date. The two paddled and necked until midnight. But a few days later he walked past her with an "adorable blonde" and uttered "a nonchalant" hello. "If he thinks he can go out with a blonde the day after he said he loves me & get away with it, he's got another think [thing] coming!" she wrote in her diary.[35] By early August she declared him "ostentatiously obnoxious" and was apparently glad to be done with the affair.[36] And with good reason: at one point Hodges had compared her habit of dating different boys to that of "a Jew in a junkpile."[37]

The relationship was the basis for the only short story Plath published during high school: "And Summer Will Not Come Again," which she wrote during the late summer of 1949 and which appeared in *Seventeen* in August 1950. The story of Celia and Bruce, a handsome, athletic older boy, closely follows Sylvia's relationship with John. When Celia pedals her bicycle past Bruce and a blond girl, he "called out airily, 'Hi there.' He didn't even look guilty, Celia thought, furious." After Bruce walks the other girl home, he catches up with Celia:

She let out a torrent of angry phrases . . . mean, cutting things she had stored up inside her. "Why, won't your girl friend play with you any more? . . . I should have known gentlemen prefer blondes . . ." But her sarcastic voice trailed off breathlessly as she saw Bruce's friendly grin vanish. A strange alien look masked his eyes as he waited for her to finish.

Too late she stopped the flood of words, frightened at the silence hanging between them. At last he said quietly, "All right, Celia. I won't bother you any more. I hadn't figured you were like this. My mistake."

He turned and walked away. Celia stood, congealed with horror.[38]

Celia then remembers lines from a Sara Teasdale poem, "An End": "With my own will I turned the summer from me, / And summer will not come to me again." The narrator likewise suggests that it was Celia's strong expression of "will" that pushed Bruce away. The story ends with Celia's despondent cries; Bruce's desertion is somehow *her* fault for expressing unfeminine anger. "And Summer Will Not Come Again" shows Plath silencing her "other" voice—the one that could be sarcastic, angry, bitter, and cruel. It is no accident that her least subversive piece of fiction from this period was her first mass-market publication.

Plath took a dramatically different approach to the relationship's end, however, in a poem she had written about Hodges on June 10, "To Ariadne (deserted by Theseus)." There, the female speaker lashes out against her lover in fury: "Oh, scream in vain for vengeance now, and beat your hands / In vain against the dull impassive stone."[39] The elegiac poem, written in careful iambic tetrameter with an *a-b-c-b* rhyme scheme, is far superior to "And Summer Will Not Come Again," which obediently conforms to the stifling gender codes of the early 1950s. By harnessing the voice of a Classical heroine, Plath was able to write a more authentic, formally impressive work about male betrayal—a strategy she would revisit in some of her strongest future poems.

Sylvia soon met another boy on the courts, John Hall, who took her mind off Hodges. She spent the last two weeks of August 1949 dating Hall, who left for his freshman year at Williams College in September. He was her physical ideal—tall and handsome with "athletic good cleanness."[40] Sylvia and Betsy used to croon over Hall during school basketball games; he had seemed unattainable then. Now she could barely believe they were dating. Unlike John Hodges, John Hall was clear about his feelings for Sylvia. He said he loved her, but he did not pressure her to have sex. He told her it "was one of the most beautiful things in the world" but was "cheapened by all the people who misused and misunderstood it."[41] She appreciated the space he gave her, and his strong, unambiguous feelings for her increased her self-confidence. "I'm glad I'm me," she wrote in her diary.[42] She had dated twenty-one different boys since the fall of 1948, but none of these relationships had taken root like the one with Hall. She spent every day with him, "playing tennis, climbing Dean's Tower, walking in the woods and admiring mansions, sitting on hilltops and strolling around Lake Waban at night with all the lights spilling reflections into the water and the trees dripping black velvet shadows over the silver wash of moonlight."[43]

On August 30, the couple drove to Cape Cod and spent the day with friends in West Falmouth. Sylvia memorialized the day in a lyrical passage in her diary:

> We battled the waves and threw ourselves on the roman-striped towels, deliciously exhausted. The sun beat down, hot on our skin. My hair was wet, smelling salty and I was oh, so happy—I can enjoy things alone, but when I have someone with me—my physical complement—someone who understands—I get the feeling of a thrilling current of fog flowing, flowing through me and John and the ocean and sky. . . . a complete circuit of electric, tingling happiness.[44]

When Hall showed her his deformed foot as they sunbathed, she gasped in shock, but decided she "liked him more for it" because it made him more vulnerable.[45]

The day before John left for Williams, he took a photo of Sylvia lounging in the grass in a halter top and skirt, looking happy and relaxed. She later pasted it in her scrapbook, noting that she looked "radiant": "he was the first person to ever make me feel quite so confident and joyful."[46] She spent the weekend with him at Williams in late October, the day after her seventeenth birthday, but the relationship was faltering. As his feelings intensified, she withdrew. He wrote her long letters, and she began to fear that he wanted to marry her. She knew she was too young to settle down: "I am afraid of getting married," she confided to her diary. "Spare me from cooking three meals a day . . . spare me from the relentless cage of routine and rote. I want to be free."[47]

Besides, by late September, she was dating yet another boy she had met at the tennis courts, Bob Riedeman, a former Crocketteer who was now a student at the University of New Hampshire. Bob—as Sylvia enjoyed writing—was six feet tall, blond, blue-eyed, athletic, and handsome. Yet he seemed to have little in common with her intellectually; he was studying forestry at a state college. Normally Sylvia was snobbish about academic pedigrees, but she gave Bob a pass. Nor did his sexist views appear to bother her. He told Sylvia he did not "go for a career woman"; when she "protested," he demurred that his future wife could have some outside interests, like painting.[48] She eventually justified leaving John Hall for this very reason—she felt he "could never enter into" her "love for books and art," which did not matter to him.[49]

Sylvia finally ended her relationship with John Hall the night before

Thanksgiving 1949, while he was back in Wellesley. After an awkward dinner, she bade him goodbye at her door. A few minutes later she looked outside and saw him in his car "hunched over the wheel, sobbing hoarsely and brokenly." It made her "sick inside," but it had to be done. "I know I managed this whole thing pretty brutally. But one emotion I can't fake is love. But I'm not the first girl in history who has told her fellow off—I don't know why I should feel so guilty and sorry."[50]

The benefits of "going steady" were, at any rate, ambiguous. Because young people were marrying earlier than they had during the previous generation—by the end of the 1950s, most women wed at age nineteen—parents encouraged their children to date in high school.[51] Aurelia was delighted when Sylvia's dates came calling, but Sylvia herself was more wary, as her short story "First Date" suggests. Prone to strong feelings, she was nonetheless ambivalent about pledging herself to one person; she often slowed things down when she suspected that her partner might be falling in love.[52] That year Plath wrote a poem titled "Adolescence," in which the speaker declares "I was not born to love one man / And him alone."[53] The poem is not about sex but power: high school boys could date as many girls as they wanted, but girls were marginalized if they "got around." Sylvia wanted the same freedom.

As 1949 drew to a close, Sylvia focused on her college applications, school exams, and SATs. She had finally broken into the November *Seventeen* with a contribution to an article about parenthood, which she hoped would help her college chances.[54] She needed to take a psychological test to be admitted to Smith, a prospect that may have troubled Aurelia, who underlined this requirement in a letter from the college. Sylvia was confident that she would be admitted to a top college; the problem was money. As she explained to Hans, for most of her peers, "their only worry is to get good marks so their parents can send them anywhere. With me it is the other way—I have the high marks, but a sad lack of funds." Yet she was optimistic, "In this land of wonderful, unbelievable opportunities," that she would win some money that would enable her to live on campus at Wellesley College, or, if she were very lucky, Smith College in Northampton.[55] As Betsy remembered, "She didn't have the father, she didn't have the money, she didn't have the clothes. She didn't have any of that. But she wanted it. And she made sure she was going to work towards that. . . . She felt beholden and did her utmost to achieve what was expected of her to achieve. Not that she wouldn't have anyway, but that was an added pressure. . . . Her mother had to scrape, and Sylvia knew that."[56]

Aurelia understood her daughter's desire for independence. With Warren away at Exeter, she had vacated the small upstairs bedroom they had shared—the twin beds had been very close together—so Sylvia could enjoy more privacy during her senior year of high school.[57] Although Aurelia knew it would be much easier, financially, for Sylvia to live at home, she wanted her daughter to live on a college campus—an experience she herself had been denied. Smith's yearly tuition was $850, while room and board cost another $750—nearly half of Aurelia's annual salary in 1949. She estimated that their home was worth $10,000, on which she owed $1,650. After doing the calculations, she decided she could afford to give her daughter $400 a year if she chose not to live at home.[58] There would be no money for Crockett's bicycle trip through Europe after graduation. As Sylvia told Hans that Christmas, "I would have given anything to sign up—but $800 was too much to pay—I could not afford it. . . . They are going to see the passion play, visit the music festival at Salzburg, cruise down the Rhine, and do all sorts of other wonderful things."[59] Eight hundred dollars was half of Smith's tuition. She would have to stay in New England, where the "dingy, snowy fields were very bare and lonely," though she assured Hans that "the barren sadness of the landscape had a strange fascination for me."[60] She tried to describe that sadness in a poem she wrote that winter, "Midnight Snow," about the snow's "cold blind silence": "And losing thus the boundary / Of the finite me, / Diffusing outward, I approach / The edges of infinity."[61]

She threw herself into her work. She received an A from Crockett for a research paper on Tolstoy's "Philosophy of History," and delivered an hour-long oral presentation on Thomas Mann's novels. Yet her favorite author remained the Norwegian Sigrid Undset, known for novels that chronicled the joys and crises of women in love. She called Undset's historical romance *Kristin Lavransdatter* "a majestic epic of womanhood . . . stark, bare and true," and declared Undset's *The Bridal Wreath* and *The Mistress of Husaby* the most "dynamic" books she had ever read. Having read mainly nineteenth- and twentieth-century male writers for the previous three years, she was excited by feminine fiction that tackled "woman as a daughter, as a mistress, and as a wife and mother." Although she normally maintained an objective scholarly tone in her work for Crockett, her paper on Undset spills over with passionate, uncritical phrases like "I was held spellbound" and "I lost myself in the personality of Kristin." Crockett noted these slips in the margin: "Be wary of such words . . . rephrase."[62]

She prepared a meticulous application to Smith. In addition to her superior academics and creative accomplishments, she listed a slew of extracurricular activities: *The Bradford*, basketball, tennis, viola, orchestra, piano, school decoration committee, school devotional committee, yearbook, Girl Scouts, Unitarian youth group, and the United World Federalists. Her SAT score in verbal was 700, math 567.[63] She amassed an impressive array of prizes, among them the top award in the *Atlantic* Writing Contest (which she won her sophomore *and* junior years), three Gold Key Awards in Regional Scholastic Art Contests, the Sons of the American Revolution History Prize, membership in the National Honor Society, and three writing awards from *The Boston Globe*.[64] She also compiled a list of authors who had influenced her, including Robert Frost, Amy Lowell, Carl Sandburg, T. S. Eliot, Edna St. Vincent Millay, Sinclair Lewis, Jane Austen, Willa Cather, Eugene O'Neill, Emerson, Shakespeare, and Tolstoy.

Crockett supplied a stellar reference—he wrote that she was the best student he had ever taught—as did her high school principal, who noted that she had achieved a fantastic record even while carrying the extra burden of "many home responsibilities" and odd jobs.[65] Her neighbor Mrs. Aldrich, for whom she often babysat, also wrote a recommendation, and she took care to mention, lest Sylvia seem *too* academic, that she was a member of a sorority and "is popular with both girls and boys."[66] There was not a hint in Plath's reference letters of any psychological troubles. Her poem "Family Reunion," which appeared in *The Bradford* on April 29, 1950, suggests that she had become adept at hiding her moods. The speaker stands at the top of the stairs as aunts, uncles, and cousins enter her house. She imagines herself a diver about to plunge into a whirlpool. "I cast off my identity / And make the fatal plunge."[67] Aurelia later wrote that Sylvia had become a "slavish admirer" of Dorothy Parker during this time, and that the poem was "cruelly satirical in the denigrating Parker manner. She was to develop this in her own style with more lethal impact later on."[68] Plath had been influenced, she thought, by Parker's 1926 poetry collection *Enough Rope*.

As graduation approached, Sylvia reflected on her life in increasingly existential terms. She contemplated the narrowing of possibilities that came with growing older, and again expressed a desire "to be free." She compared her summer of dating to "shuffling through a deck of cards to see how many new combinations you can come up with" and felt more and more distressed by the superficial Wellesley social scene: "Girls pretending to be happy with boys whom they hated. Boys leaving their dates and flirting with other girls—bottles, bottles everywhere, and the high nervous laughter." It was enough to make her want to "scream sometimes."[69] To Hans in January 1950 she wrote that the Wellesley parties were "so meaningless . . . all the noise and music can not cover up the emptiness that lies beneath. Why must people try to fool themselves by thinking that money, clothes and cars are so important? Are they afraid of facing their souls?"[70] She vowed not to let the walls of Wellesley and its culture of conventionality close in on her, to never "take such a narrow existance [*sic*] as a matter of course." Inspired by Nietzsche, she called herself "The girl who wanted to be God": "omniscient—and a bit insane." She worried, too, that she had grown too dependent on Aurelia and would have a hard time achieving "complete self-reliance." If only she could break away somehow, embrace freedom and leave behind the "constrictions and limitations" of life in Wellesley.[71]

She was talking, partly, about sex. Although she valued her virginity, she also longed for the "blind burning irresponsible delight of being crushed against a man's body." She already aestheticized sex as Lawrentian conflict: "I want to be ravished . . . to hear a man groan hoarsely, for in that moment I am the victor. In that moment only the man becomes the child, while I, yet concious [*sic*] of the stars, of the twilight, possess the wisdom of Eve, before abandoning myself to the lovely flame that eats at my insides with warm, spilling heat."[72] That fall she often cut her necking sessions with Bob Riedeman short, but doing so was a struggle. "I could kiss him forever, but I've got to be conventional, darn it."[73]

During the last few months of her senior year, she spent five "grueling" weeks rehearsing for the senior play, *The Admirable Crichton*, written by J. M. Barrie and directed by Crockett. She enjoyed playing the "proud & haughty" Lady Agatha, one of the leads: "I loved every moment of the stage (egotist that I am)."[74] Her performance received a good review in *The Bradford*, which she was editing.[75] Putting together six issues during her senior year was a stressful venture that left Sylvia and her coeditor Frank Irish "chewing their nails down to the bone."[76] But the "editors' teas" at the elegant Copley Plaza Hotel, hosted by John Taylor—a Brahmin whose family owned *The Boston Globe*—compensated for the frantic late nights.[77]

In May she learned that she had been accepted to Smith College with a full tuition scholarship of $850 for her freshman year. From the Smith Club of Wellesley she received another $450. That meant she needed only $400 for room and board—the exact contribution Aurelia had calculated she could afford. Plath turned down the full scholarship she had been offered by Wellesley College.[78] She was ecstatic:

> After countless nights and days of suspense, indecision and an agonizing weighing of pros and cons, SMITH has at last become a reality. I know my whole life will be different because of my choice . . . but I can only hope blindly that the advantages of living at Smith will in the end outweigh these I would have had if I'd accepted a town scholarship, lived

at home and gone to Wellesley. . . . I just hope I can be adequate to withstand the temptations of college weekends and keep up my marks. I just
know I'll be horribly homesick! But it's a challenge, knocking me out of a
"rut" of living alone in my own little room.[79]

In early June, Sylvia attended the senior prom with Bob. They doubled
up with Perry Norton and Pat O'Neil, but the pairing did not work well,
since Perry had wanted to go as Sylvia's date. She tried to ignore her friend's
sulking; she was going to Smith on scholarship, and she had a handsome
boyfriend she adored. (Bob had finally given her a romantic gift before
the prom—seventeen "deep red baby roses," which she saved and dried.)[80]
Though she had missed twenty school days due to illness, she again received
straight A's in all her subjects.[81] She was first in her class of 160 graduating
seniors, but, curiously, she did not receive the award for "Best Girl Student"
in the 1950 *Wellesleyan* yearbook.[82] Barbara Botsford did. (Perry Norton won
"Best Boy Student.") Louise Giesey won "Girl Most Likely to Succeed," as
well as the senior "cup" for the most outstanding student, chosen by the
faculty. "It was obvious that Sylvia and I were the two main contenders for
that," Louise recalled. "I got it. And I was very upset the minute I got it. I left
and went to the ladies' room because I was embarrassed, and because I was
worried about Sylvia." Plath, distraught, had beaten her to the ladies' room.
"We saw each other crying but we didn't have enough sense to say anything
to each other. It would have meant a lot to her to have gotten it. It meant a
lot to me."[83] Several friends inscribed notes in Sylvia's yearbook, while her
own photo caption listed the qualities she felt defined her: "Warm smile . . .
Energetic worker . . . Clever with chalk and paints . . . Those fully packed
sandwiches . . . Basketball and tennis player . . . Future writer . . . Those
rejection slips from *Seventeen*."[84]

The Class of 1950 graduation ceremony, for which Sylvia wrote the
sentimental "Senior Song," took place on June 7. Now a graduate herself,
she was "passé" and "would very soon be old," as she wrote in her scrapbook. Underneath her graduation program she pasted three photographs
of herself in her backyard looking tired and anxious. Her usual broad smile
was missing, her celebratory, optimistic outlook muted. Half her life was
already over. Emily Dickinson's "Presentiment," which Sylvia had included
in her poetry anthology for Crockett, captured something of her mood
that June:

> Presentiment is that long shadow on the lawn
> Indicative that suns go down;

> The notice to the startled grass
> That darkness is about to pass.[85]

Her urge to flee Wellesley suddenly competed with a new, uncomfortable desire to stay. But Plath was resolved. She would not become like her paralyzed characters in "Heat" and "East Wind," for, as she would later write, she was a "voyager, no Penelope."[86]

7

The White Queen

Wellesley and Smith College, 1950–1951

In July 1950, Plath began her new diary with quotes from three Irish writers—Louis MacNeice, W. B. Yeats, and James Joyce. All were politically engaged modernists who combined a broad, sweeping view of history with intimate portraits of their society. She quoted MacNeice's "Aubade," about seizing the day before the approach of war; Yeats's "We only begin to live when we conceive life as tragedy"; and Joyce's "Hold to the now, the here, through which all future plunges to the past." She began to feel burdened by time's passing, worried that she was letting too many moments slip by without seizing their artistic potential. The world was opening up to her just as she had wished, and yet she felt herself caught in flux: "With me, the present is forever, and forever is always shifting, flowing, melting. . . . I am the present, but I know I, too, will pass. The high moment, the burning flash, come and are gone, continuous quicksand. And I don't want to die."[1]

Her writing became a way to engage with the ineffable present, to pin it wriggling on a wall—like Eliot's Prufrock—before it faded into the ephemeral. "Every story, every incident, every bit of conversation is raw material for me," she wrote in early August 1950.[2] It was a theme she would return to throughout her 1950s diary. "How can I tell Bob," she wrote that summer before Smith, "that my happiness streams from having wrenched a piece out of my life, a piece of hurt and beauty, and transformed it to typewritten words on paper? How can he know I am justifying my life, my keen emotion, my feeling, by turning it into print?" He could not know, and was convinced that they could be happy together as husband and wife. But she would end the relationship that fall. Despite the glorification of married life that infiltrated every women's magazine Sylvia read, she would not settle. "Something in me wants more. I can't rest," she wrote in her journal. "Perhaps someday

I'll crawl back home, beaten, defeated. But not as long as I can make stories out of my heartbreak, beauty out of sorrow."[3]

Throughout high school, Sylvia had spent her summer days in the relaxed, privileged manner of her affluent friends. But now, while her peers from honors English toured Europe with Mr. Crockett, she faced ten weeks of full-time work to defray college expenses. Rather than return to Camp Helen Storrow as a counselor, she found a position as a farmhand at Lookout Farm in Natick, five miles from her home. The job required long hours picking and cleaning vegetables—a curious choice for a cerebral young woman who had graduated at the top of her high school class. But Lookout Farm was a respite from excessive consciousness. "Now I know how people can live without books, without college," she wrote in her journal. "When one is so tired at the end of a day one must sleep, and at the next dawn there are more strawberry runners to set, and so one goes on living, near the earth."[4] Out in the radish fields, she did not have to impress, outthink, or outperform anyone.

Lookout Farm provided Sylvia with experience for her writing and put her in closer touch with a less privileged class of people with whom, she claimed, she felt a kinship. "It is my First Job, and I'm firmly convinced I couldn't have done better," she wrote to her new friend Eddie Cohen in early August. "A ten mile bike ride plus an eight hour day picking beans, loading radish crates and weeding corn six days a week is hardly relaxation, but the people I work with—Negroes, Displaced Persons, and boys and girls my own age—are worth the low pay." Sylvia wore her laborer's status like a badge of honor, happy to find a morally unassailable way of flouting Wellesley's conventions.[5] "I'm up at six, in bed by nine, and very grimy in-between. But I just smile when my white collar acquaintances look at me with unbelieving dismay as I tell them about soaking my hands in bleach to get them clean."[6]

If her correspondence with Hans Neupert provided her with an alternative way of understanding her sheltered American existence, Lookout Farm exposed her to hardship and difference in her own backyard.[7] Sylvia had grown up in "anti-Semitic, Waspy" Wellesley, as her friend Phil McCurdy put it, where Jews and Italians were considered racially distinct.[8] Sylvia was curious about those on the fringes of the American dream; she too felt herself an "outsider," with her immigrant family background. At Smith she would not be rubbing shoulders with men like Robert, "the negroe who ran away with his wife's pay and came home from Boston the next morning at five with a taxi bill of $8 and very very inebrieated [*sic*]."[9] Or Ilo Pill, the Estonian refugee and aspiring artist who lived and worked at the farm while saving money for a new life in New York City.

Sylvia was attracted to Ilo, who was fifteen years older: she described him as "bronzed," "intelligent," "blonde," with a "muscular body." She noted in her journal that he spoke with a "thick German accent" (this alone would have been grounds for interest) and that he flirted with her. "Out in the strawberry field we were talking about German writers," she wrote Eddie, "and he suddenly burst out You like Frank Sinatra, ja? He is so sendimendal, so romandic, so moonlight night."[10] He was a man unlike any she had ever met—an eastern European artist and drifter who worked odd jobs in pursuit of loftier ambitions.

In August, Ilo invited Sylvia up to his living quarters above the barn to view one of his drawings. She was almost eighteen, with plenty of necking experience, and she probably understood what was about to happen: as she ascended the staircase her "cheeks burned." But when Ilo kissed her roughly in his room, she became flustered. "And suddenly his mouth was on mine, hard, vehement, his tongue darting between my lips, his arms like iron around me." She tried to break free, and Ilo, surprised by her protest, quickly stopped. When he saw that Sylvia was crying, he brought her some water as she composed herself. Although she resisted, the encounter had excited her—no one had ever kissed her "that way before." The kiss left her, she wrote in her journal, "warm and bruised," "flooded with longing, electric, shivering."[11] The "bruising kiss" would become one of Plath's leitmotifs. A year later, she would write about Ilo for her English class at Smith. Dylan Thomas meets D. H. Lawrence in "The Estonian" (eventually retitled "The Latvian"), about a young woman's erotic awakening: "Warm and strong his mouth moved over hers and all the young green shoots of wonder that had been growing in her since she had first seen him all of them broke free from the small cramped darkness and shot skyward into a giddy articulate blue."[12] When Plath's professor accused her of overwriting in her first draft, she removed all the references to her heroine's sexual satisfaction in the second draft. Her grade, predictably, rose from a B+ to an A–.

Lookout Farm also provided the material for Plath's first nationally published poem, "Bitter Strawberries," a piece about Cold War anxiety that appeared in *The Christian Science Monitor* on August 11, 1950. "All morning in the strawberry field / They talked about the Russians," Plath began. The women pickers try to give voice to the "vague terror" they feel in the face of a nuclear stand-off. Some want to "Bomb them off the map," while others plead for nonviolence. The strawberries turn "thick and sour"—a physical manifestation of the pestilence of war. Plath's poem suggests the powerlessness of women, whose fates are dictated by a patriarchal system they have little power to overturn. She had already explored this theme in her high school stories and would return to it in *The Bell Jar*, where she exposed the rank and rot underneath what otherwise appeared sweet and seductive. Bitter strawberries would morph into concealing cosmetics, constricting gowns, and poisonous luncheons—all metaphors for the false, conformist selves that women in the Eisenhower era were encouraged to inhabit. It is tempting to give short shrift to "Bitter Strawberries," with its Frostian overtones and awkward rhythms, yet the poem was an important, early foray into the political concerns that animated Plath's later work.

Sylvia dated a roguish Wellesley boy named Emile after her summer at Lookout Farm, but this time she played by traditional rules. "We go on dates, we play around, and if we're nice girls, we demure at a certain point. And so it goes."[13] Emile's smoking, drinking, and carousing only seemed to increase her desire for him. She began to think that "the unreasoning, bestial purity was best"—better, at least, than the teasing and flirting that only led to "soggy desire, always unfulfilled. . . . I can only lean enviously against the boundary and hate, hate, hate the boys who can dispel sexual hunger freely."[14] In her diary she wondered if she would ever find a man worthy of her intellect and literary ambitions, someone who would not "swallow up my desires to express myself in a smug, sensuous haze."[15]

"And Summer Will Not Come Again," in the August 1950 issue of *Seventeen*, followed the publication of "Bitter Strawberries." Curiously, Plath did not celebrate these milestones in her journal. In late summer she wrote that she was at a "low ebb . . . dreaming sordid, incoherent little dreams," "uneasy with fear and discontent," with "widening cracks" in her self-assurance.[16] She now thought her *Seventeen* story "trite," "syrupy," and "hideously obvious."[17] What would it take to publish in a sophisticated magazine like *The New Yorker*? The small headshot beneath the story and its sentimental caption made her wince ("Jazz makes her melt inside. Debussy and Chopin suit her dreamer moods"). She began to feel impure, and wrote about the daily cleansing rituals that "could not rinse the sticky, untidy film away."[18] She would always remain conflicted about her audience: as much as she sought recognition and payment from women's magazines, she knew that literary reputations were not made in the pages of *Ladies' Home Journal*.

In early August, Sylvia had found an uplifting surprise in her mailbox—her first fan letter. Eddie Cohen, a twenty-one-year-old English major from Chicago, had read "And Summer Will Not Come Again" in his sister's *Seventeen* and wrote to express his admiration. His tone was genuine, if patronizing. He felt the story was subtler than the usual *Seventeen* "drivel" and "offered insight into people which was a little above average."[19] Sylvia noted his condescension in her reply: "Why is it that my particular brand of drivel rates such subtle flattery? Have you a long standing bet with Ernest

Hemingway on the gullibility of would-be female writers?" He had asked her to send him a story, but she refused until he sent her *his* writing. "Now you know that my nature is far from sweet and trusting," she wrote.[20]

So began a long correspondence between two literary aspirants that Plath would later try to publish as "Dialogue of the Damned." On paper, the two had remarkably similar personalities, even similar writing styles. They were both intellectuals, passionate about literature, and increasingly skeptical of the comfortable certainties with which they had been raised. Eddie, who was from an affluent Chicago suburb, had put more distance between himself and his origins than Sylvia. "I've had my share of convertibles and sport coats, dances and socials," he told her. "I don't really care much for it now, although I can still make myself look at home in that kind of life."[21]

He was now a junior at Roosevelt College in Chicago, a liberal hotbed that was, he said, "about as far from the traditional college as one can get." He boasted that all freshmen were required to take Philosophy 101, "very anti-God and Church," a requirement that had prompted a state senate investigation. He described political science classes that verged on "free-for-all fist battles" where students were encouraged to "cross-examine" their teachers.[22] Sylvia was fascinated.

To Eddie, Sylvia described her "character" as "ice cream and pickles," a line he found particularly memorable. She told him she was slender, tall, and tan. When women asked her what brand of suntan oil she used, she replied, "None, lady, but forty-eight hours in the blazing sun per week does wonders." She described her German-Austrian background, her father's bumblebee book and his "countless scientific articles." Her brother took after her father, but she was more "subjective," like her mother. She admitted that she had a "mercurial disposition" and recounted her struggles to fit in during high school. "My biggest trouble is that fellows look at me and think that no serious thought has ever troubled my little head. They seldom realize the chaos that seethes behind my exterior." While all the other girls were attending dances, she was reading Huxley's *Brave New World*—and so on. Sylvia was slightly disingenuous when describing herself as a brainy loner, but she certainly was, as she wrote, "vulnerable."[23]

Eddie, for his part, described himself as a "semi-bohemian" in jeans and a T-shirt with "unruly" hair and a cigarette "constantly" dangling from his lips. He was a "cynical idealist" who hung out "at little jazz joints . . . or maybe just wandering the streets at four or five in the morning." He seemed a cross between James Dean and the T. S. Eliot of "Preludes." He told Sylvia he would soon be "thumbing or bumming" his way to Mexico City. The two were striking poses for themselves as much as for each other. "Don't try too hard to figure me out," he wrote. "You're liable to go neurotic too." With his dangling cigarette and his talk of "spiritual independence," Eddie Cohen was Plath's first beatnik.[24] "I wasn't aware that anyone quite like you existed," she wrote to him that August.[25]

Eddie was raised in the conservative Jewish tradition, but, like Sylvia, he viewed religious doctrine with Nietzschean distrust. "Those who believe in God are mental cowards," he wrote to her that fall. Yet he admitted that he had "clung to" the "customs, ceremonies and traditions" of Judaism even after he had "rejected the idea of God."[26] He was still very close to his rabbi, who had encouraged him to assert his independence and leave home. Plath told him she was a Unitarian "by choice" but added, "I don't like the idea of salvation being spooned out to those too spineless to think for themselves." She supposed she could be "labeled an atheist," though she had great belief in man's potential and "respect for life." She quickly deflated her rhetoric: "Sounds flowery, doesn't it."[27]

Sylvia told Eddie he was a "magnetic correspondent," and, indeed, decades later, his words still resonate with humorous, brash intelligence.[28] His letters were full of sex and death, war and madness. Though Sylvia challenged him on his "modern" morals—he believed in premarital sex and was unapologetic about his girlfriend's abortion—she could not discount his Experience. During the past year, he told her, he and his friends had been through "six illicit love affairs, two marriages, one divorce, one near-murder, one complete mental smash-up, five people winding up with psychiatrists, one sadistic-masochistic love affair, one triangle involving a male, female, and a bi-sexual."[29] His tales of sexual adventures, late-night jazz sessions in Chicago's "black belt," lunchtime conversations with Richard Wright, and his own psychoanalysis gave Plath a vicarious thrill. As did his travels: in Mexico, he wrote Sylvia about the availability of prostitutes, unexpurgated Henry Miller novels, and the "rhythm and harmony" of the open road.[30] When she wrote to him complaining that a date had called her "dramatic," Eddie responded that she was only "living intensely," as he did. "That is what seperates [*sic*] the artist from the rest of the world."[31] (Ted Hughes would later tell her much the same.)

Eddie tried to convince Sylvia that there was no shame in sex before marriage. Like her, he was bothered by the sexual double standard. "I feel that a woman has a right to her sexual life just as a man does," he wrote to her in October 1950.[32] He even laid out a sardonic list of rules for *Seventeen* heroines: they must not smoke, drink, argue, have breasts, or "be possessed of the organs of reproduction, nor of the desires which accompany same." If she breaks these rules, "the heroine must thoroughly regret such transgressions in the end."[33]

These were refreshing words for a young woman who had been troubled by these double standards, but sometimes Sylvia pushed back against Eddie's sexual freethinking. She rightly noted that men did not have to worry about pregnancy or getting a "fast" reputation ("everyone sets on the girl like buzzards"). She felt that losing her virginity before marriage would damage her chances of finding an "idealistic husband."[34] Eddie tried to reassure her that was not the case. "The only thing I can say to that is just plain old-fashioned B. S. Maybe the church-going hypocrites who so solidly support the double standard stick to that, but the guys I consider real idealists, the ones who fight for the little guy, knock down racial barriers, stick their neck out by hollering against war, get called red or crackpot for whatever they do or say—they are the ones who love a woman, not her past. As an aside, most of them wouldn't have a virgin, and the reasons for that feeling are also many and sound." Sex with the right person, before marriage, was worth it. He and his girlfriend "were never happier" than when they were sleeping together during their four-month relationship. But each solution was "individual."[35] She had to decide what was right for her.

Like Sylvia, Eddie was deeply skeptical about the hawkish direction in which America was heading. "Last night when we were riding in, I was listening to Truman," he wrote to her that September.

> I was feeling alive to the hilt with the vigor of the experience, and there he was telling me that after all this living, I'm going to die in Korea. Why WHY WHY WHY??? I want to know what the hell its [sic] all about. I'm damned if I intend to stop living for a lot of fancy slogans. Give me the reasons, in human terms, tell me why I must kill Yaakov Shmudnig and he must kill me. . . . But don't tell me I'm saving the world—from what? Are the Chinese or Koreans worse off under Communism than under our often peculiar forms of "Democracy"?[36]

He later mused that communism would triumph in the end if it was right, and he called General Douglas MacArthur "a megalomaniac, neo-Prussian."[37] He knew that these sentiments could get him into trouble, but he trusted Plath. She responded with a heartfelt letter about her own fears of war. "I guess you're a Communist nowadays if you sign peace appeals. Ed, people don't seem to see that this negative Anti-communist [sic] attitude is destroying all the freedom of thought we've ever had. They don't see that in the hate of Russia, they're transferring all the hate they've ever had. . . . I get stared at in horror when I suggest that we are as guilty in this as Russia is; that we are war-mongers too."[38] Eddie thought this letter was a masterpiece. He read it out loud to friends and continued to bring it up years later.[39]

Eddie did not influence Sylvia's feelings about the Korean War, which she had already made clear to Hans-Joachim Neupert that August in a letter about the evils of the atomic bomb and the stupidity of fighting in Korea for "a little piece of land."[40] But Eddie's antiwar stance must have made her feel less alone. That September, she wrote to him about her growing fears of military escalation: "I want to stop it all, the whole monumental grotesque joke. But writing letters and poems doesn't seem to do much good. The big men are all deaf; they don't want to hear the little squeaking as they walk across the street in cleated boots."[41]

The real point of this extraordinary correspondence was not sex or politics, but writing. Sylvia recognized Eddie's literary ability and felt that she could learn something from his "technique."[42] They began critiquing each other's work. In September 1950 she sent him "Kitchen Interlude," "Evolution," and "Bitter Strawberries," while he sent her fragments of his essays and short stories. (He eventually published her "Evolution" in the Roosevelt literary magazine, *Experiment*.) He knew he had stumbled into a correspondence with a serious talent, and he briefly assumed the apprentice's role. "Please, doctor—is the patient improving?" he asked.[43] If Sylvia had never met a boy like him, he had never met a girl like her—mature, sensitive, unruffled by talk of bisexual roommates or one-night stands. She valued their intimacy. "Don't stop talking to me, please. It's as important as if we were the only people alive," she wrote to him in September.[44]

Lines like these made Eddie want to close the distance. As early as his third letter he floated the idea of a visit: "cut me loose before I find myself in the ridiculous and embarrassing position of being infatuated with a girl I never even met. . . . if you don't stop building yourself up to me, you are liable to wake up some morning and find me sitting in a tent on your front lawn."[45] For Sylvia, however, he was a safe confidant to whom she could express both her insecurities and bold ideas without shame; he did not understand that he might as well have been a priest behind a curtained confessional. She admitted, for example, that she did not want to get married after college: "I'm not going to be disposed of so summarily."[46] Her letters to him became, like her journal, an outlet for subversive self-expression without repercussions. "You are a dream," she wrote in her journal. "I hope I never meet you."[47]

Eddie's letters provided a distraction from the looming reality of Sylvia's departure for Smith. Finally, she would be leaving Wellesley, her cramped house, her mother's and grandmother's watchful eyes. But the very thing she had desired—a spot at Smith—caused her anxiety as she pondered the effort it would take to live up to her own exacting standards. She would have to make a name for herself all over again, only this time she would be among some of the brightest and wealthiest girls in America.

One night in late August, around midnight, she left her house and walked out onto Elmwood Road. She was "sick with unfulfilled longing, alone, self-reviling," trying to find "peace inside":

> And there, miraculously, was the August night. It had just rained, and the air was thick with warm damp fog. The moon, full, pregnant with light, showed strangely from behind the small frequent clouds. . . . There seemed to be no wind, but the leaves of the trees stirred, restless. . . . Lightning, heat lightning flicked off and on, as if some stage hand were toying with the light switch. . . . The air flowed about me like thick molasses, and the shadows from the moon and street lamp split like schizophrenic blue phantoms, grotesque and faintly repetitious.[48]

The passage is full of Plathian leitmotifs—malignant moons, feverish heat, restless trees, thick fog, curious shadows, blue light—that would resurface in the *Ariel* poems. Nature's contours suddenly seemed starker, less protective, though the pregnant moon still offered respite from the burning questions of selfhood.

ALTHOUGH SMITH COLLEGE WAS FOUNDED in 1871 on conservative Christian principles, it took women's academic achievement seriously. By the 1950s, Smith was part of a group of elite women's colleges, known as the Seven Sisters, which included Wellesley, Barnard, Mount Holyoke, Vassar, Bryn Mawr, and Radcliffe. Up until the 1960s, the college embraced founder Sophia Smith's twin visions of piety and productivity. Plath's contemporaries remembered Smith at that time as a conservative school that reflected the mores of the Eisenhower era.[49] Nancy Hunter Steiner, Sylvia's senior-year roommate, wrote that the "stereotyped Smith girl of the mid 1950's was a conformist. . . . She was a doer, busily directing the activities of some prominent or obscure organization in preparation for a future role as a participating member of her community. There was about her an air of noblesse oblige." Smith, she wrote, "placed a high value on involvement."[50]

Educating oneself for the greater moral good did not hold much appeal for Sylvia, who was—though a humanist—intensely individualistic. She would repeatedly resolve not to overcommit herself to any clubs or organizations. For Plath, time alone was a necessity. She fared best in small groups; parties and small talk exhausted her. (She once fantasized about getting tuberculosis so she could take a rest cure away from society.)[51] During her second semester, she told Aurelia she needed to "conserve" her time "for a more personal and perhaps selfish line of development": "I cherish a few of my angles a bit too much to rub them off."[52] Although she would eventually be elected to academic and social committees, she did not seek such offices herself. "Sylvia did not possess the instincts of leadership," Nancy remembered. "Her pursuits were solitary."[53]

But at Smith, solipsism was self-indulgent. In the early 1950s, even educated women were encouraged to pour their ambition into family life. Adlai Stevenson, in his infamous 1955 Smith commencement speech, would tell Plath and her classmates that it was their civic duty, given the Cold War "crisis," to embrace "the humble role of housewife."[54] Stevenson, a liberal Democrat, was one of Plath's idols. But in the fifties, neither Smith nor American society at large was much interested in women's struggle for self-determination. Nancy remembered that Stevenson's address "seemed to hurl us back to the satellite role we had escaped for four years—second-class citizens in a man's world where our only possible achievement was a vicarious one."[55] Louise Giesey White, who attended Smith with Sylvia, recalled that though the college clearly "valued women, feminism wasn't a big thing."[56] One of Plath's English professors, Mary Ellen Chase, foreshadowed Stevenson's speech when she wrote in the *Smith Review* Fall 1952 issue that most Smith women did not "indulge in fantastic notions that we shall reform American society . . . or turn out many giantesses in the earth. We are, instead, inclined to look upon such presumptions as a bit ridiculous, and, on the whole, mistrust taking ourselves too seriously."[57] Sylvia's Smith friend Ellie Friedman Klein said that if you were lucky you ended up at a place like Smith "where you could do it all. But then when you started to do it all, you were called back."[58] Plath took her talents and her desires seriously, and was not about to be "called back."

Sylvia's professors, well aware of her exceptional talent, would encourage and nurture her throughout her time there. But during her college years she would also receive the message that introspection and disengagement were suspect, even un-American. Although she mocked herself for having a "persecution complex," she felt she was "paying a penalty for my individualistic ways of life." Smith could be "Heaven" but also "Hell" for "overly-sensitive" people like herself. Louise—one of a handful of Democrats on campus—found Smith intellectually stimulating but politically suffocating. She wondered if Sylvia, from a similar class background, with similar Democratic leanings, felt alienated. "I had not experienced Smith as a supportive place for people like us. We just didn't value the same things," she recalled. Sometimes Louise was astonished by the college's conservatism. She experienced significant pushback when, as president of the college's Christian association, she tried to organize a trip to an African American inner-city church in New York City. "It was very controversial," she said. Plath's determination to preserve her individuality—to maintain, as she put it, her "peculiar rough edges" and not become "a nice neat round peg in a round hole"—would be the central struggle of her Smith years.[59]

In early September 1950, Sylvia arrived at Haven House, an elegant, nineteenth-century dormitory on Elm Street with pale yellow siding, white trim, and large windows framed by black shutters. Her third-floor room was tiny, but after sharing a room with her mother, it felt like a "New York apartment." The first thing she did was position her desk, with its "velvet" maple sheen, before the window to take full advantage of the light and view across to Hopkins House.[60] Next, she bought some expensive draperies and a "deep wine" bedspread—her "dream" color.[61] Finding beautiful accessories was more than just a matter of taste. Sylvia's room was her private sanctuary where she would do most of her reading and writing. She knew the right colors would soothe and inspire.

Sylvia initially enjoyed the hallway introductions and cheerful bustle of the dorm, which she shared with forty-eight other young women. But by late afternoon on her first day, she became tired and retreated to her room. There, she lay down on her bed for half an hour listening to the ticking clock, "so rhythmic and self-assured." The meditative interlude steeled her for another round of hallway introductions and an evening cider party in the house president's room. Sylvia knew other young women from Wellesley attending Smith—Pat O'Neil and Louise Giesey, both Crocketteers. "Girls are a new world for me," she wrote Aurelia when she finally returned to her room at midnight. "I should have some fascinating times learning about the creatures."[62] She began finding her way "slowly" amid the "604 new faces, voices, screams."[63]

During her first week at Smith, Sylvia was subjected to a humiliating physical exam that involved stripping naked as female attendants snapped photos. She called it "peculiar" and may have drawn on the experience years later when she began to use Holocaust imagery in her poems.[64] At five nine and 137 pounds, her posture was deemed decent, though a nurse told her she tilted too far forward when she stood and was "in danger of falling on" her "face." "Well!" Sylvia wrote to Aurelia, next to a small drawing of herself tilting precariously forward.[65] She hoped it wasn't a prophecy of things to come.

She spent the next few days shopping, registering for classes, and attending teas and class meetings. She was pleased when two college newspaper staff members asked her to consider writing articles. Clearly her literary reputation had preceded her. Her faculty adviser, Kenneth Wright, had also heard "nice things" about her, though he told her Smith would "expect a lot"—praise that probably made her anxious.[66] The high point of that first week was the college convocation. "I never came so close to crying since I've been here when I saw the professors, resplendent with colors, medals & emblems, march across the stage," she wrote Aurelia. "I still can't believe I'm a Smith girl!"[67]

Plath carried her split sensibility about privilege with her to Smith. The only freshman on a floor of juniors and seniors, she enjoyed mocking the trivial concerns of the older students to Aurelia: "you should hear them 'Deah me, I <u>must</u> go to the Yale-Cornell game, I'll call up Bill . . .' or 'She didn't marry <u>him</u> . . . Oh, God!' "[68] As much as Sylvia wanted to fit in, she kept her distance from the wealthy young women who considered Smith an expensive finishing school, the ones who were "always talking about Europe & N.Y."[69] Jane Truslow Davison recalled that Smith was then in the throes of "the last gasp of debutantism. . . . There were a lot of class-oriented secret societies and clubs."[70] Sylvia's friend Janet Salter Rosenberg remembered, "Sylvia really was annoyed that she didn't have money." But at the same time, she mocked those who had it. "I remember Sylvia telling me with great resentment that the biggest problem these people had was which fur coat to wear on a date."[71]

Sylvia was beginning to think that dates, rather than grades, were the most valued social currency on campus. As early as the first week, she got the message when a friend told her "about how good it is not to work <u>too</u> hard, but to allot time for 'playing.' "[72] Indeed, Margaret Shook, who served on the editorial board of the *Smith Review* with Plath, remembered a popular Smith ditty, sung to a tune from *Annie Get Your Gun*:

> You're sharp as a pen point
> Your marks are really 10-point,
> You are Dean's List, Sophia Smith,
> But a man wants a kiss, kid,
> He doesn't want a Quiz Kid,
> Oh, you can't get a man with your brains.[73]

Sylvia needed confirmation that there were intellectual women at Smith, not just debutantes biding their time until marriage. As usual, she gave herself little leeway to fail: "the whole episode here is up to me," she wrote Aurelia. "I have no excuse for not getting along in all respects. Just to find a balance is the first problem."[74]

In letters home, Sylvia enthused about her yearlong classes in French literature, freshman English (with Mary Ellen Chase, among others), botany, European history, art ("Basic Design"), and phys ed. She loved the library's "quiet and refreshing" atmosphere and vowed to "spend all the hours I can during the day there." She attended her first chapel service, which she called a "Beautiful ceremony, but nothing I could ever believe in."[75] She was making friends; during her first week, a group of students had ended up in her room dancing the Charleston. One of them was Ann Davidow, who stayed long after the others left. She and Plath discussed "God and religion," and Plath sensed a deeper connection. Sylvia described Ann to Aurelia as a fellow "free thinker" who had been raised Jewish. They even complemented each other physically: Ann was almost as tall as Sylvia, "freckle-faced, short brown hair and twinkling blue eyes."[76] Later Sylvia would learn that Ann struggled with depression and suicidal thoughts, a secret that bound them closer. In late October, Sylvia met Enid Epstein, a Jewish New Yorker who had published poems and drawings in *Seventeen*. She was thrilled to meet another young woman with serious artistic ambition; the two would be nearly inseparable during her junior year. Meanwhile, she became closer to her Wellesley friends Louise and Pat.

Ann soon procured Sylvia's first date, a twenty-two-year-old Amherst senior named Bill Gallup, whom she met for dinner in early October. The blind date went surprisingly well. Bill was tall, "cleancut," and from West Newton—a familiar type. She was amused by his "observations" of her: "I live 'hard,' am dramatic in my manner, talk sometimes like a school girl reporting a theme, and have a southern accent!"[77] Yet her buoyant mood soon descended. "Today has been utterly hell-hot, sunny, and I had 4 hours of classes this morning & one this afternoon. My desk is loaded with books, all the classrooms are on the third floor, and I am physically & mentally exhausted," she wrote Aurelia. She felt "overwhelmed" by her classwork and was not sleeping well.[78] She wished she had signed on only for an eighteen-hour load instead of the more challenging twenty-four. "I find myself rather hard pressed," she wrote. She feared she would fail history with Mrs. Koffka, a six-hundred-person lecture class with a crushing reading list. English with Mr. Madeira was "strictly critical," which meant that she did not have the chance to write creatively.[79] She wanted to get outside and enjoy the brilliant foliage, but most days her classes did not end until four p.m. "I don't dare think of marks," she wrote her mother.[80] Sylvia felt that all her professors were excellent but worried she would let them down. The only class she seemed to enjoy was French, where she could focus on literature rather than grammar. "Maybe I'll get rested and balanced in a month. Just now Thanksgiving seems awfully far away."[81]

The new tone of these letters worried Aurelia, who advised her daughter to get to bed earlier and spend less time writing home. Sylvia decided she would face her dilemma with pragmatism and self-resolve: she would stay up no later than ten fifteen during the week and wake no earlier than seven. "I see a little order in the chaos already," she reassured Aurelia, and herself, in early October. "Wait for a few weeks till I build up study habits and sleep habits, and I'll have more time to breathe. . . . Rome was not built in a day, & if I accept confusion as a normal consequence of being uprooted from home environment, I should be able to cope with my problems better."[82] She soon came down with a bad cold and had to miss several classes. She tried to cancel a date with Bill, but he insisted on visiting her at Haven House. She realized that her "first enthusiasm" had "cooled completely." Later, when some of her friends wandered into her room, she "burst into tears," she told Aurelia. "Dear me, how pathetic can we get." The friends made her a pot of hot tea and served her meals in bed. Afterward, she felt "much less homesick."[83]

She tried to be "philosophical" about her frequent illnesses and treat them like a "challenge." Instead of crawling home to Aurelia, it was time, she declared, "to learn to be master of myself." She would spend weekends at Smith while most of her classmates fled, "dressed to kill," to Dartmouth and Yale. She would sit in the sun on her dorm's third-floor piazza: "Out of misery comes joy, clear and sweet."[84] Yet her mood plummeted again. She was running herself ragged trying to keep up with her "endless" class-work.[85] "Your letters, just now, are a sustaining life force," she told her mother.[86] She considered going home, but checked herself into the infirmary instead.

Sylvia was slipping into her first major depression. That October, she wrote in her journal about feeling "pathetic," "ugly," "flabby," "without identity: faceless," "mad," "a knot of nerves, without identity," "lost." She described the library's serene beauty to her mother, but in her journal she called it "a nightmare. There is no sun." While she read history assignments, she felt "pulled thin, taut against horizons too distant for me to reach." "Will I never rest in sunlight again—slow, languid & golden with peace?"[87] She felt that she would never attract a man who was her intellectual equal, and she feared herself the subject of gossip from the other students who might think her "queer" for her intense studying.[88] She was not being paranoid; peers indeed remembered that she never relaxed in the common areas after dinner but went straight up to her room to work. Her habits made her seem aloof, even arrogant to some. But those who knew her best, like Ann and Enid—and later, Marcia Brown, Janet Salter, Sue Weller, Ellie Friedman, and Claiborne Phillips—found her to be warm, sympathetic, and an astonishingly good listener, full of humor and vitality.[89] Whether they liked or disliked Sylvia, her Smith contemporaries agreed on one thing: she drove herself too hard.

Sylvia's crisis was existential as well as emotional: her dread of time passing infiltrates her journal entries. "I can hear it even through the pillow I muffle it with—the tyrannical drip drip drip drip of seconds along the night. . . . I could smash the measured clicking sound that haunts me—draining away life, and dreams, and idle reveries. Hard, sharp, ticks. I hate them."[90] Echoing Eliot's Prufrock, she wrote that she would never fulfill her goals "because there isn't time, because there isn't time at all, but instead the quick desperate fear, the ticking clock, and the snow which comes too suddenly upon the summer."[91] She wrote a sonnet, "To Time," which ended with a memorable final couplet: "Time is a great machine of iron bars / That drains eternally the milk of stars."[92]

In letters to Aurelia, this emotional crisis was coded in talk of heavy workloads, lost sleep, and weekends alone in the library. These letters marked the beginning of a literary pattern that would characterize Plath's writing life: all that was threatening and malignant was exorcised in her journal, while Aurelia received sunny, optimistic letters. It may not be the case that Aurelia demanded only good news from her daughter; more likely, mother and daughter were coconspirators in a scenario where one always tried to spare the other from worry. The novelist Janet Burroway, who knew Sylvia in London in 1960, said, "Sylvia did not invent this tone; it is the mode of the letter home." Janet referenced her own voluminous letters to her mother from 1960 to 1971: "They are plucky. They omit. They prevaricate. They lie."[93] Sylvia's Smith friend Ellie Friedman Klein agreed that the sunny tone in Sylvia's letters home was standard fifties fare. Nor was her word count excessive, she said, as phone calls were simply too expensive for scholarship students.[94] But Plath had even more reason than others to give her mother only, as she later wrote, "the gay side."[95] Sylvia, along with the rest of the family, assumed that Aurelia's ulcers were caused by stress. She likely feared that telling Aurelia what she did not want to hear could adversely affect her health. She had lost her father; she was not about to lose her mother.

Still, the gulf between the voices of Plath's letters and journals was becoming extreme. Her very first journal entry from Smith, for example, contained no grand adjectives about her new dorm, classes, or friends. Instead, it was an eviscerating mockery of the idea of "community," triggered by a fire drill. "So this is what we have to learn to be part of a community: to respond blindly, unconsciously to electric sirens shrilling in the middle of night. I hate it. But someday I have to learn—someday—" She saw the fire drill, with its military overtones, as a metaphor for blind conformity. Its screech was "inhuman," terrifying—"My nerves pained me keenly."[96] The idea of "community" terrified the iconoclast in her.

Later she would fantasize in her journal about being a man, gaining experience in bars, brothels, and battlefields, like Ernest Hemingway or F. Scott

Fitzgerald. She was frustrated by female subordination and knew she would never attain power by abasing herself:

> I don't believe that the meek will inherit the earth: The meek get ignored and trampled. They decompose in the bloody soil of war, of business, of art, and they rot into the warm ground under the spring rains. It is the bold, the loud-mouthed, the cruel, the vital, the revolutionaries, the mighty in arms and will, who march over the soft patient flesh that lies beneath their cleated boots.[97]

Her desire to conform was in constant tension with her desire to break away, to pursue artistic selfhood in experimental and risky ways. She would allude to the dilemma in her 1954 poem "Metamorphoses of the Moon," which pitted the comforts of illusion against reality:

> The choice between the mica mystery
> of moonlight or the pockmarked face we see
>   through the scrupulous telescope
> is always to be made: innocence
> is a fairy-tale; intelligence
>   hangs itself on its own rope.
>
> Either way we choose, the angry witch
> will punish us for saying which is which;
>   in fatal equilibrium
> we poise on perilous poles that freeze us in
> a cross of contradiction, racked between
>   the fact of doubt, the faith of dream.[98]

Later, in an academic paper, she wrote about the conflict between the burgher and the artist in Thomas Mann's novels. As she wrote in her journal that November, "I, too, was stunted, narrowed, warped, by my environment, my outcroppings of heredity. I, too, will find a set of beliefs, of standards to live by, yet the very satisfaction of finding them will be marred by the fact that I have reached the ultimate in shallow, two-dimensional living—a set of values."[99] Sylvia would long for freedom and escape—from Aurelia, the strictures of American middle-class womanhood, and even American men, who "worship woman as a sex machine with rounded breasts and a convenient opening in the vagina, as a painted doll who shouldn't have a thought in her pretty head other than cooking a steak dinner."[100] She began fantasizing about spending her junior year in Europe. The allure of the Left Bank literary lifestyle was strong, and it offered a liberating alternative to academic achievement, which she was beginning to find "false" and "provincial."[101]

Sylvia hated the pressure to secure weekend dates, but she played along. On a blind date that October she went to an Amherst fraternity party at Alpha Delta ("God, these Greek names are foolish") and saw through the forced gaiety to the ennui. "There seemed nothing very real about the occasion," she told Aurelia. "The boys are all rather good-looking, the girls all rather lovely or pretty or cute, as the case may be. . . . the whole system of weekends seem more intent on saying 'I went to Yale,' or 'Dartmouth.' That's enough. You've gone somewhere. Why add: 'I had a hell of a time. I hated my date.'" She was beginning to doubt that she would ever meet "a congenial boy."[102] Indeed, a Smith friend recalled that there was a widespread culture of "humiliation of women" at the elite men's colleges where Smithies socialized: on "pig nights," men would get a visiting unattractive woman drunk and make a fool of her. Sylvia would have been deeply upset by such stories.[103]

Indian summer came to Northampton in late October. Sylvia lounged in the sun, biked through the countryside, and practiced her backhand. Sun and exercise eased her anxiety. "You should see the view from my 3rd floor sunporch," she wrote her mother. "The hills are rising over the gold trees and blue and red tile roofs in a smoky blue-purple haze. Paradise [Pond] is reflecting russets & bronzes. Wellesley never had such hills!"[104] She longed to paint it all, but she had to study. Her high spirits plummeted, however, when she received a B– on her first English paper. "Now if I do my best and get B– in my 'best' subject, what chance do I have in my tough courses?" She mocked herself as a "brilliant authoress." The prospect of her upcoming history test left her "frozen," so Aurelia sent her outlines to help her study.[105] "Time ticks by relentlessly," she wrote her mother.[106] She envied the "perfect Smith girls."[107]

On October 27, 1950, Sylvia turned eighteen. She celebrated with friends over pizza at Joe's, a college hangout in town. She was an adult now, living on her own, and forging an independent life. But the milestone unnerved her. "I have little time to stop running. I have to keep on like the White Queen, to stay in the same place."[108] She felt as if she had truly left her childhood behind—"the smooth strawberry-and-cream Mother-Goose-world, Alice-in-Wonderland fable . . . to be broken on the wheel" of the "dull responsibility of life."[109]

That evening, Sylvia's house mother, Mrs. Shakespeare, joined the girls for a small party. (Aurelia had sent a cake.) Mrs. Shakespeare was upset to hear that Sylvia had decided to cancel a date with a Dartmouth boy in order to study; Sylvia repeated their conversation to Aurelia: "'But my dear, you musn't let studying blot out your social life—it's so important to keep in circulation.' I agreed with a smile, making a mental reservation (sleep, after 2 weeks of solid speed & tension, also is important.)."[110] A few days later, Miss Mensel, the woman in charge of representing scholarship students to Smith's board of trustees, met with Sylvia and "stressed the point about getting out on weekends so as not to go stale."[111] Ending up an old maid was not worth graduating summa cum laude, she implied.

Sylvia ignored her. She had so little time to socialize that she agreed to a "church date" with a Dartmouth freshman on a Sunday morning. Compared to Pat O'Neil, who started studying in the morning, skipped dinner, and finished up at ten p.m., she felt positively lazy. "It's rather a shock to realize that here <u>every</u>one studies, and often there are people more intelligent than I am."[112] She was sure her old rival Louise Giesey would receive the top academic award in her class while she barely stayed afloat with B's and C's. "I just can't stand the idea of being mediocre," she wrote to Aurelia in a burst of candor. "I am driving myself rather hard," she admitted, and wondered if she was "good enough to deserve all this."[113] Louise indeed felt tension with Sylvia at Smith, despite their friendship. "She was disciplined about how she spent her time, and also about how much of her she would show the world. . . . She didn't throw her intellect around. She didn't try to intimidate. She was always very friendly. But within narrow confines."[114]

Sylvia had recently learned that her scholarship benefactress was a famous author: Olive Higgins Prouty. Mrs. Prouty, as Sylvia always addressed her, was best known for her novel *Stella Dallas* (1923), a melodrama that was made into a film in 1937, starring Barbara Stanwyck and nominated for two Academy Awards; a popular radio series based on the novel ran from 1937 to 1955. Prouty's semiautobiographical 1941 novel, *Now, Voyager*, was ahead of its time in its portrayal of a woman with an overbearing mother on the brink of madness who is cured by a sympathetic psychiatrist. This novel, too, was made into a successful film, starring Bette Davis. The plot of *Now, Voyager* influenced *The Bell Jar*, and Mrs. Prouty inspired the character of Philomena Guinea. Prouty would influence the course of Plath's life in much more important ways, however—none of which Plath could have foreseen in 1950. The revelation of her benefactress filled her with excitement and anxiety. "If only I can meet all the opportunities," she wrote. "Just now I feel rather overwhelmed."[115] She warned Aurelia that she would look "hollow-eyed" when she came home for Thanksgiving, despite the sleeping pills Aurelia had sent her.[116]

But then she received a major boost—her poem "Ode to a Bitten Plum" appeared in the November issue of *Seventeen*. Eddie Cohen wrote to say that while he liked it, he felt it was "overdone" and too prose-like.[117] B's in English had shaken her confidence, and she was in no mood to hear Eddie's criticism.

She was also growing tired of his romantic declarations—yes, he was sexually involved with other women in Chicago, but what if he was meant to be with her? What if she was the near-perfect "Golden Woman" of his dreams, his "Love Idol," his "La Dorada"?[118] He simply had to see her. But Sylvia was not interested in serving as Eddie's muse. He was one of the few people to whom she could speak honestly, and she continued to gently rebuff his plans to visit her.

In the wake of her poem's national publication, she began to feel more secure about her abilities in English. At one point that November, her professor asked her not to speak up so much. "It's so annoying to sit back & watch people fumble over a point you see clearly," she complained to Aurelia.[119] Her art class, however, was a joy. She was studying Piero della Francesca, Michelangelo, Rembrandt, Cézanne, de Chirico, Matisse, Picasso, Henry Moore, color, texture, perspective. Three hours of woodcut printing launched a soaring, Whitmanian mood. "Oh, mumsy, I'm so happy here I could cry! I love every girl & every blade of grass."[120] She sensed "hope, opportunity, capacity" everywhere.[121]

Sylvia canceled a date on a Friday night in early November in order to see *A Streetcar Named Desire*, which she called "dynamic," with its "poetic bestiality."[122] She was steeling herself for another dateless weekend when Louise came through with a blind date from Amherst, Corby Johnson. "I threw on my clothes—all the time ranting to dear Ann on how never to commit suicide because something unexpected always happens." Her date with Corby left her feeling "terrific—what a man can do."[123]

The next week she had yet another blind date, this time with Guy Wilbor, an Amherst freshman from Chicago, set up by Ann. Guy recalled that Sylvia was "far more interesting than the average date." She was "perceptive," "intellectual," "very aware and interested in what was going on around her." Though slightly "austere" in her bearing, she warmed up once they began talking. When she spoke, he recalled, she was a "commanding presence"; she was not "girly." Their conversation centered on writing. She wanted to hear about his English class at Amherst, taught by a young professor who encouraged his students to write creatively about personal experiences. Sylvia was intrigued, and pressed him for more details about the type of "word analysis" the professor encouraged. She told Guy she wanted to become a fiction writer, though modestly omitted the fact that she had already published in *Seventeen*. When he mentioned some of his investments, she wanted to know more about the workings of the stock market. It was not the sort of serious conversation he had expected on a first date, but he was flattered by her curiosity.[124] Sylvia, for her part, felt that the night was a social triumph. Not only was her date tall and handsome, but she saw numerous friends from Wellesley at the Amherst dance. They waved and smiled as she basked in her "warm glow."[125] Now no one could say that she did not circulate.

Her friendship with Ann Davidow was deepening too. The two of them had intended to spend a few hours at the library one afternoon in late November, but when they saw the sun setting through the windows, they dashed down to Paradise Pond. There, they watched the sun sink slowly into the "glassy water & the lavender-blue twilit hill in the distance" while they talked "frankly about everything."[126] Sylvia did not have many friends who knew her well enough to break through the artificial gaiety that exhausted her, or who understood her deep connection to nature. "I could lean on her. . . . Together the two of us could face anything," she wrote in her journal.[127]

Sylvia took the bus to Wellesley at Thanksgiving. Home meant "love and security," though the house now felt small and shabby with its stained seat cushions and faded wallpaper. Aurelia had cleaned out Sylvia's old room, which left her feeling untethered. She spent time with Warren, now on scholarship at Exeter, and his roommate Clement Moore, whose novelist mother, Sarah-Elizabeth Rodger Moore, was an inspiration to Sylvia. She saw *The Red Shoes* with Bob Riedeman (who hoped to rekindle their romance) and attended a local party with a "horribly popular" date. But she felt "numb, gray" on Sunday as she headed back to Smith with a group of Wellesley friends.[128] She had hoped to sit next to the handsomest boy in the car, Bob Humphrey, but was outmaneuvered by a Smith classmate. She fumed silently all the way to Northampton and felt lonelier than ever when she arrived at Haven House.

Back at Smith, already homesick, she fell into what she herself called a "depression." "My loneliness perhaps springs from the fact that the busy routine I associate with life here is momentarily lifted & I am left spinning in a vacuum. I'm glad the rain is coming down hard. It's the way I feel inside. I love you <u>so</u>," she wrote Aurelia.[129] Routine, she said, "keeps me from thinking too much about myself."[130] She felt better when she left her room and sat down to write alongside another student in the living room: "what one human presence can mean!"[131] But to her journal she reflected more deeply:

So here I am, in my room. I can't deceive myself out of the bare stark realization that no matter how enthusiastic you are, no matter how sure that character is fate, nothing is real, past or future, when you are alone in your room with the clock ticking loudly into the false cheerful brilliance of the electric light. And if you have no past or future which, after all, is all that the present is made of, why then you may as well dispose of the empty shell of present and commit suicide.

Yet Sylvia had become adept at talking herself out of despair: "there is always the turning, the upgrade, the new slant. And so I wait."[132]

Although she had found other young women who shared her "pacifist ideals" about communist China—"none of this 'Bomb them off the map' Business!!" she wrote to Aurelia—in her journal she confided her terror of nuclear annihilation.[133] She noted how the December snow resembled "frozen ashes" and wondered how the landscape would look "if the planes came, and the bombs."[134] She imagined living "in that white world," an eternal winter, foraging and gathering from plants alongside small animals that had been spared death. All would fade into oblivion, even concepts like freedom and democracy, though she almost relished the prospect of America—"our tender, steak-juicy, butter-creamy million-dollar-stupendous land"—dying like the Roman Empire. "We all are on the brink, and it takes a lot of nerve, a lot of energy, to teeter on the edge, looking over, looking down into the windy blackness."[135] Her mood reflected the anxiety of the age.

In early December she received her first set of grades: Botany, A; French, A–; History, A–; English, B; and Art, B–. She could not understand why her lowest grades were in her two "best" subjects, but she was relieved she was on track to make honors. Now she worried about finding a date for the Haven House dance. Ann did not have a date either, and the two of them conspired to find some willing Amherst boys "by hook or crook."[136] She was still running on a sleep deficit. Her vow to get to bed by ten thirty had given way to midnight, while on Saturdays she stayed out until two thirty in the morning. She reassured Aurelia that she would start taking sleeping pills again to reestablish healthy sleep patterns. She also spoke frankly to her mother about her lack of periods since she had begun attending Smith—probably due to stress and irregular sleep. She was worried and wanted to see their family doctor when she returned home for Christmas.

Sylvia had learned some troubling news about Ann, who confided to her that she was depressed and had been contemplating suicide. Ann had gone so far as to gather a stash of razor blades and sleeping pills. Sylvia immediately wrote to Aurelia asking for advice about whether she should write to Ann's parents to tell them that their daughter was "tired." Sylvia blamed Ann's mother for making light of her troubles. "If you were her mother, she would be alright."[137] Perhaps echoing Aurelia, Sylvia told Ann that she just needed "rest."

In early December, Sylvia went on a date with an Amherst student, a twenty-five-year-old Second World War veteran. As the two walked together in the cold night, Sylvia could not help herself from asking "what its [sic] like to kill someone or be killed"—just as she had asked Hans-Joachim Neupert about bodies in the rubble of bombed-out German towns. "I said I'd like him to tell me all about the things that ever had hurt him or bothered him so I'd be able to understand him better." The vet mistook Sylvia's interest for intimacy, and he suddenly pinned her to the ground. Certain she was about to be raped, she fought him off, "all of which made a scene." Sylvia remained cool-headed and managed to defuse the situation by asking about his ex-lovers. When they parted, she felt as if she ought to apologize even though she knew her instinct was perverse. Still, she blamed herself for agreeing to go on a night walk alone with him. She did not know what to make of the experience; her mind was "in rather a fog," as she told Aurelia. She later decided that she would see the man again even though he had nearly raped her. Something about this battle-scarred ex-Marine intrigued her. And yet, she found the uniforms on the Amherst campus "sickening."[138] Plath was simultaneously revolted and fascinated by war.

Guy Wilbor accompanied Sylvia to the Haven House dance in late December after dinner and a sleigh ride. He recalled that she was more "pensive" and "reflective" this time.[139] Something seemed to be bothering her. She wrote that she had reached "the saturation point when it comes to studying," and could do no more.[140] She could not wait to see Aurelia again, and counted down the days until Christmas vacation. But once she was home, she fell into a "black mood" and felt "close to going utterly and completely mad."[141] She told Ann she had realized, perhaps for the first time, that she could no longer rely on Aurelia to comfort her:

> It was such a relief to go back and feel the responsibility slide off my shoulders on to my family's. I realize now, though, that mother can't be the refuge that she was before, and that hit me hard. . . . My mother's purpose in life is to see me & my brother "happy and fulfilled." And I can't cry on her shoulder any more when things go wrong. I've got to pretend to her that I <u>am</u> all right & doing what I've always wanted . . . and <u>she'll</u> feel her slaving at work has been worthwhile.[142]

Sylvia advised Ann to "gradually build up a philosophy of life, or your purpose in it, or something, and be reasonably jolly."

Earlier that fall, Sylvia had written a thank-you note to her scholarship benefactress, Olive Higgins Prouty, about her love of Smith and her writing ambitions. To her astonishment, Mrs. Prouty wrote back inviting her to tea over the Christmas break. Plath was extremely anxious about the meeting; to prepare, she read all of Prouty's novels, and for the tea, she dressed with great care, rechecking the seams of her stockings and clutching her white gloves nervously. On the bus ride to Brookline, a wealthy Boston suburb, she began to panic. "What if they took away my scholarship and gave it to some senior who was writing a best-selling novel? Worst of all, what if Olive Higgins Prouty was disappointed in me?"

When the bus driver called out her stop, she walked up the elegant, curved driveway to Mrs. Prouty's white mansion. A maid ushered her into the living room, where she waited stiffly by the fire. She was admiring the blue walls, French windows, and gold curtains when she heard a warm voice call, "Why, you must be Sylvia!" Over tea and cucumber sandwiches, Plath relaxed. Mrs. Prouty asked her if she had ever written about her family, but she demurred that they were just "ordinary." "For you, perhaps," Prouty said, "but not for me, not for others. Think of the material you have there!" Writing about her own family had never occurred to Plath. "I had always wanted to write about something very grand and complicated, very important and world-shaking. Home seemed so close, so familiar that I took it for granted."[143] Prouty advised her to forge stories out of the problems and conflicts that had arisen in her own life. She took this advice to heart.

Sylvia returned to Smith after the Christmas break with a bad sinus infection. Worse, she learned that Ann would not be returning to campus; she had transferred to an art school in Chicago. When she heard the news she felt "sick," for Ann had been her "one real friend." She had assumed that the two would room together. "You don't know how it is without Ann," she told Aurelia. "I loved her so!" There was no other friend with whom, Sylvia said, she could "completely be myself . . . or write in that journal of mine without having to justify myself."[144] Ann liked to study, and Sylvia had looked forward to quiet hours reading and writing alongside her in their shared room. Now she had no one to buffer her from the gossipy headwinds. She wondered how she would make any new friends given her strenuous schedule and inability to play bridge. Now, more than ever, she needed to " 'Conform in the little things': I really have to as I don't in other big things." She asked Aurelia to learn bridge with her that summer.[145] She wrote Ann a despondent letter in mid-January. "I almost wish I'd never met you—so I wouldn't feel so empty. What made me sparky & giddy was the friction of us two banging together & giving off electricity."[146] She told Ann that there were "acres of misgiving and self-doubt in me."[147]

After Ann left, Sylvia stopped writing in her journal. Her mind had become "like a wastebasket full of waste paper; bits of hair, and rotting apple cores." She felt "bereft" but chastised herself for self-pity.[148] Sylvia was compassionate toward others but bore herself little mercy. She often mistook her depression for weak-willed complaint. How could she feel so terrible when thousands of girls would give anything to switch places with her? Didn't she realize how lucky she was? What did she possibly have to complain about? Her self-contempt fed her depression in an unrelenting circle of anguish that continued to baffle her. "I have much to live for," she wrote in her journal that winter, "yet unaccountably I am sick and sad."[149]

Aurelian bromides of hope forged out of ruin frequently followed her dark journal passages. Hopkins House, which she saw every day from her window, was "smeared" and "soiled," yet she loved it nonetheless. "Such is the resiliency of man that he can become fascinated by ugliness which surrounds him everywhere and wish to transform it by his art into something clinging and haunting in it's [*sic*] lovely desolation."[150] She was not yet ready to relinquish her mother's Emersonian vision. Uplifting surprises kept her from foundering—an A– on her latest English assignment, and another publication, "Den of Lions," in *Seventeen*.

The story was based on her summer fling with Emile (Sylvia did not even bother to change his name). In the story, Marcia decides to break things off with Emile because of his playboy ways, even though she feels herself falling in love with him. "Den of Lions" is pure teen romance, but parts of the story rehearse Plath's more mature themes. The language of love is masked in the language of sacrifice, war, and violence, just as in her later poems "Purdah" and "Pursuit": "He had her cornered. No matter what she said, it would be meat for the sacrifice. The priest stood, knife raised over her chest. A flash of silver, a downward plunge."[151] (Ilo Pill would send her an illustration for the story when he read it.) "Den of Lions" had won third prize ($100) in the *Seventeen* fiction contest. When Sylvia learned the news, she "lay in bed giving little screams of joy."[152] She was not able to fall asleep until two a.m. The award boosted her confidence, and her mental health improved. "Clem's mother better watch out," she wrote Aurelia. "I'll be Sarah-Elizabeth Rogering [*sic*] her out of business in no time."[153] She called it "the best story I've ever written."[154]

She and Guy began dating again (they saw *All About Eve* in mid-January), and she was "once more eating like a pig."[155] She soon decided that Ann's departure may have been for the best, for it forced her to seek out "other freshman [*sic*] more deeply."[156] One of those students was Marcia Brown, who lived on the first floor of Haven House. "She is so alive, and we were shouting out our opinions about life while striding along into the bitter wind and antiseptic sunlight," Sylvia wrote Aurelia that January.[157] She would use similar language to describe her first conversation with Ted Hughes five years later. While some of Sylvia's Smith contemporaries remembered her as egotistical, aloof, and superior, Marcia, who became Sylvia's lifelong friend, had the opposite reaction. She recalled that when Sylvia listened to you, she made you feel like "the world's most interesting person." Whether she was speaking with a "salesman or a major in microbiology," Sylvia showed "an intent enthusiasm and a friendly, lovely smile that made them feel simply wonderful and unique."[158] Jane Truslow Davison, who got to know Sylvia in 1954, remembered that Sylvia was indeed "at her best" with Marcia, who made no "demands" and "knew instinctively how to handle" Sylvia.[159] Marcia herself recalled long, philosophical conversations with Sylvia "about what kinds of people we wanted to be and what we thought were our essential selves that couldn't be compromised and ways in which we expected to change and grow."[160] Sylvia gushed so much about the simplest things—Chinese food, French wine, even spicy pizza—that Marcia sometimes found her hard to take seriously. But she felt Sylvia's sentimental enthusiasm was "genuine" and "charming." Not everyone would.[161]

In late January, Sylvia returned home for six days of rest. Aurelia catered to her, cooking lavish meals, baking her favorite desserts, buying her perfume and silk stockings, and keeping the house quiet so that her daughter could sleep late. Sylvia made an effort to socialize and went dancing at the King Philip with Bob Humphrey. The visit home was an attempt to soothe her fraying nerves. She feared she would need to make a "Herculean" effort to keep up her relentless academic pace for another four months.[162]

When she returned to Smith she was surprised to find a three-page letter from Dick Norton waiting for her. Dick was now a senior at Yale (where Perry was a freshman) and bound for Harvard Medical School. She had spent time with both brothers over her Christmas break, when Dick began to see her in a new light. Sylvia was a college girl now, no longer just his kid brother's friend. He politely inquired whether she would like to spend a weekend with him at Yale in February. He proposed several suitable diversions—a swim meet, a chapel service, a walk in the country, a campus tour. Though Sylvia insisted to her mother that his invitation was simply a gesture of sympathy from a generous older "cousin," she wrote Ann that she was "overawed" by the invitation. "Ann, he is just the sort of boy I'd love to get to know better—a med student, good-looking, intelligent!"[163] Indeed, Dick was Sylvia's ideal: blond, blue-eyed, athletic, intelligent, ambitious, and a family friend. "He was gorgeous. He was just a catch," Louise Giesey White recalled. Louise and her Wellesley friends were surprised when Dick showed an interest in Sylvia, who they assumed was not in his league. They began to regard her with a new respect.[164] Marcia felt differently. "He looked like a caricature of an all-American boy." She was revolted by Dick's "mom and apple pie with vanilla ice cream" persona. "When Sylvia was at her most enthusiastic, adoring and worshipping of this person—which she really was—I just had to put my hand over my mouth to keep from saying, 'I don't see how you can stand him for five minutes.'"[165] But dating Dick Norton was risky. The match would have thrilled both families, who had known each other for nearly two decades. Yet if the relationship faltered, so might the close ties between the Nortons and the Plaths. Dick was a careful young man, and he must have decided Sylvia was worth the risk. He could not have known the pain and humiliation his romance with Plath would eventually cause him—or her.

Sylvia studied ferociously for her first exams at Smith. On weekends she stayed in the library from nine to six with only an hour break for lunch. She complained about her sore eyes after reading history for ten-hour stretches, and once again began relying on sleeping pills each night.[166] She joked that she would either hang herself or join Alcoholics Anonymous if she had to continue the pace. "I have a horrible feeling of tension and pressure," she wrote to Aurelia. She couldn't keep all the "Johns and Henries" of English history straight, "while dates and trends leak like water from a sieve." She often made jokes about committing suicide in the face of her massive workload—gallows humor that surely unsettled Aurelia. "Now really, I am not writing from the hospital or the morgue," she wrote in early March.[167] And later that same month, "I'll write after I pass through this week. Either that, or you will receive a little ink bottle full of ashes. Please scatter them on the waters of the ocean I loved so well in my infancy."[168]

She found a temporary escape with Marcia, who invited her to an aunt's farmhouse in Francestown, near Peterborough, New Hampshire, in early February. The girls cooked together, stayed up late chatting in bed, shopped in town, and went on a long winter hike that left Sylvia fatigued but exhilarated. The change of scenery improved her mood but made the return to Smith all the more difficult. She continued to compare her intellectual abilities to that of other girls—particularly Pat O'Neil, who had straight A's. To her surprise, a fellow student told her that her art professor had showcased Plath's work as an example of "a promising Freshman." Sylvia scoffed—"I never believe anything good about myself"—but the compliment pleased her.[169] Later that month a senior congratulated her after reading an article about her in the "Teen Triumphs" section of an Illinois newspaper, which someone had posted on the Smith College hall bulletin board. In March a student approached her and gushed, "'I hear you're writing a novel. I think that's just wonderful!'" Sylvia wrote Aurelia, "Whereupon I felt like telling her I was my twin sister and never wrote a damn thing in my life. I've got to get to work if I'm going to live up to my 'reputation.'"[170] Such encounters continued throughout the semester, and even began to bother Sylvia. "'Oh, you're the one who's writing the book?' or 'You're the one who got all A's in History?' It's too bad—because once one person knows, everybody does. The only quiet woman is a dead one."[171] (These words bring Plath's late poem "Edge" to mind, with its ironic opening image of a "perfected" dead woman.)

Sylvia was dating several different young men, but none of them satis-fied. A date with a University of Massachusetts student left her reeling. He and his friends seemed to "think of girls as a clothes-horse with convenient openings and curved structures for their own naive pleasure. . . . The Ameri-can male does not think of a woman as a friend and companion (the mature outlook) but childishly as a combination of mother and sweetheart."[172] Yet she herself was snobbish about state-school men. "It is one level of society to get plushily tight on highballs and maraschino cherries and another to get 'stewed' on beer and greasy potato chips."[173]

In February, as was tradition, Smithies trekked up to Dartmouth for the Winter Carnival. Sylvia had no Dartmouth date; nor did Marcia, whose roommate was away. She invited Sylvia to bunk with her for the weekend. Together they hiked through the countryside and shared their meals. Sylvia summed up Marcia's appeal to Aurelia: "she's the only gal around here who takes looong walks." Buttressed by a deep female friendship, Sylvia relied less on men to boost her mood. "Both of us hate women en masse. But individu-ally they are nice."[174] Around this time Grampy Schober sent Sylvia $25—a surprise windfall at a time when her savings were dwindling.

Sylvia soon learned that her midyear marks were high: all A's and A–'s except for a B+ in English ("damn").[175] Around this time she told Aurelia that her period had returned after five months, a sign that the stresses of her first semester were beginning to recede.[176] Yet she worried about Aurelia's health; her mother's ulcer was troubling her again. "I don't want you to worry about things, mummy. Is it money?"[177]

She spent the weekend of February 17–18 at Yale with Dick Norton. She stayed off campus at "the Coop" on Prospect Street, a boarding house for dates, but spent most of Saturday with Dick in his room while the rain poured down outside. She read some of his old sociology papers—she was most interested in one about his visit to a mental institution—and even his poetry. His roommates intrigued her, especially a Yugoslavian refugee who had once belonged to (but had since rejected) the Hitler Youth. They visited Perry. The weekend went well, though she was careful not to get Aurelia's hopes up: "He regards me as an indulgent older cousin would."[178] She was disappointed Dick did not try to kiss her and told Ann she had "needed a few cocktails rather badly" to get her through the weekend.[179] But Dick frowned on girls who drank, so she abstained.

Dick was an aspiring doctor, and his scientific acumen—connected, for

Sylvia, to masculinity and paternal love—impressed her. She vowed to learn more about chemistry and physics. "I don't care if I am not 'mathematically minded,'" she wrote her mother in February. "All that I write or paint is, to me, valueless if not evolved from a concrete basis of reasoning, however uncomplex it must be."[180] To Aurelia she claimed that she was intrigued by the fact that Dick did not "credit emotional expression as valuable without scientific knowledge," but in a more candid letter to Ann, she wrote that around Dick, she felt "dumb" and "brainless."[181] She adored him, yet his smugness angered her. "All in all, I was grateful to the handsome old Einstein for taking me out, but God, Ann, I never felt so shallow in my whole life. I hate being patronized. When I came back, I tried and tried to rationalize, but couldn't say that one thought in my unlogical head was worth-while." She felt his mastery of "physical & chemical laws" showed up her "slippery shifting basis of liberal arts."[182]

The following week, Dick invited her to the Yale junior prom, which was coming up on March 10. She was "thrilled to extinction" by the invitation but kept her hopes in check. "I know he's just doing it to be nice," she told Aurelia.[183] She was wrong—Dick was laying the groundwork for a relationship. After Sylvia's visit, he spoke with "Aunt" Aurelia by phone, subtly asking permission to date her daughter.[184] He need not have worried. Dick Norton (or Perry—either would do) was exactly the sort of young man Aurelia wanted Sylvia to marry. But the intimacy and mutual approval between the families would eventually prove claustrophobic. Sylvia could never be sure whether she had made the decision to date Dick independent of her mother's wishes. One can trace the beginning of the end in casual remarks from Dick's letters, such as his feeling, which he discussed with Aurelia, that Sylvia ought to learn shorthand and develop more "enthusiasm for natural science."[185] Plath would connect both ideas, in *The Bell Jar*, to Esther's breakdown.

Sylvia wore a white, half-shouldered evening gown to the prom that accentuated her slim figure and deep brown eyes. "I feel a bit like cinderella [*sic*]: a borrowed old fur coat . . . a borrowed crinoline, plus borrowed silver sandals," she wrote home.[186] Dick did not notice her insecurities. She told Ann, "evidently things took a quick turn from the platonic to the . . . well, you know. . . . As we walked up the hill to my 'house' after the dance, we stopped for a minute and let the great windy silence come at us. It was dark, the streets were quiet and bare, and the stars were clear. 'It's like being in a church,' he said. And it was." They went on a long, cold bike ride the following day; Sylvia was exhausted, though she kept up a cheerful front. "I said to myself: make the most of this kid, you may never see him again."[187] The two wrote a joint letter to Aurelia in which Dick played the awed suitor. "Need I say that Syl was her very prettiest in the new white dazzling dress? Or that she easily outshone the other pretenders?" He planned to take Sylvia to a play that night. "I just hope it will not prove to be too much for a young lady since she has had a full two days already," Dick wrote.[188] Eddie Cohen he was not.

The prom letter launched a correspondence between Dick and Aurelia that would last several years. Dick always addressed her as "Aunt A." and signed off "Your loving nephew." "As you know," he told Sylvia, "my admiration for my Aunt Aurelia defies any logical or legible writing."[189] Sylvia began to worry that she could not compare to her mother in Dick's eyes. "You better not be so capable and wonderful, because the poor boy doesn't know that I'm rather an awkward hybrid . . . like does not always breed like."[190] But that spring she was overjoyed to date a handsome Yale- and Harvard-trained future doctor; she felt "a rich sense of belonging."[191]

Now that her relationship with Dick was becoming more serious, Sylvia was in no mood to stumble on the all-too-real apparition of Eddie Cohen, whom she found waiting for her at Haven House just as she was about to leave campus for her spring break on March 21st. He had, apparently, driven all night from Chicago.

> I walked unsuspectingly into the living room and there was this strange, dark-haired guy standing with a pipe gripped tightly between his teeth. "This is the third dimension," he said, just like in a play or something. So he said he'd come to drive me home. So, fool that I am, I threw all my suitcases in his father's nash, and we were off. The funny thing is, Ann, that even though he could talk to me about my private life more authentically than any of my friends, I just couldn't get used to the idea that this physical stranger was the guy I'd written such confidential letters to. I couldn't get rid of the impression that he was just some taxi driver off the street. So all during the three hour drive home I was very nervous, not quite sure whether or not I would ever reach my destination and petrified as to what my mother would say if she saw me coming up the walk with Eddie, who she never wanted me to meet.

Sylvia told him she was dating someone from Wellesley and did not invite him into her house because she was "so scared" of Aurelia's reaction. "Turned out she was cross—not at Ed, but at my 'lack of hospitality.' I was rather shaken and surprised by the whole unexpected encounter."[192] Later, she too regretted making him drive all the way back to Chicago without offering him so much as a cup of coffee. Sylvia rightly assumed that a real-life meeting would destabilize this otherwise perfect, platonic relationship. She had given too much away to Eddie; no other young man had been privy to her deepest anxieties. Even he had admitted, just a few days before he arrived, that a meeting might result in the "destruction of the illusion."[193] He chided Sylvia for her rudeness, but after a few epistolary recriminations the two continued a mostly amicable correspondence throughout her time at Smith.

After spending her spring break with Marcia in New Jersey and New York City—her first trip out of New England—Sylvia returned to campus to learn that Dick was attending the Smith sophomore prom with Jane Anderson, who was the president of her class. (Sylvia eventually befriended Jane, who inspired the character of Joan Gilling in *The Bell Jar*, during her stay at McLean.) This development worried her. She also voiced anxiety about keeping up with her schoolwork while finding time to "<u>relax</u> & read what <u>I</u> want & lie in the sun."[194] "I really can't see too much light ahead. . . . Keep my morale up!" she begged her mother.[195] She worried that she was on the brink of another depression: "as I look ahead I see only an accelerated work-pattern until the day I drop into the grave."[196] Sylvia needn't have worried about Dick's loyalties. He visited Sylvia at Smith twice that April, and she planned a Yale visit in early May. He now addressed her as "Darling" and "Sweetie-Pie" in increasingly romantic letters, and she began to consider a life with him. When she and Marcia got summer jobs nannying for two wealthy families in Swampscott, Sylvia wrote Aurelia that the work would be "informative" since her employer was a doctor's wife.[197] She was now, as she put it, "beyond the dirndl skirt & frilly blouse stage."[198]

As the semester wound down, Sylvia began to relax. The dogwood trees were blossoming, "shading the campus with a sort of green and fragrant liquidity." She began skipping classes to read outside and felt like she was "living at a landscaped country club."[199] She spent hours tanning on the sun porch across from her room—always a form of solace and meditation—and began to plan her courses for the next year. She would major in honors English, but she could not decide what to take. Minor decisions prompted broader reflections. She asked Aurelia to get her "started secretarially next summer" so that she might apply for a United Nations job. "Shall I plan for a career? (ugh! I hate the word.) Or should I major in Eng. & Art & have a 'free-lance' career if I ever catch a man who can put up with the idea of having a wife who likes to be alone and working artistically now & then?" Mrs. Prouty thought she "had something," which cheered her enormously. She resolved to continue writing, even if it meant getting "battered & discouraged" in her courses next year.[200]

When "Den of Lions" appeared in the May edition of *Seventeen*, Dick showed the story to his Yale friends, who were full of compliments. He was proud of his "girl." Ann Davidow and Ilo Pill also wrote to congratulate Plath. Eddie was more critical: "you overdo it just a bit."[201] Sylvia admitted to Aurelia that Eddie's criticisms were insightful. In her journal that May, she wrote that rereading the story now made her "sick." What only a few months ago had seemed "so real and genuine" now "was hideously obvious," full of "lyrical sentimentality."[202] Next to a section about how her character Marcia refused to "sacrifice" her identity to join Emile's "brilliant tinsel world," Sylvia wrote in the margin of her manuscript, "How saccharine can you be?"[203] Eddie, as usual, put her deficiencies down to her lack of Experience. "You are good, Syl—mighty good. You have the eyes and ears and soul of a great writer. Sometimes, though, I wonder whether you have the heart of one." He told her that she would not achieve her full literary potential unless a man hurt her "so hard that you ache for months afterward, down where I don't think you have ever really hurt."[204] His comment was patronizing, for Sylvia had already experienced a grief beyond anything Eddie had encountered: her father's death.

Sylvia and Dick continued to see each other on weekends, mostly at Yale. They browsed in bookshops, took bicycle rides, and read Hemingway aloud to each other at Lighthouse Point. They were moving steadily toward a committed relationship. Dick's letters became more reflective and sentimental: "You are best imagined at a desk or table, neck arched foreward [sic] at an open book, blond hair about cheeks." He told her if she were with him, he would throw her over his shoulder, "Sabine-fashion," and would not be responsible for his actions.[205] He wanted her to teach him more about "artistic matters"—maybe they could even "create, as a team."[206] Sylvia told Eddie, "I won't say I'm in love. I don't believe in the word."[207] But to Aurelia she wrote that Dick was "the most stimulating boy I've ever known." There was nothing she would rather do than spend time with him, yet she felt insecure in his presence. "I can't see how any modern boy as athletic as Dick could bear a girl as uncoordinated as I am."[208] She was sure he would tire of her eventually.

When Sylvia finished her final exams in early June, she did not fret and ruminate over them as she had before. The weather was mild, and three months of freedom stretched before her. Dick and Perry picked her up from Smith and drove her back to Wellesley. "Perry drove home, while Dick explained the intricacies (sp.?) of carboxyl and hydroxyl groups, to which I listened with not as much avidity as I should have," she told Marcia.[209] Sylvia was already having second thoughts about the relationship.

Back in Wellesley, she shopped downtown for novels by Faulkner, Hemingway, Steinbeck, Richard Wright, and Pearl Buck, and tanned in her backyard. She penned a Tennysonian mock-up for Marcia:

She clasps the sun oil with hooked hands;
Close to the sun in backyard lands,
Ringed with azure halter, she stands,

The wrinkled rug beneath her crawls;
Her love for sunlight never palls,
Till with sunstroke down she falls . . .[210]

While Dick was vacationing in Maine she ambled back to her "old hunting ground," the town tennis courts. There she played against Phil McCurdy, a Wellesley High senior who was the best player on the school tennis team. She and Phil had been friendly since 1946, when he had stopped inside the Plath house on his way home from school to use the bathroom. Although Phil was younger, they quickly realized that they shared several intellectual and artistic interests (Phil would also eventually become a devoted Crocketteer). They bonded over their similar domestic situations. "We both had a solo parent, female, striving to beat poverty," he said. Phil lived only three blocks away from Sylvia and said the two of them used to sneak out at night to look at constellations. He remembered painting flowers with her at the Honeywell Fields, catching fireflies, and dancing together at Mrs. Ferguson's dance classes. "She was a delight. Whether it was a dragonfly or a line of poetry. . . . She gave it her all, whatever it was."[211] During high school, their relationship had been platonic. But as the two grew older, she called him her "protégé" and "baby doll." She ridiculed herself for trying to seduce a younger man, but she could not deny the attraction. On the courts she "maternally patted him on the shoulder & told him to come up and see me some time."[212]

There was one last academic engagement she needed to attend before the freedoms of summer—Dick's Yale commencement. The weekend portended troubles. On Saturday night she agreed to help Dick babysit his brother David, but as she and Dick read to the seven-year-old boy, she was seized by a vague distress. "I felt a preview of myself ten years hence breathe down my neck with a chilly whisper," she wrote in her journal.[213] Dick prepared an elaborate supper for her that made her feel embarrassed about her own lackluster culinary skills. On Sunday morning, Mildred Norton was up at five a.m. cleaning the house, packing lunch, and cooking an enormous breakfast. Watching Mrs. Norton, Sylvia felt "lazy," even though she had woken up at six to help. She told Ann she was impressed by Mildred's capability. "Mrs. Norton is my favorite—you would love her—very pretty in a mobile way—and terribly capable=keeps a house running and her four men well-fed, ironed, clothed and happy."[214] Sylvia would come to feel differently about Mildred Norton.

At Yale, Sylvia's mood soured in the June heat. Dick dashed off to various class events and left her to chat with his parents and other guests. "After Class Day," she wrote Marcia, "it was a two hour tea at the headmasters [*sic*] house, and I got so damn sick of making small talk with mothers of boys and fiancées and young wives that I thought my sweet girlish smile had frozen to my face." She and Mildred stayed together at the New Haven YMCA, where she slept badly. Commencement was another round of small talk and frozen smiles. She only "saw Dick in glimpses." Back in Wellesley that night, he called to tell her he had a few trips planned with friends and would not be around over the next few weeks. Sylvia was indignant. She had assumed the commencement invitation had sealed their relationship, but now Dick seemed to be backing away. "Tra la la," she wrote to Marcia. "Looks like glimpses is all we get, boy."[215] She was tired of reading his moods and ready for some distance, especially after the claustrophobic weekend with his family. She willed herself not to care. Summer by the sea, with Marcia, would salve all wounds. Or so she hoped.

8

Love Is a Parallax

Swampscott, Smith College, Cape Cod, 1951–1952

In early June 1951, Dick drove Sylvia to Swampscott, an affluent seaside town on Boston's North Shore. They were doing reconnaissance, trying to catch a glimpse of the waterfront mansion at 144 Beach Bluff Avenue where Plath would spend her summer. The house was difficult to find, and they had to ask several people for directions. Finally, just when Sylvia was convinced that the house "had been blown out to sea," they found it tucked inconspicuously behind an "aristocratic hedge" and "sweeping driveway." The Mayo family compound consisted of a large house atop a vast expanse of green lawn that sloped down to the sea, along with two smaller cottages, all white with black shutters. Plath described the "cars and shiny beachwagons parked carelessly about," while a tennis court and a yacht lay "modestly in hiding." She could not believe that she would soon be joining this world.[1]

In April, Sylvia and Marcia had been the first to respond to a post for a pair of summer nannies at the Smith vocational office. They were hired that day. Sylvia would take care of the three Mayo children—Joanne, 2; Pinny, 4; and Freddy, 6—from mid-June to Labor Day. She would earn room and board, plus $25 a week, with one day off each week. Marcia was placed with Mrs. Mayo's sister, Mrs. Blodgett, who also owned a mansion on Beach Bluff Avenue. The two friends jumped up and down when they were hired, but neither had any real sense of what she had signed up for. Sylvia began preparing for the job as if it were a professional position, telling Aurelia she wanted to learn child psychology. But Sylvia would see little of Mrs. Mayo, who spent most of her days and evenings socializing. All the child care, and many household tasks, would fall on Sylvia.

"I blithely assumed," Plath wrote later that fall, "that I would be spending most of my days lolling on the beach, swimming when the spirit moved me, writing sonnets, and keeping an occasional vigilant eye on the children."[2] Her second-floor room, with its own bathroom, balcony, and view of the sea, was enormous. But she had hardly unpacked on June 18 before she was called to help with the children's bath and bedtime. Between Pinny's night terrors and Joanne's five-a.m. rising, Sylvia did not get much sleep. Then the real work of the day began: "Picture Freddy striking Pinny and shouting and screaming," she wrote to Marcia, "while the poor girl does the same for several eons, and all the while you're pulling them apart, Joanne has been squatting cheerily in the corner stuffing her rosebud mouth with sand. God! Slight items like daily baths, helping with laundry and doing beds and such while keeping the three darlings alive—at the same time—challenge my homicidal tendencies no end."[3] On their own, the children were sweet, but together they were unmanageable, with "the most wicked combination of ages possible!"[4] Sylvia began to look forward to the "blissful silence of the cellar where I did the daily mountain of laundry."[5]

She was unprepared for fourteen-hour days of breaking up fights, mopping floors, and doing secretarial work for Dr. Mayo, and she was shocked when Mrs. Mayo "casually" mentioned that she would have to cook *all* the children's meals. Instead of protesting, Sylvia felt "guilty" and embarrassed about her inferior cooking skills. ("Ann, I <u>actually</u> don't know how to cook eggs!") She blamed Aurelia, who had "spoiled" her "by always being so capable and never <u>making</u> me work in the kitchen." In letters she mocked herself for scalding soup and burning rolls, and for poor chopping skills; she became adept at running water over her hands "to hide the dripping blood."[6] If Mrs. Mayo saw Sylvia reading a book while the children were napping, she would exhort her to try a new cake or pie recipe. "There was no time during the day when I had a legitimate hour to rest, free from disturbance," Plath later wrote.[7] Mrs. Mayo would give Sylvia a good reference ("She was an intelligent, honest, well mannered girl with a pleasing disposition," she wrote to Smith),[8] but her son Frederic later recalled that his mother "did not find Sylvia easygoing or easy to manage," and that Sylvia "did not give her the support that she needed."[9] Both women had set their expectations too high.

Sylvia had thought she would be treated as a member of the Mayo family—"presumably above the caste level of outright maid and governess." She was a Smith girl, after all. But to them, she was simply the help: "My status in the family was vague and often uncomfortable."[10] It was a depressingly familiar feeling, one she had experienced when dusting the school offices or visiting her grandfather at the Brookline Country Club. She was again learning to know her place: "I betcha I don't lift a tennis racket or sail a yacht all summer long," she wrote Marcia.[11] Sylvia watched enviously as the two college boys who lived in the compound's smaller houses took their "girls to cocktail parties, yacht club dances and sailboat rides." She would always have to work for a living—a point she emphasized in a drawing of herself with baby cereal in her hair. "I am a mess," she told Ann, "and feel most unattractive."[12]

She made light of her unhappiness to friends. "As you can imagine," she wrote Ann, "for an undomestic, un-maternal creature like I am, this 14 hour day is a wee bit of a strain."[13] She even joked about her "homicidal tendencies" in her mock-up of the *Swampscott Daily News:*

EXTRA! EXTRA!
"HIRED GIRL RUNS WILD"
A shocking event took place today in the home of Swampscott's beloved & respected Doctor M. A hitherto outwardly normal teen-age girl was found chortling hysterically over the mangled bodies of three angelic children. Our reporters rushed to the scene and found her sobbing hysterically in the kitchen. When asked what she had done to the eldest, she cried, "I fed him down the chromium-plated disposal unit in the kitchen sink."[14]

Five months later, Plath would write a real newspaper article for *The Christian Science Monitor* about her experience with the Mayos, titled, "As a Baby-Sitter Sees It." The sentimental article, filled with sweet stories about her innocent charges, gave little hint of her misery.[15] In a despairing letter to Aurelia that summer, Sylvia revisited a similar theme as she signed off: "'My head is bloody, but unbowed / May children's bones bedeck my shroud.'"[16] Sylvia felt physically and emotionally trapped by the house and all its demands: "Learning the limitations of a woman's sphere is no fun at all."[17]

Visiting Dick, who was waiting tables on Cape Cod, was not an option. "My face is a mess, all broken out, my tan is faded, my eyes are sunken. I look hideous," she wrote Aurelia.[18] The "old dungarees" and the plain shirt she wore each day were a far cry from the elegant, colorful outfits she donned at Smith.[19] She was "so dead" by eight p.m. that she went straight to sleep. "So I sit here exhausted, seeing no way out, seeing only slavery from six in the morning till eight at night," she wrote her mother after just one week with the Mayos. "I feel that I'm cut off from all humankind."[20] These letters provide, perhaps, a clue to the riddle of her suicide twelve years later, when she was a single mother in a foreign country with little help, company, or money, caring for two sick toddlers in a cold flat with intermittent electricity and hot water.

Sylvia nearly quit three weeks into the job but then began to imagine how "shut-in" she would feel in her "little room" back home in Wellesley: "How closely the trees and houses and familiar paths would crowd upon you, stifling you, smothering you, enclosing you," she wrote in her journal. "Here, the house is big and spacious and luxuriously comfortable."[21] She soon realized that the only way she would survive seven more weeks at the Mayos' was by writing about them. Once she saw herself as a writer, she no longer thought of herself as a slavey: "I must learn more about these people—try to understand them, put myself in their place. . . . I must be imaginative and create plots, knit motives, probe dialogue."[22] Life became bearable again as she recorded WASPy snippets from cocktail parties and yacht club dances. She even accompanied the Mayos on their yacht, the *Mistral*, which was staffed by a crew of three and large enough to accommodate a dozen guests. "At last I feel somewhat a master in my own domain." Looking at the sea from her private porch made her feel "infinitely placid, infinitely calm, infinitely spacious. . . . Something there is about the ceaseless, unperturbed ebb and flow . . . that heals all my uneasy questionings and self-searchings."[23] When she returned home to Wellesley for a weekend, she began to miss living amid the Mayos and their grand, carefree life:

> Somehow, I think, I have a delicious feeling of presumptuousness which comes perhaps from a secret enjoyment of living with rich people and listening to and observing them. . . . How hard it will be to return home, where the little green pine trees grow in such a close square around the house, where you can't move freely in a room without bumping into the furniture, where mother serves cranberry juice in cream cheese glasses on an old white celluloid tray. . . . How to return to the smallness, the imperfection, which is home?[24]

Like Jay Gatsby, Plath had been seduced by a fantasy of wealth. When the Mayos left for a weeklong cruise in August, she "felt the intangible steel cord of subservience loosened" and began to imagine that *she* was mistress of the house.[25] She played the piano, swam, and lounged on the porch. But when the Mayos returned, she again felt "crushed under a machine-like dictatorship."[26] She learned to hide her anger and weariness "under a necessary veneer of bright willingness."[27] It was a trick she came to master.

Marcia, only "two mansions" away, was luckier—she had no cooking or housekeeping duties and "knew about the key to the bourbon."[28] When the Blodgetts were out, she invited Sylvia to impromptu parties where the maids and cooks drank, played piano, and shot pool. The two spent their days off together on the beach, tanning their bodies over the sun-warmed rocks. Sometimes they met local boys at beach parties, but there were few opportunities for dating given their busy schedules. Sylvia was intrigued by Marcia's literary beau, Mel Woody, who sent regular letters and poems. She wrote him a flirtatious fan letter in June, urging him to marshal his "character and convictions" to succeed at Yale: "the easy way is to be avoided. Lord, how I despise the rosy path, which breeds only flabby, weak-minds [*sic*] slugs of individuals."[29] She told Mel she got "seething mad at civilization, dogma, prejudice," and quoted for him the first two stanzas of a sardonic poem she had recently written, "I Am an American." A cynical response, perhaps, to Elias Lieberman's jingoistic 1916 poem "I Am an American," Plath's version shows the influence of both Eddie Cohen and Mr. Crockett, and looks forward to *Bell Jar* themes of capitalism, advertising, affluence, chauvinism, xenophobia, and hypocrisy.[30] It was a dangerous poem to write in a nation roused by McCarthy's witch-hunts:

> We all know that we are created equal:
>> All conceived in the hot blood belly
>> Of the twentieth century turbine;
>> All born from the same sheet
>> Of purple three-cent postage stamps;
>> All spewed like bright green dollar bills
>> From the same government press;
>> All baptized with Chanel Number Five
>> In the name of the Bendix, the Buick, and the Batting Average.
>
> We all know that certain truths are self-evident:
>> That we believe in liberty and justice for all
>> Like the great green lady with the bronze torch
>> Lifted beside the door marked "Members Only."
>> That we are all free to speak our piece from the ivory soap box
>> And to letter our liberal opinions
>> In white exhaust on the spacious skies:
>> That we can all pursue happiness . . .
>> (Say, even the jets can't fly that fast, brother.)
>
> We all know the easy democracy of mind:
>> For we are averaged daily
>> And our predilections are displayed
>> On every billboard from Tacoma to Pensacola
>> From Beantown to Frisco, all along the super highways.
>> Two out of three of us prefer our ideas
>> Bite-size and pre-cooked for lasting freshness

Or you can feed them to us in ten easy lessons
With a money-back guarantee if proved unsatisfactory.[31]

Working as a nanny for the Mayos roused Plath's class consciousness. When she looked back on the summer in 1961, she wrote another poem about her time in Swampscott with Marcia, "The Babysitters," full of resentment and nostalgia:

O it was richness!—eleven rooms and a yacht
With a polished mahogany stair to let into the water
And a cabin boy who could decorate cakes in six-colored frosting.
But I didn't know how to cook, and babies depressed me.
Nights, I wrote in my diary spitefully, my fingers red
With triangular scorch marks from ironing tiny ruchings and puffed
   sleeves.

Plath ended the poem with a memory of herself and Marcia rowing out to Children's Island and reading *Generation of Vipers* aloud.

Written by Philip Wylie and published in 1942, the book may seem strange reading material for a pair of college students on their day off. It is best remembered for its vitriolic attack on overbearing mothers, who, Wylie claimed, were producing a generation of emasculated men. Marcia said "that kind of pithy, caustic, tough talk was very appealing to us."[32] He coined a term for this phenomenon—"Momism." Wylie was not the only one manufacturing this crisis. Harvard professor Anne Harrington notes in her history of psychiatry that "bad mothers" were called a "threat" to America's very "survival" by some of the most prominent psychiatrists of the day; articles with titles like "Are American Moms a Menace?" appeared in *Ladies' Home Journal* and *The New York Times* throughout the 1940s and '50s. Such fears played into Cold War insecurities about American masculinity.[33]

Wylie's radical criticisms of America's sacred cows—especially mothers—resonated with Sylvia, who would come to view Dick as a victim of Mildred Norton's "Momism." This junk philosophy also gave her a useful tool to rationalize her own complicated feelings toward Aurelia. Sylvia was so close to her mother that she sometimes did not know where Aurelia began and she ended. She had no father to provide another perspective or offer a respite from her mother's anxious hovering. Like most adolescents, she needed to differentiate herself from her parents. In her journal that summer, Plath wrote, "And you were frightened when you heard yourself stop talking and felt the echo of her voice, as if she had spoken in you, as if you weren't quite you, but were growing and continuing in her wake, and as if her expressions were growing and emanating from your face."[34] Wylie's book, and perhaps other articles Plath was reading in newspapers and women's magazines, justified her need for space. Indeed, her letters from this time suggest that she was beginning to view Aurelia's solicitousness in a more sinister way. Had her mother's need to protect her from unhappiness and tedium stunted her growth, made her soft? Had her mother pushed her into a relationship with Dick to keep her close to home? If only her mother had not taken over all the household tasks, she would be a more "capable" person—and so on. Sylvia told Marcia that she "hated" Aurelia, and in 1958, Plath would feel immense relief on hearing eight simple words from her psychiatrist, Dr. Beuscher: "I give you permission to hate your mother."[35] Wylie's book provided an earlier form of such "permission."

Anxious to see Marcia and curious about Sylvia, Mel Woody hitchhiked from New Jersey to Swampscott that summer. After Marcia showed him around the Blodgetts' mansion, he joined her and Sylvia at a nearby beach in Nahant. He was traveling light and had almost nothing with him except Rilke's *Sonnets to Orpheus*. On the beach, he read Plath Rilke's third sonnet, from Book 1 ("Where and when do we exist?").[36] In retrospect he realized this melancholy poem had been a poor choice. Mel, who had just met Sylvia, remembered that she was downcast that day.

"Sylvia was feeling very sad because she couldn't write, and I had no inkling of what clinical depression is, and I read her this poem. So my line was—and this really played a major role in my relations with Sylvia for many years—'So just stop. Give up writing.' I always had this antagonistic relation with Sylvia's poetry. I thought it was her enemy. Of course this was exactly the wrong thing to say." When Sylvia started swimming far out, Mel became afraid that she might drown. He started swimming after her, then yelled that he couldn't make it out any farther. She turned back, thus saving her own life and, he felt, his own, for he might have drowned himself trying to save her.[37]

Sylvia worried about her separation from Dick, who she imagined was working alongside pretty, seductive waitresses on Cape Cod. She had a nightmare that June that suggests some of her insecurities and unconscious conflicts:

> Seems I broke a date (trivia, trivia) with him to go out with a rakish fly-by-night male. On returning from a vile time, I was greeted by mother and Dick (who had taken Jane Anderson to the Prom.) It all ended by my holding my children (Freddy and Pinny) in my arms, and seeing Dick recede step by step, never coming back, just shaking his head sadly and saying reproachfully as he faded off, "Oh, Syl."

An amateur Freudian could pick out the relevant details: Sylvia's desire for another man besides Dick; her guilt at choosing the more dashing but dangerous date; and the silent reproach from Dick and her mother, who stand together. "My, but there is a moral to that nightmare, huh!" she wrote to Marcia.[38] Sylvia vowed to stop flirting with Ivy League lifeguards at Swampscott beach parties. She did not want to contemplate the dream's real "moral": that perhaps she did not love Dick.

He came to see her in late August. They biked to Marblehead, but it rained, and she felt physically distressed by her pent-up desire after he left. She needed some "vicious activity" to quiet her nerves and decided to go swimming. It was night, but she did not care. The water was warm from the rain. "I splashed and kicked, and the foam was strangely white in the dark." As she ran inside, still wet from the sea, the Mayos commented on the strangeness of her decision. She relished their disapproval with a new ambivalence: "What the heck do I care."[39] She counted down the last twelve days of her stay, and wrote bitter verse: "The acid gossip of the caustic wind, / The wry pucker of the lemon-colored moon . . ."[40]

Although Sylvia claimed that she had "led a vegetable existence" that summer, she was proud of herself for developing "a sense of capability and self-integrality never before felt."[41] At the summer's start, she had not known how to scramble eggs; by the end, she was making her own lamb chops, date-nut bars, and applesauce. The children now obeyed and adored her. "Something maternal awakened, perhaps, by the physical contact with such lovely young babies?"[42] she wrote in her journal.

However, the experience with the Mayos led her to again question the idea of marriage. She saw the way Mrs. Mayo waited on Mr. Mayo, and realized that even wealthy women were still responsible for managing the care of home and children. In her journal Plath acknowledged that many of her insecurities about her own future "come again to the fact that it is a man's world." She wondered why women should "be relegated to the position of custodian of emotions, watcher of the infants, feeder of soul, body and pride of man? Being born a woman is my awful tragedy." She longed to "mingle with road crews, sailors and soldiers, bar room regulars. . . . I want to be able to sleep in an open field, to travel west, to walk freely at night."[43] She sensed this was a part of her—this longing for male privilege—that Dick would not accept; she worried she might have to spend her life "cooking scrambled eggs for a man . . . hearing about life at second hand, feeding my body and letting my powers of perception and subsequent articulation grow fat and lethargic with disuse."[44] Over and over, she confided her fears of wifely subservience to her journal and guessed that Dick would expect a Mrs. Mayo, with her shantung silks and moneyed laugh. Eddie Cohen agreed:

We "radicals" believe that a wife should share her husband's life and experiences, but for most of the world a woman has a definite social role in
marriage which will not permit the existence which I am inclined to feel
you want before you start on the home and kiddies and dinner-every-
night stuff. . . . the nice clean boys of your acquaintance (you know, the
ones who want the mother of their kids to be a virgin, etc.) would probably faint dead away at the thought of their wife living in the jungles of
Mexico or on the left bank in Paris.

A man who was conventionally moral would lead a life of "conventional
morality," Eddie warned, and expect his wife to do the same. He doubted that
Sylvia could have a career and a family "within the framework of the social
structure in which you now live."[45] She began to doubt it, too.

After she left Swampscott, she visited Dick on the Cape. She had "mis-
givings" before the trip, probably because she was going with Aurelia and
Mr. and Mrs. Norton—hardly relaxing company. On the drive down, Mr.
Norton lectured her about Pilgrim history and made a detour to Plymouth
Rock, where he wanted her to bow her head "at the shrine." Skeptical about
American mythmaking, she saw only "commercialized patriotism" and con-
gratulated herself for not bursting out in laughter.[46]

The Nortons had rented a cottage in Brewster, where Sylvia spent days
at the beach with the three adults, Dick, and Perry. Dick was standoffish.
"Something was definitely tense," she wrote Marcia. It was Perry, surprisingly tanned and handsome, who drew her attention. One afternoon she
ran down the beach with him, out of the others' earshot. While "caressing"
her, he made the kinds of "honest and healing remarks" that she had been
"starving for all summer." She began to wonder if she had chosen the wrong
brother—perhaps she could fall in love with Perry after all. That night the
two of them took a long walk together "under the queer light of the stars."
They kissed "a few times," but both "felt instant mental doubts." They talked
about Dick, as well as Perry's girlfriend, and swore that they would be "lifelong comrades and confidants." Sylvia realized it was an "odd relationship"
but felt no guilt.[47] She had always been closer to Perry than to Dick. Their
physical intimacy allowed Sylvia to escape some of the tension she felt with
Dick, though it underscores the claustrophobic dynamic between the two
families.

Dick, perhaps sensing Sylvia's renewed interest in Perry, remained aloof.
For three days they barely spoke. Finally she found him alone on the beach.
He made small talk while she fumed. "I would like to level your skull with
this book; maybe you'd then say something," she declared. Dick apologized,
and the two agreed to have a "truth talk" later that night. After dinner they

headed to an open field, where they sat back to back under "a million stars, all falling or shooting." Dick had misinterpreted the tone of her last letter and assumed she was no longer interested in him. Sylvia immediately understood the reason for his "miffed attitude," and a "Great scene of reconciliation" ensued. He called her "Darling" again, and told her he wanted to marry her.[48] It was not an official proposal, she wrote Ann, "just a 'let's wait and keep our fingers crossed deal.' "[49]

Sylvia downplayed Dick's proposal in letters to friends that summer, but she was panicked.

> Am I excited, blubbering, unable to eat? Hell, no. . . . I wonder very calmly and calculatingly—Do I love him? I know him and his family too well to experience the young romantic exhilaration that I did when I first dated him last spring. But I am afraid that if I eventually did settle down to be a Doctor's wife, I would be sinking deeper into the track I was born in, leaving the world untried, as it were. . . . I'm just not the type who wants a home and children of her own more than anything else in the world. I'm too selfish, maybe, to subordinate myself to one man's career.

Yet she worried, too, about the penalty for not marrying while she was young and attractive. She thought she would "kick herself" for not settling down when it was no longer an option.[50] One of her friends, Betsy Whittemore, was already engaged and would marry in June. "I was just amazed," Sylvia wrote home. "She's my age!"[51]

The pressure to marry would only increase in the coming years. Dick, she told Ann, was "a rather absorbing problem" that had consequences for the rest of her life.[52] To Marcia she voiced similar concerns. "I'm not sure yet that he is the temperamental mate for me. I wonder if I don't need someone a little less managing and positive."[53] Sylvia was also bothered by what she called, in a letter to Eddie, Dick's "physical reticence."[54] She did not understand why he was so timid; she longed for that bruising kiss. Her mind was awhirl on the way back to Wellesley as she sat in the front seat next to Mr. Norton. While Aurelia and Mrs. Norton talked in the back, he confided to Sylvia that he would "love dearly" to have her as a daughter-in-law. He was trying to reassure her in more ways than one: the Nortons were wealthier than the Plaths, and Dick would be marrying down.[55] His remark made Sylvia "feel a little like crying." She knew, as she told Marcia, that "if it works out, a lot of people will be happy."[56] But would she?

———

"ROOMS," PLATH WROTE in her journal. "Every room a world."[57] At the start of their 1951–52 sophomore year at Smith, Sylvia and Marcia decorated their homey second-floor room with dark green bedspreads, white lampshades, bookcases, plants, and a large Georgia O'Keeffe print. They hoped the print would tie the room together, with its cool shades of green, blue, and white. Sylvia was more secure at Haven House now, and her confidence showed in her breezy, enthusiastic letters. As always, she began the year with fierce ambition. She was taking five yearlong courses: 19th- and 20th-Century Literature with Professors Randall and Drew; Introduction to Politics; Visual Expression; Introduction to Religion; Practical Writing, with Evelyn Page; and Physical Education (dance and sports). She hoped to join the Press Board and write her first story on the local mental hospital. As for money, she had a respectable $130 in the bank and planned to sell stockings on commission—a ridiculous job, she admitted, but one that might help her earn "a few dollars." The best thing about sophomore year was "NO SATURDAY CLASSES."[58] Now she could spend more time writing and trying to publish in magazines. She had close friends in Pat, Louise, Enid, and, most of all, Marcia. Before classes began, Sylvia and Marcia "took a long walk across that beautiful countryside in the autumn afternoon, lay in the grass in the sun, listening to the cows mooing, and staring in a blissful collegiate stupor at the Holyoke range of hills."[59]

Dick wrote dutifully from Harvard Medical School. His letters were full of anatomical drawings, details of cadaver and X-ray clinics, and lectures given by professors who embodied the "intense, gray suited, Man of Medicine."[60] He assumed that Sylvia was interested in his diagrams of the pectoralis minor and the serratus anterior, and invited her to a Saturday pathology lecture. He wanted her to know his world, to be as excited by medicine as he was. In theory, Plath wanted to learn more about science, a lifeline to her dead father. Yet Dick's letters may have sent another "chilly whisper" up her spine. Over time, she would grow to distrust the paternalism of male physicians—a major theme in *The Bell Jar*.

Dick reassured Sylvia that he declined to participate in high-jinks with nursing students, but she felt no such compunction to ignore male attention. His talk of marriage on the Cape had unnerved her, and she was determined to meet other men before she made up her mind. She had a feeling there was a more reckless, artistic soul waiting for her. Over the next few months, she gushed to her mother about other men the way she had once gushed about Dick.

The turning point, for Sylvia, was Maureen Buckley's coming-out party. All the women at Haven House had been invited, along with well-connected men from Amherst, Yale, and Princeton. The Buckleys were a wealthy Irish Catholic family with ten children and a mystique not unlike the Kennedys, to whom they were often compared—though they were Republicans. Like Joe Kennedy, Frank Buckley, a Texas oil baron, had serious political aspirations for his children. William Buckley Jr., Maureen's older brother, had just published *God and Man at Yale* that year; he would have a profound impact on the American conservative movement as the founder of the *National Review*. His brother James would become a U.S. senator for New York. Sylvia called the family "terribly versatile & intellectual."[61]

She described the party in lavish detail to Aurelia in a fourteen-page letter—among the longest she ever wrote to her mother. She was entranced by the spectacle when she arrived under the "white colonial columns" of Great Elm, which she thought put the Mayo mansion to shame. She had attended proms at Andover and Yale, but nothing had prepared her for this level of wealth, not even her cruise on the *Mistral*. "Girls in beautiful gowns clustered by the stair. Everywhere there were swishes of taffeta, satin, silk. I looked at Marcia, lovely in a lilac moiré, and we winked at each other." They strode out onto the lawn, where waiters served champagne underneath a grand white marquee. On nights like these, Plath could assume she was on an upward trajectory, rising always higher, away from the cramped, shared rooms of her youth. To Aurelia she wrote, "Balloons, japanese [*sic*] lanterns, tables covered with white linen, leaves, covered ceiling and walls. . . . I stood open mouthed, giddy, bubbling, wanting so much to show you. I am sure you would have been supremely happy if you had seen me. I know I looked beautiful. Even daughters of millionaires complimented my dress."

That night, she danced with the sons of privilege. Plato Skouras, whose father ran 20th Century Fox, brought her inside and compared her to a Botticelli Madonna. But the one who caught her heart was "a lovely grinning darkhaired boy" named Constantine Sidamon-Eristoff, an actual Georgian prince whose aristocratic family had settled in New York City in the nineteenth century. They danced under the marquee, then left the party and waltzed together on the lawn. Sylvia was overjoyed to find someone with whom she could "say what I meant, use big words, say intelligent things." Constantine kissed her hand like the prince he was, and admired the smooth skin on her shoulders. He drove her back to Stone House, where she was staying, while they talked of his Georgian heritage, "love, childbirth, atomic energy, . . . and so much more." Sylvia recited poetry for him as the church bells struck four. "Imagine! I told him teasingly not to suffocate in my long hair and he said, 'What a divine way to die!'" Constantine even addressed her as "Milady" as he escorted her from her car. "'Milord,' I replied, fancying myself a woman from a period novel, entering my castle." She fell into bed next to Marcia and dreamed "exquisite dreams all night, waking now and then to hear the wind wuthering outside the stone walls."

Sylvia's reference to *Wuthering Heights*, as well as other period fiction, suggests how her reading had influenced her sense of self. Such novels were often the sites of social transformation, where the penniless orphan becomes the rich mistress. They provided a framework, however dubious, for her fantasy: a scholarship girl *could* become a Russian princess. The next day, she noted, waiters brought brunch into the Buckley dining room in "great copper tureens." As they uncovered the steaming dishes, her eyes alighted on a feast of eggs, bacon, sausage, rolls, and fancy preserves. "Lord, what luxury!" she exclaimed. She may have already fancied herself Cathy Earnshaw, soon to trade Wuthering Heights for Thrushcross Grange.

The fantasy ended when she arrived back at Smith and exited the Buckleys' chauffeured Cadillac. The anticlimax was crushing. "Back here. I can't face the dead reality. I still lift and twirl with Eric, Plato, and my wholly lovely Constantine under Japanese lanterns." She wondered if she would ever see Constantine again, and feared "he was a dream." She sent Aurelia a love poem about "a bronze boy" statue she now identified with him.[62] She hoped to hear from him but assumed he would simply "melt away with the champagne."[63]

The Buckley party forced Sylvia to face her ambivalent feelings about Dick, yet she could not bring herself to end things with him—not yet. He came to Smith five days after her magical night at Great Elm. Together they went canoeing on Paradise Pond, dined at the Yankee Pedlar, then ended the night with pizza and beer at Joe's. "You were your own incomparable self, sweet and generous, understanding and thoughtful," he wrote her back at Harvard, but she began to lay out her reasons for breaking up with him.[64] To Eddie, she wrote that she could never live up to Dick's standards and did not want to spend her life emulating perfection. Eddie, with his usual perceptiveness, felt that it was easier for her to blame Dick than to acknowledge that Dick did not "measure up" to *her* standards.[65] She was becoming increasingly open with Eddie, too, about her frustration over the relationship's lack of physical progress. He felt that the situation was somewhat absurd and knew Dick was not right for her. He urged her to find someone who would fulfill her "physically and emotionally . . . not financially."[66]

Sylvia fell ill that October with a sinus infection and canceled an upcoming weekend with Dick. She was in the infirmary for a week, protected from academic and romantic responsibility as she sank into the soporific half sleep of convalescence. Though she was only a month into the semester, she already needed a break—her courses were "twice as hard as those last year," she wrote to Aurelia. She was reading the Romantic poets in her English class but felt she "had no real grasp of the subject."[67] (She again asked her mother to help her study.) Yet she was able to write creatively for English, which lightened her burden. Already she had sent a short story written for class off to *Seventeen*. She even received a fan letter for "Den of Lions" from a young woman in Hong Kong.

When she opened a letter from Constantine inviting her to visit him at Princeton in November, she let out a "loud scream" and fell to the floor. He had not forgotten her. She had so much work to catch up on, and the trip would be long and expensive, but she could justify it: "I have spent no money on social life. A prospect like Constantine is a potential. A trip like that is an experience, an emancipation, a new world." She told Aurelia that Constantine was the only boy she had met "A. D." (After Dick) with whom she could imagine spending her "future life." She signed off "your elated sivvy."[68] But Sylvia ended up canceling the trip on account of her heavy workload. "Everybody has read Constantine's letter and is urging me to go—maybe I'll marry into Russian society, etc. But wisdom has won the day."[69]

Having given up on her dreams of Constantine, Sylvia spent a late-October weekend with Dick at Harvard Medical School. She attended lectures, served as his "assistant at the microscope," and visited patients.[70] Dick felt the call to medicine as a call to service that reverberated into other areas of his life: he was now teaching Sunday school at the Unitarian church in Wellesley, and he wrote to Sylvia about his discussions of peace programs and Quaker philosophy. He planned to spend a weekend with his parents visiting veterans at the VA hospital in Framingham. He may have assumed that Sylvia shared his commitment to serving others. That fall, he wrote to her, "Syl, I am sometimes just so glad that you exist. The existences of those who know you is enriched—beyond the telling."[71] But she was an individualist, and wary of volunteering for causes that infringed on her writing time. When Mrs. Freeman sent her a box of cookies that December with a note that read, "The home is woman's paradise," Sylvia wrote to Aurelia, "No doubt she considers herself a missionary, converting the wayward."[72] Plath would always fight against the collective pressure to sublimate her creative identity.

She continued to write to Dick's parents about the goings-on at Smith, such as William Buckley's recent talk on *God and Man at Yale*. Buckley took swipes at Yale's liberal curriculum, which he felt was too secular. Sylvia enjoyed writing Dick a long "vindictive review" blasting Buckley's argument; she wrote up a piece about the talk for the Press Board.[73] Lately she considered making journalism her career. The Press Board "loved" her "tryout" news articles, and she was soon invited to join their ranks.[74] As a Press Board member, she would write for the *Springfield Daily News*, *The Springfield*

Union, and the *Daily Hampshire Gazette*. She had other reasons to be upbeat: in late October she received unexpected invitations from other young men she had met at the Buckley party, as well as a "beautiful framed pen-and-ink sketch" from Ilo.[75] She had never received so much male attention. Eddie wrote, too, saying he might visit her at Christmas. (This time, she told Aurelia, she would be welcoming.) She celebrated her nineteenth birthday with Dick and Marcia, who each gave her books by T. S. Eliot. Together they read e. e. cummings out loud over bottles of Chianti—"utmost of rapport!" she wrote in her scrapbook.[76] Yet she was beginning to feel overwhelmed. At the end of a letter to Aurelia, she signed off "your hectic Sivvy" and drew a headstone with the epitaph "Life was a hell of a lot of fun while it lasted."[77]

She felt worse in December, despite a successful date with Eric Wilson, a Yale student she had met at the Buckley party, discussing "poetry and art . . . God and moral standards."[78] Eric told her he was falling in love with her, but she considered him a "dead-end." Still, she was fascinated by his experience with a prostitute. Hungry for material, she had asked for as many details as possible—"what sort of a personality the woman had, also a little about the procedure in houses of 'ill fame.' "[79] (Years later, these details appeared in *The Bell Jar*.) To Aurelia, she confided with unusual candor, "For some reason, life seems very depressing at present. . . . am rather worn. Ah me. No sonnets till Xmas vacation."[80] Her sleep troubles plus her period had "led to a great depression"; she was enduring a series of "little hells."[81]

Her ill humor was partly a result of learning that Dick was not a virgin—a shocking piece of news he had revealed over Thanksgiving. Sylvia was infuriated by what she saw as his hypocrisy. For almost a year she had thought he was a virgin, only to learn that he was sexually experienced. Worse, he had teased *her* for being "worldly" about sex; "the shock made me sick," she wrote to Ann Davidow. She knew her anger was absurd, and admitted that she wouldn't "give a damn about any other boys being a virgin, but somehow I wanted him to be."[82]

Sylvia admitted that she was not angry with Dick so much as the double standard. "I am envious of males. I resent their ability to have both sex (morally or immorally) and a career. I hate public opinion for encouraging boys to prove their virility & condemning women for doing so." (Indeed, William Sterling remembered Sylvia's horror over a gang rape, involving members of Wellesley High's football team and a female student, that had been "hushed up.")[83] Sylvia told Ann, "I would gladly go to bed with many of the boys I have dated . . . the only thing is I'm a coward and afraid of having a baby, becoming too emotionally involved, or getting found out." She did not want to become "trapped" in a marriage to Dick, but rather to study abroad and write. Dick was too "logical, practical, planned, and scientific." She, on the other hand, was "terribly emotional, artistically inclined, romantic and impractical." Their families thought they balanced each other perfectly, but she was not so sure. "I find myself irresistibly drawn to artistic guys," she admitted. She had asked Dick how she was supposed to fulfill her "burning emotions & lusts" until she was ready for marriage. He had no good answer, and seemed "puzzled" by the question itself.[84]

Eddie had seen the denouement coming and was amused by Sylvia's revelation. "Someday, my pet, I hope you will evolve to a stage where you will let yourself fall in love rather than very calmly measuring up your men with a slide-rule and philosopher's handbook." She had written about the episode in detail, telling him that she wanted to have sex with the first handsome man that would seduce her. Eddie warned her not to "screw up your life just because you learned that there ain't no Santa Claus."[85] He predicted that the next man she fell for would not be a doctor or a lawyer, but an artist or a teacher. Yet she stubbornly continued to see Dick. She needed to keep her options open; she was not Maureen Buckley, after all.

Then a surprise letter from Constantine arrived, with another open invitation to Princeton. It seemed like a sign. She spent the early part of her Christmas break with Marcia in New Jersey, and met Constantine in New York City. They dined at his Upper East Side apartment with his parents and grandmother. Afterward, he took her to a Russian bar on 14th Street called the Two Guitars, where they danced, drank Moscow mules, and listened to a "gypsy orchestra."[86] In her scrapbook, she wrote that she felt "most wicked and worldly in black velvet suit with winsome Constantine." The evening provided a vivid contrast to her anatomy clinics with Dick. But Constantine never visited her at Smith. Later, he blamed the distractions of school, and then the Army.[87] The men she desired most seemed unattainable.

Sylvia came down with yet another sinus infection after her jaunt to New York, which necessitated cocaine packs and penicillin shots. Marcia's Christmas gift of Ezra Pound's *Pisan Cantos* helped stave off the "misery."[88] Without word from Constantine, she turned again to Dick. Over her Christmas vacation, they danced at the Wellesley cotillion, visited the Isabella Stewart Gardner Museum, and attended an evening of Charles Dickens readings. But Dick's close relationship with Aurelia continued to bother Sylvia. He had taken Aurelia on a "medical expedition" in January, to a "neuro-anatomy clinic" at Brigham and Women's Hospital—a similar "date" to one he had shared with Sylvia.[89] He wrote to Aurelia shortly afterward with ideas for future expeditions together (the Boston Medical Library, perhaps?) in a tone Plath later mocked in *The Bell Jar:* "It was last year at this time when I was plotting the many advantages that would accrue from studying near

Wellesley—and the happy prediction that I could see you from time to time has come true, oh thank heaven."[90]

By the time Sylvia returned to Smith in late January 1952, she was "praying" to make it to spring vacation "without cracking up mentally and physically."[91] Her room was a mess, Marcia was sick, and she felt "grubby" and "dateless as hell."[92] She forced herself to spend an hour playing sports in the gym every day to "un-tense."[93] Smith seemed "a damn, heartless, demanding machine."[94] A rejection from *Seventeen* brought her low, though she felt very "professional" after telephoning a news story to a Springfield paper.[95]

She opened up to Eddie about her increasing bouts of depression and anxiety. She worried that she might be schizophrenic; she most definitely had penis envy and an inferiority complex. Eddie admitted that he may have used Freudian terms "indiscriminately" in some of his past letters to her, but advised her, "Forget this stuff. My own judgment would be that whatever the nature of your difficulty is, it has nothing whatsoever to do with either schizophrenia, inferiority, or the lack of a male sex organ. If you must concern yourself about your personality, do it in terms of concrete facts, and stop agitating yourself about your sub-conscious, about which by definition you can discover nothing." She worried about her looks, her lack of money, and men. Eddie offered that these were hardly reasons "to hate yourself." He reminded her of her beauty, her astonishing intellect, and her literary achievements. He would probably fall in love with her himself if the "physical barrier between us were removed." When she despaired about her writing, he told her to compare Hemingway's *The Sun Also Rises* to *Across the River and into the Trees*. Even Hemingway had his bad days. His most helpful reassurance came on the subject of sex. He admired her for admitting desire for sex and reminded her that this desire was entirely natural—not pathological or shameful. "The fact that you have no satisfactory outlet for this stems from the fact that society is maladjusted to the welfare of the individual, and not because there is anything wrong with you. . . . you can hardly expect, at nineteen, to reject a Bostonian background in mores and arrive immediately at an objective compromise." There were few men in Sylvia's life who held such progressive views. He advised her, again, to end things with Dick; it was clear to him that she was simply using him for security. "I love you, even if you think nobody else does, and I've always got a broad shoulder to cry on, so stop worrying."[96]

Aurelia sensed that a visit might lift her daughter's spirits and came to Smith in January. Sylvia took her to an exhibit at the Smith Museum, where she finally convinced her mother that "modern art is art!"[97] She tried to influence Aurelia's thinking in subtler ways. In early February, Sylvia heard an inspiring sermon at church on love and marriage. She agreed with the pastor's advice to delay marriage until one found the right partner—"2 real people sharing common & important projects in a genuine way," as she told Aurelia. The pastor told his female audience not to settle down just "to prove you too can catch a man," and that waiting until the age of thirty gave one more time to work at a career and enrich oneself.[98] This was unconventional advice, but just what Plath needed to hear—especially as friends began announcing their engagements. Sylvia could not bring herself to tell her mother that she did not want to marry Dick. But she could, perhaps, explain her position philosophically, with a pastor's endorsement.

Sylvia returned to Wellesley for a short break in early February. She and Dick toured a maternity ward at the Boston Lying-in Hospital, where they saw lifeless fetuses in formaldehyde jars and a live birth. "I had the queerest urge to laugh and cry when I saw the little squinted blue face grimacing out of the woman's vagina," she wrote to Ann. Plath would imbue this visit with a sense of horror in *The Bell Jar* and later claim that it made her deeply fearful of childbirth. But to Ann she described her exhilaration at being a part of something so vital and primitive: "my sense of the dramatic was aroused, and I went skipping down the corridors of the maternity ward like a thoroughly irresponsible Florence Nightingale."[99]

Dick visited Sylvia at Smith in mid-February, but this time, she was distant. He wrote her soon afterward, saying that he was "very worried," wondering what the "problem" was "that wouldn't be verbalized."[100] He sent her a poem titled "Recollections," in which he celebrated "Your deeply expressive self / Your brown eye with my kaleidoscopic thoughts reflected there / Our open and honest approach to all things—so heartily a union."[101] Sylvia was not so sure, yet she invited Dick back to Smith in late February. The two spent six hours hiking through snowy fields to the Connecticut River, then decamped to the library to read together. It was a "very nice weekend," she told Aurelia.[102] The phrase captured the essence of her time with Dick. Everything they did together was pleasant and edifying. But he was not the kind of man with whom one could dance to a gypsy orchestra.

Dick became the major dilemma of Sylvia's sophomore year. The forces pushing her toward him were not only societal but familial. How could she squander the chance to be the wife of a Harvard-educated doctor? How could she face her "aunt" Mildred and "uncle" Bill? And how could she disappoint her mother, who saw in Dick the key to her daughter's financial security? As Sylvia put it to Marcia that March, her only options were to "break up our families or settle down"—neither of which appealed to her.[103] She felt trapped and enunciated her fears eloquently in her journal. The same concerns she had been weighing for several months had, with Dick's summer marriage proposal, become urgent. Her sexual attraction to him was strong, but as early as September of her sophomore year, she had organized her points against marriage with a cool-headed, philosophical rationalism. She wrote, "I am disturbed rather terribly by this sure thing. I am obsessed that it is this, or nothing, and that if I don't take this, it will be nothing, but if I do take this, I will be squeezed into a pretty stiff pattern, the rigor of which I do not like." She was determined not to become a small-town-doctor's wife: "God, I hope I'm never going to massacre myself that way."[104]

She may have underestimated Dick. In his letters, he looked forward to the time when they could spend their hours reading plays, poems, and listening to music.[105] He told her of his enthusiasm for Faulkner, Hemingway, Chaucer, Emerson, Melville, and Goethe, and often sent her clippings about art exhibits and literary readings. On a date that March, they "talked & talked & read Hemingway aloud for <u>seven solid hours</u>—without even eating."[106] He wrote her poignant, stream-of-consciousness love letters, "experiments in expression," which she inspired.[107] He danced with her in the streets of Northampton after a Smith formal in April and told her he wanted to read Wallace Stevens aloud with her.[108] "You have made my miserable tiny existence utterly throbbing and joyful," he wrote.[109]

But none of this could erase the spectral future she saw with Dick—a social life lived through civic groups and charitable societies. He would, she knew, want her to play a "town-minded, extroverted" role.[110] It was a terrible prospect for someone who dreaded the word "community."[111] She would not give up her art for a man who—she finally admitted—she did not love. "The fact remains that writing is a way of life for me." She hoped she would meet someone "better," a fellow artist who understood her need to create. "It is only <u>balance</u> that I ask for. Not the <u>continual</u> subordination of one persons [*sic*] desires and interests to the continual advancement of another's! That would be too grossly unfair."[112] When she finally met Ted Hughes four years later, she felt she had conjured him up. The wrongness of Dick confirmed the rightness of Ted, whom Sylvia would marry less than four months after their first meeting.

Sylvia and Dick continued visiting each other throughout the spring. Although she had received another "excitingly dangerous" invitation to the Princeton prom from Constantine, she declined on account of the trip's expense and her heavy workload. She worried that she might get run down and sick again. "It almost killed me to say no, but I figured a 2-day fling wasn't worth a 2-week bedrest!" She was increasingly frank with her mother about her attraction to other men, and wondered if she was "an incurable polygamist."[113]

That spring, Sylvia learned that room and board at Smith was increas-

ing by $150, an unwelcome piece of news that compounded her other wor-
ries. She would need to spend another summer working full-time as a nanny
or waitress. She asked a friend about living and waitressing at the Pines
resort, but the pay was poor and the working conditions dismal. "Of all crazy
things—money is worst," she told Aurelia.[114]

"I love this place so, and there is so much to do creatively, without having
to be a 'club woman,'" Sylvia wrote home in late April. "Fie upon offices!"[115]
Still, she was delighted to learn that she had been nominated for the electoral
board and for house president, and elected secretary of the honor board.
She was also elected to Alpha Phi Kappa Psi, the "Phi Beta Kappa of the
Arts," as well as the sophomore push committee, which was made up of the
most "outstanding" leaders in each class.[116] She even joined the prom committee. Plath had assumed that she was not well liked, and was surprised
by these honors. She had underestimated her popularity at Smith just as
she had in high school. She was now a minor celebrity on campus, known
as a straight-A student and nationally published writer. Her fame had even
spread to Amherst: Guy Wilbor recalled that by her sophomore year she was
"getting a reputation as somebody to be reckoned with" in the collegiate literary world.[117] Her poem "Crossing the Equinox" was included in the 1952
Annual Anthology of College Poetry, a compilation of the country's best undergraduate verse, while her short story "The Perfect Setup" won honorable
mention in the 1952 *Seventeen* short-story contest and appeared in the magazine in October 1952. Her poem "Twelfth Night" also appeared in *Seventeen*
in December 1952. That April two young women from the *Smith Review*
expressed admiration for her recent sonnet "Eva," and asked her to consider
joining the editorial board.[118] Many of her peers were awed by her achievements, yet she still worried that others viewed her as queer and reclusive.

She loved the novels she read in Elizabeth Drew's English class: Hardy's
Far from the Madding Crowd, Conrad's *Lord Jim*, and Lawrence's *Women in
Love*, which she finished in two days. She was also reading Dylan Thomas.
Thomas and Lawrence inspired her creatively: she began writing "Sunday at
the Mintons" on March 25, the same day she began *Women in Love*. The day
after she finished the novel she wrote another story, "My Studio Romance,"
about a student who falls for her art professor—as Sylvia was falling for
hers—on the back pages of her Dylan Thomas essay.[119] She learned that
W. H. Auden was coming to Smith the following year and began devising a
plan to meet him.

Her anti-McCarthy stance hardened that semester. In March, she heard
the Dutch mathematician and communist Dirk Jan Struik speak in the Neilson Library on "Academic Freedom and the Trend to Conformity." She
called him "Really a fascinating Marxist" in a letter home and wrote about

the lecture for the Press Board.[120] She saw Robert Frost and Senator McCarthy on back-to-back evenings in April. She, along with most of the audience, booed McCarthy. In May she heard Ogden Nash and Patrick Murphy Malin, the head of the Civil Rights Commission.[121] She told Aurelia, "As an antithesis to Senator McCarthy's 'guilt by association and hearsay' lecture, he [Malin] was an example of integrity and outstanding promise."[122]

McCarthyism wasn't simply political theater for Plath. In the late spring of 1953, her writing teacher Robert Gorham Davis was investigated by the House Un-American Activities Committee for his communist affiliation in the 1930s. Another English professor, Newton Arvin, would also be investigated. Janet Salter Rosenberg, who took Davis's writing class with Plath in 1952–53, remembered that Davis spoke frankly of the hearings to his students and even admitted that he had been pressured to name names. "He was clearly shaken by the experience." Although Janet thought Smith "80% Republican" at the time, she remembered that there was enormous sympathy for these professors who had flirted with communism as young idealists during the Depression, when capitalism seemed broken. They had all cut ties with the Communist Party once they learned of Stalin's abuses. Indeed, Janet remembered that Maureen Buckley was ostracized on the Smith campus after her sister sent a mass letter to alumnae urging them not to donate to the college because it was full of "Reds." The plan backfired—Smith received huge donations that year.[123] Plath would express her anti-McCarthyism in her short story "Initiation," later that summer.

Spring heralded a creative burst. Sylvia began teaching an introductory art class to children at the People's Institute of Northampton, and writing more poems. In early April she wrote "Go Get the Goodly Squab," with its exhortations to "Reap the round blue pigeon from the roof ridge, / But let the fast-feathered eagle fly." Yeats and Hopkins left their marks on the poem, which is full of alliteration and strong rhythms. *Harper's* accepted it in 1953, and it was the only pre-1953 poem Plath saw fit to include in her 1955 manuscript *Circus in Three Rings.* The "august" Elizabeth Drew gave her an A on an English exam, and Sylvia sent a batch of poems to Eddie that left him "gasping."[124] "A toast, lady, from this humble soul, to what I seriously think may be one of the great creative geniuses of our generation."[125] He was not wrong.

Her short stories that year focused again on the damaged and the disenfranchised. In "Marie," a short character sketch about a French Canadian cook at a women's college, Plath conveyed the working-class immigrant's loneliness and frustration with realistic poignancy. February's "Brief Encounter," with its Hemingway cadences, concerned a lonely, disabled Korean War veteran on his way home. He meets a kind college student on the train who reaffirms his faith in life, love, and family. She is changed, too—made more aware of the complacency that distracts her from the horrors of war. In June's "The New Day," a young art student overcomes her fear of mental illness after spending the day in Rockport with her art teacher's mentally disabled son. Sylvia's writing teacher, Evelyn Page, was impressed both by Plath's work and by her "nearly professional" work ethic. "She was serious about her achievement as a writer, knew that she lacked experience and bent herself to gain it. . . . though she by no means gave up her right to govern her own effects and materials. . . . [she] maintained a sound intellectual and emotional distance in revising her work." Few undergraduate writers, Page noted, possessed this quality.[126]

In each of these stories, Plath challenged herself to write empathetically about outsiders, and they showcased the secular humanism she was exploring in her classes. In a May 1952 paper for her religion class, "Religion as I See It," Plath laid out her "basic tenets": man was "born without purpose in a neutral universe," without inherent morals, and was responsible for his own destiny. There was no afterlife. "His mind may live on, as it were, in books, his flesh may continue in his children. That is all." God was not to blame for man's evils or triumphs. Plath claimed that she could "never find my faith through the avenue of manmade institutions," and called herself an "agnostic humanist." She happily admitted she was a pantheist at heart: "For my security, I resort not to the church, but to the earth. The impersonal world of sun, rocks, sea and sky gives me a strange courage." For her, the vital world was earthly and present: "the universe is non-moral, non-purposive. . . . There is no God to care."[127] She wrote that she had joined the Unitarian Church— which preached a human Jesus and the Bible as literature—on account of its tolerance, inclusion, and emphasis on reason. In her December 1951 paper "Unitarianism: Yesterday and Today," she noted that Unitarians looked to the moment Adam ate the forbidden fruit not as original sin, but as unbounded possibility—"'his greatest virtue—the way to the fullest realization of all his potentialities as a human being.'" She scorned the repetitive incantations of the Catholic Church her mother had been born into and agreed with Nietzsche's "healthy anti-Christian sentiments" in *Thus Spake Zarathustra*.[128]

Plath would not belong to any institution that trafficked in absolutes. When she studied *Paradise Lost* in the spring of 1953, she would find "Eve and Satan most absorbing"—much more so than God and his angels. She saw Eve as bold and brave rather than a narcissistic temptress. "I would have eaten the apple at once!" she declared in her exam, in which she admitted that "Satan is a favorite of mine in P.L." She added, in a "P.S.," "Among my favorite 'quotable' lines in all P.L. are his 'The mind is its own place and in itself / Can make a Heav'n of Hell, a Hell of Heav'n.' "[129]

She felt that her most important creative accomplishment of 1952 was her short story "Sunday at the Mintons," which she wrote over her spring vacation and entered in the *Mademoiselle* college fiction contest. (School breaks gave Plath precious time to write; her ability to send out poetry and fiction at the rate she did, given her heavy academic obligations, is astonishing.) The story explores the unfulfilled lives of a brother and sister, Elizabeth and Henry, living together in retirement. Before moving in with Henry, Elizabeth had lived an independent life as a librarian. The two now inhabit stuffy Victorian quarters where Elizabeth waits on Henry like a wife, longing to escape her newly circumscribed life. Her existence—the kind Plath most feared—is embodied by Henry's question "Have you finished tidying up the study?" Henry, oblivious to Elizabeth's frustration, continues to plod away with his maps and compasses, "charts and calculations"—what passes for his inner life. Elizabeth is a daydreamer while Henry is "Scrupulously exact."[130] When the two take a Sunday stroll by the seaside, Elizabeth fantasizes that Henry has been engulfed by a wave and cast out to sea. Plath constructs the scene so the reader thinks Henry has actually drowned, but at the end she reveals Elizabeth has only been dreaming. She is still trapped in a sexless life of subservience.

Sylvia told her mother that Elizabeth and Henry were based on herself and Dick, and, indeed, the connections are obvious. While she was writing the story, Sylvia jotted down each character's attributes on a piece of paper as she contrasted her emotional and subjective self against Dick's rational, scientific self: Henry was "dogmatic," "indefatigable," and "obstinate," while Elizabeth was "capricious," "volatile," "light."[131] In the story, Elizabeth imagines the inner workings of her mind to be "a dark, warm room, with colored lights swinging and wavering, like so many lanterns reflecting on the water." Henry's mind, by contrast, "would be flat and level, laid out with measured instruments in the broad even sunlight. There would be geometric concrete walks and square, substantial buildings with clocks on them, everywhere perfectly in time, perfectly synchronized. The air would be thick with their accurate ticking."[132] She would again characterize Dick as stiff and logical in her poem "Love Is a Parallax": "So we could rave on, darling, you and I, / until the stars tick out a lullaby / about each cosmic pro and con." In "Sunday at the Mintons," Plath hid in plain sight the truth she dared not admit: the thought of a future with Dick was suffocating.

Yet as Constantine receded, she drew closer to her "sure thing," and invited Dick to spend his weeklong spring break at Smith. He accepted, calling it "the happiest, most productive vacation that ever occurred."[133] They studied together in the library, biked to Mount Tom, and ate cheeseburgers at the local diner. She attended Smith's sophomore prom with him on April 26, and they continued to spend weekends together, luxuriating in the newly warm weather. "Dick & I ran barefoot on lawns, went wading in the liquid waters of Paradise, climbed trees, and generally enjoyed ourselves on our own."[134]

In mid-May the two of them, along with three other couples, drove into the Berkshire hills for a hike and a cookout. As usual, fresh air and vigorous physical activity agreed with Sylvia. "Really, though," she told Aurelia, "I am leading a gloriously country-clubby life."[135] Her relationship with Dick seemed less fraught when they were walking in the sun, drinking beer, and cooking over open fires. In May he wrote her an erotic, Joycean letter celebrating the lure of her body.[136] The new tone probably reflected their increasing sexual intimacy—"everything-but," as she put it to Eddie.[137] No longer did Dick hold back out of cousinly chivalry: "every time I see him it gets harder and harder. . . . we can't tear ourselves apart, the attraction is so strong," she told Ann. During a late-March trip to Harvard Medical School, they had spent the day in bed: "we stayed there in each others [sic] arms as it got darker and darker. . . . Time blurred, melted warmly. We had been there seven hours when we finally realized that I had to go home—plunged rudely out in the cold world again."[138] Sylvia did not know how much longer she would be able to hold back with Dick, though she knew that giving in would make it harder to extricate herself from the relationship. Still, she railed against the "customs and conventions" that kept her from fulfilling her sexual needs. "Life around here is so hypocritical," she told Ann.[139]

On May 28 she finished her final exams, and Aurelia came to collect her; they loaded the car with suitcases and cartons overflowing with books. Sylvia ended the year triumphantly with A's in her two English courses and Introduction to Politics; an A– in religion; a B in art; and a B– in phys ed. Her lower grades did not upset her as long as she excelled in English.

Sylvia spent her first weekend of summer vacation on Cape Cod with the Nortons, then headed back to Wellesley for a last idle week before returning to the Cape to work at the Belmont Inn in West Harwich. She read Virginia Woolf's *Orlando* and Gertrude Stein's *Three Lives* and wrote "The New Day" while sunning in her backyard. At night there was dinner with the Nortons and "bull sessions" with Aurelia and Dick. Eddie visited her in early June— this time, announced. The two walked the paths at Wellesley College and Lake Waban and drove around in his coral convertible discussing life and love. Sylvia made it clear to him that a physical relationship was out of the question.

On June 9, she headed south to the Belmont, a grand nineteenth-century resort that faced the West Harwich beach. After her experience with the Mayos, she had decided against babysitting. At the Belmont, she would live in the women's dormitory, work three daily two-hour shifts, and spend her nights at beach parties. Because she was inexperienced, she was relegated to "Side Hall," where the hotel's managers ate. She would make less money and have the unenviable task of waiting on her employers in a "proletarian" black waitress uniform all day.[140] She worried that amid the "loud, brassy Irish Catholics" and "wise, drinking flirts," her "conservative, quiet, gracious" demeanor would prevent her from getting much male attention.[141]

She quickly forgot her troubles when she received a telegram, forwarded by Aurelia, on her very first day of work. "Sunday at the Mintons" had won the $500 first prize in the *Mademoiselle* college fiction contest. She was ecstatic. "I screamed and actually threw my arms around the head-waitress who no doubt thinks I am rather insane!" She told Aurelia that "psychologically, the moment couldn't have been better," as she was feeling tired and depressed by her demotion to Side Hall.[142] Few things made Plath as happy as publication and prize money. She kept telling herself that *Mademoiselle* had made a mistake, or that Aurelia had made it all up to comfort her. But it was true—in August she would walk into a drugstore, buy a copy of the magazine, and see her name under her story's title. "Really, when I think of how I started it over spring vacation, polished it at school, and sat up till midnight in the Haven House kitchen typing it amidst noise and chatter, I can't get over how the story soared to where it did," she told Aurelia.[143]

Plath saw "Sunday at the Mintons" as an artistic turning point. She was proud that she had transformed Elizabeth from a thinly veiled version of herself into someone else. "I am beginning to use imagination to transform the actual incident. I was scared that would never happen—but I think it's an indication that my perspective is broadening."[144] Despite her sense of pride and fulfillment, she immediately began to doubt herself. She was worried about Dick's reaction. Would he realize that Henry had been based on him, or that the story contained "the germ of reality"?[145] Would Smith lower her scholarship when they realized she had won $500? She hoped the prize would help her win a scholarship to the Bread Loaf English seminar in Vermont the next summer, though it was "really a dream, because boys usually win those things, & my style needs to mature a lot yet." She could not shake the doubt that the prize had gone to "the wrong person by mistake."[146] Sylvia's doubts reflect the sexist mores of the time. Women were not supposed to become writers—men were.

She apologized to Aurelia for haranguing her with such concerns: "God, I'm glad I can talk about it with you—probably you're the only outlet that I'll have that won't get tired of my talking about writing."[147] No matter how tense Sylvia's relationship with Aurelia became, she knew her mother would always listen. Like Sylvia's journal, Aurelia too was an "outlet." She needed her correspondence with Aurelia to reflect her resiliency back to herself, just as she needed her journal to privately pour out her despondencies. Plath felt, at core, that she was a resourceful, capable, and vital person with faith in humanity. She would not have understood her "true" self to be the one that wanted to flee the world, give up, and commit suicide. She was not a "quitter" or a "coward"—she saw through commitments she would rather have abandoned, like the Mayo job. The ambitious, determined, optimistic self of her letters to Aurelia was not necessarily a construct, not solely a mask. Plath struggled always toward the light rather than the darkness.

Sylvia held court on the beach during her first few days at the Belmont, before most of the other waitresses arrived. One afternoon, Perry showed up unexpectedly (he was working at the nearby Latham Inn with Dick) and was "shocked at the 'competition'"—Sylvia was surrounded by five bronzed young men.[148] But she was soon brought low by the daily drudgery of waiting tables. She made an effort to get to know the new waitresses—in her calendar she recorded a long "gab session" with them on June 11—yet she still felt out of place. They all seemed so pretty and extroverted. If not for her fiction prize, she "would be pretty low."[149] Within a few days, she was "vacillating in great confusion."[150] The conditions were ripe for another depression: she had not been sleeping well; she was homesick and living with strangers; she was fatigued from hours on her feet; she had no dates; she was a terrible waitress. "I am exhausted, scared, incompetent, unenergetic and generally low in spirits," she told her mother.[151]

Aurelia came to visit, and found Sylvia in a "dangerous state of feeling sorry for myself," "tired, tense and on the verge of tears." Sylvia begged Aurelia to visit her again on her next day off ("Please, please"). The other waitresses seemed like old hands, but she could barely manage to time her food courses properly. She began to think about quitting as she had just won $500. Wouldn't her time be better spent resting and writing more stories for publication? But she would not "be a coward and escape by crawling back home."[152] She needed, as always, to prove to herself that she was "capable."

A week later, she was "a little more optimistic."[153] She saw Dick in the evenings but made an effort to date other men, including a Columbia medical student named Ray Wunderlich. She began to think of herself as a writer rather than a waitress, just as she had done at the Mayos when she reached a crisis point. "The characters around here are unbelievable, and I already have ideas churning around in my head."[154] She was devising a story called "Side Hall Girl" with an ending that would be "very positive and constructive." "Ambitious?" she asked Aurelia. "You bet."[155] She thought that she would "stick it out" until August 10.[156]

After a few late nights on the beach with Ray, Sylvia developed another sinus infection. The illness could not have come at a better time, as she had been thinking about leaving the Belmont almost as soon as she had arrived. She decided to have "one real fling" before she left, with Phil Brawner, a Wellesley Princetonian who was on the Cape for the weekend.[157] She "got all swish" in an aqua cotton dress and enjoyed a "delectable evening" at the Mill Hill Club, where they danced and drank all night. She promised to play tennis with Phil the next day, but when he came to collect her, she had a fever. She asked for a ride back to Wellesley. Phil thought the whole episode hilarious, while Sylvia was pleased with her appearance—"I looked very flushed and healthy, having both a tan and a temperature of over 100."[158]

Back home in Wellesley, Sylvia stayed in bed for a week, taking penicillin. When the Belmont called to ask whether they should hire someone else, Aurelia told them yes. Amid the get-well cards that soon arrived from friends was a letter from Knopf's editor in chief, Harold Strauss. *Mademoiselle*'s managing editor, Cyrilly Abels—for whom Sylvia would work in the summer of 1953—had been so impressed by "Sunday at the Mintons" that she forwarded the story to Strauss. Sylvia was thrilled by his words: "This struck me as an extraordinarily deft and mature story, far better than the average prize-winning short story." While he advised her not to rush into anything, he hoped Knopf would someday publish a novel by her and asked her to write him directly. "Shall I put it that I should like to watch a very gifted nature take its course?"[159] Apart from her Smith acceptance letter, this was probably the single most important piece of correspondence Plath had ever received; she promised Strauss that she would keep him informed about her writing. To round off her good fortune, Phil Brawner, who was working for Boston's Shawmut Bank as an intern, reappeared asking for dates. Together they went to double bills at the Kenmore Theater and drank Scotch and soda at the swank Copley Plaza Hotel bar. Sylvia told Marcia he was a member of the "Wellesley aristocracy."[160]

During her second week in Wellesley, however, Sylvia's heart began to sink. Her $500 from *Mademoiselle* meant she did not have to work, but the freedom that had seemed so tantalizing while she was "slinging hash" at the Belmont now terrified her.[161] She had never before faced weeks of unbroken time, and she was overwhelmed by the "awful responsibility of managing (profitably) 12 hours a day for 10 weeks."[162] In her journal and in letters, she hit on her famous metaphor. "It is like lifting a bell jar off a securely clockwork-like functioning community, and seeing all the little busy people stop, gasp, blow up and float in the inrush, (or rather outrush,) of the rarified scheduled atmosphere—poor little frightened people, flailing impotent arms in the aimless air. That's what it feels like: getting shed of a routine."[163]

Fearing that she was on the verge of another serious depression, she began scouring local classified ads for work. She wanted to go back to the Cape—she began to miss Dick terribly—but would consider all options: "Anything to give me that intangible self-respect."[164] As much as she loathed the idea of another six weeks of manual labor, she needed to get out of Wellesley, the "suburban rut."[165] Humid, still, and all but empty in summer, it was where she went to convalesce, not to grow. And she needed space from Aurelia, as she told Marcia. "I love her dearly, but she reverberates so much more intensely than I to every depression I go through. I really feel she is better without the strain of me and my intense moods—which I can bounce in and out of with ease."[166] Away from Aurelia, she could escape her guilt. She understood intuitively that working was tantamount to self-preservation. As much as deadlines unnerved her, she foundered even more when they disappeared. She longed, she told Marcia, to be "gaily drunkenly academic again."[167]

On July 12, Sylvia drove to the Cape with Mr. Norton for a few days with the family at their Brewster cabin. She had not seen Dick in three weeks. That Saturday night, she and Dick rowed out to the middle of a lake, where they "anchored, swam, watched mammoth shooting stars & a slice of red moon rising over black hills." The next night they visited a "negro cook" named Otha who worked with Dick at Latham's. It was the first time Sylvia had socialized with an African American, and she was eager to portray herself to Marcia as tolerant and progressive: "Dick & I felt right at home, drinking beer, eating sandwiches, kibitzing on canasta & merrily exchanging yarns. In twos & threes the other Negroes started leaving about midnight. But Dick & I stayed on till after 1, listening to Otha recount his experiences in New York. . . . I was entranced & went away loving them both as wonderful & sensitive people. It was a new experience for me, being in the 'minority' group temporarily."[168] As patronizing as Plath's account sounds to modern ears, she regarded her breach of the color line as daring, and enlightening.

Sylvia slept inside the same cabin with Dick and Perry—a situation that muddled her thinking about the true object of her affection. Like her, Perry was a virgin. He embodied "security" in a way that Dick, with his "competitive drives," did not. While she stayed in bed reading and napping alongside Perry, she wondered if she would end up with him after all. One afternoon she turned, half awake, to examine his sleeping body as if for the first time:

"his skin a bronze tan, and the red of his hair like strands of copper. Suddenly tender, I thought . . . : 'This is the one! After all the while and excitement and gay passionate flames, this is the one I will choose to come home to! The proverbial boy next door!'"[169] But that summer, she was still—mostly—Dick's.

After considering a job with an "admirably unscrupulous" real estate agent in Wellesley, Sylvia saw an ad in *The Christian Science Monitor* for a mother's helper in Chatham, on the "elbow" of Cape Cod.[170] Although she had vowed never to spend another summer babysitting, she was desperate to return to the Cape, with its golden promise of beaches and boys. Sylvia met with Mrs. Cantor in Chatham for an interview on July 13 and got the job on the spot. She returned home for four days, during which time she wrote the first and second draft of her anti-McCarthy story "Initiation." She sent it, along with seven poems, to *The Christian Science Monitor*. Not yet a college graduate, Plath had already assumed the habits of a professional writer.

She returned to the Cape on July 19 and began work for the Cantors, who were devout Christian Scientists. She kept house and helped care for three children: Billy, 3; Susan, 5; and Joan, 13. Her duties were more demanding than they had been at the Mayos: each day found her doing laundry, dishes, washing and waxing floors, polishing silver, food shopping, picnic packing, cooking light meals—all while supervising three children. But the Cantors were "much more friendly than the Mayos," Sylvia told Marcia, and treated her warmly.[171] She ate with the adults instead of the children, while Mrs. Cantor handled most of the cooking. Joanie helped her clean up after meals, and the two often listened to records and danced around the kitchen as they washed up. Sylvia came to enjoy packing the enormous picnic lunches she shared with the Cantors during long, sunny afternoons at Nauset Beach and Oyster Pond. She liked Mrs. Cantor, though she was bothered by her Puritan streak. Mrs. Cantor was shocked by the number of boys Sylvia met that summer and, one night, even told a date that he was holding Sylvia too close as they danced. "I felt very trapped and like shouting 'What the hell do you think I am? Red Riding Hood?' . . . Never did I appreciate mother's free rein more."[172] Still, Mrs. Cantor often invited Sylvia to socialize with their dinner guests after the children went to bed, and the two talked "companionably" after the dishes were done.[173] Mr. Cantor even paid her extra on nights they threw dinner parties. "This family is <u>so</u> different from the Mayos—so appreciative. It makes work like play," she told Aurelia.[174] Mrs. Cantor was impressed by Sylvia's ability to do what needed to be done with minimal direction. Sylvia never complained and seemed healthy and happy, though she did tell Mrs. Cantor that she took the job because she wanted to put some distance between herself and Aurelia. "Sylvia felt somewhat trapped because of her [Aurelia's] sacrifice."[175]

The Cantors lived in a large, gray-shingled house near the Chatham Bars Inn, a grand hotel with private beaches and tennis courts. Sylvia was able to use all of their facilities, a perk that made her feel like she was on vacation herself. Her room was delightfully cool, Mrs. Cantor's lobster and steak dinners were "continuously grand," and she had plenty of free time to relax at Nauset Beach.[176] She especially loved driving the children around for excursions to Orleans, Brewster, and the weekly Chatham band concert in the Cantors' "powerglide" beach wagon. She felt glamorous behind the wheel. She attended Christian Science church services and Sunday school with the family as an anthropological exercise, and began dating an eighteen-year-old Christian Scientist, Bob Cochran, who drove an MG, took her sailing, and tried to proselytize her. "It would be really fun to try to proselytize him subtly <u>out</u> of Xian Science!" she told Aurelia.[177]

Christian Science seemed to Plath an absurd religion, though she hid her skepticism around the Cantors. To Aurelia, she released her gleeful, acerbic wit—her "other" voice: "During the service I could hardly help bursting out in chortling laughter as I thought how my meek and sweetly pious face covered a wicked wicked belief in matter and how satan himself was curled up in my left ventricle chuckling at them."[178] Aurelia admonished her for being "smug"; her daughter's flair for caustic mockery worried her. Sylvia apologized. "I was really only fooling! . . . what I want is to <u>learn</u>."[179] But she could not bring herself to debunk "matter" as Christian Scientists did; she would always revel in the material world. At the same time, she was intrigued by the premise that one's attitude affected one's health, especially mental health. She had often felt that her bouts of depression were her own fault, and that a change in attitude would restore her. Mental health was much on her mind that summer; in late August she read *The Story of My Psychoanalysis: The True and Intimate Revelations of a Man Who Uncovered the Secrets of His Unknown Self*, by John Knight. She may have wondered whether she would benefit from the practice herself.

She and Dick fell into their old routine of weekly visits, though the twenty-five-mile round-trip bicycle ride to his Brewster cabin was tiring. They saw plays and ballets at the Cape Playhouse in Dennis, and spent languorous afternoons at the beach. His stories of beach parties with Latham Inn waitresses rattled her, but she too had several young men vying for her attention—not just Bob Cochran, but also Attila Kassay, a Hungarian refugee and Northeastern junior; Chuck Dudley, a Boston University freshman; and Art Kramer, a twenty-five-year-old Jewish Yale law student who worked as a security guard for a wealthy dowager in Harwich. (Art's brother, Larry Kramer, would become a celebrated playwright.) Sylvia sought out men who were as unlike Dick as possible and approached her problem with light humor in her journal: "Will I ever fling myself into the multitudinous perils and uncertainties of life with a passionate Constantine; a witty and sardonic and tempestuous Attila; a proud, wealthy aristocratic Philip?"[180]

Although Sylvia described Art as short, "very dark, swarthy and Simian," she found his unabashed intellectualism "<u>most</u> attractive."[181] He had a master's degree in English from Yale, and the two spoke of Joyce, Hemingway, Shelley, and Mann. He marked out articles for her to read in *The New Yorker* and *The Atlantic*, lent her speeches by Adlai Stevenson, and took her out to lobster dinners. She found it "exhilarating to use big words again."[182] They talked about writing, and he advised her on "textures and adverbs and restraint and so on."[183] Normally Sylvia fell for tall, blond "gods," but she was moved by his stories of childhood anti-Semitism in Connecticut, where he had been the only Jewish boy in his school and had regularly come home with bloody noses until he learned how to fight back.

The Cantors preferred Dick, but Sylvia did not care. She had written about anti-Semitism in her September 1951 short story, "The Perfect Setup," based on her time with the Mayos. In the story, the nanny's employer forbids her children to mix with Jews on the beach. The protagonist does not have the courage to challenge the summer colony's ingrained prejudices, and she obeys her employer's orders. Even as Sylvia described Art in unconsciously anti-Semitic language in her letters, she dared others to criticize her for dating a Jewish man. "I find him quite wise and brilliant and understanding and gentle and don't give a darn about his being short and ugly," she told her mother.[184] Art and Eddie, the other Jewish man in her life, seemed to be the only men who took her intelligence seriously, who spoke to her about politics and literature without condescension. So many college boys wanted a Smith girl as a status symbol. But Art and Eddie assumed that the women they dated ought to spar with them about Eisenhower and Machiavelli.[185]

Art was not the only "outsider" Sylvia met that summer. In early August she visited the Bookmobile, a roving bookshop that stopped in Chatham once a week, where she met Val Gendron, a prolific writer of pulp fiction. Sylvia was "at her feet with questions pouring out."[186] Val gave her advice and told her she would introduce her to her agent in New York if Sylvia could show her some published work. The next week Sylvia went back to the Bookmobile to "pay homage," and Val invited her to "a bull session at her shack" in South Dennis.[187] Here was another female writer, like Mrs. Prouty, whom Plath could "Hero worship."[188] But Prouty's formal manners and Brookline mansion had intimidated Sylvia. She had more fun at Val's "rickety" red barn, which she called "a dream of an artist's Bohemia." No maid opened the door, as at Mrs. Prouty's home—just Val, dressed in "an old plaid lumbershirt and paint-stained dungarees," doing her laundry at the kitchen sink.[189]

Val showed Sylvia around the yard, where she grew her own food and dried her own herbs. After coffee, grapes, and cake, she led Sylvia upstairs to her writer's studio, a cozy space littered with "stacks of manuscripts."[190] The two sat cross-legged on the floor and drank strong coffee while kittens played around them. Val let Sylvia read some of her new work and regaled her with stories from her New York days and her friendships with Rachel Carson and Ernest Hemingway's sister. Plath copied the names and addresses of "about 50" poetry and fiction magazines from Gendron's writer's handbook, which gave her a great jolt of energy. "Boy, I'll get those sonnets printed yet!"[191] A blunt practicality tempered Val's eccentricity. When Plath gave her a copy of "Sunday at the Mintons," apologizing for its "many faults," Val scoffed: "Heck, if anyone takes it apart just ask them if they could produce a prize-winner—you've got your approval. Don't apologize for it."[192] Gendron emboldened Plath to trust her aesthetic instincts. They talked until midnight, when Val drove her home in her "old jalopy—us yelling to each other all the way over the noise of the engine."[193] In her journal Plath called Gendron "my First Author."[194]

Olive Prouty and Val Gendron embodied the two forces—decorum and iconoclasm—warring silently within Plath. Throughout her life she would try to reconcile these forces in the same way that she tried to reconcile her loyalties to her mother and Ted Hughes. The two pulled Plath in different directions in a symbolic custody battle, with Plath, the dutiful daughter and wife, always trying to please both. Would she hold a proper wedding reception or elope on Bloomsday? Would she get a respectable teaching position or earn a precarious living as a freelance writer? Would she become Prouty or would she become Gendron? In her journal she pondered the question and alighted on a compromise: "I will be no Val Gendron. But I will make a good part of Val Gendron part of me—someday."[195]

Sylvia's grandparents brought her the August edition of *Mademoiselle* when "Sunday at the Mintons" finally appeared. They had all gathered at the Nortons' summer cabin in Brewster on July 30. After they ate, Sylvia spent two hours at the beach alone in Brewster, savoring peaches and cherries—and her own sense of fulfillment and joy—as she read her story. She wrote to Aurelia, "I felt the happiest I ever have in my life. . . . I read it, smoothed the page, chortled happily to myself, ran out onto the sand flats and dog-trotted for a mile far out alone in the sun, through the warm tidal water, with the foam trickling pale brown in fingers along the wet sand ridges where the tide was coming in, talking to myself about how wonderful it was to be alive and brown and full of vitality and potentialities." Dick drove her back to the Cantors' house after a "perfect day."[196]

Years later Sylvia would write to Mrs. Cantor, "I think back on that as the happiest summer of my teens—it just glows gold, the color of the Chatham sands."[197] She picked beach plums in Truro and sailed to deserted islands. She danced to records in the Cantors' kitchen and took starry night walks with dates. She wore a black dress to dance at the Chatham Bars Inn and called herself a "knockout."[198] Above all, there was Nauset Beach, the place that would become her life's touchstone for all that was holy—"over 20 miles of pure white sand and powerful bluegreen surf, low dunes," as she described it to Aurelia—"the most beautiful place on the Cape."[199] It was a stark, almost cruel contrast to the hells that awaited her the following summer in New York and Wellesley.

The Cape's thundering Atlantic beaches brought out her best self: "The tide was dead low, so for an hour I walked or ran, as the spirit moved, straight out to sea on the sand flats. . . . For 30 minutes after a vigorous 2 hour hike, I lay and basked on the sand, then the hike back to the cabin, with a brief stop at the Brewster cemetery to browse about the old tombstones. Dick biked up just as I was finishing my salad in the sun on the front steps."[200] The sea, long walks, a good meal, love: these were the things that restored Plath. They rarely came together as they did during the Chatham summer, when she finally found fulfillment in her work and her art. She wrote to Aurelia that August, "chance is strange—one feels afterward that it must have been destiny."[201]

9

The Ninth Kingdom

Smith College, September 1952–May 1953

When Sylvia returned to Wellesley in September 1952, she began dining almost nightly with the Nortons, as if she were already their daughter-in-law. Yet she was being pulled in more promising directions. In mid-September she received several letters that confirmed her growing confidence in her writing. An editor at Dodd, Mead and Co. publishers asked about the possibility of a future novel and encouraged her to apply for their Intercollegiate Literary Fellowship. One of Smith's most esteemed English professors, Mary Ellen Chase, congratulated her on her *Mademoiselle* success and invited Sylvia to her home for coffee. She wanted to discuss "Sunday at the Mintons" and Plath's "other writing."[1] Mrs. Prouty wrote, too, praising the story's technique, especially "the similes and metaphors that remain clearly etched upon my consciousness."[2] She asked Sylvia to keep her posted on her "future successes—or failures. Both." Prouty intuited that Plath needed permission to fail. Val Gendron had offered similar advice: Don't apologize, and don't let rejection equal defeat. Both knew that a woman writer's success depended as much on thick skin as raw talent.

Permission to fail was exactly what Plath needed as she began her junior year at Smith. She had spent two years building friendships and honing her social skills at Haven House. Now, with money short, she was forced to withdraw from Maureen Buckley's circle. She would be living at Lawrence House, a cooperative dorm where she waitressed at lunchtime, in uniform, to save $250 off her room and board. Sylvia tried to convince herself and her correspondents that Lawrence House was just fine—that waitressing was "not at all unpleasant," and her new roommate, Mary Bonneville, warm and homespun.[3] But on her arrival at Lawrence House, she felt "like a displaced person as yet—a bit bewildered and uninitiated."[4] She was aghast at the bright aquas and yellows Mary had chosen for the room. (Sylvia talked her into "yellow spreads and dark green furnishings, white curtains, and a harmonizing modern art picture.")[5] She told Aurelia that Mary was "a very sweet girl, in her own way" but there was no chance of a friendship. "That was a downer for her," Janet Salter Rosenberg remembered. "Mary was a science major, and she and Sylvia had very little in common."[6] Moving to a new house, Sylvia wrote Warren, "was like being a freshman all over again, only worse, because I remembered nostalgically the homey comfort of Haven House, and rooming with Marcia."[7] Still, there was some relief in living among other scholarship students; Sylvia spoke of the "delightful atmosphere of economy, and everyone understands the words, 'I can't, I'm broke.'"[8]

Lawrence House was more diverse than the other houses: Sylvia noted in letters home that some of her peers there were Jewish and African American. She had begun a tentative friendship with her housemate Janet Salter, a Jewish New Yorker and a shy, aspiring writer whom Sylvia had approached in the library the previous year when she learned she would be living in Lawrence House. "Within a half hour she had practically told me her entire life story. And she told me about her father dying when she was ten or eleven and how she was planning to be a writer and how she was already writing, and it was amazing to me. She elicited my life story in the process." Janet, who had been writing since childhood and eventually became the editor of the *Smith Review* (and, later, a professional editor), was excited to become friends with another writer. Both were taking Robert Gorham Davis's creative writing class. "More than the rest of us, she really was a writer," Janet remembered. "We were wimpy writers, and she was actually writing and selling things." They grew close during Sylvia's junior year, bonding over the books and authors they loved. "If I liked an author's work, I'd go to the library and read everything, and Sylvia had that same tendency. In that regard we were peas in a pod."[9] They rarely spoke of sex and dating; Sylvia kept this part of her life private. Plath felt less pressure at Lawrence House to "circulate," as everyone needed to maintain top grades to keep their scholarships. Sylvia's Smith friend Nancy Hunter Steiner described the Lawrence House women as many would eventually describe Sylvia herself—full of "savage industriousness."[10]

Plath was on an honors track, taking a fall semester of physical science (World of Atoms), art (which she eventually dropped), medieval literature, and creative writing (Style and Form); she was also part of the college Press Board and the struggling *Smith Review*. Both of her English professors intimidated her. Robert Gorham Davis had published in *The New Yorker* and reviewed Hemingway's *The Old Man and the Sea* on the front page of *The New York Times Book Review*. Professor Patch, a medievalist, was, Sylvia wrote home, "the most imposing literary lion I have ever seen—a great 6'5"

gray haired man who seems to live in the ruddy vitality of the middle ages."
Patch fostered a love for Chaucer that would endear Plath to the Cambridge
literary men she later met, especially Ted Hughes. He conducted his small
seminar in his home library, with his bulldog, Jeeves, sitting placidly at his
feet. Around him, Sylvia felt "pitifully stupid, inadequate and scared" but
"determined to succeed in the enormous intellectual honesty, ambition &
discipline that honoring [sic] requires."[11] She had begun to think seriously
about attending graduate school at Oxford or Cambridge after a lengthy discussion, over sherry, with Mr. Crockett. Money was "the one great problem,"
but she would find a way. "I think I will do graduate work in Philosophy. I
am going to do it," she vowed in her journal.[12] During a dinner at the Nortons' that September, when she felt trapped by the prospect of marriage,
she quelled her rising panic with thoughts of a different future. "I was going
away to England out of the warm secure circle to prove something. There
would be the going away and the coming back, and whatever would greet me
on returning, I would take stoically."[13]

In October, she plunged herself into the Press Board—to which she dedicated two hours a day, six days a week writing stories for local Springfield
newspapers—and the *Smith Review*, which was in financial crisis and barely
afloat.[14] The albatross around her neck was her science requirement. She
had hoped to fulfill it over the summer and had been unable to muster the
energy. Now she faced ten hours a week of formulae, atoms, and molecules.
Despite her earlier vow to learn more about science, she found it difficult and
dull. This was Otto's world, and Dick's; their mastery of the subject underscored her own—as she saw it—pathetic attempts at proficiency. The stress
of fulfilling the requirement would help trigger the most severe depressive
episode she had yet experienced.

That October, "The Perfect Setup" appeared in *Seventeen*. It was another
story about an outsider's harsh treatment by society—a theme that was
coming to define Plath's more serious fiction. The story was about anti-
Semitism and her summer with the Mayos. She worried about their reaction.
"I am just beginning to realize the 'position & stands' a 'writer' must take—
and the responsibility," she wrote Aurelia. When she received a letter from
the Blodgetts, the Mayos' neighbors, saying that they had read her story,
she suddenly "had visions of law courts & suits for slander."[15] To her relief,
the Blodgetts had read "Sunday at the Mintons," not "The Perfect Setup."
(*The Bell Jar*, however, would end up at the center of a courtroom battle.)

She achieved another literary success in October—"Initiation" took third
place in the annual *Seventeen* fiction contest and would be published in January 1953. The "unexpected good news" made her feel she was "maybe not
destined to deteriorate after all."[16] She had not even remembered entering

the story. Publishing her fiction was beginning to seem easier than keeping up with her schoolwork. Even fan mail was becoming routine: another young woman had written wanting to "correspond with an 'author,'" but Sylvia brushed her off, telling Aurelia, "[I] simply don't have time to get chummy with all my readers."[17]

When Sylvia learned about the prize, she thanked Aurelia in effusive, sentimental prose: "You are the most wonderful mummy that a girl ever had, and I only hope I can continue to lay more laurels at your feet. Warren and I both love you and admire you more than anybody in the world for all you have done for us all our lives. For it is you who has given us the heredity and the incentive to be mentally ambitious."[18] Later, in February 1953, Sylvia again spoke of her desire to make her mother proud and "repay" her for all she had done.[19] These passages embody the nebulous "difficulty" Sylvia mentioned to friends when she spoke about her relationship with Aurelia. Sylvia loved her mother, and felt gratitude toward her, but she also resented the pressure—real or imagined—to "lay laurels" at her feet.

Dick had driven Sylvia to Smith and helped her move into her new room. When he left, she pinned photos of him on her bulletin board. But she was still upset about Dick's sexual affairs and confided in Perry, who thought his brother's "deviances" were a rebellion against his parents' "moral standards."[20] Perry wondered if Dick was capable of love and suggested to Sylvia that she might be unhappy with someone who needed "the right gal, the right job, the right friends." Eddie Cohen had said much the same. Perry had proprietary feelings toward Sylvia, and was probably jealous of his brother. In another letter that week, he cited their "mutual love": "My grateful legions shall always provide you a sanctuary of absolute devotion in whatever crusade of yours you may ever give them the honor to protect and revere. . . . There is no truth but that we need each other."[21] Letters like this made Sylvia declare to her journal, "I am in love with two brothers, embarrassingly so," and that she would "of course marry the other brother."[22] She returned to this leitmotif many times in her journal that fall.

―――――

MIDWAY THROUGH OCTOBER, Dick's world shattered when he learned that a routine chest X-ray had revealed tuberculosis. In his letters to Sylvia, he became uncharacteristically metaphysical. "What is good? What is worth doing? Why are we here?" He would have to spend several months receiving treatment at the New York State Hospital for Incipient Pulmonary Tuberculosis (commonly known as the Ray Brook sanatorium), near Saranac Lake, New York. "Why is this happening to me (to us)?" he wrote her forlornly in

October. "Is there some happiness-credit-meter in the sugar-icing-heavens above? . . . Again and again I think 'This person cannot be me, not this character at the center of all the fuss and nonsense!' But it is."[23] He and Sylvia visited each other in the days before he left for the Adirondacks. He expected that they would carry on their relationship from a distance. "Auf Wiedersehen, my blond skier," he wrote in his last letter from home. "I'll see you in the mountains."[24]

But Sylvia was heading south. She had agreed to attend the Princeton prom with Rodger Decker, a friend of Phil Brawner's. In anticipation, she went shopping in Northampton and bought her first pair of high heels—"a lovely black-suede that had done wonders for my sense of chic."[25] She had reason to distract herself, since she was nervous that she too had tuberculosis. Luckily her chest X-ray, taken on her twentieth birthday, was clear. She celebrated with Marcia over sherry. It all "served to bring me out of the bog of lonesomeness & despair I had been wallowing in, and shot me through with new joy and love," she wrote her mother.[26] Aurelia dropped off a heart-shaped cake, which Sylvia shared with ten other girls at an impromptu house party, while Ilo Pill sent her another pen-and-ink sketch. She was thrilled that he remembered her birthday and considered visiting him in Greenwich Village. Three years after Lookout Farm, the attraction remained.

The Princeton prom was a bust. Her date, she said, was "quite intellectually stupid," and the trip had been a waste of time and money. "He served his purpose, but I never intend to see him again—I cannot abide dumb rich boys."[27] She found Princeton beautiful but full of wealthy, dull Republicans—"they are all bloodless like mushrooms inside, I am sure," she told Warren.[28] "I hope Warren goes to Harvard," she quipped to Aurelia, though she was delighted to have worn her new high heels, something she felt she could not do with Dick because of her height.[29]

At the sanatorium, Dick was pleasantly surprised by his large, en-suite room and the friendly doctors and patients. He quickly befriended another young medical school student, and he embarked on an ambitious reading course that included Hemingway, Yeats, Boswell, Dante, Aristotle, Faulkner, Salinger, Tolstoy, and others. "As for visitors, this really comes to be a *salon*," he wrote Sylvia in late October.[30] Plath had once fantasized about recovering from tuberculosis at a sanatorium so that she could spend uninterrupted months reading and writing. Now Dick, formerly scornful of the unquantifiable, was doing just that. He wrote sketches of the other patients, took music lessons, painted watercolors, corresponded with William Carlos Williams's wife, and filled a creative writing notebook with story drafts. "Don't you envy me??" he wrote Sylvia.[31] When he asked her if she thought he could make his living as a writer, she answered, "It's a hellish craft. Beautiful and bitchy."[32] He began to show greater interest in her stories' technique and autobiographical antecedents, and even sent an adventure story to *Boys' Life* magazine. He worked hard to use the uninterrupted time for personal growth, and apologized for his former rigidity. "Sylvia, I think I am trying to learn to laugh."[33] He pondered taking up smoking "to get over that smugness of purity," or joining the Navy to "mature among hardships."[34] Above all, he told her that he loved her and wanted children "as badly as I want to breathe."[35] Dick sensed that his sickness and isolation might repel Sylvia, who fetishized masculine strength. He was doing all he could to keep her in his orbit.

THAT NOVEMBER, Dwight Eisenhower defeated Adlai Stevenson in the presidential election. Plath felt "it was the funeral day of all my hopes and ideals."[36] To Aurelia, who had voted for Eisenhower, she wrote, "Well, I only hope you're happy with McCarthy . . . it wasn't Eisenhower I was against, but all the other little horrors in the Trojan Horse he rode in on. I don't envy him his crusade nor his companions, and I feel that our gullible American public may be only too sadly disillusioned. But then, variety of corruption is the spice of life. And so are red witch hunts."[37] Stevenson, she thought, was the "Abe Lincoln of our age."[38] Eisenhower's victory seemed to Plath a symbolic personal defeat, and it marked the beginning of a depression that nearly took her life.

The new world order reflected the corruption and chaos she felt in her soul. She was writing two papers a week and taking phenobarbital to sleep.[39] The competition in her classes was "cut-throat," and she was relentlessly hard on herself: "I will seek to progress, to whip myself on, to more and more—to learning. Always."[40] Plath would soon see another poem in *Seventeen*—"Twelfth Night" in December—but publication did not lift her spirits as it usually did. Enid Epstein assured Sylvia "over endless cups of tea" that her academic and creative work was brilliant. "And it always was." But Sylvia seemed "honestly unsure of everything she did."[41] In her journal on November 3, Sylvia tried to understand the reasons for her rapidly worsening state. She was baffled by her inability to control her "attitude," given all her success. "I am weak, tired, in revolt from the strong constructive humanitarian faith which presupposes a healthy, active intellect and will."[42] In a now famous passage, she analyzed the textures of her depression with Dostoevskian precision:

> God, if ever I have come close to wanting to commit suicide, it is now. . . .
> My world falls apart, crumbles, 'The center does not hold.' . . . I go plod-

ding on, afraid that the blank hell in back of my eyes will break through, spewing forth like a dark pestilence; afraid that the disease which eats away the pith of my body with merciless impersonality will break forth in obvious sores and warts, screaming, "Traitor, sinner, imposter." . . . I can see ahead only into dark, sordid alleys, where the dregs, the sludge, the filth of my life lies, unglorified, unchanged—transfigured by nothing: no nobility, not even the illusion of a dream.[43]

She wondered what had finally made Virginia Woolf and Sara Teasdale—both literary role models—commit suicide. Was their brilliance linked to their neurosis? Would she "go either mad or become neurotic" if she could not express herself creatively in marriage? She despaired of finding help—the cost and the stigma prevented her from seeing a psychiatrist.

I'll kill myself. I am beyond help. No one here has time to probe, to aid me in understanding myself . . . so many others are worse off than I. How can I selfishly demand help, solace, guidance? No, it is my own mess, and even if now I have lost my sense of perspective, thereby my creative sense of humor, I will not let myself get sick, go mad, or retreat like a child into blubbering on someone else's shoulder. Masks are the order of the day—and the least I can do is cultivate the illusion that I am gay, serene, not hollow and afraid. Someday, god knows when, I will stop this absurd, self-pitying, idle, futile despair.[44]

Although she began to feel unburdened when she allowed herself to be "unproud and cry" to Marcia in mid-November, she soon spiraled downward again.[45] She received the terrible news that a close friend of Warren's, 17-year-old George Pollock, hanged himself in his Exeter dormitory on November 18. Warren had found him in the dormitory shower and cut him down. Warren remained stoic in the face of this horror, but Aurelia suggested that the event disturbed Sylvia greatly.[46]

To Aurelia, in a letter dated November 19, Sylvia blamed her precarious mental state on her science class, which, she said, "annihilates my will and love of life." She felt like vomiting when she thought about each new week's work. "If only I wanted to understand it, but I don't!" Her letter was a cry for help. Aurelia was the only one she could confide in about her "tense emotional and mental state" and her physical symptoms. Again, she blamed her acute depression on her science course:

I have practically considered committing suicide to get out of it . . . it's like having my nose rubbed in my own slime. . . . I have become really frantic: small choices and events seem insurmountable obstacles, the core of life has fallen apart . . . I feel actually <u>ill</u> when I open the book. . . . I feel I <u>have</u> got to escape this, or go mad.

She wondered "desperately" if she should see the college psychiatrist and tell her how the course was "obsessing all my life, paralyzing my action." She hoped that she could persuade the school authorities to let her drop the second semester, but feared they would never let her. "Life seems a mockery. . . . I <u>can't</u> go on like this," she railed. She wished for a sinus infection, which would at least provide "escapism." "When one feels like leaving college and killing oneself over one course which actually <u>nauseates</u> one, it is a rather serious thing." Sylvia had never written such frank, emotional, and terrifying letters to her mother. The science course, she wrote, had become "a devouring, malicious monster." She signed off, "Love, your hollow girl."[47]

She confided her troubles to Eddie. He realized she was in the midst of a full-blown depressive crisis, but there was little he could do from Chicago. In the past, when she had written to him of "nervous tension" and other difficulties, he had been keen to "practice minor therapy" on her. This was altogether different. "Syl, honey," he wrote, "if my words and judgment mean anything at all to you, let me implore you to get yourself into some sort of psycho-therapy as soon as possible." He gave her leads for affordable clinics and told her not to let her guard down if she began feeling better. "Don't be deceived. Such a situation will merely serve to delay the ultimate reckoning, and at the same time increase its potential danger." He surmised she was finally coming face-to-face with her true feelings about Dick, which caused her guilt and anxiety. Just at the point when she had gained the courage to end things, Dick had come down with tuberculosis and entered the sanatorium. She was trapped: she could not very well break his heart as he recovered from a potentially fatal illness.

Eddie declared her science requirement a "distortion and diversion" from her "real problems." He did not assume that because she was a woman she was no good at science. He knew Plath better than that. "It would be difficult to convince me at this stage of the game, that you don't have the mental equipment to meet this subject . . . I can only conclude that you have made this course a scapegoat." He ended with a declaration of love and tried to extract a promise that she would seek psychiatric help. "I only hope that this once you will heed me <u>before</u> events prove me correct."[48]

Eddie was right: depression was the devouring monster, not Sylvia's science course. But she may not have understood the distinction. Sylvia wanted to see a psychiatrist so that she could get out of taking the course, not to seek treatment for depression. She felt that if she were released from science, she would regain her mental equilibrium. On the back of an envelope that fall she wrote, "Escape: Mary? Science? Job? Girls in House? Patch? Responsibility?" Her series of question marks underscores her confusion as to the source of her misery. Next to this list, she wrote, "Wisdom: more time, more rest, less physical danger"—as if less classwork and fewer sinus infections could cure her mental maladies.[49]

Alison Prentice Smith, from the class of '55, recalled hearing, in the fall of 1952, that Sylvia locked herself in a dormitory kitchenette and turned on the gas oven. "The college authorities were horrified," Alison said, and sent maintenance crews out to all the dormitories to remove the transoms over the kitchenette doors. Though the story was likely just a rumor, Sylvia's alleged suicide attempt became a source of dark humor among Alison and her friends: "Whenever any one of us was depressed, she would cry out, 'Ma, send me a transom!' We certainly didn't feel any sense of tragedy, just awe. Clearly there was someone next door who was even more alienated than we were, and certainly more desperate."[50]

Plath's letters and journal entries from that November show she was indeed contemplating suicide. Aurelia later alluded to this dark period to Dr. Beuscher, saying Sylvia had told her "she hadn't been able to sleep for a month and was thinking of suicide." Aurelia called Sylvia right away, extremely alarmed. Sylvia seemed calmer after they spoke, and much better when she returned home for Thanksgiving.[51] In her journal, Sylvia compared her "resurrection" to that of Lazarus, already laying the foundation for her poem "Lady Lazarus" a decade later.[52]

Plath wrote two stories around this time about her depression. "Mary Ventura and the Ninth Kingdom," which she dated December 12 and submitted to Robert Gorham Davis's Style and Form class, is a surreal allegory that gives a vivid sense of her inner turmoil that fall. Mary Ventura, a young woman, reluctantly says goodbye to her parents and boards a train heading for "the north country." On the platform newsboys yell ominous headlines about ten thousand citizens being "sentenced" for unknown crimes—possibly an allusion to McCarthy's witch hunts. A grandmotherly woman familiar with the route sits next to Mary, and makes small talk as they pass through "barren" apocalyptic landscapes of burning hills and deserted stations. Mary becomes increasingly nervous as the sun sets and her companion warns her they will soon enter the "long tunnel." When the train stops at the sixth station, a terrified lady in a fur coat begs to stay on longer. She hides her ticket, but two guards on the platform take her away. Mary watches, filled suddenly with apprehension about her destination: the ninth kingdom. "But what is the ninth kingdom?" Mary asks her companion. "'You will be happier if you do not know,' the woman said gently. 'It is really not too bad, once you get there. The trip is long down the tunnel, and the climate changes gradually. The hurt is not intense when one is hardened to the cold.'" Mary realizes that the passengers have all chosen to die. The train is suicide.

"I won't stay. I won't," she cries. "I will get the next train back home." But that, her companion tells her, is impossible. "Once you get to the ninth kingdom, there is no going back. It is the kingdom of negation, of the frozen will." Mary decides she will pull the emergency cord, to her companion's delight. "That is the one trick left," she tells her young charge. "The one assertion of the will remaining. I thought that, too, was frozen." Mary stops the train and jumps off at the seventh kingdom, where she emerges into a sunny park full of children. There, a woman resembling her companion is selling "white roses and daffodils" in the "spring of the year." "I have been waiting for you, dear," the woman says.[53] Mary has outrun her own suicide.[54]

Plath's structure is Dantean—she had been reading Dante that November—but the story's real subjects are depression, suicide, and rebirth. This was the first time Plath had faced, albeit obliquely, her mental "difficulties" in fiction. *Mademoiselle* rejected "Mary Ventura and the Ninth Kingdom" in March 1953, but it laid the foundation for 1955's "Tongues of Stone," about her stay in McLean, and, eventually, "Johnny Panic and the Bible of Dreams" and *The Bell Jar*. It shows Plath already grafting an allegorical trajectory onto her psychological struggles—mining them, even in the depth of her depression, for creative potential.

January 1953's "Dialogue," which Plath also submitted to Davis's writing class, explored similar themes. The piece, written as a script, was likely based on the real conversation Sylvia had with Marcia in November. "Alison" and "Marcia" sit in their dorm room on a Saturday night discussing Alison's troubles:

> A: I'm sick of the damn desiccated ritual: "Hello. How are you? How is he? Oh no. Oh really. Oh divine." I'm sick to death of it.
>
> M: So what are you going to do? Invent a new language? You're going to burn yourself out if you keep it up this way. Relax for a change. Get philosophical.

Marcia tells Alison that polite language "is all part of the machinery that makes life easy . . . The automatic handshake, the tilt of the hat, the dry kiss on the cheek of the maiden aunt." But Alison protests that silence would be better. "At the table sometimes, at dinner, I could go quite mad listening to the voices. Did you ever let your ears blur the sound of voices, the way your eyes, forgetful, can blur the print on a page? The voices fall apart, senseless, like the inane clucking of birds. Saying nothing in another language." Marcia presses: "You've got to have some insulation from the black vacuum, don't you?" But Alison scorns the "distractions" that people use to numb themselves from the "agony of free will"—religion, movies, television, dreams. She refuses to "numb" her pain or use "euphemisms." "Why not use the good vile words. Damn. Dung. Hell. God, they sound great. Scrawl them on the sidewalks and fences and shock the ladies and the gentlemen."[55] This is exactly what Plath would do in her *Ariel* poems, where her language becomes short and curt, as in "Lady Lazarus": "I do it so it feels like hell." In her notes from her freshman-year art class with Mr. Manzi, Plath wrote, "To hell with description—to hell with long adjectival phrases, elaborate metaphors and ornate similes—life, dirt, grime, love, sun, mud, leaves, rain—get them brightly, sharply, in short dynamic phrases."[56] In her later poems, she would invent a new language for female anger.

Alison believes in nothing but "physical deterioration" after death: "the stopping of the blood, the freezing of the mind, and all the rolls of picture film inside it." There is some relief, she feels, in "losing the identity, the ego," but nothing more. For her, heaven and hell exist only on earth, in the mind. When Marcia asks her why she thinks life is worth living, Alison replies that she is not at all sure that it is, but that she wants to "affirm life" nevertheless. How? asks Marcia. "Trying to figure the most creative way I can spend those thirty million minutes, that's all. No opium, even if the hurt is bad."

At the dialogue's end, Alison describes her depression to Marcia in a passage lifted straight out of Plath's own journal, quoted above. "God, and you didn't tell anyone. Why didn't you tell anyone?" Marcia asks. "I didn't think I could," Alison answers. "I was afraid. I was afraid that maybe they would look at me, into my eyes, and say: 'Why, I do believe you are right. There is nothing there. Nothing there at all.'" Alison finally tells Marcia she now feels "much better"—mainly because she has been able to speak honestly with a sympathetic listener. Plath's title suggests that dialogue, communication, and friendship are pathways to recovery. Sylvia was a prideful woman, and her depression embarrassed her. She did not want to burden others with her troubles. To heal, she needed friends like Marcia who would let her be "unproud." And she needed to write—to affirm her "thirty million minutes" of life through creativity.

———

TED HUGHES'S FRIEND Luke Myers later claimed that Plath's English education at Smith had been far inferior to that of a Cambridge undergraduate. Plath's English syllabi belie this assertion; honors English required intensive courses in the medieval period to the twentieth century.[57] (In her 1953 spring semester, she took only English classes: Technical Fiction and Criticism, Milton, and Modern Poetry.) Sylvia was also reading sophisticated critics, pondering the relationship between sound, rhythm, rhyme, metaphor, and image in the work of Randall Jarrell, David Daiches, Stephen Spender, Edmund Wilson, F. O. Matthiessen, Helen Gardner, and I. A. Richards, as well as the classic New Critical bibles, F. R. Leavis's *New Bearings in Modern Poetry* and Cleanth Brooks's *Modern Poetry and the Tradition*. These books prepared her for Cambridge, where Leavis taught and which was then the epicenter of New Criticism. In one English notebook from her sophomore year, she discussed the "'New' Criticism" at length, citing the approach's famous dictum, "A poem should not mean, but be." "Word=symbol valuable for itself as well as capacity of representation. Work of art=object of knowledge valuable in and for itself—Actual words are tremendously important. Great emphasis of naked poem—can't even be paraphrased because of uniqueness," she wrote, summing up the major ideas behind the critical movement.[58] Professors such as Robert Gorham Davis, Mary Ellen Chase, Alfred Kazin, and Elizabeth Drew would ensure that Sylvia was well prepared to argue the intricacies of modernist poetry with the most brilliant minds at Cambridge. (Davis told Plath's thesis advisor, George Gibian, that "he had never had a talented writer in his creative writing class who was not a little neurotic . . . except Sylvia.")[59]

In her Smith English papers, Plath circled back to a core set of intellectual themes and dilemmas that interested her personally: escapism versus "the agony of will" in Robert Penn Warren's *All the King's Men*; character versus fate in Thomas Hardy's *The Mayor of Casterbridge*; rebirth through suffering in Synge's *Riders to the Sea*; Romanticism and modernity in Chekhov's *The Cherry Orchard*; chiaroscuro in Milton; sound textures and poetic technique in Edith Sitwell; the struggle for autonomy in Nietzsche. Nearly all of these themes would resurface in Plath's poetry and fiction.

Plath wrote her senior thesis on the double in Dostoevsky. But her interest in the subject predated her thesis. A January 1951 paper, "The Dualism of Thomas Mann," was her first academic exploration of doubleness. She began with a critic's quote that could well apply to her own burgeoning sense of "dualism":

> Thomas Mann views reality as dualistic and antithetic; there is a conflict of opposites in everything. Every phenomenon has two facets. Disease looked at in one way is degrading and renders the sufferer doubly physical. In another aspect it is ennobling and heightens man's humanity. The finished product of art may be chaste and beautiful; yet how often does it have its origin in darkness and the forbidden.[60]

Plath had pondered many of these issues in her journal, particularly the "ruinous antithesis," as she quoted in her Mann paper, "between burgher and artist." All her life she tried to reconcile the subversive artist with the respectable, bourgeois intellectual. Plath noted that though Mann showed a "bourgeois desire for order . . . the artist in him realizes that when the currents cross in man there is inner turmoil and often a seething unbalance." Surely she saw the same forces working at cross-currents within herself. She was effectively trying to diagnose what she still hoped was a philosophical, rather than psychological, problem. Hers was, she thought, simply a spirit at war with itself, in need of reconciliation.

In a March 1951 paper titled "Modern Tragedy in the Classic Tradition," Plath again pondered suffering philosophically. She looked to Aristotle, Hegel, Schopenhauer, and Nietzsche for a unifying definition of tragedy, concluding that it was where "pain and exaltation become one." She was slowly discovering the themes and symbols that would flow through her best poetry: "the bleak, keen exaltation that comes from a journey through the realms of suffering toward heightened feeling; it is exaltation that may be likened to the blue steel edge of a freshly whetted knife." Tragedy was "serene agony, almost mute in its grandeur"—words that summon the dead, statuesque Greek heroine of her late poem "Edge." She considered that in Greek tragedy, like *Oedipus Rex*, the "fatal adversary is himself."[61] This was powerful, brilliant analysis from an undergraduate.

The following month, in April 1951, Plath continued along the same vein in a paper on Amy Lowell's poem "Patterns," which was one of her "personal favorites." In "Patterns," the young female speaker ponders her soldier-lover's death as she walks alone in a garden. Plath noted that at first the poem's "patterns"—the ornate garden with its precise paths, the young woman in her "stiff, brocaded gown"—seem innocuous.

> But as the poem progresses, one senses the growing rebellion which this woman feels against patterns and one realizes that it is really the stiffness of convention which is symbolized throughout the poem by the stiff, correct brocade, the bones and stays, and each button, hook, and lace. Here is a woman who was about to "break the pattern" for her lover, and he is killed in a "pattern called war."
>
> There is bitter irony in her last cry from the heart, "Christ! What are patterns for?"[62]

Plath's critical commentary on a female poet's protest against conformity and convention brings to mind the insidious ways in which the "patterns" of fashion and war would later merge in *The Bell Jar*. In Lowell's poem, the speaker longs to shed her metaphorical corset and wander naked: "What is Summer in a fine brocaded gown! / I should like to see it lying in a heap upon the ground. / All the pink and silver crumpled up on the ground." In Plath's novel, we see what Plath may have borrowed from Lowell when Esther Greenwood sheds her "corseted" identity: she stands on the roof of the Amazon Hotel and throws her slips into the "dark heart of New York."[63]

By her junior year, Sylvia had become adept at taking poems apart and putting them back together again—explaining, stanza by stanza, how the chosen form of rhymes, half rhymes, assonance, and dissonance worked in tandem with the content. She was best at recognizing the importance of sound patterns. Her papers on Yeats and Dylan Thomas bear the mark of thorough, if plodding, close reading in the New Critical tradition. In an analysis of Auden's "Fish in the Unruffled Lakes," for example, she took great pleasure in explicating Auden's rhymes: "the varied vowel sounds produce a textural pattern of bell-like cadences, now clear, now muted. The vowel level of 'gone' sinks to the duller sound of 'done,' which lengthens into the hollow clang of 'wrong.'"[64] And so on. She especially appreciated the power of poetic form to imply one meaning while carefully concealing another, as in Yeats's great elegy "In Memory of Major Robert Gregory."[65]

Plath's thirty-page paper on Edith Sitwell, which she wrote for Elizabeth Drew's Modern Poetry unit in March 1953, repeatedly returned to Sitwell's experiments with sound and form, as well as her thematic trajectory from winter to spring. Though the male modernists, Eliot, Yeats, Joyce, Lawrence, and Dylan Thomas, formed the bedrock of Plath's English education, she loved Sitwell's "bucolic eden, her rocketing jazz fantasies, her nightmare cannibal land, her wartorn hell of the cold, and her metaphysical sun-permeated universe."[66] Sitwell would become an important poetic influence on Plath's work.[67]

Although Plath wrote mostly about literature during her Smith years, she explored the philosophy of Nietzsche in several papers. Her 1954 paper "The Age of Anxiety and the Escape from Freedom," which she wrote for Mrs. Koffka's European history class, was ostensibly about Erich Fromm's *Escape from Freedom*. But Plath continually brought her argument back to Nietzsche and her desire "to climb still higher, out of the womblike security of complacent collective values into the realm of the strong, individualistic winds: 'for rather will I have noise and thunders and tempest blasts, than this discreet, doubting cat-repose.' (Zarathustra, 182)." Speaking of Auden's poem "September 1939" in the same paper, she wrote, "This verse, I think, contains the kernel of our modern problem. The insecure individual 'clings to the average.' How Nietzsche scorned and shouted against this: 'That . . . is mediocrity, though it be called moderation. . . . Ye ever become smaller,

ye small people! Ye crumble away, ye comfortable ones!' (Zarathustra, 188–
89)."[68] Plath called Auden's drinkers in the bar "pathetic weaklings" and
ended her paper by again invoking Nietzsche:

> Man wants to "alleviate suffering," in the words of Fromm, but if he is
> to achieve the fullest measure of his individual potential, according to
> Nietzsche, he must not only accept suffering (Nietzsche abhors effemi-
> nate Christian humility) but seek it! And we agree heartily here: tempting
> as it is to avoid pain, the strong individual must perceive that "pain is also
> a joy, curse is also a blessing, night is also a sun . . ."
>
> For us, this eloquent paradox expresses the full, honest, courageous
> acceptance of freedom and all its implications: an affirmation of the value
> of evil as well as good, discord as well as harmony, hardship as well as
> comfort, and pain as well as pleasure . . . rising to higher statures and per-
> spectives through conflict and suffering. (Zarathustra, 363)[69]

Plath's emphasis on pain and struggle here were significant; these ideas
would propel her later dialogue with Ted Hughes.

That same year, in a paper written for her Russian class on Dostoevsky
in March 1954, Plath again introduced Nietzsche, beginning the paper with
an epigraph from Zarathustra[70] and indulging her youthful interest in what
Ted Hughes would later call "positive violence."[71] Plath's experiments with
Nietzschean ideas in her journal and early poetry reveal that she recognized
him as an enabling literary and philosophical model: her poems "Doomsday," "Insolent Storm Strikes at the Skull," "Temper of Time," and "Song for
a Revolutionary Love" all exhibit the influence of Nietzsche, as well as Yeats.
Plath's uncollected 1955 poem, "Notes on Zarathustra's Prologue," shows
that at Smith she had already begun to incorporate Nietzsche's philosophy
into her art:

> Look to the lightning for tongues of pain
> Steep are the stairs to the Superman
>
> Go flay the frail sheep in the flock
> And strip the shroud from coward's back
>
> Till the womb of chaos sprouts with fire
> And hatches Nietzsche's dancing star.[72]

Nietzsche's melding of puritanism and Romanticism offered an appeal-
ingly subversive philosophy to Plath. Her girlhood Emersonian, Unitarian-

approved version of individualism must have seemed tepid when set beside Nietzsche's Will to Power. After all, Plath frequently called herself "The girl who wanted to be God."[73] In her journals, she wrote that she was "strong and assertive" and longed to give voice to the "masculine" elements within herself.[74] "I am jealous of men," she wrote in 1951. "I envy the man his physical freedom to lead a double life—his career, and his sexual and family life."[75] These admissions did not accord with the image of the demure, self-effacing model of fifties femininity.

Although Nietzsche has been criticized as a misogynist, he nevertheless offered Plath an ideological foundation that validated her desire for intellectual and artistic autonomy and opened up possibilities of liberation from the tyranny of gender. In Eisenhower's America, Plath was not expected to pursue her own career; subordination was the only option available to her if she wished to marry, which she did. Yet Nietzsche thought that subordination was a surrender to the enervating Judeo-Christian doctrine of humility and submission. Plath, too, vowed not to surrender. In the same journal entry in which she wrote, "I do not love anybody except myself," she swore to live a life determined by her own standards and goals. She would hatch her escape

> in the exercise of a phase of life inviolate and separate from that of my future mate . . . I am not only jealous; I am vain and proud. I will not submit to having my life fingered by my husband, enclosed in the larger circle of his activity, and nourished vicariously by tales of his actual exploits. I must have a legitimate field of my own, apart from his, which he must respect.[76]

Plath had diagnosed her situation with remarkable clarity well before second-wave feminism. Yet on account of her Emersonian upbringing and the sexist era in which she was trapped, she was conflicted about her goals, and often worried that she was selfish. In September 1951 she wrote in her journal, "I long to excel—to specialize in one field, one section of a field, no matter how minute, as long as I can be an authority there. Pride, ambition— what mean, selfish words!"[77] The words were not so much selfish as unfeminine. But Nietzsche's dramatic rhetoric of self-realization and his rejection of subservience supported Plath in the age before Betty Friedan's *The Feminine Mystique*. As he wrote, "The creation of freedom for oneself and a sacred 'No' even to duty—for that, my brothers, the lion is needed. To assume the right to new values—that is the most terrifying assumption for a reverent spirit that would bear much."[78]

DURING THE FALL of 1952 Sylvia continued to write long letters to Dick, but he had no idea how badly she was suffering. "Irony it is to see Dick raised, lifted to the pinnacles of irresponsibility to anything but care of his body—to feel his mind soaring, reaching," she wrote in her journal that November, "and mine caged, crying, impotent, self-reviling, an imposter."[79] Dick, in his illness, was free to pursue his literary interests in quiet solitude, without stigma. She, in her "health," was overwhelmed with work and near the breaking point. She smothered her resentment by sending Dick cheerful letters and packages of books she wished *she* could read. While she spent ten hours a week studying science, Dick wrote her detailed critiques of F. O. Matthiessen's *The Achievement of T. S. Eliot*.

Dick thought his literary studies brought them closer together—"I now feel more able to meet and talk with you than ever before"—but Sylvia resented the annexation of her territory, which he had heretofore been quick to dismiss.[80] She never forgot that he had once compared a poem to a speck of dust—a quote she memorialized in *The Bell Jar*. She may have preferred the old letters about blood tests and pathology clinics to this onslaught of amateur literary criticism. Sylvia had felt conflicted about turning down a marriage proposal from a Harvard-trained doctor. But now Dick wanted to be a writer. He sent her half-baked stories and poems, and a four-page paper on her own work, titled "Individualism and Sylvia Plath: An Analysis and Synthesis." He asked if he could "edit and publish" her letters as "a boon for the literary world."[81] She pretended to be flattered, but she sensed a threat. Did he expect to achieve *her* goals while she cooked him steak dinners? For her, Dick's about-face was as offensive as it was disorienting. He had no sense of the rift he sowed with each manuscript he sent her way.

The worst depressive crisis of Sylvia's life to date was punctuated, sometimes daily, by Dick's relaxed letters, which offered, as she would later write in "Tulips," a tantalizing vision of "a land far away as health." His descriptions of the calm pace of the sanatorium, which he compared to a mental hospital without locks, may have made her think more seriously about psychiatric treatment; she broached the subject for the first time with Aurelia in November.

Sylvia felt her depression recede over Thanksgiving, when she was finally able to rest in Wellesley. (She thanked Aurelia for letting her "loaf so scandalously.")[82] Cheered by a handwritten rejection from *The New Yorker* and praise from Professor Patch, she felt that she had the stamina to endure three more weeks until Christmas vacation. But it was Myron Lotz, Perry's Yale roommate, who roused her most. She met him at the Nortons' house one evening over Thanksgiving break, and was instantly captivated. She told Warren she had never "been so immediately attracted to anyone" as when

Myron stood up from the Nortons' couch and shook her hand.[83] He was tall and handsome, with an intriguing background.[84] His parents were Austro-Hungarian immigrants; his father, she told Warren, worked in a steel mill, and Myron had grown up in a rough neighborhood "with negroes, immigrants, and all kinds of people."[85] But he had defied all expectations: he was first in his class at Yale and planned to graduate in three years. He would then go on to Yale medical school. "Both of us have been so damn lucky in life." She compared his odd jobs on road crews to her own "good hard labor" at Lookout Farm.[86] "Did you ever hear of such a phenomenal character?" she asked Warren.[87]

Sylvia had fallen for both Dick and Perry, and now she was in love with Perry's college roommate. All three relationships had begun in the Nortons' living room. In the absence of a father, the Norton boys offered fraternal protection. But this desire for security competed with a penchant for eastern European refugees like Ilo Pill and Attila Kassay, who connected her, vaguely, to Otto's old-world origins. Myron was both a Norton by proxy *and* an eastern European. She arranged for him to accompany her to the Lawrence House dance the weekend of December 13. "Keep your fingers crossed that my beautiful intellectual charm will captivate the brilliant lug," she wrote to Warren.[88] When Sylvia told Dick she was dating Myron, he absorbed the news with gentlemanly equanimity, telling her that men who were "kind" to her made him grateful rather than jealous.[89] They both knew better.

She spent her first date with Myron driving around the countryside, then back to campus, where they took a long walk to the mental hospital and listened "to the people screaming." "It was a most terrifying holy experience," Sylvia told her mother, "with the sun setting red and cold over the black hills, and the inhuman echoing howls coming from the barred windows. (I want so badly to <u>learn</u> about <u>why</u> and <u>how</u> people cross the borderline between sanity & insanity!)"[90]

The next day, when Myron asked Sylvia to show him something she had written, she "calmly walked into the store and picked up a copy of <u>Seventeen</u>." It was a moment she had dreamed about, and he was duly impressed. They took a long walk into the countryside, where they spotted an airplane landing at a small airport. When they hiked over to get a closer look, the pilot offered to take Sylvia up in the air. She agreed.

I <u>didn't</u> <u>believe</u> we would go up, but then, suddenly, the ground dropped away, and the trees and hills fell away, and I was in a small glass-windowed box with a handsome mysterious pilot, winging over Northampton, Holyoke, Amherst, watching the small square, rectangular colored fields,

the toy houses, and the great winding gleaming length of the Connecticut river. "I am going to do a wing-over," he said, and suddenly the river
was over my head, and the mountains went reeling up into the sky, and
the clouds floated below. We tilted rightside up again. Never have I felt
such ecstasy! I yelled above the roar of the motor that it was better than
God, religion, than anything, and he laughed & said he knew.[91]

The pilot let Sylvia take the joystick, and she made the plane "climb and tilt"
before they landed. She never forgot the "ecstasy" of that flight; its images of
transcendence infused her poems years later.

After Myron left Smith, Sylvia came down to earth. On December 15, she
checked herself into the infirmary on account of insomnia, and finally saw the
college psychiatrist, Dr. Marion Booth—ostensibly about her science course.
She soon traveled home for her Christmas vacation, which comprised a
whirlwind of visits—Mrs. Prouty, the Cantors, Phil McCurdy, John Hodges,
and, of course, the Nortons. On Boxing Day, Sylvia traveled by train to Saranac Lake with Dick. The visit was fraught with tension.[92] Because of Dick's
illness, they could not kiss, which made it easier for her to hide her unease. She
still felt too guilty to end the relationship as she had planned, and the two simply avoided any discussion about the future. Dick wrote to her, after the visit,
that he told a friend, "I-was-fond-of-Sylvia-but-don't-know-how-she-feels."[93]

Plath based her short story "In the Mountains," published in the *Smith
Review* Fall 1954 issue, on that visit. In the story, Isobel, who no longer feels
passion for Austin, realizes she must end their relationship before she leaves
the sanatorium. The story ends with echoes of Hemingway as Austin prepares to propose to her: "Stricken, she did not move. . . . There was no wind
at all and it was hushed and still."[94]

Plath revised this story in 1955 as "The Christmas Heart," and gave it
a more sentimental ending. Sheila (formerly Isobel) realizes that Michael
(formerly Austin) has matured and grown tender during his time at the sanatorium. No longer is he "remote and self-sufficient"; and just as she has
found the confidence to embrace her own identity in Michael's absence—
shortcomings and all—so too has he embraced his weaknesses. Sheila is so
moved by his transformation that she falls in love with him again at the story's end. Plath's revised, happy ending was calculated to appeal to the wom-
en's magazine market; she instructed Aurelia to submit the story to *McCall's,
Woman's Home Companion, Good Housekeeping, Woman's Day*, and *Every-
woman's* in 1956. All presumably turned it down, as the story was never published. It is possible that Dick's increasing tenderness, similar to Michael's,
thwarted Sylvia's plans to extricate herself:

"I needed you," he confessed quite low. "I needed you very badly."

"Is that so very terrible to you, Michael?"

"No, not any more." He hesitated, then said quietly. "It is unfortunate that I can't kiss you. I need to love you now. I always will."

He put his face into the hollow between her neck and shoulder, blinding himself with her hair, and she could feel the sudden wet scalding of his tears.[95]

On December 27, Sylvia and Dick set out for nearby Mount Pisgah. It was not Sylvia's first time on skis, but she was still a beginner. "Obviously I was learning how to ski," she wrote to Myron in January. "Gaily I plummeted down straight (I hadn't learned to steer yet.) There was a sudden brief eternity of actually leaving the ground, cartwheeling (to the tune of 'You Belong to Me' blaring from the lodge loudspeaker) and plowing face first into a drift. I got up, grinned, and started to walk away. No good."[96] Plath, who had broken her fibula, would later attach great aesthetic and psychological significance to a similar scene in *The Bell Jar*, which she embellished with Nietzschean symbolism and likened to a Freudian death wish. Her own behavior may have been reckless, but the run down a small beginner's hill served by a rope tow could not have been—in practical terms—a suicide attempt. She made light of the fall in a telegram meant to soothe her anxious mother:

BREAK BREAK BREAK ON THE COLD WHITE SLOPES OH KNEE ARRIVING FRAMINGHAM TUESDAY NIGHT 7:41. BRINGING FABULOUS FRACTURED FIBULA NO PAIN JUST TRICKY TO MANIPULATE WHILE CHARLESTONING. ANYTHING TO PROLONG VACATION.... MUCH LOVE. YOUR FRACTIOUS FUGACIOUS FRANGIBLE

SIVVY[97]

Later, Dick described her departure from Saranac Lake with prescient poignancy: "You smiled weakly out over crutches, through steam, across snow, beyond trees, over frozen lakes, and disappeared."[98]

———

AURELIA WANTED SYLVIA to recuperate in Wellesley, but she refused, saying she would only be "languishing in sadness at home."[99] She returned to Smith in early January. At first, she worried that being "shut-in" in her room would make her feel imprisoned, and that Myron would lose interest in a "lame girl." She cried when Aurelia dropped her off, though she later apologized for making "such a fuss by being a baby."[100] She willed herself to abandon self-pity. "All in all," she wrote Aurelia, "my leg has made me realize what a fool I was to think I had insurmountable troubles. . . . now that I see how foolish I was in succumbing to what I thought were mental obstacles, I am determined to be as cheerful and constructive about my mental difficulties as I am going to be about my physical one."

Indeed, a physical ailment provided her with a concrete challenge that she could overcome, unlike her "mental difficulties." She knew she could impress others with her grit and courage. "Naturally I will be a bit depressed and blue at times, and tired and uncomfortable, but there is that human principle which always finds that no matter how much is taken away, some-thing is left to build again with."[101] Plath always clung to this principle—the symbolic transformation from winter to spring—in her life and her art. Even in her poem "Edge," so often interpreted as a suicide note, Plath moves from a dead body to a garden.

That January in her journal she "chalked up" her previous November depression to her new living situation, her science course, and Dick's tuber-culosis. Now that those things were behind her, and Myron was ahead, she could once again be the "cheerful, gay, friendly person that I really am inside."[102] She believed in her healthier self. She even valued the "small delights" of being stuck in her room with a broken leg: "a clear winter sun-set through the natural iron grillwork of black trees, a street lamp shining through ice-encased branches, blue sky glittering, and sun on ice-encrusted snow. Loveliness, loveliness."[103] She was carried onward by a burst of positive energy she had not experienced in several months, writing papers on *Piers Plowman* and the Holy Grail, "exercising like mad," reading *The New Yorker*, and studying for her exams. She hoped to win a coveted summer internship as a guest editor at *Mademoiselle* magazine in Manhattan, and worked hard on the trial assignments the magazine required as part of the application.[104] She was getting along better with her roommate, Mary. She came to feel that her broken leg had, ironically, widened her social circle: the women in her house were much more solicitous of her, and she had made several new friends. Above all, she looked forward to spring. "To come, and the bicycle be brought out, and the again strong legs to pedal joyous and swiftly into the green, unfolding future!"[105]

Eddie Cohen was skeptical. "I intend to nag you on the subject of a psy-chiatrist until you are at the point of tossing something other than bouquets in my direction . . . if need be, I shall fly out there and seize you by your pretty hair and drag you, cave-man style, into the office of the nearest available witch-doctor." He joked perceptively that Sylvia had broken her leg on purpose. "Incidentally, you are going to be a mighty maimed sort of person if you make a habit of substituting broken legs and other forms of violence for the colds which have been your psychological catharsis in the past."[106]

In late January Sylvia learned that she had finally gained permission to audit her science requirement for the rest of the year. With science out of the way, she could take a course on Milton, the second half of Robert Gorham Davis's creative writing class (Techniques of Fiction and Criticism), and Elizabeth Drew's Modern Poetry unit. She also audited another class with Drew that spring, Twentieth Century British Literature: Joyce, Yeats, Eliot. She opted for a second semester in medieval literature with Patch, who gave her his undivided attention at a Lawrence House dinner that month. He told her "all smith [sic] girls he knew were beautiful, compared to the other women's colleges he'd taught in."[107] His breezy sexism barely registered. On the day she finished with science, she bought an edition of Auden's poems and James Frazer's *The Golden Bough*. She was eager to earn all A's and show the college administration she deserved her scholarship.

She had good reason to be optimistic. In the fall she had received all A's, and was astonished to discover that she had received a higher grade in science (A) than she had in her creative writing course (A-). The news was welcome but troubling. How had she aced the course that had sent her into a vortex of suicidal despair? Eddie had deduced that she was perfectly capable of mastering physics and chemistry, and that she had made the science course the scapegoat for her deteriorating mental state. Her bouts of depression were tolerable if she had a reason for them. The alternative—that her affliction was completely out of her control—was too terrible to contemplate.

At Ray Brook, Dick became more despondent as he absorbed the reality of his prolonged recovery, which could take another ten months, depending on test results. "I despair of seeing you for months or even years—there being no forecast or planned meeting around which I can place thoughts and descriptions for you."[108] Sylvia felt sorry for him and continued to write, but she focused on her work and her social life: there were papers on medieval literature, Milton, Thomas Carlyle, Gerard Manley Hopkins, T. S. Eliot, W. B. Yeats, John Crowe Ransom; dates with Myron; coffee with Professor Chase; plays (*The Importance of Being Earnest*) and dinners with Marcia. She was no longer tormented by indecision over her future with Dick, which she summed up tersely in her journal: "I saw Dick, went to Saranac with him, and broke my leg skiing. I decided again that I could never live with him ever."[109] She felt liberated now that she no longer needed to "measure up to what I thought were his standards." His sickness repelled her: his mouth now seemed "poisonous" and "unclean." The sexual attraction that had kept them together for so long was gone, and yet Dick doggedly assumed that she still wanted to realign "the you and me toward the us."[110]

Sylvia made a tentative attempt to end things. She told him that their separation prevented them from having a real relationship—letters were no substitute—and hinted that she could not marry a man who would not be "self-supporting" for several more years. Dick conceded that she was right—he would not be able to go back to Harvard Medical School for at least another year. This truth depressed him most. "You have actually spoiled me, Syl, because when I ask myself if such-and-such a girl is attractive or gives satisfaction of the order and fullness that you do, the answer is invariably NO."[111] He sent her a poem about his "state of mind" that January after he learned that he would remain in the sanatorium for several more months. So much time away from his "girl" "Cuts off hope at the root / Stops jubilant creative living."[112]

In her journal Sylvia admonished herself for envying Dick's freedom; she knew quite well the sanatorium was no "Garden of Eden."[113] Negativity and self-pity were not options for the Plaths or the Nortons, yet Dick could no longer wear the bright mask of optimism. He knew he should cut Sylvia loose and continued to ask her to be honest with him about her feelings, but she could not bring herself to do so.[114] When he invited her to visit him again in February, she concocted an excuse about having to stay at Smith for Rally Day. She sent a polite letter to Mildred Norton explaining why she could not accompany them north, which she quoted verbatim to Aurelia, adding, "I am becoming an expert in the polite expedient white lie."[115] Sylvia was now completely open with Aurelia about her waning feelings for Dick. When she told her mother that Dick's old Harvard roommate was still serious about her friend Carol Pierson, she joked that she'd be happy if "Dick & I were responsible for a happy marriage . . . someone else's!"[116]

Dick's letters seemed to confirm that she had made the right decision. In late January, he wrote to her about his dislike of Virginia Woolf—symbolic proof, to her, that they would never marry. He had read *To the Lighthouse* and was baffled by Woolf's "mile-long sentences." He even typed out an entire paragraph from the novel, pointing out its flaws. He felt Mrs. Ramsay's "irritation" toward her husband was unfair since she was "basically such a little child."[117] He even noticed the "striking similarities" between the Ramsays and Henry and Elizabeth in "Sunday at the Mintons," asking Sylvia if she had read *To the Lighthouse* before she wrote her story. Not realizing that Henry was based on *him*, he quoted a Woolf sentence he thought had influenced Plath's portrayal of Henry and Elizabeth: "She set her clean canvas firmly upon the easel, as a barrier, frail, but she hoped sufficiently substantial to ward off Mr. Ramsay and his exactingness."[118] Sylvia's greatest fears about marriage to Dick were embedded in that sentence; she responded with a polite but firm letter about Woolf's genius implying that Dick simply did not understand stream-of-consciousness narrative.

Myron was the new god. "If I could build an ideal and creative life with him, or someone like him, I would feel I had lived a testimony of constructive faith in a hell of a world," she wrote in her journal.[119] He had dropped by to visit her at Smith unexpectedly in late January and asked her to the Yale junior prom in March, the most prestigious college event on the Smith social calendar. She was awhirl with plans and wanted to "look absolutely gorgeous"; she would "live in an ecstasy of anticipation" for the next six weeks. Her broken leg hardly bothered her now. In fact, she had "proved that a broken leg need not handicap a resourceful woman," she wrote Aurelia. "Oh, mummy, I am so happy. If a hideous snowy winter, with midyears and a broken leg is heaven, what will the green young spring be like?"[120]

In early February she attended a lecture by Theodore Greene on "Protestantism in an Age of Uncertainty." She was about to enter Lawrence House, pondering the relationship between philosophy and religion, when a friend told her there was a man waiting to see her in the living room. Sylvia, "Completely nonplussed," rushed up the back stairs, changed into a more flattering red sweater and skirt, and came downstairs to find "the most handsome, tall, lean, curly brown-haired boy." His name was Gordon Lameyer, an Amherst senior majoring in honors English. "What did this god want with me?" Sylvia asked Aurelia. Gordon introduced himself and told Sylvia his mother had suggested he call on her after hearing her speak at Wellesley's Smith Club.

They had what Sylvia called "an instinctive 'rapport' "—both were from Wellesley, both Unitarians with German fathers, and both shared a passion for literature and Chatham summers. He asked her out that weekend. When he left, a group of girls crowded around Sylvia, asking, "Who was _he_!"[121] She had not heard from Myron since he asked her to the prom, and the silence had affected her mood. (She would soon receive a five-page letter from him full of "God and the universe.")[122] Now she could hardly believe "the peculiar workings of chance, dropping lovely English-majoring Amherst seniors from the sky at exactly the right psychological moment!"[123]

She spent her first date with Gordon, a James Joyce "fanatic," talking about Joyce in his Amherst room as the fire roared. She had been auditing a Joyce unit that included *A Portrait of the Artist as a Young Man* and *Ulysses*, and was considering writing her senior thesis on *Ulysses*, which she called "unbelievably semantically big, great, mind cracking, and even webster's [*sic*] is a sterile impotent eunuch as far as conceiving words goes."[124] Their conversation made her all the more determined to write her thesis on the great

Irish modernist. She received another letter and postcard from Myron, and decided to ask him to Rally Day. She now had two handsome, brilliant men interested in her (three, if one still counted Dick), and her spirits ascended. Male attention, like publication, saved her from despondency and seemed to confirm her sense of self-worth. Marcia thought Sylvia's dating habits had to do with her own insecurities as a gifted woman. "She needed to be reinforced in this way. That even though she kept winning prizes and getting poems accepted and getting A's, she was still perfectly all right as a female."[125]

In the end, Sylvia called February the "Black Month"—Myron canceled his visit at the last minute, and when her cast came off, on February 19, she learned that her leg had not completely healed. The "hairy yellow withered corpse" finally released from its "coffin" repulsed her: "I felt like hell: took a razor and sheared off the worst of the black stubble and the skin of course is all coming off and raw, my ankle is swollen and blackish green, and my muscles have shriveled away to nothing."[126] The leg seemed to symbolize the rotten pestilence within her that fall. She began to consider the themes of doubleness that would animate her senior thesis and later poems such as "In Plaster."

To distract herself from her "helpless misery" she turned to poetry. On February 20 and 21, she wrote three villanelles: "To Eva Descending the Stair," "Doomsday," and "Mad Girl's Love Song." The villanelle was an elaborate French form she had rarely tried, but practicing it made her "feel a good deal better." She was so pleased with the results that she sent the poems "blindly" off to *The Atlantic* and *The New Yorker*.[127] (All three would appear in the *Smith Review* that spring.) "I am getting more proficient with the singing uncrowded lyric line, instead of the static adjectival smothered thought I am usually guilty of," she wrote her mother.[128] Writing in form was an orderly, restorative exercise. "Life is so difficult and tedious I could cry. But I won't: I'll just keep writing villanelles."[129]

"Mad Girl's Love Song" was, she said, "inspired by one myron lotz [*sic*]." Her style is typical of the time: "I shut my eyes and all the world drops dead; / I lift my lids and all is born again. / (I think I made you up inside my head.)" The speaker dreams her lover bewitches her "into bed," kisses her "quite insane," but never returns. Plath ends the poem, "I should have loved a thunder-bird instead: / At least when spring comes they roar back again. / I shut my eyes and all the world drops dead. / (I think I made you up inside my head.)"[130] Yeats's "The Song of Wandering Aengus" is the thematic—if not stylistic—influence here. Unrequited love was a major theme of Plath's Smith poems, as was the passage of time. In "Doomsday," she experiments with hard *k* consonants in an apocalyptic villanelle: "The idiot bird leaps out and drunken leans / Atop the broken universal clock: / The hour is crowded in lunatic thirteens."[131] Much of her diction from this time, though, is still genteel: in "To Eva Descending the Stair," she wrote, "Clocks cry: stillness is a lie, my dear; / The wheels revolve, the universe keeps running. / Proud you halt upon the spiral stair."[132] The future star poetry critic Helen Vendler (née Hennessy) was so impressed when she read "Mad Girl's Love Song" in 1954 that she wrote to Aurelia, who was a friend of her mother's, calling it "the only decent villanelle in the English language besides Dylan Thomas's 'Do Not Go Gentle Into That Good Night.'" Helen assured Aurelia that Sylvia would "always have a devoted audience" in her. The extraordinary letter was star-crossed; Plath would become the twentieth century's most famous American woman poet, Vendler its most famous woman poetry critic.[133]

Dick began to worry when he started receiving only one letter a week from Sylvia. He wondered if some of her letters had been lost and suggested they start registering their mail with the post office. Sylvia finally told him about Gordon and opened up about her doubts regarding their own future. College was no "way-station for matrimony"—she intended to pursue a career—and her "wound of separation" was "healing." For him it was not; he wrote to her of his loneliness and bitterness, his anxiety about death, and his own doubts about returning to medicine. The muse had departed: he stopped writing creatively and became depressed.

Sylvia reported to Aurelia in February that Dick's letters were now "pathetic."[134] She wanted to be completely honest with him about all her dates, but she knew her honesty would hurt him. In his isolation at the sanatorium, he had come to idealize her. But it wasn't her fault. She felt that she could not tell him her true feelings when he was in such a fragile state, but she did not want to waste her spring vacation visiting him at Ray Brook. She worried that he would "propose" or "try to extort a promise to him" if she saw him in person. "I know as well as I've known for a long time now, deep down, that I could never be happily married to him: physically I want a colossus; hereditarily, I want good sane stock; mentally, I want a man who isn't jealous of my creativity."[135] She felt "a great gulping breath of relief" when she thought of how she had nearly "ruined" her life by marrying Dick.[136] Myron too would have to wait: "graduate school and travel abroad are not going to be stymied by any squalling breastfed brats. I've controlled my sex judiciously, and you don't have to worry about me at all," she told Aurelia. "The consequences of love affairs would stop me from my independent freedom of creative activity, and I don't intend to be stopped."[137]

Plath's ambition to become a great artist guided her through these years of heavy dating. She had set a course, and her literary success boosted her confidence that she need not marry a man who was wrong for her. But untangling herself from the Nortons was difficult. The situation was growing increasingly awkward for Aurelia, too: Dick wrote her frequent letters that began with Thomas Mann and John Locke, and ended with questions about Sylvia's feelings for him. Aurelia replied politely, saying she did not want to meddle, but that her daughter had told her she was "not at all matrimonially minded." She tried to spell things out for Dick as plainly as she could: "I have always found Sivvy to be very honest. Should she hedge now, I am sure it would be because she were afraid of hurting you at a time when it might do you physical harm." She hoped that "no hurt comes to you through us . . . any of us. In my affections you have a place very close to that of my two who come first."[138] Dick found the suggestion that both mother and daughter were trying not to hurt him condescending. "What is hidden from view generally is more dangerous to everybody than the transient discomfort of its discovery," he wrote Aurelia.[139]

Sylvia now felt only "a great pity" and "a sad sort of maternal fondness" for Dick.[140] She finally agreed to accompany Mr. Norton on a three-day visit to Ray Brook at the end of March 1953. She would "get it over with and enjoy the rest of my vacation."[141] She tried to navigate a friendly middle ground, but Dick continued writing her love letters, some of them sexual. He had effectively become her secretary, happy to type out the handwritten manuscripts she sent to him (previously Aurelia's job). By this time Perry had become engaged to Shirley Baldwin, a Middlebury student, after a whirlwind courtship. Sylvia could no longer fantasize about marrying "the other brother."

Dick hoped that Sylvia would spend her summer waitressing in Lake Placid to be close to him, but she had no such intention—she would either work for *Mademoiselle* or attend Harvard Summer School. She began to feel pressure from the Nortons, who, she told her mother, had "no right to assume any concrete promises of plans for the future had been made. Dick was always carefully noncommittal, and so was I."[142] Sylvia was hedging—they had in fact discussed marriage the previous summer. She even contemplated telling Dick's parents that he was not a virgin so she would not look so callous in their eyes. Mr. Norton suspected that the relationship was unraveling. He wrote Dick a searching letter in February, telling him that if there was no real love between him and Sylvia, he should not "pretend," but move on.[143] Mildred Norton was less forgiving.

Meanwhile, Sylvia had found a strapless "silvery" "palish lavendar" dress that she "christened" with Myron—or Mike, as she frequently called him, even though he never went by that name—at the Yale junior prom in early March.[144] She got a pageboy cut, and buckled down on papers about Milton and Sitwell. She and Myron spent weekends together, often driving into the Vermont countryside in his Ford (a situation that worried Aurelia) and reading from his abnormal psychology book. *The New Yorker* had sent her an enthusiastic, handwritten rejection of "Doomsday" encouraging her to try again; the poem had made it to the last round. She knew that she was close to achieving her dream and immediately sent them another villanelle. An acceptance from *The New Yorker*, she wrote Warren, "would crown my life."[145] She vowed to "study the magazine the way I did *Seventeen*." *Seventeen*, in fact, accepted "Sonnet to a Dissembling Spring" in March, while "The Suitcases Are Packed Again" appeared in the magazine that month. Now that she was twenty, she hoped to publish fiction on a regular basis in *Seventeen*. Winning contests had become trite.

Springtime renewed her creative sensibilities, as did the presence of "the great W. H. Auden," who was teaching at Smith that semester. Sylvia first saw him on March 18, when he spoke at chapel. The encounter almost made up for a recent rejection from *The Atlantic*. "He is my conception of the perfect poet: tall, with a big leonine head and a sandy mane of hair, and a lyrically gigantic stride. needless [*sic*] to say he has a wonderfully textured british [*sic*] accent, and I adore him with a big Hero Worship."[146] After hearing Auden, she used her check from the *Springfield Daily News* to buy three "coveted" books: James Joyce's *Dubliners*, Sigmund Freud's *Basic Writings*, and a New Directions anthology. Sylvia worried that Aurelia would "scold" her for spending all her earnings on clothes and books. Although she hoped to earn $200—half her college expenses—as the *Springfield Daily News* correspondent during her senior year, she promised her mother that she would try to sell more writing.[147] To this end, after her late March visit to Ray Brook, she began writing a potboiler for the "True Confessions" market and finished it on April 7.

On the surface, "I Lied for Love"—at fifty-one typed pages, the longest story Plath had ever written—was a conventional morality tale: A farmer's daughter falls for a wealthy boy, bears his baby out of wedlock, and eventually marries her father's trusty farmhand (based on Ilo Pill). The farm girl, who hopes to shed her provincial life by marrying above her station, is predictably punished for her pride and materialism. Plath tried to balance the salacious with the righteous, but the story was too formulaic; besides, Plath was never one for conservative paternalism. In her journal, she admonished herself for writing such a "monstrosity" for "filthy lucre," though she came away from the exercise with a new appreciation for the "good tight plot" of the "Confessions."[148] The story was rejected. Why was it, Sylvia asked Warren, that her serious fiction sold, whereas her attempts at pulp languished in the slush pile? Plath did not yet realize that she was better at ambiguity. The sexist contours of "I Lied for Love" give a sense of the constrictive worldview Plath knew she had to uphold in her "popular" women's stories. It was this worldview she would attempt to demolish, eight years later, in *The Bell Jar*.

Perhaps inspired by Auden's lecture on April 10, Plath followed "I Lied for Love" with several poems: "Dialogue en Route" on April 12, "Parallax" and "Verbal Calisthenics" on April 16 (both dedicated to Enid Epstein), and "Admonition" on April 17. She worked on her *Mademoiselle* guest editor assignments, though she worried that twenty of the most brilliant Smith girls were her competition. She was thrilled to learn that Warren had won a national scholarship to Harvard, and decided to try for a scholarship herself at Harvard Summer School. She would apply to the Elementary Psychology course and Frank O'Connor's creative writing course—her backup plan should she not get the *Mademoiselle* guest editorship. She saw Gordon by chance after an Auden lecture in April, and the two ended up drinking ginger ale and talking "heatedly about James Joyce" and "obscure poets" in Northampton. She still referred to him as the "great God Gordon," "the best looking boy I have ever met," but she was not impressed with his career plans: he intended to become an insurance salesman after a stint in the Navy.[149]

The high point of Plath's 1953 spring semester was Elizabeth Drew's Modern Poetry seminar, which gave her the time and space to wrestle with Yeats, Eliot, Dylan Thomas, John Crowe Ransom, Hart Crane, Marianne Moore, Wallace Stevens, and Auden. She had never felt so engaged. Drew continually circled back to Yeats and Eliot, and Plath's notes suggest that she was inspired by Yeats's symbols—the mask, the tower, the gyre, blood and the moon—which she starred and underlined. Eliot's ideas about the interrelationship between time present and time future, symbolized by the "still point of the turning world" in *Four Quartets*, also excited her greatly. Plath's love and deep knowledge of Yeats, in particular, would help solidify her relationship with Ted Hughes, who shared Yeats's iconoclasm, occult interests, poetic vision, and sense of vocation. Drew's seminar inspired Plath to abandon her plan of studying philosophy or psychology. She knew now that she would "stick to writing."[150]

In April, Sylvia learned that she had been elected to Phi Beta Kappa along with twelve other Smith girls, and that she would be the editor of the *Smith Review* for her senior year—"the one job on campus that I really coveted with all my heart."[151] She got her courage up to invite Auden to dinner at Lawrence House on April 22. Sylvia, Janet Salter, Jane Truslow, and five other house English majors surrounded him at the circular wooden table in the dining hall. "There wasn't a single word about poetry," Janet remembered. "Auden just wanted to talk about current events. Basically it was a very banal conversation. . . . After dinner we went into the living room and Auden stayed a while and we sat around and talked about ordinary sorts of things. But not once did the subject of poetry come up."[152] Jane remembered that Sylvia, in her gushy manner, tried to get Auden to talk about Wallace Stevens, but Auden just questioned the young women about "blind-dating at Smith."[153] Sylvia did not seem disappointed, simply in awe. She saw Auden again a week later, on April 27, when he attended her evening Modern Poetry seminar. Over beer, he read and discussed one of his poems for two hours in Elizabeth Drew's living room, and expounded on Caliban and Ariel, "art and life, the mirror and the sea. God, god, the stature of the man," Plath wrote in her journal.[154] She called the evening "the privilege of my lifetime" and vowed to show him her poems.[155] When she finally did, Enid Epstein accompanied her to his office for moral support. Enid was sure Sylvia "would be discovered," but Auden simply told Sylvia that "she should watch out for her verbs, and that her poetry was very nice. Sylvia, dutifully, went back to her thesaurus to work on her verbs." Enid was "furious" with Auden, but Sylvia seemed to take his "criticism in stride."[156] Sylvia's Smith friend Sue Weller had a different memory. She recalled that Auden told Sylvia her work was gushy, superficial, and full of "froth." Sylvia was deeply hurt, and his words became "engraved" upon her memory.[157] This response did not surprise Sue, who said that Sylvia still complained about a bad grade she had received in her freshman English class during her senior year. Sylvia and Enid heard Dylan Thomas read at Amherst on May 20—presumably a less fraught poetic encounter.

On April 24, 1953, Sylvia learned that *Harper's* had accepted "Doomsday," "To Eva Descending the Stair," and "Go Get the Goodly Squab" for $100. They would appear in the May, September, and November 1954 issues, respectively. It was her first "Professional Acceptance," as she called it, and she boasted to Warren that *Harper's* was on par with *The Atlantic*. "Can't you just hear the critics saying 'Oh, yes, she's been published in Harper's'"—though she assured Aurelia she had not gotten "smug." The success made her all the more determined to scale those "unclimbed Annapurnas," *The New Yorker* and *The Atlantic*. She telegrammed Aurelia and offered the *Harper's* acceptance as a birthday present, dedicating her "triumph" to her mother, her "favorite person in the world."[158]

Three days later, Plath learned that *Mademoiselle* had awarded her second prize in its latest round of guest editor assignments. The news helped dispel her stress over the fifty pages of class papers due by May 20, and gave her hope that she could afford to live in Cambridge while she attended Harvard Summer School. But she blew nearly all her *Harper's* earnings on a black silk shantung dress and jacket, a navy and white pinstripe suit dress, white linen shoes, and a brown linen dress. She called the clothes "sleek and suave and stylish." Her first "professional" publication had inspired her to purchase a wardrobe befitting a professional author: "no more dirndls or baby puffs for me."[159]

As the weather warmed, Sylvia longed to leave the confines of Northampton. In early May, she joined Ray Wunderlich, her old Cape Cod beau, now at Columbia medical school, and another couple ("both very liberal jews") for a weekend in New York. Ray treated Sylvia to her first oysters at a French restaurant, followed by *The Crucible*. They finished the evening at Delmonico's, where they stayed until four in the morning discussing "Communism, racial prejudice and religion." The following day she saw her first opera, *Carmen*, and afterward, Elia Kazan's Broadway production of Tennessee Williams's *Camino Real*, which she called "the most stimulating, thought-provoking, artistic play I've ever seen in my life!"[160] She spent the evening at a Columbia dance with Ray, followed by sherry and *Swan Lake* in his room overlooking the Hudson. They danced and swooned until sunrise. She had not experienced such heady joy since Maureen Buckley's debutante party. Sylvia visited Janet Salter that spring at her family's apartment in Greenwich Village, where they made a pilgrimage to Edna St. Vincent Millay's house.[161]

Sylvia told Dick about her date with Ray because she wanted to be honest about the other men in her life now. But Dick had just come through surgery and was in no mood to hear about her gilded New York weekend. Mildred Norton wrote to update Sylvia on Dick's post-op condition. "He doesn't complain but his days look very grim. . . . Somewhere, some time, if there's justice in this life, he should have the happiest and most rewarding experiences that can come to anyone."[162] Sylvia sensed an admonishment. Shortly afterward, she heard through Perry's friend Bob Modlin that Mildred no longer wanted Sylvia to marry her "precious courageous boy." Apparently, Sylvia wrote in fury, Mildred now considered her a "Selfish Person" because she had abandoned Dick for the summer. Sylvia had also heard that Mildred thought she should contribute to her family's finances instead of going to Harvard Summer School. "As you may imagine," she told Aurelia, "I feel very chilly toward Mrs. Norton, and really don't care if I ever see her again for all the such-like rationalizations she has made about me now that she sees I'm not serious about her Baby."[163]

But Mildred's accusations struck a nerve. Blazing a trail as a woman artist was exhausting, alienating work, and Mrs. Norton had hit on Plath's secret source of shame—she feared that her artistic ambition *was* selfish. After she heard the scuttlebutt, Sylvia applied for a scholarship to Harvard Summer School and wrote to Warren that she hoped Aurelia would not have to contribute any money for his degree: "She is really down to rock bottom, and I gather from her letters that she is having ulcer trouble." She urged her brother to support himself through college and to cook for himself when he was home. Sylvia was now waging a furious campaign to ease her mother's burdens in the face of Mildred's criticisms.

> You know, as I do, and it is a frightening thing, that mother would actually Kill [*sic*] herself for us if we calmly accepted all she wanted to do for us. She is an abnormally altruistic person, and I have realized lately that we have to fight against her selflessness as we would fight against a deadly disease. My ambition is to earn enough so that she won't have to work summers in the future . . . her frailty worries me.
>
> She can't take big problems or excitements without staying awake all night, and so our main responsibility is to give her the illusion (only now it hardly seems like an illusion) that we're happy and successful and independent. After extracting her life blood and care for 20 years, we should start bringing in big dividends of joy for her.[164]

Financial self-sufficiency was easier promised than practiced, however. On the same day she lectured Warren, Sylvia wrote her mother, "PLEASE PUT A GOODLY SUM OF MONEY IN MY CHECKING ACCOUNT AS SOON AS POSSIBLE, AS I AM DOWN TO ONE DOLLAR . . . one hundred dollars would not be amiss."[165] She was also relieved that Aurelia was redecorating: "now I can bring boys home without keeping the lights down very dim and hoping they won't see the spots and tears in the wallpaper."[166]

In letter after letter that May, Sylvia honed her wrath on Mildred Norton: "I just hope that with all her resentful talk about my selfishness in not slaving to be near her son while she runs around Europe won't spoil my tentative and embryonic friendship with Myron." If she were in Dick's place, she went on, Mrs. Norton "would smile sweetly, shake her head, and say that a doctor couldn't risk the liability of a tubercular wife. And she'd also emphasize the fact that he'd never even gone steady with me, but liked me as a 'cousin.' Well, a cousin is all I'll ever be to That [*sic*] family. I really am most disgusted with them."[167]

Thus were the seeds of *The Bell Jar* sown. Sylvia would bear a grudge against Dick and Mildred Norton for the next decade; in the novel, the personal would indeed become political. Why was a woman "selfish" if she wished to spend her summer at *Mademoiselle* and Harvard rather than tending to a sick boyfriend? Plath saw the double standard clearly. She had earned $1,000 from her writing during the previous year, and wrote Aurelia, "I hardly <u>need</u> to stoop to waitressing or fileclerking."[168] She encouraged her mother to try to make money through her own writing for women's magazines and the "True Confessions" market. "I <u>forbid</u> you to work this summer! . . . Between the three of us we'll show the Norton's [*sic*] that we are all paragons of forgiving selflessness."[169]

In early May, Plath finally learned she had won one of the twenty coveted guest editorships at *Mademoiselle*. To Warren she described her joy: "I feel like a collegiate Cinderella whose Fairy Godmother suddenly hopped out of the mailbox and said: 'What is your first woosh?' and I, Cinderella, said: 'New York,' and she winked, waved her pikestaff, and said: 'Woosh granted.'" The stint lasted from June 1 to June 26 and paid $150 minus room and board. After her New York weekend with Ray, she was "excited to death" at the prospect of "4 gala weeks" at the women-only Barbizon Hotel—her first stay in a hotel.[170]

Privately, she was already annoyed by the demands being made on her. In the middle of her exam period, *Mademoiselle* assigned her a two-page spread requiring research on, and interviews with, five young male teacher-poets—Alastair Reid, George Steiner, Anthony Hecht, Richard Wilbur, and William Burford. Sylvia had a hard time finding their books, and *Mademoiselle* offered no help. (She was not able to interview Wilbur.) The assignment, which she finished on May 23, would have been stimulating if it hadn't required a wild goose chase during her exams. Dick proved a surprising ally—he sensed she was being exploited and encouraged her to ask *Mademoiselle* point blank when and how much she would be paid for the work. (He also agreed with her that his mother had no right to call her selfish.) She told the magazine she wanted to interview J. D. Salinger, Shirley Jackson, E. B. White, or Irwin Shaw. None of these requests was granted. She was assigned to interview Elizabeth Bowen at May Sarton's house in Cambridge on May 26, only a week before her Milton exam. She began reading Bowen novels at a furious pace, and complained about the timing to Warren and Dick; she also had two long stories due that week for the Press Board.

The news, in late May, that she had won two Smith poetry prizes (the Ethel Olin Corbin Prize and the Elizabeth Babcock Poetry Prize, for which she earned $120), should have pleased her. But she was tired and "harassed"; she wrote in her journal about feeling "very banal, very confused," and twice mentioned the idea of suicide.[171] Janet suspected a reason for Sylvia's darkening mood. On the last day of class that May, Robert Gorham Davis had given them some unwelcome advice as they departed: "He said he hoped none of us was going to be a writer because women writers are frequently very unhappy. This was a creative writing class where we had thought he took us seriously, and then to make that kind of statement was really devastating. I don't know how many other people experienced writers' block after that, but I certainly decided I was never going to be a fiction writer because I didn't want to be depressed. . . . Sylvia and I went back to our dormitory from that last statement and we were absolutely furious. And somewhat dazed."[172]

Janet speculated that these discouraging, sexist comments may have been a root cause of the writing block that exacerbated Sylvia's suicidal depression that August. They certainly suggest a cause for her unhappiness in May, before she went to New York. Indeed, Davis's words cut to the core of the conflict Plath faced in her young life: to heed her calling and become a great writer in a society that discouraged women from fulfilling their artistic ambitions. Plath's sense of vocation was uncommonly strong, yet such a comment from her male writing mentor reinforced the message that literary greatness was for men only; women need not apply.

Dick became worried, and offered the kind of perceptive advice that normally came from Eddie Cohen:

> You give every indication of being frightfully busy. . . . Time, you say, is in danger of pressing you back, flooding on and on and drowning you quite completely. Never a moment's rest, and always the imminence of Things to Do. Poor girl, I think you are crowded by success. For God's sake take it easy in NYC, come in by 1:00, stay moderately sober, EAT FOOD FREQUENTLY, or mark my words you'll be sick as a dog during or after. Have a good time, sivvy, of course, but take it easy.[173]

Sylvia would ignore Dick's words. She was going to New York to build a new life that did not include him. She would shed the Nortons and their conservative worldview at dances, bars, fashion shows, and cocktail parties. But such disjunction soon left Plath grasping for solidity in a city where virtue seemed but "the illusion of a Greek necessity."[174]

10

My Mind Will Split Open

Manhattan, June 1953

One of the most memorable scenes in *The Bell Jar* occurs midway through the novel, on the night before Esther Greenwood leaves New York. "Quiet as a burglar," she ascends the stairs to the roof of the Amazon Hotel just before dawn, carrying the silken sheaths and satin slips she has worn all month long in the heat. Slowly, she walks to the edge of the parapet. "Piece by piece, I fed my wardrobe to the night wind, and flutteringly, like a loved one's ashes, the gray scraps were ferried off, to settle here, there, exactly where I would never know, in the dark heart of New York."[1]

Esther's gesture was a small but aesthetically powerful protest against the phoniness of everything she had experienced that month: the worldly, uncaring men; the endless copy about lipstick and perfume; the hired dates at the magazine's ball; the poisoned luncheon at the advertising agency. There is an echo, in her reference to Joseph Conrad, of a failed pilgrimage.

During her month in Manhattan, Sylvia learned that everyone was selling something, and everything had a price. New York's fashion industry was the antithesis of Smith's austere intellectualism. Here, Professor Patch's fireside seminars and Elizabeth Drew's evening poetry discussions seemed quaint. She had imagined meeting Dylan Thomas, editing manuscripts, and attending poetry readings in Greenwich Village. Yet most of her days were filled with efforts to sell a magazine that was effectively one large advertisement. During her four weeks at *Mademoiselle*, Sylvia came to feel repulsed by the fashion industry, consumer culture, and New York City itself. Marcia Brown said Sylvia told her that "she'd met a whole lot of people she felt were phonies—really phonies—phony through and through, and that were opportunistic, exploitative, thoroughly nasty human beings with no intact integrity. The business of confusing night with day and right from wrong and good from bad had really shaken her."[2] The story of Plath's disillusion would shape the first half of *The Bell Jar:* in a 1962 progress report for the novel to the Eugene F. Saxton Memorial Trust, Plath wrote that Esther Greenwood was "beginning to crack under the pressures of the fashion magazine world which seems increasingly superficial and artificial. She is unable to connect with her destiny, or even to imagine it."[3]

A *Mademoiselle* guest editor position came with tremendous prestige. Offered annually to just twenty college students, it was one of the few literary internships available to women in the 1950s. (Most of the young women who lived alongside Plath that summer at the Barbizon Hotel were attending Katharine Gibbs secretarial school—a fate she dreaded.) Sylvia had begun dreaming about the internship in November 1952, when she attended a talk at Smith by a representative from the magazine. After she won a spot, *Mademoiselle* sent her a promotional primer on the magazine's history. Founded in 1935, it was the only American magazine that catered exclusively to "smart young women" in "the 18-to-30 age group with above average education and taste." By 1953, *Mademoiselle* was indeed recognized as the thinking women's magazine: 79 percent of its half-million readers had a college background. There were nods to sexual equality—it was the first magazine to publish a "Jobs and Futures" department where "the career girl" could search for advice, and nearly all of its senior staff members were women. Later, the magazine would publish Betty Friedan and Gloria Steinem. But in 1953, *Mademoiselle* considered itself a pioneer in other areas. Among its "long and impressive list" of firsts, Plath read the following in its promotional primer:

> "MLLE was the first fashion magazine to <u>state specific prices</u> with every fashion shown, first to tell the reader <u>where to buy</u> it country-wide."

> "MLLE was the first magazine to <u>turn an ugly duckling into a swan</u>, making completely practical application of hitherto theoretical beauty principles."

> "MLLE was the first magazine to make Christmas shopping easier by adding, in December 1940, <u>a shopping-order</u> strip at the side of each gift page."[4]

For all of *Mademoiselle*'s boasting about its literary merits—the magazine published Carson McCullers, Katherine Anne Porter, W. H. Auden, and Truman Capote—its ethos was more in line with *Ladies' Home Journal* than *The New Yorker*. Departments included "Bridal Information, Please,"

"Cooking Hints for Young Housekeepers," and "MLLE's Advance Patterns." Janet Burroway, a 1955 guest editor, remembered *Mademoiselle's* editor in chief, Betsy Talbot Blackwell, "waving her cigarette holder, adjuring us to 'Believe in Pink.'"[5] Laurie Glazer, a guest editor who became friendly with Sylvia that summer, remembered Blackwell saying, "For now, let's put all our sparkle, shall we?, into our fashion copy."[6] Jane Truslow, a 1954 guest editor, regarded these women as "a bunch of clowns." Abels seemed "foggy even then," while Blackwell was "sullen" with a "smoker's cough." Jane could not imagine "taking them seriously or being disillusioned by them subsequently."[7] But Talbot and Abels were two of the most important editors in New York, and Plath took them very seriously indeed.

Nearly all of the bulky, 380-page August 1953 issue of *Mademoiselle*, which Plath edited that June, comprised fashion ads or fashion photo shoots featuring thin white women in expensive, waist-cinching clothes. Apart from a few short features, the issue resembles a catalog. The many ads for tight girdles and cone-shaped bras suggest a throwback to the corsets of the Victorian age and its attendant restrictions. Gone are the loose clothes and androgynous looks of the flapper era, and the bold, military-cut suits of the 1940s. Only a handful of the ads in *Mademoiselle's* August issue featured women wearing pants. One ad for Jantzen showed a tightly girdled young woman playing tennis in what was supposed to be more breathable undergarments ("anyone for beautiful form in action?"). The ads reveal how difficult it was for women of this era simply to *move*.

Sylvia had assumed that literary doors would open for her at *Mademoiselle*, but she found herself corralled into fashion editing—the literary equivalent of women's work. Mary Cantwell, who worked at *Mademoiselle* in August 1953, explained the division neatly. She was too shy to approach "real" writers at cocktail parties: "Working for a fashion magazine, however distinguished its fiction, separated me, in my eyes and doubtless in theirs, from the literati."[8] Cantwell remembered her initial contempt for the young *Mademoiselle* staffers who called themselves "writers," yet she soon regarded them with more sympathy. "To survive eight hours of producing 'tangerine linen crossed with a lime-green slice of belt' . . . it is necessary to call it 'writing.'" Sylvia's senior-year Smith roommate, Nancy Hunter Steiner, remembered Sylvia calling her *Mademoiselle* work "artificial and banal."[9] In *The Bell Jar*, Esther thinks, "Fashion blurbs, silver and full of nothing, sent up their fishy bubbles in my brain. They surfaced with a hollow pop."[10]

One of the first letters the new guest editors received reminded them to bring hats and gloves, silks and shantungs, and an evening gown. The novelist Diane Johnson, Sylvia's peer that summer, remembered, "We were to be ladylike, made up, dressed up, and chaperoned as we went into the office each day, hatted of course."[11] They were told to keep to the Upper East Side and to stay away from the "jazzy" joints; the magazine recommended dancing at the Plaza or the St. Regis Hotel and dining at one of the pre-approved Italian, French, Viennese, and German restaurants on the Upper East Side.[12]

Mademoiselle's breezy talk of evening gowns and silk revived Sylvia's class anxieties. Under the stated salary of $150 on her orientation letter, she wrote, "subtract room and board," and she underlined a section on tipping waiters 15 percent and cab drivers 10 percent.[13] On the list of recommended restaurants for guest editors, she put a checkmark next to the cheapest, Hamburger Heaven, which sold burgers for fifty-five cents.[14] She underlined another section that reminded guest editors that the magazine would not pay for taxis to appointments or events before ten p.m.[15] No matter—she would walk.

———

SYLVIA ARRIVED at Grand Central Station on May 31, 1953. Two "muscular" soldiers carried her bags, called her a taxi in the "predatory crowd," and escorted her all the way to the lobby of the Barbizon Hotel. She told her mother she was "touched" by the soldiers' chivalry, though the gesture underscored the assumption that unchaperoned women needed protection in New York.[16]

As did the Barbizon itself. Located on the Upper East Side, on the corner of Lexington Avenue and 63rd Street, the seven-hundred-room hotel was a way station for ambitious young women. Opened at the height of the Jazz Age in 1927, it was supposed to function *in loco parentis*—there were curfews and sign-in sheets, and no men were allowed past the ground floor. The Barbizon was not the only hotel for women in New York City, but it was the most exclusive. One needed three letters of recommendation to secure a room, and even then prospective tenants were screened for appropriate dress and manners. The hotel promoted itself as the glamorous home of Ford models and movie stars like Grace Kelly, but most of its guests hailed from small towns and cities. The building's style pleased anxious parents and their young, freedom-seeking daughters: with its towering twenty-three stories, coral façade, Moorish curves, and Romanesque columns, it appeared both commanding and exotic. Inside there was a swimming pool, library, squash courts, recital rooms, a formal dining room, sun deck, and solarium. Delicate finger sandwiches were served at afternoon tea each day, and a social director organized bridge and backgammon tournaments. As one observer wrote,

"The hotel had the feel of a particularly luxe convent, which was hardly accidental. The expansive lobby, accented by potted ferns, Oriental carpets, and antique English lanterns, contained a sweeping staircase that led to the mezzanine, from which girls could peer down over latticed-wood railings to evaluate prospective dates below."[17]

Sylvia called the hotel "exquisite" and gushed with childlike enthusiasm about the elevator ride.[18] Her small, single room—1511—was on the fifteenth floor, with green carpet and beige walls, a dark green bedspread, and matching curtains. There was a desk, dresser, radio, telephone, and small sink. Shared bathrooms were down the hall, and there was no air conditioning. Plath would leave her windows open all day and night in what turned out to be one of the hottest summers in New York City's history. (Some of the guest editors that summer recalled that they "sat around in the nude hoping for drafts.")[19] The view impressed her more than the room: "From my window I look down into gardens, alleys, to the rumbling 3rd Avenue El, down to the UN, with a snatch of the east [sic] River in between buildings!" She relished the novelty of blaring horns, which she described to Aurelia as "the sweetest music."[20] They reminded her how far she had come from Wellesley, even though her room was next to that of Laurie Totten, who lived only two blocks away from Sylvia's home. Laurie had visited Elmwood Road two weeks before when she learned Sylvia had also won a guest editorship. They sat on Sylvia's bed talking whimsically about their ambitions as summer light streamed into the second-floor windows—two brainy young women enjoying their success before anything was demanded of them.[21]

Sylvia met the other guest editors that first night in Grace MacLeod's room, where they spoke about colleges and jobs.[22] The young women hailed from a diverse set of colleges. Barnard, Smith, and Bryn Mawr sent students, while Janet Wagner, who showed up in a long, floral-patterned "granny dress," was from Knox College in Illinois. She thought Plath looked down on her for her midwestern accent, and she called Sylvia "an Ivy League snob." Janet was not the only one who felt this way. Another guest editor from that year, Neva Nelson, felt that Sylvia assumed an aura of "Ivy League superiority" over the women from the small colleges.[23]

Sylvia had intended to wear a new suit on her first day, but a sudden nosebleed wrecked her blouse. She worried that the brown linen dress she changed into did not look professional, but her sartorial anxiety receded as she took the elevator up to the sixth floor of 575 Madison Avenue. There, she spent the day meeting various editors, including Rita Smith, Carson McCullers's sister. After Betsy Talbot Blackwell introduced "the girls" and doled out schedules for the rest of the day, the group broke for coffee. Everyone took the elevator to the downstairs lobby, "talking and laughing," Neva recalled, "to relieve the built-up tension."[24] After the break, Sylvia joined Neva in the elevator back up to the office. The two began gossiping about Blackwell—or "BTB," as she was known—and some of the other editors. Sylvia called them "a motley crew," while Neva compared Blackwell, with her fair skin and freckled arms, to an "Irish washerwoman."[25] Neva heard "a snicker" from some of the others behind them in the elevator and instantly realized her mistake.[26]

Neva and Sylvia were soon summoned to Blackwell's office, where they received a dressing down. "She seemed to be quite upset that we would be so ungrateful to say such hurtful things about her and the other editors and to say them publicly on an elevator was just not acceptable," Neva recalled.[27] Blackwell told Neva she had been against her winning a position from the beginning, and told Sylvia the only reason she won the contest was because Aurelia had sent Cyrilly Abels so many well-trained secretaries over the years. She even suggested that Aurelia had done Sylvia's assignments for her before ushering the shaken girls out of her office. "Sylvia wasn't given the chance to stand up for herself, leaving it open as to whether she'd done the work herself or not," Neva said. "We both just sat there like mute, chastised children until we were dismissed."[28] The two ran to the bathroom and sobbed. Neva did not think Blackwell was responsible for Sylvia's breakdown that August, but, she said, "we did leave that room with our self-esteem greatly diminished"; she felt Blackwell's "harsh evaluation" "drove" Plath to prove her wrong.[29] Many of Sylvia's peers agreed that she was the hardest-working guest editor that summer. Laurie Glazer thought Plath "one of the most driven women I ever knew. We were all ahead of ourselves for the era—feminists, though we didn't recognize the word."[30] Diane Johnson would credit Plath for inspiring her to take her writing more seriously, and to adopt the habits of a professional writer. "It was, in fact, the example of 'Sunday at the Mintons,' Sylvia Plath's winning story in the guest editor contest, that made that point to me and changed my life," Johnson later wrote.[31]

Neva and Sylvia were still crying in the bathroom when they were called for a photo shoot with Herman Landshoff for a "Jobiographies" feature. They got themselves "under control," then walked together to the photographer's studio, where the photo props were supposed to represent their career ambitions. When Sylvia said she wanted to be a poet, Landshoff sat her down on a sofa next to a bowl of fruit and handed her a rose. She managed to subvert the sentimental bric-a-brac: she smiled but held the rose limply, upside down.[32] Plath satirized the photographer's patronizing attitude in *The Bell Jar:* "Come on, give us a smile," he tells a distraught Esther. "Show us how happy it makes you to write a poem."[33] Roses, like the moon, would eventually become an ominous symbol in Plath's poetry. "I can still see the hurt and tears in Sylvia's and my pictures," Neva said, sixty years later.

That afternoon, Plath lunched at the Drake Hotel on Park Avenue with Blackwell and Abels. The meal could not have been relaxing, but she tried to enjoy it. The Drake Room was then one of the swankiest restaurants in Manhattan, with a dazzling belle époque interior and bustling bar. Sylvia, as always, set the scene for Aurelia: "It was thrilling: sat in dark plush room, sipped sherry, plowed through enormous delectable chef's salad, discussed writers, magazines, all sorts of exciting things."[34] Ann Burnside, a fellow guest editor, claimed that Sylvia ate an entire bowl of caviar by herself that afternoon. The story sounds apocryphal, but Plath did write about a similar episode in chapter 3 of *The Bell Jar*, where Esther devours a bowl of caviar by herself at the *Ladies' Day* luncheon. Esther explains her behavior, without apologies, in the context of her class background: "It's not that we hadn't enough to eat at home, it's just that my grandmother always cooked economy joints and economy meat loafs and had the habit of saying, the minute you lifted the first forkful to your mouth, 'I hope you enjoy that, it cost forty-one cents a pound.' "[35] Caviar was freighted with class symbolism for Plath. Her grandfather had given her small, surreptitious tastes in the kitchen of the Brookline Country Club, but she could never get enough. Now she was finally on the other side of the table. Ann felt "shocked and embarrassed" for Sylvia and avoided her for the rest of the month, but Cyrilly Abels was unfazed. Plath finished her teacher-poet assignment back at the office, then returned to the Barbizon, where she unpacked the rest of her clothes and ate a "late, exhausted supper" in the hotel coffee shop.[36]

Her second day went more smoothly. A collegiate fashion show at the Roosevelt Hotel, complete with Princeton a capella singers, delighted her; she found the clothes "exquisite" and "lush." Afterward, there was lunch at Grand Central's Oyster Bar, with its echoing, vaulted interior. So far the "plush" *Mademoiselle* lunches had not disappointed.[37] She began to hope she was shrugging off her first impression. That afternoon she attended a makeover for the guest editors at Richard Hudnut's Fifth Avenue salon, where, she told Aurelia, she "refused drastic cutting" and kept her neat pageboy intact: "still look like me. Alas."[38]

Later that day, Sylvia and the other guest editors proceeded to the *Mademoiselle* conference room, where they donned their uniforms for a group photo: long wool kilts, penny loafers, buttoned-up white blouses, and beanies. Most of them thought these "collegiate" outfits looked ridiculous. The shoot lasted for hours in Central Park in 94° heat. The women cursed and sweltered, as Laurie Glazer Levy remembered, in "prolonged humiliation" while the demanding photographer made them readjust their positions to achieve a perfect star formation.[39] Plath wrote the accompanying catchy copy, which glossed over the day's discomforts: "We're stargazers this season, bewitched by an atmosphere of evening blue. Foremost in the fashion constellation we spot *Mlle*'s own tartan, the astronomic versatility of sweaters, and men, men, men—we've even taken the shirts off their backs!"[40] Plath probably had fun with the caption, but this was not the sort of writing she wished to pursue. A verse from a popular 1950s Smith song captured her dilemma:

> We're ready to wow *Life, Time, Fortune* and Luce.
> We've energy, brains, and when we turn on the juice,
> Our style is so subtle it drives men to tears.
> But we're doing the copy of ads for brassieres.[41]

Mademoiselle had made Plath guest managing editor, one of its most prestigious positions, but she was disappointed she had not been made guest fiction editor, which would have been a more natural fit. Still, she wrote Aurelia that she had resigned herself to the work and now loved it. She was reading manuscripts by Elizabeth Bowen, Noël Coward, and even Dylan Thomas, and boasted that "the other girls just have 'busy work' to do, but I am constantly reading fascinating manuscripts and making little memo comments on them."[42] She even got to sign her own name to rejections. "Sent one to a man on the New Yorker staff today with a perverse sense of poetic justice."[43] In theory, she was getting good experience that would help her as editor in chief of the *Smith Review*. But Plath always preferred writing her own stories to overseeing the writing of others. A week into her internship, she wrote to Dick of her "aversion for fashion magazines."[44]

Plath called Abels "the most brilliant clever woman I have ever known."[45] Abels was a Radcliffe alumna with impressive literary contacts who had singled out "Sunday at the Mintons" for publication. ("Imaginative, well written, certainly superior; hold.")[46] But she was a businesswoman at heart—the "boss of the deadline," as one *Mademoiselle* memo put it.[47] Abels was "not comforting," like Olive Prouty and Val Gendron, but, as Laurie Totten Woolschlager remembered, "blunt" and "irritable."[48] Plath described her as "capable, and heaven knows what else," in her journal.[49] Abels dressed conservatively, in neutral colors, and wore her gray hair pulled up. Mary Cantwell, who worked for Abels at the time, remembered that she kept a box of Kleenex on her desk because she made so many young women cry.[50]

While most of the guest editors worked in a large communal space outside the staff offices ("the bullpen"), Plath worked in Abels's office at a card table. Abels may have thought she was doing Plath a favor by keeping her out of the bullpen and giving her real responsibility, though other guest editors noticed that by the second week of June, Plath seemed overwhelmed by her heavy workload. Such close proximity to her boss, along with the "dirty work" of "'managing'" all copy and deadlines, frayed her nerves.[51] Sylvia confided to Laurie Totten that Abels was "rather hard" on her. "She did overwork her," Laurie recalled. She guessed that Abels "thought she was contributing to her education," but in fact Abels was breaking down Plath's confidence, day by day, with her tough manner.[52] Sylvia was used to hearing only praise from her teachers and professors. Now, her first real boss—a legendary editor who seemed to know every important writer in New York—was criticizing her work. Guest editor Margaret Affleck Clark also recalled that at lunch one day, Sylvia was "upset about things, seemed to think that staff didn't treat us like intelligent people but too much like children."[53]

Guest editor Anne Shawber said that Plath was always in Abels's office "checking copy or rewriting something" while the other guest editors were out having fun. She felt sorry for her. "I don't know why they didn't make her fiction editor.... I had felt all along that Sylvia was in the wrong job, and that *Mademoiselle* had contributed to her breakdown."[54] Carol LeVarn McCabe, the inspiration for Doreen in *The Bell Jar*, also noted that Plath worked more "intensely" with Abels than the other guest editors did with their senior editors.

Laurie Totten was "depressed" when she returned home from New York because she realized she was not "ruthless" enough to make it in the magazine business.[55] She speculated that Sylvia experienced similar disillusion. In 1954, Abels wrote Plath a glowing review for her Fulbright Fellowship, calling her "one of the best young women I have had as a Guest Editor in the eleven years I have been at *Mademoiselle*. She is talented, completely responsible and a very hard and efficient worker."[56] But years later, Abels dismissed Plath. "I never found anyone so unspontaneous so consistently, especially in one so young.... She was simply all façade, too polite, too well brought up and well disciplined."[57] Sylvia, an intimidated subordinate, could hardly have behaved otherwise.

Sylvia spent her first free day in New York roaming the austere, curved galleries of the Museum of Modern Art, pondering the kind of works she had once defended to her mother and Mr. Crockett. She would have just missed an exhibit on German Expressionism and new works by Francis Bacon and Marcel Duchamp. But she probably saw the large exhibit on postwar European photography. There were familiar names like Henri Cartier-Bresson and Robert Doisneau, and less well-known figures such as the Austrian Ernst Haas. Many of the photos were disturbing: famine in India by Werner Bischof; miners in Wales by Robert Frank; returning prisoners of war in Vienna by Haas; war-torn Korea and Cockney London by Bert Hardy. There were abstract and surrealist photos by Italians and Swedes with bold geometric patterns, and haunting compositions by Anker-Spang Larsen and Vilem Kriz—broken, dismembered dolls lying in open fields or caught on barbed wire.[58] The exhibition, which was a testament to those who had risked everything to bear witness through art, was a world away from Madison Avenue.

Plath, whose poems would feature images of starvation, war, and deformity, did not mention this dark exhibit to her mother, but had cheerfully described the art fair she visited at Washington Square Park with Laurie Totten that night.[59] She and Laurie ventured into Central Park on Sunday, where they relaxed on benches and wandered through the zoo. To Aurelia, Sylvia marveled at the many different languages she heard that day. But Laurie remembered that the zoo upset Sylvia, who was "appalled by the conditions, the small cages, and the smell."[60] Sylvia later told Warren that beggars on the subway had reminded her of the zoo's caged animals.[61]

By the second Monday, after a week extolling the "astronomic versatility of sweaters," Plath yearned to return to the citadel of high literature. That was where she belonged, as Elizabeth Bowen reminded her in a warm letter congratulating her on "a brilliant start" to her writing career.[62] Plath had interviewed Bowen, but her copy was cut to a mere paragraph and placed next to a glamorous photo of the two women. An instructional memo suggested that it was the photo that mattered, not the words. ("Be sure to keep remembering that your picture is being taken. Interesting as the conversation is, keep one eye on the photographer so that he can direct you without too much interruption.")[63] Bowen asked Plath to send her more writing, a generous gesture that thrilled and terrified her.

As Sylvia buried herself in fashion copy, Frank O'Connor's creative writing class at Harvard Summer School, which started in July, took on greater significance. She submitted "Sunday at the Mintons" but worried that she would be competing against "professional writers and grown-ups" and prepared herself for the worst: "I'm dubious about getting in, as all people in the U.S. will no doubt try to."[64] Sylvia signed her letter home "your citystruck, sivvy," but her initial enthusiasm for New York had waned. "Life happens so hard and fast I sometimes wonder who is me. I must get to bed."[65] She wanted to be on the Cape, she told Dick, and she wanted to write her own stories.[66] "I just pray I get into the O'Connor course because I want to <u>write</u>

this summer," she wrote Aurelia. "Let me know what you think about my chances, also my determination to have time to really <u>work</u> at writing daily, which I have never done."[67]

Plath wanted to write about New York, yet she could not afford to experience most of it. If only she could meet men who could take her places she "couldn't go alone at night," who would treat her to oysters and champagne.[68] She hoped to find willing candidates at *Mademoiselle*'s guest editor dance, held at the posh St. Regis Hotel on 55th Street and Fifth Avenue on June 10. "Rosy ceiling, painted like sunset sky, pink tablecloths, everything washed with a rose glow and outside the floorlength windows: all the lights of the New York skyscrapers," she wrote Aurelia.[69] Two bands played simultaneously, one sinking as the other rose. There were cocktails on the rooftop deck at sunset, where a photographer captured her with her date and another couple, "daiquiri in hand, big beaming smile of joy on face."[70] The photo showed a young woman in her prime, the toast of New York, living the high life. It would appear in the August 1953 issue of *Mademoiselle*, where readers all over America would see Sylvia Plath looking gorgeous with a handsome beau at her side. ("Mad Girl's Love Song" would also appear in the August issue.) Sylvia fantasized about her name in the caption and wished she could get "the big copy of it, cause it's a great picture of me."[71] It was enough to make her the envy of even the wealthiest Smith girls.

Yet when Plath finally saw the glamorous photo in *Mademoiselle* that August, she would be appalled by its phoniness. The photo resurfaced in *The Bell Jar*: when one of Esther's fellow patients at the mental hospital sees it and makes the connection, Esther says, "No, it's not me. . . . It's somebody else."[72] The photo should have been proof that Sylvia had arrived. Instead, it reminded her that she had become a prop in her own show, her desires stage-managed to sell magazines. Even the admiring young men around her that night were showpieces, clean-cut Ivy Leaguers hired by *Mademoiselle* as escorts. Three weeks after the photo appeared in *Mademoiselle*, Plath tried to kill herself.

But that June, she was still chasing her dreams down Madison Avenue. Three Columbia men vied for her attention at the St. Regis—actors, lyricists, and composers trying to make it in New York. One (the "goodlooking one") asked her out to Jones Beach the following weekend, but canceled because of bad weather. (It rained nearly every weekend that month.) She welcomed the respite after two weeks of nonstop work and socializing. Sketch pad in hand, she walked up and down the steamy avenues of Manhattan, drawing scenes she hoped would inspire her writing. "I will make the most of being off on my own and not sulk in my Barbizon trou," she wrote to Aurelia.[73] She had little choice, since her second *Mademoiselle* check had not yet arrived, and her money had nearly run out. Aurelia sent enough to cover her hotel bill, but she needed to save the rest for her nightly fifty-five-cent hamburger. She could not even afford the bus fare to attend Warren's Exeter graduation. "Money goes like water here," she told her mother.[74]

Her strict budget made her vulnerable to pickup artists like Art Ford, a disc jockey Plath met while stuck in traffic on the way to the ballet. All the guest editors were packed into three taxis, idling in a row. Ford, in a black cowboy hat, tried the first, but Neva Nelson told him to try the car behind them. Sylvia was in that car, along with Carol LeVarn and Laurie Totten. "Too many pretty girls for one taxi," he said as he paid their fare.[75] Carol and Sylvia followed him into a nearby bar, but Laurie stayed in the cab, surprised by Sylvia's "fast" behavior. Yet Laurie admitted that she and Sylvia had drifted apart during the last two weeks of June, and that perhaps she did not know her as well as she thought.[76] Sylvia never mentioned her evening with Art Ford to Laurie afterward. They were all posturing to some extent, all trying to seem sophisticated—except Carol, who gave the impression that she had seen it all before and was not "dewy-eyed."[77] Carol and Sylvia downed a cocktail with Ford, and he invited them to a party in Greenwich Village after he finished his radio show at three a.m. His minor celebrity impressed Plath: he had been written up in *Mademoiselle* "as one of the bright young men in New York," she told Aurelia.[78]

Sylvia and Carol soon made their way to the New York City Ballet at City Center, where they saw Christensen's *Con Amore*, Balanchine's *Scottish Symphony* and *Symphonic Metamorphosis*, and Robbins's *Fanfare*. (Sylvia loved all four pieces and described them in detail to Myron.) During intermission, Sylvia ran into Mel Woody, the Yale student who was Marcia Brown's "psychic brother." After the show, the two of them ducked into P. J. Clarke's, an Irish pub, to discuss their "respective philosophies of life."[79] Mel remembered that they were both on a high after the ballet, which was one of the richest aesthetic experiences of his life. "This was the moment at which I said, 'No matter how many years go by, we're going to be just like this.' That was our conviction. We didn't really know each other, but it was very important to me. When I finally decided to give up on my first marriage, I headed to New York, I went to P.J. Clarke's, and I sat at that same table." He remembered Plath's incandescence. "Sylvia, when she was up, was *glowing*."[80] Around two a.m. Sylvia said goodbye to Mel and headed down to Greenwich Village. There, she and Carol met Art Ford at a club and stayed out until dawn. She walked all the way back to Lexington Avenue and 63rd Street.

Almost a decade later, Plath wrote about her month in New York with jaded, cynical eyes. In *The Bell Jar*, Art Ford would become Lenny Shepherd, a famous disc jockey with "a big, wide, white toothpaste-ad smile."[81] After ditching Lenny's short, unappealing friend Frankie, Esther joins Doreen and Lenny back at Lenny's apartment, where he brags about his "twenty grand's worth of recording equipment." Esther coolly observes Doreen and Lenny's rough foreplay and slips out as they are fighting ("Leggo, you bitch!"). The evening leaves her rattled, and she begins to wonder if all relationships in New York are brutal. "The tropical, stale heat the sidewalks had been sucking up all day hit me in the face like a last insult. I didn't know where in the world I was."[82] When Esther reaches her hotel, she takes a bath to wash away the "liquor" and "sticky kisses." Doreen eventually lands on her doorstep, half conscious and vomiting, but Esther closes the door and vows to "have nothing at all to do with her." The scene was based on a real event: Laurie Totten remembered finding Carol "dead drunk in her own vomit" outside her door early one morning, and summoned Plath to help.[83] In *The Bell Jar*, Esther vows to go with the "innocent" Betsy from now on, whom she "resembled at heart"—not the wise-cracking, curfew-breaking Doreen. That morning, she thinks, "I still expected to see Doreen's body lying there in the pool of vomit like an ugly, concrete testimony to my own dirty nature."[84]

Years later, Carol sobbed as she read *The Bell Jar* for the first time. She was then working for a newspaper in Rhode Island, and had asked to review her old friend's novel. She recognized herself as Doreen—a Sweet Briar society girl who is lazy about deadlines and sexually adventurous—but claimed it was a distorted portrait, a "thorough betrayal." "I was stunned. . . . This was somebody I was close to, and the whole time she had been making fun of me. . . . The pain lasted a long time. . . . It was not the Sylvia that I knew."[85] Many others who saw themselves in *The Bell Jar* felt similarly betrayed. Yet Carol's testimony underscores the fact that *The Bell Jar* is not a factually accurate chronicle of Plath's *Mademoiselle* summer. It is fiction. Plath molded the raw material of that summer to make a political point about coming of age as an ambitious woman in Eisenhower's brutally conformist America.

Carol dated Art Ford for the rest of June. Plath may have picked up some of the details for the Lenny Shepherd scene from a story she heard later, from Laurie Glazer. Laurie had performing ambitions, and asked Carol to arrange an interview with Art. Laurie remembered that when Art answered the door he was wearing only a towel. She thought of him as "very sleazy and greasy . . . a funny little man."[86] He asked her to sit on the couch with him and began pressing his knee into hers. "A star is born," she remembered him saying. "All you need to do is put yourself in my hands." He handed her a beat-up microphone and told her to start singing as he headed to the bathroom to shave. Laurie knew she had made a mistake and rushed back to the Barbizon, where she recounted the story to several others in Sylvia's room over a bottle of warm white wine. Everyone laughed, and Sylvia said, "Should I, after tea and cakes and ices, have the strength to force the moment to its crisis?" (Laurie did not recognize the quotation from Eliot's "Prufrock.") Sylvia advised Laurie to "stick to writing" rather than singing, and the conversation turned to more intellectual topics. Sylvia and Laurie began discussing Shakespeare's *Tempest*. In her diary, Laurie wrote, "S. thinks Ariel male-animal power, fiery depths. I said air, heaven, female."[87] Plath would experience a sea change herself when she began to reconsider Ariel in the 1960s. By that time, she understood the spirit as Laurie had described: "air, heaven, female." She titled her second collection of poetry *Ariel*, the name Laurie Glazer eventually chose for her daughter. Laurie wondered, when *Ariel* appeared, if Sylvia had remembered their conversation.[88]

During her third week at *Mademoiselle*, Sylvia attended a Yankees game and toured two magazine offices, *Living for Young Homemakers* and *Charm*, and attended the infamous luncheon at the Batten, Barton, Durstine and Osborn advertising agency that became the inspiration for the famous food-poisoning scene in *The Bell Jar*. On Tuesday, June 16—Bloomsday—Plath and her fellow guest editors were given a tour of the agency and treated to crabmeat and avocado salad, two of Plath's favorite foods. Sylvia began vomiting on the way home in the taxi she shared with Janet Wagner and barely made it to the hotel bathroom before another round of sickness. Soon, nearly all the guest editors were crowded into bathrooms, collapsed in misery all night long. In the morning, the hotel doctor administered intravenous treatment. Some of the women felt well enough to wander downstairs for a bite to eat, but Sylvia stayed in bed all day. She wrote to Warren that she had "wanted to die very badly for a day, in the midst of faintings and hypodermics and miserable agony."[89] The next morning, the agency sent gift baskets containing fruit and a collection of Hemingway stories. "We all joked about the poisoning of guests being distinctly bad advertising for the world's second largest advertising agency," said Laurie Glazer.[90]

The luncheon provided Plath with a perfect metaphor for the gluttonous consumerism she felt was poisoning the nation. There were echoes of Crockett's disdain for American materialism in her depiction of the event in *The Bell Jar*:

> I had a vision of the celestially white kitchens of *Ladies' Day* stretching into infinity. I saw avocado pear after avocado pear being stuffed with crabmeat and mayonnaise and photographed under brilliant lights. I saw the delicate, pink-mottled claw meat poking seductively through its blan-

ket of mayonnaise and the bland yellow pear cup with its rim of alligator-green cradling the whole mess.

Poison.[91]

Plath saw the rot festering beneath the "celestially white" façades the ad men sold—ads that had a particularly corrosive effect on women. Part of her aim in *The Bell Jar* was to expose the dark side of the fashion and beauty industries. Throughout the novel, Esther looks into mirrors and sees a distorted reflection of herself; everything she experiences at *Ladies' Day* magazine makes her question her own sense of self, and self-worth. New York made a mockery of Plath's "philosophy of life"—her optimistic belief in hard work, merit, compassion, and humanistic inquiry. Earlier that fall, Plath had wondered, "How to justify myself, my bold, brave humanitarian faith?"[92] The question was now more urgent. Yet the only things that seemed to matter in this brave new world were sex and money. At every turn, it seemed, she was encouraged to become an object for men to behold, when what she really wanted to be was the subject of her own life. "My world falls apart, crumbles, 'The center does not hold,'" Plath wrote in her journal, quoting Yeats.[93] She tried to mute her sense of "naked fear" and hollowness in a letter to Warren in late June: "Seriously, I am more than overjoyed to have been here a month, it is just that I realize how young and inexperienced I am in the ways of the world."[94]

By Thursday, June 18, Sylvia had recovered enough from the food poisoning to take a tour of the United Nations, which she felt was the world's best hope for peace. Most of June had been filled with fashion-related events—a behind-the-scenes tour of Macy's; John Frederics's hats; the Trigère fashion show; a "Fabric Talk" with Madeline Darling; a visit to Cosmetic House; and (yes) corset manufacturers. Plath needed a respite from hemlines and hat brims. The UN tour was one of the few daytime excursions that had no connection to beauty products. As Sylvia toured the sleek, modern building, she considered working there, even as a secretary.

She thought the tour well timed, for that night she had a date with Gregory (Gary) Karmiloff, a Russian-speaking simultaneous interpreter at the UN. Mildred Norton had hosted Gary on an exchange, and had told him to contact Sylvia in New York. (Sylvia sensed a thaw, and called Mildred to thank her.) She expected a dud but was pleasantly surprised by the handsome, suave eastern European sophisticate who took her to an Italian café. Gary was the only date Sylvia talked about to Laurie Totten. She felt Sylvia was attracted to him because of his "unusual avocation" and "worldly experience"—which, Laurie suspected, Sylvia deeply craved in her own life.[95]

In *The Bell Jar*, Plath changed Gary's name to Constantin and set the date in a restaurant with travel posters for Europe and Africa, candles weeping into old bottles and "sweet Greek wine that tasted of pine bark."[96] There, Esther decides she will become a war correspondent, and she will let Constantin seduce her. She returns to his apartment and waits for the moment to unfold as they listen to balalaika records. But Constantin only holds her hand tenderly and falls asleep. She leaves his apartment at three a.m. feeling hungover and unwanted. Constantin's appeal—like Gary's—lay in his old-world charm, with its promise of deliverance from American kitsch. Sylvia did not want Hamburger Heaven and its fluorescent lights and soup of the day. She wanted candlelight and figs and sweet Greek wine, surrounded by the lure of elsewhere.

In real life, Sylvia and Gary went back to his studio on Christopher Street after dinner, but Gary was not interested in sex—at least not with her. In *The Bell Jar*, Esther thinks, "This Constantin won't mind if I'm too tall and don't know enough languages and haven't been to Europe, he'll see through all that stuff to what I really am."[97] But Gary did mind. He later said Plath was "not seductive enough—a bit too provincial." He was annoyed that "she did not appreciate, as she should have," some of his Chinese furniture and his vicuña bedspread, which had cost him a week's salary.[98] Sylvia called him "the most brilliant wonderful man in the world" in a letter to Warren, but there was no second date.[99]

Sylvia walked back to the Barbizon late that night, and did not get much sleep before reporting back to work at nine a.m. She was tired and despondent over Gary's rejection. The events of the past night—indeed the past three weeks—left her feeling vulnerable that morning as she sat at the Barbizon's coffee shop and read about the Rosenberg execution.

———————

"IT WAS A QUEER, sultry summer, the summer they electrocuted the Rosenbergs, and I didn't know what I was doing in New York," Plath's novel begins.[100] The execution serves as a malingering backdrop for everything Esther experiences.

Julius and Ethel Rosenberg were sentenced to death after being convicted of passing atomic secrets to the Soviet Union in March 1951. Whether they truly deserved the death penalty—or even were guilty of the crimes attributed to them—remains a matter of debate.[101] Plath thought the couple was executed to make an example, like the women in the Salem witch trials. She was not the only one. Her Wellesley friend Phil McCurdy had driven to Washington to march in a protest proclaiming the couple's innocence. Sylvia knew Mr. Crockett and many of her Smith professors were also appalled.

Members of the international intelligentsia, including Jean-Paul Sartre, Bertolt Brecht, Jean Cocteau, Frida Kahlo, Diego Rivera, Pablo Picasso, and even Albert Einstein, called on the American authorities to pardon the couple. The incident was widely seen abroad as a modern-day Dreyfus affair, though no American Jewish organization offered to support the Rosenbergs. Julius maintained his innocence, stating before his death that the sentence was the culmination of McCarthyist hysteria.[102]

Neva Nelson was with Plath on the morning the Rosenbergs were executed. Sylvia was already seated at the counter when Neva sat down next to her and ordered a coffee and a large Danish. She seemed "much distressed about something . . . in no mood to eat anything."

> She mentioned the headlines—"Rosenbergs To Be Executed."—[and] said off-hand to me something to the effect that there wasn't enough evidence to convict them, and that they were really killing them because they were Jews. Then she turned directly to me and said, "You DO know what Jews are, don't you?" And I said, in my stock Bible-belt upbringing answer, "Yes, Christ was a Jew." And she just found that so absurd, and that's when she became so disgusted with me that she got up to leave, with me following her out the door, just as she said, "Oh, you're so stupid. Just go away and leave me alone." But I, the puppy dog I was at that time, followed her towards the subway stairs.[103]

Sylvia walked the rest of the way to work with Laurie Totten. Laurie remembered passing a newspaper kiosk and seeing the headlines about the Rosenbergs. She felt that the couple should face the death penalty: "I was fine with it." Sylvia was not. She was "vehement" that they should not be executed, Laurie recalled, and found the whole affair "hideous."[104] Other guest editors also remembered Sylvia's agitation. Laurie Glazer Levy recalled, "She said to me, 'You're Jewish and you should care.' She was always asking me about being Jewish. She said she identified with me."[105] Sylvia told Laurie Totten that she felt guilt over the Holocaust on account of her father's German background.[106] (Plath may have heard an echo of her grandmother's maiden name, Greenwood, in Ethel Rosenberg's maiden name, Greenglass.)

Many of the guest editors had never heard of the Rosenbergs. Ann Burnside Love remembered, "The serious Sylvia was agonizing over the execution of the Rosenbergs and McCarthyism; others were delighting to dream over trousseau lingerie at Vanity Fair's showroom."[107] Margaret Affleck Clark, the group's only Mormon, had the sense that Plath "contemplated these things more than a lot of girls our age." She remembered Sylvia asking her about Mormonism during a tour of the *Herald Tribune:* "She was asking about my religion and what our stance was on the afterlife and what did we think people did in heaven. I told her we go on progressing. We take the intelligence that we have and keep progressing when we get to heaven. She thought that was a wonderful idea and said it would be such a waste to just lose everything that you had in life."[108]

Plath herself probably did not have detailed knowledge of the case beyond what she read in the papers, but she knew the Rosenbergs were Jewish and that they had belonged to communist organizations. Her mind was already attuned to the ways in which outsiders and nonconformists were pushed to the margins of Eisenhower's America, and she saw the Rosenbergs as innocents paying the ultimate price for their "un-Americanism." "It is good for them to die," Plath wrote sarcastically in her journal. "So that we can have the priority of killing people with those atomic secrets which are so very jealously and specially and inhumanly ours."[109] She was appalled by her fellow guest editors' blasé attitudes, summed up by Hilda in *The Bell Jar:* "I'm so glad they are going to die."[110] Hilda's words captured American indifference, Plath suggested in her journal.

> There is no yelling, no horror, no great rebellion. That is the appalling thing. The execution will take place tonight; it is too bad that it could not be televised . . . so much more realistic and beneficial than the run-of-the mill crime program. Two real people being executed. No matter. The largest emotional reaction over the United States will be a rather large, democratic, infinitely bored and casual and complacent yawn.[111]

The Rosenberg execution provided the overarching theme of *The Bell Jar:* in 1950s America, dissidence would be punished by electric shock.[112]

There were more *Mademoiselle* commitments during Sylvia's last week: a tour of Macy's and the *Herald Tribune*, Betsy Talbot Blackwell's farewell party, and George Bernard Shaw's proto-feminist play *Misalliance* at the Barrymore Theatre. A disastrous date with a Peruvian UN delegate, José Antonio La Vias, proved to Sylvia again that New York was inhospitable to innocents. She had arranged the date at the West Side Tennis Club in Forest Hills, Queens, through Gary Karmiloff, who knew José through the UN. In her calendar, Sylvia wrote the Peruvian's name on June 20, as well as the words "Forest Hills Dance," "East Side apt.," "Latins," and "Lima, Peru."[113] In *The Bell Jar*, Esther is almost raped by her Peruvian date, Marco, at a country club dance—a harrowing scene that has caused at least one biographer to speculate that the real José did in fact rape or attempt to rape Sylvia at his apartment after the dance.[114] But Janet Wagner, who double-dated with Sylvia that night, said the two left Queens before they got into any real trouble. Janet, not Sylvia, was assaulted by her Brazilian date, though José had clearly done something to upset Sylvia. (She wrote Warren that she had spent an evening "fighting" with him, and called him "cruel" in her journal.)[115] When Janet's date wrestled her to the ground, she elbowed him in the mouth and knocked out several teeth. She fled back to Plath, who was in the clubhouse, and told her what had happened. "José had said some awful things to Sylvia," Janet remembered. "We were laughing, but we had gotten ourselves into a bit of a mess. How were we going to escape these men? How were we going to get out of Queens?"[116] Janet said the cavalry appeared in the form of a *Mademoiselle* chaperone (Leo Lerman's assistant), who had been sent out to Queens by Blackwell when she heard about the girls' plans. The two piled into the front seat of his convertible, and together they drove back to Manhattan.

Sylvia would fit in two more dates before she left New York. On Thursday night, she went out with Ilo Pill; on Friday, her last day in the city, she rode the Staten Island Ferry with Ray Wunderlich, the Columbia medical student who had treated her to champagne and oysters two months before. That day, Ray recalled, Sylvia was "ashamed because she had met indomitable things that she could not conquer, things that were conquering her. She felt that she should be better than that."[117] Sylvia *had* met unconquerable things in New York—callous men, inscrutable editors, work that bored her. The experience was supposed to have been the pinnacle of her year—her life, even—yet she had been disillusioned at every turn. Plath never met any of the literary luminaries who descended on *Mademoiselle*'s halls, like Truman Capote, Tennessee Williams, and—her biggest regret—Dylan Thomas. Each time he had visited the office, she was out. She was upset that she had not been able to interview him for the "We Hitch Our Wagons" segment—that plum assignment had gone to the guest fiction editor, Candy Bolster. Neva Nelson remembered hearing that Sylvia hung around the White Horse Tavern in Greenwich Village, where Thomas eventually drank himself to death. "Sylvia was ready to move heaven and high water to see him."[118] After the St. Regis dance, Sylvia commandeered Carol to keep vigil with her outside Thomas's room at the Chelsea Hotel.[119] But Thomas never showed up. He should have been accessible. Abels, who published *Under Milk Wood* in *Mademoiselle* in 1954, considered him a personal friend, but Plath was probably too intimidated to ask Abels for an introduction. She had failed at this, too. Crockett later recalled that Plath had sent him an uncharacteristically disconcerting letter in late June. One line stayed with him: "You'll never want to see me again, Mr. Crockett, I've let you down."[120]

On Sunday, June 21, Sylvia wrote a dark, bracing letter to Warren. The bright, cheerful "Sivvy" was stressed and fraying. "I just today felt: heavens, I haven't thought about who I am or where I come from for days. It is abominably hot in NYC . . . the humidity is staggering, and I am perishing for the clean unsooted greenness of our backyard." She would not be able to "comprehend" what had happened to her in New York until she came home to "sleep and sleep and play tennis and get tan again. . . . I am worn out now, with the strenuous days at the office and the heat and the evenings out." She admitted that she had been "horribly depressed" as well as "ecstatic," and the mood swings left her feeling wrung out. She was "soot-stained, grubby, weary," and clung to her brother's anchor:

> I love you a million times more than any of these slick ad-men, these hucksters, these wealthy beasts who get drunk in foreign accents all the time. . . . Smith seems like a simple enchanting bucolic existence compared to the dry, humid, breathless wasteland of the cliffdwellers, where the people are, as D. H. Lawrence wrote of his society "dead brilliant galls on the tree of life." By contrast, the good few friends I have seems [*sic*] like clear-icewater after a very strong scalding martini.

As for her arrival: "I will let you know what train my coffin will come in on." And her things: "All I have needs washing, bleaching, airing." This was the language of depression—Sylvia was telling Warren she felt dirty and corrupted, that *she* needed "bleaching, airing." Yet her pain was such that she spoke out of code at her letter's end, admitting the depth of her psychological distress: "oh God, it is unbelievable to think of all this at once . . . my mind will split open."[121]

On June 26, her last day, the guest editors picked up their final checks and left the *Mademoiselle* offices early. Neva met Sylvia in the Barbizon hallway after she emerged from the elevator. Sylvia was "in the midst of offering clothes" to Janet, and offered some to Neva as well. Neva did not find anything strange or dramatic about the gesture. "We jokingly told her that we'd take some of hers if she'd take some of ours (we were all so sick of wearing the same few outfits for the entire month)."[122] Carol remembered riding the elevator up to the roof with Plath that night and watching her toss clothes into the wind. "Sylvia and I were together and ready to cast off the look we'd been expected to maintain for a month."[123] But Carol said that she and Sylvia had tossed mainly their "girdles and waist-cinchers," which had caused them "misery." She noted that neither she nor Sylvia would have dared cast off their expensive outfits: "the money to pay for those clothes would have been hard earned and the dresses and gloves needed for job interviews."[124] (Carol's memory helps explain why Aurelia always maintained that the event never happened, and that Sylvia came home with her main wardrobe intact.) Sylvia would imbue this scene with somber symbolism in *The Bell Jar*, but Carol remembered it as a more "giddy" affair. "We were laughing. All this absurd phony fun we were having was over. . . . I didn't see it as Sylvia throwing off a false self. It was just fun—a 'good-bye to all that' sort of thing."[125] Neva recalled, "I heard later from Jan that Sylvia had gone up to the roof and was throwing her clothes to the wind, all a grand, funny gesture to the rest of us. . . . Sylvia was upbeat in doing this and was glad to have the whole ordeal over with."[126] Plath was shedding the corsets—literal and figurative—that had circumscribed her life that month.

Earlier that day, when Sylvia and Janet were trading clothes, Janet had offered her "anything she liked." Sylvia made a curious choice—"a green dirndl skirt, and a peasant-style blouse in white eyelet."[127] (Sylvia gave Janet her green-striped bathrobe in exchange.) This girlish outfit was the type Sylvia had told her mother, in letters home, that she had outgrown. Her choice may have had something to do with the previous day's excursions. In the morning, she watched models strut around in animal-print lingerie at the Warner corset fashion show and luncheon at the Vanity Fair showroom on 200 Madison Avenue. After the show, the guest editors were invited backstage to try on the bras and corsets. Neva remembered how Carol "pranced around" in her panties and a white merry widow corset, and, after some "negotiations," secured merry widows for all.[128] Sylvia then headed to the Pauline Trigère fashion show at the designer's Seventh Avenue atelier. There, she saw the best that New York offered in haute couture—long, narrow sheaths of crepe and grosgrain on impossibly tall, lithe models. Sylvia would never be able to afford such gowns, nor did she have the perfectly proportioned body of a fashion model. After the Trigère event, she attended two more fashion shows—Horwitz & Duberman on Seventh Avenue and Charles James at the Sherry-Netherland Hotel. Cocktails accompanied both. All told, Plath saw four fashion shows that day. The next day, she threw her girdles off the roof of the Barbizon Hotel and donned, instead, a Heidi ensemble that evoked alpine innocence. In *The Bell Jar*, Esther Greenwood would not change out of this outfit for three weeks.

11

The Hanging Man

Wellesley, July–August 1953

When Aurelia and Grammy Schober met Sylvia at the Route 128 station on Saturday, June 27, they were shocked to find her exhausted, hollow-eyed, and wearing borrowed clothes. Plath's month in New York had left her reeling and disoriented, and she was too tired to put up a front. "New York: pain, parties, work," she wrote in her journal. "And Gary and ptomaine—and José the cruel Peruvian and Carol vomiting outside the door all over the floor—and interviews for TV shows, & competition, and beautiful models and Miss Abels. . . . And now this: shock. Utter nihilistic shock."[1]

Aurelia knew something was very wrong, and "dreaded" telling her daughter that she had not been admitted into Frank O'Connor's creative writing class at Harvard Summer School. She downplayed the news, "casually" mentioning that the class was full and that Sylvia would have to wait until the following summer to register. Aurelia looked into the rear-view mirror and saw the color drain from Sylvia's face. The "look of shock and utter despair that passed over it alarmed me," she later wrote. "Sylvia was too demanding of herself."[2]

Plath had submitted "Sunday at the Mintons," her most successful story, to O'Connor, but it had not earned her a seat at his table. (O'Connor later said that Plath's writing had been too advanced for his introductory-level class.)[3] Now she was filled with doubt and self-reproach. She admonished herself for basing Henry on Dick Norton in such an obvious way, as if O'Connor's rejection were punishment for a moral lapse. It had been a cruel thing to do, she told her mother. Years later, Aurelia speculated that Sylvia experienced similar "emotional recoil" after the publication of *The Bell Jar*, which also painted a humiliating portrait of Dick.[4]

Sylvia had assumed she would spend her summer writing stories for O'Connor that she could sell. Now she considered taking a Harvard summer course in elementary psychology, but she worried that the course's tuition would leave her with little money for her senior year. In her journal she wrote that she heard "the little man in my head mocking: is this worth it, worth it, worth it, this course for $250, while your mother does all the work at home." It may have been Mildred Norton's voice she heard. Sylvia did not want to give Dick's mother the satisfaction of proving her correct, and she worried that Smith might reduce her scholarship if she did not earn anything all summer. After much internal debate, Sylvia decided to spend her summer writing creatively at home, learning shorthand from Aurelia and doing preliminary research on her James Joyce thesis. She would tell Smith she had "worked for the month of June, and took free shorthand for the rest of the summer. Logically, this is a much more politic thing to do."[5]

Sylvia had suffered a mild depression the previous summer after she had returned to Wellesley from the Belmont, and she was nervous about the bell jar descending again. Routine and discipline were the keys, she felt, to stability. "I will have to be cheerful and constructive, and schedule my day much harder than if at Harvard. I will learn about shopping and cooking, and try to make mother's vacation happy and good."[6] But she also admitted fear of paralysis. Her July journal is full of self-reproach; she called herself "an Over-grown, Over-protected, Scared, Spoiled Baby."[7] She wrote this entry on the back of her July letter to Columbia asking for more information about their graduate program. Plath drew a large slash through the letter, as if remonstrating herself for her high ambitions.[8]

Sylvia told Marcia, who was already working in Cambridge and enrolled at Harvard Summer School, that she would not be living with her after all. What she needed—or so everyone thought—was rest. But almost immediately, she knew she had made the wrong decision. "You are an inconsistent and very frightened hypocrite: you wanted time to think, to find out about yourself, your ability to write, and now that you have it: practically 3 months of godawful time, you are paralyzed, shocked, thrown into a nausea, a stasis."[9] At the same time, her calendar from early July 1953 shows that she was able to function socially. Gordon Lameyer said he saw Sylvia every day before he left for naval training camp in Rhode Island in mid-July. He had no idea she was suffering from depression and insomnia.[10] She picnicked along the Charles River with Marcia, visited New Hampshire with the Lameyers, and played tennis. But after Gordon left, the cracks that had appeared during her first few days at home widened. Her normally healthy appetite disappeared, and sleep became elusive. She wrote in her journal on July 6 that she felt "sick in the head," and was disturbed by her fantasies of "razors and self-wounds & going out and ending it all." On July 14 she wrote of her visions of herself "in a straight jacket, and a drain on the family," "murdering your mother in actuality." "Thesis panic" set in, and with it, the most paralyzing anxiety of all: "Fear of failing to live up to the fast & furious prize-winning pace of these last years—and any kind of creative life."[11]

Sylvia had other reasons to worry. In late July, Aurelia wrote to Marcia about the "state-of-emergency tension" in the house when Sylvia had arrived home in late June. Grammy was seriously ill and had almost died, she wrote, but had recovered. Aurelia's "old ulcer" also flared up again, and she was given doctor's orders to rest. Otherwise she would have to undergo a "serious and costly" surgery. Aurelia told Marcia that Sylvia had decided not to go to Harvard Summer School "for her," though she mentioned that Sylvia had been upset by some "big disappointments" that summer. She implored Marcia not to talk too much about her own exciting experiences at Harvard lest she make Sylvia jealous.[12]

Sylvia revealed nothing of these crises in her breezy letters to Gordon that July, which were full of Joycean puns, wisecracks, and questions about naval life. ("And do tell me if there are any Captain Queegs about your station, will ya, huh?")[13] She was more forthright in her letters to Dick, who told her he was disturbed by the "intense unrest" of her July letters.[14] He wondered if "accomplishing great things" while living "quietly at home" was the best way for her to spend her summer.[15]

Learning shorthand quickly became Sylvia's justification for staying at home. A woman at the Smith vocational office had told her she should learn it—"a practical skill" that would give her greater "bargaining power" after she graduated.[16] She and Aurelia began the lessons for an hour each morning, but learning this abstruse language was an exercise in futility that exacerbated Sylvia's sense of failure. She was unable to master the small squibbles "that blurred into senselessness," as she later wrote in *The Bell Jar*. There, shorthand symbolized the soft bigotry of low expectations for women in the 1950s. "There wasn't one job I felt like doing where you used shorthand," Esther says. "If I never learned shorthand I would never have to use it."[17] Aurelia later castigated herself for attempting the lessons, which she says lasted only four days.[18] But she would bristle at Plath's suggestion, in *The Bell Jar*, that she had insisted on them. This, she said, was "the biggest lie."[19]

Sylvia turned to her senior thesis. She had a brilliant academic reputation to maintain; naturally, she had chosen James Joyce's *Ulysses*. She approached her task with a determination to prove that she was capable of entering the citadel of male modernism. Her Joyce notebook from Smith shows she was well equipped to do so: she had taken extensive, sophisticated notes on *Ulysses* in Elizabeth Drew's Twentieth Century British Literature class, where she received an excellent and thorough introduction to the novel's major themes, symbols, and motifs.[20] Her classmate Nora Johnson remembered that Sylvia "could stripsearch *Ulysses* and make all the mythological connections without batting an eye."[21] Yet reading and writing about this notoriously difficult novel was probably the worst recuperative task Plath could have set herself. Instead of bolstering her confidence in her own abilities, explicating Joyce made her feel incapable. In *The Bell Jar*, Esther writes of her frustration upon reading Joyce's *Finnegans Wake*:

> Lifting the pages of the book, I let them fan slowly by my eyes. Words, dimly familiar but twisted all awry, like faces in a funhouse mirror, fled past, leaving no impression on the glassy surface of my brain.
>
> I squinted at the page.
>
> The letters grew barbs and rams' horns. I watched them separate, each from the other, and jiggle up and down in a silly way. Then they associated themselves in fantastic, untranslatable shapes, like Arabic or Chinese.
>
> I decided to junk my thesis.[22]

Plath condensed and exaggerated in her fiction what was a longer, less dramatic, struggle in her real life. Many commentators have assumed that she was no longer able to read or write coherently that July because that is what Esther implies in *The Bell Jar*. ("I can't sleep. I can't read," Esther tells her family doctor.)[23] Yet Sylvia was writing lucid, humorous letters to Gordon and Dick throughout July *about Joyce*, the very topic that stifles Esther's reading and writing. Gordon and Dick had both read *Ulysses*, and Sylvia approached them as if they were literary authorities on the subject. She asked Gordon whether he thought anything new could be said: "from your more advanced point of view, do you think the idea of a thesis on Joyce is really plausible. I thought so before I began outside reading—now I wonder."[24] Gordon ignored Sylvia's questions about Joyce in his reply, telling her about his new life in the Navy instead. Later, after Plath had attempted suicide, he realized he should have placated her fears about Joyce. In September he finally wrote her a long letter admitting that he, too, found Joyce difficult.

Dick, still ensconced on his own Magic Mountain, was only too happy to parry about Joyce. He immediately reread *Ulysses*, and found himself humbled again by Joyce's wit and semantic powers. He encouraged Sylvia to forge ahead with her thesis plans: "i [*sic*] am totally weak, worshipping, wondering and wideyed [*sic*] at the genius of James Joyce. . . . Are you really going to study that novel next year for your thesis? Because i [*sic*] think it is superbly suited to research and suited to you too." He even compared Plath's writing favorably to Joyce's. When she continued to express her doubts, he suggested that perhaps she might limit her thesis to *Portrait* or *Dubliners*. "But then again there comes the suspicion that there <u>must</u> be an unexplored area in Ulysses, be it ever so small. go [*sic*] and read over your favorite parts of the book and hunt in the keys hopefully to turn up an explanation that they have not given. but [*sic*] above all, comment [*sic*] thy soul to the One which made Heaven and Earth."[25]

Plath's inability to understand James Joyce that summer was not the reason for her depression, but rather a symptom of it; she was the top English student at Smith and perfectly capable of analyzing *Ulysses*. Her Joyce troubles seem to have been wound up with her larger worries about integrating her literary ambition with a traditional feminine role. Explicating the most difficult novel of the twentieth century was a man's game in 1953. And if Joyce was partly responsible for Plath's breakdown, he was equally responsible for her resurrection. Eight years after nearly dying during the summer of 1953, she would transform her personal tragedy into turbulent, page-turning drama in *The Bell Jar*—her subversive take on Joyce's *A Portrait of the Artist as a Young Man*. Plath's own *Künstlerroman* is darkly ironic, for it is Esther's attempt to write a thesis on Joyce's work that helps trigger her breakdown, while the novel itself was Plath's way of announcing that she *had* assimilated Joyce's forms in groundbreaking ways—even as Joyce's words throw her fictional protagonist into mental chaos.

In *A Portrait of the Artist as a Young Man*, Joyce famously wrote, "When the soul of a man is born in this country there are nets flung at it to hold it back from flight."[26] Joyce's words held a particular truth for American women in the Eisenhower era. When Plath read *Portrait* in Elizabeth Drew's Twentieth Century British Literature class in the spring of 1953, she enthusiastically underlined, in red pencil, quotes and themes about Stephen Dedalus's rejection of authority and artistic dedication, including his famous *non serviam*: "I will not serve that in which I no longer believe whether it call itself my home, my fatherland or my church."[27] Yet in *The Bell Jar*, Stephen's triumphant rejection becomes Esther's failed protest. His rebellion from oppressive cultural monoliths results in a new life; hers in a suicide attempt. There is no lighting out for the territory for women, Plath seems to say, no way to forge anew the conscience of the race using those famous Joycean weapons of "silence, exile and cunning."[28]

Like Stephen Dedalus, Esther, too, is a traitor to those forces that have shaped her; like the Rosenbergs, she is punished for rejecting American values. Yet Plath suggests that Esther's sick society—warmongering, anti-Semitic, racist, sexist, classist, and homophobic—has driven her to the brink of insanity. If her mind was maladjusted, so was the world in which she lived.

Esther enacts her own *non serviam* when she throws her wardrobe off the roof of the Amazon Hotel, freeing herself from literal and metaphorical corsets. When Buddy quotes his mother (the character based on Mildred Norton) saying, "What a man is is an arrow into the future and what a woman is is the place the arrow shoots off from," Esther counters: "I wanted change and excitement and to shoot off in all directions myself, like the colored arrows from a Fourth of July rocket."[29] (In "Ariel," Plath would write, "And I / Am the arrow.") This passage is Plath's sly take on Joyce's famous quotation, in *Portrait*, about the oppressive religious and cultural "nets" flung at the soul to "hold it back from flight." Plath, too, wanted to fly.

That July, after O'Connor's rejection and her stalled attempt at *Ulysses*, she worried that these failures would dictate her entire future, and that she might never write again. Aurelia noticed that her daughter's "joie de vivre" was gone.[30] Even neighbors noticed the change. Peter Aldrich, who lived across the street from the Plaths, had the sense of her "being distracted." "She was not the kind of smiling girl I was used to."[31] Pat O'Neil went swimming with Sylvia at Lake Waban after she returned from New York and was shocked by her friend's appearance. Sylvia's face was broken out, she was far too thin, and her eyes were "positively dogged." She seemed filled with "utter exhaustion." Pat had to convince her to go out to the raft, only a few feet offshore. "She was just too tired to swim. . . . mentally staggering from the avalanche that had hit her." When they made it out, Sylvia sat on the undulating raft, looking down at her legs in the water, and opened up about her feelings of inadequacy. "Do you know the truth, Pat?" she said. "I have sat in my room with my paper, and my mind is a big blank." She whispered the last two words. "I'm blank," she whispered again. "People think I have this great writing power and that the images just pour out, and the fact is my mind is blank." Sylvia's voice became small and pained. "How can I go back?" She said she couldn't sleep. "I keep seeing that moon go up; I keep seeing that moon go down."

Pat thought she understood. Sylvia had gone to New York "with a complete hunger to find out about life, just rushing to it, like a windstorm. It had hit her with the pace and the commercialism that she really was not prepared for. . . . at one moment she turned to me and she said, 'If Mr. Crockett only knew the ways of compromising yourself.' (Crockett had always emphasized the high ideals of the artist.) And when she said that, I thought on how many levels she'd probably been crushed. . . . by the commercial aspect of the writing, and by the sales and high pressure. . . . the chromium-plated relationships. . . . It was just a level of life that was being carried on to the clink of money, to the pressure of time and to the power of what people could get out of you."[32] Marcia had a similar sense when she saw Sylvia that July. Sylvia told her that her time in New York "had shaken her to her very foundations about hypocrisy and surface-glamour and people who were exploitative." She said she was "tremendously tired" and "had this profound problem of not being able to write."[33]

Aurelia encouraged Sylvia to relax, as she had been working at a furious pace all year. "At home, she would sunbathe, always with a book in hand, but never reading it. After days of this, she finally began to talk to me, pouring out an endless stream of self-deprecation, self-accusation. She had no goal, she said. As she couldn't read with comprehension anymore, much less write creatively, what was she going to do with her life? She had injured her friends, 'let down' her sponsors—she went on and on."[34] Sylvia's despondent journal entry from July 14 dovetails with Aurelia's account: "please, think—snap out of this. Believe in some beneficent force beyond your own limited self. God, god, god: where are you? I want you, need you: the belief in you and love and mankind. You must not seek escape like this. You must think."[35] This entry, followed by twelve blank pages, was Plath's last known journal entry until 1955.[36]

Aurelia later recalled that the only book Sylvia had "really read during the weeks before her suicide attempt was Freud's *Abnormal Psychology*."[37] This book was not by Freud, but rather a collection of essays, *Modern Abnormal Psychology*. Plath made marginal markings on 235 of the book's 880 pages. E. W. Lazell's essay, "Schizophrenia," is more marked up than any other in the collection, especially a section in which Plath likened her summer in New York City to the symptoms of schizophrenia. H. M. Graumann's "Disorders in Perception and Imagery" is also heavily marked.[38]

On July 14, Aurelia noticed red razor gashes on her daughter's legs. "Upon my horrified questioning, she replied, 'I just wanted to see if I had the guts!' Then she grasped my hand—hers was burning hot to the touch—and cried passionately, 'Oh, Mother, the world is so rotten! I want to die! *Let's die together!*'"[39] July 14 was right after Gordon left for naval training camp.[40] This was the date of her disturbing journal entry in which she wrote about killing her mother and herself. Aurelia suspected that her daughter was in free fall and immediately called the family doctor, Francesca Racioppi, a young mother of three whom Sylvia trusted. Dr. Racioppi saw Plath on July 15, and referred her to a young local psychiatrist, Dr. J. Peter Thornton.

The next day, July 16, Sylvia began volunteering for four hours each morning at Newton-Wellesley Hospital.[41] The idea was likely Aurelia's. (In *The Bell Jar*, Esther performs voluntary hospital work after her shock treatments. "My mother said the cure for thinking too much about yourself was helping somebody who was worse off than you.")[42] Sylvia called herself a "nurses' aide" in a July 23 letter to Gordon: "the environment is very new and intriguing, while, of course being very sobering at times." She told him she had fed dying patients. "I never realized or paused to think about the side of the world where the people are reaching the other end of the line: senility, even death." Sylvia was repulsed by sickness, and attending to those near death—including her old art teacher, Miss Hazelton—upset her deeply. Small details from her letter suggest the contours of nightmare: "The little woman who cries all the time and takes only liquids dies and is wheeled away rapidly. Mongoloid babies are born along with the other ones. There are whispered consultations in the halls, cautions to say nothing specific to the mothers."[43] Plath was in no condition to be ministering to chronically ill patients in a position that she understood was a cure—or rather a punishment—for self-pity.

Sylvia visited Dr. Thornton at his Commonwealth Avenue office in Boston for her first psychiatric appointment, which, according to Aurelia, took place on July 21.[44] Aurelia described Thornton as young, "handsome but opinionated."[45] Sylvia disliked him immediately—his arrogance reminded her too much of Dick. In *The Bell Jar,* Esther hopes that her new psychiatrist will "help me, step by step, to be myself again." But when she reveals to Dr. Gordon that she cannot eat, sleep, or read, he responds, "Where did you say you went to college?" Esther is "baffled" by the question, but answers him. "Ah!" he responds, "I remember your college well. I was up there, during the war. They had a WAC station, didn't they?" He tells her "they were a pretty bunch of girls," and laughs.[46] Esther has not washed or changed her clothes in three weeks, and Dr. Gordon's comment makes her feel utterly miserable. In real life, Sylvia had one more appointment with Dr. Thornton on July 27. After these visits, according to Aurelia, "she began to regress."[47] The young doctor recommended shock treatment. Dr. Francis de Marneffe, director emeritus of McLean Hospital, recalled that such a suggestion was not unusual in the early 1950s, even after only one psychiatric session. "Even then there was somewhat of a dividing line between ourselves and what we call the shock artists—people who were basically committed to shock treatment and saw that as a treatment of choice."[48] Aurelia despaired. "I felt so inadequate, so alone."[49]

Would Dr. Thornton have recommended shock therapy on a brainy but depressed Yale man after just two outpatient sessions? In *The Bell Jar,* Esther is nearly catatonic after she comes home from New York City. She refers to herself as a zombie, and tells her family doctor that she can no longer read, write, or sleep. Yet according to Plath's calendar, she did not begin to suffer from full-blown insomnia until *after* she began seeing Dr. Thornton, who seems only to have increased her anxiety. Sylvia was depressed, but she had not experienced a psychotic break with reality. Mrs. Prouty found her charming at her July 27 dinner party and, like Gordon, had no idea how badly she was suffering.

The Bell Jar exposed not only the horrors of Plath's own early psychiatric treatment but the treatment of women psychiatric patients generally. The novel is usually read as a coming-of-age tale—a female *Catcher in the Rye*—but it is also an eloquent and prescient work of social protest by an emboldened voice of dissent. (Dr. Ruth Beuscher, Plath's psychiatrist, later said the novel was a "pretty accurate" report about Plath's time at McLean.)[50] When Sylvia began seeing Dr. Thornton, 91 percent of psychiatrists belonging to the American Psychiatric Association were men, as were 85 percent of clinical psychologists.[51] Psychiatry, like much of medicine, was an inherently sexist institution in the early fifties. Medical historians have suggested that male psychiatrists were trained to regard high ambition and strong will in women as pathological: the unspoken idea was that "only men can be mentally healthy."[52] In the 1950s, women's discharge from mental hospitals often hinged on their desire to resume their feminine duties as wives and mothers. Those "who refused to function domestically, in terms of cleaning, cooking, childcare and shopping" when they returned home, as one 1961 study showed, were often recommitted.[53] Indeed, a promotional article for McLean that appeared in *The Boston Globe* in 1964 outlined a situation where a middle-class wife might benefit from a short McLean stay: "She is irritable and impatient with her husband and children. She thinks she can't cook any longer or take care of household duties." The article showed a photograph of the woman's "therapy": cooking in the McLean kitchen. She is released when she is "better able to handle" her "home responsibilities" and to continue her "voluntary job as a typist."[54] The article depicts with brutal accuracy the pre-Friedan equation of female "sanity" with domestic proficiency. Indeed, the term "depression" was not used in most British and American women's magazines in the 1950s. Articles referred instead to "nervous exhaustion," "mental conflict," or "anxiety and nervous tension."[55] These were the types of phrases Aurelia would supply to reporters from *The Boston Globe* when Sylvia went missing in August. It is probably no accident that *The Bell Jar*'s heroine Esther Greenwood shares the same name as the unjustly maligned woman in Charlotte Perkins Gilman's feminist short story, "An Unnatural Mother." Esther's literary ambitions make her appear "unnatural" to her male doctors, and Plath wrote the novel in 1961 when she herself was struggling to balance motherhood and writing.

On July 29, Aurelia's neighbor Betty Aldrich drove Aurelia and Sylvia to Valley Head Hospital, about thirty minutes north of Wellesley in the sleepy, affluent town of Carlisle. Valley Head was a genteel hospital for the well heeled, filled with private rooms, Oriental rugs, and ornate wooden furni-

ture. It was where President John F. Kennedy sent his wife, Jackie, for electroshock treatment after a particularly brutal fight about his infidelity. Dr. de
Marneffe claimed that in the 1950s Valley Head was a place where "shock
artists" practiced electroshock treatment "for profit, short term": "Valley
Head had the worst reputation among the psychiatric hospitals in the Boston
area."[56] There, Sylvia was led into the place that would remain etched in her
memory as a chamber of horrors: the shock unit.

In 1953, electroshock treatment was still in its infancy. Developed in
1938, it had been in use for only fifteen years and was, according to a McLean
Hospital historian, "crude" therapy, "often unpleasant and frightening for
patients."[57] The procedure involved placing electrodes on the temples and
shooting an electric current into the brain to induce a seizure. The hope was
that the force of the shock and accompanying convulsion would "reboot"
the brain and cure mental disease. The founder of the treatment, a neurolo-
gist named Ugo Cerletti, had observed slaughterhouse pigs being "shocked"
and anesthetized before their death and wondered if the procedure might
help humans. He eventually tried it on schizophrenic patients, with promising results—partly because the memory loss that accompanied the treatment
often wiped away patients' fear of it.

Today electroshock treatment is often used successfully to alleviate the
suffering of the severely depressed. But shock treatment was not well regu-
lated or well understood in the early fifties. The doses of electricity were
much higher than they are today, as was the frequency of treatments. And
the instruments were crude. Plath was given no anesthetic or muscle relax-
ant to help prevent the convulsive muscle spasms that often resulted in bone
fractures during shock treatment. This was not atypical for the time, Dr. de
Marneffe noted. He remembered attending several shock treatments in the
early 1950s when patients "sometimes broke their backs, quite often actually,
and fractured the vertebrae."[58]

Sylvia woke up alone after the procedure, which felt like an electrocution,
and was returned to her mother in the waiting room. There was apparently
no talk therapy between sessions, just a prescription for sleeping pills later
administered by Dr. Kenneth Tillotson, who took over the treatments after
Dr. Thornton went on vacation. (Tillotson was a former head psychiatrist
at McLean Hospital but had retreated to private practice in 1949 after a sex
scandal involving a nurse.) "Many of the horror stories the public eventually heard about ECT and lobotomy came out of institutions where such
therapies were wantonly prescribed and inexpertly administered," wrote
McLean's historian.[59] According to Dr. de Marneffe—once the most preeminent psychiatrist in Boston—Plath was a casualty of such wantonness.
Her 1961 notes on The Bell Jar—"Doctor Gordon Fictional, though botched

shock treatment real"[60]—show that she based Esther's shock treatment on her own horrific experience:

> Doctor Gordon was fitting two metal plates on either side of my head. He buckled them into place with a strap that dented my forehead, and gave me a wire to bite.
>
> I shut my eyes.
>
> There was a brief silence, like an indrawn breath.
>
> Then something bent down and took hold of me and shook me like the end of the world. Whee-ee-ee-ee-ee, it shrilled, through an air crackling with blue light, and with each flash a great jolt drubbed me till I thought my bones would break and the sap fly out of me like a split plant.
>
> I wondered what terrible thing it was I had done.[61]

Plath was not the first woman author to regard electroshock as, in Elaine Showalter's words, "punishment for intellectual ambition, domestic defiance and sexual autonomy": she was drawing on other women's asylum narratives, such as Mary Jane Ward's popular 1946 novel, *The Snake-Pit*.[62] Ward's protagonist also wonders, "Was my crime so great?" as she receives shock treatment.[63] Later, Sylvia told Mrs. Cantor that her psychiatrist had told her with "brutal frankness" "how screwed up she was—hence the necessity for shocks."[64]

In *The Bell Jar*, after her first procedure, Esther tells her mother that she is "through" with Dr. Gordon. Sylvia was not so lucky. She noted in her calendar that she had another shock treatment on July 31, the day after a family outing in Seabrook, New Hampshire, with her uncle Frank and aunt Louise.[65] Sylvia had four treatments under Dr. Thornton and Dr. Tillotson.[66]

Four months after Plath tried to end her life, she wrote lucidly to Eddie Cohen about her motivations for suicide. Her "badly-given" shock treatments had been a "traumatic experience" that shattered her sense of safety and trust in her mother.[67] Sylvia told Eddie she foresaw

> an eternity of hell for the rest of my life in a mental hospital, and I was going to make use of my last ounce of free choice and choose a quick clean ending. I figured that in the long run it would be more merciful and inexpensive to my family; instead of an indefinite and expensive incarceration of a favorite daughter in the cell of a State San, instead of the misery and disillusion of sixty odd years of mental vacuum, of physical squalor—I would spare them all by ending everything at the height of my so-called career . . . still a memory at least that would be worthwhile.[68]

Later, in May 1962, Plath wrote in a progress report on *The Bell Jar* how "Esther's shock treatment goes wrong: there is not enough voltage and she is conscious during it, feels as if she were being electrocuted, thinks shock treatments are supposed to be like that, and says nothing. She resolves to kill herself, rather than suffer another."[69] There is nothing paranoid about Plath's analysis of Esther's and her own situation. She did not know that electroshock therapy could be more safely and effectively administered, or that Mrs. Prouty would be willing to pay for her treatment at a luxurious private hospital. She saw instead a lifetime of incarceration and torture at the hands of arrogant and uncaring doctors.

After Plath's suicide attempt on August 24, Prouty wrote a scathing letter to Dr. Thornton about his botched electroshock treatment:

Unfortunately the shock treatments at Valley Head proved disastrous, as you know. Sylvia was not hospitalized during the treatments and her experience and memory of the shock treatments led to her desperate act. I realize that you left on vacation during the course of the treatments, but the fact remains that she was not properly protected against the results of the treatments, which were so poorly given that the patient remembers the details with horror. I feel very strongly that Sylvia should have been guarded against what happened, while she was undergoing the shock treatments. I think her attempt at suicide was due largely to the horror of what she remembers of the shock treatments, and the fears aroused. . . . I would like to hear from you in regard to this. . . . Have you no interest in a case that had such a disaster following your treatment of her?[70]

Prouty had hit a nerve. Three days later, a riled Dr. Thornton wrote her an angry, condescending reply. He called her "psychiatrically ignorant" and her opinions "worthless." He claimed that Plath had responded favorably to the treatments—an outrageous professional claim given Plath's subsequent suicide attempt. He hoped his letter would "stimulate" her to learn more about psychiatry, and asked her not to "burden" his office with "any further communication."[71] Still, Thornton agreed to cut his bill in half—the closest he would come to an apology.[72] Seven years later, in her poem "The Hanging Man," Plath would likewise suggest that her botched electroshock treatment led to her first suicide attempt:

By the roots of my hair some god got hold of me.
I sizzled in his blue volts like a desert prophet.

The nights snapped out of sight like a lizard's eyelid:
A world of bald white days in a shadeless socket.

A vulturous boredom pinned me in this tree.
If he were I, he would do what I did.

Dr. Thornton's and Dr. Tillotson's treatments at best had no effect on Sylvia's depression and at worst exacerbated it. She later told her Smith friend Ellie Friedman about how she had been "electrocuted": "What this was from all that she told me was terror and pain. . . . they would wheel her down, and they would electrocute her. . . . She told me that it was like being murdered, it was the most horrific thing in the world for her. She said, 'If this should ever happen to me again, I *will* kill myself.' "[73] Sylvia despised Dr. Thornton and dreaded the procedure, but she submitted to it because she had no choice, fearing that if she resisted her shock treatments she would be institutionalized; in 1953, this was a very real possibility. (Indeed, the number of American psychiatric inpatients peaked in 1953 at a little over 500,000.) She was at the mercy of a patriarchal medical system that assumed that highly ambitious, strong-willed women were neurotic. As women, she and her mother had no power to defy the system: the doctor knew best. Indeed, Aurelia allowed Dr. Thornton to administer the shock treatments despite her own misgivings about both his inexperience and the procedure itself.

Peter Aldrich remembered his mother telling him "that Sylvia really hated to go, but she knew she had to. Sometimes Aurelia had to force her into the car. I thought: What are they doing to her? . . . My only glimpse of her after a treatment was one day when she was coming out of my mother's car and she seemed uncharacteristically lifeless. It was just not like her and I thought to myself, 'That's not Sylvia.' What had they done to her?"[74] Sylvia seemed "subdued," he remembered, "out of it," almost like a "zombie."[75] Peter remembered that after treatments she would disappear inside the house for hours, which was unusual, as she normally spent so much time outside sunbathing. His mother, Betty Aldrich (Dodo Conway in *The Bell Jar*), "hated" driving Sylvia and Aurelia to Valley Head, but she felt sorry for the family and did what she could to help.[76]

Aurelia and Betty had grown friendly over the years. Both were educated women—Betty had a master's degree in literature from Radcliffe—and Sylvia and Aurelia were regular visitors to her home.[77] (Betty and her husband later visited Sylvia and Ted in England.) Aurelia was always "discreet" about her problems, but she confided to Betty about Sylvia's depression and her own financial worries. Peter remembered that Aurelia seemed lonely and did not have many friends besides his mother, who found her "sweet, but an odd duck." To him, Aurelia resembled a character out of the 1930s, with her stiff woolen suits and low-heeled, tightly laced Oxfords. He remembered her and Sylvia's grandparents as reserved and quiet. Yet Aurelia was hospitable and considerate, always bringing him homemade apple strudel on his birthday. Peter spent many afternoons at the Plath home with Warren, who taught him to make model airplanes, and he sensed that Aurelia had an easier relationship with her son. Their conversations were not marked by the tense exchanges he sometimes overheard between mother and daughter. Later, he wondered if such tension was due to Aurelia's confusion about how to handle Sylvia's "freer" instincts—her sunbathing in the driveway (which left him "agog") and her many boyfriends. When Sylvia went missing that August, Peter was one of the neighborhood kids who helped Warren search the woods around Elmwood Road.[78]

Despite her recent trauma, Sylvia continued to socialize throughout July and early August. She visited Cambridge, played tennis, attended parties, saw Marcia, danced at the nearby Totem Pole club, went to the beach with her friend Pat O'Neil, and dined at the Cantors'. In her calendar she recorded an appointment with Dr. Tillotson at four p.m. on August 12, and "cocktails, 6 pm." She was trying to keep busy. But in mid-August the calendar goes blank, except for two small words on August 17: "call marty"—her nickname for Marcia.

Still, she managed to write to Myron on August 18. Her tone was upbeat and gracious as she congratulated him on his promotion to a better baseball team. But there were hints of unease: "Life here has been very placid . . . I had to give up the idea of summer school this year because life at home demanded attention: the doctors ordered me to take time off and rest, and so I have been helping with the house, visiting Cambridge occasionally, and taking a few trips to the beach."[79] Around August 20 or 21, Sylvia had dinner with Marcia in Boston. Sylvia spoke of her "terrible frustration of not being able to write, her powerlessness before the need that she couldn't fulfill. She couldn't sleep, was miserably unhappy. . . . She had very deep circles under her eyes." She looked, to Marcia, the way she did when she had a sinus infection. "Perhaps twice each winter she was flattened by one of these things. Flat in the sense of flat on her back and flat emotionally—just lacking in everything—'Don't speak to me till I'm better—leave me alone.'" Marcia considered conferring with Aurelia, but (perhaps remembering her Wylie) she was afraid Aurelia would "smother the hell out of Sylvia." She called Sylvia often, but did not "appreciate the gravity of the situation."[80]

Aurelia told Dr. Beuscher that Dr. Tillotson, who had sessions with Sylvia from August 10–22, thought Sylvia's "problem was a sexual one and questioned her extensively about that part of her life. . . . He had numerous interviews with her and told her this was the nature of the problem." (This line of questioning came from a psychiatrist who was dismissed from his previous position for sexual misconduct.) Aurelia did not believe Tillotson's diagnosis, and felt her daughter's problems had more to do with academic pressures at Smith. Aurelia was so aggrieved by Tillotson's "sexual" line of questioning that she "insisted" upon attending Sylvia's August 21 appointment with him. Aurelia felt that her understanding of Sylvia's crisis was "vindicated" during this session.[81] In the wake of these emotional intrusions, Sylvia's depression worsened.

The following day, Saturday, August 22, Sylvia joined two friends on a double date with Dick Linden,[82] who later told Gordon, his fellow Navy sailor on the USS *Perry*, that he, Sylvia, and another couple—likely Marcia Brown and Mike Plumer—had been at the beach that day, and that Sylvia had "been probing them about the best way to commit suicide."[83] That night the two couples went dancing at the Meadows restaurant in Framingham.

Plath later wrote about this day in *The Bell Jar*, where Esther and Cal (based on Mel Woody) discuss Ibsen's play *Ghosts*—about a young man suffering from syphilis who asks his mother to kill him before he descends into madness—and the best ways to commit suicide. Esther tries to drown herself in the sea, but her body will not capitulate. Mel Woody thought the scene was based on the earlier summer day he spent at Nahant Beach in 1951 with Sylvia and Marcia during the summer they worked as nannies. On that day Sylvia had complained about her writing block; he had read her Rilke's sonnet, and she had swum dangerously far out. The episode in *The Bell Jar* actually seems a composite of both the 1951 and 1953 beach days. Sylvia later told Eddie she had tried to drown herself shortly before she attempted suicide in 1953, but that "The body is amazingly stubborn when it comes to sacrificing itself to the annihilating directions of the mind."[84]

She made a more determined attempt to end her life two days later, on Monday, August 24. Aurelia described Sylvia that day as "extremely upset and confused," and she herself as "also distraught."[85] Seeking relief from emotional turmoil, Aurelia accompanied a friend into Boston that afternoon to see a documentary about Queen Elizabeth's coronation, *A Queen Is Crowned*, at the Exeter Street Theatre. She wrote that Sylvia had encouraged her to go and that she had "looked particularly well," with a sparkle in her eyes and a new "buoyancy." Aurelia worried that the cheerfulness was "contrived" but decided to go anyway.[86] Warren was at work, but Sylvia's grandparents were home. Aurelia assumed that her daughter would be safe in their company.

She was wrong. After Aurelia left the house, Grammy and Grampy retreated to the backyard. Alone, Sylvia broke into her mother's safe and removed the bottle of fifty sleeping pills Dr. Tillotson had prescribed for her. She wrote a note in longhand saying, "Have gone for a long walk. Will be home tomorrow," which she propped against a bowl of flowers on the dining room table. She then made her way to the crawl space in the basement, whose entrance was hidden behind a pile of firewood. After hoisting herself inside, she carefully replaced the logs, one by one. She later told Eddie, "I swallowed quantities and blissfully succumbed to the whirling blackness that I honestly believed was eternal oblivion."[87] Plath swallowed about forty pills before she lost consciousness.

At the theater, Aurelia, with a mother's intuition, began to break into a cold, terrified sweat. She sensed something was wrong at home. "I wanted to get out of my seat and rush from the theater. I forced myself to remain quiet until the close, then begged my friend to drive me home at once." Aurelia probably saw the 2:10 showing, and would have returned to the house around four p.m. She waited until five thirty before she called the police and reported Sylvia missing. The Wellesley police records from that day described Plath as wearing a "blue denim skirt, blouse and jersey." "This girl depressed," the officer noted in his handwritten notes.[88]

Austrian stoicism offered no protection from this "nightmare of nightmares." The house erupted into chaos—Grampy cried while Grammy admonished Aurelia for leaving Sylvia alone, saying they had no idea she was "so ill."[89] Aurelia and Warren ventured into Boston in the heavy rain on the night of the twenty-fourth, along with Colonel Rex Gary, a family friend and former Army intelligence staffer. They hoped to find Sylvia at "one of her favorite haunts," the Boston Common or the Public Garden.[90] They returned home soaked and panicked. When Aurelia checked her safe at six forty-five the next morning, August 25, she saw that the sleeping pills were gone. "It doesn't look good," the Wellesley chief of police told the *Boston Herald*—a quote Plath later used in *The Bell Jar*.[91] Aurelia called the Wellesley police at 6:46 a.m. The log reads: "she finds a bottle containing sleeping pills missing and feels sure her daughter must of taken them with her."[92] The family also found a note in Sylvia's desk outlining what she felt were her inadequacies. Pat remembered its contents. "There was just a sheet of these things: 'I'm guilty of letting down Mr. X at Smith College. . . . I'm guilty of letting down the people who sponsored me for this editorship; I am guilty of letting down the best that's within me; I am guilty of compromising my writing.' "[93]

That day more than one hundred friends, neighbors, and a local Explorer Scout troop combed the woods and trails behind Elmwood Road, as well as the area around Lake Waban, the Dover Road, and the Sudbury River aqueduct. (A newspaper photo of a small search party, which appeared in the *Boston Traveler* on August 26, was among Plath's papers in England when she died.) Colonel Gary helped organize the search along with the Wellesley, Boston, and Cambridge police; Warren diligently recorded the searched areas on a map at home.[94] Bloodhounds were deployed, but because of the heavy rain they were unable to pick up the scent. Chief McBey searched all the garages and buildings within a one-block radius of Plath's home. After Plath was found, McBey claimed that he "thought" he had searched Plath's cellar on Monday night, and speculated that she may have entered the cellar after they searched it.[95] Neighbors gathered at the Unitarian church to pray and support Aurelia.[96] Louise Giesey White and Betsy Powley Wallingford remembered that Pat O'Neil virtually "moved in" to Elmwood Road so that she could help the family.[97] Max Gaebler also came to the house on that first day to help. When he arrived, the Unitarian minister William Rice was there; he took Max aside and told him he "feared the worst." After the minister left, Max sat with the family looking through photographs in an album, "recalling incidents from the past the way one does when someone dies, trying to reinforce whatever shreds of realistic hope we could identify."[98] Aurelia was increasingly shattered. Pat recalled, "it was as if she were dying, truly." Mrs. Cantor came to comfort Aurelia, saying over and over, "We shall find Sylvia. We shall find her. She is alive." Aurelia clung to her and prayed with her.[99]

The "Beautiful Smith Girl Missing at Wellesley" was front-page, tabloid news in the Boston papers and beyond. An astonishing 253 newspaper articles published about Plath's disappearance that August appeared as far afield as Los Angeles, Chicago, New York, and Florida.[100] Stories about Plath's disappearance also aired on the television news.[101] Most of these articles emphasized her beauty first and her brilliance second. Aurelia reported that her daughter had been wearing a summer skirt and sleeveless top the day she went missing, but *The Boston Globe* reported on August 26 that the "attractive girl" was "clad only in a strapless halter and abbreviated shorts."[102] Enid Epstein's mother cut one of these articles out of a New York newspaper and sent it to the American Express office in Paris, where her daughter was traveling with Judith Raymo. (Judith had known Sylvia at Smith, though not as well as Enid.) When Enid opened the envelope and read the news, she burst into tears. To them, Sylvia was the golden girl, completely in command of her destiny and the last person on earth who would try to end her life.[103] Plath would later be amused to find herself a media sensation; she kept at least four of these newspaper clippings, which she brought to England and which would inspire the image of the "peanut-crunching crowd" thrilled by suicide in "Lady Lazarus."

The media frenzy traumatized Aurelia, a deeply private woman who had tried to banish tragedy from the family lexicon. Now her competence as a mother was suspect. Over and over, she told the papers that her daughter had suffered from "nervous exhaustion" on account of her inability to do creative work. "There was no question of a boy in the case," she emphasized.[104] (Reporters corroborated Aurelia's explanation by pointing out Sylvia's outstanding academic reputation at Smith.)

During her days at Elmwood Road, Pat found a family disoriented from grief. As the hours ticked by with no leads, Grammy and Grampy Schober seemed fixated on their next meal, in a state of denial and in a world "unto themselves." Their numbed state troubled Pat. Aurelia, too, seemed to be withdrawing.

On August 26, the family was at the table trying miserably to eat lunch. Pat was ironing, making herself useful. Suddenly they heard a beagle howling right outside the house. Warren pounded the table and said, "Dammit, I'm going to get rid of that dog. I just can't stand it." He stood up to go outside and chase the dog, when, Pat said, "it struck him and all of us at the same instant that the dog was trying to tell us something. We all zoomed into the basement."[105] Warren found Sylvia in the crawl space. She had taken too many pills and vomited them up. "Call the ambulance!" he shouted up to them.

According to the Wellesley police report, the station received a call at 12:40 reporting that Plath had been found and requesting an ambulance. Soon paramedics, along with Chief McBey, had Plath on a stretcher and on her way to Newton-Wellesley Hospital, where she had volunteered just a few weeks before.[106] Sylvia had cut her skin under her right eye when she woke and banged her face; it had become infected in the August heat. (A friend of Aurelia's, Richard Larschan, said Aurelia told him there had been maggots—another detail that Plath used in "Lady Lazarus.")[107] Sylvia told Ellie Friedman, a few months later, that the cut was not accidental. "She talked about waking up and finding herself still alive and trying to do anything she could to kill herself. . . . She just kept smashing her head against the stone. She only succeeded in knocking herself out."[108]

Doctors treated the infection aggressively and stabilized Sylvia, whose first words on awakening, Aurelia said, were, "Oh no!"[109] Sylvia later told Eddie about waking up in the hospital, the "nightmare of flashing lights, strange voices, large needles, an overpowering conviction that I was blind in one eye, and a hatred toward the people who would not let me die, but insisted rather in dragging me back into the hell of sordid and meaningless existence."[110] Aurelia told her daughter she was loved, and how happy the family was to have her back. Sylvia answered, "It was *my* last act of love."[111]

Sylvia recovered from her infection but became more emotionally with-drawn over the eight days she spent at Newton-Wellesley. Gordon Lameyer recalled that one of the first things Sylvia asked Aurelia when she awoke was whether they still owned the house. For the next few days she made "frantic inquiries" about the cost of her medical care. "Sylvia is retreating inwardly," Aurelia wrote to Mrs. Prouty on August 29. "Her speech and comprehension has slowed down—I am thoroughly frightened."[112] The threat of ending up in a state hospital after her family's money had run out had helped drive Sylvia to suicide in the first place. Now that threat was playing out in real time as she lay in her hospital bed, worrying that she would be locked away in a padded cell forever.

Prouty suspected as much. Aurelia had admitted to her at dinner in July that Sylvia had been "depressed" "all summer" "due to her inability to write, concentrate, and accomplish mental work in connection with her senior thesis."[113] Prouty had written to Plath on August 22 from her summer enclave in Boothbay Harbor, Maine, hoping that she was "feeling better." Now she telegrammed Aurelia on August 26: "HAVE JUST LEARNED SYLVIA HAS BEEN FOUND AND IS RECOVERING AT HOSPITAL I WANT TO HELP AM WRITING."[114] Her offer of help was a godsend. Aurelia wrote to her on August 29 with "all details" Prouty had asked for. Sylvia had been treated by Drs. Thornton and Tillotson, but Aurelia had been frustrated by what she considered their lack of insight: "honestly, no one of these men seemed to realize that, while like everyone else, Sylvia's life held many yet unsolved problems, the anxiety about college was uppermost. Nor did they know—or believe—that she confided wholly in me about her long-ing for marriage, children, home, security—as well as her burning desire to develop herself to the utmost intellectually." She told Mrs. Prouty that the daughter of a friend "had had a breakdown necessitating four years of commitment" that left her parents "completely poverty stricken." Sylvia had sought to end her life "for one reason—to spare us long anguish and expense."[115]

Dr. Tillotson had left for his vacation the previous week and had not referred Plath to anyone in his absence. He did not attempt to communicate with Aurelia after Sylvia went missing, or, indeed, after she was found. As Aurelia told Prouty three days after Sylvia was found, "we have no psychi-atric help at present."[116] She resorted to contacting her Unitarian minister, Reverend William Rice, who knew one of the most prominent psychiatrists in Boston, Dr. Erich Lindemann, a Wellesley resident who had collaborated with Rice in various community service efforts.[117] Rice arranged for Dr. Lin-demann to see Plath in three days' time, on the following Tuesday, Septem-ber 1. Dr. Tillotson, who had seemed so "fatherly," abandoned his patient during the worst crisis of her life and left her distraught family to jury-rig psychiatric care.

Aurelia wanted her daughter to rest and recuperate in Provincetown, at the tip of Cape Cod, at a friend's summer home under the care of a private nurse. She wrote Smith's president, Benjamin Wright, that she had become disillusioned with psychiatrists. Wright responded that she was right to be "very wary of that profession," and that he had observed "a number of examples of mistreatment."[118] Aurelia told Prouty that she feared the "detrimental effect" the "locked doors and other patients" of a mental hospital would have on her "sensitive Sylvia." Dr. Racioppi, who saw "no trace of psychosis" in Sylvia, had approved the Provincetown plan, but Aurelia would await Dr. Lindemann's verdict. "I believe Sylvia needs most quiet, sunshine, exercise in increasing measure, and the reassurance of love."[119]

There was another reason Aurelia wanted to avoid a mental hospital: cost. She had listened to the doctors before, and the outcome had been disastrous. Her minister, Aurelia told Mrs. Prouty, "was not impressed" with the Provincetown plan. "He just said, 'Wait and see what Lindemann says.' I have never met Lindemann and do not know anything about his fees." She had an "emergency fund" of $600, which she hoped would cover the expenses at Newton-Wellesley Hospital. "That is just how far I dare let myself think. It has been the pride all my life to stand on my own feet and manage for my family with my own earnings, but this now is larger and more complex than I can handle or even understand." Her gross income, she told Prouty, was $3,900 a year. "This is a nervous breakdown—the one illness I several times jokingly said that we could not afford to have."[120] She told Prouty she would humbly and gratefully accept any help she could give. Prouty quickly reassured her that she would cover the Newton-Wellesley bill and would try to arrange further psychiatric care at her expense. "No illness is so hard for the family of the patient, so difficult to deal with wisely, and no suffering is so deep for the one afflicted," Prouty wrote Aurelia. "I speak from experience."[121]

Prouty thought the Provincetown plan was "excellent—at least as a first step," but she encouraged Aurelia to consult a "wise doctor who has had experience with a nervous breakdown such as hers." Prouty sympathized with Aurelia's desire to keep her "sensitive child" out of a mental hospital, but she herself had benefited from the care of a psychiatrist in Stockbridge, Massachusetts, where she "went to get away from home and too much solicitation and care from those dearest to me. Like Sylvia I felt I had become a burden and wanted to get away to relieve them." Prouty asked her own psychiatrist, Dr. Donald McPherson, to consult with Dr. Lindemann, though she immediately advised that Plath stay at Silver Hill Hospital in Connecticut, "a delightful country-club-appearing place, beautifully furnished with no suggestion of a sanitarium inside or out. . . . The 'guests' are of a carefully selected group."[122] Prouty hinted that she could pull strings so Plath's stay might be free; if not, she hinted that she would pay for her care. When Aurelia told Sylvia about Mrs. Prouty's offer, Sylvia replied, "That is hard to realize," but she no longer asked about the cost of her medical care.[123] Aurelia felt that the news gave her daughter some relief.

Sylvia's professors were horrified when they learned that their star student had tried to kill herself. They blamed themselves for missing the signs of her depression. Plath had sent Elizabeth Drew a long letter by special delivery that summer about her plan to change her thesis topic, and Drew now deeply regretted the short reply she had sent. "Had I known . . . that you were in a mood of despair about your creative work too, of course I should have written at much greater length, & told you how little cause you had to worry & that that is all part of the business of being creative & finely strung," Drew wrote Plath on August 28, two days after she was found. "You are by far the best student in English in the College, & you don't have to strain to be. You could do it standing on your head or in your sleep! I suspect that you were pushing yourself much too hard in the spring. . . . You just burnt yourself out for a spell."[124] Evelyn Page wrote similarly to Plath on August 29, reassuring her that she would overcome this black period and apologizing for not having spoken to her "at greater length about the strains and tensions of writing."[125] Both women told Sylvia about their own battles with depression. Robert Gorham Davis wrote to Aurelia on August 27, telling her to assure her daughter that "plenty of people have been through such crises, and come out of them strengthened."[126] All hoped that Sylvia would return to Smith and graduate.

Gordon too wrote Sylvia on August 27. Aurelia brought his letter and flowers to her daughter at the hospital on Sunday, August 30. His letter moved Sylvia deeply:

I admire you, Sylvia, I admire you more than any girl I know. More than anything I don't want you to feel differently about me now. I want to be your dearest and closest friend as you have been ever since June to me. Believe me, please believe me, I can <u>understand</u> anything. Your happiness is everything to me, so please get well as soon as you can. . . . I know what it is to face people everyday whom you think you have failed. You haven't, Sylvia dear . . . the whole world loves you. Talking to you makes living worthwhile. Sharing anything I have with you gives me the greatest pleasure, because I feel I have faith in you and you speak my language—mine.[127]

Gordon told her about the many crises of self-confidence he had endured at Choate and Amherst, and that feeling "terribly confused" at their age was normal. They were young—she still had plenty of time to develop as a writer.

She replied to him the next day, Monday, August 31, just a week after she had attempted suicide. Sylvia's letter is remarkable for its generosity and coherence at a time when Aurelia described her as retreating inwardly. She apologized to Gordon for being overly sentimental—"purple-passaging," she called it—but she wanted him to know how "tremendously important" his words were: "out of the experiences and confusions of the past it was most welcome to find some kind of constancy and friendship that I could identify with possible shared experiences in the as yet uncertain future . . ." She now knew who the important people in her life were, though she did not know why she had chosen "the hard way" to learn this. Gordon was one of the first people she wanted to see when she was ready for visitors—but not yet. Her face had not healed, she told him, and she was still "numb from all this." Sylvia expressed determination to recover: she knew the "hardest time" would be when she would

rearrange life and make a comeback, new and a year or two late, perhaps: but (I hope) worthy of you and people as strong and good as you are. . . . I mean very much and want very much to tell you that although it's a difficult and complex situation now, I will work twice as hard at recuperating so that I can again see you—and just walk and talk with you. "To learn to appreciate the green and the blue" again—and to make more of the rushing, fast, complex world become reality and part of the experience we form our lives from . . .
Gordon—please remember me smiling and thinking our way.[128]

Dick wrote Sylvia only one letter that fall, dated September 2. It was an exercise in detachment. "Sivvy, let me extend you my sympathy as a fellow patient and let me say I hope fervently for your prompt recovery. I'm so glad you're safe."[129] And with that, Dick dropped all reference to Sylvia's suicide attempt. Still locked in his own life-and-death struggle with tuberculosis, he was not equipped to deal with her breakdown.

Dick's trite words paled next to Gordon's long, anguished letters. On September 1, Gordon sent Sylvia his Amherst crew letter, one of his most prized possessions. She wrote back saying it made her "so happy I could have cried." She called it "sustenance—which I need very much just now." "I want you to know Gordy, that bearing up under the 'slings and arrows of outrageous fortune,' even if they *are* a result of one's own mismanagement . . . is incalculably easier when one has two such marvelous people as you and your mother to be so thoughtful . . ." She told him of the frequent penicillin shots she was receiving to lower her temperature, and her waning fear of needles—"which is a large step in my life—against the more minor of my fears. As for the major ones: Those remain to be knocked down, too." She implored him to think of her wherever he was, "and by some telepathic magic, I'll maybe partake of the scene—or become part of it—I only wish I could make this denouement something as poetic as scattering ashes! But it's a lot more difficult than that."[130]

Gordon wrote to her throughout the fall, mainly about his demanding new life in the Navy. He reassured her she need not respond, and, after her first two letters, she did not. He finally answered her questions about James Joyce, which she had posed earlier in July. He admitted that he found Joyce "overwhelming": "Joyce is for me a master, but for the creative instinct he is stifling and for the frustrated desire he is not exactly therapeutic."[131] There were other reassurances. Gordon knew the poet Richard Wilbur's wife, Charley Ward, who was a family friend. Wilbur had told Charley that when he heard about Plath's suicide attempt, "he wished he could talk to you and tell you about his own experiences in that almost every time he finishes a book of poems or any writing he has the horrible feeling of wondering whether he will be able to write again. It is very common amongst writers; believe me, I know. . . . Charley said by all means for me to bring you over and see them in Lincoln when I asked her if that would be all right."[132] Gordon promised that he would take her when he was on leave in November. (They eventually met Wilbur together in July 1954.)

After eight days at Newton-Wellesley Hospital, Plath was moved to the psychiatric ward of the Massachusetts General Hospital, where Dr. Lindemann oversaw her care for another eleven days. Lindemann was a famous Boston psychiatrist who had made a name for himself treating the survivors of the massive fire that broke out at Boston's Cocoanut Grove nightclub in 1942. But Sylvia made no progress at MGH; in fact, she seemed to get worse. Aurelia said that by the time Sylvia arrived there, the patients in her ward had heard all about her story. They made "derogatory," taunting comments about her mental condition, and told her she should be in a "special ward" for suicides. Sylvia then "became extremely suspicious and began to be delusional for the first time. She was demanding that the doctors prove their identities to her before she would speak to them. She became extremely self-derogatory. Openly expressed many ideas of suicide, developed considerable retardation in addition to her existing confusion."[133]

In *The Bell Jar*, Plath describes the MGH ward as a notch below Esther's previous one. The presence of Italian American patients and African American workers makes Esther, poisoned by racism, feel that she is falling "down, down, like a burning, then burnt-out star" through the mental health system. She fears, like Plath, that if she does not "get better" she will end up in a state hospital.[134] But Mrs. Prouty was not about to let that happen. She began calling Dr. Lindemann at his home for advice about Sylvia's treatment, and she encouraged Aurelia to become a more aggressive advocate. "In your place, I would call him. He is a most kind and understanding man & would not feel it an intrusion."[135] Lindemann reassured Aurelia and Prouty that Sylvia was not psychotic and would recover her mental health completely,[136] though he also ominously "warned" her that more shock treatments might "totally" alter her personality—which Aurelia later came to believe.[137] He recommended that she be moved to McLean Hospital in Belmont, with which he was affiliated. Prouty preferred Silver Hill in Connecticut, but McLean—another "country-club-appearing" place—would have to do.[138]

Waking in the Blue

McLean Hospital, September 1953–January 1954

W hen Mrs. Prouty collected Sylvia from Massachusetts General Hospital in a limousine on September 14, 1953, Plath assumed she was on her way, as she told Eddie Cohen, to "the best mental hospital in the U.S."[1] Yet McLean was foundering, and Plath's stay coincided with the end of an era. "McLean at mid-century," wrote the medical historian S. B. Sutton, "was a struggling organization, barely able to keep abreast of progressive treatment concepts, let alone serve as a model for other hospitals."[2] McLean's reputation as a backwater that indulged its patients' idiosyncrasies made it a choice of last resort for the best psychiatric residents. Austen Riggs in Stockbridge, and even the Boston Psychopathic Clinic, were more prestigious. Dr. Francis de Marneffe, who eventually became McLean's director and one of the most preeminent psychiatrists in Boston, hesitated before committing himself to McLean in 1953 as a young resident. "I knew at the time McLean was not at the forefront," he said.[3] But he also knew there would be a new chief coming in soon—Alfred Stanton, who arrived in 1955 and, according to de Marneffe, "revolutionized" the hospital. He stopped electroshock treatment and lobotomies, and prioritized formal psychotherapy. But that was not the McLean Plath experienced.

From its founding, McLean Hospital was envisioned as a comfortable retreat for the wealthy.[4] Frederick Law Olmsted, who had designed Manhattan's Central Park, created the campus on a hillside in Belmont, west of Boston.[5] When the new hospital opened in the 1890s, *The American Journal of Insanity* proclaimed that it met the "requirements for successful treatment of patients of a comparatively well-to-do class."[6] But a progressive spirit drove its founders: this was to be a new kind of retreat for the mentally ill, without barred windows, fences, or traditional wards. "When it was built it was called the City on a Hill," said McLean archivist Terry Bragg.[7]

McLean's first superintendent, Rufus Wyman, laid the groundwork for the hospital's progressive approach in 1830 when he replaced the traditional regimen of purging and bleeding with gentler "therapy": "riding, walking, sewing, embroidery, bowling, gardening, arts, reading, writing, conversation."[8] Dr. Edward Cowles, superintendent of McLean from 1879 to 1904, went further. He set up research labs and a nursing school. Though he was interested in Freudian approaches he felt, rightly, that the future of psychiatry lay in biological research.[9] The hospital would henceforth align itself with biological, rather than psychoanalytical, approaches. Cowles's compassionate, progressive approach was mirrored in the pastoral campus, which was supposed to give patients the sense that they were part of a residential community rather than an institution. Seven miles of winding lanes and underground tunnels connected the main administration building to freestanding residences. The most disturbed patients were placed on the outskirts of the campus, while the healthier ones were housed closer to the center.[10] Plath would gauge her recovery as she moved inward from the periphery.

"We are very proud of our hospital," said McLean director Franklin Wood in 1953. "It is very attractive and looks more like a college campus than a mental hospital."[11] Indeed, the redbrick Victorian buildings probably reminded Sylvia of Smith. There were tennis courts, a golf course, riding stables, gymnasiums, badminton courts, billiard rooms, and bowling alleys. Red and white oaks, sugar maples, and copper beeches dotted the hospital's sprawling 378 acres. Patients and nurses skied and skated on the grounds in the winter and played lawn games in the summer. Requests for lobster and other delicacies were routinely accommodated. Musicians from the Boston Symphony Orchestra and actors from city troupes performed in the amusement hall.

Plath was admitted to McLean at the height of its exclusivity. In the nineteenth century, it had operated on a sliding-scale fee basis; more than half of its patients paid less than the full fee. But like many institutions, McLean suffered during the Depression; afterward it moved to higher, non-negotiable fixed fees. The hospital relied on wealthy patients to survive.[12]

Promotional photographs of McLean's interior in 1953 show common spaces decorated with Persian rugs, large, ornate fireplaces, floor-to-ceiling windows, overstuffed chairs, fresh flowers, grandfather clocks, oil paintings, and, often, a piano.[13] Inside, each private room had its own bathroom, full-sized bed, bureau, writing desk, and sitting chairs. (Esther Greenwood, however, describes her Belsize living room as "shabby" with a "threadbare rug.")[14] The wealthiest residents lived in their own "cottages" and luxurious apartments. A grand staircase with intricate carved balustrades graced the entrance hall at Upham House—nicknamed the "Harvard Club" on account of the many alumnae who passed through. Robert Lowell, who was hospitalized at McLean multiple times, wrote of his experience there in 1958's "Waking in the Blue":

> This is the way day breaks in Bowditch Hall at McLean's;
> the hooded night lights bring out "Bobbie,"
> Porcellian '29,
> a replica of Louis XVI
> without the wig—
> redolent and roly-poly as a sperm whale,
> as he swashbuckles about in his birthday suit
> and horses at chairs.

In the 1960s and '70s, McLean became famous for treating poets and musicians like Lowell, Anne Sexton, James Taylor, and Ray Charles. But 1953 was still the era, as Lowell put it, of the "Mayflower / screwballs."[15] One psychiatrist who spent a summer at McLean in the early 1950s gave a damning assessment:

> There is no real therapy as we know it. . . . The chief formulae seem to have been shock, encouragement, reassurance and sublimation through activities. Because of the high rates and the luxuriousness of the place, aristocratic clientele is found, consisting of patients whose families don't want them to get really well, and want them out of the way. . . . I suspect it is a notch above state hospitals in the area, but it certainly is far from being in the same class with a psychoanalytical institution. It houses too many presumed chronics.[16]

The McLean culture seemed stagnant in other ways as well. The hospital revolved around its director and paterfamilias, Dr. Franklin Wood, which made it seem "medievalistic or feudalistic."[17] (Bragg noted that Dr. Wood had "a flower in his boutonnière, he had his Packard, he was driven around. He had a certain image to maintain."[18]) Pay was "at a stinkingly low level," and staff morale was rock bottom.[19] One physician became exasperated when Wood denied his request for funds to buy mice for his lab, telling him he should simply catch them on the McLean grounds.[20] Perhaps because of the low wages, there was an "acute" nursing shortage, which Dr. Wood admitted was a "major problem."[21] The hospital had to rely on many part-time nurses—a destabilizing situation for patients. (In *The Bell Jar*, Esther remarks that the nurses were "always changing.")[22] There were no social workers or full-time psychologists on staff under Wood's leadership, and there was no family therapy. Wood thought that patients ought to become adjusted to their families. Dr. de Marneffe recalled, "The problem was the patient, not the family, in those days."[23] Years later he was "embarrassed to admit" how little thought McLean psychiatrists gave to oppressive family dynamics in the early fifties.[24] Dr. de Marneffe remembered that there was only one part-time psychologist there in 1953, Dr. Irene Pierce Stiver.

Robert Coles, who eventually became a Harvard professor, was a psychiatric resident at McLean in the mid-fifties. He was aware of the hospital's shortcomings, but he felt that patients, allowed to remain eccentric, were treated with more dignity there than in more "progressive" hospitals. "The residents there hadn't really been regarded as psychiatric patients in the full twentieth-century sense of the phrase," he said.[25] Dr. Beuscher remembered weekly "old fashioned" teas in the "Victorian parlors" with cucumber sandwiches and a "lovely silver service."[26]

But McLean was not Baden-Baden. More dangerous therapies, like subcoma insulin and electroshock treatment, were frequently practiced. In 1953, eighty-seven patients received shock treatment and seventy received insulin. There were even four lobotomies that year—the last that were performed at McLean.[27] Sylvia could not have known the hospital would discontinue the practice, and the prospect terrified her. Electroshock treatment—only in use for about thirteen years—was a risky procedure and not well understood.[28] Some patients responded well to it and returned to a normal life. Others did not. McLean's director of internal medicine, Dr. Mark Altschule, wrote in 1953 that the hospital was testing certain drugs for use in shock treatment that would prevent "potentially fatal reactions."[29] McLean doctors were reluctant to use shock treatment on fellow physicians, which suggests their discomfort with the procedure.[30]

Dr. Beuscher remembered that hot-and-cold-water treatments in the hospital's hydrotherapy suites were common in the pre-drug era.[31] One popular therapy, practiced until the 1970s, was called the "Neptune Girdle." It involved wrapping patients in cold, wet sheets and was usually used in the "treatment of psychoneuroses." (Plath's illness fell under this diagnosis.) Another involved keeping patients in the bathtub for hours, even days.[32] While still at McLean, Dr. Tillotson, Plath's former psychiatrist, pioneered a short-lived water therapy he called "hypothermia." Patients were kept in blankets that contained a refrigerant until their body temperatures were lowered 20°, sometimes for up to sixty-eight hours. Tillotson practiced the procedure on ten patients. Four apparently showed improvement; one died. He insisted that the therapy was promising.[33]

There were milder therapies, such as occupational therapy, recreational therapy, and physiotherapy; there was a library, a coffee shop, and a beauty parlor. In the early 1950s, however, there were no scheduled activities or routines for patients. Psychotherapy was practiced, but loosely, as Dr. de Marneffe remembered. He was one of four residents in 1953 who made their rounds to the patients' rooms: "We would sit down with the patients and spend fifteen, twenty minutes, thirty minutes doing psychotherapy . . . it was not as structured as it became under Stanton. . . . Sometimes you just sat in the easy chair of the patient's bedroom and you talked and that was psychotherapy."[34]

According to McLean's 1953 "Report of the Clinical Service," "The patient is first studied thoroughly, and the situation considered in conference. Hereditary, cultural, sociological, somatic, and personal elements are considered. The problems and assets are evaluated."[35] Patients were not always interviewed. Perhaps because two-thirds of psychiatric patients were women, willingness to cooperate and serve others was considered a sign of progress.[36]

Dr. Ruth Tiffany Barnhouse Beuscher, a thirty-year-old psychiatric resident at McLean, was assigned to Plath on her admission. Dr. Beuscher had never received formal analytic training and was skeptical of the benefits of psychoanalysis, though her former colleague, Dr. de Marneffe, remembers her practicing what he called psychotherapy.[37] In *The Bell Jar*, Dr. Beuscher becomes Dr. Nolan, who evinces a similar wariness toward Freudian talk therapy. ("I never talked about Egos and Ids with Doctor Nolan," Esther says.)[38] Dr. Beuscher herself delineated the distinction: "The work that Sylvia did with me was 'therapy'—not 'analysis.' Analysis is three to five times a week on a couch, usually. This was less often, face-to-face."[39] When Alfred Stanton took over as McLean's director in 1955, Dr. Beuscher was deeply dismissive of his psychoanalytic approach, saying, "He hired a bunch of *analysts* and social workers." He was reluctant to prescribe the sedative Thorazine, which had come out in 1953–54 and which Dr. Beuscher called "God's gift to the mental hospital." She got patients to open up through art and music therapy—drawing had gotten Sylvia to talk, she said. "Others I would say, let's go for a walk, whatever. I wouldn't sit there off behind my desk asking foolish questions."[40]

Sylvia was one of the first patients that Dr. Beuscher, who arrived as a resident at McLean on July 1, 1953, treated. Plath liked Dr. Beuscher immediately—here, finally, was a female doctor to whom she could relate. Dr. Beuscher thought that Plath's depression was symptomatic of her inability to reconcile her literary ambition with marriage. She felt that Plath had been "traumatized" by her experience in New York, where her high expectations of women's professional success had met with "a low-level, stereotypical, superficial version of that." Beuscher concluded, "This left her with no place to go. She didn't have any appropriate models."[41]

In fact, Dr. Beuscher herself would become the model Plath so badly needed. She was young, stylish, intelligent, and ambitious. Sylvia compared her to Myrna Loy and later called her a mother figure.[42] But she was more of a double. Dr. Beuscher suggested as much when she told an interviewer that they "considered themselves two of a kind: Both were child prodigies with high IQs; both were ambitious and determined; both considered themselves 'intellectual snobs.'"[43] Dr. Beuscher even had the kind of marriage of true minds Sylvia coveted: her husband was a fellow psychiatric resident at McLean. Beyond offering sympathy and direction, she had something to *teach* Sylvia about successfully integrating her own seemingly conflicting desires. In *The Bell Jar*, Plath portrayed her male psychiatrists as men who doled out punishment for "unfeminine" ambition. Ruth Beuscher, alternatively, stood for everything Plath wanted in her own life.

Yet, unbeknownst to Sylvia, Dr. Beuscher had paid a steep price for her own professional freedom. Her father, Donald Grey Barnhouse, was an imposing, influential Presbyterian minister who "dominated" his family.[44] Barnhouse was famous in his day: his *Bible Study Hour* was syndicated on more than one hundred NBC stations nationally, and he founded a successful religious magazine, *Eternity*. Ruth infuriated him when, at Vassar, she eloped with a Princeton student she had met in her religious youth group. She later graduated from Barnard, then Columbia medical school. While in medical school, she divorced her first husband, with whom she had had two children. Dr. de Marneffe, who described her as "flamboyant," claimed that she had put herself through medical school by singing and playing the piano in New York nightclubs.[45] Such moonlighting may explain why her ex-husband received custody of their children. He made it difficult for her to visit them, and she eventually stopped trying; the decision would haunt her throughout her life. (She resumed her relationship with her daughter years later, but never reconciled with her son.) She met her second husband, William Beuscher, at medical school; that marriage, too, was beset by problems.

By the time Dr. Beuscher met Sylvia, she had severed ties with her father, lost custody of her two young children, and had begun to suspect that her husband was an alcoholic. She was also grieving her mother, who had recently died of cancer. Sylvia, presumably, would not have known any of this, yet the dramatic upheavals in Dr. Beuscher's life suggest that she was suffering alongside her patient. This was not a cool, clinical relationship, but—as it would turn out—something more symbiotic.

After Dr. Beuscher's second marriage ended, she left psychiatry and became a practicing Episcopal clergywoman. She had a deep interest in astrology and tarot, which she practiced regularly; she called herself a "white witch." In 1974, she brought a Plath biographer to a "professional astrologer" who could help her "find Sylvia."[46] By then, Dr. Beuscher's treatment of Plath had come under scrutiny. She would eventually divulge details about Plath's treatment to three biographers, most notably Harriet Rosenstein, who never finished her biography. Dr. Beuscher had "clandestinely read all the significant parts of her [Plath's] McLean Hospital record" out loud into a tape for Rosenstein, and given her "the last few letters" Plath sent to her—fourteen in all, including one Plath wrote a week before her suicide.[47] (Beuscher told Rosenstein she had "foolishly" burned most of their correspondence "a year or so before she [Plath] died."[48])

Dr. Beuscher's flagrant disregard for doctor-patient privacy suggests that she may have violated other professional norms. Dr. de Marneffe said that Dr. Beuscher was "not a good psychiatrist" and was "quite unprofessional and unethical in her treatment of Plath in later years." Indeed, her "poor treatment" of Plath was an open secret in the psychiatry community, he said. He speculated that Dr. Beuscher needed Sylvia's friendship as much as Sylvia needed her professional guidance, a suspicion Beuscher herself seemed to confirm when she told Rosenstein that she and Sylvia "went shopping" together and had a sisterly relationship.[49] "Whose need was being met?" Dr. de Marneffe wondered.[50] Dr. Beuscher continued to treat Sylvia on and off after she returned to Smith, and again when Sylvia and Ted Hughes lived in Boston in 1958–59. She would come to wield enormous influence. It was Dr. Beuscher who convinced Plath to seek a divorce from Hughes in September 1962, and to whom Plath wrote in February 1963 about her desire to "pull up the psychic shroud" and die.[51]

———

PLATH WAS ADMITTED to McLean on September 14. Dr. Beuscher remembered that she "spoke very little spontaneously in initial interviews" and was "preoccupied with the idea that she had been betrayed, that there was no one she could trust." She felt Plath's mind was "very active" but that Plath simply did not want to "discuss her thoughts with anyone."[52] Dr. de Marneffe remembered that Plath was initially housed on the first floor of Codman House, which burned down in 2016, and was moved "up" to Women's Belknap (now South Belknap) when she made progress. (In *The Bell Jar*, Caplan is based on Codman House, Belsize on Women's Belknap.) Plath's notes confirm de Marneffe's memory: in a 1961 outline of *The Bell Jar*, she wrote, "Drive in chauffeured car with Mrs. P. [Olive Prouty] to 3rd hospital / Codman—end of hall."[53] Dr. Paul Howard, presumably in consultation with Dr. Beuscher, first suggested a course of sub-coma insulin treatment for Plath—a procedure that required insulin injections three times a day in the hope of a "reaction."[54] The treatment had come to America from Vienna, where Dr. Manfred Sakel had hailed the calming effects of insulin on patients undergoing opiate withdrawal. He experimented with higher doses of insulin on schizophrenic patients, essentially drugging them into a stupor from which they predictably emerged less hostile. The treatment made its way to America and was widely practiced, along with shock treatment, at midcentury. Yet some doctors who prescribed it daily suspected it provided no real cure. Dr. Max Fink, who was the head of the insulin coma unit at Hillside Hospital in Queens from 1952 to 1958, called the treatment "unpleasant and dangerous," with a mortality rate between 1 percent and 10 percent.[55]

Plath's provisional diagnosis upon her admission to McLean was "psychoneurotic disorder, depressive reaction"; her determined diagnosis was "sane."[56] Dr. Beuscher's own "diagnostic impression" was "delayed adolescent turmoil."[57] On September 18, Sylvia began her three-month course of ambulatory insulin sub-coma treatment, which made her gain significant weight. Her bloated appearance depressed her, and she became listless during her unstructured days. Mrs. Prouty visited her in October and wrote to Dr. Beuscher about her frustration regarding McLean's lack of routine. "I told Dr. Wood (and I think he agreed with me) that I thought it would be beneficial to Sylvia if she had a definite schedule to follow each day—a routine which divided her day into periods. Each time I have visited her she has dwelt on the long objectless hours spent in her room."[58] Dr. Wood, however, informed Prouty that "schedules for patients was not the method now followed at McLean's."[59] Occupational therapy was available—Sylvia practiced weaving and pottery—but she was still too depressed to "plan her own day." Prouty also told Dr. Beuscher that Sylvia felt "isolated" and was "not mixing well with the other patients." A heavily marked passage in Plath's copy of William James's *Varieties of Religious Experience* suggests her sense of isolation: "And when I laid down, would say, I shall be perhaps in hell before morning. . . . I would many times look on the beasts with envy, wishing with all my heart I was in their place, that I might have no soul to lose . . ." Next to this passage, Plath wrote in the margin, "cf: McClane yard & fly & cricket."[60] (James himself was rumored to have been a McLean patient.)

When Mrs. Prouty's pleas fell on deaf ears, she took it upon herself to provide Sylvia with distractions. She encouraged her to use the weaving loom, and asked her to type part of a manuscript. Gordon wrote to Sylvia that she had once made him promise that, whatever happened in his life, he would always read. He lightly suggested that she do the same. But Sylvia was in a daily stupor due to her insulin treatment. She dressed up in a "pretty blue suit" for a drive with Prouty in October, but she seemed depressed about her lack of progress. She derided her weaving attempts as "awful," though Prouty thought her weaving "the best in the shop . . . really exquisitely done." Sylvia's typing, too, she told Aurelia, was "flawless."[61] Typing Prouty's manuscript was the one activity that seemed to lift Sylvia's spirits, and Sylvia asked her for more typing work.

Mrs. Prouty continued to press Dr. Beuscher for more information about Plath, but Beuscher was tight-lipped. She would say only that Sylvia was "a perfectionist—which accounts for her self-deprecation if she fails."[62] This was not news to Aurelia, who, like Prouty, was becoming increasingly suspicious of Beuscher's methods. "I wonder if you talked with Dr. Beuscher," Prouty asked Aurelia in late October. "I don't seem to have very satisfactory talks with her. Do you? She is always in a hurry—even though we have an appointment, she speaks only of superficial details about Sylvia."[63] Dr. Beuscher's refusal to share details of Sylvia's treatment was actually progressive for the time; Plath's male psychiatrists were much more willing to discuss her case.[64] Soon Prouty was writing to Dr. William Terhune at the Silver Hill Hospital in Connecticut about the possibility of transferring Sylvia there. Their program was much more structured, and Prouty trusted Dr. Terhune.

Aurelia remained on the sidelines that fall, shocked into submission while Mrs. Prouty managed her daughter's care. Prouty tried to include her as best she could: "You are Sylvia's mother & you are the one to decide what is best for her. I want you to express yourself freely to me and to know exactly what is going on in my mind and to share with you all the information the doctors give me."[65] But Aurelia allowed Sylvia's benefactor to make the relevant decisions. The two women took Sylvia for drives in late October—Prouty brought her out to a local farm stand, while Aurelia took her to visit her aunt Dot. Dr. Beuscher later suggested that Sylvia did not enjoy these outings, nor did she relish visitors, whose well-meaning but oppressive presence often made her feel worse. Mrs. Cantor came and lectured Sylvia about Christian Science principles, while Mr. Crockett played word games with her in an effort to regalvanize her mental agility. He remembered her as "disheveled, and very sad."[66] They did not understand the side effects of her insulin treatment, which embarrassed her.

For Sylvia, the last straw came on her twenty-first birthday, when Aurelia brought her a blooming bouquet of yellow roses, her favorite flowers. Sylvia threw the flowers away, just as Aurelia suspected she would. Plath eventually re-created the scene in *The Bell Jar*:

That afternoon my mother had brought me the roses.

"Save them for my funeral," I'd said.

My mother's face puckered, and she looked ready to cry.

"But Esther, don't you remember what day it is today?"

"No."

I thought it might be Saint Valentine's Day.

"It's your *birth*day."

And that was when I had dumped the roses in the wastebasket.

"That was a silly thing for her to do," I said to Doctor Nolan.

Doctor Nolan nodded. She seemed to know what I meant.

"I hate her," I said, and waited for the blow to fall.

But Doctor Nolan only smiled at me as if something had pleased her very, very much, and said, "I suppose you do."[67]

Aurelia later wrote to the literary critic Judith Kroll, "I knew in my bones she would in her depressed, negative state of mind find fault with that; but I knew also that if I ignored the day, she would write, 'Mother saw fit to ignore my 21st birthday' and make much of that. So I did what my heart prompted me to do—hoping for the miracle that she would understand that I saw this as an illness to be fought through and conquered and that I loved and treasured her."[68] Aurelia also told Kroll that the line in *The Bell Jar* that Esther attributes to her mother—"We'll act as if this were a bad dream"—was actually spoken by Mrs. Cantor, who drove Aurelia to visit Sylvia every Saturday.[69]

Aurelia tried to stay calm and cheerful during her visits. Dr. Lindemann, who had treated Plath earlier at Massachusetts General Hospital, told her, "You must believe in my prognosis: that she will recover completely and you must go to her with a calm center and the true conviction that she will recover—if you wish to help."[70] Under no circumstances should she enter Sylvia's room "trembling with fear."[71] Aurelia followed his advice to the letter. She tried as best she could to compose herself and suppress her anxiety; she even meditated beforehand so that she would exude strength during her visits. But her placid disposition seemed only to confirm, to Sylvia, the wide gulf between them. When Aurelia asked her daughter about the maternal resentment in her poem "The Disquieting Muses," Sylvia responded, "Well, whenever you visited me in the hospital, you were always so calm and confident that I would soon recover, I felt you had no conception of the psychological hell I was going through."[72] Aurelia later wrote, "How far my vicarious sharing of her agony went, she never knew—I didn't want her to know."[73] In fact, the stress of her daughter's attempted suicide and hospitalization caused Aurelia's ulcer to worsen. In 1955 she would have a gastrectomy in which three-quarters of her stomach was removed.

When Dr. Beuscher questioned Sylvia about the yellow roses in the wastebasket, she claimed she threw them away because she had no vase. Dr. Beuscher did not believe this explanation and began directing her psychotherapy "to getting her to realize she experiences hostility and to get her to express it some way other than directing it inward."[74] Sylvia finally confessed that she was angry with her mother, and Dr. Beuscher promptly canceled her visiting hours. The move thrilled Sylvia but infuriated Aurelia and Mrs. Prouty, who began to circumvent Dr. Beuscher entirely. Prouty now went straight to Dr. Howard with a written list of questions, which he "answered most painstakingly."[75] Aurelia also began consulting with Dr. Lindemann regularly. Lindemann—who now worked at the Boston Psychopathic Hospital, a rival clinic, but was consulting on Plath's case—was critical of Plath's treatment at McLean. He confirmed that Sylvia was inactive, getting "very little sleep," and "still felt utterly inferior and positive of the hopelessness of her condition."[76] Prouty wrote to Dr. Terhune for a second opinion regarding the treatment methods at McLean, particularly the use of insulin; she had tried to learn about the treatment at her local library, but found nothing.

Mrs. Prouty would spar with other McLean doctors over Plath's treatment that November and December. She wrote from a position of power, fame, and fortune. Prouty herself had suffered a nervous breakdown and hospitalization as a young woman, and she was determined that Sylvia should get the best treatment. Previous commentators have called Prouty "a meddler," someone "who seemed to set herself up as a mental health expert."[77] Dr. de Marneffe remembered her in 1953 as "controlling."[78] Yet it is chilling to think what might have happened to Plath had Prouty not paid her expenses at McLean and urged her doctors to give her more attention.

By late November, Mrs. Prouty suspected that Dr. Beuscher was turning Sylvia against her mother. She was deeply cynical about Freudian concepts. To Aurelia she wrote, "You said Sylvia remarked to you last time you were there, 'Why, I don't hate you, Mother!' That reveals what line is being followed—a line familiar to all of us in this age of psychoanalysis."[79] Prouty continued to complain about what she assumed to be McLean's emphasis on psychoanalysis as opposed to occupational therapy. On a handwritten note in the margin of a letter to Aurelia, she wrote, "I think her depression—attitude and ideas (by 'ideas' I mean her continued 'idea' that her mind has become 'empty' etc. etc.) continue about the same as when she first went to McLean. I feel they—McLean—should have built up her self confidence more [through] planned occupation—and less 'psychotherapy' talks about her 'mother complex' 'guilt complex' and whatnot!"[80]

Dr. Lindemann and Dr. Howard continued to reassure Mrs. Prouty that Sylvia would "recover completely," that she showed no "psychosis" or "schizophrenia"; they had "no fear the present neurosis will develop into a more serious mental condition."[81] Dr. de Marneffe later said, "I don't think one would call her borderline, the diagnosis we use these days. . . . She had no delusions. She didn't seem to be psychotic."[82] Plath's McLean diagnosis confirms that she entered the institution "sane."

In November, however, Sylvia had begun withdrawing. On November 10, her "privileges" were revoked—she was no longer allowed to leave or wander McLean's grounds as she had done previously, and her outgoing mail was censored.[83] Dr. Beuscher said Sylvia spoke with her about "the possibility of suicide . . . [she] feels hopeless about the possibility of recovery." "There is nothing in my head," she told Beuscher, who nevertheless felt "some progress is being made."[84] But Sylvia complained to Prouty that November about "her idleness and long objectless hours of nothing-to-do"; she longed "for some kind of simple occupation." Prouty wrote to Dr. Lindemann that Plath had seemed better in October, but had reverted to her earlier sadness. She told Dr. Wood that she often found Sylvia "wandering listlessly up and down the corridor and when I leave she says she will do the same, as there is nothing else for her to do."[85] Wood defended McLean's approach, responding that Plath was "an accomplisher" who was "excessively self conscious in her depressed state; and usually tries to put her worst foot forward saying that anything she is doing or thinking is 'nothing.' " He did not want to push her too hard, or make her adhere to "the pressure of a schedule."[86]

On November 24, Plath was transferred to Women's Belknap I, a ward for less disturbed patients, and put on a course of Thorazine, which had just come to McLean.[87] The drug made her drowsy and listless. Dr. Beuscher explained that these were normal side-effects, but Sylvia refused to believe her and attributed these distressing symptoms to her own worsening condition. "This makes her feel hopeless," Beuscher noted. Like her Valley Head shock treatments and her insulin course, Thorazine made Sylvia's depression worse.[88]

When Sylvia began to regress yet again, Mrs. Prouty considered practicalities. In late November, she told Aurelia that she was consulting her lawyer about "the financial situation" and that he would "probably advise a more economical place be found" should Sylvia need long-term care.[89] McLean was charging $20 a day, which did not include the price of medications—an extortionate fee, Prouty felt, given the lack of structured activities for patients. She asked Dr. Terhune if Silver Hill Hospital might consider waiving or lowering their fees for Sylvia. They reached a solution in December:

on Dr. Lindemann's advice, Mrs. Prouty and Aurelia visited the Boston Psychopathic Hospital and agreed to transfer Sylvia there. "I did hesitate to expose Sylvia to ward life when she had suffered so intensely in the ward at M.G.H.," Prouty wrote Dr. Lindemann.[90] But she could not support Plath at a luxurious place like McLean indefinitely. The Boston Psychopathic Hospital had an excellent reputation at the time—better than McLean's—but it was a brick-and-mortar urban psychiatric hospital, not a campus with a golf course. There would be no more private rooms with Persian rugs and views of the hills.

When Mrs. Prouty informed Dr. Wood of her decision, he promptly made "greater effort" to give Sylvia a routine of scheduled activities—just as Prouty had been suggesting since September.[91] Dr. Beuscher, too, finally had "a long and satisfying talk" with Aurelia.[92] Wood may have believed Plath was better off at McLean, or he may have become tired of losing younger patients to other hospitals. Dr. Howard promised Prouty, who had already paid the hospital $2,500, that McLean would bear all expenses for Plath after January 1. "He explained that they were doing this because they believed she was a very worthwhile person and they had become intensely interested in her case."[93] Howard also told Prouty that they were going to try shock treatment on Plath again. Prouty finally relented; Plath would stay at McLean. She told Aurelia, somewhat ruefully, that Aurelia was now in charge of her daughter's care.

Aurelia was relieved that Sylvia would stay at McLean, and thought Sylvia was making "good progress" there by early December. "Periodically I still have to battle with myself to combat the waves of terror I feel in connection with this continuing experience," Aurelia wrote to Mrs. Prouty on December 9. "But it is the help and understanding that you have poured forth so constantly that form the bulwark to which I hold fast."[94]

Neither Mrs. Prouty nor Aurelia balked at the prospect of another round of shock treatment. But Plath did. Dr. Beuscher knew Sylvia had a horror of shock treatment from her traumatic experience at Valley Head and that the thought of more rounds was contributing to her depression. In 1985, Dr. Beuscher offered a remarkable admission to the critic Linda Wagner-Martin: "You suggest that my reason for gaining Sylvia's trust would be to prepare her for shock treatments. This is not accurate. I hoped that shock treatment would not be necessary, but Sylvia's fear of it made her withhold much important information and many of her feelings lest I would prescribe shock treatment."[95] The psychiatrist's logic is painfully ironic: Dr. Beuscher prescribed shock treatment because Plath would not admit the depth of her depression *lest she prescribe shock treatment*. Beuscher said she and Plath "did set up the honor system" regarding shock treatment, meaning full communication and honesty, though Plath suggests otherwise in *The Bell Jar*.[96]

In December, Beuscher felt that Plath continued "to be so depressed that suicide appears to be a real risk."[97] She felt Sylvia would become "chronic" without more aggressive treatment.[98] "She was just as depressed as when she had walked in," Beuscher said. "We had talked about a lot of stuff. . . . But she had been in there for months, and Mrs. Prouty was paying the bills—this was going on and on. I discussed it with Paul [Howard], and we decided to try electroshock treatment."[99] Beuscher later revealed that she alone pushed for shock therapy over the concerns of Dr. Lindemann and Dr. Howard, who advised against it. She convinced them "that Sylvia's overriding sense of guilt and unworthiness could only be purged by the 'punishment' of shock treatments."[100]

Dr. Beuscher said she decided on the treatment in a desperate effort to break through to her patient. (In 1953 she had approved a lobotomy for one of her schizophrenic patients—an "unhappy" delusional woman who ate cat food—though she admitted that "none of us really liked that treatment.")[101] Dr. de Marneffe confirmed that Plath "did not really cotton on to psychotherapy. . . . there was a consultation with Dr. Paul Howard, and that's when she started some ECT."[102] Yet de Marneffe claimed that at least part of the reason for Plath's shock treatment had to do with Prouty's threat to withdraw financial support: "There was pressure there." Patients who could afford McLean's high fees, including his own patient Jane Anderson, "would remain a year, a year and a half in intensive therapy."[103]

In *The Bell Jar*, Esther tells Dr. Nolan about her horrific shock treatment under Dr. Gordon, promising, "If anyone does that to me again I'll kill myself." (Sylvia would say the same to her Smith friend Ellie Friedman in 1954.) Dr. Nolan reassures Esther that she won't have any more shock treatments, but then catches herself: "'Or if you do,' she amended, 'I'll tell you about it beforehand, and I promise it won't be anything like what you had before.'"[104] Esther continues to worry that Dr. Nolan will prescribe shock treatments, and begins to doubt the doctor's professional judgment. "I didn't see how Doctor Nolan could tell you went to sleep during shock treatment if she'd never had a shock treatment herself. How did she know the person didn't just *look* as if he was asleep, while all the time, inside, he was feeling the blue volts and the noise?"[105]

Dr. Nolan eventually prescribes shock treatment for Esther, but she stays with her and offers comfort before and after the procedure. When Esther awakens, she feels the bell jar has lifted. "I was open to the circulating air." Yet Esther also feels betrayed by Dr. Nolan, who does not tell her about the shock treatment until the morning of the procedure. When Dr. Nolan later tells her that she will now have the procedure three times a week, she is terrified and asks, "For how long?" The doctor's answer is slightly menacing: "'That depends,' Doctor Nolan said, 'on you and me.'"[106] Even in the best consensual relationships between doctor and patient, Plath suggests, the doctor still holds all the power. Dr. Beuscher later claimed that she had worked on preparing Plath for shock treatment "for months."[107] Yet fiction may be closer to fact: Dr. Howard had written Mrs. Prouty in mid-November, "Although electroshock therapy is . . . a possibility I do not believe, considering her improvement, that it would be good to think of [it] at this time."[108]

Sylvia had her first shock treatment on December 10. Dr. Beuscher said that after this first treatment, she "made an apparently dramatic recovery. From that time onward, she felt certain she would be well, was cheerful, thoughtful, cooperative, was no longer suicidal or depressed."[109] But Sylvia was more fearful of this treatment than Dr. Beuscher implied. On December 17, Sylvia sent Aurelia a postcard from McLean saying that she was having her sixth shock treatment "tomorrow," on Thursday, December 18. "I hope I won't have any more," she wrote.[110] Dr. Beuscher admitted that after Sylvia's sixth treatment, "she began to rebel against the shocks and refused to have any more. Was persuaded to have one more, but after that the series was discontinued. . . . Her chief complaint was the recovery period after each treatment, during which she felt keenly her loss of identity."[111]

Though Dr. Beuscher stayed with Sylvia during the procedures, as promised, Plath obviously dreaded them. She always would. Two nights before she died, in 1963, she spoke to her friend Jillian Becker about her shock treatments. "It was a horror to her," Jillian remembered.[112] Ted Hughes later wrote to a correspondent that Plath's "mismanaged" shock therapy "goes straight to the fundamental catastrophe—as she herself understood it." The experience, he said, had "pervaded everything she was & did."[113] The procedure gave her nightmares, which she described to Eddie Cohen in December: "I need more than anything right now what is, of course, most impossible; someone to love me, to be with me at night when I wake up in shuddering horror and fear of the cement tunnels leading down to the shock room, to comfort me with an assurance that no psychiatrist can quite manage to convey."[114] In her last letter to Dr. Beuscher, sent two days before her suicide, Plath wrote, "What appals [*sic*] me is the return of my madness, my paralysis, my fear & vision of the worst—cowardly withdrawal, a mental hospital, lobotomies."[115] Her nightmares and terrifying memories strongly suggest Plath developed post-traumatic stress disorder as a result of her shock treatments.

And yet, those treatments administered at McLean seemed to heal—at least in the short term. Dr. Beuscher thought Sylvia made a startlingly quick recovery, as did Sylvia herself. Five years later, Plath was still trying to understand what had made her better. "Why, after the 'amazingly short' three or so shock treatments did I rocket uphill?" she wrote in her journal. "Why did I feel I needed to be punished, to punish myself."[116] Dr. Beuscher herself was at a loss to account for the sudden change. "Nobody can explain why Sylvia got over her depression after one or two shock treatments. She just didn't want to have any more shock treatments, so she reorganized herself inside so she wouldn't have any more. I never saw it happen with anybody else."[117] (Both underestimated, looking back, the actual number of shock treatments.) Dr. Beuscher was convinced that the procedure had "a psychological significance, apart from whatever shock treatment does to people." She speculated that Sylvia needed to "be punished for something," and that when she was, the depression lifted.[118] Dr. de Marneffe's explanation was simpler—he said Plath "responded beautifully" to the treatment.[119]

AT McLEAN, Sylvia entered into a competitive relationship with Jane Anderson, a McLean patient and Smith acquaintance. Jane was the inspiration for the character of Joan Gilling, Esther's doppelgänger in *The Bell Jar*. As Plath experimented with the double, a favorite Dostoevskian motif, Jane provided a perfect example. The similarities between the two young women were uncanny. Both were high-flying Smith students from Wellesley: Jane had been president of her sophomore class and Sylvia had been elected to Phi Beta Kappa that fall. Both had attended the same Unitarian church and dated Dick Norton. Both had endured breakdowns.

Where they veered, according to Jane, was in their attitude toward treatment. Jane had been at McLean for seven months when Sylvia was admitted, during which time she had embarked on a long course of psychotherapy. She was not discharged until many months after Plath left. When Sylvia was admitted, they forged a tentative friendship; Jane recalled that they "discussed issues of psychological functioning and matters relating to suicide and death."[120] Jane gave Sylvia the newspaper clippings about her disappearance, which she had preserved. (Joan does the same for Esther in *The Bell Jar*.) But the two began to drift apart. Jane felt that Sylvia wasn't taking advantage of individual therapy. She tried to convince Plath that therapy "could be helpful to people in dealing with painful feelings so they wouldn't feel pushed to the point that they had to try to take their own life."[121]

According to Jane, Sylvia was dismissive of therapy's benefits and reluctant to use her "cognitive capabilities to understand what was going on. She seemed to be taking a very passive attitude towards her whole situation."[122]

Jane—who eventually sued the Plath estate over her portrayal as a lesbian in a film adaptation of *The Bell Jar*—felt that Sylvia had gleaned some of her "derisive" ideas about Freudian-style analysis from Dr. Beuscher. She acknowledged that after the shock treatments, Plath "was pretty well cured, as cured as she was going to be."[123] But Jane, who never had shock treatments, felt they were a quick fix that did not address the root cause of depression. Sylvia felt Jane was wasting her time with psychotherapy.

The two women judged each other accordingly, and their friendship cooled, as Dr. de Marneffe—Jane's psychiatrist for many years—remembered.[124] Jane thought that there may have been another source for their falling out, dating from a later point in their relationship: she and Sylvia parted on bad terms when Jane visited her at Cambridge in 1956 and Jane failed to show sufficient enthusiasm for her new fiancé, Ted Hughes. She felt Sylvia had still not confronted her problems deeply enough in psychotherapy, and she wanted to "rescue Sylvia from what Sylvia was doing to herself."[125] The two never spoke again. Dr. de Marneffe thought that Plath's use of Jane Anderson in *The Bell Jar* was "an incredible projection onto Joan Gilling" of Sylvia's own illness.[126]

In the novel, Esther becomes competitive with Joan about her recovery and feels superior when she makes more progress. "Ever since the shock treatments had ended, after a brief series of five, and I had town privileges, Joan hung about me like a large and breathless fruitfly—as if the sweetness of recovery were something she could suck up by mere nearness. . . . she was confined to grounds again."[127] Sylvia was similarly smug about Jane in a letter to Eddie that December, telling him, "When I entered (in the 'middle' ward) she was in the highest-ranking ward (where I am writing from now); a display of temper, however, involving her breaking several windows, involved her ending up in the 'lowest' ward, and I haven't heard from her since."[128] Sylvia dramatized Jane's relapse in *The Bell Jar*; just as Esther is due to leave the hospital, she learns that Joan has hanged herself.

Psychoanalytic readings of the novel maintain that Joan's suicide is a symbolic victory for Esther, and even for Plath herself—that by killing Joan, Plath symbolically "killed off" her depressive, life-threatening double. In real life, however, Jane pursued a rigorous course of psychotherapy at McLean, recovered her mental health, and eventually became a successful psychiatrist. Sylvia, who received little real psychotherapy at McLean and was instead prescribed insulin coma therapy and shock treatment, suffered a fatal relapse in 1963.

There may have been another reason for Sylvia's quick improvement that December. In November 1953, Gordon sent her some James Joyce poems from *Chamber Music* and apologized for a comment he had made in July when they were out walking together. His letter provides further context for Plath's suicide attempt:

> You may not remember it, but I have been haunted with the regret and ashamed that I could have said something so small and so stupid. We were talking about the great poets, and I said that the great writers had all been men. I went on to say that "Men creat [*sic*] art; women create people." When I think back on it it seems to me such a cras [*sic*] and mean statement. I was motivated I guess to strike out perversely at you, because I was jealous that you had been able to create so recently and the Muse I felt had left me bereft. As I thought back on that statement I realized that women had not been given any near approximation of the opportunity for learning as man had until practically this century. Also the opportunity to devote oneself to a life of letters was not open to women, and even today there is strong pressure to keep her in the home.[129]

He went on to say that Elizabeth Bowen was possibly the greatest living novelist, while Virginia Woolf and George Eliot were two of the best novelists who had ever written.

Gordon thought his comment about women writers had exacerbated Sylvia's sense of despair that summer. He may have been right. Sylvia had finally found a literary boyfriend with whom she could discuss Joyce for hours—and yet even he had dismissed her talent and ambition, just as Dick and Bob had. Gordon's apology may have helped alleviate her sense of hopelessness.

As Sylvia's mental health improved in late December, several of her "privileges" were restored—she was once again allowed to have visitors and go for drives and supervised walks. Although she could not leave her room unsupervised, she hoped that would soon change.[130] She became more sociable, striking up a friendship with the McLean librarian, who was a Smith graduate. Before her shock treatments she had wandered aimlessly up and down the corridors; now she spent more time in the coffee shop, "a pine-paneled den of smoky sociability," sketching for the McLean *Gazette* and writing letters.[131] Mr. Crockett visited Sylvia once a week that December at Belknap and told Aurelia that he often found her playing bridge or talking with other patients in the living room.

Gordon had been sending her letters for weeks ("He is too good to be true," she told Eddie), but she revealed more of herself to Eddie. She joked to him about her "little scandal," yet she managed to convey, in four single-spaced pages, the "hell of sordid and meaningless existence" that had prompted her suicide attempt that summer. Still, she boasted about McLean's country-clubbish features. Her peers, she told him, hailed from Vassar, Radcliffe, and Cornell; she often spent her days with "concert pianists" and "an atomic genius from MIT." McLean's reputation obviously meant a great deal to Plath. Even in "madness," she still had a foothold in the upper class.[132]

Throughout December 1953 and January 1954, Sylvia continued her sessions with Dr. Beuscher, who wrote her a prescription for a diaphragm.[133] In *The Bell Jar*, Dr. Nolan writes Esther a prescription for a diaphragm, which Esther considers her ticket to "freedom." No longer will she have to worry about "marrying the wrong person, like Buddy Willard, just because of sex."[134]

For Sylvia in early 1954, regaining her old vitality meant attracting men. Gordon was away at sea and would not return until May. Dick had stopped writing her altogether.[135] After months of hospitalization, Dick was finally free of tuberculosis and due to leave the Ray Brook sanatorium for Europe. He and Sylvia had effectively traded places, and it seems he was no longer interested in marrying her—just as she had once predicted. She felt no bitterness toward him. Indeed, she understood the new dynamic perfectly, telling Eddie that Dick "certainly owes me nothing after the way I treated him last year when <u>he</u> was down and out."[136]

With Gordon and Dick out of her life, Sylvia wrote to her Wellesley crush, Phil McCurdy, who invited her to visit him at Harvard in late December. (Plath could now leave McLean on weekends.) The two spent a day in Harvard Square, then danced that night at their old hangout, the Totem Pole. Phil drove her back to Wellesley, where they parked on a dead-end street and necked. Plath's first biographer, Edward Butscher, claimed that Sylvia lost her virginity to Phil that night. The story has been reproduced in at least three other Plath biographies, yet Phil himself rejected this claim during our interview.[137] "Let me be honest: I didn't perform well," he said. "There was not one 'magic moment.'"[138] After the close call in December, he and Sylvia had decided never to have sex for fear of ruining their friendship. She didn't talk much to him about McLean. "It never became a big issue between the two of us. I tried once to pin her down about what happened. And she said, 'I was working hard and I found my writing drying up, and the harder I worked, the less I achieved.'"[139]

Sylvia spent Christmas Day at home with her family in Wellesley, rereading all of Gordon's letters and "pounding away" a reply on Warren's "masculine" typewriter—an adjective that speaks to Plath's own gendered assumptions about writing itself. To Gordon, she cheerfully claimed that she was "feeling 100% better now," but her letter rehearsed the old, dangerous desire to excel and please. She thanked him for his Christmas gift—Edmund Wilson's *Axel's Castle*—which, she promised him, "will take me back to new depths in my dearly loved Yeats, Joyce and Eliot . . . and into new fields as well, serving as a springboard into Stein, Proust, etc. All of which will help me communicate more rewardingly with you in the future!"[140]

In January, though still a McLean patient, Sylvia began spending her weekends at home in Wellesley. On January 13, Sylvia's doctors conferred and decided to let her return to Smith on February 1 for the spring semester, as long as she saw the Smith psychiatrist twice a week. She was also advised to take a less rigorous courseload. Dr. Beuscher told Sylvia she should give herself "several years" "to decide on vocation, husband, to make other important life decisions." Sylvia was "immensely relieved" by this advice, and felt "the pressure is off." They spoke "frankly" about sex, and Dr. Beuscher tried to answer all of Sylvia's questions as best she could. She advised Sylvia not to get "too sexually involved" with anyone for the time being, as she was "not equipped to handle" the emotional complications. Sylvia would stay at McLean until "one or two days before returning" to college. "Her attitude is good," Dr. Beuscher noted. "Insight good."[141]

After Sylvia left McLean, Dr. Beuscher listed what she came to believe were Sylvia's main "problems": "1) Authority problem. 2) Difficulty with the feminine role. 3) Trouble with sense of identity. 4) Immaturity. 5) Sex. She [Sylvia] verbalized freely on all of these subjects." Dr. Beuscher's list is remarkably generic—such "problems" do not seem pathological, and might apply to many gifted young women of the era. To explain these problems the psychiatrist circles back, again and again, to what she called "the negative mother figure." Indeed, Beuscher congratulated herself for having "made" Sylvia realize that she had encouraged her mother and other "strong-minded women" in her life (presumably Mrs. Prouty) to dominate her.[142] Because of Otto's age, Beuscher felt that Aurelia and Sylvia had been locked in a "sibling rivalry" for his affection.[143] Dr. Beuscher went so far as to tell an interviewer that Esther Greenwood's "easy admission" of hatred toward her mother in *The Bell Jar* was "inaccurate." Beuscher said that "she [Plath] had spent the first month in the hospital asserting that she loved her mother." Beuscher had to "work hate admission out of Sylvia."[144]

Dr. Beuscher's psychological biases were typical of the era, when mothers were often blamed for their children's emotional problems. Psychiatry would not stop blaming mothers for their children's mental illnesses until the 1970s. (This shift in perspective gained momentum in 1970 when a group of feminist psychotherapists distributed pamphlets to their American Psychiatric Association colleagues stating, "Mother is not public enemy number one.

Start looking for the real enemy.")[145] Aurelia later wrote that several psychiatrists had questioned her about Sylvia's potty training, as if her missteps in this area led to her daughter's suicide attempt. Such accusations sound absurd now, but Freudian concepts regarding the childhood origins of neuroses still held great currency in the early 1950s before the advent of antidepressants. Philip Wylie's misogynist attack on mothers in *Generation of Vipers* was popular at the time—Sylvia had read sections of the book out loud with Marcia—and Aurelia herself blamed Wylie's "Momism" for turning her into a "scapegoat."[146] In light of these misogynistic medical and cultural biases, one might wonder how much hostility Sylvia truly expressed toward Aurelia and how much was suggested by her psychiatrist. A Plath biographer who spent six weeks interviewing Dr. Beuscher in 1970 noted that Beuscher "is clearly hostile to Mrs. Plath, Mrs. Prouty, all who might claim an equal share to Sylvia's growth and affections." She and Sylvia had "a mother-daughter's relationship."[147] Indeed, Dr. Beuscher was moved when, during their last session at McLean, Sylvia told her, "You have been like a mother, but without any of the disadvantages." Dr. Beuscher wrote, with some triumph, "This was precisely the role which the therapist had tried to assume, and it was felt that this line of approach was very successful with this patient."[148]

Sylvia's relationship with her real mother was never the same after her suicide attempt and her stay at McLean. In 1958, Dr. Beuscher would give Sylvia "permission to hate" her mother. Dr. Beuscher's notes suggest she was already nudging Plath in this direction in 1953. Aurelia, predictably, felt that Sylvia had been brainwashed by Dr. Beuscher and that the shock treatments had caused an irreparable personality change in her daughter. Janet Salter Rosenberg felt similarly; Sylvia seemed like a different person when she returned to Smith. Aurelia and Janet would each wonder if the shock treatment and the three days Sylvia spent unconscious in her Wellesley cellar had affected her brain in unknown ways.[149]

While there must have been times when Aurelia's support morphed into pressure, she was responding to a daughter who exhibited an unusually high level of intelligence from a very early age. According to a friend and Wellesley neighbor, Ora Mae Orton, Aurelia was aware of the "problem" of "maintaining both high academic standards and moral values with as little stress on all the members of the family as possible." Orton said she and Aurelia often spoke at great length "of our deep concern over this problem and our hopes that we would raise children free of emotional or mental problems."[150] Aurelia saw it as her maternal duty to encourage and cultivate her gifted daughter's talents. She did not want Sylvia to sacrifice as she had, working her way through college by "typing dull form letters eight hours a day...

from wax dictation cylinders—a grim experience I vowed no child of mine would ever have to endure."[151]

While Aurelia's concern about her daughter's future career and marriage prospects probably exacerbated Sylvia's own anxious tendencies, she cannot be blamed for Sylvia's suicidal depression any more than Sylvia herself. Plath lived in an age when there was great shame associated with mental illness, especially for someone who valued success as much as she did. She did not know how to speak to her mother about depression. Aurelia was also at a loss; she tried to coax her daughter out of her black moods with reminders of her stellar achievements, which Sylvia interpreted as pressure to succeed. In 1953, neither woman had the language to speak honestly or openly about mental illness. Aurelia had endured her husband's death, and now she had almost lost her daughter. Traumatized by grief and silenced by stigma, she fell back on platitudes.

Yet *The Bell Jar*, with its scathing portrait of Esther's mother, seethes with daughterly resentment and blame. Plath claimed that she used this trope as camouflage: Ted Hughes remembered her telling him, shortly before her suicide in 1963, that Esther's anger toward her generous and self-sacrificing mother was a symptom of her madness. In an unpublished manuscript he wrote:

> Did you know
> Who spoke in that book & what she said?
> Or did you deceive yourself
> Denying your blood issue. Christening
> Esther Greenwood a fiction?
>
> "Would I do such things? Would I ever
> Say such things?
> Against those who know how much I loved them?
> All it proves is how mad my character is,
> And how much unlike me."[152]

In the novel, Mrs. Greenwood treats Esther's mental illness as a case of weak will. Aurelia always denied that she had treated her own daughter this way, though shame and guilt would not have been unusual responses to a child's mental illness in the 1950s within an aspirational Germanic immigrant family—as the fate of Sylvia's paternal grandmother Ernestine suggests. In *The Bell Jar*, Plath writes, "My mother was the worst. She never scolded me, but kept begging me, with a sorrowful face, to tell her what she had done wrong."[153] Sylvia's neighbor Peter Aldrich remembered the great sense of shame that seemed to weigh on mother and daughter after Sylvia's suicide attempt. Hospitalization in an asylum brought shame not just to the family, he noted, but to an entire neighborhood. The stigma of mental illness at the time was so severe, he said, that those suffering from it were deemed almost "untouchable."[154]

———

IN A JANUARY 16 LETTER to Marion Freeman, Ruth's mother, Sylvia wrote of seeing *Captain's Paradise* with Aurelia and Mrs. Norton, and participating in a bridge tournament. Though Sylvia spoke pleasantly about these outings, they were not the kinds of pursuits she normally enjoyed. She disliked Dick's mother, yet in the wake of her hospitalization, her desire to return to normalcy was strong. She wrote to Mrs. Freeman with modesty, decorum, and courage:

> Perhaps mother has already chatted with you about the good news—my doctors have talked things over and decided that the best plan is for me to go back to Smith as a junior this second semester and take only 3 courses instead of 5, taking life <u>very</u> easy, with no pressure of a lot of studying or <u>having</u> to get a certain average of marks. . . . So in two short weeks I will have made the transition into the "outside" world of responsibility and independence. I expect it will be difficult in many ways—adjusting to the faster pace of normal life and activity again, but I hope I shall be able to go at it with a much more philosophic and serene attitude![155]

Sylvia would return to Smith in February 1954 as a special student for the second semester. Mrs. Prouty was furious, for McLean had assured her that Sylvia would be released to Silver Hill Hospital for a "re-education" period, which she had been willing to finance. She had spent $4,000 on Plath's treatment since September, and felt betrayed. She did not believe Sylvia was well enough to return to her regular academic routine less than six months after her suicide attempt.[156]

Dr. de Marneffe said that because Plath was at McLean voluntarily, the impetus to leave could have come, initially, from her rather than her doctors. "What happened was that twice a week the staff would meet in the basement [in] a case conference chaired by Dr. Howard. . . . Often the patient would be asked to come down, and would be interviewed by Howard as a way of both finding out how the patient felt about what was going on, but also for the purpose of demonstrating to us green residents the interviewing technique, how Howard elicited information in a nice, kind way. It could very well have been that she came down, and Howard interviewed her, and the conclusion was that you could leave."[157] Plath, maximizing the dramatic potential in her novel, wrote the corresponding scene as if Esther had been deemed "cured" by the entire staff—as if, Plath wrote in her Smith scrapbook, she had "graduated."[158]

At the end of *The Bell Jar*, Esther is poised to reenter the outside world with the full approval of her doctors, just as Stephen Dedalus stands poised on the brink of a new life away from Ireland in the final pages of *A Portrait of the Artist as a Young Man*. Indeed, in an outline Plath wrote for *The Bell Jar*, she included the phrase "going to Europe—voyage out"—a plot line she abandoned but that shows her Joycean (and Woolfian) impulse. Yet Plath leaves her readers with lingering questions. Of what has Esther been "cured," exactly? She eventually becomes a wife and mother—exactly the roles her patriarchal society expects her to fulfill. Does she decide to abide by feminine norms under the threat of more shock treatment? Is she really "better," or has she just been reprogrammed? The novel's last few paragraphs, which eerily blend Gothic elements with science fiction—Esther stares out at the "pocked, cadaverous face of Miss Huey, and eyes I thought I had recognized over white masks"—offer no clear answer.[159] And yet, the novel itself is proof that Esther has become a writer. She has managed to reconcile the parts of her identity that her doctors, and her society, did not believe could be reconciled. Plath's college notes on Joyce's *Portrait* suggest the scale of Esther's, and her own, triumph: "New life created is the final work of art: the completed book."[160]

13

The Lady or the Tiger

Smith College and Harvard Summer School,
January–August 1954

W arren drove his sister back to Smith on the last weekend of January 1954. In Northampton, they hit a "thick swirling blizzard" and spun out as they attempted to drive up an unplowed hill near campus. Sylvia saw with "blinding clarity" that death was imminent, but it held no appeal for her now. "I remember the interminable seconds as we slid, utterly out of control, and I wondered if I really was living in a deterministic universe and had displeased the malicious gods by trying to assert my will and return to Smith," she wrote to Jane Anderson, who was still at McLean. The prospect of annihilation, after all she had been through, now filled her with "horror." She thought, "this can't happen to us—we're different." Finally the car slowed and came to a stop. The experience made for a "fantastic" story, but her fear confirmed her newfound determination to live.[1]

Sylvia had returned to Wellesley from McLean in late January. At home, she played recordings of Edith Sitwell's *Façade* and Dylan Thomas reading "Do Not Go Gentle into That Good Night" over and over. His voice made her weep.[2] There was more talk of poetry at dinner with the Aldriches, where, after dessert, everyone listened to recordings of Thomas, T. S. Eliot, Ogden Nash, e. e. cummings, and Marianne Moore. Plath spent a long Sunday afternoon with the Crocketts listening to Robert Frost before a crackling fire. Only months before, she had sat stupefied with Crockett as he attempted to play word games with her. Now she spoke eloquently about Eliot and Frost.

Sylvia sounded optimistic about her recovery in letters to Gordon. She joked with him about her extra year at Smith, comparing her tenure there to "those ripe, long-maturing wines."[3] She spoke frankly, too, of the parts she had mastered: "the serious creator, the strong honest out-door type that scorns persiflage, the urbane and seductive partygoer; the eggs-and-bacon-and-coffee girl in a housecoat who can also exist somehow on olives, Roque-fort and daiquiris while clad in black velvet, and make a switch to a tanned saltwater and sunworshipping pagan. and [sic] different situations open different doors—shall we release the lady? or the tiger?"[4] At McLean, she had felt "unscholastic" as she spent her days exercising, watching movies, playing bridge, making ceramics, and "hashing out life in the coffee shop."[5] Now she was ready to immerse herself again in modern literature.

Back at Smith, Sylvia was surprised to find that the large sunlit room with three windows she had shared with Mary during her junior year was now hers alone. (The Lawrence House residents had shuffled themselves around so that Sylvia could use the room as a single.) She bought a maroon bedspread, gray curtains, blue pillows, and wall prints, and filled two book-cases with books. From her window, she could see the shops on Green Street below, and "the far gray humpback of a dark distant hill."[6] After she unpacked, Mrs. Estella Kelsey, the new Lawrence House "mother," invited Sylvia and the other girls to tea in her rooms. Plath told Jane Anderson that "everything went off very smoothly."[7]

Later, during her first meal in the Lawrence House dining room, Sylvia sat with six women whom Mrs. Kelsey had, unbeknownst to her, hand-picked for their maturity. One of them was Nancy Hunter, who would become Plath's senior-year roommate and close friend. Sylvia described her to Phil McCurdy as "tall, slender, with an enchanting heart-shaped face, green Kir-ghiz eyes, black hair and a more than figmentary ressemblance [sic] to a certain Modigliani odalisque."[8] Upon seeing the "girl-genius" she had heard so much about, Nancy blurted out, "They didn't tell me you were beautiful."[9] The others at the table balked at the "impropriety" of her remark, but Sylvia laughed. She was more relaxed now with her unhurried academic pace, and was content to adopt a "new attitude of easy-going and relaxed averageness, in contrast to my former hectic leaps for the exceptional," as she told Jane. "I feel in general very calm, philosophical, and indeed, consistently 'happy' rather than spasmodically ecstatic."[10]

Many of Sylvia's professors had written anguished letters to Aurelia after her suicide attempt and pledged their support should she return. They were true to their word, and Plath felt only admiration and warmth from the faculty. She had worried that she would be the subject of gossip, but she now experienced not a single curious stare. "No one has questioned me about my experience. . . . All of the difficulties which I was prepared to encounter have melted away like snow in the sun. . . . everybody has treated me just as if nothing had happened, and I feel most at home and casual about the whole episode, which I never thought possible," she wrote to Jane.[11] Enid Epstein Mark recalled that Sylvia was, at this point, more well-liked than she realized. "When her name was recited for being elected to Phi Beta Kappa in her junior year, she was absent. She was then hospitalized in Boston. The applause for her was deafening. Everybody knew and cared what happened to her. She never understood that."[12] Enid felt that Sylvia pushed herself too hard, and that built-up academic pressure had caused her breakdown. She remembered sitting on a bench with Sylvia during their junior year, poring over their report cards, calculating whether or not they would make it into an elite academic honor society. "This was not just icing on the cake for Sylvia. It was an imperative necessity."[13]

Janet Salter Rosenberg remembered that before Sylvia's arrival, Mrs. Kelsey summoned all the students in the house. "We had a meeting in the living room and the house mother told us that Sylvia was coming back, that she was very fragile, that we should all be very careful about what we said to her, we should not pump her for information, we should be as kind and understanding as we could." But many of the women in Lawrence House did not know what to say. "They were worried about relating to her," Janet said.[14] Sylvia stayed close to Marcia Brown, whose own mother was currently in a New York City mental hospital. Even to friends, though, Sylvia did not confide much: "we just spoke of my experiences thoroughly once, and that was that, none of the daily self-examinations and analyses that I subjected myself to with friends at McLean."[15] Plath did not want to dwell on her illness, and her friends did not probe. When Sylvia returned to campus, Louise Giesey invited her out to dinner to offer support while she readjusted to Smith. But as the two friends chatted on about "nothing," Louise could not bring herself to mention the episode. Neither could Sylvia. Still, Louise was relieved that her friend "seemed completely at ease with herself."[16] Sylvia described herself to Pat O'Neil at this time as a set of tires that had been "retreaded" for the road. But, Pat said, "she was never sure that this couldn't happen again."[17]

Plath's schedule was lighter than in previous years: Early American Literature, 1830–1900—Dreiser, Hawthorne, Melville, and Henry James—with Newton Arvin; Russian Literature—Tolstoy and Dostoevsky—with George Gibian; and Nineteenth Century Intellectual European History with Elisabeth Koffka. She was also auditing Robert Gorham Davis's Modern American Literature and a class on medieval art with Phyllis Lehmann. Before her classes, she chopped vegetables in the Lawrence House kitchen, which she preferred to waitressing. She enjoyed bantering with the kitchen workers, who provided snippets of dialogue she stored away for her stories.

In her Russian Literature class, Plath read *The Idiot, Crime and Punishment,* and *Notes from Underground.* "I felt conspicuous at first during the discussions of suicide in these books," she told Jane, "and felt sure that my scar was glowing symbolically, obvious to all (the way Hester's scarlet letter burned and shone with a physical heat to proclaim her default . . .). But now I am really so adjusted to my attempt of last summer that I may even write my Russian paper on the theme of suicide." She had, she felt, "a personalized understanding of the sensations and physical and mental states one experiences previous to the act."[18] A Smith friend from this period, Connie Taylor, remembered that suicide was, philosophically, "a big general topic. Everyone sat around drinking sherry, listening to Bartok, discussing the void. Kierkegaard [was] very big. Dostoevski big too. It was almost as if everyone was trying to drive himself crazy. . . . all of us were being pushed in so many different directions that the attraction of nothingness was very real."[19]

Plath lost some friends and found others. Janet was surprised to find that Sylvia no longer seemed interested in her company. "Of all the people in the house, she and I were closest. She had casual relationships with the other seniors. The relationship with me was much closer, and I can't say that I wasn't quite hurt by the way she was acting. But I understood that this was a different person." No longer did they discuss their ambitions to become great writers; no longer did Sylvia declare she was going to be famous, as she had many times during the previous year, or that someday someone would write her biography. "And so this openness had stopped."

Janet thought Sylvia was determined to make a new set of friends to correspond with her new self. "She cultivated people in the dormitory who she had not known, which was sort of strange. . . . But to us, she'd been Jekyll and Hyde, and we'd seen only the Jekyll and suddenly she was Mr. Hyde. And she walked all over people, she didn't fulfill her responsibilities, she would not show up for her job she was supposed to be doing and someone else would have to do it." Sylvia gained a reputation for "bird-dogging"—stealing other women's boyfriends. Janet said Sylvia never would have flouted this taboo before her breakdown. "I think she thought that the psychiatrist she had been being treated by had given her permission to do anything she wanted."[20]

Sylvia's closest confidantes now were Marcia Brown, Pat O'Neil, Nancy Hunter, Jane Truslow, and the "unconventional" Claiborne Phillips, who would rush into Sylvia's room at two in the morning and suddenly talk of "free will and destiny and objective and subjective worlds."[21] With these women, Sylvia discussed "every field from sex to salvation," often over bottles of Chianti at Joe's or martinis at Rahar's bar.[22] Sylvia shared a dark bond with Jane Truslow, who had also spent time in an asylum and received shock treatment the year before. Though Jane later came to feel that Sylvia manipulated those at Smith to get special privileges ("if you had the good luck to have a little nervous problem, then you were really treated like a queen"), her February 10, 1954, journal entry suggests Sylvia's warmth and humor: "We found so many laughable things in common that few others would be able to understand. I didn't think we talked as sensationalists, but to anyone else it would have been so. It was the first time I have talked to anyone who really understood."[23]

Sylvia also spoke of her suicide attempt to Claiborne, now her best friend in Lawrence House. "She had some vague memories of a hospital that were very strange and terrible, but like a dream, unreal. Then, at the sanatorium she said she just sat as if dead, numb and unfocused on a lawn where they would wheel her in a chair." She told Claiborne she "had really been helped" by Dr. Beuscher.[24] Later, in a June 1954 letter, Sylvia made a generous gesture Claiborne would never forget: "I want you to know also that if ever things look black and ominous, I am always here, wanting you to come visit or stay any time at all. (If I'd been sure of someone being 'there' any time I wanted, I might not have felt so frightfully isolated last summer.)"[25]

To Nancy Hunter, Sylvia detailed the "frustrations" that had led to her suicide attempt.[26] She did not discuss her therapy and shared just a single story with Nancy about her time at McLean: one afternoon she had stormed into her psychiatrist's office and demanded a lobotomy because she felt so hopeless about her prospects for recovery. "You're not going to get off that easily," the psychiatrist joked.[27] Sylvia found humor in the anecdote, Nancy recalled.

Sylvia grew closer to Sue Weller (a "great girl") and the "brilliant music major" Dorri Licht.[28] Sue remembered long, pleasant afternoons at Rahar's nursing a single martini and listening to Sylvia talk about men.[29] Sylvia was keen to experience as much of life as she could now, she told Gordon:

> Life is so largely eating and sleeping and going places without ever getting there: my "experiences" with the quantity of "action" seem so few and outstanding in comparison. . . . I can count them off: seeing a baby born, breaking rules and going up spontaneously for the first time in a small private airplane, cutting up the lungs of a human cadaver, being the only white girl at an all-Negro party, battling high waves in a storm in trying to climb aboard our little tipping sailboat, squatting in the blazing noon sun setting strawberry runners and wishing for water, racing my favorite golden retriever along the hardpacked shore at Nauset beach. . . . little things, large things, that all are somehow very important in the formative scheme of living. I want to do more, so very much more: to bike and hike through Europe, to travel out West, to meet and know and

love people with that intense rapport, transient and elusive though it may be, which I have felt so strongly in so many separate instances: I want to condition myself to hear, and not just listen; to see, and not just look; to communicate, and not just talk; to feel, and not just touch. . . . It is so disastrously easy to settle down into the smooth undemanding rituals of the trite sheepish conformist life. . . .[30]

She was eager to date again after her nunnish interlude at McLean, and went out with eight different boys, mostly from Amherst, during her first month back at Smith (though she thought the Amherst boys "so young and weak and 'sheepish'").[31] She told her mother she was "'getting back in Circulation'" with "the greatest success."[32] Mel Woody humorously recalled that Plath "assaulted" him one February night when he came to visit her in Northampton. "We were walking someplace to have a beer and she pinned me against the wall and started kissing me! I was taken aback because there'd never been any hint of that sort. But of course I enjoyed it. We ended up on a rooftop at Smith. So that got that going."[33] It was all good fun, Sylvia felt, as her "marital future was far from being at stake."[34] Myron Lotz still called, but she now found him "dull"—"so damn sad, depressed, spongy."[35] George Gebauer, an Amherst chemistry major, was her new favorite. All the male attention, she wrote Jane, had convinced her that she was not damaged goods after all: "I feel that my escapade has in no way made a lasting scar on my future associations, but is of advantage in deeping [sic] my understanding of self and others."[36]

She saw the Smith physician, Dr. Marion Booth, once a week, but did not feel the same rapport she had with Dr. Beuscher. Their talks were more "philosophical"; she wrote Jane, still at McLean, that "psychiatric help is really superfluous" now that she had "several close friends to confide in, and no problems."[37] Booth was probably not much help; she was a professor of bacteriology and public health. Janet worried that Sylvia was seeing her regularly. "We all thought that was a mistake, but not one of us was willing to say that to her. Dr. Booth was unqualified to tell anything about psychology or psychiatry. She didn't have the training."[38]

Sylvia received good news from *Harper's* again: in late January she learned it would publish one of her poems in the spring, though the editors had not yet decided which one. She joked to Aurelia that they probably thought she was dead and that any poems of hers would appear inside a "black border."[39]

Dostoevsky was beginning to replace Joyce as Plath's favorite author. "I'll never get over the experience of reading 'The Idiot' and 'Brothers Karamazov,'" she wrote Gordon that March.[40] She wondered if eternity was like Mephistopheles described it in *Crime and Punishment*—"one little room, like a bath-house in the country, black and grimy and spiders in every corner."[41] Her letters were intensely literary, full of quotes from Williams's *Camino Real*, Eliot's *The Confidential Clerk*, Sherwood Anderson's *Winesburg, Ohio*, and Christopher Fry's *The Lady's Not for Burning*.

Sylvia attended I. A. Richards's lecture, "The Dimensions of Reading Poetry," in early March.[42] Richards, a professor at Cambridge, was one of the most famous critics of his day. President Wright held a reception for him after the lecture, where Sylvia "sat on the floor at his feet" before the fire and listened to him read his poetry aloud.[43] Richards had pioneered New Criticism, which, by the 1950s, had become the standard analytical method in English departments. Plath had mastered this technique of vigorous close reading in her Smith literary essays. But New Critical ideas also influenced her poetry. Her college style is marked by intricate formality and literary allusions meant to amplify a poem's complexity. She enjoyed showing off her formal skills by writing villanelles, sestinas, and other rhyming verse. Her vocabulary, too, in these college poems, bears the mark of her thesaurus—unlike her later work, which used simpler, direct language and the rhythms of natural speech. Plath was aware that some of her work had an artificial, almost stilted quality; she would later write in her journal that she was trapped inside a "glass caul."[44] These were affected, apprentice poems calculated to please professors and editors. They were, in the parlance of the time, superbly "well-made." But her Smith-era poem "A Sorcerer Bids Farewell to Seem" reveals her longing to free her poetic lines from elaborate artifice and structure:

> I'm through with this grand looking-glass hotel
> where adjectives play croquet with flamingo nouns;
> methinks I shall absent me for a while
> from rhetoric of these rococo queens.

It would be some time before Plath was able to "vanish" "alone to that authentic island where / cabbages are cabbages; kings: kings."

———

DICK'S DEPARTURE from Sylvia's life—he was traveling in Europe, looking for a new girlfriend, she quipped to Jane Anderson—provided an enormous psychological release. Gordon was away at sea, writing long, descriptive letters about Joyce's Dublin and Odysseus's Greece. He would not return until June. His missives resembled travelogues more than love letters, and Sylvia told Aurelia she was secretly glad he was away.[45] Meanwhile, George

Gebauer's views on women's rights had begun to anger her, and she no longer considered him a serious prospect. She was beholden to no one now. She was free.

In early March, Cyrilly Abels invited Sylvia to lunch in New York City. Sylvia wanted to "reconquer" the "old broncos that threw me for a loop last year" and planned to stay with Ilo Pill, now a "fatherly" thirty-five years old.[46] She unwisely brushed aside the arrangement's romantic complications and began planning a visit over her spring break. This time, she vowed to know the city on her own terms, "from the Village to Harlem by walking and looking and more walking."[47]

She spent the first weekend of her two-week spring break at Harvard with Warren and his friends—Luigi Einaudi, the grandson of Italy's president; Clem Moore, the son of writer Sarah-Elizabeth Rodger Moore; and Alec Goldstein. (Clem Moore would later marry Susan Alliston, one of the women Ted Hughes was seeing when Plath died.) Back in Wellesley, Sylvia met Dr. Beuscher for a long cup of coffee in Framingham. Dr. de Marneffe considered such a meeting an unethical blurring of the lines between treatment and friendship. Any meeting over the standard one-hour session, he said, was not good psychiatric practice—and, according to Plath's calendar, many of her "comradely" sessions with Dr. Beuscher lasted two, sometimes even three hours.[48] As Sylvia told Gordon that April, Dr. Beuscher was "now one of my best friends . . . only 9 years older than I, looking like Myrna Loy, tall, Bohemian, coruscatingly brilliant, and most marvelous." When Plath ran her plans for a New York trip and Harvard Summer School by Dr. Beuscher, she "approved heartily."[49]

Around this time, on March 27, Sylvia attended a cabaret dance at Harvard's Adams House with Phil McCurdy. There, she danced with Scotty Campbell, the assistant director of the summer school. Sylvia "boldly" told him, as they danced, that she had been "hesitant" to apply for a scholarship this summer as she had been rejected the previous one. Scotty assured her she should apply again as he "whirled" her away from Phil and whispered compliments in her ear. She figured Scotty would forget all about her in the morning, but she soon received a letter from him all but promising a scholarship if she signed "on the dotted line."[50] She was thrilled, and seems not to have resented the manner by which the funds had come about. This, she knew, was how the game was played.

Sylvia flew from Boston to New York on March 28 with an overstuffed suitcase and Dostoevsky's *The Possessed*. Ilo met her at LaGuardia Airport, and his aunt's "roué escort" drove them back to the Pills' "dark, dingy 3rd floor walkup" in an Estonian section of Harlem.[51] The family prepared a "ceremonial dinner" for Sylvia, who then posed for formal portraits with Ilo's mother and aunt. Ilo, now an architect's draftsman, had always regarded Sylvia as more than a friend, and her visit likely sent mixed messages. Aurelia and others had advised her not to stay with him, but she dismissed their misgivings, insisting, "I could manage myself equally well in Ilo's apartment as at Smith."

Everything went according to her "calculations," she told Gordon, until Ilo "startled" her early on Monday morning as she lay in bed. He announced that he was staying home from work to spend time with her. "I told him coldly, in a flash of inspiration, that I was engaged to be married in a few months, and so was to be considered as a friend, and absolutely nothing more . . . which information succeeded in making him behave with utmost solicitude and tact for the rest of my stay." (She may have been less startled than she let on to Gordon.) After Ilo left, she walked from 123rd Street all the way to Midtown, where she met Cyrilly Abels for lunch at the Ivy Room of the Drake Hotel. They spoke mainly of Dylan Thomas, and Abels confirmed that Thomas had been "drinking to excess on an empty stomach" in the days before he died. Against her better judgment, Sylvia met Ilo at the Met that afternoon. He came bearing a half-dozen red roses, "a combined apology and farewell present." Together they toured exhibits on Sargent, Whistler, Cassatt, and medieval art. The paintings did not appeal to her as much as the abstract expressionists. She realized that her tastes were "arrantly modern!"[52]

That night, she adorned her hair with one of Ilo's roses and met up with Atherton "Bish" Burlingham, a Cornell graduate who was now attending Union Theological Seminary. Bish was the boyfriend of a Lawrence House friend, Mary Derr, who described him then as a blond Cary Grant. Janet was close to Mary, and remembered Mary's fury when she learned that Sylvia had arranged to meet Bish.[53] Sylvia, indifferent to the heartbreak she had caused, accompanied Bish to lectures by Paul Tillich and Reinhold Niebuhr at the seminary, dined with him at breakfast and lunch, and played the piano at a practice room while he sang opera—"gay fun." She had strong feelings for him, but the relationship did not outlast her spring vacation. He remained just "a potential."[54] Janet thought the entire escapade "ridiculous." "He was a theological student! She was going to be a minister's wife? Not Sylvia. This was not in her wildest dreams."[55]

Sylvia left Ilo's apartment midweek to stay with Janet downtown in Greenwich Village. Janet thought she was arriving by train at Grand Central, but she did not appear as scheduled. When Sylvia did not get off the next train, Janet called Aurelia, who became filled with anxiety. Plath had only been out of McLean for three months, after all. Around six p.m., Sylvia finally called Janet, cheerful and oblivious of the worry she had caused. She had stopped off uptown to see Bish and said she'd be "right down," but it was another two hours before she showed up to Janet's apartment. "She finally waltzed in, didn't say, 'I'm sorry I inconvenienced you.' Didn't say anything. We sat down and ate dinner, my father in the grumpiest silence I'd ever seen him in. Sylvia settled into a supposedly social conversation until it was time to go to bed." Janet called Aurelia to tell her Sylvia had materialized, but Sylvia would not get on the phone to speak to her mother. She asked Janet to tell Aurelia that she had come back earlier, but Janet refused. "The next day she told me she had to go see some people who she had met when she was at *Mademoiselle*. Fine. Go ahead. I didn't know whether I believed her or not. I was still so unnerved." Janet said she and her family felt used. "She just wanted a bed. She really wasn't visiting me."[56]

Abels surprised Plath by inviting her to dinner at her Fifth Avenue apartment before she left the city. Plath got along well with Abels's husband's nephew, a "young Jewish news reporter" for Voice of America. After dinner, she joined him for drinks at the Albert Hotel, which she called a "Greenwich dive."[57] Janet recalled that Sylvia came home that night at one a.m., again angering her parents, who normally slept in the living room. Sylvia spent Friday with Janet and Dee Neuberg, another Smith friend, lunching at the Time & Life Building and watching the end-of-season skaters at Rockefeller Center. Sylvia had lost her wallet at the Albert bar, and Janet's father lent her $25 to get home. "I'll never see that again," he told Janet after Sylvia left. He didn't, though someone later returned Plath's wallet to her at Smith with all the money in it. (She was overjoyed to be "solvent for the rest of the year!")[58]

The trip marked the true end of Sylvia and Janet's friendship. Janet was upset that Sylvia had stolen Mary Derr's boyfriend and had largely ignored her, while Janet's parents now considered Sylvia "persona non grata." The trip would have social ramifications for Plath, too. Mary was "very vocal" about telling people back at Lawrence House what Sylvia had done to her, and house seniors retaliated by calling her "Silver Plate" in private, a reference to her phoniness.[59] Jane Truslow thought that some of Plath's behavior was brazen and selfish; Jane even called her "cheap." "People who knew her in the house were always glad to hear something bad about her."[60] Even Claiborne, too, was troubled by what she felt was Sylvia's hedonistic nature that spring. "She seemed to feel somewhat defensive and to anticipate my disapproval by referring to her psychiatrist and being emancipated from old hang-ups about sex."[61] But shaming had little effect on Plath. Sylvia told a Smith friend after her breakdown that she now felt "less compelled to conform," adding, "I used to have to play bridge but now I don't."[62] Later, at Cambridge, she would "bird-dog" Ted Hughes. She wanted what she wanted.

On the train back to Boston, Sylvia stopped off for an overnight visit in New Canaan, Connecticut, with Sarah-Elizabeth Rodger Moore. Mrs. Moore, the mother of Warren's roommate Clem, was one of Plath's "ideals," and the two women discussed her writing career as they toured the mansion. Sylvia marveled at her study, "separate, all windows looking out into trees and lakes, walled with books and files, with the typewriter the central talisman on this writer's altar," as she told Gordon. Warren and Clem, also on vacation, joined them for dinner. Sylvia left the next morning rested and hopeful that she too might someday write her own fiction in "a modern dream house in the plushest part of the New Canaan woods."[63]

The next day, April 3, she met Mel Woody for lunch in New Haven. She had written to Mel before she left for New York City to arrange a date with him on her way home. She sent a poem with her letter:

> sun aslant along blue blotter . . . flesh sunwarm
> clean air greenlucid and spattered with
> sundrops . . . tender sproutings of spring
> . . . .
> somehow I will and must
> see you [64]

After a romantic interlude at Yale, Mel agreed to accompany Sylvia back to Wellesley on the train. She still had five days of vacation left before she had to return to Smith. "Sylvia said, 'You've got to come home with me to protect me from my mother.'" He understood that Elmwood Road had become stifling for her and that she needed a buffer. He gave her a poetry book by Hart Crane and D. H. Lawrence's *The Man Who Died*. He spent the night sleeping in Warren's room, and read the entire Lawrence book to her out loud the next morning before he departed to visit another erstwhile girlfriend in Newton. Sylvia had told Mel about what she termed "The Resurrection"— her rebirth after near death—and he thought Lawrence's book would be fitting. "She was hungry for life all along. She had a terrible time putting it all together because there was so much she wanted to embrace."[65]

Smith seemed sleepy after the buzz of New York, but Sylvia tried to take advantage of the college's many cultural opportunities. She was particularly impressed by a lecture on Ibsen by Hans Kohn, a visiting professor from Columbia. "I'll never be the same again. It was absolutely explosive—vital— soul-shattering!" she wrote Phil McCurdy. After the lecture, she rushed to the bookstore, bought Ibsen's collected plays, and "read them immediately." "Phil, I'm worried—what I've got is worse than epilepsy or syphilis! I went to that damn store and came back having bought TWELVE (12!)

books!" Among them were plays by Shaw and O'Neill, poetry by Whitman and Delmore Schwartz, Fry's *Venus Observed* and Sterne's *Tristram Shandy*. "My bookcases are overflowing—shelves of novels, poetry, plays, with lots of philosophy, sociology & psych. I am a <u>bibliomaniac</u> (with a slight touch of nympho thrown in!)."[66]

Plath's sexual hunger was wound up with her "resurrection," and her new embrace of life—though she was still a virgin. She was finally operating at full capacity, deeply fulfilled, challenged, and stimulated by new ideas and authors. "Doomsday" had appeared in *Harper's*, and she encouraged Phil to pick up a copy: "ah vanitas, vantitatum," she wrote him. "I'm only human: & did so want to share my happiness." When Phil wrote to her of the loss of Harvard's Adams House master, she replied philosophically, "if we could be clairvoyant and see the date of our own doom, the bloodclot in the vein of our existence—how differently we might proportion our time . . . and yet, perhaps all one can do is go on and on 'making the best of a bad job . . .' and loving life the more for its individual ephemeral quality."[67] Plath had come a long way since August.

ALL OF HER READING was preparation, she felt, for great work—and great love. In April, Sylvia met Richard Sassoon, the Yale roommate of Mel Woody and Nancy Hunter's "psychic brother" Dick Wertz. Sylvia first saw Sassoon—as she usually called him—while visiting Mel at Yale. Mel remembered that he, Sylvia, Dick Wertz, and Sassoon all went out together on that occasion. Later, Sassoon arranged a date with Sylvia despite the fact that she was seeing Mel. Sassoon and Sylvia spent the afternoon together in the Northampton countryside, where they "raced each other over the green fields" and "meandered along by the river."[68] After dinner, they drove out to Mount Tom and climbed an 830-foot-high firetower in the dark. Sylvia was nervous as her legs shook beneath her, but she was eager for the small adventure: "a victim of vertigo, I shuddered in ecstasies of terror all the while pretending to be brave," she wrote Phil.[69] After, they drank in a pub in Amherst and spoke to each other in French. Sassoon complimented Plath on her accent, and she felt like the "belle of the bar."[70]

Sylvia first mentioned Sassoon to Aurelia in an April letter. His father, she noted, was a cousin of Siegfried Sassoon, the famed World War I poet. The Sassoons, of Persian Jewish descent, had married into the Rothschilds to become one of the most powerful and wealthy Jewish lineages in Europe. Sassoon, born in Paris to British parents, had attended Lawrenceville in New Jersey, but Mel found him Continental in manners and British in attitude.

He was "neurasthenic" and extremely "class-conscious." "He complained that in America you don't know how to deal with people because you can't tell what class they are."[71] Plath likely knew about Sassoon's heritage, for she told Claiborne he had "money."[72] Later, she referred to him in her journal as a "Persian Jew."[73] To others she described him as "a thin, slender Parisian fellow who is a British subject, and a delight to talk to . . . a very intuitive weird sinuous little guy whose eyes are black and shadowed so he looks as if he were an absinthe addict."[74] (At five feet eight inches, Sassoon was an inch shorter than Sylvia.) She would cast Sassoon, who was a French major and an aspiring writer, as Rimbaud and Baudelaire—much as he would cast himself. Mel thought he was "brilliant," though Sassoon always tried to hide his vast intelligence. "He was lounging around all the time, then he'd sit down and type at sixty words a minute and write an A paper and I'd say, 'How'd you do that?' And he said, 'I've been writing it all week.' Kind of like Mozart with symphonies, he had it all finished." Mel claimed that Sassoon's French was so good the Yale French department invented courses for him.[75]

By late April, Sassoon was writing frequently to Plath, partly in French, happy to play the world-weary sophisticate: "I am a cultural mongul [*sic*]—decadent & lazy."[76] His missives were full of exclamations and non sequiturs that sounded straight out of Baudelaire: "I am master and actor. Will you play?" "I am God. I damn you for my pleasure!"[77] "I am as chained to you as you are to your dreams." "There is no oblivion!!!" "I had to run to the all night café . . . in order to be a little alone."[78] He called Sylvia his "enchant-ress" and "sorceress" and told her that she was "the artist," he the critic.[79] Dick had invited Sylvia to Yale with neatly copied train schedules. Sassoon took a more dramatic approach: "Saturday? Sunday! Shall I come? Shall I come—when the Sun you so love and I so loath (it—he is my rival; I prefer my appetite!) Shall I come when the sun still strives to murder myth?"[80] Plath played along: "ANNIHILATE SUN. COME SATURDAY. WIRE WHEN. TOMORROW & TOMORROW."[81] (She signed off "Eva," invok-ing her poem "To Eva Descending the Stair.") Together they drank French wine on hilltops and quoted French poetry: "great rapport—charming little chap—diversion," Plath wrote her mother.[82] But Sassoon proved to be much more than that. He later said that their relationship was "very adolescently hysterical, egotistical. We did not attend to each other so much as to our effects on each other." Yet he admitted it was also "magical," "tremendously significant for both of us and extremely rich," and rightly noted that "Sylvia had a strong mixture of puritanism and passion."[83]

Sylvia sent Aurelia two new sonnets that April—"Doom of Exiles" and "The Dead." These were the first proper poems she had written in nearly a year. The third stanza of "Doom of Exiles" struck a tragic tone:

Backward we traveled to reclaim the day
Before we fell, like Icarus, undone;
All we find are altars in decay
And profane words scrawled black across the sun.[84]

The two poems were full of sleep and death, but Sylvia reassured Aurelia that she was still seeing the Smith doctor regularly, and that she was "continually happy in a steady fashion, not ricocheting from depths to heights, although I do hit heights now and then."[85] She toed the same line with Eddie Cohen, who admitted that he was a little jealous of her fireside chats with Auden and I. A. Richards. Eddie was by now married and working full-time for a Mexican import-export company—a "dull and dusty" job he loathed. He had become a "pitchman" in order to support his family and had realized— hopefully not too late—that he would "rather be a starving, happy anything than a successful drudge." He was not sure how he had lost hold of his bohemian principles, and his youth:

I regard my evolution towards a typical middle class citizen as somewhat alarming. I am rapidly developing into a good bridge player; I am a dedicated Cub-master; I have built-in book shelves instead of brickand-boards; I belong to the Book-of-the-Month Club; I am looking for a house in the suburbs; and I am starting to hate myself. What the hell ever happened to all night wanderings in the honky-tonk areas, weekends lost in sex and drink, radicals, and camping trips? . . . The problem is whether it is possible to properly integrate the raw passions and desires and interests of the "free" soul with the necessary demands of raising a family. It is a problem which is, I venture, as old as copulation . . .[86]

This was exactly the sort of bourgeois sea change Sylvia feared. She smugly suggested that one could always find time to write if one tried hard enough. Eddie thought her naive. "And you, my charming little optimist? How much free-lancing will you be doing when there are three kids around the house wanting, respectively, to be diapered, fed and have the funnies read to them? After they're asleep, you say? . . . You can't plan your life out on paper and expect it to behave that way. I suspect that this tendency of yours contributed to your trouble. You didn't know what to do when something happened that wasn't in the blueprint."[87]

Sassoon reassured Plath that it was possible to outwit conventional expectations. In a late-April letter, he invoked the symbol of the comet moving through the universe and back again. He advised Plath to "flie [sic] with it! Move with it! Rise with it! Burn with it! Charge with it!"[88] It was as if Sassoon had invoked "Ariel" and "Stings" nearly a decade before their composition. Here was someone who would not just tolerate Plath's literary ambitions—he expected her to achieve them. When "Doomsday" appeared in *Harper's* that April, Sassoon gushed with enthusiasm: "It is Art! What an effort it must have been. Yes—work! And I did not know you were capable of t's and k's! Or had so strong a fist. You will crack poor nature yet!"[89] Sassoon understood that Plath was struggling to be the "brave" artist they both wanted her to be even as she fulfilled her academic duties to family, teachers, and benefactors. He knew she was the burgher and the artist both, yet he effortlessly reconciled the contradiction for her: "truths or lies, you or the actress—not much matter, one lives some lies, they are quite as much a part."[90]

Sylvia had never met anyone who so thoroughly inhabited a literary pose and who expected her to inhabit one in turn. He was the only man she had yet met who possessed a "soul" she considered "holy." Sassoon allowed her to transcend the model of 1950s femininity she found so claustrophobic. To him, she wrote in a style that was experimental, erotic, and languorous—part D. H. Lawrence, part Gertrude Stein.

Words revolve in flame and keep the coliseum heart afire, reflecting orange sunken suns in the secret petals of ruined arches . . . so sylvia burns yellow dahlias on her dark altar of the sun as the sun wanes to impotence and the world falls in winter. . . . do you realize that the name sassoon is the most beautiful name in the world. it [*sic*] has lots of seas of grass en masse and persian moon alone in rococo lagoon of woodwind tune where passes the ebony monsoon. . . .[91]

Sassoon did not care whether Sylvia was a virgin, attended church, or did good works. As she told Phil, "my frenchboy is not the outdoor type . . . he prefers cloistered velvet rooms, pale with roses, light wine, a volume of baudelaire or vigny or rimbaud [*sic*] and a nuit d'amour."[92] His nonconformist, intellectual personality and his Continental, laissez-faire attitude appealed to the part of her that sought to experiment with darker, more taboo modes of experience. In January 1956—just a month before she met Ted Hughes—she would write to Aurelia,

Naturally I am sorry that none of the "nice" boys who've wanted to marry me have been right. . . . I shudder to think how many men would accept only a small part of me as the whole, and be quite content. Naturally, all of us want the most complete, richest, best parts of us brought out, and in turn will do this for another. Actually, as you probably know, Richard

Sassoon is the only boy I have ever loved so far; he is so much more brilliant, intuitive and alive than anyone I've ever known. Yet he pays for
this with spells of black depression and shaky health which mean living
in daily uncertainty, and would be hard over any long time. But he is the
most honest, holy person I know. . . . ironically enough, he "looks" not
at all like the kind of man I could be fond of; but he is, and that's that.[93]

Sassoon was not interested in marriage or children—at least not yet. He
excited and frustrated her; she called him "the child of the devil and dionysus
[sic]."

Jane Truslow found Sassoon "foreign, dark, broody" and silent when he
came to visit Sylvia.[94] Connie Taylor, who was dating Sassoon's friend Alec
Holm at Yale, remembered that during train rides to New Haven with Sylvia
they would discuss the burdens of loving ambitious, literary men. Sassoon
had "vast aspirations . . . to be great," Connie said, but Sylvia had published
more—much more—than he had.

We used to sit on the train and talk about facing these young men who
were, I suppose, afraid of us. . . . the puzzlement of how one dealt with
wanting to be somebody important, of going whole hog in one's profession, the emotional problem of being a woman in this situation. She was
very conscious of this. And being faced with a young man who had ambitions and who was not as successful maybe made it worse.

Like Sylvia, Connie was ambitious; she would go on to become an influential
historian. She was not surprised that Sylvia had "cracked-up" the previous
year; doing so "seemed more normal than abnormal. That she had a disease
is obvious. But that the tensions she was living under were unreasonable is
also very very obvious."

At Yale, they congregated at the Elizabethan Club, where men drank
sherry, smoked clay pipes, and made witty conversation; the atmosphere was
that of an Oxford Common Room. Connie felt this milieu inspired Sylvia to
study in England, where she could be a part of "a cosmopolitan intellectual
life." As for Sassoon himself, Connie found him "witty, melodramatic" with
"no sense of humor about himself." She recalled him sitting on a low ledge at
Calhoun one evening "saying he couldn't stand life any longer. . . . complaining of melancholy; impossibility of fulfillment." The ledge, however, was just
a few feet off the ground. Connie told Sassoon that if he jumped, he wouldn't
die—but he would probably hurt himself. He climbed down.

She and Sylvia never found a solution, on those long train rides, to the "problem" of driven young men. But "there wasn't any question" that they would take the train back to New Haven.[95]

———

SYLVIA GUESSED THAT she would probably receive a mix of A's and B's that semester; she did not mind as long as she did not get any C's. She claimed that she no longer experienced a nauseating insecurity after finishing exams; she wrote Aurelia that she "really enjoyed" her Early American Literature exam, and "got quite inspired with my own spontaneous eloquence!"[96] The weather was turning and she looked forward to long afternoons on the sun porch rereading *War and Peace*—her major pastime that spring. Things were beginning to settle into place: she decided to write her thesis on Dostoevsky and room with Nancy—now her "dearest friend"—during her senior year.[97] Her poems "Admonition," "Verbal Calisthenics," "Never Try to Know More Than You Should," and "Denouement" appeared in the *Smith Review* that spring, and she became an unpaid correspondent at the *New York Herald Tribune*.

That April, Smith awarded Plath a nearly full scholarship of $1,250 from Olive Higgins Prouty's fund. Sylvia would be responsible for only $300 during her 1954–55 senior year. It was the largest scholarship Smith had ever awarded, for the college did not want their prize student to feel any "financial or other pressure this spring or summer." The committee hoped Plath would attend summer school rather than waitress, especially in light of her "superb recovery" and "beautiful adjustment."[98] Sylvia immediately telegraphed the good news to Aurelia, presenting it as a birthday present. For Aurelia, this truly was "a boon," as she had paid full tuition for the spring 1954 semester.[99] For Plath, too, the news came at the right time—she had just $1 left in her account that May.

She began to think about applying for a Fulbright Fellowship to Oxford or Cambridge, or graduate school at Radcliffe or Columbia. She even considered joining the Women's Naval Reserve so she could finance graduate school on the GI bill. Her experience at *Mademoiselle* had convinced her she did not want "a job in business," even for "a magazine or for a publishing house." As she wrote Gordon, who was trying to decide between a career in business or academia, she would probably still experience "a nucleus of conflict" even if she did manage to combine writing and motherhood: "it's damn hard to keep whipping yourself out of some comfortable bourgeois complacency . . . but I want to do just that . . . to keep on learning and thinking and feeling intensely even if it hurts like hell."[100]

To Mrs. Prouty, Sylvia wrote of her "joy" over her *Harper's* publication, her courses, her scholarship, her election to Phi Beta Kappa, and "the new boy with dark eyes in elegiac purple hollows." "What a girl you are!" Prouty replied. "Your illness must seem to you now like a bad dream. I'm so glad you waked up. My dearest love."[101] But Prouty was worried by Sylvia's emphasis on her achievements, and asked Aurelia if she had any "misgivings" about her daughter's health: "I realize there may be other anxieties. In fact I <u>know</u> that there are."[102]

Aurelia did have misgivings. Her daughter seemed changed, her old "sunny optimism" muted:

> After Sylvia's return to college, she made me think of deep-sea plants, the roots firmly grasping a rock, but the plant itself swaying in one direction then another with the varying currents that pass over and around. It was as though she absorbed for a while each new personality she encountered and tried it on, later to discard it. I kept saying to myself, "This is only a stage; it will pass."
>
> Her memory grasped and held to discords and seemed to have lost recollections of shared childhood and early girlhood joys. Kindnesses and loving acts were now viewed cynically, analyzed for underlying motives. We all strove to be patient, helpful, and understanding through this very difficult period of self-rediscovery on her part.[103]

Sylvia had become more frank in her letters to friends about her increasingly difficult relationship with Aurelia. She mocked her mother for placing demure photos of her around the house "for propaganda,"[104] and told Gordon in late June that she was experiencing "forays with the maternal monolith . . . conflict."[105] Therapy with Dr. Beuscher had unleashed Sylvia's anger, and Aurelia bore the brunt. Yet Plath would later characterize her behavior as typical, if delayed, adolescent rebellion.

Throughout that spring Sylvia and Sassoon spent much of their time picnicking in the countryside around Northampton and drinking bottles of Bordeaux. He admitted that he was falling deeply in love with her: "You will never know how wonderful I feel when you say I make you happy. It is so much better than being a God."[106] Mel was still under the impression that he and Sylvia were dating, and she was amused to receive "passionate metaphysical love letters" from both men in her mailbox.[107] When Mel wrote to her that spring urging that they consummate their relationship, she told him she was a virgin, and that if she slept with him "lacerations and pathos" would follow. She would become especially attached to him, she warned.[108] He told her of his "deep revulsion for anything that smacks of a strategy of caution," and Sylvia, now in love with Sassoon, responded with a scathing diatribe:

> Really, now, do you accept the fact that your "total commitment to earth" involves more than a brief spasm of irresponsible ecstasy? Do you accept the fact that the demand of fertility is fertility, creation (not of male euphoria) of babies, and the care of such? Can you deny that the end of fertility is reproduction, not just the hedony which you condone as "a ritual act of fertility" . . . ? . . . I am hardly ready or willing to produce the children which nature would endow me with as the understood reward of my actions.[109]

She resented his implication that she was a "puritan pragmatist" and told him she never wanted to see him again. Two days later, she informed him that she would be coming to Yale to visit his roommate Sassoon. She would return the Crane and the Lawrence books; he should "feel free" not to be there. But her tone was light as she acknowledged the "intricate" and "interweaving web of circumstance" that tied her friends to his (Mel had dated Marcia and was becoming close to Nancy) and humorously suggested a "family barbecue."[110] Jane Truslow Davison remembered Sylvia delighting in her dates' "Don Juan-ish quality" and the "high drama" that ensued when Sassoon's and Gordon's visits almost overlapped.[111]

Sassoon finally told Mel, "I'm dating your girlfriend." Mel responded that he never considered Sylvia his girlfriend, and soon realized the arrogance of his sexual request. Her letter set him straight. She would only sleep with someone she intended to marry, she told him.[112] Sylvia continued writing Mel long, cerebral letters about Lawrence, Hemingway, Nietzsche, Fromm, Joyce, and Dostoevsky, and while he did not feel proprietary about her, he felt she was not a good match for Sassoon. "I remember saying to myself, 'He's not strong enough to handle Sylvia.'"[113]

In early May, before Sassoon left for a summer in Europe, Sylvia accompanied him to New York City. They saw Chekhov's *The Seagull*, starring Montgomery Clift, in Greenwich Village, then headed back to their 44th Street hotel for "the inevitable french [*sic*] poetry and wine" and a "nuit d'amour."[114] The night seemed to mark a new phase in their relationship. Sassoon wrote to her shortly after, "And if all memory should perish—we have known each other—it is deeper than memory. . . . 'darling' is a new word and so is 'love'—I love you, darling."[115] That Sunday, they "spent two hours gourmandizing" at the Steuben Tavern in Times Square, where they feasted on herring in sour cream, onion soup, éclairs, and white wine before heading back to New Haven. Sylvia told Phil the trip was "a much needed bohemian respite to my more academic obligations."[116]

Those obligations now included studying ten hours a day for her final exams in late May; her joints became stiff from sitting for such long stretches, and she was "so cerebralized" that she had difficulty falling asleep. She remembered the days at Lookout Farm when she was "struck with an uncomplicated physical exhaustion which swallowed me in a dark and dreamless sea of sleep until I woke refreshed and rejuvenated at dawn."[117] She knew she needed "physical exercise" for "balance," but she felt she could not afford the time away from studying. Among the books and authors she had to master were, as she listed in her scrapbook, "War and Peace, Anna Karenina, Portrait of a Lady, The Ambassadors, The American, Erich Fromm, Nietzsche, Hegel, Marx, et al."[118] But she was relieved that she was still capable of intense studying: "exams and papers proved I hadn't lost either my repetitive or my creative intellect as I had feared," she wrote.[119]

Sylvia felt she was leaving on a high note: "A semester of reconstruction ends with an infinitely more solid, if less flashingly spectacular flourish than last year's."[120] She thought she had aced her final Early American Literature exam on Melville, James, and Hawthorne. She was elected president of the college arts society, Alpha Phi Kappa Psi, and awarded a gold and ruby pin from Tiffany's. She was delighted, if not surprised, to receive the Ethel Olin Corbin Prize for "Doom of Exiles." All augured well for her senior year. "Look-out," she wrote in her scrapbook, "for next year most optimistic—great courses, Nan for roommate, exciting thesis topic, and who knows what tall man!" Her ebullience manifested itself in a new blond bob. It was the start of her "Platinum Summer," which she hoped would be her best yet.

Aurelia was "shocked" when Sylvia returned from Smith in late May with her bright yellow hair, though she admitted "it was becoming." She felt her daughter "was 'trying out' a more daring, adventuresome personality, and one had to stand by and hope that neither she nor anyone else would be deeply hurt."[121]

ON JUNE 1, Sylvia received a formal letter from Scotty Campbell, her erstwhile Harvard dance partner, that she had received a full scholarship to Harvard Summer School.[122] She had already lined up a job at the Southward Inn on Cape Cod in case the scholarship did not materialize, and was relieved that she would not have to spend another summer "slinging hash." Aurelia was having ulcer trouble again, and, to convalesce, she and her parents rented a cottage on the Cape for the summer. (Sylvia would tell Gordon that September that Aurelia was "very sick," and that she was "worried always" and "scared" about her mother's health.)[123] Sylvia decided to divide June between the Cape and Wellesley, where Nancy came to stay during the first week of the month. Nancy was from Ohio and had never seen the ocean; she was astonished by Nauset's pristine sand, undulating dunes, and rhythmic surf. Sylvia set the scene in a July letter to Mel: "ten mile strolls along the fantastic solitude of nauset [*sic*] beach, with powerful surf crashing on hardpacked sand, and a treacherous undertow sucking back into itself with a low chuckle of rocks and pebbles."[124]

Sylvia and Nancy called on Mrs. Prouty in Brookline, where they giggled like schoolgirls and devoured so many cucumber sandwiches they felt sick. Nancy was moved when Sylvia woke her up on her twenty-first birthday with breakfast on a tray and a copy of *Alice in Wonderland* in which she had inscribed, "A classic, read-aloud heirloom to be taken in small, mirthful doses at bedtime."[125] In the evenings, they double-dated with Phil McCurdy and his Adams House tutor, Norman Shapiro, who was pursuing a doctorate in French poetry. On one of these dates, Sylvia asked Norman to recite some Old French poetry for her; he recalled that he "needed no prodding":

> As the stars, in exquisite dispassion,
> View my tribute to the May,
> I fancy I may fashion
> Stars of my own, to condone
> The reckless fancy of my play . . .

Sylvia loved the poem, and relished the phrase "exquisite dispassion."[126] As they dined on Armenian cuisine and watched Turkish belly dancers, Nancy was struck by Sylvia's easy cosmopolitanism and worldly friends, who seemed to speak "seven languages fluently."[127] At Smith, Sylvia was always holed up in her room studying. Now, released from the pressure of maintaining her grades and her scholarship, she was hungry for new, even taboo, experiences.

Sylvia went to bimonthly appointments with Dr. Beuscher and attended the wedding of Marcia Brown to Mike Plumer, in Hanover, New Hampshire, on June 15.[128] Marcia remembered that the night before the ceremony, Sylvia, who was in the wedding party, "drank too much and made a complete ass of herself. She was ridiculous, falling all over men. She didn't know how to handle liquor at all. She was uncoordinated, mentally and physically. Finally, we had to haul her home and put her to bed." Sylvia was weepy, hungover, and abashed the next morning, but Marcia wasn't angry. Rather, the episode made her worried that Sylvia might get herself "into sticky situations" with men, especially without a girlfriend by her side.[129]

Claiborne Phillips married Avrom Handleman, at Smith, on June 7. Sylvia, though invited, did not attend, citing a conflicting date with Gordon; the snub upset Claiborne greatly. Two other close friends, Louise Giesey and Enid Epstein, also wed that June, shortly after their Smith graduation. The pressure was on. Her own wedding, Sylvia told Phil, would be held atop a vast cliff overlooking the ocean, "sort of a pledge of honesty, relating one to the huge natural forces of procreation and life: a kind of pagan ritual, in some respects, clean and unadorned."[130] This Lawrentian fantasy did not come to pass—Plath, too, would marry in a church.

In late June, Sylvia learned that Ruth Freeman's father had died suddenly. She and Aurelia rushed to the Freemans' Winthrop home to "sustain, support, solace." As soon as they arrived, Sylvia embarrassed herself by drinking out of the last glass Mr. Freeman had used before dying. It was just like her, she told Gordon, with her "infallible instinct for doing the tabu thing in all innocent accidence."[131] She kept busy washing dishes and comforting Ruth's grieving brother, David, yet she secretly thought that Mr. Freeman's death at seventy was merciful. He was, she told Gordon, a "victim of skin disease which had stopped his one creative outlet—painting—so wasn't deadness better quick than a slow paralytic stroke, or a slow decaying senility?"

For Plath, the journey back to Winthrop evoked a deep nostalgia and a fleeting sense of loss:

Sweltering heat, blowing hot air in sweat stenched subways, a bus jolting through narrow streets, crowded houses, increasingly familiar—and then, suddenly, the blue blast of ocean between bleak buildings—a walk down a street woven with the rich, plumcake associations of ten years of creative and imaginative childhood. . . . lawns that were continents, rocks that were fortresses, alleys that were secret passages to magic worlds: all seemed now strangely shrunken and denuded of myriad mystic meanings—like talismans become impotent . . .

She took a walk by her old house and saw "the golden rain trees and shrubs that my botanist father planted now flourishing giants, though the house and yard had shrunken as if unsanforized through years of rain."[132]

Six months later, she would write a story based on that afternoon, "The Day Mr. Prescott Died" (heavily influenced by James Joyce's "The Sisters"), in which the narrator also drinks out of the dead man's glass.[133] Like Plath, the unnamed narrator assumes Mr. Prescott's death was a blessing to his family—that, as an old curmudgeon, he "had it coming" and "nobody's sorry."[134] The narrator resents spending the day with the Prescotts cooking and cleaning and comforting, and her mother admonishes her for her "nasty" words. The narrator silently mocks her mother, who comforts Mrs. Prescott with platitudes. Yet when the narrator is alone with Mr. Prescott's son, Ben, she realizes the enormity of his loss. "I thought of Mama, and suddenly all the sad part I hadn't been able to find during the day came up in my throat. 'We'll go on better than before,' I said. And then I quoted Mama like I never thought I would: 'It's all the best of us can do.' And I went to take the hot pea soup off the stove." The narrator learns the value of social convention in the face of loss. Plath, who had also lost a father whom illness had made irascible ("disease twisted an otherwise good nature," she told her mother), understood that relief could coexist with grief.[135] "I wonder, are you really sorry," the narrator asks Ben. He replies, "Not really sorry, now, but I could have been nicer." She tells him that he carries a piece of his father with him; the story seems an oblique reflection on Sylvia's own mourning for Otto.

In June, Gordon finally came home on leave from the Navy. Sassoon was in Europe, allowing Sylvia ample time to become "reacquainted" with her old boyfriend. Gordon, six foot four and dashing in uniform, was a stark contrast to the "slender, dark, enigmatic, poetic" Sassoon.[136] The men Sylvia loved came to personify the writers they most admired: Gordon preferred the Joycean Yes to the Baudelairean *cri de coeur*. Joyce, more than any other author, became Gordon's and Sylvia's touchstone. Over the coming weeks, they tried to outdo each other with their witty Finneganian puns. Sylvia wrote to Gordon in July: "Vraught by the sveldtering noonday headt, Absinned hears the dingle of a sturm nearby und yearns for a drang of vatever iss in it, HomoChinEyezed or uddervise. Liddle doss she know that this sturm is 100% mescalin flowing from a leak in a hidden moundand still."[137]

As Sylvia began spending more time with Gordon, whose destroyer was docked in Newport, Rhode Island, her old feelings came rushing back with a new intensity. He inspired her to write again, to "invent new ways of expressing the richness of life." She told him she was "at war psychically" over how best to invent this language: "one earthy part in me preferring bodily sun-worship and physical prowess and power, the other cerebral part preferring the sedentary construction of aesthetic artifices to order in form the artless chaos of content in the flux of time."[138] She invited Gordon to stay with her family in Eastham, on the Cape, telling him that he no longer had the title of "'visitor'—which implies all sorts of formalities." She fantasized about the two of them someday spending their summers in a quiet beach cottage, writing, surrounded only by "pines, sand and sea." (She would, in fact, enjoy such a honeymoon in Eastham with Ted Hughes.) She told Gordon she would be his "cook-secretary" and begged, "do let me be your typist!"[139] Sassoon receded across the Atlantic.

But Sylvia had unfinished business. In late June, after a long walk down

Nauset Beach, she decided to visit Dick in Orleans. To Gordon, she compared the experience to her journey back to Winthrop the previous week:

> dick [*sic*], too, seemed to have shrunk, telescoped up, like alice-in-w, both physically and psychically . . . I had lived so hard and much and deep that never again could I go back to the same small country of his personality which once, years ago, I had seen as vast and flittering with promise . . . [. . .] sue [*sic*] and I swam with him and saw the infirmary he'll run, and he loaned me his bike for the rest of the week . . . and I left, feeling a mingled relief and pity—at his everpresent, inverted snobbery, puritanically directed against smoking, drinking, women with short hair and lipstick— all excesses of comfort and artistry and imagination.

There must have been much she wanted to say to Dick, but she would save that conversation for her fiction.

Seeing Dick only intensified Sylvia's feelings for Gordon. She declared that they would have a different kind of relationship: "teaching and sharing on a mutual plane—<u>not</u> in a rigid teacher-student character—but rather as if we both were perpetually students—<u>both</u> learning, discovering and creating life . . . and maybe even art . . . [. . .] we will be hobo and hoyden, duke and duchess . . . [. . .] oh, I love you more than the alphabet and Roget's thesaurus combined."[140] It was the sort of pledge she would later make to Ted Hughes. But Gordon avoided talk of love and a future together; instead, he filled his letters with detailed descriptions of naval life. His words threw little heat: "I wonder how it is possible for me to like you better but I constantly do."[141]

Sylvia, hedging her bets, resurrected her correspondence with Mel, to whom she wrote a platonic but passionate five-page letter in early July. She was at home for her last weekend before summer school started, becoming "unbelievably domestic" as she cooked steaks, folded laundry, and sunbathed in her Wellesley backyard. Mel was her "psychic brother," she said, and they were connected by an "ectoplasmic umbilical cord." She hoped he would visit her soon, "whenever you felt there was no one to commune with; which is naturally an arrogant attitude for me to have for it implies that I am a damn good high priestess of the intellect (which, by the way, I am)." She spoke to him of her suicide attempt:

> oh, mel [*sic*] (which devilishly enough means honey in latin [*sic*]) there is so much to talk to you about . . . [. . .] because the cataclysmic downward gyre I plummeted to symbolic death in last summer, when the center did not hold because there was none, or rather (as you wrote), too many, has given me an understanding of the black and sustained hells a mind can go

through . . . and the enormous insulated loneliness when you feel that no human hand or love could reach or move you.

She told Mel that she was moving to Cambridge and starting "a potentially vital and intellectually valuable summer."[142] By then Mel had started dating Yoko Ono, whom he met at a Sarah Lawrence mixer. ("She was clearly the most beautiful girl, but she was Japanese so no one was dancing with her.") Mel described himself at the time as "a young man on the make" and ended things with Yoko before they got too serious. She was shy, and told him she had attempted suicide at fifteen. He did not want to hurt her. In a last bid for his affection, Yoko invited him to visit her at Cambridge University, where she planned to spend the summer. He declined, but later reflected, "I might have introduced Sylvia and Yoko."[143]

————

ON JULY 6, 1954, Sylvia moved to #4 1572 Massachusetts Avenue, a one-bedroom apartment in a collegiate redbrick building a block from Harvard Square. She had three roommates: Nancy Hunter, Joan Smith, and Kay Quinn. Joan and Kay were friends from Lawrence House who had secured summer jobs in Boston and who obligingly slept on a pull-out sofa in the dining room when Sylvia and Nancy insisted that they needed the private bedroom to study. In exchange, Sylvia and Nancy promised to cook. Plath had registered for Elementary German with William Oldenbrook and the Nineteenth Century Novel with Frank O'Connor, from whom she was still eager to learn. She spent her first week exploring Cambridge with Nancy, and meeting various young men for coffee and beer. But she missed Gordon "like hell." In a letter that July she wrote to him of the "eversoaring intense love I have for you," and looked forward to the "naked wonder of living with you every day." Sylvia held little back with Gordon, and fantasized about what their married life might look like, "pretending that this is <u>really</u> *our* apartment, and that I am shopping for you, saving up daily vignettes to share with you, buying books with the intention of reading them aloud together before bed." She could hardly contain her emotion: "darling, I shall simply explode like a feminine H-bomb if you don't let me right now tell you very hard again and again that I love you love you love you love you love you!!"[144]

"We had a gluttonous appetite for the attractions of the city and little money to indulge it," Nancy wrote of that summer; the two "pledged" to accept any dates they were offered.[145] Sylvia finally had the chance to spend a leisurely summer without the crushing weight of maintaining a straight-A average; Nancy remembered that the dates ran through their summer "in a motley procession." Sylvia treated the men as "dalliances" and told Nancy she would marry Gordon.[146] Dating different, overlapping men was not unusual during the 1950s, yet Nancy found Sylvia's behavior unnerving. She remembered that Plath was attracted to older men, especially professors.

One in particular caught Sylvia's attention: Edwin Akutowicz, a thirty-one-year-old mathematician who had received his PhD from Harvard in 1947. Sylvia first mentioned Edwin in her calendar on July 7—her very first day of summer school.[147] Nancy said the two met him on the steps of Harvard's Widener Library, which is also where the meeting between Esther and Irwin (the character based on Edwin) occurs in *The Bell Jar*. Nancy claimed she disliked Edwin immediately—she described him as bald and "myopic-looking" with thick glasses.[148] But he was also tall with blue eyes, and he introduced himself as a biology professor at an eastern college. (Akutowicz actually worked at this time for MIT in their Division of Defense laboratories.) Plath's 1961 notes on *The Bell Jar*, where she likens Edwin to a "Dream-father," strongly suggest that what she may have seen that day was a young version of Otto.[149] Few of Sylvia's friends remembered her ever mentioning Otto—except Nancy. She said Sylvia spoke of him as a father whom she "adored." Sylvia told her he was a true intellectual, as she was, but that her mother was "vacuous." She also told Nancy, cryptically, that "she felt responsible for his death when he died."[150]

Nancy, Sylvia, and Edwin went out for a beer at the Oxford Grille in Harvard Square, where, Nancy wrote, Edwin "wooed" them with his "awesome understanding of subjects we hardly knew existed" and "elaborate theories."[151] "He had not spoken more than ten sentences when both Syl and I knew that he was probably the most brilliant man we had ever met," Nancy wrote. Sylvia was "dumbstruck" by him.

The two women returned to their apartment giddy and a little drunk, wondering which one of them Edwin would call. The phone rang later that afternoon—for Nancy. She agreed to come to Edwin's apartment on Sunday night, a little over a mile from their place. Nancy wrote that Edwin got her drunk and chased her around his couch. Deeply shaken, she demanded that he take her home, which he did. She wrote that she "collapsed inside the door of our apartment, sobbing my fear and rage" to Sylvia. Nancy refused Edwin's calls, and he finally asked Sylvia out instead. Sylvia met him for an "evening of talk" on July 13, and began seeing him regularly: she wrote that she "studied" at his apartment on July 14, 19, and 22.[152]

Nancy's accusations against Edwin are serious ones, yet she may have misremembered these events' chronology. According to Sylvia's calendar, she and Nancy met Edwin on July 7. Nancy said that Sylvia began seeing him after her own disastrous date; Sylvia's first date with him was July 13.

This means that Nancy's first date must have occurred between July 7 and July 13. Yet Sylvia wrote to Gordon on July 19 that Nancy had come home at midnight from a steak dinner prepared by Edwin, adding, "he'll make some strange woman a wonderful cook!"[153] The letter also suggests that Nancy continued seeing Edwin after their first date. In 1971, Nancy referred to Edwin as her then boyfriend, and claimed, bitterly, that Sylvia had only shown interest in him "so she could supersede me in that relationship."[154]

On Friday, July 23, Plath finally realized her dream of meeting the poet Richard Wilbur, whom she had written about for *Mademoiselle*. Wilbur's mother-in-law, Mrs. Ward, lived in Wellesley and was friendly with Aurelia and Mrs. Lameyer. In her calendar, Sylvia recorded the meeting with an excited star: "Evening with Gordon at Mrs. Ward's. Met Dick Wilbur at last!" In 1972, Wilbur would publish a poem about the meeting, "Cottage Street, 1953":

> I am a stupid life-guard who has found,
> Swept to his shallows by the tide, a girl
> Who, far from shore, has been immensely drowned,
> And stares through water now with eyes of pearl.
>
> How deep is her refusal; and how slight
> The *genteel* chat whereby we recommend
> Life, of a summer afternoon, despite
> The brewing dusk which hints that it may end.[155]

Wilbur—who misdated Plath's visit by a year and called her poems, in his last stanza, "unjust"—presents Plath as weak and scared, yet she may simply have been quiet and nervous before her idol. Nancy remembered that in 1954, Wilbur was "the one man in the world whom Syl most admired . . . she talked of him often. She read every word he wrote and showed me every article about him and every photograph of him that appeared anywhere in print."[156] The poem would bother Elizabeth Bishop when she read it. "A very *neat* poem by Wilbur about Sylvia Plath makes me angry," she wrote to Robert Lowell in 1973. "I think it is very bad—really unfeeling." What should have been "deep & sad" simply seemed "smug." Lowell responded, "The Wilbur poem annoyed me too."[157]

Sylvia spent the weekend of July 24 on the Cape with Gordon, then returned to Cambridge for a date with Edwin on Monday. She met him at eight fifteen that night but left no more details in her calendar about the traumatic events that would inspire a famous scene in *The Bell Jar*. In the novel, Esther, who is living in Cambridge with her asylum friend Joan, meets Irwin, a math professor, on the steps of Widener Library. Esther decides to lose her virginity to him because he is older, experienced with women, and intelligent. "Then, to be on the safe side, I wanted somebody I didn't know and wouldn't go on knowing—a kind of impersonal, priestlike official, as in the tales of tribal rites."[158] Esther hemorrhages after sex with Irwin and nearly bleeds to death before she is saved at the hospital.

Nancy provided more details in her memoir, which was published almost twenty years after the event. One morning, she said, she woke up to find that Plath was not in her bed. Soon, Edwin called, explaining that Sylvia had hemorrhaged at his apartment the night before and that they had seen a doctor. "But she's fine now," he said, and hung up.[159] According to Nancy, when Sylvia returned to the apartment in the late afternoon, she began to bleed again. Nancy asked what had happened, and Sylvia told her that Edwin had "masturbated" her.[160] Nancy barely had time to react; before long she was on the phone with Dr. Heels, a local gynecologist, who told her how to stanch the bleeding. Nancy, untrained "in the techniques of the midwife," as she put it, sat with Sylvia from seven to ten p.m. and thought she had stopped the bleeding. But when Sylvia stood up, Nancy saw a large pool of blood on the plastic tablecloth they had spread on top of the bed. As Sylvia swayed and careened into a wall, Nancy panicked.[161] She called Edwin, who picked them up within five minutes and drove them to Mount Auburn Hospital. There, Dr. Heels finally stopped the bleeding.

Sylvia's cryptic calendar jottings provide furtive clues about what transpired. She drew an arrow from July 26 into July 27, where she wrote "Dr. Heels." Her dates suggest that she saw him, as she told Nancy, in the early-morning hours of the 27th. The next day, July 28, she wrote "Mt. Auburn Hospital," "recuperation," and "cleaned apartment" in her calendar. She called Dr. Beuscher at nine a.m. on July 29, then met her for an appointment on July 30. (Sylvia told Nancy that Edwin drove her to all her appointments with Dr. Beuscher.) The meeting was probably an emergency one, as Sylvia normally saw her psychiatrist every two weeks. On August 4 and 5, she wrote "Call Dr. Heels." On August 6: "Dr. Heels check-up."[162] Ted Hughes later testified in his *Bell Jar* trial deposition that "the hemorrhage business" in the novel had really happened to Sylvia.[163] Sylvia herself said in her journal that she lost her virginity to Edwin and that the sex was consensual and passionate: "Never felt guilty for bedding with one, losing virginity and going to the Emergency Ward. . . . I had feelings and found out what I wanted and found the one only I wanted and knew it not with my head but with the heat of rightness, salt-sharp."[164] In *The Bell Jar*, Esther also describes her sexual experience with Irwin as a deliberate choice.

Sylvia had obviously changed her mind about losing her virginity to the man she would marry. She had almost died during the previous summer; *this* summer, post-resurrection, was about embracing life. She may have tried to save face with Nancy, whom she regarded as an innocent, by telling her she had been "masturbated." After all, this was 1954, and Sylvia was unofficially engaged to Gordon—she wrote about their looming marriage in an August 7 letter to him—and she was likely nervous about gossip. She had not counted on such a public aftermath of so private an event. Sylvia's two appointments with Dr. Beuscher on July 29 and 30 suggest that she experienced emotional pain after her night with Edwin. Still, in her scrapbook, Plath described her time with him in affectionate terms: "A cool study, beer and intrigue provided by assistant physics professor Edwin Akutowicz at MIT, and a casserole of life, love and learning."[165] Nancy herself said the hemorrhaging did not cause Sylvia any "emotional trauma," and seemed more traumatized by the ordeal than Sylvia did. "I kept seeing her blood on the regular white tiles of the bathroom and hearing her anguished voice as she pleaded with me to keep her from dying," she wrote.[166]

During the weeks that followed the night in question, Plath did not withdraw—on the contrary, she led a dizzying social life. To Nancy's astonishment, Sylvia saw Edwin again that summer and invited him to Smith that fall. She and Edwin spent several hours drinking and discussing Machiavelli at Rahar's, in Northampton, on October 31. Nine days later, Sylvia spent the afternoon at his apartment in Cambridge: "Lovely fire, beer, talk and very dear time—reading and pipe smoke," she wrote in her calendar.[167] There would be more dates with Edwin in April and May of 1955; that year, she even sent him some of her poetry. In 1975, Edwin wrote to Frances McCullough, the editor of Plath's abridged journals, about his impressions of Plath. He noted that they spoke of poetry and probability, and that she told him about her grief for Otto. She had been frank with him about her suicide attempt, as well, but he did not see any "deeper tensions" within. He said Plath seemed more balanced than many young women he had known at the time.[168]

Sylvia dated other men that summer of whom Nancy did not approve. Chief among them was Dr. Ira Scott, a married instructor at Harvard who provided afternoons, as Plath joyfully recorded, of "sailing in Marblehead, beach and sun in Duxbury, garden grandeur at Castle Hill, champagne and steak at charming inns."[169] Sylvia's behavior alarmed Nancy. "She was not depressed or alienated; in fact, she was racing from experience to experience with a recklessness that asserted her invincibility."[170] On one Saturday,

August 21, Sylvia breakfasted with Gordon, saw Harvard's famous glass flowers with Ira, then attended a cocktail party on Beacon Hill with her "enigmatic, handsome" neighbor Lou Healy and some medical school students. They stayed up until dawn drinking and discussing "Satanic Sadism."[171] Plath was on furlough, trying to experience as much as she could before the window closed again.

In early August, Sylvia told Gordon that she had hemorrhaged after being "manually attacked" by Edwin—though she assured him they had gone no further.[172] She downplayed the event, framing it as a misunderstanding for which she was partly to blame. She had thought her friendship with Edwin was strictly "platonic," she wrote Gordon on August 5, "but I lost my eve-like naïvté [sic] with a traumatic shock last week, when I realized that I might have only comradely intentions, while my 'comrade' might have totally different expectations of our meetings."[173] Gordon accepted her version of events at the time.[174] She promised him she would no longer hold tête-à-têtes with young men.

Sylvia told Gordon she had an upcoming appointment with Dr. Heels for a pelvic exam. "Even if I regret the unsavory way I discovered about my manyarteried [sic] insides, I'm glad to get the deluge over with so that I will be healthily prepared for a natural and completely understood sexual life."[175] Two days later, she wrote him that Heels had pronounced her "intact, healthy, and generously normal." But the ordeal had exhausted her: she returned to Wellesley for the weekend, went to bed at five p.m. and slept for fifteen hours. She hoped Gordon would understand her need to use the time to "rehabilitate," "repair my wardrobe and my serenity."[176] He reassured her that he loved her.[177]

She spent the short break reading and writing in her backyard and luxuriating in "the minor-keyed daily delights" of a suburban summer. "I cherish the lunging roar of the powermower as peter aldrich [sic] mows our lawn, the blasé drone of the cicada, the junior greek [sic] chorus of children playing hide-and-seek in the foliage, sunlight incandescent on blue and pink cornflowers." Even the sound of her mother's voice beckoned. She was getting along with Aurelia after a period of "belated" adolescent rebellion, which she compared to the American colonies' desire for independence from mother England. With her "revolution" over, she felt "loving, benevolent, without fearing for my ever-strengthening newfound independence and self-reliance."[178]

Sylvia worked hard at her German. Gordon, whose father was from Germany, helped her study, but she received a B on her exam. She began to regret taking the course, which turned her into a "beast of burden, with blinders." It pained her to see "shaw, ibsen, o'neill [sic], and the rest, languishing unread on my bookshelves."[179] However, she chose to spend most of her free hours drinking and dining with friends and dates—sharing hot toddies with Nancy or sherry-soaked fruit compote with her German class. She reveled in "the 'Joy of Cooking' social life centered around charming intimate dinners."[180] Few would have guessed that the platinum blonde whipping up consommé in champagne glasses had tried to kill herself a year before.

In mid-August Sylvia spent the weekend in Jaffrey, New Hampshire, with Gordon and his family. They canoed on Thorndike Pond and climbed Mount Monadnock. She was as close to the Lameyers now as she had been to the Nortons, and they considered her part of the family. But three days after she returned to Cambridge, she again saw Ira. "Bourbon & waters—Louis Armstrong—Jon Dos Passos & steak & candlelight" she wrote of her date on August 19. The next night, she went out with Gordon, who may have suspected she was seeing another man: "long tense bull session," she wrote in her calendar, "problems." A week later, she ran into Gordon unexpectedly when she was out with Ira. She wrote in her calendar that a "scene" ensued.[181]

The anniversary of her suicide attempt was on her mind: in her calendar she drew a border, in red pencil, around August 24–28. On the 22nd, she took a sedative—phenobarbital—after what she enigmatically called a "crisis of suspended animation." Gordon, with his "mending talk," had helped.[182] But it was Ira she turned to that week. Sylvia saw him almost every day from August 23rd to the 26th; they enjoyed long walks, daiquiris, and steak dinners. She spent the anniversary day itself—August 24—sailing in Marblehead with him. She relished the salt spray on her skin, the "warm, choppy" water, the "roaring" ride back to Cambridge in his convertible, and the "exquisite" pink Brooks Brothers shirt he gave her that morning.[183]

Aurelia called Nancy on the 24th and became extremely anxious when Nancy told her Sylvia was out. Could Nancy guarantee that Sylvia was not at that very moment trying to kill herself? Nancy finally located Sylvia, who promptly called home and reassured her panicked mother. Plath made sure to see Dr. Beuscher on August 27. The two had a "long good talk" about "domination, paternalism, sadism."[184] Something—whether it was a memory of Otto, Edwin, Sassoon, or the "cruel" Peruvian—triggered these connections, which would later find their way into the black heart of Plath's most famous poem, "Daddy."

Nancy saw Sylvia's behavior that summer as dangerously promiscuous, but Sylvia had finally found the courage to flout the repressive sexual double standard she described with such anger in her high school and early college journals. Dr. Beuscher had sent her off from McLean with the diaphragm prescription. Sylvia's affairs with Edwin and Ira—one married, both professors rather than college boys—suggest that she was determined to use it. The fact that these men were *not* serious prospects was, as Esther hints in *The Bell Jar*, part of their attraction. Sex that summer was something Plath wanted on her own terms, with men to whom she was not committed. Men treated sex casually until they were ready to marry. Now that pregnancy was no longer an issue, why shouldn't she?

On the last day of August, Hurricane Carol struck New England. Safe from the storm's coastal ferocity in Wellesley, Sylvia reveled in the strafing winds and churning skies. The power went out, and she wrote a poem, "Insolent Storm Strikes at the Skull," by candlelight. After clearing up the wreckage the next day, she headed back to her apartment in Cambridge, where she would stay until mid-September, then to the Cantors' home in Chatham for a weekend with Gordon. There, the two swam in the "iced champagne surf," picnicked on the outer sand bar, and danced at the Chatham Bars Inn.[185] Over the next two weeks, she saw Gordon nearly every day, and they began sleeping together. Feeling renewed, she wrote several poems before returning to Smith on September 20. She spent more time on the Cape visiting the Cochrans, the Cantors, Aurelia in Eastham, and Warren at the Pines resort.

Sylvia and Gordon had spent the last weekend of August alone in Wellesley, and she became worried in September that she was pregnant. Gordon was ready to marry her, and did not regard the pregnancy as a crisis. Sylvia did. She saw Dr. Beuscher three times during the second week of September; one session lasted for three hours. The scare clarified her priorities after weeks of idealizing married life. She was not yet ready to become a wife and mother, and she saw with vivid precision what such a turn would mean: no Smith degree, no Fulbright, no bohemian sojourn in Europe. A life with Gordon suddenly seemed the antithesis of all she wanted, and she was overwhelmed with relief when she realized she was not pregnant. As she wrote to Enid Epstein, she had "put off all thought of marrying him to a very indefinite future . . . he is amazingly young yet (or I am amazingly old) and I am Machiavellian enough to want to grow to the fullest."[186] She had walked a fine line that summer between sophistication and dissolution, and she had nearly imperiled her future. But she was lucky, and her luck made her confident that she could continue to assimilate such experiences into her writing. She told Gordon, "I can like jazz, blatant syrupy love lyrics, dirty jokes, bartenders, taxi drivers without any sense of superiority or patronizing pride, quite honestly, and simply talk that language . . . but in the final analysis I guess I want, like Eliot, to refine the dialect of the tribe."[187] Plath's decision not to marry Gordon Lameyer had consequences she could not yet envision. In six years, she would be T. S. Eliot's dinner guest.

14

O Icarus

Smith College and Wellesley,
September 1954–August 1955

Sylvia began her senior year at Smith in "a siege of activity."[1] On top of the usual academic pressures, she was applying for a Fulbright Fellowship to England, a Woodrow Wilson Fellowship, and admission to Oxford, Cambridge, Radcliffe, Yale, and Columbia.[2] Her goal, she told Mel Woody, was a graduate degree at Radcliffe or Harvard "eventually," but only after she had traveled "around the world." She wanted to see England, Italy ("where I am a daughter—body-and-soul"), France, and Africa; to escape, for a time, "the land of the chromium plated bathroom, the ivory soap opera and the league of women voters!"[3]

She rushed between appointments with professors, nurses, and college officials as she gathered the necessary documents for her applications: "12 letters of recommendation, 3 health exams, 12 statements of purpose, etc."[4] She took her Cambridge University entrance exams at Mary Ellen Chase's home. Chase, George Gibian, Newton Arvin, Elizabeth Drew, and Alfred Kazin would write Plath glowing recommendation letters. All said she was the best student they had ever taught, and emphasized her graciousness, maturity, humor, and good manners.[5] (Chase noted, "She has not the slightest trace of conceit or arrogance.")[6] Kazin spoke for all of Plath's mentors when he wrote that she was "not merely the most gifted student in the class but perhaps the most interesting student writer I have seen in years. . . . I have even heard it said that she is the most gifted student Smith has seen for many years."[7] No one mentioned Plath's suicide attempt or stay at McLean.

Sylvia told Aurelia that because these professors were "all very big names in their field internationally, I should have an advantage there that might compensate for my mental hospital record."[8] She had heard that Oxford and Cambridge "aren't hospitable to lady-suicides," and so she asked Dr. Beuscher for a recommendation, hoping that she would attest to "the completeness of my cure."[9] Dr. Beuscher did just that: "at the time of hospitalization Miss Plath was suffering from a state of mental turmoil which is highly unlikely ever to recur. Some of the qualities most obvious in her illness were the very ones which, properly channeled and maturely balanced, contribute to her undoubted superiority as a person. She has a great sense of responsibility, not only to others who may depend on her, but also to herself, and to her integrity."[10] Sylvia's only negative recommendation came from her house mother, Mrs. Kelsey, who felt that though her "character," "appearance," "voice," and "deportment" were all "pleasing," her devotion to writing made her "selfish" and "difficult."[11]

Sylvia decorated her Lawrence House room in "Harvard" crimsons and "Yale" blues, hung sketches from Ilo and snapshots of Gordon. She felt more at ease there now that a cliquey contingent of seniors had graduated. Sylvia was still a breakfast waitress six days a week, and noted, optimistically, that the commitment would force her to go to bed early each night; she knew that fewer than eight hours a night could start her on a precipitous downslide.

She had a relatively light class load due to her six-credit thesis tutorial. Shakespeare with Miss Dunn was "magnificent," as was her Short Story Writing course with Alfred Kazin. But she found her intermediate German conversational course "terribly difficult."[12] Like science, German was psychologically fraught territory, for it was bound up with Otto's legacy. Despite her Harvard summer course, Sylvia felt unable to "stammer" out a single sentence.[13]

Her Dostoevsky thesis made up for her struggles in German. Her adviser George Gibian encouraged her to pursue the thesis topic she had chosen: "several pairs of the 'double' personality in dostoevsky [sic]," as she explained to Gordon.[14] She limited her social activities, including weekends with him, and devoted all her free time to her thesis. "I must read like fury," she wrote.[15]

Her monkish devotion to scholarship required a new look. With her platinum summer and its men behind her, she dyed her hair back to its natural brown in September. "I feel that this year, with my applying for scholarships, I would much rather look demure and discreet," she told Gordon:

in a sense, I'm rather sure that my brown-haired personality will win out this year . . . gone is the frivolous giddy gilded creature who careened around corners at the wheel of a yellow convertible and stayed up till six in the morning because the conversation and bourbonandwater [sic] were too good to terminate . . . but it is good for me, and this is really the most honest part of myself, I think.[16]

Plath, excited to finally find herself in command of a challenging literary topic, was now energized rather than crushed by her workload. She revisited *The Picture of Dorian Gray, Dr. Jekyll and Mr. Hyde*, Freud, Jung, Poe, and Frazer; she hoped to read Otto Rank in German—"all fascinating stuff about the ego as symbolized in reflections (mirror and water), shadows, twins . . . dividing off and becoming an enemy, or omen of death . . . or a warning con- science."[17] For once, she did not downplay her analytical ability: "perhaps it's all abominably bad, but I secretly don't think so," she told Aurelia.[18] This was the most serious scholarly work she had ever done. She hoped to write "an adolescent story about doubles" after she had finished her thesis—"every incident in my life begins to smack of the mirror image."[19]

She found an outlet for her creative work in Kazin's fall semester fiction class. When Kazin arrived at Smith in the fall of 1954 as a visiting professor, Plath was eager to meet him. She couldn't believe her luck when the *Smith Alumnae Quarterly* asked her to interview him. Mr. Kazin, she wrote, "does not like to consider himself as any one particular type of writer," and when pressed about his teaching style, "he would only say that the important thing is 'not to have theories.'"[20] He emphasized discipline over raw talent, though talent was important, too. To Plath, he embodied the world of the heroic intelligentsia. Kazin was a public intellectual involved in the major theoreti- cal and political debates of his age. He, along with Hannah Arendt, Karl Sha- piro, Saul Bellow, and Lionel Trilling, contributed regularly to the magazine *Commentary*, which was founded after the war to address "public opinion of problems of Jewish concern."[21] Esther Greenwood's horror of the Rosenberg execution suggests Plath's sympathy for the radical literary and political New York Jewish circles to which she was connected, tangentially, through Kazin.

During her interview, Plath found Kazin "brusque" at first. When she revealed that she had worked her way through college and had literary aspi- rations, he warmed to her. He had thought she was "just another pampered smith [*sic*] baby," and invited her to audit his creative writing class—the only class he taught that year—where she made a strong first impression. She was "appalled at the weak, mealy-mouthed apathy of the girls, who either were just too scared or just too stupid to have opinions."[22] Plath was soon refer- ring to Kazin as "the great god Alfred," and began writing fiction for the first time in nearly two years.[23] She called him "the light that incandesces my year,"[24] and loved the way he flouted dry academic convention: "he told me it's my holy duty to write every day, spill out all, learn to give it form, and is going to let me go off on my own every week, only asking that I turn in lots and lots and not to bother with the regular class assignment."[25]

In Kazin's class, Sylvia got to know Ellie Friedman, a young Jewish woman from Longmeadow, Massachusetts, in the Class of '56. Ellie felt Kazin took

Plath seriously—here was "the Big Man teaching writing and here's a student who he knows immediately is better than he'll ever be. That's the feeling I had when I was there." Ellie, who called herself "snobbish" about her taste in friends, said she "fell in love" with Sylvia over dinner one night at Martha Wilson House, where she lived. "She was never a mad, obsessed poet when I knew her. She was *happy*, and she was *funny*." The two became close that year as they whiled away afternoons in each other's rooms. Sylvia would read Ellie her poetry and flaunt her rejection letters, saying, "'Look at my rejections, it means I'm a writer!'" Ellie added, "She was always interested, always welcoming."[26] They spoke often of their love for Russian literature and Yeats, their dreams of becoming a writer and an actress. Ellie thought Sylvia romanticized her Jewishness, partly in reaction to her own "arid" WASP identity. "I think that the idea of these people who went through great trial and who wandered a great deal and yet had a central core on which they could rely was a big source of fascination. Jews seemed to have a relationship to self that I think she always felt was missing." She had the feeling that Plath wanted to "dissipate" her "whiteness."[27]

Eventually Sylvia opened up to Ellie about her traumatic experiences at Valley Head and McLean, telling her "many times" about the horrifying details of her shock treatment. "She told me about her sessions . . . She told me what would happen, it was like being murdered, the electroshock therapy. It was the most horrific thing in the world for her. That's when she said to me, 'If this should ever happen to me again, I *will* kill myself.'" Ellie said Sylvia was "referring to the madhouse" and shock treatment, but also to "her madness, her loss of self, her inability to do anything. Because that's what you are. You sit there and you can't do anything." Sylvia told Ellie, "When you're crazy, that's all you ever are." She did not portray McLean as "a good place," but spoke positively about Dr. Beuscher: "She felt that she understood. . . . she gave her herself back."[28] But mostly Sylvia spoke about what the psychiatrists *did* to her: how the nurses had strapped down her hands and placed electrodes on her temples before turning on the electric current.[29]

Ellie's brother's disappearance from Dartmouth in 1954 meant that she understood great pain. "We had something of pain to share. . . . We held it to be like pleasure: it is our own, it is not for everybody. 'I don't want anybody's pity. And I'm not going to talk about it in tears, either.'" She and Sylvia shared moments of black humor, joking about a student who hanged herself near Paradise Pond. They told each other they knew what was on "'the far side of Paradise': the Northampton State Asylum for the Insane."[30]

Sylvia, Ellie noted, divulged these details from a place of health. Yet these conversations also suggest the lingering trauma of Plath's mismanaged shock treatment at Valley Head, and perhaps other shock treatments at McLean. Sylvia's depression had abated, but the repercussions of her disastrous "cure" haunted her. Still, her improved mental health was not simply a façade. Her painful memories of Valley Head and her anxieties about a relapse did not cripple her as her depression had in 1953. In the past, writing a lengthy thesis, mastering German, and impressing a famous writer would have left Sylvia exhausted and full of self-doubt. Now she was able to function at a high level without a struggle. She had never been so enmeshed in a scholarly paper before: "the best thing is that the topic itself intrigues me, and that no matter how I work on it, I shall never tire of it."[31]

Meanwhile regular exercise helped her stay balanced. At Smith, Sylvia's frequent colds and sinus infections, Marcia said, would just "flatten" her. She "was really seriously ill for a substantial period of time. . . . She would withdraw, simply go to bed and stay there feeling dreadful."[32] When she was not laid low, however, Sylvia always seemed to be on the go. Many Smith friends recalled her love of the outdoors and her attention to colors and patterns in nature—a stone wall, or bark on a tree. Pat remembered her saying, "Let's get out in a bike and ride. Let's go skating. Let's *do* something."[33] Professor George Gibian recalled that Sylvia looked "always as if she had just come back from skiing in Vermont or swimming in Bermuda—healthy."[34]

In September Sylvia again joined the Lawrence House crew team, which practiced three times a week. She had rowed during her sophomore year and "luxuriated in the exercise."[35] She told Gordon, "it does me no end of good to be out on the water in a shell . . . the feeling of pulling hard and skimming along in a unanimous sweat of stroking is really potent!" Her health seemed to improve after she began taking iron for anemia; she suddenly felt "strong and ironic."[36] She thought she would "explode" with new poems and stories in the spring, and sent a humorous greeting card to Gordon, whose preprinted message made light of her breakdown: "To bundles of nerves / And strange complexes / To all of those / With wrong reflexes / Whom drugs won't help / Or antibiotics / Let us celebrate / Being neurotics."[37] She felt she could have written the verse herself.

————

A SUMMER OF REST and restricted diet on Cape Cod had not healed Aurelia's duodenal ulcer; by late September, she was back in the hospital. After her release she was put on bed rest and instructed to take a leave from Boston University. Sylvia had grown used to Aurelia's medical crises and did not dwell on them ("does 'bed rest' mean you'll be at home in bed & not teach the rest of the year, or what? let me know if I can be of any use whatever. One thing, I'm desperate for cotton clothes—all I have up here is woolens").[38] But Olive Prouty was alarmed. "I know that many ulcers are the result of anxiety—or mental stress," she wrote to Aurelia. Prouty guessed that the "terrible experience" Aurelia had endured the previous year had caused the trouble and thought a change of scenery might help.[39] She invited Aurelia to stay with her at the Plaza Hotel in Manhattan. She was glad, she added, that Sylvia's hair "was again its natural color . . . she herself seemed so natural and unstrained."[40]

Mrs. Prouty took the surprising step of confiding in Sylvia about her worries regarding Aurelia, whom she thought might benefit from a talk with a psychiatrist. Prouty felt Aurelia needed to hear, from a professional, that she was "no longer necessary to her children."[41] She wrote perceptively to Sylvia, "I feel sorry that Dr. Beuscher couldn't have included her in her treatment of your illness. It seems to me that psychiatrists should treat their patient's nearest relative . . . as well as the patient himself—for often he, or she, is the cause of the patient's maladjustment and illness.—& his treatment is beneficial to all concerned."[42] The idea of family therapy seems to have appealed to Sylvia. When Warren visited her that fall, she suggested, lightly, to Aurelia that he begin therapy with "some respected doctor or social advisor" who "could point out more specific and constructive ways to develop in warren [sic] an articulate, active and participating delight in life . . . a sense of 'fun,' which I think has been a family weakness." Sylvia felt that she had worked hard to grow over the summer in Cambridge, and she wanted Warren to experience a less restricted life, as she had. "I know that underneath the blazing jaunts in yellow convertibles to exquisite restaurants I am really regrettably unoriginal, conventional and puritanical, basically, but I needed to practice a certain healthy bohemianism for a while . . . I needed to associate with people who were very different from myself."[43]

Henry James had replaced James Joyce, for the moment, as Sylvia's and Gordon's literary touchstone: "Sometimes I see you as a Jamesian heroine like Isabel Archer being exposed to life," Gordon wrote. Sylvia liked the comparison, despite its ambiguous prophecy, and signed off a letter as "Isabel." But she started to pull away, telling Gordon that they faced a "hard future" together should they marry. He dismissed her doubts. "I love you, I love all of you, and your thorns are the best part of you."[44]

Gordon spent three days with Sylvia in October to celebrate her twenty-second birthday, but the visit did not go well. She was upset with him for interrupting her work. He gave her a brown cashmere cardigan sweater, while his mother sent her an apron—a gift that probably sent a "chilly whisper" up her spine. She was more excited by Ira Scott's baby-blue Brooks Brothers shirt to match the pink one he had given her over the summer, and some coral jewelry from Sassoon. Edwin Akutowicz visited her on November 2 and took her out to dinner in Northampton. "He is very peculiar and archaic, but amusing," she told Aurelia.[45] Though Sylvia and Nancy Hunter were now roommates, their friendship had not survived the events of the previous summer, when Sylvia had felt the cold glare of Nancy's disapproval. Now Sylvia was annoyed that Nancy had literary ambitions and fancied herself a campus "Poetess." "The stardust has long gone out of my eyes," she wrote to Mel. "We speak, that is all."[46]

Sassoon, back from Europe, continued to write Sylvia Wertherian love letters full of *Sturm und Drang* throughout the semester. "God! My darling, darling did you hear the thunder last night, beating and banging at the beauty of a mottled sky . . . it was only my love raging at the distance between me and my love."[47] Sassoon knew about Gordon but felt less threatened as the weeks passed. "My darling—my rival begins to bore me—at least I am not jealous anymore and I am sure you would not enjoy going through Italy with him because he only agrees with what a hundred people have said and it is all wrong."[48] Sassoon's devastating portrayal of Gordon as a bourgeois fop struck a nerve with Sylvia. His letters pulsed with a Romantic sublimity that made Gordon's Joycean puns seem dry and irrelevant. Sassoon unintentionally summed up her predicament: "when you have lived the beauty of Mallarmé you do not wish to read Sandburg."[49] Her "Frenchboy" enjoyed portraying himself as base, depressed, cruel—much like the compelling characters she was reading in Dostoevsky, whom she now declared "the greatest philosophical influence on my life . . . along with nietzsche, huxley, fromm [*sic*] and a few others."[50] As Dostoevsky replaced Joyce, Sassoon replaced Gordon.

Sassoon played with tropes of violence in his letters, a French literary posture meant to conjure de Sade: "And I know I teach girls to be women and I teach them how to taunt me and then you are far and cannot be punished. . . . you are the only one I have wished to please and to punish."[51] He told her in December that in New York "it will be rather fun to play daddy to a naughty girl if you are naughty."[52] But he also wrote of his love and wrote intelligently about her poems. When she sent him "Verbal Calisthenics," "Admonition," and "Ice Age" that fall, he replied, "I am so terribly proud of you, darling. . . . The Americans are saying that poetry should sound natural, and I never heard anything more absurd in my life. Poetry is a great discipline, a torturous discipline, a perversion."[53] He probably knew about Plath's suicide attempt, but he assumed that his soul was the more troubled.

"At times I am a very depressed man—I have tried to hide it—but you must know this of me."[54]

With her other boyfriends, Sylvia had to deny the iconoclast within. Sassoon, alternatively, required her to disavow anything that smacked of middle-class morals. "I think original sin is vulgar, and self-denial disgusting, and the conception of a personal deity cowardly," he wrote to her that fall, effectively demolishing the bedrock of Aurelia's moral philosophy.[55] But Sassoon could not shield himself from the strong emotion he felt for Plath. He was, despite himself, falling deeply in love with her and felt he was on the brink of madness.[56] He told her that he would no longer write to her unless she made a greater effort to see him.

When Sylvia told Gordon about Sassoon out of "frankness," he asked that she stop seeing him. Sylvia balked: "I do not plan to refuse reunions with my old friends . . . ira and sassoon [sic] among them," she wrote to him in late November. She broached ending the relationship: "obviously, darling, I would never think of calling anything 'quits.' even [sic] if you decide to marry someone else in a few years from now, I hope we shall always be good friends."[57] Although she spent Thanksgiving with Gordon, the next day Ira picked her up in Cambridge. Together they drove to Concord, where they drank champagne at the historic Colonial Inn. The following day she had a "grand talk" with Dr. Beuscher—"need for being & experiencing—who knows what's 'good' in the long run anyhow? Trial & error . . . maturity— necessity of paradox—need for wait for 'ebb-tide'—look up 'Psychology & Promethean Will'—for sustenance."[58] By Sunday she was back with Sassoon for a steak dinner followed by "cognac on Mount Tom."[59] Gordon began to understand. A few days after declaring his love for her and looking forward to "a future of knowing you for what we call 'ever,'" he spoke plainly: "your attitudes toward me have changed and mine toward you."[60]

Sylvia had again left one man for another whose literary and intellectual interests dovetailed more closely with her own: Dick was a scientist with a passing interest in poetry; Gordon an English major and a Joyce fanatic; Sassoon a Dostoevskian darkling. She moved through these men and others as she moved more confidently toward her own literary destiny, increasingly determined not to settle for a conventional marriage. Yet Sylvia, still her mother's daughter, found extracting herself from her unofficial engagements to Dick and Gordon difficult. She had boxed herself into a corner with Gordon, just as she had with Dick. Studying for a graduate degree abroad seemed an increasingly attractive option.

———

SEVERAL LITERARY ACCEPTANCES BOOSTED Plath's confidence in November. "Go Get the Goodly Squab" and "To Eva Descending the Stair" appeared in the September and November issues of *Harper's*, while her story "In the Mountains" and poem "Circus in Three Rings" were published in that fall's *Smith Review*. Cyrilly Abels wrote Plath that her "Triad of Love Lyrics" had won honorable mention in *Mademoiselle's* Dylan Thomas poetry contest. Abels also bought "Parallax" for $30, money Plath badly needed (she was elated she could finally buy a girdle, brush, comb, and slippers). By this time, winning literary contests was almost passé. She was more excited by her A– in German, which she had brought up from a B through weekly tutoring sessions. She began translating Rainer Maria Rilke poems, using the same rhythm and rhyme scheme—"very difficult for me, but terribly stimulating," she told Gordon.[61] She was thrilled, too, by an airplane ride she took that November. She had asked Aurelia to give her permission to fly, as Smith required, but Aurelia was too nervous to allow it. Sylvia took matters into her own hands. As she explained to Gordon, "Icarian lust" came upon her, and she sweet-talked one of the pilots at the small local airport into taking her on a flight: "and we are up, tilting over hamp, me screaming about how this is the fourth dimension and god isn't it a fantastic day."[62] Sylvia neglected to mention the flight to Aurelia, but assured her she was "most happy"—"busy and occupied, of course, but oh! With such a healthy, philosophical outlook!"[63] Mrs. Prouty was not convinced, and asked Sylvia candidly whether she was "<u>really</u> as happy as you <u>seem</u>. I was so so doubtful—unsure—and lonely—at your age—temperamentally. Is your joyousness real or assumed? I wonder sometimes."[64]

By early December, Plath had nearly finished her thesis—two months early. "I am so proud of myself!" she wrote her mother. Now she had time to enjoy her Christmas vacation and revise stories she had written for Kazin, who had enjoyed "Superman and Paula Brown's New Snowsuit." Sylvia wrote Aurelia, "every time one sits down to the blank page, there is that fresh horror, which must be overcome by practice and practice."[65] She was looking forward to her upcoming tutorials with Alfred Fisher, a Shakespearean scholar who had offered to take her on as a private poetry student. (Plath came up with a "classy" title for the tutorial: "The Theory and Practice of Poetics.")[66] Janet Salter Rosenberg recalled that Fisher was a "handsome, nice, absolutely good teacher" but "had a reputation" for getting involved with students.[67] Sylvia described him as "very British, with keen blue eyes, white hair and mustache, and most tweedy clothes." Fisher wanted Plath to help him research the Elizabethan poet and playwright John Ford, and asked her to turn in a "batch" of poems each week. To Aurelia, Sylvia compared the practice to "prospecting for gold: you know the raw nuggets are there, but you have to sift through a hell of a lot of sludge to get at them!"[68]

In early December, Plath rendezvoused with Sassoon in New York City. They saw *The Bad Seed* and dined on escargots, oysters, shrimp, and wine at Le Veau d'Or.[69] Sassoon bantered in French with the waiters, and a couple next to them whispered that the two young lovers could not be a day over eighteen.[70] While they downed more oysters at Steuben's on Sunday, some-one stole Sylvia's suitcase from Sassoon's car, parked just off Fifth Avenue. Nearly her entire wardrobe was gone, plus many of her favorite poetry books and her Chanel No. 5. "I'm trying to keep this secret from mother," she wrote her friend Jon Rosenthal, "because when one is supporting oneself, one does not replenish wardrobe, one wears dungarees for a year. so [*sic*] I will wear dungarees for a year. and [*sic*] pretend I have become an ascetic. you [*sic*] know just cawn't beah cashmeah sweatehs, so vulgah."[71] A visit to the police station did little good, but Sylvia was fascinated by the details of the cases she overheard. Sassoon mailed her a check before he knew whether his insurance policy would cover the loss, and she replaced her wardrobe. She even got a poem out of the incident: "Item Stolen: One Suitcase."

Sylvia turned in a first draft of her thesis on December 17; the next day, she celebrated with Warren and Gordon at Robinhood's Ten Acres, a cocktail lounge west of Boston. She was now on her Christmas vacation, and would soon join Jon Rosenthal on a skiing trip to Stowe. Jon, an Amherst gradu-ate who was now in the Army, had bunked with Sylvia's old boyfriend Bob Riedeman at Fort Dix. Someone had pointed Sylvia out to Jon at an Amherst fraternity party in April 1954, when she was George Gebauer's date, and told him that she had tried to kill herself. Jon was struck by Sylvia's beauty and dynamism, and could hardly believe she had been suicidal. On leave that November, he called on a friend at Lawrence House; when she was not home, on a whim, he asked for Sylvia, who was surprised to find him in the living room. The two immediately began bantering about her poem "To Eva Descending the Stair."[72] They dated briefly in November before he was reas-signed to El Paso, but he returned to see her in December. He remembered her as radiant, bursting with ideas and energy. When he offered to take her either skiing in Vermont or to New York City, she wrote him that New York was "intellectualized and sedentary and most daiquiri-saturated," and decided she needed "a more elemental communion with nature on snow slopes."[73] He picked her up in Wellesley on Monday, December 20, bound for Stowe. Aurelia fretted over the practical details of their trip. Sylvia had told Jon that Aurelia was a "nervous mother, whom I see as little as possible. . . . in case she dies unexpectedly, she wants to be able to send me a telegram. (seriously [*sic*] though, I do love her, and am not contemplating matricide)."[74]

Jon had romantic hopes for the trip, though he booked separate rooms. At first, all went well. Plath wrote in her calendar on December 21 that she had a "magnificent 2 hour ski class on Toll House slopes . . . snow plow, turn and rope tow—victory & power."[75] She was pleased to have made a "comeback" on the slopes, and called it the "last bronc broken." But Jon hurt his ankle during a late-afternoon run, and the injury dampened their moods. They left Stowe midmorning on the 22nd. Sylvia wrote in her calendar, "enormous feud with Jon—silent drive back through Grandma Moses Landscape."[76] Jon remembered some of the details: on the way back, Sylvia felt he was driving too fast and jumped into the back seat, where she curled up in silence for two hours—sleeping or thinking, he did not know. Eventually, he said, she jumped back into the front seat and kissed him. She explained that she had once been close to death and that she never wanted to get that close again; she felt she had a better chance of surviving an accident in the back seat.[77] Sylvia then opened up to him about her suicide, explaining that "people had put her on a pedestal," and she felt compelled to maintain her achievements, even though doing so had cut her off from "the nourishment that she needed."[78] None of this frank talk alarmed Jon, who felt Sylvia was simply less conformist than the other Smith girls he knew. She was "very out-front" about her feelings.[79] He found this aspect of her personality refreshing. He would see her one more time in September 1955, and then never again.

Despite their recent quarrel, Sylvia saw Gordon frequently over her Christmas vacation. She saw Dr. Beuscher the day after Christmas, and may have discussed how to end her relationship with him: "long talk: impossibility of argument or logic—retirement in dignified silence—moral honesty—each situation judged in itself," she wrote in her calendar.[80] Her vacation was productive—she polished her thesis and revised "Mary Ventura and the Ninth Kingdom," "The Day Mr. Prescott Died," and "The Smoky Blue Piano," a screwball comedy and jab at Nancy Hunter that she had written earlier in the term for Kazin. Sylvia told Enid Epstein the story had "'plot' (very unusual for me) and a frothy sense of humor (more unusual)."[81] It concerns two summer school roommates who are both romantically interested in a mysterious neighbor, Lou (an amalgam of Sylvia's real neighbor that summer, Lou Healy, and Edwin Akutowicz), who owns a blue piano. The narrator, based on Sylvia, assumes that Lou wants to date her beautiful and brilliant roommate, Lynn, based on Nancy. She imagines Lynn walking down the aisle with him while she plays maid of honor, despite the fact that Lynn already has a boyfriend. Yet at the story's end we learn that Lou is really interested in the narrator, and simply using Lynn to get close to *her*. "I had a lovely vision of Lynn preceding me down the aisle in a peacock-green dress while somebody played the chorus from 'Lohengrin' on a smoky blue piano," the narrator says.[82] The story shows Plath exploring the theme of her thesis in her fiction. The narrator triumphs over her double, just as she would in *The Bell Jar*. Plath was thrilled when *Ladies' Home Journal* returned "The Smoky Blue Piano" in mid-January 1955 with requests for changes. She immediately rewrote the story to their specifications (dropping the "diary" format) and sent it back, hoping for an $850 acceptance. Mel suggested that she had sold her "integrity down the river," but Sylvia defended herself. "I just played up my sense of humor, that's all. It's much harder than being tragic and depressing, you know!"[83] The revised story was rejected, but it shows how efficiently Plath functioned as a professional writer even before she had graduated from college.[84]

Plath's other major story from January 1955, "Tongues of Stone," was based on her experience at McLean. The writing is bleak and somber, entirely devoid of the black humor that marks the mental hospital scenes in *The Bell Jar*. The young protagonist describes her depression as Plath had in her journal:

> she would drag out her nights and days chained to a wall in a dark soli-
> tary cell with dirt and spiders. . . . she was caught in the nightmare of the
> body, without a mind, without anything, only the soulless flesh that got
> fatter with the insulin and yellower with the fading tan. . . . She had gone
> on circling at the brink of the whirlpool, pretending to be clever and gay,
> and all the while these poisons were gathering in her body, ready to break
> out behind the bright, false bubbles of her eyes at any moment crying:
> Idiot! Imposter!

The young woman fantasizes about killing her mother—as Plath did in the days before her suicide attempt—and regrets that "They had raised her like Lazarus." She attempts to hang herself with a cotton scarf she has hidden, but "her hands would slacken and let go." She breaks a glass and hides the shards for future use, the sensation "voluptuous."[85]

In the story's first draft, Plath had left her protagonist languishing in depression in what she called "eternal night." But Kazin was distressed by the story's unrelenting hopelessness, and told her that "writing was invented to give more joy." She decided to change the ending "from life to art," to "a conclusion of dawn."[86] In the final draft, the protagonist has a reaction to the insulin. "I feel different," she tells the nurse in a scene that she later rewrote in *The Bell Jar*. That night, she is filled with a new hope: "And in the dark the girl lay listening to the voice of dawn and felt flare through every fiber of her mind and body the everlasting rising of the sun."[87] Plath thought the story was "naked and depressing," but "the best work of 'art' I've ever done . . . beautifully written."[88] She was right—the story, with its vivid depictions of mental hell, was her best since "Sunday at the Mintons." "I have a feeling that I may be destined to be more successful in writing than I thought at first," she wrote Aurelia.[89]

Only five days after returning to campus after her Christmas break Sylvia checked herself in to the infirmary with a sore throat, cough, and cold. She used this time "off" productively, as was her habit: she wrote five new poems, which she promptly sent off to *The New Yorker*, and had a surprise visit from Peter Davison, an assistant editor at Harcourt, Brace.[90] Peter was visiting Alfred Kazin, who had sent him over to cheer Sylvia up. She was impressed by Peter's pedigree: a Harvard degree, a Fulbright to Cambridge, a British poet father, and a position at a major publisher. To her astonishment, Peter asked to see any novel she might write in the next few years. They would be dating by the spring.

By now Gordon had left for Guantanamo Bay, Cuba, where he wrote Sylvia long letters about keeping America safe from Russia. She was secretly relieved. She assumed that she would confront a "deluge" of thesis revision in January, but George Gibian thought her manuscript was excellent, and, by the first week of January, she was ready to send her thesis to the typist, nearly a month early. She was delighted by the "professional results" when it came back, and cut classes to proofread all seventy pages. "I was so proud, it is an excellent thesis, I know it in my bones," she wrote Aurelia. She had already heard rumors that Gibian had pronounced it a "masterpiece."[91] He later called Plath "a brilliant student . . . a wish fulfilment student. . . . Before she was even in my course, everybody would talk Sylvia Plath, Sylvia Plath."[92]

Titled "The Magic Mirror: A Study of the Double in Two of Dostoevsky's Novels," the thesis had the potential to be the *pièce de résistance* of Plath's college experience. Yet there was more at stake. Her earlier attempt, the previous year, to begin a thesis on James Joyce's *Ulysses* was partly to blame for her breakdown, suicide attempt, and subsequent hospitalization. In the wake of what she had endured, she sought a theme that resonated with her own experience, and would carry her through the long months of solitary reading and writing. In *Ulysses*, Joyce has much to say about Ireland, Catholicism, colonialism, literature, history, class, grief, love, and sex, but not much about mental illness and its attendant destructions and illuminations. For that, Plath turned to Dostoevsky.

She wrote about the connection between doubling and insanity. Plath dedicated the first half of her thesis to an analysis of Golyadkin and his double, Golyadkin Jr., in *The Double*, an early work dating from 1846. She ended with a more sustained discussion of Ivan and Smerdyakov's doubleness in *The Brothers Karamazov*. She wanted to show that the double was an integral component of Dostoevsky's work as a whole. But she implies early on that Dostoevsky's interest in the double was a function of his interest in mental illness: "Indeed, literary critics and psychoanalysts alike point out that Dostoevsky's remarkable penetration into the depths of the human mind anticipated the discoveries of modern psychoanalysis."[93] Her own path toward recovery mirrored Dostoevsky's increasingly complex understanding of the "schizophrenic personality," as she described Golyadkin, from *The Double* to *The Brothers Karamazov*.

While Plath drew heavily on James Frazer in her discussion of the double's literary and anthropological antecedents, Otto Rank's and Sigmund Freud's psychoanalytical viewpoints interested her more. She promises her reader that she will not "diagnose mental maladies" but will instead "stress the intrinsic technique of the stories themselves."[94] Yet throughout her thesis, Plath continues to circle back to psychoanalytic readings. She compares Golyadkin's "personality structure to that of a victim of acute schizophrenia" and discusses Freud's idea that the Double is a "'ghastly harbinger of death.'"

> By creating a Double, the schizophrenic no longer needs to castigate himself or to feel guilty for harboring these corrupt urges; at last he can blame someone else for these transgressions which he once felt were his.
>
> However, the advantages of this radical division involve danger as well as distinct relief. The double alleviation of tension, which frees the victim from responsibility for his repressed desires and yet satisfies those desires, is countered by a new fear of attack from the outside. The Double becomes an ever-present liability, for it increases the vulnerability of its creator; it may even betray or kill the very personality which gave it life.[95]

This was not simply literary criticism—Plath was also examining, from a safe, objective distance, her own experience with mental illness. Plath was not schizophrenic; she never hallucinated, never lost track of her identity or her location, and never fell into trances. But her mood swings, which she frequently acknowledged, may have caused her to believe that she shared certain symptoms with the schizophrenic. She had written in her journal of a similar "double"—a voice that wrecked and ridiculed her fragile self-confidence, "screaming, 'Traitor, sinner, imposter.'"[96] When Plath wrote, in her thesis, "The mystery of the second self becomes a menace; the inner duality becomes a duel to the death," or when she described "the seductiveness of suicide as a release from prolonged torment," she was writing as much about herself as about Dostoevsky.[97]

Plath's scholarship on Lawrence, Emerson, Nietzsche, Dostoevsky, and others was intertwined with her search for a guiding life philosophy that would help her manage and mitigate the blunt blows of depression. Through the act of analyzing Russian literature, Plath had come upon a cure of sorts. As she wrote, "Dostoevsky implies that recognition of our various mirror images and reconciliation with them will save us from disintegration."[98] Like Dostoevsky himself, Plath would someday distance herself from her own menacing doubles by giving them voice on the page. Dostoevsky had suffered from epileptic fits (often associated with madness in the nineteenth century) and helped Plath understand that it was possible to converse with the devil and emerge unscathed, even enlightened: "Although, at the last, Ivan succumbs to insanity in court, Dimitri, Katarina, and Alyosha all affirm the strong likelihood of his recovery. 'Ivan has a strong constitution,' remarks Alyosha. 'I, too, believe there's every hope that he will get well.' "[99]

————

SYLVIA FINISHED her exams on January 20 and returned to Wellesley for a brief interregnum between semesters. She lounged around the house in her pajamas, playing the piano "for hours soupily crooning in bad french [*sic*], and getting a hell of a kick out of it." She had a "fun" "bull session" with Dr. Beuscher at her house, where they discussed, she told Gordon, "religion, philosophy, honesty, selfishness, and a lot of other potent, perhaps more intimate, topics." She and Aurelia were "getting along much better," though in a letter to Gordon, she hinted that she managed her anger toward her mother by imagining her dead.[100] Aurelia had written to Sylvia about an "attack" she had experienced due to stress, and Sylvia was beginning to suspect that she may have inherited her own anxiety not from Otto (as Aurelia thought) but from her mother. "I don't know whether it is an hereditary characteristic, but our little family is altogether <u>too</u> prone to lie awake at nights hating ourselves for stupidities."[101]

Sylvia still had one more academic hurdle to overcome—the interview for a Woodrow Wilson Fellowship, which was held at Harvard on January 22. In her calendar, she wrote, "grueling—4 men: barrage of questions."[102] The "smug" all-male committee, headed by Harvard's dean, had intimidated her, asking her if she would "give up teaching for marriage without a fuss, what about babies, would I marry a teacher . . . and on and on."[103] Plath had never experienced such blatant academic sexism. The men twisted her every remark "to their purposes, tossing it back, asking loaded questions, until I felt like a painted wooden toy at the rifle booth in the circus."[104] When she learned that she had been turned down for the fellowship a few days later, she struggled to understand what had gone wrong. To Aurelia she wrote, "this is the first time I have been really rejected after having all the chances, and I have been terribly sad all morning."[105] In her calendar, she wrote, "shock!"[106]

She now assumed that she would not get into Radcliffe, but the college assured her that the Wilson interview would not affect her chances for admission: "not at all," Radcliffe's friendly dean wrote to Plath, and told her, bluntly, that the Woodrow Wilson Fellowships were "given mostly for men who might otherwise go into business, law, medicine etc."[107] This shockingly sexist explanation made Sylvia feel better; she was relieved the rejection had nothing to do with her hospitalization or "character blots."[108]

She consoled herself by writing, but her subject matter reflected her anxieties about whether she could—or should—achieve her professional goals. The fellowship interview had reminded her, once again, that American patriarchal society frowned on female trailblazers. At Smith, strong academic women like Mary Ellen Chase, Evelyn Page, and Elizabeth Drew had nurtured her; she was not used to defending her ambitions to a wall of stone-faced male professors. Sylvia saw herself through the men's eyes—a woman and a former asylum patient—and was suddenly filled with doubt.

"Home Is Where the Heart Is," which Plath wrote a few days after the interview, explores the consequences of self-repression. She described it as a story about a housewife "who comes to mental crisis, faced by a family who seems to be seeking life outside the home. She manages creatively to bring them all back together."[109] Plath was exploring her own future in the story, in which Mrs. Arnold, once the top English student and writer in her college, ruminates on her decision to sacrifice her career for housewifery and motherhood. Plath emphasizes the drudgery of Mrs. Arnold's days—her life has been curtailed by dirty dishes, "mountains of laundry," a howling baby, sullen teenagers, and a distracted husband. While Mrs. Arnold listens to the radio, she dreams about going to Paris, and begins to wonder what her life would have been like had she fulfilled her own ambitions rather than her lawyer husband's. Yet that night, on cue, her children treat her respectfully and her husband is offered a higher-paying job. "Now I know what I was really meant for, Michael. . . . That Arch of Triumph they talk about . . . coming up the walk this afternoon, I knew deep down inside all the while that it was really our own front door!"[110] Plath wrote other versions of this story: "The Visitor" and, later, "Day of Success" were both variations on the theme of the martyred, triumphant housewife. These stories reflect not what Plath wanted but what she was expected to want. She told Aurelia that "Home Is

Where the Heart Is," which she submitted to a Christian writing contest, was "tailored to specifications . . . very plotted, and noble, but not preaching."[111] Yet the story was written just a few days after she had faced a skeptical panel of male academics.[112] She may have begun to wonder whether Mrs. Arnold's life represented the more realistic course.

After the Woodrow Wilson interview Sylvia boarded a night flight to New York, where she rendezvoused with Sassoon. She felt that her Manhattan weekends were a winter "tonic" that helped her through her "periodic slackening times."[113] She and Sassoon dined decadently on caviar, pear tart, and vermouth cassis at Toffentetti's, Le Gourmet, Le Veau d'Or, and Chez St. Denis, and saw performances that made a lasting impression—the "Russian-Jewish" "absorbing fantasy" *The Dybbuk*, and several foreign films, including the Japanese *Gate of Hell*, which she called a "color poem . . . not a superfluous gesture in the whole thing."[114] She and Sassoon spent an afternoon viewing the Picassos and Braques at the Museum of Modern Art, where she saw the silent French film *The Temptation of St. Joan:* "excruciatingly beautiful silent symbolic," "the most shattering work I've ever endured."[115] She described it in detail to Mel:

> I'll never forget the final scene at the pyre, a strong and terrible masterpiece of understatement, with the flames licking the wood, smoke rising, the faces of the peasants. . . . I was physically unable to stop looking, even though my mind screamed for release. With the final tension of the film dissolved, I went for a long walk in the cold dark of Central Park, crying and crying, those cold pure tears of Greek tragedy. . . . Human kind cannot bear very much reality. That kind of reality.

Images of martyrdom, torture, and fire would all feature in her late poems. The trip fortified her. "I returned to Smith gladly (which last week I thought was both physically and psychically impossible) and will subsist happily for months on cold water and brown bread."[116]

Sylvia was taking three English courses this semester: the Twentieth Century American Novel with Kazin; an English review unit with her sophomore year writing teacher, Evelyn Page; and her poetry tutorial with Alfred Fisher. Under Fisher's guidance, she began writing poems at a rapid rate: "my typewriter won't be still."[117] "I am obsessed by writing as the first thing in life, and the poems come more and more," she wrote to Gordon that February.[118] During the first two weeks of the spring semester, she wrote nine new poems;[119] by the semester's end, she would "pound out" nearly fifty new poems—about five new poems a week.[120] Her confidence was growing. "I have felt great advances in my poetry," she told Aurelia, "the main one being a growing victory over word's [sic] nuances and a superfluity of adjective."[121] Her burgeoning poetry collection began to take shape in her mind.

Sylvia was correct about her weaknesses. As Mrs. Prouty put it in a letter to Aurelia, "I am often puzzled by her underlying meaning. Many of her poems are to me like abstract paintings—bright, vivid, colorful." But Prouty did not know "what the lovely words and rhythmic sounds are saying."[122] Many poems from Plath's Smith period are, as Plath later admitted in a 1962 interview, "desperately Audenesque." (Consider "Yet astronomic fountains / Exit from the heart" in "Parallax.") Others, such as "Advice for an Artificer," are full of Sitwellian wordplay and aural effects ("Shall we spell summer with tricks of rhetoric / till thoughts like purpling plums grow grandly rich / and glut the feigning brain").[123] Still others, such as "Love Is a Parallax," are New Critical exercises in Marvellian poise and conceit. Yet alongside the thesaurus vocabulary are the images for which Plath would become known: bones, mist, ice, sun, blood, stone, skulls, hags, moons, stars, hearts, flames, wind, and flowers. She continued to write about spring (and false springs), unrequited love, time passing, ennui, storms, and death—just as she had in high school. But her language could be brittle. Plath's poems had not yet achieved the spare grandeur of her mature voice.

The most successful poems from this period—"Two Lovers and a Beachcomber by the Real Sea," "Go Get the Goodly Squab," "Epitaph in Three Parts," "Morning in the Hospital Solarium," and "Lament"—were about loss. They are the antecedents of "Sheep in Fog," "Words," and "Edge." Their muted cantations forced Plath to tone down the aural fireworks that overwhelm many of her "thesaurus" poems from this period. Yet she achieved success with some of what she called her "giddy" verses as well. "Circus in Three Rings" foreshadows "Aerialist" and "Lady Lazarus" ("a rose of jeopardy flames in my hair / yet I flourish my whip with a fatal flair") while "The Suitcases Are Packed Again" looks forward to the ebullience of "Ariel" ("with a jerk / We zoom up into lunatic black sky / Where little epileptic comets smirk / And giddy asteroids go whizzing by").[124] Several of her Smith poems feature young female speakers in the midst of a circus, taming lions, walking tightropes, and performing daredevilish tricks—a metaphor, perhaps, for her own attempts to transcend patriarchal obstacles set before an ambitious young woman in the mid-fifties.

In early February, Sylvia made one such attempt when she and her friend Sue Weller interviewed for a one-year position teaching fifth-grade English at the American School in Tangier, Morocco. "I can think of nothing else," she told Gordon.[125] Aurelia was less excited, and told Sylvia she would be better off taking education courses or learning shorthand, despite her previous failed attempt. Furious, Sylvia issued a *non serviam:*

> Now with me, writing is the first delight in life. I want time and money to write, both very necessary. I will not sacrifice my time to learn shorthand. . . . I do not want the rigid hours of a magazine or publishing job. I do not want to type other people's letters and read their manuscripts. I want to type on my own and write on my own. . . . I realize that my goals in life may seem strange to you. . . . Do consider what I say seriously.

The job would enable her, she wrote Aurelia, to "counteract McCarthy" and serve her "religion, which is that of humanism."[126] But the job did not come through.

Sylvia began dating Peter Davison in late March. Peter had been to Cambridge on a Fulbright and also had literary ambitions; he was the closest she had yet come to finding a male "double." Even if the romance did not bear fruit, Sylvia knew that Peter, with his publishing connections, could help her professionally. She probably did not tell Sassoon about Peter, or Edwin Akutowicz, whom she saw twice at Smith in April and again in Cambridge during May and June.

Sassoon would have made light of his rivals. He continued writing Sylvia dramatic love letters from Yale, sometimes playing a character out of *Les Liaisons Dangereuses*. He spoke of spankings, beatings, and adultery, and may have given Plath the idea for her later poem "Pursuit" when he wrote, "I love you and my love lies in waiting still and stealthy and hateful as a tiger."[127] Most of his letters were unabashed declarations of love, but he offered his thoughts on her poetry, too. His critique of her sonnet in an April 20 letter likely made an impact:

> I very tinily but unmistakably wince and am not sure why except there is too much maybe strictly structure . . . it remains a plan and one does not see it or move with the movements (except in the matter of sound and rhythm you are so good at) . . . and yet it is not PRESENT and worse it is not a present because it has wit's lack of generosity.

This loyalty to structure over nature—what Plath would later call "the glass caul"—was something Ted Hughes and his friends would mock when they read Plath's early poems at Cambridge. Yet even as Sassoon criticized her poems, he emphasized his ignorance and offered unconditional support. He ended this same letter, "darling, I am so proud of all you do and say . . . and you do not stop, but always something better or something new. . . . it makes me proud of you and proud that I fell in love with you."[128] The couple rendezvoused in New York City again in late March. Sylvia told Aurelia she was staying with Smith friends, but in fact she stayed with Sassoon before he returned home to Tryon, North Carolina, and she to Wellesley, for the spring vacation.

On April 1, Plath received a letter from Columbia appointing her as a graduate residence scholar for the 1955–56 academic year. The appointment came with free room and board, plus a $500 scholarship toward tuition. With her $1,000 graduate fellowship from Smith, the year at Columbia would cost her nothing; she would even have spending money left over. Yet Sylvia, still hungry for Experience, was determined to go to England even if she had to spend the summer waitressing, and within a week she had turned down Columbia's generous offer. She had been accepted to Newnham College, Cambridge, in February and had heard rumors through Mary Ellen Chase that her Fulbright application had made the final round. She was confident about her chances.

In mid-April, Sylvia learned she was one of six finalists for the Glascock Poetry Prize, held at Mount Holyoke College. She gave a reading there and lunched with Marianne Moore, one of the judges; Plath called her "as vital and humorous as someone's fairy godmother incognito." She shared a guest room with Lynne Lawner, a contestant from Wellesley College, with whom she would continue to correspond. She had her photograph taken with Moore by *The Christian Science Monitor* and *Mademoiselle*, and spoke on the radio. Sylvia enjoyed the spotlight, especially the poetry reading attended by (she guessed) two hundred people. "I loved doing my poems," she wrote Aurelia, "because they all sounded pretty polished and the audience was immensely responsive, laughed in some of the witty places, even, which made me feel tremendously happy." (She was so pleased with her performance that she considered becoming a "humorous public speaker.")[129] Plath eventually tied with a young man from Wesleyan for first place, for which she received $50. In the judges' notes, she read that Marianne Moore "commends your spirit, patience, craftsmanship and strong individuality. Her main adverse criticism is of a too adjectival manner at times bordering on formula."[130] The other judge, John Ciardi, called her "a real discovery" and "a poet," and offered to help her publish in little magazines. Sylvia gushed to her mother, "so it's not a completely indifferent world, after all!"[131]

Good news followed on April 18 in the form of a twenty-five-dollar check for "Circus in Three Rings" from *The Atlantic*. Plath was thrilled to have scaled another of her "Annapurnas." The editors wanted her to revise the first and last stanzas, however, and change the title to "The Lion Tamer" or "The Tamer."[132] She called the suggestion an "aesthetic rape" and, after a long talk with Alfred Fisher decided not to tamper with her poem.[133] "I did resent this attempt at butchering to fit their idea of it," she told Aurelia. "Prose, I wouldn't mind, but a poem is like a rare little watch: alter the delicate juxtaposition of cogs, and it just may not tick. . . . I battle between desperate Macchiavelian [*sic*] opportunism and uncompromising artistic ethics."[134] Opportunism won the day. After downing two martinis and sleeping for twelve hours, she revised the poem and sent it back to Edward Weeks, along with five other poems she hoped he would prefer. She would learn, on May 21, that *The Atlantic* took her original, unrevised "Circus in Three Rings." "Such bliss! That fortress of Bostonian conservative respectability has been 'charmed' by your tight-rope walking daughter!" she wrote Aurelia.[135] *The Nation* would publish "Temper of Time" in its August 6 issue, while Plath earned $15 from *Mademoiselle*, which published "Two Lovers and a Beachcomber by the Real Sea" that August. The poem, with its beach setting and existential quandaries, shows the influence of Wallace Stevens's "The Idea of Order at Key West." Plath writes:

> We are not what we might be; what we are
> Outlaws all extrapolation
> Beyond the interval of now and here:
> White whales are gone with the white ocean.

Sylvia decided to drop German in late April—she needed to focus on her comprehensive exams surveying the whole of English literature, and her growing poetry collection. She explained her decision to her mother: "I am in my cycle of ebbed energy and know that at these times I must pare my demands to a bare minimum."[136] Sylvia now knew the consequences of trying to "do it all," and she was wise to reduce her obligations in the face of mounting academic pressure. "It seems my life is a constant readjustment between my psychic demands and my physical supply. I need three long months of sun and sand and tennis and time (to read and write as I choose or do not choose) to recover from the academic trials of this year," she wrote Gordon.[137]

May, too, was a month of bounty. Plath won the Ethel Olin Corbin Prize, the Marjorie Hope Nicolson Prize for her senior thesis, and the Clara French Prize, awarded to the top senior in English. She was accepted to Radcliffe and won the Academy of American Poets Prize as well as an honorable mention in the *Vogue* Prix de Paris. The *Vogue* prize came with $25 and a tentative job offer at a Condé Nast publication—but Plath had already decided against a career in media. Her year's earnings from writing and prizes came to an astounding $465, "plus much joy!"[138] The best news came on May 20, when she learned that she had won a Fulbright Fellowship to Newnham College, Cambridge. Sylvia was ecstatic and immediately called Aurelia at Newton-Wellesley Hospital, where she was again being treated for her ulcer. She celebrated with Sassoon in New York, where she "wept buckets" watching Laurence Olivier play Heathcliff in *Wuthering Heights*.

Sylvia passed her grueling comprehensive exams—a "hot hell of 12 hours"—to graduate summa cum laude on June 6, Sassoon's twenty-first birthday.[139] That morning, before the ceremony, she was suffering from severe abdominal cramps. Nancy Hunter told Sylvia to ask a Lawrence House beatnik, whom Sylvia disliked, for some rum. But Sylvia and this student had been feuding all year: she had taunted Sylvia about her conventional values, and Sylvia had threatened to report her secret stash of alcohol. Still, she gave Sylvia the rum without hesitation. Sylvia was grateful and wrote her a note that read, "Thank you for teaching me humility."[140]

Aurelia, still recovering from her recent stomach surgery, arrived at Sylvia's commencement on a mattress stretcher.[141] Sylvia was one of only four summas in her entire college class, and the accolade cemented her standing as one of the most gifted academic students of her generation. Kazin and his wife blew kisses as she received her degree, and President Wright gave her a firm handshake. Mary Ellen Chase promised to be her "Chase bank" in England should she ever run short of funds. It was "a magnificent send-off," Sylvia wrote in her scrapbook, for a young woman who once thought she would not graduate.[142] Adlai Stevenson, erstwhile Democratic presidential candidate, gave the commencement speech. He famously—and condescendingly—told the class that they should aspire to be superlative mothers and housewives and that their main role was to support their husbands. Afterward, Sylvia picnicked at Quabbin Reservoir with her mother, who was helped along by her grandparents and Mrs. Cantor. (Warren and Mrs. Prouty had not been able to attend.) She wrote her new friend Lynne Lawner that Stevenson was "most witty and magnificent as commencement speaker" but quipped that he was "operating on the hypothesis that every woman's highest vocation" was marriage.[143] She knew now that marriage and children could wait: "writing is the first love of my life."[144] To that end, she assembled her first poetry collection, *Circus in Three Rings*, which included most of the 1955 poems she had written in Alfred Fisher's tutorial. She ended the collection with Sassoon's favorite, "Doomsday."

Sylvia spent her summer in Wellesley, reading, writing, gardening, and painting old furniture while Aurelia recuperated from stomach surgery. Her doctors had instructed her not to take on any summer teaching. Her weight was still dangerously low, and, after she left the hospital in late June, Sylvia drove her to medical appointments. Mrs. Prouty wrote frequently, and paid at least one of Aurelia's hospital bills.[145]

When not tending to Aurelia or attending weddings—Sylvia served as maid of honor at Ruth Freeman's wedding on June 11 in Winthrop—she applied herself to "the slicks." She "saturated" herself in old copies of *The Saturday Evening Post* and *Ladies' Home Journal* in the hopes of gauging that "'indefinable something' which makes a $1000 story."[146] In July and August she wrote a short story, "Platinum Summer," which she had originally entitled "Peroxide," based on her experience waitressing at the Belmont, and featuring dueling male leads.[147] The rich playboy Ira Kamirloff, who "seldom had anything but dishonorable intentions," dates the Plath character, Lynn Hunter, after she dyes her hair blond. But it is the "intellectual" medical student and fellow waiter, Eric Wunderlich, whom she truly loves. After some scandalous adventures with Ira, which Eric observes disdainfully, Lynn wins over Eric by dyeing her hair back to its natural brown. The moral is conventional: the girl gets the hero only after she has tamed herself and her "wild" impulses. Plath ends the story:

> "Will you ever," she returned, "want me to act like a kaleidoscope?"
>
> "You already do," Eric grinned down at her. "That's what worries me. With that impulsive streak of yours, you'll always need someone masterful around to keep you from going quite wild."
>
> "Someone like a lion tamer?"
>
> "Someone," Eric illustrated by kissing her masterfully on the mouth, "exactly like me."[148]

That July she sent off a more staid, brown-haired piece, "Tea with Olive Higgins Prouty," to *Reader's Digest*, and learned that *The New Orleans Poetry Journal* and *Lyric* accepted three poems.[149] Yet *Mademoiselle* turned down three of her new stories, which she had entered in the College Fiction Contest.[150] She wrote Gordon, "I keep reading about this damn adrienne cecile rich [*sic*], only two years older than I, who is a yale [*sic*] younger poet and regularly in all the top mags; and about 23-year old blondes from radcliffe [*sic*] who are already selling stories plus climbing alps. occasionally [*sic*], I retch quietly in the wastebasket."[151] The rivalry with Adrienne Rich made Plath more determined to succeed, and she mailed out her poetry collection to the Borestone Mountain Poetry Award that summer. Plath had been inspired by an article she had read in the *Writer's Yearbook*, advising her to think of herself as a woman first, and a writer second—otherwise, every rejection would throw her "into depression." If she identified herself too closely with her craft, the failures would seem like "grievous wounds" to her sense of "personal worth."[152] "I would like to memorize this article forever etching it in my head. It is a directive to live by," she wrote Aurelia.[153]

In early August, Peter Davison, now assistant to the director at Harvard University Press, invited Sylvia to Martha's Vineyard. (He had been dating her since March; he later remembered lying on his apartment floor with her "listening with rapture" to Dylan Thomas reading "Fern Hill.")[154] She and Peter had drinks with the Irish poet Padraic Colum and his wife Mary at the Landfall Restaurant, across from the ferry landing in Woods Hole. It was not the first time Plath had met Colum; she had shared drinks with him when visiting Phil McCurdy, who was teaching at the Children's School of Science in Woods Hole that summer. Phil remembered, "It was amazing to me how the two lit up the evening wherever they were. I've often thought that there was a kind of spiritual radio wave between the poets. He was a remarkable man, but actually very reserved, very reticent. But when Sylvia was with us, he became extremely animated." He remembered Colum reciting his poem "King Cahill's Farewell to the Rye Field" in Plath's honor. "We were sitting there with our mouths open."[155]

Sylvia and Peter took the ferry to Vineyard Haven and arrived "up-island" at Chilmark after dark. The couple stayed at a rustic compound on South Road near Lucy Vincent Beach that had been set up by several families after the First World War. The visitors—a count and countess from Bonn, writers, psychoanalysts, lawyers, and academics—impressed Sylvia, and she washed dishes alongside the president of Rutgers University. They sailed and swam in Menemsha, dined on lobster and champagne, and careened down the dunes at the nude beach near Gay Head. Peter soon put Sylvia in touch with Henry Volkening of the venerable Russell and Volkening literary agency. Volkening wrote to her asking her to stop by for a drink "and a leisurely talk" before she sailed for England.[156] Plath left no record of the meeting, but she met with Constance Smith at the Harold Ober agency before she left America. Smith made a bad impression, and Plath became wary of agents.

Meanwhile, Sassoon had taken the improbable step of accepting a sales job with a heating company after graduation. He spent his days inspecting furnaces and selling "cleanouts"; his hands, he said, were "irrevocably stained with soot and my chest is branded with the name of a firm. . . . Dearest, forgive me for being tired and a little depressed and bothered, but I have never journeyed so far into banalite [sic]."[157] Sylvia tried to reassure Sassoon that he was building character, but he dismissed her easy bromides: "and you have the damned idiotic audacity to say this is the sort of thing that matures one! My dear, how very foolish. How very foolish indeed." Yet he relished the

irony of playing the American salesman, which he called "the very foundation of American life and economy." He was, he said, a "smashing success"
at the job and declared it all "a great cosmic joke."[158] Sylvia was unsettled by
his plebeian adventure.

She had gently suggested that Sassoon try to find another line of work,
but he was a good salesman—he was promoted within just a few weeks—and
decided to stay with the firm until he came up with a better plan. (He would
eventually decide to take classes at the Sorbonne that fall.) Much like Frank
Wheeler in Richard Yates's *Revolutionary Road*, Sassoon discovered that he
was not immune to life's bourgeois pleasures; he enjoyed drinks after work
and the easy backslapping camaraderie of his colleagues. But Plath was not
about to marry a furnace salesman. She was not about to marry anyone—not
while her shining Cantabrigian future awaited. As she had advised Warren
that July, "your security and love of life don't depend on the presence of
another, but only on yourself, your chosen work, and your developing identity. then [*sic*] you can safely choose to enrich your life by marrying another
person, and not, as ee cummings says, until."[159]

Nevertheless, Sylvia invited Sassoon to Wellesley for the Fourth of
July weekend. The invitation suggests the seriousness with which she now
regarded the young man she had once called a "diversion." They spent time
at the beach, relaxed on her porch, took walks in the moonlight—"two days
of comfort and sun," as Sassoon put it. His letters became more pressing and
ardent—he spoke continuously of his love for her, his loneliness without her,
his fear that he was wasting his life while she sailed off to Europe. "Took the
afternoon off today. I went to the beach and it made me very sad, I am too
old to play alone in the sand. I will not go until I can take you with me."[160]

Sylvia had the house to herself again as Aurelia spent most of July and
August on the Cape. She hoped to see Dr. Beuscher "a few times" before
she set sail, but Beuscher was busy with her new baby boy. Sylvia called,
but Dr. Beuscher did not call back. The silence was discomfiting, especially
as Sylvia was not getting along with Aurelia. She wrote to Sassoon of the
"hatred and frustration" in her home, and hinted that he was partly to blame;
Aurelia resented the slightly foreign, dissolute young man who had stolen
her daughter away from Gordon. ("I thought I had succeeded at being the
picture of charming young innocence," Sassoon wrote to Sylvia.)[161] This was
the second time Sylvia had broken off an informal engagement to the son of
Wellesley friends, and Aurelia was at a loss to explain her daughter's capri-
ciousness. Plath would later write in her journal, "She necked and petted and
flew to New York to visit Estonian artists and Persian Jew wealthy boys and
her pants were wet with the sticky white filth of desire. Put her in a cell, that's
all you could do. She's not <u>my</u> daughter. Not my nice girl. Where did that

girl go?"[162] Sassoon encouraged Plath to set aside her grievances. "Just say she is a hell of a bitch and then determine to get along with her for the last month. . . . Just accept all the enormous evils and get on with the business of family life."[163] He later recalled, "Sylvia was both very rebellious toward her mother and very attached."[164]

Sylvia spent another weekend with Sassoon in mid-July, but it did not go well; he spent the whole time trying to "reach" her, and suspected the end was at hand. "I will no longer strain against the limits of both our healths of mind and body. I take with me the memory of all the joy it is possible for me to have had with a woman."[165] He told her he would not always be a furnace salesman—that he might become a publisher or professor, or travel overland to Baghdad. He hinted that someday he would be a wealthy "future gentle-man." Whatever happened between them, he would wait for her until she was "ready."[166]

In August, it appears, Sylvia ended the relationship. Sassoon was crushed. "I only hope you know what you do, and what you are about to do. . . . It is possible that you strangle as decent, as honest and as faithful a heart as will ever have beat so proudly and profoundly for you alone."[167] He accepted her decision, yet he continued to build up her confidence: "Sylvia, you are a great big, healthy, powerful woman! Remember it."[168] Sylvia had also ended things with Peter Davison. Peter had begun to feel himself just "a symbol" to Sylvia, someone who could give her "literary respectability." Sex between them was "very melodramatic" and "athletic"; she played "big parts in bed," he said, with "big talk," which stood in the way of real intimacy. But their relationship seemed to deepen when she opened up to him in August, after sex, about the reasons behind her suicide attempt and her terror of electroshock therapy. It was a breakthrough. He would never forget these two hours "of spontane-ous tenderness" when she described her depression as an "organic, existing, live thing."[169] She told him that after her father died, her mother had to work to support the family and that she felt "driven to succeed, that with each year the pace of achievement quickened." After she returned from New York, she said, she did not sleep for a month. "The only way she could get any respite from the wakefulness was to die." She had tried unsuccessfully to drown herself and had considered guns and hanging, but couldn't bring herself to try them. She called Mrs. Prouty "my patron" with "a real sense of gratitude." She spoke of her shock treatment at McLean as an "expurgation," and described how she gradually came back to life. She was deeply grateful to those who had helped her.[170]

Peter was so "overwhelmed" by these revelations that he took to his bed for two days. He had fallen in love with Sylvia and was "shocked and hurt" when she broke up with him later that month during a walk after dinner at Elmwood Road. He sensed that he had been used as "a trophy brought home for mom," and remembered that she delivered the blow with "the air of an executioner."[171] He felt she had "dismissed" him precisely because of her honesty: "it was somehow coldly unforgivable" that she had told him her suicide story.[172]

Gordon suddenly seemed the more solid prospect, still her "sure thing." She wrote to him in early August: "I Must See You Before I Sail. I simply can't leave this country without seeing you. I am damn ritualistic, I know, but you are woven so into the tissue of my life."[173] This was an unexpected swerve. Sassoon had spoken of his depression and hinted at his alcoholism—afflictions that had initially increased his Baudelairean appeal but now seemed more alarming. Gordon had no such demons, as far as Sylvia knew. She wrote him that she was going "off without a chart or friend to stabilize transition."[174] She invited Gordon to London: "you kind of symbolize the home continent."[175]

In late August, Hurricane Connie dumped a deluge of rain on the Boston area for two days. Sylvia had always loved a good storm and told Gordon she "couldn't resist driving to cambridge [*sic*]" in the heavy rains to see the destruction: "the harvard stadium stood like a greek arena on the mediter-ranean [*sic*]. . . . somehow I was most exhilarated by all this. . . . there is an ancient grandeur to it which I love, in contrast to the killing manmade devas-tation of war, which only sickens me."[176] Aurelia had given her private danc-ing lessons at the Fred Astaire Dance Studio in Boston as an early birthday present, and Sylvia spent the end of August learning the tango with another blond god, Richard Hanzel ("tall, lean, with a white-blond crew cut and the most fantastic teutonic bone structure"). They spent their Coke breaks dis-cussing Plato. Sylvia had been hesitant to learn to dance, but she soon looked forward to the lessons. "I've just Got to Express all this life I have inside me somehow in rhythm and patterns, freedom in discipline."[177]

She spent the last weekend of August visiting Sue Weller in Washing-ton, D.C. She toured the Mall, the National Gallery ("I love the Flemish school"), and the Lincoln Memorial, which impressed her "emotionally & intellectually, most of all. Such a colossus, in such clean, enormous, simply carved white stone. I felt shivers of reverence, looking up into that craggy, godlike face."[178] The memorial may have been an unlikely inspiration for her later poem "The Colossus."

She returned to Wellesley and prepared, emotionally, for her departure.

She tried to make peace with her mother and quell the rising tide of fear. To Gordon, she wrote philosophically about the future:

> I grow old, I grow old. already [sic] my pre-departure homesickness has set in and I am growing ineffably nostalgic. two [sic] years, so crucial, and will I know what to do with them? the horror, to be jamesian, is to find there are plenty of beasts in the jungle but somehow to have missed all the potshots at them. I am always afraid of letting "life" slip by unobtrusively and waking up some "fine morning" to wail windgrieved around my tombstone.[179]

She wondered, "will I grow, like my favorite Isabel Archer, through struggle and sorrow?" In a sonnet, "Ennui," she wrote about her fear:

> The beast in Jamesian grove will never jump,
> compelling hero's dull career to crisis;
> and when insouciant angels play to God's trump,
> while bored arena crowds for once look eager,
> hoping toward havoc, neither please nor prizes
> shall coax from doom's blank door lady or tiger.[180]

Mrs. Prouty offered practical advice Sylvia probably did not want to hear: "I hope you don't expect too much from it. I hope you are ready to be disappointed—and perhaps lonely.... You may feel pretty forlorn."[181] Prouty told her to find a trusted adviser, someone with whom she could discuss "any sort of problem that may arise." Yet Sylvia was confident that she was embarking on the right course. Though she felt "rootless and floating," she knew England was "the best and only thing for me."[182] As she told Warren, "staying in new england or even new york [sic] would suffocate me completely at this point. my [sic] wings need to be tried. o icarus [sic]."[183] To Gordon, her peregrinating counterpart, she wrote, "you must speed this female ulysses [sic] on her way with a kind of creative blessing. I'll need it. I certainly will."[184]

Part II

15

—————

Channel Crossing

Cambridge University, September 1955–February 1956

Plath boarded the *Queen Elizabeth II* on September 14, 1955, en route to Cherbourg, France. From there she would travel to England. At Cambridge, she would be cut off from the voices and embraces of those who cared most for her as she navigated a new social scene and a challenging, unfamiliar academic system that was entirely male dominated. But the blank slate of a new country was precisely what Plath needed in 1955. Home was the place she had tried to die, where everyone knew of her problems, and where her brilliance would always be shadowed by her attempted suicide. She felt that a new life abroad, away from Aurelia's hovering, would allow her to shed her old self. "I am fighting, fighting, and I am making a self, in great pain, often, as for a birth," she wrote Aurelia. "I am being refined in the fires of pain and love."[1]

Although American power was rising as England's waned in the mid-1950s, the British regarded Americans as unsophisticated colonials with little talent for nuance or irony. Britons were still coming to terms with their nation's diminished influence, and America's prosperity was a source of resentment. As one of Ted Hughes's American friends, Luke Myers, wrote, "Americans were rich; the products of Europe's long traditions and ruined wealth had to watch crowds of untutored but confident Yanks eat in the best restaurants and tramp through their museums making ludicrous observations."[2] Yet, even after the devastations of war, London still possessed the kind of cultural cachet to which New York or Boston could then only aspire. T. S. Eliot, the most famous American poet of his day, chose to live in London, where he ran the poetry division at the prestigious literary publisher Faber and Faber. Sylvia understood that she would seem like a vulgar Roman in the eyes of cultured Greeks.

The five-day crossing was not glamorous—the cabins were tiny, the floors too hot for bare feet, and the bathrooms hidden away at ends of long halls. Salt-water baths were by appointment, even if that meant midnight ablutions. Sylvia mentioned none of these hardships to correspondents. In a breathless postcard to Ellie Friedman, she wrote about "a tragic shipboard romance with a young Jewish nuclear physicist" named Carl Shakin.[3] Carl, an engineering student at New York University, was on his way to take up a Fulbright at the University of Manchester. (The boat was full of Fulbrighters.) He had been married for two months, but that didn't deter him from exploring France with Sylvia when the ship arrived in Cherbourg. A fellow passenger on the ship was shocked that Sylvia and Carl "didn't try to hide the fact that they were, indeed, sleeping together."[4] Carousing about with a married Jewish man was exactly the kind of scandalous "European" behavior that suited Sylvia's newly liberated self. She did not, however, mention this transatlantic tryst to Aurelia, just a "genial" new friend named Carl with whom she enjoyed "tea and long bull sessions on deck."[5]

In Cherbourg, Sylvia wrote, the ancient churches and flower markets were a welcome change from the "eightlane [sic] highways and mass markets" of America. Here the "streets are made for bicycles and young lovers, with flowers on the handlebars and around the traffic lights!"[6] To Ellie, she added with dramatic flourish, "there the men know how to look at one."[7]

After a rough crossing from France, Sylvia finally arrived by train in London. The experience was heady: she "walked miles through green queen's parks" and discovered, she told Ellie, "sin & shashlik in Soho."[8] She toured the National Gallery and the British Museum, wandered among the bookstalls on Charing Cross Road, and became a "devotee of café expresso with foaming white cream."[9] She saw four plays in a week, including *Waiting for Godot,* and marveled at Piccadilly Circus and Trafalgar Square at night with their "lighted fountains and flowerbeds and regiments of pigeons." She told Aurelia she already felt "stirrings of loyalty" whenever she heard "God Save the Queen," and pronounced herself most "capable" handling the new bills and coins.[10] After saying goodbye to Carl, she ran into an ex-boyfriend of Sue Weller's and alighted with him to the Doves, a "fascinating Dickensian pub . . . in a court overlooking the dark, low-tide Thames, where in the moonlight, pale swans floated in sluggish streams that laced the mudflats."[11] London was living up to her literary expectations.

She stayed first at Bedford College in Regent's Park, then moved to the YWCA across from the British Museum, where she experienced "a keen aesthetic satisfaction" staring at the museum's Ionic columns through the bathroom window. The sense of possibility was overwhelming. "I have lived years in the space of hours," she wrote in her first letter home. The Fulbright

Committee sponsored lectures on politics and economics, where she heard members of Parliament and prominent editors. She also attended several "impressive receptions," including a party hosted by the American ambassador at the U.S. embassy. "Never have I seen such a palace!" she gushed home in language that recalled Maureen Buckley's debutante party. "Such elegance." At the English Speaking Union, she met the countess of Tunis and had "a most intriguing talk"—and several glasses of wine—with a member of the Queen's Royal Horse Guards. The Fulbright reception for English literature students at Bedford College, however, was disappointing. There, she felt, "atrocious" hostessing prevented her from meeting famous guests such as Stephen Spender, John Lehmann (the influential editor of *The London Magazine*), and C. P. Snow. She hadn't realized she was in such esteemed company; the gray-suited men had simply looked "like respectable professors."[12] At least she managed to meet the critic David Daiches, whose lectures she would attend at Cambridge. Her New York stint in the world of women's fashion magazines had literally sickened her, but in London she was energized by the presence of prominent literary critics and writers.

On October 1 she left London for Cambridge by train. From the Cambridge station, with her massive trunk in tow, she made her way to Whitstead, a building on the Barton Road that housed twelve foreign Newnham College students. She found Whitstead's white stone walls, red-tiled roof, small yard, and resident ravens quaint. The Scottish housekeeper, Mrs. Milne, showed her up to her "atticish" room on the third floor, which she immediately decided would make a cozy writer's garret.[13] Over the next few weeks, she decorated her room with two enormous bookcases, a tea set she had ordered in London, an oblong walnut coffee table, fresh fruit, handmade rush mats, brightly colored pillows, and "great bouquets of Van-Gogh-type yellow chrysanthemums, vivid postcard reprints of Picasso ... candles in wine bottles."[14] The room was full of yellows, holly greens, chestnut browns, and accents of black and white. Plath created a haven where she could proudly hold small "salons"—"as yet, all is poised on the threshold, expectant, tantalizing, about to begin," she wrote home.[15]

Although she described her new digs enthusiastically in letters, she hinted at the shortcoming that would later stand for all that was wrong with England: there was no central heating at Whitstead. It was only October, yet her room was "cool enough to keep butter and milk in (!)" and she could see her breath "in frosty clouds" each morning in the bathroom.[16] She told Aurelia that "the damp here is continuous."[17] To keep warm, she put a shilling in a small gas fireplace, which, she told Marcia, "scalds the side nearest it & leaves the other as cold as the back of the moon."[18] By February, Sylvia would wear gloves while typing, but she would still feel "an intense pain" when she tried to bend her freezing fingers. Each night she took a hot-water bottle to bed, and wore wool socks and sweaters over her flannel pajamas. Mornings were excruciating—she had never experienced "such cold" as she hacked a thin layer of ice off her windows "to make a kind of porthole so I could see out."[19] Plath was not overdramatizing; the biting cold that winter was a ubiquitous theme in other Whitstead residents' memoirs.[20] Indeed, Whitstead itself was so cold that there was no need for a refrigerator—all food was kept in the buttery.[21] Two of the wealthier girls bought oil heaters for their rooms. Jean Gooder, who graduated from Newnham with a BA in English in 1956, remembered the "dismalness" of those years: "you'd use your gown as a draft blocker at the bottom of the door. . . . Rooms were spartan, meals were terrible, rationing went on until 1953. There were no pleasures."[22]

Still, there was a window-seat sofa Sylvia could "curl up in and read with a fine view of tree-tops," and a gas ring where she could make tea.[23] Eventually, she managed three-course dinners—sherry, salad, steak, wine, and fruit compote—on the small stove. It was a skill born of necessity, for she found the food served in Newnham's dining hall—whose "ornate white woodwork" made her feel as if she were "sitting inside of a frosted wedding cake"— bland and full of starch.[24] Breakfasts at Whitstead consisted mainly of fried bread and scrambled eggs from powder. There were not even paper napkins because of a postwar paper shortage. "I am getting used to going around feeling rather sticky and jam-ish!" Sylvia told Aurelia.[25]

The food in Hall, however, was positively gourmet compared to what she encountered in Newnham's tiny infirmary when she came down with her annual autumn sinus infection: "No greens, no fresh fruit or red meat!" she wrote home. Sylvia had expected cocaine sprays, penicillin, and wholesome meals like she had received at Smith. "Well, what a rude awakening!" She was given only aspirin and told that no doctor would see her unless she ran a temperature. When she asked the "one stony-hearted and absolutely 'rule-bound' nurse" for a Kleenex, the nurse offered to tear up an old sheet: they had no tissues.[26] Sylvia walked out after one night, preferring the comforts of her room to "Newnham Hospital." She ended up seeing a private doctor in town.

Yet for every British inconvenience, it seemed, there was something quaint or traditional that made up for the discomfort. She enjoyed hearing the Latin grace spoken in Hall before each meal, and she was overwhelmed by the selection of tropical fresh fruit "from the colonies" in the town's open-air market.[27] She relished the challenge of biking down narrow cobbled lanes and dodging double-deckers; Cambridge contemporaries remembered the determination and speed with which she cycled.[28] She walked to Grantchester through "meadows full of cows and brooding white horses" and took tea by a roaring fire.[29] Even the raw weather, which she often described as silver and luminous, had its Gothic charms: "Heavy morning and evening mists make me feel I'm moving about in a ghost-play."[30]

Her immersion in British life was complete when, on October 20, she was amazed to find herself in a receiving line for Queen Elizabeth, "within touching distance," at Newnham.[31] (Sylvia's friend Isabel Murray Henderson remembered that before the visit, "we were all summoned to the main Hall and taught how to curtsey.")[32] Few Americans had the honor of meeting the Queen of England in 1955. This was a major moment for Sylvia, who had worked as a maid, nanny, and waitress. Now she was introduced to royalty. "Oh mother," Plath wrote, "every alleyway is crowded with tradition, antiquity, and I can feel a peace, reserve, lack of hurry here which has centuries behind it."[33] She was moved by the grand, imposing architecture of the Cambridge colleges; the punts moving luxuriously down the River Cam; the stunning interior of King's College Chapel; and the quiet backstreets and squares where she rode her bicycle, her black subfusc gown flowing behind her. "A kind of golden promise hovers in the air along the Cam and in the quaint crooked streets," she wrote home in early October. "I must make my own Cambridge. . . . I have to begin life on all fronts at once again."[34]

American, South African, and Scottish students at Whitstead kindly showed Sylvia around town during her first few days, but she was eager to meet more English students—especially English men.[35] She was dismayed that there was no new student orientation, as there would have been at an American college. "No official 'big sisters' come up to one here . . . everything here is so lackadaisical and de-centralized," she told Aurelia.[36] Newnham, despite its impressive Queen Anne–style buildings and eighteen acres of grounds and gardens, was a less heavily endowed institution than Smith. It had been founded in 1871 as a house for five female students who wished to audit university lectures, yet it was not until 1948—only seven years before Plath arrived—that women were allowed to take a Cambridge degree. Cambridge would be the last university in Great Britain to extend full equality to its female students.

Women's colleges at Oxbridge were overshadowed by the men's colleges. They were poor in comparison, lacking centuries-old endowments and wealthy alumni, and begrudged their place within the larger, all-male university. Their food and lodgings were drastically inferior, as Virginia Woolf famously noted in *A Room of One's Own*. Cambridge women were encouraged to focus exclusively on their studies and behave with ladylike decorum. There was no Seven Sisters glamour and little sense of empowered female fellowship—the mood was serious and stoic. Jane Baltzell Kopp, a fellow American and one of Sylvia's few close friends at Cambridge, claimed that

Newnham was not a "supportive community" in the way that Smith had been for Plath—"absolutely not."[37] Jean Gooder, who knew Plath at Newnham and attended the famous party where Plath met Hughes, agreed that students who came from proud American women's colleges had to adjust their expectations. "I encountered two things for the first time in my first few weeks in Cambridge: anti-feminism and anti-Semitism. Both were a real shock. I don't mean that they were everywhere but they certainly existed, and Sylvia must have found herself brought up against them too."[38] The bigotry was both invisible and omnipresent.

At Smith, Plath had been the most celebrated student of her year, a celebrity on campus and the pet of the English faculty. But until she met her supervisor Dorothea Krook during her second term, she felt no rapport with any female Newnham dons. She considered them, she told her mother, "such grotesques!" They seemed to her straight out of Dickens: she described one as "cadaverous," another like a "midget." "They are all very brilliant or learned (quite a different thing) in their specialized ways, but I feel that all their experience is <u>secondary</u> and this to me is tantamount to a kind of living death."[39] In her journal, she wrote, "The men are probably better, but there is no chance of getting them for supervisors, and they are too brilliant to indulge in that friendly commerce which Mr. Fisher, Mr. Kazin and Mr. Gibian were so dear about."[40] Women with PhDs at that time were largely single and childless, like a troupe of academic nuns.

Jean Gooder, who eventually became director of studies at Newnham, remembered, "It was not easy being at a women's college then. I found it really peculiar to be working only with women, who were comfortable with their situation, formal. There was no give. . . . They never taught us that women had only been admitted to full membership of the university in 1948. They said nothing. They were tame. They were dutiful scholars. They knew their texts and topics, but God where was the interest, where was the chutzpah?" She found the quality of teaching at Newnham low, with the exception of Dorothea Krook, who, she said, "was by *far* the most interesting teacher."

Newnham refused Jean and two other friends permission to attend F. R. Leavis's weekly seminars at Downing College—but they went anyway, the only women in a roomful of male undergraduates. Jean felt lucky to be a part of the seminar, which was much more rigorous than what she experienced at her own college. She had some sympathy for Sylvia's desire not to be like the female Newnham dons. ("One wouldn't!") When Jean went to the Cambridge career services department for advice, they tried to steer her into teaching. She did not want, as she put it, to be "stuck in the education system," and told them she wanted to join the diplomatic service, or the World Health Organization. "Forget it, you'll only ever be a secretary" was the response. She ended up spending her career teaching at Newnham, where she helped change the culture to one of strong female fellowship.[41]

Plath's revulsion toward the Newnham dons was not entirely due to sexism. She felt the life of an academic was too remote from the living world. "It is often tempting to hide from the blood & guts of life in a neat special subject on paper where one can become an unchallenged expert, but I, like Yeats, would rather say: 'It was my glory that I had such friends,' when I finally leave the world."[42] May Collacott Targett remembered that Sylvia had come to Cambridge "wanting to be a star writer rather than an academic expert on English literature."[43] While there were few women academics Sylvia could look to in her search for a life that combined art, marriage, and motherhood, there *were* female writers who had successfully integrated all three. "Don't worry that I am a 'career woman,'" she wrote Aurelia that January. "I am definitely meant to be married & have children & a home & write like these women I admire: mrs. moore [Sarah-Elizabeth Rodger], jean stafford, hortense calisher, phyllis mcginley [*sic*] etc."[44] She had a horror of ending up alone, a "career girl." In her journal she wrote, "Save me from that, that final wry sour lemon acid in the veins of single clever lonely women."[45]

Sylvia, along with her contemporaries, had been socially conditioned to think this way. Dr. Marynia Farnham, the psychiatrist who cowrote the bestselling *Modern Woman: The Lost Sex* (1947), cautioned that women should hold no "fantasy in her mind about being an 'independent woman.'" Career women, she wrote, pursued their ambition "at terrific cost to themselves and society." They had "unhappy" children and husbands, who "do not have real women as partners. Instead, their wives have become their rivals."[46] Plath would have absorbed this message in other ways. Cambridge men, it was said, preferred dating the student nurses at the nearby Addenbrooke's Hospital to the Newnham and Girton bluestockings. (In 1953, the future sociologist Hannah Gavron wrote to a friend while visiting Cambridge, "Newnham is vile, it looks like a gas works and all the men utterly despise Newnham and Girton.")[47] Sylvia overheard snippets of conversations in hall attesting to such preferences: "'I always thought they expected girls to do worse than boys at things. . . . But here, you know, it's quite the opposite; there's such a competition for girls to get in the boys are quite terrified of them.'"[48] The women students may have discussed their intellectual ambitions over tea, but they were not encouraged to question the established hierarchies.

Plath did. As she wrote to her mother in February 1956, "it seems the Victorian age of emancipation is yet dominant here."[49] Sylvia's Newnham friend Isabel Murray Henderson recalled that the sexism at Cambridge was "more obvious" than what she had experienced at the University of Aberdeen, but that "One had simply to despise the perpetrator and move on."[50] Plath took a harder line. In May 1956, she would publish an article in Oxford's *Isis* about sexism at Cambridge:

> the most difficult feat for a Cambridge male is to accept a woman not merely as feeling, not merely as thinking, but as managing a complex, vital interweaving of both. Men here are inclined to treat women in one of two ways: either (1) as pretty beagling frivolous things (or devastating bohemian things) worthy of May balls and suggestive looks over bottles of Chablis by candlelight, or, more rarely, (2) as esoteric opponents on an intellectual tennis court where the man, by law of kind, always wins.... A debonair Oxford P.P.E. man demurred, laughing incredulously: "But really, talk about philosophy with a *woman*!" A poetic Cambridge chap maintains categorically: "As soon as a woman starts talking about intellectual things, she loses her feminine charm for me."

Plath countered that the American coeducational system made for a more equitable atmosphere, and she hoped that a Cambridge woman would be able, in the future, to "keep her female status while being accepted simultaneously as an intelligent human being."[51] Later she would tell an interviewer how at Cambridge she had been criticized for beginning a poem "just like John Donne, but not quite managing to finish like John Donne, and I first felt the full weight of English Literature on me." Other women poets at Cambridge, she said, had approached her and asked her how she could bear to publish "because of the criticism, the terrible criticism."[52] Indeed, just showing up for an exam could be reason for criticism, as Jean Gooder remembered. "We girls streamed in, and the men who were the functionaries, who guarded the portals of the Divinity School, looked on us with such evident disapproval. It was a morning exam, and when we came back in the afternoon [for another exam], absolutely unrehearsed and undiscussed, we had all put on makeup."[53]

That October, 1955, Sylvia still imagined nothing would hold her back. She was excited to meet her academic supervisor, Miss Kathleen (Kay) Burton, and looked forward to attending her lectures and tutorials. She expected to feel "a bit strange and lonely," as Mrs. Prouty had warned, and asked Aurelia to send her oatmeal cookies. "I shall probably sound quite homesick these first few weeks; I always enjoy giving love, and it is slightly painful to have it shut up in one until deep friendships develop . . . Do bear with me."[54] There was no party for her on her twenty-third birthday, though some Whitstead students left an earthen vase filled with yellow flowers in her room. She splurged on expensive art books thanks to her generous book allowance, and walked with a date, Ken Frater, to Grantchester, where they had tea by the fire at the Orchard.

Sylvia's closest girlfriend that term was Jane Baltzell, an American Marshall scholar from Brown University who was also an English literature student and aspiring writer. The two got to know each other during walks across the back fields from Whitstead to Newnham's dining hall each evening. Sylvia also became chummy with Evelyn Evans, who lived in a neighboring room in Whitstead. Both Jane and Evelyn remembered Sylvia "incessantly working," pounding away at her typewriter at 6:30 a.m., more focused on her studies than "chit-chat in rooms over coffee." Sylvia gave Evelyn the impression that her writing earnings helped keep her family afloat. Once, when Evelyn was nursing her during a bad cold, Sylvia told her she felt guilty about having a German father on account of the Holocaust. Evelyn found the conversation "morbid." When she was well, though, Sylvia "had enough energy for umpteen people." Evelyn often helped her choose her outfits for London jaunts as Sylvia posed in front of the full-length mirror in the corridor.[55]

But Sylvia spent more time with men. Soon she was receiving "surprise visits" from Americans, including Dick Wertz, Sassoon's Yale roommate, who was studying theology at Cambridge; Myron Lotz, now studying medicine at Oxford; and a young man she had met at the Glascock Poetry Contest in Massachusetts. Dick took her punting along the Backs, which Sylvia described romantically for her mother: "swans and ducks bobbing for the apples fallen in the water from border gardens, innumerable crew shells and quaint low bridges, and weeping willows trailing over crenellated walls and the lacy spires of St. John's College."[56] Myron's visit was less enchanting: he bragged about his Yale summa degree and his new car, and Sylvia found herself "really disgusted by his american [*sic*] materialism which has degenerated into a disagreeable self-satisfaction and conceit."[57] She felt just the opposite—ignorant and unread compared to her sophisticated British peers.

Sylvia was eager to begin translating her experience onto the page, and wasted no time researching the English literary magazine market. Just five days after arriving in Cambridge she sent off her poems "Ice Age" and "Danse Macabre" to *The London Magazine*. She would soon publish in *Chequer*, one of the Cambridge literary magazines, though the quality of university poetry did not seem to her very high.

There were societies for nearly every imaginable activity, even tiddly-winks. She wanted to write for the university newspaper and join the Labour Club so she could become better informed about politics; she was curious about the far left, too. "I shall also investigate the Socialists, and may, just for fun, go to a meeting or two of the Communist Party (!)"[58] She wished she could join all the extracurricular clubs that interested her, but in the end she settled on the Cambridge Amateur Dramatic Club, or ADC. She auditioned with parts from *As You Like It* and *Camino Real*, and boasted to her mother that she beat out more than one hundred others for one of nine female spots in the troupe. That October, she played the "mad poetess" Phoebe Clinket in Alexander Pope's *Three Hours after Marriage*, an "absurd farce," but she did not get a major part in the next play, *Bartholomew Fair*. She was inspired by the avant-garde films she saw with her new ADC friends, films that brought Poe and Kafka to mind. *The Cabinet of Dr. Caligari* was, she told Aurelia, "the sort of movie I enjoy most: it shocks one into new awarenesses of the world by breaking up the conventional patterns and re-molding them into something fresh and strange."[59] Sylvia's Downing College beau Christopher Levenson recalled that films were serious business at Cambridge "in the era of Truffaut and Godard, Buñuel and De Sica . . . subject to endless discussion and interpretation, on par with traditional theatre."[60]

In many ways, Cambridge conformed to Sylvia's expectations. She walked among the grand, imposing colleges and spent afternoons in Grantchester taking tea beneath the shady blossoms of an apple tree just as Rupert Brooke and Virginia Woolf had. She sat by the fire reading *The Tempest* aloud with ADC men and hosted sherry parties in her Whitstead garret. But in other ways, Cambridge was utterly foreign. Unlike at Smith, men outnumbered women ten to one; she was a second-class citizen. Women were not even allowed in the hallowed halls of the Cambridge debating society, the Union, unless escorted by a man. Sylvia also had to navigate the British class system, and she needed to assimilate quickly lest she be labeled a naive, unsophisticated Yank—which was how Jane remembered her during that first term. Jane was embarrassed when Sylvia asked a Cambridge bobby where they could find somewhere "picturesque" to eat. She remembered her English friends ridiculing Sylvia's Samsonite luggage (which Sylvia had gotten on sale), and her use of the term "enjoy." "In her room at Whitstead, for example, she had a favorite piece of furniture, a coffee table. . . . She apparently would often remark on how much she 'enjoyed that table,' thereby unconsciously regaling her English visitors, for I heard that anecdote more than once."[61] One of Sylvia's Whitstead contemporaries, Philippa Forder Goold, thought Sylvia was "the epitome of what we non-Americans imagined an American coed to be," and admitted to "disliking her fairly intensely."[62] Plath's adoption of a mid-Atlantic accent by 1958 suggests that she felt such pressures and tried to conform. (Jane said that when she listened to Sylvia's later poetry recordings, she did "not recognize her voice." At Whitstead, Sylvia had spoken with a strong American accent.)[63] Ted Hughes's friend Michael Boddy, who met

Sylvia at a Cambridge mixer in 1955, remembered that she was "very obviously an American College Girl, nodding her head, doing a hair-flipping laugh, and saying 'Wunnerful! Wunnerful!'"[64]

Plath's academic program—a second BA in English, for which she was allowed to skip the first year's examinations—also presented new challenges. Cambridge was much less structured than Smith, with no annual midterms or final exams. Each week that fall, she would attend two one-hour "supervisions"—Tragedy and Practical Composition & Criticism—an hour of French language tutoring, and twelve hours of lectures. Her only required assignments were essays for her two weekly supervisions. But such freedom was illusory. Plath's entire degree would be based on her performance on her final Tripos exams in June of her second year. She had chosen the topics for Part II of the degree herself: Composition and Criticism, Ancient and Modern Tragedy, French, the English Moralists, and the History of Literary Criticism. At Cambridge, no one would take attendance or formally grade her tutorial papers. It was up to Sylvia alone to make sure she was reading and learning enough to succeed on her final exams.

Sylvia—like her father—relished the challenge of mastering new fields. Still, she felt like a "novice compared to the specialized students here."[65] After less than a month in her Tragedy supervision, she wrote Aurelia that she felt "enormous handicaps reading . . . in a vacuum where I have had no background."[66] Normally Sylvia was the A student who intimidated others. But at Cambridge she accepted being behind in a way she never would have at Smith, and saw an opportunity for self-improvement—spreading "pathways and bridges over the whistling voids of my ignorance."[67] She challenged herself to read more until she was an expert in sixteenth-, seventeenth-, or eighteenth-century literature.[68] Her anonymity in Cambridge seems to have liberated her, at least for a time, from the competitiveness that marked her academic career, though she felt "claustrophobic at the piles and piles of books rising up around me that I 'must read.'"[69] She was proud of herself for tackling her weakest literary subjects. As she wrote to Mrs. Prouty, who often prodded her to lower her academic expectations, "The constant struggle in mature life, I think, is to accept the necessity of tragedy and conflict, and not to try to escape to some falsely simple solution which does not include these more somber complexities. . . . One doesn't get prizes for this increasing awareness, which sometimes comes with an intensity indistinguishable from pain."[70] Prouty replied that she had known Sylvia would be "disappointed & disillusioned—but you are standing up to it and taking it."[71] Plath had lately received only rejections from magazines, and was bitterly disappointed that she had not won the Borestone Mountain Poetry Award, an annual contest nearly as prestigious as the Yale Younger Poets prize. She vowed to write for two hours a day so that she could send out more material for publication and "get rid of this sense of a financial deadend."[72] (She was $50 in debt to Dr. Beuscher.)

Prouty understood the homesickness, alienation, and sense of inferiority Sylvia might experience alone in England. While Sylvia's family and friends assumed that she was living an enchanted life in Cambridge, Prouty worried that her Grand Tour would end in sorrow and ruin, as it had for Isabel Archer. She was skeptical of Sylvia's cheerful letters—such as her claim that "the cold air (which blows directly from the russian [sic] steppes) makes me feel simply grand: clean, fresh and strong."[73] Prouty guessed the truth: the damp cold made her sick. Sylvia appreciated her candor. "I feel I can talk to you like a second mother, perhaps even more frankly!"[74] Even Mary Ellen Chase warned, "My one anxiety is that you are whirling about too rapidly. . . . rein in your Bay Horse and Hound a bit lest you burst into radiant particles!"[75] (Chase's image brings the end of "Ariel" to mind.)

Plath attended morning lectures by Basil Willey and Dorothea Krook on the moralists; Muriel Bradbrook and Enid Welsford on tragedy; Theodore Redpath on the history of tragedy; F. R. Leavis on criticism; and Joan Bennet on the metaphysical poets.[76] Her Tragedy and Practical Criticism supervisions with Kay Burton met in the afternoons on Tuesday and Thursday, respectively. She hoped to attend David Daiches's lectures the following term on the modern English novel. Plath told her mother the writers Daiches taught were "Really 'modern,' I think, instead of the usual concept of 'modern' here: e.g. 'modern poets' are considered to be Wordsworth, Arnold, and Coleridge!"[77] Daiches was the critic who helped resurrect Virginia Woolf's reputation. But Sylvia seemed most excited about attending the "pithy deadpan" F. R. Leavis's lectures on literary criticism.[78] After applying for special permission, Plath audited Leavis's weekly classes at Downing College.[79] (Christopher Levenson recalled that Leavis disliked Americans, and once "mocked an American visitor by climbing into the study through the open window rather than by the door, commenting that that was the custom in Cambridge.")[80] Leavis—who had, along with I. A. Richards and William Empson, introduced the concept of New Criticism—was one of the most influential literary critics of the twentieth century, and shaped Cambridge's English department in ways that still resonate today. Leavis was disturbed by the rise of the dime-store novel and other "low" culture, such as (in his opinion) women's magazines. As a scholarship student, Plath could transcend her middle-class upbringing by mastering high culture—by attending Smith and Cambridge, winning literary prizes and scholarships, reading the right books, and publishing in highbrow publications like *The Atlantic*. But Plath was also steeped in what Leavis, in the sexist context of the day, would have considered low culture: she had spent much of her high school and college years breaking into the women's magazine market. This division between high and low was something Plath always straddled; while she would prefer to publish in *Harper's*, she did not turn down *Ladies' Home Journal.*

Apart from her lectures and the ADC rehearsals, there was another activity that required several hours each week: dating. An attractive, clever, confident American woman did not suffer from lack of male attention at Cambridge in 1955. Many contemporaries remembered that Sylvia cut a dramatic figure on the quads with her perfectly coiffed hair, infectious laughter, and fashionable clothes; Christopher Levenson recalled her as "fresh and outspoken."[81] In her letters home, she often reassured Aurelia and Mrs. Prouty that she was not a "career girl," but lamented the fact that the right man had not yet appeared: "I sometimes despair of ever finding anyone who is so strong in soul and so utterly honest and careful of me," she wrote the night before she met Ted Hughes.[82] She longed to find a "strong" man who could "match" her own strength, who would not be intimidated by her talent and her accomplishments, someone who would create art alongside her. If she could not find such a husband at Cambridge, with its ten men for each woman, she thought, she would not find him anywhere.

Meanwhile, Sassoon had abandoned his career in furnace sales for philosophy at the Sorbonne. He visited Sylvia at Cambridge on December 4, and they decided to meet again in Paris over her Christmas vacation. Sylvia spoke of Sassoon constantly to Jane Baltzell. He was her main "preoccupation." "She was obsessed with Sassoon—and she called him Sassoon. She lived for his letters, she relished them very obviously. She would read them at the breakfast table, laughing out loud. She romanticized him tremendously. She saw him as a Rimbaud."[83] Yet Sylvia dated several Cambridge men during 1955 and early 1956: Winthrop Means, Isaac (Iko) Meshoulam, John Lythgoe, Brian Corkery, Richard Mansfield, Martin Deckett, Ken Frater, Tony Smith, David Buck, Mallory Wober, and Christopher Levenson, who felt Sylvia was drawn to him because he had done "relief work after the 1953 Dutch floods" and traveled in "war-ravaged Germany"—experiences that made him seem "more cosmopolitan," in her eyes, than his contemporaries.[84] (He was also the editor of *delta*, a Cambridge literary magazine.) Christopher thought Sylvia "physically very attractive in an exotic, very un-English way." He came to find her "too glossily sophisticated, too worldly-wise," but also, when she let down her guard, too effusive with her gee-whiz American mannerisms.[85] Sylvia hadn't yet mastered the art of English understatement.

Early in the term, she wrote to Ellie that she had had dates with three young men in a single day; she was soon juggling so many dates for tea and sherry parties that she longed to hide in her room.[86] One young man caught and kept her attention—Mallory Wober, who was studying natural science at King's College. She had met him at a Labour Club dance on October 10, and he quickly became Sassoon's rival. (He was, in fact, distantly related to Sassoon.)[87] When Sassoon visited her in early December, he and Sylvia had a "long sad talk" about how "you can't go home again."[88] Compared to Mallory, Sylvia wrote Ellie, Sassoon had "shrunk, like gregor samsa [sic], to an insect."[89]

Mallory had lived for nine years in India, where his father was in business, before moving back to London. He was Jewish—"amazing family background: Moorish Jews, Russian Jews, Syrian Jews, etc."—cultured, and charming.[90] In the afternoons he invited Sylvia to his room for tea or sherry. ("Seeing young men make tea is still a source of silent mirth to me!" she wrote home.)[91] She lounged before his fire while he played Beethoven and Scarlatti on his small Hammond organ. In the evenings they attended concerts and dined at the Taj Mahal, where he spoke Hindustani with the wait-staff and introduced her to mangoes and Indian cuisine. She introduced him, in turn, to Dylan Thomas, whom she read aloud, "practising some experimental ideas of mine in getting people to like poetry by hearing it without analytic fanfare."[92] He took her to a candlelit Evensong service at King's College Chapel, where she was overwhelmed by the grandeur. She described this "mystical" night over and over in letters to her friends and family, calling it one of the most profound experiences of her life.

Sylvia found Mallory immensely civilized, and exoticized his Jewishness, which, she said, gave him "a subtle strange other-world aura."[93] She spoke of him as she later would Ted Hughes: "a young Hercules," a giant of the earth from the time of the "Old Testament prophets . . . strong and peaceful as the Rock of Gibraltar."[94] To Ellie she wrote, "he is dmitri karamazov [sic] and I made him all myself. god, elly [sic], he is the kind one could create a superman with." Sylvia was falling in love with him and opened up to Mallory about her breakdown and suicide attempt, telling him about "going into hospitals and meeting mad doctors and being treated in incomprehensible ways."[95] She was dismayed by his age: at nineteen, he was four years her junior. To friends she wrote that he was much more mature than men her own age—"compared to gordon, to ira, to mr. kazin's harvard-pressboy [sic] he is a MAN,"—but she saw his age as an impediment to a relationship: "to think I'm making him ready for some girl who is teething innocently in her cradle!"[96] She told Sassoon about Mallory to rouse his jealousy: "a rugged jewish hercules [sic], hewn fresh from the himalayas [sic]."[97]

By December, Sylvia had earned an invitation from Mallory's mother to stay with the family in London over the Christmas break. She told Aurelia, "it is an Event to have a 'christian' [sic] girl accepted, I gather. Ironically enough, I am not really a christian [*sic*] in the true sense of the word, but more of an ethical culturist: labels don't matter, but I am close to the Jewish beliefs in many ways."[98] (In "Daddy," Plath writes, "I think I may well be a Jew.") However, she had to turn down Mallory's holiday invitation because she had already accepted one from John Lythgoe, a "shy Botany student" who came from an aristocratic family. Sylvia did not say much about John in her letters home, but she enjoyed telling correspondents about her tea date with his grandmother, Lady Tansley, in Grantchester.

Sometimes Sylvia's dates crossed paths, and farce ensued. In mid-November, she canceled a trip to Ely with John in favor of a tea date with Mallory. John did not get her message, and showed up at her room while she was entertaining Mallory. Sylvia made the best of an awkward situation:

> well, nothing remained but to have them both for tea. . . . believe it or not they both stayed from 4 till 10 at night, talking about everything from "is there a purpose to the universe" to the Belgian Congo—no mention of supper! john [*sic*] left only after I invited him to tea today, and mallory [*sic*] took me to a lovely late steak dinner at the Taj. My first "salon," and most stimulating.[99]

Mallory said that Sylvia was always "fighting off" men who wanted to date her. (Indeed, she told Dick Wertz, perhaps exaggerating, that she had received several marriage proposals at Cambridge.)[100] He remembered Sylvia's bright clothes, make-up, "big skirts," and "flamboyant" nature. Heads turned when she walked into a room. This "genius-person comes to subdued England and is four times more vivid than the culture." One afternoon, when he was in Sylvia's room at Whitstead, there was a knock on the door. Sylvia said, "Go away." The door opened and a hand dropped a bouquet of flowers on the floor. Mallory made motions to leave, but Sylvia said, "You don't have to. He's gone."[101]

Sylvia managed to spend a day with Mallory's family over the December break at his London home at 71 Wentworth Road. In a later letter to him, she described the afternoon's scenes in "snapshots": "dream-walk through mist, underground,—to lights, carols, hot roasted chestnuts, conversational Bobby, surrealist mushrooms in Trafalgar Square—all this is Christmas—wrapped in my heart—and will be with me in Paris to sustain me till the New Year which will really begin when I am with you again."[102] She would write Mallory love letters from Paris even as she shared her hotel room with Sassoon.

In December, she had a double tea date with Mallory and a young man named Nathaniel LaMar, who had attended Harvard and known Warren at

Exeter. Nat, as Sylvia called him, had published a story in *The Atlantic* ("Creole Love Story") that impressed her, and she begged a mutual friend for an introduction. She told Aurelia that he was "a lovely, light-skinned negro, and I look most forward to talking to him about writing, etc."[103] Sylvia mentioned numerous tea and coffee "dates" and satisfying conversation with Nat—"American talk." She found him a "strong contrast to the Englishmen, who have a kind of brittle, formal rigidity and . . . a calculated sophisticate pose."[104] By January she called him her "dearest friend in Cambridge . . . a blessing; the true friend, warm, dear, and emotionally very much like me."[105] Like Perry Norton, Nat became a "psychic brother," and she told Aurelia she would join him in Paris for Christmas.[106] She later wrote, more suggestively, "I have a greater faith that if I work and write now, I will have a rich, inner life which will make me worth fine, intelligent men, like Sassoon, and Nat."[107]

Sylvia's labeling of Nat as a "light-skinned negro" reveals the prejudices of her era. But such easy camaraderie between a black man and a white woman would have been impossible in segregated 1950s America. Jane recalled that Cambridge was much more diverse than American campuses on account of the presence of so many Commonwealth students, and that Nat was regarded as a "wunderkind."[108] Still, Cambridge was not free of racism or anti-Semitism. Both Mallory and Nat were "others" whose religion and race kept them outside the mainstream of English life. Ted Hughes was a Yorkshireman, a provincial who did not belong to the highborn set that still filled Oxbridge in those days. Plath, also an outsider, seemed drawn to those on the fringes. As she wrote to Jon Rosenthal that term, she felt no "rapport" with "the delicately boned frosty-eyes, terribly proper English. My best friends here are Jewish or negro."[109]

Sylvia had more trouble making close female friends in England, a fact that worried her mother. She treated Aurelia's concerns lightly, but, after four years at Smith, she missed having girlfriends in whom she could confide. Sylvia thought that English women, whom she described as "hysterical and breathless," ignored and looked down on Americans.[110] To Ellie she wrote, "the women here are ghastly: two types: the fair-skinned twittering bird who adores beagling and darjeeling tea and the large, intellectual cowish type with monastically bobbed hair, impossible elephantine ankles and a horrified moo when within 10 feet of a man."[111] Jane felt similarly. "The English women at Newnham (both faculty and students) . . . all seemed humorless and deliberately—aggressively, even—unattractive, physically as well as otherwise. I found them incomprehensible, and didn't make a single friend among them."[112] Jane said that Whitstead's distance from Newnham's main buildings meant that Whitstead's foreign residents were isolated geographically from the English women undergraduates: "they just had no interest in us."[113] She and Sylvia would befriend only Canadian, South African, and Scottish women at Newnham.

Jean Gooder, who shared a Tragedy supervision with Sylvia, remembered thinking, "There's this beautifully dressed blond sitting in the corner, dumb. She never uttered a word, and I paid her no attention." Later, Jean—with the benefit of her perspective as director of studies at Newnham—realized what a difficult situation the college had put Sylvia in. "I would never have put a first-term student onto the Tragedy paper like that. It was a crazy way to begin. You want to give them some sense of what Cambridge English is about, what it means. It was very bad management." But in 1955, Jean was wary of Sylvia. Her conversational style, as many Cambridge contemporaries recalled, was "gushy," "easily satirizable."[114] She seemed to many a walking cliché of the clean-cut American girl. But she could also be nasty, making "awful, sour comments" about people and exhibiting "appalling rudeness" in shared supervisions.[115] Jean said, "One of the things that put me off Sylvia was her notion of being extremely well turned out, beautifully made up, aggressively so." Jean had spent time at the Sorbonne in Paris before she went up to Cambridge. "My idea of chic was Left Bank, black." Sylvia, on the other hand, wore "clothes of a hard cut, very clear primary colors. . . . She was very American. It was very effective. She compelled attention."[116] Sylvia's Newnham contemporary Felicity Meshoulam said Sylvia developed a reputation for "cheap flirtatiousness" that fall. And yet, Felicity thought, Sylvia also seemed to like Cambridge's "Puritan atmosphere."[117]

Isabel Murray Henderson shared Sylvia's wariness of the English undergraduates, who could be "flippant and unserious." But this was an act—the most clever students often appeared, out of pride, to be the most "indolent." (Iko Meshoulam remembered that this was especially true of Ted Hughes and his friends.)[118] This facet of Oxbridge culture, which still exists today, was completely foreign to Sylvia, Isabel remembered. "She rightly saw this deficiency as a real social disadvantage. . . . The very clever could be stand-offish at meals and minor encounters. This was not being competitive but more like conceit." Americans did not know what to make of the English students' more casual demeanor, while the English women could be similarly nonplussed by the Americans. For example, Isabel remembered, Americans at Newnham knew how to type, whereas the British students "were advised never to learn to type or we would end up being secretaries."[119]

Sylvia and Jane's dim view of English women may have been colored by their experience in Kay Burton's Tragedy supervision with A. S. Byatt, the future writer of *Possession* and other novels. Byatt was known as Antonia (Toni) Drabble then, the elder sister of the novelist Margaret Drabble;

she had a terribly clever reputation, and would take a first-class degree in English in 1957.[120] Jane remembers that she and Sylvia found Byatt rather "annoying in her mannerisms"—lounging on the floor, for example, rather than sitting properly in a chair. It was clear to them that Byatt was Kay Burton's favorite—probably, they thought, because she was English and they were American. The Yorkshire-born Byatt admitted, years later, that it was essentially so: she remembered Plath wearing "bobby socks and totally artificial bright red lips and totally artificial bright blonde hair . . . a made-up creature with no central reality to her at all, always uttering advice like a woman's magazine column. She wrote beautiful words, but there wasn't anybody inside there." Byatt claimed Plath "didn't show any signs" that she would become a major poet at Cambridge. "She just seemed silly."[121]

Jane was, in Sylvia's words, "as close to a 'best' friend as I have."[122] But she admitted that she felt a sense of "rivalry" around Jane, and Jane's burgeoning friendship with Isabel also upset Sylvia. Jane did not know Sylvia had thought of her as "a potential best friend" and felt "rather sad in retrospect."[123] The two quarreled, and by the end of her second term Sylvia would not have a single close girlfriend at Cambridge. She longed to see old Smith friends like Ellie Friedman and Sue Weller, with whom she could "be wholly woman," and counted down the weeks until their visits to Cambridge.[124] Ellie, who had also spent time in England, felt that class dynamics were partly to blame for Sylvia's isolation. British women at Cambridge, she said, "closed you off, they never asked you in. They're generally from a higher class—a moneyed class—and they're not going to ask you to come for the weekend. You're left with the men."[125]

Writing, like love, was a constant source of elation and anxiety. During the nine-day staging of Ben Jonson's *Bartholomew Fair* (November 24 to December 3), in which Plath had only a small role as the whore Punk Alice, she experienced a period of writer's block. While she boasted to several correspondents that the play had been reviewed in *The Times* and that the costumes had been made in Stratford-upon-Avon, she was disappointed with her marginal role—"five short speeches and a cat-fight in Act 4, Scene 5."[126] (Jonathan Miller, who played Troubleall, remembered Plath as "this rather big, blonde girl standing with one hand on her hip in what she thought was a traditionally 'whorish' posture," while Jane remembered that Sylvia pronounced "the word 'whore' with peculiar gusto.")[127] Sylvia was also upset about the toll the play had taken on her writing. After the play, she quit the ADC; the commitment was simply too demanding, and she was not prepared, as she put it, to give "blood." "I am no Sara Bernhardt," she admitted to Mrs. Prouty in mid-December.[128]

To Aurelia she was more frank: "'muteness is sickness' for me, as richard wilbur [*sic*] says, and I felt a growing horror at my inarticulateness; each day of not-writing made me feel more scared."[129] Although Plath cared a great deal about publishing her work, she insisted to others that she was "dependent on the process of writing, not on the acceptance." She wrote Aurelia, "When I say I <u>must</u> write, I don't mean I <u>must</u> publish. There is a great difference. The important thing is the aesthetic form given to my chaotic experience, which is, as it was for James Joyce, my kind of religion, and as necessary for me . . . as the confession and absolution for a Catholic in church." Writing was purgation and fulfillment, even if "the actual story never lives up to the dream."[130]

Later, Plath's first-term Cambridge experiences found their way into her more mature poems. "Whiteness I Remember" was partly based on a wild ride she took on December 10 on a horse named Sam. Dick Wertz suggested the outing and Sylvia agreed, though she had never ridden a horse. She was in "ecstasy" until Sam began to gallop through a busy intersection and down the wrong side of the street. As cars pulled over and women on the side-walk began to scream, her feet fell out of her stirrups. She knew she should have been terrified—Dick, pursuing her in horror, thought she was going to die—but she felt invigorated: "I find myself hugging Sam's neck passion-ately. . . . such power: like the old gods of chance: I feel like one human, avenging thunderbolt."[131] The images would reappear in "Ariel."

Sylvia found more experiences to write about in France that Christmas. Her December 20 arrival in Paris was "nightmarish": her flight was canceled due to bad weather, and she had to take the ferry instead. Then Jane, with whom she shared a Left Bank hotel room, accidentally locked her out.[132] (Sylvia ended up sharing a room with two Swiss girls from Cambridge.) The next morning, Sylvia greeted Jane coldly; in a postcard to Mallory, Sylvia called her "thoughtless."[133] The incident did not bode well for their burgeoning friendship, although Sylvia, Jane, and Sassoon enjoyed a companionable meal together in Paris after the lockout. Jane liked Sassoon, whom she thought "small and wiry," and recalled that the couple behaved "appropriately" at the restaurant; after hearing Sylvia's rhapsodic affections, she had half expected them to fall over each other.[134] Jane left for Italy, and Sylvia eventually moved to another hotel on the Left Bank with Sassoon, between the Boul'Mich and the Boulevard St. Germain. She was delighted with her blue velvet room and its view of the Seine.

Sylvia stayed with Sassoon in Paris for ten days. Nat LaMar, who had offered to be her Parisian "escort," joined her for the first few days. Sylvia told Ellie that during this time she "had a brief affair with him." But she had come for Sassoon; when Nat left, she reunited with her great love.[135] Together the couple walked for hours along the Seine browsing through the bookstalls and lingering in cafés. They saw plays and ballets—Plath's favorite was Georges Simenon's "surrealistic 'La Chambre', cyclic, detective, drama with vampire woman . . . god, what a dance; seduces him and murders him; convulsions great."[136] She could hardly contain her joy at seeing so many Parisian landmarks, both high and low: "saw hundreds of whores, thanks to dear Richard, who obligingly quoted price ranges," she wrote Ellie.[137] She saw the *Mona Lisa* and *Winged Victory* at the Louvre, and sought out her "favorites": "the 'Virgin of the Rocks' and several thin, torturous El Grecos, a marvelous anonymous Pieta d'Avignon, Breughel, and my beloved Flemish school."[138] She marveled over the Cézannes, Van Goghs, and Gauguins at an Impressionist exhibit at the Orangerie, and wrote Aurelia about the Parisian faces, so "beautiful" compared to those in London, where everyone struck her as "un-chic, dowdy and formal."[139] To Mallory she wrote that Paris was "like the combination of heaven and hell in one colossal surrealistic dream."[140] Outside the cafés there were oysters and snails on ice, and artists—always artists. At one café she saw the manager give a toothless beggar soup and bread. The man had once been a clown in the circus and had gone mad, the manager explained. To Sylvia, the gesture epitomized the Parisian spirit.

On Christmas Day she and Sassoon spent the morning in bed, lingering over croissants, coffee, and oranges. Sylvia proclaimed the Christmas service at Notre Dame an "an aesthetic feast"—she marveled over the "blazing jeweled colors of the windows" and the "mammoth organ," which "sounded really like the voice of god." They wandered along the Île de la Cité and the Palais de Justice, and through the Tuileries, where they watched an "utterly enchanting" puppet show.[141] When Sylvia checked her mail at the American Express office, she found twenty-five letters and cards—including $25 from Mrs. Prouty—waiting for her. News from home tended to make her homesick, though she was determined to stay in England for another year. Ruth, her oldest friend, was pregnant, and Dick was engaged to Joanne Colburn, whom Sylvia considered too "quiet and delicate" for him.[142] (They would wed in June 1956.) This news made her anxious about her own future. Nearly all of her close friends had married, and some were beginning to start families. Aurelia, meanwhile, wrote her about "the relief of engaged girls."[143] Yet she would not apologize for her unconventional path. "I believe one has to live alone creatively before being ready to live with anyone else."[144] She told Aurelia, "as blake [sic] says: 'the road of excess leads to the palace of wisdom.'"[145]

She could not have found a better guide than Sassoon, a decadent aesthete who understood her appreciation for "the daily texture of life with a keen awareness and joy in small, colorful things: from the sight of a flicker on the grass to the sound of rain on a tin roof."[146] The two traveled by train to the French Riviera on New Year's Eve. Plath had brought her Smith-Corona typewriter so she could record her impressions. Sassoon slept on her breast while, with a painter's eye, she wrote about the "Van Gogh stars" and "Cubist" landscape. With each mile they put behind them, she was distancing herself from her real life and entering into a dream life with Sassoon. She wrote in her journal:

> lifting my head sleepily once, suddenly the moon shining incredibly on water. Marseille. The Mediterranean. Sleep again, and at last the pink vin rosé light of dawn along the back of the hills in a strange country. . . . and the red sun rising like the eye of God.[147]

She was, she told Mallory, "practically screaming with joy at the feast of color."[148] Plath would write about this dawn in "Southern Sunrise":

> A quartz-clear dawn
> Inch by bright inch
> Gilds all our Avenue,
> And out of the blue drench
> Of Angels' Bay
> Rises the round red watermelon sun.

Like her description of her ride on Sam, the language here prefigures the "red // Eye, the cauldron of morning" of the sunrise in "Ariel," as does the theme of transcendence through movement. She was already becoming a poet of apotheosis.

In Nice, Plath and Sassoon stayed in a small, iron-balconied room with a view, and spent their days traveling on a Lambretta through Beaulieu, Villefranche, Menton, Cap Ferrat, and Monte Carlo (where they played roulette). In the evenings, she drank wine, ate pastries and fruit, and read *The Autobiography of Alice B. Toklas* in bed. This was her life as she had dreamed it. "Sassoon and I shared all this, all life, crying, kicking each other, madly in love, growing, and all that. God, what a life," she wrote to Ellie.[149] But her relentless enthusiasm alarmed Mrs. Prouty. "She seems to see everything through pink-lavender glasses. Everything—even the tawdry and so often (to me) ugly Riviera—is beautiful to her," Prouty wrote Aurelia. "Isn't Sylvia a little starry-eyed about it all? I'd like to hear her tell about something that disappointed her."[150]

For Sylvia, the pinnacle of the trip was her visit to the small hillside village of Vence, the burial place of D. H. Lawrence and the site of the Chapelle du Rosaire, designed by Henri Matisse in 1951. Sylvia had seen photographs of the chapel in art books over the years, and had always dreamed of seeing it in person. When she and Sassoon arrived, however, she learned that the chapel was closed. Distraught, she walked away down the hill. Meanwhile, the mother superior saw Sassoon, still standing by the chapel, and beckoned him inside. He looked around for Sylvia, but did not see her. After his brief tour, he found her at the bottom of the hill, sitting on a rock and crying. She was furious that he had gone in without her and demanded that he take her back inside.

In the chapel, finally, she basked in the white and blue light shining through Matisse's stained-glass windows. "I just knelt in the heart of sun & the colors of sky, sea, & sun, in the pure white heart of the chapel," she told Aurelia.[151] It was the closest thing to grace she had ever experienced; "epiphany . . . weeping—vision of Love," she wrote in her calendar.[152] But she could not forgive Sassoon's selfishness, as she saw it, and the two had a heated row on the sunny hillside.

Both Plath and Sassoon made this argument the dramatic centerpiece of short stories they later wrote about the Rosary Chapel. Sassoon's 1962 story "In the Year of Love and unto Death, the Fourth—an Elegy on the Muse," was, he claimed, "pretty biographical."[153] It concerns a young man who reminisces about an old girlfriend. At once remorseful and nostalgic, the narrator remembers the early days of their relationship: "an unbelievable protraction of the instant of first sight love—with all its magical lightening of perfected creation, of Eden regained, and all the profound agonies of doubt."[154]

Sassoon's description of the Plath character's wonder as they drive to the Rosary Chapel has the ring of authenticity: "I got a crick in my neck from turning to all she told me to look at. Her excitement in one instance nearly caused an accident. This made us laugh heartily. Her laughter had a wonderfully sonorous note; it was elemental." She was, he wrote, "as various as the sea, and I as the sun."[155] But they quarreled at the chapel:

"Let's go now."

"I won't go! I won't go until I've been inside. I'll stand here and starve until they open to me."

"Oh, the hell . . ."

"Hell! Why do you say that? Why do you say hell?" Her eyes flashed and she brought clenched fists abruptly to her chest in a motion of terrifying violence; she seemed possibly about to cry. "Why do you say hell? Because it's *I* that will go there, not you! I!"

"I forbid you to say such an absurdity! I forbid it. Do you hear!"

"No, no! I hear nothing! Your voice and words mean nothing, in this thing! Because there, *there* is the place of sacredness. And there you avoided me. For that you had to be alone."

. . . She sobbed a little, and then she sat quietly on a rock in the road-side ditch. "I will wait until they let me in."

"Very well! I will see to it."[156]

And in Plath's 1956 short story "The Matisse Chapel," the character of Sally accuses Richard:

"You are so selfish that you went to see it without me. You knew that reporting about it wouldn't mean anything. You wouldn't even tell the Mother Superior: 'No, I will not see it without my girl.' You didn't even have the courage for that."

"Remember, I got you in," Richard said.

"They let you in because you looked miserable," Sally said. "And they let me in because I was crying. Simply because I was crying."

The radiance of the day was going. It was getting colder, approaching four o'clock, and the sky was thickening from blue to gray, curdling over with clouds. Animosity rankled between them. Stubbornly, Sally made the decisive gesture and withdrew her hand from Richard's arm.[157]

Sally wonders "if anything could save them now, after they had turned their backs on the colored chapel and fallen to squabbling."[158]

In real life, the two parted after "good farewell love."[159] Mallory—to whom Sylvia had written romantic letters from Paris—met her at Victoria Station, and she spent the night at his London home. But her feelings for him had receded; she would soon find excuses to turn down his invitations at Cambridge. England itself seemed paler after the riotous colors of the Mediterranean. She was disgusted with the "harsh Cockney" accents she heard, and the "bored, impersonal, dissatisfied faces of the working class, the cold walls between people in train compartments."[160] She felt better once she reached Cambridge on January 9, where she fortified herself with fresh fruit and flowers from the market.

She would soon receive a crushing letter from Sassoon. He felt she wanted more from him than he could give. Sylvia quoted his letter to Ellie: "'two years of army . . . and I must make a fortune and only then found a family, and always in the holy skies our love is and will be: someday; meanwhile, I must be noble and give you your freedom.'" Heartbroken, she begged him to reconsider—or at least agree to see her in Paris over the coming spring break. He responded with "a kind of promise to come crashing out of the aether in countless years hence and claim me amidst blood, thunder, and apotheosis as his woman and all the rest of it."[161] Sylvia was distraught. She wrote Sassoon, "I have found that it is beyond your power ever ever to free me or give me back my soul; you could have a dozen mistresses and a dozen languages and a dozen countries, and I could kick and kick; I would still not be free."[162]

Her world began to diminish. Her reading list was so arduous she felt she could read for the next ten years and still not complete it. Yet she kept up a "spartan siege": during the last week of January she read eighteen Strindberg plays and wrote a fifteen-page paper.[163] The following week brought supervisions and lectures on Chekhov, Racine, Woolf, Aeschylus, and the Jacobeans. "So you see," she wrote home, "the pressure is constant."[164] If only she could write more—when she wrote she felt a "spiritual calm": "I would smother if I didn't write."[165]

Jane never saw Sylvia depressed at Cambridge, and only later learned about her breakdown and suicide attempt from a Smith graduate, May Collacott, who arrived at Whitstead in the fall of 1956. But Sylvia was more depressed than she let on. "Moon—sad—destructive—lonely," she wrote in her calendar as the weather raged. Throughout January, her calendar entries shared a disturbing despondency: "snowy, rainy sickish day"; "rain, smoky fog"; "miserable cold still—frost—bitter"; "tired, wet day." A film about unrest in Northern Ireland, *Odd Man Out*, caused her "catharsis" and "tears"; two days later, on January 29, she wrote, "Tremendous sense of Guilt & pressure."[166]

Sylvia's burgeoning depression began to take a physical toll. On January 31 she awoke with "excruciating pains and was violently sick." She was taken by ambulance to Addenbrooke's Hospital, where she was put under watch for acute appendicitis in a large, crowded ward. She told Aurelia she felt "deserted and precarious (no medecine [*sic*], not even water)" and went home the next day with a diagnosis of "colic," which meant "absolutely nothing" to her.[167] In her calendar, she described the experience as a "nightmare," but she assured her mother that she was resilient: "I know I have already faced The Worst (total negation of self) and that, having lived through that blackness, like Peer Gynt lived through his fight with the Boyg, I can enjoy life simply for what it is: a continuous job, but most worth it. My existence now rests on solid ground; I may be depressed now and then, but never desperate."[168] Yet the next day she wrote in her calendar, "life miserable—suicidal."[169]

Mallory and Nat no longer interested her. She was, she told Mallory, a "disagreeable, idiosyncratic, pseudo-misanthrope."[170] Mallory's Israeli friend, Iko Meshoulam, recalled that Mallory experienced "great agony" after Sylvia dropped him, for he had been "in love like a schoolboy. . . . Very tragic."[171] Despite his heartbreak, Mallory considered himself "pretty lucky. To meet somebody rare—in some ways nasty—but still a rare person, is not everybody's lot."[172] But Sylvia, too, was desolate. She wrote her McLean friend Jane Anderson, "there have been very dark days, however rosy a mere skimming summary may sound."[173] The only Cambridge man who interested her now was Christopher Levenson, who was on sherry-drinking terms with Stephen Spender and E. M. Forster. She and Christopher spent the weekend of February 17–18 together in London, where they saw, at her suggestion, W. S. Merwin's play *Darkling Child*. But the weekend only reminded her that he was not Sassoon.

As Sassoon receded, she attached herself more fiercely to his image. She would wait for his return as if he were a sailor on a long voyage, and keep herself pure for him. In her journal, she wrote,

> I am rather high, and distant, and it is convenient to be led home across the snow-fields. It is very cold, and all the way back I am thinking: Richard, you live in this moment. You live now. . . . I want to write you, of my love, that absurd faith which keeps me chaste, so chaste, that all I have ever touched or said to others becomes only the rehearsal for you, and preserved only for this.[174]

Not only was Plath losing Sassoon, she was losing ground as a college poet. The Cambridge literary scene, dominated by the *Granta*, *delta*, and *Chequer* cliques, was intensely competitive and entirely male. Sylvia was naive about the obstacles she would have to overcome to break into these small, privileged worlds. Philip Hobsbaum, Ted Hughes's Cambridge contemporary and Seamus Heaney's mentor (and, in 1955, a *delta* editor), ran a writing group that Hughes attended. When Sylvia applied, she was refused admittance. She sent Philip four "meticulously typed" poems, but they seemed to him immature, like "college girl stuff."[175] He later admitted that he had made a sexist mistake.[176] Christopher agreed that the sexism at Cambridge was pervasive, but Sylvia seemed to transcend it: "because of her personal energy and vivacity I doubt if that in itself would have created literary obstacles for someone like Sylvia." Yet his words suggest the very sexism she had to overcome—and that Plath was welcomed into the *delta* and *Chequer* fold because she was an attractive, clever young woman, not because she was a respected campus poet: "She wrote articles for *Varsity*, the weekly newspaper and altogether her flair for publicity, and her self-assertiveness seemed much more professional than most of our fellow would-be writers. She appeared very self-assured and glamorous . . . but almost too clever, too sophisticated in our eyes."[177]

Chequer had published two of Plath's poems, "Epitaph in Three Parts" and "Three Caryatids Without a Portico by Hugh Robus: A Study in Sculptural Dimensions" in its Winter 1956 issue. Now, at the end of January, she was horrified to see that Daniel Huws, a close friend of Ted Hughes, had mocked her poems in a review. Daniel and his friends scoffed at the New Critical tricks Sylvia had mastered. They subscribed to a Neoromantic aesthetic that sought to resurrect the incantatory rhythms of Yeats and Dylan Thomas. Sylvia had expected to take Cambridge poetry by storm; instead, she had become a laughingstock. In her calendar that February she wrote repeatedly of her doubt about her literary career.

Sylvia's physical and mental health continued to deteriorate. She feared an impending breakdown that January as she read Shirley Jackson's 1954 novel *The Bird's Nest*, about a young woman with multiple personalities.[178] She was, she told Aurelia, "stoically inured to the winter, and working hard so that the spring will be a true and deserved flowering."[179] But privately she was haunted by the prospect of another depression—"The fear that all the edges and shapes and colors of the real world that have been built up again so painfully with such real love can dwindle in a moment of doubt, and 'suddenly go out' the way the moon would in the Blake poem."[180] She did not want to return to America, which seemed to her now provincial and materialistic. She fantasized about a writing fellowship, living in Italy, reporting for an international newspaper—anything that put her in the midst of "vital" people and events. "I am just about through with the academic community," she told her mother.[181] But she knew she had little chance of joining a newspaper with no practical experience. She had won nearly every prestigious academic prize it was possible for a young woman to win, yet she had few career prospects outside the field of education. Without the salve of Sassoon's love, and with the harsh review of her poems still ringing in her ears, she feared the emptiness would engulf her again: "The horror is the sudden folding up and away of the phenomenal world, leaving nothing. Just rags."[182]

She felt better—briefly—after she learned that her Smith friend Sue Weller had received a Marshall Scholarship to Oxford. She also learned, in early February, that her Fulbright Fellowship had been recommended for renewal. "Complete reversal of desperate & depressed mood" she wrote in her calendar on Valentine's Day.[183] She reassured Aurelia, "I am solidly, realistically joyous; I like living in hope of publication; I can live without the actual publication."[184] Her hope was rewarded that week when *The Christian Science Monitor* bought one of her drawings and an article about Cambridge life.[185]

She and Christopher Levenson saw each other nearly every day in February, and she made time for tea and coffee dates, films, and plays with friends—among them *The Bacchae* (in Greek), Dalí's *L'Age d'Or*, and Cocteau's *La Belle et La Bête*. Yet by mid-February she was rehearsing her "old doubts re superficiality in expression (words) & in experience": "cold inferior feelings re writing & thinking"; "very depressed & antagonistic & hollow . . . close to blackness again."[186] She longed for "stoic courage," and made a "new resolution to be accessible and sweet."[187] Between February 20 and 23 she was able to channel her suffering into art; she wrote "Winter Landscape, With Rooks," "Tale of a Tub," and "Channel Crossing." But on February 24, the day before she met Ted Hughes, she wrote in her calendar, "miserablest of days—awful wet cold—drugs—far off—no sleep—great depression."[188]

Sylvia missed her mother's healing hand and her grandmother's chicken soup; the English food disgusted her. At Cambridge, no one made a fuss over her. "I miss that very subtle atmosphere of faith and understanding at home where you all knew what I was working at, and appreciated it, whether it got published or not," she wrote Aurelia on February 24 in an unusually despondent letter. She apologized to her mother for "overflowing," but it was necessary to "spew out those thoughts which are like the blocked putridity in my head."[189] Other areas of her life started to fall apart; she couldn't prepare for her new classes, and she couldn't rouse herself to socialize. Her professors, she felt, thought she was stupid, and the students in her college surely thought she was mad. Years later, Jane wrote that Sylvia had been wrong. "None of us knew anything at the time about her history in America and in the general array of psyches in Whitstead at the time, she seemed decidedly one of the healthy ones."[190]

Sylvia wrote desperate letters to Sassoon, asking him "to tell me if he would <u>not</u> see me in paris, italy [*sic*], etc."[191] His response was "disquieting," but he promised that he would return for her someday. She ignored him, and declared she would visit him in Paris during her Easter vacation regardless of whether he wanted her there or not. As she told Ellie, "I have from somewhere got the guts to go to paris [*sic*], stand in his door, rouse him from whatever mistress it is now, and say, smiling 'here I am darling. How about coffee?'" But even as she concocted plans to see him, she longed, she told Ellie, for someone to "break richard's [*sic*] image & free me": "I am committed, until some big, brilliant combination of all the men I have ever met . . . comes and transforms me into the Woman I am with richard [*sic*]: writer, poet, reader, sleeper, eater, and all."[192]

Sylvia did not mention that she had already met such a man the week before. His name was Ted Hughes.

16

Mad Passionate Abandon

Cambridge University, February 1956

Before Sylvia Plath knew Ted Hughes, she knew his poems. She had read them in the November 1954 issue of *Chequer*, and in the short-lived *Saint Botolph's Review*.[1] Plath was struck by Hughes's brazen voice, so radically different from the well-wrought verse then fashionable in English and American literary circles. This poet wrote of seething jaguars and dark figures who obeyed the laws of nature, not man:

> When two men meet for the first time in all
> Eternity, and outright hate each other,
> Not as a beggar-man and a rich man,
> Not as cuckold-maker and cuckold,
> Not as bully and delicate boy, but
> As dog and wolf because their blood before
> They are aware has bristled into their hackles,
> Because one has clubbed the other to death
> With the bottle first broached to toast their transaction
> . . . .
> Then a flash of violent incredible action,
> Then one man letting his brains gently to the gutter,
> And one man bursting into the police station
> Crying "Let Justice be done. I did it, I."[2]

This was the voice of *King Lear* rather than *The Faerie Queen*. Hughes preferred, as a Cambridge friend later wrote, "the strong stress patterns of native Anglo-Saxon poetry. He was an intensely English poet, whose England is a tough country of snowfalls, mud and biting tempests. Its farms cling perilously to barely fertile hillsides, scraped from the eternal rocks beneath."[3] Plath recognized in Hughes an explosive talent at a time when he had published fewer than a dozen poems in college magazines. Her belief in him was uncanny, and prescient.

By the time Plath read "Law in the Country of the Cats" in the 1956 *Saint Botolph's Review,* Hughes had graduated from Cambridge, but he was still a regular presence there. He famously camped out in a tent in the garden of the Saint Botolph's rectory, where his friend Lucas (Luke) Myers—a Tennessee man and distant relation of the poet Allen Tate—bedded down in an old chicken coop.[4] Most of Ted's friends were outsiders who, like him, felt disdain for the clipped accents of the British upper class: Luke Myers and Bertram (Bert) Wyatt-Brown were American; Daniel Huws was Welsh; Colin White was a Scottish communist; Terence McCaughey was Irish. Daniel Weissbort, whose Polish parents had brought him to England from Belgium in the 1930s, was Jewish, as was the medical student Than Minton. Despite the fact that several of these young men had gone to elite private schools, Wyatt-Brown remembered "lengthy discussions about the mannered snobs in various colleges," the "crumbs" they "despised."[5] (The Duke of Buckingham's son, who once served sugared violet petals at a tea party, was a favorite target.) David Ross called his friends "a sort of socialist group" and remembered Hughes being "very well aware of class . . . it was virtually impossible not to notice it."[6] Indeed, when Christopher Levenson went round selling issues of his literary magazine *delta* at "certain colleges," he was struck by "the number of Lords and Viscounts on the nameplates beside their doors."[7]

Hughes was friendly with several Englishmen, such as Ross, Peter Redgrove, Philip Hobsbaum, and Brian Cox, but his Yorkshire background marked him as northern and, in the prejudice of the day, provincial. Redgrove, a poet, was amazed that Hughes did not try to tone down his Yorkshire accent, which could be a professional liability; when Redgrove later submitted an early recording of Hughes reading his poems to the BBC, they rejected it because of Hughes's regional cadences. His refusal to change his accent was a gesture of indifference rather than defiance, Redgrove felt; Hughes simply "lacked" the sense of himself as inferior.[8] Hughes later told a friend, "I lay low, because I felt, I suppose, that I was in enemy country."[9]

———

HUGHES HAD COME UP to Pembroke College, Cambridge, in October 1951 after winning an Open Exhibition. Like Plath, he came from a family that worked hard to make ends meet—his father was a journeyman carpenter turned newsagent, his mother a thrifty homemaker. Both sides of the family were from the Calder Valley in West Yorkshire, near Brontë country. While Plath's family had fallen down the class ladder after Otto's death, Hughes's family had worked its way up. Hughes's paternal Irish grandfather, John Hughes, had come to Yorkshire around 1870 from Manchester with a wave of Irish laborers to build a local reservoir. Because he lived in Cragg Vale, he was nicknamed "Cragg Jack," and he married a local woman named Polly Major. Polly's father had been a major in the British Army, stationed in Gibraltar; her mother was Spanish.

Hughes's paternal grandparents moved into a small row house on King Street, across from the Calder River, in the mill town of Hebden Bridge. Cragg Jack frequented the nearby Stubbing Wharfe pub, where he was known for his Irish ballads. The Calder River flooded often, and with it the family's low-lying home. Jack died in 1903 at forty-seven of a respiratory infection, leaving Polly to raise three children—including Hughes's father, William, almost ten—on her own, while cleaning houses. Money was so tight that Hughes's father once had to attend school wearing a pair of ladies' boots, a gift from one of Polly's employers. Polly brought in extra income by selling sweets out of her living room, where she made her young customers read a Bible passage before they could buy their "spice."[10]

Hughes's mother Edith was a Farrar. The family featured prominently in English literary history. Nicholas Ferrar, after whom Hughes would name his son, published George Herbert's *The Temple* and helped found the village of Little Gidding, which inspired T. S. Eliot's famous poem in *Four Quartets*. The Puritans eventually destroyed the contemplative community; Hughes traced his opposition to English Puritanism, in all its forms, to this ancestral rupture. The Farrars would rise to prominence in West Yorkshire, too. Hughes's mother and her siblings grew up on the edge of poverty—Edith was one of six children raised in a tiny rented two-bedroom cottage in Hebden Bridge (two siblings died in infancy)—but her brothers, Walter and Thomas, became two of the wealthiest men in the Calder Valley. Hughes's uncle Walt, whose eldest son died of pneumonia, developed a close relationship with his teenage nephew, whom he took on driving trips to Ireland and the Continent; he occasionally stuffed wads of cash into Ted's pocket.

Walter and Thomas Farrar fought in the First World War, while Edith left school at the age of thirteen to become a machinist at a local mill. She met William (Billy) Hughes when he was home on leave from the war in 1916, and they married in 1920. The family settled in Hebden Bridge in a row house by the railroad tracks, where Gerald was born; Olwyn followed eight years later. The family then moved to Mytholmroyd, where several other Farrar relatives were already living. Ted was born there on August 17,

1930, at 1 Aspinall Street in a second-floor bedroom overlooking a muck-filled lane.[11]

A few miles east of Hebden Bridge, the smaller village of Mytholmroyd lay at the base of the Calder Valley, surrounded by rolling green hills and high moorland that promised respite from the factory smog below. Hughes would later mythologize this area as Elmet, Britain's last Celtic kingdom, in his collection *Remains of Elmet*. Here, among the steep hills and shifting light, young Ted spent hours hunting and exploring with his older brother, Gerald. Together they scrambled up the footpaths to the imaginary grave of the "Ancient Briton" in Redacre Wood, slid down the steep packhorse slopes in winter, and listened to their echoes under the "long tunnel ceiling" of the nearby canal bridge. Ted's boyhood friend Donald Crossley remembered Ted's propensity for mischief: he put mice and frogs down girls' backs, threw rocks at the derelict Empress Foundry, and once tied Donald up to a tree for hours during a game of "Red Indian." Ted and Donald fished in the Rochdale Canal, just a few feet from Ted's house, with homemade nets made from old lace curtains. (They tried to keep the fish as pets in jam jars, but they always died.) Once Ted painted a skull and crossbones on the outside of his house and, upon completion, let out a booming laugh. That laugh, and the bravado of its timbre, astonished and delighted the neighborhood boys. The memory of it stayed with Donald all his life.[12] He recalled his friend's magnetism: "Ted had that great lock of black hair when he was younger—Errol Flynn he was, really. Smart looking lad. So we can understand that lots of women would fall for him. Even myself, I must admit—goodness knows what it was like for a woman; if you fell in love with Ted it were God help them, really. . . . if a room were full of people it was much more valuable when Ted was in that room."[13]

Hughes always remembered the Calder Valley as a childhood paradise, the Heaneyesque *omphalos* of his psycho-geography. He eventually purchased a home there in 1970 called Lumb Bank (now the Ted Hughes Arvon Centre). But his relationship to the area grew more complicated as he matured. He encouraged Donald's teenage daughter Ruth to get out of the Calder Valley and see the wider world. "I remember him telling me that if I was curious about something, I should get on a bus and go and see it first hand—get experience of it myself, even if my parents couldn't take me," Ruth said. "My overwhelming memories of him were of a very generous, caring and locally well-liked man, but who had a definite mysterious side."[14] Wilfrid Riley, the son of "Dick Straightup," a local character Hughes immortalized in *Lupercal*, remembered Ted as warm, "not at all standoffish," good company in the pub. But he seemed to have a different set of "morals" and "ways" that set him apart from the locals.[15] As much as Hughes's family and community drew him back to the Calder Valley, they prevented him from living freely and anonymously. In later years, after Plath's death, Hughes would turn to the west of Ireland, and Irish friends like Barrie Cooke and Seamus Heaney, for restoration and solace.

Gerald Hughes, ten years older than Ted, remembered the Depression years in Mytholmroyd as a "desperate period, which cannot be imagined by anyone who has not experienced it. . . . How we managed to exist on such a low income I do not know."[16] The textile industry that had been the area's main economy for centuries had collapsed, and the whole of the Calder Valley—decimated by horrific losses during the First World War—seemed to Hughes a graveyard. Nearly half the thirty thousand local men who had joined the Lancashire Fusiliers never came home. He captures the gloom in "First, Mills":

> The whole land was quietly drained.
> Everything became very quiet.
>
> Then the hills were requisitioned
> For gravemounds.
>
> The towns and the villages were sacked.[17]

Ted's father, Billy, was one of only seventeen regimental survivors of Gallipoli (a book in his shirt pocket had stopped a bullet). He was later awarded the Distinguished Conduct Medal at Ypres, where he rescued wounded men from no-man's land. In his poems, Hughes sometimes portrayed his father as a stoic, taciturn Yorkshireman, though Gerald remembered him "casually" telling war stories.[18] Contemporaries remembered Billy Hughes as talkative and gregarious. He was a legendary local footballer—Wilfrid Riley remembered him as "a great sportsman in his day, very well known about here."[19] He might have played professionally, but chose the steadier (and, at that time, better paying) route of work and family. He was traditional, and considered his son's literary achievements with a mixture of pride and skepticism. Wilfrid Riley remembered Billy talking about how he had grown up working with his hands and complaining that the new generation wasn't "producing something in a solid form." Referring to Ted's writing, Billy said, "I don't understand getting all this pay for such little effort after the way we worked."[20]

Gerald remembered that the family "ate lots of porridge" and the occasional rabbit he shot. Hunting was not for sport: it was a necessity. Gerald left school at fourteen to work at his uncle Walt's clothing factory. Walt had joined forces with a partner, John Sutcliffe, to found one of the most successful businesses in the area, while Edith supplanted the family's "sparse budget" by taking in extra sewing.[21] There was no plumbed bathroom or central heating at 1 Aspinall Street, but there was a large bathtub in the small kitchen. Ted and Gerald shared the attic room, with its skylight overlooking Scout Rock, a local landmark that exerted a strong pull on Hughes's imagination. The immense stone bulk of the Mount Zion Primitive Methodist Church, where the family worshipped, sat across the street. It blocked the sun and moon and provided Hughes with a perfect metaphor for Christianity's antagonistic relationship to nature. As a child in the 1930s, he longed to get up the valley and escape the pollution of the dark satanic mills below. The air grew clearer and quieter the higher he climbed. Up near Sugarloaf, the sounds of birds, sheep, and cows replaced lumbering trains and mill clatter.

When Ted was young, there were children's encyclopedias on the family bookshelf and not much else. But Edith had a literary bent—she loved Wordsworth and told elaborate stories to her children. Later, Ted would impress Sylvia with his ability to "spin a yarn" in the Irish tradition. He inherited, too, his mother's interest in the sixth sense. Her family believed that she had the "second sight": she had seen a cross burning in the sky on D-Day. Edith, whom Gerald described as selfless and "marvellously even-tempered," wrote poetry about the Yorkshire countryside, while Billy enjoyed reciting Longfellow's *Hiawatha*.[22] (Ted would later recite it to local tuberculosis patients.) Gerald remembered that his mother was "always keen to try and develop our artistic abilities."[23] When one of Ted's teachers told Edith of his writing ability, she bought him, he remembered, a "whole library—second hand—of classic poets."[24] She was nearly as ambitious for her talented son as Aurelia was for her daughter.

Billy Hughes had worked for his brother-in-law at the Sutcliffe-Farrar textile factory, but his hours were cut during the Depression. He then worked as a migrant joiner in Wales, coming home once a month to see his family. Though Edith's mother, sister, and brother all lived in Mytholmroyd, hers was a difficult life. As a child, Ted sometimes heard her weeping to herself as she sewed. In 1938, after carefully considering several local opportunities, the Hugheses bought a newsagent's shop in Mexborough, in southeast Yorkshire, with a family loan of £340.[25]

Mexborough—surrounded by mining pits and inhabited by colliers prone to drink and violence—was so polluted that the stars in the night sky were always obscured. (Ted was amazed by his first clear, star-filled night during a school trip to Switzerland.) Yet its location in "England's Ruhr Valley" meant that it had almost no unemployment during the late 1930s. It was home to twenty thousand people, most of whom worked in the coal, steel, and rail industries and had some disposable income to spend on candy, magazines, and tobacco. The Hughes children were never hungry, even during wartime rationing, when Billy Hughes bartered tobacco for meat. Poorer local boys envied Ted, who sat on his family's store counter sucking on candy and reading magazines while they delivered newspapers for his father.[26]

The move from Mytholmroyd to Mexborough shocked Ted's siblings. His older sister, Olwyn, cried for two weeks. Gerald had no intention of living in a place where the air still reeked of the emptied pits and old men spat black phlegm onto the streets. He headed south for Devon to become a gamekeeper and would eventually immigrate to Australia. Ted, just seven, was less troubled by the move. Boys' adventure magazines and cowboy films replaced hunting expeditions in the Calder Valley, though he soon found country retreats around Mexborough—the pastoral farmland near Old Denaby and the secluded private park of the Crookhill sanatorium, where he became close with the caretaker's family, the Wholeys. There, he would shoot, fish, or relax under a shady tree with a book. Edna Wholey, whom he courted in the 1940s, remembered idyllic summer days at Crookhill spent with her head in Ted's lap as he read to her from Greek translations.[27]

Edith Hughes was determined to send her gifted son and daughter to Mexborough Grammar School, which charged a modest fee and catered to the area's brighter pupils. There, Ted thrived under the tutelage of two English teachers, Pauline Mayne and John Fisher, who taught him about poetry and tutored him for the Cambridge exams. Fisher's influence was as important to Hughes as Crockett's was to Plath—perhaps more, as Ted was a rather lazy student who did his best work for teachers he liked. Hughes's biographer Steve Ely described Fisher, an ex-Navy man, as "quirky, unconventional . . . a non-conformist" who often wore a "bohemian" turtleneck instead of the usual schoolteacher's jacket and tie. Fisher wore his hair in "a floppy fringe that frequently fell across his forehead," which lent him an air of "Byronic frisson"—a look Hughes made his own.[28] On Sunday evenings, Ted and Olwyn often visited the Fishers, with whom they discussed art and literature and listened to Beethoven, much as Plath did with the Crocketts. As a teenager, Hughes took up Fisher's aesthetic obsessions—"Shakespeare, Yeats, Beethoven, Hopkins, the Bible, mythology, the war poets."[29] It was Fisher who presented Hughes with Robert Graves's *The White Goddess*, which, Hughes later told Graves, became "the chief holy book of my conscience" before he went up to Cambridge.[30]

Ted, who had been obsessed with Henry Williamson's *Tarka the Otter* as a boy, had also been "swallowed alive by Yeats"; discovering *The Wander-*

ings of Oisin in the Mexborough school library had been something akin, he said, to "trauma"—such was the force of the revelation. "From that point, my animal kingdom, the natural world, the world of folktales and myth, and poetry, became a single thing—and Yeats was my model."[31] He eventually learned all of Yeats's poems by heart. D. H. Lawrence was Hughes's other "holy" writer in his teens. "His writings coloured a whole period of my life," Hughes recalled.[32] Lawrence's poem "Glory" left a foundational mark on some of Hughes's most famous animal poems, "The Hawk in the Rain," "Hawk Roosting," and "The Jaguar":

> Most of his time, the tiger pads and slouches in a burning peace.
> And the small hawk high up turns round on the slow pivot of peace.
> Peace comes from behind the sun, with the peregrine falcon, and the
>   owl.
> Yet all of these drink blood.[33]

Ted liked to present himself as a maverick, but at Mexborough he became a school proctor and sub-editor, along with Olwyn, of the school literary magazine, *The Don and Dearne*, where he published his work from 1946 to 1950. He also wrote, cast, and directed the annual Christmas revue in 1948, which featured the kind of "Pythonesque" humor that Fisher favored.[34] Hughes's high school record shows, if not a stellar performance like Plath's, a concentrated effort to succeed where it mattered most. Like Sylvia, he valued success.

After Gerald left home, Ted "came under the influence," as he put it, of his older sister—precocious and literary, with a "forceful personality."[35] Olwyn gave him Jung's *Psychological Types*, which, like *The White Goddess*, deeply influenced his burgeoning aesthetic. From Jung, Hughes learned, as he later told a critic, "that most neuroses, of individuals and of our cultures," were the result of "loss of contact" with the "primitive human animal."[36] He later owned seventeen volumes of Jung.

Between Olwyn's influence and his teachers' prodding, Ted grew "totally confident" that he would become a poet.[37] By high school he had devoured the work of Lawrence and could recite long stretches of Shakespeare, Kipling, Yeats, Longfellow, Shelley, Eliot, Thomas, and Hopkins by heart. He filled teenage exercise notebooks with Irish folklore, proverbs, and myth ("If a warrior drinks the milk of a fairy woman he is invulnerable") and wrote, like the young Sylvia, a considerable amount about fairies.[38] He was writing his own poetry too, "long lolloping Kiplingesque sagas." When his teacher Pauline Mayne singled out his description of a gun "breaking in the cold 'with frost-chilled snap,'" Hughes thought, "well, if that's poetry that's the way I think so I can give you no end of it."[39] He became known as the school poet; he and another friend called themselves "the intelligentsia."[40]

Despite the headmaster's skepticism, Mr. Fisher decided to put Hughes up for a spot at Cambridge in 1948. Hughes passed the Cambridge entrance exams, but Fisher included a book of Ted's poems with his Pembroke College application for good measure. Hughes always felt that his poems tipped the balance, and credited Fisher with his admission to Cambridge. Recent scholarship has debunked this myth: Ted had to earn his place at Cambridge just like everyone else.

Hughes spent the next two years, October 1949 to October 1951, fulfilling his national service as a Royal Air Force ground wireless mechanic at a remote radar station in Patrington, East Yorkshire. The work was "undemanding, solitary, often nocturnal," and left him with many hours to read.[41] Little action came to Patrington: one night Hughes panicked after he heard what he thought was the sound of a nuclear bomb exploding over the radio, later to learn it was the sound of sheep being sheared. He wrote short stories and an early Gravesian poem, "Song," which he dedicated to a young local woman who remembered him as "moody," "a thinker."[42] (He signed it "Disciple of the Daemonic.") He wrote the poem before he read Graves's *The White Goddess* and before, as he later told a friend, "I stepped into the actual psychological space of contemporary literature, smogged as that is by the critical exhalations and toxic smokestacks and power stations of Academe. . . . It is the one song I sang in Arcadia."[43] He devoured Shakespeare, but also Yeats and Irish folklore. His sense of his Celtic roots and identity deepened in Patrington, where he became close friends with three young servicemen from Ireland and Scotland.

> The fact that my father's father, whom I never knew, was Irish, had never figured in the family mythology. . . . However, once out of Yorkshire I found myself drawn to Scots and Irish, but particularly to Irish people. . . . When after National Service I moved to Cambridge University, and found myself a "guest" of a people that were every bit as strange to me as they were to any Irish or Scotsman, I immediately, the first day, attached myself to an Irishman [Terence McCaughey].[44]

As the critic James Underwood has noted, Hughes arrived at Pembroke College, Cambridge, in October 1951 "already resistant to what he found there"—and willing to challenge the very foundations of the English literary establishment.[45]

IN FEBRUARY 1952, Ted described Cambridge to Olwyn as at turns "wonderful" and a ditch "where all the frogs have died."[46] He had already decided to become a poet, even if it meant poverty, and experienced none of the torturous, gendered conflicts that made Plath doubt her literary ambition. Writing was holy discipline to him, just as it was to Plath, yet he cared little about his future prosperity. Nor did he make much attempt, unlike Plath, to publish his poetry at Cambridge. When *Granta* finally published his poem "The Little Boys and the Seasons" in June 1954—his first acceptance—he used a pseudonym, Daniel Hearing. He published "Song of the Sorry Lovers" that same month in *Chequer* under another pseudonym, Peter Crew.[47] He did not have, as his friend Daniel Huws put it, "American expectations."[48]

While other Cambridge undergraduates imitated Sebastian Flyte from *Brideshead Revisited*, Ted loathed flashiness. Contemporaries like Brian Cox, who later founded the influential literary journal *Critical Quarterly*, remembered him as tall and "craggily handsome." (Anne Sexton would later call him "Ted Huge.") He wore gray flannel trousers and a black corduroy jacket, or, in inclement weather, his uncle's World War I leather jacket. Cox said he "radiated an extraordinary dynamism."[49] He was already adept at the Ouija board, and developed a college reputation for his forays into the occult. Jean Gooder, who was close to Ted's then girlfriend Shirley, remembered him as a "very striking person": "You'd notice him if you walked into a room. He had an immense capacity for being still. He was just immensely intelligent. . . . a man who thought for himself. He was absolutely uninfluenced by fashion, or the current Cambridge scene. In that sense, Sylvia was a black-and-white contrast. She wanted to suss out the entire map, and read her way through it. He didn't give a damn what the map was. He was creating his own."[50]

Christopher Levenson similarly recalled, "Like almost everyone else I found Ted broodingly impressive, physically overpowering. . . . someone one could easily see as Heathcliff."[51] Christopher's Downing College room was next to Luke Myers's, and he often heard Luke, Ted, Huws, Danny Weissbort, and a few others bellowing out Irish ballads. Patrons at the Mill or Anchor pubs along the banks of the Cam would have heard much the same around closing time, led by Terence McCaughey.[52] No one had any idea, of course, that they were in the company of the future poet laureate of England, the man to whom Prince Charles would one day create a shrine at Highgrove.[53]

Though Hughes suffered trauma after the suicides of Plath and his lover Assia Wevill, and the death of his daughter Shura, the blackness never swallowed him. He had, as Cox put it, "Enormous potency."[54] Still, as his friend Helder Macedo remembered, "There was something dark about Ted."[55] His life, as his biographer Jonathan Bate noted, was hardly less scandalous than Lord Byron's. Huws, one of Ted's closest friends, understood how the dark legend took hold. "Ted was given to wild and fantastic and exaggerated talk and action—his friends expected it of him. A colouring of cruelty might at times be part of it. He could use it to shock people. And his manner was naturally blunt. But in this there was already a large element of acting a part, as though he wished to conceal his tender side."[56] Another Cambridge friend, D. D. Bradley, agreed that Ted "delighted to play Heathcliff" and that his speech was "gnomic . . . designed to startle."[57]

Terence McCaughey remembered evenings spent listening to Beethoven in Ted's Pembroke room, watching Buster Keaton and Marx Brothers movies, or sitting outside in the dusk while Ted hooted at owls. Ted, a year before his death, wrote to Terence that at Cambridge he'd been "going through some curiously controlled nervous breakdown. . . . Without you, I doubt if could have lasted the first year out."[58] Than Minton, who suffered anti-Semitism at Cambridge, found in Ted a "deeply human" friend who was outraged by such slights.[59] Than felt he owed his Cambridge degree—and hence his future medical career—to Hughes: after a wild party, Ted roused him from his hangover and persuaded him to show up for his final biochemistry exam.

Luke Myers, an American, became one of Ted's best friends at Cambridge. They met through a mutual friend, James Affleck, who edited *Chequer*, and were soon exchanging poems. The first (and worst) poem that Luke remembered receiving from Hughes was "Money, My Enemy." Later, he wondered how the author of such verse could be swept away by (in his opinion) a high-maintenance American woman.[60]

Ted's Pembroke College room, above the College Library, was, as he described it, full of medieval "worm-eaten" beams, crannies, and deep recesses. There was a sloping roof, windows facing out over busy Trumpington Street, and an imposing oak fireplace in which he sometimes roasted raw meat. He painted giant leopards in "black, yellow, and green, big as alsations [*sic*]" on one wall, a "great-headed stopping hawk, bison and horses" on the other. (His college senior tutor made him repaint the walls white.) Beethoven's death mask hung on a beam; Ted once played Beethoven's pieces, loudly and in chronological order, from eleven p.m. until five a.m. on his gramophone. There was a settee and chairs, but visitors preferred the floor. His desk was covered with papers and was therefore "inaccessible." He used candles rather than electric light. "The mice were so plentiful that I grew tired of trapping them," he wrote Plath in 1956.[61]

The room was down a long hallway, cut off from the rest of the college—a perfect place for parties. Ted later boasted to Sylvia that he'd had so many parties during his undergraduate years that empty bottles filled "half the corridor" outside of his room. Even English faculty dons attended his parties, he said, playing "bawdy songs" on his hired piano.[62] Hughes told Plath these "parties were never interrupted until the police complained of the bottles coming out of the windows and the people hanging by their hands which happened once." (One drunken visitor had scaled the windows to enter.) The dons, Hughes felt, were Cambridge's true eccentrics—F. R. Leavis, reciting to himself on his bicycle, and George Rylands, "the only man left alive who slept with Rupert Brooke."[63] But he felt only scorn for the grammar school boys who tried to cultivate their eccentricities. In a long letter to Sylvia in early October 1956, he described different types of Cambridge men with anthropological precision.[64] "The whole of Cambridge was regarded as a big joke," Huws recalled.[65] They tried to avoid anyone wearing a blazer and tie.

Harold Bloom, who later became the preeminent literary critic in America, sometimes joined Hughes and his friends at the Anchor pub. The discussions, remembered Iko Meshoulam, were "tremendously earnest." ("These boys could drink 12 Guinness without moving an eyelash.")[66] Harold impressed everyone with his encyclopedic knowledge of English literature, though Ted did not much care for him. Hughes ignored his studies to while away hours at the Anchor talking politics and philosophy; Bloom lectured him about becoming more organized, and less lazy.[67] The men were, Luke recalled, "temperamentally incompatible" but equally adept at identifying obscure lines of verse. One night, over pints, someone recited a poem that stumped even Bloom. "That's Meredith," Hughes answered casually. "One of his sonnets."[68]

Although Hughes read English during his first two years at Cambridge—tutored by the sympathetic and approachable Matthew Hodgart, who encouraged his interest in James Joyce and Irish ballads—he was appalled by what he considered the excoriating, life-denying analysis practiced by Leavis and his ilk. Hughes's frustration was not misplaced: the joke then was that the point of the Cambridge English Tripos was to allow students to understand "The Waste Land." Leavis did not endorse the kind of bardic, Gravesian approach to literature that Hughes and his friends valued. And though Leavis loved D. H. Lawrence, he excoriated the Bloomsbury writers. Christopher Levenson remembered, "T. S. Eliot he termed 'a male spinster' while at times he would simply say 'Well, I mean, Virginia Woolf . . .' whereupon the class would join in the sneer." A friend told Levenson he was the only student he ever heard ask Leavis a question that dared to imply that "a different interpretation was possible."[69]

After a long night spent writing a literary essay during his second year,

Hughes famously dreamed that a fox put a bloody paw on his paper and said, "Stop this—you are destroying us."[70] The dream inspired him to switch his course of studies, in his third year, from English to archaeology and anthropology. (Luke made the same decision.) It also inspired one of Hughes's most famous poems, "The Thought-Fox":

> Across clearings, an eye,
> A widening deepening greenness,
> Brilliantly, concentratedly,
> Coming about its own business
>
> Till, with a sudden sharp hot stink of fox
> It enters the dark hole of the head.
> The window is starless still; the clock ticks,
> The page is printed.[71]

Hughes later told the critic Keith Sagar, "I connected the fox's commands to my own ideas about Eng. Lit., & the effect of the Cambridge blend of pseudo-critical terminology & social rancour on creative spirit & from that moment abandoned my efforts to adapt myself. . . . it seemed to me not only a foolish game, but deeply destructive of myself."[72] Plath would reach a similar conclusion. As she wrote to her mother in March 1956, "I am going to revolt from this critical world (which can dry one's blood, if one isn't careful: I see it in all the women around me). . . . I fly to the saintly, religious, intuitive."[73]

Hughes graduated from Cambridge in 1954 with a third-class degree—a "Gentleman's C." He had submitted a satirical poetry collection in partial fulfillment of his degree, titled, "The ear-witness account of a poetry-reading in Throttle College, before the small poets grew up into infinitesimal critics." It bears heavy traces of Jung. The key to sanity, Hughes argued throughout the collection, was getting back in touch with our primitive instinct; we must "meet the beast halfway" lest we be "devoured" by our neuroses.[74]

Hughes's Cambridge degree could have led to a professional career in education, publishing, or journalism. Instead, he worked at a steel factory as a night security guard and washed dishes at the London Zoo. He fantasized about working on a North Sea trawler but knew his family expected more. "I shall have to get a proper respectable job, because if I don't Ma will just worry herself away," he wrote to Gerald in 1954.[75] During the summer of 1955, he traveled to Paris and dabbled in the Left Bank life, writing poetry in cafés and subsisting cheaply on wine, baguettes, and cheese. Like Plath, he dreamed of traveling and writing his way through Europe, though applying for grants and fellowships would not have occurred to him. It was not until he met Sylvia, who acted as his agent, that he made a reputation outside of Cambridge. Without her managerial zeal, as he later told Aurelia, he would have been little more than a minor poet.

By the autumn of 1955 Ted was living at Daniel Huws's father's flat at 18 Rugby Street (where Dylan Thomas had once slept) in London's Bloomsbury district. Hughes's friend Philip Hobsbaum, who had published Hughes's poem "The Woman with Such High Heels She Looked Dangerous" in *delta*, eventually secured him a job reading novels at London's Pinewood Studios for a film company, J. Arthur Rank. Hughes was supposed to write up synopses of the novels he thought would make good films, but he worried that the potboilers were contaminating his creative impulses. He told Terence McCaughey, "Everybody there is . . . as far up everybody else's arse as they can get." He quit in the spring of 1956, admitting to Terence, "I'm not very well equipped really to live outside a college."[76] He came up to Cambridge on weekends and stayed at Queens' College with his friend Michael Boddy or camped on the Saint Botolph's rectory lawn. He sometimes dropped in on Hobsbaum's London Group, which met at Philip's bedsit off the Edgware Road. Philip remembered Ted's booming renditions of "Lord Randall, My Son," and his recitations of Gerard Manley Hopkins. "Ted was the lyric poet par excellence and we all knew how good he was."[77] By this time, Hughes had written "The Thought-Fox," though he did not attempt to publish it until he met Plath.

Hughes would eventually apply for a postgraduate diploma in education, but he did not want a "proper" job that would interfere with his writing. He made serious plans to start a mink farm in Yorkshire and tried to lure Gerald back to England with promises of mink fortunes. Gerald was unswayed, and Ted applied for a visa to join his brother in Australia.[78]

Bert Wyatt-Brown came to Cambridge from America, like Plath, in the fall of 1955 to read English. Suitcases in tow, he found his way to the Saint Botolph's rectory, where his childhood friend Luke Myers had talked Mrs. Hitchcock, the former rector's widow, into renting him a broom closet.[79] Bert found a "band of poets" in the back garden smoking Gauloises and Woodbines, dressed in the "workingman's style" of grays, blacks, and browns. He joined them, a bit intimidated, and passed around his American Marlboros; the friendship was sealed. Getting to know this group would prove "intoxicating"—literally and figuratively.[80]

By the time Sylvia arrived in Cambridge in the fall of 1955, Ted, Bert, Luke, Joe Lyde, Daniel Huws, Danny Weissbort, Than Minton, and David Ross formed a loose, literary "gang" based around the Saint Botolph's rectory—"a gang around Ted in many ways," as David remembered. Not all of them lived at the rectory, but it was, in a sense, their spiritual home. The Anchor and Mill pubs were their other gathering places. Philip Hobsbaum, who presided over a rival literary faction, called them a "rough crowd": "there were poets such as [Peter] Redgrove and myself who wore suits and ties, and poets such as Hughes and his associates who, to put it mildly, did not."[81] (Daniel Huws countered that he had no interest in conversing with Philip, who was an ardent Leavisite. "He was just too earnest . . . deadly serious.")[82] During Hughes's second year at Pembroke, Redgrove invited him to one of a series of poetry readings that he and Hobsbaum had set up. Hughes based his farcical "Throttle College" poem on this experience. "He was so horrified," Huws said. "There's nothing Ted would have regarded more absurd than undergraduates reading each other's poems."[83] The Botolphians, as Bert called them, shared his antipathy. When a swan that the Chinese government had presented to the university disappeared, Jean Gooder recalled, "We knew very well that it was roasted in the vicarage garden. That was such an embarrassment to the university. But that was the kind of absolute daredevilry—recklessness—that they could get up to. They were anarchic."[84]

If the weather was warm, the Botolphians would gather in the garden and read aloud from whatever book was at hand: Michael Boddy remembered Orwell, Joyce, Rimbaud, Dylan Thomas, Blake, Hemingway, Graves, Salinger, and Ovid. When Ted wasn't drawing up horoscopes, he was writing poetry, or commenting on his friends' work. Sometimes Ted took Michael to the university library and pointed out the "occult books" that interested him; he taught Michael "about astrology and how to cast horoscopes." At night there was hypnotism, more reading aloud, and drink. Iko Meshoulam thought "Ted believed he had powers." His presence was so powerful that others thought he had powers, too.[85] Ted was generally reserved, but he relished the stray shocking phrase. He joked with Michael that his passion for literature was erotic, telling him about a young woman with whom he had "a root" at the Brontë Parsonage. They had started against a glass case holding memorabilia and then, "with increased confidence," moved to Emily Brontë's death couch. He told Michael, who thought Ted was "embellishing," that he hoped to do the same in the Jane Austen museum. Hughes also joked that he got an erection every time he walked into the Cambridge University library.[86]

Friends remembered that Ted could switch easily from "'bloke' to 'bard.'"[87] Michael remembered his "tremulous expressive tone when reading" and was surprised to learn that Hughes recorded himself reading Shakespeare in order to perfect his own reading technique.[88] Ted always considered Michael's poems with "care" and diligence—an observation many of Ted's friends shared. "He was very good at that—responding," Peter Redgrove said.[89] But there was another side. When Michael spent the night at 18 Rugby Street in 1956, he remembered Ted settling into his room to write, "A bit like a resting volcano, collecting itself for a blow."[90]

———————

THE IDEA TO START a new literary magazine came to the Botolphians in 1955 as they drank wine in Huws's Peterhouse College room, awaiting news of a disciplinary proceeding involving a young woman caught in Daniel's bed. He was innocent—he had been in London when a friend had parked his girlfriend in his vacant room—but the details did not much matter to those in charge. Banished from Peterhouse, the woman would spend the night with Hughes in his tent on the Saint Botolph's lawn.

The young men were tired of Cambridge's Victorian prohibitions. There were penalties for breaking curfew, forgetting to wear one's subfusc gown, or entertaining women in college rooms—particularly galling to men who had already spent two years fulfilling their national service. Cambridge was then, as Daniel remembered, "like a monastery."[91] Following the Peterhouse incident, the young woman's boyfriend was expelled, Daniel and David Ross were suspended, Luke was told to leave his shed at the Rectory, and Ted was forbidden from setting foot within a three-mile radius of Great Saint Mary's University Church—a decree he promptly ignored. (Luke simply moved from the rectory chicken coop to the rectory dining room.) They wanted to rebel without getting into more trouble, but in those days, subversive pamphlets could get one expelled, or "sent down"—as Mark Boxer, the editor of *Granta*, had been, for publishing a poem the university deemed blasphemous. (Boxer staged a mock funeral procession on the day he left, complete with a hired hearse, coffin, and eulogies.) But Cambridge's conservatism gave them something to rebel against, and in that way, it shaped them. Jean Gooder remembered, "It was a terrible place, Cambridge, then, except there were very extraordinary things happening, and very brilliant people."[92]

None of Cambridge's literary magazines—*Chequer*, *Granta*, or *delta*—appealed to the Botolphians, who felt that a new magazine would provide a platform for *their* kind of poetry. They shared Christopher Levenson's sentiment that *Granta*, the university's oldest literary magazine, "represented . . . the whole ethos of flowered waistcoats, effeminancy and extravagant living."[93] Peter Redgrove, who felt *Granta* was "very snooty and very exclusive," decided to start his own literary magazine, *delta*, whose editorship Philip Hobsbaum eventually passed on to Levenson.[94] But *delta*, as Levenson said, "took itself very seriously, indeed solemnly," as if protesting the extravagance of *Granta*.[95] The Botolphians solidified plans for their own new literary venture on a trip to the East Anglian coast in January 1956.[96] "In a freezing cottage belonging to David Ross's parents," wrote Bert, "we ate fish and chips wrapped in newspaper, drank the local brew, and planned a new chapter in the history of English literature."[97]

This was a time when Movement poets such as Donald Davie, Elizabeth Jennings, John Wain, Philip Larkin, and Kingsley Amis dominated the postwar British poetry scene. Luke would later describe the Movement as "an expression of logic rather than myth, 'classical,' and esteemed principally as an instrument of stability."[98] Hughes felt similarly. He associated Movement poems with "the post-war mood of having had enough":

> enough rhetoric, enough overwhelming push of any kind, enough of the
> dark gods, enough of the id, enough of the Angelic powers and the heroic
> efforts to make new worlds. They'd seen it all turn into death camps and
> atomic bombs. All they wanted was to get back into civvies and get home
> to the wife and kids and for the rest of their lives not a thing was going
> to interfere with a nice cigarette and a view of the park. . . . Now I came
> a bit later. I hadn't had enough. I was all for opening negotiations with
> whatever happened to be out there.[99]

Bert remembered many conversations at the Saint Botolph's rectory about the "crabbed and moribund" Movement poetry.[100] Indeed, Ted wrote to Olwyn in 1956 about the "meanness and deadness of almost all modern English verse—with which I feel not the slightest affinity."[101] English poetry after Auden, he felt, had abandoned "the whole historical exploration into spirit life . . . religion, myth, vision" and had embraced in its place "pedantic, frivolous, tea-and-biscuits Oxford High Anglicanism . . . which seems to me closer to the pride, pomp and circumstance of the High Table than to any altar of uncut stones."[102]

The Botolphians' contempt for the Movement was a manifestation of their obsession with Graves's *The White Goddess*. Hughes said he "soaked the book up" during his three years at Cambridge and recalled his "slight resentment to find him [Graves] taking possession of what I considered to be my secret patch."[103] It became a talismanic text for Ted, Daniel, and Luke, who carried *The White Goddess* "in their hands as if it were their version of Holy Scriptures," Bert remembered.[104] Graves believed that the source of the poet's inspiration was a seductive but ultimately dangerous muse, the White Goddess, and that poetry was "magically potent in the ancient sense."[105] Authentic poets were acolytes to this cruel muse, and the more one gave in service to the White Goddess, the larger the literary return. Poems were, in effect, offerings, though true devotion required complete sacrifice: "she will gladly give him her love, but only at one price: his life. She will exact her payment punctually and bloodily."[106] Graves's themes of sacrifice, martyrdom, and primitive ritual resonated with the Boltophians' Romantic understanding of the poet's spiritual function. Hughes would have gleaned similar ideas from James Frazer's *The Golden Bough*, which he read and annotated at Cambridge.

Graves thought women were meant to be muses, not writers: "Woman is not a poet: she is either a Muse or she is nothing."[107] Plath was destined to become, for Hughes, the human embodiment of the White Goddess—a role she played happily for a time, but which she eventually chafed against.[108] Yet Graves's influence on Plath, too, should not be underestimated. According to Luke, he and Ted were in the process of "rereading" the book when Sylvia came into their lives.[109] Daniel also remembered Sylvia's interest in the book. Everyone's fascination with Graves, Yeats, and Lawrence, Daniel said, was "taken for granted."[110] In a July 1957 journal entry, Plath contemplated inventing a heroine for her novel who is "a bitch: she is the white goddess. Make her a statement of the generation."[111] Many of Plath's later poems show Graves's influence—some ironically.[112]

But in the winter of 1956, Plath's fashionable verse was very much a product of the New Critical aesthetic, full of the symmetry and preciousness that so riled the Botolphians. Ted and his friends wanted to resurrect the exuberant bombast of Thomas, the apocalyptic intensity of late Yeats, the ritualistic wisdom of Graves, the passion of Lawrence. Plath's poem "Three Caryatids Without a Portico," in the Winter 1956 issue of *Chequer*—studded with words like "tranquil," "regal," "serenity," and "grace"—was an easy target:

> In this tercet of torsos, breast and thigh
> slope with the Greek serenity
> of tranquil plaster;
>
> each body forms a virgin vase,
> while all raise high with regal grace
> aristocratic heads; . . .[113]

"Cruel laughter greeted a reading of her work," wrote Bert, who remembered the poets gathering in Luke's room that winter to dissect the latest issue of *Chequer*. "We deplored her efforts as trivial and immature. After all, what women could ever write lasting poetry? . . . How hopelessly misguided and wrong we were."[114] Luke remembered that Ted stayed silent during the discussion. In his *Birthday Letters* poem "Caryatids (2)," Hughes remembered how they "had heard / Of the dance of your blond veils, your flaring gestures,

/ Your misfit self-display. More to reach you / Than to reproach you [. . .] we concocted / An attack, a dismemberment, laughing."[115] Hughes later wrote that he found Plath's poem "thin and brittle, the lines cold."[116]

Bert knew Sylvia through his girlfriend Jane Baltzell, and "feebly defended" her "braininess, striking good looks, and lively personality" to the Botolphians. But the others could hardly contain their glee as they delivered a "scathing appraisal" of Plath's genteel verse. Luke later called Sylvia a "flashy target" whose poems they disapproved of "in spite of their being well made, or rather partly because of it. Her ambition shined through them, or so we thought, and we also thought it was peculation to write poetry, which should come down on the poet from somewhere, out of sheer will."[117] Hughes wrote about the male condescension Plath experienced at Cambridge in his *Birthday Letters* poem "God Help the Wolf After Whom the Dogs Do Not Bark":

> The Colleges lifted their heads. It did seem
> You disturbed something just perfected
> . . . And as if
> Reporting some felony to the police
> They let you know that you were not John Donne.
> . . . .
> Nobody wanted your dance,
> Nobody wanted your strange glitter . . .[118]

Sylvia had been fêted for her writing at Smith, but her American accolades held little currency among the Botolphians. Bert remembered that they "grumbled ceaselessly how she was demeaning the poetic profession by publishing in *The New Yorker*, *Ladies' Home Journal*, *Mademoiselle*, and other middle-brow and popular outlets."[119] The playwright Michael Frayn, who worked on the Cambridge *Varsity* editorial team, recalled her approaching him confidently and asking for assignments. "She was a fantastic chatterer. She talked very fast and very continuously. She was a very bright person." He "warmed to her."[120] She also asked for an introduction to Ben Nash, who had a literary reputation as well as "a formidable reputation as a seducer of women." Sylvia seemed "aware of this." Michael took her to Ben's room at King's College, but he was out. Sylvia met Ben eventually, and, according to Michael, they became romantically involved.[121] (Sylvia's calendars suggest as much.) At one point, Sylvia lectured Michael and some other young men about how they could support themselves by writing for American magazines like *Mademoiselle*. They found her advice well intentioned but hilarious.[122]

Jane shared the men's "Botolph" attitude, claiming that Sylvia seemed overly preoccupied with "commercial success." She was so good at "marketing," Jane felt, that Ted would never have become a successful poet without Sylvia's help. But Sylvia did not seem, to Jane, interested in "the mystery and mysticism" that was "the primary thing" for the male poets in the group.[123] Daniel put it more bluntly. "Sylvia wrote to publish. Ted didn't. . . . She had what I think of as American self-publicity. You noticed it."[124] Hughes's letters suggest he was hardly ambivalent about success, but he cultivated an air of indifference. Plath's ambition was held against her.

Bert was the initial link between Sylvia and Ted.[125] He sold Sylvia her copy of the *Saint Botolph's Review* on February 25, 1956, from the corner of King's Parade and Silver Street. (He could hardly believe he had passed off seventy-five copies by then, "some to clergymen misled by the title.")[126] Michael Boddy remembered that he and his friends "fanned out" to sell copies, hawking it at the women's colleges in hopes of luring them to the launch party they had planned that night. He recalled how, on that cold, foggy day, a Heathcliffian Hughes would "loom out of the gloom" to ask a harried passerby for a shilling. "Invariably the apprehensive punter would pull out a shilling to get away, and Ted would give him a copy of the Review."[127] When Sylvia saw Bert hawking the pamphlet, she approached him; he promised she would like the poetry inside. She bought a copy for one shilling and six pence (the print run had been underwritten by David Ross's father) and dashed back to Whitstead on her bicycle.

Bert was "still shivering" in the cold February dusk outside the Anchor pub when Sylvia returned to speak to him, flushed and pedaling "furiously."[128] Did he know Ted Hughes, author of "Fallgrief's Girl-Friends," and E. Luke Myers, who had written "Sestina of the Norse Seaman"?[129] He did, and he invited her to meet them herself at the magazine's launch party that night. As it turned out, Hamish Stewart, a Canadian at Queens', had already invited her to the party as his date.

By evening, a strong, chilly wind was blowing through Cambridge. Sylvia, back at Whitstead, was excited and rattled by the poems she had just read in the *Saint Botolph's Review*. Hughes, Myers, Huws, Weissbort, and Ross had all written poems that resonated more deeply with her aspiring creative vision than the neat, well-mannered verse she was then writing. Hughes's "Fallgrief's Girl-Friends" had especially impressed her:

> . . . he meant to stand naked
> Awake in the pitch dark where the animal runs,
> Where the insects couple as they murder each other,
> Where the fish outwait the water.[130]

Hughes's poem "Secretary" probably also struck her, with its portrait of a woman afraid of her sexuality, trapped in a loveless life of servitude (at night she "lies with buttocks tight"), as reminiscent of the stories she'd written about lonely, single women in high school.[131]

Reading Hughes's and Myers's poems in the *Saint Botolph's Review* was a moment of reawakening for Plath, a return to the swaggering poetic instincts of her adolescence—to poems like "Sea Symphony," "I Have Found the Perfect World," and "I Am an American." This poetry was unadorned, unabashed, slightly savage—"vital," as she might have put it. She felt something was missing from her own verse, and that the Saint Botolph poets had found it. In her journal she fixated not on Ted but on Luke. She compared his technique to "an athlete, running, using all the divine flexions of his muscles in the act" and predicted that he would "be great, greater than anyone of my generation whom I've read yet." Later, she predicted the same for Ted. But it was Luke who drew her to the party, Luke she would approach first. She called his poems "tight and packed and supple and blazing." *This* was how she wanted to write: "until I make something tight and riding over the limits of sweet sestinas and sonnets . . . they can ignore me." She was right: Christopher Levenson remembered thinking that her verse "displayed great technical virtuosity but was brittle, not 'serious' enough."[132] Sylvia wrote how these poets' "magnificent" writing made her own poems seem superficial, filled with "glib, smug littleness"—though she reminded herself that this diminutive tendency was "not me. Not wholly." She knew that if she wanted to be taken seriously at Cambridge, she would have to abandon her poetry's well-wrought decorum.[133]

———

ON FEBRUARY 25, 1956—in the hours before she read the *Saint Botolph's Review*—Sylvia saw a university psychiatrist, Dr. Davy, whom she liked and thought fatherly. Her decision to seek psychiatric treatment spoke to the seriousness of her growing depression. She felt unburdened as she told Dr. Davy about her "past." Sitting with him, she realized how few adults she really knew at Cambridge. She had no mentors like George Gibian or Mary Ellen Chase, no family friends like the Aldriches or the Cantors, and no one like Mrs. Prouty with a vested interest in her writing. "I am going to talk to this Dr. Davy again in a couple of weeks," she wrote Aurelia, "because he is the first <u>adult</u> I've spoken with in Cambridge, and it is an immense relief to get away from these intense adolescent personal relationships."[134] Just knowing he was there made her feel better. Still, she was at a very low point in the hours before her life changed. To Aurelia she wrote,

Sylvia Plath and Dick Norton at the Yale Junior Prom, March 9, 1951. Above this photo in her scrapbook, Plath wrote, "A photo of the very young, very gay collegiates after a rather exhilarating evening."

Sylvia Plath with the Mayo children, Joanne, Freddie, and Pinny, on the North Shore of Massachusetts, summer 1951

Sylvia Plath sunbathing on the North Shore of Massachusetts, summer 1951

The Mayo mansion, Swampscott, Massachusetts. Plath took this photo and pasted it in her scrapbook. She lived on the top floor, with her own balcony, during the summer of 1951.

Sylvia Plath, Marblehead, Massachusetts, July 1951

Sylvia Plath and her "psychic brother," Perry Norton, at Yale, spring 1953

Sylvia Plath and Myron Lotz, spring 1953

Sylvia Plath interviewing Elizabeth Bowen, May 1953

Sylvia Plath at a *Mademoiselle* dance at the St. Regis Hotel, New York City, June 1953. Plath later mocked this photo, which appeared in the August edition of *Mademoiselle*, in *The Bell Jar*.

McLean Hospital, Belmont, Massachusetts

Dr. Ruth Beuscher, late 1950s

Sylvia Plath, Northampton, Massachusetts, 1954

Sylvia Plath with her mother and brother, Christmas, 1953. Plath was still a patient at McLean Hospital when this photograph was taken. She pasted it in her scrapbook, along with a Christmas card from McLean, and provided a caption: "1953—fall—a time of darkness, despair, disillusion as black only as the human mind can be—symbolic death, and numb shock—psychic regeneration—McLean Christmas and memory of mental alma mater from which, at last, I graduated 'summa.'"

Sylvia Plath at Chatham, Cape Cod, July 1954

Sylvia Plath and
Gordon Lameyer,
Chatham, Cape Cod,
July 1954

Sylvia Plath in her Wellesley
backyard, c. 1954–55

Sylvia Plath's room at Lawrence House, Smith College, April 1955, where she typed more than fifty poems for her poetry tutorial with Alfred Fisher

Sylvia Plath interviewing Marianne Moore, April 15, 1955, at the Glascock Poetry Contest, Mount Holyoke College

Warren and Sylvia Plath, Wellesley, Massachusetts, 1955

Newnham College, Cambridge

Whitstead, where Plath lived at Cambridge. Ted Hughes and Luke Myers threw stones at her top-floor, four-paneled window to get her attention.

VARSITY — Saturday, May 26th, 1956

Sylvia Plath tours the stores and forecasts
MAY WEEK FASHIONS

WITH May Week just around the corner like some fair Country of Cockaigne — but barely visible through the present smog of Tripos exams—we set out to discover what the well-dressed Newnhamite or Girtonian might wear for punting, cocktails and balls.

From large department stores to small specialty shops, Cambridge offers a fine, colourful selection of spring fashions which should enable our Cambridge undergraduates to rival the most chic and charming of imported London models.

We chose a different Cambridge shop to outfit us for each occasion and picked featured and favourite styles for photographs. While aware that our assignment was for a newspaper article rather than for private purchase, department managers kindly donated advice, information, and much time, treating us,

Strapless white cocktail dress.

indeed, like a Saturday Cinderella.

bathing suits

To begin with bathing suits, perfect for beach holidays and very safe punting. At Robert Sayle's on St. Andrew's Street we found this bright white one-piece (pictured right), peppered with black polkadots, bow-tied over each hip, by Aqualine in elasticated rayon batiste (at 79/6). Also on the rack and worthy of note: a vivid red swimsuit by Slix in rayon lastex, bordered narrowly at bodice and hem by a woven cotton design of blue hearts and red rickrack on a white ground (67/9).

For the sleekest of black suits to set off a tan, we liked a rayon lastex model by Trulo, cut close with straight princess lines and two small darts sliced in the cuffed top (89/6).

Valuable beach accessories also at Robert Sayle's: a wide-brimmed raffia sun-hat, gaily beaded in red (27/9); a stylish Italian beachbag in black straw, embroidered with white raffia flowers, to carry every-

Strapless Frank Usher ball gown.

thing from picnic to sunglasses (12/6); a flamboyant red-and-white striped towelling stole with big pockets and black-tasseled fringe (24/6); and finally, to complete the whole ensemble, a white terrycloth beachcoat with attractive full circular yoke (73/6). Happy swimming, everyone!

cocktail dress

Our cocktail and dance dress featured at Joshua Taylor's (see picture) is a strapless white cotton by Jean Allen, patterned with pink rosebuds and green leaves; the marvellous pouf skirt billows most bouffant over its triple crinoline petticoats (£10 12s. 6d.). Draped from the front to a pert bow in back, this gala outfit sports its own cover-up bolero and so becomes suitable for afternoon garden parties or champagne soirées overlooking Great Court, Trinity.

Runners-up: A poppy-red button-down jumper dress in French cotton put out by Continentals (at £4 7s. 6d.), with square open neck and cool, clean-cut flared skirt; also, a green-and-white striped cotton dress by Estrava, fresh as a mint julep, with off-the-shoulder boat neck, cuffed pockets at hip (£4 19s.).

Rembrandt Originals are showing a versatile tan cotton dress, its skirt printed in a stunning black design; definitely to be seen in motion, the accordian pleated skirt flares out, changing the pattern with every walking step; sleeveless, buttoned neatly down the front and trimmed by a slim black belt, this dress is fitted for casual afternoons

White one-piece, with black polka dots, bow tied over each hip.

about town (£5 19s. 6d.).

For the ultimate in exquisite ball gowns, we visited Vogue's elegant shop just opposite Emmanuel and chose a strapless Frank Usher model in floating white nylon sketched over lightly with a

delicate black pattern and banded once about the bodice, twice about the full skirt, with black lace and velvet ribbon (17 guineas).

Pick your partners, men; we propose a toast to the best May Week yet.

Sylvia Plath posing in the Cambridge University paper, *Varsity*, in May 1956. "She made her impact," Daniel Huws said of this spread.

Sylvia Plath in Venice, spring 1956

Sylvia Plath in Paris, spring 1956

Ted Hughes, 1960

Tonight I am going to a party celebrating the publication of a new literary review which is really a brilliant counteraction to the dead, uneven,
poorly written 2 lit. magazines already going here, which run on prejudice and whim; this new one is run by a combination of Americans and
Britains, and the poetry is really brilliant, and the prose, taut, reportorial,
and expert. Some of these writers are Jane's friends, and I must admit I
feel a certain sense of inferiority, because what I have done so far seems
so small, smug and <u>little</u>. I keep telling myself that I have had a vivid,
vital good life, and that it is simply that I haven't learned to be tough and
disciplined enough with the form I give it in words which limits me, not
the life itself.[135]

Plath had been devastated when she read Daniel Huws's review of her
Chequer poems in *Broadsheet* that February. "Of the quaint and eclectic art-
fulness of Sylvia Plath's two poems," Huws wrote, "my better half tells me
'Fraud, fraud'; but I will not say so; who am I to know how beautiful she
may be."[136] Daniel's review reveals the flippant but deep sexism that permeated Cambridge literary circles. Sylvia hardly registered the "beautiful";
what upset her was Huws's aesthetic judgment. She told Aurelia, "they abhor
polished wit and neat forms, which of course is exactly what I purpose [*sic*]
to write, and when they criticize something for being 'quaintly artful' or
'merely amusing,' it is all I can do not to shout: 'that's all I meant it to be!' "[137]

Frank O'Connor's rejection had been private, but this rejection was public, and more humiliating. Worse, Plath believed it was true. Daniel Huws,
she wrote in her journal, had been right to mock her poem. She turned her
anger at him inward and prepared herself to fall at the feet of the "brilliant"
male poets she would meet that night. Full of sadness and self-contempt,
Plath was a disciple in search of a master the night she met Ted Hughes.

The Botolphians, too, were in a state of confusion. They felt "rejected"
by *Granta* and *Chequer* and, despite their bombast, doubted their ability to
"open up a new era in literature." "Our desperation was acute—each of us
with a different source of anguish," Bert remembered. A spirit of "intense
disillusion," even "near violence," haunted them, a postwar "fear that we
were not up to the mark of our older, veteran brothers."[138] Alcohol quelled
the panic. That night, Sylvia had dinner with Nat LaMar, Jane Baltzell, and
Win Means, then met Hamish at 8:45 at Miller's, where they got drunk on
Whiskey Macs. (She described Hamish as "a rather impossible Canadian
who drinks & smokes too much, but is aware of a certain pub-life & pub
characters in Cambridge which I find occasionally refreshing after weak
intellectual tea.")[139] The two eventually stumbled to the party at the Cambridge Women's Union in Falcon Yard, where the Botolphians had rented a

hall on the second floor. They, too, had been drinking all afternoon at the Anchor, and had shared a fifth of bourbon in the Saint Botolph's rectory dining room before heading to the party.

"The birth of the *Review* should have inspired a bright festival of song and dance," Bert later wrote. "Instead, it became a sinister affair, far out of control."[140] The party, like the poetry it celebrated, was raucous, even "unwholesome." David Ross, too, remembered it as a "roaring affair."[141] Iko thought it "very wild," and Ted "very drunk, very rambunctious."[142] The young poets were making a stand against the dryness and dullness of modern English verse, and they knew they must play the part. By night's end several Victorian-era stained-glass windows would be smashed and at least one argument about poetry would come to fisticuffs. The next day Michael Boddy told the police that some football "yobs" were responsible for the vandalism. (Iko remembered that it was in fact "the *delta* people" who had crashed the party and started the fight.) Luke was nevertheless disciplined by his Downing College tutor for the damage to the hall and forced to leave the rectory, though Ted told David years later that he was the one who had broken the windows. Jean, who was at the party with Ted's girlfriend Shirley, recalled less chaos but lots of drink. "Speeches were made. Short and informal, and not in the least London manner. They weren't launching something very grand. No, it was much more alternative."[143]

Jane remembered the "mood of dejection" until the "manic rhythms of a first-rate jazz band filled the rooms." She had been to an earlier rowing party where drunken students had set crew shells on fire. There was "latent violence" in the air that night, she wrote her parents.[144] Ted wrote to Terence McCaughey, now in Dublin, about the new magazine—he was proud some thought it "obscene." The "best thing about it," he wrote, was the launch party. "Mac played, all drank, more women than men, we left the place smashed, windows out, polished floor like a dirt-track. The bill will come one day."[145] Indeed it would.

As the Irish ballads grew louder and off-key, Bert and Jane watched the Saint Botolph's "bacchanalia" at an American remove. Jane put down the debauchery to the terrible winter that had left "everyone's nerves . . . cranked up pretty tight."[146] The party was likely the wildest Sylvia had ever attended, and she too was eager to play her part. Bert remembered that her "fervor immeasurably intensified the Dionysian air."[147] Sylvia wrote in her journal that she was already "very, very beautifully drunk" when she ascended the stairs and entered the hall "with brave ease."[148] Jane recalled her wearing a black subfusc gown—a detail Sylvia included in her short story about the night, "Stone Boy with Dolphin." Jane was surprised to see her there, as Sylvia did not know anyone in the Saint Botolph circle besides Bert. Ted,

Jane thought, looked like an "eagle in a pet shop . . . bored, melancholy, discontent."[149] She had been so impressed by Hughes's poems in the *Review* that she had come to the party to meet him. But his "dyspepsia" put her off, and she avoided him. "He was large and alarmingly powerful, both physically and in psychological presence."[150] Contradicting Hughes, she remembered that the crowd was mostly male.[151] Sylvia, Jean Gooder remembered, "was pretty sloshed. But she was gunning for what she thought was the top poet"—Ted. "She'd done her homework." Jane remembered Sylvia's bright red hair band, a "scarlet streak."[152]

Fortified by drink, Sylvia first approached Bert, then found Daniel (Hamish introduced them) and spoke the "immortal line of introduction" she had planned ever since she read his "clever precocious slanted review": "Is this the better or worse half?"[153] Daniel remembered her tone of "friendly aggression" as she defended her poem.[154] She moved on to Luke, whose poems she had singled out in the *Review*. They began dancing the twist while she quoted his lines from his poem "Fools Encountered." Luke's English girlfriend Valerie sat alone as he and Sylvia bantered, and he worried that Valerie "must have been thinking that I had deserted her in favour of a more aggressive compatriot, but Sylvia tired of me and asked where Ted Hughes was."[155] Sylvia was likely less interested in Luke once she heard his American accent.

Ted's girlfriend Shirley was a Newnham student reading English. Luke described her as "a serious and attractive young woman, intelligent, reserved and very English." (Ted had dated another woman at Cambridge, Liz Gattridge, a nurse, before Shirley; he had written Liz passionate love letters and considered marrying her, but the relationship ended when she moved abroad.) Shirley was the inspiration for the "beautiful" girl in "Fallgrief's Girl-Friends." "Ted's friends thought he would do well to marry her," Luke said.[156] Presumably so did Ted, who had brought her to Yorkshire for a week to meet his parents. She, too, had introduced Ted to her parents. Jean remembered, "She came from a relatively humble northern background, and faced with some of public school self-confident casual manner, retreated into herself, didn't like it. She was absolutely smitten with Ted. It went very, very deep."[157] In the fall of 1955, Ted had asked her to come with him to Spain; the plan seemed impractical, and she declined. But whatever commitments Ted may have made to Shirley receded as he approached the tall, vivacious American woman dressed in red and black, her eyes "a crush of diamonds."[158]

This was not the first time Ted had seen Sylvia. Daniel recalled that there were some women at Cambridge who were "very glamorous," "public figures . . . a bit like film stars . . . you knew some of them by sight."[159] Sylvia was one of those women. She and Jane cut such a striking pair that Shirley—

who had seen the two around Newnham—pointed them out to Ted, who thought they looked "Swedish."[160] Christopher Levenson said that Sylvia "seemed to possess all that easy social charm and savoir-faire that as diffident, awkward Englishmen we expected from Americans."[161] Indeed, Jane recalled that Sylvia's fashionable, American clothing set her apart, as trendy collegiate styles had not yet crossed the Atlantic.[162] The poet David Wevill, Assia Wevill's husband, had just one memory of Plath while he was at Cambridge, "walking in Trinity Lane, standing out in her spring dress among students in their rumpled clothes."[163]

Sylvia asked Luke to point out Ted Hughes. And suddenly there he was, looking straight into her eyes. She began quoting his poem, "Fallgrief's Girl-Friends"; they "shouted as if in a high wind" above the music.[164] In an unpublished draft of his poem "St Botolph's," Hughes wrote that he and Plath retreated to the quieter "stove-room" where crates of alcohol were "hoarded from the rabble."[165] Ted reassured her that Daniel would never have written so harshly about her poem if she had not been beautiful. Sylvia already suspected that her gender had made her an easy target, and she told Ted that a woman practically had to sleep with the editor to get a poem published at Cambridge. Ted, amused, said she was "all there," wasn't she. They spoke of his dull job in London, and he told her he had "obligations" in the next room—Shirley.[166] But then he kissed her and grabbed her earrings and red hair band. When he tried to kiss her again, this time on the neck, she bit his cheek. Hughes later wrote:

> Behind the door, I poured more brandy. We drank.
> I kissed you. Whether you were drunk
> Or concentrated for a masterpiece, suddenly
> You fastened to me, your limbs steely,
> Like a trap. Our kiss developed
> Till my left cheek was in your teeth
> And your screwed-up ball-face of joy
> Bit & held with all your strength. I broke free,
> I was laughing & you were laughing . . .[167]

Luke, Daniel, and Bert did not see the kiss or the bite, which suggests that it happened in a more private space. Jean, who had come to the party with Shirley, saw it but remembered the scene differently: "I saw Sylvia coming in. She'd been in a different room. It was in full swing and Ted was standing very centrally in the room. Shirley was standing in the doorway. Sylvia went straight up to him and bit him on the cheek. I literally saw it happen. Shirley was right behind. Ted had his back to her. She didn't see what had happened, but I could see her face framed in the doorway." Jean had lent Shirley some earrings, and she had lost one. When Shirley returned to the room to retrieve it, Jean said, "She knew something had happened. It was just one of those electric moments."[168]

Plath recorded her own version of events in her journal in Wagnerian prose:

> Then the worst happened, that big, dark, hunky boy, the only one there huge enough for me, who had been hunching around over women, and whose name I had asked the minute I had come into the room, but no one told me, came over and was looking hard into my eyes and it was Ted Hughes. I started yelling again about his poems and quoting: "most dear unscratchable diamond" and he yelled back, colossal, in a voice that should have come from a Pole, "You like?" and asking me if I wanted brandy, and me yelling yes . . . and I was stamping and he was stamping on the floor, and then he kissed me bang smash on the mouth and ripped my hairband off . . . and my favorite silver earrings: hah, I shall keep, he barked. And when he kissed my neck I bit him long and hard on the cheek, and when we came out of the room, blood was running down his face. His poem "I did it, I." Such violence, and I can see how women lie down for artists. The one man in the room who was as big as his poems, huge, with hulk and dynamic chunks of words; his poems are strong and blasting like a high wind in steel girders. And I screamed in myself, thinking: oh, to give myself crashing, fighting, to you. The one man since I've lived who could blast Richard.[169]

This was a relationship that was, from its first violent, theatrical moments, soldered on the work of D. H. Lawrence, W. B. Yeats, Dylan Thomas, Emily Brontë, and Fyodor Dostoevsky.[170] Plath was already conducting a literary dialogue with Hughes—proving herself as his reader, playing a role out of one of his poems, and daring him to play back. Her performance succeeded. Hughes thought he recognized a fellow traveler who was as disdainful of propriety as he was. What other woman would dare to draw blood with a kiss? He saw in Plath the same things she had found in his early poems—a fascination with what he would later call "positive violence," and a contempt for gentility.[171] Critics have often assumed that Plath adopted such poses after she met Hughes, but in fact both poets embarked on their courtship with a mutual sense of aesthetic purpose. A deep interest in poetry and violence marked Plath and Hughes's relationship from their first meeting. Their understanding of positive violence—a vital, elemental, and liberating force—evolved through their engagement with the work of Arthur Schopenhauer, Friedrich Nietzsche, Sigmund Freud, and Carl Jung; the war poetry of Wilfred Owen and Keith Douglas; and modernist literature by Gerard Manley Hopkins, T. S. Eliot, W. B. Yeats, Dylan Thomas, and, especially, D. H. Lawrence.[172] When Plath says she will give herself "crashing, fighting" to Hughes, she presciently describes the central role that the themes of violence and competition would play in their poetic dialogue.

Plath and Hughes would each come to see the other as an embodiment of an aesthetic as much as a real person—"chapters in a mythology," as Hughes once put it.[173] They saw themselves as Cathy and Heathcliff, Oliver Mellors and Connie Chatterley. As Plath wrote in her journal in April 1956, "I lust for him, and in my mind I am ripped to bits by the words he welds and wields . . . and glory in the temporary sun of his ruthless force."[174] Sylvia sensed immediately that he was "the only man I've met yet here who'd be strong enough to be equal with."[175] For Ted, Sylvia's American identity was connected to her sexuality from the start: as he recalled in his *Birthday Letters* poem "St Botolph's," her "long, perfect, American legs / Simply went on up."[176] Later he told an interviewer "To me, of course, she was not only herself: She was America and American literature in person. I don't know what I was to her."[177] To Ellie Friedman, it was obvious who Ted was to Sylvia. When Ellie met Ted in 1956, she was not surprised by Sylvia's choice of husband. She recalled that the 1939 film *Wuthering Heights*, in which Laurence Olivier played Heathcliff, had made an enormous impression on her and Sylvia, and, indeed, many young women of her generation. At Smith, the two had often spoken dreamily about someday finding their own Heathcliff.[178]

Plath became "obsessed" with Hughes almost immediately. "Ted Hughes—mad passionate abandon" she wrote in her calendar on February 25.[179] Hughes later wrote his own version of events in "St Botolph's":

> Falcon Yard:
> Girl-friend like a loaded crossbow. The sound-waves
> Jammed and torn by Joe Lyde's Jazz. The hall
> Like the tilting deck of the *Titanic*:
> A silent film, with that blare over it. Suddenly—
> Luke engineered it—suddenly you.
> First sight. First snapshot isolated
> Unalterable, stilled in the camera's glare.
> . . . .
> You meant to knock me out
> With your vivacity. I remember
> Little from the rest of that evening.

I slid away with my girl-friend. Nothing
Except her hissing rage in a doorway
And my stupefied interrogation
Of your blue headscarf from my pocket
And the swelling ring-moat of tooth-marks
That was to brand my face for the next month.
The me beneath it for good.[180]

Ted returned to Shirley—whom he still called his girlfriend in a letter to Terence a few weeks after the party—and Sylvia decided to leave. In yet another literary re-creation of this night written three years later, "Stone Boy with Dolphin," Plath wrote that the kiss and bite happened, as Hughes remembered, in a smaller, quiet back room. When Leonard (Ted) tells Dody (Sylvia) that he has obligations in the next room, she bites him. He shakes her off, turns his back on her without a word, and leaves her alone. Plath's language is ambiguous, and suggests that Leonard pushes Dody to the ground. Hamish (Plath did not bother to change his name in her story) peers through the door and asks if she is all right. He tells her they are going and quickly grabs her coat. Dody is deeply embarrassed as she leaves and imagines everyone talking about what she has just done. The story is much less triumphant than Plath's journal passage.

There, Sylvia wrote that Hamish told her Ted was "the biggest seducer in Cambridge" before he swept her away from the "orgy."[181] (Daniel and Luke both heard that Ted had punched "a protesting Hamish," though they did not see it happen.)[182] Sylvia was now very drunk, and, as they approached Queens' College, she found herself surrounded by five young men asking if they could kiss her. Hamish drove them off but persuaded her to climb Queens' locked, iron gates. She tore her tight skirt as she scaled the iron spikes "in an act of sublime drunkenness and faith."

In Hamish's room, Sylvia was too drunk and exhausted to stop what was about to happen and blamed herself for the evening's progression. She lay under him, "damn grateful for his weight," and "begged" him to scold her— didn't he know she was a "whore" and a "slut"? He remonstrated her for being a "silly girl"; he "kind of liked" her. He asked her when she would learn her lesson. "When? When?" Sylvia chided herself in her journal.[183] He walked her back to Whitstead before dawn through the dark, silent campus. Sylvia was freezing and terrified as they crossed the iced-over Cam, which she thought would break under their weight. Back in her room at last, she made hot milk to warm her frigid hands.

Plath's fictional—but autobiographical—account of this night in "Stone

Boy with Dolphin" suggests that she regretted sex with Hamish. During the act, Dody tries to dissociate herself from what is happening:

> What I do, I do not do. In limbo one does not really burn. Hamish began kissing her mouth, and she felt him kiss her. Nothing stirred. Inert, she lay staring toward the high ceiling crossed by the dark wood beams, hearing the worms of the ages moving in them . . . and Hamish let his weight down on top of her, so it was warm. Fallen into disuse, into desuetude, I shall not be. (It is simple, if not heroic, to endure.)[184]

It would take Sylvia two days to "recuperate" and feel anything but "worthless and slack." She hoped to see Ted again, she wrote in her journal. "But I want to know him sober."[185]

Sylvia's bite left marks on Ted's cheek for a month. "The next day everybody gossiped about Ted's bloody cheek," Bert remembered. "One and all we dismissed Sylvia as overly dramatic, un-English, and, who could deny it, stereotypically and vulgarly American. But a measure of ferocity had been lurking in all of us, not just Sylvia."[186] Christopher Levenson also recalled that "the next morning everyone knew about it," but that "the bite and ensuing relationship seemed to us at the time entirely 'right,' they deserved each other, and I remember wondering out loud as to which of them would influence the other most. Would Sylvia tame and domesticate Ted and introduce neat, witty mannerisms into his poetry or would he rather liberate Sylvia's previously repressed passions?"[187] Hughes would not soon forget Plath, though she assumed that he would. In a draft of "St Botolph's," he wondered:

> What is quietening [sic] to remember
> Is the speed of your express
> And the speed of mine and our meeting
> Not knowing if we were one express, two become one,
> Or one following the other, or one
> Overtaking & somehow all in the one line
> And maybe none of these, maybe collision . . .[188]

17

Pursuit

Cambridge and Europe, February–June 1956

Sylvia recovered slowly. The day after the *Saint Botolph's Review* party, hungover, she wrote a despondent entry in her calendar that bears little resemblance to the blazing prose of her journal: "weary & gray—chills—simply spent—desperate / re-work—obsessed re Ted—dark giant—lust & anger—nap."[1] She felt bad about the sex with Hamish—Dody feels "stained" in "Stone Boy with Dolphin"—and worried that Ted was lost to her.[2] She began to sketch a story in her journal about shock treatment, which she intended to submit to the *Review*. It would be bold and taboo. She embarked on a bolder kind of poetry, too.

Sylvia told her mother that she had met a "brilliant ex-Cambridge poet at the wild St. Botolph's Review party last week, will probably never see him again (he works for J. Arthur Rank in London) but wrote my best poem about him afterwards."[3] This poem, "Pursuit," was about sexual arousal and "the dark forces of lust," as Plath put it in her journal. "It is not bad," she admitted to herself. "It is dedicated to Ted Hughes."[4] She felt it was superior to the "small, coy love lyric" she had been writing, and sent it, along with "Channel Crossing" (written on February 23), to Aurelia. "I am most scornful of the small preciousness of much of my past work," she wrote home on March 9. Now, she was "making a shift."[5]

Plath had been reading Jean Racine's plays for her Tragedy supervision with Kay Burton in late February—she would finish her Racine paper on March 5—and the material inspired her. (Burton herself remembered that Plath displayed a "mature and wise" "grasp of human values.")[6] She used an epigraph from Racine's *Phèdre*—"Dans le fond forêts votre image me suit"—to launch "Pursuit," finished on February 28:

> There is a panther stalks me down:
> One day I'll have my death of him;
> . . . .
> Insatiate, he ransacks the land
> Condemned by our ancestral fault,
> Crying: blood, let blood be spilt;
> Meat must glut his mouth's raw wound.

The poem continues for three more stanzas in which the speaker, "Appalled by secret want," tries to "rush / From such assault of radiance." She shuts the "doors on that dark guilt."

"Pursuit," with its "taut thighs" and "black marauder," was the most sexually charged poem Plath had ever written. Yet she thought it literary enough to send to Aurelia with a detailed explication:

> It is, of course, a symbol of the terrible beauty of death, and the paradox that the more intensely one lives, the more one burns and consumes oneself . . . I am hypnotized by this poem and wonder if the simple seductive beauty of the words will come across to you if you read it slowly and deliberately aloud. Another epigraph could have been from my beloved Yeats: "Whatever flames upon the night, Man's own resinous heart has fed." The painter's brush consumes his dreams, and all that.[7]

In her journal, Plath wrote that "Pursuit" was "triggered" by Ted, "but written for Richard."[8] The poem's style is of a piece with the searing, dramatic love letters she wrote Sassoon on March 1 and 6, begging to live with him in Paris and pledging to give herself to him forever. "More than anything else I want to bear you a son and I go about full with the darkness of my flame, like Phedre, forbidden by what auster [sic] pudeur, what fierté?"[9] Yet "Pursuit" also answers back to Hughes's "The Jaguar" (itself influenced by Rilke's "The Panther") and his "Law in the Country of the Cats." The themes of competition, erotic struggle, and violence at the heart of "Pursuit" would become touchstones of Plath and Hughes's poetic dialogue. This decidedly ungenteel poem was a breakthrough for Plath and heralded the beginning of a new creative direction.

Despite her vow to Sassoon to become a "consecrated single woman," Sylvia dated several men that March. She joined Christopher Levenson for tea with Stephen Spender on March 1, and saw films with Hamish and Iko, the Israeli friend of Mallory Wober's. Although she had struck sparks with Hughes, her journal is full of anguish over Sassoon. Indeed, Iko said that around this time, Sylvia came to his room "in a state of upheaval" (she had been drinking) and told him she was "confused" by her feelings for both Ted and Sassoon. She said she "needed a man to lean on" as she kissed him and asked him to make love to her. Although he was "highly stirred," he declined—he was still loyal to Mallory—and she fell asleep on his bed. When she awoke, she was calm. Neither ever mentioned the incident again.[10]

Sylvia had come down with another sinus infection that made her "despair" (she longed for cocaine sprays), and she was frustrated by her professors' inaccessibility.[11] Daiches, Leavis, Willey, and Redpath all impressed her, but she complained to Aurelia that "there is no personal interplay," no "reciprocal current of ideas" as there had been at Smith. She had met one "vivid, brilliant, opinionated young woman"—Dr. Dorothea Krook—whom she wanted as a supervisor. "I feel I could 'grapple with' her mind, she seems the kind one would work like mad for, and I miss this among the women here so much: their grotesqueries and sublimations as people undermines a really deep complete admiration of them."[12] Plath read D. H. Lawrence's *The Man Who Died*, a novella about Christ's resurrection, with Krook that March. She "felt chilled" as Krook read parts of it out loud, "as if [an] angel had hauled me by the hair in a shiver of gooseflesh." It was the same feeling she had experienced reading Joyce's "The Dead." "I have lived much of this," she wrote in her journal, for she too had come back from the dead. The story made her think of Otto, and how he had "gone into the dark; I rail and rage against the taking of my father . . . I would have loved him; and he is gone. . . . I lust for the knowing of him." After a coffee session with Professor Redpath at the Anchor, she had "practically ripped him up to beg him to be my father."[13] She warned herself not to marry an older man as a father substitute.

Ted returned to Cambridge on March 9, consumed by thoughts of Sylvia. He had asked Luke (who asked Bert) to find out her address. It was not like Ted, Luke thought, to show so much interest in a woman. Late that night, the two threw stones up at what they thought was Sylvia's Whitstead window, though they were mistaken. She was not home anyway; she was out drinking with Hamish.[14] When Bert told Sylvia about Ted and Luke's visit the next day—after she had seen her psychiatrist, Dr. Davy, that morning—she was overjoyed. "HE is here; in Cambridge," she wrote in her journal. "Please let him come; let me have him for this British spring. . . . Oh, he is here; my black marauder; oh hungry hungry. I am so hungry for a big smashing creative burgeoning love . . . The panther wakes and stalks again." She "lay, burning, fevered with this disease" as she waited for Ted and became furious as she watched the hours tick by.[15] Luke and Ted returned the next night, again throwing clods of dirt at the wrong window while Sylvia slept and dreamed of Winthrop. Hughes could have left Plath a note in her pigeon-hole at the Newnham porter's lodge, but that was not his style. His gestures were more Shakespearean.

With her Fulbright renewed, she could now afford to visit several European cities over her spring break. She had decided to visit Sassoon in Paris (invited or not), but meanwhile made plans to spend her spring vacation with Gordon, who was touring German universities in April. Young women generally did not travel alone through Europe at the time, and she admitted to Aurelia that she felt she needed Gordon's protection.

In any case, Sylvia had no close female friends at Cambridge with whom she could travel. "I really long for a woman confidante," she wrote Aurelia that term.[16] Jane was perhaps her closest friend, but they had quarreled after Sylvia saw that Jane had underlined passages in some books she had lent her. They were both "American girls who write," as Sylvia put it, and each thought of herself as the "queen" among men. Sylvia knew Jane was connected through Bert to the Saint Botolph's men, and it is clear that she wanted no competition from the other tall, attractive, literary American. (Jane, indeed, admitted she was attracted to Ted at the time.)[17] Sylvia also understood that she had to align herself with a man, whether it was Ted, Christopher, Nat, Luke, or *Granta* editor Ben Nash, to gain entry to literary Cambridge. There was no comparable female group of "rebel-poets," as Bert called the Botolphians, with whom Sylvia could while away afternoons over pints at the Anchor.

In mid-March, Sylvia got a splinter in her eye and had to undergo emergency surgery at Addenbrooke's Hospital. She was fully conscious during the operation, which fascinated and horrified her. "I looked on (couldn't help it) and babbled about how Oedipus and Gloucester in King Lear got new vision through losing eyes, but how I would just as soon keep my sight and get new vision too." Sylvia put up a brave front for Aurelia and her friend Gary Haupt, who stood by her during the ordeal, but she must have been terrified; she now felt she deserved "Paris and pampering."[18] She would write a poem about the experience in 1959, "The Eye-Mote."

Around this time, Sylvia got to know Luke better. Together they saw *Juno and the Paycock*, ate at the Anchor, shared supper in his flat, and spoke of Wallace Stevens.[19] She called him a "nice guy" in her calendar.[20] He was likely doing reconnaissance for Ted, who wrote Luke on March 18 asking him to invite Sylvia to Rugby Street in London. Ted was thinking of postponing his departure for Australia for another nine months, presumably on account of Sylvia, who was ecstatic about the prospect of seeing him again.

She arrived at 18 Rugby Street on March 23, the night before she was due to leave for Paris. It had been nearly a month since she and Ted had seen each other. Sylvia was alarmed by the conditions at the sagging Bloomsbury townhouse, which were considerably worse than those at the rectory. She called it a "slum."[21] Hughes lived on the second floor of the old Georgian building in a flat with no electricity or running water and only a coal fire for heat. There was no place to bathe, and the building's only toilet was in the coal cellar underneath the street, "always black with coal dust," as Ted's friend and neighbor Jim Downer remembered.[22] There was no sink in the bathroom, just a cold-water tap on the landing. The kitchen was a bucket and a single gas ring, which, Jim said, leaked so badly that visitors often grew lethargic. Plants died within a few days.

A small band of artists congregated at Rugby Street: Ted; Jim, a visual artist; the French filmmaker Jacques Tati; Lucie Rie, a potter whose work Plath admired; and Peter O'Toole, studying at the Royal Academy of Dramatic Art and supremely confident in his future. The others were not, though they pretended otherwise. Everyone was broke, and they spent their nights discussing art over candlelight, drinking instant coffee and, when someone was "flush," bottles of Bulls Blood beer. They all pitched in for radio batteries when the BBC's Third Programme aired Richard Burton reading Dylan Thomas's *Under Milk Wood.* Jim remembered Peter O'Toole singing songs from *West Side Story* and practicing his lines from *Juno and the Paycock.* Michael Boddy, a sometimes visitor, was struck by O'Toole's dapper appearance, "very much out of place in Rugby Street." One night O'Toole taught them all how to rip up phone books—an "old vaudeville trick"—which they burned for heat in the fireplace.[23]

Ted was as impatient for Sylvia as she had been for him at Whitstead. In his *Birthday Letters* poem "18 Rugby Street," he wrote, "I invoked you, bribing Fate to produce you":

> I can hear you
> Climbing the bare stairs, alive and close,
> Babbling to be overheard, breathless.
> . . . A great bird, you
> Surged in the plumage of your excitement,
> Raving exhilaration. A blueish voltage—
> Fluorescent cobalt, a flare of aura
> That I later learned was yours uniquely.

About her arrival, Plath later wrote in her calendar: "recited Panther—acted same—disturbing."[24] In an unpublished draft of "18 Rugby Street," Hughes wrote, "Imagining / It was written for me, I tried to live up to it. / You held off. I recited / Graves' full version of Tom a Bedlam's song. / We got wilder, but you would not stay."[25] In the final version, he wrote, "I held you and kissed you and tried to keep you / From flying about the room."[26]

After a supper of wine and eggs, they spoke of poetry and listened to verse recordings. Michael was spending the night and remembered entering the flat to find the two sitting close to each other in the living room in separate chairs. Sylvia had her knees drawn up in an armchair as she touched Ted's face and looked into his eyes. Ted's knees touched Sylvia's chair. The two whispered to each other, oblivious of him, then left without saying good-bye. "It was like a vision, here one minute, gone the next."[27]

Ted walked Sylvia back to her hotel, the historic Clifford's Inn on Fetter Lane, where she smuggled him into her room. "Wild wandering night," she wrote in her calendar the next day, "wounded and shaken from ruthlessness of Ted who called me wrong name at 5am."[28] In her journal: "sleepless holocaust night with Ted."[29]

Just before sunrise, Ted returned from Fetter Lane to Rugby Street. In an unpublished poem, he described hearing "blackbirds and thrushes," "Their dawn chorus awash through the whole city." He was "floating / On air . . ."[30] Michael awoke to Ted "shaking" him and shouting "in fierce triumphant tones: 'When a man's been with a woman he must eat! Cook me the sausages!'" Michael had never seen Ted so "agitated." "He was always pretty calm. But he was restless, couldn't settle." Michael cooked breakfast while Ted continued to move about, muttering phrases he "couldn't catch." When Ted finally relaxed and sat down to eat, he spoke lustily about the sexual satisfaction he had found with Sylvia the night before. He seemed to be in an altered state.[31]

Much later, Hughes, with his deep-seated beliefs in astrology and fate, would recall the night differently. In a *Birthday Letters* poem, "18 Rugby Street," he conjured a latent doom:

> Opposite the entrance
> On a bombsite becoming a building site
> We clutched each other giddily
> For safety and went in a barrel together
> Over some Niagara. Falling
> In the roar of soul your scar told me—
> Like its secret name or its password—
> How you had tried to kill yourself. And I heard
> Without ceasing for a moment to kiss you
> As if a sober star had whispered it
> Above the revolving, rumbling city: stay clear.[32]

SYLVIA LEFT TED for Paris the following morning, March 24, with a fellow Fulbright scholar who dropped her at the Hotel Béarn on rue de Lille at dusk.[33] Exhausted, she washed her "battered face, smeared with a purple bruise from Ted and my neck raw and wounded too."[34] The sex, she suggested, had been rough—though perhaps not so different from what she had enjoyed with Sassoon. As Hughes wrote in his draft of "18 Rugby Street," he was trying "to live up" to "Pursuit," which Plath had recited upon entering his lair. They seemed determined to shock each other, to prove how far they had traveled from the traditional mores of their respectable upbringings. Yet Sylvia also wrote, in the night's aftermath, of Ted's "big iron violent virile body, incredible tendernesses & rich voice which makes poems."[35] Still, she was furious that he had called her "Shirley" before he left her hotel room. She was annoyed, too, that Michael had shown up at 18 Rugby Street unannounced. She wouldn't have "minded just Luke," but now she worried that Michael would gossip about her back at Cambridge. Above all, she was upset with herself for not spending more time with Hughes. "He suggested we go to Jugoslavia; if only he knew me rightly! I foolishly did not give him time. . . . Such mistakes I make."[36]

But Hughes was not yet a serious prospect, for Plath was still trying to resurrect her relationship with Sassoon. She believed that she could talk him out of joining the Army if he would only see her in person. When she arrived in Paris, she forced herself not to run straight to Sassoon's apartment and instead went in search of dinner. On the street, she met Giovanni Perego, the Paris correspondent for an Italian communist newspaper. They dined together, and Sylvia went to bed early feeling "terribly alone."[37]

In the morning, when she arrived at Sassoon's flat, the curt landlady told her that Sassoon had left and would not be back until after Easter. Sylvia wept as she wrote him a letter in the living room. "He had left no address, no messages, and my letters begging him to return in time were lying there blue and unread. I was really amazed at my situation; never before had a man gone off to leave me to cry after."[38] Distraught, she headed to the brasserie where Sassoon had taken her on her first night in Paris. She ordered a drink and read *Antigone*.

She tried to forget him as she sketched along the Seine, drank in cafés, and explored Montmartre. She ran into her Cambridge friends Tony Gray and Gary Haupt, and other Fulbright scholars she knew—Ted Cohen and Carl Shakin, her "shipboard romance." This time Carl's wife was in tow, and the encounter was brief. It seemed incredible to her that she should meet so many men by chance, yet Sassoon failed to appear. To Aurelia, she "gave" only "the gay side" of things, but she was lonely.[39] She and Tony ended up in bed together at her hotel, though he drew back at the last minute. Sylvia thought that she had "scared" him with her "need and volcanic will."[40] She resolved to "Be chaste" and not drink too much, for she now bitterly regretted her drunken behavior at the *Saint Botolph's* party and her wild night with Hughes in London. In her journal, she worried constantly that she would be the subject of gossip at Cambridge: "let no one verify this term the flaws of last!"[41]

Back in London, Ted could not stop thinking of Sylvia. He wrote her on March 31 that if she did not come to London to see him on her way back, he would return to Cambridge to see her: "Sylvia, That night was nothing but getting to know how smooth your body is. The memory of it goes through me like brandy."[42]

On April 3 Sylvia ran into Gordon at the American Express office—a fortuitous coincidence, as the office had been sending her mail back to Whitstead and she had no way of communicating with him. Relieved, they made plans to leave for Germany on April 6, and saw Cocteau's ballet of Racine's *Phèdre* at the opera, which revived the "black marauder" fantasy of "Pursuit." Before they left, they toured Notre Dame and Sainte-Chapelle. She was "brave & desolate" without Sassoon, whom she willed daily to appear.[43]

Sassoon later wrote a short story, "The Diagram," based on his 1956 Easter vacation in Spain. The narrator claims that he has left Paris in order to make a clean break with a serious girlfriend:

> I was at the time running north-south, east-west and diagonally over Spain . . . because I was trying to make up my mind about a girl I most genuinely loved who was coming to Paris to see me, where I wouldn't be because of having gone away to try to make up my mind, and from whose letters I understood was going to start having an affair with a certain fellow so as to make me jealous and give me a mind to marry her, which I was unwilling to do just because of this imminent unfaithfulness—all very complicated. I kept writing her telegrams and not sending them.[44]

Sassoon would, in fact, send several "long letters" from Spain to Plath at Whitstead, where she received them, as she wrote her mother, "too late."[45]

In February, Sylvia had practically begged Gordon to travel with her around the Continent. Now she had misgivings. She felt awkward about letting him pay for her meals and hotel, and insisted on paying her train fare and some of her plane ticket home.[46] But she was desperate to see Italy and knew she could not travel there alone. She had become so "sick of dark sleazy men at my elbow" that she had stopped leaving her hotel for dinner.[47]

Gordon served a useful purpose, even if, as she claimed, she preferred the company of her typewriter.[48]

Together they left Paris by train on the morning of April 6. Sylvia felt desolate: "terrible sick sorrow re Richard—temptation to jump," she wrote in her calendar.[49] In Munich, she was embarrassed by Gordon's stammering attempts to speak German; his father was from Germany, and he had often intimated that he knew the language well. Now she knew his German was no better than hers. As the mutual goodwill dissolved, they left Munich on April 7 and traveled by train through Austria and the Tyrolean Alps. Sylvia had wanted to see her grandparents' hometown of Innsbruck, but there was no time to stop. She pressed her nose to the window and "almost cried" as the train rushed through the city.[50] In Venice, they took gondola rides past pink palaces and beheld the gilded grandeur of Saint Mark's. "How ridiculous this is. It must look to others as if we were lovers," Sylvia said to Gordon.[51] They stayed only one day, leaving for Rome on the 9th. Sylvia lounged on the sunny Spanish Steps and toured the Vatican and the Sistine Chapel, at whose ceiling she "stared for hours in reverence."[52] At the Colosseum, she ate oranges and bananas in the sun "while speculating on Christians & wild beasts."[53] She and Gordon ran into her old Wellesley friend Don Cheney, who had gone to Choate with Gordon and was on a Fulbright in Rome. Sylvia was relieved to have an escort who spoke Italian and provided a buffer between her and Gordon, with whom she was now barely on speaking terms. Drunk after "too much wine for lunch," Sylvia and Gordon fought; "barbs," she wrote in her calendar on April 11. "I should know by now that there is always bound to be a hidden rankling between the rejector and the rejected," she told Aurelia.[54] Gordon, too, was relieved to say goodbye; he never wanted to see Sylvia again. (He later apologized for his behavior during the trip and assumed all responsibility for things turning sour.)[55]

She felt "joy" leaving "Rome & Gordon" for Ted and London.[56] She had found another letter from Hughes at the American Express office in Rome. This one came with a poem:

> Ridiculous to call it love.
> Even so, fearfully did I sound
> Your absence, as the shot down feels to the wound,
> Knowing himself alive
>
> Only by what most frightens, the suddenly
> Anxious and kneeling sky, clouds, trees,
> The headlong instant that halts, stares, comes close
> With an incredulous ghastly eye.

. . . .

Wherever you haunt earth, you are shaped and bright
As the true ghost of my loss.[57]

Ted expected her at his flat at nine p.m. on Friday the 13th, with a bottle of smuggled brandy.

On the plane from Rome to London, Sylvia met a "charming" South African man, Michael Butcher, who took her out to a steak dinner at his "posh London club."[58] There, she washed up and made herself presentable. Michael paid the bill and bought her a carnation, but she had other plans. Scrubbed and sated, she took a taxi to 18 Rugby Street and presented Hughes with his brandy, which they promptly drained. "Exhilaration," she wrote in her calendar. "Bloody exhausting night of love-making."[59] In the morning, they ate steak and eggs while they listened to recordings of poems. And then: "back to bed in dirty gray rain twilight—sleep & longing for magnificence of Ted—lovely horizontal talk."[60]

Plath later wrote about this night in a fragmentary chapter called "Venus in the Seventh," likely an early draft of *Falcon Yard*, one of her lost, unfinished novels. The fragment hints at the erotics of violence the couple enjoyed. The first few pages recount the escapades of Jess Greenwood, an American Cambridge student and poet, as she travels through Munich and Venice during her Easter vacation. Jess travels with her old boyfriend Winthrop, who is based on both Gordon and Dick. Winthrop annoys her, and she looks forward to her reunion with her British lover Gerald back in London. Jess's language echoes Lawrence's in *Women in Love*: "The newness of Gerald caught at her. She knew nothing much. But he was hard, and cruel. And if she could take it without whimpering . . . then she might take life, after a fashion. . . . Just feel, stride along with him, until he bashed her head in and went off with the next."[61]

At his flat, the Hughes character opens the door and "hulked there, in his black sweater, with the collar up, unshaven. He stepped back to let her in. . . . And his voice. UnBritish. Refugee Pole rather, mixed with something of Dylan Thomas: rich and mellow-noted. Half sung." They talk with his neighbor Jim upstairs, but Jess is impatient. "She could swim in him: that incredible violent presence of his: leashed. Too much man for this island. The only man on it. He didn't think: he was." Later, the Hughes character tells Jess about his dreams of white leopards and foxes, while Jess describes her "black dreams . . . Nightmares, all dark and sultry with the air yellow as sulphur." They speak haltingly of the violent passion that gripped them during their first night together, before Jess left for Paris.

"If you hadn't come back, I would have come to Cambridge to find you again. To make up for that last time . . ."

She shivered, holding herself up against him, their toes touching. "Oh," she laughed ruefully. "It was terrible, that. I went to Paris all scarred. Black and blue . . ."

"But you liked it?"

"Yes."

"I was furious with myself. I don't know what happened to me . . ."[62]

Jess recites her poem, "Conversation Among the Ruins"—an actual poem by Plath—which she has dedicated to him. This poem is a strange choice, as it foretells the lovers' doom. He says, "You like one-syllabled words, don't you? Squab, patch, crack. Violent." She answers, "I like words to sound what they say: bang crash. Not mince along in iambic pentameters." Plath suggests in "Venus in the Seventh" that she was attracted to Hughes not only for his "incredible violent presence" but for the force of his language.

Sylvia returned to Cambridge on April 14 to find news of her grandmother's rapidly deteriorating health and several letters from Sassoon. She wept as she read, wishing she had received them in Paris. But she refused to descend into emotional turmoil again. She must accept her grandmother's imminent death, forget Sassoon, and give all of herself to Ted Hughes. The next day, Sunday, April 15—which she called the "Best day in World"—Ted came to her in Cambridge.[63] They walked to Grantchester under a sunny sky, proclaiming Chaucer to the cows. At Luke's flat, they dined on steak and caviar, brandy and wine. After "good violent love," they read poems and spoke of Isis and horoscopes; at night they drank and talked at the Anchor. The morning was a "dawn of tenderness & miracle."[64]

Ted stayed in Cambridge most of that week, but by Tuesday Sylvia was already feeling as if "he'd slept with 5 girls since I last saw him."[65] She had spent less than a week with Ted and still barely knew him. He exaggerated his misanthropic side for her, just as she exaggerated her Dionysian side for him: "cold Grey night by starlit river—revelation of his lack of care—horror, revulsion sad walk by self in cold," she wrote in her calendar on April 17, just four days after their reunion night in London. She ricocheted between feelings of exhilaration and fear. Just as Hughes refused to "stay clear," so too did Plath. In her calendar on April 18, she declared, "incredible feeling of own faith & integrity that will come through—Ted cannot ever annihilate me—I can see his flaws—egoism, bombast & lack of care for others are worst."[66]

On April 17, Sylvia revealed her new love to her mother, and thereby made it real:

> The most shattering thing is that in the last two months I have fallen ter-
> ribly in love, which can only lead to great hurt: I met the strongest man in
> the world, ex-Cambridge, brilliant poet whose work I loved before I met
> him, a large hulking healthy Adam, half French, half Irish, with a voice
> like the thunder of God; a singer, story-teller, lion and world-wanderer
> & vagabond who will never stop. The times I am with him are a horror
> because I am then so strong & creative & happy, and his very power &
> brilliance & endless health & iron will to beat the world across is why I
> love him and never will be able to do more, for he'll blast off to Spain &
> then Australia & never stop conquering people & saying poems. It is very
> hard to have him here in Cambridge this week & I am terrified even to
> have known him, he makes all others mere puny fragments. Such a tor-
> ment & pain to love him.[67]

Sylvia had nearly settled for Dick, then Gordon, "in a splurge of contrived social-conscience."[68] She had humiliated herself with Sassoon, grovel-
ing at his doorstep like a "begging-dog" in March.[69] All that was behind her
now. The man she had waited for like a messiah had come to deliver her. And
yet, two days after she had revealed her love for Ted to Aurelia, Sylvia wrote
a letter to Sassoon that suggests how forcefully his "desertion" of her in Paris
had determined her fate—and the course of literary history:

> something very terrifying too has happened to me, which started two
> months ago and which needed not to have happened, just as it needed
> not to have happened that you wrote that you did not want to see me in
> paris [sic] and would not go to italy [sic] with me. when [sic] I came back
> to london [sic], there seemed only this one way of happening, and I am
> living now in a kind of present hell and god knows what ceremonies of
> life or love can patch the havoc wrought. I took care, such care, and even
> that was not enough, for my being deserted utterly.[70]

SYLVIA SLEPT LITTLE while Ted visited her at Cambridge. She busied herself during the day writing articles for *Varsity* and poems she sent off to *The
Atlantic*, *Harper's*, *Poetry*, and *The New Yorker*. She was experiencing a "tremendous creative surge," and resented having to "read philosophy" when
there were "poems, articles, stories—nudging at fingertips."[71] On April 17,

the day she told Aurelia she had fallen in love with Ted, she sent off seven poems to *Poetry*.

She wrote another seven poems, most of them about Hughes, between April 18 and April 29: "Faun," "Ode for Ted," "Song for a Summer's Day," "The Queen's Complaint," "Firesong," "The Glutton," and "Strumpet Song."[72] Plath portrayed Hughes as a creator and destroyer of worlds, who spared little sentiment for the women he loved and left. In the Hopkinian homage "Ode for Ted," Hughes is a Yorkshire Adam: "For his least look, scant acres yield . . . / at his hand's staunch hest, birds build." "Complaint of the Crazed Queen," like "Pursuit," imagines a strong man full of "fury," "on his prowl," who leaves his love crazed and her world diminished. Sylvia boasted to Aurelia that these poems would "hit the critics violently" and that her voice was "taking shape, coming strong; Ted says he never read poems by a woman like mine: they are strong and full and rich, not quailing and whining like Teasdale, or simple lyrics like Millay: they are working sweating heaving poems born out of the way words should be said."[73] She and Ted were, she wrote, each other's best critics. She would not be dismissed as a lady poet, and felt she was finally leaving the preciousness of her earlier poems behind. But Plath's comments ("working sweating heaving") also suggest that she believed she needed to write like a man in order to make her mark. After all, men controlled the Anglo-American literary and academic worlds, and they took few women poets seriously. Even Virginia Woolf was mocked in Leavis's classroom. The odds against Plath were staggering.

In her letters home that April, Sylvia described Ted in a torrent of wild emotion. He was, she told Warren,

> tall, hulking, with rough brown hair, a large-cut face, hands like derricks, a voice more thundering and rich than Dylan Thomas, a force that breaks windows when he stalks into a room, half-Irish and half-French with a gift of story-telling that spellbinds; he writes poetry that masters form, bangs and smashes through speech to go better than Yeats, better than Hopkins at its best: none of this pale niggling cerebralizing. We are both strong and healthy as blazes. He throws the discus, hunts, shoots, plows, grafts roses, writes for film studios, knows the name of every bird and beast hopping over the moors: I am learning a new vocabulary from him. He hikes into the room, yanks out Chaucer or Shakespeare or Hopkins or Blake and begins to read in a voice that shakes the house.[74]

Variations on these themes colored nearly all Sylvia's letters home that spring. "I shall never again find his like in the world. . . . never have two people, too strong for most in one dose, lived so powerfully & creatively!" It was "a lifelong fight to forge a vital life," and she hoped she had "the guts and grace to do it."[75] She and Ted, she told Aurelia, were meant for each other; she promised that "the world will come to see him in the light of my look, even as I shall be the most beautiful woman in the blazing sun of his belief in me."[76]

Together they read Siberian and Magyar folk tales, took long walks to Grantchester "yelling poetry and words and stories at each other."[77] They punted down the Cam amid "arabesques of bird trills," and made love in hidden spots in the meadows.[78] They searched for owls in the night. When the weather turned raw, they cooked trout on Sylvia's gas ring, listened to Beethoven, discussed horoscopes, Cuchulain, and Snatchcraftington. He drew witches, wolves, and ghosts; she sketched landscapes and cottages. Her letters overflowed with a joy she could not contain. "I've never been healthier: radiance and love just surge out of me like a sun," she wrote Aurelia.[79] "I love others, the girls in the house, the boys on the newspaper. . . . I give and give; my whole life will be a saying of poems and a loving of people and giving of my best fiber to them."[80]

By late April her mind was "racing." In her calendar she wrote, "love for Ted still astounding—inner dialogues—whole future gathering—accelerating—taut balance."[81] She reached a crescendo in May. "All the blood spilt, the words written, the people loved, have been a work to fit me for loving Ted," she wrote Aurelia.[82] Sylvia warned her mother that Ted "may shock you at first, unless you imagine a big unruly Huckleberry Finn: he hasn't even a suit of clothes, he is so poor."[83] If he seemed "rough" on the outside, he was "lovely" on the inside.[84] "Oh, mother," she pleaded, "rejoice with me and fear not."[85]

Hughes's Australian voyage receded as the couple planned a summer writing together in Spain. He was now bunking in Cambridge again, at Alexandra House in an upstairs bedroom that he shared with two young women who ran a soup kitchen below. In his poem "Fidelity," he claimed that he shared a bed each night, naked, with a "lovely girl" for a month. But they never made love. "It never seemed unnatural. I was focused, / So locked onto you, so brilliantly, / Everything that was not you was blind-spot."[86] Sylvia, though, dated other men throughout April. On April 28, Michael Butcher, the South African she had met on the plane from Rome, took her out to the Mill, where she had two "fatal" cocktails, then to Miller's for wine and lamb chops despite her "pang at vision of dear Ted." There were "dozens of kisses" with the future historian Keith Middlemas and a "disastrous debach [sic]" at Alexandra House that night.[87] The next day Keith visited her; she also saw *Granta* editor Ben Nash. But she felt guilty and wrote a "long ecstatic letter" to Aurelia about Ted.[88] Soon after, the two committed themselves to each other for good: "miraculous switch & promise of life together," Sylvia wrote in her calendar on April 29, a little over two weeks since reuniting with Hughes in London.[89] This was the same day Sylvia learned that her grandmother, always a source of comfort and stability, had died.

On May 5, Betty and Duane Aldrich—Sylvia's Wellesley neighbors— visited Sylvia and Ted on their trip to England. Betty had once driven Sylvia to her disastrous shock treatments at Valley Head; now Sylvia and Ted took her punting to Grantchester on a sunny spring day. That night, Betty and Duane treated the young couple to roast duck, cheese, Chablis, and cognac at Miller's. The Aldriches liked Ted, and Sylvia began to hope that her other American friends—Marcia, Claiborne, Louise, Pat—would "accept this man of mine" despite his poverty.[90] And of course, she hoped that Betty would bring back a good report to Aurelia. In her calendar, Sylvia wrote that after dinner with the Aldriches, she "got guts to face Ted in honest brave statement of concern for next year." She also noted that she had written a "long letter" to Dr. Beuscher that morning (since lost), which suggests she was seriously considering marriage.[91]

Still, Sylvia hedged her bets: during the first week of May she recorded two evening dates with Ben Nash in her calendar, and on May 5, she reminded herself to write to Michael Butcher. But after May 7, the names of the men who had crowded her calendar since October all but disappear. "Sweet dear Ted: god I love him," she wrote that day. On May 10, she wrote for the first time of a wedding in her calendar: "Afternoon of best love yet: created wedding plans—great joy—planning."[92]

Ted told Luke that Sylvia had asked him to marry her, and he agreed. Luke was worried but not surprised. "I had seen it developing force since he said to me several times . . . in April and May of 1956 that he was falling 'too much' in love with Sylvia." Luke thought Ted was strangely "passive" about it all, though he noted that Ted had a similarly passive relationship with his "gifted and strong-willed elder sibling" Olwyn.[93] Sylvia was anything but passive. After so many years of searching for a supportive, literary husband— time wasted on Dick, Gordon, Sassoon, and Mallory—she was quick to act. She spelled out her desire for Hughes as plainly as she could to Aurelia, the last hurdle: "For the first time in my life, mother, I am at peace; never before, even with Richard, did I cease to have little opportunist law courts in session in my head whispering: look at this flaw, that weakness; how about a new man, a better man? For the first time I am free."[94]

Sylvia continued to press her case in letters that May: "All the social questions about money, family position, bank accounts, blow off like chittering irrelevancies in a cyclone before two people who depend solely on their native talent and love of honesty."[95] She vowed that they would live simply and write in a cheap Mediterranean outpost, where they would support themselves by teaching English. They needed nothing more than their typewriters and each other. Sylvia asked Aurelia not to judge Ted on the basis of "wealth, or a slick 10-year guarantee for a secure job, or a house & car."[96] Yet she herself worried about introducing him to the American ambassador and the Duke of Edinburgh (Queen Elizabeth's husband, Prince Philip) at an upcoming Fulbright reception in his "ancient" eight-year-old suit.[97] Sylvia claimed that she did not care what it looked like: "I look at him and he is dressed in purple and gold cloth and crowned with laurel."[98]

Ellie Friedman thought Ted's unsuitability as a husband—at least from Aurelia's perspective—made Sylvia "run straight into his arms."[99] Meanwhile, Hughes's old friends could hardly believe that their "wild ruffian," as Pembroke's dean had once called him, was engaged to an American.[100] They assumed that Sylvia came from money, and that she would expect Ted to produce more of it; they even made up a ditty that went "I'd rather my Ted as he used to be / Than with Sylvia Plath and her rich Mammy."[101] Bert Wyatt-Brown and David Ross rather liked Sylvia—she struck David as "one tough lady . . . determined, strong."[102] But to Luke she personified American materialism; he was skeptical that Sylvia was the right wife for the author of "Money, My Enemy."

Ted had no such doubts. He felt Sylvia understood his literary vocation, which she shared, and would not pressure him to become a conventional breadwinning husband—just as Sylvia felt he would not pressure her to abandon her writing for homemaking. His life, too, had changed. That summer he told Olwyn that he had committed himself to Sylvia and his writing, whatever the cost.

> I have met a first-rate American poetess. She really is good. Certainly one of the best female poets I ever read, and a damned sight better than the run of good male. Her main enthusiasm at present is me, and she thinks my verses are as good as I think they are and has accordingly and efficiently dispatched about twenty five to various immensely paying American Mags. So. She has published stories and poems in some of the top American journals. If you're in Paris on the 22nd I'll introduce you. . . . has her Mars smack on my sun, which is all very appropriate.
>
> My life is peaking, and my writing at last going with me [sic] method. . . .

> Postscript: Later tonight. For the last month I've lived about the strongest life I ever did live. The main thing about it—and the thing that has saved it from being just absurd—is that I've written quite a bit. As I'm

miserable and fit for nothing if I don't write continuously, I shall from now on shape my life round writing instead of squeezing writing into my life where I can.[103]

Ted canceled his autumn passage to Australia. He now planned to teach in Spain while Sylvia finished her final year at Cambridge; then they would marry and teach in America together. Sylvia reassured her mother that she would soon be "a proud grandmother yet!"[104] She began drawing up a wedding invitation list that included Mrs. Prouty, Dr. Beuscher, the Cantors, the Aldriches, the Crocketts, and Mary Ellen Chase. Pat O'Neil was her choice for maid of honor. If Pat's Catholicism precluded her from serving, Ruth, Marcia, and Ellie were her second, third, and fourth choices; otherwise, they would be bridesmaids, along with Joan Cantor. They were people who "really know what this means to me; sort of an apocryphal dedication to a tough, honest, creative life full of love and giving to the world of books and babies."[105] Aurelia's reaction might be guessed. Sylvia and Ted had been dating continuously for less than a month.

Newly engaged, Sylvia traveled to Rugby Street on May 11 and, after "love," cleaned Ted's "greasy filthy kitchen."[106] That night she and Ted attended the Fulbright reception, where they spoke with Prince Philip. When the Duke asked Ted his occupation, he replied, "Chaperoning Sylvia." "Ah," the Duke smiled, "the idle rich."[107] Sylvia brought up this meeting years later in 1962 when an English friend, Elizabeth Compton, tried to explain the "terrible, crushing" British class system to her, and how Hughes had "suffered" under it in ways that were not always obvious to Americans. "I asked her if she didn't think that, somewhere, Ted had a feeling of inferiority," Elizabeth wrote. Sylvia answered with a bitter laugh. "'Ted has lunched with the Duke of Edinburgh,' she said."[108]

Sylvia got so drunk on "countless sherries" at the reception that she blacked out and vomited; she wrote of "Ted's care & solace through bad night."[109] Back at Cambridge, she paid for her leisurely weekend by staying up all night on Monday to finish her Plato paper for Dr. Krook. As the birds began their morning song, she felt "tense, tired—electric wires trilling in blood—green milky dawn."[110]

Sylvia and Ted had sexual freedom at Whitstead, where they spent long afternoons in Sylvia's room. But Ted's presence did not endear Sylvia to her fellow Whitstead residents. Philippa Forder Goold felt less free to wander the halls in her dressing gown for fear of running into Ted, and she grew annoyed at how Sylvia commandeered the kitchen's "common stock" to cook for him.[111] She resented, too, the way Sylvia expected her fellow residents to hide Ted's presence from the house mother. Jane Baltzell Kopp remembered that one afternoon after Ted and Luke had been "lying in a field" dreaming up a Utopian society, they rushed back to Whitstead in a "brain fever" with a bottle of wine. Sylvia had no corkscrew, so Ted went round knocking on doors. When the house mother, Christine Abbott, told him she did not have a corkscrew, he opened the wine by "wildly" smashing the bottle's neck on her door handle. Abbott, shocked into silence, simply shut her door. Jane was astounded there were no repercussions.[112]

If Sylvia noticed the resentment building around her, she probably felt that the trade-off was worth it. She always referred to sex as "love" and described these times in her calendar with words like "tender" and "quiet," though in late May she and Ted had a row—"wrong love & hard talk." They made up quickly, "another step front—sense of growing through hardness & hurt."[113] She spent lazy afternoons lying on the banks of the Cam with him, reading poetry, sketching, or drinking outside at the Anchor. Throughout that May, a "wonderful well being" descended on her, and she told everyone she had never been happier.[114] She had at last found the place, she wrote Aurelia, "that whistling desert where human beings stand naked before the sun and the earth and give in full honesty and faith of all their being."[115]

Sylvia felt she knew enough about philosophy now to impress Dr. Krook, who, as she admitted to Aurelia, had become a substitute for Dr. Beuscher. She was sailing effortlessly through her supervisions, "now coming into the full of my power."[116] Discussing Plato's *Gorgias* with Krook, Plath felt "pure delight"; she had never felt so "whetted" and "keen."[117] Years later, Krook remembered those supervisions with particular pleasure. She called Plath "one of the most deeply, movingly, responsive pupils I had ever had. I felt the things I said, we said, her authors said, mattered to her in an intimate way, answering to intense personal needs, reaching to depths of her spirit."[118] With Plath, Krook "let herself go" and pursued Plato "further than I had done with any other student." She remembered that there "was nothing wild, feverish or defiant" about Sylvia, whom she found "extraordinarily modest, self-effacing, unassuming, unspoilt." When Krook eventually met Hughes—whom she described as "very shy, very taciturn, very much a Yorkshireman"—she was unnerved by Plath's ecstatic happiness and shuddered to think what might happen should something "*go wrong* with this marriage of true minds."[119]

Sylvia's academic confidence spilled over into her creative life; she worked furiously on her poetry manuscript, which she hoped to enter in a contest judged by Richard Wilbur and May Sarton. To Aurelia, she claimed, "I am learning and mastering new words each day, and drunker than Dylan, harder than Hopkins, younger than Yeats in my saying."[120] She wrote several poems—"Bucolics" on May 5, "Wreath for a Bridal" on May 17–18, and "Two Sisters of Persephone" on May 24. "Aerialist" followed on May 30, "Dream with Clam-Diggers" on June 1, "Ella Mason and Her Eleven Cats" on June 2, "Tinker Jack and the Tidy Wives" on June 7, and "Letter to a Purist" on June 8.[121] These were minor poems, but they pleased Plath. She told Warren, "I am writing poetry as I never have before."[122]

She was getting better reporting assignments, too: on April 24 she "gorged" herself on caviar at the "posh" Claridge Hotel, where she reported on Khrushchev and Bulganin's visit for the Cambridge paper *Varsity*.[123] She met the Soviet ambassador and British Prime Minister Anthony Eden, and discussed Dostoevsky with Russian officials. She shook Bulganin's hand and invited him to Cambridge, then sang along to "For He's a Jolly Good Fellow" while a British guest joked that she would never be let back into America. Two weeks later, she published a more serious piece in Oxford's *Isis* about the difficulties women faced at Cambridge, followed by an article on May Week fashions for *Varsity* for which she modeled a bathing suit, a cocktail dress, and a ball gown (which showed "how hard up they are!" she quipped to Aurelia).[124] *Varsity* also published Plath's impressions of Paris, with her accompanying sketches.[125] When Luke suggested to Ted that *Varsity* had published this piece to mock Sylvia's American sensibility, his eyes "took on a protective, hurt expression at the thought of Sylvia being set up for mockery."[126] (Indeed, Michael Boddy remembered the *Varsity* editors "snickering" about Plath's "Caryatids" poem and her fashion spread.)[127] Meanwhile, Hughes taught her about horoscopes, and she began planning a novel about Cambridge. She awoke each morning to "thrushes caroling" on the branches of a pink cherry tree in full bloom just outside her window.[128] "God, such a life!" she wrote home.[129]

In mid-May, Sylvia's Smith professor Mary Ellen Chase and her partner Eleanor Duckett visited Cambridge and took Sylvia out to long "divine" lunches.[130] Chase had worked tirelessly to secure Plath a spot at Cambridge, and was happy to see her star pupil thriving. Chase hinted that Smith would hire Plath as an English instructor after she graduated from Cambridge. The prospect thrilled Sylvia, and made her reconsider her earlier plan of "world-wandering" and itinerant English teaching. She hoped, despite herself, that Ted would get a job at Amherst.

Sylvia continued to tell Aurelia she did not mind that Ted was "penniless," yet in the same letter she asked for help choosing the nicest "stainless steel patterns" for her pans, and hoped that the couple would receive enough wedding gifts in Wellesley "to start us on a home."[131] She wondered whether they could get summer waitressing and bartending jobs on Cape Cod, or whether Ted might be employed as a "chauffer with a millionaire family."[132] She soon had another idea: she began sending Hughes's poems out to American magazines in May. "I want the editors to be crying for him when we come to America next June."[133] Ted had "commissioned" her his "official agent," she joked, but it was true; he would owe his career to her. She typed Hughes's poems in Whitstead's sunny backyard as he sat beside her, revising his now famous poem "The Jaguar." She felt his work was, like him, "fierce, disciplined with a straight honest saying," and predicted that "the world will be a different place" once he began publishing.[134]

Sylvia was upset that she could not return to Wellesley for her grandmother's funeral and worried Aurelia would cancel her June visit to Cambridge. Sylvia had never been apart from Aurelia for so long and was desperate to see her mother again. She asked Warren to "convince her subtly" that it was her moral duty to come, and she told Aurelia that out of sorrow would come strength.[135] ("If anyone had asked me what time of my life was most invaluable, I would say those 6 terrible months at McLean: for by re-forging my soul, I am a woman now the like of which I could never have dreamed of.")[136] Sylvia mustered all of her rhetorical force to convince her mother not to cancel her trip, guessing correctly that the language of martyrdom would be most effective:

> You, alone, of all, have had crosses that would cause many a stronger woman to break under the never-ceasing load.
>
> You have born daddy's long hard death, and taken on a man's portion in your work; you have fought your own ulcer-attacks, kept us children sheltered, happy, rich with art & music lessons, camp and play; you have seen me through the black night when the only word I knew was No and when I thought I could never write or think again; and you have been brave through your own operation. . . . Think of your trip here as a trip to the heart of strength in your daughter who loves you more dearly than words can say.

Together, Sylvia assured her mother, they would "walk through green gardens and marvel at this strange and sweet world."[137] Aurelia booked her trip.

If Aurelia had reservations about Ted, she kept quiet. Mrs. Prouty was more candid. Sylvia's and Ted's backgrounds were too different, she wrote Aurelia, and they hardly knew each other. Prouty asked Sylvia not to make a decision about marriage until she was less infatuated, and reminded her that other boyfriends had once stirred similar feelings. She should regard them all as "warning examples."

You anticipated that I would feel skeptical. I think "skeptical" isn't quite the word. Fearful more closely describes it. He sounds too much like Dylan Thomas for me to think he would make a satisfactory husband and father. Dylan Thomas's attitude towards women was much like that you describe . . . Thomas's wife was marvelous about his various love affairs and came to his rescue when he broke down physically and morally. Are you ready to do this for this second Dylan Thomas?

You don't really believe, do you, that the characteristics which you describe as "bashing people around," unkindness and I think you said cruelty, can be <u>permanently</u> changed in a man of 26?[138]

Sylvia was very much in love with Ted, but she relished shocking the dowagers in her life. Her early depictions of Hughes were perhaps encouraged by his own attempts to strike a misanthropic pose. But they were also self-consciously literary: Plath had spent her first two terms at Cambridge engrossed in tragedy, reading Ibsen, Strindberg, Chekhov, Synge, Yeats, Racine, Corneille, and Marlowe. She read more than fifty tragic plays in her second term alone. She told others she was fascinated by the "destructive love-hate relations between men & wives" in the plays, and intrigued, in Ibsen, by "the need for the artist to sacrifice life to his creation and the deadly retribution he must pay, laying waste to the creative lives around him, yet having to follow his call."[139] Plath's reading influenced her perception of Hughes, which she dramatized for maximum effect in her letters. When she told Aurelia he was "a violent Adam," "a breaker of things and people," "arrogant, used to walking over women like a blast of Jove's lightning," she had spent less than a week with him.[140]

The work of D. H. Lawrence, especially, had inspired Plath to look for a partner who, like Oliver Mellors in *Lady Chatterley's Lover*, would match her strength.[141] The writer Claire Tomalin left Newnham a year before Plath, but remembered the impact "Lawrence via F R Leavis" had upon romantic relationships of her literary generation, of "sex within marriage being passionate, serious and sacramental. . . . something entirely different from the bloodless, easygoing style of Bloomsbury."[142] Indeed, Lawrence's novels had convinced Plath that, as Rupert Birkin put it, man and woman could exist in "mystic conjunction" without sacrificing themselves to the other's ambitions or desires.[143] It was as if Lawrence himself had predicted Ted Hughes. Echoing a scene from *Women in Love*, Plath had written in her journal in 1952:

two over-lapping circles, with a certain strong riveted center of common ground, but both with separate arcs jutting out in the world. A balanced tension; adaptable to circumstances, in which there is an elasticity of pull, tension, yet firm unity. . . . I do not believe . . . that artistic creativity can best be indulged in masterful singleness rather than in marital coopera- tion. I think that a workable union should heighten the potentialities in both individuals.[144]

Dick, Gordon, and Sassoon had all been gods. Now Sylvia applied ele- ments of her Sassoon mythology to Ted: he was her Byronic hero, her Man- fred, whom she would save from himself. She told Aurelia she would "teach him care."[145] Later, she congratulated herself: "You should see how Ted is changing under my love and cooking and daily care! Gone is the tortured black cruel look, the ruthless banging gestures; he is mellowing, growing rich and kind and dear and tender and caring of me as he would be of a delicate bird." Without her love, she wrote Aurelia, he would have become "bitter & cynical, and destructive."[146] But Sylvia also wanted Ted to save *her*—and her poetry—from dull conformity. She would find the "guts" to rise to Hughes's challenge and devote her life to writing. The ascetic in her relished the idea of living frugally, while the Romantic in her sought a stance against the world. Together, they would fly close to the sun: "no precocious hushed literary circles for us: we write, read, talk plain and straight and pro- duce from the fiber of our hearts and bones."[147] Yet Claire Tomalin recalled how "those Lawrentian marriages of total commitment worked out uncom- fortably . . . I don't recall that many of our supposedly Lawrentian husbands took on the cooking."[148]

Sylvia boasted of Ted's contempt for convention the way her Smith peers boasted about their fiancés' Ivy League pedigrees. But Jane Ander- son, Sylvia's friend from her McLean days, thought she detected hints of unease when she visited Sylvia in Cambridge midmorning on June 4. In her *Bell Jar* trial deposition, Jane said that as soon as she got off the train, Syl- via began telling her about her new love, Ted Hughes. Jane remembered that Sylvia called him "sadistic," but she assured Jane that she could "man- age" him.[149] Jane thought this was a strange way to introduce one's fiancé, but she kept quiet while Sylvia continued talking in a "pressured" way. To Jane, Sylvia seemed tense, anxious, and "ambivalent" about her decision to marry Hughes; she sensed that as much as Sylvia enjoyed the drama of play- ing Cathy to Ted's Heathcliff, she wanted someone to talk her out of the marriage.

According to Jane, who had no desire to involve herself in Sylvia's roman- tic affairs after their disastrous shared history with Dick Norton, Sylvia soon dropped the subject and began pointing out historical buildings. They stopped in a pub for a quick sherry, where it became clear to Jane that Sylvia resented her silence. Sylvia left brusquely, saying she had to meet Mary Ellen Chase (Plath recorded a 1:15 lunch date with Chase in her calendar that day). In the past, the two had always parted on good terms and exchanged addresses. This time, Sylvia simply said goodbye and walked away, leaving Jane to explore Cambridge on her own. For weeks Sylvia had longed for a female friend to confide in about her love for Ted and her wedding plans; "I miss a good woman," she had written in her journal that April.[150] Now, someone with whom she had shared a harrowing, intimate history declined to listen. Jane knew Sylvia was angry with her, and sensed, correctly, that they would never see each other again.

The idea of a Wellesley wedding receded as the weeks passed; Sylvia and Ted could not wait. The couple wanted to marry at Westminster Abbey, but the dean there informed Hughes that the ceremony must be performed at his parish church of Saint George the Martyr, tucked inside a charming Bloomsbury square. There was some hassle with the marriage license, and arrangements were rushed. They spied a priest near the church, and Ted shouted, "That's him!" He then followed the sixty-nine-year-old Reverend Wilson home (across from Dickens's house, Plath noted) and learned that "he was the right one."[151] Ted spent the night before his wedding with Michael Boddy and Joe Lyde at their flat in Cambridge. He said nothing to them about what awaited him the next day.[152]

On Bloomsday, June 16, at one thirty in the afternoon, Sylvia Plath and Ted Hughes married. The hushed interior of Saint George's, with its red and gold finery and gleaming icons, was unusually bright in a nation of damp, gray stone churches. Outside it was raining, but inside, the candlelight illuminated the yellow walls and stained-glass windows, while above the gilded columns, painted saints stared impassively from the golden reredos.

Aurelia, who had arrived in London only three days before, stood in disoriented attendance. Sylvia and Ted had announced their "decision to get married" to her at dinner at Schmidt's, a German restaurant, on the night she arrived in England.[153] She had been sick during dinner the night before and still felt unwell. Now, impossibly, her daughter was about to be married to a man she had just met.[154] Sylvia, dressed in a new pink wool knitted suit she borrowed from Aurelia, had bought gold wedding rings and new shoes and trousers for Ted. Yet he still felt, as he later wrote in "A Pink Wool Knitted Dress," like a "post-war, utility son-in-law" with his "drab" old tie and corduroy jacket, "thrice-dyed black, exhausted, / Just hanging on to itself."[155] He had given Sylvia a pink ribbon and a pink rose and thought she looked "transfigured" in the "echo-gaunt, weekday chancel":

So slender and new and naked,
A nodding spray of wet lilac.
You shook, you sobbed with joy, you were ocean depth
Brimming with God. . . .
Levitated beside you, I stood subjected
To a strange tense: the spellbound future.[156]

Only Aurelia and Warren were to know of the secret marriage, for Sylvia feared the Fulbright Commission would rescind her scholarship if word leaked. The risk and the secret ceremony heightened the drama.

Afterward, the three adjourned to Schmidt's, where they had, as Sylvia put it, their "wedding breakfast."[157] They also celebrated Hughes's first magazine acceptance, by the prestigious *Poetry*—"Bawdry Embraced," which he dedicated to Sylvia—as if poetry itself had blessed their union. Plath would speak of the coincidence often.[158] "Sylvia is my luck completely," Ted wrote his brother.[159]

Husband and wife returned to 18 Rugby Street, where Sylvia was once again disgusted by "the dust & grease and carrot peels."[160] It was not the wedding night she had once imagined, as she slow-danced under white marquees in America. Yet she had escaped a suburban life as a doctor's wife. Her instinct to flee had been correct, she now felt sure. Her desire to please had almost killed her, and now Hughes would give her a gift more precious than cars and houses: freedom to write. He expected her to out-earn him.[161]

Six years later, in her 1962 review of *Lord Byron's Wife*, Plath wrote that the author "begins, as might many a shrewd marriage counselor, with a meticulous investigation of the bride's mother."[162] Plath was writing suggestively about her own marriage. Her wedding was meant to be a surprise "gift" to Aurelia, but in fact it was Sylvia's checkmate. Ted knew he was the antithesis of the all-American Wellesley boys Aurelia had quietly encouraged her daughter to marry. He described himself that day as "the Swineherd / Stealing this daughter's pedigree dreams / From under her watchtowered searchlit future."[163] He was not wrong. Ted's joblessness worried Aurelia and would remain a source of grievance for years to come. She did not trust him to care properly for her daughter, who was more vulnerable than he knew.[164] "You will be kind to her?" she asked him, just before the ceremony.[165] Sylvia knew Aurelia would frown on Ted's manners, his poverty, and his shaky prospects. She could not give her mother time to voice her doubts, lest she herself become dissuaded.

18

Like Fury

Spain, Paris, Yorkshire, Cambridge, July–October 1956

A t last I have found my native country," Sylvia wrote her mother in July 1956 on a train bound for Madrid. Just four months earlier, she had wept for Richard Sassoon in Paris as he traveled through southern Spain.[1] Now she hurtled through the same dry landscape alongside her "magnificent handsome brilliant" poet-husband, sharing wine with Spanish soldiers.[2] As she stared out the window, she marveled at the "violent colors" and the "blinding white pueblos."[3] In Andalucía, workers lounged with jugs of wine beside donkey carts, and widows covered El Greco faces with black lace mantillas. In the small seaside village of Benidorm, Sylvia and Ted would walk along dirt lanes through hills of almond groves, barter with fishermen at the morning market, and buy their milk straight from a neighbor's goat. For Sylvia, no other European country would compare to Spain's "primitive unspoilt dreamland."[4]

After their Bloomsday wedding, Sylvia, Ted, and Aurelia had returned to Cambridge until June 21. The three of them then traveled to Paris on the 22nd.[5] Ted established a friendly rapport with Aurelia, and did not seem to mind spending the first part of his honeymoon with his new mother-in-law. Sylvia minded more, but she could hardly leave Aurelia behind after begging her to come to England.

In Paris they met up with Luke, and Sylvia was treated to drunken ballads on the banks of the Seine. She found Aurelia a surprisingly relaxed traveler— "she was like a young girl—taking pictures, drinking wine, etc.," she wrote Marcia.[6] Hughes was more somber. "Your Paris, I thought, was American," he later wrote in "Your Paris":

Under the chestnut shades of Hemingway,
Fitzgerald, Henry Miller, Gertrude Stein,
I kept my Paris from you. My Paris
Was only just not German. The capital
Of the Occupation and old nightmare.

His wife, he thought, saw none of this, just "frame after frame, / Street after street, of Impressionist paintings."[7] Yet she was less giddy than he knew. Newly married to her creative and physical ideal, she had expected happiness at full tilt. Instead, Paris exhausted her—"felt drugged & slow," "Absolutely wicked, futile day," "sad day," she wrote in her calendar throughout late June and early July. She had not counted on sharing her honeymoon with her mother, who traveled with them until June 29, and Luke, who kept "barging in" on her and Ted.[8]

To complicate matters, she found a long, bitter letter from Sassoon waiting for her at the American Express office on July 2. He had felt "shock" when he received her letter telling him about her engagement, and he mourned the end of their relationship. "There is really no reason for me not to believe that you are happier now than you ever were or could have been with me . . . Except that your letter to me was not the letter of a happy woman." Sylvia had earlier reminded him that he had abandoned her in Paris—she referred to it as "the crime"—and told him she was doing what was best for *her*. Sassoon accepted the new reality, along with dawning awareness of the life they might have lived together. "I shall have my years to live in the structure of less, in regret and even in shame. For the angel is dead, the red god dead, and I am like a carcass from whom the interior has been taken."[9] He reassured her that he would soon be out of her life for good when he sailed to New York that June. There he would find work until the Army called him up.

Reading this dramatic letter from Sassoon in Paris—on her honeymoon—must have been deeply discomfiting for Sylvia. Only four months had passed since she had traveled to Paris for Sassoon's sake and found herself "deserted" for the first time in her life. Heartbroken, she flew back to Ted. But Sassoon's letter suggests his own heartbreak and regret; Mel Woody and Dick Wertz said that it took Sassoon years to get over Plath, who had been his first love.[10] His letter likely upset Sylvia's equilibrium, and helps explain the melancholy she noted in her calendar that July. Ted knew about Sassoon—he testified in his *Bell Jar* trial deposition that Sylvia had mentioned him—but he would not learn of her despondent search for Sassoon in Paris until he read her journals after her death. Shortly after Sylvia received Sassoon's letter, she wrote "The Shrike," a poem about a wife who is jealous of her husband's dreams; it was the first iteration of a story—"The Wishing Box"—that she would start in Benidorm and finish in Cambridge.

Sylvia had once longed to visit the great capitals of Europe, but now she found that traveling produced "great fatigue." She and Ted needed "several hours" of quiet writing time each day. Otherwise, she told Aurelia, who was traveling in Amsterdam, "we get cold on paper, cross, or nervous. . . . We are really happiest keeping to ourselves, and writing, writing, writing."[11] They could hardly afford to gallivant across Europe, and her Olivetti typewriter was heavy.

The couple arrived in Madrid on July 7. The city's "eerie hot night streets" and throngs of evening crowds heightened Plath's sense of Spain as a surrealist spectacle.[12] In the "dry blazing heat" her sinus problems abated, leaving her, she wrote, with "a light clear head that I never knew was possible."[13] Ted was amazed by their hotel's private shower, as his last bath had been "in a public hole in London" on his wedding day.[14] Sylvia wrote home that he yipped with glee at the prospect of private ablutions.

Following in Hemingway's footsteps, they attended a bullfight at Las Ventas, but they left "disgusted and sickened by such brutality."[15] Sylvia was almost happy to see the bull gore the matador in the thigh. She later wrote a story, "The Black Bull," about a chauvinistic husband and an angry, patronized wife.[16] It was a theme she had already used to good effect in "Sunday at the Mintons" and would explore again in "The Wishing Box," "The Fifty-Ninth Bear," and "The Perfect Place." But it was an unusual honeymoon story.

After five days in Madrid, they traveled eight hours south to Alicante, which Sylvia thought "worse than any Coney Island." But the seaside fishing village of Benidorm, an hour north of Alicante on the Costa Brava, exceeded her expectations with its "blaze of blue sea, clean curve of beach, immaculate white houses and streets, like a small sparkling dream town." Dry, ochre hills framed white Moorish buildings atop cliffs that fell dramatically to the sea, where fishing boats listed on a wide sandy beach. The village seemed to have escaped the twentieth century; donkeys pulled wooden carts past women washing clothes in the public fountain. There were flowers and palm trees everywhere. "I felt instinctively with Ted that this was our place," Sylvia wrote home.[17]

A woman on the bus to Benidorm who overheard Sylvia and Ted talking introduced herself as Señora Mangada, and offered to rent them a room in her house overlooking the beach. The señora's colorful garden and large, well-stocked kitchen charmed Sylvia, as did the señora herself as she spoke, in French, about the romance novels and poems she had written and the Spanish lessons she could offer. Though Sylvia found the room itself "too small," its French doors opened onto a large, private balcony terrace with a stunning view of the sea.[18] The balcony convinced them to stay. On July 12, they settled in for ten weeks of creative discipline.[19]

In the mornings they breakfasted on café con leche, brandy milk, and bananas. Lunch—often on the beach—was bread, butter, tomatoes, herring, eggs, potatoes, sardines, and fruit; dinner was fresh fish and cheap wine on their balcony. In the evening sea breeze, they fantasized about buying their own villa in Benidorm. "We have such fun," Sylvia wrote Aurelia, "and both agree that we don't feel we're living with 'another' person, but only the perfect male and female counterparts of our own selves, very whole and happy."[20] Her children would be "lucky" to be "bred on original fables!"[21]

As usual, Sylvia gave her mother the "gay side." In her journal she called her first morning in Benidorm "a nightmare."[22] The señora's kitchen was infested with ants; there was no hot water or refrigeration; the small single bathroom had temperamental plumbing; the tap water was not potable. Sylvia had to boil milk and clean dishes with cold water and straw. "But how I long for a good american [sic] kitchen," she despaired.[23] They soon realized that the balcony, which had seemed so quiet during the siesta hours, overlooked a crowded boulevard. Ted took to writing inside the small bedroom to avoid the tourists' stares. The lack of refrigeration meant that food spoiled easily, and the two were often sick with fever and diarrhea. Both suffered terribly from sunburn. Their Lawrentian fantasy was coming apart at the seams.

Money, too, was a constant concern. Sylvia told Warren she had almost nothing until her next Fulbright check came in September, while Ted had only the £50 Olwyn owed him. Yet Sylvia told others she was "daring to live the way most people dream of living when they are fifty: to sacrifice all for our ideal of a good life, not other people's cars & securities & 10-year leases."[24] She boasted to Aurelia that they ate "perfectly well" on one dollar a day—but then admitted her anxiety. "I hope never again in my life I will have to be so tight with money. We will one day have a great deal, I am sure of it."[25] She claimed that they had no money for air-mail stamps and could not send out manuscripts. Aurelia, who was traveling in Europe and would join Mrs. Prouty in London in early August, promptly sent her $100.

Surprisingly, Sylvia asked her mother to come to Benidorm. It was an odd request for a honeymooning daughter, yet she longed for the comfort and security of her mother's presence as she tried to make the best of a deteriorating situation. Hughes later wrote of Plath's unease in his poem "You Hated Spain": "Spain frightened you," he wrote. He thought Plath recognized a familiar darkness—"the blood-raw light," "the Goya funeral grin"—

and "recoiled."[26] Yet Plath was as fascinated as she was disturbed. Hughes would come to feel that Federico García Lorca's *duende*—the otherwordly force of pain, blood, and lust that pulsed within Spanish music and poetry—was the antidote to "colorless" English poetry, which he and Plath intended to shock out of submission.[27]

After one week, Señora Mangada told Plath and Hughes they needed to leave so she could rent the whole house to another family. Sylvia excoriated her in a letter to Aurelia, but that night, she and Ted went for a walk and, on a hunch, followed a road into the mountains. There, they came upon a large white stucco house for rent. They promptly secured the ground floor for the same price the Señora had charged for just one room—about $175 for ten weeks. The house, in the "native quarter" at 59 Tomás Ortuño, had a private kitchen and seemed to them "a grand mansion" with its three bedrooms, dining room, living room, and lovely vine-covered porch.[28] They were farther from the sea, and there were cockroaches, but they had escaped the noisy bustle of fishmongers and tourists.

The change benefited their writing. The two worked in cool, quiet solitude facing each other from the ends of the large dining room table. The floor was tiled with stone, "giving the effect," Plath wrote, "of living at the cool bottom of a well."[29] They wrote until noon, then lunched, sketched, and swam until the late afternoon, when they wrote again until dinner. Sylvia was increasingly proud of her sketches, and thought she was developing an original "primitive" style.[30] She sold several pieces to *The Christian Science Monitor*. Hughes worked on the fables "How the Animals Became" and "O'Kelly's Angel."

Plath was determined to write prose rather than poetry, for she thought she had not written a good story in three years. Between July 22 and 27 she wrote two drafts of "The Black Bull" but felt her mind "an impressionist blur." (Whereas Hughes's vision, she said, was "photographic.")[31] She began "The Hypnotizing Husband" on July 24, a story based on Hughes's hypnosis of her when she was ill; she would publish a darker version in *Granta* later that year as "The Wishing Box." She also worked on an outline for her Cambridge novel; a doppelgänger story about Nancy Hunter called "The Fabulous Roommate"; and a story outline, "Remember the Stick Man." She finished a poem on August 19, "Epitaph for Fire and Flower," and a twenty-five-page piece about their former landlady, "That Widow Mangada." She hoped to sell the stories to *Ladies' Home Journal* or *McCall's*.

Ted read her Shakespeare while she cooked (he was "shocked" that she had read only thirteen of his plays) and set her concentration and observation exercises as he had for Luke and Daniel.[32] Sylvia appreciated the exercises at first, but she would come to resent them. When he awoke each morning, he told her of his dreams about animals and William Blake—a detail that found its way into "The Wishing Box." Her nightmares receded, but she wrote little in Spain—at least, by her standards. She had composed more poems during her busy last term at Cambridge. Plath's imagined ideal conditions for writing had ironically produced writer's block, a pattern that would continue—with the exception of her Yaddo residency—whenever she set aside full weeks to write.

In her journal, she wondered whether Ted's presence was to blame for her block. She began to think of their configuration at the writing table as a face-off. In her short, ironic vignette "Mr. and Mrs. Ted Hughes's Writing Table," Plath portrayed Hughes as the more serious writer:

> At the head of the table, Ted sat in a squarely built grandfather chair with wicker back and seat; his realm was a welter of sheets of typing paper and ragged cardboard-covered notebooks . . . A bottle of blue ink, perpetually open, rested on a stack of paper. Crumpled balls of used paper lay here and there, to be thrown into the large wooden crate placed for that purpose in the doorway. All papers and notebooks on this half of the table were tossed at angles, kitty-corner and impromptu.

In Plath's description, her side of the table "was piled with tediously neat stacks of books and papers, all laid prim and four-squared to the table corners . . . a ragged brown covered Thesaurus . . . a bottle of jet black ink, scrupulously screwed shut."[33] She needs a thesaurus; he does not. Her ink bottle is shut; his is open. He sits at the head of the table; she seems strangely disembodied. Despite Sylvia's exclamations of marital bliss in her letters home, "Mr. and Mrs. Ted Hughes's Writing Table" suggests that she was aware of the partnership's creative complications—the potential for both influence and rivalry—from the earliest days of her marriage.

Plath returned to the image of the writing table again in "The Other Two," written in 1958–59 but set during the Benidorm honeymoon. The poem speaks to creative tension as much as it does to a lovers' quarrel. The speaker feels haunted by a pair of lovers she sees in the wood of the "baronial" dining room table:

> He lifts an arm to bring her close, but she
> Shies from his touch: his is an iron mood.
> Seeing her freeze, he turns his face away.
> They poise and grieve as in some old tragedy.

This ghostly couple follows the real lovers, invading their dreams. They seem harbingers of trouble.

At night, Plath and Hughes studied languages and translated *Le Rouge et le Noir*, then walked amid the almond trees toward the shadowy, purple hills. They fantasized about a future in Spain or teaching Spanish at an American university. Yet Sylvia's calendar reveals fatigue, creative frustration, and discontent throughout July and August. She recorded her fury over a letter from Olwyn, her bouts of fever and diarrhea, sleepless nights, and "depressing" siestas.[34] At Cambridge, she had eaten in hall and had a housekeeper. Now she did all the daily shopping, cooking, laundry, and cleaning. In her calendar she wrote of her exhaustion after boiling sheets and towels and scrubbing the bathroom and kitchen floors on her hands and knees.

The couple quarreled on July 23. "Bad evening after Ted's letter home," Sylvia wrote cryptically in her calendar. "Wild, full moon-walk toward mountains in glare of moonlight—sour wrongness continuing through morning of shopping—tears, synthesis & good dear love—day of recovering."[35] Her journal entry is equally ambiguous as to the cause of the row:

> No sleep, smothering. Sitting in nightgown and sweater in the dining room staring into the full moon, talking to the full moon, with wrongness growing and filling the house like a man-eating plant. The need to go out. It is very quiet. Perhaps he is asleep. Or dead. How to know how long there is before death. The fish may be poisoned, and the poison working. And two sit apart in wrongness. . . . Two silent strangers.[36]

This was the first time Sylvia had written so despairingly about her relationship with Ted. In the letter that troubled her, Ted told his parents he and Sylvia would be married by the time they visited Yorkshire in September. He added, "Don't be frightened of Sylvia being a drag. It's obvious from what's happened since I met her that she is anything but." He reassured them that Sylvia was "very very bright," "a very fine cook and a much more certain money-earner than myself."[37] Sylvia's calendar entry suggests that she had come across this letter before Ted sent it. She may have been angry about his decision to reveal the secret marriage, and troubled by her in-laws' skepticism about her character.

Hughes later wrote a poem about this quarrel called "Moonwalk." In an early, more personal draft that differs considerably from the final poem, he wrote that Plath had run outside in a "dumb rage," and he had followed, bewildered. "I came after you to catch you, maybe / As you walked into the sea / Or off the edge of a cliff." They walked along on a "moonlit hill with its contorted olives" overlooking the harbor. In the poem, he tries to calm her. "'Look,' I said, 'the lamps of the sardine fleet.'" He felt as though they were floating in space. "Your mask was bleak as cut iron," he wrote.

> I had no idea what was going on behind it.
> I still hardly knew you. No idea
> What might come flapping out of your cupped hands.
> I watched.
> Doctor of all difficulties, I humored.
> Your attempt to kill yourself long since
> Was meaningless to me as my own death.
> I tended the life of the survivor which had nothing to do with the dead one's.[38]

This quarrel seems to have troubled Sylvia for the next two weeks. On July 27 she wrote in her calendar of her "relieved decision to leave Spain early," and on August 9 she noted her "inability to write poetry—sad and sick—view of uncertainties."[39] She often rocked herself calm in a favorite chair on the house's "viny porch."[40] One afternoon, she had a "talk with self in water alone" while Ted was at a Spanish lesson.[41]

On August 14, they hitched to Alicante, where Ted applied to teach English at the Instituto Vox. He impressed the faculty, who practically promised him a position beginning that fall. Sylvia was relieved that they would be able to support themselves while she finished her last year at Cambridge, and began to feel more secure about their future; she wrote in her journal that she had never experienced such "Perfect mental and physical well-being."[42] When she suffered food poisoning that August, Ted sat vigil through the night, cooling her body with damp cloths and cradling her head as he fed her watermelon and broth. She had never been so sick, and she called Ted "an absolute angel."[43] But Hughes had been unnerved by his wife's panic. In his *Birthday Letters* poem "Fever," he wrote,

> You cried for America
> And its medicine cupboard. . . .
> . . . "Help me," you whispered, "help me."
> . . . Your cry jammed so hard
> Over into the red of catastrophe
> Left no space for worse. And I thought
> How sick is she? Is she exaggerating?
> And I recoiled, just a little,
> Just for balance, just for symmetry,

Into sceptical patience, a little.
If it can be borne, why make so much of it?
"Come on, now," I soothed. "Don't be so scared.
It's only a bug, don't let it run away with you."

What I was really saying was: "Stop crying wolf."
Other thoughts, chilly, familiar thoughts,
Came across the tightrope: "Stop crying wolf,
Or else I shall not know, I shall not hear
When things get really bad."[44]

If Hughes sensed a more lethal depression to come, he seems to have underestimated the severity of Plath's "bug" that August. She would remember it as one of the worst illnesses of her life and would tell others she had almost died. Ted was used to the spartan conditions of postwar British life, but Sylvia was tired of pretending she found such conditions quaint. She began dreaming of "refrigerators & pasteurized milk and drinkable tap water . . . Now that I have lived without icebox or variety of food or any convenience whatsoever, any place in America will seem like luxury to me," she wrote Aurelia that August. "I only hope that subtly I can convince Ted to love it as much as I do."[45]

Their money was running out, and they had already decided, in July, not to stay through September in Spain. They would spend four days with Warren in Paris, then September at Hughes's parents' home in Yorkshire. By their last week in Benidorm, both felt attuned to the town's rhythms, which Plath captured in her detailed, black-ink sketches of peasant markets and sardine boats. Yet the brutal Spanish heat had begun to fray her nerves; she now claimed she preferred the "gray weather" of Paris, telling Aurelia that under "the blank blazing sun . . . there is a lack of intellectual stimulus in countries as hot as Spain."[46]

On August 21 the couple traveled by train to Paris through Barcelona, where they stopped off to see the monkeys and crocodiles at the zoo. In Paris, they met up with Warren and saw Sergei Eisenstein's *Battleship Potemkin*. Warren told Aurelia he was "Very, very pleased" with Ted, and thought the couple looked brown and healthy.[47] Sylvia had not needed Aurelia's $100 check after all, and returned it to her through Warren.

Sylvia sat on the banks of the Seine and remembered why she loved Paris; she had missed "the continuous fine movies and plays and art exhibits."[48] Ted wrote a pleasant letter to Aurelia about their travels, and how Spain had released his wife's creative imagination. "I try to keep her writing and drawing—the more she does, the more she can do, and the better she feels."[49]

They hoped to sell everything they had written and drawn; he was optimistic that Sylvia's sketches would fetch a considerable price. Sylvia, too, wrote to others of her idyllic honeymoon. But when she returned to Cambridge that fall, she would finish the story she started in Benidorm, "The Wishing Box," about a wife who commits suicide rather than endure another day in her magnificent husband's shadow.

———

"I WISH YOU COULD see your daughter now," Sylvia wrote Aurelia from West Yorkshire that September. She was staying at the Beacon, Ted's parents' home, just outside the small hilltop village of Heptonstall, high above the mill town of Hebden Bridge where the Hugheses now ran a tobacconist and "fancy goods" shop.[50] Heptonstall, with its commanding views and plentiful light, was the most desirable place to live in the Calder Valley.[51] Billy and Edith Hughes were proud of their upward trajectory, but when Aurelia visited them in 1961 she would find that years of soot pollution had blackened the town's gritstone homes, and the sky seemed tombstone gray. Several of the village's cottages were derelict, abandoned for the warmer, plumbed council houses built nearby in the late 1930s. Ellie Friedman, who visited Sylvia in Heptonstall in September 1956, was unsettled by the town's quiet insularity. Ted told Ellie that villagers watched what was going on outside their homes in strategically placed mirrors. He may have been joking, but she began to feel watched as she walked along Heptonstall's narrow cobbled lanes.[52] Indeed, a longtime resident whose family had known Sylvia and Ted remembered that when strangers came to the town "the curtains would twitch open."[53] Sylvia told Ellie she felt "very tall and blond and foreign" amongst the villagers.[54] Young American women were rare visitors in that high country.

Where Aurelia saw soot stains, Sylvia saw Gothic charm. The Beacon, perched atop one of the highest points in Heptonstall, had heart-expanding, panoramic views of the Pennine hills and moors: Shackleton, Crimsworth Dean, Colden, and the wooded valley of Hardcastle Crags. Sylvia set the scene for Aurelia soon after arriving: "a wicked north wind is whipping a blowing rain against the little house and coal fires are glowing." Outside her bedroom window she could see "an incredible wild green landscape of bare hills" covered with stone walls, sheep, cows, and clear streams. She said she had become "a veritable convert to the Brontë clan, in warm woolen sweaters, slacks, knee socks."[55] Rooks' caws and wingbeats punctuated the silence as she wandered around the ruins of the thirteenth-century village church and its Gothic graveyard (coincidentally full of Greenwoods, her grandmother's Anglicized maiden name). The atmospheric church grounds—along with the cemetery at nearby Haworth—would help inspire a fine poem, "November Graveyard," which Plath began on September 9.[56] She did not know, when she wrote the last stanza of "November Graveyard," that she was contemplating her own burial ground:

> At the essential landscape stare, stare
> Till your eyes foist a vision dazzling on the wind:
> Whatever lost ghosts flare,
> Damned, howling in their shrouds across the moor
> Rave on the leash of the starving mind
> Which peoples the bare room, the blank, untenanted air.

Sylvia was condescending toward Ted's family, calling them "dear, simple Yorkshire folk." She described Edith as the "plump" mistress of a "tiny kitchen" where she made "starchy little pottages and meat pies."[57] By the end of her stay, she would abandon her reserve and tell Aurelia that Edith was "a messy pottering kitchen-keeper and atrocious cook . . . it is all I can do not to rearrange her sloppy cupboards etc."[58] Yet she wanted Edith's approval. After the couple separated, Edith expressed sadness to Aurelia and praised Sylvia's strength of character. Yet she also told Ted's brother Gerald she thought Sylvia had been "strong-willed" and "possessive." Gerald and his wife always seemed to be surrounded by sunshine, she said, but Ted and Sylvia were more "sober" together.[59] Edith thought Sylvia's German heritage accounted for her serious disposition, yet she never doubted that Ted and Sylvia were happy together in the early years of their marriage.

The couple spent their mornings walking on the moors, which Sylvia began to love as much as the ocean, "striding on top of the world . . . with the great luminous emerald lights changing always."[60] Hughes's uncle, Walt Farrar, led them over the moors to Top Withens, the ruined farmhouse reputed to be the site of the original Wuthering Heights. Sylvia was more impressed with the landscape than the broken-down building itself, but she reread *Wuthering Heights* and told her mother she "really <u>felt</u> it this time more than ever."[61] The relics at the nearby Brontë Parsonage Museum in Haworth moved her. "They touched this, wore that, wrote here," she wrote in her journal.[62] She described herself and Ted as "a happy Heathcliffe [*sic*] and Cathy! Striding about in the woods and over the moors."[63] In late September the two again hiked over the moors behind the Beacon to Top Withens, but this time, without Uncle Walt, they got lost. They made love in the heather, and then flagged a bus home.

Sylvia had received good news on September 1—*The Atlantic* had taken "Pursuit" for $50; it would appear in the January 1957 issue.[64] But she felt depressed and restless for nearly her entire month at the Beacon. The word "weary" appeared often in her Yorkshire calendar that September. She was jealous of her mother-in-law, to whom she seemed to have temporarily "lost" her husband; "no good love since Paris—growing sense of suffocation & loneliness," Sylvia wrote in her calendar on September 4. She walked out onto the moors alone, weeping, filled with "fury at Ted's lack of understanding." The next day was "grim warped blocked," "mind caught in cog somewhere," "depressed and sterile." She took a walk with Ted to a ruined mill through "green glooms of heather" but felt "wet, never-cheerful." She began to fear she was losing herself—to Hughes, to the vast weather of his person and his horizonless home: "sick, sterile fear in face of his great creativeness," she wrote in her calendar on September 6.[65] On September 7, Plath began what she called a "secret story, slight & subversive" titled "Hardcastle Crags" (the title refers to a wooded trail and park near the Beacon):

> Cold, she resolved, I shall go cold as he. She lay in the grass, not daring to get up for fear Gerald would spot her and spoil her perfect fury of self-pity. Daylong he sat tousled in his mother's parlor in his old RAF sweater, writing poems about water drops and martyred bishops and playing his battered, cracked Beethoven records over and over. Beethoven's deathmask hung waxen and eerie in their bedroom. She had married a genius. . . .
>
> . . . Oh, she would make him sorry this last time. She heard the police demanding sternly: "Gerald, what have you done with your wife?" "Why," Gerald said, gnawing absent-minded on a slice of buttered malt bread, "she lost herself on the moor one day about a week ago. Careless girl." Perhaps, Olwyn thought, she would only stay out overnight. She tried to remember the direction back to Gerald's mother's house.[66]

While Sylvia frequently bragged to others about Ted's "genius," here it is a source of irony.

Plath wrote another "secret" "subversive" work around this time.[67] In "On the Difficulty of Conjuring Up a Dryad," Plath frames her speaker's sense of artistic inadequacy through the metaphor of psychoanalysis:

> "My trouble, doctor, is: I see a tree,
> And that damn scrupulous tree won't practice wiles
>   To beguile sight:
>   E.g., by cant of light
>   Concoct a Daphne;
>   My tree stays tree."

The relationship between doctor and patient here parallels that of the male and female writer as Plath slyly challenges Hughes's Neoromantic, shamanistic version of artistic creation with her own less "visionary" style. "On the Difficulty" suggests creative tensions within the marriage even at a time when Plath told her mother, "There is no question of rivalry."[68] To Aurelia, Sylvia wrote blithely from Yorkshire, "I can't for a minute think of him as someone 'other' than the male counterpart of myself, always just that many steps ahead of me intellectually and creatively so that I feel very feminine and admiring."[69] Given that it was Plath, in fact, who was "ahead" of Hughes professionally, her comment suggests the gendered tightrope she was walking. Plath had hoped that this ideal marriage of true minds would help her writing, but this poem, and her stories "Hardcastle Crags" and "The Wishing Box" suggest that she was already anxious about sublimating her talent and ambition to Hughes.

But she was productive in Yorkshire. She typed up "Remember the Stick Man," "The Black Bull," "That Widow Mangada," and "Hardcastle Crags" and sent the latter three to *Mademoiselle* on September 17. (She also typed up Hughes's stories and poems.) She wrote another short story there, "All the Dead Dears," and at least two poems, "November Graveyard" and "Obstacle Course" (since lost). Still, Hughes remembered her weariness:

> When we walked North
> Across Crow Hill Moors to Wuthering Heights
> You were still learning what I was like.
> I was still learning the same. You weren't sure
> What you felt about the Blackstone West Riding.
> It amused and depressed you. It was color
> For a novelist's eye, you diligently noted—
> But your soul shrank from it. And I was part of it.
> Your salt-scoured, Cape-Cod spinnaker sparkling spirit
> Was depressed. Sometimes appalled. But we walked
> Out across that ocean of skylines
> Not all that much unlike North Dakota.
> It was prairie wide, and wild, & good.
> And Wuthering Heights was there romantically
> Somewhere ahead. And the sky
> Was vast gulfs of blue, and the air
> Lifted us like alcohol[70]

Hughes recalled that on one of these walks, they came across a half-dead grouse that had been wounded by a fox. He crushed the grouse's head with a stone, "gently," in an "instant." But Sylvia was appalled. Ever since a stranger on a bus had told her about "heather-birds" on the moors—a detail she used in her story "Initiation"—the grouse had symbolized the artist's solitary path. Hughes later wrote, "I saw you saw in what I had just done / Something incredible, inconceivable."[71] Plath wept, horrified.

At the Beacon, Sylvia was no longer Isis but a duty-bound daughter-in-law. She felt suddenly alienated from her husband, and missed America and her family as she realized the enormity of the step she had taken. Wilfrid Riley grew up in Heptonstall and became close to the Hughes family. He used to visit the Beacon when Ted and Sylvia were staying there and remembered Sylvia's difficulty fitting in.[72] She was, he recalled, "a very clever person, but you couldn't be at ease with her some way. She wasn't with you. She was up in the clouds, always studying poetry, what have you. . . . You couldn't sit with her and converse with her like you can normal people." It wasn't pride, he thought, that made her this way. "Shyness came into it. She couldn't lend herself to people. She was a little bit aloof from people, and I don't think she intended to be."[73]

As usual, Mrs. Prouty saw straight into the heart of things. She wrote Sylvia on September 12, "So often a girl has to go through a disturbing period when visiting her fiancé's people—& many an engagement goes onto the rocks after such an upsetting test." Prouty admitted that she had been worried, when Sylvia first wrote to her about Ted, "that there might be a tragedy ahead," but that Aurelia had reassured her he was "a most gentle and understanding person." She did have one lingering concern: "It is most interesting that you find that satisfied love is conducive to writing. I think most creative writers are spurred more by unsatisfied love, unfulfilled yearning and untold wants than by the satiating effect of complete emotional happiness."[74]

Plath's moor poems, which she wrote in the late fifties and early sixties, reflect an ambivalence about Hughes's home ground. In "Hardcastle Crags" (1957), a young woman walks out alone to confront a violent, alienating landscape. The cottages she sees are "dark, dwarfed" as in a sinister fairy tale, while the "long wind" pares "her person down / To a pinch of flame." Plath writes, "the weight / Of stones and hills of stones could break / Her down to mere quartz grit in that stony light . . ." In "Wuthering Heights," the sky is "pale," the sheep stare blankly, and the speaker feels the wind "trying / To funnel my heat away." The air communicates only two words: "Black stone, black stone." In "The Snowman on the Moor" (1957) the speaker flees onto the moors after quarreling with her lover. There, she meets a surreal snowman wearing a belt of women's skulls—women whose "wit made fools / Of kings, unmanned kings' sons." The speaker returns home "humbled," "crying"—silenced for her feminine rebelliousness as she makes her way through a landscape haunted by Lear, Heathcliff, and Hughes himself. In 1961 Plath would write "Wuthering Heights," where the horizons "ring" the speaker, then "dissolve and dissolve / Like a series of promises." The dissolving promises, constricting "ring," and doomed love story suggest, perhaps, something more than the poet was willing to admit.

Ellie Friedman's visit to Heptonstall that September cheered Sylvia. Ellie and her friend John met Sylvia for tea at the grand, Tudor-style Sutcliffe's Inn, where Ellie updated Sylvia on Smith gossip. (When Sylvia heard about the recent affairs between students and professors, she vowed not to let Ted teach there.) Ellie found Ted "warm and somewhat withdrawn." She did not quite know what to make of him. He insisted that the four visit a witch in the valley at midnight, but all they found was a "gnarled" old woman sitting by the fire. "We talked about farming, neighbors and wildlife rather than eye of newt and mandrake root," Ellie said.[75] He worked on her horoscope while she was there but refused to share the results before she left. He didn't like what he saw. "It was an odd thing to do," she recalled.

One day they visited Haworth parsonage, then hiked to Top Withens. Ellie remembered Sylvia sitting down to sketch the ruined farmhouse and its lone, bare tree. On the way back to Heptonstall—a much longer trek—Ted got them lost. Ellie was surprised, as Ted had intimated he knew the wild terrain well.[76] As darkness dropped, they found a farmer who offered them tea and directions home. "That night," Ellie remembered, "Sylvia made rabbit stew and we ate like starved prisoners." Ted had hunted and killed the rabbit, an act that seemed both to repulse and attract Sylvia. "It bothered her," Ellie recalled, "but she liked the fact of it. . . . Freed at last of our intellects, of addressing ourselves to logic."[77] (Plath drew upon this experience in her later poem "The Rabbit Catcher.") They spent the next few days taking long walks in the high country. Ellie had never seen Sylvia "so delighted with life, love and optimism dangling from her like jewels." Sylvia told her that Ted was the most magnificent man she had ever met, " 'Aside from the fact that he's not a Jew,' she winked."[78] Ellie understood what Sylvia saw in Ted. "*Wuthering Heights*, the movie, with Laurence Olivier—that was our idea of the 'great love.' . . . The brooding genius who would die for us. . . . That was formative in our lives."[79]

Despite the pleasant days with Ellie, Sylvia's "dull dead feeling" soon returned.[80] Edith blundered in on the couple while they were making love, and Sylvia felt a "growing sickness & jealousy & oppression—sense of rivalry with women—cut off from proper privacy."[81] On Edith's birthday, September 18, Sylvia recorded a "smothered chocking [*sic*] feeling of frustration & uncertain future just out of reach . . . horrid imaginings of rivalry & sickening voodoo forces."[82] She took a long walk with Ellie on September 21, and wrote in her calendar, "tears & cows . . . sloppy dominating intruding mother—tears, sickness, final relief & blame on intolerable <u>situation</u>." She felt better the next morning—"depression lifting"—and spent her last few days in Yorkshire reading Hemingway, revising her story "All the Dead Dears" (based on stories she had heard from Hughes's parents), and sitting before the fire listening to Beethoven, "the only music big enough for Ted."[83]

BEFORE THE NEW TERM at Cambridge began, Sylvia accompanied Ted to a poetry-reading audition at the BBC in London on September 27 that had been arranged by Peter Redgrove.[84] She was full of wifely pride—"eager, alive talk with dear Ted—Optimism & excitement," she wrote in her calendar.[85] At the studio, Sylvia encouraged Ted to read one of his own poems in addition to Yeats and Hopkins. She sat in the listening room with Donald Carne-Ross, who nodded along as Hughes spoke, muttering "superb" and "perfect." He offered Hughes a spot on the BBC's "erudite" Third Programme reading Yeats.[86] This opportunity almost made up for the separation the couple was about to endure. The marriage was still a secret, lest Plath lose her Fulbright, and so she returned to Cambridge to finish her final year alone while Hughes returned to his parents' house in Yorkshire. He still had vague plans to teach in Spain.

On October 1, Sylvia's first day back at Whitstead, she learned that *Poetry* had accepted "Two Sisters of Persephone," "Metamorphosis," "Wreath for a Bridal," "Strumpet Song," "Dream with Clam-Diggers," and "Epitaph for Fire and Flower." She was pleased that these were mostly "<u>happy</u> poems" that celebrated her love for Ted. *Poetry* was, she told Aurelia, "a magazine of <u>poets</u> . . . and not commercial!"[87] Christopher Levenson had told Plath that she "wouldn't sell much of such poetry," and she was thrilled to prove him wrong. "So there is a god afterall [*sic*]; and it isn't, praise be, Stephen Spender," she wrote Ted in Yorkshire. She told him the *Poetry* acceptance was "the consecration of my new writing, which, properly, began with you and 'Pursuit.'"[88] Ted congratulated her without jealousy: "Joy, Joy as the hyena cried. Now you are set. I never read six poems of anyone all together in Poetry. . . . It will spellbind every Editor in America. It will also be a standing bottomless battery to charge what you write from now on . . . Joy, Joy."[89] He predicted she would win the Borestone poetry award, but worried that her success would make her "open to every knave's nice manners and charming conversation while I sit here and stare at the skyline like an old stone."[90] Away from her in Heptonstall, he felt paralyzed. "I love you, Sylvia, all day, all night when I can't sleep. Thinking about you and just blankly missing you has brought me to a standstill. I love you I love you I love you."[91]

Alone in Cambridge, Sylvia found her fellow students abrasive and the food more "gruesome" than she remembered.[92] But she forced herself to work, and began to write again—"Monologue at 3 AM" on October 3, "Street Song" on October 4, and "Touch & Go" on October 5. She tried to settle into "this queer ascetic way of life," and spent much of her time walking in Grantchester, drawing birds and cows.[93] She told Ted, "it gives me such a sense of peace to draw; more than prayer, walks, anything. . . . It is as if, by concentrating on the 'inscape', as Hopkins says, of leaf and plant and animal, I can know the world in a new and special way."[94]

Jane Baltzell and Isabel Murray had grown closer in Sylvia's absence, and their tight friendship gave her an "outside feeling."[95] Jane remembered that Sylvia was quieter, more self-contained, after she met Ted. He "had reached her very deeply." Sylvia was used to being in control in her relationships, but now, Jane thought, "she might have been a little amazed and perhaps slightly alarmed at how much he meant to her."[96]

Sylvia avoided the other students, especially the Americans, whom she now saw as "extrovert, surface, blithering."[97] She told Ted she felt sick without him. She wept; she couldn't eat; she had terrifying nightmares about tribal ceremonies and purifying rituals. "I think if anything ever happened to you, I would really kill myself," she wrote to Hughes on October 9. "I shall never leave your side a day in my life after the exams."[98] Before bed each night, she knelt by the window and threw all her "force and love" toward Ted's bed in Yorkshire. "I can't believe any body ever loved like this; nobody will again."[99] The ritual made her feel more connected to her husband: "my whole life, being, breathing, thinking, sleeping, and eating, has somehow . . . become indissolubly welded to you."[100]

Sylvia lived chastely, but it was during this time that she committed herself to a poetry of the body. She called herself "a female lyricist who sings the glory of love . . . We shall be living proof that great writing comes from a pure, faithful, joyous creative bed. . . . I love you like fury."[101] She was reading Augustine and Saint Paul, but found their stances against the body ("flesh means sin") "intolerable." "The blind leap" of Christianity appalled her, and she called God "a rat."[102] But she was enjoying herself: "God how these writings stimulate my thinking."[103] She quoted "blessed Yeats" in defense of her new "strong blood-faith," and invoked Chaucer's Wife of Bath as her model: "Bless the strong loving body."[104] She was impressed, too, with Sartre's concept of existentialism. Hughes advised her to maintain her skepticism about academia in general and Christian authors in particular, and to read Blake as "antidote" to Augustine—

"all your christian [*sic*] philosopher trash, and it is trash, all completely crooked." The entire church, he felt, was "the perch of avarice, greed, cruelty, and tyranny."[105] She was forging a creative philosophy in the crucible of love.

From Yorkshire, Ted wrote loving letters addressed to his "Puss-Kish Ponky." He sympathized with Sylvia's desire to read for pleasure, but he exhorted her to buckle down on her tutorial reading and try for a First Class degree. He was ambitious for her; he knew she was capable, though he warned her the effort would entail hours of boredom. He predicted that she would become famous, and told her to read poetry aloud while walking back and forth in her room timed to "the metre" of her steps—if she did not think such advice "too ridiculous."[106] (Later, Plath would tell others her *Ariel* poems must be read aloud.) Without her, he felt "amputated," like he had lost a "vital interior organ."[107] He promised to keep working on television plots, and told her to get three solid hours of thinking in a day—one hour for "remembering," another hour for "discovering plots and themes," and a last hour thinking about "some part of a theme" that interested her. He advised her to "think straight to the thing" without any "mental intervention" when she was composing.[108] Hughes wanted her to keep her mind open, always, to "the demon, the poem dictator"—the *duende*.[109] He was still convinced he had to work in Spain on his own before reuniting with Sylvia after she had finished her degree. "Then we shall have our lives."[110]

That October, Hughes sent Plath several BBC radio and television play plots about unhappily married couples and spouse murderers. Many of these plots concerned marriages that self-destruct on account of jealousy. One, for example, revolves around a woman trapped in an abusive marriage who tries to poison herself but, on second thought, decides to poison her husband instead.[111] Another tells of a husband who flies into a jealous rage after finding his wife with another man.[112] And still another is uncannily prophetic: a newly married couple decides to move to the country in order to find solitude and escape the adulterous temptations of the city. Soon, however, they grow tired of the country and decide to start an inn. Before long, their city friends flock to the inn, and old lovers tempt both husband and wife. In the end, the couple buys a cottage closer to the city so that they will no longer feel so isolated.[113] Was this plot a kind of warning, both to himself and Sylvia, of the potential dangers that awaited them? How could Hughes have known that he and his wife would move to Devon, that their city friends would later descend on them and wreak havoc on their marriage? The plot may have expressed Hughes's subconscious anxiety that lovers who depended solely on one another, who did not allow others into their world, would soon find that world stifling rather than liberating.

In Heptonstall, Hughes spent his days in listless tedium, distracted with longing for Sylvia. He walked the moors, reading Yeats aloud and watching the tumultuous weather that would mark some of his best poems. In addition to the plots, he sent Sylvia long descriptions of moody skies. One evening, a policeman stopped him as he walked toward Hebden Bridge. They had been searching for a criminal and "checked me over as if I were some wild man," he wrote Sylvia. "The fact is, I'm unrecognisable and look like a strange beast unless you're with me."[114] Two young girls had run screaming away when they saw him approach. Sylvia wrote back, "Darling, you're the wildest love-liest piece of flesh walking. If little girls scream, it is only in a kind of Bacchic ecstasy; the police are just jealous."[115]

Alone at Cambridge, Sylvia felt the same sense of "abnormality."[116] When she was not studying, she was writing, typing out Ted's and Luke's manu-scripts, sending out their work to magazines, reading up on the tarot, and walking along the Backs. She wrote to Ted almost every day, a young revo-lutionary plotting to overthrow the established order. Sylvia thought *The London Magazine* and *The New Yorker* were within their sights. "They'll be begging for us yet," she wrote Ted in early October.[117] Though she ridiculed typical *New Yorker* poems—"no blood and guts, just goldenrod and wist-ful crayfish"—she longed for an acceptance there and submitted her work often.[118] Hughes had not yet published in a British magazine, but Plath had faith that he was on the brink of fame. She told him not to tear up his TV play or "go black" if his poems didn't find a home: "THEY WILL."[119] She advised taking advantage of any opportunity, even if unpaid: "we are new, green yet, in their tremulous eyes . . . forget about the money, for god's sake."[120] She urged him not to write "to sell," yet sniffed out contests in *The Observer* and *The Atlantic* with her "incorrigible american [*sic*] weather-eye cocked for windfalls" and nagged Hughes to enter: "I have a project for you to work on this year, for the next 5 or 6 months, and I want you to give it all you've got."[121] She fantasized about fans and TV producers "flocking to the dock in hundreds" when they sailed into New York Harbor. She was only half jok-ing. She suggested they find New York agents that summer, for they would soon need, she wrote, "movie rights, TV rights."[122] Plath was well ahead of her time in her explorations of other media forms beyond poetry. Her confi-dence in their future was astounding, and prescient. "Darling, be scrupulous and date your letters. When we are old and spent, they will come asking for our letters; and we will have them dove-tailable."[123] She told Hughes, "some-day, I will be a rather damn good woman writer."[124]

Plath criticized Hughes's poems insightfully and confidently. "How about another word for 'hideous'? I'd like better something that <u>showed</u> the eyes hideous, as in the fine 'Snake's twisted eye.' "[125] At times she sounded professorial. "I don't think 'horrible void' is the best you can do; I'm eternally suspicious of editorializing with horribles, terribles, awfuls and hideouses; <u>make</u> the void horrible; let your reader have the sweet joy of exclaiming" 'ah! Horrible!' " "Explicate this, please." "Couldn't you do better for either 'vegetative' or 'immensity'? Try like you showed me in Shakespeare, some monosyllabic concrete word to wed one or the other of those four-syllabled colossi."[126] She praised his lines that were "athletic," musical, and psychologically arresting, and encouraged him to attack her own poems "brutally" in return.[127]

Hughes responded in kind. He liked her lines that were "firm, discreet, passionate . . . not tortoised in imagery."[128] He was wooing her away from the elaborate rhyme and syntax she had mastered at Smith. He knew she was capable of less imitative verse, and he wanted her to find her own voice: "If you write whatever attracts you, and you write it as hard as you can, and as rich, then you can't miss. . . . Just write it off, in your own way, and make it stand up off the page and jump about the room."[129] As she had done for him, he advised her to dispense with unnecessary adjectives ("fierce flaring," for example, should be changed to simply "flaring") and encouraged her to move beyond "smooth manners": "Everything goes perfectly here until 'Pierced side' . . . Something like 'Open' would give a much rawer more vulnerable terrible sense." Her lines should be, above all, "clear and vivid."[130] He questioned language like "watery radiance" and "verdant" as too "vague" and "18th century."[131]

In late October, Hughes assured her that her poems were "masterly" and that her current verses were the best he had ever seen. His praise underscored his generation's biases—"Your verse never goes 'soft' like other women's"—but he never doubted that Plath had the talent and the drive to become one of the best poets of the era.[132] He exclaimed at her brilliance in letters to his brother in 1956: "As a result of her influence I have written continually and every day better since I met her. She is a very fine critic of my work, and abuses just those parts of it that I daren't confess to myself are unworthy."[133] He wrote Olwyn from Spain that Sylvia was "as fine a literary critic as I have met."[134] Hughes's praise of Plath, and his admission of her influence on him, was unusual in an era when women poets were not taken as seriously as their male contemporaries.

He delighted in her gossip from Cambridge, especially when it concerned pompous literary types—"midden metre-farters" he called them. When Sylvia told him about the "Cambridge Makers," a new literary society run by Christopher Levenson, he could hardly contain himself.

> O delicious, succulent, what a prime plum for my vindictive and most contemptuous critical palate. . . . All these phoney sub-spender people

have the naivest sense of what the ancient poets were really like, and what they underwent to get that name. . . . So any modern poet who feels he can be an important man in society by divine operation of his metrical genius, arrogates the old title.[135]

She should not be fooled: "You, believe it or not, are more famous, and more respectably established as a poet, and with more real authority . . . than anyone at Cambridge certainly since I went up there."[136] Even Thom Gunn and Auden, he now thought, were "95% trash."[137] Levenson recalled that Plath and Hughes indeed kept their distance from the more established literary cliques at Cambridge: "as far as I could tell both Sylvia and Ted were *sui generis*, not part of the scene except for the one Ted created for himself with the single issue of St Botolph's Review."[138]

Sylvia did not need to be reminded of her superior résumé: "how free I feel . . . having direct commerce with the best editors in the world—America, America, God Shed His Grace On Thee."[139] She was more worried about the "death of an inner life"; "that obsesses you," Hughes wrote.[140] She was reading about schizophrenia and "manic-depressive geniuses" like Beethoven, Dickens, and Tolstoy in her abnormal psychology book.[141] When she asked Ted what he thought about "mental cases," he told her that Keats, Chaucer, and Shakespeare were all "delicately mad," and that "going nuts" meant "your thoughts have autonomous life, whereas sane people have them in harness, under their will, in slavery, depersonalized with convict number and shaved head, not themselves."[142] This unconventional view of mental illness probably reassured Sylvia, who had worried about the "lasting scar" McLean would leave on her "future associations."[143] The British psychiatrist R. D. Laing would soon popularize a similar sentiment.

Plath never mentioned her history with suicide in her love letters, though she was writing about it, obliquely, in her stories. On October 7, she finished "The Wishing Box," in which a woman loses her power to dream in the face of her husband's superior imagination, and eventually kills herself. Plath thought the story "rather good," while Hughes, seemingly unperturbed by this fictional turn of events, thought it excellent material: "This is the kind of poetic theme you could make exclusively your own ground."[144]

Each morning, Harold relays his vivid dreams to Agnes, the story's narrator, who listens with envy and bitterness since her own dreams cannot match the radiance of her husband's, which are "meticulous works of art."[145] While Harold tells her of evenings spent in the company of William Blake, Robert Frost, and William Carlos Williams, Agnes simply "smoldered in silence."[146] She confesses to Harold that her dreams are dull and mundane, and he directs her in an imaginative exercise. But his efforts only make matters worse; soon Agnes turns to sherry, the cinema, and television to distract herself from her imaginative void. The story ends with Agnes dead on the sofa, an empty pillbox by her side, dressed in an emerald evening gown.

Plath outlined the plot to Hughes in amusing terms, calling the husband "a complete escapist who accepts his vivid dreams as reality," while Agnes's dream life is "sordid and sparse." There is a sinister edge to the story, for Sylvia herself had gone through a similar depression—Agnes "gets worried about her powers of imagination," loses her power to sleep and read, and commits suicide with sleeping pills. Harold seems partly to blame for Agnes's breakdown, which begins directly after he says, "Every day, just practise imagining different things like I've taught you."[147] Ted sometimes hypnotized Sylvia using similar language.[148] He told Olwyn in 1957, "I practise huypnotising [sic] Sylvia, and am gradually getting better. I can now remove slight pains, relax her so completely that after five minutes she feels to have had a night's sleep,—and soon I shall move onto other things, such as make her write poems and stories, then to write them down without difficulty."[149]

Agnes is not Sylvia, but rather the woman Sylvia vowed not to become. To Ted she admitted that Agnes, "poor thing, is certainly an aspect of one of my selves now," and vowed to drink only one glass of sherry a day so as not to become like her. Plath apologized to Hughes for "plagiarizing" his "magnificent" dreams. "Are you angry? It's actually a very humorous terrible little story."[150] She was also at this time writing "The Invisible Man" (since lost), about a young man named Oswald McQuail who becomes invisible at the height of his college career. That story, too, featured a suicide. "It must be funny, but terribly serious," she wrote Ted; indeed, black humor would animate The Bell Jar.

When Sylvia heard that J. D. Salinger had entered a mental hospital, she wrote to Ted, "I am sure insanity is the most necessary state for a fine artist—that 'divine madness' where the terror & piercing insights he has daily are not locked in retreat or raving but made into works of art."[151] These words suggest that she had begun to absorb Ted's more positive view of "madness" as creative vision, and perhaps regard her own experience with mental illness with less shame. Yet she was suffering terribly from nightmares as she worked on "The Wishing Box." "God, it's terrible; the daily world I can wrest, amid great hurt and void, more and more to my will, but I get to dread the night so."[152] Ted tried to reassure her that they were manifestations of the duende: "peaceful sleeps go with minds shut to the visitation." He too was beginning to fear the loss of his poetic powers, away from Plath, for he had read in Freud that the loss of a loved one could dry the well. "I can't stay in England and not be with you. I do nothing here. And I try. I think of you constantly and just don't sleep any more."[153]

IN EARLY OCTOBER the BBC formally accepted the Yeats program that Hughes had proposed during his September audition. Sylvia was triumphant. "MY HUSBAND IS A GENIUS AND WILL READ YEATS ON THE BBC!" she wrote Aurelia.[154] She hoped the reading would help him get a teaching job at Amherst and told Ted not to sail for Spain just yet. Now that he had his foot in the door, she coaxed, he might get more work. After a "tearful reunion" on October 12, the couple returned to Rugby Street, where Sylvia had her "first deep sleep in 2 weeks—all knots dissolved." She was seized by a "new polished potential feeling."[155] The couple wandered through Charing Cross and browsed at an occult book shop, where Sylvia bought *Painted Caravan*, a book on tarot, which would inform her poem "The Hanging Man."[156]

Hughes's BBC work raised his profile, as Plath had predicted. The editor of *Nimbus*, a respected English literary magazine that published Auden, asked Hughes to send poems, while Peter Davison at the Atlantic Press invited Hughes to submit his book of fables. Plath spent two days typing it into a neat manuscript and sent it off to Davison in mid-October. The couple learned that *The Nation* had accepted Hughes's "Wind" on October 22. To Aurelia, Sylvia wrote, "we <u>are</u> different from most couples . . . our writing is founded in the inspiration of the other, and grows by the proper, inimitable criticism of the other, and publications are made with joy of the other; what wife shares her husband's dearest career as I do? except maybe Marie Curie?"[157] She continued forging her own aesthetic: "my poems and stories I want to be the strongest female paean yet for the creative forces of nature, the joy of being a loved and loving woman; that is my song; I believe it is destructive to try to be an abstractionist man-imitator, or a bitter sarcastic Dorothy Parker or Teasdale."[158]

Plath wrote more poems—"Spinster" on October 19, "Sheen & Speck" and "Evergreens" on October 22, and "Sonnet After Squall" and "On the Plethora of Dryads" on October 24—and *The Christian Science Monitor* bought her Benidorm article and accompanying sketches. But she had little real social life now that dating was out. The monasticism was good for her writing; she told Aurelia that she had only scorn "for those that are drinking and calling themselves 'writers' at parties," when they "should be home writing and writing; everyday, one has to earn the name of 'writer' over again, with much wrestling."[159] Still, she saw Ben Nash on October 19 for tea; the next afternoon they saw two art house movies together, followed by wine and dinner. She may have felt the expectation of a quid pro quo since Ben, whom she had dated before Ted, had recently accepted her story "The

Day Mr. Prescott Died," which appeared in *Granta* on October 20. Sylvia would have found herself in an awkward situation, as her marriage was still a secret. She could not reveal it; neither could she alienate an important editor.

Sylvia did not tell Ted that she had spent the afternoon with Ben, though she mentioned she had given him "The Wishing Box" and "The Invisible Man" for consideration. The day after her date with Ben, she typed up ten of her poems for Ted to give to Donald Carne-Ross at the BBC, and wrote Ted a "frenzied tearstained letter begging him to come to Camb."[160] Later that October, Sylvia wrote in her calendar, "terrible afternoon of sorrow & anguish over Ben Nash episode—microcosm of nightmare of lax faithlessness." In the same entry she quoted someone—either Ben or Ted—admonishing her: "only one way to come across."[161] Ted may have been aware of temptations at Cambridge. In early October he had written, "You keep watch on our marriage Sylvia as well as I shall and there is no reason we shouldn't be as happy as we have said we shall be. Don't let any stupid thing interfere. Good night darling darling darling darling."[162]

The nightmares receded, but Sylvia still had "queer dreams" in which she levitated to the sun, feasted in the streets of Winthrop, and slept with Ira Scott. Warren gave her a birthday card that read, "join me in sin," and Dr. Krook became a witch.[163] In another dream, she and Ted

> found a very vivid green lawn, with a dark willow, squat dark trunk, smack in the middle, and I was showing this to you, with our manuscripts laid out under the tree, as the place of peace where at last we could practice rising together.... it came as close to any dream I've had for years in giving me the delight and breathless soaring I used to have in my flying dreams.[164]

She was finding their separation increasingly intolerable. "It is so hard for me to be deprived of doing all the woman-things for you—cooking & bedding & listening & telling you how fine you are & how all my faith is in you." Yet in the next breath, she wrote of her annoyance with Schopenhauer's "ridiculous essay" "On Women": "what poverty of experience he must have had to deny us minds & souls—& make us mere procreating animal machines!"[165] Plath's embrace, in the same paragraph, of both wifely servitude and female equality may sound irreconcilable, but she didn't see it that way. Subservience, for her, meant renouncing a husband, children, and rich domestic life in order to write. She refused; she wanted it all. "I am amazed you live," she wrote Hughes in late October, "that I didn't just make up your being warm and talking and being my husband."[166]

In late October, she told Aurelia, she read through the Fulbright roster and saw three married women; she got up her courage to reveal the marriage. Isabel Murray Henderson remembered a different story. When Sylvia received mail addressed to "Mrs. Sylvia Plath Hughes," the college secretary and house mother, Christine Abbott, asked her to report the change to her "moral" tutor, Irene Morris.[167] On October 23, Sylvia sent Ted a "desperate telegram" asking him to come to Cambridge. When he did not answer, she sent another.[168] Ted finally responded by telegram: "DANGEROUS TO RING LETTER FOLLOWING."[169] (He thought the college porters would eavesdrop.) He wrote that he too had decided that their separation "seems mad."[170] He worried that her Fulbright money would be confiscated or at least halved, but he was hopeful. "If I were to stay in England and earn wouldn't all our problems be solved? It will be time to go to Spain etc when we both go together and are not faced with a financial steeplechase." They would discuss their future on Saturday. "I can hardly remember you without feeling sick and getting aching erections. I shall pour all this into you on Saturday and fill you and fill myself with you and kill myself on you."[171] But neither could wait until Saturday. Ted phoned and told her he would come to Cambridge that very night to "hash this out."[172] Sylvia was ecstatic. "DAY OF TRAUMA, DECISION & JOY," she wrote in her calendar on October 23: "Ted's coming like a miracle—inarticulate—decision to make marriage public & live together—steak dinner, warm love & release—weary love."[173]

Sylvia soon revealed the secret to Dr. Krook, who told her not to worry about giving up her scholarship. Krook was correct: the Fulbright officials "scolded" Sylvia for worrying, and joked that the marriage was a boon for Anglo-American relations; they treated Sylvia "like Grace Kelly having just been married to a Dark Foreign Prince."[174] Irene Morris likewise reassured her that nothing would change on account of the marriage, and was surprised when Sylvia hugged her in a decidedly American display of affection.[175] Both Morris and Kay Burton invited the couple out for a celebratory sherry, and Sylvia was given permission by the College Council to continue her studies on November 10. Sylvia dramatized the confession, telling Ted's parents, "I felt like an orator on the creative virtues of marriage before a jury of intellectual nuns."[176] She realized that she should not have been so anxious, yet "the ingrained English maxim that a woman cannot cook and think at the same time had me dubious."[177] She told Aurelia to make an announcement about their engagement in *The Wellesley Townsman*, and instructed her to send out engraved invitations to a "gala party" in June. There would be "no strain" on Aurelia "to keep up pretenses any more."[178] Ted moved, unofficially, into Sylvia's Whitstead room, where he hung his Beethoven death mask above her map of Boston.

19

Itched and Kindled

Cambridge University, October 1956–June 1957

O n Sylvia's twenty-fourth birthday, she and Ted splurged on sherry, smoked salmon, duck, pheasant, and chablis at Miller's—"an orgy of optimism and self-encouragement," Ted wrote Aurelia, "which will carry us for months."[1] That autumn, he had secured more BBC work, and learned that *Poetry* had accepted "The Drowned Woman" and *The Atlantic* had taken "The Hawk in the Storm" (later retitled "The Hawk in the Rain"). Sylvia's red sleeveless velvet dress was a revelation to him—"She looked as I've never seen her . . . magnificent magnificent nine-times magnificent."[2] He gave her a tarot pack, a gift she thought would start her "on the road to becoming a seeress."[3]

Sylvia hoped to read horoscopes and practice astrology alongside Ted. They even made their own Ouija board and, when they were not trying to contact the dead, asked about potential poetry acceptances. Sylvia told her mother that she and Ted would "become a team better than mr. & mrs. yeats [*sic*],"[4] but in her calendar that October, she wrote that the struggles with the Ouija board filled her with "depressing exhaustion."[5] Sue Weller, who visited the couple in Cambridge in 1957, felt that Sylvia did not believe in the Ouija board but was "catering" to Hughes's "idiosyncrasies."[6] Hughes remembered how the nightly sessions with Pan, as they named their guiding spirit, unnerved her. In a *Birthday Letters* poem, "Ouija," he wrote that when he asked Pan whether they would be famous, Sylvia began weeping. "Don't you see—fame will ruin everything," he remembered her saying through tears.

> I was stunned. I thought I had joined
> Your association of ambition
> To please you and your mother,

To fulfil your mother's ambition
That we be ambitious. Otherwise
I'd be fishing off a rock
In Western Australia. So it seemed suddenly. You wept.
You wouldn't go on with Ouija. Nothing
I could think of could explain
Your shock and crying. Only
Maybe you'd picked up a whisper I could not hear,
Before our glass could stir, some still small voice:
"Fame will come. Fame especially for you.
Fame cannot be avoided. And when it comes
You will have paid for it with your happiness,
Your husband and your life."[7]

———

OLWYN CAME TO VISIT in mid-November, slightly suspicious of her broth-er's new bride. Ted had written to her about Sylvia in May, calling her his "secretary in chief" and assuring Olwyn she was "Very unpretentious, very German in some ways—works herself till she drops. And she certainly has a startling poetic gift."[8] Sylvia thought Olwyn a beautiful "changeling" and half forgave her for the money she still owed Ted.[9] Yet when Olwyn returned to Paris on November 18, Sylvia felt "queer," "locked in," and distant from Ted, as if Olwyn meant more to him.[10]

Indeed, Sylvia's calendar suggests tension in the marriage that fall. Her notes there hinted that her birthday was a less joyous affair than Ted had described to Aurelia. That night, she wrote cryptically about her "sorrow & anguish" over the Ben Nash episode, and, two days later, "fight w. Ted re our lurid pasts."[11] On October 31, Sylvia wrote of a "lousy afternoon" in a London pub after announcing their marriage to the Fulbright officials: "utter waste—tearful dinner at Schmidt's—hectic, sick trainride back... sense of tension insecurity & longing for love expressed."[12] November 1 was a "rough day"; November 2, "grueling worst day"; November 3, "Exhausting aftermath day"; November 4, "uneasy day"; November 5, "Horrible day"; November 7, "tedious tense day ... jealousy, feeling of division—tightrope walking steps—wish for wisdom of Eve"; November 10, "grim day ... casu-alty ward—back Xrays—slipped disc ... grim rainy evening & pain." And so it continued as the winter weather began its yearly onslaught on her health. Still, there was usually good "love" even during these low times.

Though Plath was deep into Hume, Hobbes, Mill, and Bentham that term and enjoying her supervisions with Dr. Krook, she quickly found herself "back in obsessive state of writing poems under pressure to put off work."[13] Between November 17 and 19, she wrote the marvelous "Black Rook in Rainy Weather," one of her strongest early poems. It was likely influenced by Hughes's "The Hawk in the Rain," in which the hawk becomes an emblem of humanity in its futile attempt to master the elements, while nature is a malevolent force bent on extinguishing life:

> I drown in the drumming ploughland, I drag up
> Heel after heel from the swallowing of the earth's mouth,
> From clay that clutches my each step to the ankle
> With the habit of the dogged grave, but the hawk
>
> Effortlessly at height hangs his still eye.
> His wings hold all creation in a weightless quiet,
> Steady as a hallucination in the streaming air.[14]

Escape is impossible; the hawk, like the speaker, will eventually "mix his heart's blood with the mire of the land." Plath's "Black Rook in Rainy Weather," on the contrary, exhibits an optimistic hope for grace—or poetic inspiration—in a "dull, ruinous landscape":

> . . . I only know that a rook
> Ordering its black feathers can so shine
> As to seize my sense, haul
> My eyelids up, and grant
>
> A brief respite from fear
> Of total neutrality. With luck,
> Trekking stubborn through this season
> Of fatigue, I shall
> Patch together a content
>
> Of sorts. Miracles occur,
> If you care to call those spasmodic
> Tricks of radiance miracles. The wait's begun again,
> The long wait for the angel,
> For that rare, random descent.[15]

Plath borrows elements of Hughes's poem to quietly dismantle his vision. While Hughes's understanding of nature resembles Shelley's in "Mont Blanc," Plath's here is closer to Thoreau's *Walden*. Her American "Emersonian" vision positions itself against Hughes's British Romantic sublime.[16] It was another literary face-off, like "Mr. and Mrs. Ted Hughes' Writing Table," "The Black Bull," "The Fifty-Ninth Bear," and "On the Difficulty of Conjuring Up a Dryad." They had been married for less than six months, but Plath had already written several works that speak to her anxiety about her own role within the marriage. By "doubling" Hughes's poem with her own, she outwardly paid homage to Hughes; by undermining his poem's premise, she asserted her own artistic vision.

She wrote another five poems during this November 17–19 period— "Soliloquy for a Solipsist," "April Rhapsodies," "Letter to a Purist," "Ode on an Onion," and "On the Extra"—and sent all six to *The New Yorker* (all were rejected). On November 21 she wrote the poems "Item" and "Megrims," which Peter Steinberg, who discovered the poem, called a "monologue addressed to a 'Doctor' by a paranoid, yet fairly casual speaker."[17] "Natural History" followed on November 23. "Black Rook" was the best of the surviving group. Plath had recently begun work on her Cambridge novel, and polished the fifty-odd poems in her poetry manuscript, *Two Lovers and a Beachcomber*, which she intended to enter in the Yale Younger Poets Contest that February. Hughes "experienced something like a bang on the head" after he read it. "It's a wonderful book," he told Aurelia and Warren, "and when it's published I shall write a long review, and make sure that its excellencies are what hit the public first, and set the tone for a dizzy enthusiasm."[18]

Sylvia, in turn, had her own plans for Ted. On October 18 she had met John Press, who worked for the British Council, at a Fulbright reception. Plath asked Press if he knew the poet Ted Hughes. He did not, but he invited her to dinner with his wife, where they discussed various strategies for getting Hughes published, and gossiped about Auden, Spender, and MacNeice ("oh god," Plath wrote Hughes, "how I chortled inside and begged them to go on").[19] They told Sylvia about an American first book contest sponsored by Harper's publishers and the New York Poetry Center at the YMHA (now known as the 92nd Street Y in Manhattan). She wrote to Ted immediately, "I'm sure you'll win this; I feel very queer about it."[20]

A month later, Plath typed up Hughes's poetry manuscript and entered it in the contest.[21] She did not enter her own manuscript, which she felt was not yet complete. She thought that Ted's poems were more accomplished, riskier, and less imitative than her own. She continued writing poems throughout the next week, but her calendar showed the strain of reconciling married life with her academic requirements: "tired," "very depressed," "bad tempered," "exhausted," "caffeine tense numb day," she wrote throughout the last week of November. But her days often ended happily once she reunited with Hughes: "steak, mushroom & string bean supper, red wine, good love."[22]

In early November the couple settled on a cheap ground-floor flat in a Victorian terraced house at 55 Eltisley Avenue, a short walk from Newnham. The flat was close to Grantchester Meadows but still convenient to town. After a winter in wool sweaters at Whitstead, Sylvia vowed to keep the new flat "extravagantly warm!"[23] She was overly optimistic—the house had neither central heating nor hot water, and they had to share a bathroom with a Canadian couple. Sylvia hated the small kitchen, "a little dank cell smelling suspiciously of mushrooms."[24] Even Ted found the house dispiriting. In his *Birthday Letters* poem "55 Eltisley," he wrote about how he had "looked for omens" when they first moved in, and found blood on a pillow sheet. He knew a widow had lived there, and he began to worry that the former couple's "old griefs" would hang like "a miasma" around their new married life.[25]

They set about banishing the old ghosts. They covered kitchen shelves in white-and-red-checkered oilcloth and painted the living room walls a cool blue-gray. Sylvia hung her Braque still life over the mantel and bought a blue secondhand sofa; together they built five large bookcases and decorated the living room with yellow lampshades and pillows. Hughes remembered Plath in "a fury of scouring"; she resolved to "make it like an ad out of house and garden [*sic*]."[26] She asked Aurelia to call as soon as they moved in "to bless it."[27]

Ted wrote Aurelia chummy letters about Sylvia's writing and cooking, and he thanked her for sending an American bounty—steak knives, meat thermometers, Flako pie crust, a vegetable peeler, a shaving kit. Sylvia planned to move out of Whitstead in December, at the end of term. A Smith alumna, May Collacott, would move into Sylvia's old room and hear that Sylvia "cut quite a swath through Whitstead."[28] May became friendly with Jane and Isabel, taking over Sylvia's old spot in the trio.

Plath hardly noticed. She was deeply in love with her creative and physical ideal, a man she had practically conjured. She was also distracted by politics. The Suez crisis and the Hungarian revolution that autumn appalled her. She felt that Britain and France were aggressors, and that "Eden is, in effect, helping murder the Hungarians." She and Ted went for long walks along the Cam feeling "stunned and sick; the whole world, except us, we felt was utterly mad, raving mad."[29] The Suez crisis resurrected Sylvia's old pacifism and her growing contempt, fueled by Ted, for England. "Britain is dead," she wrote Aurelia that November. Everything seemed "so old and dirty; soot of centuries worked into every pore," and the food "without any nourishment whatsoever."[30] Even chicken was "a luxury" in England—"you should see the scrawny, bony 'boiling' chickens that appear in butchers [*sic*] windows—how I miss our lovely delicate toasty golden-brown fryers!"[31] To Marcia, she complained of the two hours it took to heat hot water for their baths. "Oh God

Bless America, land of the Cookiesheet, Central Heating & Frozen Orange Juice!"[32] She "secretly" hoped that Hughes would find "America the wonderland I feel it is." She told Aurelia, "I would never want to live in England or bring up children here; it is a dead, corrupt country."[33]

Sylvia could hardly wait to show off her new "roaring hulking Yorkshireman" who wrote poems with "raging power & violence."[34] He was, she told Marcia, "the only man I've ever met whom I could never boss; he'd bash my head in." Still, she missed "woman-talk"; she had only one real "woman friend," Dr. Krook, who was "incandescent with brilliance," her "salvation among the grotesque female dons at Newnham."[35] Ted suspected that Sylvia had pulled away from her few female friends on his account. Only Dr. Krook was exempt. In "55 Eltisley," he wrote, "I pitied your delirium of suspicion."[36] Yet Sylvia's dwindling circle of Newnham friends was a natural consequence of her marrying and moving out of Whitstead.

Hughes sold poems to *The Atlantic*, *Poetry*, and *The Nation* that November, but he wasn't making much money. He nearly took a "laboring job" but then instead accepted a position teaching English at the Coleridge Secondary Modern School for Boys in Cambridge.[37] The students' poor test scores had kept them out of the more academic grammar schools; many would leave before graduation to work in the trades. Hughes had grown up with similar working-class boys, and he tried hard to inspire them. He read them W. H. Auden and Robert Frost, assigned poetry-writing exercises and World War II history readings, and asked them to close their eyes while he told stories. "But what an experience! Life purely as a writer would be suicidally narrow," he told Aurelia.[38]

Sylvia officially moved to 55 Eltisley Avenue on December 7, after Michaelmas term ended. She gushed about cooking a shoulder of lamb with her new meat thermometer; swishing around in her new aqua silk bathrobe; and polishing furniture with her new duster.[39] "I am regarded as a Phenomenon by the virginal victorians [sic] at Newnham—'Think & cook at the same time?' They titter incredulously."[40] Her *Joy of Cooking* was "a blessing," and she included intricate descriptions of her meals in nearly every letter home.[41]

> Ted is so appreciative about my cooking it makes kitchen work a joy; we have steak, fish-in-milk; rich vegetable stews; marvellous Italian spaghetti with meat-sauce; pork & sweet breads, fruit all the time heaped on the sideboard (we take your super-vitamins religiously). But I can't wait to make him cakes, feathery pies, broiled chicken, parfaits etc etc.[42]

There was no irony—yet—in her blissful depictions of housewifery. But she was already tiring of "practical business" that crept up on her.[43] She had not counted on the three-mile round trip to the laundromat, or the long daily walks to the grocer and butcher. Money was a constant worry; she hoped life would become "less hand-to-mouth" soon, she told Aurelia.[44]

Her sinus troubles returned, and the flat's spare electric heater did not provide much warmth. She found the coal fire "filthy," "either too hot or too cold," and waxed nostalgic to Warren about "America's material conveniences."[45] She still bundled up in wool socks and multiple sweaters. Ted told Aurelia that it was "like living at the bottom of a stagnant swamp."[46] He knew the prospect of America kept Sylvia's courage up, as he wrote in a later poem:

> But you were happy too, warming your hands
> At the crystal ball
> Of your heirloom paperweight. Inside it,
> There, in miniature, was your New England Christmas,
> A Mummy and a Daddy, still together
> Under the whirling snow, and our future.[47]

Mrs. Prouty wondered whether Sylvia was telling the whole truth about her perfect marriage in her letters. To Aurelia, Prouty confessed, "I'm always a little fearful that Sylvia's high spirits have flagged—come down from her high altitude, & that she may be going through a downward dip."[48] Both women hoped the couple would end up like Elizabeth and Robert Browning, but they had their doubts. "I wonder how you really feel about it," Prouty wrote.[49]

Sylvia and Ted spent Christmas 1956 at the Beacon in Yorkshire. When they returned to Cambridge, they found gifts waiting for them: checks from friends and family; more modern kitchen tools from Aurelia; and, alarmingly, chocolates, fruits, and crepes from Sylvia's old beau Ira Scott. All the tangible reminders of home made Sylvia long to return to Wellesley and surround herself with people who believed in her, like the Cantors, the Aldriches, and the Crocketts.

The couple soon settled into a writing routine. They went to bed at ten p.m. and rose at six a.m. to write for two hours before Ted left for work. ("The moral boost it gives outweighs an hour's sleep," he told Aurelia.)[50] Plath was writing short stories for women's magazines—"I will slave & slave until I break into those slicks"—and applying for teaching positions for herself and Hughes at New England colleges.[51] She had not realized how difficult it would be to obtain a teaching position without a PhD, a published book, or any real teaching experience, "brilliant and rare as we are." When Aurelia lightly suggested that Ted pursue a PhD, Sylvia reiterated their disdain for more academic qualifications. "Ted does not want to be a university professor for a career. He wants to write, now & for the rest of his life. And in marrying a writer, I accept his life." Yet she hinted that she too had hoped for "the American dream of a secure sinecure writing on campus . . . *I* know Ted's mind is magnificent, not hair-splitting or suavely politic—but employers may find Phd's more convincing."[52] Sylvia was torn between supporting her husband and pleasing her mother. "Our problem is that we are primarily writers . . . and only secondarily academic."[53] When Mary Ellen Chase came to Cambridge in January, she told Sylvia that she and Ted would "be crazy to get doctorates!" "They would rather have me have poems & essays published in the Atlantic than a Phd," Sylvia wrote Aurelia after the visit.[54] Chase told Plath not to apply to any other colleges before she had written to the head of Smith's English department about an appointment. Chase also hinted that Smith might take Hughes on in a year.

Sylvia had heard that Jane Baltzell was her "main rival" for the Smith position, and began to wonder whether Chase was "playing" her off against Jane because she had committed the sin of marrying. Plath knew Chase lived with a woman, Eleanor Duckett, and she started to resent what she interpreted as her "peculiar dismissal of men." She was angry when Chase told her that she and Hughes could see each other on weekends if they taught in different cities. "That is not the kind of woman I want to fix up our jobs," Sylvia told Aurelia.[55] She began to hope Jane would get the position so she would not have to turn it down. "I was not interested," Jane recalled.[56] She had been "chilled" by the "proprietary way" in which Chase and Duckett had spoken of Sylvia one day at tea. They had called her marriage to Hughes a "blunder." Chase had nothing against Hughes, but thought "for a woman of Sylvia Plath's stature this is simply a disaster of the first order."[57] At a garden party that May, Sylvia would confide to Jane her "apprehensions about letting herself into their grips, being put in a bottle."[58] Jane thought Sylvia was right to hesitate about working with "sponsors and benefactors to whom she owed much."[59] Yet Jane also knew there was "a side of Sylvia that cared a great deal about security," and an offer from Smith "easily validated success."[60]

In January, Hughes had his first acceptance from a British magazine, *Nimbus*, though the editor informed him the magazine might well collapse before his poem was published. (Indeed, it never appeared.) The couple hardly cared—the attention from the British literary world after so many rejections put them in a "gay mood," as did the January publication of Plath's "Pursuit" in *The Atlantic*, her six poems in *Poetry*, and "The Wishing Box" in *Granta*.[61] *Gemini*, an Oxford-Cambridge literary magazine, had also accepted two of Plath's poems, "Spinster" and "Vanity Fair," and a short story, "All the Dead Dears," while *The Antioch Review* had accepted "Black Rook in Rainy Weather." Four other poems of hers appeared in *Chequer* that winter; "our fame has spread around Cambridge," she told Aurelia.[62] Ted made her memorize a poem a day and drew up a "huge chart of English writers & their dates," which he hung on the wall of their bedroom in preparation for her exams.[63]

She eased the pressure of reviewing the whole of English literature by writing more poems—in January 1957, "Sow," "The Snowman on the Moor," "Mayflower," and "The Lady and the Earthenware Head." The last poem, which she called "the best verse I've ever written," was based on a clay model that her former Smith friend, Mary Derr, had made of her head.[64] (Sylvia had brought it with her to Cambridge and, on Ted's advice, placed it high up in a tree near Grantchester Meadows.) Hughes did not like the poem, but he was otherwise encouraging. "Her book is startling," he wrote to Aurelia that January. "The individual poems are dazzling and disturbing enough, but more than that, they add up to each other—most books of poems stale their effect because the poems somehow break each other down, betray each other, outyell each other—Sylvia's are cumulative. This is especially surprising because her individual poems have such a brilliant and emphatic finish."[65] In mid-February, Plath sent her fifty-five-page poetry manuscript *Two Lovers and a Beachcomber* to the Yale contest, judged by Auden.

Sylvia hoped that Ted would fall in love with America and want to stay, especially as American magazines continued to show more interest in his poems than British ones did. She and Ted were disgusted, she wrote, by "the trash published by the Old Guard, the flat, clever, colorless poets here."[66] Sylvia's dislike of England became even more pronounced in her letters home that spring. "I gather, from reading Blake & D. H. Lawrence, the deadness has been growing for a long time. Everything is frozen, stratified. . . . I can't wait to get Ted out, & he can't wait to go."[67] Yet she conceded that England had given her the one thing she treasured most: "the husband of my whole life & love & work."[68]

That January, a new couple moved into the upstairs flat at 55 Eltisley Avenue. Sylvia was taken aback when the young husband introduced himself as George Sassoon. She asked him "idly" if he were related to the First World War poet Siegfried Sassoon. "It turned out that the boy was his son. And a pale, sick looking runt of a wealthy stock he is, too," she wrote Aurelia.[69] This quiet, unassuming young couple ("pathetically eager to please," Sylvia wrote) would become the target of Sylvia's wrath over the next few months.

She lashed out at them in letters, berating them for their "pampered, paid life" and their health problems.[70] She raged to her mother about the couple's wealth, and wrote self-righteously about her own need to work for money: "we despise the Sassoon couple upstairs. They live like pigs . . . They are unbelievable & don't deserve to live."[71]

Sylvia's nastiness was out of all proportion. The target, of course, was not George but Richard Sassoon, with whom George shared a family connection, a slight frame, and a fragile constitution. George's presence was a constant reminder of Sylvia's old lover, and, perhaps, her unresolved feelings for him. She had never given herself the chance to properly mourn Sassoon; instead, she had headed straight to Hughes's flat the day she returned to London from her disastrous spring break. It was the first time she had been left by a man—normally she did the leaving. Ted had been a life raft in a sea of potentially suicidal misery, and she had clung to him tightly. Indeed Sylvia had written Sassoon that her relationship with Ted need not "have happened" had he not abandoned her.[72] Her malicious comments about George's wife's miscarriages suggest jealousy of a woman who *had* become a "pampered" Sassoon. Such comments foreshadowed those she would make about Assia Wevill.

Mrs. Prouty noted Sylvia's tendency to mock barren women in her poems that spring, and warned her that this line of thinking showed no "kindness." She was distressed by Plath's poem "Two Sisters of Persephone," in which one sister "works problems on / A mathematical machine" and ends up a virgin, "bitter // And sallow as any lemon," while the other sister "Burns open to sun's blade" and "bears a king." Mrs. Prouty told Sylvia she was too "scornful" of the childless sister. "I felt sorry for her—& if I were writing a short story <u>she</u> would be my heroine—<u>not</u> her fruit-bearing sister. Most women who bear no children are victims and are to be treated with compassion."[73] Sylvia ignored her. Channeling Lawrence, she continued to write poems that extolled fertility and sexual love, and mocked barrenness.

––––––––

ON FEBRUARY 23 at ten thirty in the morning, Sylvia and Ted received a life-changing telegram. Hughes's manuscript, *The Hawk in the Rain*, had won the Harper's/YMHA First Book Contest out of the 387 manuscripts submitted. The judges—W. H. Auden, Stephen Spender, and Marianne Moore, whom Plath thought "the 3 best living & practicing poets in the world today"—had recognized Hughes's "poetic genius" without being "scared of it as small jealous poets & frightened poetry editors are."[74] A pot of milk burned on the stove as the two danced deliriously around the flat. They called their mothers, and Aurelia burst into tears. That night, they celebrated over turkey, lemon mousse, and chablis at Miller's. Sylvia vowed to return for venison and snails when her own book won a prize.

To Luke Myers, who hardly needed persuading, Sylvia wrote that *The Hawk in the Rain* was a book "to read in wild reverence, & built [*sic*] a great rock altar for in the middle of wild islands."[75] She told Aurelia it would change the direction of British poetry:

> Ted writes with color, splendour & vigorous music about love, birth, war, death, animals, hags & vampires, martyrdom—and sophisticated intellectual problems, too. His book can't be typed: it has rugged violent war poems like "Bayonet Charge" & "Griefs for Dead Soldiers," delicate, exquisite nature poems about "October Dawn," & "Horses," powerful animal poems about Macaws, Jaguars, & the lovely Hawk one. . . . He combines intellect & grace of complex form, with lyrical music, male vigor & vitality, & moral commitment & love & awe of the world.
>
> O, he has everything.[76]

Plath soon sent Hughes's manuscript to Faber and Faber, who returned it with a brusque note saying they did not publish first volumes by American writers. When she replied that Ted Hughes was British, they accepted the manuscript. It was another triumph for Ted—and for Sylvia. She had helped him choose the final poems for *The Hawk in the Rain*, and would limit his revisions for the Faber edition. She told Aurelia that if not for her restraining hand "he would rewrite a poem to eternity."[77] Edits in Plath's handwriting to "Griefs for Dead Soldiers" and "The Ancient Heroes and the Bomber Pilot" appear on the Faber proofs, while Plath helped Hughes with many short story and drama plots around this time. In one letter he apologized for stealing her material,[78] while elsewhere he wrote that she supplied the "exercise" that inspired his short story "Snow."[79] Letters also reveal that Plath suggested major revisions to Hughes's children's book, *How the Whale Became* (originally entitled *How the Donkey Became*).[80] It's little wonder Sylvia felt proprietary pride in his work.

Christopher Levenson remembered how the Harper's prize opened doors for Hughes, whose success in Britain had been "only sporadic" beforehand. "It was a salutary early lesson in literary disillusion to see how quickly the leading London magazines and the quality Sunday newspapers changed their tunes once Ted won the award."[81] The book's phenomenal success was due, in part, to its highly charged aesthetic. Hughes's magnificent poem "Wind" embodied his first collection's sensibility:

This house has been far out at sea all night,
The woods crashing through darkness, the booming hills,
Winds stampeding the fields under the window
Floundering black astride and blinding wet

Til day rose; then under an orange sky
The hills had new places, and wind wielded
Blade-light, luminous black and emerald,
Flexing like the lens of a mad eye.[82]

Hughes has traveled far from William Wordsworth's bucolic, restorative Lake Country, where man and nature achieve mutual harmony. Here, as in "The Hawk in the Rain," nature is an amoral, primeval force that mocks faith in shelter.

The Hawk in the Rain would be published by Faber and Faber in London, and Harper's in New York, in mid-September 1957.[83] It marked a watershed in Anglo-American postwar poetry. Peter Davison remembered that the "book's reception was extraordinary and changed the couple's life."[84] In the British and American papers, W. S. Merwin, Philip Booth, Al Alvarez, and Edwin Muir compared Hughes to Hopkins, Dylan Thomas, and Rilke. Muir's review in *The New Statesman* would set the tone for Hughes's critical reception: "Mr. Ted Hughes is clearly a remarkable poet and seems to be quite outside the currents of his time. His distinguishing power is sensuous, verbal and imaginative; at his best the three are fused together. His images have an admirable violence."[85] Merwin, too, wrote of the poems' "capacity for incaution" and "strength and brilliance" in *The New York Times Book Review*.[86] Robin Skelton of *The Manchester Guardian* noted Hughes's "masculine vigour," while in *The Observer* Alvarez, fast becoming England's most important young poetry critic, drew attention to his "anti-poetical toughness," "belligerent ugliness," and "heroical, misanthropic swagger."[87] John Press, who had told Plath about the contest, compared Hughes's words to "a hard, relentless assault-weapon" in *The Sunday Times*.[88]

These terms would later come to haunt Hughes, who critics would increasingly identify as a "poet of violence." In 1959, for example, Tony Dyson expounded on Hughes's fascination with power in an article for the *Critical Quarterly*:

For Ted Hughes, power and violence go together: his own dark gods are makers of the tiger, not the lamb. He is fascinated by violence of all kinds, in love and in hatred, in the jungle and in the arena, in battle, murder and sudden death. Violence, for him, is the occasion not for reflection, but for *being*. . . .[89]

By the early sixties, the morality of Hughes's "violence" was frequently debated in the pages of magazines, academic journals, and anthologies. After Plath's death, in an essay called "Poetry and Violence," Hughes situated himself as one in a line of poets who glorified the primal energy that animates the life force:

> . . . does it make any sense whatsoever to say that in these poems—Blake, Yeats, or Popa were "celebrating violence"? Or does it make more sense to say: "these sacred animals emerged into the field of vision of these poets, charged with special glamour, 'terrible beauty' and force, and the poets simply felt compelled to make an image of what they saw—at the same time trying to impose some form of ethical control on it." In this sense, such poems simply bear witness. And I would have thought, any culture that would prefer to be without poetry of this kind—one would prefer to be without.[90]

Hughes asserted that "positive violence" is "a life-bringing assertion of sacred law which demolishes, in some abrupt way, a force that oppressed and *violated* it." He mocked the notion of "humanitarian" values, which he believed had prevented humans from facing "our extraordinary readiness to exploit, oppress, torture and kill our own kind." Hughes understood why his poems might be interpreted as glorifying violence, yet he insisted they did not: "If the Hawk and the Pike kill, they kill within the law and their killing is a sacrament." He later defended his collection *Crow* along similar lines in one of his notebooks: "That he explodes is positive. It is not an image of 'violence' but an image of breakthrough. . . . That he pushes to the point where he is annihilated means that now nothing remains for him but what has exploded him—his inner link with his creator, a thing of spiritfire."[91]

Feminist critics would nevertheless remain skeptical of Hughes's intentions. Jacqueline Rose, for example, criticized Hughes poems like "Hawk Roosting" and "Thrushes" as verse that appeared "pure identity in its fascist mode," "complicit with what it condemns."[92] Yet Hughes was not venerating the fascist mind-set—he was exposing it, and exploring its traces in ourselves.

Though Hughes would later rue some of these early reviews, in 1957 he and Plath were thrilled that his poems—and his "capacity for incaution"—had been received in such crashing terms. He frequently quoted his reviews in letters to his siblings and friends, while Sylvia carefully saved each cutting in a scrapbook. "You see how honest talent & faith work out!" she wrote

Aurelia, reveling in her triumph. "Neither Ted nor I married for money, social position, or family heritage. Just love, & worshipping the gifts in each other & wanting to spend our lives fulfilling them in each other. & now we will have money, social position, & belong to the aristocracy of practicing artists, with our families, too!" Ted, she continued, was relieved that his father no longer needed to apologize for his son's artistic ways: "Writing is looked down upon as 'arty'—until it brings publication & Money [*sic*]. Well, the money doesn't matter to us."[93] But of course, it did. Later, when they received the book's contract, Sylvia calculated that with their royalties they would make only about ten cents a copy.[94] They could make much more by selling poems to magazines. Ted's next book, she decided, would not go to a publisher until all the poems had been sold off individually.

Plath elegantly sidestepped the issue of marital rivalry in a letter home, though her comments suggest that it hung in the air. "I am more happy than if it was my book published!" she told Aurelia.

> I have worked so closely on these poems of Ted's and typed them so many countless times through revision after revision that I feel ecstatic about it all. I am so happy <u>his</u> book is accepted <u>first</u>. It will make it so much easier for me when mine is accepted—if not by this Yale Series, then by some other place. I can rejoice then, much more, knowing Ted is ahead of me. There is no question of rivalry, but only mutual joy & a sense of us doubling our prize-winning & creative output.[95]

Still, Plath had published much more than Hughes, and may have been surprised to find herself the trailing spouse. In the same breath with which she declared the rivalry nonexistent, she began to ponder how she might catch up. Indeed, on the day she learned about Hughes's prize, she bought Virginia Woolf's "blessed diary" and "a battery of her novels."[96]

Plath was suddenly seized by another writing block. "I am stymied, stuck, at a stasis," she wrote in her journal on March 4.[97] In the wake of Ted's triumph, she worried about carrying even more of the household burden. Now all her blithe talk about "Books & Babies & Beef stews" seemed terribly naive as she saw her future as a series of "domestic chores" that had, throughout history, prevented all but the wealthiest women from fulfilling their creative potential.[98] She resented having "3 jobs—writing, cooking & housekeeping" and vowed to "have children only after I have a poetry book & a novel published, so my children fit into <u>my</u> work routine & don't overthrow mine with theirs."[99] Yet in her journal she worried that she would simply give up, "escape into domesticity & stifle yourself by falling headfirst into a bowl of cookie batter."[100] She likely doubted that she could ask her husband to share those chores now that he was famous. If she did not win an equally prestigious prize—and soon—she would never reclaim her poetic equity within the marriage.

Sue Weller visited Sylvia and Ted at Eltisley Avenue that spring and remembered Sylvia weeping copiously over her stove as she cooked. "Ted did nothing to console her," and Sue, taking her cue from Ted, likewise said nothing. Sylvia had told her she was upset about receiving a middling grade on a moral philosophy paper, but Sue had the sense that Sylvia's unhappiness had more to do with the "artistic rivalry" between her and Ted. Though Sue thought Sylvia was full of life and vitality, she also found her friend's need for constant reassurance exhausting. "It was an enormous burden to be really close to her," she said.[101] She speculated that Ted may have decided, by that point, that he would not—or could not—deal with Sylvia's "emotional problems" anymore. He could not be her Leonard Woolf.

Mrs. Prouty, perceptive as always, warned Sylvia not to push herself too hard: "the person who wants to write enough will make time. So will you. But I hope you won't have to make it at dawns, before breakfast. . . . Someone remarked to me after reading your poem in the Atlantic—'How intense.' Sometime write me a little poem that isn't intense. A lamp turned too high might shatter its chimney. Please just glow sometimes."[102]

When Mary Ellen Chase learned of Ted's success, she told Sylvia she would "stake her reputation" on them and so earned her way back into Sylvia's good graces.[103] A few days later, on March 12, Robert Gorham Davis offered Sylvia a one-year, renewable position teaching three sections of freshman English at Smith for $4,200. (The class, George Gibian noted, was "the very bottom bottom of the pecking order.")[104] Chase had written a four-page letter to Davis full of praise for Plath and Hughes in early February. She had spoken with Morris, Burton, and other Cambridge professors who had taught her. "All write in highest praise of her." She said Sylvia would be "a fine addition to our staff" and implied that she had made a complete recovery from her breakdown.[105]

Despite her earlier reservations about returning to Smith, Sylvia felt enormous relief: "I am just walking on air."[106] The dynamic within the marriage had shifted again; Sylvia was now the earner. She hoped that Ted might get a position at Amherst, but she noted that with her "good salary," he need not teach at all.[107] To Marcia she wrote, "I know now that if I want to keep on being a triple-threat woman: wife, writer & teacher (to be swapped later for motherhood, I hope) I can't be a drudge, the way housewives are forced to be here. . . . no promising jobs, starvation wages."[108] Her future was looking brighter, and Hughes's book would make them the talk of the "poetry-conscious university communities."[109] Aurelia had given Sylvia and Ted a summer cottage rental in Eastham, on Cape Cod, as a wedding present. "I can't wait to run up my beloved Nauset beach in the sun," Sylvia wrote.[110] She told her mother again about her "secret campaign to make Ted love America": "one must never push him: he'll come round of his own accord."[111]

That March, Plath worked "daily" on her Cambridge novel, provisionally entitled *Falcon Yard*.[112] She wanted to have "300 single-spaced pages" by the time she sailed for America, then to rewrite the novel over the summer and send it to Peter Davison at the Atlantic Press. She worried about achieving a "subtle structured style" that would be both literary and suspenseful.[113] Ideally, the novel would be a best seller about "the voyage of a girl through destruction, hatred and despair to seek and to find the meaning of the redemptive power of love."[114] It would be a paean to Hughes. In her diary she outlined the plot, which was based almost entirely on her own experience and the people she had met at Cambridge. She called the female protagonist "a femme fatale in her way."[115] But she was racked by insecurity about her ability to make the work come together: "the horror is that cheapness and slick-love would be the result of the thing badly written."[116] For "courage," she read Virginia Woolf's diary. "I feel very akin to her . . . Her moods & neuroses are amazing."[117] In her journal she admitted that she felt she had been "reduplicating" Woolf's suicide "in that black summer of 1953," but that she now looked to her as a guide. "Bless her. I feel my life linked to her, somehow. I love her."[118] Yet Plath did not want to emulate Woolf's writing style. Her own voice would be more like J. D. Salinger's or Joyce Cary's—wry, dry, and self-deprecating. She wanted her prose style to be poetic, too, "Like Stephen Dedalus walking by the sea: ooo-ee-ooo-siss."[119] By early April 1957 she had written eighty single-spaced pages of the novel.

D. H. Lawrence was still her biggest prose influence. Plath was studying his novels with Dr. Krook that term as she worked on *Falcon Yard*. In February, she had written a paper titled "D. H. Lawrence: The Tree of Knowledge Versus the Tree of Life," which suggests that she had begun to read Lawrence through the lenses of Hughes and Graves.[120]

> Science has robbed the sun and moon of magic, leaving a spotted ball of gasses and a dead crater-pocked world in place of gold god and silver queen: a poor trade. Worse, men and women no longer live by intuition, but by ideas. The chittering dictums of the head and the will block out the spontaneous voices of the blood and the impulse. . . . Deprived of the rhythm of savage song, the meaning of the animal yell, we exist for the mechanical screak of steel on steel. . . .
>
> We must get back "in touch."[121]

She went on to praise Connie Chatterley, who "identifies herself with life. She chooses the spontaneous, intuitive expression of her own woman's nature. And becomes linked again with the creative rhythms of the universe."[122] These were ideas that Plath hoped to incorporate into her poetry and "female aesthetic."[123]

Plath's alliance with Hughes deepened her allegiance to Lawrence. In her 1957–58 teaching notes for freshman English at Smith, she would discuss Lawrence's "great religion . . . belief in the blood" and quote from one of his essays: "Life is only bearable when the mind and the body are in harmony, and there is a natural balance between them."[124] In February 1958, she would reread Lawrence's novels and linger on the parallels between his fictional lovers and herself and Hughes.

> I opened The Rainbow which I have never read & was sucked into the concluding Ursula & Skrebensky episode & sank back, breath knocked out of me, as I read of their London hotel, their Paris trip, their riverside loving while Ursula studied at college. This is the stuff of my life . . . I felt mystically that if I read Woolf, read Lawrence—(these two, why?—their vision, so different, is so like mine)—I can be itched and kindled at a great work: burgeoning, fat with texture & substance of life. . . .[125]

Hughes would later write, "If SP and I managed to get through it all, it was because for crucial years we defended each other, we were a sufficient world to each other: our poetic folie à deux saved us from being isolated, surrounded and eliminated."[126] Lawrence sanctioned and sanctified the couple's passionate commitment to love, art, sex, nature. Plath, Hughes once said, was "Laurentian" rather than "women's lib."[127] Yet *Lady Chatterley's Lover*, like *Wuthering Heights*, was a strange marital touchstone. Plath could not have foreseen that Lawrence's "belief in the blood," upon which her marriage and her artistic partnership was built, would also provide—for Hughes—the justification for its dissolution.

THE CAMBRIDGE SPRING bore fruit. *Poetry* accepted four of Plath's poems and four of Hughes's.[128] The symmetry pleased her. She noted that out of the forty-two poems in her new book, twenty had been published, "10 of these in blessed <u>Poetry</u>."[129] John Lehmann at *The London Magazine* accepted "Spinster" and "Black Rook in Rainy Weather," and Hughes's "Famous Poet." *The London Magazine* was, according to Hughes, the "true sanctum sanctorum of English letters," the British equivalent of *The Atlantic*.[130] The influential

London critic G. S. Fraser wrote to Hughes "cursing himself" for not having discovered him.[131] (Ted told Olwyn that Fraser thought him "the Jesus Christ come to redeem Modern Poetry.")[132] Sylvia gloated to Aurelia, "Ted's leaving just as London realizes (too late) that they've been ignoring a genius & their only true living poet (young) is perfect."[133] Hughes's poem "The Martyrdom of Bishop Farrar" was broadcast on the BBC's Third Programme *The Poet's Voice* on April 14 (and rebroadcast two days later), which perhaps prompted Plath to write to Carne-Ross at the BBC on April 21, asking if *she* could try out for a spot on *The Poet's Voice*. When the couple's work appeared in the same issue of *Granta* that May, they became the talk of literary Cambridge.[134] Ted chalked his success up to Sylvia, telling his brother Gerald in May, "Marriage is my medium. Also my luck thrives on it, and my productions. You have no idea what a happy life Sylvia and I lead . . . We work and walk about, and repair each other's writings. She is one of the best critics I ever met and understands my imagination perfectly, and I think I understand hers. It's amazing how we strike sparks."[135]

Hughes's contract for the British publication of *The Hawk in the Rain* came with an astonishing note from Charles Monteith: "Mr. Eliot has asked me to tell you how much he personally enjoyed the poems and to pass on to you his congratulations on them."[136] All of Plath's predictions about Hughes's success had come true. "I guaranteed 15 poems sold in a year if he let me be his agent when I first met him & he's written his best since we've been working together."[137] Hughes had indeed sold fifteen poems since June, plus "a broadcast poem and a book to two countries." He had already started his second collection. Plath, too, had sold fifteen poems since their wedding, and begun her novel. "If only I can get my book accepted in the next few months it will be perfect," she told Aurelia.[138]

Given the good fortune that had come their way that year, both were surprised when Marianne Moore, one of the judges of the Harper's contest, asked Hughes to cut "The Little Boys and the Seasons," "Bawdry Embraced," and "The Drowned Woman" from *The Hawk in the Rain*. (The word "whore" appeared in the latter two poems.) To her mother, Plath invoked Lawrence as she defined herself and Hughes against the prevailing modes of British and American poetry, especially the Movement:

> We feel, strongly, that to cut these two out would be to silence a large part of Ted's voice: which is raised against the snide, sneaking, coy weekend-review poets whose sex is in their head, & the prissy abstract poets who don't dare to talk about love in anything but mile-distant abstractions. . . .
>
> Ironically enough, I opened Marianne Moore's book of critical essays to see if she ever treated poets who wrote about sex directly & honestly,

and the page fell open to this letter from D.H. Lawrence to Miss Moore when she edited the Dial: "I knew some of the poems would offend you. But then some part of life must offend you too, and even beauty has its thorns and its nettle-stings and its poppy-poison. Nothing is without offense & nothing should be: if it is part of life, & not merely abstraction."

Naturally, Ted & I agree with Lawrence. I think he puts his finger on her blind spot most eloquently.[139]

Three days later, Sylvia wrote again to her mother, "We want logic, but not without blood feeling; music without vague emotion. . . . They think they can ignore us in their magazines, because we are too disturbing. In a year, the whole picture will be changed." She told Aurelia that she and Ted were "alone, really alone . . . among young modern poets"—few shared their commitment to "the great subjects of life: love, death, war."[140] Yet in the end Hughes agreed to cut the three poems, chastened by how they "would read to Ma & Pa."[141]

When the Poetry Book Society chose *The Hawk in the Rain* as one of its top choices for 1957, Hughes would famously write in its bulletin, "What excites my imagination is the war between vitality and death, and my poems may be said to celebrate the exploits of the warriors of either side."[142] He was staking out his poetic territory; he and Plath would continue to position themselves against the Movement. Sylvia wrote to Aurelia that spring of the "cheap, flat 'new movement poetry' . . . the meanings are dull, often superficial 'top-of-the-head' philosophizing, and there is no music, no sense picturing."[143]

That May, Plath spent long days at the university library "steadily reading . . . Corneille, Racine, Ibsen, Strindberg, Webster, Marlowe, Tourneur, Yeats, Eliot."[144] Her letters home were all about America. To Ted's brother Gerald she wrote of her dream landscape: "I am dying to show Ted Cape Cod . . . scrub pines, lakes, sand cliffs & tons of icy green-blue Atlantic ocean pounding 20 miles of almost deserted shoreline."[145] Dreams of the Cape sustained her. "I will not feel at all 'guilty' in indulging in sun & sea there," she wrote Aurelia.

You know, I think that through our years of family scraping to get money for scholarships etc. we three developed an almost Puritan sense that being "lazy" and spending money on "luxuries" like meals out, or theater or travel was slightly wicked! And I think all three of us are being given the rare chance of changing into people who can experience the joys of new adventures and experiences.[146]

Aurelia now had her driver's license and had been promoted to associate professor at Boston University. Sylvia began to feel that her grandmother's death, painful as it had been, had forced her mother to grow. She wrote Marcia that Aurelia was now "entertaining, driving to work," adding, "I am so proud. . . . she is making a life at the age of 50." Sylvia hoped for a new chapter in their relationship when she returned to America as a married, professional woman, able to share her "active life" with Aurelia.[147]

In late May, Sylvia sat six three-hour exams for the English Tripos II—a second bachelor's degree—and submitted her poetry manuscript, *Two Lovers and a Beachcomber*, as an "original composition" in partial fulfillment of the degree.[148] When she returned home her fingers were so cramped she could hardly bend them. Ted heated hot water and prepared her bath, and served her steak and wine in bed. Her French, Tragedy, and Chaucer exams had been "stimulating" and "fair," but the Criticism & Composition and English Moralists exams were, she felt, "horrors."[149] She was too exhausted to feel much excitement upon learning that her poetry collection had made the final round of the Yale Younger Poets contest. Ted, too, was tired; he had recently finished his teaching duties and felt despondent about the fate of his working-class boys. There had been small successes, like the Elizabethan play he had directed, yet the daily drudgery of keeping order had depleted him. When he left the school he felt as if he were abandoning a sinking ship with the most vulnerable passengers still on board.

Sylvia would not receive the First she had hoped for but, instead, a 2.1—essentially, magna cum laude. She was disappointed, but reminded herself that she had completed her second BA in two years while most British undergraduates did it in three. (This was false logic—Fulbrighters were allowed to skip the first year of the degree entirely—but it boosted her morale.) The couple packed up their belongings, including more than three hundred books, and left for Yorkshire on June 5, shunning her graduation and Cambridge's extravagant May Balls. Sylvia would later tell Jane Baltzell that she felt "much more partisan" about Cambridge than Smith. The "misery & weariness & confusion" of her first year had receded, leaving only memories of "a green Eden . . . that delicate baby blue sky and the ducks at the mill race and every detail bright and haunting as stained glass. . . . I still endow it with the light of gone, very gone youth."[150]

Sylvia spent her entire first day at the Beacon in bed, recovering from the "desperate tenseness of the past month" as well as from a vitriolic attack on one of her poems by a "young don" who had pronounced her verse "hollow" compared to John Donne.[151] The anonymous writer tore into Plath's poem "Epitaph for Fire and Flower," which she had published in the Winter 1956–57 edition of *Chequer*, saying that she had produced "disconnected sparks" rather than a "richness of meaning."[152] Sylvia thought the John Donne comparison absurd, as did Ted. The "vicious abuse" left her spent and shaken. Once she regained her strength, she and Ted took long walks on the moors. "We walk for miles & meet not a soul: just larks & swallows & green green hills and valleys."[153] Olwyn, who was home on a ten-day visit, remembered the couple reading the war poet Keith Douglas together outside on a blanket in a nearby field. "Two poets communing with a precursor whose work had many affinities with their own . . . I always saw this as an image of Sylvia and Ted's central shared allegiance to poetry."[154]

Sylvia had not read half the novels on the syllabus for Smith's freshman English, and was already worried about the number of books she would have to master for her new teaching job. Her anxiety and homesickness led to some antisocial behavior. According to Olwyn, Sylvia left abruptly when Ted's old English teacher, Mr. Fisher, stopped by the Beacon one afternoon. Sylvia's behavior probably had nothing to do with Fisher, but rather a perceived slight from Olwyn. Ted later apologized to his sister en route to America: "The days at home were ill-starred." Sylvia was still wound up from her exams, he said, and the house was too small for five people. Ted sympathized with his wife's sense of displacement, and he asked Olwyn to give her another chance:

> Her immediate "face" when she meets someone is too open & too nice—"smarmy" as you said—but that's the American stereotype she clutches at when she is in fact panic-stricken. Or perhaps—and I think this is more like it—her poise & brain just vanish in a kind of vacuous receptivity—only this american [*sic*] stereotype manner then keeps her going at all. She says stupid things then that mortify her afterwards. Her second thought—her retrospect, is penetrating, skeptical, and subtle. But she can never bring that second-thinking mind to the surface with a person until she's known them some time. She's hard to bring out, in fact. You saw how much better she was the last day. Don't judge her on her awkward behaviour. I'm sure you see what she's really like.[155]

Hughes suggested that Plath's "real" self—the self that was "penetrating, skeptical, and subtle"—was at odds with her "false" American self.[156] He seemed to understand that American culture, and the limitations it placed on women, was poisonous for her.

On the morning of their first wedding anniversary, Ted presented Sylvia with an enormous bouquet of pink roses. They packed a picnic of chicken, steak, and wine and spent the afternoon on a shady hillside overlooking the moors, reading and talking about "the tough times past & good times to come." This was the only place Sylvia did not miss the ocean: "the air is like clear seawater: thirst-quenching & cool, and the view of spaces, unlike anything I've seen in my life." She sketched out her future to Aurelia. They would support themselves teaching while they published books and won Pulitzers, Saxons, and Guggenheims and have "3 or 4 children."[157] Sylvia skipped over the challenges that awaited: Ted had no job, and they had barely $100 between them. But she had reasons for optimism. She was returning to America with a Cambridge degree, a poet-husband on the verge of real fame, an academic position, and more publications to come. "All from now on should be literally clear sailing!" she wrote Aurelia on June 20, the day she left England. She boarded the *Queen Elizabeth* filled with visions of Nauset, the black edges of her past dissolving in the clean emerald surf of her future.

20

In Midas' Country

Cape Cod and Smith College, June 1957–June 1958

Photographs show Sylvia Plath and Ted Hughes smiling and at ease on the deck of the *Queen Elizabeth* as it sailed into New York Harbor on June 25, 1957. But the crossing had been difficult. Sylvia became seasick after indulging in martinis and lobster Newburg, and vomited all over the coffin-sized bunks in the tiny cabin. Ted began to worry that life on the luxury liner was a preview of what awaited him in the land of plenty. He felt sickened by all the rich food—"three five course meals a day," which he could not stop himself from eating. He found the Atlantic "uninteresting" and compared the voyage to living on a "desert island with a thousand howler monkeys." By the third day at sea, his "depression was black and absolute. It was difficult even to speak." The couple's mood improved after they spotted a whale alongside the ship. They ran to the bow and finally felt "the sensation of crossing the Atlantic—the heroic bid."[1] Plath took descriptive notes of her fellow passengers, jotting down snippets of dialogue for later use. She wrote long, painterly passages of the ship and sea: "blue swimming light . . . Clear blue shadows on white paint . . . a wake of rainbows—."[2] She was going home.

Ellie Friedman, Lynne Lawner, Russ Moro, and Robert Bagg were waiting for the couple when they docked in Manhattan at Pier 92.[3] Ted got off the boat without Sylvia, who was, Robert remembered, "badly sunburned, and still ministering to herself in their cabin." Robert, who knew Russ, Ted's Cambridge friend from Amherst, was impressed with Hughes's dramatic cadences. "Sylvia's arms are 'BLISTERED LIKE BULLION,' he told us." Manhattan seemed "'MASSIVE AS MADRID.'" Sylvia soon disembarked. "She was also tall," Robert remembered, "her blonde hair reined in under a kerchief, and all business in dealing with officialdom. My impression of

Sylvia that day was of her hyper-intensity, her unconcealed sensuality, and her fierce devotion to Ted."[4] Ellie knew Russ through the media and publishing world, and wanted to introduce him to Sylvia. She thought he could be helpful.[5]

Hughes later wrote home about the skyscrapers that made "terrific dark caverns of their streets. And all the streets are crawling with these gaudy cars."[6] Even Sylvia felt that "everything seemed immensely sparkling & shiny & fast-paced & loud after my bucolic existence on the Backs and the Bronte moors."[7] Ted walked to the pier-side bulletin board full of messages for arriving passengers, and found, under "H," a telegram informing him that *The Hawk in the Rain* had been chosen as a selection by the Poetry Book Society.[8] But the celebration would have to wait. When a suspicious customs officer asked Sylvia to open a trunk packed with three hundred books, he unearthed *The Nude*, by Kenneth Clark, and the banned *Lady Chatterley's Lover*.[9] She wept as she explained that she was teaching Lawrence in her college course. The customs officer told her she looked much too young for such a job but let them through with the books. It was not the homecoming she had imagined, but she was relieved to be back in America after two years. "God shed his grace," she told Lynne. "We are here."[10]

Sylvia squeezed into the back of a yellow cab between Robert and Russ and immediately drew Robert into a conversation about young poets. "Who did I think was the best of the new ones, she prodded, after stating with conviction that her husband was already the best of 'our generation.'" When Robert told her that he liked James Merrill and W. S. Merwin, she dismissed Merwin as "much too vague and dreamy." She pressed on. "Who won the Glascock this year?" she asked. "I did," Robert said. "Who were the judges," she wondered. "Nemerov, Hecht, and Andrews Wanning of Bard." "Lucky you," she said.[11]

They headed to Russ's family townhouse on the Upper East Side for Hughes's first American dinner, served by an Italian maid. There, Sylvia met the future sinologist David Keightley, Russ's Amherst classmate, who was then editor of World Publishing.[12] She eagerly agreed to send him her poetry manuscript. Robert recalled that Ted already had something of a reputation in America, and that "The Martyrdom of Bishop Farrar" had made a deep impression on him and his literary friends. Struck by Ted's "spondaic detonation" of "charged verbs," he wondered about the effect it had on Sylvia's poems. "That's what she heard daylong, his staccato speaking habit, which sought out arresting alliterative combinations."[13] He gave Ted a sheaf of his poems that night and asked him to take a look.

Four days later, in the cool, late-afternoon hours, Aurelia held a small, catered wedding reception for her daughter and son-in-law under a white tent in her Wellesley backyard. Sylvia wore a green-blue linen dress with a full skirt and a white stephanotis corsage on her shoulder. Aurelia thought she looked radiant as she greeted her seventy guests. Perry and Shirley Norton remembered her as "gorgeous," introducing "my Ted," holding tightly to his arm.[14] But Wilbury Crockett was not impressed. He sensed a "hauteur," an arrogance in Ted, and wanted to kick him.[15] Ted was, no doubt, out of his element, but he had not married down. He stood by his wife's side, struck speechless by the wealth he observed. "What a neighborhood!" he wrote to his parents. "All the houses are in their own little grounds." He described the wedding party in great detail, recounting their gifts and the probable cost—a "very elite looking" tray, a "huge" pressure cooker, a salt and pepper shaker that was "very modern and pleasant to handle." He loved his new silk suit, made, he noted, of "Wonderfully expensive material."[16] Hughes was not immune to bourgeois pleasures. "Imagine how I enjoy this," he wrote, after tallying all the fifty-dollar bills they received.[17] "This land literally does flow with milk and honey."[18] Robert, who was at the reception with Russ, cornered Ted and asked what he thought of the poems he'd given him earlier. Hughes said he admired one about a Great War soldier, then he changed the subject to astrology. He told Robert that if he knew the exact minute he had been born, he could predict whether or not he would become a successful poet. Russ, meanwhile, looked on the proceedings with dismay. He did not like Sylvia and thought "the coupling risky, a Fitzgerald-esque time bomb."[19]

Karen Goodall, who lived next door to Sylvia's aunt Dot and uncle Joe in Weston for many years, remembered that the Plath-Schober family hoped Ted, as husband, would now "shoulder the nervous burden of Sylvia." No one in the "quiet, conservative" family seemed to know how to handle this brilliant, "not sufficiently placid" young woman. There was still bitterness about her suicide. "What people would say is, 'That ungrateful child. She does so well in school. She has a family that adores her. Everything was going right. Why does she have to do this?'" The family "wrongly invested" their expectations in Ted as "caretaker."[20]

A few days after the reception, Sylvia and Ted drove to Northampton to look for an apartment. They ended up renting a furnished one-bedroom on the top floor of a stately white house at 337 Elm Street, an elegant block near Smith. It was a cut above their student digs, Sylvia thought, and "very cool in the sun-swelter."[21] Dan Aaron, director of Smith's freshman English course, treated the couple to gin and tonics later that day at his home. There, for the first time, Sylvia saw books and engravings by Leonard Baskin, an artist and Smith professor who would eventually become Ted's lifelong friend. Hughes warmed to Aaron, who knew some of his Cambridge friends, and the prospect of a social life at Smith. Plath liked Aaron, too, but she felt awkward about teaching alongside her former professors and worried about meeting their high expectations.

The couple was thrilled that the Poetry Book Society chose *The Hawk in the Rain* as a top selection. Hughes—whose first poem had been published only a year before—wrote his parents, "It means my book will . . . challenge everything being written in England."[22] His poems had been accepted by the "posh intellectual" *Sewanee Review*, *The Spectator*, and, finally, *The New Yorker*, which took "The Thought-Fox." Sylvia marveled at how a reputation could open doors: a year before, *The New Yorker* had rejected the same poem. She had been publishing her poems since she was eight, but Ted, after less than two years, already had a prize-winning poetry collection and a *New Yorker* acceptance—her two life goals. "I knew this would happen from the minute I read his first poems, but it is blissful to have it come so soon," she wrote Marcia. "And he just sits, unshaved, his hair every which way, munching raw steaks & writing more."[23]

Plath took her role as Hughes's agent seriously. She sent his poems, and hers, to dozens of magazines, and tried to muster up as much free publicity as she could. She asked Ellie, now working for CBS, if she knew any New York editors who might want to publish an article about him. "How about a real dark Heathcliffe [sic] picture of Ted in 'People are Talking About' with all his book prizes???" And yet, Sylvia maintained that she and Ted were above such hustling. When the 92nd Street Y wanted to make a short film about Hughes, she wrote airily to Ellie, "Ted wants no personal circus, only poem readings & whatever magazine notes will help the book. Peace & Cape Cod."[24] But even on Cape Cod, peace would prove elusive.

———

ON JULY 13, Warren drove the couple to Eastham, a small village on the outer Cape, near Nauset Beach. Aurelia had rented them a shingled cottage amid the pines at the Hidden Acres Cottage Colony for six weeks.[25] Nauset was three miles to the east, Cape Cod Bay three miles to the west. They had no phone and no car, just their bicycles, Sylvia's new Olivetti Lettera 22 typewriter (a gift from Aurelia), some books, and clothes. Ted found the two-bedroom cottage comfortable and modern. He especially liked the screened-in porch. "When you step from the doorway pine needles touch your head, and as you sit there you see chipmunks & little red squirrels among the house-high trees," he wrote Olwyn.[26]

For the first few days, they luxuriated in silence and ate simple meals Sylvia prepared in their single frying pan. She was delighted to see four of her poems in that July's *Poetry*.[27] Yet soon a neighbor began playing his radio too loudly, and the biting horseflies became a nuisance. "God has to remind us this isn't heaven," Sylvia wrote in her journal.[28] The cottage itself proved rather too rustic—Sylvia sent Aurelia a long list of "suburban" supplies they needed (eggbeaters, pillowcases, facecloths, nail clippers, coffee mugs), while the lack of a car proved a major inconvenience. They had to rely on the colony's caretaker, Mrs. Spaulding, for frequent rides into town. Mrs. Spaulding, in turn, felt free to drop by for coffee and conversation—just the kind of suburban mingling they had longed to escape. And even in paradise, Sylvia had disturbing dreams, all "diabolically real." "Why these dreams?" she wrote in her journal. "These last exorcisings of the horrors and fears beginning when my father died and the bottom fell out. I am just now restored. I have been restored for over a year, and still the dreams aren't quite sure of it. They aren't for I'm not. And I suppose never will be."[29]

Everything would be better, Plath reassured herself, once she began "the painful process of getting writing again after nine months."[30] Her first day back at the typewriter produced only one "good image": "This bad beginning depressed me inordinately." As she and Hughes walked to the beach along busy Route 6, the cars seemed to her "deathly . . . like killer instruments from the mechanical tempo of another planet." The "badly begun poem" weighed on her all day.[31] She vowed to "never get in this rusty state again, for writing is the prime condition of both our lives & our happiness: if that goes well, the sky can fall in."[32]

As in Benidorm, this American honeymoon yielded little in the way of new writing. She had not published a story in a women's magazine in five years, and she spent much of her time in Eastham trying to write fiction that would sell. She wanted to show the editors at the "slicks" that the twenty-year-old adolescent writer had transformed into a more mature literary voice. But she feared that creative paralysis would bring on another depression.

While Hughes began writing the poems that would go into his second collection, *Lupercal*, Plath worked on four stories.[33] None would be published, but it was during this time that Plath outlined the plot and themes—in "The Trouble-Making Mother"—that would become the basis for *The Bell Jar*:

Get tension of scenes with mother during Ira and Gordon crisis. Rebellion. Car keys. Psychiatrist. Details: Dr. Beuscher: baby. Girl comes back to self, can be good daughter. Sees vision of mothers [sic] hardship. Yes yes. This is a good one. A subject. Dramatic. Serious. Enough of the hyphenated society names. Mental hospital background. Danger. Dynamite under high tension. Mothers [sic] character. At first menacing, later pathetic, moving. Seen from outside first, then inside. Girl comes back: grown bigger, ready to be bigger. Like mother, yet furious about it.

Wants to be different. Bleaches hair. Policemen. Annoying her. Story in newspapers. After suicide attempt. Earthy Dr. Beuscher. . . . MOTHER-DAUGHTER. Troubles. Graphic. A real story.[34]

The girl's name would be Judith Greenwood—like Esther Greenwood, the future heroine of *The Bell Jar*—and she would be "a statement of the generation. Which is you."[35] After starting this story during the third week of July, Plath felt the "old fluency" return "at last, at last." The story, as her confident, fast-moving outline suggests, was writing itself. In her journal she wrote, "I must say, I'm surprised at the story: it's more gripping, I think, than anything I've ever done." She finished on July 25 and sent the piece off to *The Saturday Evening Post*, where it was quickly rejected. Yet the writing restored her faith: "And now, aching, but surer and surer, I feel the wells of experience and thought spurting up, welling quietly, with little clear sounds of juiciness. How the phrases come to me." Plath thought it her "first good story for five years" and later realized that it contained the seeds of a novel.[36]

Each afternoon, after four hours of writing, Sylvia and Ted biked to Nauset. There, they swam along a sandbar halfway between Nauset Light Beach and Coast Guard Beach, with "clear level water & long rollers."[37] The sand and the blue horizon stretched in both directions for miles; Sylvia had fantasized about such summer afternoons during the long Cambridge winters. In the evening, they read. Plath immersed herself in Virginia Woolf's diary, *The Waves*, and *Jacob's Room*. She reread and underlined the end of *The Waves*, which chilled her as much as the end of James Joyce's "The Dead." "Virginia Woolf helps," she wrote in her journal. "Her novels make mine possible." Woolf's writing inspired her to believe in her own vocation and even to "go better than she." She promised herself: "No children until I have done it. . . . My life, I feel, will not be lived until there are books and stories which relive it perpetually in time."[38]

When it rained, Sylvia cooked and baked cakes. She knew she tended to "escape into cooking," as Hughes put it, when "faced by some tedious or unpleasant piece of work."[39] Now she mined her baking habit for dramatic potential in "The Day of the Twenty-Four Cakes," which she outlined in her journal:

> woman at end of rope . . . quarrel with husband: loose ends, bills, problems, dead end. Wavering between running away or committing suicide: stayed by need to create an order: slowly, methodically begins to bake cakes, one each hour. . . . Husband comes home: new understanding. She can go on making order in her limited way: beautiful cakes: can't bear to leave them.[40]

Plath was aware of her story's parodic elements, and she wondered whether she should use a "Kafka lit-mag serious" tone, or a style more appropriate for *The Saturday Evening Post*.[41] In the end she decided to experiment with both. The story has not survived, but its outlines point to Plath's unsettled approach to domesticity. In her stories about housewifery and motherhood— "The Visitor," "Sunday at the Mintons," "Home Is Where the Heart Is," "The Wishing Box," "Sweetie Pie and the Gutter Men," "Day of Success"—wives respond to their subordination with murderous fantasies, suicidal unhappiness, or smug superiority over "career women." They are painful referendums on dreams deferred.

These tensions came to a head in "Dialogue Over a Ouija Board," the first poem she had written in six months. She found the form liberating: "strict 7 line stanzas rhyming ababcbc," which she challenged herself to make sound "like conversation."[42] The poem had a biting undercurrent. Just as she had written about unhappy, ghostly doubles in Benidorm ("The Other Two"), she now wrote about another glowering married couple.

Although Plath frequently gave the impression to others that she shared Hughes's interest in the occult, "Dialogue Over a Ouija Board" reminds us that she was more ambivalent.[43] In the poem, the wife, Sybil, is skeptical of her husband Leroy's ability to interpret "messages" from Pan. (The couple's names add a layer of irony to the proceedings: Sybil suggests a divine seer, while Leroy loosely translates, in French, to "the king.") "Pan's a mere puppet / Of our two intuitions," Plath writes, a "psychic bastard / Sprung to being on our wedding night." The couple fights about the meaning of Pan's "messages":

> How can we help but battle
> If our nerves are the sole nourishers
>
> Of Pan's pronouncements, and our nerves are strung
> To such cross-purposes?

The poem speaks to creative tension within the marriage. To others, and herself, Sylvia always described Ted as her ideal. In her journal that July she wrote, "he sets the sea of my life steady, flooding it with the deep rich color of his mind and his love and constant amaze at his perfect being: as if I had conjured, at last, a god from the slack tides."[44] But her work suggests a more complex professional relationship, even a burgeoning rivalry. As Sybil says, "I glimpse no light at all as long / As we two glower from our separate camps, / This board our battlefield."[45]

By creating fictional doubles of herself and Hughes, Plath simultaneously addressed and contained her anxieties about the creative partnership. She refused the role of muse; like the heroine of her unfinished novel *Falcon Yard*, she felt herself a "voyager, no Penelope."[46] Many Hughes poems from this period, too, display anxiety over a powerful female rival.[47] While Sylvia worried that she would remain the trailing spouse, especially once a baby arrived, Ted would increasingly worry that underneath his wife's freewheeling Lawrentian exterior lurked a bourgeois desire for respectability and financial security. And he was all too aware of Robert Graves's warning, in *The White Goddess*, that one cannot serve Goddess and wife at the same time.[48]

As July turned to August, the couple became listless in Eastham. The temperature was in the high nineties, "terribly still and sultry"—and Sylvia longed for the "nip" of fall weather.[49] The laundry came back dirty; she could not make sense of Faulkner. In late July, a pregnancy scare brought on "a black lethal two weeks" as bad as the weeks that had preceded her suicide attempt.[50] She was paralyzed with fear; if she were pregnant, there would be no Smith job, no traveling, no novel: "clang, clang, one door after another banged shut with the overhanging terror which, I know now, would end me, probably Ted, and our writing."[51] She felt she would resent her child for closing the doors she had pried open. The couple biked through a driving thunderstorm to a doctor in Orleans on August 4 for a blood test. The next day her period came. But she had lost her momentum.

Ted, too, became restless. He was "paralysed" by the cost of the cottage Aurelia had rented for them—"Dowry almost" at $70 a week.[52] He developed an ear abscess, which caused pain, fever, and severe facial swelling. "Conditions haven't been as ideal as they've seemed," he wrote Olwyn that August.[53] Sylvia endured another setback in early August when she learned that her manuscript had not won the Yale Younger Poets contest. (John Hollander had won.) For over two months she had fantasized about her own moment in the sun—the introduction by Auden, the ensuing *New Yorker* acceptances. She confided in her journal:

> Worst: it gets me feeling so sorry for myself, that I get concerned about Ted: Ted's success, which I must cope with this fall with my job . . . feeling so wishfully that I could make both of us feel better by having it with him. I'd rather have it this way, if either of us was successful: that's why I could marry him, knowing he was a better poet than I and that I would never have to restrain my little gift, but could push it and work it to the utmost, and still feel him ahead.[54]

Now she would have to begin again. She reread the manuscript with a newly critical eye, hating the poems for what she now saw as "bland lady-like archness or slightness."[55] She could hardly believe Adrienne Rich and Donald Hall, with their "dull" poems, were ahead of her. She had not worked hard enough, "Not one tenth hard enough." She must become "stoic" again, and "fight."[56] There would be no more stories with "phony plots," "the old lyric sentimental stuff."[57]

By late August, Sylvia had begun counting down the days until they could leave the Cape. She felt lazy and unproductive, and hardly realized that she had experienced two creative breakthroughs. In July, she had sketched a rough outline of a major plotline of *The Bell Jar*, and, in late August, she had pondered a coastal scene in her journal that would inspire her fine poem "Mussel Hunter at Rock Harbor," which *The New Yorker* would accept in June 1958: "the weird spectacle of fiddler crabs in the mud-pools off Rock Harbor creek.... An image: weird, of another world, with its own queer habits, of mud, lumped, under-peopled with quiet crabs."[58] Hughes would later write of their coastal explorations in his *Birthday Letters* poem "Flounders." "Was that a happy day?" he wondered, remembering how he and Plath had been swept out to sea in their dinghy by a strong current.[59] They eventually rowed to a sandbar, where "big, good America found us"; a powerboat towed them back to the dock. Back in the shallows, they caught flounders "big as plates." For Hughes, the day symbolized the life of adventure, beauty, and bounty they might have led had they not sacrificed their marriage to art:

> And the day
> Curled out of brilliant, arduous morning,
> Through wind-hammered perilous afternoon,
> Salt-scoured, to a storm-gold evening, a luxury
> Of rowing among the dream-yachts of the rich
> Lolling at anchor off the play-world pier.
>
> How tiny an adventure
> To stay so monumental in our marriage,
> A slight ordeal of all that might be,
> And a small thrill-breath of what many live by,
> And a small prize, a toy miniature
> Of the life that might have bonded us
> Into a single animal, a single soul—
>
> It was a visit from the goddess, the beauty
> Who was poetry's sister—she had come

To tell poetry she was spoiling us.
Poetry listened, maybe, but we heard nothing
And poetry did not tell us. And we
Only did what poetry told us to do.[60]

————

HUGHES WAS INITIALLY EXCITED to live in America: he wrote repeatedly to Olwyn in 1957 that he was tired of England, which he described as "rotten," "complete death."[61] Yet by the time he traveled to Cape Cod, he had become alarmed by American culture, wrapped, as he saw it, in "cellophane."[62] American food was "not fresh living stuff but a ten-year preservative, a chemical concoction."[63] Bread was "de-crapularised, re-energised, multi-cramulated, bleached, double-bleached, rebrowned, unsanforised, guaranteed no blaspheming. There is no such thing as bread."[64] He complained to his sister that "everybody's so friendly, and nobody knows anybody else's family history, and nobody ever bothers to get to know anybody except on purely temporary and facetious terms."[65] He spoke of the average American living on credit, mocked the "city man's" naturalist pretensions ("Expensive rods and fat paunches")[66] and wrote to Danny Weissbort of "greed, vulgarity, & the horrible superficiality of a race without any principles."[67] He admired only the sharp honesty of American literary reviews, so unlike the vituperative tones of British reviewers, and the wildlife. Echoing Leavis, he told Olwyn that "women's magazines & men's paper-backs, newspapers . . . make up the shared consciousness of the American people."[68] He reckoned that the "indigenous literary form" was "the advertisement."[69] All the best Americans lived in Europe, he wrote his sister. "I think America will destroy the world, slowly."[70]

Wellesley gave him—and Sylvia—the "jimjams." That June he wrote Gerald, "a comfortably housed life in America is an officially entered numbered trap in the rat-race. . . . The food, the general opulence, is frightening. My natural instinct is to practise little private filthinesses—I spit, pee on shrubbery, etc, and have a strong desire to sleep on the floor—just to keep in contact with a world that isn't quite so glazed as this one. . . . It's good too for me to be surrounded by a world from which I instinctively recoil."[71] He and Sylvia busied themselves moving to Northampton, which struck him as more "English—all the shops & streets huddled together—so maybe that will be more congenial."[72]

After paying their deposit and first month's rent on the apartment, Sylvia worried about scraping by until her first paycheck and went over her bills in meticulous detail with Aurelia. Sylvia was still dependent on her mother, whom she constantly asked for favors. Would Aurelia withdraw money for them at the bank? Could she send their bookcase to Northampton? Could she call the dentist to ask about Sylvia's swollen gum and make doctor appointments for herself and Ted in December? Did she have advice about driving lessons for Ted?

Aurelia sensed her daughter's anxiety and advised her to take "deep breaths," while Sylvia calmed herself with the knowledge that she would "never be anything less than conscientious."[73] She would teach the same syllabus to three different classes and share her office with an older scholar, Miss Hornbeak (Sylvia loved her name), on the top floor of the Neilson Library. All three of her classes met in nearby Hatfield Hall and Seelye Hall, a suitably collegiate brick building with large, light-filled classrooms.[74] She bought two new blouses to boost her "morale," as Aurelia had advised.

As September drew to a close, Sylvia began to realize that class preparation, grading, and regular conferences with sixty-six students would leave her little time to write. Yet she was ready to immerse herself in academic life again, for she knew the bell jar descended when she was listless: "How I long to be busy!" She felt she functioned more "happily & efficiently" when she had "a hundred things to do."[75] Ted reassured her that she would inspire her students, and she was grateful to him for making meals and doing the dishes while she prepared her classes. On the day *The Hawk in the Rain* was published in America, September 18, the owner of a local bookshop sent the couple two bottles of champagne. They shared one bottle by candlelight and saved the other for the end of Sylvia's first teaching week.

Sylvia could not sleep the night before her first class, and for many weeks after it, she battled to maintain her poise before the lectern. She had hoped that teaching would stimulate her and help her writing. Instead she found it an exhausting juggernaut that left her "always deathly nervous."[76] She thought of herself as a "hopeless extempore speaker" without sophisticated knowledge of the subjects she was teaching—an absurd comment from someone who had just earned a 2.1 on the Cambridge Tripos exams. She even worried that she did not know how to teach grammar properly, for she had always intuited correct usage by ear. Teaching at her alma mater, where she had been the star of the department, only intensified her anxiety. She recounted her struggle in her journal—"Letter to a demon"—on October 1. The demon within was her "murderous self":

> It is there. I smell it and feel it, but I will not give it my name. I shall shame it. When it says: you shall not sleep, you cannot teach, I shall go on anyway, knocking its nose in. It's [sic] biggest weapon is and has been the image of myself as a perfect success: in writing, teaching and living. As

soon as I sniff non-success in the form of rejections, puzzled faces in class when I'm blurring a point, or a cold horror in personal relationships, I accuse myself of being a hypocrite, posing as better than I am, and being, at bottom lousy.[77]

Thanks to the therapy she had undertaken in 1953–54, Plath was now better equipped to stop these cycles of negative thinking. She reassured herself that she could not be expected to teach as well as a published scholar with a PhD. She would do her best, and that ought to be enough. She had quit her job at the Belmont, and nearly quit her first nanny job with the Mayos. This time, she would not quit. "I'll fight it . . . that black cloud which would annihilate my whole being with its demand for perfection and measure, not what I am, but of what I am not."[78]

Hughes captured something of Plath's terror in his *Birthday Letters* poem "The Blue Flannel Suit."

> . . . Now I know, as I did not,
> What eyes waited at the back of the class
> To check your first professional performance
> Against their expectations. What assessors
> Waited to see you justify the cost
> And redeem their gamble. What a furnace
> Of eyes waited to prove your metal. I watched
> The strange dummy stiffness, the misery,
> Of your blue flannel suit, its straitjacket, ugly
> Half-approximation to your idea
> Of the proprieties you hoped to ease into,
> And your horror in it.[79]

She would not always be so nervous; confidence would come with experience. And she knew, as she told Marcia, that she could learn something from teaching her "favorite writers, who stimulate my own writing"—Lawrence, Joyce, James, Dostoevsky, Woolf—to smart, disciplined women.[80]

Plath's syllabus was deeply personal. In September and October, she taught two chapters from William James's *Varieties of Religious Experience* and five Hawthorne short stories, including her old favorite "Rappaccini's Daughter."[81] In November, she followed these texts with Henry James's "The Pupil" and "The Beast in the Jungle" and D. H. Lawrence's "The Rocking-Horse Winner," "The Blind Man," "The Prussian Officer," and "The Princess"; she ended the semester with Joyce's *Dubliners*. During the spring semester, she would teach Dostoevsky's *Crime and Punishment*, Joyce's

A Portrait of the Artist as a Young Man, and a miniature version of her Cambridge tragedy course (Webster, Aristotle, Ibsen, and Strindberg).[82] She used selections from Louis Untermeyer's 1955 *Modern American and British Poetry* on Hopkins, Yeats, Eliot, Thomas, Auden, Crowe Ransom, and e. e. cummings.[83] She planned to teach poems by Marianne Moore, Wallace Stevens, Elizabeth Bishop, Richard Wilbur, and Edith Sitwell if she had time.

This was, as one of her former students recalled, "heavy, depressing stuff."[84] To her students, looking back, it must have seemed that Mrs. Hughes—as Plath's students called her—already had a morbid obsession with death. Yet her interest in this theme reflected a sound and current approach to literary modernism. "Death-in-life," alienation, and paralysis were prominent themes in discussions of modernist texts by critics like Edmund Wilson, Harry Levin, Hugh Kenner, David Daiches, I. A. Richards, F. R. Leavis, and Elizabeth Drew in the 1950s.[85] Plath often quoted these critics' works in her teaching notes, especially as they pertained to Joyce, Yeats, and Eliot. Her teaching notes on Eliot's "The Love Song of J. Alfred Prufrock," for example, were typical of her era: "helpless consciousness of having dared too little . . . Fear of life. Hesitation: fatal: suspension of decision." Again, on "The Waste Land": "paralysis of man," "life dead, love dead, nature dead, culture dead, no integration." On Joyce: "modern man's exile from the old vital relationships with family, country and religion. STERILITY. ISOLATION."[86]

On the last day of class, Plath's students would ask her why there was "so much death, so much living death in the stories, poems, plays & novels we've read." Her response, as she wrote in her lecture notes, probably struck her students as unusually passionate. "DEATH IS ONE OF THE MOST MOVING & TROUBLING EXPERIENCES OF LIFE: DEATH-IN-LIFE IS ONE OF THE MOST TERRIBLE STATES OF EXISTENCE: NEUTRALITY, BOREDOM become worse sins than murder, worse than illicit love affairs: BE RIGHT OR WRONG, don't be indifferent, don't be NOTHING." Poetry, she went on, could help us "re-create worlds." "MANY POETS, MANY READERS live by poetry as people have lived by religion: BOTH ARE RITUALS, PATTERNS" that give "special meaning to the most profound experiences of human life."[87]

Plath's teaching notes suggest that her reading of modernist texts—Joyce, Lawrence, Eliot, and Yeats—gave her the aesthetic tools and thematic confidence to transform her suicide attempt into high art in *The Bell Jar*. Her mouthpieces would not be working-class Dubliners, as in Joyce, or shell-shocked veterans, as in Woolf, but women who suffocate within a sexist society. Plath called Manhattan a "dry, humid, breathless wasteland" in a June 1953 letter to Warren; as the critic Amanda Golden has noted,

Esther's descriptions of herself as "numb," "hollow," and "dead" speak to the "death-in-life" that Joyce and Eliot wrote about in *Dubliners* and "The Waste Land."[88] ("The Waste Land," after all, was in large part about Eliot's nervous breakdown.) In other ways, *The Bell Jar* was an ironic reworking of Joyce's *Portrait of the Artist*.

Edmund Wilson's depiction of London in "The Waste Land" in his landmark book of literary criticism *Axel's Castle*—which Gordon gave Sylvia at McLean—resonated with her own experience of Manhattan. In the margin, she wrote, "1953—yes! June—NYC" next to the following passage: "The terrible dreariness of the great modern cities is the atmosphere in which 'The Waste Land' takes place. . . . all about us we are aware of nameless millions performing barren office routines, wearing down their souls in interminable labors of which the products never bring them profit—people whose pleasures are so sordid and so feeble that they seem almost sadder than their pains. And this Waste Land has another aspect: it is the place not merely of desolation, but of anarchy and doubt."[89] Plath probably made these markings during her teaching year, when she consulted *Axel's Castle* regularly. Even Henry James gave her an idea when he described May Bartram, in "The Beast in the Jungle," as "under some clear glass bell"—a phrase she underlined. She would return to Eliot, Joyce, James, and Wilson when she wrote *The Bell Jar*: "these are the sunk relics of my lost selves that I must weave, word-wise, into future fabrics."[90]

But in the fall of 1957, Sylvia could not see more than one or two days ahead of her syllabus. She spent her free time correcting papers and trying to get a handle on "what the hell I'm teaching."[91] In an early November letter to Warren, she wrote of her frustration:

> I sometimes wonder if I can live out the grim looming aspect of this year without despairing. . . . I am simply not a career woman, and the sacrifice of energy and life blood I'm making for this job is all out of proportion to the good I'm doing in it. My ideal of being a good teacher, writing a book on the side, and being an entertaining homemaker, cook & wife is rapidly evaporating. I want to write first, and being kept apart from writing, from giving myself a chance to really devote myself to developing this "spectacular promise" that the literary editors write me about when they reject my stories, is really very hard.
>
> . . . I am sacrificing my energy, writing & versatile intellectual life for grubbing over 66 Hawthorne papers a week and trying to be articulate in front of a rough class of spoiled bitches. If I knew how to teach a short story, or a novel, or a poem I'd at least have that joy. But I'm making it

up as I go along, through trial and error, mostly error. . . . it's easier for the men . . .[92]

Plath's teaching style drew mixed reviews. One former student, Sally Lawrence Kauder, called her "one of the best teachers at Smith," who inspired in her a lifelong love for Henry James. Another student, Martha Resnik Siderowf, recalled, "As a teacher, she was unusually sensitive to her students." Martha was impressed that Plath knew all her students' names and nicknames—a rarity in a large freshman English class. Plath was "graceful, gracious, and always seemed ready to smile. She was not at all intimidating and encouraged us to express ourselves without the fear of being chastised." Martha and another student, Judy Hofmann, invited Plath and Hughes to dinner at their dorm one night and found the couple "delightful guests." Sylvia regaled them with stories of freezing Cambridge lecture halls and cake-baking mishaps, while Ted joked that he preferred the cakes that didn't come off to those that did.[93]

Another former student, Ellen Nodelman, had a completely different experience. "Everyone in the class hated her," she said, echoing Plath's own sense that the students in her nine a.m. section did not like her. "She didn't joke with us. She didn't encourage us. She just walked into the classroom, put her things down on her desk, fixed a steely gaze on us, laid down the law for an hour, gathered up her things and stalked out."[94] Other students recalled her as "conservatively and sternly dressed, with her hair pulled back,"[95] "cold,"[96] "extremely controlled," "clipped," with a slight British accent.[97] Plath did most of the talking, sometimes using the Socratic method of cold-calling, which intimidated some of her students. Yet Ellen also said the consensus was that Plath was "a very good teacher. . . . She was rigorous, demanding, and thorough in her approach both to her students and to the literature we were reading."[98]

Plath's "impersonality" in the classroom reflected not only the masculine pedagogy of Cambridge, but a central tenet of the modernist texts she was teaching. T.S. Eliot, in "Tradition and the Individual Talent," had argued for the separation of personality and poetry: "Poetry . . . is not a turning loose of emotion, but an escape from emotion; it is not the expression of personality, but an escape from personality."[99] Plath—who would, ironically, be labeled an emotional, "confessional" poet—adhered rigidly to this dictum in her classroom. Only six years older than her students, and without the protective armor of a PhD, she believed she had to embody decorum and gravity. Another former student, Phyllis Chinlund, remembered her as "the image of bottled up energy. Total control and intellectual discipline."[100]

Plath's own description of her teaching resonates with her students'. In late September, she outlined her pedagogical strategies to Dorothea Krook, reflecting on what had worked and what had not:

> I am, by philosophy, I think, more dictatorial than is proper for an American. After I managed to work out a reasonably forceful discussion-maneuvering, I had an exciting time. Many of the girls will never need to take another English course; many of them would perhaps never read a poem again; I felt, now and then, like a missionary among the heathen. My texts were my salvation.[101]

On November 6, Plath learned that one of her students, Deborah Coolidge, had hung herself by Paradise Pond. (News of the suicide appeared in *The Sophian*, which carried Plath's article about Cambridge in the same issue.)[102] Plath said nothing about it in class. "She just forged on ahead," Ellen remembered.[103] Plath did not mention the incident in her journal.

Ellen remembered knowing about Ted Hughes's existence, but she recalled that he was by no means the Famous Poet on campus—that title was reserved for Anthony Hecht (though Hughes was "considered madly sexy").[104] Plath never discussed her own work, or anything remotely personal, in class.[105] She could have benefited from the bump in status that came with publishing in *The Atlantic* and *Poetry*, but to make such facts known would have been immodest and, by the standards of the day, unfeminine. Although she participated in one college poetry reading, students were much more aware of the male professors who "wrote," like Hecht and Fisher.[106] Ellen recalled that most of the women in Plath's class would have preferred a male professor.

Hughes had a second poem accepted by *The New Yorker* ("Bull Frog"), while *The Hawk in the Rain* had already sold more than one thousand copies in America. He read at the 92nd Street Y Poetry Center in New York that October, where Plath thought he looked like a "Yorkshire god." She guessed there were about 150 people in the audience, many of whom asked Hughes to sign copies of the book. (Plath lent him her "shoulder for a writing desk.")[107] Hughes was disappointed that no one of importance came. He began to feel trapped and unable to write once they returned to Northampton.

Plath was thrilled to learn that she had won the Bess Hokin Prize from *Poetry* magazine for her ten poems published in 1957, but she was too exhausted to enjoy her success. She tried to hide her anxiety, "To bear my Visitor alone."[108] She took sleeping pills throughout October. Hughes noticed her unhappiness and told Olwyn she was "creaking under her burdens" and "works every hour she wakes almost."[109] Sylvia again poured out her frustrations to her brother: "How I long to write on my own again! When I'm describing Henry James [*sic*] use of metaphor to make emotional states vivid and concrete, I'm dying to be making up my own metaphors."[110] By Thanksgiving she had heard that her Smith contract would likely be renewed and that she would be promoted, but she had already decided to "get out while the gettings [*sic*] good." The "security and prestige of the academic life" was not worth the death of her imagination.[111]

————————

THOUGH SYLVIA FELT STYMIED all semester, she made important literary connections on several trips to Boston that fall. Foremost among them was the genial Jack Sweeney, head of the Woodberry Poetry Room at Harvard, who, as Dido Merwin remembered, "liked nothing better than to bring poets together in his home on Beacon Street in Boston."[112] Sweeney invited Hughes to record some poems for the Poetry Room at Stephen Fassett's Beacon Hill studio around Thanksgiving; afterward, Plath and Hughes dined with the Sweeneys and the Merwins at Sweeney's home. The poet Bill Merwin, who had written an influential review of *The Hawk in the Rain* in *The New York Times*, had wanted to meet Hughes when he learned he was living in Massachusetts, and Sweeney had arranged the dinner. Plath described Merwin to her mother as "the most lucrative & machiavellianly-succesful of young (30) American poets, rather unpleasant in many ways." But he was worth cultivating: he knew "all the producers, poets etc. of London & America," called Robert Lowell "Cal," and had recently refused the position of poetry consultant to the Library of Congress.[113] Ted described both Bill and Dido, in a long letter to Olwyn, as a literary couple that had met on Majorca, where they had been part of Robert Graves's entourage. He called Dido "bumptuous garrulous upper class . . . very amusing." She struck him as someone who liked to profess. Bill Merwin he found too serious. "No play in his mind . . . No irony."[114] Merwin was equally put off by Hughes during their first meeting, when he sat "very gloomily in the corner and was silent." Sylvia seemed to him "charming, rather nervous and bubbling . . . slightly tinkly and high-pitched."[115]

The Merwins invited the Hugheses to lunch the next day at their fifth-floor walk-up on West Cedar Street (rather a challenge for Hughes, who was on crutches after jumping out of a chair and fracturing his foot). There, Dido recalled, "the all-absorbing topic" was "how to survive without having to teach."[116] Bill supported himself through freelancing jobs, though he and Dido would soon move to London, where the BBC provided more regular work; the Merwins' presence there would help convince Sylvia and Ted to follow. That day, as Sylvia admired their "rickety heavenly" apartment with its distant view of the Charles River, she wondered if the "slummy" side of Beacon Hill might be turning into Boston's Left Bank.[117] She became determined to hold court in her own Beacon Hill apartment.

Sylvia and Ted spent their Thanksgiving break in Wellesley. They dined with Mrs. Prouty, who, Sylvia told Warren, was now "obsessed with Ted," and spent Thanksgiving at Aunt Dot's home in Weston. Sweeney invited them to the Woodberry Poetry Room on November 27 to hear poetry recordings, including Hughes's own. Sylvia was angry that she had needed "special permission" to enter Harvard's Lamont Library, which housed the Poetry Room; "it's ridiculous they don't allow women, isn't it?" she wrote to Warren.[118] Her letter to him was sunny, but in her journal she called the week in Wellesley "a black-wept nightmare."[119]

Back in Northampton, the couple felt "the jinx of depression" break—at least, that is what Sylvia told Aurelia, who was recovering in the hospital from a hysterectomy. They had been at her bedside while she recovered, and the experience spooked Ted. "She's just a bag of nerves," he told Olwyn, "like someone permanently in a desperate situation & with 5 minutes to think her way out of it."[120] Sylvia plied her mother with good news, as always: Ted had written six new poems, had a third *New Yorker* acceptance, and had a first prose acceptance from a children's magazine, *Jack & Jill*. Best of all, *The Hawk in the Rain* had been chosen by *The New York Times Book Review* as one of the best books of the year. It was probably around this time that Plath wrote "The Thin People," a surreal nightmare poem that draws on imagery of famine, war, and depression. Although Plath wrote the poem in rhyming couplets, her rhymes are subtle; the overall effect is, as Plath might say, "ugliness": "They were wrapped in flea-ridden donkey skins, // Empty of complaint, forever . . ." Indeed it was the "ugliest" poem Plath wrote that year, and thus a triumph for a poet who was trying to shed her decorous, well-mannered tics.

Near the end of the fall semester, Sylvia came down with pneumonia and spent her Christmas vacation recovering while Ted rested his fractured foot. Exhausted and moody, neither wrote much. "I get more & more bored with these Smith people," Ted wrote Olwyn. "They dare not say a word that would not be admired & let pass by the whole assembled committee for advancement & faculty promotion."[121] After a fitful convalescent break, Sylvia returned to Smith in January and informed her department chair that she would be leaving at the end of the year. She wrote Warren, "he was very sorry & surprised but I practically skipped out."[122] When Alfred Fisher heard the news he summoned Plath to his office. He told her, as a friend, that she was expected to stay for two years and that if she left early, "the Institution will regard you as irresponsible." He himself had resigned twice (due to gossip about "sleeping with students"), but each time the president had asked him back. Now he was trying to extend the same favor to Plath. "It's all in your mind," he told her, "about anxiety. I have it from various sources."[123] He had heard she was an excellent teacher.

Plath's old thesis adviser George Gibian also questioned her decision. "What do you need to write?" he asked her over tea. Plath knew that her old professors "mean vaguely well," but they had "no idea what is for my own good."[124] Fisher and Gibian had wives (or ex-wives) who took care of their children and domestic affairs while they pursued their writing. Plath did not have the same luxury; teaching, writing, and running a home left her spent. Another female professor, Marie Borroff, confessed to Plath that she, too, felt teaching "a great psychic exhaustion"—as did Edna Williams, who had been teaching English for decades.[125] Plath now understood why so many female professors remained unmarried.

In late February, Dan Aaron took her to lunch and entreated her to stay at Smith, conjuring up visions of a part-time position for her, a position for Hughes, even a grant. Perhaps she could find, as Gibian suggested, a way to reconcile writing and teaching, like Anthony Hecht. She began having second thoughts, which she admitted to Olwyn:

> Ironically, now that I feel casual and masterful about the whole thing . . .
> one part of me feels sad to leave. I love the power of having 70 girls
> to teach, & get what is surely a dangerous enjoyment from shocking
> them into awareness, laughter & even tears. . . . But it's only been since I
> decided officially to leave that I've enjoyed it.[126]

She later told Dorothea Krook that she and Ted were invited to house dinners by the students in her classes once a week—"and only with effort did we keep it down to this."[127] In her journal she admitted she felt a "great nostalgia for my lost Smith-teacher self" and anxiety about starting over in a new city "at the one trade which won't be cheated."[128] Yet she still maintained to Olwyn that teaching was "dangerous" to her "own writing":[129] "What is it that teaching kills? The juice, the sap—the substance of revelation . . . I am living & teaching on rereadings, on notes of other people, sour as heartburn, between two unachieved shapes: between the original teacher & the original writer: neither."[130] Paul Roche, a British poet on the Smith faculty, thought that what decided Sylvia, in the end, was Ted's lack of reputation at Smith. "He was totally ignored, and that upset her." She told Paul, "Ted is being just wasted here."[131] His wife Clarissa agreed. Sylvia always gave the impression that her work "was of less importance" than Ted's.[132]

Her love for Ted, with his "queer electric invisible radiance," still burned.[133] "I need Ted to smell & kiss & sleep with & read by as I need bread & wine," she wrote in her journal. "He is my life now, my male muse, my pole-star centering me steady & right."[134] That winter, they hiked up a Hadley hill, tracking rabbit and fox prints in the snow, "breathing rarer and rarer air" until they ascended the summit. There, they found "a vast god's eye view . . . Of all this, the world in our heads, we word-stitch and make fabrics."[135] Aurelia had warned her she was "too critical" and would end up "an old maid," but she had proven her wrong. "I feel, miraculously, I have the impossible, the wonderful—I am perfectly at one with Ted, body & soul . . . our vocation is writing, our love is each other," she wrote in her journal. "What other husband would cook her veal chops, bring her tea and coffee and iced pineapple, do the dishes, nurse her through her sicknesses?"[136] When *Mademoiselle* accepted a poem from each of them on the second anniversary of the day they met—her first acceptance in almost a year—Plath saw it as symbolic confirmation of their literary future.[137] They ransacked Graves's *The White Goddess* for "subtle symbolic" names for their children. Yet the prospect of a baby still seemed "too strange and fearful."[138] Sylvia knew how easily she might surrender her dreams to motherhood.

In April they had an "absurd" quarrel—Ted accused Sylvia of throwing away his old cuff links, coat, and book about witches (she hated the parts about torture). Sylvia denied it all and ran out of the apartment "sickened." She headed to the park next door, where she sat until she spied him walking along a nearby path. Furtively, she paralleled his course, hiding behind pine trees, wagging their branches with humorous flair until he came to her. They forgot their quarrel over oysters and white wine at Wiggins Tavern, though the supper itself was "spoiled by our extreme budget consciousness. . . . Lucky we're both puritans & great misers."[139]

She had a harder time reconciling with her Smith colleagues, who, she was sure, resented her for leaving. After an uncomfortable run-in with some faculty members, Sylvia could barely contain her anger. But, she noted in her journal, "In polite society a lady doesn't punch or spit." She calmed herself preparing dinner for Ellie and her friend Leonard Michaels:

Violence seethed. Joy to murder someone, pure scapegoat. But pacified during necessity to work. Work redeems. Work saves. Baked a lemon meringue pie. . . . Set table, candles, glasses sparkling crystal barred crystal on yellow woven cloth. Making order, the rugs smoothed clean . . . tables cleared. Shaping a meal, people, I grew back to joy.[140]

She vowed to find "Salvation in work" and busied herself with various plots, some set in Yorkshire, some in New England, that included versions of herself, Hughes, and Ellie Friedman.[141] She planned a short story for *The New Yorker* about coming of age and "Ilo's kiss," the memory of which still moved her.[142]

The new title of her poetry manuscript, *The Earthenware Head*, was Lawrentian. For her, it symbolized "Rough terracotta color, stamped with jagged black and white designs, signifying earth, & the words which shape it."[143] As always, she wanted to write in a "bigger, freer, tougher voice: work on rhythms mostly, for freedom, yet sung . . . No coyness, archaic cutie tricks." It was the same determination that had gripped her at Cambridge after she had read the poems in the *Saint Botolph's Review*. Her voice, she surmised, was "Woolfish, alas, but tough. Please, tough, without any moral other than that growth is good. Faith too is good. I am too a puritan at heart."[144] Plath dreaded the label of "lady poet."

THE "BLACK YEAR" had turned out to be "the most maturing & courage-making year yet—I could have dreamed up no test more difficult." Yet Sylvia's subconscious continued to drag her under. Throughout the winter and spring she suffered "miserable tense knotted sleepless nights," punctuated by nightmares of the London Plague and the Holocaust.[145]

Ted, for his part, found Northampton stuffy and insular, and had spent much of the fall trying to conquer a writer's block that made his "days as dull as an empty house." Smith girls, "Chromium dianas" with their "machined glaze of hyper-health," unnerved him.[146] "I shall not quickly be caught in a small American town again," he told Luke Myers in early 1958.[147] Clarissa Roche remembered that Hughes "wasn't interested in charming anybody. . . . Nobody disliked him—everybody liked him, it was just that nobody considered him anything special." It was Plath, their "most famous graduate," they fawned over. Clarissa remembered one night toward the end of 1957, after dinner at their Elm Street apartment, when Ted "went completely silent . . . just made the atmosphere so heavy. Sylvia was talking more and more quickly, louder and louder. She was sitting on the floor, which we often did, and he literally snuffed out the evening. And apparently he did that—Sylvia called them 'white hot silences.'"[148] George Gibian, too, remembered Ted as a "hulking silent dark Yorkshireman."[149] Marcia and her husband Mike visited the Hugheses in Northampton and Boston, and found Ted witty and garrulous, "devastatingly charming, booming laughter." But Marcia also felt "that he could really turn off and tune out, sit in a black funk with Sylvia embarrassed and saying, 'Now, Teddy, be nice.'" Sylvia and Ted seemed very happy together—she was her usual "affirming" self—but Marcia sensed "great intensity and great volatility, just under the surface, and that might explode." It bothered her how "absolutely worshipful" Sylvia was of Ted and his work. "She felt her poetry was inferior." And she saw that Sylvia "was carrying a great deal of the marriage," not just in terms of the housekeeping, but "the nuts and bolts—the plans and the filling out of forms and the taxes."[150]

Ted may have been bothered by the same dynamic. In America, Sylvia was in the driver's seat, and he was along for the ride. By early January, when Ted accepted a fourteen-week position at the University of Massachusetts at Amherst for $2,200, he was ready for a distraction: "it will be to the mortification of idleness."[151] He saw the value in teaching himself new works and felt it was "a great means of coming at a type of maturity. . . . especially if you're a younger brother."[152] Sylvia wrote Aurelia that the position had been offered "out of the blue," though Sylvan Schendler, who was teaching at Smith, claimed he helped get Ted the job. He would teach a creative writing course, Freshman Composition, and two sophomore Great Books classes ("Milton, Moliere, Goethe, Dostoevsky, Eliot, etc").[153] Plath had the more prestigious, full-time position, yet she wished she could teach a creative writing course. This was not an option until she published her own book. But to do so required time, and money. She earned $100 for grading sixty exams for Newton Arvin's American literature class. (Arvin, she quipped, was "too august" to do it himself.)[154] She later regretted taking on the extra work, which she had thought paid $300. "I'd have been better off writing two poems for that price," she wrote Warren.[155] Sylvia frequently plundered reams of Smith College memorandum paper to save money. She would grow so fond of the pink sheets that they became "a fetish": "somehow, seeing a hunk of that pink paper, different from all the endless reams of white bond, my task seems finite, special, rose-cast," she wrote in her journal.[156] She also entered jingles in numerous contests sponsored by Dole Pineapple, Heinz Ketchup, French's Mustard, and Libby Tomato Juice in hopes of winning cars and cash. For the first time, though, she and Ted were not living hand to mouth; they would manage to save $1,400 by the summer.

Ted found teaching at UMass surprisingly pleasant: "I do it so easily and confidently . . . the whole lesson just pours into my head," he wrote to Olwyn. "I wonder where all this was when I was at Cambridge."[157] Yet he was wary of becoming too comfortable. Like Plath, he felt that full-time work "is the death of the artist."[158] Hughes still found most American poetry—apart from John Crowe Ransom and Wallace Stevens—too precious. But he told Olwyn that he was "enjoying America more" since he had started teaching and learned to drive. They became determined to leave Northampton for Boston. Sylvia asked Aurelia to look into the possibility of a job at Boston University for Ted, who already had full-time job offers from Amherst College and Mount Holyoke College. To Olwyn he wrote, "They are graves."[159]

Plath's productivity suffered during her teaching year: in 1957, she wrote about half the number of poems she had written the previous year. But Hughes's writing picked up during the spring of 1958. He devoured old issues of the *Journal of the Society for Psychical Research* and wrote more of the poems that would eventually end up in *Lupercal*. "Pike," one of his best-known poems, came to him one day in bed at Elm Street. "All the poems for my second book," he wrote Olwyn, "are a little hard-headed. I have tried so hard to take nothing for granted in matters of cadence & rhythm, that sentiment & warmth has seemed like a proscribed outlaw. In an effort to express myself trenchantly & controlledly, I have kept out softness."[160] He would encourage Plath, too, to keep softness out of her own poems, to make them "direct and 'unliterary.'"[161] By early February, Hughes had written twenty new poems, but he was in no rush to publish a second book when he could earn more money publishing the poems in magazines.

Sylvia sought inspiration in the modern art class she audited that spring at Smith, mining the paintings for images she could use in her poetry. An art magazine, *Art News*, had asked her to contribute poems about paintings. The assignment galvanized her. She told Aurelia that her "deepest source of inspiration" was "the art of primitives like Henri Rousseau, Gauguin and Paul Klee and De Chirico. . . . Once I start writing, it comes and comes."[162] During her spring break, March 22–28, she wrote eight new poems, which she proclaimed to be the best she had ever written. She felt that she had broken through the "rococo crystal cage" to describe her "real experience." They were "thunderous."[163] "I feel like an idiot who has been obediently digging up pieces of coal in an immense mine and has just realized that there is no need to do this, but that one can fly all day and night on great wings in clear blue air through brightly colored magic and weird worlds," she wrote Aurelia that March.[164]

Plath's "art poems"—"Virgin in a Tree," "Perseus: The Triumph of Wit Over Suffering," "Battle-Scene," and "The Ghost's Leavetaking," all based on Paul Klee paintings—were syntactically dense and elaborately formal. Klee expressed a lucid, minimalist aesthetic that Plath wanted to imitate in her poems, but she was still caught in syntactical webs and faulty lines, as in "The Ghost's Leavetaking": "the raw material / Of our meat-and-potato thoughts assumes the nimbus / Of ambrosial revelation." Still, she reiterated her belief in her vocation and destiny that March. "Arrogant, I think I have written lines which qualify me to be The Poetess of America (as Ted will be The Poet of England and her dominions)." The only women poets who rivaled her were "Sappho, Elizabeth Barrett Browning, Christina Rossetti, Amy Lowell, Emily Dickinson, Edna St. Vincent Millay—all dead. Now: Edith Sitwell & Marianne Moore . . . May Swenson, Isabella Gardner, & most close, Adrienne Cecile Rich—who will soon be eclipsed by these eight poems." In her mind, only women were her competitors, as if men and women played in different leagues. She was "eager, chafing, sure of my gift, wanting only to train & teach it."[165]

If Klee led Plath further into the rococo labyrinth she meant to escape, Giorgio de Chirico led her out. Plath's most successful art poem from this period was "The Disquieting Muses," inspired by an abstract, surrealist painting of that title by de Chirico—"three terrible, faceless dressmakers' dummies in classical gowns," as Plath told the BBC, "seated and standing in a weird, clear light."[166] Plath compared the women to Macbeth's weird sisters, the Three Fates, and de Quincey's Sisters of Madness. In the poem, the speaker suggests that these sinister muses have haunted her since birth, when her mother failed to invite an "illbred aunt" or "unsightly / Cousin," who "sent these ladies in her stead." Her mother has tried to banish the muses—her "witches always, always / Got baked into gingerbread"—but the muses cast their heavy shadows across her life:

> Day now, night now, at head, side, feet,
> They stand their vigil in gowns of stone,
> Faces blank as the day I was born,
> Their shadows long in the setting sun
> That never brightens or goes down.
> And this is the kingdom you bore me to,
> Mother, mother. But no frown of mine
> Will betray the company I keep.

"The Disquieting Muses" hurt Aurelia deeply. "Oh the way she said it, it broke my heart: '*Mother, mother.*' Oh it was awful."[167] She thought Plath's lines about being forced to take piano lessons were particularly galling. In reality, Aurelia claimed, Sylvia had begged to take piano lessons at the New England Conservatory as a child, and Aurelia took on weekend tutoring to pay the tuition. When she confronted Sylvia about the poem, she laughed

("Oh, that,") and told Aurelia she had been angry at her for making light of her depression at McLean.[168]

That spring Hughes was writing some of the best poems of his career, yet he found life in America increasingly hard to bear. He fell ill; Plath wrote that there was "no clear malady, no clear remedy."[169] She described him as "flagging in discontent" in her journal; he told her, "I want to get clear of this life: trapped."[170] He complained to Gerald again that American culture was "anti-mental, anti-solitary-study, anti-thinking for yourself."[171] His dismal spirits affected Sylvia, who now reversed course. "America wears me, wearies me," she wrote in her journal. "All America seems one line of cars, moving, with people jammed in them, from one-gas-station to one diner and on. . . . I am, in my deep soul, happiest on the moors—my deepest soul-scape, in the hills by the Spanish Mediterranean, in the old, history-crusted & still gracious, spacious cities: Paris, Rome."[172] In England, she had longed for America. Now in America, she longed for Europe. Hughes had already decided they would move back to England at the end of their Boston year. "Neither country is fit to live in," he wrote Daniel Weissbort. "Yet who wants to be an exile."[173] When Sylvia asked Luke Myers, in a 1957 Christmas card, when he was coming back to America, Hughes wrote underneath, "She doesn't mean 'will you ever come home,' she means 'will we ever get back to Europe.' Our hope."[174]

Hughes feared the fate Graves had laid out in *The White Goddess:* "the woman whom he took to be a Muse, or who was a Muse, turns into a domestic woman and would have him turn similarly into a domestic man."[175] By December 1959 he would write to Daniel Huws of Graves's influence on his new collection: "I was noting the other day which ones had reference to Graves' White Goddess, and out of 41 pieces there are only about 6 that are not direct representation of her or her victims."[176] He added that his "exile" in America "has driven me to nostalgic themes." Most of the poems in *Lupercal*, though set in British landscapes, were written in America; living in Massachusetts had not dulled Hughes's senses as much as he suggested to others. (Plath would later use the same word—"exile"—to describe her life in England in the early sixties while she was writing *The Bell Jar*.)

Jack Sweeney invited Ted to give a poetry reading at Harvard on April 11. He and Sylvia drove through a storm with one broken wiper; as the sleet blurred their vision, each passing car seemed to Sylvia "a possible death." They arrived nervous and jittery to the deserted "sepulchral" Longfellow Hall on the Radcliffe campus. Soon a steady stream of familiar faces entered— Peter Davison, Mrs. Cantor, Mrs. Prouty, Marcia and Mike Plumer, Phil McCurdy (now married with a baby son), Aurelia ("thin & somehow frail"), and Gordon, whose presence rankled Sylvia. She thought he was "jealous as hell, but noble, in his way, to come."[177] Sylvia also noted the presence of Philip Booth, Harry Levin's wife (Levin, ill, had sent her in his place) and, "at last," Adrienne Rich and her husband, the Harvard economist Al Conrad.[178] Sweeney introduced Hughes, telling the audience that before he had won the Harper's contest he had been employed as a night watchman at a steel factory. (There would be no mistaking Hughes for a Cambridge fop.) Hughes read "The Thought-Fox," "To Paint a Water Lily," "Acrobats," and "The Casualty," among others, while Sylvia felt "the foolish tears" spring to her eyes. She thought the applause had been "warm and genuine," though Aurelia observed that because there was no microphone, no one beyond the second row could hear him.[179]

After the reading, Hughes, Plath, Adrienne Rich, and Al Conrad decamped to the Sweeneys' apartment, where Plath drank two bourbons on ice and admired original paintings by Picasso, Juan Gris, and Jack Yeats. She described Rich as "little, round & stumpy, all vibrant short black hair, great sparkling black eyes and a tulip-red umbrella: honest, frank forthright & even opinionated."[180] Plath left no record of what she and Rich discussed; the silence suggests Rich impressed her, as Plath was usually unkind to rival poets. She felt ill at ease, almost "feverish" as the bourbon kicked in, and wondered whether her "trusted" lavender tweed dress was gauche.[181] Later they headed out to Felicia's Café on Hanover Street in the Italian North End, where Plath sat between Conrad and Sweeney. Everything seemed a blur until Sweeney asked her to make a recording for Harvard's Poetry Room in June.[182] That got her attention, though she noted ruefully that the date he suggested was Friday the 13th.

———

ON APRIL 18, at the invitation of Lee Anderson, Plath recorded some of her poems in Springfield, Massachusetts, for the Library of Congress files.[183] Plath read with a deliberate, clipped, mid-Atlantic accent, graced with the Kennedy cadences of Boston ("stubborn" is "stubbohn," "rare" is "raheh"). The recording is the closest thing we have to Plath's *ars poetica*, and worth quoting at length. When Anderson asked her what poets she read for pleasure, she answered, without hesitation,

Yeats, Ted Hughes continually, and Yeats, Eliot, John Crowe Ransom especially. I have started reading Robert Lowell. I like a good deal in Robert Lowell. . . . Shakespeare, Chaucer, who else, Thomas Wyatt, who else, Ted, you know, Hopkins. Let's see, what others, I think Yeats I like very very much. . . . I learned my first changing in sound—assonance and consonance—from Yeats, which actually is technical. I was very excited when I discovered this. I also read Dylan Thomas a good deal for the subtleties of sound. I'd never worked with anything except rhyme before, and very rigid rhyme, and so I began developing schemes and patterns of sound that were somehow less obvious, you get them through your ear if not through your eye. And I think that I just happened to learn this from Yeats, Thomas too in a way.

When she taught Yeats, she told Anderson, she finally felt a synthesis between her teaching and writing: "the scalp crawled, the hair stood up," as she prepared the poems for class. Yeats was "genuine: an anti-type of Eliot, and I do enjoy Eliot, Yeats is lyrical and sharp, clear, rock-cut." But teaching her favorite poet only reminded her that she was not fulfilling her potential. "The kind of analysis I do with my classes is somehow inimical to the kind of work I do by myself."

Anderson asked her if it was "necessary to write in a strict form to get music." Plath answered:

I like to work in forms that are strict, and yet the strictness isn't uncomfortable. Sort of like a comfortable corset or something, I suppose [laughs], that isn't really noticeable and obvious, but it's there. There's some bone, some skeletal structure to the poem. And I think that for me at least I'm very much lyrically inclined, and I lean very strongly toward forms which are, I suppose, quite rigid in comparison certainly to free verse. I'm much happier when I know that all my sounds are echoing in different ways throughout the poem than if I just forget about it.

After Plath read "On the Difficulty of Conjuring Up a Dryad," Anderson asked, "What is your working philosophy?" Plath seemed surprised.

PLATH: [laughs] My working philosophy? You mean as far as writing poetry goes?

ANDERSON: Your own.

PLATH: About what poetry should be?

ANDERSON: Yes.

PLATH: Well it's hard to say. My own poetry technically, as I said, I'd like to be extremely musical and lyrical with a singing sound. I don't like poetry that just throws itself away in prose. In other words I don't like poetry that you could, that is bad prose, and I think a lot of poetry is bad prose. I think there should be a kind of constriction, a kind of tension which is never artificial, and yet keeps in the meaning, and a kind of music too. And again, I like the idea of managing to get wit in with seriousness, and contrast, ironies, and I like visual images, and I like just good mouthfuls of sound which have meaning. I think that's another thing. I don't like just ramping about in sound but having a very strong meaning come through the first time. . . . But I have really no idea, I haven't read aloud enough, very few people have read my poems anyway. [laughs] So I have no idea how they affect other people.

Plath's self-deprecating remarks suggest that she was unused to being asked about her "working philosophy." But someone was finally taking her thoughts on poetic composition—especially the important relationship between form and music—seriously. She had come a long way since 1953, when a *Mademoiselle* photographer had posed her on a sofa with a rose.

Plath knew she had poems waiting to be unleashed that would put "the neat prosy gray-suited poems of Donald Hall, et. al. [*sic*]" to shame. Ted knew it, too. He wrote Gerald that May that Sylvia was "one of America's brightest" poets.[184] She was upset that she remained "unrecognized," despite an acceptance that spring by *Ladies' Home Journal*, which took a sonnet, "Second Winter," that she had written at Smith. *The New Yorker* rejected her latest submissions in April, causing "sobs, sorrow: desire to fight back," but she was confident that in a year (or two) she would be "'recognized.'" She was "all itch & eager fury" to write again, and teaching continued to drain her, despite her new confidence at the lectern.[185] She wrote to Warren that her colleagues "depressed" her more than ever: "it is disillusioning to find the people you admired as a student are weak and jealous and petty and vain as people."[186] Academics, she told him, would always treat writers with suspicion. Aurelia, too, needed convincing.

I can talk to you freely about our plans, if not to mother: she worries so that the most we can do is put up an illusion of security: security to us is in ourselves, & no job, or even money, can give us what we have to develop: faith in our work, & hard hard work which is spartan in many ways. Ted is especially good for me because he doesn't demand Immediate Success & Publication, and is training me not to. We feel the next five years are as important to our writing as medical school is to a prospective surgeon.[187]

More popular modes of poetic expression bothered Plath and Hughes. That spring, Paul Roche and his wife Clarissa invited them to tea with the poet George Abbe, who combined a beatnik spirit with a confessional sensibility. He seemed to Plath "slick," a "huckster," telling them "anyone can write." He improvised poetry onstage, "fished up a mood poem in his unconscious & wrote it on the blackboard . . . Ted & I got sicker and sicker." In her journal Plath wrote that his poems were "about his boyhood, sob. . . . As if poetry were some kind of therapeutic public purge or excretion. Ted & I left, disgusted, to go home to our private & exacting demons who demand every conscious and deep-rooted discipline, and work, and rewriting & knowledge."[188] They liked Roche, but Abbe had struck a nerve. Plath was hesitant to equate poetry with therapy, yet she admitted in her journal, "Fury jams the gullet & spreads poison, but, as soon as I start to write, dissipates, flows out into the figure of the letters."[189]

Abbe was one of several poets Plath demeaned in her journal that year, in addition to Roche, Hecht, and Merwin. In a mean-spirited passage, she even dismissed Roche's and Hecht's wives as boring and their children as "idiots."[190] Plath felt herself a student or rival around the other woman professors—Mary Ellen Chase had retired, and younger faculty like Joan Bramwell and Marlies Kalmann were formal and distant—and admitted, in April, that she had "few friends."[191] She still saw Ellie and Marcia sometimes, but even these relationships had cooled. She felt that Marcia had settled into "dogmatic complacency" and had "shrunk so small" as a wife.[192] When Ellie came to visit in early April, dressed in high black heels and a black cocktail dress, Sylvia fumed quietly while Ellie, she thought, "played to Ted."[193] Ellie had landed a plum position at the *New York Herald Tribune*, and Sylvia was full of sour grapes. She was "sick of everything."[194] Their social life was so monotonous that when Sylvia heard sirens she almost hoped "for an incident, an accident."[195]

Paul Roche remembered that they all spent a lot of time at the Ouija board together. Ted and Clarissa, he said, were "serious," but Sylvia was not. "She was slightly ironic. . . . almost as if it were a kind of game."[196] The only thing Ted and Sylvia seemed to enjoy together that year, besides their walks in Child's Park and the surrounding countryside, was watching Leonard Baskin at work in his studio. Baskin remembered impassioned discussions with Plath and Hughes about "images of elemental force" and felt there was a "symbiosis going on among the three of us." He found Sylvia "totally happy . . . in great harmony with Ted. . . . There was no demonic, obsessive quality to Sylvia." It was Ted, he remembered, who could fill a room with "the most unalterable silences. . . . He had a grey, hulking, brooding quality. What this did to Sylvia I'm not sure." Baskin wondered whether Ted was the right kind of husband for a sensitive woman who needed, he felt, "continual reassurance."[197] Plath would dedicate her 1958 poem "Sculptor" to Baskin.

As April turned to May, Sylvia felt increasingly exhausted. She called herself "weary" and "depressed" in her journal; she wrote of her fear of death and childbirth, her "slipshod part time" scholarly ways; she fretted about her novel and looked to George Eliot and Henry James for a model of "social surface, decorum."[198] She wanted her novel's protagonist, Dody Ventura, to be "complex," a moralist who was also a rebel. James's heroines were "so noble: she sees and sees and will not flinch or be mean, be small . . . she will not indulge 'the vulgar heat of her wrong.' With which, under which, I should explode."[199]

Yet as the end of the semester neared, Sylvia vacillated between her contempt for teaching and her desire for security, prestige, and money: "teaching 3 or 4 days a week with over 3 months of paid vacation seems a gift, now I think of it."[200] She knew Aurelia was deeply skeptical of her decision to leave Smith, and wondered if this accounted for her sudden coolness. "Queer mother—stiff about helping us come to Boston . . . her guarded praise at our getting poems published, as if this were one more nail in the coffin of our resolve to drown as poets and refuse all 'secure' teaching work."[201] Aurelia indeed began to resent Ted for encouraging Sylvia to trade a promising teaching career for the elusive art of poetry.[202] She knew that her daughter needed structure and routine. She had seen Sylvia shifting listlessly around the house, her self-hatred intensifying day after day, during the black July and August of 1953.

There were a few high points that May—dinners with Leonard and Esther Baskin (the only faculty couple that escaped Plath's scorn), the novels of Henry James, and a reading by Robert Lowell in Amherst on the 6th. Lowell's poems had struck her just as Hughes's had when she first read them in the *Saint Botolph's Review*: "taste the phrases: tough, knotty, blazing with color & fury, most eminently sayable."[203] After the reading, she drove Lowell around Northampton "looking for relics of his ancestors, and to the Historical Society & the graveyard." She described him to Warren as "the mad and very nice poet Robert Lowell (the only one 40ish whom we both admire, who comes from the Boston Lowells & is periodically carted off as a manic depressive) . . . He is quiet, soft-spoken, and we liked him very much."[204] Hughes too emphasized Lowell's manic depression and asylum stays in a letter to Olwyn, but he found him "very congenial" and thought Lowell's new poems, from the forthcoming *Life Studies*, "more exciting poetry than anything he's ever written."[205]

That May, after Lowell's reading, Plath began writing "Full Fathom Five," another elegy for Otto:

> I walk dry on your kingdom's border
> Exiled to no good.
>
> Your shelled bed I remember.
> Father, this thick air is murderous.
> I would breathe water.

"Full Fathom Five" is an important thematic precursor of Plath's more achieved paternal elegies, "Electra on Azalea Path," "The Colossus," and "Daddy." She was pleased with her allusions to Shakespeare's *The Tempest* and decided to rename her entire collection *Full Fathom Five*. "It relates more richly to my life and imagery than anything else I've dreamed up" she wrote in her journal, "the association of the sea, which is a central metaphor for my childhood, my poems and the artist's subconscious, to the father image—relating to my own father, the buried male muse & god-creator risen to be my mate in Ted, to the sea-father neptune—and the pearls and coral highly-wrought to art: pearls sea-changed from the ubiquitous grit of sorrow and dull routine."[206] *The Earthenware Head* seemed too glassy and brittle a title after hearing Lowell.

Sylvia's mood descended as she moved closer to a life without regular income or structure. Her doubts manifested themselves in various physical ailments (colds, rashes), and on May 14 she wrote that she felt shut in a "prison of highstrung depression."[207] Ted, too was depressed; both stopped eating. She hinted obliquely at suicide in her journal: "I feel about to break out in leprosy: nervous: hearing stairs creak: dying of cowardice—ready for all the lights to mysteriously go out and the horror of a monster to take me: nightmares haunt me."[208] "All's polished to a dull luster // In the sulfurous noon," Plath wrote in her 1958 poem "In Midas' Country."

She pushed through and finished teaching on May 22, ending with Edith Sitwell, e. e. cummings, and John Crowe Ransom. She told Warren she "felt honestly sorry to say goodbye to my girls" and was "amused" to "get applause in the exact volume of my own feelings toward every class: a spatter at 9, a thunderous ovation at 11 which saw me down two flights of stairs, and a medium burst at 3." She was proud of herself for fighting through "those first black weeks of teaching," to have "won over" her most difficult students and "taught them a good deal." She could hardly believe she had eloquently unpacked "The Waste Land" and other difficult works. "But I have."[209]

When she emerged from Seelye Hall, finally free, she expected to find

Ted waiting for her. Suddenly she saw him walking up the road from Paradise Pond ("where girls take their boys to neck") with a pretty young student who quickly turned away as Sylvia approached. "I gagged at what I saw," she wrote in her journal. Distraught and enraged, she confronted Ted, who told her the woman was one of his students, and that they had run into each other by chance. Hughes later engaged in extramarital affairs, but that day—so early in their marriage—he probably told the truth. Sylvia did not believe him, and she poured out her despair and fury in her journal. "I made the most amusing, ironic & fatal step in trusting Ted was unlike other vain and obfuscating and self-indulgent men. I have served a purpose, spent money, mother's money, which hurts most, to buy him clothes, to buy him a half year, eight months of writing, typed hundreds of times his poems. Well, so much have I done for modern British & American poetry."[210] She could no longer sleep "for shaking at horror."[211]

She had suspected that something strange had been going on because of his "late comings home," but seduction was much on her mind that afternoon when she saw Ted with this young woman. Just before her last class, she had seen a Smith professor, Bill Van Voris, flirting with a student at a coffee shop; this scene made her remember her own meetings with Alfred Fisher, "sitting in the same seat, & me opposite, that official sexual rapport . . . students made mistresses."[212] She was also in the throes of a depression that, as she herself had admitted, heightened her sense of paranoia and insecurity. Back at Elm Street, they fought it out: she left bloody claw marks on Ted's cheeks and sprained her thumb. In her journal she referred to bites and snarls. Some have assumed, from this entry, that Hughes hit her, but Plath's syntax is ambiguous: "I remember hurling a glass with all my force across a dark room; instead of shattering the glass rebounded and remained intact: I got hit and saw stars." Plath's colon suggests that she "got hit" by the ricocheting glass, not by Hughes. She felt the fight had helped bring them closer. "Air cleared," she wrote afterward. Nothing, not "even total possession," was "worth jeopardizing what I have which is so much the angels might well envy it."[213]

If the bell jar had lifted, so had the veil on their marriage. Sylvia would spend the summer and much of the fall of 1958 battling depression and writer's block, for which she partly blamed Ted. The shared sense of vocation that had helped bind them together suddenly seemed, by that summer, more problematic. Mrs. Prouty had warned her about the difficulties of a creative marriage, and she now worried she was becoming "too dependent" on Ted. She began to admit that the union had as much potential to hold her back as it did to propel her forward. The fury of May had unlocked other resentments:

It is as if I were sucked into a tempting but disastrous whirlpool. Between us there are no barriers—it is rather as if neither of us—or especially myself—had any skin, or one skin between us & kept bumping into and abrading each other. I enjoy it when Ted is off for a bit. I can build up my own inner life, my own thoughts, without his continuous "What are you thinking? What are you going to do now?" which makes me promptly and recalcitrantly stop thinking and doing. We are amazingly compatible. But I must be myself—make myself & not let myself be made by him.[214]

Two days after she wrote this passage, Sylvia experienced another kind of grief. Earlier that month, she and Ted had found a baby bird that had fallen from its nest, "convulsed in what looked like a death-shudder."[215] They brought it home, fashioned a rag-and-paper nest in a cardboard box, and fed it ground hamburger for a week. But the bird did not recover, and each dawn they awoke to its miserable scrabble and wheeze. "We couldn't sleep or write for days, nursing it & hunting vainly for worms, identifying with it until it became gruesome," Sylvia told Warren. "Finally, we figured it would be mercy to put it out of its misery."[216] Ted put the bird to sleep—"fixed our rubber bath hose to the gas jet on the stove & taped the other end into a cardboard box"—while she watched, distraught and weeping. When its small legs finally stopped shaking, Ted brought it to her, "composed, perfect & beautiful in death."[217] Plath would use similar language, five years later, to describe the dead woman in "Edge."

Together, they walked outside into the cool dusk of Child's Park and buried the bird under a "druid stone."[218] For Sylvia, it was "a shattering experience. Such a plucky little bit of bird. I can't forget it."[219] She had taught her students about the significance of birds as an augur of hope and creative inspiration in Joyce's *Portrait of the Artist*. This bird was a different kind of symbol. "We left ferns & a green firefly on the grave, felt the stone roll of our hearts."[220]

21

Life Studies

Northampton and Boston, June 1958–March 1959

Sylvia ended her last semester on a final, sour note when the faculty decided to replace the low grade she had given a student's senior thesis with a summa cum laude. Outraged and baffled, she saw it as another sign that she did not belong in academia. Some members of the faculty were not sorry to see her go. "She disappointed Miss Drew enormously when she came back to teach at Smith," Janet Salter Rosenberg recalled. "I went to my fifth reunion, the year after Sylvia and Ted had been there. She said, 'It didn't matter whether the girl had emotional problems, she didn't fulfill her responsibilities at Smith,' and that was that. I really got quite an earful."[1] Mary Ellen Chase, too, was "very disappointed at her leaving the faculty."[2] Charles Hill, another English professor, felt Plath "owed" it to the department to stay because of all the support, financial and otherwise, she had received as a student. She had not been, he thought, sufficiently "considerate."[3] Plath had alienated Smith friends like Janet, Jane Truslow, Claiborne Phillips, and Nancy Hunter with her determination to fulfill her own desires in 1954–55; now a similar dynamic played out with her Smith professors. Because Plath was a woman, she would always pay a social price for putting her own needs first. But for her the cost was worth it. No longer would she extemporize about symbolism and irony in James Joyce and T. S. Eliot: "like a soldier, demobbed, I am cut loose of over twenty steady years of schooling & let free into civilian life."[4] Sylvia and Ted left Northampton for New York City after she finished grading her last exam on June 3. In her journal, she wrote, "I start, like a race horse at the bugle."[5]

The campaign began at the Biltmore Hotel, where the couple lunched with two of London's most powerful literary men: Charles Monteith, chairman of Faber and Faber publishers, and vice chairman Peter du Sautoy. They promised to introduce Sylvia and Ted to "'Tom' Eliot" when they returned to England.[6] This was the life Plath had dreamed of—not teaching Eliot, but knowing him. Later they called on their editor friend David Keightley, the critic Babette Deutsch, and Oscar Williams, who had included Hughes in a recent anthology.[7] Williams shepherded them to a party on Fifth Avenue, where, after sharing an elevator with Lionel and Diana Trilling, Sylvia mingled with Ralph Ellison, John Farrar, "endless boring professors from Columbia," and others Williams had published.[8] This was Alfred Kazin's crowd, and Sylvia was out of her element. (She disparaged the Jewish businessmen she met at a party that same day in a letter to Warren.) The couple also made a pilgrimage to Brooklyn Heights to visit Marianne Moore, who, Sylvia wrote, served "strawberries, sesame seed biscuits & milk & talked a blue streak."[9] Moore, one of the judges for the Harper/YMHA contest, would champion Hughes's work but grow to dislike Plath's.

To save money, the couple stayed with Sylvia's old friend Pat O'Neil, who lived near Columbia at 523 West 121st Street. They wandered through Central Park and Harlem (Hughes admitted he had once thought only African Americans lived in New York City) and saw Lorca's *Blood Wedding* at the Actors' Playhouse in Greenwich Village. Afterward Sylvia ran into Dick Wertz, Sassoon's old roommate, as she headed to the subway. She was about to say hello when she suddenly saw Sassoon himself. His back was turned, and he did not see her. She told Aurelia about the moment, but not Ted. "I kept quiet & passed by. . . . Of all the people in NYC!"[10] The encounter rattled her.

On their last night in New York, they saw two "experimental" Ionesco plays at the Sullivan Street Playhouse—*The Bald Soprano* and *Jack*.[11] Hughes enjoyed them, but he was ready to leave the city, which he compared to "living in an underground terminal. Soot, noise, weariness, cheapjacks." He thought the Village's bohemianism contrived and "pathetic." "If Chelsea is 5 removes from the Left Bank," he wrote Olwyn, "this is 50 from Chelsea."[12] Manhattan embodied the brash American materialism, flashiness, and excess he had come to loathe. He was most interested in the Bowery bums.

Hughes preferred smaller university cities like Boston and Cambridge, where he and Plath were quickly becoming part of the literary establishment, thanks to Jack Sweeney. After the couple returned to Northampton, Sweeney asked Plath to record several of her poems for the Harvard Poetry Room on June 13.[13] Plath worked hard to be worthy. She had culled everything she had written more than two years ago from her collection and hoped to have fifty strong poems to send out to publishers by the winter. "I feel I've got rid of most of my old rigidity & glassy glossiness & am well on the way to writing about the real world," she told Warren in early July.[14] Ted pushed her in this "unsentimental" direction, telling Aurelia in July that Sylvia had written "two or three first class poems, as strong as anything she has done, and I think the unbroken practise is necessary—her style and self are changing so rapidly that it is a continuous labour to bring the two together."[15] Plath was cheered when "Spinster" and "Black Rook in Rainy Weather" appeared in the influential *London Magazine* in June—no purveyor of "glassy glossiness"—while her "Sow" and Hughes's "Thrushes" would appear together in the next British PEN anthology. Each also had two poems in the forthcoming Borestone anthology—a reassuring symmetry.

It was probably in early June that Plath wrote "Mussel Hunter at Rock Harbor," which she proudly sent to Warren on June 11. In the "syllabic" poem, which comprised seven lines of seven syllables, Plath writes of finding "The husk of a fiddler-crab, / Intact, strangely strayed above // His world of mud . . ." The speaker ponders whether the crab "Died recluse or suicide," and comes to her stunning, lyrical conclusion:

> The crab-face, etched and set there,
>
> Grimaced as skulls grimace: it
> Had an Oriental look,
> A samurai death mask done
> On a tiger tooth, less for
> Art's sake than God's. Far from sea—
> Where red-freckled crab-backs, claws
> And whole crabs, dead, their soggy
>
> Bellies pallid and upturned,
> Perform their shambling waltzes
> On the waves' dissolving turn
> And return, losing themselves
> Bit by bit to their friendly
> Element—this relic saved
> Face, to face the bald-faced sun.

The artist-speaker admires the "relic," which, even in death, has "saved" itself. It has not perished: it has become art. The poem is elaborately formal, yet its highly structured meter does not distract from its imagistic power. Moore's syllabic verse and Hughes's "Relic" ("I found this jawbone at the sea's edge: / There, crabs, dogfish, broken by the breakers or tossed . . .") were both major influences.[16] But there is no place for a meditative encounter between the self and nature in Hughes's "Relic": "The deeps are cold: / In that darkness camaraderie does not hold: / Nothing touches but, clutching, devours."[17] As in "The Hawk in the Rain" and "Wind," Hughes's version of nature is more brutal and amoral than Plath's. She may have used "Relic" as a philosophical foil when she wrote "Mussel Hunter at Rock Harbor," which inaugurated a new creative phase.

Hughes had applied for a Eugene Saxton fellowship, which he and Plath assumed he would win with a letter of support from Moore. But he soon learned that the fellowship was run by trustees of his American publisher, Harper & Brothers. The conflict of interest made him ineligible—a "supreme & rather distressing irony," Sylvia wrote Warren.[18] She decided that *she* would apply for a Saxton and would also ask Moore for a letter, while Hughes would apply for a Guggenheim, "marshal [*sic*] TS Eliot et al. behind him."[19] She and Ted were still determined to spend a year writing in Italy or Germany before starting a family, and she hoped to finish a novel there. She asked Warren not to tell Aurelia about any of their plans.[20]

By the summer of 1958, *The Hawk in the Rain* had sold 1,700 copies in America and 1,600 in England, earning the couple about $1,500. Sylvia knew that they needed a steadier income. Neither wanted a full-time job—she thought of applying to the MacDowell Colony for writers and artists, or house sitting on the Cape for free rent—but they resigned themselves to waitressing and bartending if necessary. Their money problems vanished for the moment on June 25, when *The New Yorker* accepted Plath's poems "Mussel Hunter at Rock Harbor" and "Nocturne."[21] The couple jumped up and down after reading poetry editor Howard Moss's words: "Mussel Hunter" was "a marvelous poem" and "Nocturne" "extremely fine." After ten years of rejections and "the usual New Yorker coolness," Plath had finally scaled her Annapurna.[22] The acceptance gave her "great courage" to continue writing full-time. She earned $377 for the two poems, nearly four times what she had made for "half a year of drudgery" correcting papers for Newton Arvin. They had recently signed a lease to move into a small sixth-floor apartment in Boston's Beacon Hill on September 1. "You see what happens the minute one worships one's own god of vocation & doesn't slight it for grubbing under the illusion of duty to Everybody's-Way-Of-Life!" she wrote triumphantly to Aurelia in June.[23] She noted that her *New Yorker* check would cover three months of rent in Boston.

By early July, Plath and Hughes had earned more than $2,000 from their writing since September 1957—"magic money" they kept in a separate bank account and did not spend.[24] Money no longer meant new clothes, but freedom to write. When *Poetry* bought three of Plath's poems in late July for $44, she "added up the lines right away: two more weeks groceries."[25] Hughes had written twenty-eight poems for his second collection, *Lupercal*, by mid-July, and had already sold seventeen. He was making such a name for himself that a university in New York offered to buy some of his manu-scripts for their archive, while his children's story "Billy Hook and the Three Souvenirs" appeared in the mass-market magazine *Jack & Jill* that July. The couple always hoped to break into the children's market and use the proceeds to subsidize the less lucrative practice of poetry. That September, Hughes would check "stacks" of children's books out of the Boston Public Library with the aim of writing one himself.[26] (Faber and Faber published *Meet My Folks!* in 1961.)

They spent their final weeks in Northampton hiking on Mount Holyoke and walking in nearby, fragrant Child's Park, the setting for Plath's poems "Child's Park Stones" and "Fable of the Rhododendron Stealers." Plath wrote the latter poem after confronting two girls picking rhododendron blossoms in the park that June. Although she had stolen a rose from the park that very day, the girls' copious pilfering enraged her. "I have a violence in me that is hot as death-blood. I can kill myself or—I know it now—even kill another," she wrote in her journal. She wanted to tear one of the girls "to bloody beating bits." Yet she also pondered her "split morality," which she made the central question of her poetic "fable."[27]

Free from grading and teaching prep, Sylvia read Shakespeare and Rachel Carson, and dabbled in anthropology, Aztec history, books on wild-life, demoniacal possession, spiders, and scorpions—all "fascinating and ter-rible."[28] The titles reflect Ted's interests, which she was starting to share. Together they visited Wellesley and its environs, calling on Sylvia's child-hood friend Ruth Freeman Geissler, now mother to three young children, and Mrs. Prouty, who was uncharacteristically optimistic about Sylvia's full-time writing plans. She had fallen under Ted's spell, Sylvia frequently told others, and now believed that their future would be "dazzling."[29] But Sylvia knew that Aurelia did not approve of their plan to embark on a life of free-lance writing, and tension between mother and daughter mounted through-out the summer. Sylvia told herself to "keep clear of confiding in mother: she is a source of great depression—a beacon of terrible warning."[30]

In early July, Sylvia told Aurelia she wanted to visit Winthrop with Ted. Though the town was "run down," memories of the weather-beaten streets still moved her. "I am writing some good poems about it, I think," she wrote her mother.[31] Plath was speaking mainly about "Green Rock, Winthrop Bay," in which the speaker revisits one of her childhood totems to find the old landscape diminished.

> No lame excuses can gloss over
> Barge-tar clotted at the tide-line, the wrecked pier.
> I should have known better.

Still, thoughts of Winthrop made her nostalgic for her childhood, and she tried translating her German copy of *Grimm's Fairy Tales*, a gift from Aurelia. "I feel extremely moved [by] my memories of my German background, & Austrian, and also my ocean-childhood, which is probably the foundation of my consciousness," she wrote her mother that July. Germanic and oceanic themes merged in her new, dark poem "Lorelei." Aurelia had once sung her a German song about the Lorelei—the folkloric Rhine maidens—though Sylvia claimed that the poem came to her during a session at the Ouija board that July: "Pan" had called the "Lorelei" her "own kin." She wrote Aurelia, "This had never occurred to me consciously as a subject & it seemed a good one: the Germanic legend background, the water-images, the death-wish and so on."[32] Plath wrote the poem quickly, and it became one of her favorites. Like "Full Fathom Five," it is written in *a-b-a* tercets, and gives a glimpse of the more mature poetic voice of "Elm" and "Edge." Plath begins hopefully, "It is no night to drown in: / A full moon, river lapsing / Black beneath bland mirror-sheen," but ends on a darker note:

> O river, I see drifting
>
> Deep in your flux of silver
> Those great goddesses of peace.
> Stone, stone, ferry me down there.

Along with "Mussel Hunter at Rock Harbor" and "Full Fathom Five," "Lorelei" was among the best poems she wrote that year.

Back in Northampton, Plath was restless as she worked on a story, "Bird in the House," about a dead baby bird that became "a tormenting spirit & by its small sick pulse darkens & twists two lives."[33] Editors were on vacation, and the couple's single fan—a gift from Aurelia—provided little relief from the humidity. Sweltering, Sylvia walked around the apartment in her bathing suit. Marianne Moore had written her a "queerly ambiguous spiteful letter" in response to her request for a Saxton grant reference.[34] Plath thought she could count on Moore's support, for she had awarded her co-first prize in the Glascock Poetry Contest in 1955. Moore had even written a generous and admiring inscription in Plath's copy of her *Collected Poems*. ("Sylvia Plath's turned down corners and underlinings make me feel that there was some reason for the collecting of these poems. I am grateful to have a reader.")[35] Now Plath felt that Moore's cryptic messages were "resonant only with great unpleasantness."[36] Moore had written, "you are too unrelenting" about "Mussel Hunter at Rock Harbor," which, ironically, Plath had written in Moore's syllabic style. "Sylvia, don't be quite so grisly," she advised.[37] Plath wept bitterly. She understood what it meant to lose support from one of America's most influential women poets. Moore would eventually balk at *The Colossus,* writing to Knopf editor Judith Jones in April 1962 that Plath's poems were "bitter, frost-bitten, burnt-out, averse."[38] When Plath applied for a Guggenheim in 1961, Moore criticized her for having a baby and told the committee to give the award to Hughes instead of Plath, saying he had "twice the talent she has."[39] Hughes never forgot that Moore made Plath doubt her talent. In his poem "The Literary Life," he described Moore as spiteful and washedup, her cheeks like "the crumpled silk / Of a bat's wing."[40]

Sylvia ran an intermittent temperature that summer and had X-rays taken to rule out lingering complications from her December pneumonia. Although she was pronounced healthy, she did not mention her checkup to Aurelia, who heard about it from her dentist and wrote a hasty, worried letter to Sylvia. Mother caught daughter off guard, and Sylvia wrote candidly about her doubts concerning her new freedoms:

> I am finding it rather difficult to adjust to this sudden having-nothing-to-do. I realize that this is the first year of my life I haven't "gone to school" & thus haven't an imposed purpose to give direction to my days. My prose is quite painful & awkward to begin with, as my poetry is much more practiced & advanced: I haven't written a proper story for several years & work each morning a few hours on exercises in description. I have always expected immediate success & am gradually inuring myself to slow progress & careful practise. I think I will need a part-time job in Boston to give my life a kind of external solidity and balance. I hope I can slowly & painstakingly develop writing as a part-time vocation, because I think I need a sense of purpose beyond cooking and cleaning house, and there is no other career I can feel really useful in and drawn toward that would combine with children.

She added the old, baleful coda: "I miss having any girl-friends to talk to & exchange gossip & advice with."[41]

In her journal she was more forthright about her unhappiness. She understood its origin. "I have been, and am, battling depression," she wrote plainly on June 20, and made an astute self-diagnosis:

> It is as if my life were magically run by two electric currents: joyous positive and despairing negative—which ever is running at the moment dominates my life, floods it. I am now flooded with despair, almost hysteria, as if I were smothering. As if a great muscular owl were sitting on my chest, its talons clenching & constricting my heart.

She knew why the talons clenched—she was "'completely free'" for the "first time" in her life. "So I have all this, and my limbs are paralyzed." She thought again of having a baby "to elude my demanding demons & have a constant excuse for lack of production in writing."[42] But she vowed to wait.

Throughout July she wrote of "this queer suffocating hysteria on me," the "sick feeling which won't leave," the "absolutist panic."[43] She continued to work on her novel, but the words would not come. "I must cure this very destructive paralysis & ruinous brooding & daydreaming. If I want to write, this is hardly the way to behave—in horror of it, frozen by it. The ghost of the unborn novel is a Medusa-head."[44] Plath saw poetry, which came easier, as "an excuse & escape from writing prose."[45] And, indeed, the summer of 1958 was a productive one: she wrote "Above the Oxbow," "Fable of the Rhododendron Stealers," "Child's Park Stones," "Incommunicado," "Owl," "Moonrise," "Sculptor," "Night Shift," "Two Views of a Cadaver Room," "The Beggars," "The Goring," "The Net-Menders," "Memoirs of a Spinach-Picker," and "Frog Autumn." But none of these poems had the force of "Lorelei," "The Disquieting Muses," or "Mussel Hunter at Rock Harbor." She felt "rejected by an adult world, part of nothing—of neither an external career of Ted's . . . nor a career of my own, nor, vicariously, the life of friends, not part of motherhood."[46] She was emotionally and professionally adrift. Some days, she felt the "strangling noose of worry, of hysteria, paralysis" loosen; other days it returned, this "queer deathlike state" that brought continual exhaustion, self-doubt, and panic.[47]

Money was the worry that never disappeared. Sylvia realized that if she wanted children, she and Ted needed to "sacrifice." "I find myself horrified at voicing the American dream of a home & children," she wrote in her journal, fantasizing about an artist's estate on the Maine coast. But she reminded herself of "the great fault of America . . . expectancy of conformity."[48] She knew that she needed routine and structure, and considered court reporting, which meant learning the stenotype. Aurelia, who made her living teaching secretarial skills, stood ready to help. But Sylvia was wary. She didn't want to be "a conventional regular secretary," and decided against the course.[49] She knew that her mother, aunt, and uncle resented Ted because he would not get a job. Hughes was adamant. "I refuse to work for somebody else, merely to earn cash to keep alive to go on earning cash perhaps to keep alive infants for the same meaningless round," he wrote his brother that summer. "When we have children, I want them to be rooted in a life with meaning."[50] Sometimes Sylvia resented him, too, but those moments were fleeting. "I know he is the great poet of our generation & feel that the most important thing is to somehow clear these next five years for a tough & continuous apprenticeship to writing," she wrote Olwyn in late June.[51] She understood that Ted's refusal to conform to American "pressure" allowed her to opt out as well.[52] For she too had her "own dream, which is mine, & not the American dream. I want to write funny & tender women's storys [*sic*]." She admired Ted's single-minded dedication to poetry and vowed in her journal to support him as he would her: "there are no rules for this kind of wifeliness—I must make them up as I go along & will do so."[53]

When "Mussel Hunter at Rock Harbor" appeared in the August 9 issue of *The New Yorker*, Sylvia's friend Florence Sultan—the wife of Stanley Sultan, a visiting writer at Smith—invited her over to read it. Plath was "awestruck"— "the first poem in the magazine, page 22, taking up almost a whole page," she wrote in her journal. The two women drank wine and played with Florence's baby, who did not interest Sylvia nearly as much as her poem, which she pondered "in a rapt contemplation."[54] She regarded the prospect of her own baby "fearfully, dimly."[55]

Sylvia, Aurelia, and Grampy Schober celebrated Ted's twenty-eighth birthday on August 17 in Eastham. Ted enjoyed himself more on Cape Cod this time around, even though he and Sylvia were almost swept out to sea one day in their rowboat—an occasion he later memorialized in his *Birthday Letters* poem "Flounders." Sylvia had asked Aurelia, who had a discount at the Boston University bookstore, to buy Ted Robert Lowell's *Lord Weary's Castle* as a birthday gift. (Unable to find Lowell's book, Aurelia bought him a fishing rod instead.) Ted later gave Sylvia a copy of *Lord Weary's Castle* for her own birthday that year. Both poets held Lowell in high regard, and hoped to meet him again soon in Boston.

The other book Sylvia asked Aurelia to buy for Ted was Rachel Carson's *The Sea Around Us*. He had already read it, but he loved the book so much that Sylvia wanted him to have his own copy. The Carson request suggests Plath and Hughes's growing awareness of environmental issues. In later years, Hughes told others he had been shocked into becoming an environmentalist in late 1959 when he read an article in *The Nation* about radioactive waste dumped into Boston Harbor. He was also enormously influenced by Carson's *Silent Spring*, which he and Plath read when it was serialized in *The New Yorker* in summer 1962. After Plath's death, Hughes founded one of the earliest environmental magazines, *Your Environment*, along with his old Saint Botolph friends David Ross and Daniel Weissbort. He used his literary celebrity to fund various environmental causes for the rest of his life, with some success. In 1985, a year after he became England's poet laureate, he sent John Elkington's *The Poisoned Womb* to then prime minister Margaret Thatcher, who took it under consideration. Prince Charles, another environmentalist, became a trusted friend. Plath shared Hughes's environmental concerns; their daughter's first outing would be to an anti-bomb protest march in London.

When the couple returned to Northampton from Cape Cod, they found their landlady furious that they had left their windows open. Mrs. Whalen even dared to criticize Sylvia's meticulous housekeeping. Plath, seething, vowed to "caricature" her in a story. "All fury, grist for the mill."[56] It was a strategy she revisited in the years to come.

―――――

MRS. WHALEN BECAME "a flat memory only" as Sylvia and Ted left Northampton behind for Boston on September 1, 1958.[57] Their Willow Street apartment, in the charming, historic Beacon Hill neighborhood, delighted with its forest-green walls, hardwood floors, and plush couch. The rent was high, at $115 a month, and only a curtain separated the "pigmy" galley kitchen from the living room, but there were spectacular views over the Charles River from the two bay windows, which Sylvia called their "writing corners," "luminously light."[58] She told others she found the apartment's small size "hostile to any elaborate housewifery, and that to the good."[59] Her "workroom" was the main living room; she loved to gaze across the gables and chimney pots of Back Bay to the Charles River, sparkling mesmerically in the autumn sun. To her left was the gleaming John Hancock building; to her right, the "pruned & plumed trees of Louisberg [sic] Square."[60] Ted worked in the pale blue bedroom, where he set up a desk of two large wooden planks before the bay window. Sylvia treasured her new anonymity, telling Ellie Friedman, "Nobody here has heard of Smith, or us, which is magnificent."[61] She wrote more candidly to Dorothea Krook of how "in America, privacy is suspect; isolation, perilous."[62]

They spent their first few days exploring the city's less genteel quarters. They wandered by wharves and dark waterside taverns that seemed straight out of Melville, and open-air markets in the Italian North End. Sylvia even ventured inside a tattoo parlor, but she nearly fainted as she watched the artist ply his trade. (She later wrote about the experience in a story, "The Fifteen-Dollar Eagle," which would be published in the fall 1960 *Sewanee Review*. Ted boasted to Olwyn that the editor called it a "marvelous tour-de-force.")[63] They rode the famous swan boats in the Public Garden. Both decided that Boston was their favorite city, especially Ted: "he claims, everywhere, that the heavy stone buildings, the scraggly brick flats, the green park full of swans, remind him of England," Sylvia wrote Dr. Krook.[64]

But within two weeks, Sylvia's old panic, "absolute & obliterating," was back.[65] Ted's ability to concentrate and produce made her feel lazy. He later told the critic William Scammell that his "influence" at this time amounted to "a relentless application to the job . . . a general pressure towards concrete language and direct statement." He told Sylvia that when she had finished a poem, she should feel "exhausted . . . utterly spent" like the discus player who collapses on the field after his third throw, and he taught her exercises "to release her mind from the dreadful panic lock it used to get into."[66] But Hughes, too, was mired in a "black depression," according to Sylvia, for much of September.[67] The apartment had come with an aquarium and two goldfish, and he felt that the tank was too small. He became distraught at how the fish were "suffering, almost dying."[68] They changed the tank water every day, hoping that the fish would not die, as the drama of the baby bird played out all over again. Plath continued working on her short story about the bird throughout September, but it, too, refused to fly.

Aurelia's calls, filled with "unspoken nervousness" about her own troubles and their joblessness, did not help.[69] Whole days slid by with nothing to show. The two listened to Beethoven sonatas late into the night, woke late, ate at odd times, and sat in silence. "Stop & ask why you wash, why you dress, you go wild—it is as if love, pleasure, opportunity surrounded me, and I were blind," Sylvia wrote in her journal.[70] She and Ted bickered. He could nag *her* about her cooking and writing from his "superior seat," she complained, but not the other way around. "No criticism or nagging," she wrote in her journal on September 11. "Shut eyes to dirty hair, ragged nails. He is a genius. I his wife." She vowed not to let Ted see her work, so that her life would not "hang on" his. She was annoyed when *The Atlantic* rejected her "Snakecharmer," while Ted received a $150 check for "Dick Straightup." "The famed & fatal jealousy of professionals," she observed drily in her journal. "Do we, vampire-like, feed on each other? A wall, sound-proof, must mount between us. Strangers in our study, lovers in bed."[71] She spoke of "Ted's depression" and her "disease of doldrums."[72] She wondered again and again how she would fill her days, thinking she might "rush to Harvard, to Yale" and "beg" them to admit her into a PhD program—anything to "take my life out of my own clumsy hands."[73] Smith had asked her back for a third time, sweetening their offer with a writing course. "I have nightmares about accepting," she wrote Ellie, "so must refuse."[74]

A visit from Luke Myers, who was teaching in Paris that year, seemed to rouse Ted. He read children's books for ideas and began working on his play *The Wound* and two Yorkshire stories, "Sunday" and "The Rain Horse." He also learned, on September 4, that "The Thought-Fox" had beaten more than three thousand other poems to win the 1958 Guinness Poetry Award for the best poem published in England. The award came with £300—enough,

Plath wrote Krook, to "see us fed for ten months."[75] T. S. Eliot wrote personally to Hughes, "I have heard that you have won the first prize for the year in the Guinness Poetry Award and am writing to congratulate you. I should also like to tell you, not having had any communication with you before, how delighted I was when I first read the script of The Hawk in the Rain and how happy I am that you should be on our poetry list."[76] The note meant more to Hughes—and to his prospects—than the prize money.

Plath, meanwhile, was still trying to make headway on her Cambridge novel, *Falcon Yard*, reading the notebooks of Henry James for inspiration. She could not decide whose influence to follow—that of James or D. H. Lawrence. She had decided that Virginia Woolf was not the right model for her after all, telling Lynne Lawner that September that Woolf never "writes more than about tremulous party-dress emotions, except in the odd Mrs. Ramsey." Even some of Lawrence's stories, Plath felt, were "potboilers."[77] Her strongest influence, in many ways, was working in the room next door.

By late September, Sylvia could bear no more freedom. She wrote to the Smith vocational office asking for suggestions about a part-time job, or anything full-time that "involved newspaper, publishing, or editing work."[78] She also sent her résumé to three Boston temp agencies. She got the first job she interviewed for and started secretarial work in the outpatient psychiatric clinic at Massachusetts General Hospital. The pay was low and the hours longer than she wanted, but the position came "with compensations of fascinating work & no home work."[79] Sylvia had been treated at this hospital after her suicide attempt in 1953, a fact she omitted in her breezy letter to Ellie: "I type fascinating records, meet troubled people who think they are going to give birth to puppies or that they have lived for three centuries or that they will go mad if they leave an ingredient out of a cake."[80] She loved reading the patients' strange case histories—"as if I had my wish & opened up the souls of the people in Boston & read them deep." Their fears and anxieties—death, snakes, elevators, loneliness—made her feel less alone, and "paradoxically" her "panic-bird" began to recede.[81] Yet Sylvia quit her job at the clinic after only two months and took a part-time job later that spring, three days a week, as a secretary to the head of the Department of Sanskrit and Indian Studies at Harvard. Her short story "Johnny Panic and the Bible of Dreams," which she wrote while working at the clinic, suggests that the hospital brought back painful memories.

"Johnny Panic" came easily to Plath in the midst of a writing block. The story is a reworking of an earlier mental hospital piece based on her stay at McLean, "Tongues of Stone," now told from the perspective of a secretary at the adult outpatient unit at the City Hospital. In the story, widely considered Plath's most successful, the narrator collects patients' dreams in her own manuscript—a transgression for which she is punished by shock treatment at the story's end. "Johnny Panic" contains surrealist touches; the end sequence, when the narrator enters a dungeon-like basement filled with howling mental patients, may be a dream. Yet elements of the final shock treatment scene come straight from Plath's shock sessions at Valley Head. Doctors are more threatening than patients; shock treatment is an instrument of torture. Plath had found her métier, "queer and quite slangy," but her subjects—fear, anxiety, depression, mental hospitals—were not decorous.[82] The now-classic story would be rejected by *Sewanee Review* in 1961 by an editor who seemed confused by Plath's experimental prose. Her narrator, he said, was "too removed" from the "normal world." The story amounted to "little more than notes," but could she please tell her husband to send more poems?[83] (The story was eventually published in *The Atlantic* in September 1968.)

Plath's novel in progress, *Falcon Yard*, was more traditional. Her notes suggest the direction the book might have taken: "Denise Peregrine: Heroine, kinetic. Voyager, no Penelope. Leonard: Hero. God-man, because spermy, creator. Dionysiac. Pan. How to lead pan into world of toast and nappies? Falcon Yard: Love, bird of prey. Victors and victims. A fable of faithfulness. Risen out of depravity and suffering."[84] She desperately wanted to write celebratory prose about her Cambridge experience and love for Hughes, but she could not seem to sustain a long, exuberant Lawrentian narrative. Work on the novel continued to stall, and her depression deepened.

In mid-December, Sylvia decided to resume her therapy sessions with Dr. Beuscher, who convinced her that Aurelia was the source of her depression. "Better than shock treatment: 'I give you permission to hate your mother,'" Plath wrote in her journal.[85] In her notebooks about her sessions with Dr. Beuscher that winter, Sylvia mocked Aurelia for encouraging her to settle down with someone like Dick or Gordon:

> a nice little, safe little, sweet little imitation man who'll give you babies and bread and a secure roof and a green lawn and money money money every month. Compromise. A smart girl can't have everything she wants. Take second best. . . .
>
> She slept with people, hugged them and kissed them. Turned down the nicest boys whom <u>she</u> would have married like a shot & got older and still didn't marry anybody. She was too sharp and smart-tongued for any nice man to stand. Oh, she was a cross to bear.[86]

The dam had broken. There must have been some relief in finding a reason and a target for her depression, and Sylvia began to blame the insidious "demon" voice inside her head on Aurelia: "she doesn't know she's a walking vampire"; "I have ulcers, see how I bleed"; "I'd kill her, so I killed myself"; "She's deadly as a cobra"; "She wants to be me: she wants me to be her"; "You won't kill him [Hughes] the way you killed my father"; "Her daughter tried to kill herself and had to disgrace her by going to a mental hospital: bad, naughty ungrateful girl."[87] Sylvia wrote in her journal that she loved Aurelia, too, but Dr. Beuscher encouraged her to vent her anger. That December, Plath was reading Freud and was deeply swayed by his ideas regarding childhood trauma as the root of mental maladies. She did not need much prodding from modern psychiatry, which traced mental maladies, from shyness to schizophrenia, back to a "bad mother." Sylvia believed that Aurelia lived through her accomplishments—and doled out her love through them—but was secretly jealous. Dr. Beuscher encouraged her to believe that her suicide attempt had been "An accusation that her love was defective. . . . I felt I couldn't write because she would appropriate it. . . . if you don't love me, love my writing & love me for my writing."[88]

Aurelia and Otto did have high expectations for their children, but Sylvia's accusations were influenced by Dr. Beuscher and the sexist Freudian and "Momist" rhetoric of the time. Dr. Beuscher had become a mother substitute, as Sylvia admitted in her journal, and wielded enormous influence. Plath's depression may indeed have been exacerbated by the death of her father and her difficult relationship with her mother. But Dr. Beuscher's strategy, which encouraged rage rather than understanding or forgiveness, was a Pyrrhic victory.[89]

Hating one's mother was especially difficult when one secretly agreed with her. Over dinner in Wellesley that fall, Aurelia had told Sylvia that she wished *she* had been offered a teaching job at Smith. Sylvia bristled and became even more defensive about her unconventional marriage and career aspirations. Yet she shared Aurelia's ambivalence. Ted, she felt, "is as pathological as I am in his own way: compulsive against society so he envisions 'getting a job' as a kind of prison-term. . . . What is so terrible about earning a regular wage?" she wrote in her journal.[90] The couple's bickering continued. Ted told Marcia and Mike Plumer, when they visited that winter, that Sylvia had ripped up his torn socks and never mended his shirts. "So he thought by shaming me, he could manipulate me," Sylvia wrote in her journal. "My reaction: a greater stubbornness than ever . . . Both of us must feel partly that the other isn't filling a conventional role: he isn't 'earning bread and butter' in any reliable way, I'm not 'sewing on buttons and darning socks' by the hearthside. He hasn't even got us a hearth; I haven't even sewed a button."[91] Incredibly, Plath began to wonder if Mildred Norton had been right after all about "a man supplying direction and a woman the warm emotional power of faith and love"—a bromide she would famously mock in *The Bell Jar*.[92]

Sylvia felt that she and Ted were "directionless"—"we belong nowhere"—and she was angry at herself for caring about society's judgments.[93] "Who am I angry at? Myself. No, not yourself. Who is it? It is my mother and all the mothers I have known who have wanted me to be what I have not felt like really being from my heart."[94] Her feelings toward Ted, Aurelia, and her writing all became intertwined: "Now all I need to do is start writing without thinking it's for mother to get affection from her! How can I do this: where is my purity of motive? Ted won't need to get out of the house when I'm sure I'm not using his writing to get approval too and sure I'm myself and not him."[95] She again vowed not to show him any more of her work and hinted at the creative marriage's challenges in a *Mademoiselle* article in January 1959: "The bonuses of any marriage—shared interests, projects, encouragement and creative criticism—are all intensified. Both of us want to write as much as possible, and we do."[96] Yet Sylvia had also written lovingly about Ted in December when Dr. Beuscher asked her if she had "the guts" to ever admit she had married the wrong man. Plath responded in her journal:

> I would. But nothing in me gets scared or worried at this question. I feel good with my husband: I like his warmth and his bigness and his being-there and his making and his jokes and stories and what he reads and how he likes fishing and walks and pigs and foxes and little animals and is honest and not vain or fame-crazy and how he shows his gladness for what I cook him and joy for when I make something, a poem or thing so I can fight out my soul-battles and grow up with courage and a philosophical ease. I love his good smell and his body that fits with mine as if they were made in the same body-shop to do just that.[97]

She had not been "afraid of marrying Ted, because he is flexible, won't shut me in"—he never expected her to give up her literary aspirations, which he took as seriously as he did his own.[98]

By late December 1958 Plath had hit on a new subject. In "The Shadow," a young German American girl's father is sent to an internment camp during World War II. The story was loosely based on her own experience and that of Gordon's father, who had been sent to an internment camp in Bismarck, North Dakota. Sylvia wrote to Gordon, who was now married, asking him for details regarding his father's experience for an "article" she was writing.[99] The creative swerve back to childhood may have been prompted by therapy.

She was also beset by memories of her experiences with Dick—the traumatic birth scene, his sexual hypocrisy, his "conventionalism"—and sketched out a story about him on December 28 that would later provide the backbone of *The Bell Jar*. "The modern woman: demands as much experience as the modern man," she wrote in her journal.[100]

She celebrated Christmas 1958 in Wellesley with Ted, Aurelia, and Warren. After caroling around Beacon Hill, the four drank glühwein before the fire at Elmwood Road in what should have been a perfect holiday tableau. Sylvia had always been deeply invested in the aesthetics of Christmas—she loved the brilliant reds, greens, and golds, the carols and ringing bells. Yet, finally surrounded by friends and family, she still felt alone. In England she had authored an ideal life in her letters home. Now her quotidian struggles with career, marriage, and money were on full display. (Aurelia called Sylvia's Boston apartment "tiny" in her Christmas letter to friends and family that year.) Many of Sylvia's Wellesley and Smith friends were now mothers who had settled into the conventional suburban life she purported to disdain. She began to worry that she would "go soft" if she isolated herself too much and wished Ted would join a church with her. "If only Ted wanted to do something. Saw a career he'd enjoy. But I wonder: he says 'get a job' as if it were a prison sentence. I feel the weight on me. The old misery of money sweeping away. . . . I need a flow of life on the outside, a child, a job, a community I know from the preacher to baker. Not this drift of fairytales."[101] Plath had a healthy vision of what a balanced and integrated adult life ought to look like, and, troublingly, it was not the sort of life Hughes wanted.

PLATH AND HUGHES'S ARRIVAL in Boston coincided with momentous developments in American poetry. Boston in 1959 was the unlikely epicenter of an aesthetic revolution. Robert Lowell was about to publish *Life Studies*, Anne Sexton *To Bedlam and Part Way Back*. Lowell, Sexton, Maxine Kumin, Adrienne Rich, Stanley Kunitz, Elizabeth Hardwick, George Starbuck, Sam Alpert, Richard Wilbur, and John Holmes all lived in or around the city. The Poets' Theatre was thriving. "Being a 'poet' in Boston is not so difficult except that there are hoards [*sic*] of us living here," Sexton wrote to the poet Carolyn Kizer in February 1959. "The place is jammed with good writers—it's very depressing."[102]

Sexton complained to W. D. Snodgrass about Boston's literary parties—"It is politics and as bad as the University itself. . . . 'who do *you* know' and 'do you have a new book in process'"—but Plath enjoyed them.[103] She and Hughes socialized with Philip Booth, the Fassetts, the Sweeneys, and Richard Wilbur. Stephen Fassett remembered that Sylvia did not speak of herself as a poet at first; she came "trailing along as Ted's wife." But he soon got to know her as a brilliant "scholar who knew everything . . . lots of fun to talk to—together they were marvelous." He especially remembered her "eagerness towards life: a not unpleasant greed for good things."[104] Lowell and Hardwick came to dinner at Willow Street and told chummy stories about Dylan Thomas over slices of Plath's lemon meringue pie. Lowell was one of the few poets Plath did not regard with contempt or jealousy. Compared to "the gimmicky Cummings" and the "bland" Wilbur, she found him "like good strong shocking brandy after a too lucidly sweet dinner wine."[105] She was thrilled to call him a dinner guest. The couple also sometimes saw Stanley Kunitz, who remembered Plath as "amiable but secretive during the course of her visits with Ted to my Cambridge apartment—he did the talking." Kunitz would later recommend Plath's first book, *The Colossus*, for publication, barring "one or two poems that were too clearly derivative from Roethke."[106] In late October, Plath and Hughes spent the evening at Lowell's place, along with Robert Frost, a living legend who, Hughes said, "monologued very pleasantly until about 2 a. m." and was "very amusing, extremely human, a bit tough."[107] They met Frost again at Peter Davison's attic apartment on November 11. At the end of the evening, Plath, Hughes, and Davison walked Frost back to his home. Davison remembered that Frost "clearly took a shine to Ted," but that Plath "kept very quiet while the two male poets spoke of Edward Thomas and the English countryside, of Ezra Pound and T. S. Eliot."[108]

Plath saw Adrienne Rich occasionally in these circles. Like Kunitz, Rich felt Plath "was Ted's wife first, and a poet only after that."[109] Rich wrote to Jack Sweeney in late February that she was looking forward to spending an upcoming evening with "Ted and Sylvia Hughes," though she mentioned only Hughes's poetry.[110] Plath once asked Rich, who had two small children, whether it was possible to combine writing and motherhood. Rich told her, "Yes, but it's hellishly difficult."[111] Plath expressed similar anxieties about writing and motherhood to Ruth Whitman, a Jewish poet and mother of two she had met through the Fassetts. "Dare she have children? She was terrified that it would get in the way of her poetry." They spoke of "practically nothing else" when they got together. Whitman encouraged Plath to have children, saying, "If you stay in your narrow space, you'll find yourself writing about the same things over and over again."[112] Rich later admitted, "What I wanted to tell her was 'Don't try,' because I was in such despondency . . . I couldn't foresee a future different from the past two years of raising children and being almost continuously angry."[113]

In a less sexist time, Rich might have been Plath's ally and confidante, but in 1959 Rich was too much a rival. And perhaps Rich herself was less welcoming to Plath than she might have been, for Rich admitted that she felt "threatened" when she met Anne Sexton in 1959: "There was little support for the idea that another woman poet could be a source of strength or mutual engagement . . . if she was going to take up space, then I was not going to have that space."[114] Plath rarely mentions Rich in her letters or journals, but she admired her poems: "they stimulate me: they are easy, yet professional."[115] If she did not work more "philosophy" into her poetry, she felt, she would always "lag behind ACR."[116]

Although Plath had poems published in *The Spectator* and accepted by *The London Magazine* in early January 1959—"The Disquieting Muses," "Lorelei," and "Snakecharmer" would appear in the March issue—she was troubled by her poetry manuscript's rejection that month from David Keightley's World Publishing. She blamed herself for writing about "too many dreams, shadowy underworlds." It was another reason to follow Rich's lead, yet she longed to stay true to her own voice. She admonished herself for writing poems about "the baby gods . . . the moon-mothers, the mad maudlins, the lorelei, the hermits," rather than the "real world" of "blood, lust and death."[117] In her best poems, Plath would fuse both strategies, and use the power of myth to illuminate personal triumphs and sorrows.

While Plath was trying to sound like Rich, Rich herself was following Lowell's lead and attempting to find "a new freedom of expression," as she told Sweeney in February 1959.[118] Just as Hughes and his friends had become impatient with the genteel verse of the Movement in Britain, American poets had grown weary of elaborate form. "Young poets in the mid-1950s," Peter Davison remembered, "still overshadowed by the sequoias of Frost, Pound, Eliot, Stevens, Cummings, Marianne Moore, and William Carlos Williams, had taken refuge in a formal elegance that they were beginning to outgrow."[119] Rich agreed: "In those years, formalism was part of the strategy—like asbestos gloves, it allowed me to handle materials I couldn't pick up bare-handed."[120] Rich and Lowell, by the late fifties, knew something needed to change. As Lowell wrote, "Poets of my generation and particularly younger ones have gotten terribly proficient at these forms. They write a very musical, difficult poem with tremendous skill. . . . It's become a craft, purely a craft, and there must be some breakthrough back into life."[121]

Lowell's *Life Studies*, which Davison called "the most influential book of American poetry for a generation," provided that breakthrough.[122] *Life Studies* was the answer to the dilemma Lowell had posited to Elizabeth Bishop in 1959: "My trouble seems (just one angle for looking at it) to be to bring together in me the Puritanical iron hand of constraint and the gushes of pure wildness. One can't survive or write without both but they need to come to terms. Rather narrow walking."[123] Lowell's collection was published in the spring of 1959, but Plath and Hughes had already read some of his new poems that winter.[124] Hughes's similar desire to "break through" probably made Plath more responsive to Lowell's work. Daniel Huws remembered Ted "pointing out in *The Colossus* a couple of poems which he thought were the beginning of something new. 'Mushrooms.' I think he helped liberate her from the models she'd followed before."[125]

In *Life Studies*, Lowell—who would experience at least twenty manic episodes and hospitalizations—wrote about depression, suicide, mental hospitals, and familial inheritances. In "Skunk Hour," his most famous poem, he channels Milton: "I hear / my ill-spirit sob in each blood cell, / as if my hand were at its throat. . . . / I myself am hell; / nobody's here—."[126] He wrote of McLean's "locked razor" in "Waking in the Blue," lobotomized jail mates in "Memories of West Street and Lepke," and returning "frizzled, stale and small" from the asylum in "Home After Three Months Away."[127] Plath had endured similar experiences but had never dared confront them in her poems. Lowell dared.

Hughes kept himself at a slight remove from Boston's poetry scene. Yet he found Lowell's new verse "exciting."[128] The two were close enough that Lowell gave Hughes the manuscript of *Life Studies* to read before it was published, and confided in him about his anxieties regarding its reception.[129] Ted told Olwyn he thought parts of *Life Studies* "marvelous," though he noted that it was "autobiographical" and predicted that "not many people will like it."[130] To his parents he called Lowell "easily the best of all the Americans under fifty—easily and far away. He goes into the mental hospital now and again. . . . However he's about the most charming and likeable American I've ever met."[131] (Indeed, after meeting Lowell in Boston in 1958, he had written to Luke Myers, "his whole tempo is perfect Botolph.")[132] Although Hughes's enthusiasm for Lowell would wane over the years, in 1959 he shared Lowell's belief that modern poetry needed to be revitalized from an inner source, whether traumatic personal experience or nature's primal life force.[133] He boasted to his parents and sister that Lowell considered his poem "Pike" " 'a masterpiece,' 'immortal,' and 'a new way of writing.' "[134] Al Alvarez, poetry critic at *The Observer* from 1959 to 1977, noted Lowell's influence in his review of *The Hawk in the Rain* ("Lowell prowls about").[135]

Boston in the 1950s was, as one contemporary observed, a well-mannered society in which gay men were "clubbed to death in the bushes" and lesbians were "unthinkable": "Mental hospitals flourished."[136] That the man writing poems of madness and mental hospitals hailed from one of the most prominent families in Boston mattered. (The joke went that Harvard was a

Lowell "family business.") Lowell gave others courage, and permission, to follow his example. Elizabeth Bishop explained the dilemma in a 1960 letter to Lowell. It bothered her, she wrote, that so many women writers—Virginia Woolf, Elizabeth Bowen, Rebecca West, Katherine Anne Porter, and Anne Sexton—belonged to "'our beautiful old silver' school of female writing . . . They have to make quite sure that the reader is not going to mis-place them socially, first—and that this nervousness interferes constantly with what they think they'd like to say." They had to mitigate their unwomanly literary calling by confirming that they were "nice," Bishop said.[137] Her perceptive comment cuts to the heart of Plath's dilemma at mid-century.

The poet Kathleen Spivack, a Lowell protégé, recalled the obstacles for women writers in a Puritan city overshadowed by Harvard. "The field was full of misogyny."[138] Even Lowell, one of Elizabeth's Bishop's best friends, chose women for his poetry workshop on the basis of looks, Spivack said; in class, he spoke of all women poets, even Bishop, as "minor."[139] The situation had hardly improved a decade later in 1971, when Lowell told the British critic Ian Hamilton, "Few women write major poetry. Can I make this generalization? Only four stand with our best men: Emily Dickinson, Marianne Moore, Elizabeth Bishop and Sylvia Plath." Such condescension angered Bishop, who told Lowell, "I'd rather be called '*the 16th poet*' with no reference to my sex, than one of 4 women—even if the other three are pretty good."[140] Spivack, who attended Lowell's 1959 creative writing seminar, thought that both Plath and Rich had managed not to offend "Boston propriety and male prerogative" by "being worshipful and self-effacing."[141] Rich had won the Yale Younger Poets prize when she was a Radcliffe undergraduate, but at Harvard she was not allowed to take upper-level English classes, which were only for men.

Lowell was not the only poet breaking taboo in the late 1950s. There may have been a less obvious "confessional" poetic influence on Plath—the Beats. In 1959, Allen Ginsberg, Peter Orlovsky, and Gregory Corso visited Lowell for the first time in his Boston apartment. Lowell and Ginsberg began corresponding, each accusing the other of missing the point of good poetry. They would not meet again until 1977, when they gave a joint reading at Saint Mark's Church in Greenwich Village. By then, the two seemed more like collaborators than antagonists. Each had helped loosen the parameters of American poetry and popularize the "raw" over the "cooked," as Lowell famously put it in his 1960 National Book Award acceptance speech for *Life Studies*.

Plath, in England, would have missed most of the publicity that surrounded the publication of *Howl* in 1956 and its obscenity trial in 1957. By the time she returned, however, the Beats were famous, their outrageous poetry readings and Benzedrine-fueled road trips frequently described in the national papers and middlebrow magazines such as *Time* and *Life*. Plath never mentioned Allen Ginsberg or Jack Kerouac in her letters and journal, but she would have known about *On the Road*, published in 1957, and *The Dharma Bums* in 1958. Articles about "the Beat Generation" had appeared in *The New York Times* as early as 1952.

The Beats had access to areas of underground experience that were mostly off-limits to middle-class white women in the 1950s. Columbia's proximity to Harlem meant that Kerouac and Ginsberg spent many evenings in bars and jazz clubs.[142] Theirs was the free life Plath had dreamed of in her journal when she fantasized about living as a man and visiting bars and brothels. Despite her boasting about Jewish and African American friends at Cambridge, Plath's race and gender meant she had little contact with these American subcultures. All of her poetic training had been through the university rather than the street: martinis at the Ritz were about as daring as Plath got during her year in Boston. Plath's Germanic work ethic and sobriety bore little resemblance to the Beats' infidelities, addictions, and dishevelments. Indeed, literary critics typically frowned on the Beats, who, says Louis Menand, were considered "not serious" by 1950s intellectuals.[143] Alvarez mocked the Beats' pretensions and "self-pity" in *The Observer* in November 1958, declaring them a "joke."[144] That same year, Norman Podhoretz published a scathing article about the Beats, "The Know-Nothing Bohemians," in *The Partisan Review*.[145]

But Plath shared the Beats' contempt for the middlebrow (televisions, station wagons, payment plans), which she encoded into her fictional depictions of suburbia. Corso and Ginsberg had both been patients at mental hospitals. "Johnny Panic and the Bible of Dreams," with its surrealist elements, suspicion of authority, and vision of holy madness, has a Beat sensibility, as does *The Bell Jar*'s suggestion that insanity is a sane response to the repressions of Cold War America. The 1953 electrocution of the Rosenbergs symbolized, for Plath, other victims of repression—radicals, Jews, homosexuals, dissidents, artists.

In 1961 Plath would try to include Corso's "A Dreamed Realization" in a selection of American poetry for the *Critical Quarterly*. (In the end, she could not obtain permission.) She would also include Robert Creeley, a poet of the Black Mountain School, in the anthology. She wrote that her selection would range "from Gregory Corso to Richard Wilbur (i.e., encompassing the Beats and the Elegant Academicians). Over 15 poets. Over 20 poems."[146] Her use of the term "Elegant Academicians" was not necessarily gracious. She saw the Beats and polished poets like Wilbur on opposite poles of the aesthetic spectrum, and may have found the former a refreshing antidote to the latter by the early sixties. Like her, Beat writers sought to break out of the glass caul; they counted themselves enemies of New Criticism, which Ginsberg and Kerouac had loathed as undergraduates at Columbia. Ginsberg felt that "true art" was "uninfluenced, unrepressed, uninhibited"—not so very different from the practice that Hughes preached.[147]

————

SYLVIA'S TEAR-FILLED SESSIONS with Dr. Beuscher, which she called "a cleansing and an exhaustion," left her "happy."[148] But the peace was temporary; she continued to suffer from depression and nightmares—dead babies, half-decayed corpses, graveyards, shock treatment at Valley Head—throughout January 1959. "The old sickness on me," she wrote in her journal on January 8. She considered, again, a PhD in English at Columbia, and questioned whether she was really "the sort to stay home all day and write."[149] She read Saint Therese's autobiography and looked up the requirements for a psychology PhD, but six more years of study was too wearisome a prospect. Lynne Lawner's letters from Rome did not help. Lynne was living Sylvia's dream life—attending literary salons, writing and translating poetry, learning Italian with seemingly endless amounts of money and time. Yet a surprise letter from Eddie Cohen moved her. He had vowed "to stay away," but had read so much of her recent work he could not resist congratulating her—and apologizing for forgetting "the meaning of friendship when you needed it most.... You've come a long way since Seventeen, but your first fan is still one of your fondest."[150]

Sylvia's depression began to lift somewhat once she began socializing. On New Year's Eve, she and Ted attended a masquerade party at Stephen and Agatha Fassetts' home, where Sylvia dressed as Little Red Riding Hood and Ted as the wolf. (Agatha had let Sylvia roam through her attic until she found an old sealskin coat, from which Ted made an alarmingly realistic wolf mask.) Sylvia also spent a lot of time with Marcia, who had adopted three-month-old twins. Marcia remembered that Sylvia visited her almost daily for two or three months that spring and was enormously helpful. "She was thoroughly saturated in the experience and loved it."[151] She and Marcia cooked together and discussed motherhood and infertility—which Sylvia worried about—and Marcia taught her how to use a sewing machine. Sylvia braided a rag rug and spoke "easily about babies, fertility, amazingly frank and pleasant" with Perry Norton's wife, Shirley. With Shirley, Sylvia felt "part of young womanhood. How odd, men don't interest me at all now, only women and womentalk."[152]

That January, she attempted a sonnet about the dead bird and finished her poem "Point Shirley," about her grandmother—"Oddly powerful and moving to me in spite of the rigid formal structure. Evocative."[153] In February, she made another recording of her poems at the Fassett Recording Studios, and began another Winthrop poem, "Suicide Off Egg Rock." But the poem didn't seem to work, initially. In her journal she wrote, "set up such a strict verse form that all power was lost: my nose so close I couldn't see what I was doing. An anesthetizing of feeling."[154] Plath did not need Robert Lowell to point out that she was using form as a crutch: "What inner decision, what inner murder or prison-break must I commit if I want to speak from my true deep voice in writing . . . and not feel this jam up of feeling behind a glass-dam fancy-facade of numb dumb wordage."[155] She rewrote the poem until it contained, she felt, "the neat easy ACRich lyricism."[156] Hughes thought "Suicide Off Egg Rock" inaugurated "the first phase where she began to sound a 'natural' (as opposed to 'artificial') note."[157] Plath was grappling with her own trauma, writing obliquely about her attempt to drown herself in August 1953:

> No pit of shadow to crawl into,
> And his blood beating the old tattoo
> I am, I am, I am. . . .
>
> Everything shrank in the sun's corrosive
> Ray but Egg Rock on the blue wastage.

The couple marked the third anniversary of their Saint Botolph's meeting over trout, duck, and French wine at the Blue Ship Tea Room, perched at the end of a sagging Boston wharf. But they celebrated in the shadow of a quarrel. "Last night a miserable dowie dowie fight over nothing, our usual gloom," Sylvia wrote cryptically in her journal.[158] They had decided to move back to England at the end of the year to a "big house in the country outside London."[159] Sylvia's newly unearthed anger toward her mother gave her the momentary confidence to leave home, and anyway, she assumed the move would be temporary, just a year. But Ted's increasing antipathy toward American life decided the matter. "There is something suspended about my life here," he wrote to Olwyn in January, "like the beginnings of blindness & deafness."[160] Sylvia treated the move as another Fulbright gambit. In her journal she wrote, "Am happy about living in England: to go to Europe at the drop of a channel-crossing ticket: I really want that." Yet in the same journal passage, she vowed to become less dependent on Hughes. "Must try poems. DO NOT SHOW ANY TO TED."[161]

By February, Sylvia had decided that she was not making enough progress writing at home, and she enrolled as an auditor in Lowell's creative writing seminar at Boston University. The class met at 236 Bay State Road on Tuesdays from two to four p.m. and had an official roster of five students. About fifteen others audited the class, including Anne Sexton and, occasionally, George Starbuck, then a junior editor at Houghton Mifflin.[162]

Plath initially called the seminar "a great disappointment." Lowell, in his "mildly feminine ineffectual fashion," let his students say things she would not let her Smith freshmen get away with. "Felt a regression," she wrote in her journal after the first class. But she continued to attend throughout the spring. Despite her misgivings, she sensed she needed a more structured, academic setting to conquer the feeling that she had become "a recluse who comes out into the world with a life-saving gospel to find everybody has learned a new language in the meantime and can't understand a word he's saying."[163] Plath's words were prescient; in Lowell's class, she would indeed start to learn a "new language." Lowell encouraged Plath to write about experiences Dr. Beuscher had persuaded her to resurrect and her mother had wanted her to bury—experiences too painful to probe with Hughes. Indeed, Lowell's poem about McLean, "Waking in the Blue," which he read out loud in his seminar, moved Plath deeply.[164] But it would take time for Plath to make the imaginative leaps Lowell and Sexton had already begun. "She was a dutiful student of poetic tradition of the time," Kathleen Spivack remembered. "She was watchful and very careful, holding herself back."[165]

In class that spring, Lowell hovered restlessly on the verge of a breakdown. By April, he would check himself into McLean; during his last class, his students were terrified he was going to throw himself out the window. Sexton recalled how everyone smoked and used their shoes as ashtrays while Lowell read poems "soft and slow" in his formal New England manner. Sitting at a window seat overlooking Commonwealth Avenue, Lowell performed cerebral, sometimes "maniacally elliptical" textual analysis. He discussed form as much as meaning, always prodding the class to investigate how the formal structure enhanced what was being said—or not said—within. "Poetry was meant to be understood," Spivack remembered; he "had little patience" for students who wrote "obscure" verse. "What does this poem really *mean*?" he would repeat, going around the table, meeting silence.[166]

In class, Plath was formal, proper, confident in her superiority, Spivack thought, as she announced on the first day that Wallace Stevens was her favorite poet. Spivack never saw Plath crack a smile, even when Lowell joked. "She was precise, analytical, and could be quietly devastating to another student poet."[167] She remembered Plath nodding at whatever Lowell said, though she could match his ability to tease out obscure poetic influences. "'Reminds me of Empson,' Sylvia would say . . . 'It reminds me of Herbert.' 'Perhaps the early Marianne Moore?'"[168]

Lowell returned the favor, in his own deflating way. When Plath work-shopped "Sow," he declared it almost "perfect," but then quickly moved on. "Everyone senses that Lowell has damned with faint praise and has managed to sidestep real engagement with the poem," Spivack remembered. Low-ell seemed more "dazzled" by Sexton, who approached her poetry from the opposite end of the aesthetic spectrum.[169] Plath was an academically trained poet, Sexton, intuitive; Plath's poems were formal, cerebral, while Sexton's were personal and raw. Lowell helped Sexton prune her manuscript *To Bed-lam and Part Way Back* and then shepherded it to poetry editors at Knopf and Houghton Mifflin. He did not extend the same assistance to Plath.

Plath often went to the Ritz with Sexton and George Starbuck after the seminar ended. Their triple-martini afternoons are now legend, as is Sex-ton's quip that they parked in the hotel's loading zone because they were there to get loaded. Starbuck remembered their "hilarious conversations comparing their suicides and talking about their psychiatrists."[170] Sexton and Plath became literary doppelgängers in the public imagination: both attractive, young female poets with Wellesley roots, both students of Low-ell, both McLean "graduates," as Plath put it, victims of mental illness and suicide.[171] Yet Sexton was a much wilder figure than Plath, and outwardly more unstable. She left her children largely in the care of her mother-in-law and battled addictions to pills, booze, and—as she put it—suicide. (She attempted suicide twelve times between 1957 and her death—from suicide—in 1974.)[172] Her devoted fans felt that her unguarded lyrics spoke truth to power in the heady days of early feminism. But that very rawness led Elizabeth Bishop to believe Sexton was not in the same league as Low-ell. "She *is* good, in spots," Bishop wrote to Lowell in 1960, "but there is all the difference in the world, I'm afraid, between her kind of simplicity and that of *Life Studies*, her kind of egocentricity that is simply that, and yours that has been . . . made intensely *interesting*."[173] In 1962, Hughes told Alvarez that Sexton was "good"—to a point. "When Lowell holds his breath, she wilts. Surely she's very thin, surely the writing's pretty undistinguished. Very direct, unloading her life & all its paraphernalia, but the short sharp poems are the best."[174]

Sexton had no formal education past high school, and by her own admis-sion she was not widely read. Each time she was given the chance to teach literature at the university level, she balked, claiming she was no good at critical analysis. As her biographer Diane Middlebrook noted, "if someone floated an allusion to Yeats or Hardy, Eliot or Pound, she often had to bluff."[175] Even after Sexton won the Pulitzer Prize in 1967, the English department at Boston University, where she taught as an adjunct, refused to grant her a tenure line for several years. A former English professor there remembered, "It mattered a lot that she had absolutely no education—that outraged people."[176]

Plath was less snobbish about Sexton's lack of education than she might have been—though in a March letter to Lynne Lawner she mentioned that Sexton had published in *The New Yorker* and the *Partisan Review* "without ever having gone to college."[177] Yet Plath was pleased to be paired with Sexton during Lowell's workshop. "He sets me up with Ann [*sic*] Sexton, an honor, I suppose. Well, about time. She has very good things, and they get better, though there is a lot of loose stuff."[178] Plath's criticism of Sexton's "looseness" comes as no surprise given her New Critical biases, which she had not yet purged.

Like Lowell, Plath recognized Sexton's revolutionary talent at just the time she was trying to shed her formalist tics. For years Plath had castigated herself for not getting more "life" into her poems. Here, suddenly, was another Wellesley housewife-poet, suicide survivor, and asylum patient who had effortlessly achieved the aural and emotional effects she herself tried so hard to create—and, more importantly, who wrote with confidence from a woman's perspective. Musing on her decision to cut "Electra on Azalea Path" from what would eventually become *The Colossus* (though she later changed her mind and included the poem), Plath wrote in her journal, "Too forced and rhetorical. A leaf from Ann [*sic*] Sexton's book would do here. She has none of my clenches and an ease of phrase, and an honesty."[179] Plath told Lynne Lawner that she admired Lowell "immensely" and that Sexton had "the marvelous enviable casualness of the person who is suddenly writing and never thought or dreamed of herself as a born writer: no inhibitions."[180] (Indeed, Sexton wrote to a friend that year, "I am kind of a secret beatnik hiding in the suburbs.")[181] Sylvia felt she had few such female models, she told Lynne that March. "Except for M. Moore & Elizabeth Bishop what women are there to look to? A few eccentrics like Edith Sitwell, Amy Lowell. And the perennial Emily, I suppose."[182]

In Lowell's seminar that spring, Plath read Sexton's "You, Doctor Martin," about Sexton's experience in a mental hospital, as well as "Music Swims Back to Me," "The Bells," and "Some Foreign Letters."[183] Most searing was "The Double Image," a seven-part sequence about Sexton's mental breakdown, her separation from her infant daughter, and her mother's death. Plath singled out "The Double Image" in her letter to Lynne Lawner as her favorite Sexton poem. It was inspired—like many of Lowell's new poems—by W. D. Snodgrass's "Heart's Needle," a poem about divorce. Sexton read "The Double Image" and "You, Doctor Martin," aloud in class in early March. The latter poem ended in the "honest" voice Plath so admired:

> . . . I am queen of all my sins
> forgotten. Am I still lost?
> Once I was beautiful. Now I am myself,
> counting this row and that row of moccasins
> waiting on the silent shelf.[184]

The effect of Lowell's and Sexton's poems on Plath was intoxicating. In a 1962 interview, Plath suggested the extent of their influence:

Robert Lowell's *Life Studies*, this intense breakthrough into very serious, very personal, emotional experience . . . interested me very much. These peculiar, private and taboo subjects, I feel, have been explored in recent American poetry. I think particularly the poetess Anne Sexton, who writes about her experiences as a mother, as a mother who has had a nervous breakdown, is an extremely emotional and feeling young woman and her poems are wonderfully craftsman-like poems and yet they have a kind of emotional and psychological depth which I think is something perhaps quite new, quite exciting.[185]

Lowell later claimed he had thought Plath and Sexton "might rub off on each other" and that "Sylvia learned from Anne."[186] His instincts were good. As Sylvia wrote Lynne that March, "I am leaving the rather florid over-metaphorical style that encrusted me in college. The 'Feminine' (horrors) lavish coyness. The poems I have written in this last year are, if anything, 'ugly.' I have done many in syllabic verse which gives freedom of another sort & excited me for a good while, but they are pretty bare. The ones in the London magazine are the last of the lyric florid picture-poems."[187] (She was talking about "Snakecharmer," "Lorelei," and "The Disquieting Muses," which had appeared in the March issue.) Inspired by Lowell's and Sexton's "honesty," and pushed toward a tougher voice by Hughes, Plath thought she was finally breaking out of her "glass caul."[188]

The autobiographical explorations of both Lowell and Sexton dovetailed with the work Plath herself was doing in therapy with Dr. Beuscher, who encouraged Plath to visit her father's grave in Winthrop. She did so, for the first time, on March 9. She was disgusted by his small, flat stone on Azalea Path, barely visible among the throngs of "crude block stones, headstones together, as if the dead were sleeping head to head in a poorhouse." She wanted to "dig him up. To prove he existed and really was dead."[189] Afterward, she and Ted walked along the seawall to Deer Island, where they chatted with a prison guard. Hughes, in his black coat, walked out onto a long sandbar; his image inspired Plath's poem "Man in Black" in March, eventually published in *The New Yorker*. Sylvia called it a love poem in her journal, yet admitted to Otto's hovering presence.

Shortly after visiting her father's grave, Sylvia began to doubt Dr. Beuscher's methods. "I am getting nowhere with RB. . . . What good does talking about my father do?" she wondered in her journal. "It might be a minor catharsis that lasts a day or two but I don't get insight talking to myself."[190] Something about her relationship with Dr. Beuscher was not quite right—she admitted in her journal that her "extra-professional fondness" for her psychiatrist "inhibited" her during their sessions.[191] She also scoffed at Dr. Beuscher's claim that the pain of her menstrual cramps was all in her mind, and that she had "killed and castrated" her father. Did that mean that all her nightmares of defaced and deformed people were her "guilty visions of him or fears of punishment for me?"[192] That seemed absurd. These journal entries suggest how blurred the patient-doctor lines had become and show Plath's deep critical intelligence at work in the face of dubious psychoanalysis.

But surely Plath's regular sessions on the couch influenced the new poems she wrote that spring. Most of the poems Plath wrote in Lowell's seminar—"Suicide Off Egg Rock," "Electra on Azalea Path," "The Beekeeper's Daughter," "The Eye-Mote," "Watercolor of Grantchester Meadows," "The Ravaged Face," "Man in Black," "Aftermath," "A Winter Ship," and "Metaphors"—were formal and precise. But now there were chinks in the armor. Several of these poems delved into autobiography much more profoundly than her earlier work. Consider "Electra on Azalea Path," written in late March after her visit to Otto's grave, and probably influenced by Sexton's elegiac portrait of dark inheritances in "The Double Image."

> I am the ghost of an infamous suicide,
> My own blue razor rusting in my throat.
> O pardon the one who knocks for pardon at
> Your gate, father—your hound-bitch, daughter, friend.
> It was my love that did us both to death.

Although Plath had hinted obliquely at her suicide and depression in previous poems such as "The Disquieting Muses," "Lorelei," and "Full Fathom Five," this was the first time she had addressed it in such direct, personal terms. The phrase "hound-bitch" was a huge leap—Plath had never before used a curse word in her poetry. Although "bitch" here describes a dog, she plays with its double meaning; the shadow curse gives the end of an otherwise conventional elegy an edge of rage. Plath was starting to shed her decorum; indeed, Hughes noted that in Lowell's class, "For the first time, she tried deliberately to locate just what it was that hurt."[193] By "Daddy," three years later, she would write in a much angrier voice. Sexton helped usher in this transformation. "Daddy," Plath's most well-known poem, is heavily indebted to Sexton's "My Friend, My Friend," which Sexton published in the summer 1959 issue of *The Antioch Review* and probably workshopped in Lowell's class. Plath would pilfer Sexton's cadences and tropes of Jewishness to buttress her own poem of vengeance and sorrow, while Sexton would draw on Plath's Nazi imagery in her later work.[194]

Houghton Mifflin accepted Sexton's *To Bedlam and Part Way Back* in May as Plath struggled to find a publisher. "I was too determined to bet on myself to actually notice where she was headed in her work," Sexton later admitted.[195] Indeed, in an April 1959 letter from Sexton to Snodgrass, Plath—whom Sexton had known for two months—hardly seems worth mentioning: "Ted Hughes and his wife (Sylvia Plath) are in Boston this year (he is an english [*sic*] poet)."[196] Plath resented Sexton for publishing in *The Christian Science Monitor*—her domain—and doing poetry readings at McLean. Plath called her a "copy-cat," though she admitted that Sexton was the "more successful copy-cat."[197] Sexton eventually wrote a famous elegy, "Sylvia's Death," about their shared fascination with suicide ("what is your death / but an old belonging").[198] In 1967, she told Hughes that she had "little to add" to a biographical portrait of Plath. " 'Sylvia's Death,' " she said, "makes everyone think I knew her well, when I only knew her death well."[199]

Plath seems not to have invited Sexton to 9 Willow Street, but she did invite her Lowell classmate Kathleen Spivack to tea. Spivack was immediately struck by Hughes, whom Sexton had now started calling "Ted Huge." He seemed tall, taciturn, "darkly handsome," and "formidable." He "folded himself into a sagging armchair and lounged in an exhausted manner" while Sylvia "fluttered nervously about with hot water, a kettle, pot, real tea (not tea bags!), cups and saucers." She felt Sylvia wanted her to notice how she first warmed the pot and poured milk into the teacups in the proper "English way." The erudite couple intimidated her, and conversation flagged until Sylvia and Ted began describing their young, British contemporaries, who were mostly unknown in America:

They were soon off on a conversation of their own, discussing the merits of the poems. Ted's accent grew thicker, Sylvia's too. They were more articulate for having an inarticulate audience, me. They said very "British" things like "Nonsense!" and "Rubbish!" to each other, clipping their consonants as they disagreed. This impressed me no end! It was an occasion for each of them to shine. I felt perhaps they did not talk this way when they were alone together. But here they seemed companionable, lively, interested in each other's opinions, and also in besting each other in front of me. Ted munched a lot of shortbread. Sylvia kept pouring the tea. I was filled with the sense of all I had not read, and admired this literate, cultivated couple.[200]

Hughes was not much impressed with contemporary American poets other than Lowell and John Crowe Ransom. He had told Olwyn in summer 1958, "American poetry—there are hundreds of writers producing poems that look at first sight impressive, but this common brilliant style is at second reading a poor cheat—there is a glaze of impermeable plastic cleverness laid over a general nothing. So that, after a year at close quarters with it, I begin to see clearly that the good poets since Robert Lowell are mostly English, still."[201] He wrote Luke Myers in May 1959 that he found e. e. cummings the "chief Christ" of "that most brainless American romanticism" that was "verseless, styleless," full of "irreverence for poetic tradition."[202] Although he wrote Olwyn in 1959 that he found Lowell's style "utterly new,"[203] he told a critic in 1998 that he "despised" the confessional genre, and considered it "reprehensible, not truly creative." He felt that true experience ought to emerge "obliquely, through a symbol."[204] He was still firmly ensconced within a British tradition that found such a poetics slightly embarrassing, slightly uncouth—as Sylvia herself had been perceived during her first few months in Cambridge. Hughes, as he told Daniel Weissbort in 1959, felt that "AutoBiography is the only subject matter really left to Americans. The only thing an American <u>really</u> has to himself, & <u>really</u> belongs to, is his family. Never a locality, or a community, or an organization or ideas, or a private imagination."[205] Indeed, he would tell Daniel Huws in December 1959, "Another year in America would have worked a permanent petrification on my glands." Yet during his "exile" in America Hughes wrote what many critics consider to be his finest book: *Lupercal*.[206] He later admitted that the year had been good for Plath, too. In 1966 he would write Lowell, "without the combined operation of you and Anne Sexton Sylvia would never have written what she finally did."[207]

22

The Development of Personality

Boston, America, Yaddo, April–December 1959

Robert Lowell's seminar broke up in April. Ted described the last class, as relayed by Sylvia, in a letter to Olwyn:

Usually he is very quiet, shy, whispers (a real mad whisper) but this time he burst in, flung the tables into a new order, insulted everybody, talked incessantly. . . . He told them, elegiacally, that he hadn't been able to see any of them much outside class because he had to see his psychiatrist so often, as he had only just come out of McLean's (the mental hospital he came out of over a year ago). Then he went on, like a deathbed speech, how he had loved teaching them, that he never wanted any of them to publish a ragged line that he wouldn't be proud of, because he didn't want any one to say that he was an incompetent teacher—etc. He drove straight from the class, we heard afterwards, to McLean's—where he now is, under supervision. This was the day before his book came out. He gets quite homicidal.[1]

Hughes's writing was going unusually well. "I'm in a good year I think," he wrote Olwyn, "the pieces I've got lately have the right sort of fire—a couple of them more deeply & brilliantly colored than anything in my book." He'd written "Hawk Roosting" at Willow Street, and would publish "Thrushes," "The Bull Moses," and "Nicholas Ferrer" that summer. They would all go into *Lupercal*. D. H. Lawrence's influence was as strong as ever, but Hughes was also reading Lowell's new poems, as well as Crowe Ransom, Lorca, and Baudelaire. Lorca's essay on the "Duende" perfectly encapsulated his new poetic strategy, he told his sister that spring: "It's deeper than Dionysiac—it's the direct voice of the blood, & speaks only directly into the face of death."[2] Poems like "View of a Pig," "Hawk Roosting," and "Pike," which Hughes called "the most inspired poem I've ever written," had come easily to him.[3] ("I really believe Goethe's remark that no amount of thought can correct or improve a work of genius," he wrote Olwyn in August.)[4] They became some of Hughes's most famous poems.

On April 11, Hughes learned that he had won a $5,000 Guggenheim Award with T. S. Eliot's support. He and Sylvia were in bed when they heard the door buzzer, and exchanged a look of hope. He retreated to the bathroom while Sylvia took the envelope and "gasped out in her suppressed excitement, 'They've given you 5000 dollars.' . . . I went on pacing, but weeping with relief."[5] It was more money than they had expected; to calm himself, he went for a walk along the Charles River with George Gibian, Sylvia's old Smith professor, who had also won a Guggenheim.

Sylvia felt that they were finally receiving their due. *The New Yorker* accepted her "Watercolor of Grantchester Meadows" and "Man in Black," while a visit from photographer Rollie McKenna, who had also photographed Dylan Thomas and T. S. Eliot, confirmed a certain status. Plath's new collection, which she had retitled *The Devil of the Stairs* (after a line by T. S. Eliot), now comprised "40 unattackable poems," mainly recent work; she felt that her old Smith poems were "miserable death-wishes."[6] Only ten poems remained of the book that had been rejected by Auden for the Yale prize two years ago, and only thirteen remained unpublished. She still felt "blocked about prose" and thought of her poems as "an evasion," an excuse not to begin a children's book and finish her novel.[7] She sought inspiration in Philip Roth's *Goodbye, Columbus*, Virginia Woolf's *The Years*, and E. M. Forster's *A Passage to India*, which she found full of "miraculous flow and ease."[8] She wavered in her estimation of *The Years*. "The recreation is that of the most superficial observer at a party of dull old women who have never spilt blood." Woolf's "childless life" accounted for what Plath saw as her preference for "lighting effects" instead of "potatoes and sausage": "she shows no deeper current under the badinage."[9]

By early May she felt stronger, and finally wrote *The Bed Book* in one day, after contemplating its plot line for six months. The children's book was only eight pages long, but she felt an immense relief when she mailed it on May 3 to the Atlantic Press. (It was rejected, and remained unpublished until 1976.) "Suddenly it frees me—and Ted too." She could finally read *The New Yorker* without feeling "drowned or sick."[10] She mailed Hughes's children's book, *Meet My Folks!*, to Harper's and Faber and Faber in mid-May, and finished a story, "Sweetie Pie and the Gutter Men," which she had begun earlier in the month. (The story remained unpublished until 1977, when it was collected in *Johnny Panic and the Bible of Dreams*.)

"Sweetie Pie and the Gutter Men" recounts a brief afternoon reunion between two old college friends, Myra, who is childless and married to a sculptor, and Cicely, the wife of an obstetrician and mother of two. Although Myra is based on Sylvia herself, Cicely is a version of Aurelia, or what Sylvia might have become had she married Dick: "prudish" and "provincial." Her home is polished to perfection, conventionally decorated, and cold. Over lemonade in the backyard, the two discuss Cicely's husband's new obstetrical practice and Myra reveals that she saw a birth at a charity ward that left her shaken. ("They had to cut into her, I remember. There seemed to be a great deal of blood.") Cicely would rather not speak of such things, and instead disciplines her daughter, Alison, who imagines dramatic scenarios for her doll, Sweetie Pie: "She pokes people's eyes on the sidewalk. She pulls off their dresses. She gets diarrhoea in the *night*." Myra is drawn to the little girl, and out of Cicely's earshot she asks Alison what she does to her doll when she is "*very* bad." "I knock her down. I spank her and spank her. I bang her eyes in," Alison answers. "Good," Myra responds. "You keep on doing that." Myra finds the child's fantasies of violence refreshing after the stultifying atmosphere of Cicely's home, yet she is aware of her own "hurt" as she encourages the child to lash out. "She turned only once, and saw the child, small as a doll in the distance, still watching her. But her own hands hung listless and empty at her sides, like hands of wax, and she did not wave."

Myra's despondency stems from her awareness of women's limited choices: she does not want Cicely's stable, bourgeois life, yet she envies the spoils of suburban womanhood. Plath makes a subtle point here about how the sparks of female independence are snuffed out by a sexist culture that will not tolerate deviation from convention, and how women often dole out punishment because they are constantly punished themselves. Cicely punishes her naughty daughter, who then punishes her rebellious doll. Plath hints at the story's proto-feminism when Myra considers the anesthetic given to women in childbirth: "It was barbarous. It was a fraud dreamed up by men to continue the human race; reason enough for a woman to refuse childbearing altogether."[11] (A similar line would appear in *The Bell Jar*.)

Ambition was much on Sylvia's mind that spring. She planned to discuss it in her upcoming sessions with Dr. Beuscher: "driving Ambition; how to harness it, not be a Phaeton to its galloping horses."[12] Sylvia did not want to become Myra or Cicely; she wanted to serve her art above all else, "to keep in that state of itch which is comfortable: go as far enough ahead to be stimulating, near enough to be attainable with discipline and hard work."[13] She had begun to realize that she was "furious" with anyone who got "ahead" of her professionally, and worried that she would fall forever behind once she had children. She was also fighting with Ted that spring after he had pronounced her nonfiction "too general."[14] She refused to speak to him for a day and again vowed to show him no more of her work. (The unflattering portrait of Myra's husband, Timothy, may have been a result of this argument.) For solace, Sylvia turned to Perry Norton's wife, Shirley, her rag-rug-braiding partner, with whom she felt the "anger flow harmlessly away into the cords of bright colored soft wool."[15]

Between the early winter of 1958 and late May 1959, Plath wrote six stories: "Johnny Panic and the Bible of Dreams," "The Fifteen-Dollar Eagle," "The Shadow," "Sweetie Pie and the Gutter Men," "Above the Oxbow," and "This Earth Our Hospital" (retitled "The Daughters of Blossom Street"). The last three she wrote in May alone. When she took stock of her work in her journal, she felt her "panic bird" recede: "I weep with joy."[16] The routine of part-time work benefited her writing—as did Lowell's creative writing class. She felt that she had finally broken through her writer's block to produce good prose worthy of publication and prizes. "My poems are so far in the background now. It is a very healthy antidote, this prose, to the poems' intense limitations." She dreamed that two stories were published in *The New Yorker* and that Dr. Beuscher congratulated her as Aurelia turned away and muttered her indifference. "Which shows, I think, that RB has become my mother."[17]

Surveying her work, she pronounced "This Earth Our Hospital" her best story—an "amazing advance from 'Johnny Panic'" "Full of humor, highly colored characters, good, rhythmic conversation."[18] The piece overflows with the snappy dialogue Plath had always longed to write; narrated by a secretary in a psychiatric clinic of a hospital, it contained a conventional moral and took fewer aesthetic risks than the subversive and surreal "Johnny Panic." She sent it to *The Atlantic* on May 31, convinced that "It should be a Best American Short Story."[19] She loved the title so much she decided she would use it for a future book of her collected short stories. (She would wait a year to see it in print, in *The London Magazine*.)

A week later, however, she was brought low by the news that her poetry manuscript had again lost the Yale Younger Poets prize "by a whisper." The winner: George Starbuck, in her opinion "a rank travesty." Dudley Fitts, editor of the series, wrote that her manuscript had lacked "technical finish," and was too "rough."[20] (He did not tell her that Maxine Kumin's manuscript had come in second after Starbuck's.) Plath fumed at the absurdity of his criticism—she had tried hard to break out of the "machinelike syllabic death-blow" that she considered her poems' "main flaw." "Will I ever be

liked for anything other than the wrong reasons?" she despaired in her journal. "My book is as finished as it will ever be. . . . I have no champions. They
will find a lack of this, or that, or something or other. . . . How ironic, that all
my work to overcome my easy poeticisms merely convinces them that I am
rough, anti-poetic, unpoetic. My God."[21]

Fitts, she continued, was a "fool, who wouldn't know a syllabic verse if he
saw one," while Starbuck was a writer of "glib light verse with no stomach to
them."[22] Yet Fitts did Plath a favor—in June he sent her manuscript, along
with Maxine Kumin's, to Stanley Burnshaw, vice president at Henry Holt
Publishers. Fitts asked Burnshaw to consider both manuscripts for publication. Burnshaw sent these manuscripts, plus another from Lee Anderson—
who had recorded Plath in Springfield—to Robert Frost for his opinion.
Burnshaw told Frost that "the girl," Kumin, "might have got" the Yale prize,
and recommended that they offer contracts to Anderson and Kumin.[23] But
he had his doubts about Plath. "The more I think of her writing," he told
Frost, "the less excited I become in the prospect of adding her to the Holt
list. So she would be third on my list. I'm not even ready to recommend
that we publish her."[24] (Frost presumably agreed; Henry Holt Publishers
would reject her book later that fall.) Meanwhile, two days after the Yale
blow, Plath, with her usual stoicism, sent her manuscript to Knopf.

After reading two mental health stories in *Cosmopolitan* on June 13, she
vowed to write an asylum story along the lines of *The Snake Pit:* "I must write
one about a college girl suicide. THE DAY I DIED. . . . There is an increasing market for mental-hospital stuff. I am a fool if I don't relive it, recreate
it."[25] She thought of another title, "LAZARUS MY LOVE." Plath was still
working on her Cambridge novel, *Falcon Yard;* on her third wedding anniversary she decided to call her protagonist Sadie Peregrine—a name that
conjured up peregrinations, wanderings, sadism, and, of course, her own initials. Yet she felt she would not be able to complete a novel until she was sure
her short stories were "salable"; she told Ann Davidow she could not "cope"
with the rejection of a three-hundred-page manuscript after all the "time,
sweat and tears" it would require. "Nothing stinks like a pile of unpublished
writing, which remark I guess shows I still don't have pure motives (oh-it's-
such-fun-I-just-can't-stop-who-cares-if-it's-published-or-read) about writing. . . . I still want to see it finally ritualized in print." She did: "Night Shift"
was published in London's *Observer* on June 14—the first of many to appear
in that paper. Poems continued to come: "Slowly, slowly, I write poems and
they are about cadavers, suicides, Electra complexes, Ouija boards, hermits,
fat spinsters, thin spinsters, ghosts, old men of the sea, and, yes, fiddler crabs
and mammoth pigs." Her book, she told Ann, was "deeper, if more grim"
than Starbuck's, and she knew she should have won the Yale prize.[26] Mean-

while, Hughes sent the completed manuscript of *Lupercal* to Faber and Faber in mid-June.

In late June, a doctor told Sylvia she was not ovulating. The prospect of barrenness filled her with horror. She saw childless women as cursed, symbolic of the empty life she so feared, and she treated them cruelly in her poems. To think of herself among their ranks was a prospect that made her want to die. "My god. This is the one thing in the world I can't face. It is worse than a horrible disease," she wrote in her journal. She thought of herself as "part of the world's ash. . . . I want to be an Earth Mother in the deepest richest sense." She feared Ted would want to leave her. Barrenness was even connected to *Lupercal*, whose title described a Roman fertility ceremony. "All joy and hope is gone."[27] Sylvia assumed that she would now have to undergo a regimen of injections and hormones, a "horrible clinical cycle" of "becoming synthetic."[28] However, the prognosis soon proved misleading; after having her tubes flushed (a common gynecological procedure to increase fertility), she became pregnant in early July.

The couple had decided to spend some of Hughes's Guggenheim money on an eight-week cross-country trip that summer before they hunkered down at Yaddo, the prestigious artist's colony, in September. They planned a route to Pasadena, California, where they would visit Sylvia's paternal aunt, Frieda Plath Heinrichs, and her husband, Walter.[29] Before they left, Sylvia and Ted camped in the backyard at Elmwood Road in their new tent, which was large enough for four people and tall enough for Ted to stand in. This was the night, Hughes later suggested in a poem, of their daughter's conception.[30] Aurelia bought them an air mattress and two light, comfortable sleeping bags, and lent them her 1953 gray Chevy sedan—a considerable sacrifice for eight weeks. Throughout the trip, Aurelia kept them informed of their literary acceptances and rejections.

The couple left Boston on Tuesday, July 7, and spent the night at Whetstone Gulf State Park in upstate New York; the next day they drove into Canada, where they pitched their camp on the edge of Rock Lake in Algonquin Park, Ontario. They caught perch and picked blueberries. (Sylvia caught more, and bigger, fish than Ted throughout the trip.) Plath would later write in "Two Campers in Cloud Country" (July 1960) that she had wanted to get away from the Public Garden, "the labeled elms, the tame tea-roses," and "The polite skies over Boston." Yet the poem's speaker suggests that the "big, brash" landscape is disturbing, too, with "neither measure nor balance." In Canada, the "colors assert themselves with a sort of vengeance":

These rocks offer no purchase to herbage or people:

They are conceiving a dynasty of perfect cold.
In a month we'll wonder what plates and forks are for.
I lean to you, numb as a fossil. Tell me I'm here.

Just as her old landscape poems conveyed a hidden, often painful, emotional truth, so too does "Two Campers in Cloud Country." Plath's talk of frozen conception links the poem to her anxieties about her potential barrenness. Nearly two years after "Two Campers," she would write another ambiguous poem about Rock Lake, "Crossing the Water" (April 1962), in which both the water and the poem reflect the thoughts of barrenness and the dark impulses that were tormenting her. In a characteristically cheerful postcard to Aurelia, she wrote that she and Hughes had been the only ones rowing on the "huge lake" at night "under the stars & new moon on mirror-clear water."[31] But Plath's poem presents a different version of the experience: "Black lake, black boat, two black, cut-paper people" rowing to nowhere. "Cold worlds shake from the oar. / The spirit of blackness is in us, it is in the fishes."

They left Rock Lake on July 11, alternating time at the wheel. Sylvia reported to Aurelia on "the unbelievable stretches of country, unpeopled, green, with lakes and rivers everywhere," but was equally "amazed at the terrible shoddiness of Canadian towns," which mainly consisted of gas stations, tar-paper shacks, and aluminum trailers.[32] Four hundred miles later, they arrived at Brimley Park in Michigan. After a sponge bath, Sylvia faced her typewriter toward Lake Superior and wrote Aurelia about the many "tests" she had "passed."[33] For two people who had no camping experience, they were getting along very well—the equipment made cooking and washing simple and she had no trouble making pancakes and bacon for breakfast.

On July 14, on their way to Wisconsin, they saw their first bear, which, Sylvia told Aurelia, "made our day." She said they had "fallen in love with Wisconsin—it is so uncommercialized—unlike Michigan—all bluegreen woods & lovely farms."[34] There, they visited Northwestern College, where Otto had been a student, and camped for two nights on the Nozal family's hilltop in Cornucopia, with its view of Lake Superior through the birch trees.[35] A phone call to Aurelia yielded good news—*The London Magazine* had accepted Plath's "In Midas' Country" and "The Thin People" while *The Times Literary Supplement* had taken "The Hermit at Outermost House" and "Two Views of a Cadaver Room." She was proud of her first acceptance by the *TLS*.

Next came the Badlands of North Dakota, the state Sylvia's paternal grandparents had once called home. She described the eerie landscape to Aurelia as a "beautiful spot" that "literally lept [*sic*] at us out of the prairies." They camped in a grove of cottonwoods that offered a view of the Missouri River and the rocky, striated hills. Yet Hughes described this setting in Dantean terms in his poem "The Badlands": "A landscape / Staked out in the sun and left to die." Plath, he claimed, was "overwhelmed / By the misery of the place, like a nausea. . . . 'This is evil,' / You said. 'This is real evil.' "[36] She could not settle into the landscape, so far from the ocean.

Montana proved more welcoming. They camped on the grounds of a Congregational church and feasted on steak and flaky boysenberry pie. Sylvia described the landscape to her mother as "yellow wheat & black earth fields stretching in alternate ebony & gold bands to the purple mesas on the horizon."[37] At Yellowstone, they dined on trout they caught themselves and marveled at the geysers. But a bear smashed their rear car window one night at three a.m. and ransacked their food supply. The couple waited nervously in their tent until dawn, when a park ranger ran the bear off. They moved to another campsite, smeared their car windows with kerosene, and took a tranquilizer each (Sylvia had been "saving" them for the Donner Pass).[38] She gave Aurelia and Warren a detailed account of the incident, which she drew on in "The Fifty-Ninth Bear," a story she wrote that fall at Yaddo. She would add one important detail to her fiction: the bear kills the husband. In his *Birthday Letters* poem "The 59th Bear," Hughes wrote that he had not understood "what need later / Transformed our dud scenario into a fiction," and attributed the ending to Plath's need to exorcise her own death wish.[39] The couple camped at Yellowstone for five days, and eventually saw a total of sixty-seven bears during their trip.

The drive across America unsettled both of them. Sylvia's worries about infertility, plus the actual symptoms of a first-trimester pregnancy—nausea, exhaustion, and mood swings—had increased what Ted called her "worsening nerves."[40] He was disturbed by the vast, impenetrable rock formations at places like Karlsbad and the Badlands. Yet he wrote Aurelia, "This is the greatest experience I ever had. America doesn't really start before about Wisconsin—from there on it's true Paradise."[41] Sylvia gives no hint of marital tension in her letters home, but her poems and story from this time suggest that traveling had become increasingly stressful. The couple often camped for free on church grounds, behind gas stations, on beaches, and in farmers' fields without access to bathrooms. Sylvia did laundry in lakes. Though she was an experienced Girl Scout, "roughing it" while pregnant—and in heat that sometimes topped 100°—was exhausting.

In Utah they swam in the Great Salt Lake and heard an organ concert at the Mormon Tabernacle before camping "among Sagebrush & grazing bulls."[42] Plath learned in Utah that Knopf had rejected her poetry manuscript, and she instructed her mother, via postcard on July 25, to mail it immediately to Harcourt, Brace. Publishing her manuscript was now more important than ever, as she worried she could not have a baby. Aurelia encouraged her to tinker with some of her poems before sending the manuscript out again, but Sylvia dug in. "PLEASE don't worry about my poetry book but send it off. . . . I also have gone over it very carefully and am not going to try to change it to fit some vague abstract criticism. If an editor wants to accept it and make a few changes then, all right. You need to develop a little of our callousness and brazenness to be a proper sender-out of mss."[43] They drove on to Nevada, Sylvia's "least favorite state," and passed through Reno, the site of Otto's divorce and her parents' marriage, without stopping. Sylvia told her mother she thought it an "awfully ugly place."[44]

After a stop in Lake Tahoe, they camped on the beach near San Francisco. They drove over the Golden Gate Bridge, called Aurelia from Drake's Bay, and learned that Faber and Faber had accepted *Lupercal*. Hughes was staring out over the Pacific when he received the news, which he thought fitting.[45] They drove down the coast through Big Sur and Los Angeles to Pasadena, where Aunt Frieda welcomed the weary couple with a feast. Aurelia had secretly sent Frieda money to entertain the couple after Frieda had written to her of their "limitations."[46] (Frieda thanked Aurelia profusely and, abashed, admitted that she felt like a "cheat" for keeping Aurelia's "indulgence" to herself.)[47] Sylvia loved Frieda's "little green eden of a house," which was "surrounded by pink and red and white oleander bushes" and avocado, persimmon, fig, and peach trees. She marveled at her aunt's resemblance to her father—"the same clear piercing intelligent bright eyes and face shape."[48] Sylvia felt a connection with her "young-spirited" aunt in the short time she was in Pasadena.[49] Frieda, too, was extremely moved by her brief meeting with her brother's child. She sensed that there were deeper things Sylvia wanted to discuss with her, yet those things were "somehow lost in the scramble."[50] After two nights in a "luxurious" Pasadena hotel, the couple headed south again. Sylvia told Aurelia she wept when saying goodbye to Frieda and remarked again that she "looks like a feminine version of Daddy."[51]

Private showers soon became a distant memory as Sylvia and Ted began pitching their tent again. Near Needles, California, they "sweltered among hordes of huge rubber-eating crickets" who ate holes in their mattress and sleeping bag.[52] The heat during the day could reach 115°. It all became too much for Sylvia; after their tent nearly blew away in a sweltering wind and thunderstorm, they began staying "on occasion" at $5 motels.[53] She would capture the desert's disquieting surrealism in July 1960's "Sleep in the Mojave Desert":

> The desert is white as a blind man's eye,
> Comfortless as salt. Snake and bird
> Doze behind the old masks of fury.
> We swelter like firedogs in the wind.

They continued on to the Grand Canyon, Tucson, El Paso, and Juarez, Mexico, and Sylvia stopped writing detailed letters. She and Ted had been on the road for nearly six weeks. In the French Quarter in New Orleans, Ted sent Warren and Aurelia a poem that made light of their exhaustion:

> As we crawled over Nevada's oven top
> Honky tonks & mirages drank our drop;
> God knows California was one itch
> Of sunburn lotion, bugs and the lousily rich.
> Burned black, bled white, we fled fast into Texas,
> There dust & dullness came near to annex us . . .[54]

Years later, he recalled their true weariness in a *Birthday Letters* poem, "Grand Canyon":

> We were numbed by the shock-waves
> Coming off the sky-vistas at us—
> The thunder-beings that swept against us and through us
> Out of the road's jackrabbits and the beer-can constellations
> We drove into after dark.[55]

They rested for a week in Sewanee, Tennessee, where they stayed with Luke Myers's mother in her mansion, Bairnwick, and met the editor of *The Sewanee Review*, Monroe Spears, at a party. The connection was an important one, as Spears had published Plath's "Point Shirley" and "The Departure of the Ghost" in their current issue, and would accept her short story "The Fifteen-Dollar Eagle" in late August. They headed back to Massachusetts through Washington, D.C., and Philadelphia, where they stayed with Sylvia's uncle Frank. When Sylvia and Ted finally arrived in Wellesley on August 28, Aurelia "sensed a great weariness" in her daughter, who had begun to hope she was pregnant.[56]

ON SEPTEMBER 9, Plath and Hughes arrived at Yaddo, America's preeminent artists' colony, set on four hundred pine-filled acres in Saratoga Springs, New York. Since the colony's founding in 1900, a stint at Yaddo had become a rite of passage for American artists, many of whom had gone on to win Pulitzer and MacArthur prizes. Sylvia and Ted would stay until November 19. "They were very fond of each other, very quiet, kept much to themselves. Pleasant, hard working and appreciative of the kind of life Yaddo offered them," the poet Pauline Hanson, Yaddo's resident secretary, remembered.[57]

Yaddo's director, Elizabeth Ames, had heard about Plath from Alfred Kazin, who had written to her in 1955, "The best writer at Smith, and a very remarkable girl in every way, is Sylvia Plath, she is the real thing."[58] Four years later, Sylvia and Ted moved into a large first-floor bedroom, Room 1, at West House, the wood-and-stucco guest house just a short walk from the main mansion. Its grandeur impressed Sylvia: "The libraries and living rooms and music rooms are like those in a castle, all old plush, curios, leather bindings, oil paintings on the walls, dark woodwork, carvings on all the furniture. Very quiet and sumptuous."[59] Each day after breakfast, the couple parted: Sylvia to her sunny third-floor studio, Room 8, in West House; Ted to his small, one-room cottage, "Outlook," in the woods. From nine to four, Sylvia sat at her "huge heavy dark-wooded table," typing on her new Swiss-made light green Hermes 3000 typewriter, before four east-facing windows overlooking the "tall dense green pines."[60] The acres of Norway spruce, balsam firs, and white pine suggested the Black Forest more than the Adirondack woods. Former resident Hortense Calisher thought the towering pines looked like something out of a German opera.[61]

Sylvia read in the Yaddo authors' library and took breakfast and dinner communally in the mansion's baronial dining room, with its "diamond-paned windows overlooking green gardens and marble statuary, golden, deep rugs and antique velvet cushions, heavily gilt-framed paintings, statues everywhere."[62] The meals were rich; she had not eaten so well since the Sassoon days. "Honey oozing out of the comb, steaming coffee on the hot-plate," she wrote in her journal, "sweetbreads, sausages, bacon and mushrooms; ham and mealy orange sweet potatoes; chicken and garden beans."[63] Elizabeth Ames was the grande dame of Yaddo at the time, and she required guests to dress formally for dinner. The erudite and witty conversationalists who gathered after cocktails around the long dining table intimidated the painter Howard Rogovin, the youngest guest that season. "I don't think I can do this," he confessed to the English writer Martin Green, who sat next to him on his first night. He thought he might have to leave Yaddo. Green told him not to worry, and to follow his lead. "This was nothing," Green told him, compared to High Table at Cambridge.[64]

Sylvia and Ted, both Cantabrigians, were more comfortable in the gilded surroundings. Yet Howard recalled that Ted wanted him to know that he was very much a Yorkshireman. On one of their daily walks through the woods, Ted told him that as a member of the British working class, he would never have ended up at Cambridge if not for a government Education Act that broadened school access. Sylvia felt no such compulsion to discuss her own scholarship years and basked in the "great countryhouse, a fine library, fine grounds, fine cooking," as she wrote Ted's parents.[65] Memories of Yaddo may have influenced the couple's decision to later purchase their own "great countryhouse," Court Green, in Devon.

Yaddo's monasticism allowed Plath to focus on her art. "The only sound is the birds, and, at night, the distant dreamlike calling of the announcer at the Saratoga racetrack," she wrote home. "I have never in my life felt so peaceful and as if I can read and think and write for about 7 hours a day."[66] Hughes, too, relished the solitude as he worked on his play "The House of Taurus," a modern version of Euripides' *The Bacchae*. A five-minute walk separated the couple during their working hours, but it was enough to make Sylvia feel a new independence. "I am so happy we can work apart, for that is what we've really needed," she admitted to Aurelia and Warren.[67]

There were only twelve other artists at Yaddo that fall, and the grounds were quiet.[68] Sylvia and Ted walked the winding, wooded trails through the estate, and lingered in the European-inspired rose garden. Each morning Ted woke early to go fishing; he caught bass in the small lake but threw them back since the estate's food was so fine. Sylvia was still trying to learn German, "painstakingly" studying the language for two hours a day.[69] The outside world intruded only by mail—rejections and acceptances, and letters from Aurelia full of anxiety about her heavy teaching load.

Sylvia, Ted, and Howard formed a trio. They did not socialize much with the poet May Swenson, who arrived in November, and the other two West House guests. Swenson met Plath only once, when she was curled up in bed recovering from a sinus cold. "Books and notepads, papers, pens, magazines" were strewn across the blankets, along with apples and grapes. Swenson was struck by how "well paired" the tall, attractive couple was, and how Plath "sounded very British." "A handshake and the flash of smile, then Sylvia's head drooped, her blue eyes lidded, and she looked down into her lap."[70]

Howard became especially close to Ted. They went fishing together on Yaddo's lakes, and walked down to the Saratoga racetrack to watch the horses. (Once, when a horse had to be put down, Ted stayed to watch the whole drama, telling Howard he was going to write a poem about it.) Ted was always "congenial, friendly, very open, very smart." He did not often talk about poetry, but he mentioned his admiration for Robert Lowell, Theodore

Roethke, and his friend Leonard Baskin. Howard found Sylvia much quieter, and less relaxed. She never joined them for walks, although she was invited. Howard, who stayed on the second floor at West House, heard Sylvia's typewriter going all day long above him. She dressed smartly, "like a Smith girl," he remembered, in sweaters and wool skirts. He found her calm, serious, and beautiful. He was attracted to her, but her demeanor warned him off. She never spoke to him of anything personal.[71]

In the evenings, the three retreated to West House's ornate sitting room, a luxurious retreat with a grand fireplace, immense Persian rug, stained-glass windows, art deco lamps, and grand portraits. There, they sometimes listened to music with the composer Gordon Binkerd. One evening, Howard remembered, Sylvia read her poem about a Brueghel painting, "Two Views of a Cadaver Room," which she had written the previous summer, out loud to them. Ted sometimes drew up astrology charts of great writers and Yaddo guests. (He saw something he didn't like in Howard's chart and never finished it.) But the three of them—and sometimes Pauline Hanson, Yaddo's secretary—spent most of their time sitting at the Ouija board. Ted was the ringleader; Sylvia seemed less excited but went along. Howard was sure that Ted cheated—his answers were too interesting.[72]

Ted convinced Howard to paint portraits of himself and Sylvia.[73] She was reluctant, but Ted finally persuaded her. She sat for three or four sessions of about forty minutes each, dressed conservatively in a sweater and wool skirt. Ted recited poems and read D. H. Lawrence aloud while Howard painted in the style of contemporary German painters Max Beckmann, Lovis Corinth, and Ernst Kirchner. At one point Sylvia became frustrated. "I don't know what we're doing here," she said. "Why *do* it?"[74] Howard joked that one of them might become famous. Plath was a talented visual artist and had painted self-portraits. But she did not like ceding control of her image and instinctively recoiled before the male gaze. Hughes later wrote the poem "Portraits" about the sessions, published in *Birthday Letters*. According to Howard, Ted added several ominous details, like the dark human figure in the painting's background, which he interpreted as Sylvia's "demon." "He thought I sensed her instability, but I was just swirling some paint around," Howard said. Nor did Howard remember the appearance of a snake, which Hughes turned into a dark symbol in his poem. "There was no snake. That's Ted."[75]

Sylvia told Aurelia that Yaddo was heaven, but her journal records a different truth. She was still experiencing pregnancy-related nausea and mood swings, as well as depression and anxiety; in late September, she had a long, heart-shuddering panic attack that lasted on and off for two days. She diagnosed "the old fall disease."[76]

Plath wrote "The Fifty-Ninth Bear" during her first week at Yaddo but felt only "disgust" for the "stiff artificial piece."[77] (It would be published in *The London Magazine* in 1961.) She spent hours in the library reading *The Sewanee Review*, the *Kenyon Review*, *The Paris Review*, *The Nation*, *Art News*, and *The New Republic*. She made a point to read female writers such as May Swenson (whose birdwatching before breakfast made her feel lazy), Katherine Anne Porter, Jean Stafford (Robert Lowell's first wife), Iris Murdoch, and Eudora Welty, as well as Lowell, Roethke, Freud, Jung, and Paul Radin.[78] She finally sat down with Elizabeth Bishop's poetry, and was impressed by her "fine originality, always surprising, never rigid, flowing, juicier than Marianne Moore."[79] All of it made her wonder when she herself would "break into a new line of poetry" that was not "trite."[80] In her journal she vowed to begin writing in the first person—to "forget" John Updike and Nadine Gordimer.[81] While brainstorming on September 26, she wrote, "A mad story: college would-be suicide. A Double story: involvement with roommate."[82] It was the fourth time she had written about such a plot. All of these elements—the first-person narrative, doubles, and suicide—found their way into *The Bell Jar*.

In her journal, she remonstrated with herself for her inability to get outside her own subjectivity: "Always myself, myself," as she put it.[83] She sent stories to *The Atlantic* knowing that Peter Davison would reject them (he did, as well as Hughes's "The Courting of Petty Quinnett," that October). If only she could write "meaningful prose, that expressed my feelings, I would be free."[84] Even "Johnny Panic and the Bible of Dreams" was just a fantasy; she wished she could have made it "real."[85] Nearly all of the other poems she published that summer and fall appeared in the middlebrow *Christian Science Monitor*.

Her creative anxiety finally subsided on September 30 after she began a story titled "The Mummy," a "mother story," since lost, that she called "a simple account of symbolic and horrid fantasies."[86] She finished it on October 4 and was amazed at how her language dovetailed with passages she had read in Jung's *The Development of Personality*, which she found in the Yaddo library.[87] Jung's book included case histories of mother-daughter relationships, and Plath was struck by how her "instinctive images" related to Jung's "psychological analysis": "The word 'chessboard' used in an identical situation: of a supposedly loving but ambitious mother who manipulated the child on the 'chessboard of her egotism': I had used 'chessboard of her desire.'"[88]

Plath read Jung's book, full of mother blame, at a crucial point in her poetic development. She was already attuned to Jung through Hughes and Dr. Beuscher, who considered herself a Jungian analyst. Now it was as if Jung had read her mind: "Mother," he wrote, "projected all her phobias onto the child and surrounded her with so much anxious care that she was never free from tension."[89] Neuroses in children were "more symptoms of the mental condition of the parents than a genuine illness of the child." Children "suffer from the unlived life of their parents" and the parents' "repressed problems . . . secrete an insidious poison which seeps into the soul of the child through the thickest walls of silence."[90] And so on. Plath took several pages of notes on the "insidious" influence of mothers in the chapter titled "The Development of Personality," including the following passage:

> parents set themselves the fanatical task of always "doing their best" for the children and "living only for them." This clamant ideal effectively prevents the parents from doing anything about their own development & allows them to thrust their "best" down their children's throats. This so-called "best" turns out to be the very things the parents have most badly neglected in themselves.

Under this quotation, Plath quoted more of Jung's words: "There is no human horror or fairground freak that has not lain in the womb of a loving mother."[91]

Jung gave Plath permission, as Dr. Beuscher had, to blame her mother for her mental maladies. This was entirely in keeping with the psychiatric biases of the day. Jung's book made Plath feel, she said, like a "victim." "My 'fiction' is only a naked recreation of what I felt, as a child and later, must be true," she wrote in her journal.[92] Such permission seemed to release something in Plath, who was herself on the brink of becoming a mother and alarmed by Jung's statement that "neurotic states are often passed on from generation to generation."[93] She dreamed that her own mother was "furious with my pregnancy, mockingly bringing out a huge wraparound skirt to illustrate my grossness."[94]

The Development of Personality also contained a lengthy disquisition on "fidelity to the law of one's own being" and standing apart from "the herd."[95] Those who achieved "greatness," Jung wrote, have "never lain in their abject submission *to* convention, but, on the contrary, in their deliverance *from* convention." Developing one's personality was lonely, isolating work, Jung wrote, especially if one had a vocation: "He must obey his own law, as if it were a daemon whispering to him of new and wonderful paths."[96] Jung's ideas resonated with Plath, who had refused a comfortable life as the wife of Dick Norton or Gordon Lameyer, against her mother's wishes and her culture's expectations. It was a moral imperative, Jung wrote, to honor the "Promethean" and "Luciferian" aspects of her own personality. His ideas dovetailed with those of Lowell, Sexton, and Hughes, who all sought to break with convention in their work and their lives. These influences coalesced at Yaddo, where Plath, uninterrupted—finally—with a room of her own, found courage in "walking naked," as Yeats once wrote. Soon she began to confront, rather than sidestep, her psychic pain in her poems.

Several were published that fall: among them "I Want, I Want" in the *Partisan Review*; "On the Decline of Oracles," "The Death of Myth-Making," and "A Lesson in Vengeance" in *Poetry*; "Yaddo: The Grand Manor" in *The Christian Science Monitor*; and "Two Views of a Cadaver Room" and "The Hermit at Outermost House" in *The Times Literary Supplement*. But she had not published a story since the summer of 1957, when "All the Dead Dears" appeared in *Gemini*, more or less a student publication. The only stories Plath could bear to reread now were "Johnny Panic and the Bible of Dreams," "The Wishing Box," "The Mummy," and "The Tattooist" (later retitled "The Fifteen-Dollar Eagle"). All the others, she wrote in her journal, were "duller than tears," even "The Daughters of Blossom Street," which she had thought her best story just a few weeks before.[97] She was still reading Ted's stories, typing up some of his manuscripts, and sending both their work to magazines. Her husband seemed completely free of "the phantom of competition" that plagued her, and she vowed to "forget salable stories," like him. She would write about moods and incidents, like her search for Sassoon in Paris and her fever in Benidorm. She echoed Hughes when she wrote in her journal of her desire "Not to manipulate the experience but to let it unfold and re-create itself with all the tenuous, peculiar associations the logical mind would short-circuit."[98]

October was largely a month of rejections. Sylvia wept when Henry Holt turned down her poetry manuscript, but she sent it to Viking the next day, and then to Farrar, Straus on October 30. Ted offered her some radical advice: "start a new book."[99] She was determined to do so, but the rejection sent her back into a black state. Even *The New Yorker* acceptance of "A Winter's Tale" on October 7 (it was published on December 12) could not rouse her. Knopf rejected her children's book *The It-Doesn't-Matter Suit*, about a group of Germanic brothers loosely based on her father's family. She seemed to hit a new low in mid-October:

> Very depressed today. Unable to write a thing. Menacing gods. I feel outcast on a cold star, unable to feel anything but an awful helpless numbness. I look down into the warm, earthy world. Into a nest of lovers' beds, baby cribs, meal tables, all the solid commerce of life in this earth, and feel apart, enclosed in a wall of glass. Caught between the hope and promise of my work—the one or two stories that seem to catch something, the one or two poems that build little colored islands of words—

and the hopeless gap between that promise, and the real world of other peoples [*sic*] poems and stories and novels. My shaping spirit of imagination is far from me.[100]

Harcourt's rejection of *The Bed Book* on October 19 made her even more determined to abandon her old manuscript. "Ted says: You are so negative. Gets cross, desperate. I am my own master. I am a fool to be jealous of phantoms." But she could not shake her anxiety. She had forgotten all her Joyce and Plato; she needed to master German; she ought to get a PhD. Ted alone was her "salvation." "He is so rare, so special, how could anyone else stand me!" she wrote in her journal. He seemed immune from the "vision of success" she held out for herself, "As if the old god of love I hunted by winning prizes in childhood had grown more mammoth and unsatiable still." She told herself to "Keep away from editors and writers" and write for satisfaction alone. "Take a lesson from Ted," still "the ideal, the one possible person."[101]

Ted practiced deep-breathing and stream-of-consciousness "concentration" exercises with Sylvia in mid-October, and she was able to write two poems that "pleased" her: "The Manor Garden," about her unborn child (whom she called Nicholas during her pregnancy), and "The Colossus," on "the old father-worship subject."[102] These, along with "Medallion," about a dead snake, would comprise the beginning of her new book.[103]

In "The Manor Garden," Plath took a new approach to inheritance and birth, what she called the "Fable of children changing existence and character as absurd as the fable of marriage doing it. Here I am, the same old sourdough."[104] Despite her professed enthusiasm for babies and beef stew, she feared the vortex of motherhood: "Must never become a mere mother and housewife," she wrote in her journal. Now that Sylvia was actually pregnant, she admitted that she was scared of the "Challenge of baby" coming when she still had not fulfilled her literary potential. "I will hate a child that substitutes itself for my own purpose," she wrote.[105] Dr. Beuscher had warned her that she would most likely suffer from postpartum depression after her first baby if she "didn't get rid of it [her depression] now."[106] She tried to focus on the pleasures, rather than the unknowns, of motherhood, but she could not help but envy the "Independent and self-possessed" May Swenson: "My old admiration for the strong, if Lesbian, woman. The relief of limitation as a price for balance and surety."[107]

"The Manor Garden" is a dark twist on Yeats's beneficent "A Prayer for My Daughter." Plath hopes to bestow a blessing, but she cannot deny the forces that threaten her baby. The poem is modern, existential, and bereft, a Cold War pietà that borrows from Eliot's "The Journey of the Magi." It begins grimly: "The fountains are dry and the roses over. / Incense of death."

Plath sees trouble ahead: "You inherit white heather, a bee's wing, // Two suicides, the family wolves, / Hours of blankness." Though the poem is set in Yaddo's garden, it anticipates the lifeless garden of her late poem "Edge," inhabited by "blue mist" "dragging the lake," crows, worms, and "broken flutings." "The Manor Garden" reflects Plath's depressed state of mind and the fear of motherhood that surfaced in her nightmares of dead and deformed babies—intensified by Jung's descriptions of monster children growing in the wombs of loving mothers.

"The Colossus," too, subverts traditional expectations. It is an angry yet tender paternal elegy—a freer, less reverent revision of her earlier "Electra on Azalea Path." The surrealist poem envisions a daughter-caretaker who tends to her father's immense statue on a deserted island. Plath incorporates elements of *The Tempest*, *Robinson Crusoe*, and *Gulliver's Travels* ("Scaling little ladders with gluepots and pails of Lysol / I crawl like an ant in mourning / Over the weedy acres of your brow") to create a proto-feminist elegy. This was the poem that the poetry critic Helen Vendler—who had joined Plath for stroller walks as an infant—would later declare Plath's first real poetic triumph.[108] Plath jettisons decorum with a vengeance:

> I shall never get you put together entirely,
> Pieced, glued, and properly jointed.
> Mule-bray, pig-grunt and bawdy cackles
> Proceed from your great lips.
> It's worse than a barnyard.
>
> Perhaps you consider yourself an oracle,
> Mouthpiece of the dead, or of some god or other.
> Thirty years now I have labored
> To dredge the silt from your throat.
> I am none the wiser.

"The Colossus" is a metaphorical rejection of all Fathers and their monumental authority. Plath mocks patriarchal tradition, which she cannot or will not master: the father's language sounds like a series of grunts. She has traded elaborate, "glossy" lines for plainer diction, and dispensed with the self-blame of her earlier elegy for Otto ("It was my love that did us both to death"). Yet at the end of the poem, the daughter refuses to abandon the father's stony legacy. "No longer do I listen for the scrape of a keel / On the blank stones of the landing." The lines suggest the loneliness of her mourning and, at the same time, the plight of the female poet who clings to the approval, and language, of her literary fathers. Jung had warned that such dutiful daughters would leave no legacy of their own. "The Colossus" and "The Manor Garden" offer neither comfort nor blessing to dead father and unborn child. They are the antithesis of the sentimental feminine homily. Finally, Plath was fulfilling her Jungian destiny, as she wrote in her journal at Yaddo that November, "To be true to my own weirdnesses."[109] These subversive, ironic poems helped free Plath to confront the taboo of her breakdown and suicide.

Sylvia enjoyed sketching the Yaddo greenhouse, a short walk down the hill from her studio.[110] On October 22, she mulled over an idea during a walk with Ted: "dwelling on madhouse, nature: meanings of tools, greenhouses, florist shops, tunnels, vivid and disjointed. An adventure. Never over. Developing. Rebirth. Despair."[111] The next day they brainstormed on a single piece of paper. Several themes that found their way into Plath's "Poem for a Birthday" sequence appear in Hughes's handwriting: "Witch-burning," "Change of vision of a maenad, as she goes under the fury," "The stones of the city," "Person walking through enormous dark house," and "Flute notes from a reedy pond." Plath noted the ideas she liked in a small square in the right-hand corner: "Maenad," "The Beast," "Flute notes from reedy pond," "stones of city—the city where men are mended MOULTS," "witch burning."[112] These would all become titles in the seven sequences that Plath called "a series of madhouse poems."[113]

On October 23, Plath wrote that the poetic exercise she had tried the day before, which had begun in "grimness," had turned "into a fine, new thing."[114] Between October 22 and November 3, she used the Yaddo greenhouse and tool shed to conjure the mental hospital in spare, arresting language:

> This shed's fusty as a mummy's stomach:
> Old tools, handles and rusty tusks.
> I am at home here among the dead heads.
>
> Let me sit in a flowerpot,
> The spiders won't notice.
> My heart is a stopped geranium.

Several memorable lines from "Poem for a Birthday" would resurface, in slightly different guises, in her *Ariel* poems: "These halls are full of women who think they are birds"; "Now they light me up like an electric bulb. / For weeks I can remember nothing at all"; "My ankles brighten. Brightness ascends my thighs. / I am lost, I am lost, in the robes of all this light." In the sequence's final, strongest section, "The Stones"—written in a form that gestures to Dantean terza rima—Plath faces her experience less obliquely. Using the same Swiftian, surrealist imagery she had discovered while writing "The Colossus" only a few days before, she describes the mental hospital as factory and assembly line: "This is the city where men are mended. / I lie on a great anvil."

> A workman walks by carrying a pink torso.
> The storerooms are full of hearts.
> This is the city of spare parts.
>
> My swaddled legs and arms smell sweet as rubber.
> Here they can doctor heads, or any limb.
> On Fridays the little children come
>
> To trade their hooks for hands.
> Dead men leave eyes for others.
> Love is the uniform of my bald nurse.
>
> Love is the bone and sinew of my curse.
> The vase, reconstructed, houses
> The elusive rose.
>
> Ten fingers shape a bowl for shadows.
> My mendings itch. There is nothing to do.
> I shall be as good as new.

As in the end of *The Bell Jar*, the final declaration of recovery is ironic and ambiguous: we are not at all sure the speaker is cured. Indeed, the surrealist fantasy and the explicit "weirdness" of the sequence suggest that perhaps she is not.[115] In June 1961, Plath discussed "The Stones" on the BBC: the speaker, she said,

> has utterly lost her sense of identity and relationship to the world. She imagines herself, quite graphically, undergoing the process of rebirth, like a statue that has been scattered and ground down, only to be resurrected and pieced together, centuries later. Her nightmare vision of waking in a modern hospital gradually softens as she recovers and accepts the frightening yet necessary ties of love which will heal and return her whole again to the world.[116]

"Poem for a Birthday," "The Manor Garden," and "The Colossus" show that children, fathers, and doctors are not to be idolized in Plath's new poetic universe. They are harbingers of anxiety, infantilizing and fallible. These revolutionary new poems were a personal *cri de coeur* along the lines of Lowell and Sexton, but buttressed—as Hughes later noted—by surrealism, history, and myth.

Ted wrote to Olwyn from Yaddo, "Sylvia has suddenly begun to write in a completely new style—obviously her own at last."[117] The irony is that the style was borrowed from Theodore Roethke's "The Lost Son." Hughes later wrote that "the sequence began as a deliberate Roethke pastiche," yet Plath knew this new note was also hers.[118] "The absence of a tightly reasoned and rhythmed logic bothers me. Yet frees me," she wrote in her journal.[119] Though Sylvia would later complain that Yaddo was too monastic—a "nunnery"—this was the first time in her life she was completely free of both academic and domestic obligations. Even during her previous stretches of uninterrupted writing time in Benidorm, Boston, and Cape Cod, she had been responsible for the cooking, shopping, cleaning, dishes, laundry, ironing, mending, typing, bookkeeping, and the myriad other tasks that fell to women in the 1950s. At Yaddo, she was able to separate from Hughes, literally and figuratively. Her new pregnancy, her freedom from domestic chores, and her private studio helped her inhabit a less circumscribed psychological space that enabled her to make daring creative leaps. After Plath's death, Hughes would write that in "The Stones" he heard, for the first time, the "real" or "reborn" voice of her deep self.[120] He later remembered, "Bowed over your desk at Yaddo / Moored in some psychic umbilicus / Writing your Poem for a Birthday. / You thought it was your birthday, / Your rebirth. You wanted to be reborn."[121]

As if confirming her new aesthetic direction, James Michie, a young half-Scottish, half-American editor at the British publisher Heinemann, contacted Plath that October expressing admiration for the poems she had recently published in *The London Magazine* ("In Midas' Country" and "The Thin People"), where he was a member of the editorial board.[122] He asked her to send him her poetry manuscript; a year later, Heinemann would publish *The Colossus*, the only collection of her poetry Plath ever saw in print.

By November there were only six guests left at Yaddo, all living in West House—Plath, Hughes, Howard Rogovin, May Swenson, Gordon Binkerd, and Arthur Deshaies. Plath wrote "The Burnt-Out Spa" on November 11, and, two days later, "Mushrooms." But by mid-November her adrenaline subsided, and she wrote nothing new during her last week. "Paralysis again," she wrote in her journal. "How I waste my days. I feel a terrific blocking and chilling go through me like anesthesia." She wondered if she would "ever be rid of Johnny Panic."[123] She had barely achieved anything, she felt, in the past ten years. She was convinced that she had written no good story since "Sunday at the Mintons" and felt that she needed more space from Ted. "Dangerous to be so close to Ted day in day out," she wrote in her journal on November 7. "I have no life separate from his, am likely to become a mere accessory." They must "Lead separate lives." She did not "dare open Yeats, Eliot."[124]

She was ready to leave Yaddo, tired of the "drifting uncertainty of our lives," and Saratoga Springs, another college town, reminded her too much of Northampton. She missed Boston, museums, and theaters, but she knew that Ted would stay another year if given the chance. He had met a Chinese composer, Chou Wen-chung, with whom he had begun collaborating on the *Bardo Thodol*, the Tibetan Book of the Dead. The production was to involve a chorus, "Buddhas and Demons and Hells and landscapes of rebirth flashed up onto the screen," and priests and dancers. ("Pity we never went ahead with our spectacular," Hughes later wrote a friend, "we'd have preempted the Timothy Leary Beatnik expropriation of all that business in the mid-Sixties.")[125] In her journal, Plath wrote that Hughes's "vocation of writing is so much stronger than mine."[126] Her horror, at twenty-seven, was to find herself "well-educated, brilliantly promising, and fading out into an indifferent middle age."[127] The lesson of Henry James's "The Beast in the Jungle" was never far from her thoughts.

As the end of their Yaddo stay approached, Plath began to feel an "Odd elation," which she attributed to their upcoming departure for England.[128] John Lehmann had accepted "The Daughters of Blossom Street" for *The London Magazine*, news that made her skip through the grounds like a child (although he had rejected "The Wishing Box" and "The Shadow"). She was particularly pleased by this acceptance, as the magazine's editorial board included Elizabeth Bowen. Lehmann himself had helped Virginia and Leonard Woolf run the Hogarth Press. Plath was cheered, too, by the publication of "A Winter's Tale" in the December 12 *New Yorker*. She hoped the three stories and eleven poems she had written at Yaddo would help make her name in England.[129] "My tempo is British," Plath wrote, and, indeed, British magazines and editors seemed more amenable to her dark wit. She thought that in England she would be less afflicted by her "commercial American superego."[130] She despaired of "breaking" the "drawingroom [sic] inhibitions" in her prose, but in her poems, she knew, "There I have."[131]

Still plagued by nightmares of dead babies and "puritannical" [sic] mothers, she mustered her old optimism. "Whenever we are about to move, this stirring and excitement comes, as if the old environment would keep the sludge and inertia of the self, and the bare new self slip shining into a better life."[132] She was moving to England to find this new life—a "pioneer / In the wrong direction," Hughes later wrote—but her desire for reinvention was American.[133] From now on she would live, she wrote, in a "blithe, itchy eager state where the poem itself, the story itself is supreme."[134]

Part III

23

The Dread of Recognition

London, 1960

Sylvia Plath crossed the Atlantic for the third and final time, aboard the SS *United States*, in mid-December 1959.[1] The voyage was colder and less pleasant than her previous crossings. The decks were closed for most of the day and she felt "confined" in the narrow cabin at the water line, where rough seas slammed against the hull and broke her sleep. Drunken revelers paraded through the halls, screaming and laughing until dawn. She took sleeping pills, and Dramamine for seasickness. She and Ted dined on lobster Newburg and rare steak, yet the service was so terrible they resolved to "tip no one."[2] (Ted called the ship "the worst boat on the Atlantic.")[3] A photograph from the voyage shows an unsmiling couple dressed formally for dinner—Sylvia in a blue silk, kimono-style blouse, her hair swept back in a bun, Ted in tweed jacket and tie.[4] Exhausted and seasick, Sylvia found nothing to catch her interest, not even Pasternak's *Dr. Zhivago*, which "disappointed" her.[5] There were no painterly word sketches of sea and wind in her letters. She did not try very hard to mask her despondency and homesickness to Aurelia, who was filled with anxiety about the move.

Ted wrote a cheerful letter to Aurelia at sea, but his parting advice suggested the strains of the previous months. "Look after yourself. As Frost says, 'Something has to be left to God'—so don't take every anxiety onto yourself, that's a form of pride and unfaith. Just relax."[6] Sylvia too advised Aurelia to take sleeping pills, and to "treat" herself to "naps & relaxings, hot milk & honey."[7] Even Edith Hughes, writing to Aurelia from Yorkshire, tried to "extend some comfort" on the eve of the young couple's departure from America. "I do try not to penetrate, in thought too deep where my children are concerned," Edith wrote. "One has to form a kind of self protection against distress because as one grows older it doesn't do any good at all." She advised Aurelia to "wish them well and pray for them. . . . When you feel overcome just go and make a pot of good black coffee and have a cigarette. I promise to keep you informed how Sylvia looks and little details we like to hear about them. So keep smiling. They love each other you know."[8] Edith's kind words probably did not reassure Aurelia. In the margin of the letter, she wrote, "Sylvia, 5 months pregnant, leaves for England—to look for a home in London & to get a midwife to 'take her on'!"

After their first night in London with Daniel and Helga Huws, at 18 Rugby Street, the couple traveled to Yorkshire, where an exhausted Sylvia reported a "black sky all day." They had planned to travel to Corsica and Rome on the Guggenheim money, but now had second thoughts. "Ted's as tired of traveling as I am," she wrote Aurelia before Christmas. As usual, Sylvia criticized Edith's cooking and housekeeping, and she spoke of the superior meals she would make in her American-style kitchen. But she would overlook these annoyances for a two-week visit. "The main thing is that the family is loving & closeknit." She was cheered, surprisingly, by Olwyn, who was home from Paris. "I like her a great deal," Sylvia wrote Aurelia, describing her as "chic," "a nice ally," and "much more sophisticated & critical than even I."[9] Yet Olwyn remembered their time together as tense, marked by a feud over an old bathrobe.[10]

Plath got to work immediately, and spent the next two weeks typing her eighty-six-page poetry manuscript, *The Colossus and Other Poems*, to send to James Michie at Heinemann. She socialized with Ted's relatives and played tarot cards with Ted and Olwyn. The stormy weather did not stop the young couple from taking long walks on the moors to escape the crowded quarters at the Beacon. (Sylvia told Aurelia to "reread Ted's poem Wind, it's perfect.") On Christmas Day, Aurelia's American gifts inspired collective sighs of admiration, though Sylvia's favorite gift was from Olwyn—a pair of cinnamon colored gloves from Paris that fit her "like a second skin." Sylvia and Ted prepared the Christmas meal, but even an eight-pound turkey could not dispel Sylvia's homesickness. "No tree, which I missed," she wrote Aurelia.[11] The next day she wrote her aunt and uncle, "No snow for Christmas, just about a foot of water."[12] There was no central heating at the Beacon and Sylvia complained that she could see her breath if she sat more than "a few feet away from the fireplace." The raw, damp weather seeped into her bones, and she lashed out at Edith to her aunt Dot. "Mrs. Hughes is a very simple, but nervous woman, who can't imagine that hospitals in the city are better than drunken country doctors & it will be a relief to get away from her worrying."[13] To Aurelia, though, she admitted that she "must really be a terror of a daughter-in-law," and acknowledged her own tendency to over-criticize.

Edith was "really very warm & good-hearted & if anything, I think, inclined to be a bit frightened of me."[14]

A few days after Christmas, Ted and Sylvia walked down to Heptonstall village to buy bread to make French toast. Hughes wrote in his notebook, "The sky clear, a wind beginning, the landscape bright. Not a feeling of the new year, but a definite respite day." Later, when he and Sylvia went for a country walk, she talked to a young calf and tried to pet it, but Ted thought her new calfskin gloves repelled it. "We waded," he wrote, "through the ankle deep hoof-churned mud behind that farm & went along toward the piggery. The bare hawthorn on the brim of the hill, over the trough—the clear still water—like ice water—in the trough. . . . We grunted, squealed & addressed them."[15]

The couple sounds content, but Hughes's later *Birthday Letters* poem "Stubbing Wharfe" hints that he knew of his wife's unhappiness. The poem recalls a night when they sat inside the Stubbing Wharf pub alongside the canal in Hebden Bridge, amid the "shut-in / Sodden dreariness of the whole valley, / The hopeless old stone trap of it" and "the moorland / Almost closing above us."[16] Hughes's description is a far cry from Brontë country, as Plath had once described it to her mother. He recalled a somber mood:

> You having leapt
> Like a thrown dice, flinging off
> The sparkle of America, pioneer
> In the wrong direction, sat weeping,
> Homesick, exhausted, disappointed, pregnant.
> Where could we start living? Italy? Spain?
> The world was all before us. And around us
> The gloomy memorial of a valley,
> The fallen-in grave of its history,
> A gorge of ruined mills and abandoned chapels,
> The fouled nest of the Industrial Revolution
> That had flown. The windows glittered black.[17]

They returned to London in early January 1960 and stayed with Daniel and Helga Huws again for the next two weeks, as they hunted for a suitable flat of their own. Helga's enormous German meals of bratwurst and sauerkraut made Sylvia feel "at home"; she nearly wept when Helga produced an exquisite gingerbread covered with glazed almonds.[18] "I must say all her Germanic-ness, her German talk . . . & her rigorously clean housekeeping has sustained me through a very difficult period," she wrote Aurelia.[19] Sylvia had spent her wedding night at 18 Rugby Street and was all too familiar with its shortcomings; in a letter to Dr. Beuscher, she called it a "condemned slum." There was no bathtub, and the only toilet—unfortunate for a woman in her seventh month of pregnancy—was in a "dark, dank" coal-filled cellar.[20] She admired the way Helga endured these indignities with "Germanic stoicism."[21] Not to be outdone by a fellow Prussian, Sylvia displayed no discomfort with the primitive conditions. Helga was impressed. The two became close—partly, Daniel thought, because there was "no literary rivalry." He remembered Sylvia's exhaustion, but also her forays to London bookshops; one day she came home "full of enthusiasm with a copy of Philip Larkin's *The Less Deceived*."[22] The choice surprised him, as Hughes did not care for Larkin. But the flat hunt soon became "very tiring."[23] The couple wanted to live in central London near a park, but the only places they could afford, at about $24 a week, were unfurnished dumps without heat or hot water. It was, Sylvia wrote Lynne Lawner in Rome, a "Dickensianly grim & chilblain-ridden" time.[24]

Apart from the Huwses, the couple's only other friends in London were the Merwins, whose tales of subsisting off BBC commissions had helped lure Sylvia and Ted back to England. Bill and Dido Merwin were now living in north London at Saint George's Terrace in an elegant townhouse that faced the grand, green expanse of Primrose Hill. "They seem to have become our amazingly close friends in no time at all," Ted wrote to Aurelia and Warren in January.[25] Bill, who had written a glowing review of *The Hawk in the Rain* in *The New York Times*, felt that Ted was on his way to becoming one of the most important poets in Britain. Sylvia and Ted preferred Bill to Dido, whom Ted described as a "slightly jewish [*sic*] hyper-charged upper middle class Scorpio of about 45." Sylvia told Dr. Beuscher Dido was "middle-aged, thrice-married."[26] But when Dido contacted friends about vacancies, they knew they were in her debt. Ted called the Merwins "our saviours."[27]

Sylvia made inquiries through Dido about obstetrical care and was told she would not be able to give birth at a hospital, as those beds were "spoken for at least eight months ahead of time."[28] She would have to give birth at home, without anesthesia, with a midwife—though a doctor would swoop in at the end to "catch" the baby. Sylvia assured Aurelia that midwifery was "a respected profession here": "I shall be all set, & very glad to escape the crowded labor wards & hospital food, etc."[29] Better yet, it was all free. But to Marcia she wrote more candidly that she "shuddered at the word 'midwife,'" and was "sceptical" of natural childbirth, which her American doctor had advised against.[30] In her copy of Grantly Dick-Read's *Childbirth Without Fear*, Plath marked up the chapters about diet in pregnancy, the pain of labor, fear of childbirth, and mental preparation. One heavily annotated passage suggests her fears: "How many women, therefore, who hear that one in a thousand dies in childbirth, can disregard the fact that they are not likely to be the one?"[31] And also: "Depression and disappointment are potent pain intensifiers."[32] Next to Dick-Read's assertion that "childbirth is not a physical function," Plath simply wrote "!"[33] She wrote Dr. Beuscher, "I don't have any GrantlyDickRead illusions, but I feel I have made the best arrangements for my own odd psychic setup. . . . Do let me know what you think about this!"[34] Aurelia admitted in a letter to a friend that she was not reassured by her daughter's bright talk.[35]

Sylvia settled on her obstetrician, the young, Cambridge-educated Dr. Christopher Hindley (referred to her by Dido), and they narrowed their hunt for a flat to his neighborhood near Primrose Hill. After a couple of false leads, Dido "smelt out" a third-floor flat in a four-story townhouse at nearby 3 Chalcot Square.[36] It was just a two-minute walk from expansive Primrose Hill, with its large fields and walking paths, and beyond, Regent's Park, where Sylvia had first stayed, at Bedford College, when she arrived in England in 1955. They had found the flat just in time; after six months of peripatetic living, Sylvia had very nearly reached her breaking point. To Olwyn she wrote, "I don't think either of us has sustained such a prolonged period of crammed exhaustion & despair before—& physical cold, hunger & all the misères."[37] It had all convinced her, she told Marcia, that the English were "the most secretly dirty race on earth."[38]

The one-bedroom flat was small but filled with light. Best of all, it overlooked a gated green square that could serve as the baby's play space come spring. Indeed, the setting was "Ideal," Sylvia told Aurelia: "like living in a village yet minutes from the center of London."[39] They could hear the animals from the nearby London Zoo. Today the neighborhood is pristine and affluent, as it was in the late nineteenth century, but in 1960 Sylvia described it as "slummy-elegant," "rapidly up & coming."[40] Hughes called Chalcot Square "decrepit."[41] Their landlord assured them that the neighborhood would soon be another Chelsea. "I think I shall be a very happy exile & have absolutely no desire to return to the land of milk & honey & spindryers," Sylvia wrote Lynne Lawner.[42]

In truth, the flat was far from ideal, and Sylvia only planned to stay a year before finding a larger dwelling. The townhouse, which had previously housed Irish laborers, was being renovated. They could not move in until February, and they would have to buy their own appliances and heaters. Still, Hughes knew that they had been lucky to find it, after a week of losing flats to others. And it was "cheap"—"18 dollars a week, not including electricity."[43] The Merwins would lend them furniture until they could purchase their own.

From the Guggenheim, the couple had set aside a year's rent, six months' food budget, and $650 to buy furniture. But the future was precarious. Even with the looming publication of *Lupercal* and Ted's inclusion in a new Faber and Faber anthology, Sylvia wrote to Marcia, "nothing makes any money." She hoped to "stretch" the Guggenheim until early September.[44] After that, they would have to live solely on income from their writing and the BBC— and some help from Aurelia and Mrs. Prouty, who was concerned enough to send Sylvia a $300 check that fall for a private doctor. After the January 30 publication of "Two Views of a Cadaver Room" in *The Nation*, Plath would not see another poem in print until April.

Back at the Beacon (the "express" train from London to Yorkshire took nearly six hours, with three connections), Sylvia took her first bath in two weeks and marveled at the sun shining on the "dazzling, snow-covered moortops."[45] She finally felt warm in the thick wool bathrobe Edith Hughes had knit for her. Her baby was due on March 27, in about six weeks, and her thoughts turned to motherhood. She and Ted, guided by the stars, were sure the baby was going to be a boy, Nicholas. If a girl, she would be Frieda Rebecca. Sylvia asked Aurelia to send her the *Harper's* acceptance letter for "Mushrooms"—"I need to see that kind of mail now."[46] She was thrilled to learn that another Yaddo poem, "Medallion," had tied for a first-place award from the *Critical Quarterly*.[47] Plath was then unknown to the editors, Brian Cox and Tony Dyson, but the magazine would become an important promoter of her work. When she met Dyson and Cox—who had known Hughes at Cambridge—by chance at a 1960 Guinness prize party, she expressed delight that they did not know she was married to Ted Hughes. "Because obviously," Cox remembered, "we *might* have given her the prize for that reason." Philip Larkin was one of the judges, and Cox had the impression that the prize buoyed Plath, for she hadn't "had a lot of success" yet.[48] *Mademoiselle* and *The Atlantic* had recently rejected three "slangy" stories, which she dared not now send to Faber and Faber—Ted's publishers—for inclusion in one of their anthologies lest she "embarrass" him, and them.[49] The fact that Plath was now holding her work back from the most prestigious publisher in England for fear of embarrassing her husband suggests how the creative marriage was beginning to stymie her own ambitions. Indeed, she had inaugurated this worrisome trend in 1956 when she chose to enter Hughes's manuscript in the YMHA/Harper Brothers contest rather than her own. She had apparently decided, early on, not to leverage Ted's poetry contacts at Faber, either, and sent the manuscript of *The Colossus*—forty-eight poems, nearly one-third of them written at Yaddo—to James Michie at Heinemann on January 25.

She had written only one poem since arriving in England, "You're," about the child she was carrying. The baby is like "A creel of eels, all ripples. /

Jumpy as a Mexican bean," yet there is a Gothic tinge. The baby is also "moon-skulled," "Trawling your dark as owls do," "Mute," "Vague as fog." The skulls and owls add heaviness to a poem that wants to lift and jump. The speaker grasps at buoyancy, but cannot elide the undercurrent of fear that presses at her from another angle. The next poem Plath wrote, nearly five months later in June 1960, was "The Hanging Man."

Sylvia and Ted moved into their Chalcot Square flat on February 1 and began a three-week frenzy of scrubbing, waxing, and painting. Ted built cupboards, kitchen shelves, counters, and bookcases, and did all the heavy lifting. Tools and timber littered the staircase and living room. "The place looks like a railroad station now," Sylvia told Aurelia. But she loved "the spanking newness of everything . . . nobody's old stove to clean or toilet to scrub!"[50] They put up rose-colored wallpaper and green cord curtains in the bedroom, and hung a large print of Isis and the illustrated Gehenna Press broadside of "Pike" on their living room wall. They painted the floorboards gray. Sylvia checked in with the sympathetic Dr. Hindley and wept in his office. She had endured much strain over the past month, and she was tired. He prescribed a sedative. Aurelia, meanwhile, worried about her daughter's exposure to paint fumes.

Sylvia's kitchen was the flat's pièce de résistance. They purchased a new gas oven at a discount and, her "pride and joy," an American-sized refrigerator. She was smug about its superiority—"The British are still afraid of Big things"—and kept rubbing the stove and refrigerator with a cloth "just to see them sparkle."[51] All of it amounted to a little over $500. Dido Merwin would later chastise Plath in a vicious essay, included in Anne Stevenson's biography, for buying new appliances instead of getting them secondhand. In fact Sylvia fretted over the cost of these big-ticket items, asking Aurelia several times to compare their prices to American models and to reassure her that she was not overspending. She had considered getting them secondhand but worried that she did not have enough mechanical knowledge to judge their true condition.

They met their upstairs neighbor, Mrs. Morton, who worked as a French interpreter for a telephone company. Sylvia described her as a "warm-hearted," "widowed older woman . . . an aged Bohemian" in her "Russian-novel antique attic."[52] Spinsters, along with barren women, were one of Plath's targets, for these were the two fates she herself feared. That September, Plath would satirize Mrs. Morton and her gentlemen callers in a mean-spirited poem, "Leaving Early."

The Merwins, when they visited, were alarmed to see that Ted's only writing space was a small windowless foyer in which he had set up a rickety card table. They assumed that Sylvia—who now seemed, in the wake of her appliance purchases, a spoiled American—had commandeered the rest of the apartment. They offered Ted the use of Bill's study while they were away in France from late April through the summer, in exchange for his mowing their lawn. As they lived around the corner, the situation was ideal. Yet Ted told Olwyn he liked his hallway study, with its "3 doors & red walls." "The result is very good—no distractions whatsoever, and the proof is the enormous amount I've got through."[53] Twenty-five years later, he still remembered the "windowless cubicle just big enough for a chair" as one of "the best places I ever had" to write in.[54] Although the Merwins had not thought to extend their study offer to Sylvia, Ted did: the poets would share the quiet retreat after Frieda was born. (Bill Merwin later expressed outrage that Sylvia had used his study.)[55] Sylvia wrote there in the morning, Ted in the afternoon.

About a week after moving into their new flat, Plath received the letter she had been waiting for all her life. Just two weeks after she had submitted her manuscript to Heinemann, James Michie wrote on February 5 to accept *The Colossus*.

Dear Miss Plath,

I have your poems and Heinemann would like to publish them.

Can you ring the line and drop in to see me any time, any day this month?[56]

A few days later, on February 10, Sylvia dressed carefully in a black wool suit and cashmere coat, and donned her Parisian gloves and Italian calfskin bag. She looked, she wrote, "resplendent" as she walked into the York Minster pub on Soho's Dean Street to meet with Michie, who presented her with a contract for *The Colossus and Other Poems*. "She signed it on the glass-crowded bar-top," Ted wrote Olwyn. "You can't imagine how euphoric she is."[57] Afterward, she and Ted celebrated over champagne, veal, and mushrooms at Bianci's Italian restaurant on Frith Street in Soho—the same restaurant in which she had sat "in misery a month back, homeless & cold & very grim." Everything had changed. Ted brought her *The Complete Poems of D. H. Lawrence* to mark the occasion.[58]

The Colossus, dedicated to Ted, would come out in October. Plath would receive 10 percent of the royalties, which she knew would "amount to nothing."[59] Yet the prestige of signing with a firm that published Lawrence, Evelyn Waugh, and Somerset Maugham mattered more to Plath than money; Hughes thought Heinemann "one of the most powerful publishers in England."[60] On that February day, it must have seemed that she had achieved nearly every goal she had set herself—she had married a brilliant poet; she was soon to become a mother; she had found a charming flat in central London; she had just signed a contract for her first book. She took much satisfaction in succeeding where Aurelia had quietly predicted failure. In her letter home, Plath exulted in her triumph, describing every detail of her exquisite outfit, the "notorious" pub, and the signature itself. She was finally in command of her personal and professional destiny.

As February drew to a close, Plath learned that the *Critical Quarterly* had taken "Blue Moles," "The Beggars," and "The Manor Garden" (they would appear in the summer issue) while *The London Magazine* had accepted Hughes's story "The Rain Horse." She and Ted now traded full days in bed; one read, wrote, and slept while the other handled all domestic duties. In the evenings they socialized with the Merwins or attended plays. "Now we are 'at home,' London is a delight," she wrote Aurelia. Sylvia was excited to see Ibsen's *Rosmersholm* in late February, her first staged Ibsen play, and Racine's *Phèdre* in early March. "I find I am made much happier by tragedy, good tragedy, classic tragedy, in movies and on stage than by so-called 'hilarious musicals and/or farces,'" she wrote home. Tragedy, she wrote, "really purifies & liberates me."[61] Hughes, too, wrote of the play's "tremendous" effect in terms that suggest discontent with an increasingly bourgeois life: "Totally cathartic. I have not often felt it. Catharsis is what we more & more lack. There is less & less in our lives that satiate our spiritual powers. . . . As our lives grow drier & more timid, our art does not compensate. . . . Something like this Phèdre, every other day, would cure me."[62]

Hughes's first copies of *Lupercal* arrived on February 23 (the official release date was March 18), and while Plath was displeased with the jacket's color combinations, she felt that it was "a handsome affair."[63] Ted inscribed a copy to her: "To Sylvia, its true mother, with all my love, Ted," dated February 25, 1960. (He noted in the inscription, "4th anniversary of St Botolph's.")[64] Already, publicity was building. Hughes was written up in *Queen*, which Sylvia called "a sort of Harper's Bazaar," as one of Britain's most important new writers.[65] Meanwhile, Sylvia whiled away long hours reading Bill Merwin's American history books. The two couples spent many nights drawing up their astrology charts; Bill remembered that Sylvia, a Scorpio, took pride in hers.[66] "Hope to be writing soon again, too," she told Aurelia. "I feel much freer (and appreciated, by publishers at least) here to write than I ever did in America."[67] Since she had signed her contract with Heinemann, two other British publishers, including Oxford University Press, had asked to see a manuscript. She told Marcia that April that the British were "much kinder & open to poetry than in America, where loss of money is such a phobia."[68] Yet she still wanted a homecoming for *The Colossus*—"it is a good, fat solid 50-poem book now & deserving of print there. I naturally would be very happy to be recognized in my own country!"[69] She instructed Aurelia to keep sending their manuscripts out to American magazines.

Luke Myers visited Chalcot Square in March, but he spent only one night at the Hugheses' flat before retreating to the other Huwses at 18 Rugby Street. He remembered Sylvia as tense and testy during the visit. While she cooked dinner, he and Ted stepped out to a local pub, where Ted, he later remembered, said he had a hard time working through all of Sylvia's interruptions. They returned from the pub to find half-filled bowls of lukewarm clam chowder waiting for them. Sylvia seemed angry and "demanding," Luke said, in the "style of some American women of the period."[70] (He apparently was oblivious about why a heavily pregnant Sylvia might resent making dinner while they relaxed at the pub.) Daniel Huws remembered that Sylvia preferred socializing in small, intimate, "domestic" gatherings: "She relaxed. She became herself."[71] "The timeless, anarchic nature of pubs—a quality of Irishness . . . something Ted loved, in his younger days, was anathema to Sylvia, with her strong need to feel that everything was under control, even her social pleasure, and with her businesslike dedication of her time."[72] Indeed, British pubs at that time were mostly the domain of men, a fact that might also account for Sylvia's preference for dinner parties and explain her annoyance at being left behind by Luke and Ted that night.

There was more aggravation to come. When Olwyn visited Chalcot Square that March with a girlfriend, Janet Crosbie-Hill, the two women chain-smoked. Sylvia suspected that the smoke was not good for her or her baby, and opened the windows. Olwyn thought her rude. But the child-care authority Dr. Spock had recommended limiting visitors in his book *Baby and Child Care*, which Sylvia consulted regularly; she underlined his passage about the importance of time alone and rest. As she told her mother after Luke's and Olwyn's visits, "Ted is, if anything, too nice to his relatives and friends, and I get weary sitting for 8 hours at a stretch in our smokefilled rooms waiting for them to leave—impossible to nap or relax with so many people around. I feel very unlike entertaining anyone just now, simply 'inwaiting,' wanting to read, write in my diary, & nap."[73] Sylvia was now the most important person in Ted's life, and his sister and close friend resented her coup (Olwyn and Luke exchanged letters about Sylvia's "aggression" in March of 1960). Sylvia *was* hospitable to friends she liked—in March she threw three separate dinner parties for the Huwses, the Merwins, and the Rosses. She would later offer an apology to Olwyn in a friendly April letter after the baby's birth; she said she had been under a "cloud" during her visit, about to come down with a flu and sinus infection that would keep her in bed for the last two weeks of March.[74]

Sylvia finally got the attention she yearned for at Selfridge's flagship

department store, on busy Oxford Street, where she ventured alone by bus in
March. The bubbly salesladies sat her down and displayed their wares. Sylvia
bought practical rubber sheets but indulged in a handmade Scottish shawl.
This was the closest she would come to an American-style baby shower in
London, as she had no close friends or family of her own to make a fuss. The
baby was coming soon: at her next doctor's appointment, she finally heard its
heartbeat and was reassured that "Frieda/Nicholas" was in the correct position. Aurelia sent diapers and many other gifts, while Sylvia picked out a pale
pink crib. "I keep wondering what it will be like to see a breathing infant in
it. This seems an enormous milestone to pass: three of us instead of two."[75]

Lupercal was published on March 18. Ten days later, on the baby's due
date, Al Alvarez delivered a resounding review in the *Sunday Observer* titled
"An Outstanding Young Poet." Sylvia quoted it proudly to Aurelia: "'Hughes
has found his own voice, created his own artistic world & has emerged as
a poet of the first importance . . . What Ted Hughes has done is to take a
limited, personal theme and, by an act of immensely assured poetic skill, has
broadened it until it seems to touch upon nearly everything that concerns
us. This is not easy poetry to read, but it is new, profound & important.' We
cooed & beamed all day."[76] *The Daily Telegraph* agreed: "Mr Hughes at 30
is . . . the most strikingly original, technically masterful, poet of his generation."[77] Another review, in *The Observer*, compared Hughes to Thom Gunn
and used language that would set the terms for Hughes's future reception:
"a tall, craggy Yorkshire poet of thirty, who is not afraid of Strong Feelings,"
in "romantic revolt against the dry, cerebral verse of the 'Movement' of the
fifties (Conquest, Larkin, Amis, Wain, etc.)." Hughes was "earthy and emotional; more close to the land and farm."[78]

Lupercal contains many of what are now regarded as Hughes's best
poems, and best lines—"Hawk Roosting" ("I am going to keep things like
this"); "View of a Pig" ("Scald and scour it like a doorstep"); "Thrushes"
("More coiled steel than living"); "Relic" ("Nothing touches but, clutching,
devours"); "Mayday on Holderness" ("The nightlong frenzy of shrews");
and "Pike" ("deep as England"). The poems had mostly been written in
New England, but their imaginative hinterland is Yorkshire—Old Denaby,
Crookhill, Roche Abbey. Nearly all the book's reviewers regarded it as a
watershed in postwar British poetry. Ted's success made Sylvia wonder, again,
if her own book would ever appear in America. At least the short *Observer*
article had included, she told Aurelia, "a note about me 'his tall, trim American wife . . . who is a New Yorker poet in her own right.'"[79]

There was more good news that month: on March 24 Hughes learned
that he had won the Somerset Maugham Award for *The Hawk in the Rain*—
about $1,400, to cover three months of travel abroad. Sylvia began dreaming

of the French Riviera, Rome, the Greek Islands—"all sorts of elegant sun-saturated schemes."[80] The prize gave Ted great confidence, he told Olwyn: "the awful abstract murderous supersonic brain-paralysing tension which I was under in America & until this last month seems to be lifting. I'm writing with a new sort of energy & a heat that reminds me of myself again. . . . I have never had more ideas."[81] The BBC offered him more work, and Sylvia was relieved by the prospect of "very good fees."[82] They stopped worrying about money for the moment when an editor at *Harper's Bazaar* offered Hughes $275 for the American publication of "The Rain Horse."

Sylvia's due date, March 27, came and went. She spent "cosy" days indoors cooking, reading Sartre and Camus in French, and watching children play cricket in the square through her window. "We hear the clear song of a certain thrush at dawn each morning. . . . The daily icecream truck jingles to a stop & the little ones all rush up. Oh, I am so impatient!"[83] Their Irish midwife and Dr. Hindley came round every few days to reassure her that "everything was ripe & ready." She would be glad to have an April baby, for April was the "Plath month" (Warren, Aurelia, and Otto were all born in April) and offered more promise than March, "an exhausted, grubby end-of-the-year month." She and Ted took an evening walk to Primrose Hill on the last night of March "under the thin new moon . . . all blue & misty, the buds a kind of nimbus of green on the thorn trees, daffodils & blue squills out on the lawns & the silhouettes of wood pigeons roosting in the trees."[84]

Ted was unsettled when Sylvia's due date passed. He suffered what appeared to be a panic attack at the BBC on March 29. He was speaking to the critic George MacBeth "for the first time" about the possibility of a program as they drank pints in the BBC cafeteria. Suddenly he broke out "in a cold sweat." He excused himself to the bathroom, where, he wrote in his journal, he "felt like fainting, fought to keep consciousness. . . . I was in a bad way." He returned to the lobby and fell to the ground "in a sitting position. Instantly felt better, & the pain vanished . . . from the pit of my stomach. My consciousness cleared and I said, 'How extraordinary!'" He then rejoined MacBeth at the table. He thought that the attack was brought on by an account of Wilfred Owen's death he had read that morning, as well as his own growing fame. "Also, last night, I read the first scenes of Julius Caesar. I connected it with (a) the extraordinary excitement of Sunday—the reviews, the Somerset Maugham Award precisely analogous, in my mind, to the offering of the crown to Caesar. My own dread of recognition, my immense satisfaction with it."

There were domestic anxieties, too. "The great excitement I am living under—Sylvia expecting her baby today, my writing, my euphoria," as well as "The hangover of exhaustion from the last nine months, which, for the first time in my life, showed me my health crack via nerves. My deep worry over this." He remembered similar attacks in previous weeks before meeting John Lehmann, or anticipating a review by Roy Fuller, when his anxiety rose and his heart had begun to race. "I believe the most violent hidden reactions in me are connected with 'literary public life' as it threatens me. . . . I have no doubt that involvement in all that would eventually kill me. . . . Whoever owns me detests all that, and I pray to be able to obey her." He believed the collapse at the BBC "was punishment" from "her," the White Goddess. "I hope this was a genuine lesson."[85]

———

SYLVIA'S WATER BROKE on April 1 at 1:15 a.m. Ted had been hypnotizing her "to have 'an easy quick delivery.' "[86] The labor would be short—less than five hours—but not easy. When she began vomiting and "contracting violently," Ted called the midwife, who arrived at two a.m.[87] Sylvia was disappointed to see an unfamiliar midwife, Sister Mardee, rather than "the blond golden-voiced Irish one" she had come to know. But Sister Mardee soon proved herself most "capable"—the highest of Plath's accolades.[88] The midwife assumed that she would return to deliver the baby after breakfast and was astonished to see that Sylvia was nearly at the pushing stage. The pain, Sylvia wrote Marcia, was "very severe," and she did not know how she "could last through 20 more hours."[89] She asked for anesthesia, but neither Sister Mardee nor Dr. Hindley could offer it. Ted and the midwife gave calm, soothing encouragements. A husband's presence at the delivery bed was unusual in 1960, but Ted stayed by her side all night, "holding my hand, rubbing my back & boiling kettles—a marvelous comfort." By five a.m. Sylvia was fully dilated and ready to deliver. Dr. Hindley arrived at five thirty, "just in time," to deliver a baby girl, seven pounds, four ounces. "I looked on my stomach & saw Frieda Rebecca white as flour with the cream that covers new babies, little funny dark squiggles of hair plastered over her head, with big dark blue eyes."[90] The blue eyes were Otto's, she told Aurelia.

The midwife sponged the baby in a Pyrex mixing bowl and wrapped her in a blanket before handing her to Sylvia for her first feeding. The "minute" they left the room, Sylvia called, as she wrote Lynne Lawner, "my nerve-wracked mother."[91] Ted assumed that Aurelia was worried about her daughter "in the hands of Europe's mediaeval obstetricians," though he himself thought the home birth more humane than the "chemically controlled occurrence" it would have been in an American hospital.[92] Sylvia agreed, writing to Marcia on her typewriter a few hours after the birth about the "intimacy" and "privacy" of a home birth, and how she had feared the "nightmare of labor wards, deep anesthesia, cuts, doctors bills etc. in American hospitals."[93] She had been traumatized, she wrote Dr. Beuscher the next day, by her experience with Dick Norton, the "nightmare vision of that delivery I saw at the Boston Lying-In—the mother too doped to know what was happening, not seeing or holding the baby, cut open and stitched up as if birth were a surgical operation & sent off on a stretcher in the opposite direction from her child."[94] For two weeks before the birth, she had been unable to sleep through the night and had been taking sleeping pills. She told Lynne she had "deeply feared" childbirth and had been "as nervous as possible." She recommended a home birth—blessedly free of "surgical instruments, masks etc"—"to anybody with my particular set of nerves." She had not torn or needed an episiotomy. Now, as she gazed on her sleeping infant, she was filled with relief. "Have one, it's incredible," she told Lynne. "The whole experience of birth and baby seem much deeper, much closer to the bone, than love and marriage. . . . Frieda is my answer to the H-bomb. I never gave a damn about babies till I had her; now I still don't give a damn about other people's, but regard her as a strange private miracle."[95] That night the new parents lit candles and "played with" their new baby. "I don't know when I've been so happy," Sylvia wrote Dr. Beuscher on April 2, "being tired, bloody & without apparent stomach muscles is just a stage to be grown out of, no real bother."[96]

Nearly all Plath's letters that April included news of the other long-awaited arrival. "LUPERCAL preceded Frieda Rebecca by exactly two weeks but she arrived in a hurry to make up for it," Sylvia joked to Ted's brother Gerald in Australia. "Both productions have been well-received by the world at large & are, we hope, destined for brilliant futures."[97] Plath, too, would have several professional successes that spring: "Man in Black" and "Watercolor of Grantchester Meadows" ran in *The New Yorker* on April 9 and May 28, respectively. *The London Magazine* would publish "The Daughters of Blossom Street" in May, and "The Sleepers" and "Full Fathom Five" in June.

Sylvia spent her first ten days with Frieda (whom she called Rebecca for several weeks) at home, as midwives descended twice a day to help her bathe and care for the baby—all for free. Sylvia breastfed her every four hours with ease. Dido sent veal casseroles, trout in aspic, and hearty stews, and the small flat filled up quickly with flowers, cards, and telegrams. Sylvia was oddly "moved" by Mildred Norton's baby gift from Harrods and annoyed that Aurelia's congratulatory letter did not arrive until a week after Frieda's birth. She was also upset with Warren, who still had not written, and she made sure Aurelia knew that Dick's mother had taken the time to write to her before her own family had. She was angry with Aurelia, too, for suggesting that they give the baby something to curtail her height.

> I'm surprised at you. Tampering with nature! What an American thing to feel measuring people to ideal heights will make them happier or not interfere with other things. Whatever height Frieda Rebecca is, I shall encourage her to be proud of it.[98]

Bill Merwin was the baby's first visitor, followed by the Huwses a day later. Bill arrived with a silver thimble for Frieda, and daffodils and *New Yorkers* for Sylvia. She was grateful for the gifts, but told Aurelia, "The one infuriating thing about the general euphoria around here is that I have no relatives or friends of <u>my own</u> to admire the baby in person. Ted's people & friends are dear . . . but it isn't the same."[99] Still, she appreciated the Merwins' meals, attic furniture, books, gifts, and company, and was touched when Dido gave her a piece of pearl jewelry she had received for her own christening.[100] Sylvia and Ted decided that the Merwins would be the baby's godparents.

Ted temporarily took over the day-to-day burdens of domesticity that Sylvia was expected to bear while writing and, now, caring for a baby. She praised Ted for his attention to Frieda. "You should see him rocking her & singing to her!" she wrote home. "She looks so tiny against his shoulder, her four little fingers just closing around one of his knuckles."[101] Ted wondered if Frieda was "precocious"—"She already looks at things, your finger for instance,—with a ferociously intent expression."[102] He too felt that the baby had settled Sylvia, and that she took to motherhood naturally. "Sylvia is wonderful with her—serene, casual, full of solid sense," he told Aurelia.[103]

After two weeks, Sylvia was discharged from the midwives' care, though Sister Mardee still dropped by to check on her. Spring, with its warm "lambish" winds and tentative greens, had finally displaced the raw, wet winter.[104] Sylvia bought a large, luxurious baby carriage with a check Mrs. Prouty had sent to cover her doctor. ("<u>Don't</u> tell her my home confinement was free!" she instructed Aurelia.)[105] They took Frieda for her first walk in Regent's Park on April 14. Three days later, Sylvia brought her infant to the CND anti-bomb protest in Trafalgar Square, "an immensely moving experience."[106] She told Aurelia about the long column of protesters marching in silence with their "Ban the Bomb" banners, and how she wept as she watched them file past, "proud that the baby's first real adventure should be as a protest against the insanity of world-annihilation—already a certain percentage of unborn children are doomed by fallout & noone [*sic*] knows the cumulative effects of what is already poisoning the air & sea."[107] She hoped that neither Aurelia nor Warren would vote for Richard Nixon in the upcoming American presidential election, a wish that became a command as the summer progressed. In July she told Aurelia she would "disown" her if she voted for him.[108] She asked her mother to find out if she could vote in absentia for Kennedy and told her to get them a subscription to *The Nation* "to keep up with American liberal politics."[109]

Sylvia was deeply concerned about the effect of nuclear war and fallout, but there was another reason she attended the march. Ted and Dido had gone off together to meet Bill Merwin there, and no one had thought to ask Sylvia to come along. Angry, Sylvia called Peter Redgrove, one of Ted's old Cambridge friends, and asked him to accompany her. They carried Frieda in a cot between them. When Ted and Dido returned to the flat, they found no note and became worried. Dido speculated that this had been Sylvia's way to exact "revenge" on her and Hughes for leaving without her.[110] She was probably right. Yet Redgrove "detected no tension whatsoever" between Sylvia and Ted.[111]

By late April Frieda had dropped her early-morning feeding, which meant that Sylvia could sleep straight through from two to seven a.m. "My whole philosophy of life is dependent on getting enough sleep: without it, one gets completely demoralized," she wrote to Aurelia. Although she was "eager to begin writing & thinking again," she could not imagine being separated from Frieda. She fretted about leaving the baby with a sitter's service during an upcoming cocktail party at Faber and Faber, where she would "presumably meet Eliot." Since Sylvia was breastfeeding, it was difficult for her to leave Frieda for more than a few hours. "I wish I could carry her like a papoose," she wrote.[112] But she went ahead and employed the service anyway.

In the end, she was glad to escape the flat, however briefly, without the baby. They met Hughes's Cambridge contemporary Karl Miller, literary editor of *The Spectator* (soon to move to the *New Statesman*), and a BBC producer for lunch, and had dinner with Lee Anderson, who had recorded Plath in Massachusetts for the Library of Congress. She gorged on performances: Laurence Olivier in Orson Welles's version of Ionesco's *Rhinoceros*, Harold Pinter's *The Caretaker* ("how much better, profounder, Ted could do it"), and the Royal Ballet's performance of *Antigone* ("tragic, wordless").[113] She would later persuade Ted to see Arnold Wesker's "Roots" trilogy that summer, which he reviewed for *The Nation*. Hughes had little patience for the Angry Young Men of the 1950s, but Plath felt that Wesker was the inheritor of the American playwright Clifford Odets, whose plays she described as "also about Jews & Communists."[114] This kind of left-wing, vaguely socialist drama still interested Plath, who had once written a similar kind of play,

Room in the World. Wesker's work connected her back to American politics, and resonated with her interest in outsiders.

Only Ted spoke to T. S. Eliot at the Faber and Faber cocktail party in Russell Square on April 21. Sylvia spent most of her time talking to Janet Burroway, a 1955 *Mademoiselle* guest editor and Cambridge Marshall scholar now living below Sylvia's old room at Whitstead. Faber and Faber was publishing her first novel, which put Plath on guard; Burroway was another doppelgänger, whose academic and literary trajectory resembled Plath's.[115] The two had mutual friends (Jane Truslow, Peter Davison) and had briefly crossed paths in America. Janet told Sylvia she had feared that her boyfriend would fall in love with her on his Oxford Fulbright—such was Sylvia's brilliant reputation. Janet recalled, "She was in a postpartum glow. I remember her glee at being a retrospective object of jealousy, and her impulsive invitation to supper."[116] Janet thought that Sylvia regretted the invitation, for on May 3 she received a short note inviting her and her friend Zulfi—Zulfikar Ghose, the distinguished Pakistani writer—over for a "very simple spaghetti" supper.[117] Veal scallopini, apparently, was for the Huwses; chicken tetrazzini for the Merwins.

Sylvia had joked that Janet would find her flat among the "squalidia" of Chalcot Square. Janet deconstructed the cute term years later: "It would be impossible to infer from England today the England of the fifties. Swinging London was not so much as a twinkle in anybody's eye, and the culture shock for the daughters of Betty Crocker was of a grimy kind—dour, fusty, crusted with the penury of spirit that a whole country had learned in war."[118] She thought Sylvia's décor—much of it inherited from the Merwins—"shabby" but "chosen with a good eye, care, and flair." She remembered "the stingy lighting and the sense of the ceiling's being too low for this high couple and their energy." She and Zulfikar found Sylvia busy with preparations, and Ted "cordial enough." Sylvia tried to hold her crying baby, only five weeks old, in her left arm as she cooked with her right. Janet saw that Sylvia was becoming "increasingly brittle, taut." When Frieda cried, Sylvia brought the baby into the living room and "shoved her" at Ted.[119] "He was pacing, gesturing with one simian arm, the baby held in an elbow-out crook of the other, while he described, intense and intent, how the animals woke him at night and how he lay listening to them."[120] Janet wrote her parents soon after the dinner that she found Ted "capable and slightly tough-looking . . . articulate and interesting and strong." He described for her the "English Attitude": "A fellow asked me: what do you think of being a father? What do you *think* of it—isn't that just like an Englishman?"[121]

Janet assumed that the Hugheses thought she and Zulfikar were a pair of "chattering hopefuls," though both were already quite successful.[122] The situation, with its rivalrous tension, "was dangerous," she wrote years later. She wished she could have "known Sylvia better."[123] Not long after the dinner, Sylvia wrote Lynne Lawner about Janet. "I find her cold & very clever, but feel—whether wrongly or not—that you & I are emotional sisters on the other side of the moon."[124] Sylvia could have used an American girlfriend who shared her intellectual firepower and literary aspirations. Back in Boston, Anne Sexton and Maxine Kumin read their poems to each other over the phone almost daily. Sylvia had no such female collaborator; in 1960, she had few friends in London at all. Her resentment of "doubles" like Janet stemmed partly from the sexist literary climate of the time and the scarcity of literary opportunities extended to women.

Over fifty years later, reflecting back on the dinner, Janet wrote, "All of us were floundering through new ideas of what marriage was . . . how far the writer's need for solitude could be allowed in the life of a wife and mother."[125] No one in her 1958 Barnard class, she said, had heard of feminism "except to describe antiquated efforts to win the vote. 'Liberation' was a word we used for 'Europe' and 'the Jews.' "[126] Barnard's president, Millicent McIntosh, had told Janet to call her "Mrs." rather than Professor, Dr., Dean, or President, as it was the title "she's proudest of." The messages were indeed mixed, and their effect on ambitious young women was destabilizing. Like Sylvia, Janet veered between visions of herself as a writer and herself as a mother. "I knew these two images were in conflict. What I didn't understand was that the choice might never be made, that my life could unroll, or lurch, or cascade, with the tension between them constant."[127] Sylvia had convinced herself, when she married Ted, that there was no conflict. But when the marriage began to dissolve, so did the glue with which she had fixed together these two seemingly irreconcilable selves.

———

IN THE SPRING OF 1960, Plath and Hughes made an influential friend: Al Alvarez, the young poetry critic at *The Observer*. Alvarez was well on his way to becoming his generation's kingmaker, that rare critic who would change the course of twentieth-century poetry. While the New Critical mantra was that poems should "not mean, but be," Alvarez felt poems should both mean *and* be. "Movement" poets were targets, as were "loose" Americans like William Carlos Williams and Allen Ginsberg. Technical skill was still highly valued, yet there was a new urgency: poems should engage, even if that engagement took the form of the death of a pig, or the shadows of a yew tree.

As an undergraduate at Corpus Christi College, Oxford, Alvarez had formed a trio with George Steiner—who would later write influentially about Plath—and the American poet Donald Hall, who was there on a Henry Fellowship.[128] Hall became Alvarez's mentor, and introduced him to contemporary American poetry.[129] After Oxford, Alvarez spent a year at Princeton. America was "a relief," he recalled. "England was all balled up in those days. It got its jaws a bit looser, but it took time. There was no American literature taught, which was rather stupid."[130] By the time he met Hughes and Plath at age thirty-one, he had published two academic books: *The Shaping Spirit* (1958), about modernist poetry; and *The School of Donne* (1960). He was an early champion of Thom Gunn, whose first book, *Fighting Terms*, he declared in the *Partisan Review* "the most impressive first book of poems since Robert Lowell's."[131] He would be partly responsible for the "twinning" of Gunn and Hughes.[132]

Like Hughes and Plath, Alvarez was obsessed with D. H. Lawrence; he had even made a pilgrimage to New Mexico to visit Lawrence's widow Frieda in 1956. He ended up marrying Frieda Lawrence's granddaughter Ursula Barr that same year, a fact that impressed Sylvia and Ted immensely. Alvarez, who described himself as a "London Jew," had been trained as a Leavisite but had decided to pursue freelance criticism rather than scholarship; he abandoned his fledgling doctorate at Oxford in 1956 to begin his influential ten-year stint at *The Observer*.[133] He later wrote, "if the young woman I was marrying was to be my Frieda, then I wanted to be her Lawrence, not her Professor Ernest Weekley."[134]

Alvarez was not keen on "the Group," the creative writing group Philip Hobsbaum had once run in Cambridge and now ran in London. "I don't think I ever went to one of their meetings, which was really an achievement," Alvarez recalled.[135] He thought the most exciting new poetry was coming from America in the form of Lowell's *Life Studies*, which he had praised highly in his *Observer* review of April 1959.[136] "I was useful," he recalled.[137] Indeed, Alvarez's review helped shore up support for Lowell in Britain.[138] (Lowell wrote to Elizabeth Bishop in April 1959, "I've gotten a rave review from Alvarez in England, so I guess the book won't be ignored.")[139] The two eventually became friends.[140] More than fifty years later, Alvarez still rated Lowell as without question the most important American poet of his era.[141]

The Group had been moving in a similar aesthetic direction. At their meetings, Edward Lucie-Smith wrote, "Very frank autobiographical poems—the poetry of direct experience—have been frequent."[142] As were dramatic monologues, which members often read aloud. It was the dawn of the 1960s, and a freer aesthetic was in the air. But there were more personal reasons Alvarez was drawn to the new poetics of Lowell and Sexton. "Nineteen sixty was, I suppose, the worst year of my life. My marriage was on the rocks, I was chronically depressed, and I celebrated Christmas by attempting to take my own life," he wrote in a memoir.[143]

Alvarez had already pronounced Hughes "a real poet" in his review of *The Hawk in the Rain*. He praised *Lupercal* even more highly that March.[144] In December, he would single out *Lupercal* in *The Observer* as one of the best books of 1960, indeed "the best book of poems to appear for a long time" and "a first true sign of the thaw in the dreary freeze-up of contemporary verse."[145]

Alvarez came round to Chalcot Square not long after Frieda's birth to interview Hughes, who immediately reminded him of Heathcliff: "He was a man who seemed to carry his own climate with him, to create his own atmosphere, and in those days that atmosphere was dark and dangerous."[146] Yet Hughes also seemed to Alvarez "quiet-spoken, shrewd and modest. He was not a man to give himself airs and never came on as a poet. It was not a line of work that would have cut much ice with his neighbours in Yorkshire or Devon and he had no taste for the literary world. But he was utterly sure of his talent."[147] When Alvarez entered the Chalcot Square flat, he had no idea that the woman who greeted him was Sylvia Plath, whose poems he had already published in his newspaper. When Plath—whom he described as "briskly American: bright, clean, competent, like a young woman in a cookery advertisement"—shyly revealed her identity, both were embarrassed. Alvarez thought that his mistake "depressed" her.[148] The three forged a tentative alliance that day with ramifications none of them could foresee.

In early May, Frieda emerged out of her "bleak world of cries, hungers & air bubbles" to give Ted her first smile. Plath's proofs for *The Colossus* arrived on May 4, and she lingered over every detail in a letter to Aurelia: "The poems look so beautifully <u>final</u>. The printers-publishers page says: William Heinemann Ltd. London Melbourne Toronto Cape Town Auckland The Hague. c Sylvia Plath 1960 All rights reserved. And of course says For Ted on the dedication page. I can't get over it."[149]

That same evening, Sylvia and Ted dined at T. S. Eliot's home with Stephen Spender and his wife, Natasha Litvin. Eliot put them "immediately at ease" as they spoke of America and sipped sherry by the coal fire.[150] Hughes found him mild, traditional, and impeccably mannered; he wrote to his old teacher John Fisher that Eliot had a habit of looking at the floor while he spoke in "funereal & measured" tones.[151] But he could also be "whimsical & pleasant," Spender "almost congenial."[152] Plath thought Spender "Wonderfully wry & humorous.... Talk was intimate gossips about Stravinsky, Auden, Virginia Woolf, D. H. Lawrence . . . I was fascinated. Floated in to dinner, sat between Eliot & Spender, rapturously & got along very well."[153] Hughes was overwhelmed by the gestures of support from the world's most famous poet. He wrote Olwyn, "I felt to get on so well with him though he's charitable & tactful & no doubt gives most people the feeling—that I must send him my play then go talk to him about it, as he invited me to."[154]

Eliot et al., as their elders, posed no threat, but Plath and Hughes were competitive with their contemporaries. In early 1960, the poet David Wright, who had won a Guinness award that year, turned down *Lupercal* for the Poetry Book Society choice. Hughes ran into him at the Lamb pub one night in Bloomsbury, where Wright told him he thought his book "too American," and "oughtn't to be encouraged." "This to my face," Hughes wrote to Luke Myers. "What a dim muddy glow there is lighting this goldfish bowl of the English intelligentsia. Nothing exists for them later than 1948. . . . America— the word itself, pronounced, acts on them like an obscene private joke."[155]

Sylvia saw several American friends that spring. Most cherished among them was her old Smith friend Ann Davidow. "I have so missed a good American girlfriend," she told Aurelia, an oft-repeated sentiment that suggests Sylvia's relative isolation in London.[156] Ann was visiting her fiancé, Leo Goodman, a math professor on a Guggenheim at Clare College, Cambridge. Together the two couples drove out to Stonehenge that May in balmy spring weather and picnicked among the buttercups near the "ominous upright stones." Sylvia called it an "exquisite day."[157] She also saw her old beau Myron Lotz, who annoyed her, as did Peter Davison and his wife, Sylvia's Lawrence House peer Jane Truslow, who, like her, had endured a breakdown and shock therapy. Over dinner at an Indian restaurant in Soho, the couples spoke about the BBC, T. S. Eliot, and American friends. Ted, who had seemed so silent in Boston, was now in good humor, telling the Davisons that advertising slogans were much simpler in the North than in London. ("In the North there's a great sign: 'Drink Wells Beer. Makes You Drunk.'") Though Sylvia began the evening "very gushy" ("Oh, how in-teresting!"), Jane remembered that as the night wore on, Sylvia became increasingly worried about Frieda, who was back at the flat with a sitter. The two women spoke about "this Great Experience of Motherhood," and Sylvia extolled the virtues of breastfeeding. "I thought she would bend over backward not to have this coming into the conversation. I was really surprised to find a sort of LaLeche-y League thing going on." When Sylvia's milk came in, the four cut the meal short so that Sylvia could get back to Frieda as quickly as possible.[158] Sylvia wrote to Aurelia that as they left Jane and Peter on the bus, "he yelled desperately after us: 'Look for the Hudson Review, I have a long poem coming out in it.' Pity & shame compelled me from yelling back 'I have four coming out in it.' "[159] (Davison would have the last word when, as an editor at Houghton Mifflin, he published Anne Stevenson's hostile Plath biography *Bitter Fame*, which was coauthored by Olwyn Hughes and advertised as a "Peter Davison Book.")

After entertaining the Davisons, Janet Burroway, Ann Davidow, Myron Lotz, and Lee Anderson, Sylvia implored Aurelia not to give out their address to London-bound Americans, "all but Ann a distraction & expense." Hiring sitters was also expensive, and they decided that Ted would no longer give readings unless he was paid. Now time was truly precious: the new baby and Ted's growing fame meant that Sylvia's workload had doubled.

> The baby's feedings & keeping the house clean & cooking & taking care of Ted's voluminous mail plus my own have driven me so I care only for carving out hours where I can start on my own writing. . . . even a modest fame brings flocks of letters, requests, schoolgirls asking for "the author's own analysis of the symbols in his stories" etc. ad nauseam. If Ted didn't have his study he'd be distracted by the phone, the mail, & odd callers so he'd get no work done at all. And as his secretary and my own I have a personal reason for being strict. So please help us by not steering anyone our way.[160]

Exceptions would have to be made for Ted's family, however. When Edith Hughes finally visited, more than two months after the baby's birth, Sylvia could sense her storing up every detail for a letter to Aurelia, which she indeed sent: "They both looked very well, Sylvia tall & slim & said she felt fine. She is so efficient handling the baby, no fuss or flurry, just goes quietly on. They both look very comfortable and happy." Edith noted that the flat was "spotlessly clean. She makes a lovely mother."[161]

Ted's career had "rocketed"—*Lupercal* sold so well that Faber and Faber did a second printing just two months after the first.[162] "My one aim is to keep Ted writing full-time," Sylvia declared to her mother.[163] He had finished a new verse play, *The House of Aries*, which the BBC's Third Programme accepted for production in the fall.[164] (T. S. Eliot had offered to "read & discuss" any more plays he wrote.)[165] Sylvia noted that nothing like the BBC existed in America, and that it had become a lifeline for them; it had paid Ted $3 a minute for various broadcasts since February.[166] He had begun a novel about Yorkshire (apparently never finished), which she was convinced would be a success if he were spared the deadening routine of office work. But she expected something for her sacrifice—namely, commercial success that would allow them to buy a London townhouse.

Sylvia knew that they would be worth much more someday, but they needed money now. The $5,000 nest egg in their American bank account was savings for a down payment on a house, to be touched only in an emergency.[167] They were "stretching" the Guggenheim—which officially ended on May 31—until September. Ted had even set up a meeting with a rare-book dealer, Ifan Fletcher, to sell some of his manuscripts to Indiana University for $450. Sylvia wanted nothing more than to buy her own house in London, but knew they would not get a mortgage unless Ted had a "'regular job.'" "Damn his uncle anyway," she wrote to Aurelia. She resented Walt Farrar for not helping them with money as her own mother did, and wished Ted "could adopt Maugham as uncle"—likely reflecting on her own financial relationship with Mrs. Prouty.[168]

When Sylvia saw a charming townhouse for sale around the corner at 41 Fitzroy Road, she began hatching plans. It was £9,500—about $25,900 (roughly $257,000 in 2020 dollars)—which they could just manage with a $5,000 down payment. But Ted was reluctant; the house was expensive, they had no regular income, and he did not want to be tied to a large mortgage at 5 percent interest. Sylvia knew he was right, and her initial elation subsided. She wrote of the house to Aurelia, who she probably hoped would offer financial assistance. But Aurelia was skeptical; at the bottom of Sylvia's letters, Aurelia calculated the price in dollars, and the interest. "$1295.00 int alone annually," she wrote.[169] Sylvia decided that it was a good time to send a letter to Mrs. Prouty, and instructed Ted to write, too. His ten-page explanation of his poems delighted Prouty, who asked Aurelia, on cue, what they were living on.

Sylvia had a practical solution to their financial dilemma: *she* would get a job. This was an audacious decision for a breastfeeding mother in 1960. But no bank would give them a mortgage without a steady income. She needed a break from child care and housework, and felt that part-time work might stimulate her writing again as it had in Boston. She enjoyed office life— she liked dressing up, gossiping, observing, and performing practical tasks. Though the set-up likely infuriated Aurelia, it was a progressive arrangement that many husbands of the time would not have sanctioned. Sylvia wrote to the Smith vocational office asking for references and transcripts, and began scanning ads.

On a hot and humid June 23, the Hugheses traveled to Faber and Faber in Bloomsbury's Russell Square, where they were ushered inside a high-ceilinged room with long windows that opened out onto a balcony. The evening soiree was in honor of W. H. Auden, who had left Britain for America under a cloud before the war. Now London's literati offered an apology of sorts. "I drank champagne with the appreciation of a housewife on an evening off from the smell of sour milk and diapers," Sylvia wrote Aurelia.[170] At one point, Charles Monteith called Sylvia over to see Ted, "flanked by TS Eliot, WH Auden, Louis MacNeice on the one hand & Stephen Spender on the other, having his photograph taken." " 'Three generations of Faber poets there,' Charles observed. 'Wonderful!' " Sylvia added, "Of course I was immensely proud."[171] A *Sunday Times* photographer took a now-famous photograph of the distinguished lineup, which was captioned "A Pride of Poets." Plath told the Merwins she thought MacNeice "a bit of a mess, but nice," Spender "very drunk," Eliot "amiable."[172] To Dr. Beuscher she was more starstruck over Eliot: "I honestly felt in the presence of a holy being."[173]

The poet Ruth Fainlight, who became close to Plath, later wondered how Plath truly felt as she watched her husband assume his place—literally and figuratively—in the twentieth-century British poetic tradition, which was solely male. "And of course you could feel proud, but more importantly and much more onerously, 'Where do I fit into this? What does this have to do with me?' " Fainlight felt that she herself had no poetic role models at the time, and certainly no female poet friends until she met Plath. "Eliot, Yeats, Graves, and Lawrence. . . . It was dispiriting, the fact that there weren't any women, actually. I mean, Edith Sitwell? No." She acknowledged that there was Teasdale, Millay, Bishop, and Moore, "but they weren't as thrilling to me as Lawrence or Yeats."[174] The literary sexism of the time was pervasive. "No matter what one thought, no matter how critical one's thoughts, it still saturated one, sank in, and was horribly influential."[175]

Hughes's anxieties were different. In his notebook, he revealed his view of the photo shoot:

Auden just inside the door, reptile wrinkles lively warm brown eyes, shortish, thick. Face almost immobile in its heavy wrinkles. Said hello—too much noise etc to comfortably say more and he quickly turned to some new person (which turned out to be Cyril Connolly). Later had photo taken on stairs: spoke with his wife, & Eliot joined. Asked when he did his reading while he worked at Lloyd's—he said most of it he had done before, but he continued to read for the Criterion articles. I asked if he had more of the landscape poems—no they were all. I said I imagined this was the sort of poem he worked on all the time—no they came to him some time after visiting the places. Spoke of jobs. He has been ill. Herbert Read told someone that Eliot has always been the ill one of the group—from the beginning. Chest trouble—or trouble breathing.[176]

The photo and the diary entry suggest Hughes's desire for recognition from an establishment he ostensibly rejected. T. S. Eliot would become Hughes's main living literary model. When Hughes learned of Eliot's death in 1965, it affected him deeply: "like a crash over the head, exactly, followed by headache. Heavy after-effects. I've so tangled him into my thoughts, as the guru-in-chief & dreamed of him so clearly & unambiguously that this will have consequences for me. At once I felt windswept, unsafe. . . . His being my publisher simply sealed his paternity. How often I've thought of going to ask for his blessing—and I would have once if I'd done as much as I could."[177]

Sylvia was gratified to see her husband "enshrined between The Great."[178] But with the arrival of her newborn daughter, the prospect of matching Ted's achievement had diminished. When a reporter at the Faber party asked her about Ted's Maugham award—"My dear, I'm so pleased your husband won the award. When are you going abroad to celebrate it?"—she answered, "Well, not till the baby can appreciate Europe a bit better."[179] Horizons were no longer boundless. They had imagined a utopian marriage in which they would both produce from the fiber of their being—and, indeed, after the Faber party, they gave a joint reading at the Institute of Contemporary Art—but their positions were becoming stratified along traditional lines. Jetting off to Italy with a toddler was not an attractive option. Sylvia's domestic workload was much heavier now, and her letters make clear that Ted's career took precedence at this time despite her casual mentions of *New Yorker* acceptances, first-book proofs, and requests for poems from the BBC. Still, Sylvia felt she was lucky. She wrote Aurelia in June that Ted was "wonderful" with Frieda, helped with housework a good deal, "& is strongly behind my having 3-4 hours of writing & study time a day."[180] Other Newnham gradu-ates, such as the authors Claire Tomalin and Jessica Mann, recalled their isolation and hopelessness raising children in the 1950s as they watched their husbands advance professionally. This was a time, Mann noted, when fathers refused to push strollers ("regarded as a symbol of unmanliness"), much less mind their own baby.[181] Hughes did so every day.

With the Merwins in France for the summer, the Hugheses socialized with the Huwses, Leo Goodman, and a local young couple, Ben and Sally Sonnenberg. (Ben and Ted would eventually grow close.) Sylvia and Ted celebrated Ted's thirtieth birthday on Hampstead Heath, picnicking on his favorite food: Fortnum & Mason's chicken pie, white wine, and salad. Sylvia gave him a witch figurine and an oil painting of an Aztec king from a local art gallery. To Aurelia she downplayed her disappointment about losing the Yale Younger Poets prize again, and American publishers' lack of interest in *The Colossus*, which she thought "better than most first books."[182] But the couple's recognition in America was growing. Harper's publishers, after reading her short story "The Daughters of Blossom Street" in *The London Magazine*, had expressed interest in a novel or short-story collection, while the editor of the *Texas Quarterly* hosted lunch for Plath and Hughes, and bought $200 worth of their work on the spot.[183] Six of Plath's poems appeared in major magazines that summer, including "A Winter Ship" in the July *Atlantic*, "Mushrooms" in the July *Harper's*, and "The Net Menders" in the August 20 *New Yorker*.[184]

Although Plath felt her days sliding into housework and baby-minding, she managed to write what she called several "light poems" that summer, including "Sleep in the Mojave Desert," "Two Campers in Cloud Country," and "On Deck."[185] (She sent them all to *The New Yorker*, along with "You're," on July 9; two were accepted.) But other summer poems were anything but light. In late June's "The Hanging Man," a poem about her shock treatment, one hears the chilly, authoritative voice of later poems like "Elm" and "Edge": "By the roots of my hair some god got hold of me. / I sizzled in his blue volts like a desert prophet." "The Hanging Man" set the tone for July's "Sleep in the Mojave Desert," which rehearsed similar imagery of deserts and lizards from Plath's American cross-country trip. "Stillborn," written in July, refers not to a baby, but to her poems, which refused to come to life:

> O I cannot understand what happened to them!
> They are proper in shape and number and every part.
> They sit so nicely in the pickling fluid!
> They smile and smile and smile and smile at me.
> And still the lungs won't fill and the heart won't start.

Plath continues, in the final stanza, "they are dead, and their mother near dead with distraction, / And they stupidly stare, and do not speak of her."

Sylvia wrote frequently in her letters about Frieda's merriness, and her delirious love for her daughter. But her poems that summer were filled with images of deformity, numbness, sterility, and terror. Gone were the playful invocations of "You're"—"O high-riser, my little loaf." Instead, there is "Stillborn," with its imagery of jarred, pickled fetuses, and references to exhaustion ("their mother near dead"), guilt, and boredom. These poems hint that Plath may have experienced some form of postpartum depression, which was a deeply taboo subject in 1960. Fear of being separated from one's baby—as chronicled in Charlotte Perkins Gilman's classic story "The Yellow Wallpaper"—kept the illness almost entirely underground. Postpartum depression was not even recognized in the psychiatric *Diagnostic and Statistical Manual* until 1994. Today the psychiatric community agrees that women with a history of depression are at a much higher risk for postpartum depression—indeed, Dr. Beuscher had warned Plath of that risk as early as 1959—and that mothers may experience postpartum depressive symptoms throughout the year following birth.[186] (Sylvia would tell her friend Catherine Frankfort in 1962 that she thought she was suffering from postpartum depression in the wake of Nicholas's birth.)[187]

Plath would have had no way to express feelings of postpartum depression in letters, and her journals from this time are lost. She may have turned to poetry to say the unsayable, with "stillborn" results: perhaps certain poems did not come because they were too terrible to write. There are some clues in her letters—the "ghastly July: rain every day," her aimless, "helterskelter" days, the "10 and 2 day feeds which so broke up my time."[188] In August she wrote Aurelia, "I really hunger for a study of my own out of hearing of the nursery where I could be alone with my thoughts for a few hours a day. I really believe I could do some good stories if I had a stretch of time without distractions."[189] Her pleasure reading included Alan Moorehead's *Gallipoli*. Ted wrote that it was around this time the two of them "with a great shock, discovered Emily Dickinson," whom he called "America's greatest poet, without a doubt."[190] Plath was already familiar with Dickinson, who was one of Aurelia's favorite poets, yet her surviving college essays show no evidence that she had studied Dickinson in any depth. The omission suggests the lack of academic attention women poets received—even the "greatest" of them.

The English summer was proving as dismal as she had expected, and Sylvia longed for sunny blue skies and a tan. "I am a horrid pale yellow. O England."[191] Yet for all the "raw and chilly" weather, she was relieved to live in England's welfare state. Her labor and delivery had been virtually free, as had all her postpartum treatment and Frieda's pediatric care. A bad infection in her lower lip that month, which required several visits to the doctor and two boxes of penicillin shots, cost only twenty-five cents. (She still was not ready to "risk" a Health Service dentist, however, and paid out of pocket for private dental care.) Health care would have cost much more in America, while the state-funded BBC made it possible for them to live in London without teaching. The two had earned more than $1,000 from their writing since moving there in February, thanks mainly to the BBC. Ted had made $330 for his hour-long *The House of Aries*, while George MacBeth at the BBC had asked Sylvia to contribute some poems to "a program of New Poetry."[192]

Aurelia's own finances—always Sylvia's safety net—became less secure when Boston University decided to fold its secretarial teaching department. Although she had tenure, she was now, she told her daughter, "working twice as hard" to earn an income—hoping for piecemeal work teaching German or medical shorthand.[193] Sylvia told her she was disgusted by BU's tactics, but she also sounds weary of her mother's penchant for martyrdom. "And don't think you should take courses to show them you're 'game' for anything." Sylvia had an answer to her mother's dilemma—a fascinating piece of advice that sheds light on the complicated symbiosis between the two women:

> I wish you'd spend half as much time in your afternoons playing with women's magazine stories, with feeling. Get a plot, imagine it in several scenes, with a character changing through events & finding something out about life & resolving problems. I'll edit anything you do for what it's worth. I bet if you pretended <u>this</u> was the way you had to earn some money, you'd turn out two or three things in the year. Why don't you try?[194]

Sylvia was all too aware, it seems, of her mother's unfulfilled literary ambitions.

In August, Sylvia and Ted returned to Yorkshire for a week. Hughes wanted to escape London's "incessant grinding wheel," which lately had caused him more "anxious pains."[195] His torpor dissipated as soon as he reached the moors. "The silence here is overpowering—because the hills seem to embody it—you can see it—everything is spellbound to it."[196] He was beginning to think that if he were ever to write anything of substance, he needed a real study and "spells of rural peace & isolation. . . . One visitor puts me off for the day before & the day after."[197] Sylvia got Ted's father talking about the First World War, and his stories amazed them both. She told Aurelia she was finally able to unwind after "months of half-fatigue." They took long walks while Edith watched Frieda, cooked their meals, and did their laundry. Sylvia expressed her gratitude for this "vacation of sorts" begrudgingly (she had resolved not to cook).[198] But the time away from the baby and the walks in the "pure clear air" widened her perspective. "All the frustrations of habit fell away & we made several long-range plans."[199] They spent a day at the seaside resort of Whitby after Uncle Walt stuffed $150 into Ted's pocket at the pub. Whitby did not impress Sylvia: "there is something depressingly mucky about English sea resorts. . . . the sand is muddy & dirty. The working class is also dirty—candy papers, gum [sic] cigarette wrappers. My favorite beach in the world is Nauset & my heart aches for it. I don't know, there is something <u>clean</u> about New England sand, no matter how crowded."[200] In her 1961 poem about the English seaside, "Whitsun," she would write, "And we picnic in the death-stench of a hawthorn. / The waves pulse and pulse like hearts. / Beached under the spumy blooms, we lie / Seasick and fever-dry."

Back in London, they began looking for a new study. They had tired of the "obligations" and "giddy hairdresser sublessees" that came with use of the Merwins' study, and had decided that the Merwins would not, after all, be Frieda's godparents.[201] (In December they would ask Leo Goodman and Ann Davidow-Goodman.) Sylvia wrote Aurelia that they now had "large reservations" about the friendship with the Merwins: "both of us feel the need to free ourselves from this uncomfortable dependency. . . . Ted's work is so good he doesn't need 'contacts' of any sort."[202] In December, they would use a $150 check from Mrs. Prouty to replace the Merwins' furniture, still in their flat. Mrs. Morton upstairs allowed them to use her attic flat while she was at work, though Hughes only used it a few times before retreating, again, to the windowless cubicle in his entryway.

Success continued upon success. Stanley Kunitz published another glowing review of *Lupercal* in *Harper's*, and Hughes appeared in the September 9 issue of *The Times Literary Supplement* in an article about the "British Imagination," along with a photo and two poems, "Thistles" and "A Fable."[203] (He would publish the same two poems, for $50, in *Mademoiselle*, of all places, in March 1961.) Hughes now had various paid speaking engagements in schools and colleges around London. Plath published "The Manor Garden" in *The Atlantic*, "The Beekeeper's Daughter" and "The Colossus" in the *Kenyon Review*, and other poems and stories in *The Hudson Review*, *The Listener*, the *Texas Quarterly*, and *The Sewanee Review* that fall.[204] She began taking Italian lessons at Berlitz twice a week in anticipation of their Maugham travel award; despite a toddler in tow, she had talked herself into going either to Corsica or Italy (her friend Lynne Lawner was still living in Rome) in the spring of 1961.

The Yorkshire visit had prodded them to start house hunting in the countryside. They now considered Cornwall, where Sylvia fantasized about buying a house with an orchard and a view of the sea. Still, she would have preferred to stay in London; it seemed a mistake to leave just as their reputations were taking off. In late September, Ted lunched with Thom Gunn and Charles Monteith—who reported T. S. Eliot's delight with his children's book, *Meet My Folks!*—and he and Sylvia drank champagne with their publishers, a BBC producer, and John Lehmann at his "posh Kensington house."[205] If Ted ever became rich from his writing, Sylvia said, she would buy a home on Hampstead Heath and divide their year between London and the country. "I am much more a city-dweller than Ted," she told Aurelia.[206]

In November, Sylvia would spend a day in a real estate agent's office educating herself about "mortgages, rent controlled tenants and other details." She collected lists of houses for sale in her district and presented herself, with a letter of introduction from her new doctor, Dr. Horder, to the owner of a nearby townhouse selling for £7,000 at 4 Chalcot Crescent. Sylvia told

Aurelia it was her dream house, and felt that they would be able to afford it in another year or so. She put her name down for "first refusal." "Oh mother for the first time I saw us living in a house perfectly suited to our needs!"[207] She vowed to write more women's magazine stories in hopes of making money, and signed with a London agent, Jennifer Hassell, who she hoped would help her break into the market. But Sylvia bet on Ted's plays as the surest moneymaker. "Maybe someday you'll be able to go see his plays on Broadway!" she wrote her aunt, uncle, and grandfather.[208] She knew that the townhouse was "impossible to manage at this point, but who knows what Ted will have written in a year's time."[209]

Sylvia often dramatized their financial situation, telling others they were living on next to nothing when in fact they had managed to save $7,000 by November 1960—an astonishing sum of money for two freelance writers. It was enough to pay for a country house in cash. Sylvia's American dream of home ownership dovetailed with Ted's desire for a quiet rural retreat. And she wanted Ted to be happy. "There he is, after him a huge gulf, and then the rest of the little people," she wrote her mother that fall.[210] In the meantime, they lived frugally. They held off on a *New Yorker* subscription until Aurelia finally bought them one in September. Nor did they buy a radio, despite all of Hughes's BBC broadcasts, until September. Sylvia began making Frieda's clothes with a sewing machine (lent to her by Marcia's London friend, Marcia Momtchiloff), boasting to Aurelia that she could save $3 on a nightie. The savings were almost an afterthought once she began designing; the outfits filled her with pride.

The Colossus was published on October 31, her birthday week. The print run was small—just five hundred copies—and Plath was upset by two typeset errors that had somehow slipped through. But she was delighted with the cover: a light green rectangle with her name and the title, in small black letters, surrounded by a delicate, Victorian floral pattern against a white background. It was a more feminine cover than the Faber jackets of Hughes's books, with their bold colors and large typeface. But the poems inside were not delicate and feminine. Plath had mostly jettisoned her cerebral, reflective, formally intricate work—only three poems from 1956 or before remained—for an art that was looser and more ominous. The weather of these poems was gray-green storm light, their mood apprehensive. Ted was impressed. He wrote to Olwyn that week, "I've been living with her poems for 4 years now & am very critical, but they remain absolutely fresh & unique."[211]

In the collection's best poems, "The Colossus," "Lorelei," "Full Fathom Five," "The Manor Garden," "Hardcastle Crags," "The Disquieting Muses," "Mussel Hunter at Rock Harbor," and "The Stones," Plath builds up a pressure she never quite releases. In her manuscript's previous incarnations (*Cir-*

cus in Three Rings, Two Lovers and a Beachcomber, The Bull of Bendylaw, The Earthenware Head, The Devil of the Stairs, Full Fathom Five), most of the poems were tightly reined in and controlled, more metaphysical than Romantic in spirit. In *The Colossus*, a master draftswoman has begun to paint abstracts. In her title poem, the dead father's "pig-grunt" is "worse than a barnyard." Plath conjures the *Oresteia* in the poem, but she has gained the confidence to question and subvert the elegiac tradition. These were courageous poems for a woman to publish in 1960. Still, despite Plath's risk taking, no poem in the book truly shattered convention. "The Colossus," with its anger toward the Father, and "The Stones," full of asylum imagery, come close; but for all the thinly veiled anger toward Otto and Aurelia in "The Colossus" and "The Disquieting Muses," the resentful daughter remains dutiful in both poems. Luke Myers knew that Plath was holding back. In his 1962 *Sewanee Review* analysis of the collection, he noted, "I can not help wondering what will happen if, in Miss Plath's second volume of poems, the emotional distance is shortened." He asked for fewer phrases like "Mark, I cry," and more of "the pressure of 'Lorelei.'"[212] In *Ariel*, Plath would let the pressure build, and release: "Off, off, eely tentacle!" she would write in "Medusa"; in "Daddy," "you bastard, I'm through."

Plath wrote at least six poems between late September and December 1960. The BBC asked her to record two of them, "Leaving Early," set in Mrs. Morton's attic flat, and "Candles," on October 26. "I am just slowly surfacing," she wrote to Lynne Lawner that fall.[213] She was inching her way toward the *Ariel* voice. The end of October's "Love Letter," for example, rehearses the rising, "pure acetylene / Virgin" of "Fever 103°": "From stone to cloud, so I ascended. / Now I resemble a sort of god / Floating through the air in my soul-shift / Pure as a pane of ice. It's a gift." She conjured up a glass bell jar in November's "A Life," and examined its "inhabitants." This was a stark portrait of depression:

> A woman is dragging her shadow in a circle
> About a bald, hospital saucer.
> It resembles the moon, or a sheet of blank paper
> And appears to have suffered a sort of private blitzkrieg.
> She lives quietly
>
> With no attachments, like a foetus in a bottle,
> The obsolete house, the sea, flattened to a picture
> She has one too many dimensions to enter.

"Candles" and its companion poem "Magi," both written that October and inspired by Frieda, are gentler poems set in soft, golden light, but with ambiguous blessings.[214] In both poems, Plath deconstructs the religious imagery surrounding the Christ child. (That year, Plath called herself and Hughes "two grim atheists.")[215] The wise men in "Magi" are "dull angels" who have nothing to teach her daughter: "Let them astound his heart with their merit. / What girl ever flourished in such company?" In "Candles," the mother is full of doubt about her nursing infant's future as the candles weep and glow around her. "How shall I tell anything at all / To this infant still in a birth-drowse?" Sylvia told Aurelia that the poem was "about candles & reminiscences of grammy & grampy in Austria spoken while nursing Frieda by candlelight at 2 am. I'm very fond of it."[216] The candlelight conjures up a gentler world that no longer exists, symbolized by the mother's memory of her Austrian grandmother presenting roses to Emperor Franz Josef. Candles now "Drag up false, Edwardian sentiments." The speaker knows a different reality—two world wars since Franz Josef, and the threat of nuclear annihilation.

Sylvia never mentioned her doubts and fears for her child in her letters, where Frieda squeals in delight over her teddy bear and beats on a book like a drum, as Ted taught her. Sylvia told Aurelia she would have three more children: Megan, Nicholas, and Jacob. But to the just-married Ann Davidow-Goodman she wrote of never-ending sinus colds, which Ted told her she could cure if she put her mind to it. (He prescribed brandy, which, she joked, was her preferred medicine.) After the "crisp blue American weather" of September, Sylvia knew that she needed courage for the darkening months ahead.[217] "Winter is here, the long wet grey half-year, and the leaves afflicted with jaundice and raining down from the trees," she wrote Ann that October.[218] An uncollected poem from autumn 1960, "Home Thoughts from London," sounds a melancholy note. "Milk-fog's indigenous to Regent's Park," Plath writes. "Where are the trenchant autumns I knew— / The sumac-maple war paint of outer Boston?"

> O blueness, crispness, O superlatives—
>
> Call up those Lincoln-Concord clear days I
> Let slip like football games, without a look.
> I'm smothered by a fuzzed gentility,
> Mopish in my black coat as any rook.

"Together with some dozen welfare mothers," the speaker wheels her baby daughter to Primrose Hill in the mist. The poem ends, "we're strangers here."[219]

AS SYLVIA STRUGGLED to find time to write, Ted became more determined to protect himself from the distractions of literary life. "Very strange & very unpleasant because you feel you're being turned into something, saturated with people's thinking about you," he wrote to Olwyn in the summer of 1960.[220] In November, the BBC's Third Programme aired his play *The House of Aries*, and he turned down the chance to appear on television as part of a show, hosted in Leeds by John Betjeman, on northern writers.[221] Sylvia had written excitedly to Dr. Beuscher about the invitation, "I hope he gets his face on the screen!"[222] In December, despite protest from his mother, he passed on another invitation to appear on British television as "poet-of-the-year." He had begun to dread the critical commentary that followed his radio broadcasts, positive though they were. By year's end he had decided to refuse all speaking engagements and "cumbersome commissions": "public life appalls him," Sylvia wrote.[223] She began telling others he was a "hibernant."[224] Ted explained his predicament in more detail to Aurelia and Warren in a December letter, calling the previous year "the busiest, most preoccupied year I've ever spent":

> when I got back here (having left in 1957 as a complete unknown) I found myself really quite famous and was deluged by invitations to do this, give readings, do that, meet so-and-so, etc, and many doors were comfortably wide open that I had never dreamed of being able to enter and places such as the B.B.C., which I had been trying to penetrate for years, suddenly received me as guest of honour. . . . To enter "literary life" is in fact to enter a small windowless cell, empty, under a stunning spotlight, and left to your own devices in the knowledge that millions of invisible eyes are watching through the walls. It's not "life" at all, you see. And it cuts you off from life.

He admitted that "it had to be tasted at first hand" and had given him some "real advantages"—contacts with the BBC, influential editors, and grant givers. "Though I might have had these anyway."[225]

Plath, however, was still vying for recognition. *The Colossus* received good reviews from prominent critics like John Wain in *The Spectator*, Roy Fuller in *The London Magazine* ("The language of this poetry is unusual but not eccentric, with a great gift for the right epithet, the metaphoric noun"), Austin Clarke in *The Irish Times*, Thomas Blackburn in the *New Statesman*, and Al Alvarez in *The Observer*.[226] Richard Howard, in *Poetry*, perceptively noted that Plath wanted "to make you *hear* what she sees, the texture of her language affording a kind of analogue for the experience she presents."[227] The book would be reviewed prominently alongside collections by Boris Pasternak, e. e. cummings, and John Betjeman on the BBC in late December.[228] But it won no prizes, and Heinemann, according to Plath, did not "advertise" it.[229] The couple's friends could not find it in London bookshops.[230] Plath worried that she would never find her readers, and that *The Colossus* would remain merely a "gift book" for her friends and relatives.[231] At least Mrs. Prouty had sent her another check for $150—the only money, she joked dryly, the book would ever earn. Still, she proudly sent an inscribed copy to Mr. Crockett with an accompanying letter about dinners with T. S. Eliot and Stephen Spender.

Sylvia awoke on her twenty-eighth birthday to German coffee cake, complete with flaming candle, and gifts wrapped in brown paper. They celebrated at home with a Fortnum & Mason chicken pie, German chocolate, Brie, Stilton and cheddar, pink champagne, and the *Lord of the Rings* trilogy. Sylvia declared it her best birthday yet and told Aurelia with her usual hyperbole that she was "happier living in London than anywhere else in the world."[232] Yet in the same letter she spoke tentatively of returning to America and asked Aurelia to help organize Ted's application to reenter the U.S.

Stephen Spender had written the Hugheses a letter after Eliot's dinner party in May, apologizing for having talked too much. He invited them to dinner that October, along with Louis MacNeice and Rosamond Lehmann (John Lehmann's sister). Hughes barely tolerated the evening. He told Olwyn he found Spender "poisonous," chatting on about Churchill ("Winnie") and other British politicians. "You constantly have the feeling of being permitted to look into this brilliant ballroom full of shining heads who are all exclaiming 'Stephen, darling.' . . . MacNeice comes off much better,—though he's terribly slimy, he's slimy in his own way."[233] Hughes grew impatient of the talk surrounding poetry and politics, especially the poetry of the 1930s. Sylvia wrote Olwyn that she was "more tolerant of Spender than Ted—or corrupt enough to be amused by him & a bit fond of him."[234] Plath delighted in the literary gossip and felt herself a witness to history. "Their conversation is fascinating—all about Virginia (Woolf), what Hugh (Gaitskell) said to Stephen in Piccadilly that morning, why Wystan (WH Auden) likes this book or that, how Lloyd George broke Spender's father's heart."[235] On such evenings, Plath felt that she had arrived.

Spender procured Plath a press ticket to the last day of the *Lady Chatterley's Lover* obscenity trial at the Old Bailey on November 2. The issue at the heart of the trial was D. H. Lawrence's use of the word "fuck." In her journal, Plath quoted Dame Rebecca West, the bishop of Woolwich, and Dame

Helen Gardner of Oxford on the novel's merit and moral message, which resonated with her own: in short, the novel was "a bold experiment trying to study sex. [*sic*] situation more openly." Graham Hough from Christ's College, Cambridge, told the judge (in Plath's words), "No proper language to discuss sexual matters—either clinical or disgusting—secretive, morbid attitude. L tries to redeem normally obscene words."[236] The verdict in Lawrence's favor came to symbolize the beginning of the swinging sixties, with its attendant loosening of restrictive social mores.[237]

The trial was a victory for literature in general, and Plath and Hughes's vision in particular. Plath wrote to Dr. Beuscher about her surprise at the "not guilty" verdict from the "unpromising prosperous middleclass [*sic*] looking jury after a very biased, sneering summing up by the judge who tried to influence the jury against the 'egghead' witnesses."[238] Those impeccably credentialed "egghead witnesses" argued that the infidelity at the heart of the novel was "sacred," "highly moral," and "spiritual"—that this was, as the bishop of Woolwich put it, "a book Christians ought to read." In her journal Plath recorded Mrs. Bennet of Girton College, Cambridge, saying, "physical life impt. & is being neglected—people live poor & emasculated lives, living with half of themselves. . . . a marriage can be broken when it is unfulfilled."[239] Sylvia agreed wholeheartedly. Yet, when infidelity occurred in her own marriage, Hughes would look no further than Lawrence for his imprimatur.

Sylvia spent much of November house hunting and working on stories she could sell to American women's magazines (she and Ted had started collaborating on plots again). Ted felt that there was greater potential in such writing than the "art stories" she had previously been trying to sell. Instead of shoehorning her poetic sense into women's-magazine fiction, Ted thought she was better off facing real life—particularly birth and marriage—head on.[240] Meanwhile, he worked on the *Bardo Thodol* and a handful of poems. Sylvia told Olwyn she was "suffering late autumn exhausture & blues"; Frieda was teething, waking up two or three times each night and leaving her "haggard."[241] She dreamed about selling enough stories to pay for a regular part-time babysitter who would release her from "the drudge-work" of child-rearing, though she also felt that "children seem to be an impetus to my writing." She was heartened by the BBC broadcast of "Candles" and "Leaving Early" on November 20 for *The Poet's Voice*, as well as BBC commentator Owen Leeming's request for her stories (she sent him one of Ted's, as she felt she had nothing worth showing). But broadcasting work would not secure a mortgage. She needed to find a "queer parttime" job.[242]

On weekends, she and Ted explored art museums and bookshops. They were struck by the Picasso exhibit at the Tate. Sylvia bought and inscribed the exhibition book, while Ted wrote to Olwyn, "Everything after Bathers playing with a ball about 1930 to Guernica, really gave me a shock." He thought Picasso "A sadistically abusive wit at bottom, a great noise in the street," though he preferred Klee's work.[243] Plath found a new muse in the paintings of Leonor Fini, an Italian-Argentine painter whose work was exhibited at the Kaplan Gallery in London from November 2 to December 3 that year. Sylvia wrote to Olwyn of her enthusiasm for Fini's "jewel-like misty otherworldish damsels & cadavers with a weird, terrifying beauty, like necrological mannequins."[244] She fantasized about "paying pilgrimage" to her Corsican monastic home. Fini's paintings of women and corpses—some of them ironic depictions of women out of mythology and Romantic poetry—resonated deeply with Plath's own "weird" aesthetic instincts. Indeed, there is an echo of Fini's statuesque "necrological mannequin" in "Edge."

On December 18, the day after Hughes's short story "The Harvesting" was broadcast, Plath listened to Edward Lucie-Smith's good review of *The Colossus* on the BBC's Third Programme.[245] Lucie-Smith, a member of the Group, was an important young critic. But Alvarez outdid him. His December 18 review of *The Colossus* in *The Observer* would help make Plath's name. Alvarez was candid about the biases Plath faced in London:

> Sylvia Plath's *The Colossus* needs none of the usual throat-clearing qualifications, to wit: 'impressive, considering, of course, it is a *first* volume by a *young* (excuse me), *American* poet*ess*.' Miss Plath neither asks excuses for her work nor offers them. She steers clear of feminine charm, deliciousness, gentility, supersensitivity and the act of being a poetess. She simply writes good poetry. And she does so with a seriousness that demands only that she be judged equally seriously. . . . most of her poems rest secure in a mass of experience that is never quite brought out into daylight. . . . It is this sense of threat, as though she were continually menaced by something she could see only out of the corner of her eye, that gives her work its distinction.

This was not fey ladies' poetry—it was "serious." Plath's language was "no-nonsense," "bare but vivid and precise, with a concentration that implies a good deal of disturbance with proportionately little fuss." Even her weaker poems, which Alvarez likened to "fairy stories," were intriguing: "here her tense and twisted language preserves her and she ends with something ominous, odd, like one of the original tales from Grimm."[246] Still, the poet Richard Murphy sensed the entrenched sexism behind even this review. "Sylvia got pats on the head from Alvarez for being such a good woman poet that you wouldn't think she was a woman: 'it's wonderful to think that there's at last a woman poet that you don't have to make allowances for!' She must have felt this."[247]

Alvarez reviewed three other books that day, including Merwin's *The Drunk in the Furnace*, but he gave pride of place to *The Colossus*. Plath was quietly jubilant that her review was twice the length of Merwin's, though she knew that the attention would create trouble with Dido: "it would be difficult to toss off such a review where my book got first place, most space & best notices."[248] On the following page, Plath and Hughes saw Alvarez's pick for the best poetry collection of the year: *Lupercal*.[249] Alvarez, "the bright young critic," as Plath called him, had singlehandedly secured their reputations in reviews that were practically side by side.[250] Their poetic and personal partnership had never been so strong.

24

Nobody Can Tell What I Lack

London, January–March 1961

By mid-December 1960, Sylvia knew that she was again pregnant. She looked forward to "the deep dreamless sleeps of Yorkshire," where they would spend Christmas.[1] Ted, too, was ready to leave London and return to the moors—"the air like solid clear glass we can walk through miraculously," Sylvia wrote to the poet Philip Booth.[2] Yet the journey north was ill-starred. After Christmas, on December 30, Sylvia and Olwyn—"fresh from Paris"—had a terrible row.[3] "Olwyn made such a painful scene this year that I can never stay under the same roof with her again," Sylvia wrote Aurelia.[4] She had left the Beacon at dawn with Ted and Frieda without a word.

The women's previous two meetings had been fraught and tense, and their relationship had devolved during the past year. Sylvia thought that her book's good reviews had made Olwyn jealous, while Olwyn claimed Sylvia overreacted to something she said and lost her temper. Both may have been looking for a fight. On New Year's Day, Sylvia wrote a furious letter to Aurelia about the argument, and another long letter to Dr. Beuscher a few days later. She had always hoped that Olwyn would "accept Ted's marriage and forgive me for being a person with marked opinions, feelings and 'presence,' but this Christmas some small spark touched off the powderkeg & she made obvious to Ted & his mother what I've known all along: that her resentment is a pure and sweeping and peculiarly desperate hatred."

In her seven-page letter to Dr. Beuscher, the longest of Plath's fourteen surviving letters to her former psychiatrist, she continued, "Olwyn had been nagging at us for being too critical of people ever since she came up & finally I asked her to lay off & said she was as critical as the two of us put together." This was the first time she had ever "confronted" Olwyn.

She started to fume and shriek and the stream of words ran more or less "youre [*sic*] a nasty bitch, a nasty selfish bitch, Miss Plath" (she calls me by my maiden name as if she could unmarry me) "you act as if our house were your palace, I watched you eat Christmas dinner & you certainly stuffed yourself, you think you can get away with everything, you're trying to come between Ted & me, you bully me and my mother and Ted. I'm the daughter in this house.... you're a bitch, an immature woman, inhospitable, intolerant..." and on and on.... Ted's mother did say blandly that the two of them slept in the same bed till Olwyn was 9 and Ted 7. So she does have a five year lead on me.

Sylvia thought that Olwyn's "fury" had to do with her visit to Chalcot Square the previous spring, when she had brought a guest and expected a heavily pregnant Sylvia to wait on her. Sylvia "had visions of a sisterly interest in my feelings," but Olwyn had ignored her and talked astrology with Ted. It turned out, Sylvia told Dr. Beuscher, that Olwyn had wanted to stay with them. Sylvia told her the flat was too cramped already, and she was about to have a baby. Olwyn brought up the issue again at Christmas, claiming "you had plenty of room." That night, Sylvia left the house.

I put the baby to bed and went for a long walk in the full moon over the moors, utterly sick. What upset me most was that neither Ted nor his mother <u>said</u> anything. I simply said, "Go on, Olwyn, tell me all of it." Ted appeared with his nice sane art-teacher cousin in a car as I was nearing Scotland. He had evidently hit his sister & told her off after I'd gone. Later, he said what we'd just witnessed was a pathological case & that we'd better steer clear of Olwyn till she got married. Luckily I remembered your wise advice that the woman who shouts her head off most seems in the wrong regardless of who's right & I was glad I hadn't retorted to Olwyn in kind.

Olwyn told Sylvia she would never again return home for Christmas if Sylvia was there. "The morning we left—neither Ted nor I having slept & his mother having cried all night—she threw her arms around me, smiled, said 'I'm sorry' & ran back to bed."[5] Sylvia thought Olwyn's apology was a show to mollify her brother. She told Aurelia that Olwyn had also taunted Gerald's wife, Joan, into leaving the Beacon in tears; Ted had to retrieve her from the train station with her bags packed for Australia. Sylvia wrote Beuscher, "As Ted said, 'if she did that to Joan, not caring much about Gerald & never writing to him, you can imagine how much more she resents you.' I certainly can. . . . I remember your saying when I spoke of their childhood intimacy that this sort of thing never ends or undoes itself."[6] (The fact that Ted and Olwyn had shared a bed as young children led Sylvia—and others—to speculate about incest. But this was a then common practice in cramped, working-class households like the Hugheses' in Mytholmroyd.) Sylvia asked Beuscher for advice, as she did not want to "drive" Olwyn and Ted to have "clandestine meetings." Should she keep quiet about what happened? "What attitude should I take when we meet again? Generous, I suppose." She had acted like a "goody-goody" around her "pseudo-mothers—Mrs. Prouty, Mary Ellen Chase, Mrs. Cantor ad inf, but I am not prepared to regress & efface myself with Olwyn."[7]

Whatever happened that night, the two women resented each other deeply; Olwyn later called Sylvia "straight poison," "a monster," "hurtful and bloody rude," and "a complete bitch."[8] These two confident, literary, and cosmopolitan women might have been natural allies. Olwyn graduated with a 2.2 degree (cum laude) in English literature from Queen Mary College, London, in 1950, and then worked in Paris as a secretary at the British embassy and the Martonplay literary agency. In Paris, as Hughes's biographer Jonathan Bate wrote, "She was having the time of her life, with French food and wine, freedom and boyfriends."[9] This was the kind of life Sylvia, too, had once dreamed about. But their similarities, and their love of Ted, pushed them toward rivalry. The cramped quarters at the Beacon could not have helped family harmony, and Olwyn may have sniffed out Sylvia's snobbishness toward Edith. (Sylvia and Ted would stay in a separate cottage next door during a future visit.) The two women, as Sylvia predicted, would never meet again, though they would exchange a few friendly letters.[10] In fact they met on only six occasions while Plath was alive; Olwyn admitted in 1976, "I really didn't know her well at all."[11] Yet as Hughes's literary agent, Olwyn would effectively control Plath's copyright, and story, for almost four decades.

Ted could have tried to broker a peace between the two women, as he did in the summer of 1957, but he chose to leave the Beacon with his wife without saying goodbye. He told Sylvia Olwyn's "outburst derived from an idiotic jealousy."[12] In his diary on January 3, 1961, he wrote, "Olwyn's attack on Sylvia, like her attack on Joan. In the animal world the attacker always wins."[13] He tried to comfort Olwyn, too. "Don't get too depressed about Xmas—we feel how we feel, apparently," he wrote her on January 10. But he defended his wife; he didn't agree that Sylvia had been "crusading."[14]

After the drama at the Beacon, Sylvia and Ted welcomed the clean slate of the new year. "Last year was a sort of death-march, except for Frieda," Ted wrote Luke Myers in January. He had written "nothing," been plagued by "exhaustions, nervous tics" and nightmares about being trapped inside "falling houses"—"the classical dream of the breakdown." Sylvia, too, had "been going through a poor time, with bouts of flu . . . & sundry malicious planetary foistings."[15] Back in their warm flat, life seemed more bearable. They were on good terms with the Merwins again—Bill had secured them more reviewing for *The Nation*—and Sylvia described them to Aurelia as "really the nicest people we know here."[16] Meanwhile, Hughes's old Pembroke friend Brian Cox, now running *Critical Quarterly* with Tony Dyson, asked Plath to select and edit a supplement of American verse for the magazine.[17] She was delighted by the invitation and began planning her selection. She finally found a temporary part-time afternoon job doing copyediting and layout work at *The Bookseller*—work she enjoyed so much that she thought about becoming an editor when her children were school age. She hoped that the extra money would help them through "this bare time between grants."[18] Although she tried to write as much as possible while tending to the baby, it was difficult to find consecutive hours in which to concentrate. She was determined not to be an overindulgent mother, for her own sake as much as Frieda's. "I want her to be a self-sufficient creature who can read or color or play with toys while I work nearby," she told Aurelia, "none of this holding her on the lap all day as Mrs. Hughes did which was nearly the ruin of her."[19]

Their social lives grew busier. Early in the year, they met the critic M. L. Rosenthal, poetry editor of *The Nation* (he had recommended that Macmillan publish *The Colossus*, which he thought "very good"). The first time they met, Sylvia seemed quiet, in the background, "effaced by her very powerful husband. . . . It was he who did all the talking. . . . One would never have guessed the power behind that rather overpolite façade." She struck him as "Very American, very well-scrubbed." Rosenthal remembered meeting the Hugheses again at a dinner party at Alvarez's house in June 1961. He, Hughes, and Alvarez initially did most of the talking, but Plath "brightened up" when Rosenthal began speaking about his ideas regarding "Confessional" poetry. "She remarked on studying with Lowell, knowing Sexton, the openings for her own verse that their examples had provided." She spoke about *Life Studies*. "She was terribly interested in Lowell but characteristically she didn't say anything about him personally. What she was interested in and what she talked about quite a lot was the question of putting yourself right into the poem. And the problem of aestheticizing it, of transcending the material, of getting beyond the personal. We agreed about that: it could be done, it had to be done, it wasn't worth it unless you get past the personal." (By this time, Rosenthal had coined the term "Confessional poetry," with which Plath's name would be forever linked.)[20] He also remembered Sylvia's telling him about her shared child-minding arrangement with Ted, which he felt was "certainly unusual for that time and indicated an unusual flexibility in Ted . . . or an unusual will in Sylvia."[21]

Eleanor Ross Taylor and her husband, Peter, both American writers close to Robert Lowell, invited Plath and Hughes to dinner at their Kensington Gate home that January. Thom Gunn came for lunch early in the month while he was traveling through London on his Somerset Maugham Award. Plath called him "a rare, unaffected & kind young chap."[22] He was Hughes's Cambridge contemporary (Faber and Faber would publish a joint anthology of their work in 1962). But Plath was more excited to finally meet Theodore Roethke, whom she called "my Influence," at a party on February 1.[23] (Ted had given her Roethke's *Words for the Wind* for Christmas.) Roethke told Hughes to "give him a nod" if he ever wanted to teach at the University of Washington, and Plath soon began planning "another American year."[24] Hughes was probably less excited about such a plan. The Poetry Center at the 92nd Street Y—the cosponsors of the first book prize Hughes had won— asked Plath that spring to give a reading in New York. The opportunity for literary parity with her husband appealed to her, and she hoped to accept at a later date.[25]

Such parity was beginning to seem within her reach. On January 18, Plath and Hughes recorded *Two of a Kind: Poets in Partnership* on the BBC (it was broadcast on January 31).[26] The program offered a fascinating account of their shared creative life, and suggests that Plath was becoming better known. Still, an internal BBC memo hinted that Hughes was the main draw: "What do we have on his wife?" someone wrote in the margin of Hughes's letter confirming that he and Plath would record the program.[27] The previous July, after Plath had sent the poet and BBC producer George MacBeth some of her poems, he told Anthony Thwaite she was "like her husband on an ordinary day"—that her best poems only matched Hughes's average ones.[28]

Hughes spoke in broad Yorkshire cadences tempered by Cambridge while Plath, with her mid-Atlantic accent, sounded like Katharine Hepburn in *The Philadelphia Story*. Old American friends would be astonished by this voice when they heard recordings of Plath reading her work. This affected accent was perhaps a new strategy in the old struggle to transcend her class. When the program's host, Owen Leeming, asked her about her background, she mentioned that she was born in Boston but was "in England to stay now." The transformation from Smith girl to wry British poet was nearly complete.

Leeming was fascinated by this marriage. Did they need to write separately or together? How did they influence each other? Plath's and Hughes's answers were ambiguous, sometimes conflicting, and suggest a difficult balancing act. They presented a united aesthetic front and campaigned for a new direction in British poetry, yet they took pains not to present themselves as collaborators. When Leeming asked them whether their temperaments were "parallel or in conflict," Hughes answered, "I think superficially we're very alike . . . we live at the same tempo, have the same sort of rhythm in every sort of way, but obviously this is a very fortunate covering for temperaments that are extremely different but that lead secret lives, you see. They content themselves in an imaginative world so they never really come into open conflict." Plath averred that she was "much more distractable" and needed to separate from Hughes, who could write anywhere. Hughes seemed more at ease with this line of questioning than Plath:

> Apart from the experiences of your own life and my experiences of my life, I also have in a way Sylvia's experiences of hers, and all the experiences she's had in the past. . . . and in this way, two people who are sympathetic to each other . . . who are compatible in this sort of spiritual way, they in fact make up one person, they make up one source of power which you both use and you can draw out material in incredible detail from this single shared mind. And I'm *sure* that this is certainly a source of a great deal in my poetry. I don't know whether it works the other way around. I suspect it does.

"It's a very hard thing to put into words, isn't it," Leeming said. "Yes," Hughes answered. "It's a complicated idea to get across because you first of all have to believe that this sort of telepathic union exists between two sympathetic people, which of course a lot of people don't believe." Hughes would always believe that Plath had access to his unconscious. He later suggested it was no coincidence that they had written about similar themes in *The Bell Jar* and the *Bardo Thodol* while they were both working in Bill Merwin's study during the spring of 1961: "for about three months we were both every day soaking our heads in the same death and expiation and rebirth myth, in the same cubic yard of space, she in the mornings, me in the afternoons."[29]

Plath told Leeming she was more "practical" about mutual influence. Ted's interest in animals had made her think more about her father's interest in bees; as a result, she said, "the image of beekeeping has become part of my poems. And I think this is a direct result of knowing Ted. I somehow know more about my own past through him than I would otherwise. But I'm also influenced by art, by paintings and sculpture. . . . A lot of my poems describe paintings and take off from a visual image."

Leeming pressed on: "Don't you find, the two of you, that being married, being in close contact like you are, and also having a basic similarity of approach, that there's a great danger that your poetry will tend to almost collapse, the one into the other?" Plath protested, dropping her accent and sounding much more American. "I've always thought that our subject matter in particular and the form in which we write—the forms—are really quite, quite different, and I'd be interested to know where they coincide." Leeming countered, "I don't think they're as different as all that." He noted their "technical trick of vigor," similar subjects (animals, rural landscapes), their frequent use of enjambment. Plath, clearly agitated, responded that this was true of their poems before they knew each other, not "a result" of their meeting. They were "writing for ten years" before they had ever heard of each other: the "toughness and knottiness that we both admire is something again we've always admired and perhaps that's why we met in the first place."

Hughes was more inclined to agree with Leeming. "I think it's something we share with several other writers too, several other people writing now." Plath conceded that they shared a "distaste for slack lyrical quality or floweriness," as did all their young poet friends. But they reminded Leeming that they treated similar subjects differently, as in Plath's "Sow" and Hughes's "View of a Pig." Plath laughed nervously as Hughes explained how his poem "was the complete reversal of Sylvia's theme."

Plath was breaking new ground in her marriage, yet *Poets in Partnership* revealed fissures of unease. Her literary ambitions and identity could have easily "collapsed" under the weight of Hughes's fame. In 1961, married mothers' artistic outlets did not extend much further than the church choir or the watercolor class. But Plath was determined to keep writing in the face of conservative societal expectations. Hughes allowed her that space; he believed that "she was a genius."[30] When Plath told Leeming, "I'd never be writing as I am and as much as I am without Ted's understanding and cooperation," she was expressing gratitude for what was in 1961—six years before abortion was legalized in Britain—a progressive marriage. Plath declined to add that Hughes probably wouldn't be writing "as much" without her "cooperation," for she brought a professional know-how to the creative marriage. She knew how to get published; Hughes did not. It was Plath, in her role as Hughes's agent, who jump-started his career. They were both, equally, in each other's debt.

———

IN FEBRUARY, Anne Sexton sent Plath *To Bedlam and Part Way Back*. Plath's response was flattering but brief. She seemed, already, to sense that Sexton would become for her what Thom Gunn was for Hughes. Plath thought it "terrific" to have her "favorites back again together with the newer ones you were doing when I left ('Elegy in the Classroom' among them!)." She thanked Sexton for her encouraging words about *The Colossus*, which she had sent to her. She and Ted were aware of "great burbles of success from Boston," which included a third book and a Guggenheim for Adrienne Rich. (Sylvia would hear in March from Dido that Robert Lowell had been hospitalized for mania—"interned again.")[31] Sylvia made sure to include her own "burbles": they were thriving in London; Frieda made them want to "found a dynasty"; they socialized with Spender, MacNeice, Auden, Gunn, Roethke, and Eliot. She wrote, "We thrive so in London we'll probably stay forever & my children will no doubt talk back to me with clipped Oxford accents till I knock their jaws into proper shape for the old broad A."[32]

Ted now had so much regular BBC work, Sylvia told Aurelia, that he earned as much as he would at a nine-to-five job. She was probably exaggerating, but the extra income had come just in time. Nicholas Farrar or Megan Emily (Emily for Otto's middle name, Emil, as well as Brontë and Dickinson) was due on August 17, Ted's birthday. Sylvia asked Aurelia to come over for the birth. "Oh, how I look forward to your coming! My heart lifts now that the year swings toward it."[33] With a second child on the way, she was even more determined to buy a London townhouse.

But Sylvia miscarried on February 6. "I lost the little baby this morning & feel really terrible about it," she wrote to her mother. She estimated that she had been four months along. Ted tried to distract her with poems to type; work, he felt, was "a good cure for brooding." Sylvia knew miscarriages were common, and her "lady" doctor assured her she would have another healthy pregnancy. "I am in the best of hands, although I am extremely unhappy about the whole thing," she wrote Aurelia. She tried to move on, though they postponed their Italy trip until the fall. (In the meantime, they had applied for money from a Royal Literary Fund set up for "distressed authors" in financial hardship.) She told Aurelia to tell Mrs. Prouty about the miscarriage "in a casual way": "I always make it a point to sound cheerful & wanting for nothing when I write her."[34]

Sylvia was soon back to her daily routine, walking Frieda in the park—the weather was unusually sunny that February—reading *The New Yorker*, enjoying the theater and cinema. But she was bereaved and anxious; she dreaded an impending appendectomy at month's end, and later wondered whether her bad appendix, which had been troubling her for months, was to blame for the miscarriage. And there was something else, an allegation she kept to herself until the fall of 1962.

In January, Hughes had written to Moira Doolan, the head of Schools Broadcasting at the BBC, with a proposal for a new radio series aimed at schoolchildren.[35] Doolan was intrigued, and she called the Chalcot Square flat to arrange a lunch meeting with Hughes in early February. Sylvia answered the phone and was allegedly surprised to hear an Irishwoman's voice. When Hughes returned, according to him, "1/4 hour late" from his lunch with Doolan, he found Plath furious. In 1974, Hughes told Frances McCullough, who edited Plath's abridged journals, that Plath "had torn up all his writing into strips, his writing and his notes." He said this was one of the times when he had seen Sylvia's "rages," her "demonic side, destructive, like 'black electricity.'" Immediately after he told the story, he admitted, as McCullough recorded in her notes, that "he used to try slapping her out of her rages, but it was no good. And once she turned into his slap and got a black eye, and went to the doctor and told him Ted beat her regularly. But then as it began to heal, she decided it looked dramatic, and began to mascara the other eye to match."[36]

Seamus Heaney unkindly described Moira Doolan as middle-aged and "dumpy," and could not understand Plath's jealousy.[37] Yet Doolan was, according to Jonathan Bate, "a powerhouse of ideas at the BBC in the early sixties."[38] Suddenly, Hughes was on the cusp of an important relationship with a powerful female collaborator and patron. The meeting came at a time when Plath, among the most highly educated women of her generation, was knee-deep in laundry, dishes, and dirty diapers. As she had told Leeming in the *Poets in Partnership* interview, she spent her days on "shopping, dishes, and taking care of the baby and so forth. I think very few people have an idea I do anything at all except household chores."[39] Ted, she told the Merwins, was "relatively impervious" to the "innumerable little umbilical cords" that tied her to "icebox, phone, doorbell, baby and so on."[40]

With time, Plath had a different story to tell. On September 22, 1962, about three weeks before Hughes left her for good, and in the midst of a volatile separation, she would write to Dr. Beuscher,

> Ted beat me up physically a couple of days before my miscarriage: the baby I lost was due to be born on his birthday. I thought this an aberration, & felt I had given him some cause, I had torn some of his papers in half, so they could be taped together, not lost, in a fury that he made me a couple of hours late to work at one of the several jobs I've had to eke out our income when things got tight—he was to mind Frieda. But now I feel the role of father terrifies him. He tells me now it was weakness that made him unable to tell me he did not want children, and that his joyous planning with me of the names of our next two was out of cowardice as well. Well bloody hell, I've got twenty years to take the responsibility of this cowardice.[41]

Sylvia had dated the miscarriage to Monday, February 6, in her letter to Aurelia but suggested that it had been going on throughout the weekend of February 4–5. The fight, then, probably occurred during the first few days of February.

There are no references to this disturbing incident in Sylvia's surviving journal entries of February and March 1961, which date to her time at the hospital and are extremely loving toward Ted. On the day she told Aurelia about the miscarriage, she called Ted "the most blessed kind person in the world" and noted how he was "taking wonderful care of me."[42] But then, one of Sylvia's favorite words for herself was "tough." Her passing, almost blasé reference to this incident in her letter to Dr. Beuscher suggests that she probably did not think of herself as a victim at a time when slapping a "hysterical" woman was culturally sanctioned, even glamorized in Hollywood films. In the same letter, Sylvia told Beuscher that she and Ted had had "six stormy but wonderful" years together—more ambiguity. When Aurelia witnessed the couple quarreling in Devon in the summer of 1962, she told Warren their troubles were "not new, but erupted afresh."[43] Paul Roche had dinner with the couple in London in 1961 and remembered them as tense and bickering. Ted seemed to goad Sylvia with purposely "uncouth" table manners, as if playing up his working-class background. She reprimanded him and yelled at him throughout the evening to stop speaking so loudly or he would wake Frieda.[44]

The American author Susan Fromberg Schaeffer, who was close to Ted and Olwyn, published a long novel about Ted Hughes called *Poison* in 2006. Her friendship with the Hugheses obviously, but secretly, supplied many of the details in this book. In one scene, the Hughes character tells the Dido Merwin character a version of the same story that Plath told Dr. Beuscher in her 1962 letter:

> I came back from a meeting in London. . . . and there she was, shredding my manuscripts. . . . No apologies. No regrets. . . . So I struck her. And the pity of it was, that night she miscarried. . . . I would have left her then, if she hadn't miscarried, if I hadn't given in and gotten her pregnant again as soon as the doctor gave the word, I had to give her back what I thought I had taken from her.[45]

Either Olwyn, Ted, or Dido herself must have confided this story to Susan Schaeffer. Indeed, Olwyn felt so betrayed by Schaeffer after she published *Poison* that she cut off all contact with her.[46] In 2006 she wrote to Schaeffer's husband, "I'm reading POISON—in bits—as much as I can stand at a time.

It has made me ill. I considered you and Susan good friends so the book is nightmarish."[47] A furious Olwyn listed many incidents in the book—which she called an "infantile willful atrocity"—that she said Schaeffer had made up. The incident surrounding the miscarriage was not among them.[48]

Sylvia had written in her journal about scratches, sprained thumbs, and broken crockery after she had confronted Ted about his student in Northampton in 1958. She had also written about bruises after her first "holocaust" night of sex with Ted. Courting violence, as Plath's early drafts of *Falcon Yard* show, was something of an aesthetic stance, and part of the couple's shared mythology. Indeed, the relationship began with violence on the night they met. Sylvia and Sassoon had experimented with rough sex, and, according to one source, Gordon Lameyer believed that his own relationship with Sylvia fizzled out because he refused to "beat her up" in the bedroom.[49] Ted recalled that Sylvia once smashed his mahogany writing table, made from his "mother's heirloom sideboard," with a stool in a fury when he was late to mind Frieda.[50] (He told Frances McCullough that this occurred on a different day from the Moira Doolan incident, though his drafts of "The Minotaur" suggest it happened on the same day.) Hughes saw, in Plath's rage, a deeper potential for her poems. He laughed when he witnessed the table's destruction: "That's what you should have put into *The Colossus*, all that energy," he told her. "She began to laugh and stopped. . . . it was like a revelation to her. . . . she did begin to do that."[51] Hughes wrote about the incident in "The Minotaur":

> "Marvellous!" I shouted, "Go on,
> Smash it into kindling.
> That's the stuff you're keeping out of your poems!"
> And later, considered and calmer,

> "Get that shoulder under your stanzas
> And we'll be away."[52]

But by February 1961, the couple's erotics of violence—itself a manifestation, perhaps, of their poetic war on gentility—seems to have morphed into something uglier.

While there is no surviving contemporaneous account of this fight, both Plath's and Hughes's recollections suggest that there was a physical altercation when Hughes found Plath ripping his manuscripts. Frieda Hughes has noted that we will never know exactly what happened. While she was not surprised by her mother's fury toward her father as the once passionate marriage burned itself out, her mother's accusation of violence did not resonate with the loving, devoted father she knew: "In all my life with my father, I had never seen this side of him. What, I asked myself, would qualify as a physical beating? A push? A shove? A swipe?" For Frieda, the "context" of her mother's destroying her father's manuscripts—the thing, apart from Frieda herself, that was most "precious" to them—was "*vital*, and it confirmed in my mind that my father was not the wife-beater that some would wish to imagine he was."[53] Whatever happened between Sylvia and Ted that day, it was unusual enough that both poets singled it out, as, in Sylvia's words, an "aberration" in their marriage. Ted felt guilty enough about what he did that he later unburdened himself to someone, probably Olwyn. According to Sylvia's September 1962 letter to Dr. Beuscher, nothing like it ever happened again.

Sylvia's London friend Suzette Macedo remembered that this period had marked a "real cooling" in the marital relationship. Sylvia "wasn't at ease" with Ted's BBC work, she said, because "there were a lot of women at the BBC, and those were the kind of women who went to bed." They had a "loose" reputation at the time, she said, though such a claim sounds sexist now. Plath was married to the most famous young poet in England. "She was not crazy," Suzette said, to think that a successful BBC producer might find Ted attractive—or he her—while Sylvia folded diapers. Indeed, Sylvia later wrote Dr. Beuscher, "movie stars have nothing on a handsome male poet."[54] Suzette said that Ted had begun to feel that Sylvia "pushed too hard." He "became passive"—and resentful—about her sending his poems out. They had begun "wanting different things." Pregnant again, Sylvia dreamed of a larger home, more children, and more money, while Ted, sensing an ambush, began to retreat from domestic demands and public literary life. "She was always trying to encourage Ted to do more commercially, and he was not really interested," Suzette said, though she pointed out that he enjoyed writing children's books, plays for the BBC, and translations. But, according to Suzette and her husband, Helder, who knew Ted well, he still had qualms about turning poetry into profit. "He hated the idea of selling his stuff more than necessary." Sylvia, meanwhile, was writing to family in America about her hopes that Ted's plays would bring them wealth. Suzette remembered that there had been "a reconciliation between them" that June and July when Aurelia visited and babysat Frieda while they went to France together. Nicholas, their second child, she said, was "a peace-making baby."[55] Suzette's memory dovetails with Susan Schaeffer's suggestion, in *Poison*, of Ted's strong sense of guilt and need to atone for his act.

This marital crisis likely inspired Plath's poem "Zoo Keeper's Wife," written on Valentine's Day, about two weeks after the fight, in which a wronged wife suffers from insomnia: "I can stay awake all night, if need be— / Cold as an eel, without eyelids. / Like a dead lake the dark envelops me." The speaker alludes to a miscarriage, and asks, sarcastically, "But what do you know about that / My fat pork, my marrowy sweetheart, face-to-the-wall?" Something has disturbed the marriage; a reckoning seems possible, if just out of reach. The wife bitterly describes their "courtship" in a clear allusion to Hughes. The London Zoo was an important part of the couple's life—they had chosen Chalcot Square partly because of its proximity to the zoo, where they frequently took Frieda, and Ted had once worked there as a dishwasher. Also, around this time, Ted was considering an advanced degree in Zoology.

> You wooed me with the wolf-headed fruit bats
> Hanging from their scorched hooks in the moist
> Fug of the Small Mammal House.
> . . . .
> You checked the diet charts and took me to play
> With the boa constrictor in the Fellows' Garden.
> I pretended I was the Tree of Knowledge.
> I entered your bible, I boarded your ark . . .

"Zoo Keeper's Wife" sounds a new note in Plath's poetic lexicon. It uses the voice of the wronged, avenging woman in language that prefigures later *Ariel* poems like "The Jailor" and "The Courage of Shutting-Up." Suddenly, Plath unleashes anger normally reserved for mothers, fathers, barren women, and spinsters upon a husband figure. Plath had already done this in her short stories "The Wishing Box" and "The Fifty-Ninth Bear," but never in her poems. Something had inspired her to use this caustic voice against Hughes.

Plath also wrote a short story, "Day of Success," between February and August of 1961, that alluded to the Moira Doolan incident.[56] A housewife, Ellen, spends her days pinching pennies and minding her six-month-old baby girl while her playwright husband, Jacob, retreats to his private study to write. (The furniture, drapes, and wallpaper are exact duplicates of those in the Chalcot Square flat.) The self-sacrificing Ellen is a model of mid-century femininity. But Ellen lacks confidence. "*I'm homespun, obsolete as last year's hemline,*" she says. She begins to worry that the assistant of a high-powered television producer, Denise Kay (a "real career girl" and a redhead, like Moira Doolan), will seduce Jacob. She imagines Jacob and Denise together at rehearsals, "author and producer collaborating on the birth of something wonderful, uniquely theirs." Tellingly, Ellen's anxiety has to do with Jacob and Denise "collaborating"—creating art together.

In the story, Jacob remains true to his wife. He blasts Denise Kay for drinking martinis at lunch and ridicules her for being a "career woman with a mind of her own," a "highpowered" "diesel engine." Plath too was a woman with a powerful engine. But the *Ladies' Home Journal* ethos of the day demanded that the career woman must lose to the happy homemaker. The story ends as Jacob tells Ellen he has bought her a home in the country with his advance. When a divorced friend gives Ellen a recommendation for an expensive hairdresser, she says, "Braids are back in style this season, love— the latest thing for the country wife!"[57] (Later, after she and Ted separated, Sylvia wrote to Aurelia that she was going to "face" her literary friends in London and tell them "happily" that she was "divorcing Ted, so they won't picture me as a poor, deceived country wife.")[58]

Doolan's phone call may have aroused Plath's jealousy—most BBC producers were men—but "Day of Success" suggests that it also made her feel powerless. As the critic Luke Ferretter has noted, Ellen's successful, literary husband possesses an "absolute sovereignty against which there is no appeal."[59] Plath had absorbed this sexist power structure. It is perhaps no accident that in retaliation she attacked the source of Hughes's financial and professional power: his manuscripts.

Plath turned to her writing as a way of restoring order. Poetry demanded concentration, precise language, and a philosophical outlook; it could contain experiences that seemed chaotic and sprawling. The two poems Plath wrote that month about motherhood, "Parliament Hill Fields," completed on February 11, and "Morning Song," on February 19, are among her finest.

"Parliament Hill Fields," her elegy for the lost baby, is tender, brave, and beautifully crafted. Miscarriage was a taboo subject in the 1960s—or at least, as the poet Ruth Fainlight said, "unseemly."[60] Even the word "pregnant" was deemed indelicate, and it was banned from 1950s television shows like *I Love Lucy*. There was no female elegiac tradition mourning the unborn—an astonishing omission from the literary canon given that a quarter of all pregnancies end in miscarriage. Plath was writing in uncharted territory, giving voice to an experience shared secretly by millions of women. In June, she would read "Parliament Hill Fields" on the BBC. She began with a short introduction that did not obscure the poem's devastating subject: the speaker is caught, Plath says, "between the grief caused by the loss of a child and the joy aroused by the knowledge of an only child safe at home. Gradually the first images of blankness and absence give way to images of convalescence and healing as the woman turns, a bit stiffly, and with difficulty, from her sense of bereavement to the vital and demanding part of her world which still survives."[61] Rarely was miscarriage given such a public forum. "Your absence is inconspicuous; / Nobody can tell what I lack"; "I suppose it's pointless to think of you at all. / Already your doll grip lets go," Plath reads, her voice faltering.

"Morning Song," with its memorable first line, "Love set you going like a fat gold watch," is more joyful: the living baby's "clear vowels rise like balloons." Yet the poem is not sentimental. Plath treats the pious culture of motherhood ironically when she writes, "One cry, and I stumble from bed, cow-heavy and floral / In my Victorian nightgown." As in other poems, Plath registers unease with her massive new responsibility: "I'm no more your mother / Than the cloud that distills a mirror to reflect its own slow / Effacement at the wind's hand."

Other poems from February rehearse themes and images Plath would return to in her *Ariel* poems. "Barren Woman" seems a premonition of "Edge": "Marble lilies / Exhale their pallor like scent" and "nothing can happen." At the poem's end, "The moon lays a hand on my forehead, / Blank-faced and mum as a nurse." "Barren Woman" was likely inspired by Dido Merwin, as was "Face Lift," another poem in this group, which merges hospital imagery and the language of rebirth that Plath had used in "The Stones": "Mother to myself, I wake swaddled in gauze, / Pink and smooth as a baby." Sylvia had been fascinated by Dido's descriptions of the procedure, but, as she wrote Aurelia, "I have a very moral attitude that one should earn good wrinkles & face up to them."[62]

―――――――

SYLVIA ARRIVED AT Saint Pancras Hospital for her appendectomy on February 26 carrying a suitcase full of books. She had taken the bus to Camden High Street, but got lost soon after it dropped her off. An older woman took pity on her and summoned her husband to drive her to the hospital. "I sat in the back among oil cans & promptly started bawling," Sylvia wrote the Merwins.[63] Both fascinated and repulsed by hospitals, she was extremely nervous about the procedure. She brought a notebook, at Ted's and Aurelia's suggestion, to "occupy" herself with notes for poems.[64] *The Atlantic* had recently taken "Words for a Nursery," and Plath was writing poetry again in earnest. That February, "The Fifty-Ninth Bear" appeared in *The London Magazine*, and "A Winter Ship" in *Encounter*.

Her surgery on February 28 went smoothly, and she was filled with "immense relief" when it was over. "You were absolutely right about the anesthesia, Dido—just my thing.... they gave me heavenly pain-killing injections which caused me to 'float' over my inert body feeling immensely powerful & invulnerable."[65] She spent her days drowsing "pleasantly" and reading Agatha Christie novels in the new, pink-walled ward, an "immense improvement over that grim ward at Newton-Wellesley."[66]

By her third day she was walking around "gossiping" with her fellow patients.[67] Ted came round in the evening with grapes, rare steak sandwiches, freshly squeezed orange juice, and tollhouse cookies. When he visited, she wrote in her journal, "I felt as excited & infinitely happy as in the early days of our courtship. His face which I daily live with seemed the most kind & beautiful in the world."[68] One evening he arrived with a letter from *The New Yorker* offering her their "coveted" first-reading contract for the next year. She earned $100 simply for signing the renewable contract, which stipulated a 25 percent "bonus" on the price of each poem accepted, plus other financial perks, in exchange for right of first refusal.[69] Sylvia was only too happy to sign, "under the influence of morphia, but genuinely."[70] She had been dreaming about joining this rarefied company for years. She thanked Bill Merwin, who had written to Howard Moss at *The New Yorker* earlier in the month on the couple's behalf.[71]

Once she could eat again, she told Aurelia, her days were restful. "I haven't been free of the baby one day for a whole year & I must say I have secretly enjoyed having meals in bed, backrubs & nothing to do but read." Ted had been "an angel," though she sensed he was ready for her to come home: "little remarks like 'I seem to be eating a lot of bread' & 'Doesn't the Pooker make a lot of dirty pots' tell me he is wearying of the domestic routine." Sylvia's own "domestic routine" had no end in sight, but she was not about to complain. On the contrary: "Poor dear, I'd like to know how many men would take over as willingly & lovingly as he has!" She told Aurelia she admired the "table of flowers sent by Ted's parents, Ted, Helga Huws & Charles Monteith, Ted's Editor at Faber's."[72] The bouquet of red tulips from Helga would soon inspire one of her best poems.

Plath's hospital stay is the subject of one of only a few surviving journal entries after 1959. The entry is darker than what she wrote to Aurelia and suggests that the hospital brought back memories of Valley Head and McLean: "I feel curiously less worried about losing my appendix than being electrocuted."[73] Her details contain more wit and black humor than her letters home ("Snoring: the worst horror of all"); still, after a year of waiting on her husband and child, others were finally waiting on her.[74] "I feel more fresh & rested than I have for months," she wrote in her journal.[75]

Sylvia meant to be productive, even in the hospital. She enjoyed talking with the other women, whose fortitude made her feel that it was "impossible to indulge in mopes of self-pity, a very good thing."[76] She felt camaraderie with the infirm and filled her notebooks "with impressions & character studies." She admitted, "I learn a great deal." Her "pet" was a "suicidal Scorpio secretary": "All morning talked to Jay Winn across the way about her office & private life & nervous breakdown—cannot congratulate myself too much on this confidence because I blabbed about my own breakdown & misapplied shock treatment."[77] She tried to "cheer up" a patient in a leg cast, and spent time at the bedside of a woman named Joan from South Devon in a full-body plaster cast who became the inspiration for her poem "In Plaster."

Sylvia was discharged from the hospital on March 8. Her doctors ordered her not to lift a finger and to "behave 'like a lady' " for two weeks. Ted told her not to worry—he insisted that he enjoyed caring for the baby and doing housework, which he had taken over since the miscarriage. The hospital stay seemed to ease some of the tension in the marriage; Sylvia refers to Ted in many March letters as an angel and a saint. Hughes's get-well gifts included "a stack" of D. H. Lawrence books ("the only diet I felt like"), a bouquet of yellow primroses, and *The Oxford Book of Wildflowers*. "I must say that the last 6 months I have felt slapped down each time I lifted my head up & don't know what I'd have done if Ted hadn't been more than saintly & the baby adorable & charming," she told her mother, who had supplied the check that paid for Hughes's gifts.[78] The couple hoped that the removal of her appendix would have a positive effect on her mental and physical health. "That appendix really must have been plaguing her for years—a steady drain of toxins into her system possibly for the last five years," Ted wrote to Aurelia and Warren. "Anyway now she's renewed."[79] Sylvia felt resilient, "very close to a self I haven't been for sometime & full of hope."[80]

The flowers, the plaster cast, the patient's stories, and the presurgical rituals would keep Plath writing for months. In her journal she wrote, "I shall have a story out of this, beginning, 'Tonight I deserve blue light, I am one of them.' "[81] The line sounds like something out of "Johnny Panic and the Bible of Dreams" and lends credence to Hughes's claim that *The Bell Jar* began to take shape while she was in the hospital. Yet when Plath began a prose sketch of her time at Saint Pancras in her journal, titled "The Inmate," it had the sound and texture of her somber late poems, like "Sheep in Fog" or "Words": "Still whole, I interest nobody." "This is a religious establishment, great cleansings take place. Everybody has a secret. I watch them from my pillows, already exhausted." The flowers are "sweet-lipped as children. All night they've been breathing in the hall dropping their pollens, daffodils, pink & red tulips, the hot purple & red eyed—anemones."[82]

Her notes were preparation for "Tulips," which she wrote on March 18, ten days after leaving the hospital. The poem's driving force is desire for dissolution:

The tulips are too excitable, it is winter here.
Look how white everything is, how quiet, how snowed-in.
I am learning peacefulness, lying by myself quietly
As the light lies on these white walls, this bed, these hands.
I am nobody; I have nothing to do with explosions.
I have given my name and my day-clothes up to the nurses
And my history to the anesthetist and my body to the surgeons.

The speaker is content in her inertia: "I have never been so pure." The smiles of her husband and her children stare out from a photograph like "little smiling hooks," catching her skin. "I only wanted / To lie with my hands turned up and be utterly empty." But the vivid, blooming red tulips assault her senses. They "are too red in the first place, they hurt me." They break through her wish for death-in-life, and remind her of love, beauty, and obligation. Her heart beats, finally, "out of sheer love of me." Tears stream down her face, and the poem closes with its famous lines: "The water I taste is warm and salt, like the sea, / And comes from a country far away as health." In "Tulips," restoration defeats oblivion. Three days after her surgery, Plath had written in her journal, "I am myself again: the tough, gossipy curious enchanting entity I have not been for so long."[83]

Remarkably, on the same day Plath wrote "Tulips," she also wrote "In Plaster." The poem plays with the idea of the double that had fascinated her since her Smith days; here, the saintly white cast duels with the "ugly and hairy" body within. Both poems were long and written in a similar sestet form. Plath realized that she was at the start of a new phase in early March. She wrote in her journal that reading Boris Pasternak's late poems had unlocked something: "they excited me immensely—the free, lyric line & terse (though sometimes too fey) idiom. I felt: a new start can be made through these. This is the way back to the music. I wept to lose my new tough prosiness."[84] Ted likewise wrote to Aurelia, "Sylvia's been writing a great pace ever since she's been out of hospital & has really broken through into something wonderful—one poem about 'Tulips' . . . is a tremendous piece. Her poems are in demand more & more."[85] He told Olwyn that "Tulips" was "absolutely inspired . . . a real torrent."[86] He later told Anne Stevenson that it was Plath's "first spontaneous poem," which she wrote "quickly, without recourse to her thesaurus."[87]

Those tulips unsettled Hughes, too. On April 12, some weeks after Plath had written "Tulips," he wrote in his journal, "The red tulips—hearts terrifyingly vivid terrible. Organs pulsing something red and uncontrollable . . . Tulips the colour of blooded yolks."[88] Aurelia, who had lost her husband and nearly lost her daughter—and who had endured several ulcer-related surgeries—understood the poem intuitively. When "Tulips" appeared in *The New Yorker* on April 7, 1962, she wrote to Mrs. Prouty: "It recalls to me the times when, after major surgery, I just floated thankfully, yet in clouded consciousness, reluctant to take up the business of full return to living—too weary yet to assume responsibility. Anything that compels one's return to that awaiting struggle is, at first, a rude intruder—be it a well-meaning friend or, as here, a vase of vibrantly red tulips."[89]

Eighteen Rugby Street, Bloomsbury, London, where Plath and Hughes spent their wedding night

St. George the Martyr, the Bloomsbury church where Plath and Hughes married in secret on June 16, 1956

Ted Hughes and Sylvia Plath on their honeymoon in Paris, August 1956

Ted Hughes and Sylvia Plath in Yorkshire, England, 1956

Moorland around Haworth, home of the Brontë sisters and the setting of *Wuthering Heights*. Plath liked to compare herself and Hughes to Cathy and Heathcliff, and the couple often walked these moors when they visited Yorkshire. Plath told her mother it was the only place she did not miss the ocean.

The Beacon, Ted Hughes's family home, sitting high atop the Calder Valley in Heptonstall, West Yorkshire

Sylvia Plath writing on a stone wall near the Beacon, Heptonstall, September 1956

(below) Top Withens, the reputed model for Wuthering Heights. Plath and Hughes often walked here, and Plath set several poems in the area.

Heptonstall village center. One long-time resident remembered that when strangers walked through town, "the curtains would twitch open."

The commanding hilltop village of Heptonstall, which Hughes later characterized as the center of the Celtic kingdom of Elmet

Ted Hughes and
Sylvia Plath,
Cambridge,
England, 1957

Ted Hughes,
Wellesley, c. 1957

Sylvia Plath sailing into New York Harbor on the *Queen Elizabeth II*, June 1957

Ted Hughes and Sylvia Plath,
New York City, June 1959

Sylvia Plath reading her poems in
The New Yorker, August 1958

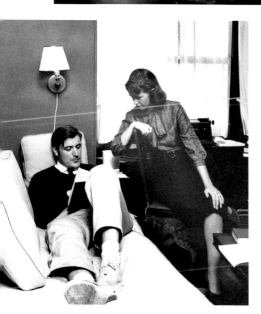

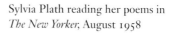

Ted Hughes and Sylvia Plath inside their
apartment at 9 Willow Street, Boston, 1958

Sylvia Plath at Jackson Lake, Grand Teton National Park, Wyoming, July 1959

Ted Hughes on the North Dakota prairie, July 1959

Ted Hughes in Wisconsin, July 1959

Sylvia Plath and Ted Hughes stopping for a break during their drive across America, summer 1959

Sylvia Plath, Algonquin Provincial Park, Ontario, Canada, July 1959

Sylvia Plath rowing at Yellowstone, summer 1959

Plath's study on the top floor of West House, Yaddo. Here she learned to be true to her own "weirdnesses."

Hughes's study, "Outlook," at Yaddo, a five-minute walk from West House

The rose garden at Yaddo, Saratoga Springs, New York, which may have served as a model for the garden of "Edge"

West House, Yaddo, where Plath and Hughes spent the fall of 1959

25

The Moment of the Fulcrum

London, March–August 1961

The English spring heralded the end of what Sylvia called, in a letter to the Booths, "a manic-depressive winter full of flu, miasmas, near bankruptcy, nights full of teething yowls from our changeling." Ted chalked it all up to "starry malevolences."[1] The March weather was warm and sunny, "real June days," Sylvia wrote to Aurelia.[2] Sylvia spent hours on a blanket with Frieda on Primrose Hill, just as Aurelia had once taken her to the Arnold Arboretum and laid her out in the sunshine. In late March the news came that *Lupercal* had won the prestigious Hawthornden Prize, awarded to the best book published in England by a writer under the age of forty-one; a week later, Plath's "Magi" appeared in the *New Statesman*. Hughes had earned about $1,500 since January for his BBC work. Sylvia told Aurelia, "they seem eager to take anything he does."[3]

Sylvia's health returned in time for Frieda's first birthday on April 1.[4] Sylvia and Ted began the day for Frieda with a rousing rendition of "Happy Birthday," followed by balloons, books, a "blue fairytale landscape" painting by a local artist, stacks of new clothes from America, and a homemade cupcake. The balloons scared Frieda at first; she preferred the books, which she immediately pretended to read. Her parents were delighted. "She is mad for books," Sylvia wrote home, "probably because we read all the time."[5] Frieda had "suddenly become a little girl," and Sylvia loved brushing her hair and dressing her in fine Polly Flinders frocks from Aurelia.[6]

In the wake of the Hawthornden Prize announcement, there seemed an endless stream of publicity. Plath and Hughes were slated to record a joint program on April 6 for *The London Echo* on the BBC, "reading poems & talking about our childhoods. It's supposed to come out over a lot of networks in America."[7] The BBC hoped to capitalize on the success of *Poets in Partner-*

ship, which had been rebroadcast twice that winter. (No known recording of *The London Echo* program survived, if indeed it was ever made.) Alvarez published six new Hughes poems in *The Observer* on April 16.[8] Around the same time, Hughes appeared on BBC television's *Wednesday Magazine* to promote his new children's book, *Meet My Folks!*[9] Sylvia watched the interview at the studio, "very proud," and reported home that Ted had received another request to appear in a television feature, reading his poems in Yorkshire.[10] The handsome poet would have been a magnetic presence on television, but he declined. His decision likely frustrated Sylvia. In November 1960 she had written to Dr. Beuscher about her hope that Ted would get "his face on the screen" when he appeared on John Betjeman's program. "To Ted's mother, appearing on television with that best-selling nonpoet Betjemann [*sic*] would be the height of Ted's career."[11] Sylvia kept her frustration to herself, exclaiming to Aurelia in late April, "It is so marvelous having married Ted with no money & nothing in print & then having all my best intuitions prove true!"[12] She continued to hope for a windfall. By the end of the month, Hughes had nearly finished his five-act play, *The Calm*, which had been tentatively commissioned by Peter Hall, one of Hughes's Cambridge contemporaries and, he thought, "the best director in England."[13] Sylvia felt this was their real break—"Oh you wait," she told Aurelia, "we'll be wealthy yet."[14] But *The Calm* was a flop. When it was staged in Boston at the Poets' Theatre that November, Peter Davison wrote Hughes that he "left the theatre baffled but reflective," and it received a harsh review in the Harvard student newspaper.[15] The script later achieved fame as the scrap paper on which Plath wrote "Daddy."

Still, Sylvia had reason to hope for a commercial breakthrough, for both enjoyed the privileges that came with membership in literary London's old boy network. Ted explained the value of their connections to Aurelia: "All the posts of power—or the main ones—in the literary world over here are now filled by people who were my contemporaries at Oxford or Cambridge & many of them vague acquaintances. It's the first time, I imagine, the very youngest generation has ever had such complete control. They're all eager to promote their own 'age-group,' luckily for us."[16] This group included Alvarez at *The Observer*; Hall, artistic director of the Royal Shakespeare Company; Brian Cox and Tony Dyson at the *Critical Quarterly*; Karl Miller at *The Spectator* and the *New Statesman* (Miller would found the *London Review of Books* in 1979); Charles Osborne, assistant editor of *The London Magazine*, future director of the Arts Council of Great Britain, and the main theater critic for *The Daily Telegraph*; Edward Lucie-Smith, Peter Redgrove, George MacBeth, Philip Hobsbaum, and others. Plath benefited from this network, but the strongest ties were among men. After her marriage ended, she would try to forge bonds with women writers like Stevie Smith and Doris Lessing, to little avail.

For all her success in Britain, Plath still coveted an American publisher. In late March, she received encouraging news: her Heinemann editor James Michie wrote from New York to say that Knopf was interested in publishing *The Colossus*.[17] She called his letter a "drunken note" and refused to believe him.[18] That very week, though, she received a letter from Judith Jones at Knopf offering her a contract. Stanley Kunitz had read her manuscript and advised Knopf to publish the book if Plath would cut the "Poem for a Birthday" sequence, which he thought plagiarized Roethke's "The Lost Son." Plath admitted to Jones that several of the poems in the sequence were "too obviously influenced" but asked to keep "Flute Notes from a Reedy Pond," which she felt "stable and quite formal." She was "delighted" to cut five other poems from the American edition but told Jones she was "most concerned about the chance of ending the book with 'The Stones,'" a poem of ambiguous, perhaps ironic, rebirth. "The whole experience of being broken and mended, together with the ending 'Love is the uniform of my bald nurse' etc., seems to me the way I would like to end the book." She argued that the cadence of "The Stones" "is nothing like Roethke."[19] This was the poem—or so Hughes had told her—that contained the first echoes of her "real poetic voice."[20]

Jones had doubts about keeping "Flute Notes from a Reedy Pond," but she finally gave in; Plath had persuaded her that it "prepares you for 'The Stones.'" They cut "Black Rook in Rainy Weather," "Metaphors," "Maudlin," "Ouija," and "Two Sisters of Persephone"—which Jones had agreed were "the least successful poems in the book."[21] Jones thought *The Colossus* would be the best first volume published in America that year. "I cannot remember when I have been as impressed by any collection of a young poet," she wrote Plath.[22] However, its earlier publication in England disqualified Plath from major American poetry contests.[23]

Plath quickly sent Theodore Roethke the Heinemann edition of *The Colossus* and offered a bashful apology for falling "too in love" with his work. "I hope you won't hate me for the last sequence of 7 poems which show me so far under your influence as to be flat out." She reassured him that she was removing the poems in the American edition, then asked if he would write her a reference for a Guggenheim fellowship "if you think any of these are any good." She told him she would "rather have you than anybody so I ask you first."[24] (In fact she had already asked Philip Booth.)[25] Sylvia's pivot from alleged plagiarist to humble acolyte was as graceful as it was coy. She possessed a keener sense of how the literary game was played than did her husband; and her efforts were beginning to pay off: she would win a Eugene Saxton fellowship that year, though not the Guggenheim.

Sylvia broke the Knopf news to Aurelia on May Day. "GOOD NEWS GOOD NEWS GOOD NEWS!" she began her letter home. "ALFRED KNOPF will publish THE COLOSSUS in AMERICA!" She hadn't told anyone except Mrs. Prouty, afraid to "jinx" her chances until she knew it was true.[26] Knopf was "THE publisher." Plath was giddy. "It is like having a second book come out—this one the Ideal. Ever since their first letter came I had a 'night of inspiration' and then started writing 7 mornings a week at the Merwins [sic] study and have done better things than ever before."

The acceptance of her poems by an American publisher was indeed a major breakthrough which inspired her to home in on her novel. She had started working on something longer, she told Ann Davidow-Goodman, in late April. She was "one-third through a novel about a college girl building up for and going through a nervous breakdown."

> I have been wanting to do this for ten years but had a terrible block about Writing a Novel. Then, suddenly, in beginning negotiations with a New York publisher for an American edition of my poems, the dykes broke and I stayed awake all night seized by fearsome excitement, saw how it should be done, started the next day & go every morning to my borrowed study as to an office & belt out more of it. I'll have to publish it under a pseudonym, if I ever get it accepted, because it's so chock full of real people I'd be sued to death and all my mother's friends wouldn't speak to her because they are all taken off. Anyhow, I have never been so excited about anything. It's probably godawful, but it's so funny, and yet serious, it makes me laugh.[27]

Plath here suggests that she began *The Bell Jar* sometime between March 30 and April 6, the week that marked the beginning of her correspondence with Knopf. Hughes later claimed that she had started the book in late February.[28] "She didn't really talk to me about it. She simply said, she was writing a novel," he testified in his 1986 deposition in the *Bell Jar* lawsuit. He "didn't know until afterwards" what she was writing about.[29] In an unpublished poem he wrote during the trial, Hughes remembered,

> Morning after morning, you wrote it out
> In Bill Merwin's study—
> (While I patrolled the zoo, introducing
> All the creatures to Frieda, morning after morning).

You imparted no bulletin, only, "I am
Having a terrific time." I recoiled from
My notion of your novel—how much more
Uneasy, manipulative prose!

I still dislike it. But now I understand it.

You were changing so fast—your every poem
I heard as a fuller, surer rehearsal
Of your voice—I never thought your novel
Might be producing the whole drama. Hindsight
Fastens on those poems you ventriloquized
In that appendectomy interlude
During your days in hospital, mid-novel.

That poem "In Plaster" epitomized
The moment of the fulcrum—the moment
Between Life & Death as you crossed from Death.
There you are: Prisoner & Jailor,
Perfectly parabled.
And for the first time (not quite the first)
The prisoner speaks the speech
And stays centre-stage
The jailor, no more voice than a straitjacket
Dangling on a tree, never after
Got a word in.[30]

Hughes may have been wrong about Plath's dates of composition, but he was likely right about "In Plaster" releasing the voice of the "prisoner," a voice Plath would graft onto Esther Greenwood. Another trigger, perhaps, was Alvarez's essay "Beyond the Gentility Principle," published in *The Observer*—the only newspaper Plath read regularly—on February 19, 1961. The essay was the basis for his introduction to his influential 1962 anthology, *The New Poetry*. He argued that English gentility ignored the horrors of "Two world wars, the concentration camps, genocide and the threat of nuclear war," a criticism that surely resonated with Plath and her fledgling novel's underlying message:

This is not to say that English poets should write exclusively of psychoanalysis, or the concentration camps, the H-bomb or any of the other contemporary horrors. Heaven forbid, for the results would be propaganda, not poetry. But they should give up the pretence that life, a few social distinctions apart, goes on the same as ever, that gentility, decency and all the other social totems and taboos will eventually muddle through.[31]

Released from the never-ending routine of housework and baby care; flooded, suddenly, with memories of her earlier hospital stays in Massachusetts; and nudged in an "ungenteel" aesthetic direction by Alvarez that February, Plath quickly began to sketch the outlines of *The Bell Jar*. As she had written in her journal in January 1958, "I wonder if, shut in a room, I could write for a year. I panic: no experience! Yet what couldn't I dredge up from my mind? Hospitals & mad women. Shock treatment & insulin trances. Tonsils & teeth out. Petting, parking, a mismanaged loss of virginity and the accident ward, various abortive loves in New York, Paris, Nice."[32] Ideas that had been lying dormant for almost a decade suddenly took flight.

By mid-April, she told her mother, she was "working like mad" in the Merwins' study seven mornings a week from eight to one. Afterward, she could face her housework: "I find I enjoy all the little niggly jobs like ironing & floor scrubbing when I've had my Morning."[33] Sylvia's friend and neighbor Lorna Secker-Walker remembered being impressed by Ted's willingness to look after Frieda in the mornings while Sylvia wrote, which was highly unusual for husbands in those days.[34] (Though he likely wasn't ironing and floor scrubbing.) This arrangement, plus a quiet study outside of the flat, created the right creative environment for Plath. She would spend the next few months writing efficiently, finishing the novel by August. (She produced only four poems that spring.)

Plath hardly spoke of her novel in her letters to her mother. She knew the devastation it would wield, yet she pressed on. She later claimed that the novel was a potboiler, but she was deeply excited by her progress. Her letter to Ann shows that she believed in her work and the new voice she had found. That discovery had been made possible, in part, by distance: she was writing about events that had taken place in America in 1953 from London in 1961. During the intervening years, the Cold War had intensified. The Bay of Pigs invasion took place in April 1961 and the Berlin Wall was erected in August—the very months Plath was writing *The Bell Jar*. Russia and America continued to test nuclear bombs. In May, *The Observer* ran a series on "America and the Cold War." Sylvia had attended the CND Ban the Bomb march in April 1960, and become anxious about the effects of nuclear fallout on the environment. *The Bell Jar* would reflect these political anxieties. While she was alarmed by contemporary developments, time had dulled the personal pain surrounding her breakdown. She had achieved the very ambitions that had, in 1953, seemed the source of her malaise. Secure in her position as a writer, mother, and wife, she could look back without turning to salt.

Sylvia's London social circle was widening. She had befriended two of her neighbors who were also educated mothers. Lorna Secker-Walker was an alumna of Saint Anne's College, Oxford, who had recently finished a PhD and would eventually become an esteemed professor of medicine. She had a little girl named Joanna and lived at 5 Chalcot Square, not far from Catherine Frankfort, a former nurse, who had two little boys at 18 Chalcot Crescent. Lorna's and Catherine's husbands had known each other at Oxford, and the Secker-Walkers had followed the Frankforts to Chalcot Square; Lorna moved just two doors down from Sylvia and Ted in March 1961. Catherine got to know Sylvia first and remembered her as "gay, warm and easy . . . a complete extrovert."[35] Lorna thought Catherine warmer and perhaps easier to talk to than she herself was. "She was a very, very sweet person. She wasn't an academic in the same sense. She was a practical kind of person." But Lorna, too, became Sylvia's friend. "I would be coming out of my front door and she would give a great wave . . . just straightaway very friendly as we said in those days, 'as Americans *are*,' not the sort of rather more reserved British approach."[36]

Lorna remembered Sylvia's happiness during this period, and was equally struck by Ted's. He seemed to her "the gentlest of men." One night, over a long, relaxed dinner at their flat, Ted told the story of the bear at Yellowstone that broke into their car. He entranced everyone with his deep voice; as darkness fell, his small audience was so rapt that no one got up to turn on the lights. "It was that kind of a night," Lorna said. She remembered, too, Sylvia's intense desire to buy a flat in the neighborhood. When 9 Chalcot Square went up for sale, Sylvia immediately arranged a tour with Lorna. The townhouse had been used as a halfway house for Borstal boys—juvenile prisoners—for a number of years. One of the boys had supposedly murdered the warden in the bathtub before the house was closed. During the tour, Lorna remembered, Sylvia was "fascinated" by the bathroom where the murder had allegedly occurred. It was one of the first rooms she wanted to see. She was unfazed by the building's history but still could not afford it.

Sylvia and Ted now had more than $6,000 in their American bank account, yet Sylvia wrote home several times that spring about how their London neighborhood was gentrifying and in five years they would not be able to afford anything. It made her "sad," she wrote, because she wanted to spend the rest of her life there. Leaving would simply be "unbearable."

Perhaps Ted's uncle Walt might lend them £1,000? The unwritten request was to Aurelia herself, who would eventually lend Sylvia half that amount. "I know I'm boring about this, but it's the main big step ahead and somehow it seems the one problem: we have all the rest: love, work we love & that supports us, a wonderful baby etc. etc."[37]

Ted had other locations in mind. He wanted to explore the countryside in Cornwall and Devon, for he and Sylvia had felt "imprisoned" at home with the baby for the past year.[38] They purchased a new black Morris Traveller station wagon with a light wood frame and red upholstery for about $1,900. (Neither trusted used-car salesmen.) The car seems to have been Ted's idea; Sylvia felt that it would make "a big dent" in their American savings account. He told Aurelia they paid for it with poetry prize money but later wrote to Daniel Huws that the money had come from "one of Sylvia's fairy godmother's [sic]."[39]

Just four years before, they had arrived in America with $100 between them. Since then, their currency, in all its forms, had risen. Their professional prospects looked ever brighter. Plath's "A Life" appeared in *The Listener* on May 4 and "Morning Song" in *The Observer* on May 21; *The London Magazine* would soon publish Hughes's story "The Harvesting," while *Harper's Bazaar* accepted his "Snow." They were making important new connections, too. Sylvia wrote home that Eric Walter White, secretary of the British Arts Council, "has taken an interest in us," treating them to a private box at Covent Garden's *Rigoletto*.[40] She enjoyed the publicity Ted disdained, and gushed to Aurelia and Warren about the Hawthornden Prize ceremony, presided over by Cecil Day-Lewis, on May 31.[41] There, she and Ted met Ruth Fainlight, an American poet, and her husband Alan Sillitoe, a previous Hawthornden winner (for *The Loneliness of the Long-Distance Runner*), who presented Ted with his award.

Ruth, who described herself as "a New Yorker and a Jew who had 'married out,'" became one of Sylvia's closest friends in England.[42] Fainlight was the daughter of a Ukrainian-American mother and British-Polish father; she had moved to Britain at fifteen and married her first husband at eighteen. She "ran away" with Sillitoe at twenty and lived with him in France and Spain for several years. In Mallorca, she became close to Robert Graves, whom she considered her mentor. ("That was my education.")[43] She had been "thrilled" by the connection to Laura Riding as well. Like Plath and Hughes, she was enormously impressed by *The White Goddess*, which she called "the poet's handbook."[44] Ruth, like Sylvia, was an aspiring poet married to a more successful writer, who also happened to be a working-class northerner. Sillitoe's *The Loneliness of the Long-Distance Runner* was an international best seller and established him as, in Ruth's word, "a media 'star.'"[45] Ruth thought that she and Sylvia "were both very lucky because we had very lovely, obliging husbands": they simply assumed that Ted and Alan would share the housework and child care, and give them time to write. "What other people were doing was neither here nor there. We were young, we were artists, and we thought we were different than anyone else." Although Fainlight came to believe that her own career "suffered" as a result of Sillitoe's fame, she thought Plath and Hughes's poetic relationship was "exemplary."[46]

Ruth's first impression of Sylvia was "of a burningly ambitious and intelligent young woman trying to look like a conventional, devoted wife but not quite succeeding. There was something almost excessive about that disguise."[47] "I empathized with her immensely because we were both in such similar situations, and it was so bizarre," she remembered. "We were both Americans, both married to these charismatic men from the North who were very much in the public eye, and we were nobodies. I was more of a nobody than her because she at least had a book and a child. I didn't have either. . . . We had an enormous amount in common. And we were both suffering under the 'Oh, you write as well, do you, Mrs. Sillitoe?' She less of course. She was more assertive than me. She was very good at holding her own."[48]

Ruth recognized Sylvia as someone who, like her, abided by "then-current ideas of femininity" but who also "shared profounder self-destructive traits."[49] They dined together at Chalcot Square or at the Sillitoes' flat in Notting Hill that summer. Ruth remarked, like many others, that Sylvia and Ted were "too large-scale and long-limbed for the small crowded rooms." She remembered "heaps of books and papers" around the flat, Sylvia's bright chatter as she cleared the table, and Ted's playing with Frieda. Both seemed to her "equally, and touchingly, youthful. It was galling to have met such a congenial pair just before they left London."[50]

New friends also included Helder and Suzette Macedo, whom Sylvia often described as a Portuguese literary couple, though only Helder was from Portugal (Suzette was from South Africa). They met that June at the Primrose Hill home of a mutual Faber and Faber author, Sylvester Stein, and his wife, Jenny. The Steins, who were part of a South African literary expatriate community—anti-apartheid dissidents—lived in a large house on Regent's Park Road, close to Chalcot Square. They were wealthy and well connected in the literary world, and threw a party—a "Faber to-do," Suzette said—to celebrate Hughes's winning the 1961 Hawthornden Prize. Jenny, who was friendly with Suzette, told her they had already met Sylvia and Ted. She had found Sylvia "very nervous, very American, there was a bit of gush, gush, gush," and Ted "just gorgeous."[51] Jenny wanted them all to meet.

At the Steins' party, Suzette found Sylvia "overdressed" and "nervous," but warm. They soon realized that they were both "starry students" of

English literature with a deep love of Yeats. Ted and Helder took to each other immediately and would become, in Suzette's words, "seriously good friends." When Suzette asked Sylvia what she did, she said, "Oh, I write a bit." "She said she was writing little stories for magazines"—she mentioned *Woman's Own*—"and then she said, 'And I write some poetry.' Really playing herself down . . . She was being modest. She said 'Oh, but Teddy's a genius.'" When Suzette pressed her, asking if she had published in Britain, Sylvia revealed that she published under the name Sylvia Plath. Suzette was astonished, as she had read Sylvia's poems and reviews of *The Colossus* in the London papers. But she was troubled by Plath's modesty. "I thought, What is all this about? 'Teddy's a genius.' It was over the top."[52]

Not long after the Steins' party, Sylvia made a serious social blunder. When Jenny Stein came round to call at Chalcot Square, Sylvia did not invite her in. Sylvia, newly pregnant with her second child, had heard that one of the Steins' children had the measles, and she was afraid of the risk the illness posed to her pregnancy. But Sylvia explained none of this to Jenny, who told Suzette and Helder that Sylvia just shut the door with a brusque "We're busy." Helder remembered that the Steins were astonished by Sylvia's rudeness. Visits between friends in their social set at the time were, he recalled, "very informal, the door had no key, just walk in, there was always food. Ted and Sylvia didn't want to be mixed up in that sort of thing."[53] Sylvester Stein was a politically engaged writer—his second novel, critical of apartheid, was banned in South Africa—and on Sundays he and Jenny held a literary salon of sorts where exiled South Africans congregated; Doris Lessing was also part of this set. Jenny Stein's visit to Chalcot Square marked a symbolic invitation into this world, especially for Sylvia, who was still largely known as Ted's wife. The Steins never invited the Hugheses to any of their parties again, and Plath was frozen out of what might have been, for her, a supportive and influential circle.

But Suzette grew close to Sylvia. Both of them, she said, had "monster mothers," and both had attempted suicide. She was struck by Sylvia's love of cooking and her "adoration" for Ted. "She had huge respect for him as a mentor and felt he knew far more about literature than she did. . . . She had Wagnerian fantasies about Siegfried and Brunhilde." Suzette found Ted's willingness to split the child care "astonishing at that period."[54] She would never have expected "such collaboration" from her own husband. "He believed in her. She owed a lot to Ted. A lot. Ted was a very generous person. He was the first man I'd ever seen change a nappy, or look after babies, because men did not do that at that time, I can promise you. . . . He shared with her, he boxed and coxed with Dido about Merwin's studio, and he really did the chores." Helder said, "He really encouraged people. He was very generous, very giving."[55]

Plath had sensed that moving to England would be good for her writing, and it was. Living as an expatriate in London gave her a freedom she did not possess in America, where she had felt great pressure to live up to the feminine ideals touted by magazines like the *Ladies' Home Journal* and *Mademoiselle*. Plath was too conservative for Greenwich Village, too free-thinking for Wellesley; London offered just the right kind of cosmopolitanism. She could escape her class anxieties, too, in England, where, as her Cambridge contemporary Michael Frayn noted, no one could place her mid-Atlantic accent, and where her Smith and Cambridge pedigrees suggested affluence.[56] The American exuberance of *Falcon Yard*—a dead end, she now realized—soon gave way to the drier tone of *The Bell Jar*. Yet she would continue to look to American poets who broke taboos and wrote about their mental breakdowns as she assimilated her own experience into her work.[57] She had absorbed Hughes's and Crockett's disdain for "cellophane" American values, but American poets like Lowell and Sexton, whose poems chronicled the self in crisis, offered her a new way forward.

Still, *The Bell Jar* is as much a work of social protest as it is the chronicle of a breakdown. Plath had read Erich Fromm's *Escape from Freedom* at Smith, and was probably familiar with his 1955 book, *The Sane Society*, which had chapter titles like "Are We Sane?" and "Can a Society Be Sick?—The Pathology of Normalcy." Fromm argued that "a whole society can be sick" and that those "of greater integrity and sensitivity" who were "incapable of accepting the cultural opiate" often went crazy:

> Many psychiatrists and psychologists refuse to entertain the idea that society as a whole may be lacking in sanity. They hold that the problem of mental health in a society is only that of the number of "unadjusted" individuals, and not that of a possible unadjustment of the culture itself.[58]

This, Plath's shadow argument in *The Bell Jar*, would come to dominate the anti-psychiatry movement in Britain, led by R. D. Laing, in the early 1960s. Suzette said she was "sure" Plath "was aware" of Laing's 1960 groundbreaking book *The Divided Self: An Existential Study in Sanity and Madness*, which contains many images and ideas that resonate with the *Ariel* poems. Plath, with her deep interest in doubles and doppelgängers, would have been hooked by the title alone. Suzette read *The Divided Self* soon after it came out in 1960 and "was fascinated" by it. She said she "talked about it to Sylvia," as psychoanalysis was a fashionable topic within their leftist circles. These

circles included Laing himself, who met the Macedos and Doris Lessing at
Ruth Fainlight and Alan Sillitoe's home in the 1960s.[59] Fainlight remembered
that Laing was "one of the hot properties . . . people wanted to meet him."[60]
This circle also had communist ties, though its members were appalled by
Stalin's abuses. Lessing had been an active communist in her youth, while
Sillitoe's works often portrayed working-class heroes; he was invited to the
Soviet Union many times in the '60s.[61] Plath was not exposed to leftist ideas
so openly in America, where none other than Robert Lowell had denounced
Yaddo's director Elizabeth Ames in the late 1940s for communist ties. In the
spring of 1961, Plath's London friends provided an incubator and a receptive
audience for the Cold War concerns of *The Bell Jar*.

Indeed, Suzette remembered conversations with Sylvia about the Cold
War and "the Jewish question." "She did talk about the politics . . . how awful
the putting to death of the Rosenbergs was. And she had very strong liberal opinions." Sylvia also complained to her about "the narrow-mindedness
of the American dating system, and petting"—"the demands made on a
girl . . . the difficulties of proving oneself. All of that. She did criticize very
much the emphasis on virginity. . . . She said it was such a difficult world to
be a young woman." She told Suzette, too, about her general anxieties during her summer in New York: "When she got to New York, this was her first
time confronting an unknown world. She had to confront it. The world she
came from was this small world of her mother's and preconceptions of what
society was, and she was really stunned by the sophistication, and the experience of the *Mademoiselle* prize, and it made her . . . well, she didn't want to
stay alive for a while because she didn't fit in. There was always this need to
fit in, which must have been there from when she was young."

Fitting in was still a challenge, Suzette said, in England. "When she
wanted to be accepted she went into this gushing mode. . . . She didn't quite
know how to fit into the English village. Where she felt comfortable was
with poetry groups, with poetry intellectuals, because she didn't know how
to fit in the dining circles of Primrose Hill."[62] Suzette was thinking of the
Steins.

Moving amid these left-leaning intellectuals, Plath was free to criticize
America without being blacklisted. Earlier, in the summer of 1960, her first
in Chalcot Square, she had produced an extraordinary satirical collage that
suggests the ideological position she had adopted. On a photo of President
Eisenhower sitting at his desk in the Oval Office, she pasted a woman in a
swimsuit lounging provocatively next to a caption that read, "Every man
wants his woman on a pedestal." (The line anticipates "Every woman adores
a fascist," in "Daddy.") Other elements include a large fighter jet aimed at the
woman's vagina, controlled by two giddy young men in the corner cut from

an ad for "Electric Scale-Model Racing," and, in the right-hand corner, a couple sleeping with masks over their eyes. Plath pasted the word "SLEEP" onto Eisenhower's lapel and fitted his hand with a deck of cards.[63] As the critic Robin Peel has written, "The 'toys for boys' message is explicit, as is the somnambulism of America."[64]

Plath had created a visual outline of the themes she would tackle in *The Bell Jar*: America, symbolized by Eisenhower, is an oppressive patriarchy in thrall to the Cold War's military-industrial complex. Its consumer-citizens are asleep to the dangers its leaders pose, while those who see through the smoke and mirrors (as Esther Greenwood would) are marginalized and ignored. Plath suggests, with her phallic warplane poised to impale the sleeping beauty, that such a society is particularly dangerous for women. "The trouble was, I hated the idea of serving men in any way," Esther Greenwood says in *The Bell Jar*.[65]

Had this collage been on the novel's first cover, *The Bell Jar*, considered "an unhealthy celebration of death" by some, might have been read in a different way—its author more Beat than beaten down.[66] It has survived to give us a deeper sense of the anti-military, anti-patriarchal, and anti-American feelings Plath possessed as she embarked on her novel in 1961. She had originally used the title "Diary of a Suicide," but then changed it to the more ambiguous *The Bell Jar* when she wrote the second draft.[67] She had encountered the phrase in work by Elizabeth Bowen, Philip Wylie, and in her favorite short story, "The Beast in the Jungle," by Henry James. Yet it is perhaps no accident that she chose for her title a symbol shaped like an upside-down mushroom cloud.

————

THAT MAY, Plath finished her short American poetry anthology for the *Critical Quarterly*, which encompassed "the Beats" to "the Elegant Academicians."[68] She had included Howard Nemerov, William Stafford, Denise Levertov, Richard Wilbur, George Starbuck, Lucas Myers, Adrienne Rich, W. S. Merwin, Anthony Hecht, Robert Creeley, Anne Sexton, and W. D. Snodgrass. Stafford, Rich, and Merwin had the most poems in the selection; Robert Lowell and Theodore Roethke were notable exclusions. Plath's choices related to her own preoccupations—the American landscape, love, sin, art, childhood, nostalgia—yet few of the poems seem direct influences on her own work. Most of her selections gave a nod to formalism. Though she had tried to include a poem by Gregory Corso, she otherwise ignored the Beats.[69] Her picks were, essentially, conservative. The anthology would eventually sell twelve thousand copies—a staggering number for a one-off poetry imprint. The editors, Cox and Dyson, later acknowledged that Plath helped introduce a new generation of university students to American poetry.[70]

Plath knew that she was catching up with her husband. That summer several poems appeared in major publications, including "You're" in June's *Harper's*, "On Deck" in the July 22 *New Yorker*, and "Words for a Nursery" in the August *Atlantic*, while another eight poems were published in the highbrow *London Magazine* (including "Zoo Keeper's Wife" and "Parliament Hill Fields") and the *Critical Quarterly*.[71] She mentioned to Aurelia that Ted had typed up more than one hundred pages of his play *The Calm* himself, a significant detail that suggests a new dynamic within the marriage. Plath's Knopf contract probably boosted her confidence, for Knopf was the most prestigious literary publisher in New York, the American equivalent of Faber and Faber. Her rising stock meant that she may have no longer felt obligated to play the perfect hostess to Hughes's friends. Leonard Baskin, who stayed for ten days that May while launching a European exhibit of his work, tried her patience.[72] The "ghastly arrangement" forced her to move Frieda into the kitchen and cook separate meals for Leonard, who was picky. She said he "used" her like a servant: "about all I saw of him was dirty dishes, unmade beds and piles of dirty shirts and socks which he left for me to do," she complained to Aurelia.[73] Near the end of Leonard's stay, they all took a day trip to the countryside, at Ted's suggestion. Sylvia was upset she had been pulled from her writing yet again. Baskin remembered her "glacial, punitive fury"; she refused to speak to him for twenty-four hours.[74]

Leonard did not understand what had angered Sylvia, and he asked Ted in a late-June letter whether he had been "somehow responsible" for the "cold un-generosity of that day."[75] Hughes explained the understandable source of Plath's anger: "the main cause" of the "unpleasant" last day, he wrote, "was that Sylvia hadn't been able to do any work all week in the middle of her first longish work which had been going like gunpowder up to that point, and she was upset at the same time at taking no part in your visit except to cook and so on. So your sharp remarks to her on that Friday hit her with a special irony."[76] The "longish work" was *The Bell Jar*. Plath was in the middle of writing a classic American novel, yet she was expected to drop everything to be a hostess and maid.

Still, Leonard was one of Ted's closest friends, and Sylvia knew that amends would have to be made. Almost a year later, in April 1962, she wrote Baskin a heartfelt letter inviting him to their home in Devon. Leonard had asked Ted to write the foreword for his new book of engravings—"an honor," Sylvia admitted.[77]

O Leonard I have so many times thought of writing & written in thought: it is incredible what wounds & damages a few silly hours can do. I can only say, not in explanation or apology, but simply in fact, that when you came . . . I was very much worried at being in the middle of a first novel & living in that tiny hole with no place or time to finish it & having to forgo the art galleries & green breathing space & time to write which is my life blood & makes it possible for me to be domestic & motherly.

She graciously thanked him for serving as a character reference for her Eugene Saxton grant.[78]

On June 5, Plath recorded a twenty-five-minute BBC Third Programme broadcast of her poems for *The Living Poet* series, which would air on July 8. Plath was excited by the invitation and felt it was about time. "There is a Living Poet every month," she told Aurelia, "and I am on the list of Americans among Robert Lowell, Stanley Kunitz and Theodore Roethke, which I find quite an honour."[79] Anthony Thwaite, who invited Plath to perform on *The Living Poet* series, also felt the broadcast was an important milestone for her, as she was getting "well-known among poetry-reading circles." Plath had the freedom to write the script, choose her poems and her coreader. She chose Marvin Kane, an expatriate American playwright and actor with whom she and Hughes had crossed paths in London. Thwaite told Plath she should choose poems that rhymed for the show. "And she said, 'Why, every one of them rhymes!' And she pointed out that there was this tenuous, very off, off-rhyme in every one of them." They all had "great structure." Thwaite was impressed with Plath's professionalism. "She was always very quick on the up-take . . . extremely businesslike. She knew what she wanted and there was no show or temperament about it."[80]

Before reading "The Disquieting Muses," "Spinster," "Parliament Hill Fields," and "The Stones," she gave each poem its own concise, poetic introduction. Plath said that her poems "attempted to re-create definite situations and landscapes" and were "quite emphatically, about the things of this world": "fear," "despair and barrenness," domestic love, and delight in nature. Dark emotions took the guise of "unworldly things such as ghosts or trolls or antique gods."[81] Heeding T. S. Eliot's call for impersonality, Plath distanced herself from the poems' speaker, careful to call each of them "a person," despite the autobiographical details. Yet her decision to explain the poems at all was anathema to the expected New Critical approach to the text. Kane read "Sleep in the Mojave Desert," "Suicide Off Egg Rock," "Magi," "Medallion," and "You're." Both Americans read with British accents.

Sylvia and Ted desperately needed a break from "babytending" and were relieved when Aurelia visited in June. Sylvia's letter to Warren captures an intimate moment at Chalcot Square: "Mother is at the moment bathing Frieda, I halfway through making a strawberry chiffon pie & Ted typing a letter to T. S. Eliot."[82] The truth was probably more complicated. Sylvia could pour her heart out to her mother as long as she was far away; now, in person, she distanced herself. She was relieved when a friend of the Merwins took an interest in Aurelia. The woman "filled a gap" Sylvia was "no good at—a sort of chatty solicitous companion."[83] But she needed Aurelia's help with Frieda if she was to have a holiday. They ate their lunches and suppers together and saw several plays. "We took her to see 'Ondine,'" Sylvia wrote to Warren, "just her thing, all magic & fairytale."[84]

On June 28, Sylvia and Ted headed to France to spend two weeks with the Merwins. They arrived in Boulogne and drove down the coast, through Berck-Plage and Rouen, then on to Mont Saint-Michel and Douarnenez in Finisterre. Sylvia swam in the Atlantic, explored rocky points at the western edge of Brittany—the Pointe du Raz, the Pointe du Van—breakfasted on crepes, and ate huge plates of lobster and mussels. She was struck by a statue of Our Lady of the Shipwrecked at the Pointe du Raz; "She is in love with the beautiful formlessness of the sea," she wrote that September in "Finisterre." The trip would yield another, longer poem, "Berck-Plage," in June 1962.

They arrived at the Merwins' farm in Lacan on July 5. Sylvia spent most of her time happily sunbathing on a geranium-filled terrace and eating Dido's excellent meals. Dido had insisted that Sylvia rest—"she won't let me wash a dish," Sylvia wrote home. The farm had "a superb view, plum trees, country milk, butter & eggs, a billion stars overhead, cow bell's tinkling all night softly." After a few days, Sylvia felt "so renewed."[85]

Dido remembered the holiday rather differently, and she later complained to Anne Stevenson that, among other things, Sylvia ate too much. Dido probably did not know that Sylvia was pregnant again and in her first trimester—normally a time of increased appetite. She complained, too, that Sylvia acted rudely toward her society friend Margot Pitt-Rivers, the Spanish wife of the anthropologist Julian Pitt-Rivers and the former duchess of Lerma. Dido claimed that Sylvia would not let Ted out of her sight around Margot and accused her of a "Liaisons Dangereuses phobia."[86] Margot was wealthy, titled, sophisticated, in her forties, and on her second husband—just the sort of woman Sylvia did not trust. She was also a glamorous martyr who had narrowly evaded imprisonment for her role in the Spanish Civil War.[87] Bill Merwin had dedicated poems to her. Sylvia mentioned the duchess in a postcard to Aurelia, but also wrote, "I am ready & <u>eager</u> to come home."[88] Ted later told Frances McCullough that Sylvia had "exploded" in one of her "rages" at the Merwins' farm, "where she wrote *The Bell Jar* very fast, and got very upset doing it."[89]

Plath would write a poem about her time in Lacan, "Stars Over the Dordogne," which suggests unease with this aristocratic set. As the speaker looks up into the night sky, she feels embarrassed by the "luxury" of stars.

> The few I am used to are plain and durable;
> I think they would not wish for this dressy backcloth
> Or much company, or the mildness of the south.

Plath ends, "I shut my eyes / And drink the small night chill like news of home." Hughes, too, would rue the holiday. In July he wrote to Daniel and Helga Huws, "I wish we had gone almost anywhere else. I'm sure now that I detest the French, France & everything touched by them."[90] But he apologized to the Merwins later that month. "Since we came back we've regretted some things." He and Sylvia should have come to them "fresh" rather than after the Brittany excursion. "Perhaps we were unlucky with Margot too—things seemed to fall apart somewhat at that point, didn't they."[91]

The couple returned to England on July 14. The next day, Plath read from a selection of contemporary American poetry by Galway Kinnell, Anne Sexton, Robert Creeley, Denise Levertov, Charles Olson, and others on the BBC program *Possum Walked Backwards*. The program did not feature her own work—a reminder of the shadowy liminal space she now occupied without a strong reputation in America or England.

But that was changing. In June, she had been chosen for the BBC's *Living Poet* series. On July 17, Plath and Hughes read their poems at the "Poetry at the Mermaid" Festival at the Mermaid Theatre in London. Hughes was given the more prominent billing—he read twice, first at one with Geoffrey Hill and Clifford Dyment, then again at eight in the evening in a lineup of eight poets that included Plath. (All the poems had been commissioned by Guinness; the best would win "Thirst Prize.") Hughes read "My Uncle's Wound" and Plath read "Tulips." Introducing her, the festival director, the poet John Wain, remarked, "We have such a predominantly masculine week here, a fact that didn't really strike me until the programming was complete.... I'm very glad we have at any rate, one very fine woman poet this evening, Miss Sylvia Plath, as I refer to her by her maiden name before she was Mrs. Ted Hughes."[92] The introduction, like Alvarez's review of *The Colossus*, reveals the sexist barriers Plath had to scale to be taken seriously. Yet loud applause welcomed her onto the stage. In the surviving recording, she sounds nervous at first, then settles confidently into her rhythms. Jack Sweeney, in the audience, was deeply impressed. To the Fassetts he wrote, "It was, for me, very moving to hear and see Sylvia as the only woman on the stage that evening and the only American on the stage! She read with great grace and clarity and command and the poem she read is a humdinger."[93] Over dinner that night with Eric Walter White, Sweeney asked Plath to send him her poem's drafts for Harvard's Lamont Library. She would send them to him about a month later, saying that she had "specially saved" them out of her weekly draft sheets.[94]

The other poets who read that night included R. S. Thomas, Michael Hamburger, Thomas Blackburn, and Richard Murphy, who had recently written his first poetry collection, *Sailing to an Island*, which would be published by Faber and Faber in 1962. Murphy, who was Anglo-Irish and five years older than Plath, joined Sylvia and Ted for lunch after Hughes's afternoon reading. Ted "made a strong, silent impression" as Richard told stories about his home on the west coast of Ireland, where, from the small fishing village of Cleggan, he ferried passengers to the nearby island of Inishbofin on his traditional Galway hooker.[95] To Ted and Sylvia, it seemed that Richard lived a Yeatsian dream life where peace came dropping slow. A friendship took root. Ted later wrote to Daniel Huws, "He's unexpected—English Public School finish, manners & appearance of a fastidious cleric, but very fresh, & very nice."[96] When their marriage started to fall apart a year later, Sylvia and Ted would turn to Richard, and Ireland, to heal the wound.

The following day, July 18, the couple headed to Yorkshire for a week with Aurelia. Ted returned to his grammar school in Mexborough with Sylvia to deliver a lecture on Speech Day, arranged by his old teacher John Fisher. But the car broke down on the way, and they were late to the proceedings. Though the headmaster introduced Hughes as "*the* poet of his generation" he was privately upset by his tardiness. Hughes approached the lectern and said, "I suppose it has taken me thirty years to get here" and admitted that he "had always set his mind against giving an 'address' and certainly did not intend to do so to this captive audience.'"[97] He read his poems, explaining their links to Old Denaby, before sitting down. While the applause, one reporter claimed, was "the longest & loudest ever heard in Mexborough Grammar School," several members of the school's senior staff were angry Hughes had not delivered a more traditional speech.[98] Fisher, however, was "delighted" with Hughes's unorthodox style.[99] Plath helped smooth things over by "graciously" presenting some of the school prizes and mixing eas-ily with guests at the reception afterward.[100] Later that day, they visited the Wholeys at Crookhill.

Aurelia wrote to Warren from Heptonstall sounding very much like her daughter: "I've never been happier than I have been since I've come to this strange, wild part of England." Yet she did not seem happy. She mentioned her "cell-sized room (very quaint & I <u>like</u> it!)" and complained how her daughter just "<u>can't</u> maintain American standards of cleanliness." Aurelia was impressed with the moorland scenery but disturbed by the less romantic parts of Yorkshire: "The seven-hour drive up here was horrible—we passed through town after town of blackened brick-stone house attached to stone house—not a tree or blade of grass . . . the ugliest cities in the world, I'm sure, and the robot-like people one saw about made me shudder." Heptonstall vil-lage itself she found "mean and ugly," and she described Edith and William Hughes's home condescendingly; like her daughter, she could not resist a jab at the tiny, "jammed" kitchen. But she liked the Hugheses, whom she found "earthy, warm-hearted." As for English "middle class living," it had taken her two weeks to "adjust," but she was beginning to see its strengths. "Our American way of life is efficient, comfortable, but makes us soft," she wrote. Sylvia cooked most meals, and the group made excursions to the Brontë Par-sonage Museum in Haworth, Hebden Bridge, and the surrounding moors. The visit tired Aurelia, who told Warren she walked "several miles of <u>steep</u> climbing a day" between Sutcliffe's Inn and the Beacon, sometimes pushing Frieda's pram.[101]

Back in London, Sylvia and Ted headed to Devon on July 28. (Aure-lia, who was staying in the Merwins' flat, babysat.) They knew they needed more space, but they could not afford a London home. Ted preferred a rural retreat, and Devon, with its moorland, rivers, and direct train to London, was affordable; Clarissa Roche said Sylvia told her the move "was entirely Ted's idea."[102] Hughes later claimed that their goal was also eventually to purchase a London flat so that they could have two bases. They had looked at a house in Yorkshire (Lumb Bank, which Hughes eventually purchased after Plath's death), but it was eight hours by train and, as Ted later explained to Anne Stevenson, "full of my relatives." The main reason they chose Devon over another rural part of England, though, had to do with their fear of a nuclear accident. "What decided us was that in 1961 the world seemed closer to nuclear war than ever since—and the panic was greater because the threat was really coming up for the first time. Nuclear business preoccupied us a good deal," Hughes told Stevenson. They had secured a map in 1960 that alerted them to the locations of nuclear waste dumps and illnesses like leukemia. They worried about fallout, and decided that "if we were going to move we might as well be upwind of likely accidents—which brought us to Devon."[103]

They had been combing through Devon's real estate listings since early spring and narrowed the search down to eight homes, but only one enchanted: Court Green, a centuries-old manor house with a thatched roof, nine rooms, a wine cellar, attic, stable-cum-garage, servants' cottage, and tennis court. The house was surrounded by three walled-in acres of apple and cherry trees, blackberry and raspberry bushes, and large elms. There was even a twelfth-century castle *motte*, about two meters high, on the grounds. Court Green was in the small rural village of North Tawton, near Dartmoor, on the River Taw, which meant good fishing for Ted. Sylvia was happier about the four-hour express train to London, while Exeter and the coast were just an hour's drive. She was impressed by Court Green's former inhabitants, Sir and Lady Arundell. Sir Robert Arundell, governor of Barbados, had grown up in the house, which seemed to Sylvia "as if it had been full of warm fires, and flowers, and happy children."[104]

They returned to London at midnight on July 29, "exhausted" but full of enthusiasm for the home.[105] They had agreed to pay £3,600 (about $10,000; $88,000 in 2020 dollars) for it.[106] Aurelia offered to lend them the entire amount, but Ted refused. She and Edith would eventually lend them £500 each so that they would avoid the "terrible interest rate" of 6½ percent. Despite Aurelia's generosity, her letter to Warren that week suggests tension. "I wish I could see it," she wrote wistfully the day after Sylvia returned from Devon, "but Ted and Sylvia are glad (I sense) that the distance makes this impossible right now. They don't mind your seeing it; but said that I would find flaws that they intend to eradicate by the time I come to visit next summer. (!)" She added that if Warren came to visit he should plan to stay at an inn: "truly you will be happier."[107] Aurelia returned to Boston on August 5.

Sylvia continued to fantasize about a London townhouse, but she also wanted a spacious home where, she had told Owen Leeming, "I can shout to Ted from one end to the other and he won't be able to hear me."[108] And here was an ancient manor home, a veritable British estate with its own aristocratic lineage. If Court Green seduced Ted with its privacy and orchards, it lured Sylvia with its suggestion of grandeur; indeed, she had often dreamed about living in mansions like Olive Prouty and Sarah-Elizabeth Rodger. Court Green satisfied both her American Dream of home ownership and her American fantasy of British gentry life. Yet the decision to move to Devon— like the marriage itself—was romantic and impulsive; neither Sylvia nor Ted realized how isolated they would become in the deep country.

Ted hoped that Court Green would provide a grounded, earthy respite that would refocus his energies. He had not been producing much poetry over the past year. His "open ticket" at the BBC, as Sylvia described it, meant that he worked mainly on more lucrative plays and children's programs.[109] Ironically, his desire to support himself through writing meant that he had little time for the writing he valued most—poetry. He would write to Thom Gunn after the move about how pleased he was to be free of London and its paralyzing "smog of static."[110] He looked forward to fishing in the River Taw, his "main dream come true," Sylvia wrote Jack Sweeney in August.[111]

Frieda was now walking and beginning to talk. She would point to the picture of Isis on the wall and say "I-see," and sit on her mother's lap as she typed. The couple still planned to use Ted's £500 Maugham Award to go to Italy, but by mid-August, on the cusp of their move and expecting a second child in January, they decided to cancel the trip. "We've had enough of moving around to last for years," Sylvia informed Aurelia.[112] She had little desire to trot around Italy pregnant, with a toddler in tow. The forfeiture may have increased Ted's sense, as he later wrote to Olwyn, that he was becoming imprisoned within the marriage.[113] Plath was less in need of a writing holiday now that she had finished *The Bell Jar*. That month, revisiting her journals, she noticed a despondent 1958 passage. "Why don't I write a novel?" she had written then. Next to it, in pen, she wrote, "I have! August 22, 1961: THE BELL JAR."[114] She likely finished the novel on this day.

Now that Ted was leaving London, he could afford to give himself over to it. During their last weeks in the city, the couple visited the British Museum and the National Portrait Gallery. Sylvia wished that they'd taken off more afternoons together to explore. They made arrangements to sublet their flat. Two couples came round, and both wanted it. One was, Sylvia wrote, "a young Canadian poet, the girl a German-Russian whom we identified with." They had originally promised the flat to the other couple, who had produced a check on the spot. But after reconsidering, they tore up the check and offered the flat to David and Assia Wevill. "The couple are coming to supper this week," Sylvia wrote Aurelia.[115] Ted told Al Alvarez he did not know David but that he had already "met her glancingly." David showed sixty of his poems to Ted, who sent Alvarez three he thought "first rate" for *The Observer*.[116] Sylvia seemed fascinated by Assia. She told Ruth Fainlight, shortly after meeting the Wevills, about "this marvelous, intriguing woman and this young poet."[117] Suzette was similarly struck by Sylvia's fascination with Assia, whom she thought "wonderful, beautiful . . . with a passport on her face."[118] She called Assia "the Wandering Jewess. She's lived everywhere, done everything; I know her; she's my alter-ego."[119]

The forthcoming Knopf edition of *The Colossus* distracted Plath from thoughts of leaving London. Filling out the author's forms gave her a thrill, as did her seventy-five-pound first prize for "Insomniac" at the 1961 Guinness Poetry Competition at the Cheltenham Festival of Art and Literature. Anthony Thwaite had helped judge the prize. When Plath and Hughes had first come to London, he remembered, Plath had been "an obscure figure" associated with Hughes. "One saw odd poems of hers around . . . good, but nothing great." With "Insomniac," however, "I recognized it was a Sylvia Plath poem. . . . She had established a voice after *The Colossus*."[120]

Sylvia hoped that she and Ted would still see their London friends in Devon since they were "on the holiday route to Cornwall," but claimed once a year was enough. "I shall look forward to the solitude."[121] Ted hoped that the move to a real home might help repair the family breach, and he took the unusual step of asking Olwyn to soften her stance toward Sylvia. "Since you mis-posted your letter to Sylvia at xmas you haven't directly acknowledged her again, & it would be generous & quite timely for you to do so now. She wonders rather miserably if you ever will. If you didn't think you had such a monopoly on temperament, we could be perhaps picturing pleasant meetings in Devon."[122] But Olwyn did not visit Court Green until after Sylvia's death.

26

The Late, Grim Heart of Autumn

Devon, September–December 1961

The Hugheses arrived in the quiet country village of North Tawton, Devon, on September 1. Court Green was just a short walk from the town center, with its small clock tower, post office, shops, and red-brick town hall. Local footpaths offered stunning views of the surrounding moors. Their home was, and still is, one of the grandest in the village. "But the space! And the orchard! And the garden!" Ted exclaimed to Olwyn.[1] The house conferred status on its new owners, whose grandparents had waited tables and cleaned houses. Sylvia joked to Helga Huws that she and Ted were the new "lords of the manor."[2]

Sylvia immediately filled the house with flowers from the garden, "great peachy-colored gladiolas, hot red & orange & yellow zinnias." Frieda loved "tramping through the big rooms" and got so much exercise that she needed two naps a day. Sylvia was thrilled to see her daughter so happy in the fresh country air. She felt calm and content. "My whole spirit has expanded immensely—I don't have that crowded, harassed feeling I've had in all these small spaces I've lived in before," she wrote Aurelia.[3]

On the ground floor were a dining room, living room, playroom for Frieda, kitchen and laundry, and storage rooms. Upstairs were two large bedrooms, a smaller bedroom, and a bathroom. The third floor was attic space. A cobblestone court surrounded the buildings, while large trees loomed over both sides of the property, which abutted Saint Peter's Church, its graveyard, and farmers' fields. Plath and Hughes finally had their own separate studies; his was in the attic, hers on the second floor facing the churchyard, "the best front bedroom." An Aga coal stove warmed the large kitchen, and hot water came from an immersion heater. The dining room was "the heart-room of the house, with light-green linoleum, light pink walls, and shoulder-high wood paneling." They ate on the Wevills' large round dining table, which they were holding for them at Court Green. "The place is like a person: it responds to the slightest touch & looks wonderful immediately," Sylvia told her mother.[4] Ted was delighted by the starlings that "live over our bedroom under the thatch, thump & chirp in the mornings, fly into the cherry tree & whistle at each other."[5]

One of the first letters Plath received in Devon was from Howard Moss at *The New Yorker*, suggesting revision to "The Rival" and rejecting "Stars Over the Dordogne" and "Face Lift." Moss was confused but intrigued by "The Rival." Plath explained the poem as "a contrast between two women: the speaker, who is a rather ordinary wife and mother, and her 'rival'—the woman who is everything she is not—who obsesses her. This woman terrifies the speaker and dominates her thoughts, seeming almost superhuman . . . and, in the third section, grows impressive and omnipresent as a sort of goddess."[6] Moss would reject the poem in late September. The Rival, with her messages like "carbon monoxide," was a personification of Plath's perfection-demanding demon. In Devon, she set about protecting herself with her lares and penates—flowers, painted hearts, bright red curtains. She would not be turned to stone, would not find herself waking, as she wrote in the poem, in a "mausoleum."

Warren visited in September after a conference in London. Frieda peered at him shyly on the car ride from the train station back to Court Green, where Sylvia plied him with refreshments and homemade banana bread. He described the property enthusiastically to Aurelia, though he remarked that the town was so small he could hardly believe the London train bothered to stop there. Sylvia happily reported that he made "himself useful," mowing the lawn and chopping wood. He and Ted sanded a large elm plank (which had been meant for a coffin) into her first "real capacious writing table."[7] Together they picked blackberries in the surrounding fields, explored Exeter Cathedral, picnicked over the sea at Tintagel, and ate at the local inn, the Burton Hall Arms. Sylvia and Ted split their days between child-minding and writing as they had in London—she had the mornings, he the afternoons—but she still bore the brunt of the housework. She decided to keep the Arundells' cleaning lady, Nancy Axworthy, who helped with housework for three hours on Tuesdays and Thursdays. Nancy, she told Aurelia, was her "best news"; she had always dreamed of hiring help to free her from domestic drudgery. Nancy said Sylvia and Ted always treated her with kindness and decency: Sylvia "was good to work for." She gave Nancy free rein to do her job and never complained. Ted and Sylvia brought her cups of tea while she cleaned and Sylvia encouraged her to use the Bendix washer for her own laundry. Nancy remembered that Ted "genuinely" shared the child-care duties, even nappy changing. "He did a lot for those children. . . . He did a lot to give her the time to write."[8] Sylvia felt Ted, too, had found the right balance: "I never have known such satisfaction just seeing him revel in this place and leading at last exactly the life he wants."[9]

Ensconced in her own manor home with her cherished family, a book of poems, and a novel to her name, Plath too finally had all that she wanted. And yet, the first poem she wrote at Court Green depicted ruin rather than promise. "Wuthering Heights" is a portrait of the abandoned Yorkshire farmhouse, Top Withens, on which Emily Brontë allegedly based *Wuthering Heights*. Sylvia and Ted had often hiked there over the moors in 1956 when they had blithely identified themselves with Cathy and Heathcliff. Plath's depiction of Top Withens in 1961, however, is a rueful backward glance. The poem, set on Hughes's ground, is filled with images of a home—and perhaps a marriage—coming apart: "The horizons ring me like faggots," the skies "dissolve / Like a series of promises," "Lintel and sill have unhinged themselves." The old farmhouse deteriorates more with each passing year on the high, lonely moor. The move to Court Green symbolized a new chapter; "Wuthering Heights" was an odd benediction.

More bleak images were to come. "Blackberrying," finished on September 23, follows a speaker down a dead-end hill "That looks out on nothing, nothing but a great space / Of white and pewter lights, and a din like silversmiths / Beating and beating at an intractable metal." "Finisterre," written six days later, also begins with an image of "the land's end," filled with cliffs, rocks, and mists. Between September 29 and October 29, Plath wrote five other poems that cast a baleful note—"Last Words," "The Moon and the Yew Tree," "Mirror," "The Babysitters," and "The Surgeon at 2 a.m.," another surreal hospital poem. "The Moon and the Yew Tree" is among her finest. Hughes wrote that he suggested the poem as an exercise one night when she could not sleep. He told her to write about what she saw when she looked out of the window—Saint Peter's Church, a graveyard, and a large yew tree. The result, he later said, greatly "depressed" him.[10]

The poem announces itself as a portrait of depression: "This is the light of the mind, cold and planetary," Plath writes in her most memorable first line. "The trees of the mind are black. The light is blue," she continues. Lines like "I simply cannot see where there is to get to" and "I have fallen a long way" suggest a terrible despondency. The speaker muses on the nearby church, which offers community and solace. Yet she feels unworthy:

> The moon is my mother. She is not sweet like Mary.
> Her blue garments unloose small bats and owls.

> How I would like to believe in tenderness—
> The face of the effigy, gentled by candles,
> Bending, on me in particular, its mild eyes.

She ponders the saints in the church, "stiff with holiness." She stands apart. "The moon sees nothing of this. She is bald and wild. / And the message of the yew tree is blackness—blackness and silence."

The last poem Plath wrote in 1961 was "The Babysitters," about her summer with her old friend Marcia Brown (now Marcia Plumer) in Swampscott. "It is ten years, now, since we rowed to Children's Island," she begins. She recounts the mansions, the Mayo children, the yacht, the day off at the island. Apart from the very early "Betsy and Sylvia," which was never published, "The Babysitters" is the only poem Plath ever wrote about friendship. Its nostalgic, intimate tone stands out in an oeuvre full of myth, symbol, dramatic landscapes, and psychic interiors:

> The bold gulls dove as if they owned it all.
> We picked up sticks of driftwood and beat them off,
> Then stepped down the steep beach shelf and into the water.
> We kicked and talked. The thick salt kept us up.
> I see us floating there yet, inseparable—two cork dolls.
> What keyhole have we slipped through, what door has shut?
> The shadows of the grasses inched round like hands of a clock,
> And from our opposite continents we wave and call.
> Everything has happened.

Plath wrote this poem just a week after "The Moon and the Yew Tree." The two poems sound very different, yet both speak to isolation, loneliness, and exile.

Plath probably also wrote her short story "Mothers" around this time. The story concerns a young mother, Esther, who lives with a writer-husband in a manor house clearly based on Court Green. She is an American transplant searching for community, but her options are limited. The town rector visits her at home and asks her if she believes in "the efficacy of prayer." Plath writes, "'Oh yes, yes I do!' Esther heard herself exclaim, amazed at the tears that so opportunely jumped to her eyes, and meaning only: How I would like to. Later, she wondered if the tears weren't caused by her vision of the vast, irrevocable gap between her faithless state and the beatitude of belief."[11] The language is very similar to that of Plath's artful mindscape in "The Moon in the Yew Tree," while the story itself, which chronicles Esther's attempt to assimilate, suggests a root for such emotions.

Hughes sensed his wife's unhappiness. He later wrote in his poem "The Beach" how that autumn Plath "needed the sea."

> England was so filthy! Only the sea
> Could scour it. Your ocean salts would scour you.
> You wanted to be washed, scoured, sunned.
> That "jewel in the head"—your flashing thunderclap miles
> Of Nauset surf.

"The Beach" becomes a meditation upon England and America. "England / was so poor!" Plath says in Hughes's poem. "Were English cars all black—to hide the filth? / Or to stay respectable, like bowlers / And umbrellas?" English art was "depressionist." Hughes tells her they had "never recovered" from two world wars. They drive to Woolacombe Sands, a wide and expansive beach on the north coast of Devon, but the November afternoon is cold and rainy. "So this was the reverse of dazzling Nauset." In the poem, Plath refuses to get out of the car. Hughes writes, "You sat behind your mask, inaccessible— / Staring toward the ocean that had failed you."[12]

The autumn weather was "crisp and clear," and the accolades kept coming Hughes's way.[13] In July, *Vogue* had published an article about Hughes, Louis MacNeice, Thomas Kinsella, and William Empson. (Hughes, looking serious and swarthy, had the largest photo.) He was asked to co-judge the next two years' Poetry Book Society Selection and learned that Faber and Faber was putting together a dual *Selected Poems* of him and Thom Gunn. His work would appear in October's *Harper's Bazaar* alongside poems, Plath marveled, by Robert Lowell and Marianne Moore. Likely reflecting on her experience at *Mademoiselle*, Sylvia wrote Aurelia that the editors at *Harper's Bazaar* "are generally very brainy women & the fashion blurbs written by Phi Beta Kappa English majors. Poor things."[14]

Yet Hughes's poetic output was dwindling as his prestige grew. He was recording short programs for the BBC *Woman's Hour* in a local station in Plymouth while completing other small assignments for the BBC and *The Sunday Times*. He had yet to make real money from his plays, as Plath had hoped. They had spent nearly their entire savings—$5,880—on Court Green, and had about $1,200 left. (Thanks to several generous housewarming checks from America, the balance grew to a little over $2,000 by late October.) Ever practical, Sylvia wrote a chummy letter to Peter Davison, who had been corresponding with Hughes, at September's end. She waxed lyrical about her spacious rooms at Court Green and invited him and Jane to stay as if their last tense meeting had never happened. She enclosed several of Hughes's poems, including "Wodwo," "in case you want to publish it in America."[15] Her own career continued to gain momentum as Hughes's plateaued. Her Heinemann contract for *The Bell Jar* is dated October 21, 1962, and states that the novel was "finished and submitted."[16] She had finally sold her first story, "My Perfect Place," to a woman's magazine, *My Weekly*, and was back to wondering if short stories were the route to steadier income. Ted encouraged her, and the two of them started collaborating on plots they intended to sell to women's magazines, just as they had as Cambridge students.

Sylvia's letters during this period move deftly between talk of potty training, home renovations, *New Yorker* acceptances, and meetings with James Michie at Heinemann. She was considering a new poetry collection called *Tulips & Other Poems* and organizing copyright permissions for her "American Poetry Now" *Critical Quarterly* supplement.[17]

The Macedos were the first London friends to visit Court Green that fall, after Warren's visit. Suzette remembered little Frieda grabbing Helder's hand, saying, "Show you my house!" as they entered Court Green. "It was lovely staying there, and Sylvia was very happy, but also there was an undercurrent that it hadn't been quite the decision of both of them." Suzette thought that the house suited Sylvia more than Ted, who seemed "restless . . . like a trapped animal."[18] "He used to say he hated London, but he didn't really. He liked London. . . . It was Sylvia who wanted the big house, the children. . . . But it was too big a house. Too cold. When I came back, I thought, '*Not* a good idea.' "[19]

Sylvia did start to miss London. Although she extolled the bucolic virtues of Court Green to acquaintances, to closer friends she expressed her frustration with rural life. "I long to go to London, even for a movie or for a play," she wrote to Ruth Fainlight less than two weeks after she arrived.[20] She told Helga Huws that North Tawton was "ugly," the yard full of nettles, the plaster "crumbling ominously," and "a billion birds living in our thatch." All this when they had "solemnly sworn No Thatches (fear of fire, expense, rain, predatory birds, etc.)."[21] When her Knopf editor requested a publicity photograph for the American edition of *The Colossus*, Plath was embarrassed to admit that she was "so buried in the country" she knew no one with a camera. She understood the importance of the publicity photo from her *Mademoiselle* days, but hoped that "the public can get by without anything until I again return to civilisation."[22] She thanked Howard Moss at *The New Yorker* for sending her literary clippings from America. "Buried as we are among Devon hedges and livestock, we don't get a chance to keep up on these at all."[23] The only newspaper they subscribed to was *The Observer*.[24]

They owned a radio and a record player (all of Plath's records were Classical) but not a television.[25]

To London friends, Sylvia mocked her neighbors. Mrs. Sibyl Merton Hamilton, who lived across the street at Crispins Cottage, was the "wife of the dead coffee plantation owner & local power. . . . She is old, booming, half-deaf, with a dachshund named Pixie."[26] (She would in fact come to like Mrs. Hamilton, whose sensible British demeanor struck just the right note.) There was also a young mother, Sylvia Crawford, whom Plath thought pleasant but "dumb." (The vicar, she told Helga Huws, had sent Crawford round "to be my friend.")[27] The midwife seemed suspicious of them "as artists and outlanders" until her son, away at boarding school in London, informed her that Ted Hughes was a famous poet. After that, she treated Sylvia "with surprising warmth."[28]

Fireside chats with T. S. Eliot became a distant memory. There were, Sylvia told Helga, "no soul-mates."[29] She expanded on this problem to Marcia: "What I miss most is (I don't quite know how to put it) 'college-educated' mothers. I got to know several nice, bright girls in London whom I miss, but there is nobody like that round here."[30] She put on a brave face: "I don't require the intimacy of other people to keep me happy."[31] But Sylvia had always flourished in the company of close female friends and foundered when those friendships receded. There were other hints of tension. To Ruth Fainlight she joked that she had one study, while "Ted has 3 or 4 in case he wants a change." She asked Ruth and Helga to visit her "in the late, grim heart of autumn."[32]

Kenneth Davies, the local midwife's son, was sixteen when the Hughes family moved to North Tawton. He remembered that no one in the town of eleven hundred had any idea who Sylvia Plath and Ted Hughes were and no inkling of who they would become. Most of the townspeople were farmers, factory workers, or employees of the North Devon Water Board. "There were very few educated people," he remembered, "and I am pretty certain that none could match the Hugheses' intellect. Add to that that she was an American, so Sylvia was going to find it difficult." He noted, "word soon got around that a personality had arrived."[33]

Sylvia knew the villagers found her and Ted "quite outlandish," and she soon realized that if she wanted to fit in she needed to attend the local Anglican church. She found the Irish rector "a little dull simple man," and his sermons slightly absurd.[34] "When he talks of sinfulness, I have to laugh," she wrote Aurelia. She would always remain a "pagan-Unitarian," but she wanted to give Frieda a "spiritual" grounding.[35] She had envied her mother, growing up Catholic and having "a rich & definite faith to break away from"—this seemed preferable to no religion at all, which might make Frieda feel "curious and outcast."[36] To Aurelia, she wrote, "I know how incredibly powerful the words of that little Christian prayer 'God is my help in every need' which you taught us has been at odd moments of my life."[37] She was not simply humoring her mother; on the same day she wrote this letter, she wrote "The Moon and the Yew Tree," with its sense of loneliness and yearning for communion. Evensong would come closest to fulfilling her spiritual needs, such as they were: "it's a peaceful little well on Sunday evenings, & I do love the organ, the bellringing & hymn-singing, & muse on the stained-glass windows during the awful sermons."[38] She could see the church windows through the trees from her house.

She and Hughes had about fifty children's books between them to review, at $50 an article.[39] ("My acquisitive soul rejoices," Plath wrote home.)[40] But she was deep in domesticity that fall and seemed most excited about her new Bendix washing machine. She planned to start her birthday week "with a bright white Monday wash." On her twenty-ninth birthday, Ted presented her with "a lot of fancy cans of octopus & caviar," two R. S. Thomas poetry books, a wicker basket, and a Parker pen. She also received a letter from Howard Moss at *The New Yorker*, accepting "Blackberrying." Aurelia sent a check that would pay for a nice meal in London, where Sylvia, nearly seven months pregnant, traveled that week despite feeling "very ponderous."[41] She spent two nights in early November with the Sillitoes. Ruth Fainlight had written to her about a threatened miscarriage earlier that autumn, and Sylvia offered her support and sympathy: "noone [*sic*] can ever really identify deeply enough with someone else's special predicament to make the words 'I know how you feel' carry their full weight. But our sad & confusing experience of losing a baby last winter has made me feel much closer to the difficulties & apprehensions of childbearing."[42]

In London, Plath attended the Guinness award ceremony at Goldsmith's Hall, where she read "Insomniac" and collected her seventy-five-pound prize.[43] The next day she met with the editor at *My Weekly* and sold some old poetry manuscripts to Indiana University through the same seller who had bought Ted's.[44] She saw two Edward Albee plays, *The American Dream* and *The Death of Bessie Smith*—interesting choices for someone who had recently described herself as an "exile." It was an exhausting trip for a woman in her third trimester of pregnancy. "London is very tiring when one doesn't have a place of one's own, and the getting about a Herculean task," she wrote Aurelia.[45] She was relieved to find Ted and Frieda waiting for her at the station on her return.

Diversions in North Tawton were simpler. Sylvia described the family's early-morning walks among the "hedgerows a tapestry of oak leaves, holly, fern, blackberry leaves all intertwined, the green hills dotted with sheep and cows, and the pink plaster farms very antique."[46] One fall day they watched a fox hunt. The aesthetics fascinated Sylvia "in spite of our sympathy for foxes"—"red jackets, brass buttons & velvet caps drinking whiskey on horse-back . . . sulphurous dogs."[47] It was another American fantasy of British life, like punting on the Cam, striding across the moors, tripping through Tra-falgar Square. She could almost imagine that she was indeed the wife of a country squire with an ancient farmhouse every bit as impressive as Dido Merwin's. There was occasional snow, but she wished for more. "I miss my crisp white 6 foot American blizzards," she wrote to Ted's brother, "we used to have such fun sledging & building igloos. I suppose I'll be telling Frieda about 'the old days in the old country' where everything was just slightly legendary."[48]

———

WHEN TED AWOKE on November 9, he turned to Sylvia and said, "'I dreamed you had won a $25 prize for your story about Johnny Panic.'"[49] Sylvia went downstairs to find a letter from the Eugene Saxton foundation telling her she had won a grant for $2,080 to work on *The Bell Jar*.[50] She was ecstatic, and relieved. The foundation had awarded her the exact amount she had requested—enough, she calculated, to pay for a full-time nanny and house-keeper. She had bought herself time to write a second novel. She hadn't told them that she had already finished and signed a contract for *The Bell Jar*. "Just between the two of us (and don't tell anyone)," she wrote Aurelia, "I fig-ured nothing was so sure to stop me writing as a grant to do a specific project that had to be turned in at the end, with quarterly progress reports—so I finished a batch of stuff this last year, tied it up in 4 parcels, & have it ready to report on bit by bit as required."[51]

In early November, Hughes finished his play *The Wound*, which Plath described as "a poetic drama for voices (not acting) about the delusions of a soldier with a wound."[52] He typed it up himself. *The New Yorker* had taken "Tulips"; "Sleep in the Mojave Desert" appeared in *The Observer*; her *Ameri-can Poetry Now* selection was almost ready for the printer; and "The Perfect Place" (originally titled "The Lucky Stone" and written in the fall of 1960) appeared in the October 28 issue of *My Weekly*. Plath called the story "very stiff & amateurish,"[53] but she hoped it might help her get published in *Ladies' Home Journal*, "a much more advanced and professional magazine than any of the women's weeklies over here."[54] The British magazines were full of rec-ipes, she complained, "for things like Lard & Stale Bread Pie, garnished with Cold Pigs Feet, or Left-Over Pot Roast in Aspic."[55] Indeed, she "rejoiced" at the arrival of two issues of *Ladies' Home Journal* from Aurelia that November.

"It has a special Americanness which I feel the need to dip into, now I'm in exile."[56]

"The Perfect Place" concerns a young Canadian woman, Joanna, whose parents have died in a car accident. Engaged to a fastidious British lawyer named Kenneth, Joanna is on holiday at a British seaside resort planning their upcoming wedding. Joanna knows that she is supposed to feel lucky: "I should be loving this . . . yet I feel stifled, hemmed in."[57] She has begun to find Kenneth too "exacting," and his mother insufferable. She tells herself that his "career comes first," but she can't quite convince herself. "*Why must I feel so rebellious? What's happening to me?*" she wonders. Kenneth would rather work than take a walk on the beach, which Joanna thinks is her "native habitat." When Joanna realizes that she is falling for a local artist, Simon—who personifies the "rough country"—she finds the courage to call off the engagement to the fey, urbane Kenneth and return her large diamond ring, a "cold emblem of security and affluence." Joanna's North American heritage, her love of the sea, her confusion surrounding the life she is supposed to want versus the life she actually wants—all of this brings the story back to Plath herself. Simon is based on Ted, while Kenneth, "a solid, commonsensical object blocking out the view of everything that mattered to her"—is yet another iteration of Dick Norton, who had become Sylvia's improbable male muse.

She would send the editor at *My Weekly*, Helena Annan, two more stories in late December 1961—"Shadow Girl" and "A Winter's Tale." Both were rejected in early January 1962. "Shadow Girl," written at Court Green, is set in London and concerns a young woman with a famous publisher father who is exploited by striving male authors. She finally finds love with a documentary filmmaker by escaping her father's shadow. (An interesting detail, given the shadow Otto cast over Sylvia's own life.) "A Winter's Tale," set in Hughes's Yorkshire, is about a young woman, Kate, whose husband has recently died. She moves from London to a moorland cottage where she can mourn his absence in peace. The story involves a visit to Wuthering Heights with visiting London friends, and her meeting a local young widower who bears more than a passing resemblance to Heathcliff; Kate (whose name suggests Cathy) embarks on a tentative relationship with him at the story's end.

Plath wrote "A Winter's Tale" around the same time that she wrote her poem "Wuthering Heights," in the fall of 1961. Certain words and images appear in both. Set side by side, the two pieces show how constrained Plath was in her stories, and how much more freedom she allowed herself in her poems. The powerful, bleak, imagistic poem and the cloyingly formulaic story seem written by two different authors. As the editor of *My Weekly* wrote to Plath in January 1962, they wanted stories with "nice, ordinary, recognizable homeliness."[58] Hughes had encouraged Plath to write for this commercial market as a way of "learning how to write about life directly and boldly and full-scale."[59] Yet he also maintained that her best work—and the work that mattered most to her—was her poetry.

In November, Sylvia received an alarming letter from James Michie at Heinemann about "the libel issue" in *The Bell Jar*. Plath had originally called her main character Victoria Lucas, which was also her pen name. (Sylvia's friend William Sterling claimed this was the same name she used on her fake ID to get into Rahar's as an underage Smithie.)[60] Michie reminded her that this was not good practice, and she quickly changed the heroine's name to Esther Greenwood. She admitted to Michie that the "whole first half of the book is based on the Mademoiselle College Board Program for Guest Editors," but she called nearly all the main characters in the novel "fictitious." Her arguments were spurious: "Presumably any old Doctor Gordon could sue me for saying he gave a bad shock treatment."

The only characters that Plath admitted were based on real people were Buddy Willard ("indistinguishable from all the blond, blue-eyed boys who have ever gone to Yale") and Mrs. Greenwood. "My mother is based on my mother," Plath wrote in a revealing slip, "but what do I say to defame her? She is a dutiful, hard-working woman whose beastly daughter is ungrateful to her. Even if she were a 'suing' mother, which she is of course not, I don't see what she could sue here." Plath cited Lowell's use of McLean in *Life Studies* and claimed, "All I say about it is laudatory anyhow." She seemed not to take "the libel issue" seriously. The only concession she made was to change the name of Jane Anderson's character, "Jane," to "Joan." She wrote breezily to Michie, "There are so few people or institutions that I can be said to 'defame' in any way, and the few I criticize I certainly don't think are recognizable." She asked him to keep a "Hush" about the book being finished, as she needed to keep its completion a secret from the Eugene Saxton foundation until her last installment.[61] Michie agreed to stay mum. But he had been right to warn Plath about potential problems ahead. The novel would upend the lives of Dick and Mildred Norton and Aurelia—and Jane Anderson, who would sue the Plath estate for libel in 1982.

Winter was fast approaching, and Court Green had no central heating. In December, Sylvia was troubled to find that most of the house was at 40°; portable heaters got it up to "50-55."[62] She bought two more electric Pifco heaters and spent $750 on rugs—an extravagance for two poets with no regular income. But rugs lent softness to a hard life: "it makes an immense difference in our morale. Living on dirtyish bare boards in very cold weather is grim."

She prized the living room Oriental—a wool Wilton, "rich red background & green & white figured border & center medallion."[63] The children would be kept off. She spent much less on furniture: they bought a chair, table, antique mirror, and dresser for under $2 at a local auction. (Sylvia boasted to Aurelia that they had paid just twelve cents for the table.)

All of this determined nesting may have been a way to ward off other, more nebulous fears. On December 7, the anniversary of Pearl Harbor, Sylvia wrote Aurelia a long letter about nuclear war. She had been "so awfully depressed" by two articles on the subject she had read in *The Nation*:

> Juggernaut, the Warfare State, about the terrifying marriage of big business and the military in America, and the forces of the John Birch society etc., and another about the repulsive shelter craze for fallout, all very factual & documented & true, that I simply couldn't sleep for nights & with all the warlike talk in the papers such as Kennedy saying Kruschev [*sic*] would "have no place to hide," & the armed forces manuals indoctrinating soldiers about the "inevitable" war with our "implacable foe," I began to wonder if there was any point in trying to bring up children in such a mad self-destructive world.

She was glad to be living in England and was disgusted by the commercialism surrounding the sales of fallout shelters in the U.S. "I think the boyscouts [*sic*] & the American Legion & the rest of those ghastly anti-communist organizations should be forced to sit every Sunday before movies of the victims of Hiroshima, & the generals each to live with a victim."[64] This is the language of *The Bell Jar* and her Eisenhower collage. She and Ted worried about the poison in the atmosphere and strontium-90 levels in the milk; she was "very gloomy about the bomb news," though she claimed that she felt safer in the country.[65] The political anxiety added to other stresses. She had begun taking sleeping pills, she said, on account of pins and needles in her arms, a pregnancy symptom. And she worried about the upcoming delivery, which would again take place at home.

Still, Plath and Hughes ended the year with reason for optimism. G. S. Fraser gave Plath's *American Poetry Now* supplement a favorable review in *The Times Literary Supplement*, an endorsement that carried nearly as much weight as Alvarez's.[66] In mid-December, Plath was invited to judge the 1962 Guinness contest at the Cheltenham Literature Festival. *The New Yorker* accepted "The Moon and the Yew Tree" and "Mirror Talk" (later, "Mirror") and renewed her contract. She delved excitedly into *Frieda Lawrence: The Memoirs and Correspondence*, which Knopf had sent to her, and she and Hughes paid off their £600 mortgage at month's end. Hughes wrote to Theodore Roethke turning down a chance to teach with him at the University of Washington, telling him that they planned to stay in Devon for at least three years before moving.[67]

They celebrated a relaxing and festive Christmas, the only one they would ever spend together at Court Green. "It is the first one we 'made ourselves,' from start to finish," Sylvia wrote Aurelia in a happy letter. Frieda's eyes lit up when she entered the living room, with its beautifully trimmed tree and stacks of presents. Ted had made her a wooden cradle for her baby doll, which Sylvia painted white with red and blue flowers and birds.[68] She was determined to continue the Plath family traditions: steaming oatmeal followed by presents, then a mid-afternoon feast of turkey, gravy, stuffing, brussels sprouts, roasted chestnuts, and apple pie. Afterward, they sat by the fire and enjoyed candy, nuts, and fruit from their new neighbors. "I look so forward to our doing this every year," Sylvia wrote home. "Our house is a perfect 'Christmas' house."[69] Next year she planned to have a piano, and play carols, and sing. For now, she was content with her blessings: "The merest dust of snow on everything, china-blue skies, rosy hilltops. New lambs in the fields."[70]

27

Mothers

Devon, January–May 1962

Nicholas Farrar Hughes was born on January 17 at five minutes to midnight in the guest room at Court Green. "I had a lot more work with him than her," Sylvia wrote home, hinting at the trials of delivering a nine-pound-eleven-ounce baby. Frieda, in comparison, had been a "ladylike" seven pounds, four ounces. "He looked very swarthy to me when he arrived, like a wrinkled, cross old boxer."[1] Ted thought he looked like Otto.

Her due date, January 12, had passed uneventfully. She felt exhausted and "cowlike" in "layer after layer" of wool; at 170 pounds, four hours on her feet was like "a day's work in the fields."[2] She rested, baked, and played with Frieda. Then, on the 17th, the contractions began "in earnest" in the late afternoon. Ted called the midwife, Winifred Davies, at eight thirty p.m. when they became regular. The two sat by Sylvia's bed and "gossiped pleasantly" as she tried to follow their conversation between contractions. She felt more in control of her labor this time, with the help of gas. "Instead of the mindless crawling about and beating my head against the wall as with the worst cramps with Frieda, I felt perfectly in possession of myself, able to <u>do</u> something for myself," she wrote in her journal.[3] But her equanimity collapsed when the gas ran out and the pain grew unbearable near midnight. Winifred worried that the waters had not yet broken and sent for Dr. Webb. Later she told Sylvia it had been an emergency.

Winifred finally broke the membrane herself, and Sylvia began to bear down. In her journal Sylvia later described the pain as "a black force blotting out my brain and utterly possessing me. A horrible fear it would split me and burst through me, leaving me in bloody shreds. . . . 'It's too big, too big,' I heard myself say. . . . I felt panic-stricken—I had nothing to do with it, It [*sic*] controlled me. 'I can't help it,' I cried."[4] But within a few seconds the baby emerged "in a tidal wave of water . . . howling lustily."[5]

> "Here he is!" I heard Ted say. It was over. I felt the great weight gone in a moment. I felt thin, like air, as if I would float away, and perfectly awake. I lifted my head and looked up. "Did he tear me to bits?" I felt I must be ripped and bloody from all that power breaking out of me. "Not a scratch," said Nurse D. I couldn't believe it. I lifted my head and saw my first son, Nicholas Farrar Hughes, blue and glistening on the bed a foot from me, in a pool of wet.[6]

Exhausted, Sylvia thought that the baby looked "angry," his head slightly misshapen during delivery. "I felt no surge of love. I wasn't sure I liked him," she wrote in her journal.[7] She had been expecting a girl and was shocked at first by this swarthy, screaming boy. Ted, too, was shocked. He told Leonard Baskin that the baby had a "terrifying expression of ferocity" and had seemed to him "ugly" in the moments after birth.[8]

Nurse Davies washed and swaddled the baby, then handed him gently to his mother. Soon enough, Sylvia was flooded with love. "It felt like Christmas Eve, full of rightness & promise."[9] She was calm and joyful as she watched Frieda hold her brother with Winifred's help. Even the elm tree outside seemed a portent of blessings. "Beautiful clear dawn & full moon tonight in our huge elm," she wrote Aurelia.[10] Ted was reassured in the morning when the baby's head had recovered its shape: "Now he's thriving," he told the Baskins, "a very calm, steady child."[11] Later, Plath would write of her son's birth:

> You stuck & would not come.
> The pain grew black & contained me like the mouth of a flower,
> Black, blood-sweet.
> So we fought our first fight.
>
> It was so quiet.
>
> You came in spite of it, a rocket
> Sailing, in a wall of water, on to the sheet.
> Head, shoulders, feet, dragging three shrieks
> After you like ripped silk. Blue, irrefutable
> As a totem.[12]

Ted helped with Frieda and the washing-up. The bank manager's wife, Marjorie Tyrer, stopped in with oranges and custard; their neighbor, Rose Key, brought a roast beef dinner. Other neighbors brought baby clothes. Sylvia was touched by their solicitousness, as she barely knew most people in North Tawton. Yet a "10 day misery" followed. Winifred Davies had to leave town to care for her ailing father, and Sylvia's milk took a week to come in. In her journal she described the crisis: "the baby starving & crying all night, culminating in two nights of 103° milk fever followed, with me at war with the two substitute midwives & Doctor Webb." Penicillin cured her fever, and her milk finally came in. Winifred returned, and she assisted the doctor with the circumcision—"a trauma for me," Plath wrote in her journal. Nurse and doctor tried to shield the screaming baby with their bodies while Sylvia, weeping, nearly fainted.[13]

Sylvia told Aurelia that Ted had been "a saint" through it all, making her fresh green salads and chicken soup while minding Frieda. She hoped to give him "a 6 week holiday from any babycare" when Aurelia came to visit in the summer.[14] She did not question the assumption that such care was largely her responsibility. Court Green's housekeeper, Nancy Axworthy, was now working extra hours, scrubbing, vacuuming, and ironing, but there was always more for Plath to do. "Even as it is, I have my hands full, with cooking & two little babies—I don't know what I'd do without her."[15] Frieda, now a rambunctious toddler, needed "watching every minute": she peeled wallpaper, threw things down the toilet, tore up papers, drew on walls with coal, uprooted flower bulbs, and gorged herself on hidden candy.[16] Sylvia wondered how her own mother had ever managed without help when she and Warren were small, and congratulated herself for writing her novel ahead of the Saxton deadlines: "the day is a whirlwind of baths, laundry, meals, feedings & bang it is time for bed."[17] (She told Dr. Beuscher she had written the book "in under 2 months.")[18] Still, Frieda's high jinks amused her. "Who did that?" Sylvia would ask, pointing to a patch of ripped wallpaper. Frieda would shake her head "chidingly" and say "bad girl." "Who's the bad girl?" Sylvia would ask again, barely containing her grin: "& she points to herself and says 'ME' and burst into uproarious laughter. She is such a sunshiney thing."[19] She was grateful that Nicholas did not have colic, as Frieda had. He was a calm baby, and Sylvia thought him a "darling." "I imagine he will have a rather dark handsome craggy face, although now he is soft as a peach."[20]

The unremitting labor of child care and household chores became a familiar refrain in Plath's letters that winter, as did lack of sleep. When a book publisher asked her for a brief biography she listed her occupation as "Housewife & mother of two small children," rather than "writer," above a list of her considerable publications.[21] (Most recent was "The Rival" in *The*

Observer on January 21.) Plath was well on her way to becoming one of the foremost poets of her generation, but she would not allow herself to claim that lofty mantle.

They listened to Hughes's *The Wound* on their new radio on February 1; "In Plaster" and "Context" appeared in *The London Magazine*, and "Sleep in the Mojave Desert" in *Harper's*, that month. The proofs for the American edition of *The Colossus* arrived on February 2. Plath made just three small corrections. The book would be published on May 14, 1962, "in time for your birthday," she wrote Aurelia. "I have got awfully homesick for you since the last baby—and for the Cape & deep snow & such American things. Can't wait for your visit."[22] She had just one request: new bras and underwear from Filene's in Boston. Her old ones had fallen apart, and she could not bear the thought of shopping for undergarments in Exeter. "If this is too extravagant, don't bother," she wrote her mother. "I'm slightly dazed & have no notion of common sense at the moment."[23]

An underwear purchase was hardly extravagant against the background of a life lived at full tilt. Against all odds, Sylvia and Warren had switched filial roles: she had left home to marry in secret, while he had spent every weekend with Aurelia for the past eighteen months. He, not she, had involved Aurelia closely in his wedding preparations even as he was finishing up his PhD at Harvard.[24] Sylvia had done nothing wrong by leaving America and marrying a foreigner, yet Aurelia could never shake the feeling that something *was* wrong. She had seen her daughter's limp body crouched in a basement crawl space, and she worried constantly about a recurrence. And so Aurelia sent the bras and panties, along with sweaters, dresses, and gift cards to posh London toy stores. Sylvia sometimes resented the gifts even as she showed them off to neighbors. The largesse represented another form of obligation, while the gifts could embarrass her. "Honestly, you must go slow, mother!" Sylvia wrote to her in early March. "You have been so generous with things for Frieda and Nicholas I am concerned about your budgeting!"[25] A Devon friend, David Compton, remembered Sylvia making fun of her shining Bendix washing machine: "Aurelia organized delivery of the biggest, grandest Bendix you'd ever seen in all the world. Elizabeth and I were taken in—to show it to us, you'd think, proudly—but basically to show how awful Aurelia was, how American and overdone. Poor Aurelia couldn't get it right." Sylvia, he said, "found it necessary to apologize for her mother. . . . 'Oh that's terribly Aurelian.' " He said Sylvia spoke of her mother with the superior air of an educated English person mocking a vulgar, rich American.[26] She would read Aurelia's letters out loud to the Comptons, saying, "Oh you must see what my mother says here. Oh, my God!"[27] Yet to Aurelia, Sylvia waxed lyrical about her Bendix. Her letters from Devon are full of reassurances and homely asides that seem calculated to distract her mother from her life's radical decisions. "How I envy girls whose mothers can just drop in on them," she wrote Aurelia in early February.[28]

Such sentiments were not outright lies, despite the way Sylvia mocked Aurelia to her British friends. She was attached to Aurelia and was still her mother's daughter—appearance, respectability, and good manners mattered. Her thank-you notes to the Wellesley neighbors she would mock in *The Bell Jar* were prompt and decorous. "Ted joins me in sending best wishes and in admiring the lovely blanket and potholders," she wrote to a family friend in early February after a full paragraph extolling the gifts' virtues.[29] Ted wrote many gracious, good-humored letters to Aurelia that bear no trace of the hatred he later told Olwyn he bore her. The Cruickshanks and the Aldriches and the Freemans all received pleasant updates after Nicholas's birth. Sylvia delighted most of all in news of the Nortons and asked Aurelia to keep her informed. "I was fascinated to hear about Dick Norton's starting a practise— how perfectly Dickensian! I would love to know details about David. Why does he find his parents difficult??? How is it Perry didn't save any money? O I love hearing all these bits of personal detail about the people I used to know. New people are never as interesting as the ones one grew up with."[30]

———

FOR SYLVIA, the gray, rain-clogged winter was "a grubby time with little children, indoor washing, and no snow to play in."[31] But by mid-February, snowdrops began to appear along with "a scattering of primroses & countless daffodil sprouts."[32] She fantasized about lying in the apple orchard all day with her children once the trees were in bloom. For the first time since her Wellesley years, she was gardening again; she filled her letters with excited talk of buds and sprouts. "I find being outdoors gardening an immense relaxation," she wrote Aurelia in late February.[33] "I think I will go just wild when our trees start blooming—there are fat buds on the lilac. I think the most exciting thing to me is <u>owning flowers and trees</u>!"[34] Ted had planted plum, pear, peach, and nut trees, while Sylvia and Frieda prepared the flower beds. They had been taking the vitamin C pills Aurelia had sent all winter, and, "miraculously," none of them had caught a cold.[35]

But it was a false spring. Winter dragged on stubbornly through March, and Sylvia became disconsolate. Letters home alighted on a familiar theme. "I miss the American snow, which at least makes a new clean exciting season out of winter, instead of this 6 months cooping-up of damp & rain & blackness we get here. Like the 6 months Persephone had to spend with Pluto."[36] Court Green was still very cold; the temperature was at freezing in the "drafty halls," and the east wind blew the heavy back door wide open. The skies remained "grey tombstone."[37] That March, Sylvia told Marion Freeman, was reputed to be the coldest in seventy years. The whole family slept in Nicholas's room, the warmest in the house. In the evenings, they huddled around the fire. Sylvia suffered chilblains, a skin condition caused by prolonged exposure to cold. To Clarissa Roche, she wrote, "the word Chilblains undid me. . . . I got very grim."[38] She had always thought it "a Dickensian disease" and felt "morbid" about living in Victorian conditions when central heating was ubiquitous in America.[39] She was determined to make the house warmer, and drew up plans to lay a stone foundation. "Wuthering Heights" appeared in the *New Statesman* in mid-March; the poem reflected her mood that spring.

She struggled to be optimistic: "Life begins at 30!" she told Aurelia in late March.[40] When the weather improved, she vowed to spend six months outdoors and learn to ride. That March she wrote Dr. Beuscher an upbeat, cheerful letter asking if she could dedicate *The Bell Jar* to her—it was "seriocomic . . . fictionalized, but not so much that doing it & coming back to life is due so much to you that you are the only person I could dedicate it to."[41] (Beuscher replied that September, "I would love to have the dedication to RB," though Plath eventually dedicated the novel to Elizabeth and David Compton.)[42] Sylvia wrote of her beautiful "Manor," the birth of Nicholas, her pride in her land and gardens. The letter contains no hint of the unhappiness she had confessed to other friends. Dr. Beuscher had indeed become a mother figure—and as she did for her real mother, Sylvia was trying to put up a good front.

She had few visitors from outside North Tawton, and so she made a concerted effort to visit her neighbors: Mrs. Hamilton across the street at Crispins; Mrs. Macnamara, with her nineteen-room rectory, Cadbury House; Rose Key, in the Court Green cottages, whose husband, Percy, was suffering from lung cancer; the "humpbacked" Elsie Taylor, and Mr. and Mrs. Watkins, also in the cottages; Dr. Webb and his wife, Joan; Major and Mrs. Billyeald; the old widower Mr. Ellis, with his "fusty" piano; George Tyrer, the local bank manager, and his wife, Marjorie.[43] These older, provincial villagers comprised Sylvia's new social set. Although she made fun of their stodgy décor ("Yes, it <u>was</u> all brown and cream"), she spared them the unkindness she routinely launched at writers.[44] Sylvia's closest Devon friend, Elizabeth Compton Sigmund, remembered that she was "so interested in people. She used to absolutely buttonhole them and say, 'How does your husband do the bell ringing?' And, 'Was he a fireman?' She wanted to know about people's lives."[45] Elizabeth's husband at the time, the writer David Compton, felt that both Sylvia and Ted shared this passion for the quotidian. "They were always so, so aware of the significances of things. Everything in life was large and important . . . they lived an exhausting intellectual and emotional life because they cared."[46]

Sylvia's midwife, Winifred Davies, became fond of her after Nicholas's birth and helped her acclimate to village life. Winifred recalled, "North Tawton is rather a conservative place and she used to dress oddly—which put people off to begin with. . . . Sylvia's appearance—black stockings, long braid down her back—suggested the college girl far more than the mother of two."[47] Winifred's son Kenneth remembered, too, that "Sylvia was a bit like a fish out of water in the quiet market town of North Tawton. She wanted to fit in and to meet people but there were few of her level of intellect. My mother by virtue of her job knew everybody and was able to make introductions and suggestions."[48] Though Sylvia would complain to Dr. Beuscher later that fall that Winifred was unimaginative and unintellectual, David remembered her as a steady hand during Sylvia and Ted's 1962 marital crisis. "She was of the village, but she was a larger person, and Sylvia could talk to Winifred. So could we. She was perfectly comfortable with our concerns, was aware that there were other things than North Tawton. . . . In the best sense, she was motherly. Winifred was special. Sylvia was very lucky to have her."[49]

Sylvia tried to impress the matrons of North Tawton over tea and sandwiches. These afternoon tête-à-têtes revolved around ailments, distant relatives, home renovations, and upcoming holidays. "Talked of the wallpaper," she wrote in her journal about an afternoon at the Tyrers', without a trace of irony.[50] She was sounding for story material, yet these encounters filled a real need for female companionship. Sylvia liked being fussed over by these older women. "My very pleasant sense of warmth, hot tea, and being neatly dressed for a change," she wrote in her journal after tea with Marjorie Tyrer. "Felt refreshed, enlivened, renewed. Very at home."[51] Her efforts speak to her loneliness, and her desire for respectability. Clarissa Roche remembered, "Doctors, nurses, midwives, these words peppered her conversation and letters. . . . they took the place of nonexistent family and friends."[52] When Winifred's son told his mother that Ted was a famous writer, Sylvia wrote in her journal, "We were 'placed.' I felt very pleased."[53]

Yet even as Sylvia drank from their steaming pots of tea and ate their herring on toast, she felt a "curious desperate sense of being locked in among these people, a cream, longing toward London, the big world. Why are we here?"[54] She later wrote of "the flat malice of people I keep dreaming into friends."[55] She sometimes called them "Jewy."[56] In her short story "Mothers," she described the village women: "Burdened by their cumbersome woolens and drab hats, they seemed, without exception, gnarled and old."[57]

Hughes later wrote, in an early draft of his poem "Error," "Old women, / Brueghelish, earth-worn, / Stump-warts, you called them, — / Sniffed at your strangeness . . ."[58] To Aurelia, Sylvia wrote of their small kindnesses, but she described them as "provincial" to Ruth Fainlight. "I am very happy with Court Green, my study, the babies, but mad for someone to talk to."[59] She begged Clarissa and Paul Roche to visit before they headed back to America.

"Mothers," probably written in the autumn of 1961, was the best short story Plath wrote in England. Esther is an American wife and mother married to a poet who lives in a house just like Court Green. She has become friendly with a London transplant, Mrs. Nolan, the pubkeeper's wife. At first it seems like Esther and Mrs. Nolan, with their sophisticated urban values, will form a natural alliance. "What do you *do* here?" Mrs. Nolan asks Esther conspiratorially. Esther says she cares for her baby and types her husband's work. Plath does not reveal whether Esther has any artistic ambition herself, but she suggests that such ambition would be met with skepticism in the village.

Esther and Mrs. Nolan, both newcomers, hope to join the town's Mothers' Union, but at a church tea the rector humiliates Mrs. Nolan by announcing that she is a divorcée. Tension builds as Esther's desire to assimilate into this provincial community threatens to annul the burgeoning friendship. "If Mrs Nolan, an Englishwoman by her looks and accent, and a pubkeeper's wife as well, felt herself a stranger in Devon after six years, what hope had Esther, an American, of infiltrating that rooted society ever at all?"[60] At the story's end Esther allies herself with a local woman (probably based on Rose Key) who agrees that divorcées should be barred from the Mothers' Union. The ending conforms to *Ladies' Home Journal* ethics, yet read in light of *The Bell Jar*, Esther seems to betray her own values when she shuns an outsider to fit in. Plath's use of the name Esther suggests that "Mothers" may have been part of a new novel, a sequel to *The Bell Jar* based on her life in Devon with Hughes.

Sylvia appreciated her neighbors' attention, but she balked when they called on her unexpectedly. One morning in February, she was "stunned" when Ted led Mrs. Hamilton up to her study, her "symbolic sanctum." Fuming silently, Sylvia invited her in. After she left, Sylvia and Ted had a "great Fratch." Why, Sylvia wondered, could Ted not have turned Mrs. Hamilton away with a polite "She's working"? She would never have interrupted him while *he* was working. "My anger at Ted being a man, not at Mrs. H. really," Sylvia wrote in her journal.[61] Three days later there was a more upsetting surprise visit from sixteen-year-old Nicola Tyrer, the daughter of the Tyrers. Sylvia again recorded her fury in her journal: " 'I'm not too early?' Oh no, said

Ted. He made her a cup of tea and she stood in the kitchen while I finished my coffee and Frieda her bacon. . . . I kept wanting to get to work. Furious that Ted had invited anyone in. The morning gone. . . . She is shrewd, pushing, absolutely shameless. . . . I <u>must</u> have my mornings in peace."[62]

Sylvia and Ted had socialized with the Tyrers that winter, but Sylvia had come to resent Nicola's interest in her husband. Ted initially assumed the role of Nicola's mentor ("Ted's Biblical need to preach," Sylvia wrote dryly), inviting her to come round to "sample our books."[63] He lent her *Orlando*—pretentiously, Sylvia thought—while she recommended *The Catcher in the Rye*. But the relationship soon morphed into something more charged. Ted wrote Nicola letters about poetry when she returned to her boarding school in Oxford; on vacations, she showed up at Court Green dressed elegantly, her hair perfectly coiffed. Sylvia tried to match her: "I managed a girdle & stockings & heels and felt a new person," she confided to her journal that February.[64] During one visit, when Nicola complained that she wanted to trim her shape, Ted said, "What's wrong with your shape?"[65] Another time, Nicola said that *The Seven Samurai* bored her, and Ted agreed. But Plath knew that *The Seven Samurai* was her husband's favorite film. Sylvia directed her anger at Nicola rather than Ted. "She will of course take anything from him & who doesn't love to have bright young youth listen to pontificatings." She vowed vigilance. "I shall be omnipotent—chauffeur, entertainer, hostess, if the occasion arises. A charming ignorance as to any difference between us. Her models: Bridgette Bardot & Lolita. Telling."[66]

Nicola had unwittingly arrived at the Hugheses' doorstep during the most difficult period of their marriage. Winifred remembered that before Nicholas's birth, Sylvia and Ted had established an orderly and productive writing routine. "Sylvia would work early in the morning while Ted tended Frieda in the garden. Then they would exchange roles. But after Nick's birth that's when things began to break up. Sylvia used to interrupt his train of thought with cooking or the children." Ted "resented the interruption." Sylvia, meanwhile, felt that "Ted should enjoy the little baby as much as she did." "My impression is that they both demanded too much of each other," Winifred said. Sylvia, especially, demanded too much of herself:

> Sylvia wanted lots of children, and yet she didn't want to give up her writing for the children. . . . She wanted to *do* everything herself, you see. . . . Sylvia wanted to *grasp* everything, not just know about it. . . . She wanted to ride. And she wanted a cow so she could learn to milk. She wanted bees so she could keep bees. And she wanted her roses-round-the-door Devon cottage. . . . And she wanted her man who would be *her* man and nobody else's.[67]

Sylvia hinted at her frustration to Aurelia: "I long to have a day or two on jaunts with just Ted—we can hardly see each other over the mountains of diapers & demands of babies."[68] The stresses of trying to write and keep house with a new baby were hard to bear alongside visits from a besotted high schooler. Sylvia felt that she, "a scatty mother of almost 30," could not compete with the "young girl's complete flowerlike involvement in self, beautifying, opening to advantage." She wrote in her journal of her desire "to unclutch the sticky loving fingers of babies & treat myself to myself alone for a bit. . . . To purge myself of sour milk, urinous nappies, bits of lint and the loving slovenliness of motherhood."[69] Whenever she heard Nicola's voice at the door, she "flew down" the stairs. By April, Sylvia began turning Nicola away. One day, when she showed up and asked to read in their garden, Sylvia, "aghast," made up an excuse: "so, No." Another time when Nicola stopped by and asked to play with Frieda, Sylvia told her that she had been bitten by a crow. "To give the illusion of sweet loving charm while refusing. A marvelous art I must develop."[70]

On April 19, Ted joined the Tyrers for tea, and Nicola accompanied him back to Court Green. Sylvia opened the door to find them "under the bare laburnum like kids back from the date, she posed & coy."[71] Nicola remembered Sylvia standing at the door with Nicholas in her arms, saying, "Oh Nicola, are you seeing Ted home?" in a "steely" voice.[72] Nicola asked if she could come inside and listen to Sylvia's German records, whereupon Sylvia "rushed" inside, got the records, and, as she wrote in her journal, "thrust them into her hands. 'This way you can study them to your heart's content all the rest of your vacation.' . . . For some time I seriously considered smashing our old & ridiculous box victrola with an axe. Then this need passed, & I grew a little wiser."[73] Nicola thought Sylvia's jealousy absurd—she did not think that Ted had feelings for her—yet she was "euphoric" that Sylvia saw her as a threat, because Ted Hughes, she told Anne Stevenson, was her "adolescent fantasy."[74] Even if the teenager's solicitous attention did not tempt Hughes, it unquestionably strained the marriage.

There were other strains. David Compton remembered Ted bringing a young woman back from London that spring and putting her up in the guest room at Court Green. Ted explained that they had met at a poetry reading and that she was "simply a fan" who wanted to learn more about his poetry; he had obliged by offering to show her Devon. David and Elizabeth had dinner with Ted, Sylvia, and the young woman—whom David thought in her late teens—at Court Green. "She was so evidently besotted with him . . . very worshipful. It showed. And Elizabeth and I did say afterwards, 'You know, I was surprised that Sylvia put up with that!' . . . But Sylvia did not appear to be noticing."[75] This young woman was not, David insisted, Nicola Tyrer but someone who had accompanied Hughes back on the train and who had no connection to North Tawton. She may have been Siv Arb, the Swedish journalist who arrived after Easter to take photographs, though David's memory of this woman's arrival dovetails with specific details in Plath's calendar: there she noted that Ted went to London alone on April 16 and that the Comptons came over for "tea" the following day.[76] Olwyn later told Anne Stevenson she remembered lines from Sylvia's lost journals from that spring: "We answer the door together. They step over me as though I were a mat, and walk straight into [Ted's] heart."[77] Later, in a frank letter to Olwyn, Ted admitted, "Something began to happen to me in April or so, & since then this marriage, house, Sylvia etc have seemed just like the dead-end of everything."[78]

PLATH'S STUDY WAS her sanctuary. Her mornings there were "as peaceful as churchgoing—the red plush rug and all, and the feeling that nothing else but writing and thinking is done there, no sleeping, eating or mundane stuff."[79] *Poetry* published five of her poems in its March issue; "Tulips" appeared in the April 7 *New Yorker*; and "The Colossus" in the April *Encounter*.[80] The *New Statesman* sent her a batch of books to review. And she had begun a new novel, she told Aurelia—"something amusing . . . but may just be happy piddling . . . I find long things much easier on my nature than poems—not so intensely demanding or depressing if not brought off."[81] Plath had told her Knopf editor Judith Jones that she was working on a novel in February 1962, and the word "novel" also appears in Plath's 1962 calendar during the week of March 4. (In her surviving 1962 journal, she wrote that Dido Merwin appeared in her novel under the name Camilla.) Aurelia later said this novel was about Sylvia's life in England with Ted—a continuation of the unfinished "Falcon Yard," and a sequel to *The Bell Jar*—but that Sylvia burned the manuscript in summer 1962 after she learned of Ted's affair with Assia Wevill.

Political anxieties shaped Plath's work that winter. In her essay "Context"—published in *The London Magazine* in February 1962—she described her preoccupations as "the incalculable genetic effects of fallout" and "the terrifying, mad, omnipotent marriage of big business and the military in America." She had been deeply disturbed by Russia's test explosion of a huge nuclear bomb on October 30, 1961—the biggest explosion to date, which dwarfed all World War II explosions combined. In December 1961 and January 1962, Plath would have read graphic accounts of violence in Algeria in *The Observer*; a January 13 article in *The Times* described "stealthy throat-cutting" and "lynching."[82] In "Context," she wrote of "the tortured Algerians," "Hiroshima," and "mass extinction" as contexts for her poems, but claimed that these events influenced her work only in "a sidelong fashion." Her images—"the moon over a yew tree," "a child forming itself finger by finger in the dark"—might be "deflections," but never "an escape." Poetry was not "political propaganda," she wrote. "I do not think a 'headline poetry' would interest more people any more profoundly than the headlines."[83]

Cold War anxieties found expression in a long poetic sequence about childbirth, which she wrote from December 1961 to late January or early February 1962. "All night I have dreamed of destruction, annihilations—/ An assembly-line of cut throats," she wrote in "Waking in Winter," the first poem.[84] The unpublished sequence, containing sections with variant titles— "Woman as Landscape"/"The Ninth Month"/"Waking in Winter"; "Fever in Winter"/"Fever"/"Fever 103°" (not to be confused with the later *Ariel* poem of the same name)—features images of annihilation and atrocity that look forward to "Elm" and other *Ariel* poems.[85] The first line of "Fever," for example, is, "The elm is a clot of burnt nerves, the sky is tin."[86]

The "Fever" sequence and "Context" laid the groundwork for *Three Women*—Plath's proto-feminist verse play written in March 1962—produced by Douglas Cleverdon and broadcast on the BBC's Third Programme on August 19.[87] *Three Women* was inspired by a 1958 Ingmar Bergman film, *So Close to Life*, which is set in a maternity ward and follows the lives of three women: one who has a miscarriage early in her pregnancy; another whose full-term baby dies shortly after delivery; and an unmarried mother who considers giving up her baby.[88] Sylvia probably saw Bergman's film in February or March 1961 after her own miscarriage and hospital stay in London. But she had set off in a different direction that spring, choosing to write *The Bell Jar*. Now Plath was drawn back to maternity and childbirth, a subject she could mine for dramatic potential as Hughes could not. Plath's three women differed from Bergman's: the first is a married mother who has a healthy baby; the second a secretary who has a miscarriage; the third an Oxbridge student who gives up her baby after considering an abortion.

Anne Stevenson has called *Three Women* "the first great poem about childbirth in the language."[89] There are no speaking roles for men, who function primarily as oppressors. The play was a turning point for Plath, who harnessed and honed the freer, more intimate voice of "The Moon and the Yew Tree" to explode female taboos surrounding miscarriage, postpartum depression, and abortion.[90] She was in uncharted territory, inventing a new tradition. Her previous poems, with the exceptions of "The Colossus" and "Parliament Hill Fields," could not have been called feminist. But that February Plath was writing up her first Saxton progress report for *The Bell Jar*, with its condescending boyfriends, unsympathetic male doctors, vicious workplaces, mental hospitals, electric shocks, and sexual assaults.[91] Prose was a better vehicle for her scathing, cynical indictment of Eisenhower's America than poetry, whose formalist grace notes had, until now, largely checked Plath's anger and resentments.

Plath's neat, symmetrical stanzas muted the subversive material within. The first woman in the play who gives birth to the healthy son is initially smug, transformed by her painful labor and the massive anxiety that attends motherhood. This First Voice most closely resembles Plath's:

> How long can I be a wall, keeping the wind off?
> How long can I be
> Gentling the sun with the shade of my hand,
> Intercepting the blue volts of a cold moon?

Plath had written about maternal anxiety before, but here the theme finds its full expression. "It is a terrible thing / To be so open," the new mother says as she watches the dawn light up "the great elm outside the house." "I am reassured. I am reassured," she says, though the phrase's repetition suggests the opposite.

The Second Voice belongs to the secretary who suffers a miscarriage. Plath had already written about miscarriage in "Parliament Hill Fields," full of private, lyrical anguish. Here, self-blame ("I have tried and tried") gives way to blame against patriarchal power. As the secretary watches the men who run her office, she thinks of the "flatness from which ideas, destructions, / Bulldozers, guillotines, white chambers of shrieks proceed":

> Governments, parliaments, societies,
> The faceless faces of important men.
>
> It is these men I mind:
> They are so jealous of anything that is not flat! They are jealous gods
> That would have the whole world flat because they are.

Plath aligns death and destruction with the male, life-giving with the female—a dichotomy that would resurface later that year in the *Ariel* poems.

In writing the Third Voice, of the Oxbridge student who gives up her baby girl for adoption, Plath again draws on her own experience—she had pregnancy scares as a young wife, and earlier. "I wasn't ready. / I had no reverence," she writes. The student charges her male doctors with a gross double standard: "They are to blame for what I am, and they know it. / They hug their flatness like a kind of health. / And what if they found themselves surprised, as I did? / They would go mad with it." Most shocking, in this section, is the student's regret: "I am not ready for anything to happen. / I should have murdered this, that murders me." This speaker decides, finally, to give up her baby, yet she knows that she will carry the loss for the rest of her life. "She is a small island, asleep and peaceful, / And I am a white ship hooting: Goodbye, goodbye."

To approach abortion with some sympathy at a time when the practice was still illegal in Britain was radical, as was the play's focus on the darker aspects of maternity.[92] Plath had first explored this theme in her journal when she wrote about the distressing birth she had seen in the Boston Lying-In Hospital with Dick Norton in February 1952.[93] She probed it again in "Sweetie Pie and the Gutter Men," and later in *The Bell Jar*, where Esther claims that men had invented drugs to make women forget the terrors of childbirth. Why are women forbidden to speak of such things, Plath asks in *Three Women*, while mass murder and nuclear annihilation make headlines? After her miscarriage, the secretary says, "This woman who meets me in the windows—she is neat. // . . . How shyly she superimposes her neat self / On the inferno of African oranges, the heel-hung pigs." The "heel-hung pigs" stand as a more authentic symbol of the "inferno" she has been through than her "neat" reflection.[94] *Three Women* opened up new poetic pathways for Plath, setting her on a course toward "Daddy" and "Lady Lazarus," where superhuman female heroines wrest control of their destinies from the patriarchy. The play stands as a bracing antidote to a subject that is still routinely sanitized and sentimentalized.

———

BY LATE MARCH, Sylvia told Aurelia, the daffodils were "coming out in their heavenly startling way, like stars." Frieda followed her mother around the garden with a toy lawnmower, calling "Mummy's Oodle-Ooo." "It is so soothing & kindly to work in the earth, pruning, digging, cutting grass," Sylvia wrote home.[95] They planned to sell the daffodils at the local greengrocer, along with other crops.

Nicholas was an easier baby than Frieda. He smiled all the time and cried only when he was hungry. Sylvia, too, was now a more confident mother. "I really enjoy him—none of the harassment & worry of Frieda's colic and my inexperience."[96] They began teaching Frieda to read, and they joked that she already knew "the tiny bird on the New Yorker masthead is an 'Ow.' "[97] They delighted in her unfolding personality, "very squirmy & active."[98] Sylvia told her mother, "I have the queerest feeling of having been reborn with Frieda— it's as if my real rich happy life only started just about then."[99] She was still sending her poems out regularly. *Harper's* accepted two poems; *Poetry* published five poems in March. She sent George MacBeth at the BBC Talks Department several new poems, remarking that two of his poems, "Mother Superior" and "Ash," "make my hair stand on end."[100]

Money was becoming less of a worry. Plath's Saxton grant had enabled them to furnish the house, replace the old wood floors, and repay their loans to the Hugheses and Aurelia. Ted earned $730 for two broadcasts of his radio play *The Wound*, which aired for the second time that winter, on February 17—almost a third of their expected yearly earnings. His poems were now being translated into Swedish and included in more anthologies. But he continued turning down lucrative television appearances. Sylvia toed the family line: "Ted has just made another stand for integrity & privacy by refusing to do a TV program on the Poet in the Process of Composing a Poem from Start to Finish."[101] She probably would have jumped at such an opportunity herself.

Nicholas and Frieda were christened on March 25—he in a gown of Limerick lace Sylvia borrowed from Marjorie Tyrer, she in a delicate white and blue dress with a matching blue French coat. Sylvia held no admiration for the rector, William Lane, but she wanted her children to be part of their new community. She had stopped going to church after Lane gave "a ghastly H-bomb sermon" about how the parishioners would ascend to heaven in the event of a nuclear explosion, unlike the "pacifists & humanists & 'educated pagans'" who would fear "being incinerated etc. etc." Sylvia wrote Aurelia, "I felt it was a sin to support such insanity even by my presence." Marcia had sent her a copy of a Unitarian sermon on fallout shelters that made her weep. "I'd really be a church-goer if I was back in Wellesley or America—the Unitarian church is my church. How I miss it!!! There is just no <u>choice</u> here."[102]

In late March, Marvin Kane, the American playwright who had worked with Plath on her BBC *Living Poet* program the previous year, invited her to contribute to a BBC Home Service program about Americans in England called *What Made You Stay?* Plath agreed so long as Kane would interview her at Court Green; she could not leave the baby to go up to London, though she told him, "I miss London a lot more than Ted does!" To Kane she described herself with just the right amount of irony as a "loyal American housewife," raising a garden of "Country Gentlemen corn, Kentucky wonder beans" on her two and a half acres.[103] Intrigued, he arranged a visit with his wife in early April.

Plath was upbeat during the interview. She laughed frequently as she described how she "had always idolized England . . . especially as an English major." She had been "immensely excited by the historic sense of London in the first place, and then the look of it"—the black, hearse-like taxi cabs and the double-decker buses, the "Old World formality about everybody from the bobbies to the postman." Many things about England were superior to their American counterparts, she said. English butcher shops, with the "pigs at close quarters," were much more interesting than American supermarkets with their meat wrapped in cellophane and background Muzak. (Though she *had* nearly fainted the first time she saw the pigs strung up in rows.) She and Ted preferred England's "Victorian" child-rearing sensibilities: "In America, the children have almost completely free reign [*sic*]," while in England, "children have to fit into the adults' life." Best of all was the English "ability to be eccentric." She described her first visit to an English home (possibly Mallory Wober's or John Lythgoe's), where she watched her friend's mother embroider a tapestry of a rattlesnake. Plath laughed as she recalled how, at bedtime, the woman offered her the choice between a hot-water bottle and a cat.

And then there was the weather, which "infected" her. She meant to say "affected," caught the Freudian slip, and then laughed: "It really does infect me!" She continued, "Weather affects me *intensely*. I find that I just don't observe it, I can't make the best of it the way many people can." She had heard "with joy" that no place in England was more than seventy miles from the sea, but she described her disappointing journey to Whitby, in Yorkshire, in the "pouring rain," past rows of "very depressing" redbrick houses: "It rained perpetually, and there was a kind of litter underfoot of little gum wrappers and so on and I was so intensely depressed [laughs] by this vision of the sea that I retreated inland rapidly." But there was one aspect of English life she valued unequivocally. "England seemed a great deal more hospitable to a couple of artists who wanted to be artists and at the same time lead a very normal and rather placid family life." She could live in "the deep country" and still "get to London in a day." In America, "The pressure for an artist, especially one that's not commercial, to get a job, to get a regular job that then turns out to exhaust his energies, to take all his time and so on, is so great that it's almost impossible to resist it."[104] There was no BBC in America.

Charming remarks aside, Sylvia continued to write home about the cold and the rain, and the endless housework and baby care. These burdens, the weather, and her predisposition to postpartum depression suggest that Plath was suffering both physically and psychologically during that "cold mean spring," as she called it.[105] Her housekeeper, Nancy, left in mid-April for two weeks and would not return until early May. Frieda was acting up; Sylvia told Gerald and Joan Hughes that her daughter had a "rapid, hysterical temperament."[106] The "graveyard" weather intensified her bone-weariness.[107] "I have said to myself: I will write tomorrow, then it is sure to be a sunny day & how cheerful I will be. Believe it or not, we havent [*sic*] seen the sun for <u>three weeks</u>."[108] She had taken the children out for only one day in nearly a month.

April 1 was Frieda's second birthday; April was also Otto's birthday month. On April 2, Plath finished "Little Fugue." The yew tree became, again, a resonant symbol, this time for her father:

> Such a dark funnel, my father!
> I see your voice
> Black and leafy, as in my childhood,
>
> A yew hedge of orders,
> Gothic and barbarous, pure German.

It was another exercise in elegy writing, one that would bring her closer to the Nazi imagery of "Daddy." The charges were muted, but the familial reflections were darkening.

Ten days later, she turned again to the great shadows of the trees outside her window. During a restless early dawn on April 12, she began one of her best poems, "Elm," which she finished on April 19.[109] (The poem went through at least fifteen drafts.)

> I know the bottom, she says. I know it with my great tap root:
> It is what you fear.
> I do not fear it: I have been there.

Familiar images appear: the sea, galloping horses, hooves, echoes, poisons, hooks, clouds, shrieks, the moon, "malignity." The voice of the elm mocks and taunts: "Love is a shadow. / How you lie and cry after it." Plath alludes to shock treatment ("My red filaments burn and stand, a hand of wires") and depression ("I am terrified by this dark thing / That sleeps in me"). The poem ends with a startling image of a "murderous" face in the branches of the elm that "petrifies the will" and kills.[110] When Plath submitted "Elm" for the second time to *The New Yorker*, she told Howard Moss, "The whole poem is the elm talking & might be in quotes. The elm is talking to the woman who contemplates her—they are intimately related in mood, and the various moods, I think, of anguish, are explored in the poem. . . . I realize it is a rather wild & desperate piece. But, I hope: clear, clear."[111]

"Elm" was influenced by Ruth Fainlight's "Sapphic Moon," a poem about miscarriage that moved Plath when she read it in the February 18, 1962, issue of *Encounter*. In an April 16 letter to Fainlight—written while she was working on "Elm"—Plath expressed her deep admiration for "Sapphic Moon": "It is a real White Goddess poem, and a voice on its weird fearsome own."[112] Plath no doubt recognized the poem's "weirdness" as akin to her own. In Fainlight's poem, the moon—an agent of infertility and miscarriage—

appears through a window and "enters the womb like an instrument" to sow the "seeds of death." Plath practically lifts Fainlight's lines for the voice of the miscarrying secretary in *Three Women:* "There is the moon in the high window," she writes, midway through the poem. "I feel it enter me, cold, alien, like an instrument. / . . . I, too, create corpses." The word "malignity" in "Elm" echoes Fainlight's phrase "cold malignancy," while the third draft of "Elm" contains the excised line "a lunar Xray of barrenness," not unlike Fainlight's moon, which "Passes like X-ray through lovers' caresses."[113]

Plath dedicated "Elm" to Fainlight, perhaps to acknowledge her borrowings.[114] But the dedication also suggests the poem's original connection to miscarriage, which Ruth had experienced three times before the birth of her son in 1962, and Sylvia once. There is a hint of elegy, in "Elm," for Plath's lost baby: a line from the second draft of the poem reads, "Grieving & flat, as a mother with no children."[115] But Plath needed to differentiate her White Goddess poem from Fainlight's; the references to grief, miscarriage, and infertility did not make the final cut. Instead, Plath gave oblique voice to her own private hells—her traumatic memories of shock treatment and debilitating depression. "Elm" was the last poem Plath wrote before Assia Wevill's arrival at Court Green.

On the afternoon of April 17, the Hugheses' neighbor Percy Key had a stroke. Percy's wife, Rose, rushed to Court Green to summon Ted. Sylvia thought that she might wait at home, "and then something in me said, now, you must see this, you have never seen a stroke or a dead person." She followed Ted, where they found Percy in front of the television, shaking and twitching. "Rose clutched Ted," Sylvia wrote in her journal, until the doctor came. "He said Thank you, and we melted back to the house. I have been waiting for this, I said. And Ted said he had, too." They "hugged each other," and Sylvia was "seized by a dry retching" over what had just happened.[116] All of this occurred as Plath was revising "Elm"; the imagery of petrification, perhaps inspired by Percy's stroke, was added late, to the penultimate draft, on April 19.

That same day, Sylvia had tea with Elizabeth Compton, who had offered her and Ted the use of her Devon farmhouse after she heard the BBC *Poets in Partnership* interview. Ted had remembered her offer, and invited her and her husband, David, to tea at Court Green. Elizabeth recalled, "We went and sat at the playroom. . . . Ted talked to David about money, like authors do. Sylvia was chatting to me and she said, 'What do you do?' And I said, 'I go canvassing for a liberal democrat.' She said, 'A what?' I said, 'It's a political party.' She said, 'Ted, I've found a committed woman!' And I felt foolish, because I didn't think of being committed, it was just something I did occasionally. But no, she was very lively, she kept dashing out because Nick was in his pram outside . . . it was a very sunny day. . . . She took me round and showed me some of the rooms. 'I'd like to have five children. I'll have three boys up in the attic, and the girls will be down below.'" Sylvia did not speak of her own poetry to Elizabeth, who remembered, "No, she talked about Ted's writing, and she said she'd been copying, typing them out, sending them off. But when I said to him, 'I didn't know Sylvia wrote poetry,' he said, 'She doesn't, she *is* a poet.'"[117] David, too, remembered Sylvia in those early days of their friendship as "an impressive, dependable, loving mother" with a well-thumbed copy of Dr. Spock. "She insisted" on this demarcation, he said, and presented Ted as "the poet."[118]

That day, Sylvia and Elizabeth "discussed the military and industrial links between Britain and the US."[119] North Devon was a very conservative area, and the women found they shared liberal political views. "I could see that she could be savage because of the way she talked about big business and armaments in the States: her fury, her rage that men could exist in this corrupt way."[120] Elizabeth later introduced Sylvia to Mark Bonham Carter, the local Liberal candidate for Parliament, with whom she became friendly. Elizabeth would go on to receive an honorary doctorate from Plymouth University for her activism against chemical and biological weapons—she was profiled in *The Independent* in 1995 as "one of Britain's most remarkable campaigners"— and later expressed sadness that Sylvia hadn't been able to join her.[121] "She would have been fascinated. She would have joined in. She would have taken over."[122]

Elizabeth, who became Sylvia's closest friend in Devon, lived with her husband and three children, with little money and no electricity. She lit her house with oil lamps and candles. Sylvia romanticized these hardships and "became enamoured" of Elizabeth's "earth-mother" image.[123] She, too, was a mother married to a writer, with a complicated relationship with her own mother. Elizabeth remembered that Sylvia confided her apprehensions about Aurelia's impending June visit, after Warren's wedding, but did not discuss any tension in her own marriage.[124] On the contrary, Sylvia and Ted seemed "incredibly close." One spring afternoon the two couples took a walk near the Comptons' home and paused on a bridge over a trout stream. Sylvia glanced down at the water and said to Ted, "See the color." They exchanged looks, then both eyed the water below. "There was no need for words," Elizabeth said. "They both knew; they both saw; they both felt it." She sensed "a tremendous feeling of peace between them."[125]

David likewise had no idea that there was any real strain on the marriage that spring. Although he knew Ted was a famous poet, it was clear that Ted

abhorred pretension. "He was a good pub guy. He handled the English villager *extremely* well. He was, after all, not at all upper class. He was closer
to us socially than she [Sylvia] would ever be." Sylvia was, he said, "The
most American person I'd ever met." He remembered her gushiness, but "it
seemed genuine." She was "all light." In hindsight, David felt that Sylvia's
"bright American sensible no-nonsense" manner was at odds with Ted's disposition. Ted "needed her discipline. He needed her direction. He needed all
sorts of things that he resented." And David remembered, too, Sylvia's "delicate nastiness" toward Ted. The inside of Court Green—her domain—was
"spotless," but the garden—Ted's department—"was a shambles. She would
make little jokes that weren't altogether kind. . . . She would say, 'Oh you
must go and see what Ted's been doing in the vegetable garden. It's absolutely marvelous.'" Upon inspection, they saw that Ted had done "about two
square inches in one corner."[126]

But David recalled a mostly easygoing friendship before Sylvia and Ted's
marriage broke up: "We were two young couples with children, and we
were in many ways just bourgeois, making a life, a couple of fathers working
at home. Most of our shared life was domestic—visits to the beach, taking the children up on Dartmoor. We both as fathers were very involved in
our children's upbringing, as was becoming a lot more fashionable in our
group—certainly men were involved in that—and just meeting in the evenings. . . . We'd come over in the kitchen with a bottle of wine and play
poker for matchsticks. And nobody talked about their art. Occasionally there
would be a reference between them. . . . One I do remember was a dispute
between them as to which poems were going to go into his next book. One
didn't intrude. . . . They talked about his work, but not hers, not at all. . . . We
agreed on so many matters, of raising children. It was important. We were
parents. It wasn't all talk about existentialism."[127]

Soon David realized that Sylvia was a writer too. He was writing avant-
garde, German-influenced radio plays for the BBC, some of which Plath
read and commented on. She seemed to understand what he was trying to
do. "They were both very, very good to me. They took me seriously. Nobody
else I think ever had, you know. They sponsored me for Arts Council grants
and things." Sylvia, he remembered, "had a great openness. What came into
her head, she said." She was warm and personable, "and more physical than
the British are. She would come out and grab your hand and touch you. . . .
She was an enormous enthusiast for everything. Everything she was doing
was just so exciting and interesting to her." Ted, too, "would lean forward
with blazing eyes and really listen to what you were saying and say a fascinating thing back. He was my height and dark, dark, and cadaverous and
just terribly romantic." It was hard not to be swept away by this intense,

erudite couple. "I was enormously aware that I was touching the hem of greatness."[128]

————

"ON EASTER SUNDAY the world relented & spring arrived," Sylvia wrote to Aurelia. The Easter holiday had always marked her own symbolic rebirth, and she filled her letters home with joyous proclamations. "I have such spring fever I can hardly think straight"; "O it is so heavenly here I can hardly speak"; "I wouldn't leave this place for a billion dollars."[129] The daffodils were blooming in earnest now—she had picked six hundred in one week. The family spent whole afternoons gathering bunches, which they sold for a shilling. Sylvia felt intoxicated by Court Green's beauty and thought her yard "More beautiful than the Cambridge backs."[130] Ted began to worry that their property was so idyllic the villagers would begin to regard it as "a public promenade."[131]

Just after Easter, a "lady" Swedish journalist, Siv Arb, took a now-famous series of photographs of Sylvia and her children among the daffodils at Court Green. Sylvia complained about Arb, but she was grateful for a visit from Ted's aunt Hilda and her daughter Vicky over the Easter holiday— they "pitched right in with the dishes & cleaning, so were no extra work."[132] Hosting visitors was much more taxing now that she had to keep up with housework, gardening, renovations, two children, and her writing.

Neighbors, too, got on Sylvia's nerves that spring. Percy Key had cut down some of the Japanese creeper at Court Green, which outraged Sylvia and Ted. Sylvia became annoyed at Rose's requests to buy daffodils while knowing full well that she would not be charged. Plath finally told her they were "a bob a dozen. She looked stunned. Is that too much for you, I asked dryly?" Sylvia felt "sick" about going to tea at Rose's, "because Percy makes me sick." He became so weak that June that Ted had to lift him in and out of bed every day. For Sylvia, the contrast was startling. "And all about the world is gold and green, dripping with laburnum and buttercups and the sweet stench of June. In the cottage the fire is on and it is a dark twilight." She could hardly believe that Percy had been healthy just a few months before and was now plagued by "'something on the lung,'" as she wrote in her journal.[133] She would use the phrase in her April poem about Percy, "Among the Narcissi."

Sylvia had written to Ruth Fainlight in mid-April congratulating her on her new baby boy, who she hoped would be a companion for Nicholas. She invited them all to stay at Court Green and told Ruth's husband, Alan Sillitoe, that she had an extra study where he could work. (She did not extend the same invitation to Ruth.) The Sillitoes arrived with baby David on May 2 after an eight-hour drive. Both seemed fatigued when they appeared in the doorway at Court Green, but it was Ruth's birthday, and they had brought a bottle of champagne to celebrate. Ruth remembered Sylvia dressed in a plaid skirt and sweater, very much "an English country lady. . . . I'm sure it was a self-conscious role."[134] The two women nursed their babies together while Plath read "Elm," which she dedicated to Fainlight, out loud. Ruth thought the poem "extraordinary" and did not hear the similarities between it and her own "Sapphic Moon." She remembered during the visit that Sylvia and Ted seemed tense around each other. "It wasn't good. But we didn't discuss it at all. I wouldn't have initiated a discussion about it. And she didn't. So that was that. . . . We wanted just to talk about poetry and be poets. The difficulties of everyday life we were glad to put to one side. We didn't have complaining coffee-klatch conversations."[135] Sylvia wrote to Ruth after they left asking if she should use Ruth's married or maiden name in the dedication. Sylvia admitted that she preferred the latter, writing, "I had thought of the poet-self first." Ruth was slightly troubled by the question, whose answer seemed obvious: "we were two poets, Sylvia Plath and Ruth Fainlight, not Mrs. Hughes and Mrs. Sillitoe, and our friendship was centred on this crucial reality."[136]

Ruth later admitted that she felt oppressed by Sylvia's "impression of great confidence as a mother," even if this confidence had been a show. Sylvia had begun painting hearts and flowers on the backs of chairs and cupboards, and the impulse and the symbolism troubled Ruth. "Sylvia painting those little Germanic hearts and flowers all over Court Green . . . trying to be the perfect everything. I know, I've gone through it, of wanting to be the best at it, and it's a total waste of time and energy." But the pressure to embrace domesticity was "absolutely" a force in the mothers' lives.[137]

Sylvia and Ruth spent hours gathering daffodils and laid them carefully in cardboard boxes for the grocer. There were hundreds, thousands, it seemed. Ruth became dizzy from the effort. The flowers began to appear almost menacing, with their "eye-like" black dots and "sulphur" yellows. "Too many sexual organs. Looking down the trumpets of the daffodils again and again and again, it absolutely freaked me after a while," Ruth said.[138] "Sylvia laughed, but I hurried back into the house."[139] On May 3, Hughes and the Sillitoes drove to Dartmoor. A constable stopped them and warned them that a prisoner had recently escaped from the local prison. On the moor, Ruth stayed in the car, tired, while Ted and Alan walked through the heather. They came to a dirty stream near an old army camp, and saw rusty shell cases and "torn holes" in the grass. Something bleak had occurred there. Ted was disturbed by "The black scrubby cattle. The lamb's head in the grass, which I dared not mention to Sylvia."[140]

Ruth continued to feel "a palpable tension" between Sylvia and Ted during this visit, which was around the time Sylvia had stopped allowing Nicola Tyrer into her home. The couple avoided looking at each other, or even speaking to each other; the air between them seemed much more strained than it had during their companionable meals in London. The air had been strained between Sylvia and Alan Sillitoe, too. After Sylvia's death, David Compton—then living at Court Green with Elizabeth at Ted's request—found a letter from Alan Sillitoe to Sylvia in her desk. "He had obviously somehow said something that she had misunderstood. There had been an unpleasant note and he really thought that she was being oversensitive. . . . Apparently something had gone wrong and he felt it necessary to write and apologize. He said, 'You overreacted.' But very lovely."[141] (David found similar letters from Al Alvarez and Christopher Logue in her desk.)

Ruth, Alan, and their three-month-old son would leave England to join Jane and Paul Bowles (and, sometimes, Tennessee Williams) in Tangier during the spring of 1962, partly, Ruth said, to avoid Sylvia and her aspirations of perfect motherhood. Ruth felt an immense relief in Tangier, where she could afford a maid who cooked, cleaned, and watched the baby while she wrote. Ruth did not return to London until February 1963, after Sylvia's death. She would wonder if her presence there could have saved her.

———

IN EARLY MAY there was a spate of "Cape Cod August weather," as Ted wrote. Letters home were full of cherry trees and daffodils. He told Aurelia, "Twenty or thirty times a day Sylvia staggers & exclaims—hit by a fresh wave of the wonders of this place."[142] They spent long sunny afternoons planting flowers and sowing rows of beans and peas, and reviewing children's books.[143] "I think Sylvia's happier here, now the good weather's come, than she's been since I've known her," Ted wrote to Aurelia that May. "Also, she's writing very well, which seems to be the main thing. Since she left America, she's lost the terrible panic pressure of the American poetry world—which keeps them all keeping up on each other. As a result, she's developing her own way & will soon be a considerable genius." He told Aurelia that Howard Moss at *The New Yorker* had made a "stir" over "Tulips," which appeared in the April 7 issue. (Plath quoted Moss: "I have heard nothing but the most extravagant praise of TULIPS. Everyone I know thought it extraordinary. So do I.")[144] Ted sounded deeply content in his letter to Aurelia, but, like his wife, he was used to telling Aurelia what she wanted to hear. "This is a very satisfying life—producing steadily, in these surroundings, and with all this to work at. And we both needed it, since we'd got to be such outstandingly fleet rats in such a hectic pace. . . . One needs to provide substance & duties to the life—as we've done by coming here."[145]

Faber's *Selected Poems of Ted Hughes and Thom Gunn* came out in early May; Hughes inscribed his copy "To darling Sylvia" on May 10. Four days later, the American edition of *The Colossus* was released. Plath was pleased with it, and she wrote Knopf's Judith Jones to express her gratitude. She felt that it was "the 'final' first book. The English one being a trial run."[146] Ted wrote Aurelia with pride about how "fantastic" the book was, though he denigrated the American poetry scene. "While all those busy clamourous American whippet poets race round in circles after their stuffed fashionable hare (and the publishers all betting drunkenly on them) Sylvia is beginning to produce some really permanent poetry."[147] Yet *The Colossus* would practically sink without a trace in America. No major paper reviewed it, and it did not sell out its small print run.[148] The book's lackluster sales would contribute to Knopf's decision later that year to pass on an American edition of *The Bell Jar*. Plath still equated an American reputation with success, and she was bitterly disappointed as the months ticked by and her book remained unnoticed.

But that May, she was hopeful. The BBC had contacted her about doing a literary program, *The World of Books*. The Tyrers had left town for good—Nicola with a tearful goodbye—and Sylvia now found North Tawton "with the T's departure, an easier much more restful place."[149] She felt more relaxed than she had in months. "Now it is spring, it is just heaven here," she wrote Aurelia on May 4. "I never dreamed it was possible to be so happy."[150]

28

Error

Devon, May–June 1962

I n his poem "Error," Ted Hughes suggested that the move to Devon had marked the beginning of the end of his marriage:

> What wrong fork
> Had we taken? In a gloom orchard
> Under drumming thatch, we lay listening
> To our vicarage rotting like a coffin,
> Foundering under its weeds. What did you make of it
> When you sat at your elm table alone
> Staring at the blank sheet of white paper,
> Silent at your typewriter, listening
> To the leaking thatch drip, the murmur of rain,
> And staring at that sunken church, and the black
> Slate roofs in the mist of rain . . .[1]

Years later, it seemed to Hughes, "The trans-continental dream-express / Of your adolescence" had "Slammed to a dead-end, crushing halt, fatal . . ."

The move to Court Green was Hughes's bid for imaginative freedom, away from the distractions and squabbles of London literary life. As he wrote to his friend Ben Sonnenberg in October 1961, "Life in London was no longer possible. For over a year I have written more or less nothing and finally just stopped trying—waiting for London to pass off somehow, like a headache. . . . I thank London for nothing."[2] He had been delighted to leave the city for Devon, he told Sonnenberg. Yet in an early draft of "Error," Hughes recalled the sense of apprehension he felt on his arrival at Court Green:

When the lane narrowed—winding in and down,
Tighter & tighter—my prophetic stone
Tightened in me. The black Morris Traveller
Rigged with our Czechoslovakian kitchen chairs
Wobbled into the ambush. What had we done?
How would we ever get out of it? . . .
    For the first time
We owned something & it was an orchard.
It was an ancient home. And ancient ground.
It was the end of freedom, of careless freedom.
It was entering the alien, rooted society
Of the dead. It was serious. I was not
Sure we could measure up to it. The church
Waited, blocking the sunset. A wall of gravestones
Stood above us, like a reception committee
Reading our credentials. What had we done
With our lives?[3]

Court Green seemed an "old evil house reeking / Of Rentokil."[4] Hughes's diary suggests the poem's accuracy. On October 11, 1961, he wrote, "awake all night . . . my brain by 5 a. m. like a rusted ball & socket joint, creaking & aching." The next day brought little relief. "Bright day, windy fresh—blue sky, bright yard, but no settled feeling."[5]

The rural idyll did not, as he had planned, improve his imaginative faculties. By midyear, 1962, Hughes was in the midst of a serious writing block; the real drought that afflicted Devon that summer became a mockery of the creative drought afflicting him. He blamed his wife, in part. He wrote Olwyn in the summer of 1962, after he had fallen in love with Assia Wevill, that the only good work he had produced since moving back to England was while Sylvia was in the hospital for her appendectomy.[6] (It seems both writers needed space from each other at that time, for Sylvia, too, had experienced a renewed period of heightened creativity during her hospital separation from Hughes.) In addition to being a famous writer, Plath wanted to be the ideal wife and mother—thrifty, hardworking, and faithful, like Jenny in "Day of Success." And the harder she tried to inhabit these roles, the more constricted Hughes felt. Both would have recognized D. H. Lawrence's observations in his poem "Both Sides of the Medal":

Since you are confined in the orbit of me
do you not loathe the confinement?

Is not even the beauty and peace of an orbit
an intolerable prison to you,
as it is to everybody?[7]

The idea of constriction would surface in Plath's poem "The Rabbit Catcher" that May: the "tight wires" trapping the prey was an apt metaphor for the forces binding the unhappy couple. The poem has often been interpreted as a diatribe against Hughes, yet the last line of the poem is "The constriction killing me also." The arrival of their second child had dashed the couple's freewheeling ambitions; they had given up the Maugham Award and scrapped their plans to live in Italy. They both found themselves locked into traditional gendered roles that had once terrified them. "I'm aghast when I see how incredibly I've confined & stunted my existence, when I compare my feeling of what I could be with what I am," Ted wrote Olwyn in late summer 1962.[8] In some respects, Sylvia settled more comfortably into her role as wife and mother. For her, living with her beloved children and husband among the daffodils at Court Green was, as she later told Elizabeth, like living in Eden. But as Sylvia found her place in the world, Ted became gripped by anxiety that he had succumbed to the sedate, genteel life (living in a manor house, no less) that he had tried so hard to avoid. Later he told Anne Stevenson that after they left London, he and Sylvia became "well aware of the possible mistake of our move—isolating ourselves too far and finally, narrowing the children's options of good schools, losing easy access to libraries & lively friends. But we did want the isolation. We wanted to block off all other ways out except by writing." The error "made itself felt in bizarre and alarming ways, in both of us. But at least we had life on our own terms in our own place."[9]

In his poem "The Lodger," Hughes writes of what he called "heart trouble," but which sounds very much like panic: "The pangs. The poundings."[10] (It was not unlike the attack he'd had at the BBC in March 1960.) He thought he "was going to die." At night he went to bed "with fingers that throbbed so hard / They jerked the book I clung to and stared at." He had been experiencing such attacks for almost three years, he wrote in the poem, yet had never told Sylvia. In Devon, they grew worse.

I was already a discard,
My momentum merely the inertias
Of what I had been, while I disintegrated.
I was already posthumous. . . .
My new study

Was all the ways a heart can kill its owner
And how mine had killed me. . . .[11]

Sylvia told Winifred Davies that Ted "wanted out" that summer because he was upset that "he could no longer write in the afternoon when he had to assume domestic chores."[12] His resentment probably angered Sylvia, who assumed far more domestic duties than he did and had even less time for writing. Winifred thought his frustrations with the marriage were creative rather than sexual: "Ted was jealous of Sylvia's work." Hughes had not written much since *Lupercal*. He was busy with BBC work and editing an American poetry anthology, which he never completed.[13] Plath, meanwhile, had written a novel, a radio play, and poems that seemed stronger by the week. His wife was again the breadwinner, as she had been in America; her Saxton grant provided their main source of income. His poetry was no longer flowing; Sylvia was no longer his "luck"; marriage was no longer his "medium."

Hughes's later writings hint at the isolation he felt in Devon, away from the distractions of London he claimed to disdain. In 1986 he wrote to his son, Nicholas, that in America, he and Sylvia had "made hardly any friends, no close ones, and neither of us did anything the other didn't want wholeheartedly to do. . . . Since the only thing we wanted to do was write, our lives disappeared into the blank page." Years later he speculated that he and Sylvia should have realized that "one person cannot live within another's magic circle, as an enchanted prisoner."[14] He believed, as he told Owen Leeming in 1961, that he and Sylvia had telepathic access to each other's thoughts. He thought his wife possessed "clairvoyant divination," and he later claimed that she had stolen an image of the goddess Nehamah, based on Assia Wevill, from his brain for her poem "The Munich Mannequins."[15] The once fulfilling symbiosis now seemed claustrophobic: "Our telepathy was intrusive."[16]

After Sylvia's death, Ted told his brother Gerald that she had become intensely concerned, "even paranoid," about *The Bell Jar* in the fall of 1961 and winter of 1962. She worried that it would not be successful and would hurt her friends and family in America. "Again and again Ted had tried to reassure her, but her anxieties grew, and the emotional tension between them and the increasing marital strains reached an unbearable pitch," Gerald wrote in his memoir.[17] Sylvia was indeed under much stress during this period. She was trying to write new work and reassuring Heinemann that she would not be sued for libel, all while caring for a toddler, a new baby, and a large home. But the end of the marriage, when it came, was also bound up with Hughes's writing block and his hope for imaginative regeneration with a new muse many called "the most beautiful woman in London": Assia

Wevill.[18] As Ted's later lover Susan Alliston would write in her diary in 1963, "He says he's never in his life found someone so physically attractive. Also she releases his imagination.... She is a rare person. He might be able to save her and she him."[19] Hughes's images of panic in "The Lodger" suggest that he experienced a private breakdown in the spring and summer of 1962—one that would have very public consequences.

———

WITH HER "RAVEN" HAIR and kohl-lined gray eyes, Assia Wevill struck many as "Babylonian"; admirers compared her to Scheherazade and Aphrodite.[20] Luke Myers thought she bore a "strong likeness to Elizabeth Taylor."[21] Suzette Macedo remembered, "Everybody was in love with her; she was magnetic; she told stories, she was *beautiful*. And, also, death to men. . . . She needed to be loved, she wanted to be loved." The Macedos met the Wevills around Christmas 1961 at a party thrown by a South African literary friend. By then the Wevills had taken over Sylvia and Ted's Chalcot Square lease. Suzette had already heard about Assia from Sylvia, who had told her that Assia was "wonderful."[22] Assia's history of exile and her command of German, Hebrew, and Russian intrigued Sylvia. Jillian Becker, another of Sylvia's London friends, was less charitable. She thought Assia "capable of immense malice, of idiotic and cruel intrigue for the fun of it but a kid playing what she thought to be a femme fatale."[23]

When Assia walked into the party, Suzette thought, "That must be the beautiful girl. She was stunning." Suzette sat down next to Assia and told her she was friendly with the Hugheses. "Oh," Assia said suggestively, in her deep, alluring "cut-crystal English" voice. "You know them, do you? What do you think of him?" Suzette answered that Ted was "a very good poet." "But, *him*," Assia pressed. Assia and David were "much more available socially" as a couple than Sylvia and Ted, who were more "ambitious" and moved in more "prizewinning" literary circles. Suzette would become close to both women, though she remained closer to Assia.

Assia Gutmann was born in Berlin in 1927, the child of an atheist Russian Jewish father and a devout German Lutheran mother. She and her sister Celia were brought up in a Berlin teeming with cabarets and cafés. Assia's father, a doctor, had treated members of the Bolshoi Ballet, a romantic detail Hughes would later include in poems about her. Until the Aryanization of the German health services, the Gutmanns enjoyed an affluent lifestyle, complete with white damask tablecloths and fine silver cutlery. But by the early 1930s, with the Nazis in power, Assia's father could no longer practice medicine. Jewish and married to a Christian, he began to fear for his family. When Assia turned six, the Gutmanns fled to Pisa, Italy, among the first group of Jewish refugees to leave Germany. After six months, the family fled again, to Palestine, where in 1933 they settled in Tel Aviv. "We were driftwood, post-war driftwood," one of Assia's Israeli friends later remarked.[24]

In Palestine, there were no damask tablecloths. Dr. Gutmann found himself among a surplus of doctors in a land of mostly healthy young people. Assia's mother became a dressmaker and cooked lunch for paying customers; Assia once allowed the local butcher to "fondle her" to get meat at a discount.[25] There were other indignities. Assia's father was indulgent, but her mother could be cruel. She would hit the girls with a violin bow, tie them to windows for minor infractions, and break their toys. The hardships of exile made her moods even blacker, and the sisters reacted with wild, dark moods of their own. Assia's father often calmed them with tranquilizers. Assia's family, however, was luckier than others in their extended family; the Nazis killed her paternal uncle, his wife, and their young daughter. (Her maternal cousins, meanwhile, joined the Hitler Youth.) She knew that her own escape from the horror had been close. On a 1954 trip to Germany with her second husband, she stood before the gates of Dachau but could not bring herself to enter.

The half-German Assia experienced a sense of persecution in Tel Aviv that was similar to what Sylvia had experienced in 1940s Winthrop. Just as Sylvia had feared that her father might be sent to a detention camp for Germans, Assia feared that her mother might be detained as an "enemy sympathizer."[26] A native German speaker, Assia was told to hide her German background. She picked up Hebrew at her first school, but she was no Zionist; while Assia's teenage friends were eager to work on a kibbutz over their holidays, she was happiest—like Sylvia—lying on a beach.

The Gutmanns wanted a European education for their daughter and took on extra work to pay her tuition at a local British school. There, Assia learned the Queen's English and immersed herself in British literature. She dreamed of moving to England and establishing her own literary salon. She later told her closest female friend in England, Pam Gems, that she wanted to marry an English poet who looked like Rupert Brooke. Pam told her that she would have been better off in the nineteenth century, a muse to "Shelley and Browning and Keats." She thought Assia had "an artistic temperament but no specific talent to express it."[27] The Irish writer William Trevor, who worked with Assia in London, remembered her constructing elaborate plots for novels "someone else might care to write."[28]

In 1946, Assia left Tel Aviv for London, where she had secured a spot in the Regent Street Polytechnic School of Art, and married John Steele, a British soldier she had dated in Tel Aviv. (Assia's parents had practically demanded the match, desperate for British passports.) She quit art school to play the part of a suburban wife but grew lonely and isolated. Hoping to improve his prospects, John decided to emigrate to Canada—a decision that appalled Assia, who could not face another upheaval. Canada, a friend recalled, "meant intellectual death for her."[29] She followed him but tried to commit suicide in 1948 by taking fifty aspirins; she was saved at the hospital. The couple divorced.

In Vancouver, Assia met the future economist Richard Lipsey. They married and moved to London, where Assia stood out amid the gray postwar drab in her fashionable bright reds and purples. "We were stopped in the streets—one man clutched at her sleeve, and stared and stared before apologizing," a friend remembered.[30] The couple lived on tinned sardines and potatoes while Richard studied for a PhD at the London School of Economics. Assia's visions of a glamorous literary life receded. She tried to kill herself twice, again with pills. Both times her husband saved her.

On a voyage back to England from Canada, where the couple had been visiting Richard's relatives, Assia met the Canadian poet David Wevill. A shipboard romance ensued, with her husband's full knowledge. The affair continued in England, where David was studying at Queens' College, Cambridge. Assia finally left Richard for David and found satisfying work with Reuters, translating Hebrew broadcasts about the Suez Crisis from the Middle East. The assignment eventually led to a copywriting position at Notley's advertising agency, where she worked with the writers Peter Porter, William Trevor, and Edward Lucie-Smith. Suzette remembered that Assia was a talented copywriter and "very happy in her advertising world."[31]

Through Edward Lucie-Smith, Assia and David fell in with the Group and began attending their weekly meetings in mid-1957. She was thrilled to join a salon, even if it was not her own. It was here that Assia encountered Ted Hughes's poems for the first time.[32] She herself wrote poems but did not submit them to the Group. One that survives, "Magnificat," has the ring of Dylan Thomas's "The Force That Through the Green Fuse Drives the Flower," one of Plath's favorite poems: "And I do praise the force that falls / With loosened stones and plunging force / Of clear ghost-rivers in dried beds."[33] Philip Hobsbaum would write that he found, in Assia's work, "a community of vision linking Hughes, Plath, and Wevill." Assia's later translations of the Israeli poet Yehuda Amichai would earn her praise.[34]

In London, Assia developed a reputation as both a tragic muse and a femme fatale. When she and David arrived in Hobsbaum's Stockwell flat for a Group session, Peter Redgrove whispered to Hobsbaum, "I know who she is. She has killed two men already, and will be the death of David."[35] Hobsbaum remembered her posh accent, her wit, and her skill with language.

Together, she and David cut slightly tragic, glamorous figures. The novelist Fay Weldon remembered that when they entered a room, heads turned. William Trevor thought Assia looked like Sophia Loren, and David, Gary Cooper. They were beautiful and damned, he thought, like "Scott Fitzgerald people, sixties-style."[36] Assia played the part especially well; she once tried to stab her second husband, Richard Lipsey, with a Burmese dagger near the entrance to the South Kensington tube station.[37]

In 1958, Assia followed David to the University of Burma, where he had accepted a two-year teaching contract. She was still married to Richard, but they had agreed to divorce shortly before she left. Richard was now on the brink of a professorship at the London School of Economics, but Assia, like Sylvia, followed the drifting poet. The divorce took nearly two years.

In Burma, Assia and David met Michael Mendelson and his wife, Pat. Michael belonged to a prominent, wealthy Jewish family who had fled Belgium for England at the start of the Second World War. Educated at Cambridge and the University of Chicago, he was an anthropologist who studied the Maya in Guatemala and, later, Buddhist culture in Burma. He would adopt the pen name Nathaniel Tarn when he began writing poetry. Patricia Mendelson remembered that in Burma, Assia "presented herself as very glamorous, and was quick to adopt the colonial etiquette, wearing wide-rimmed hats, puffing on her cigarette."[38] Assia once shocked a group of expatriates at a dinner party with her impersonation of Eva Braun. On a memorable 1962 Boxing Day, she donned full Burmese costume and danced for the Macedos, Doris Lessing and her son Peter, and David. Suzette remembered that Doris was "fascinated" by Assia, while the men were left speechless. "I thought, My God, she's just, what is she?" Suzette said.[39]

After her divorce from Richard finally came through in 1960, Assia and David married in Rangoon and then headed back to London. (The British Council had refused to extend David's teaching contract in Burma when they learned that he was living with a married woman.)[40] Assia was pregnant and had decided to keep the baby—she had had several abortions over the years—but she miscarried. David worked as a porter at Harrods, then as a copywriter at the Ogilvy, Benson, and Mather advertising agency. Assia returned to Notley's, where she grew more successful as a copywriter. A famous 1961 Notley's ad featured Assia, William Trevor, and another well-heeled couple punting on the Serpentine, drinking champagne and typing on a typewriter. Notley's did not need a professional model when they had Assia, who looked glamorous and sophisticated holding a champagne flute in one hand, a pencil in the other. She soon moved to a higher-paying position at another agency, where she impressed her superiors with her "unconventional, often wild and stimulating ideas." She headed up several successful ad campaigns, including a now iconic television commercial for Sea Witch hair dye, part James Bond, part Homer. She was so talented that she was able to keep her job despite frequent tardiness and absences, and what one supervisor remembered as a "wild temper": "it always puzzled me why she was in advertising, when she could have been a diva; our world was too limited for her."[41]

The Wevills were looking for a less expensive flat when they saw Plath and Hughes's sublet ad in the *London Evening Standard*. "I didn't meet or know Hughes or Plath while at Cambridge, though I did read some of their work," David recalled.[42] All three had contributed to *delta* and *Chequer* around the same time, and were all published in Christopher Levenson's *Poetry from Cambridge* in 1958.[43] Poems by Plath and David Wevill had even appeared in the same issue of *delta* in the summer of 1956.

The Cambridge poetry connection helped Assia and David beat out the other interested party for the Chalcot Square flat. After meeting Sylvia and Ted, Assia remarked to William Trevor, "Heavens, the coincidence of it! All three of them being poets!" Trevor thought he heard a more plaintive cry, that of "the outsider": "she had no lines to offer in that charmed poetic circle. One day she might have the right to be there, but for the moment she possessed little more than beauty and an imagination she could not properly make work for her."[44]

The two couples socialized "a few times" over the next three weeks, before the move to Devon, David remembered. "We got on with them like a house on fire." According to Ted, Assia even gave Sylvia a handmade wooden snake from Burma. David ascribed "no subtle reasons behind it." ("Assia was indifferent to the occult, and for her, it was just a decorative object.")[45] The two couples kept in touch by mail and phone after the Hugheses moved to Court Green; they invited the Wevills to stay in the spring of 1962. In a May 14 letter to Aurelia, Sylvia described them as "a nice young Canadian poet & his very attractive, intelligent wife coming down for this weekend."[46] Sylvia simply wrote "The Wevills" in her calendar that weekend, along with a menu of beef stew, corn chowder, and gingerbread. She left no star, as she often did on happy occasions.

WHEN ASSIA RECEIVED the invitation, she told her supervisor that she planned to "seduce Ted" in Devon.[47] Suzette also recalled her rhapsodizing about Ted's good looks and asking, "Shall I wear my war paint?" "I said, 'What for?' Because it was a bit of a joke. She *was* naughty, and she adored making an impact. But it didn't cross my mind that she meant it when she was invited to Court Green."[48] Such declarations seemed out of character to some who knew her. Edward Lucie-Smith felt that she was unaware of her beauty and "often panic-stricken when men misinterpreted her warmth and friendliness." He suspected that it was her naivete that "created so many explosive situations around her."[49] David Wevill himself thought her "Brave, resourceful, warm" but with "many shadows" from her displaced past.[50] Neither thought her manipulative. Ruth Fainlight, who hated Assia after Sylvia's death, eventually became very close to her.

Yet many who knew Assia agreed that she could be dramatic. An old boyfriend from Canada remembered that she "thought that ordinary life was contemptible" and tried to live the values of the modernist poets she admired.[51] Assia's ad agency colleague Julia Matcham recalled that she "had an original, entertaining mind . . . coloured by an exaggerated romanticism, which in its rather tenuous relationship to reality allowed her free rein to be quite ruthless in the pursuit of anything she wanted, without the burden of a bad conscience." When Assia had told her about making a play for Ted, she had been "perfectly unashamed."[52] Ted Hughes was Britain's most famous young poet in 1962, and his celebrity impressed Assia. Lucie-Smith said that Assia was "an intellectual snob. She was very influenced throughout the Hughes business by the fact that this was <u>Hughes</u>."[53] One of Assia's colleagues remembered overhearing Assia, after the Hugheses separated, tell her hairdresser that she was carrying the child "of a very famous poet."[54] Ted came to believe that Assia arrived at Court Green with a plan. "We didn't find her—she found us. She sniffed us out," he wrote in his poem "Dreamers," eliding his own role in the affair.

Ted picked David and Assia up at the train station on the evening of Friday, May 18. They dined together on the Wevills' round wooden table and "talked a lot," David remembered, "satirizing people we knew. It was a lively conversation."[55] Assia told stories from Burma, Sylvia "anecdotes of her life in the States." In "Dreamers," Hughes wrote that in the morning, at breakfast, Assia told him that she had dreamed of "A giant fish, a pike." Plath, in the poem, was "astonished, maybe envious." This was the moment, he suggested, that he fell in love with Assia:

> I saw
> The dreamer in her
> Had fallen in love with me and she did not know it.
> That moment the dreamer in me
> Fell in love with her, and I knew it.[56]

Ted did not realize that Assia would have seen the Gehenna Press broadside of "Pike" that hung on the wall at Chalcot Square; he viewed the dream as a sign.[57] The conversation put Sylvia on guard. As early as 1957 she had contemplated writing a story about a "poet husband" who writes about his "Dream Woman Muse" rather than his wife.[58] And as Suzette, who was privy to both Sylvia's and Assia's confidences, noted, Sylvia was at the time breast-feeding, sleeping little, and looked like—in her word—a "shlumper."[59] It was a term, Yiddish in origin, that Suzette had learned from her Jewish friends to describe women who let themselves go after having children. Sex that had once been, according to Suzette, "wild and demanding" was now on the wane after the birth of their second child. "Assia had no pity for that at all. Her attitude was she [Sylvia] had no right to let herself go like that. Assia was always perfumed and manicured."[60] Indeed, Sylvia would tell Dr. Beuscher that fall that sex had become so infrequent after Nicholas was born that she thought Ted was ill.

The next day, Saturday, David and Ted drove to Dartmoor with Frieda while Sylvia and Assia weeded together in the vegetable garden and pre-pared the day's meal. Plath would later include images from this afternoon—variations of "black boots among the cabbages"—in her July 1962 poems. Ted thought that Sylvia, half German herself, found a doppelgänger in Assia. "She fascinated you," he wrote in "Dreamers." "Her German the dark under-current / In her Kensington jeweller's elocution / Was your ancestral Black Forest whisper—" "Warily you cultivated her, / Her Jewishness, her many-blooded beauty, / As if your dream of your dream-self stood there."[61] Ted, too, was fascinated by this Jewish-German-Russian refugee. Both reduced Assia to a cipher, and a cliché: she would become a Germanic black goddess in Plath's work, a "slightly filthy" seductress in Hughes's. "Her black-ringed grey iris, slightly unnatural, / Was Black Forest wolf, a witch's daughter / Out of Grimm," Hughes wrote in "Dreamers." There, he called her, notoriously, a "Lilith of abortions."[62] The real woman, according to those who knew her best, was generous and talented, but troubled.

After dinner that Saturday night at Court Green, the four spoke of Roethke, Sexton, and Lowell and listened to a recording of Lowell read-ing "The Quaker Graveyard in Nantucket." Sylvia went up to bed first and called for Ted to join her, but he stayed downstairs.[63] The Sillitoes had felt tension between the couple during their spring visit, but David noticed nothing amiss. "She and Ted gave the impression of a very close and devoted couple that had worked out a life for themselves," he told Assia's biogra-phers.[64] Sometimes Sylvia's face would betray an odd expression, "as though she were looking inward," but for the most part she was a "gracious" con-versationalist.[65] Assia, though, silently judged her surroundings. In her diary she later mocked the hearts and flowers Sylvia had painted on furniture. The rooms, she thought, were too red, "childishly furnished. Naively furnished. The whole look of it improvised, amateurish."[66]

David recalled that he was "chatting" with Sylvia outside on Sunday afternoon while Assia and Ted made potato salad in the kitchen. "We could hear Assia and Ted's muffled voices, and suddenly Sylvia went very still. She touched me on the knee and said, 'I'll be back.' She jumped from her chair and ran into the kitchen as if she remembered that she had left some fire burning." She did not return, and at lunch he noticed that she was withdrawn, "as if a door had slammed down on her."[67] He sensed that she was tired of hostessing or had fought with Ted. Assia told Suzette that Sylvia had asked her to peel the potatoes—"now, Assia was not a potato peeler, ever," Suzette said—and that Ted had gone in to help her while Sylvia was somewhere else in the house. When Ted stood behind her, Assia "could feel his eyes" boring into her.[68] Ted said, " 'You're a Taurus, aren't you?' At this moment she turned round, their eyes met and . . . le grande passion!"[69] Assia told Suzette there was an "enormous current between them" in that moment.[70] Sylvia had then "walked in, slammed something down on the table and said 'What are you talking about?' " Ted answered, "Just our signs." Sylvia turned to Assia and said, "I think you should leave after lunch."[71] Assia told Suzette, "She'd sent them off unceremoniously. . . . They were marched off to the train, practically. . . . Poor darling David said, 'What have we done?' "[72] Sylvia told her own slightly different version of the story in a July 11, 1962, letter to Dr. Beuscher as the marriage was falling apart. "I'd walked in on them (Ted & she) Tête-à-tête in the kitchen & Ted had shot me a look of pure hate. She smiled & stared at me curiously the rest of the weekend."[73]

David remembered that Sylvia drove them to the train station after lunch. She had not kicked them out, exactly, but "she was very nervous, clashed the gears, and was on edge." On the train, he asked Assia whether she had noticed the change in Sylvia's behavior—she had been so friendly but had "changed completely" after lunch. Assia then told him, "Ted kissed me in the kitchen, and Sylvia saw it."[74] Assia offered no further details, and David tried to push the event from his mind. He hoped that it was just a harmless flirtation.

Back in London, Assia and David both confided in Michael Mendelson, who now went by his pen name, Nathaniel Tarn. Nathaniel was also a Jewish refugee whose childhood had been interrupted by war, and Assia trusted him. He and his wife had been Assia and David's closest friends in Burma, and they remained close in London, where Nathaniel now taught at the London School of Economics. Suzette recalled that he was Assia's "confidant," and throughout the spring and summer of 1962, Nathaniel kept notes on his conversations with both Wevills, whom he often met (separately) for lunch.[75]

These notes, archived at Stanford University, offer a contemporary account of Assia's and David's perspectives about Sylvia and Ted as they unfolded in real time.

Assia told Nathaniel that the stay at Court Green had been "full of difficulties." "Sylvia, a witch, hated her, wanted her out early. Sylvia's clairvoyance. Hughes hates her. Has been unable to write for 4 years. Wrote Lupercal in 10 days she was away (?)," Nathaniel wrote in his notes. Assia did not mention a kiss to him; she may have lied about it to make David jealous. Nathaniel noted that Assia was frustrated by David's passivity. "D. doesn't react. She wants to make him react."[76] Assia's word "clairvoyance" to describe Sylvia may have come from Ted, who likely mentioned his belief that Sylvia had such powers.

Sylvia had indeed sensed the attraction, as she told Dr. Beuscher. She did not write to her mother between May 14 and June 7—an unusually long stretch of silence. While the flirtation between Ted and Nicola Tyrer had angered her, Nicola was a teenager. This was different. The two poems Plath wrote the day after the Wevills left suggest a change in marital weather. "The Rabbit Catcher" reads, "And we, too, had a relationship— / Tight wires between us, / Pegs too deep to uproot, and a mind like a ring / Sliding shut on some quick thing." In "Event" (originally titled "Quarrel"), Plath wrote, "Love cannot come here." "Who has dismembered us? // The dark is melting. We touch like cripples." The same day she wrote these two poems, she sent them, along with "Elm" and *Three Women*, to Howard Moss at *The New Yorker*. She would later send "Event," "The Rabbit Catcher," and "Elm" to Al Alvarez at *The Observer*. Plath was writing about a marriage in trouble, and these angry poems were not meant to be private. They upset Hughes: in a draft of "The Minotaur, 2," he wrote about "Event": "'What's this?' I asked. 'Hey wait a minute / This is breaking the rules. / Do we blab about each other, about our secret life / To amuse poetry fanciers?'"[77]

Assia's visit reawakened Ted. Two days after meeting her, he suggested to the Merwins that he felt close to breaking through his writing block. "I'd got to the point of writing purely out of nerves—so now I'm quite content to let that tension relax & smooth itself out. Then maybe I'll be able to hear myself speak."[78] He wrote to Olwyn later that summer that "just as the climax was arriving," he had been doing "quite a burst of writing."[79] On May 24, he told the Merwins that he was "writing a morality play 'Difficulties of a Bridegroom'—moral, 'What you are afraid of overtakes you,' something of a joke."[80] The play was about a young man, Sullivan, who runs over a hare with his car on his way to London to see a girlfriend. Hughes had told Plath the hare was her totem, a fact that she had exploited in her poem "The Rabbit Catcher."

On May 22, Assia sent Sylvia a letter that included a small tapestry kit Sylvia had mentioned she liked. Assia had sought out the "Rose Bouquet" pattern at Harrods and told Sylvia that she would change the wool thread colors for her if she didn't like them. Assia did not mention the weekend in the letter, which concerned the technical aspects of tapestry. She told Sylvia she might become "seriously addicted" to the needlepoint work. ("Please, please don't let it possess you.") She signed her letter, "Much love, Assia."[81] Sylvia wrote "tapestry" in her calendar one or two days a week up to July 1, which suggests that she worked steadily on it for about five weeks. "I'm learning to do gros point tapestry for cushion & seat covers. Wonderfully calming," she told Aurelia.[82] Assia's polite note and generous gift seem to have mitigated Sylvia's suspicions.

Alvarez stopped by briefly on June 8 on his way to Cornwall. To him, Sylvia seemed confident and secure in her marriage, "her own woman again."[83] But Alvarez had his own reasons to steer clear of the unfolding drama. Assia told Nathaniel Tarn that she and Alvarez were lovers, but that by February 1962 she had tired of him. She said Al had begged her to accompany him to America, but she declined. Undeterred, he would, according to Assia, propose marriage to her in late July 1962. In 2016, Alvarez denied the affair, dismissing Tarn's notes and calling Assia "a nightmare, a very unpleasant woman," among other things. Anne Alvarez, whom Al married in 1966, disliked Assia intensely. She remembered that when she and Al used to go out together with Assia and Ted, Assia tried to erode her trust in Al. Anne called Tarn "Assia's drunken friend" and also dismissed his notes.[84]

David Wevill was less surprised by the revelations in Nathaniel Tarn's notes. "Tarn was a good friend in those years, and 'drunken' doesn't fit him at all. . . . Al was drawn to Assia as were many."[85] Assia told Nathaniel that Ted was "terribly jealous" of Al in 1963, four months after Sylvia's death.[86] Nathaniel considered himself Assia's main male confidant and wrote with some satisfaction of the "many gaps" in other friends' knowledge of her dramas, particularly "Alvarez being attracted to A. [Assia] at the same time as Hughes."[87] Ted wrote about a London assignation with Assia in his diary: "The first meeting at Al's flat: the Joan Baez records on—the strange bliss. The spicey suspicions that she knew the place too well, that she had visited Al there."[88]

THAT JUNE, Sylvia enjoyed showing off Court Green to Ted's parents, who, she told Aurelia, were "immensely impressed & proud."[89] Six laburnum trees—her "favorite tree"—bloomed right outside her study window, drip-

ping "gold everywhere," she told Joan and Gerald Hughes.[90] The weather
was "halcyon clear." She apologized to Aurelia for her three-week silence,
claiming, "This is the richest & happiest time of my life."[91]

It wasn't all hyperbole. The BBC had accepted *Three Women* and had
asked her to do a talk on "The World of Books." She was excited that Douglas
Cleverdon, the same producer who had worked with Ted, was now producing *her* work.[92] (When *Three Women* aired on August 19, Eric Walter White,
secretary of the Poetry Book Society, called it "absolutely first class," and he
invited the Hugheses to dinner in London.)[93] Ted had just finished recording
a program about the war poet Keith Douglas, and his play *The Wound* would
be rebroadcast a third time on July 14, netting them "another blessed $300
out of the blue."[94] Sylvia hoped that with Aurelia about to arrive she could
get back to work on her new novel. She wrote Alfred Fisher, her old Smith
professor, to ask whether she could buy some pads of pink Smith memoran-
dum paper. "My muse is mad for them!" she wrote. She also sent him a copy
of *The Colossus*, writing, "I got to remembering those fine afternoons in my
senior year at Smith under your office gable. The book is your due." She told
him how wonderful it was to live in the country on their "ancient smallhold-
ing" amid the apple trees and laburnum, writing "in shifts, balancing babies
in between." She had started a second book of poems "much freer than this"
and had a first novel accepted: "It is wonderful to discover one's destiny."[95]

Sylvia put Assia out of her mind and set about fulfilling her dream of
raising bees and harvesting her "own daffodil-apple blossom honey."[96] In
early June, she and Ted met with the local beekeeper, Charlie Pollard, who
demonstrated his techniques. Neither Sylvia nor Ted had brought any protective clothing, and Sylvia half-jokingly prayed to the spirit of her dead
father to shield her. The other beekeepers, who included the rector and Sylvia's midwife, lent them hats. Plath would draw deeply on this day in her bee
poems, especially "The Bee Meeting," in which she transformed this enthusiast club into something more sinister. In her June 7 journal passage about
the event, she sounds excited about a new adventure with her husband: "We
were interested in starting a hive, so dumped the babies in bed and jumped in
the car and dashed down the hill past the old factory to Mill Lane."[97] Pollard
gave them a hive, which they painted white and green and filled with Italian
hybrid bees. Ted got stung many times, Sylvia noted, but she did not.

The fine weather and the outdoor work in the garden improved Sylvia's
spirits. She told the Kanes she was in the garden "from morning till night
digging & hacking the huge weeds from square after square of vegetables."
By evening, she was "stupid-cow-tired," but the work calmed her. (Ted, she
wrote, was "a wonderful planter but does not see weeds. I see weeds.")[98]
When she was not in the garden, she was painting furniture white or black

with hearts and flowers "to make 'sets' for this room or that."[99] David Compton remembered that she used to joke excitedly to Frieda that the bees had landed on the Germanic folk-art flowers she had painted around the front door at Court Green.[100] The furniture painting, the gardening, and the honeybees were a reflection of a personal and artistic philosophy that Sylvia described to Olwyn as "this William Morris making & designing of things, babies & incipient books."[101] But so much making added to the many domestic burdens she already carried.

Sylvia and Ted celebrated their sixth wedding anniversary on June 16. "*ANNIV*," Sylvia wrote in her calendar. She made a celebratory dinner of roast beef, mushrooms, peas, potatoes, and her pièce de résistance, lemon meringue pie. The anniversary seems to have given her a new burst of energy. That week, her calendar was much fuller than it had been since the Wevills' visit; there are long lists of tasks again, nearly all of them checked off. Two days later, she wrote Olwyn, "I just feel to be lifting a nose & a finger from the last 3 years cow-push of carrying, bearing, nursing & nappy-squeezing. My study is my poultice, my balm, my absinthe."[102] Yet she wrote just one poem in June, "Berck-Plage," completed on the 30th. "When you come I really must sit in my study in the mornings!" she told Aurelia.[103] Sylvia told no one about her marriage's difficulties that spring. Yet there was a telling aside in her June letter to Olwyn: she praised Thom Gunn's recent collection, writing that she was also "very sympathetic to Alvarez's poems, some of them, because I like him & know something about how his wife's knocked him about & gone off."[104]

Sylvia wrote to Dr. Beuscher in July that just when she thought she had "stepped into" her dream life, something changed. Ted began to "leap up" in the morning to get the mail.

> He began to talk, utterly unlike him, of how he could write & direct film scripts, how he was going to win the Nobel Prize, how he had been asleep all the time we were married, recoiling, as the French say, so he could jump the better. How he wanted to experience everybody & everything, there was a monster in him, a dictator. . . . He would come out with these things after spurts of lovemaking as in our honeymoon days, asking me like a technician, did I like this, did I like that. Then round on me for holding hands & being jealous of other women.
>
> I just felt sick, as if I were the practice board for somebody else.

When she told Ted that she intended to start a second novel, adding, "laughingly," that she needed six weeks of peace and happiness, he "flew" at her, saying, "Why should I limit myself by your happiness or unhappiness?"[105]

Hughes's outbursts and actions suggest that he was, as he hinted to his brother, seeking his own rebirth. He wrote about freedom and morality in his journal that June: "How free?" "What are the elements of wholeness?" "Since life must be lived in bondage, can it be, by choice & discipline & cultivation, a bondage to joy?"[106] On June 14 he recorded the outlines of a dream: "after some lively time in Paris, with attractive girls, back here. Postman comes. I run down, receive from him a note & take it into front room. On it is written the address, in Paris, of the most attractive of the girls—and 'there is a room for you here if you still want it.' "[107]

29

I Feel All I Feel

Devon and London, June–August 1962

"*MOTHER ARRIVES*," Sylvia wrote in her calendar on June 21. Starred entries were happy ones, though Sylvia confided to Elizabeth Compton that she had mixed feelings about Aurelia's visit. She was excited to see her mother, but the visit came in the midst of a marital crisis. While she looked forward to the "free mother's help, babysitter & part-time cook all of which I am desperate for," she would have to contain her emotions.[1]

Aurelia's arrival was inauspicious. She did not know that she needed to open the train door herself when it arrived at the station, as train doors opened automatically in America. By the time she managed to open the door, the train had begun moving and she turned her ankle as she jumped onto the platform with her luggage. Sylvia instantly blamed herself. The swelling went down that evening, but the accident cast a pall over Aurelia's arrival. While she thought North Tawton "plain," she surveyed her daughter's ancient manor home approvingly. "Here our land begins," Sylvia said proudly as they approached Court Green. Sylvia had "wanted everything perfect" for her mother's visit, Winifred Davies remembered. "She wanted to make that house rather like the picturebook Devon cottage with roses round the door. . . . And of course she couldn't do it. She couldn't get the roses round the door."[2] Such trellises took more than one season to grow. Instead, Sylvia had placed a hand-drawn "Welcome Home" sign in the guest room, along with a blue and black Liberty silk scarf—the last gift she would ever give her mother.

To Warren, Aurelia described her first week at Court Green as her "happiest in many, many years."[3] Frieda wandered into Aurelia's room each morning to play, and Aurelia enjoyed helping Sylvia with the house and garden. Plath described an idyllic scene to the Kanes: "We are writing again, both of us, and she gets on beautifully with the babies, minds them, bakes cookies. O it is lovely."[4]

Aurelia's help gave Sylvia more time to write, but it also gave Ted the freedom to pursue Assia in London. On June 26, Ted and Sylvia went up to London together to record for the BBC and have lunch with Douglas Cleverdon. That day Ted left the BBC studio for Assia's advertising agency in Mayfair. "She got a fright when she heard that Mr. Hughes was downstairs," Suzette recalled. Assia told her secretary to tell Ted she was in a meeting. Soon after, Assia called Suzette and announced, "Pub. 1:00." They met at the pub halfway between their offices, and Assia gave Suzette a "very dramatized, Assia-like account of this enormous current." Assia did not mention a kiss at Court Green, but she showed Suzette a note. "It said, 'I must see you in spite of all marriages.'" Ted had left it for her at the advertising agency when she did not appear. "He definitely wants to see me. What am I going to do?" she asked Suzette.[5] Assia told Suzette she was going to send him a flower or a leaf, with no note. According to Nathaniel Tarn, Assia showed Ted's note to David to make him "react." David was unconcerned and remained "v. sweet & loving." Yet David later hinted to Nathaniel that he knew about his wife's burgeoning affair with Ted Hughes. (Assia "gagged" when Nathaniel told her.)[6] Ted was the senior poet, and had the ear of Faber and Faber, the publisher David hoped to land. He would have to tread carefully.

One June afternoon when Assia was sitting in London's Grosvenor Square with her colleague William Trevor, she told him about the May weekend at Court Green. She said she had been making a salad in the kitchen when Ted Hughes wandered in, "how they'd talked, and how she'd been attracted to him." There was no mention of a kiss. She had thought Plath "A brisk, hard, magazine-editor kind of American"—"an assessment considerably at odds with the opinions of those who knew Sylvia Plath well," Trevor pointed out.[7] Assia reached down with her manicured fingers and picked up a blade of freshly mowed grass. "I think I'll send him this," she said. "Just by itself." Trevor asked her if this was a good idea. "Not really," she replied. He remembered her addressing the envelope and dropping the blade of grass into it, an attempt, he thought, to "enter the charmed circle by playing with fire for the sake of it."[8]

Assia told Trevor that within three days she received a reply from Court Green: "beside the scrap of London grass lay one from Devon."[9] Trevor was never sure if this part of the story was true, though Hughes later wrote about it in a poem, "Chlorophyll": "She sent him a blade of grass, / but no word."[10] If Sylvia suspected that Ted had been to see Assia, she did not let on. She was cheerful during a June 28 lunch with the Comptons at Court Green, just two days after Ted had left his note for Assia. Elizabeth had no idea anything was wrong.[11]

Sylvia visited Percy Key one last time on his deathbed, and found him, as Ted put it, "a bag of bones."[12] "I was very sick at this and had a bad migraine over my left eye for the rest of the day," Sylvia wrote in her journal. "The end, even of so marginal a man, a horror."[13] Percy died on June 25. Three days later, Sylvia and Ted attended his funeral—Sylvia's first. The funeral offered a surprising respite from marital troubles; she felt the "awful" urge to grin throughout. "A relief; this is the hostage for death, we are safe for the time-being." They stood as Percy's coffin was brought to the cemetery by cart. "Heard priest meeting corpse at gate," Sylvia wrote in her journal, "incantating, coming close. Hair-raising." She felt an urge to throw dirt into the grave, but stopped herself—she did not want to hurry Percy "into oblivion." As she and Ted walked away, she felt an "unfinished feeling. Is he to be left up there uncovered, all alone? Walked home over the back hill, gathering immense stalks of fuchsia foxgloves and swinging our jackets in the heat."[14]

Details of Percy Key's funeral would find their way into Plath's art. "I have written a long poem, 'Berck-Plage' about it," she wrote in her journal. "Very moved. Several terrible glimpses."[15] The seven-part poem in unrhyming couplets, completed on June 30—the same day as Percy's funeral—merges imagery from the funeral with memories of the French seaside town Plath and Hughes had visited in 1961 on their way to the Merwins' farm. Anne Stevenson has perceptively suggested that the poem is full of images Plath associated with her father: "the sea, the maimed man, the black boot, the crutches, the dying man and mourning wife, the corpse, the burial." She argues that Plath wrote "Berck-Plage" to "create," or re-create, her own father's funeral, which she had not attended.[16] Indeed, in the final section of the poem, Plath imagines a group of children "barred" from the funeral, turning "wordless and slow" from their play:

> Their eyes opening
> On a wonderful thing—
>
> Six round black hats in the grass and a lozenge of wood,
> And a naked mouth, red and awkward.
>
> For a minute the sky pours into the hole like plasma.
> There is no hope, it is given up.

The associations in "Berck-Plage" are deeply private. Sylvia may indeed have been exorcising her own ghosts, trying to reinvent the end of Otto's story. Where "Elm" took eight days and fifteen drafts, the much longer "Berck-Plage" came quickly. In earlier drafts, Plath included a more hopeful section about the birth of her son. But she cut it from the final version.[17] By the poem's end, the "wonderful thing," the transubstantiation from flesh to soul, is impossible. The sky balks; the children turn away.

Sylvia's ability to finish "Berck-Plage," one of her longest poems, in three days suggests that she had set her worries about Ted and Assia aside. But Assia's envelope with its blade of grass, mailed sometime after June 26, likely arrived around the time of the funeral. Ted's sudden desire to intercept the morning mail, along with his other "queer" behavior, may have roused her suspicions.[18] Sylvia herself may have intercepted the letter with the blade of grass; after July 1, references to Assia's tapestry disappear from her calendar. On July 1 she wrote "novel" in her to-do list. This was probably not the celebratory sequel to *The Bell Jar* set in Cambridge, Boston, and Devon and based on her life with Ted—which she discussed with Aurelia during her visit—but the beginnings of a new, third novel about marital betrayal. There was also a dramatic shift in the tone and subject matter of Plath's poems after July 1. Her May poems "Event" and "The Rabbit Catcher" describe a couple in crisis, but no blame is apportioned. Her July 2 poem, "The Other," clearly implicates Assia. Ted himself suggested a dramatic domestic shift when he wrote to his brother Gerald on July 2 that he was gathering him-self "for a new putsch. . . . It's a good thing every ten years or so to smash your life to bits—whatever's alive in it will survive and you're well rid of the rest."[19]

Sylvia had a horror of "barren" women, and now one had seduced her husband; Assia's barrenness would become part of her mythology. In 1970, Winifred recalled, "Sylvia told me once that Assia was making a set at Ted because she wanted children. Her own husband couldn't give her any chil-dren. And that she wanted to take the children."[20] It is unlikely that Assia was attracted to Ted because she wanted to "take" his children. Nevertheless, Syl-via became fixated on Assia's history of abortion, which she may have heard about from Suzette or Ted himself. The first draft of "The Other"—written on the back page of her earlier "The Rival"—sets up a comparison between the fertile Sylvia and the barren Assia: "I am thick with babies, ribboned with milk. / You carry seven small corpses in a handbag."[21] These lines, which judge a rival severely for her abortions, complicate Plath's status as a femi-nist icon. Later drafts mention a woman in "silk" with "shoe-black hair"—clearly a reference to Assia. But Sylvia also suspected that Ted was attracted to Assia precisely because she had no children. "And now you are inserting yourself like glass / Between me & him," she writes in another draft of "The Other." Lines from earlier drafts of this poem suggest a marriage in turmoil: "Deranging my nerves, my nerves." "And you say you have feelings." "Mornings there is a pallor he cannot shake off."[22]

On July 6, Sylvia and Ted helped Elizabeth celebrate her thirty-fourth birthday. Sylvia brought a homemade cake with thirty-five candles. "'One to grow on,' she said," Elizabeth remembered. "She was chatting and laughing and saying 'I have swallows come and steal my thatch and put it in their nest.' "[23] She charmed the other couple at the party and playfully chastised Elizabeth for asking whether she had made the cake from scratch or from a packet. ("What? A packet cake? Do you really think I would? I beat those whites for a quarter of an hour. I *timed* it.")[24] But Elizabeth remembered Ted as "quiet and sullen."[25] Elizabeth and David still had no idea the couple was having problems. Back at Court Green, Aurelia had "felt tension and had shuddered under the oppressive silences during the past week," she wrote in her travel diary, but Sylvia had also, at times, seemed "almost hysterically gay."[26]

On July 9, Sylvia was relaxed and calm as she drove Aurelia to Exeter for a day of shopping. "I have everything in the world I ever dreamed and longed for—my husband, my babies, my writing," she told her mother. They had wine with their lunch at the Clarence Hotel and returned to Court Green in "high spirits."[27]

Then the phone rang. Sylvia wrote to Dr. Beuscher on July 11, "I picked up the phone & a nasty man's voice asked if Ted could take a call from London. Ted always wants me to find out who it is, so I asked, & the man said he was sorry, the person didn't want to say. I felt thick with my own dumbness & called Ted. It was a woman, saying 'Can I see you?' He said she didn't say her name & he had no idea who it was. I was pretty sure who it was." Assia Wevill. "She is very destructive—had so many abortions when she was young she only miscarries now, wants to die before she gets old, tried to kill her first husband with a knife." Sylvia claimed in this letter that Assia had been "calling for a while, for no apparent reason, seeming almost speechless when she got me." When Sylvia went to clean Ted's study, as she usually did, she found "empty envelopes in her hand lying around, dated during all the time he'd been leaping up for mail."

Ted said "No," she couldn't see him, over the phone. But I was standing there, stunned. Then the next day, after a night of no sleep & horrid talk (me asking him for god's sake to say who it was so it would stop being Everybody), he took the train to London for a "holiday." He assured me, in a flash of his old self, that me & the children were what he really loved

& would come back to & he was not going to London to lie about & had not touched another woman since we were married. I have discontinued the phone, for I can't stand waiting, every minute, to hear that girl breathing at the end of it, my voice at her fingertips, my life & happiness on her plate.[28]

Aurelia provided the only other eyewitness account: "Sylvia went to it, put the receiver to her ear and the few seconds silence led me to look over at her. Her face was ashen and she called shrilly, 'Ted!' He must have been just at the top of the stairs, probably expecting that call, for he fairly fell down in his haste to get to the phone. Sylvia dashed upstairs. From this moment on, the whole atmosphere within Court Green changed."[29] Sylvia later pulled the phone cord out of the wall. The phone would not be in working order again until November. Ted's friend, the critic Keith Sagar, thought Assia knew what she was doing. "Telephone calls—he'd never pick up the telephone." It was, he thought, a "ruthless tactic."[30] Elizabeth agreed. "That wasn't a way of contacting Ted, that was a way of destabilizing Sylvia."[31] Sylvia also told Suzette that Assia would often call pretending to be a man; Suzette said Assia's voice was naturally very deep, though "she was perfectly capable of being very devious."[32]

After Ted hung up the phone, he went upstairs to join Sylvia in their bedroom. They talked while Aurelia watched the babies. Sylvia told Suzette that when she confronted Ted, "He denied everything. . . . She ranted, she screamed, she pulled the phone from the wall. She told him to get the hell out. He got the hell out."[33] Suzette's memory dovetails with Sylvia's own description in her letter to Dr. Beuscher. Aurelia later recalled the scene with bitterness. "I had him [Nicholas] all day in my arms and I was going to leave—I wasn't going to stay in that house. I wanted them to fight it out or do whatever they wanted to do. I wanted to get off the scene and be away from the whole thing and I wanted very much to go home." Nicholas was "screaming and screaming," so she knocked on their bedroom door and asked Sylvia to take the baby while she went to dinner at Winifred's. "I opened the door and they were in bed together—not in any embarrassing position—and I just handed her Nick and I didn't even give them a good look and disappeared. And I think on the basis of that one thing she wrote that poem 'Medusa.'"[34]

The next morning, Aurelia got up early with the children and cooked them breakfast. Later, Sylvia came downstairs in her robe and made herself a cup of coffee. "She looked over toward me, her hand holding the mug shook, her lips trembled, and she then put the mug down and fled upstairs." Sylvia could no longer pretend that her life was on an ascending trajectory. Aurelia felt she should "keep out of the way," and took the children outside. She knit to "steady" her "thoughts," and hoped that she was wrong about the source of her daughter's unhappiness. "Sylvia and Ted came out and went to the far end of the vegetable garden, apparently talking earnestly. In my naivete, I thought that perhaps they had had bad news concerning some work sent out for publication." Frieda approached her parents, then ran back to Aurelia, "shaking her head, Saying 'Mummy cry; Daddy cry . . .' (omitting the 'r')."[35] Later that afternoon, Aurelia and Ted drove to the train station in silence. Hughes was leaving for London, where he would stay with Alvarez.[36] Aurelia remembered how Ted gave "a strange little laugh. 'Well, I don't know just when I'll see you again, Aurelia, but have a good time.'" Ted later told Elizabeth, a few months after Sylvia's death, that Aurelia had driven him to leave Sylvia for Assia. "My effort to get away from her [Aurelia] was a large part of my leaving Court Green last summer & starting the fire I wasn't able to put out."[37]

After Ted left, Sylvia told her mother the phone call had been from Assia Wevill, "with whom Ted had been having an affair for some time, whenever he went to London, ostensibly only on BBC engagements." Sylvia had felt "a growing change in Ted, and with this telephone call all disturbing indications, evasions, and events fell into one indisputable, shattering revelation."[38] The hurt, when it came, was a blow comparable to her father's death. "She felt that she had been thrown out of Eden," Elizabeth said.[39]

Before Assia's phone call, Sylvia's letters had been mostly pleasant and witty. Now there was anger. To the Kanes, she blamed her distress on her mother, a convenient shield. "We have been up in a heaval with my mother here (she stays way into August) as with no matter what good will & fortitude mater's [*sic*] turn to witches after a certain amount of days if left in the sun."[40] In her six-page letter to Dr. Beuscher on July 11, she mocked her "happy" letter of March 27, in which she had extolled her husband and their joy at Court Green. She had learned of Ted's affair, she wrote, and was now "at sea." "I suppose all this sounds very naive to you. It is, after all, what seems to happen to everybody. Only I am not, as Ted says, blasé enough, I care to a frenzy." She could never revenge herself by having affairs with other men, for none possessed Ted's genius and beauty.

> Ted is so fantastically unique—beautiful, physically wonderful, brilliant, loving, eager for me to do my own work, without (as I thought) a lie or deceit in his body. It is the <u>lying</u> that kills me. . . . I am sure a possessive wife would have driven most men mad before this. But I just don't have the ability to care nothing about other women chasing Ted. . . . He

seemed to want to flee all big publicity—TV & so on, & was furious when I let any cameramen into the house. But now it is different: I have been a jinx, a chain.

The thought of his being with another woman, especially one who "is dying to stop my creative work," made her "retch." "I cannot sleep. I cannot eat. . . . I keep having to run off to cry and be dry-sick as each image of that girl assaults me, and her pleasure at hearing me nonplussed on the phone, of taking my life and joy. I can't imagine a life without Ted. But I am not like other wives who tolerate all—marriage to me is a kind of sanctity, faithfulness in every part, and I will not ever be able to love or make love again in happiness, with this looming in front of me. It is his wanting to <u>deceive</u> me that is so like this girl & unlike him." She asked Beuscher, "What can I <u>do</u>?"

She refused to get a divorce. "I honestly do believe I am wedded to Ted till death. Other men seem ants compared to him. I am physically attracted to no-one else. All the complexities of my soul & mind are involved inextricably with him." She was

> simply not cool & sophisticated. My marriage is the center of my being,
> I have given everything to it without reserve. Worst, my writing is killed
> by this mess. I write, not in compensation, out of sorrow, but from an
> overflow, a surplus of joy, & my ability to criticize my work & do it well
> is my objectivity, which stems from happiness, not sorrow.

She felt such joy upon receiving the first proofs of *The Bell Jar* the day after Ted left. "It saved the day for me: I roared and roared, it was so funny and good." But she could not face the empty bed at night. She imagined Assia and Ted together, and fantasized about "breaking her nose & knocking her teeth out." Assia was "sophisticated, so mocking"—unlike her: "I break up in pieces, cry, rave. I am proud." She would not play the "part of the wronged wife," and she would be damned if Ted thought he could come home from his London trysts "refreshed" to a "wife-secretary-mother-dishwasher-housekeeper. . . . I can't be any sort of sweet homebase for stuff that makes me gag. I feel ugly and a fool, when I have so long felt beautiful & capable of being a wonderful happy mother and wife and writing novels for fun & money. I am just sick."

She knew that others would tell her to let the affair run its course, let Ted get Assia out of his system—David Compton remarked that "wife-swapping" had by then entered the consciousness of the bourgeoisie—but she couldn't.[41] "Well, what about my system? How do I get this other It out? The jealous retch, this body that comes, laughing, between my body & his body."

"To make things worse," Sylvia continued, her mother had witnessed it all. Aurelia was "a real help & I make her feel this. But you can imagine how images repeat themselves—here I am, alone with my mother & the children! I am so numb I am only glad she looks after Frieda, because I am hollow as a zombie inside & without motion." At least Aurelia was "good, doesn't pry, makes herself scarce." Sylvia implored Dr. Beuscher to write back to her. "I can talk to no-one about this—mother, of course, least of all."[42]

After Ted left, Sylvia fled to Elizabeth's house with baby Nick for a night. Elizabeth was "shocked" by her state. "She wept and gripped my hands, saying, 'Ted lies to me. He lies. He is having an affair and he has become a *little* man.' She said that she couldn't feed Nick: 'My milk has dried up.'" Elizabeth insisted that she sleep upstairs, but Sylvia slept on their sofa. She told Elizabeth, "I gave my heart to Ted. If he doesn't want it, I can't take it back. It's just gone." She said, "I cannot live without him."[43] David remembered that the two women spent most of the night in the kitchen and that he heard Sylvia weeping, "a wrung-out, reluctant, dry, ashamed sort of convulsive thing. . . . She was absolutely shattered and remained so. But it wasn't a disproportionate reaction considering what she'd put into the relationship. . . . This drive toward integrity, this drive to love, this drive to the occult, this drive to art. . . . to become bigger in every way."[44] He stayed in the background, "wary of emotionality," as Elizabeth consoled Sylvia, who kept gripping her hands and saying, "Help me!"[45]

The next morning she was somewhat calmer. "She was bending over this basket of kittens we had. 'Look at them, they're so new, they can't even see.' You'd think that nothing had happened, really, but she was very distressed."[46] She began weeping again as she left. Elizabeth begged her to stay but she would not. David was surprised that Sylvia had come to Elizabeth instead of seeking support from her own mother back at Court Green and felt that the gesture spoke to the increasingly dysfunctional relationship between Sylvia and Aurelia. Winifred, too, remembered Sylvia's distress during this time. "Frieda was in her bed and Sylvia didn't just cry quietly. She used to open her mouth and howl as a child would howl. Poor Frieda was terrified."[47] The week of July 9 is uncharacteristically bare in Plath's 1962 calendar.

Sylvia wrote to Clarissa Roche on July 11 asking her to come to Court Green, saying that Aurelia had arrived "out of the blue," which was false, and that "things are hectic." "I get homesick for you just writing to you."[48] Plath also wrote a poem on this day: "Words heard, by accident, over the phone." ("Speak, speak! Who is it?") Meanwhile, Suzette had gotten wind of the developments. When Assia learned that Ted had left Court Green, she called Suzette, who remembered her saying, "'Disaster . . . she has thrown him out . . . and it's terrible . . . and he is pushing me to leave David and I don't want to. I'm not going to leave David.' "[49] Assia asked Suzette and Helder to come meet her, her husband David, Ted, and Al Alvarez at a local London pub one night that July. When Suzette arrived, she found Ted "looking absolutely black," standing at the counter with Al. The Wevills, Ted, and the Macedos then went to a party at Nathaniel Tarn's "palatial" house in Hampstead. On the way to the party, Ted sang a mournful Irish ballad, "The Brown and Yellow Ale," about a husband who lies down and dies because of his wife's unfaithfulness. Helder noticed the "current" between Ted and Assia that night.[50] Indeed, Assia seemed to enjoy playing Ted and David off against each other. "These people were in an extreme state of tension with each other," Edward Lucie-Smith said, speaking of the larger "network" that included the Wevills, the Hugheses, the Macedos, Al Alvarez, and the Merwins.[51] Helder Macedo agreed, adding that "Ted was himself in crisis. . . . they all behaved very extremely—in destructive ways, self-destructive and otherwise."[52]

Suzette phoned Sylvia in late October or early November, when the phone had been reinstalled at Court Green. Sylvia was angry, and hung up on her. Suzette called again, and this time Sylvia stayed on the line. "And she said, 'What are you phoning for? You're *her* friend.'" Suzette said, "Sylvia, just stop. I can't help it if I'm a friend of Assia's." She told Sylvia she was concerned about her. "She was in a terrible state." Suzette asked her to come stay, which she did, in early November. Sylvia spoke of how she had come to realize that Ted was having an affair: "She'd known it from the beginning, when she saw them in the kitchen when they were supposed to have been peeling potatoes. . . . She knew it was rubbish that he was going for the BBC," she said. When he returned to Court Green from London, Sylvia told Suzette, he "smelled different." Sylvia said she ransacked Ted's study and burned his papers, and that the name "Assia" came out of the flames—and that was how she knew. It was the sort of story she liked to tell, Suzette said. She could be dramatic, like Assia, that way.[53] Sylvia had also found love poems written to Assia in Ted's study.

Aurelia claimed that Sylvia also burned the new version of her unpublished *Bell Jar* sequel (likely based on drafts of *Falcon Yard*), parts of which Sylvia had read to her out loud that June. Aurelia had come into the living room during her first night at Court Green to find her daughter sitting in "her favorite chair, by the fireplace." She was editing some pages in her hand.

> As I sat down opposite her, she announced excitedly, "I have written two novels, mother; one is complete [*The Bell Jar*] and one almost done in first draft, and a third planned in my head." She scowled for a moment, quickly made a note on the page she apparently had been reading, then looked at me and continued with a note of triumph in her voice. "This

second one I'll show to Ted as a birthday surprise; he's the 'hero' and it's dedicated to him." Smilingly she held up a page with just the words "To Ponter" neatly centered on it. "It's autobiographically based, more or less—facts serve Art, you know."

From her answers to my questions, I learned that this novel was woven about her student life at the University of Cambridge, her romance and marriage, the combination of married life and teaching at Smith, the Beacon Hill year following, the return to England—all ending with the birth of Frieda. "I feel I have been living a series of novels, really, and this is, so far, the most exciting part." She paused, then added, slowly and thoughtfully, "It is Life seen through the eyes of health,"—a statement I did not fully understand until after her death and after my reading of *The Bell Jar*.[54]

Sylvia began reading Aurelia "parts at random" until Nick began to cry. Sylvia went upstairs to tend to him and never mentioned the novel again to Aurelia until the day, shortly after Assia's phone call, when she stood "helplessly in the doorway" of Court Green and watched her daughter "furiously" tear apart the thick manuscript: "piece by piece she burned this sequel to *The Bell Jar* in a blazing bonfire she had built at the end of the cobbled courtyard. . . . Later that night I brought up the subject of the destruction. All Sylvia would say was that the manuscript had symbolized a period of joy that now proved to have been built on false trust—the character of the hero was dead to her—this had been his funeral pyre."[55]

———

THAT SUMMER, Ted wrote to Olwyn, his fiercest protector, with the "Grave news" of the separation. Since April, the marriage and Court Green had seemed a "dead-end":

So I blew up—very mildly—and went on the spree, but that was no substitute for the real thing, which is to go & live where I like alone, working uninterruptedly, choosing my friends as I please & seeing them as often as I like, & generally changing myself without the terrible censorship of somebody like Sylvia confining my every impulse & inclination. . . . I came awake, & find myself in the old folks' home. And I have come awake. I know in rough outline what I want, I feel it's in my power, & the 10,000 desires which in a gentlemanly considerate way I've repressed for 6 years have suddenly appeared in full bloom, absolutely insatiable. So, I'll give Sylvia the house, the car, & and send her cash. The less I own, the better. I shall live in London till December, because I have numerous engagements to read etc, then I shall go to Germany, live there till I speak fluent German, then Italy, till I speak fluent Italian, & so on. My centre of gravity has suddenly become internal, so I need no outer guidance or stabiliser. Besides, I've suddenly acquired, along with the rest—a great power to work along purposeful lines. I don't know what will happen. Sylvia has more or less helped—refusing to have me near the place, since I became so sinful. She made some terrible mistakes, and I let her make them.

But it seems insane to me that I shouldn't try to make something of myself & my life. And the only things that change me are situations & relationships & a fairly emotional carry-on—not this tepid routine of reading & sinking back into the family circle. I would like to be at least one English person of my generation that will have broken the shell—I'm so sick of the sight & sound of them.[56]

He felt as if he were suffocating with Sylvia under her bell jar. His only alternative was "suicide by wishy-washiness." He would work to fulfill his promise; he would not become a drifter. He was writing more than ever: "I seem to thrive on upset." Nicholas, only about six months old, was still "quite strange" to him, but he worried about living without Frieda—"a problem," he wrote. As for his wife: "Sylvia's tough, she'll be O. K."[57]

On July 10, the day after Assia's phone call, Ted "dropped in" on the Wevills at his old Chalcot Square flat carrying four bottles of champagne.[58] He said it was his birthday, though it was not. When David left to buy cigarettes, Ted told Assia he was leaving Sylvia and that he wanted to spend the next day with her. Assia agreed, and the two spent the afternoon of July 11 at Al Alvarez's flat.[59] After that first night, Assia told Nathaniel Tarn that Ted was "very virile, 'does things a man does,' decides etc. everything D. has stopped doing."[60]

Assia returned to Chalcot Square later that afternoon, where she met David. The two of them joined Alvarez for drinks in the pub. Tarn noted that Alvarez had by this time "guessed about" Hughes, who had told him "he has left S[ylvia] & is in love." Ted spent the night at Al's flat, oblivious of his friend's feelings for Assia. Two days later, on Friday the 13th, Ted took Assia to the Ritz, where, Assia told Suzette, she ordered champagne and peaches to mark the beginning of the love affair. Assia told Nathaniel he made "violent & animal" love to her: "he ruptures her. A. turns against him, goes quite cold." Assia phoned Suzette on the Sunday after their "tryst" and asked to meet at the Cosmo Restaurant. "She had expected peaches and champagne but Ted had ripped the nightgown off her . . . she had been really frightened by his physicality," Suzette remembered. Sylvia, she noted, "could handle it." Assia told Suzette she never wanted to see Ted again and spoke of her husband's gentleness. Suzette remembered that though Assia sounded "horrified" as she told the story, "it was as if there was something there she needed and wanted."[61] Sylvia would hear about all of it. Her London friend Jillian Becker said, "she lamented to me that his need to sin in such luxurious settings—The Ritz, the shores of the Mediterranean—so depleted their joint bank account."[62]

David Wevill could no longer contain his rage. Tarn recorded that when Assia told David, that night, that she was seeing Ted off at the station, he grabbed a knife and walked toward Waterloo. But he turned back and returned to the Chalcot Square flat, where, in despair, he swallowed eighteen sleeping pills. When Assia arrived back at the flat at twelve thirty, she found him half conscious. She was terrified, and, at the same time, struck by how young and sweet he looked in contrast to "fierce H." She woke him and told him Hughes had raped her. An ambulance brought them to the hospital, where his stomach was pumped. "She walks him around all night," Tarn wrote. "They leave. She sees him again in afternoon. He still wants to kill H. Doctors quiet him down. D. writes to H. 'if you come near my wife again I will kill you. D. W.'" (Assia also told her colleague Julia Matcham about David's suicide attempt, and Sylvia spoke of these events in letters to her mother.) When Assia told Ted that David had tried to kill himself, Ted let out a groan, "says he [David] was straightest man in the world," Tarn wrote.

According to Tarn's July 19 journal entry, Ted told Assia that Sylvia had "been having hysterics, child also."[63] Ted also told her Sylvia had crashed her car and ordered him to send back the Wevills' dining room table. Tarn's journal suggests that Plath drove her Morris Traveller off the road into a nearby clearing in mid-July. Hughes later told Alvarez that Plath had "blacked out" while driving and that the accident was minor. But he was troubled by the event, Alvarez recalled. "His dark presence, as he spoke, darkened an even deeper shade of gloom."[64] Alvarez said Plath told him in autumn 1962 that the accident had been a suicide attempt.

> It had been no accident; she had gone off the road deliberately, seriously, wanting to die. But she hadn't, and all that was now in the past.... The car crash was a death she had survived.... there was neither hysteria in her voice, nor any appeal for sympathy. She talked about suicide in much the same tone as she talked about any other risky, testing activity: urgently, even fiercely, but altogether without self-pity. She seemed to view death as a physical challenge she had, once again, overcome.[65]

Still, Hughes's claim that the accident was partly caused by a feverish black-out seems plausible, especially as the site of the crash was a flat airfield where local adolescents learned how to drive. Nancy Axworthy, Elizabeth Compton, and Winifred Davies had no memory of this event. Sylvia herself told Suzette Macedo, in late summer, that "she had got into the car in a black mood and found herself driving it straight into a tree. . . . it was not a conscious attempt at suicide but a blind destructive urge over which she had no conscious control. . . . She said she had cried for hours afterwards."[66]

Assia told Nathaniel that David's meekness made her long again for Ted, but she decided to stay with her husband "until he can get back on his feet properly." Assia thought that Ted was going to stay with Sylvia; she told him she didn't want "a slinky affair in London."[67] But David was not so sure, and he contemplated living in Portugal. Assia felt they had reached an impasse—David wanted children, she told Nathaniel, while she wanted to "keep independence" and have a career.

Nathaniel had lunch with David near the end of July and tried to counsel him "about keeping on top of one's woman." He thought that David had a "completely mythical view of his marriage & this will blow up in his face one day." Nathaniel was beginning to feel overwhelmed by the love quadrangle—Ted, Assia, Al, David—and vowed to stop attending the Group. The gossip was simply too much; Assia, he wrote, had told him "a whole stack of lies about the [Peter] Porter & [Peter] Redgrove party." David was equally tired of gossip and also vowed to stop attending. Alvarez, meanwhile, was, in Tarn's words, "cashing in on all this." Assia told Nathaniel that Al proposed marriage to her in July. She refused, though she thought him "rather sweet." Tarn noted that Alvarez retaliated by publishing a column of poems in *The Observer* on August 5, "starting with Sylvia, then Ted, then, immediately under this, a good Wevill poem about cuckolds! A fine piece of family history."[68]

———

AURELIA HAD MOVED INTO Winifred Davies's house in mid-July, a week after Assia's phone call. Ted had wanted her to stay at Court Green, but she knew the couple needed space. He had returned from London by then. Aurelia told Warren that Ted and Sylvia "must work out their problems—not new but erupted afresh from a touching off of incidents." Aurelia's comment suggests that the marriage was already in distress before the Wevills' May visit, and that Sylvia had confided in her about those troubles. "Sivvy has taken on too much again. Well, I gather this isn't the first time—so that's that." She signed off sadly. "I hate writing all this—I am just holding on to my belief that we each have to live out our many lives in as much dignity & carefulness as possible."[69] Winifred remembered that Sylvia spoke to her about Ted and Assia during this time but that she never "referred to suicide nor breakdown." Nor did Sylvia "express strong anger," only sadness. "I didn't get the impression that Sylvia was self-pitying."[70] But her behavior became more erratic. She lost track of time. "She'd ask you to dinner at seven and she wouldn't have even started to cook it when you arrived."[71] Winifred's son would wait four hours for lunch when he visited Sylvia in London that winter.

Sylvia leaned on female friends like Elizabeth Compton and Sylvia Crawford, but kept her earlier commitment to accompany Ted to Bangor, Wales, during the last week of July to give a poetry reading for the *Critical Quarterly*. They spent a night en route with Daniel and Helga Huws at their home near Aberystwyth. (Daniel was now working at the National Library of Wales.) Sylvia and Helga had a long conversation in Helga's bedroom, where Sylvia "unburdened." She was angry about Assia, "in turmoil" and seeking "consolation."[72] Neither Sylvia nor Ted expressed a wish to separate to the Huwses, who thought the affair a typical marital difficulty they would work through. Tony Dyson and Brian Cox took them out to dinner in Anglesey the night before the reading. "At first they seemed strained, but as the red wine flowed we all relaxed, and the laughter and conviviality of our earlier dinners were restored."[73] But the bad feelings returned at the reading, where, Sylvia told Dr. Beuscher, she saw Ted eyeing a young blond secretary.

In her three July letters to Dr. Beuscher, Sylvia wondered if she had been too possessive. She had always been terrified something would happen to Ted and had never wanted him to leave her alone in Devon. She now questioned her former assumption that "We would experience Everything together. . . . both of us must have been pretty weird to live as we have done for so long." And she admitted, "any husband of mine would have a large flow of my feeling for my father to complicate our relationship."[74] She did not want Ted to see her as a "puritanical warden." She still thought about having two more children with him—though he did not want any more—and mentioned that he wanted to "hire a live-in nanny to free me."[75]

At least he had finally revealed the identity of the "femme fatale": Assia Wevill, whom Sylvia dubbed "Weavy Asshole" to Dr. Beuscher. She had known it was Assia, of course, but to hear Ted confirm her suspicions at last was freeing. "It was very like the old shock treatments I used to fear so: it broke a tight circuit wide open, a destructive circuit, a deadening circuit, & let in a lot of pain, air and real elation. I feel very elated." She had been in "wild agony," but now that she knew it was Assia, she felt less threatened. "I didn't die. I thought my capacity for conventional joy & trust & love was killed, but it wasn't. It is all back." Ted had told her that Assia "wasn't very sensual." Moreover, Sylvia wrote Beuscher, "she can't make a baby (and really isn't so sorry), can't make a poem, just ads about bad bakery bread, wants to die before she gets old and loses her beauty, and is <u>bored</u>. Bored, bored, bored."[76] Plath felt herself intellectually and sexually superior:

> One thing about sex. I hate comfortable rituals. I like all sorts of positions at a lot of odd times of day, & really feel terrific and made new from every cell when I am done. I actually wondered at one point if Ted was sick. Well, of course, how can one keep up that intensity & variety every day & night for over 6 years. A biological and psychological impossibility I would think. And I have my pride. I mean, I was not schooled with love for 2 years by my French lover for nothing. I have in me a good tart, as distinct from a bad tart: I feel all I feel, which is a lot, & which I think men like to feel they can do, and I do not need to pretend I feel, or to feel only in my head. Well I want this tart to have a good life again. I'm damned if I'm going to be a Wife-mother every minute of the day. And as I am a pretty faithful type, and have no desire left for malice or revenge on Ted, to "get back at him," I'd just as soon make love with Ted. But coming from a distance, from a space, a mutual independence.[77]

Despite Plath's open and mature attitude, notable in the age before second-wave feminism, she admitted that the thought of her husband with other women "nauseates me horribly." How could she feel joy making love to him knowing that he was "registering them under my name in hotels"? She mocked her homey gestures of love—"baking bread, making pies, painting furniture"—as "silly and empty" now. And she could barely tolerate Aurelia's presence. "I think in one way she hates me for having deprived her of her vicarious dream-idyll, and in one way she is viciously glad: 'I <u>knew</u> men were like that,' I feel her thinking. 'Horrid, selfish bastards, just like my husband. And Sylvia thought hers was an exception!' It has been humiliating for me to have her here through this."[78]

Above all, she hated her new status as the wronged woman. "I realise now he considered I might kill myself over this . . . and what he did was worth it to him. I have always admired him for this inner pride and energy—most people just haven't got the power in them. But I would like to break my life, & go ahead with him, not be relegated to the homefront: the suffering & pitied but very repugnant mother-wife."[79] Ted had told her he had been faithful to her before Assia, but this was little consolation:

Am I to cheer him off onto one infatuation after another now? I have too much pride to say: O please God, it kills me to think of all these other women knowing you and your body and laughing at me, doing the dishes & wiping noses in Devon. My other impulse is to say: O fuck off, grab them all. What seems civilized & sophisticated to the people we move among seems stupid and boring and selfish to me. Am I an idiot to think that there is some purpose in being bodily faithful to the person you love? . . . I simply can't laugh and blow smoke-rings.[80]

Ted, she told Beuscher, was "handsome & fantastically virile & attractive. I am not beautiful." She thought he still loved her, "in a way," but she wondered how she could make "these women <u>unnecessary</u> to him. . . . I don't want to be sorrowful or bitter, men hate that, but what can I do in the face of these prospects? . . . I want Ted to understand I am not a doll-wife who can be lied to & kept happy. . . . What I am <u>not</u> is a Penelope type."[81] She had begun to love living in North Tawton, but Ted had told her "freedom" to him meant travel. She understood, in a way.

I am damned if I want to sit here like a cow, milked by babies. I love my children, but want my own life. I want to write books, see people & travel. . . . I refuse the role of passive, suffering wife. . . . I get a terrific sensual pleasure in being pregnant & nursing. But I must say, I get a terrific sensual pleasure in being light & slender & fucking as well. . . . What I don't want to be is an unfucked wife. I get bitter then, & cross. And I feel wasted. And I don't just mean the token American what-is-it twice a week, front to front, "thank you darling" either.[82]

There were no other men she admired intellectually or physically "in cow country." She was "a feeling & imaginative lay, & probably can write quite funny & good books." This letter, and others like it, reveal how brave and self-aware Plath truly was; her evolved attitude toward her own sexuality and desire is especially remarkable for someone who had come of age in 1950s America.

Ted trading her and the children in for "a better family model" would be, she told Beuscher, "the real worst." Sylvia told him she had saved him from "ever getting mucked up with a wife & children again. . . . And he does genuinely love us. He says now he dimly thought this would either kill me or make me, and I think it might make me. And him too." She still thought he was a "genius" and a "great man."[83] She found it "funny" that he was working on a radio play called *Difficulties of a Bridegroom*, about his encounter with a "dream femme fatale."[84] She asked Dr. Beuscher in her July letters to bill her, as she needed her counsel now more than ever. What should she do when Ted made passes at a woman at a party? "Smile & vanish? Smile & stand by? What I don't want to be is stern & disapproving or teary. But I am only human."[85] She considered flying to America to see Dr. Beuscher in person, but she felt she could not afford it. Beuscher, for her part, never formalized a long-distance doctor-patient arrangement with Plath. Indeed, she dismissed the paid session idea.

On July 21, the day after she wrote the searing "Poppies in July," Plath contacted Alvarez to ask if he had made a decision about three new poems she hoped he would publish in *The Observer*: "Event," "The Rabbit Catcher," and "Elm." Her accompanying letter was brusque but confident. "I like your opinions. I don't mean, agree. But like. And I am tough enough, so don't be ginger. I'd be grateful to have a whole No, or whatever, soon, because I need to flog round what I've got. Money money. You know. Please don't be 'nice.' "[86] By now Plath had probably read Alvarez's polemical essay, "Beyond the Gentility Principle," in his controversial 1962 anthology, *The New Poetry*.[87] In the now-famous introduction, Alvarez argued that gentility had achieved a stranglehold on British art and life. Plath's brusque tone reflected Alvarez's sentiment; she, too, was done being "nice." She signed the card, "Love, Sylvia," a term of endearment she normally reserved for family and close friends, not poetry editors. Alvarez, who replied three days later, responded in kind. "They seem to me the best things you've ever done. By a long way." He thought "The Rabbit Catcher" "flawless," and told her, "The last half of 'Elm' is superb." He promised to persuade *The Observer* to take all three. He signed off warmly. "Again: I think these poems very fine. Love, Al."[88]

On the same day she contacted Alvarez, she wrote to the Anglo-Irish poet Richard Murphy to tell him that the epilogue of his poem "The Cleggan Disaster" had won first prize in the Cheltenham contest she had helped judge that year.[89] Her decision to contact two eligible literary men the day after she had written to Dr. Beuscher about creating a new life for herself seems more than coincidental. But her request to Murphy was also about healing. She asked him if she and Ted could visit him in Ireland in late August or early September. "I desperately need a boat and the sea and no squalling babies. . . . The center of my whole early life was ocean and boats."[90] She had known the truth about Assia for less than two weeks, but she was already contemplating a reconciliation with Ted in Ireland. Her July letters to Dr. Beuscher, angry as they are, show that she wanted the marriage to survive.

Aurelia left Court Green on August 4. Sylvia and Ted drove her to the station with the children. They had not resolved their marital problems, and Aurelia suspected that her presence over the past six weeks had made things worse. Elizabeth remembered, "She didn't want to upset her mother. She was impatient with her, I think. I understood because my father left us with very little and I remember the desire to protect my mother, and it did annoy me, and you felt very sorry, but also impatient. We both felt that about our mothers."[91] Winifred was kind to Aurelia but had found her, that summer, "so precise and time-tabley." In later years Aurelia would complain to Winifred that Frieda was not being "stretched enough at school." Winifred remarked, "I think she would have pushed. And I wonder whether she pushed Sylvia too much like a piece of elastic that never got a chance of going back again and being herself. And committing suicide"—the attempt in 1953—"was a sort of rebellion against being stretched too far. You've just got to break at some stage."[92] Clarissa Roche had a different view: "It was her mother who nursed her through the impossible summer of 1962 and restored order in her life, perhaps restored life itself."[93]

Three weeks after Aurelia returned to America, Sylvia would write to her full of apologies. "I can never say how sorry I am you did not have the lovely reveling and rest I meant you to have."[94] But that day at the station, baby Nick was the only one who smiled. As the train pulled away, Aurelia locked eyes on her daughter, who returned her gaze "stonily."[95] They never saw each other again.

30

But Not the End

Devon and Ireland, August–September 1962

Three days after Aurelia left Court Green, Sylvia traveled to the nearby town of Crediton to seek legal counsel regarding a separation from Ted. A new financial arrangement was on her mind—she wrote notes regarding checking accounts and tax statements in her calendar—and she set up horseback riding lessons with her new friend Joan Webb, the doctor's wife. In riding she would find a metaphor of motion that would propel some of her best poems. She was trying to wrest back control of her life.

On August 9 she went to London to record "The Surgeon at 2 a.m." for the BBC's *The Poet's Voice*. (Ted had returned to care for the children in her absence.) Ideas began to coalesce in London, away from Hughes. On August 10, she wrote in her calendar, "Start Int. loaf!!!"—a reference to her third novel, which she would start later that summer and first titled *The Interminable Loaf*, then *Doubletake*, and finally, according to Hughes, *Double Exposure*.[1] It would chronicle the dissolution of her marriage. The 130-page draft (or partial draft) of this book, like most of Sylvia's late journals, disappeared after her death—though not before Assia, Olwyn, and possibly Ted had read it. Ted may have destroyed it, as Assia wished him to; it may have burned in a 1971 fire at his Yorkshire home, Lumb Bank; or it may have been taken. Alvarez said Plath told him she was "deeply involved" in it during the fall of 1962 and that it "was the real stuff." He remembered hearing that she had shown seven chapters to her Heinemann editor.[2]

In London, Sylvia saw Marvin and Kathy Kane, who had recently been threatened with eviction. Seizing the opportunity, she offered them free rent at Court Green for six weeks in exchange for help with child care and cooking. Ted picked them up at the station on August 13. The Kanes lived in

the guest room and were, Sylvia thought, "fantastically neurotic." She told
Aurelia she had "grave doubts as to their staying power."[3] Marvin Kane, for
his part, felt the tension in the house and thought that the children had
"absorbed this unhappy atmosphere. . . . They weren't docile." Sylvia had
difficulty with Frieda, especially, who was in a "highly charged state." He and
Kathy felt "uncomfortable" around the couple, though Marvin found Ted on
his own "extremely pleasant to be with. . . . He emanated a sense of stillness
and peace."[4] Ted did not confide in Marvin about his marital difficulties, and
Marvin did not probe. But Sylvia, full of anger and sorrow, opened up to him
about the rift.

Sylvia left the Kanes in charge while she and Ted went up to London on
August 15 to see Mrs. Prouty, who treated them to dinner, Agatha Christie's
The Mousetrap, and a night at the posh Connaught Hotel. The two played the
part of a loving married couple; Mrs. Prouty told Aurelia that Sylvia looked
"so pretty—& Ted—handsome."[5] This charade initiated a thaw. Sylvia later
told Dr. Beuscher in a September 22 letter, "I never had such good loving, felt it was the consecration of our new life."[6] The couple breakfasted in
bed together, but when Ted emerged from the bath, dressed, "with a funny
pleased smile," he told her he was going out for a drink with some friends.
Sylvia assumed that she would join him, but he told her to "go home on the
next train." She soon heard "by accident" that the affair was not over and he
was going to see Assia.[7] To Mrs. Prouty she wrote that September, "I will
remember it as the last happy night with Ted, now happiness, the word, has
ceased to have meaning for me."[8]

Richard Murphy wrote in mid-August, inviting Sylvia and Ted to Connemara in September. Sylvia imbued the trip with promise. "I simply must go
to Ireland and sail for a week," she replied. "I don't know when I've looked
so forward to anything. I am sick of the bloody British sea with its toffee
wrappers & trippers in pink plastic macs bobbing in the shallows, and cara-
vans piled one on top of the other like enamel coffins."[9] The trip was to be a
reprisal of her American summers; a final chance to right the marriage.

On August 25, the Canadian poet and critic John Malcolm Brinnin called
on Court Green during a driving tour of Devon with his partner, Bill Reid.
Brinnin, who had met Plath and Hughes in Boston, had been the director of
New York's 92nd Street Y Poetry Center until 1956; he wanted to include
Plath and Hughes in a poetry anthology, *The Modern Poets*, which he was
editing. He also wanted Hughes to replace him for a year at the University
of Connecticut while he went on teaching leave. Brinnin spoke to Hughes
about the anthology and the job offer. He spoke, too, about his recent visit
to a morgue.[10] Plath and the children were present in the room, and Hughes

told Brinnin they needed to discuss the matter outside. Brinnin later told Peter Davison, "Ted said he couldn't think about accepting any offer until certain matters (unspecified) in his life had been resolved."[11]

Plath would base the two characters in her mid-November poem "Death & Co.," which included imagery of dead babies "in their hospital / Icebox," on Brinnin and Reid. The poem portrays the couple as devilish harbingers of death. Plath blamed Brinnin for Dylan Thomas's death, as Brinnin had brought Thomas to the United States on the four-year tour that culminated in his demise.[12] This fact, combined with her own recent car crash and Brinnin's talk of morgues, made him a model for her emissary of doom.[13] Hughes thought her reasons were more personal. Plath, he said, was "outraged" that Brinnin had tried to hire Hughes, despite the fact that the job offer was "lucrative." "She regarded it as an attempt to sabotage our experiment"— their creative marriage and writerly life at Court Green.[14]

By late August, Sylvia had come down with the flu and was rapidly losing weight. Ted stayed in London during the week while the Kanes nursed Sylvia at Court Green. On August 27, Sylvia told Aurelia she'd had enough.

> I hope you will not be too surprised or shocked when I say I am going to try to get a legal separation from Ted. I do not believe in divorce and would never think of this, but I simply cannot go on living the degraded and agonized life I have been living, which has stopped my writing and just about ruined my sleep and my health. I thought I would take almost anything to give the children an illusion of home life, but I feel a father who is a liar and an adulterer and utterly selfish and irresponsible is worse than the absence of a father, and I cannot spend the best years of my life waiting week after week for the chance returns of someone like this. What is saddest is that Ted has it in him to be kind and true and loving but has just chosen not to be. . . . I have too much at stake and am too rich a person to live as a martyr to such stupidity and heartlessness. I want a clean break, so I can breathe and laugh and enjoy myself again.[15]

Sylvia was heartbroken, but she was also clear-eyed and self-aware enough to fight for her independence. She believed in her ability to rebuild her life, for she had already risen from the ashes, Lazarus-like, in 1953. She would do it again. She wrote what must have been a difficult letter to Edith Hughes revealing "Ted's desertion," "& his utter faithlessness & irresponsibility," though she assured Ted's family that she "deeply" loved them.[16]

Plath finished only one poem that August, "Burning the Letters," about a ritual bonfire she had made of Hughes's manuscripts and the name— Assia's—that had supposedly floated above the charred papers:

And here is an end to the writing,
The spry hooks that bend and cringe, and the smiles, the smiles.
And at least it will be a good place now, the attic.
At least I won't be strung just under the surface,
Dumb fish . . .

Her "love" now has "nothing to say to anybody. / I have seen to that."

After Plath's death, Hughes told others Plath had been practicing "witch-craft" that fall.[17] Suzette, who saw Sylvia mainly in London in December and January, claimed Sylvia believed in "the supernatural."[18] But in Devon, Elizabeth said Sylvia "never talked about astrology . . . psychic powers, receiving signs." She made a "passing historical reference" to tarot, nothing more.[19] Clarissa Roche remembered Sylvia had told her the bonfire story "as a big, big joke," while laughing.[20] David Compton said the real story was much less dramatic—Sylvia was simply cleaning out the fireplace and randomly saw a piece of "charred paper" with Assia's name on it.[21] (Presumably, then, Ted had tried to destroy Assia's letters.) But whenever Sylvia told this story, she added, with absolute sincerity, "Truth loves me."[22] Indeed, she tacked a Stevie Smith poem, "Magna Est Veritas" (Great Is Truth), above her desk that fall:

With my looks I am bound to look simple or fast I would rather look
    simple
So I wear a tall hat on the back of my head that is rather a temple
And I walk rather queerly and comb my long hair
And people say, Don't bother about her.

The poem's speaker says that she has picked up more facts over time than the people in "smart hats" and does not "deceive" because she is "simple." Smith ends the poem, "Great is Truth and will prevail in a bit."[23] This poem seems to have become a self-help mantra: Plath likely imagined herself as the honest, "simple" woman, Assia and Ted the deceptive ones in "smart hats."

In "Burning the Letters," Plath's poetic speaker sounds strong and satisfied, but the real bonfire suggests rage and powerlessness. Without Hughes's ballast, Plath's career prospects and social position wobbled. She worried about the stigma of a broken home. Her next poem, "For a Fatherless Son" in late September, was an elegy for the lost family: "One day you may touch what's wrong / The small skulls, the smashed blue hills, the godawful hush." Though she would have been cheered by the BBC broadcast of *Three Women* on August 19, her letters around this time reveal a penchant for black humor. She sent George MacBeth two poems for inclusion in his *Penguin Book of Sick*

Verse, "In case they strike you as being darker than my other darks, sicker than the old sicks."[24]

She considered closing Court Green in November, moving to Spain, and renting a villa through March. "I have just recovered from a bad bout of flu, which the babies caught too, and my weight has dropped after this worrisome summer, and I do not think it wise to try to undergo another English winter just now," she told Aurelia.[25] She wrote similarly to Ruth Fainlight. Ted, she said, "will set us up for 3 months in Spain this winter," near Málaga, where his friend Ben Sonnenberg lived. Hughes still had to take up the Maugham grant, she explained, "so this is an excuse to do it." She asked Ruth, who was living in Morocco, to give her practical advice about traveling by car with children: "What route did you take, where stay, did you reserve ahead, etc. etc. Ted never will make a plan till the day ahead, but I would like to know what I can expect. Are there Paddipads [diapers] in Spain. Strained babyfoods? Is there a God? Where is Franco?" She fantasized about meeting Ruth in Spain and arranging playdates for their little boys. Nick, she wrote, "is gorgeous now. . . . I adore him." She hoped that it would be easier to find a nanny there, as it was "almost impossible" in Devon. "Have a 2nd novel I'm dying to write [*Double Exposure*] and no time. Which I suppose is better than lots of time & no novel." She signed off, "please write," and enclosed a copy of "Elm" dedicated to Ruth.[26] Sylvia did not mention her looming separation in her light and chummy letter. She may have hoped that she and Ted could return to each other in the place they had honeymooned, far from Devon's gray skies.

The late-summer weather was "ghastly—nothing but rain."[27] Sylvia had her first riding lesson at a stable near Okehampton in late August on an older, plodding mare named Ariel.[28] She would come to love her riding lessons, her bees, and her honey ("delectable stuff"). These activities made her feel capable again. She tried to exude confidence in her letters home: "I love you all very much and am in need of nothing, and am desirous of nothing but staying in this friendly town & my beautiful home with my dear children." Once she had a live-in nanny, she said, she would be able to "lead a freer life."[29]

As for money, they were barely scraping by, living on the last of her Saxton grant and piecemeal BBC and poetry earnings. Ted had been withdrawing cash from their account since early July; Sylvia assumed that he was wining and dining women on his London jaunts.[30] She retaliated by taking out a £173 life insurance policy on Ted on August 22, leaving them with only £10 in their British checking account.[31] Hughes began borrowing money from the Kanes, who by late August had had enough of Court Green and decamped to Cornwall. "They took over the day we were in London and it nearly killed them," Sylvia wrote Aurelia. She now had no one to watch the children while she and Ted were in Ireland and would have to hire someone. She planned to renovate a small cottage in her yard for a live-in nanny. "A business arrangement, with money paid, is the only thing I can count on," she told Aurelia.[32]

Not all the news was grim. Plath took great pleasure in a letter from Anne Sexton that included her new collection *All My Pretty Ones*. "I was absolutely stunned and delighted with the new book," she told Sexton. "It is superbly masterful, womanly in the greatest sense, and so blessedly <u>unliterary</u>. One of the rare original things in this world one comes upon." She had thought to buy Sexton's book the day before, and was amazed to find it in the mail that very morning.

Plath singled out "The Black Art" as her favorite and also praised "Letter Written During a January Northeaster," "Letter Written on a Ferry While Crossing Long Island Sound," "Water," "Woman with Girdle," "Old," "For God While Sleeping," and "Lament." Sexton's letter made Plath nostalgic for Boston, and she became hungry for details about the road not taken. What was it like to be a "Lady Poet Laureate"? Had the Radcliffe grant freed her from the "drudge of housework"? How were Maxine Kumin and George Starbuck? Who did she "see, know, now"? Sylvia did not mention Ted in the short letter, just Frieda and Nicholas, and "keeping bees and raising potatoes and doing broadcasts off and on for the BBC." Sexton had already beaten her to a second poetry publication, and Plath felt no need to admit her marriage's failure. If she was jealous, she didn't let on. "More power to you, although you seem to need nothing—it is all there."[33]

All My Pretty Ones arrived at an auspicious time. Plath was poised to make a break with her husband, which would coincide with a new style of writing that would be, like Sexton's, "womanly" and "unliterary." Plath wanted to shed what remained of her formalist tics and write about vital experience—especially women's experience. She recognized Sexton as a pioneer and fellow traveler. Her themes fascinated Plath: hospital stays, transcendence, the yearning for death, Icarian flight, birth, babies, maternal anxiety, abortion, atheism, doubles, mother anger. Indeed, some of Sexton's phrases could have been written by Plath: "I soar in hostile air / over the pure women in labor"; "My nurses, those starchy ghosts"; "Now you rise, / a city from the sea." Sexton's "The Starry Night" would influence "Ariel," while Plath's "pure acetylene / Virgin" rising up to "Paradise" in "Fever 103°" owes something to the nuns in Sexton's "Letter Written on a Ferry While Crossing Long Island Sound."

Disparate influences coalesced: Plath's break with Hughes and desire for personal rebirth coincided with a growing interest in Alvarez's polemic against gentility in *The New Poetry* and the arrival of *All My Pretty Ones* on her doorstep. Alvarez's essay and Sexton's verse emboldened her to push her voice to extremities, as Hughes himself had, ironically, encouraged her to do. Plath knew that Lowell, the most important contemporary American poet, favored Sexton's verse, and that Sexton had won a prestigious grant from Radcliffe. The evidence, which Plath would have weighed shrewdly, suggested that Alvarez was right: the most exciting American poetry was not by the "Elegant Academicians," as she had once called them. Not Wilbur, Merwin, Stevens, or Moore, but Lowell, Snodgrass, and Sexton. Sexton pulled Plath closer to the short lines, quick cadences, and bursts of *Ariel*. Ten days after receiving Sexton's letter, Plath sent off a new batch of poems to *The New Yorker:* "Berck-Plage," "The Other," "Words heard, by accident, over the phone," "Poppies in July," and "Burning the Letters." Nearly all of them concerned Ted's affair with Assia, which was out in the open now. Sylvia's desire for public retribution was strong.

Hughes spent much of August in London. When the Kanes left for Cornwall on August 31, he returned to Court Green to look after Sylvia, who was still ill with flu. Ted wrote to Eric Walter White in early September that he and Sylvia would have to forego a London meeting with him, Jack, and Máire Sweeney as Sylvia had come down with "a most severe bout of flu—quite knocked out, temp 103° etc. . . . and I shall have to stay here & nurse."[34] He resented the sacrifice. But Sylvia told Elizabeth that it was the sickest she had ever been—"double pneumonia was nothing to this."[35]

Just when Sylvia began to regain her strength, she received another blow. Judith Jones at Knopf wrote to explain why more reviews hadn't appeared of *The Colossus*, complaining that the "self-involved" poets to whom she had sent copies had not bothered to respond (though she did, at least, express interest in publishing *The Bell Jar*).[36] Marianne Moore had written to Jones criticizing the American edition of *The Colossus;* it was in this letter that she stated Plath's poems were "bitter, frost-bitten, burnt out, averse."[37] Jones forwarded the letter to Plath. "I am sorry Miss Moore eschews the dark side of life to the extent that she feels neither good nor enjoyable poetry can be made out of it," Plath replied to Jones. "She also, as I know, eschews the sexual side of life, and made my husband take out every poem in his first book with a sexual reference before she would put her name to endorse it. But she is a scrupulous letter writer, so bless her for that!"[38] Plath had once called Moore "the most famous American poetess."[39] She would have a hard time shaking off her criticisms.

Sylvia wrote another distressed letter to Dr. Beuscher on September 4. Beuscher had sent one reply in response to Plath's previous letters about Hughes's affair but had not yet made clear whether the letters would count as paid therapy. Sylvia was desperate for a more structured, doctor-patient relationship. "I wish to hell I could have a few talks with you. Nobody else is any good to me, I'm sick of preamble. That's why I thought if I paid for a couple of letters I might start going ahead instead of in circles."[40]

The home situation, she explained, had deteriorated. "Any kind of caution or limit makes him murderous." After spending the week in London, Ted had come home to "lay into us: this is a Prison, I am an Institution, the children should never have been born." When she was ill with flu she had started having blackouts; she asked Ted to stay home and help her, and he accused her of "blackmailing him with my health." When he returned from London she was even sicker with flu and a 103° fever for three days, and the doctor had lectured Ted "about manly responsibilities, the old red flag to the old bull."[41] Ted had told the doctor that she was "unstable" because she said she had "canine influenza"—a joke, as she had caught the sickness from the Kanes. Such talk between husband and doctor scared her; Sylvia well knew that these were the sorts of discussions that could lead to involuntary asylum commitments. (Indeed, the mid-fifties saw the peak of asylum inpatients in Britain.) "I honestly think they might try to make my life such a hell I would turn over Frieda as a sort of hostage to my sanity," she would write Dr. Beuscher on September 22.[42] She wrote to Aurelia, too, of her worries that Ted would try to use her mental health issues to get custody of Frieda. As terrible as the end of her marriage was, the idea of being committed to an asylum and losing her daughter was much worse. Sylvia had good reason to maintain a front of "sanity" that fall—to broadcast optimism, reasonableness, and proactiveness. Ted's perceived line of attack both terrified her and filled her with fury. "I am so bloody sane," she wrote Beuscher. "I am not disaster-proof after my years with you, but I am proof against all those deadly defences—retreat, freezing, madness, despair—that a fearful soul puts up when refusing to face pain & come through with it. I am not mad; just fighting mad."[43]

On September 9, Sylvia hosted Mrs. Prouty for dinner at Court Green—an occasion that required more theater. Her thoughts turned to Ireland. She spoke of the upcoming trip with Ted happily to Elizabeth. "She was very excited then because she felt like it was a real rapprochement. It was the first time they'd been together for a long time," Elizabeth said.[44] Sylvia told Elizabeth she would try to regain her health on the trip and asked her to send David's 1962 novel, *Too Many Murderers*. "I'm dying to read it, it looks just the thing to cheer me up, all about murder."[45]

THE JOURNEY TO CLEGGAN, a small, isolated fishing village on the Connemara coast, was long and tiresome. Sylvia and Ted took the night ferry from Holyhead, Wales, to Dublin. There they met Jack and Máire Sweeney, who plied them with oysters, brown bread, and Guinness. On Thursday, September 13, they traveled west by train to Galway, and from there another sixty miles west to tiny Cleggan. The Connemara village was set on the west coast amid pristine beaches and dramatic cliffs where waves broke over daggerhead rocks. In this remote part of Ireland, peat smoke trailed out of white thatch cottages, sheep held up traffic, and men in Aran sweaters gathered in pubs, speaking quietly in Irish. Electricity had only recently arrived. To Sylvia and Ted, it was paradise.

Richard Murphy greeted them warmly and escorted them to their twin-bedded room at the Old Forge, his small cottage behind the waterfront Pier Bar. Richard noted that when Ted signed the guest book, he wrote his address as "Halifax, Yorkshire," while Sylvia listed hers as "Court Green, North Tawton, Devon." Bad weather prevented them from sailing on Friday, so Murphy and his young assistant drove them instead to Yeats sites. They stopped first at Coole Park, the estate of Yeats's patron Lady Gregory. There they inspected the famous copper beech tree where Yeats had carved his initials. Plath told Hughes he should carve his initials beside Yeats's, as "he deserved to be in that company" more than the other Irish writers whose names appeared there.[46] But a spiked fence surrounded the tree, and Hughes declined to make his mark.

They drove on to Thoor Ballylee, Yeats's tower, the destination of the pilgrimage. Richard remembered that Sylvia spoke often during the drive, while Ted remained quiet.[47] The tower was then a ruin looted by locals, and the grounds were empty. "Jackdaws fled protesting as we climbed the spiral stairs. From the top, Sylvia threw coins into the stream," Richard remembered. "There they were—the two of them—for the first time really confronting Yeats in his tower."[48] They noticed an apple tree bearing fruit, which they hoped dated from Yeats's time. Sylvia and Ted "insisted" that they take some apples, and so they gathered "more than a hundredweight."[49] They saw this as a kind of "rite," Richard said, appropriating Yeats's apples.[50] Murphy worried about the repercussions if an Anglo-Irishman, an Englishman, and an American were caught plundering the grounds of Ireland's greatest bard. "Why are you doing this?" he asked Ted. "When you come to a place like this," Hughes answered, "you have to violate it." On their return to Cleggan they dropped in on Murphy's wealthy aunt, who showed Plath the nineteenth-century prints of Rangoon that would reappear in her poem "The Courage of Shutting-Up." Hughes, who called Murphy "decayed aristocracy," was uncomfortable in the local "Big House."[51]

Though Sylvia and Ted did not argue in front of Richard, both opened up to him privately about their troubles. Sylvia told him that Ted's "lies upset her." She wanted a legal separation, not a divorce. "Their union had been so complete, on every level, that she felt nothing could really destroy this." Like the Huwses and the Macedos, Richard thought the affair would blow over, for he had never encountered a couple whose minds were so "incredibly interlocked," who had "a closer, more creative relationship" than Sylvia and Ted. He was astonished that Sylvia was ready to leave Ted on account of one adulterous lapse, and tried to persuade her that she was a "sophisticated, highly intelligent writer" who should not "go back to these innocent, puritanical notions and apply them to your life and Ted's."[52] He told Sylvia that if she was serious about ending things, she should get a divorce. A legal separation would not allow Ted to remarry and would be "cruel."[53] Ted told him that the marriage had "been marvelously creative for him" for six or seven years, but that now it had "become destructive, and he thought the best thing to do was to give it a rest by going to Spain for six months." Ted did not mention Assia, but, Richard recalled, "her role was implied."[54] Hoping for reinforcements, Richard phoned the Irish poet Thomas Kinsella in Dublin and asked him to come to Cleggan to help defuse the tension.

On Saturday, the trio sailed to Inishbofin on Murphy's sailboat, a traditional Galway hooker, the *Ave Maria*. Richard remembered Sylvia's happiness that day. "During our passage of six miles across open water with a strong current and an ocean swell, Sylvia lay prone on the foredeck, leaning out over the prow: a triumphal figurehead, inhaling the sea air ecstatically." He dropped them off at the pier and told them he would return at five p.m. Inishbofin, remote, quiet, and beautiful, was an ideal place for the couple to reconnect. Sylvia and Ted spent the day wandering the dirt paths that traced the island's hilly ledges, and eating lunch at Day's harborside pub. Sylvia asked the pub's proprietor, Margaret Day, if she would "dig up the roots of an arum lily" for her to bring home. The islander liked Sylvia but didn't take to Ted. "He was one person you brought to the island whom I didn't like," Margaret told Richard.

The craggy Connacht coast was straight out of a Hughes poem, but it was Plath, Murphy said, who fell "in love with Connemara at first sight." She told him she wanted to rent his cottage even while he lived there. "Alarmed" by this proposal, he introduced her to a local woman, Kitty Marriott, whose nearby cottage in Moyard, "Glasthule," Plath agreed to rent from November 1. Richard was struck by the "astonishing decisiveness" with which Sylvia made her plans.

Thomas Kinsella arrived for dinner on Saturday night and impressed the company with his wit. That evening, Murphy wrote in 1988, Plath rubbed his leg "provocatively" under the table at dinner.[55] By the time he wrote about the same incident in his later 2002 memoir, the gesture had lost its force and become, simply, "a gentle kick under the table"—allowing for the possibility that this "kick" might have been accidental.[56] Elizabeth was always skeptical of Richard's story. "This ridiculous thing that people seem to believe—the man they stayed with in Ireland, he told people she was playing footsie with him under the table! She knew he was gay! She wasn't that kind of woman at all. She just would have thought it ludicrous." Elizabeth said Sylvia told her, before she left for Ireland, that she was going to visit a "gay poet," and that when she returned, she hinted that Richard had designs on Ted.[57] It is possible that Plath knowingly put Murphy—who was not "out"—in a very awkward position. (Murphy was divorced with a daughter, yet his homosexuality was an open secret in certain circles.)[58] Or she may, indeed, have been making a pass at a wealthy, aristocratic, and handsome poet who could give her refuge in Ireland. Accidental or not, Richard took Sylvia's kick as an invitation. But he had just been through a painful divorce and had no interest in getting involved with Ted Hughes's wife.

After dinner, Sylvia and Ted made a Ouija board and held a séance. Richard did not participate, and Sylvia went to bed early. Hughes and Kinsella stayed up late; in the morning Murphy found scrap verse notes, in the manner of a Hughes poem, littering the table. Kinsella admitted he'd helped the spirits along.

The next day, Sunday, Ted left Sylvia in Cleggan while Richard was out. He told her he had decided to go fishing with his painter friend Barrie Cooke in the village of Quin, in County Clare, for a few days and that he would meet her again on Wednesday at the Dublin boat.[59] This was the same day the BBC broadcast Plath's poems "The Moon and the Yew Tree" and "The Rabbit Catcher" as part of their New Poetry series, though it is unclear whether Ted and Sylvia heard the broadcast in rural Ireland. The airing of such a personal poem as "The Rabbit Catcher" would have complicated their fragile rapprochement. "Blackberrying" appeared in The New Yorker that week, in the September 15 issue. It was the last poem of hers Plath saw in the magazine.

Cooke took Hughes to the rocky, lunar landscape of the Burren, and then fishing on a nearby river. They slotted themselves into the limestone slabs near Mullah Moor, and watched the geese flying overhead "off Slieve na

Maun to their watering ground."[60] It was a cathartic, reinvigorating experience for Hughes, who spent that night with Cooke and his wife, Harriet.[61]
Ted felt suffocated in his marriage, and the Irish landscape—and Barrie's
company—somehow freed him. "All understood without need for explanation," Cooke told Sweeney of Hughes's response to the Burren. He continued cryptically, hinting at Hughes's marital troubles:

> His intensity is literally frightening. I don't mean this in the romantic,
> hair-wild, wild-eyes, moody way of course. I mean his ruthless search
> to expose himself. He is quite dedicated to extracting everything out of
> himself and that doesn't just mean ART. He's also the only person I've
> met yet who is as serious as myself about IT. Maybe more, to be honest—
> perhaps that's why he is disturbing. He is more ruthless than me by far
> and that I find terribly admirable.[62]

Cooke's perceptive letter reveals something of Hughes's mood that weekend.
Hughes later wrote to his son Nicholas in 1998, "going to Ireland broke me
out of that arid sterile alienation from myself that my life at C.G. [Court
Green] had trapped me into, and with a single stride plunged me right into
the productive, fruitful thick of my best chances. And in Ireland I did make
a big breakthrough—in my writing and in everything to do with myself."[63]
Seven years later, when Ted visited after Assia's suicide, Barrie felt he had
misjudged him. He wrote to Sweeney, "He is a good man and not the ruthless man that everyone thinks he is and even I thought he was (though I
admired and liked him). He is a very honest man. And, inside his rocks, has
great loving warmth."[64] Richard agreed. He felt Ted's "craggy" demeanor
and "tough Yorkshire" manner concealed "marvelous tenderness . . . extraordinary gentleness."[65]

When Richard realized that Ted was gone, he "panicked." He knew
he could not spend a night alone with a married woman in rural, Catholic
Ireland. He, "a divorced Protestant with a British accent," did not want to
jeopardize the alliances he had built with Cleggan's villagers. The kick the
night before made him worried Sylvia had encouraged Ted to leave. And
so he asked Plath to return to Dublin with Kinsella the next day. Sylvia, he
said, "was enraged. . . . She scarcely spoke to me, and when she did, she put
a strained, artificial distance between us." Instead, she opened her heart to
Mary Coyne, Richard's neighbor and cook, who remembered her as "a lovely
person" but "tearful, very highly strung."

The next day, Sylvia was polite but stony in her goodbye. Richard said
that she had made him feel, in her silence, that he "had been mean, and was
partly to blame for her misery." She drove back to Dublin with Kinsella, and

spent Monday and Tuesday night with him and his kindly wife, Eleanor, who comforted her. Kinsella wrote Murphy that when Plath boarded the boat to Holyhead, Wales, on Wednesday, September 19, she was "in fair form, giving the impression (to the casual observer at least) that no fears need to be entertained by anyone."[66] But Sylvia was seething. Ted failed to meet her at the Dublin boat as promised. This, for her, was the point of no return.

Back in Devon, Plath would write an angry, intimate letter to Murphy on September 21. She had been "appalled" to realize that she had upset him when she joked about writing *New Yorker* poems about Connemara, "his" territory. She was still determined to spend the winter in Ireland and was unsure whether his initial support of that plan had been genuine. To Richard she wrote,

> May I say two things? My health depends on leaving England & going to Ireland, & the health of the children. I am very reluctant to think that the help you gave with one hand you would want to take away with the other. I am in great need of a woman like Kitty Marriott & if there is one thing my 30th year has brought it is understanding of what I am, and a sense of strength and independence to face what I have to. It may be difficult to believe, but I have not and never will have a desire to see or speak to you or anyone else. I have wintered in a lighthouse & that sort of life is balm to my soul. I do not expect you to understand this, or anything else, how could you, you know nothing of me. I do not want to think you were hypocritical when showing me the cottages, but it is difficult to think otherwise. Please let me think better of you than this.

Plath had not actually wintered in a lighthouse—she was speaking metaphorically, letting Murphy know that she was strong enough to brave the Connemara wilds on her own. He had seemed so supportive of her plan to stay in Ireland, only to send her unceremoniously packing because she was a woman and her presence could make trouble for him. Plath was more widely published than Murphy, and his dismissal outraged and humiliated her. She rescinded an earlier invitation she had made for him to visit Court Green for the same reason he had expelled her from Cleggan: "My town is as small & watchful as yours."[67]

Sylvia returned to Court Green on September 19, alone, a day early. She found the children rested and happy, and their agency nanny, Miss Cartwright, "wonderful." For once, her child-care arrangements had gone smoothly, "everything in applepie [*sic*] order." There was a telegram from Ted, sent from a London address, telling her that he "might be back in a week or two."[68] Sylvia, who would later learn that he was in Spain with Assia for ten days, was furious. (Hughes told Anthony Thwaite some months after Plath's death that he felt very guilty about what he had done to Sylvia in Ireland. He told Murphy, too, in 1968 that "leaving her alone in Cleggan was cruel.")[69] She wrote that day to Kathy Kane, "the end has come. It is like amputating a gangrenous limb—horrible, but one feels it is the only thing to do to survive."[70] Plath chose a simile tangled up with her father's death to describe the decision to end her marriage—a confluence of symbolism she would revisit in "Daddy." After she put the children to bed, she walked to Winifred's house for comfort. Sylvia told Aurelia that "she was a great help. She more or less confirmed my decision."[71]

ASSIA AND TED HAD RETURNED from Spain and were back in London. Assia had decided to leave David and asked Suzette if she and Helder would go round to "comfort" David after she broke the news. The Macedos agreed and were shocked when they arrived at the flat. David had smashed a hole in the wall with his fist and slashed "to ribbons" one of Assia's leather hand-bags. Assia was there, too, and told Suzette, "I'm afraid he's going to kill me." Helder calmed David down, and they went out to the pub. Assia and Suzette stayed behind. Assia, now calmer herself, spoke of her "fabulous" time in Spain with Ted and, "in the same breath," her second thoughts about leaving "poor David." She told Suzette she had destroyed letters from Sylvia to David.[72]

Sylvia now had a reply from Dr. Beuscher, dated 17 September, to her anguished July 30 and September 4 letters.[73] "I just don't see you as a second Caitlin," Beuscher responded, referring to Caitlin Thomas, Dylan Thomas's wife, who had endured his infidelities and abandonment until his death. "I much prefer your 50-yr. image with wisdom and blue hair." Beuscher dismissed Sylvia's notion of paying for letter sessions as "irrelevant" and asked on what grounds she was being consulted—as "woman (mother) (witch) (earth-goddess), or as a mere psychiatrist?" She hoped that it was not the latter, as "in spite of much effort on my part, I am totally unable to function solely as a psychiatrist in this crisis. Too much of my own past," she admitted, "too much of my own feelings about my mother, my sister-in-law . . . my every personal experience, plus my general beliefs about women, their status as it is, was, has been, and should be, enter into whatever I might say to you.

I cannot pretend my viewpoint is objective. Frankly, I am furious at Ted. You thought you had a man, and perhaps you do, but he is certainly acting like a little child."

Dr. Beuscher, then, would not treat Plath as a patient, but she tried her best to fill Plath with confidence about her future: "do not give up your own personal one-ness. Do not imagine that your whole being hangs on this one man. . . . Just don't get out of the driver's seat in your own life. Has he left you? OK, sad, tragic, stupid, unfortunate, anxiety-provoking, BUT NOT THE END." Beuscher thought Hughes was "a man in crisis" and that Plath should not get sucked down "in a whirlpool of HIS making. . . . Don't be anyone's doormat. Do your crying alone. Hold your head up, and your heart will follow." She warned Sylvia against repeating her "mother's role—i.e., martyr at the hands of the brutal male." Resist the temptation to go to bed with Ted, she said—"Stand back and be an old-fashioned lady." She should get a lawyer and discuss child support. She told Sylvia to write to her again. "If I help you, it is my reward. . . . I have often thought, if I 'cure' no one else in my whole career, you are enough. I love you."[74]

Dr. Beuscher's dismissal of Sylvia's "paid sessions idea" seems generous, but it allowed her to disentangle herself from a messy situation. She realized that she had crossed an ethical line, and probably had legitimate misgivings about treating a patient across the Atlantic. She apparently made no plans to speak to Sylvia by phone once it was reinstalled at Court Green, nor, in her surviving letters, did she instruct Sylvia to seek help from a mental health professional in England.[75]

Sylvia replied to Dr. Beuscher with an update on September 22. "I am really asking your help as a woman, the wisest woman emotionally and intel-lectually, that I know. You are not my mother, but you have been the midwife to my spirit." Beuscher, she knew, would not advise her to "diminish" herself. Things had changed irrevocably since her September 4 letter. The Ireland trip had not saved the marriage, but hastened its demise.

> I have been very stupid, a bloody fool, but it only comes from my think-ing Ted could grow, and grow up, not down, and my wanting to give us a new and better and wider start. I was prepared for almost anything—his having the odd affair, traveling, drinking (I mean getting drunk)—if we could be straight, good friends, share all the intellectual life that has been meat and drink to me, for he is a genius, a great man, a great writer. I was ready for this, to settle for something much different and freer than what I had thought marriage was, or what I wanted it to be. I changed. I have a rich inner life myself, much I want to learn & do, and this blessed gift made me feel capable of quite another life than the life I had felt at

heart I really wanted. Even our <u>professional</u> marriage—the utterly creative and healthy critical exchange of ideas and publication projects and
completed work—meant enough to me to try to save it. But Ted, his
attitudes and actions, have made even this impossible, and I am appalled.
I am bloody, raw, nerves hanging out all over the place, because I have
had six stormy but wonderful years, bringing both of us, from nothing,
books, fame, money, lovely babies, wonderful loving, but I see now the
man I loved as father and husband is just dead. . . . I realize, stunned, that
I do not <u>like</u> him.[76]

Sylvia told Dr. Beuscher that when Ted had returned from his first London
tryst with Assia, he told her "the affair was kaput." But he needed his freedom, he explained to her, and wanted to spend more time in London "on
drinking bouts with a few friends." Sylvia promised him that she "wouldn't
be tearful or try to stop him from anything." He spent half his weeks in London, and when he returned he "would lay into me with fury—I looked tired,
tense, cross, couldn't he even have a drink, what sort of a wife had he married
etc. I was dumbfounded."[77]

She had hoped that Ireland would restore her health, but, she explained,
Ted had left her one morning—he said "he was going grouse shooting with
a friend"—and she hadn't "seen him since." It all made sense, suddenly. Ted
had stopped sleeping with her and had been "groaning this other woman's
name in the night." She had been "in agony," but now understood he was
"being faithful" to Assia. The few times they had sex, Sylvia felt degraded—
"he made so sure I felt nothing, and was tossed aside like a piece of dog
sausage. Well I am neither my mother nor a masochist; I would sooner be a
nun than this kind of fouled scratch rug." Sylvia wrote that she was going to
London to see a solicitor about a legal separation. She would no longer allow
Ted to come back to Court Green "every week to make my life miserable,
kick me about & assure himself that he has a ghastly limiting wife." He had
let Nicholas fall out of his pram, she claimed, and called him a usurper. She
added that Ted "beat me up physically" in February 1961, two days before
her miscarriage. Now, she told Beuscher, "He means well—says all he wants
is to live his own life & send us ⅔ of what he earns." But she still worried that
Assia wanted to take Frieda from her.

The marriage was over. "Call solicitor," Plath wrote in her calendar on
September 21.[78] Spain, she told Aurelia, was now "out of the question."[79]
Ireland became the stay against confusion. She wrote Beuscher about her
plan, to begin the separation somewhere else so that she would not be "left,
passive. I need to act . . . to fatten and blow myself clear with sea winds &
wild walks." She would not sacrifice herself to her children as her mother had

done, nor would she move in with Aurelia, who had already started lecturing her: "'<u>Now</u> you see how it is, why I never married again, self-sacrifice is the thing for your two little darlings etc. etc.' till it made me puke." She would not burden her own children with the "lethal deluge of frustrated love which will lay down its life if it can live through the loved one, on the loved one, like a hideous parasite. . . . I don't want Frieda to hate me as I hated my mother, nor Nicholas to live with me or about me as my brother lives about my mother, even though he is just married." She had once asked her mother "why, if she discovered so early on she did not love my father, that her marriage was an agony, she did not leave him. She looked blank. Then she said half-heartedly that it was the depression & she couldnt [sic] have gotten a job. Well. No thanks." Ted would not turn her "into a doggy sobby stereotype . . . My sense of myself, my inner dignity and creative heart won't have it. . . . I think when I am free of him my own sweet life will come back to me, bare and sad in a lot of places, but my own, and sweet enough."[80]

"I am afraid the news from Court Green is not good," Winifred wrote Aurelia on September 22. Sylvia had been "in great distress the other night when Ted did not come back." She felt better the next day, when she told Winifred she had "made up her mind to get a separation." But Winifred was skeptical. "She has a hard hill to pull, I am afraid." The midwife understood the need for a good nanny. "If she can write she will be able to loose [sic] herself for a few hours." Winifred blamed Ted, whose unconventional writer's life seemed to her too much like loafing. "Ted has never grown up, he is not mature enough to accept his responsibilities, paying bills, doing income tax looking after his wife & children, so Sylvia has taken over all that practical side of the partnership of necessity & no man really likes that. He wants to be free for parties, travelling etc." She thought success had "gone to his head." She assured Aurelia that Sylvia seemed "calmer" after their evening heart-to-heart: "I made her eat supper & we had some good laughs as well as some tears."[81] Sylvia continued to keep up a front with Nancy Axworthy, her cleaner, who detected almost no change in her employer throughout the summer and fall of 1962. Sylvia remained upbeat and cheerful on the mornings Nancy cleaned. When Ted did not return with her from Ireland in September, she told Nancy in a "breezy, casual" way that he was away lecturing at a university.[82]

Ted, meanwhile, felt as if he were emerging from a crisis he barely understood. "Things are quite irrevocable. . . . I'm aghast when I see how incredibly I've confined & stunted my existence, when I compare my feeling of what I could be with what I am," he wrote to Olwyn in late summer. "I've had the most terrific labours to get back the flow of mind & memory that used to be quite spontaneous, & should be." His writing was suddenly taking off; he was "creating two other poets. One experimental & lyrical, one, very rigid formalist. . . . My own poems barge midway . . . exploiting the qualities of the extremes without reducing myself to or losing myself in either." This letter suggests how closely Hughes linked his new life to a new phase of writing: his personal and aesthetic choices seemed to reaffirm one another. He told Olwyn he was trying to set Sylvia up in Spain while he renovated the cottage for a nanny: "as soon as I clear out, she'll start making a life of her own, friends of her own, interests of her own. If she wants to buy her half of the house gradually fair enough."[83] He had heard that Sylvia was trying to track him down through her solicitor. "Yes, it's just like her, to employ a snoop." Ted knew that Olwyn would sympathize with him; his letters to her, with their dismissive comments about Sylvia, suggest that his sister was now his strongest ally. He seemed excited about the looming separation and the prospect of freedom:

> Sometimes she wants a legal separation, sometimes a divorce at once. I've left her in Ireland, while I attend to one or two small things, & I shan't be back at Court Green until Oct. 1st—by then she'll probably be wanting a divorce, & have started it up.
>
> In her manner with other people she's changed extraordinarily—become much more as she was when I first knew her & much more like her mother, whom I detest. You're right, she'll have to grow up—it won't do her any harm.[84]

Both Plath and Hughes wanted the other to "grow up." Plath's love now seemed, to Hughes, a stranglehold. He wanted her to accept his need for erotic freedom, which he felt would enhance his creativity. The romantic patterns of his later life—he would never be faithful to a woman after he left Plath—suggest that for him, fidelity was a struggle. But Plath was too dignified to stay married to an adulterer. She had made sacred vows to Hughes, and she wanted him to "grow up" into the faithful husband and father he had promised to become.

Perhaps what finally doomed the marriage was neither Plath's possessiveness nor Hughes's adultery, but fame and its legendary temptations. There were other factors, obviously: depression, rivalry, disillusion, violence, class, to name but a few. But fame gave Hughes sexual and professional opportunities to expand at exactly the time Plath wanted him, as he saw it, to contract—to settle into a predictable, domestic life. Plath had suggested as much when she told Dr. Beuscher that movie stars had nothing on handsome male poets. And, indeed, Hughes was now secure enough in his professional success to tell his sister, with some bravado, "I'll gradually become the guiding taste at Faber's, when Eliot retires."[85] Fame made Hughes even more determined, as he had told Olwyn in 1958, to sacrifice everything to his poetic vocation: he would "pursue it at all costs." For it would be "miserable," he wrote, "to feel that your gifts have somehow fallen to pieces & come to nothing . . . through neglect."[86] This was the fate he was trying to avoid now that the walls of domesticity and fatherhood were closing in. Assia was his new muse—perhaps a directive from the Goddess herself—and he felt he owed it to his "gift" to pursue her.

The marriage that had begun as a bold creative experiment ended in the most predictable of clichés. Plath was all too aware of this sad devolution, and her disillusion was nearly as painful as Ted's abandonment itself. The tawdriness of the affair—that someone of Ted's intellect could be seduced by a "whiff of Chanel," as she put it—compounded her humiliation.[87] It also disoriented her; maybe she did not know Ted at all. "Perhaps if Ted was that person that was enamored by Assia, then she had invented Ted," Helder Macedo observed. But the Stevie Smith poem Sylvia tacked above her desk that fall suggests she saw herself in a new light, too—as honest, virtuous, and resilient. She was ready to make a new life.

———

MISS CARTWRIGHT, the agency nanny, returned to Court Green on September 24 to spend the night with the children while Sylvia traveled to London to see her solicitor. She still did not know Ted's whereabouts and would have to "trace him." "He is utterly gutless. Lies, lies, lies," she wrote Aurelia.[88] The solicitor told her that a wife was only allowed one-third of her husband's income, and that if the husband did not pay, suing him would be "long & costly." "The humiliation of being penniless & begging money from deaf ears is too much," she wrote Aurelia. "I shall just have to invest everything with courage in the cottage & the nanny for a year & write like mad. Try to get clear. I'm sure the American laws aren't like this." She hoped that Ted would settle out of court and agree to a decent "fixed allowance." She said she had contributed a third of their joint $7,000 income that year. "Now it is all gone. I am furious. I threw everything of mine into our life without question, all my earnings, & now he is well-off, with great potential earning power, I shall be penalized for earning, or if I don't earn, have to beg. Well I choose the former."[89]

Sylvia stayed with the Macedos on this trip, and Suzette remembered that she and Sylvia grew closer. Suzette had also attempted suicide, and the two women spoke frankly about their breakdowns. "She kept nodding & saying 'Yes' when I described my emotional state." They spoke of their emotional and sexual lives like college girls in a dorm. Sylvia wanted to hear more about Suzette's "intimate relations" with Helder and asked her if she had "ever been out of the body in love making." Suzette added, "Sylvia had."[90]

There was another reason, besides Sylvia's solicitor's appointment, for her London visit. She called unannounced on Al Alvarez, who had published her poem "Crossing the Water" in *The Observer* on September 23 and so given her a pretense for dropping by.[91] Alvarez lived in a modest, sparsely furnished studio in an old converted barn in literary Hampstead, on Fellows Road, not far from where Sylvia was staying with the Macedos. The studio was quaint, but the only source of heat was a coal stove; the toilet was in a cold garage, and the water ran lukewarm.[92] Sylvia suspected that Ted had been staying with Al in London; Ted later thought she had come to sniff out his lair.

Alvarez remembered that Plath arrived looking neat and prim, her hair in a bun, like "an Edwardian lady performing a delicate but necessary social duty." The studio was sparsely furnished, and she sat cross-legged and comfortable on the floor as she clinked the ice around in her whiskey. (The sound was the only thing, she remarked, that made her "homesick for the States.") She told him, with "polished cheerfulness," that she was living on her own with the children. Alvarez later wrote that he was shocked to hear "that anything could have disrupted the idyll" of the Hugheses' marriage.[93] But his surprise was disingenuous. Ted had been staying with him on and off since July; he knew of their marital problems. Sylvia told him she had been writing "a poem a day" and that she possessed a "new drive." She read him "Berck-Plage," "The Moon and the Yew Tree," "Elm," and some others. They must be read aloud, she said. Alvarez had been receptive to her poetry in the past, and, with Hughes gone, she needed a sympathetic ear. She also understood the need for another male patron. Newly separated from England's most famous young poet, she was trying to forge an alliance with London's most famous young critic.

By 1962, Alvarez was a kingmaker whose influence stretched across the Atlantic. His April 1962 anthology, *The New Poetry*, became one of the most influential anthologies of the postwar period. The book promoted a new style of poetry, later dubbed "extremism," whose exemplars were Hughes and Lowell.[94] Hughes had given Plath an inscribed copy of the anthology ("For Sylvia All My Love Ted"), and she starred or underlined twenty passages from Alvarez's introductory essay, "Beyond the Gentility Principle," including parts that discussed "the poet's ability and willingness to face the full range of his experience with full intelligence; not to take the easy exits," and Berryman and Lowell's practice of dealing "openly with the quick of their experience, experience sometimes on the edge of disintegration and breakdown."[95] Alvarez remembered that Sylvia "spoke of it often and with approval, and was disappointed not to have been included among the poets in the book."[96] Daniel Huws called the anthology "very, very influential" and said it "changed the general climate a lot." He felt that Alvarez was trying to dethrone Robert Graves.[97] The book made such an impression on a young Seamus Heaney that he brought it on his first date with his future wife, Marie. He hoped that its modern sensibility would impress her. The poet Michael Longley remembered that every aspiring poet he knew seemed to have a copy in his back pocket.[98]

Ted told Olwyn that *The New Poetry* sold ten thousand copies in its first month. "There must be a poetry boom," he wrote.[99] And, indeed, there was, thanks in part to the cheap paperback *Penguin Modern Poets* series, launched that same month, that introduced a generation of British readers to postwar poetry.[100] More Britons than ever before were educated, and they were hungry for culture. But Alvarez had tapped into something deeper: the 1960s were dawning, and with them came a new impatience with British gentility and its American cousin, conformity.

Alvarez chose a Jackson Pollock painting, *Convergence*, for the cover of the book's second edition, and scholars have traced ideas and language in the book's introduction to Harold Rosenberg's 1959 major work on abstract expressionism, *The Tradition of the New*. Rosenberg thought "A painting that is an act is inseparable from the biography of the artist."[101] Alvarez absorbed Rosenberg's ideas, and co-opted his term "extremist." This alignment with both abstract expressionism and psychoanalysis symbolized the new poetry's effort to break boldly and radically from literary convention: to shock, to flaunt taboo, to live the values of one's art. The book's guiding spirit was Lowell, whom Alvarez praised for "trying to cope" with his "disturbances" "nakedly, and without evasion."[102]

Alvarez argued that gentility had sterilized British life and that "the makers of horror films are more in tune with contemporary anxiety than most of the English poets."[103] Behind and ahead stood the specter of mass extermination; it was the poet's responsibility to bear witness and sound the alarm. "Theologians would call these forces evil, psychologists, perhaps, libido," Alvarez wrote. "Either way, they are the forces of disintegration which destroy the old standards of civilization. Their public faces are those of two world wars, of the concentration camps, of genocide, and the threat of nuclear war."[104]

Plath's *Ariel* would become, for Alvarez, the high-water mark of "extremist" verse. But in 1961, when he was assembling his anthology, no other

British poet exemplified this "new poetry" better than Hughes. To Philip Hobsbaum and Peter Redgrove, too, it seemed "that the future of poetry in Britain was dependent on Hughes's work being established as the true model for the age."[105] Hughes, Hosbaum said, "was writing accomplished verse when the rest of his generation was still wondering whether to be barbaric like Dylan or sophisticated like Empson."[106] Edward Lucie-Smith recalled Hobsbaum's London Group members crashing rival literary parties at G. S. Fraser's Chelsea flat and "baiting the company" by reciting Hughes's poem "The Martyrdom of Bishop Farrar"—declaring their "faith in Hughes" in front of the "appalled" guests.[107] "The Martyrdom of Bishop Farrar" describes Farrar's burning in graphic detail ("Hear him crack in the fire's mouth") and represented what Alvarez felt a modern poem ought to achieve. *This* poetry did not keep its distance from atrocity or violence: in Hughes's poem, as the critic Will Wooten has written, "sincerity, extreme suffering and extreme death intersect."[108] "The Martyrdom" became the London Group's banner poem, though Hughes attended its meetings only sporadically.[109] Plath's "Lady Lazarus," which was influenced by Hughes's poem, would sound a similar note.

Alvarez said that including Plath in the first edition "never crossed my mind. She was an American in England, and ergo we couldn't have her."[110] Yet Alvarez *had* included two other Americans, Lowell and John Berryman. The clear reason for Plath's exclusion was her gender; there were no women poets in the first edition. (In *Poetry from Cambridge 1958*, Plath had been one of only two women represented in the selection of twenty-two poets.)[111] The new poetry itself, as Wooten notes, could at times "be self-consciously masculinist" and "define itself in ways hostile to women."[112] Though Plath had not yet written the majority of her *Ariel* poems, much of her work at that point fit Alvarez's criteria: "The Stones," "Lorelei," or "Tulips" would have been obvious choices. But Alvarez had ignored a whole swath of American poets: the Beats, the Black Mountain Poets, the New York School. *The New Poetry* seemed to confirm that Lowell and Hughes had single-handedly saved Anglo-American poetry from gentility.[113] Alvarez would include Plath and Anne Sexton in his second edition in 1966, realizing too late that it was not Hughes but Plath whose work best articulated the sound and sense of the new poetry. He later called her exclusion from the first edition a "terrible mistake. Stupid."[114]

The Holocaust was a particular obsession of several of the anthology's poets, who, fifteen years after the war, felt a moral imperative to speak the unspeakable. In the wake of Adolf Eichmann's capture and trial in 1960–61, there was a new desire to come to terms with the horror. Alvarez, who was Jewish, admitted that his experiences with depression and suicide influenced his interest in the Holocaust: "my own suicidal behaviour had given me a personal stake in the idea of a murderous century reflected in murderous art."[115] His feelings suggest the reasons Plath, too, was drawn to the Holocaust. Shortly after her visit to Alvarez, she criticized her mother for ignoring the horrors of Belsen and Auschwitz in favor of happier stories.

When Plath first visited him, Alvarez was working on a BBC radio production, *Under Pressure*, about the legacy of the Holocaust and the Cold War in eastern Europe. The program was based on his visits to Poland, Hungary, and Czechoslovakia in 1961 and 1962.[116] Plath, the daughter of German-speaking parents, was interested especially in Alvarez's attempt to understand how, as he wrote, "the concentration-camp experience has been coped with in imaginative terms."[117] Alvarez said he had "become obsessed with the concentration camps" in 1960—"they were all I read about while I was working myself up to my overdose. . . . Later Sylvia Plath also became obsessed with the camps during her last months and we talked about them continually."[118] He remembered speaking with her about his visit to Auschwitz, in the fall of 1961. Concentration camp imagery and eastern European geography appeared in many of Plath's October 1962 poems, most famously "Daddy" and "Lady Lazarus."[119]

Plath was hardly alone in her use of Holocaust and Nazi imagery, for which she has been much criticized. As *The New Poetry* shows, the theme was in the air by the early 1960s. Peter Porter, George MacBeth, Anthony Hecht, and Geoffrey Hill all wrote poems around this time that referenced the Holocaust.[120] MacBeth remembered Plath saying to him in 1960, "I see you have a concentration camp in your mind too."[121] Indeed, Plath had included Hecht's "More Light! More Light!" in her 1961 *American Poetry Now* anthology. These poets did not, presumably, think they were exploiting or appropriating the Shoah. The Eichmann trial was ongoing, Hannah Arendt had published *The Origins of Totalitarianism* (1951) and Erich Kahler *The Tower and the Abyss* (1958). Both books, which influenced Alvarez, argued that "mass evil accompanies 'mass society.' "[122] Arendt's image of Lazarus to describe this phenomenon suggests that Alvarez may have recommended these books to Plath. The stakes had never been higher for poets, Alvarez argued in his anthology. The new poetry had a responsibility—not to "confess," but to lift the veil; to bear witness to atrocity. Plath's use of Holocaust imagery must be considered in this particular literary-historical context. In an *Observer* review on October 14, 1962, Alvarez picked out Vernon Scannell's "Death of a Jew" and "Elegy," about nuclear annihilation, for particular praise and dismissed Roy Fuller's poetry as "laudably sensible."[123] Plath read this piece the week before she wrote "Lady Lazarus." Her poem would be courageous and unflinching according to the terms Alvarez had helped set.

In late September 1962, when Plath visited Alvarez in Hampstead, she was on the verge of writing some of the greatest poems of her life. Some of the poems she had written before she read *The New Poetry* contained graphic images of radium and fire, "destruction, annihilation, ash"—oblique comments on horror and extremity.[124] But Alvarez's anthology upped the stakes and nudged Plath further in the direction she was already moving. He "was sure" that the anthology had influenced her poems ("My guess is she was pissed off not to be in it").[125] Plath read many *Ariel* poems to Alvarez before she read them to Hughes, and she considered Alvarez's advice when revising them.[126] The imagery and themes in the *Ariel* poems corresponded almost uncannily with Alvarez's concerns—the Holocaust, nuclear war, suicide, totalitarianism—which he discussed with her during her four visits to London in the fall of 1962.[127]

———

SYLVIA ARRIVED BACK at Court Green from London on September 26. Pain, anguish, and physical exhaustion were taking their toll. "To chemist for pills," she wrote in her calendar that day.[128] To Aurelia, she wrote of her troubles with Ted. "He is a vampire on my life, killing and destroying us all. We had all the world on tap, were even well off, now this insanity on his part will cost us everything." She asked Aurelia to tell Mrs. Prouty about "the situation." "It is difficult, I feel, & not my place, for I want nothing from her, but I would like her to know the truth, that I am deserted" with "a mountain of bills."[129] She probably hoped for financial help from Prouty, but she knew she could not depend on it. She instructed Aurelia to withdraw $500 from her Boston account and send it to her by check.

She made an effort to visit friends every afternoon with the children to keep herself busy. But she began to suspect that the villagers' attitudes toward her had changed now that she was living alone. She lashed out at Aurelia, with whom she was furious for telling Winifred about her "nervous breakdown." "Any ordinary doctor treats a former 'mental case' as a 50% exaggerator." Neither Winifred nor Dr. Webb believed, she said, that her temperature had reached 103° in late summer. And Ted, she said, had tried to convince Dr. Webb that she was "unstable" because of her jokes about "canine influenza." "So you see how your blabbing has helped me." Aurelia offered to visit, but Sylvia balked. "I do not want you to waste your money coming here, and I shall never come to America again."[130]

Miss Cartwright's efficiency gave Sylvia hope—"she is a whiz, and I see what a heaven my life could be if I had a good live-in nanny." Her dreams spilled out in letters—skiing in the Tyrol with Warren and Maggie, a Guggenheim in Rome with the children. She planned to write *New Yorker* stories and BBC plays in Ireland, though at the moment she was broke. Nearly all her Saxton grant money was gone, and the couple rarely had more than £300 in their checking account that summer. Ted had said she could take £300 from their joint account "as some recompense for my lost nanny-grant, to build over the cottage. This is a <u>must</u>." If she were truly "lucky," her writing would pay for a London flat and "fine free schools" for the children, and she would return to Court Green on holidays and during the summer. "I would <u>starve</u> intellectually here," she told her mother.[131]

Winifred found her a temporary nanny to come nine hours a week. She suggested that Sylvia work on her novel in the early morning when she couldn't sleep, and go to bed early in the evening after she put the children down. Plath took this advice and worked slowly on her novel—just three pages on September 28, but better than nothing. "It is the evenings here, after the children are in bed, that are the worst, so I might as well get rid of them by going to bed," she wrote Aurelia. "I feel pretty good in the morning, & my days are, thank goodness busy." She still had no appetite, but she made a point to eat with Frieda in the kitchen. She forced herself to leave the house in the afternoon to see people "who know nothing, or at least who are darling, like the Comptons." Her sleeping pills—"a necessary evil"—allowed her to "sleep deeply & then do some writing & feel energetic during the day if I drink lots of coffee right on waking."[132] She told Aurelia she would take them as long as she had to.

Sylvia's solicitor had told her that, since Ted had "deserted" her, she could deplete their joint savings, and she instructed her mother to send another $500 from their American account at Christmas. It would all go to renovating the cottage for the nanny. "I don't break down with someone else around," she confessed to Aurelia.[133] To Kathy Kane, on September 29, she wrote, "The evenings are hell. I can't sleep without pills. Well, if I can just live through this fall, & try to get my novel done somehow, then go to Ireland for the worst three months & come back with the daffodils, maybe this spring & summer will bring new life & new plans."[134]

She was more candid with Dr. Beuscher, whom she also wrote that day.

I think I am dying. I am just desperate. Ted has deserted me, I have not seen him for 2 weeks. . . . Tonight, utterly mad with this solitude, rain and wind hammering my hundred windows, I climbed to his study out of sheer homesickness to read his writing, lacking letters, and found them— sheafs of passionate love poems to this woman, this one woman to whom he has been growing more & more faithful, describing their orgasms, her ivory body, her smell, her beauty, saying in a world of beauties he married a hag, talking about "now I have hacked the octopus off at my ring finger." Many are fine poems. Absolute impassioned love poems—and I am just dying.

Even in the midst of heartbroken despondency, Plath was clear-eyed about the quality of her husband's love poems to another woman. She was an artist before she was a wife.

Compared to Assia, who was "beautiful," she felt herself "haggish & my hair a mess & my nose huge & my brain brainwashed & God knows how I shall keep together. . . . If I had someone living with me, I would not break down & talk to myself, cry, or just stare for hours." She had considered "begging" her aunt Dot to come until she went to Ireland, which she hoped would help her heal. She had about $2,000 left in savings, and the house, which was in her and Ted's names. But she worried continually about money, and felt that the British divorce laws were "so mean." Still, she told Beuscher she wanted to remain friends with Hughes. "I mean my God my life with him has been a daily creation, new ideas, new thoughts, our mutual stimulation." Plath still valued the artist in Hughes, even as he cavorted about in London and Spain, "passionately in love," while she was "stuck with two infants." But:

> Every view is blocked by a huge vision of their bodies entwined in passion across it, him writing immortal poems to her. And all the people of our circle are with them, for them. I have no friends left except maybe the Alan Sillitoes who are in Morocco for the year. How and where, O God do I begin? I can't face the notion that he may want me to divorce him to marry her. I keep your letters like the Bible. How should I marshal my small money? For a nanny for a year, O God, for what. And how to stop my agony for his loved body and the thousand small assaults each day of small things, memories from each cup, where we bought it, how he still loved me then, then when it was not too late. Frieda just lies wrapped in a blanket all day sucking her thumb. What can I do? I'm getting some kittens. I love & need you.[135]

There were no more façades or bluffs, but the lines between doctor and patient had become disastrously blurred. Dr. Beuscher hardly knew how to respond. She had already declined to offer Sylvia "paid sessions." She later recalled that these fall letters had showed "that her depression had deepened and that there was a return of the somatic delusion (or only metaphors?) which she had had in her first illness. . . . this was to the effect that her brain was turning to mush." Sylvia's letters had "alarmed" her, and she *had* thought, as she later admitted, of telling her to "get on the next plane and come to see me."[136] But she did not think that Sylvia should return home to her mother.[137] She knew Plath did not have enough money to stay in a hotel, and she thought about inviting her to stay in her own guest room. But this would have gone against "the general protocol" for psychiatrists. "I thought of breaking that rule, but my own circumstances at the time were such that I knew it would be impossible."[138] Beuscher replied to Plath with a clear directive: Do not return to America.[139]

On the same day that Sylvia wrote Dr. Beuscher, September 29, she finally admitted the truth to Mrs. Prouty. "Of course there is another woman, who has had so many abortions she can't have children & is beautiful and barren and hates all I have created here." She claimed that Ted had never wanted children but had not had the "courage" to say so. "I feel I am mourning a dead man, the most wonderful person I knew, and it is some stranger who has taken his name." She hoped to finish her new novel, which she worked on in the mornings before the children woke, by midwinter. "It is funny, I think. At least I hope so." The night with Prouty in London had been her "happiest night" "for months," and was "the last happy night with Ted." She would stay in England—"I love it here." She asked Prouty to stay in touch. "I am so glad you have seen the dream I have made—as far as it got."[140]

Sylvia received Dr. Beuscher's response to her previous letters on September 30. She advised Sylvia to go "the whole hog" and get a divorce. "You can certainly get the goods on him now while he is in such a reckless mood," she said; it might be harder later, once he realized that she was trying to procure evidence. (The remark lends some credence to Assia's claim, in October, that Sylvia had set detectives on her.) Beuscher reminded Sylvia to keep Ted out of her bed. She cited a practical reason for this: in America, she said, wives lost the right to sue for divorce if they slept with their husbands after they had admitted to adultery. She added, "The other reasons you already know." She also advised Sylvia to cut contact with Ted's family until the custody issue was settled. Beuscher had already been through a "bitter" divorce and lost custody of her two children.[141] She was speaking from experience.

Sylvia took Dr. Beuscher's advice. "Bless you," she wrote her. "There is a dignity & rightness to it. I was clinging to dead associations." Sylvia did not want people thinking she would not allow Ted to remarry. "I do know he's a lousy husband & father—to me at least. And I may, at 50, find a better." She still loved Ted, but she could see a brighter path ahead. She was writing poems between five and eight a.m. each day before the children woke, "An immense tonic." The divorce, she said, would be like "a clean knife. I am ripe for it now. Thank you, thank you."[142] She broke the news to Aurelia in early October:

I am getting a divorce. It is the only thing. He wants absolute freedom, and I could not live out a life legally married to someone I now hate and despise. Ted is glad for a divorce, but I have to go to court, which I dread. The foulness I have lived, his wanting to kill all I have lived for six years by saying he was bored & stifled by me, a hag in a world of beautiful women just waiting for him, is only part of it. I am sure there will be a lot of publicity. I'll just have to take it . . . there is no honor or future for me, chained to him. . . . If I am divorced, he can never be unfaithful to me again, I can start a new life.

Ted had agreed to pay a £1,000 yearly allowance, which was higher than the average yearly wage of £800. "I want no loans, no mercies. If Mrs. Prouty feels like any concrete help, fine. She can afford it, you can't," Sylvia wrote Aurelia. Ugly language surfaced: she worried that Hughes's "working class family & sister" would tell him the allowance was too much. "I pray he will sign the maintenance before they get him to Jew us. The courts would give me nothing. They are bastards in England." Yet she bristled when Aurelia sent $50. "For God's sake, give me the feeling you are tamping down, taking care of yourself. Just sold a long New Yorker poem. I'll get by." She had heard that David Wevill had threatened Ted with a knife, then attempted suicide, and she worried that "he might come down here & do us in if Ted wasn't found."[143] But she refused to ask Aurelia for help. "I haven't the strength to see you for some time. The horror of what you saw & what I saw you see last summer is between us & I cannot face you again until I have a new life." Although she said she would "move heaven & earth to have a visit from Aunt Dot, or Warren & Margaret," moving back to America was out of the question. "I want to make my life in England. If I start running now I will never stop."[144]

31

The Problem of Him

Devon and London, October 1962

In early October 1962, Sylvia wrote a warm, witty letter to Richard Murphy that bore no trace of her earlier bitterness. She reminisced about their visit to Yeats's tower, "the first pure clear place" she had been "for some time." She spoke of wintering in Ireland and joked that she might find a "good Catholic" to help her—"only I suppose I am damned already. Do they never forgive divorcées?" Plath described her decision without anger, connecting it to rebirth. "I am getting a divorce, and you are right, it is freeing. I am writing for the first time in years, a real self, long smothered. I get up at 4 a.m. when I wake, & it is black, & write till the babes wake. It is like writing in a train tunnel, or God's intestine."[1] Plath may well have been "damned" as a divorcée in early-1960s Britain. But excommunication empowered her to survey her new poetic landscape with the eyes of a fallen angel.

Four days after returning from London—and Al Alvarez—on September 30, Plath wrote "A Birthday Present." The poem reads like a grim, surreal mockery of her 1959 Roethkian "Poem for a Birthday," whose themes of healing and resurrection now seemed quaint. Here, the poet longs to break through an artificial, cellophaned world to what is real and terrible: "Only let down the veil, the veil, the veil." The poem's savage irony set the tone for what was to come—Plath's grand *non serviam*.

During the month of October, Plath wrote almost a poem a day—one of the most extraordinary literary outpourings of the twentieth century. In four weeks she would produce nearly as many poems as she had written in 1960 and 1961.[2] These were the poems that would, as she predicted, make her name. Plath lifted the veil to reveal ugly realities about her own life, and her society. She filled these poems with images of torture, murder, genocide, war, suicide, illness, revenge, and fury—but also spring, rebirth, and triumph. Her language would shock and startle, but her path was well trodden. For Plath, as for Yeats and Dante, the fires of hell were purifying.[3] Hughes understood. He called *The Bell Jar* "the map / Of your Commedia," and the *Ariel* poems "the total song: / Inferno, Purgatory & Paradiso."[4]

The risk she had taken when she married Ted now revealed itself. She had lost her husband to a thrice-married woman with a history of abortions—all slightly scandalous to Sylvia, who was still her mother's daughter. The poetry she wrote in October cannot be cleaved from this reality. The loss of Ted meant emotional turmoil and domestic chaos, but also freedom. In her work she reinvented Classical heroines like Clytemnestra, Antigone, and Medea. She flouted deeper taboos than Lowell and Sexton, killing off fathers, mothers, children, and the self in poems of annihilation, flight, and transcendence. These furious, urgent, and sometimes reckless poems defied formal meter, yet their stanzas were symmetrical and rhythmic. This poetry was veering off in a new direction, just as Plath was in her life. She would define them for the BBC: "These new poems of mine have one thing in common. They were all written at about four in the morning—that still, blue, almost eternal hour before cockcrow, before the baby's cry, before the glassy music of the milkman, settling his bottles. If they have anything else in common, perhaps it is that they are written for the ear, not the eye: they are poems written out loud."[5] Suddenly unmoored from the certainties of her life, she left behind certainty in her art. There was no need to hold tight anymore. She was in free fall.

Both Alvarez and Hughes felt at the time that Plath was facing personal demons she had repressed for years. Hughes realized that Plath was answering back to him in intimate code. He thought that as she wrote *Ariel* she was influenced by several of his poems that she had kept with her after he left Court Green, including "Out," "The Green Wolf," "New Moon in January," "Heptonstall," "Full Moon & Little Frieda," and "The Road to Easington."[6] And, indeed, many of Plath's *Ariel* poems engage with Hughes's work in a game of one-upsmanship. But neither Hughes nor Alvarez recognized how much farther Plath had actually gone, how much wider her context. For these poems engaged not only with personal horrors, but cultural ones. Just as First World War poets like Wilfred Owen and Siegfried Sassoon blew apart notions of honor and chivalry with irony and black humor, Plath dealt a similar blow to postwar gentility. Like Allen Ginsberg's "Howl," like Wilfred Owen's "Dulce et Decorum Est," hers are poems of personal grief transmuted into public protest.

The deluge began on October 1 with "The Detective." An abandoned wife and her children have disappeared, and a detective speaker tries to reconstruct events. The poem is clearly aimed at Hughes:

> This is the smell of years burning, here in the kitchen,
> These are the deceits, tacked up like family photographs,
> And this is a man, look at his smile,
> The death weapon? No one is dead.

"There is no body in the house at all," Plath wrote. "It is a case of vaporization." Allegations of abuse, murder, and dismemberment hang in the air. The trail has gone cold: "There is only the moon, embalmed in phosphorous. / There is only a crow in a tree. Make notes." Metaphor, history, and autobiography merge surrealistically.

"The Courage of Shutting-Up," which reads like a companion piece to "The Detective," came the next day. There are more surreal images about a truth that must be silenced; there is talk of death and torture. "Must it be cut out?" she writes of the tongue. "It has nine tails, it is dangerous. / And the noise it flays from the air, once it gets going!" Eyes and tongues witness everyday atrocities they are forbidden to express. Silenced, they become "a country no longer heard of, / An obstinate independency / Insolvent among the mountains." The poem is about the marginalization of the powerless by the powerful, embodied by the aristocratic British library with its exotic colonial prints and male totems. The wagging tongue appears "Hung up in the library with the engravings of Rangoon / And the fox heads, the otter heads, the heads of dead rabbits." Plath was remembering the Rangoon prints Murphy had showed her in Ireland, while the foxes, otters, and rabbits allude obviously to Hughes. Both men had hurt her, and both embodied different types of male violence (colonialism; the hunt). Neither decorum nor femininity permit the tongue to reveal, the eyes to suggest: "Their death rays folded like flags." But Plath's tongue refuses to be governed. Just a few days after seeing Alvarez, she wrote in this poem of "tits / On Mermaids." "Tits" was the coarsest word she had ever used in a poem.

Around this time, Plath received a letter from Howard Moss at *The New Yorker* accepting "Elm" but rejecting "Burning the Letters," "Poppies in July," "Words heard, by accident, over the phone," "The Other," and "Berck-Plage" ("none of them seemed to us quite as splendid as ELM," he wrote).[7] Moss's rejection of her angry, personal poems—and praise for the more symbolic "Elm"—may have pushed Plath in the latter aesthetic direction. She gave up, for the moment, the rebellious, proto-feminist voice of "The Detective" and "The Courage of Shutting-Up" for more surreal poems inspired by the nature in her backyard. She called these poems, written mainly between

October 3 and 9, "the Bee sequence" in letters to editors that fall: "The Bee Meeting," "The Arrival of the Bee Box," "Stings" (begun on August 2), "The Swarm," and "Wintering." All were based on her experience of beekeeping in Devon that summer. But they also resurrect the ghost of the *Bienen-König*, Otto Plath. She wrote in her journal that she hoped the spirit of her dead father would protect her from her stinging bees.

Indeed, Otto's *Bumblebees and Their Ways* is an important, frequently overlooked, influence on Plath's *Ariel* poems. Consider the following by Otto:

> The way in which the Psithyrus queen proceeds in order to ensure the success of her atrocious work has all the appearance of a cunning plan, cleverly conceived and carried out by one who not only is a mistress of the crime of murder, but also knows how to commit it at the most advantageous time for herself and her future children, compelling the poor orphans she creates to become her willing slaves.

Describing a moment when the queen bee attacks other bees around her, he writes that she

> now went on the warpath herself. She quickly seized one worker after another, whether attacked by them or not, rolled them below her abdomen and stung them to death. This done, she seemed to feel quite at home in the jar, and began to lap up the honey which was oozing from the bodies of her victims.[8]

The personification of the queen bee as a calculating murderess left its mark on Plath's October 1962 poems.

Introducing "the Bee sequence" for the BBC, Plath wrote, "Recently I took to keeping bees. I was intrigued from the start by this ancient art of stealing sweetness, and by the heraldic regalia—the bee hats, the screen visors, the cheese-cloth breastplates and gauntlets."[9] Plath's BBC comment about "The Bee Meeting" belies its sinister tones: "In this poem a novice is being initiated by the village beekeepers and a visiting expert."[10] Scenes of torture haunt "The Bee Meeting," with its Gothic assemblage. Plath welds memories of her shock treatment with medieval sacrificial rite, and hints that the speaker has been "damned" by the villagers, and must be punished. In "The Bee Meeting," T. S. Eliot's "Little Gidding" meets Shirley Jackson's "The Lottery":

> I am exhausted, I am exhausted—
> Pillar of white in a blackout of knives.
> I am the magician's girl who does not flinch.

The villagers are untying their disguises, they are shaking hands.
Whose is that long white box in the grove, what have they
    accomplished, why am I cold.

Hughes's work was another important influence. He later suggested that his poem "The Road to Easington," with its similar rhythms and question-ing lines, had "brought on the first of the Bee poems," "The Bee Meeting." To him, its message was clear, as he wrote William Scammell in 1998. "She deliberately adopted the manner of pieces of mine that she interpreted as evidence of my perfidy, then reversed them onto me as replies in the same code (i.e. that I could not fail to recognize and read)."[11] The first line of "The Road to Easington" reads, "Is there anything along this road, are there answers at the road's end?" Plath adopted the same long, questioning lines in "The Bee Meeting":

Who are these people at the bridge to meet me? They are the
    villagers—
The rector, the midwife, the sexton, the agent for bees.
In my sleeveless summery dress I have no protection,
And they are all gloved and covered, why did nobody
    tell me?

Plath knew this was fruitful territory. "The Arrival of the Bee Box" fol-lowed on October 4. For the BBC she wrote, "It is literal and descriptive: I have just received my bee colony. It is written for anyone who has ever tried to keep a genie in a too-small bottle."[12] Plath's speaker becomes the captor, bending an ear to the "furious Latin" of the angry hive. The speaker muses on her power: "They can be sent back. / They can die, I need feed them nothing, I am the owner." But she is "not a Caesar." She vows to set them free. "The box is only temporary."

Plath knew that bees often functioned in English literature as a tradi-tional symbol of the well-run state. But in "The Swarm" she upends this association, linking them with the territorial conquests of Napoleon and the bloody wartime history of "Russia, Poland and Germany!" The observer-speaker exults in the swarm's threat of destruction as it morphs through the air, "A flying hedgehog, all prickles." She is almost saddened when a villager breaks up the swarm with a shot, for she is on the side of the bees, flying for their freedom.

"Stings," too, traffics in power. The speaker ponders the hive's queens as she handles the honeycombs—"winged, unmiraculous women, / Honey-drudgers." Then the poem takes a more personal turn.

Ted Hughes and Sylvia Plath at Marcia Brown Plumer's home in Concord, Massachusetts, December 1959, shortly before their departure for England

3 Chalcot Square, with its blue plaque commemorating Sylvia Plath. Plath and Hughes lived on the top floor.

Sylvia Plath and Ted Hughes with baby Frieda, Hampton Court Palace, London, May 1960

Sylvia Plath with Frieda, nine months, January 1961

"A Pride of Poets." From left: Stephen Spender, W. H. Auden, Ted Hughes, T. S. Eliot, and Louis MacNeice, at a Faber and Faber party, London, June 1960

TED AT FABER PARTY WITH MR. & MRS. T. S. ELIOT

Plath's photos of Hughes with Valerie and T. S. Eliot, London, c. 1960-61

Court Green, North Tawton, Devon, as it appears today. Plath's study looked across the old graveyard.

North Tawton village center

The Devon countryside where Plath went riding on Ariel, 1962

Sylvia Plath and Frieda at Court Green, fall 1962

Sylvia Plath and her children, Frieda and Nicholas, among the daffodils at Court Green, April 1962

Yeats's House, 23 Fitzroy Road, London. This was Plath's last residence. The second-floor windows looked out from her living room; the top two windows belonged to the children's room (right) and the au pair room (left). Plath's bedroom study faced the back garden.

The view from Sylvia Plath's bedroom study at 23 Fitzroy Road

Sylvia Plath's grave in Heptonstall, England

Assia Wevill, Great Hormead,
England, May 1959

Ted Hughes, Assia Wevill, and Shura Hughes,
mid-1960s

Assia Wevill and baby Shura, Court
Green, Devon, c. 1965–1966.

Assia Wevill with Frieda, Nicholas, and Shura Hughes,
December 1966

Sylvia Plath, "Woman
with Halo," c. 1950–51

Sylvia Plath's 1960 collage
of the Eisenhower era

Sylvia Plath, "Triple-face Portrait," c. 1950–51

Sylvia Plath, "Two Women Reading," c. 1950–51

Sylvia Plath, "Self-portrait," 1951

I am no drudge
Though for years I have eaten dust
And dried plates with my dense hair.

And seen my strangeness evaporate,
Blue dew from dangerous skin.

The speaker rejects effacement, and the poem ends with some of Plath's most famous lines:

> . . . I
> Have a self to recover, a queen.
> Is she dead, is she sleeping?
> Where has she been,
> With her lion-red body, her wings of glass?
>
> Now she is flying
> More terrible than she ever was, red
> Scar in the sky, red comet
> Over the engine that killed her—
> The mausoleum, the wax house.

On Tuesday, October 9—two days before Hughes left Court Green for good—Plath finished "Wintering," a personal meditation on her struggle.[13] It begins in darkness as the speaker imagines her jars of honey lined up in Court Green's cellar. Plath's BBC notes offer no hint of the poem's connection to her life: "This year the bee season was poor, I started my colony late, and to make up for the six jars or so of honey I extracted, I had to feed my bees sugar syrup till they slowed into their annual coma."[14] But this is dangerous terrain for Plath, whose first suicide attempt occurred in the dark cellar of her Wellesley home. (She would write her first draft of "Edge" on the back of this page.) "This is the room I have never been in," Plath writes. "This is the room I could never breathe in." The dark cellar becomes a metaphor for the speaker's troubled state of mind.

> The black bunched in there like a bat,
> No light
> But the torch and its faint
>
> Chinese yellow on appalling objects—
> Black asinity. Decay.

Possession.

It is they who own me.

Suddenly the speaker refocuses her attention on the bees outside, "all women," keeping their "long royal lady" warm and alive. "They have got rid of the men," Plath writes. This female emblem of resilience distracts the speaker from death and darkness. Her questions and hopes about the hive's survival apply also to Plath herself:

> Will the hive survive, will the gladiolas
> Succeed in banking their fires
> To enter another year?
> What will they taste of, the Christmas roses?
> The bees are flying. They taste the spring.

Plath ended *Ariel* with "Wintering," making the last word "spring"—the symbol of rebirth and regeneration that had been an aesthetic leitmotif and touchstone since childhood.

If Plath's poetic vision was triumphant, her reality was bleak. She wrote to Dr. Beuscher on October 9—the day she finished "Wintering"—that Ted "has nothing but shattering things to say to me, seems to want to kill me . . . I long for the divorce, for my independence, like clear water." Ted had told her he had been "a hypocrite for at least the last 3 years of our marriage, I have been eating not real bread, but a delusion of love." The past six years had been "sentimentality."[15] He seemed so different to her now—he had always been a "steady driver" but was now driving at "suicidal" speeds through the narrow Devon lanes, chain-smoking, and lying.[16] She told Beuscher he had left the hotel where he spent his first night with Assia without paying, after breaking a sink and burning curtains. "Our marriage had to go, okay. But she makes the going foul." Still, Sylvia knew that she had to play a certain part. "I have to be <u>nice</u>, can't afford the luxury of a fury even. Be good little doggy & you shall have a penny. It is the last degradation. Right now I hate men. I am stunned, bitter." She dreamed of moving to London to start her own life. "I have the consolation of being no doubt the only woman who will know the early years of a charming genius. On my skin. Like a Belsen label."[17]

She told Aurelia, too, of Ted's preparations to leave her life. "Ted is in love, humming, packing, leaving this week. He'll live with the woman, I think marry her, though he won't admit it." She worried he would change his mind about the £1,000 yearly allowance. "He is very pleased with himself and whenever he wants to be very very pleased sort of hums & says, 'I think £1,000 is too much. You can economize, eat less roasts,' etc., etc.'" She feared that his family would turn him against her, though Edith, upset and bewildered by her son's behavior, wrote to Aurelia expressing sympathy for Sylvia.

Sylvia longed intermittently for the "culture & libraries" of city life and the rural peace of Connemara. "I am dying to get to Ireland. I need three months away to recover. Everybody leering and peering," she told Aurelia. "In spring I'll have strength to cope with the rest, the return, holding my head up. I can't sleep without pills & my health has been bad." She looked to Warren now that she had "no man." Her own husband "laughs at me, insults me, says my luck is over, etc. He goes tomorrow." She went on:

> Everything is breaking—my dinner set cracking in half, the health inspector says the cottage should be demolished, there is no hope for it, so I shall have to do over the long room instead. Even my beloved bees set upon me today when I numbly knocked aside their sugar feeder & I am all over stings. Ted just gloats.[18]

Now that Ted's marriage was ending, Assia had doubts about ending hers. She and David were traveling to Germany together in early October, and she didn't want to leave him until their financial prospects improved. She told Nathaniel Tarn on October 10 that Sylvia had named her "as correspondent in a divorce suit" and was "setting detectives onto her." If true, this was rather more than Assia had bargained for. Things with Ted were moving too fast, while David was finally fighting for her. "D. [David] is countering the danger in a 'magnificent way,' doing all the things he should do to save the marriage," Assia told Nathaniel. He was skeptical they would stay together, though he noted on October 26 that the Wevills seemed close on the way to a Peter Redgrove reading. "D. [David] is in a pathetic state doing some kind of marking act: opening car doors for A., lighting her cigarettes etc. She keeps on looking dramatically at him, as if he were going to break. They are very lovey-dovey, arm in arm all the time."[19] David later said that during this time, "We didn't want our marriage to end, and I didn't feel it was ending." Assia told her husband she "regretted" her affair with Ted, which continued to appall Nathaniel.[20] "For me, this is like watching a Greek play," he wrote in his diary on October 1.[21]

On the same day Assia expressed her doubts about Ted to Nathaniel, Sylvia wrote "A Secret," another surrealistic nightmare poem. She then wrote a pleasant letter to Howard Moss, delighted that *The New Yorker* had taken "Elm." "I am happier about your taking this than about any of the other poems of mine you've taken—I was afraid it might be a bit too wild and bloody, but I'm glad it's not."[22] She approved of the new title he'd suggested, "The Elm Speaks," and sent him a new batch of poems on October 12: "A Birthday Present," "The Detective," "The Courage of Quietness" (retitled "The Courage of Shutting-Up"), "For a Fatherless Son," "The Applicant," "Daddy," and her five bee poems. Moss would reject them all.

TED HAD RETURNED to Devon while Assia traveled with David in Germany. But he moved out of Court Green on Thursday, October 11, and did not return until after Sylvia's death. She chose to commemorate his leave-taking by writing "The Applicant," her devastating mockery of marriage. In the poem, the speaker makes a pitch to a potential groom. Plath called him "an executive, a sort of exacting super-salesman. He wants to be sure the applicant for his marvelous product really needs it and will treat it right."[23]

> Come here, sweetie, out of the closet.
> Well, what do you think of *that*?
> Naked as paper to start
>
> But in twenty-five years she'll be silver,
> In fifty, gold.
> A living doll, everywhere you look.
> It can sew, it can cook,
> It can talk, talk, talk.

The poem recalls fashion ads from *Mademoiselle*, as well as the long, sentimental verse Aurelia had sent to a very young Sylvia about a doll named Rebecca who was never sick or angry. This compliant model of womanhood was now the subject of Plath's satire.

Alone in the home she had once shared with Hughes, Plath's cynicism about marriage turned to sadness and anger. But it was Otto, rather than Ted, who would bear the brunt of her rage in verse. It was time for the reckoning she had first attempted in poems like "Full Fathom Five," "Electra on Azalea Path," and "The Colossus." Plath knew how to take advantage of a creative burst, and she rode the waves of her fury. She wrote five drafts of "Daddy" on October 12, the day after Hughes left Court Green.[24] The poem famously begins:

> You do not do, you do not do
> Any more, black shoe

> In which I have lived like a foot
> For thirty years, poor and white,
> Barely daring to breathe or Achoo.

"Daddy, I have had to kill you," Plath continues. "You died before I had time— / Marble-heavy, a bag full of God." As in "The Colossus," the father is a "Ghastly statue" with

> . . . a head in the freakish Atlantic
> Where it pours bean green over blue
> In the waters off beautiful Nauset.
> I used to pray to recover you.
> Ach, du.

The father becomes a Nazi, the daughter a Jew bound for the camps. "Here is a poem spoken by a girl with an Electra complex," Plath wrote for the BBC. "Her father died while she thought he was God. Her case is complicated by the fact that her father was also a Nazi and her mother very possibly part Jewish. In the daughter the two strains marry and paralyze each other—she has to act out the awful little allegory once over before she is free of it."[25]

Fantasy was spun from reality: Otto was no Nazi, but he possessed the habits of a rigid Teuton. "I think I may well be a Jew," the speaker says. Aurelia almost certainly told Sylvia she suspected her maternal grandmother was Jewish or part-Jewish. Plath perhaps wondered whether she had other Jewish relatives on her mother's side, for her maternal grandmother's maiden name was Grünwald, a common Jewish surname in early-twentieth-century Austria and Hungary.

There is another possible source for "Daddy." Elizabeth Compton's father had abandoned his family when she was three to join the fascist Blackshirts. Her mother told her he became a bodyguard for Oswald Mosley. Elizabeth used to dream about him "in his black uniform with black boots. I think I really must have seen him like that when I was a child. My mother said I did, that he used to come home wearing those horrible big black boots and the full regalia."[26] Elizabeth was Sylvia's only close friend in Devon that autumn, and she said that she and Sylvia discussed being raised by single mothers. Did Elizabeth tell Sylvia the story of her own father's fascism, and the dream of his terrifying black boots?

After Daddy's daughter admits that she tried to commit suicide to "get back, back, back to you," she changes tack. Now Plath unleashes her fury at Hughes:

> I made a model of you,
> A man in black with a Meinkampf look
>
> And a love of the rack and the screw.
> And I said I do, I do.

Daddy and his "model" are little Hitlers in a twisted, Wagnerian libretto. In the end, the speaker "kills" both men, and stands among the corpses. The poem ends as the daughter delegitimizes her father—"Daddy, daddy, you bastard, I'm through."

"Daddy" has become one of the most notorious poems of the twentieth century, blasted by prominent literary critics like Harold Bloom, Irving Howe, Helen Vendler, and even Seamus Heaney for what they considered Plath's exploitative appropriation of the Holocaust. But the force of Plath's rhetoric cannot be denied. As Maggie Nelson notes, "the injunction to behave appropriately . . . is but a death knell for art-making, especially for women."[27] Despite its blasphemies, the critic George Steiner famously declared "Daddy" the *Guernica* of modern poetry, even as he expressed his own skepticism about its "subtle larceny."[28] Hughes seemed to defend the poem:

> Her reactions to hurts in other people and animals, and even tiny desecrations of plant-life, were extremely violent. The chemical poisoning of nature, the smiling pile-up of atomic waste, were horrors that persecuted her like an illness—as her latest poems record. Auschwitz and the rest were merely open wounds, in her idea of the great civilised crime of intelligence that like the half-imbecile, omnipotent, spoiled brat Nero has turned on its mother.[29]

"Daddy" became a rallying cry for feminists in the 1960s and '70s. In one fell swoop, Plath seemed to have metaphorically killed off all the Fathers that had silenced and oppressed generations of women. And she had suggested women's complicity in their own devaluation: "Every woman adores a Fascist, / The boot in the face, the brute / Brute heart of a brute like you." For these second-wave feminists, the poem was a potent blend of social commentary and autobiography.

But the drafts of "Daddy" show that the climactic ending did not come easily to Plath. The last stanza of the first draft of "Daddy" reads:

> If I've killed one man, I've killed two—
> The vampire who said he was you
> And drank my blood for a year,

> Seven years if you want to know.
> Daddy, daddy, lie easy now.[30]

With "lie easy now," the poet offers the dead father comfort in the manner of a traditional elegy, and defuses her earlier rage. By the second draft, however, Plath changes her mind. She crosses out "lie easy now," then replaces it with the more perfunctory, "it's over." She then crosses out "it's over" and writes, "I'm through, I'm through"—then adds, "with you." This too she excises. "There's a stake in your fat black heart," she writes, and then she is off, ending, "Daddy, daddy, you bastard, I'm through." Daddy will not be avenged—*she* will. Even if the daughter's victory seems forced by the poem's end, the poem itself has triumphed. Plath has overturned centuries of elegiac—and feminine—convention in a single stanza.

The curse word "bastard," which Plath uses here for the first time in her poetry, suggests the ungenteel influences of Hughes, Lowell, Alvarez, and most of all Sexton, whose "My Friend, My Friend" provides much of the tonal and thematic architecture for "Daddy." Plath's poem echoed the rhythms of Sexton's first stanza:

> Who will forgive me for the things I do?
> With no special legend of God to refer to,
> With my calm white pedigree, my yankee kin,
> I think it would be better to be a Jew.[31]

"Daddy" shows that Plath had her finger on the pulse of contemporary poetry. Lowell and Sexton were pushing the boundaries of Brahmin propriety with poems about madness and suicide. Hughes had encouraged her to channel her more violent instincts into her verse. Alvarez thought poetry ought to deal with extremities of human experience and emotion, particularly the Holocaust and nuclear war. These voices were at her back, helping her navigate as she wrote "Daddy." But this is Plath's moment. "Bastard" announces Plath breaking from a male-centered, high literary tradition into something original. She becomes a Dadaist who rejects logic, good manners, and high rhetoric and lets the surrealist impulse of early poems like "The Disquieting Muses" flourish unchecked. "Bastard" sounds the confidence of a new aesthetic suddenly divined. Rivulets had appeared in "The Colossus," "The Stones," "Elm," and "The Moon and the Yew Tree." Now the geyser has blown. Clarissa Roche wrote that after Plath read "Daddy" to her at Court Green that fall, the two fell on the floor in fits of laughter. It was the laughter of liberation. Plath had introduced female anger into the poetic lexicon.

And yet, for all of its hatreds and grievances, Alvarez would perceptively call "Daddy" a love poem.[32] Indeed, the poem is written in the cadence of a nursery rhyme. The vowels in the poem's first stanza sound oddly like an attempt to comfort a child. "You do not do, you do not do / Any more, black shoe," Plath writes. The "ooo" continues like a twisted leitmotif for the rest of the poem. It sounds a plaintive note at odds with the poem's wild accusations. Even the title is affectionate. The ghost of form, too, gestures toward the decorous elegiac manners she has abandoned: Plath's symmetrical five-lined stanzas just contain the rage expressed within them. The poem overwhelms with its rhetorical and performative brio, but a quieter message hums underneath the tantrum: only love deeply felt causes such pain. "Daddy" may appear a dead end of vengeance, but it is nakedly vulnerable. The speaker has been damaged—she sounds jilted—and the effort to turn weakness into strength may falter. Plath never reveals whether she admires or pities this little girl lost, wailing for retribution.

The repercussions of "Daddy," however, extend beyond the Freudian family romance. Plath expresses horror at how an entire male humanist tradition, epitomized by her German professor father, has failed. While "Daddy" seems to emerge from a voice that is barely coherent, it is highly literary and historical. The poem draws not only on a photo of Otto Plath standing before a blackboard but also on a modernist masterpiece Plath had been taught to venerate—"The Waste Land." As in Eliot's poem, there are false prophets, an outworn religion, images of war and industrialization, nostalgic memories of prewar Europe, allusions to the restorative powers of water, references to suicide, images of bones and corpses, an inability to communicate, different polyphonic registers and shifting identities, the use of German, repetition, verbal tics, apostrophe, and nursery rhymes. Yet there is no chance for regeneration in "Daddy," no hopeful possibility as in "The Waste Land" that the land will be set in order. There is only murder and "wars, wars, wars." Here Plath does something akin to Picasso in his early Cubist drawings. What seems facile at first glimpse shows itself as a calculated, radical gesture born of impatience with a tradition that had run dry. Because Picasso could no longer imitate, he innovated. Plath does the same in "Daddy," her surreal poem of rupture. The poem is not just a radical kind of elegy but an elegy for a bankrupt culture.

Read as public elegy rather than private confession, "Daddy" ironically conforms to Theodor Adorno's famous statement that "it is barbaric to write poetry after Auschwitz," for in trying to describe the horrors of Belsen, the poem implodes. The European humanist and aesthetic tradition has failed to humanize, and the speaker's language has been reduced to metaphorical rubble. Plath positions her speaker as the waste product of the twentieth century, filled with a violence and rage that will trump reason and beauty. She is the heir of Brueghel, whose paintings of war, death, torture, and public executions appeared in the October 7 edition of *The Observer* just a few days before she wrote "Daddy." The article claimed, with persuasive illustrations, that Brueghel's works were "more relevant to modern war and to the concentration camps than almost any painted since."[33] Plath had loved Brueghel's *Landscape with the Fall of Icarus* since high school, and had written of his art in her 1959 poem "Two Views of a Cadaver Room." She would have read this piece with interest.

Another overlooked influence on "Daddy" is Hughes's poem "Out," about a son's inability to reach a father traumatized by his experience in the Great War. Plath had sent "Out" to the BBC and *The Observer* in the summer of 1962; Hughes would find a copy of it on Plath's desk after she died, among a group of his poems he thought she was responding to, bitterly, in her own work. Indeed, "Out" shares certain words and images with "Daddy." Hughes uses the phrase "Atishoo!," and Plath uses "Achoo"; while he writes that the war held his speaker's "neck bowed to the dunkings of the Atlantic," Plath describes Daddy as having a "head in the freakish Atlantic." The poems are also connected thematically. Both "Out" and "Daddy" deal with a child's relationship to a distant soldier-father who has alienated or disappointed that child. The speakers of both poems are their fathers' "luckless doubles"—inheritors of their psychic wounds, victims of their fathers' wars.[34] Both poems declare a renunciation.

But "Daddy" mocks the genteel pieties of "Out," replacing them with an angrier and less reverent criticism of the father. Plath's words are stronger, louder, more self-consciously vulgar (and, perhaps, American) than Hughes's: where Hughes writes with Gravesian eloquence, "Goodbye to all the remaindered charms of my father's survival," Plath ends with "Daddy, daddy, you bastard, I'm through."[35] She one-ups Hughes by taking elements of his own work and grossly distorting them, giving him an exaggerated reflection of the world and world order he has presented.

Plath's "tantrum of style," as Helen Vendler once called it, is, more accurately, the style of ruin.[36] But if the poem is diagnosing the modern condition in the manner of "The Waste Land," Plath's diagnosis is closer to that of Samuel Beckett's "Nothing to be done" than to Eliot's "shantih shantih shantih." Surrealism allowed Plath to reinvent the elegy and change the course and current of twentieth-century poetry.

————

"DADDY" LEFT a luminous afterglow. After Plath wrote it, she composed a dutiful letter to her mother, telling her to "tear up" her previous letter, as it had been written at her "all-time low." "I have an incredible change of spirit, I am joyous—happier than I have been for ages. Ted left yesterday, after a ghastly week, with all his stuff, clothes, books, papers. Instead of returning home to blueness & gloom, as I expected, I found myself singing, washing Frieda's hair, rubbishing out junk, delighted." She was "full of fantastic energy, now it is released from the problem of him."[37]

Her appetite returned; she ate her "first good meal in months" after she returned from driving Ted to the train station. She was full of plans, flush with a $300 check sent by Mrs. Prouty and happy about her poem "Blackberrying" in the September 15 *New Yorker*. There would be a new nanny, a new nanny's quarters, a new phone, and a holiday in Ireland ("heaven, utterly unspoiled . . . thank God I found it"). She would stay at her "darling cottage" from early December to late February with the children and, she hoped, Ted's aunt Hilda; she would gaze at the sea, milk her own cows, make bread and butter, and drink "honey-tasting whisky." Meanwhile, Nick was "an angel" and feeding him was no problem. "He's just like me, greedy," she told Elizabeth.[38] Frieda was in love with her new kittens, Tiger-Pieker and Skunky-Bunks. Most importantly, Sylvia told Aurelia, she was writing again:

> Every morning, when my sleeping pill wears off I am up about 5, in my study with coffee, writing like mad—have managed a poem a day before breakfast! All book poems. Terrific stuff, as if domesticity had choked me. As soon as the nanny comes & I know I've got a stretch of guaranteed time, I'll finish the novel. . . . I miss brains, hate this cow life, am dying to surround myself with intelligent good people. Shall have a salon in London. I am a famous poetess here—mentioned this week in The Listener as one of the half-dozen women who will last—including Marianne Moore and the Brontes![39]

This vote of confidence from the literary establishment buoyed Plath's spirits. The psychic weight of performing the role of the perfect wife was gone, and her writing became her salvation: "thank God I have my own work. If I did not have that I would not know what I would do," she wrote to Warren and Maggie.[40]

Even at the height of her fury toward Hughes, Plath never renounced his writing. On the day she wrote "Daddy," she told Warren, "The one thing I retain is love for & admiration of his writing, I know he is a genius, and for a genius there are no bonds & no bounds. I feel I did discover him, worked to free him for writing for six years." But now she was "looking forward" to

the divorce.[41] Her letters to friends and family all contained the same grievances: Ted's hypocrisy, the irony of his move to London, her cultural death
in North Tawton. She looked forward to a freer intellectual life in London,
better schools for her children, new friends, freelance work, and proximity
to the BBC. She tried to be hopeful, and told her brother that "the release in
my energy is enormous."[42]

Yet there were outward signs of distress. She had taken up smoking when
her solicitor in London offered her a cigarette, and she told Warren on
October 12 that she was "a wreck, bones literally sticking out all over & great
black shadows under my eyes from sleeping pills, a smoker's hack."[43] (Suzette
Macedo found Sylvia in a similar state when she visited her in London that
autumn: smoking, which alarmed her, and "very up and down.")[44] Sylvia told
Warren to "tactfully convey" to Aurelia that she should not plan a visit for a
year and a half—not until she was settled and "happy" in her "new London
life." She hoped that he and Maggie would come instead, or that she might
accompany them to Austria. "I <u>must</u> really learn German. I want above all
to speak it," she wrote on the same day she called the language "a barb wire
snare" in "Daddy."[45]

Four days later, her tone grew more alarming. She could not go home,
she wrote Aurelia, but "must get out of England." Ted had told her, she
claimed, "how convenient it would be" if she were dead. "I need help very
much just now," she wrote. Her "old fever" had returned, and she had the
chills. Could Maggie quit her job and fly over? She must make a new start. "I
am a genius of a writer, I have it in me. I am up at 5 writing the best poems
of my life, they will make my name. I could finish the novel in <u>six weeks</u> of
daylong work." She admitted to Aurelia that her first novel, "a secret," was
"finished & accepted." She was working hard on her third novel (what would
have been *Double Exposure*), and a fourth novel idea had come to her that
very week. "Ted is dead to me, I feel only a lust to study, write, get my brain
back & practice my craft. . . . I must not go back to the womb or retreat." She
made plans for the future—"a year of creative writing lecturing in America
& a Cape summer"—when the children were older and her second book of
poems finished.[46] Her aunt Dot had written to say the family would pay for
her to come home at Christmas, but Sylvia could not face them. She asked if
they would instead "chip in" to send Maggie to England.

> Do I sound mad? Taking or wanting to take Warren's new wife? Just for a
> few weeks! How I need a free sister! We could go on jaunts, eat together,
> I have all the cleaning done & someone who'll mind the babies 9 hours
> a week.
>
> I need someone from <u>home</u>. A defender.[47]

She implored Aurelia to "have a family powwow & answer this as soon as possible!"[48]

Plath's urgent letter refers obliquely to themes she wrote about that day in "Medusa," the companion poem to "Daddy." Aurelia was now the target:

> Did I escape, I wonder?
> My mind winds to you
> Old barnacled umbilicus, Atlantic cable,
> Keeping itself, it seems, in a state of miraculous repair.
>
> In any case, you are always there, . . .

Aurelia is "a placenta // Paralysing the kicking lovers"; "Cobra light / Squeezing the breath from the blood bells / Of the fuschia." The poem's ending names the old source of conflict: "your wishes / Hiss at my sins. / Off, off, eely tentacle! // There is nothing between us." Does "nothing between us" mean severance or closeness? In an earlier draft, Plath made clear she was playing with the double meaning of "Aurelia," which also refers to a jellyfish genus: "That stellar jelly-head! / And a million little suckers loving me!"[49] The double meaning of her name had been a private joke between Aurelia and Sylvia, but "Medusa" suggests that Aurelia's judging gaze could turn her daughter to stone.[50] It is a more personal poem than "Daddy," the distance between speaker and poet smaller.

Indeed, according to Suzette, Sylvia spoke bitterly about her relationship with Aurelia around this time, calling her a "demon mother" who was "controlling, demanding, difficult."[51] She lied to Suzette, perhaps for dramatic effect, saying that as a child she had gone on a seaside holiday and found her father disappeared when she returned. She claimed Aurelia had not told her about her father's death until she was sixteen and that "Her burden as a child was to figure out why he was gone."[52] "The father was the dead hero . . . she hated her mother. She told me so many things about this mother to the point where she didn't want to live anymore, the mother who had pushed her beyond endurance, who wanted her to win all the prizes, all of this. And so when *Letters Home* was published, I was absolutely stunned, because on days when I remember her being with me and telling me how awful her mother was, it was 'Darling Mummy, I've met T. S. Eliot,' like a cat bringing little tidbits."[53]

———

IN HER POETRY, Plath found a way to use the emotional contradictions she experienced toward her mother and husband. The day after Plath finished

"Medusa," she wrote "The Jailer," which imagines a woman "drugged and raped," kept by a Bluebeard figure. As in "Daddy" and "Medusa," the speaker fantasizes about liberation from a tyrant. "I die with variety— / Hung, starved, burned, hooked," she writes. "I wish him dead or away. / That, it seems, is the impossibility. // That being free."

Plath's first "independent act," as she put it to Aurelia, was a weekend visit to the Kanes (now a "horrid couple") in St. Ives, Cornwall, on October 13–14.[54] She wrote about the visit in "Lesbos," whose first line—"Viciousness in the kitchen!"—sets the shrill tone for the rest of the poem. Just as Plath had rewritten the traditional elegy the week before, she now rewrote the feminine domestic tableau. The kitchen is no longer the warm heart of the house; instead, it is a place where "potatoes hiss" and "there's a stink of fat and baby crap." "The smog of cooking, the smog of hell / Floats our heads," Plath writes. "Lesbos" attacks sentimental feminine ideals of hospitality, friendship, and motherhood. At the poem's end, the speaker leaves in a huff, vowing never to return:

> Now I am silent, hate
> Up to my neck,
> Thick, thick.

Marvin Kane remembered Plath's unhappiness during the visit. "There was still this clinging to this feeling of why-should-this-happen. One felt that the old hadn't been swept away yet: there was still too much rubble there." Kathy urged Sylvia to rebuild her life in London, where she had friends and important professional contacts.[55]

On October 19, Plath wrote "Stopped Dead," about Hughes's wealthy uncle Walt—"Uncle, pants factory Fatso, millionaire." She no longer trusted Ted's relatives, and she decided that seeing Ted's aunt Hilda, who had offered to come to Devon, "would be insanity."[56] Ted's mother, meanwhile, wrote to Aurelia that she was "shattered by the events at Court Green in the last few months," though looking back, she remembered that Ted had been "very quiet" during the couple's last trip to Yorkshire. She had "great faith in Sylvia's future happiness—she is a brilliant woman, famous in her own right, and a very strong assertive person." She told Aurelia they would always be there for her daughter if she needed them. "If they could have kept together I felt there was nothing they could not do, and those two lovely children. It breaks my heart."[57] But Sylvia's relationship with Ted's family had deteriorated. That month, Sylvia called Edith a "Yorkshire-Jew skinflint."[58]

Neighbors in North Tawton were sympathetic. "Everybody here [is] very good to me," Sylvia wrote home, "as if they knew or guessed my problem."[59]

(Ted tried not to burn bridges. Before he moved out of Court Green that October, he inscribed first editions of *The Hawk in the Rain*, *Lupercal*, and *Meet My Folks!* to Winifred.)[60] But as autumn wore on, the villagers' well-meaning inquiries began to bother Sylvia. She told Elizabeth that she practically had to chase the rector away with a broom when he called to offer counsel. Villagers brought up her situation in the local shop and gossiped that she was not married, since she received mail under her maiden name.[61] Sylvia was appalled by such small-mindedness. It was as if she had become the stigmatized divorcée of her story "Mothers."

Sylvia continued to rage against the Hugheses in ugly anti-Semitic language, though admitted to Aurelia in mid-October, "I have a fever now, so am a bit delirious. I live on sleeping pills, work from 4 a.m. to 8 a.m."[62] She cursed in letters to her mother as she never had before: her "bastardly" nanny, who refused to cook and charged double the standard fee, and "This bitch of Ted's" who was "barren" from all her abortions. Ted was "an absolute bastard." He had told her before he left Court Green that "it was not living in London that he hated, but living with me! too bad he didn't tell me then!"[63] She claimed that he wanted her to return to America, but she would not surrender so easily.

Her relationship with Ted had reached a new low, marked by a disturbing refrain in her letters to Aurelia, Warren, and Dr. Beuscher: "Ted's fantastic thoughtlessness, almost diabolic—he keeps saying he can't understand why I don't kill myself, it would be so convenient, & has certainly tried to make life hell enough. . . . I think he actually counted on my committing suicide."[64] It is hard to judge the veracity of this claim in the heat of marital war, for Sylvia exaggerated in other letters. (For example, she claimed, outrageously, that the Hugheses would have her put her children "in an orphanage" while she worked so that Ted would not have to support her. In fact Edith Hughes wanted to see more, not less, of her grandchildren.)[65] If Ted did utter such callous words, were they a response to Sylvia's goading threats that she would kill herself if he left her? Or were they as heartless as Plath alleged? The context of such conversations is unrecoverable, and only Plath's contemporary side of the story survives. But she repeated this claim often. Normally formal and decorous in her letters to Mrs. Prouty, she now let loose—on October 18 she told her of Assia's abortions, Ted's wish that she kill herself, his "meanest, most materialistic" working-class family, and so on. Aurelia and Mrs. Prouty would remember these letters, and, when the wound was raw, they would privately blame Ted for Sylvia's death. Ted would blame himself.

Sylvia regained her composure when she talked about her work. "Miraculously, and like some gift, my writing has leapt ahead and not deserted me in this hour of need," she wrote to Prouty. "I have devotion to it—what else but my babies could get me up at 4 in the morning! I have, too, great joy in my work."[66] Prouty sent Sylvia an encouraging letter in November, admiring her "fighting spirit and endurance" and reassuring her that friends and relatives in America loved her. She told Sylvia they could talk on the phone, and she promised that she could fly over in just a few hours if necessary.[67]

Sylvia wrote to Clarissa Roche on October 19 about her "flickery" 103° fever, Ted's desertion, the divorce, her early-morning writing, and her need for companionship.[68] The following day, she wrote "Fever 103°."[69] The letter proves that Plath's real fever—and anger—provided a metaphorical backdrop to one of her most iconic poems. The opening line tackled a question women had wrestled with for generations: "Pure? What does it mean?" Plath explained in her BBC introduction, "This poem is about two kinds of fire—the fires of hell, which merely agonize, and the fires of heaven, which purify. During the poem, the first sort of fire suffers itself into the second."[70] Dante is the obvious influence, but this is a modern woman's journey. The poem went through five drafts, all written on October 20, on the backs of chapter 3 of *The Bell Jar*, Hughes's *The Calm*, and blank paper. Like "Daddy," it borrows heavily from Anne Sexton, this time from "Letter Written on a Ferry While Crossing Long Island Sound."

"Fever 103°" proceeds through the feverish speaker's disjointed imaginings—the smoke of hell becomes "Isadora's scarves," which threaten to choke the "weak"; a baby becomes an orchid turned white by Hiroshima's radiation. The speaker says she has been "flickering off, on, off, on" for three days and nights. But she has gained clarity. "I am too pure for you or anyone. / Your body / Hurts me as the world hurts God." The poem ends with a vision of the speaker rising, "a pure acetylene / Virgin / Attended by roses, // By kisses, by cherubim, / By whatever these pink things mean." Her "selves" dissolve, "old whore petticoats" "To Paradise." In her delirium, the speaker believes she is becoming pure again. Yet her wish to achieve purity through "dissolving" also makes an ironic point that would secure this poem a place in the feminist canon. "Fever 103°" foreshadows "Edge," where a perfect woman is a dead woman.

The furies Plath had released in her poems made their way into several letters home that fall. Alarmed, Aurelia had sent Winifred a telegram: "Please see Sylvia now and get woman for her. Salary paid here." (Mrs. Prouty would contribute, too.)[71] When Sylvia got wind of this plan she wrote an angry letter to Aurelia on October 21:

> Will you please, for goodness sake, stop bothering poor Winifred Davies! You have absolutely no right or reason to do this, and it is an endless embarrassment to me. . . . It was incredibly foolish of you to send <u>her</u> a

telegram. . . . Why didn't you wire <u>me</u>? And to imply that money is available from over in America is the <u>worst</u> thing you could do—it completely falsifies my hard-up predicament, everybody thinks Americans are rich and my problems are magnified. I can't see how you could be so silly! Just like telling them I had a nervous breakdown when I have a fantastic job to get this stupid doctor to <u>admit</u> I have a fever even when he takes it on his office thermometer. This is one of the reasons I find your presence so difficult. These absolutely scatty things! My business in this town is <u>my</u> business, & for goodness sake learn to keep your mouth shut about it.[72]

Aurelia's assumption that her daughter needed to be managed from afar infuriated Sylvia, while her attempts to comfort with Victorian platitudes backfired. Sylvia continued,

Don't talk to me about the world needing cheerful stuff! What the person out of Belsen—physical or psychological—wants is nobody saying the birdies still go tweet-tweet but the full knowledge that somebody else has been there & knows the <u>worst</u>, just what it is like. It is much more help for me, for example, to know that people are divorced & go through hell, than to hear about happy marriages. Let the Ladies' Home Journal blither about <u>those</u>.[73]

Yet Aurelia was only trying to give her daughter what she asked for in letter after letter—a nanny. Indeed, Aurelia and Mrs. Prouty's help in this regard would prove crucial to Sylvia's well-being that fall.

By this point, Sylvia had jettisoned decorum. She wrote to Dr. Beuscher that same day, October 21, about her "intensified . . . dislike" of Aurelia:

She has identified so completely with me or what she thinks is me, which is really herself, that she can't eat, sleep etc. What I see now I despise about my mother is her <u>cravenness</u>. Her wincing fear, her martyr's smile. <u>Never</u> has she taken a bold move, she has always stuck quietly in one place, hoping noone [*sic*] would notice. Her letters to me are full of "one can't afford <u>one</u> enemy," "the world needs <u>happy</u> writing". Basta![74]

Plath's poetic and epistolary voices had begun to reflect each other. As she told Dr. Beuscher, "All during my 6 years of marriage I wondered what to write <u>about</u>, my poems seemed to me like fantastical stuffed birds under bell jars." That had changed. "I am doing a poem a day, all marvelous, free, full songs." Everything she had "experienced is on tap."[75]

She was aware that Ted was seeing other women now—he "takes them to hotels" and bars, she wrote Dr. Beuscher. Hughes, too, seems to have reached new levels of fury. There were no more reassurances from him, as there had been before Ireland, that he would find his way back to her and the children. The couple was now at war:

> He told me openly he wished me dead, it would be convenient, he could sell the house, take all the money & Frieda, told me I was brainless, hideous, had all sorts of flaws in making love he had never told me, and even two years ago he had not wanted to live with me. . . . Why in God's name should the killing of me be so elaborate, and the torture so prolonged! . . . Two years of hypocrisy, just waiting for the right bed to fall in? I can't believe it. It just seems insane to me. . . . He was furious I didn't commit suicide, he said he was sure I would! . . . He says he thinks I am "dangerous" toward him now. Well, I should think so![76]

Sylvia admitted to Dr. Beuscher that, though she got a certain satisfaction from "hanging out a clean laundry in the apple orchard," she hated housework—"domesticity was a fake cloak for me." She joked about sailing off to Lesbos, but told Beuscher she was not attracted to women and—still—could barely imagine herself attracted to anyone who wasn't Ted: "few men are both beautiful physically, tremendous lovers & creative geniuses as Ted is." Incredibly, she now thought "the ethic of faithfulness, is essentially boring. Ted made much better love while he was having these other affairs & the tart in me appreciated this." But philanderers were boring too. Though she longed to see the "one man" who had attracted her as much as Ted (probably Sassoon), the only option was never to marry again—to be her own woman. "I am so bloody proud & particular." She would write novels that would fund a life of plays, dinners, and affairs with "men friends" in London. "I want my career, my children, and a free supple life. I hate this growing-pot as much as Ted did." Yet she had enough self-awareness to understand the psychological risks and perils of a future alone. "I guess I haven't really been 'cured,'" she told Dr. Beuscher. "I seem to have acted, in a different key, my mother's relation with my father—and my joy in 'getting rid' of Ted is a dangerous one."[77]

Sylvia loved her children passionately, yet she admitted to her mother, "I have so much writing in me, the children are a kind of torture when on my neck all day." The villagers were friendly, but "everybody eventually comes round to 'Where is Mr. Hughes.' I hate Ted with a passion." The painting, the sewing, the cooking, the planting—it had all been for naught: "Years of my life wasted," she told Aurelia on October 21.[78] That day Plath wrote

"Amnesiac," which she told Mrs. Prouty was "about a man who forgets his wife & children & lives in the river of Lethe. Guess who!"[79]

And yet she was almost cheerful in a letter she wrote on October 22 to Ruth Fainlight, reminiscing about how they had talked of "less-famous, or even infamous wives of famous husbands."

> Psychologically, Ruth, I am fascinated by the polarities of muse-poet and mother housewife. When I was "happy" domestically I felt a gag down my throat. Now that my domestic life, until I get a permanent live-in girl, is chaos, I am living like a spartan, writing through huge fevers & producing free stuff I had locked in me for years. I feel astounded & very lucky. I kept telling myself I was the sort that could only write when peaceful at heart, but that is not so, the muse has come to live, now Ted is gone, and my God! what a sweeter companion.[80]

THAT OCTOBER, Sylvia reread D. H. Lawrence's *Complete Poems*, which Ted had given her on the day she signed her contract for *The Colossus* in 1960. She underlined much of "The Mess of Love" and wrote "Oct. 22, 1962," in the margin. ("We've made a great mess of love / Since we made an ideal of it.") She dated and starred several other poems, including "Lies" ("Lies are not a question of false fact / but of false feeling and perverted justice"), "Poison" ("What has killed mankind . . . is lies"), "Commandments" ("faked love has rotted our marrow"), "Laughter" ("Listen to people laughing / and you will hear what liars they are / or cowards"), and "Retort to Jesus" ("And whoever forces himself to love anybody / begets a murderer in his own body").[81] Lawrence's poems, with their images of love, truth, lies, poison, Lucifer, moons, knife edges, and rising phoenixes, gave Plath plenty of material to consider the day before she wrote the first drafts of "Lady Lazarus."[82]

The poem, more ironic than "Daddy," explores similar surrealist territory. Plath's BBC introduction suggests her admiration for her creation: "The speaker is a woman who has the great and terrible gift of being reborn. The only trouble is, she has to die first. She is the phoenix, the libertarian spirit, what you will. She is also just a good, plain, very resourceful woman."[83] Lady Lazarus seeks to exploit her audience's love of the freak show: "Peel off the napkin / O my enemy. / Do I terrify?— // The nose, the eye pits, the full set of teeth?" No image is too grotesque or offensive for Plath—bad breath, corpses, Nazi lampshades made of human skin, maggots on wounds. The speaker, who taunts in irregularly rhyming tercets, performs a striptease before a "peanut-crunching crowd," regaling them with tales of her previous suicides, promising them the ultimate spectacle—her own death. Finally she reaches her famous crescendo:

> Dying
> Is an art, like everything else.
> I do it exceptionally well.
>
> I do it so it feels like hell.
> I do it so it feels real.
> I guess you could say I've a call.

Plath had been intrigued by female martyrs at least since seeing *Joan of Arc* with Richard Sassoon in New York City. In the poem, Lady Lazarus knows that she has already become a relic. "And there is a charge, a very large charge / For a word or a touch / Or a bit of blood // Or a piece of my hair or clothes." The lines are uncanny—as if Plath foresaw her own after-life. But in the moment, she was answering back to Hughes, offering him exactly what he had conjured up in his early poem "The Woman With Such High Heels She Looked Dangerous": a woman "painted for the war-path," who kills men. Indeed, Hughes could be describing Lady Lazarus when he writes:

> And when the sun gets at her it is as if
> A windy blue plume of fire from the earth raged upright,
> Smelling of sulphur, the contaminations of the damned,
> The refined fragile cosmetic of the dead.[84]

Hughes thought that Plath possessed occult powers, an identity she takes up ironically in her poem when she plays with the idea of witch burning and witchcraft, answering back, perhaps, to Hughes's famous poem "The Martyrdom of Bishop Farrar." Plath's grotesque femme fatale is in part a rebuke to Hughes's obsession with Gravesian motifs; as Plath's friend Jillian Becker remembered, "Ted who Knew [*sic*] desired her to be Robert Graves' Muse-Witch-Goddess."[85]

By the end of the poem, Lady Lazarus seems indeed to have died again as she transforms herself into a Jewish Holocaust victim. The lines are meant to shock:

> Ash, ash—
> You poke and stir.
> Flesh, bone, there is nothing there—

A cake of soap,
A wedding ring,
A gold filling.

Herr God, Herr Lucifer
Beware
Beware.

Out of the ash
I rise with my red hair
And I eat men like air.

What is one to make of this woman ambiguously poised between the mighty Classical heroines of myth and the doomed victims of the twentieth century's greatest conflagration? Like the speakers of "Daddy," "Stings," "Fever 103°," and "Purdah," Lady Lazarus seeks revenge against her patriarchal tormenters. Yet there is something cartoonish about her—a whiff of cinematic melodrama that mocks Hughes's obsession with the White Goddess and the femme fatale.

Plath was also drawing on current events. The October 21, 1962, edition of *The Observer* carried articles about the mass suicide of Jewish martyrs at Masada; Anna Kindynis's haunting charcoal drawings of World War II famine victims; unethical drug experiments on humans; the Berlin talks between John F. Kennedy and the Soviet foreign minister, Nikita Khrushchev; and American atomic bomb tests. Indeed, as the critics Paul Giles and Robin Peel have noted, the worst of the Cuban missile crisis occurred during the last two weeks of October 1962; the period from the 22nd to the 27th marked the most terrifying phase of brinksmanship between Kennedy and Khrushchev, when Americans and Russians confronted the prospect of nuclear annihilation on a daily basis. Plath's letters during this period reflect more personal anxieties, but she must have been all too aware of the apocalyptic threat on the horizon. The despair and fury Plath felt toward Hughes was likely exacerbated by this life-threatening geopolitical reality. "It is easy to forget how all-consuming the fear of nuclear catastrophe was," Giles notes, "and *Ariel* speaks cogently to this condition of terror and paralysis."[86]

War, martyrdom, suffering women, nuclear annihilation, sinister doctors, and male political leaders—all of this found its way into "Lady Lazarus." If Plath could not rise up in her real life and exact her revenge, she could do it in her poems.

On October 23, after writing the first few drafts of "Lady Lazarus," Sylvia again apologized to her mother in a familiar refrain. "<u>Please</u> forgive my grumpy sick letters of last week. The return of my fever, the hideous nanny from whom I expected help, and my awareness of the 'Hughes position' combined to make me feel the nadir had been reached. Now, everything is, by comparison, miraculous. I hardly dare breathe."

The miracle was a twenty-two-year-old local nurse in training named Susan O'Neill-Roe, whom Winifred had found for Sylvia. She was a natural with the children, whom she watched daily from eight thirty a.m. to six p.m., and full of energy; "the difference in my life is a wonder," Sylvia wrote. After Susan retreated to her second-floor bedroom and the children were in bed, Sylvia took a tray of supper upstairs and ate at her desk while she worked, "surrounded by books, photos, cartoons & poems pinned to the wall."[87] Her appetite returned, her health improved, and she caught up on professional obligations. "I feel, with health, I can face anything, and am in excellent spirits. This nurse is so capable & sweet!" she wrote Mrs. Prouty.[88]

Susan's presence righted Sylvia's life. Winifred reported to Aurelia that Sylvia was now "full of the joys of spring."[89] Sylvia wrote of her study to Mrs. Prouty, "this quiet center at the middle of the storm. If I have <u>this</u>, the rest of my life will settle into pleasant lines." She placed brilliant red poppies and dark blue cornflowers on her desk alongside Warren and Maggie's wedding portrait. "I shall forge my writing out of these difficult experiences—to have known the bottom, whether mental or emotional is a great trial, but also a great gift."[90] She felt she was undergoing the symbolic rebirth she was describing in her poems.

Susan indeed remembered that Sylvia seemed mostly happy throughout the six weeks she worked at Court Green; she did not detect any extreme emotional states, as Winifred had. (Though she noticed Sylvia had a strange habit of locking her room whenever she left it.) Sylvia seemed very loving toward the children and tended to them immediately if they cried in the night. Susan never saw Sylvia weep. On the contrary, she seemed full of energy and plans, taking control of her life in small but significant ways. Sylvia had given up lighting fires in the drawing room when Ted left—she told Susan hauling firewood was a husband's job—but now the two women collected the wood and enjoyed great, crackling fires in the evening. Together they visited St. Ives with the children, picnicking near the sea. Sylvia bought herself pottery and jewelry in one of the local shops.[91]

Since Susan had arrived, Sylvia had written most of "Lady Lazarus" and "Cut," about a recent kitchen accident. Plath had nearly severed her thumb with a knife, an event she described in shape-shifting quartets: "What a thrill— / My thumb instead of an onion." A cascade of violent, male metaphors set within a feminine kitchen interior follow: the thumb becomes a "hinge," "hat," scalped pilgrim, Redcoat soldier, "Kamikaze man," Russian babushka, and, finally, "Dirty girl, / Thumb stump."[92] The speaker shames herself for the unfeminine "thrill" she feels as she watches the blood jet, which she transforms into poetry. The poetic speaker seems fascinated by her injury, but Susan remembered that in actuality Sylvia had been very "frightened" by it. The cut itself took a long time to heal; Sylvia told Susan the local doctor had "botched" her treatment with "bad stitching."[93] Suzette Macedo recalled that when Sylvia stayed with them in London in early November, her hand was covered in a "stinky" and "dirty" bandage. The wound looked gangrenous. "She said it was like a fever, she was just writing these poems. . . . All this fever of creation, she was in a terribly heightened state."[94] Suzette noted Sylvia was not just speaking in metaphors—she was physically feverish from her infected wound. And yet she hardly seemed aware of the dirty bandage, so confident did she seem of new beginnings.

With Susan at the helm, Sylvia wasted no time planning another London trip. She wanted to see Al Alvarez, Clem Moore's father, and Patric Dickinson from the Royal Court Theatre, who was organizing a poetry festival and wanted her to help present the festival's American night. Dickinson's invitation made her optimistic about the glorious London life that awaited, and she used a birthday check from Aurelia to buy a stylish dress at a posh local shop. She would, she wrote home, have "the Salon that I will deserve," and her children would converse with London's greatest minds.[95] She wrote Clarissa Roche, urging her to visit Court Green from November 15 to 20, when Susan would be away on holiday. She asked Clarissa to bring a copy of Sappho with her ("I must read her—a fellow lady poet!"). Clarissa had hinted in her previous letter that Ted may have become jealous of Sylvia's talent, and that his decision to leave was based on "ego." Sylvia agreed. "Ever since I wrote my novel for example (which Ted never read) Ted has been running down the novel as a form—something 'he would never bother to write.' "[96]

Finally released from Sisyphean domestic drudgery, Sylvia grew more confident about her future, and she resented Aurelia's doubts about her chosen course. "For goodness sake, stop being so <u>frightened</u> of everything, Mother!" she wrote on October 25. "Almost every word in your letter is 'frightened'! One thing I want my children to have is a bold sense of adventure, not the fear of trying something new." The Irish winter would be no worse than winter in Devon. Now that Susan had agreed to accompany her to Ireland, Sylvia's optimism returned. She was eating three healthy meals a day—"Probably a lot more than you do!" Aurelia had admitted that she felt helpless to protect her daughter. Sylvia's response was brisk. "Now don't you feel helpless any more. I am helped very much by letters, the birthday checks. If Ted gives me £1,000 I shall manage very well, with just an 'au pair,' the car & his insurance to pay." She added that she was making headway in her riding lessons, "'rising to the trot' very well now. . . . My riding mistress thinks I'm very good."[97]

Warren and Maggie had offered to come to England, but with Susan's help there was no need of that now. Sylvia was resigned to seeing Ted's friends during her upcoming trip to London and would hold her head high. She believed in "going through & facing the worst, not hiding from it." Two days after writing "Lady Lazarus," she told Aurelia, again, "Now stop trying to get me to write about 'decent courageous people'—read the Ladies Home Journal for those! It's too bad my poems frighten you—but you've always been afraid of reading or seeing the world's hardest things—like Hiroshima, the Inquisition or Belsen."[98] After this letter, she would not write to Aurelia for almost two weeks—and then even more infrequently as autumn turned to winter.

Some of the anger in this letter comes through in "The Tour," which Plath wrote on the same day she wrote her mother, October 25. The poem concerns a maiden aunt shocked by the speaker's unkempt appearance and lifestyle.

> Toddle on home to tea now in your flat hat.
> It'll be *lemon* tea for me,
> Lemon tea and earwig biscuits—creepy-creepy.
> You'd not want that.

The poem takes aim at the symbols of passive femininity—maiden aunts, reading glasses, and tea, which the hostess-speaker fails to serve—as well as Marianne Moore, who had criticized Plath's work and asked Hughes to remove poems with sexual references from *The Hawk in the Rain*. The speaker dares to expose herself unguarded, "in slippers and housedress with no lipstick!" Her house is "a bit of a mess!" Like "Lesbos" and "Cut," "The Tour" is both a fantasy of release from oppressive feminine roles quietly enforced by other women and an aesthetic manifesto ("creepy-creepy") proudly at odds with Moore's ("You'd not want that."). Plath found in Alvarez's war against gentility a kind of proto-feminism, for women had the most to gain—and the most to lose—by shedding decorum.

Mrs. Prouty was relieved to hear that Sylvia had dropped her request that Warren and Maggie fly to England. "For it troubled me that she could seriously ask it," she told Aurelia. "It seemed so unreasonable that I feared perhaps her grief & despair & shock of Ted's desertion had affected her in some mental way beyond her control." She agreed with Aurelia that the Ireland trip was a terrible idea—Sylvia had no friends or "connections who would keep her in a crisis," no doctor for herself or the children. But she knew that there was no way either of them could change Sylvia's mind if she was determined. "I know how you go on suffering. But it may come out all right," Mrs. Prouty told Aurelia.[99] She wrote Sylvia that she would pay for a permanent nanny, but Sylvia gently rebuffed the offer in an October 25 letter; she could manage the $15 a week from her own *New Yorker* earnings, and with Ted's alimony she would stay afloat. Prouty ignored her and sent a $500 check ($4,300 in 2020 dollars) in late October to cover Susan's salary, and told Sylvia to spend the previous $300 she had sent on new clothes that would boost her morale.[100] If there is an unsung hero in Sylvia Plath's life, it is Olive Prouty.

On October 27, Sylvia turned thirty. She wrote two poems that day: "Poppies in October" and "Ariel," one of her best.[101] "Poppies in October" juxtaposes alarming images of emergency—carbon monoxide, a woman in an ambulance—with the disquieting presence of poppies and cornflowers. There is something of Lowell's "My mind's not right," from "Skunk Hour" here ("O my God, what am I"), but the poem is more impressionistic.[102] "Ariel" strikes a more exuberant note. There are three handwritten drafts, followed by three typed drafts. Most of these drafts are dated October 27. Plath used fresh paper for "Ariel"—there is nothing on the backside—which suggests that the poem she sat down to write on her thirtieth birthday was too important for scrap paper.

Plath's BBC introduction to "Ariel" is spare: "Another horseback riding poem, this one called 'Ariel,' after a horse I'm especially fond of."[103] The poem combines images of Plath's recent horseback rides with her memory of a runaway journey on a faster horse at Cambridge years before, which she wrote about in "Whiteness I Remember." In reality, Ariel was an old and slow mare, but her name was full of Shakespearean possibility; she is also Pegasus, long associated with poets and poetry in Greek mythology.

"Ariel" begins on the moors at dawn with a stanza full of assonance and sibilance:

> Stasis in darkness.
> Then the substanceless blue
> Pour of tor and distances.

The ride begins, and the mare becomes "God's lioness":

> How one we grow,
> Pivot of heels and knees!—The furrow
>
> Splits and passes, sister to
> the brown arc
> Of the neck I cannot catch

The poet-speaker invokes Lady Godiva, who rode naked through Coventry to protest her husband's ill-treatment of the townsfolk. "White / Godiva, I unpeel— / Dead hands, dead stringencies." The allusion suggests female rebellion against male perfidy, as Lady Godiva's decision was prompted by her husband's dare. Plath may have imagined herself reenacting this dare in "Ariel," stepping up to Hughes's poetic challenge and proving to him that in her metaphoric nakedness she is empowered rather than humiliated. Indeed, Plath wrote and double-starred the date, "27 October," into her copy of *Homage to Mistress Bradstreet* by John Berryman, suggesting that the American poetry collection, with its considerations of infidelity, was an influence on "Ariel."

There are other allusions to Hughes throughout "Ariel," which draws on his earlier poems "Phaetons," "Constancy," "The Horses," and, most explicitly, "The Thought-Fox." By the fall of 1962, "The Thought-Fox" had become Hughes's most famous poem. Hughes spoke of his pride in it during a 1961 BBC broadcast: "long after I am gone, as long as a copy of the poem exists, every time anyone reads it the fox will get up somewhere out in the darkness and come walking towards them."[104] "The Thought-Fox" established Hughes's reputation as an animal poet who tracked his creatures through his poems with the surefooted instinct of a hunter.

> I imagine this midnight moment's forest:
> Something else is alive
> Beside the clock's loneliness
> And this blank page where my fingers move.

The poet links the fox's spirit to his own creativity: "Till, with a sudden sharp hot stink of fox / It enters the dark hole of the head. / . . . / The page is printed."[105] "The Thought-Fox" had become emblematic of Hughes's poetic persona and thus an inspiring foil for Plath as she contemplated her new life, alone, on her thirtieth birthday.

Plath had experienced a major poetic breakthrough on her twenty-seventh birthday, at Yaddo. There, she had written the seven-part "Poem for a Birthday," which recounted a troubled woman's recovery from mental illness—partly prompted by Hughes. When Plath finished the sequence, she knew that she had hit a new note, and she confided to her journal that the poems had freed her.[106] Now, three years later, Plath wrote another successful birthday poem—this time, without Hughes's help. Such a poem, if good enough, would confirm that Ted's abandonment had freed her to become an even better poet than she had been before.

Both Plath's horse and Hughes's thought-fox are vessels of creativity. Each poem begins in darkness: Hughes's opens at "midnight moment's" while Plath's first line is "Stasis in darkness."[107] Although this darkness defines a natural landscape—for Hughes a forest, for Plath "tor and distances"—the poet is not actually situated in these landscapes but inside a room, where the poet-speaker is writing. Hughes makes this explicit in "The Thought-Fox," in which the speaker describes himself "Beside the clock's loneliness." In "Ariel" we do not discover this detail until Plath writes of the child's cry sounding through the wall, suggesting that the speaker has been, like Hughes's, alone in the act of writing. These dark spaces represent, for both poets, the stasis of the imagination in the moment before creation. Like "The Thought-Fox," which begins in a midnight forest, expands into a "widening deepening greenness," then contracts again to a "hole of the head," "Ariel," too, moves from stasis to the more expansive "tor and distances" to finally contract into the "red // Eye" of the rising sun. (The word "eye" appears twice in both poems.) Each poem expands and contracts from beginning to end. Both poets break through a barrier: for Hughes the moment occurs when the fox "enters the dark hole of the head," while Plath's speaker aims straight into the sun. In each case, the deepest corners and furthest reaches of the imagination are penetrated.

But horses are larger, stronger, and faster than foxes; Plath's poem is the stronger of the two, the one with the more intensely rhythmic momentum, the more resounding final crescendo. Unlike Hughes's speaker, she will not wait passively for the poem to sneak into the mind; she will ride after it (or ride with it) as an active participant in the creative process. Hers is the more daring of the two speakers, willing to take more risks with her poetry: riding a galloping horse requires more courage than tracking a fox. Whereas Hughes's fox displays what could crudely be called female characteristics—it is timid, quiet, moves "delicately" while setting "neat prints" on the snow— Plath's horse, although referred to as "God's lioness," displays stereotypically male characteristics of strength, agility, speed, and recklessness. Plath's poems, as Marianne Moore lamented, were not decorous; at any moment they could rise up, throw the reader off, and pursue their own course. They were, especially now, poems that could not be tamed.

The short lines, enjambment, and dashes of "Ariel" keep the poem moving at a quick clip; Plath creates a drama of speed and rebirth imagined as a metaphor for the flight of writing. The speaker shape-shifts, becomes pure motion, "a glitter of seas." But then the fantasy, and the act of writing the poem, halts: "The child's cry // Melts in the wall." The cry interrupts both poet and reader, who realizes, abruptly, that we are not on the moors after all, but enclosed, indoors. The speaker, presumably a mother, ignores the cry, and resumes her flight.

> And I
> Am the arrow,
>
> The dew that flies
> Suicidal, at one with the drive
> Into the red
>
> Eye, the cauldron of morning.

Plath here inverts Mrs. Willard's assertion—originally spoken by Dick Norton's mother—in *The Bell Jar* that "What a man is is an arrow into the future and what a woman is is the place the arrow shoots off from."[108] Mildred Norton's comment embodied the life Plath had rebelled against. Her fear of that life had led her to flee Dick, Gordon, Wellesley, America. The final lines of "Ariel" are a referendum on the unconventional path she had chosen as she took stock of her life on her thirtieth birthday. She had always been the arrow—until suddenly, as a single mother, she wasn't. But Plath could still take flight in her poems. In "Sailing to Byzantium," Yeats asks the "holy fires" to purge him so that he might escape the obligations of the body and become his art.[109] This—as well as Hughes's "The Thought-Fox"—is the shadowy subtext of "Ariel." Yet Yeats never had to stop writing to tend to an infant. Plath is flying blind as she tries to reconcile her life as an ambitious poet with her life as a mother.

The desire for dissolution at the end of "Ariel" has often been read in triumphant, transcendent terms, but the child's interruption presents a larger problem: either the woman stops writing poetry to tend to the child, or she ignores the child for the sake of her art. For years Plath had abhorred barrenness and boasted that children would enrich her creative life. Now, alone with two toddlers in a drafty old house in a remote country village, she began to acknowledge the difficulties that came with motherhood. "Ariel" offers a brief respite from the dilemma as the mind soars in Parnassian Romantic flight over sublime landscapes. Plath could have removed the reference to the crying child and made "Ariel" a different kind of poem. In her first draft, there was no child. Instead, "Ariel" ended with an image of orgasm: "One white melt, upflung // to the lover, the plunging / Hooves I am, that over & over."[110] But in the second draft, Plath replaced the lover with a child. If the poem began as a way for her to take flight from the pain of abandonment, its final form was driven by the desire to escape the demands of mothering. And so "Ariel" became the first poem in English that confronts the risks and burdens of maternity for the woman poet. (In an ironic twist, it is the baby who nearly prevents the poet from giving birth to the poem.) "Ariel" is partly about the competing "drives" of creativity and maternity. Plath had begun to realize that the two were not so easily reconcilable, and that her creative drive was, as her friend Lorna Secker-Walker observed, as strong as her maternal one.

Other poems Plath wrote in late October and early November—"By Candlelight," "Nick and the Candlestick," and "The Night Dances"—display more confidence in the child as a sublime poetic subject. In these poems, the child commands the mother's attention, while nature becomes a spectator. In "Nick and the Candlestick," Plath writes:

> Let the stars
> Plummet to their dark address,
>
> Let the mercuric
> Atoms that cripple drip
> Into the terrible well,
>
> You are the one
> Solid the spaces lean on, envious.
> You are the baby in the barn.

Her short BBC introduction to this poem illustrates the tradition she was working against: "In this poem . . . a mother nurses her baby son by candle-light and finds in him a beauty which, while it may not ward off the world's ills, does redeem her share of it."[111] In "The Night Dances," Plath writes that the calla lily cannot compare to the breath of a sleeping infant, while the comets, full of "coldness, forgetfulness," stand in contrast to the "Warm and human" baby. In "By Candlelight," "haloey radiance" bathes mother and child in the night nursery—though the critic Paul Giles has noted that Plath's reference to "mercuric / Atoms that cripple" in "Nick and the Candlestick" suggests anxiety surrounding the Cuban missile crisis, which was in its "most intense phase" when the poem was written in late October.[112]

These poems, writes the poet Eavan Boland, changed the nature poem forever: "This is no longer a poet being instructed by nature. This is a poet instructing nature."[113] Boland, one of Plath's most influential poetic inheritors, argues that in these poems about Nicholas, Plath pushed back against the masculine sublime and reconfigured the poetic hierarchy. The poems gave Boland, and other women poets, the confidence to believe that "Standing in a room in the winter half-light before the wonder of a new child is aesthetics"—that transcendence could alight in the nursery as well as upon the mountaintop.[114] Yet even in her tender poems about Nicholas, such as "By Candlelight," Plath uses unsettling and even macabre imagery. The bells that tongue the hour are "dull," the candle is a "yellow knife," its shadows "violent giants." The baby is "Small and cross," a roaring prisoner behind his "bars." In "Nick and the Candlestick" the nursery becomes a Hadean underworld, full of "Black bat airs" and "Cold homicides." Plath is often at her best when she is writing about her children, but she is never at ease. The intimacy between mother and child, in her poems, is always shadowed by something threatening and ominous—perhaps the burden of the mother's poetic calling itself.

The New Yorker would reject every poem Plath sent to it in October, November, and December 1962 except for "Amnesiac." Rejection letters from Howard Moss—seven in all—arrived with depressing regularity that fall and winter, as he passed on some of the greatest poems of the twentieth century: "Ariel," "Purdah," "Daddy," "Lady Lazarus," "Fever 103°," "Poppies in October," and "Sheep in Fog," among others. *The New Yorker* still thought of itself as a family magazine, and these poems were too shocking for a publication that sat on living room coffee tables. Once the rejections arrived, Plath's optimism and creative momentum became harder to sustain. She had told her mother the poems she was writing that autumn would make her name. Now she wondered if they would be published at all.

32

Castles in Air

Devon and London, October–November 1962

I n early October 1962, Sylvia wrote to Al Alvarez to ask whether he would like to hear some of her new poems when she traveled up to London at the end of the month. "For heaven's sake, yes, I'd like nothing better," he replied. Ted had told him "rather smugly" that her new poems were even better than the last batch she had sent to him—which he thought "superb."[1] "God knows you're the only woman poet I've taken seriously since Emily Dickinson," Alvarez wrote. "And I never knew her." The invitation was just the slightest bit suggestive. "Come over to my place. I have lots of drink."[2]

Although Sylvia had professional appointments in London in late October, she had more personal reasons for the visit. After years of knocking distantly at the door of Howard Moss at *The New Yorker*, she had managed to forge a strong personal connection to the most important poetry critic in England. Now her poems would skip the line and get a face-to-face audition. She could hardly contain her excitement. To Mrs. Prouty, she wrote, "the top poetry critic in England and poetry editor for the Observer (the big Sunday paper here, twin to the Times) will hear me read all my new poems aloud at his home! He is a great opinion-maker & says I am the first woman poet he has taken seriously since Emily Dickinson!"[3] "Needless to say, I'm delighted," she told Warren.[4]

Plath wrote most of the poems that made her famous in a single month—October 1962. She claimed to correspondents that fall that Ted's leave-taking had freed her writing, that domesticity had choked her. Yet as her summer and fall letters to Dr. Beuscher show, Ted's departure caused Sylvia deep emotional anguish and plunged her even deeper into domestic drudgery until Susan O'Neill-Roe's arrival. Sylvia lost so much weight that September that she worried Elizabeth and Winifred. It was not until her late-October

1962 trip to London, when she shared whiskey and poems with Al Alvarez, that she began to hope that a real rebirth was possible. After this visit, she changed course, abandoned her Ireland plans, and decided to move to London. She had just written some of the greatest poems of her life, poems of revenge and empowerment. The woman who visited Alvarez in late October, and again in early November, was ready to act. Her poems had broken through; so would she.

When Sylvia arrived in London on Monday, October 29, she headed to the BBC to record "Berck-Plage" for *The Poet's Voice*.[5] Afterward, she went straight to Al Alvarez's studio in Hampstead. She read him her new poems out loud, and he had the feeling that she was used to "being listened to properly"— presumably by Hughes.[6] Although later Alvarez could not remember when Plath read specific poems that fall, he remembered hearing, over the course of her four visits, the bee poems, "A Birthday Present," "The Applicant," "Getting There," "Fever 103°," "Ariel," "Poppies in October," "Lady Lazarus," "Daddy," and "Letter in November." The poems astonished him. "It was as though Lowell had opened a door which had previously been bolted against her."[7] Before *Life Studies*, Alvarez said, she had mastered "Stevenesque cadences and Empsonian ambiguities," building poems "grudgingly, word by word, like a mosaic. Now all that was behind her."[8] They spoke of the exhilaration she felt while riding her mare, Ariel, and also of suicide. They were both a "member of the club," Alvarez wrote: "Suicide, in short, was not a swoon into death . . . it was something to be felt in the nerve-ends and fought against, an initiation rite qualifying her for a *life* of her own."[9] Her poetry, he felt, had finally become true to "the forces that really moved her: destructive, volatile, demanding, a world apart from everything she had been trained to admire. . . . She turned anger, implacability and her roused, needle-sharp sense of trouble into a kind of celebration."[10] He felt she was "completely off in her own direction" with these new poems. And she was "great fun, clever and amusing."[11]

Alvarez was most impressed with "Ariel," which Plath had written just two days before. He took it and "Poppies in October" for *The Observer*. "I told her it was the best thing she had done, and a few days later she sent me a fair copy of it, carefully written out in her heavy, rounded script, and illuminated like a medieval manuscript with flowers and ornamental squiggles."[12] Apart from her handmade cards to relatives, this copy of "Ariel" is the only illustrated, dedicated poem in Plath's vast archive. Alvarez's high estimation of the poem may have influenced her to call her second collection *Ariel* rather than the other titles she had considered: *The Rabbit Catcher, A*

Birthday Present, The Rival, and *Daddy*.[13] She was thrilled by the recognition. "The Observer critic thought my poems were marvelous & took two on the spot," she wrote Mrs. Prouty on November 2. "I feel I am writing in the blitz, bombs exploding all round."[14]

Alvarez's praise gave Plath confidence to hold her head high at the PEN party on October 29. The party was to celebrate the publication of a new PEN poetry anthology that two of her poems—"Candles" and "You're"— had appeared in.[15] She felt stares and judgments, and described to Prouty the "malicious questions, the gloating nastiness" of others.[16] But Edward Lucie-Smith remembered no "nastiness." People were "concerned" about Sylvia, talking among themselves before she arrived about how best to help her and get her work. When she did arrive, late, she spoke to Lucie-Smith of her desire to live an "independent existence." She gave the impression this had nothing to do with Assia, "that she had left because she wanted, in a sense, to become herself. She said that she couldn't cope with the demands of her own talent and with the demands of running the household at Court Green. That was the only time I ever saw the poise a bit disturbed. She was certainly keyed up. Higher color than usual."[17] Michael Hamburger had a long conversation with Sylvia and was "struck by her hectic desperation."[18]

Daniel Huws, who talked to Sylvia "an awful lot" that night, had a different memory. He was surprised that she was there, and equally surprised to find her smoking. She was the most relaxed she had ever been around him, and he felt that she had finally dropped her grudge from the Saint Botolph's days. When she asked him how he felt about divorce, which she was considering, he answered that as a Catholic he believed marriage was until death. She responded, "Absolutely, that's what I believe too." Daniel knew nothing of Sylvia's psychiatric history. "Ted was utterly loyal. He never ever talked about Sylvia's problems . . . never even hinted she'd been suicidal."[19] He remembered embracing Sylvia as he helped her into a taxi, "sitting bolt upright and staring ahead as the taxi vanished down the Kings Road." It was the last time he saw her. Like so many others, he later thought he had "let her down."[20] But Sylvia felt that she had faced "the spotlight with dignity." She wrote Mrs. Prouty, "Being the wife of the most famous poet in England is not easy, but I felt I did best to see the lot of people at once."[21] Ted was conspicuously absent.

On this trip, Sylvia stayed with Eric Walter White and his wife Dodo— not the Macedos, who she now thought too close to Assia. Sylvia wrote to the Whites on October 26 thanking them for rescuing her from "enforced purdah in the West Country."[22] The image would resurface in "Purdah," which she finished on October 29, possibly on the train to London. In the poem, Plath channels the shrill voice of Clytemnestra, who murdered her husband,

Agamemnon. Like "Daddy," "Purdah" is a dramatic poem of female revenge. At the poem's end the speaker imagines "The shriek in the bath, / The cloak of holes." During her visit, Sylvia spoke frankly to the Whites about "her troubles."[23]

The next day, October 30, brought two important professional opportunities. At eleven a.m., Sylvia met Patric Dickinson at The Running Hare pub on Davies Street, where she agreed to help organize the "American Night" at the Royal Court Theatre's poetry festival in mid-July. Dickinson remembered, "She was open, lively, and attractive," and drank two lagers.[24] The offer boosted her confidence; she saw it as a gambit. "It means I'd have to be an actress-hostess of sorts," she wrote Aurelia. "A fantastic challenge—me, on the professional stage, in London."[25] At twelve thirty she made her way to Albion House to meet Peter Orr, who interviewed her for the British Council's *The Poet Speaks* series. She used the interview—at least in part—to broadcast her independence from Hughes's circle. She told Orr she found "writers and artists" "the most narcissistic people." She claimed to prefer the company of "doctors, midwives, lawyers, anything but writers. . . . As a poet, one lives a bit on air. I always like someone who can teach me something practical."

Plath read a selection of poems that reflected Alvarez's aesthetic preferences: "The Rabbit Catcher," "Ariel," "Poppies in October," "The Applicant," "Lady Lazarus," "A Secret," "Cut," Stopped Dead," "Nick and the Candlestick," "Medusa," "Purdah," "A Birthday Present," "Amnesiac," "Daddy," and "Fever 103°." When Orr asked her about the themes she liked to write about, she spoke of Lowell and Sexton. "I must say that the poets who excite me most are the Americans. There are very few contemporary English poets that I admire."[26] Plath left Orr wondering if her husband was among those "very few"; Hughes's name was never mentioned. Instead Plath spoke of Alvarez and their shared aesthetic preoccupations. English poetry, she said, was "in a bit of a strait-jacket, if I may say so. There was an essay by Alvarez, the British critic: his arguments about the dangers of gentility in England are very pertinent, very true. I must say that I am not very genteel and I feel that gentility has a stranglehold: the neatness, the wonderful tidiness, which is so evident everywhere in England is perhaps more dangerous than it would appear on the surface." Sylvia was keeping her distance from Ted in more ways than one.

She brought the conversation back to the preoccupations of Alvarez's *The New Poetry* again and again. She had felt more freedom starting out as a poet in America, she said, where she did not feel the full weight of English literature on her. When Orr speculated that few Americans possessed the historical awareness that inspired a poem like "Daddy," she averred that she was "a rather political person" and "fascinated by history." She was reading about Napoleon and the First World War, she said. And her German-Austrian background gave her a "uniquely intense" perspective on the concentration camps. She quietly defended her use of the Holocaust, claiming that she had no time for

> cries from the heart that are informed by nothing except a needle or a knife. . . . I believe that one should be able to control and manipulate experiences, even the most terrifying, like madness, being tortured. . . . I think that personal experience is very important, but certainly it shouldn't be a kind of shut-box and mirror-looking, narcissistic experience. I believe it should be *relevant*, and relevant to the larger things, the bigger things such as Hiroshima and Dachau and so on.

Her new poems, she said, were meant to be read aloud: "In a sense, there's a return isn't there, to the old role of the poet, which was to speak to a group of people, to come across."[27] When Orr mused that poetry writing "has been a great satisfaction to you in your life," she responded, "Oh, satisfaction! I don't think I could live without it. It's like water or bread, or something absolutely essential to me. I find myself absolutely fulfilled when I have written a poem, when I'm writing one. . . . the actual experience of writing a poem is a magnificent one."

When Sylvia returned to Court Green at the end of October, Ireland was out of the question. "You are <u>absolutely right</u> about the need for me to strike London <u>now</u>. Ireland was an evasion," she wrote Mrs. Prouty on November 2. If she did not "return to London <u>now</u>, when it is most difficult," she would "be more & more outside the literary business circle." She was determined "to shirk <u>nothing</u>. To flee <u>nothing</u>."[28] She would return to London on Monday, November 5, to look for a new flat in Hampstead, not far from Al Alvarez.

———

SHORTLY BEFORE her London trip of November 5–7, Sylvia visited a beauty salon in Winkleigh to have her hair done. She told others it was the first time she had visited a professional hairdresser in seven years. She had her bangs cut in a fringe "in the most fashionable style—high on top, curling down round the ears," and kept her "long coronet in the back." The new haircut improved her "morale": "Ted didn't even recognize me in the train station!" she wrote Aurelia. "Men stare at me in the street now, I look very weird & fashionable."[29] After years of scrimping, she used Mrs. Prouty's and Aurelia's recent checks to buy an exquisite camel suit and a few other fine pieces at the Jaeger shop in Exeter. Like her "platinum summer," her new look reflected a new direction in her life, and also, perhaps, a new love.

In his autobiography, *Where Did It All Go Right?*, Alvarez wrote of how he "slept around" after the breakup of his marriage in the summer of 1961. "After all, this was swinging London and everyone was doing it." Alvarez, like Plath and Hughes, revered D. H. Lawrence, whose ethos of sexual freedom was in the air: "for perhaps the first time since the 1920s, it was possible to be young in England and feel free." Even while he dated his girlfriend Jill Neville, he slept with other women, he admitted, "to prove my attractiveness." "Now I was 30-something and divorced and it was my turn to misbehave. I chased women, drove too fast, played high-stakes poker and spent more time than I could decently afford off in the hills, climbing rocks with the boys."[30] Alvarez—like Hughes—tried to live the principles of the poetry he admired.

Sylvia herself liked risk, and she was attracted to powerful literary men. Although the Macedos did not think that Alvarez was "her type," he may have reminded her of her other "type"—Richard Sassoon—who was also short of stature, Jewish, fiercely intelligent, and prone to black moods.[31] Her independent career in London, and the quality of life for her two children, depended on her literary success and promotion. Plath, Ruth Fainlight remembered, was a networker, and Alvarez, as Plath told correspondents again and again, was "*the* critic." Suzette Macedo remembered that when Plath stayed with them in London that fall she was always dashing off to see Alvarez. Suzette did not think that Sylvia was attracted to him as passionately as she was to Ted, but she understood why Sylvia was interested. "I got the feeling there was something with Alvarez, that she admired him a lot. . . . I suspected she would have liked something to happen. . . . Alvarez was a very powerful figure, he could get you BBC jobs, he could get your poems in *The Observer*."[32]

When Sylvia returned to London on November 5, she read a Carolyn Kizer poem, "The Great Blue Heron," for George MacBeth's program *The Weird Ones* at the BBC.[33] The nostalgic poem about ephemeral childhood summers at the seashore sounded like something Plath herself might have written about Winthrop or Nauset. The program featured new American poetry by several poets Plath had known in Boston: Robert Lowell, Philip Booth, John Holmes, and Richard Wilbur. Kizer herself had become close to Anne Sexton. Once part of this group, Plath had cast herself out of the magic circle and tied her destiny to Hughes and England. The program helped cement Alvarez's idea that, as Plath had recently told Orr, the best new poetry was coming out of America. It may have made her wonder where her own work now stood. She was too American, it seemed, for

Alvarez's anthology, but too British to be included in the BBC's American poetry programs.

This time, Sylvia stayed with the Macedos in Hampstead, at Fitzjohn's Avenue. The choice was strategic, for though she was still friendly with Suzette, she considered her "a best friend of Ted's girl friend."[34] Indeed the Macedos had become close to both David and Assia Wevill.[35] On this visit, Sylvia tried to exude confidence and optimism, which she hoped Suzette would relay back to Ted and Assia. She wrote Aurelia, "they see how I am, full of interest in my own life, & are amazed, as everyone is, at my complete lack of jealousy or sorrow. I amaze myself. It is my <u>work</u> that does it, my sense of myself as a writer."[36] Suzette was only half aware that she was walking a "tightrope." "I was having confidences with both of them. It took me years to understand that I had been used as a postbox."[37]

Sylvia may have exuded control in her letters home, but Suzette remembered her "distress" during the visit. "She was hyper. She was obviously taking pills." Suzette thought that Sylvia was on some sort of amphetamine.[38] She seemed "up," hardly aware of her badly infected, stinking cut thumb. She told the Macedos she "did not care" about Ted anymore—she was going to set herself up and become independent, start her own salon—and that she had nearly finished a novel "about IT." Affairs were not uncommon in literary London, and the Macedos, like nearly all of Sylvia and Ted's friends, assumed that Ted and Assia's "bourgeois" liaison would run its course. They were troubled by Sylvia's assumption that the marriage was over. "He's become a tailor's dummy to me," Sylvia told Suzette, who remembered that "she talked as if she really despised him." Sylvia also told Suzette about how cruel Olwyn had been to her, and how much she "loathed" her sister-in-law, who she felt had "a hold over Ted."[39] Suzette assured Sylvia that Assia did not want to leave David, and she advised her to "hold on" until the affair was over. Sylvia was unmoved by this revelation. "She couldn't forgive him, because that was the one thing that had been absolutely no no no between them . . . any kind of adultery. . . . She was absolutely adamant . . . hell-bent, furious."[40] Sylvia would not consider the possibility that there may have been other women before Assia, whom she blamed completely. She "hated Assia" and admitted to Suzette that she was not sure she could trust *her*. "She was very up up up up up. And then we put her to bed."[41] Sylvia slept on the couch in the living room.

After Suzette had tucked her in (Sylvia thanked her profusely), she retired to her bedroom and told Helder, "She's in such a state. . . . She's mumbling like mad. She can't forgive." Sylvia had earlier told Suzette she was "seeing Alvarez," and was going to "transform herself with a new outfit, a camel suit from Jaeger. . . . She was high and flirtatious and enchanting."[42] She said Alvarez was "wonderful: without him she couldn't have survived."[43] But Sylvia's talk of independence made Suzette anxious—she could not imagine how Sylvia would cope on her own with two small children. Later that night, when she went to check on Sylvia, Suzette saw that she was "fast asleep, and crying."[44] "There was a kind of wildness that was held in check by this enormous will that was holding her up. She held herself very tall. . . . She wouldn't even cry when she was conscious. She had to be asleep."[45]

On that visit, Sylvia showed Suzette drafts of some "poisonous" poems about Assia.[46] She told Suzette "she was writing at white hot intensity, in a trance, until all hours of the morning. She was not afraid of it—she welcomed it. She talked of the fever of possession, but there was exaltation, a sense of privilege of being near the real thing."[47] She gave the Macedos a copy of her poem "Poppies in October," which she dedicated to them. She left it for them on the table—along with a replacement tin of Nescafé, Suzette remembered, which Sylvia particularly liked—before she headed out in the early morning on November 6.[48]

On her way to see Dr. Horder in Primrose Hill about her cut thumb (so infected it was almost amputated), Sylvia stopped at a two-story, three-bedroom flat on Fitzroy Road, around the corner from her old place at Chalcot Square. The house was adorned with an official blue plaque stating that W. B. Yeats had lived there as a child. Suzette remembered that Sylvia had deliberately gone to see if there was a flat available at the Yeats house, though in a November 7 letter to Aurelia, Sylvia suggested that the discovery was accidental. "By an absolute fluke I walked by the street & the house (with Primrose Hill at the end) where I've always wanted to live," she wrote. "Flew to the agents—hundreds of people ahead of me, I thought, as always. It seems I have a chance!" The flat, which was £10 a week, symbolized the fulfillment of her literary promise—"my work should be blessed"—and the dream of independence. "I shall be a marvelous mother & regret nothing. I have two beautiful children & the chance, after this hard, tight year, of a fine career—schools & London in winter, Court Green, daffodils, horse-riding & the beautiful beaches for the children in summer," she wrote Aurelia. "Pray for this flat coming thru."[49] For Plath, Yeats's house meant another rebirth.

When she returned to the Macedos' later that day, she was full of enthusiasm. Suzette remembered her taking out a Yeats book and letting it fall to a page that read something like, "Prepare the house for George." Helder felt she "took this magic business quite seriously," though much less so than Ted.[50] Jillian Becker had the opposite feeling, that she took none of it "seriously." It was simply "fun . . . the fashion among poets, specially propagated by Robert Graves."[51] For Sylvia, near the end of her life, "magic" was Yeatsian—bound up with metaphor, allegory, symbol, mysticism. It was a force to be used creatively. Sylvia would repeat the "experiment" back at Court Green with Susan; that time, she opened up her *Collected Plays of W. B. Yeats* to a page from *The Unicorn from the Stars*, as she told Aurelia, and blindly pointed to "'Get wine & food to give you strength & courage & I will get the house ready.'"[52] In the margin she wrote the date, November 13, 1962, and "The prophecy—true?"[53]

Plath rushed straight from the Yeats flat across "dark, blowy" Primrose Hill to tell Alvarez about her discovery. He remembered how on that "gloomy November afternoon she arrived at my studio greatly excited."[54] Her call was not spontaneous: Suzette remembered that she wore her new Jaeger suit that day and had done up her hair fashionably.[55] It was probably during this visit that Plath read him "Daddy" and "Lady Lazarus," which she called "some light verse."[56] Poems full of Holocaust references needed the blessing of a prominent Jewish critic, but the material was familiar to Alvarez for another reason. He may have heard an echo of his own poem, "Back," in "Lady Lazarus." "Back" is about his suicide attempt in 1961, when he enacted "the whole performance again. . . . Three times," after leaving the hospital.[57] But Plath's approach was different; he recognized immediately that nobody had ever written poems like these before. He was "appalled" at first: "the things seemed to be not so much poetry as assault and battery." Still, he thought them extraordinary. He was amazed, too, by Plath's composure. "There was no trace of the poetry's despair and unforgiving destructiveness in her social manner. She remained remorselessly bright and energetic." When she asked him what he thought about "Lady Lazarus," he told her to remove a line, "I think I may be Japanese." She did so, though he later realized this had been bad advice. "I was over-reacting to the initial brutality of the verse without understanding its weird elegance," he admitted.[58] By erasing the reference to Hiroshima, the poem lost its wider sense of cultural horror and seemed to appropriate the Holocaust.[59] She also told him she was "deep into a new novel." While she spoke of *The Bell Jar* "with some embarrassment . . . this new book, she implied, was the genuine article."[60]

On November 7, Sylvia wrote to Aurelia from London with a new exuberance. She told her mother Ted had helped show her around flats and that he was "behind" her now. She claimed that the anger on both sides was dissipating. "Now he sees he has nothing to fear from me—no scenes or vengefulness—he is more human." She considered borrowing a table for her new flat from "Ted's girl—I could be gracious to her now, & kindly. She has only her high-paid ad agency job, her vanity & no chance of children & everybody wants to be a writer, like me. . . . let them have affairs & parties, poof! What a bore." This attitude toward Ted and Assia was new. Since July, she had been writing furiously about them both in her letters home. But now, she felt a growing sense of resilience. "I am no longer in his shadow, & it is heaven to be liked for myself alone, knowing what I want," she wrote. "I envy them nothing."[61]

Why "now" could Sylvia be "gracious" and "kindly" to Assia? Suzette remembered, "One day she went from the flat to meet Alvarez. And she came back and she was very revved up and it wasn't to do with having got a contract for another program at the BBC!"[62] Helder, too, remembered that when she returned from Alvarez's studio, "She was pink and glowing. And warm. . . . She contrasted the current rejections of others who had been her friends with Al's 'absolutely marvelous' treatment."[63] Something happened during this London trip that inspired Plath to write "Letter in November," a love poem for Alvarez, three days after she returned to Court Green. In her BBC introduction she described the poem as "a love letter—a tribute to that alchemical power which can turn the rattiest, deadliest season to fine, sheer gold."[64] The "alchemical" was a witty reference to Alvarez, who was the addressee, the "Love" of a poem that describes a new, life-affirming happiness: "Love, the world / Suddenly turns, turns color." "I am flushed and warm. / I think I may be enormous, / I am so stupidly happy," she writes. Abandoned in the country with her art and her children, she, like a soldier of Thermopylae, thrives in the space where she has been metaphorically left for dead. Plath dedicated "Letter in November" to Alvarez, and sent it to him with a rose petal.[65] Years later, Alvarez said, "She was in love with me."[66]

Unlike most of Plath's autumn poems, "Letter in November" describes real feelings in real time, largely unobscured by symbol and myth. But Sylvia's timing was unlucky. She dated the poem November 11—the very day Al met his future wife, Anne Adams, a psychotherapist, who was staying with friends around the corner from his studio. He wrote that when he met Anne, he was "seeing someone else—or rather, I was gloomily playing the field."[67] He pursued Anne, inviting her to stay in his studio over Christmas when she was kicked out of her flat. By mid-January, she was living with him. The relationship stalled and restarted; they would marry in 1966.

Sylvia knew nothing about Anne when she wrote "Letter in November." Other poems she wrote in early November, in that first flush of deep feeling, reflect what she thought was a burgeoning romance. "Gulliver," too, is an oblique love poem. Plath finished it on November 6 in London, on the day she had seen Alvarez. (On the same day she also finished "Getting There," with its eastern European themes and imagery, and "The Night Dances.") Sylvia had long had a habit of describing her boyfriends in larger-than-life terms. Just as Ted had been Adam and Mallory Wober Hercules,

Al was Gulliver—gigantic to the Lilliputians, who here stand for the quarreling, pretentious members of London's literary society. The poem imagines Gulliver lying down, staring up at the clouds, tied to earth by his small captors, the "spider-men." "Winding and twining their petty fetters, / Their bribes— / So many silks. // How they hate you. / They converse in the valley of your fingers, they are inchworms." These little people are filled with contempt for the giant among them. Plath commands, "Step off! / Step off seven leagues," "Let this eye be an eagle, / The shadow of this lip, an abyss." The simile is clear: Alvarez was the most important critic in London, a metaphorical giant who might grow even bigger if he cut the sycophants and supplicants loose. Plath may even allude wittily to their relationship: clouds float over Gulliver's horizontal body "Unlike you, / With no strings attached."

Two days after "Gulliver," Plath finished "Thalidomide" with its nightmarish imaginings of deformed babies. Thalidomide, a drug prescribed to pregnant women with morning sickness, was licensed in Britain in 1958. In 1961 the drug was withdrawn after doctors realized that it was deforming babies' limbs. Two articles about the dangers of thalidomide appeared in *The Observer* in October 1962.[68] Sylvia had given birth to Frieda in 1960 during the brief window between the drug's licensing and ban. While the theme of doctors harming their patients had personal relevance for Plath, certain lines in the poem go further, and suggest that she may have taken the drug. Nightmares of deformed babies had haunted her when she was pregnant with Frieda at Yaddo in 1959. The speaker wonders, "What glove // What leatheriness / Has protected // Me from that shadow—" the "dark / Amputations." "Thalidomide" is a meditation on the anxieties of mothering:

All night I carpenter

A space for the thing I am given,
A love

Of two wet eyes and a screech.

The lines suggest the burden of the infant's endless demands, and the mother's sacrifice. All seems out of a woman's control, fated by a cold moon, which Plath connects to miscarriage and menstruation. "The dark fruits revolve and fall. // The glass cracks across, / The image // Flees and aborts like dropped mercury." Plath's final images hint at the specter of an unplanned pregnancy—which would have been disastrous for her—and the relief of menstruation. She began the poem on November 4 and finished it on November 8—just before and after she saw Alvarez in London. It also came between two poems whose subject was obviously Alvarez. Thalidomide babies, like the camps, were the kind of modern horror Plath and Alvarez might have discussed during her visit, while fears of pregnancy may have resurfaced if she had planned to become—or, indeed, had become—sexually active again.

While "Gulliver" and "Letter in November" suggest a deepening relationship with Alvarez, the other two poems Plath wrote the following week, "Death & Co." and "Years," speak to a new hopefulness. In "Death & Co." Plath personified death coming for her speaker. But she resists: "I am not his yet." And in "Years," which echoes "Ariel" and foreshadows "Words," Plath embraces Alvarez's love of speed and risk:

> What I love is
> The piston in motion—
> My soul dies before it.
> And the hooves of the horses,
> Their merciless churn.
>
> And you, great Stasis—
> What is so great in that!

Both poems reject the stasis of nonbeing, of death: "Eternity bores me, / I never wanted it." Plath's despair had lifted.

———

ALVAREZ NEVER DENIED that his relationship with Plath deepened during the fall of 1962. Indeed, he wrote poignantly about their afternoons together in his later memoirs. He sensed that she was interested in him, yet he always maintained that the relationship was platonic. But Olwyn Hughes, one of three people known to have read Plath's 1962–63 journals, disputed Alvarez's version of events. Before her death, Olwyn told Hughes's biographer Jonathan Bate that Plath had written wittily in her journal about a sexual encounter with Alvarez during this November 5–7 visit (it probably took place on November 6, her only free full day in London, according to her 1962 calendar). Olwyn had earlier revealed this information to the Hughes critic Mark Wormald and Hughes's biographer Elaine Feinstein.[69] Such an encounter would explain why Plath felt bold enough to send Alvarez a love poem with a rose petal. Alvarez spoke of sleeping around during this time, but for Plath, sex was Lawrentian, sacred.

During our 2016 interview, Ted's closest lifelong friend, Daniel Huws, said that Ted himself had told Luke Myers—who in turn told Daniel—that Sylvia had written in her journal that she had "spent the night" with Al once during the autumn of 1962.[70] Myers confirmed this in a 2001 letter to Elaine Feinstein, in which he told her that his previous supposition that Plath and Alvarez had not slept together was wrong.[71] Ted had told him of the details in Sylvia's journal. Daniel said that the brief affair was why, for much of Ted's life, "Alvarez was a dirty word. He felt betrayed."[72] Elizabeth Compton, who knew Alvarez in 1962, said he told her he had been involved in a romantic relationship with Plath at the time; he was the first person Elizabeth phoned when she learned of Sylvia's suicide.[73] When the matter of sex with Plath came up in our 2016 interview, Alvarez gave a small smile but stayed silent, neither confirming nor denying what his wife, sitting next to him, called "gossip." Moments later, however, he vehemently denied any romantic involvement with Assia Wevill. "I was all sorts of things, but mad for her I never was."[74] In a 1970 letter to a Plath biographer, he called Assia a "bitch"; his bitterness toward her was still plain nearly fifty years later.[75]

A sexual encounter, however brief, casts a new light on Plath's *Ariel* poems. Plath wrote nearly all of the poems for which she is now remembered—including "Daddy," "Ariel," "Lady Lazarus," "Purdah," "Fever 103°," and the bee poems—in the month of October, between her first visit to Alvarez in late September as a newly single woman and her second and third visits to him in late October and early November. Al, not Ted, was her new sounding board. It is possible that she was writing poems she knew would please Alvarez—not only because she respected his aesthetic judgment and shared his aesthetic preferences but because she needed, very badly, to sell her poems. Her future and that of her children depended on her financial independence, and Alvarez was an emotional and professional lifeline for Plath in the winter of 1962. But because he always understated his romantic involvement with Plath, his role in her creative breakthrough that fall has been largely ignored.[76] In his memoir *The Savage God*, he portrayed himself as someone who recognized the genius of Plath's new poems, restored her confidence, and secured her posthumous reputation. All of this is true enough, but a sexual affair complicates that narrative. Sex raised the stakes, and raised Plath's hopes.

Olwyn claimed that part of the reason Ted burned Sylvia's last journal was because he did not want her children to read about their mother being damaged by other men. Olwyn's claim seems accurate in light of Ted's own admission to a critic, Jacqueline Rose, in the 1990s. "First you must believe me when I tell you—I have never told this to anyone—I hid the last journal, about two months of entries, to protect—possibly to my utter foolishness—

somebody else."[77] That "somebody else" could have been Assia but was likely Alvarez. Hughes felt obligated to "protect" him because he had been a friend and because his own actions had led to Alvarez's entanglements with his wife. Ted was fiercely private, but he tried to tell Al, in his oblique way, that he knew. "What I didn't find out in my nearly daily visits to her I found in her diary—complete details," he wrote suggestively in a furious 1971 letter to Alvarez.[78]

Hughes's knowledge of the affair helps explain his white-hot rage at Alvarez in this letter and others he wrote to him in the early 1970s, when Alvarez was about to publish *The Savage God*, a memoir of his friendship with Plath, and of her suicide, in serialized form in *The Observer*. Ted had not yet told his children that their mother had committed suicide, and he raged against Al for revealing intimate details about her death to the "peanut-crunching crowd." Daniel Huws believed that the affair between Sylvia and Al fueled "Ted's grievance" with *The Savage God*. "Alvarez must have felt almost as guilty as Ted in a way, and that writing that book was . . . he was driven by a bad conscience."[79] Hughes never made explicit accusations of an affair in his letters to Alvarez, though he alluded to it. He wrote that Alvarez's book must have started "in a sacred way by one part of you, as a private, personal document," but had become beholden to the "greedy demand of that empty public."

> Whatever Sylvia may be for your readers & you, for her mother & me & her children she is something different, she is an atmosphere we breathe. This is something apart from remembrance, it is a world imposed on us by the public consciousness of her and of our inevitable relationship to her. Your memoir has simply increased that atmospheric pressure intolerably . . . for your readers it's five interesting minutes, but for us it is permanent dynamite.

He reminded Al that he had been "false to the facts," and that Al didn't know "half" of what had really been going on with Sylvia during the last week of her life.[80] Ted also told Al that he knew he had "faked" some of the details of his memoir.[81] "I can only think Sylvia's death has become a theme for some involvement of your own—some private thing that's fouled your judgment. If so, for Christ's sake step back & see what you're doing."[82] Alvarez himself admitted that he had destroyed most of Plath's letters to him because he "was so upset and guilty about what had happened that I wanted to have done with it all."[83]

Al replied to Ted that he wrote his memoir as "a tribute" to Sylvia. He had kept all of her angry revelations about her marriage out of the book, and thought that his account of her last days was more accurate than many of the "rumors" making the rounds. And he reminded Ted of the role he'd played in making both of their reputations:

> For the last ten years or more I have taken a lot of trouble to get both your poetry and Sylvia's read with understanding and a proper respect. I have done so not because you happened to be friends of mine but because I think you the most gifted poets of this generation. Sylvia knew this and knew I understood in some way what she was trying to do. That, presumably, is why she came to me with her poems after the separation.[84]

The Observer published the first serialization of *The Savage God* in 1971 but decided to "cut short the story" in light of Hughes's angry letter to the paper casting doubt on its accuracy. On November 7, 1971, the paper published Alvarez's response under Hughes's comments. "I was writing about Plath as a person—I think, a genius—in her own right," Alvarez wrote, and added, pointedly, that at the end of her life she was no longer living with Hughes.[85] In other words, Ted had forfeited his right to outrage when he left Sylvia, who had turned to Al for comfort and companionship in late 1962. Hughes and Alvarez did not speak for six years after this incident. Ted finally broke the silence in 1977, dropping by Al's place unannounced. "Believe me, I've really missed you," he later wrote.[86]

If Hughes knew about the encounter, why did he not mention it in these furious letters? Perhaps because Hughes could hardly bring up the affair as he criticized Alvarez for publicizing details about *his* private life. Alvarez suggested the nature of this unspoken pact in a 2004 interview about the film *Sylvia:* "the scriptwriter has me telling Ted that Sylvia has made a pass at me. Treachery posing as confession and gossip may be the lifeblood of soap opera, but in the real world friends don't behave like that, especially friends who know each other's secrets and wish each other well."[87] In an unpublished, undated note in the British Library, Hughes wrote angrily:

> Al hurt by my reaction to his account
> Of S's death . . .
> his irresistible need to tell
> How he too tended the final days
> How he too performed on that stage
> And shall now forever perform.[88]

Hughes felt doubly betrayed—not only had Alvarez kept quiet about his own romantic involvement with Plath, he had positioned himself as Plath's champion when feminists began to attack Hughes, calling him a murderer. For decades no one doubted Alvarez's side of the story because Plath confided only in her journal. She never confirmed the Macedos' suspicions. But then, they noted, Sylvia wasn't the kind of woman who spoke openly about such matters—unlike Assia, who reveled in her romantic dramas.[89]

Ted may have resisted the urge to reveal his hand, but Olwyn did not. In 1972, she wrote to Alvarez asking him to write to the president of Random House to protest the publication of Robin Morgan's *Monster*, which included the controversial poem "The Arraignment" that accused Hughes of Plath's "murder." Doris Lessing and Richard Murphy had already written to Random House in protest, Olwyn said. Olwyn wrote dismissively, showing a lack of understanding of Plath's work, "I think the day that girl discovered the Confessional School was a black day."[90]

Alvarez, stung by his recent feud with Hughes, declined to help. "Naturally I think the poem is worthless," he wrote to Olwyn. "But after Ted's extraordinary behaviour last year it would be inappropriate for me to get into the act. My own reaction would be to take no notice of Robin Morgan's carry-on. But you and Ted must do what you think best."[91] Olwyn, furious, suggested that he might want to think twice about withholding support, given his own involvement with Sylvia.

> I find your attitude extraordinary. . . . The issues are so very different and this poem so truly vile, I was sure you would have no hesitation attempting by brief cable to sway Random House away from the ignominy of publishing it.
> I was wrong.
>
> PS You will be interested to know that the old red herrings—novel that tells all, piles of unpublished and damning late poems and all that piffle are given as basic reasons for Morgan's disgusting piece. So you see in a way it concerns you more than you seem to think.[92]

Sixteen years later, she wrote to Alvarez again. This time she quoted a line from Plath's 1962 journals about their sexual encounter, and asked him to elaborate for Anne Stevenson's forthcoming biography of Plath, which she coauthored.[93] He replied curtly: "Thanks for the invitation to tell all. The answer—of course—is a definitive no."[94] He added that he was struck that she was quoting Plath's 1962 journals, which "Ted said were lost or destroyed. Does this mean that they have been found again and will eventually be available in print? If so, that is fascinating news." Olwyn responded soon after, asking, "Would you like to go over the end chapters and see if you feel you want to add anything? Not about the brief laison [sic], necessarily. Just any touches or corrections." Olwyn had lived in Paris and spoke French fluently; she was using "liaison" as the French use it. She elaborated on this "brief laison [sic]" in a condescending postscript:

> JOURNALS: No, I read them 63-64. I suppose the line I mentioned was in the last one (which was only for a few months). The only other mention of you I recall was a full page of tense instructions to herself (just before yr. Xmas 62 meeting) to be patient, to be casual, not to show her feelings and scare you off) [sic] After that, with the January freezze [sic] up, she spiraled down. Its [sic] a pity they are lost, though—apart from more bitching than usual—they are very much a continuation of the others. Nightmares and struggle, jubilations on her work. And as usual little of the sort of simple information one would expect from a Journal.[95]

Olwyn went on, speculating that when Richard Murphy had "rebuffed" Sylvia's alleged advances in Ireland, she had turned to Al in London.

> Meanwhile she had the odd couple of days in London where the episode with you occurred and around that time switched her plans for a move to London. It seems both Murphy's silence and your involvement may have played here. She then spent Dec. getting the flat to rights (did you see her during this time?) and the Xmas Eve meeting put an end to her hopes of a relationship with you. . . . So you see for a real mapping of this period, her involvement with you is one of the keys. And why I finally asked you to think about indicating it in some way. But I see how you wouldn't want to descend to such indiscretion.

At the end of the letter Olwyn added in a handwritten line, "Sylvia confided in no one about your relationship—except on 'influential critic' lines." Later, Olwyn told the poet and critic Elaine Feinstein about the episode. When Feinstein wrote about it in an early draft of her 2001 Ted Hughes biography, Olwyn scribbled in the margin, "Please, Elaine OUT. This conveyed to you in confidence."[96] With nothing of her own to gain, Olwyn changed her mind about conveying this explosive information about Plath's last lover to the public. Feinstein removed the passage.

SYLVIA'S LONDON HIGH did not last long. She returned to Court Green to find a letter, dated November 5, from Howard Moss at *The New Yorker* rejecting all ten of the new poems she had sent him: "A Birthday Present," "The

Detective," "The Courage of Quietness," "A Secret," "For a Fatherless Son," "The Bee Meeting," "The Arrival of the Bee Box," "Stings," "The Swarm," and "Wintering." He also rejected "Poppies in October," "Ariel," and "Purdah." Wasting no time, Plath sent her old beau Peter Davison "Fever 103°," "Nick and the Candlestick," "Purdah," "A Birthday Present," "The Jailer," "The Detective," "The Courage of Quietness," "Lesbos," "Eavesdropper," and the bee poems.

On November 8, just after returning from London, Sylvia promptly wrote to another influential male ally, Bill Merwin. Dido had refused to speak to Sylvia when she had called in August with questions about a child psychiatrist for Frieda, and she felt that she needed to secure Bill's support—especially now that she was moving back to London. "I was simply stunned. Ted has since told me that Dido is no friend of mine & to forget her. My one thought was—was it an illusion, an hypocrisy, all that love & friendship I thought was for me as well as Ted?" She told Merwin of her plans to move to London and hire an au pair so that she could write. "Domesticity always bored me, & I will simply buy myself a foreign girl. . . . All I want is my own life—not to be anybody's wife, but to be free to travel, move, work, be without check." She still thought Ted "a genius & the best living poet," and she wished him "joy"—"Ted is getting me writing jobs, I am delighted to be free of the need to crop my life to his will or that of any man." But she was filled with sadness that Bill might side with Dido against her. "Must I give you up too? . . . Was I wrong in thinking you were real as well?"[97]

Hughes also wrote to Merwin in the fall of 1962:

Sylvia's much better off now—it's thrown her onto her better self. There are definitely two of those selves. The main difficulty is Frieda, I wouldn't like to lose her. . . . Your judgment of what was happening to my writing was exactly what I thought too. Marriage wasn't entirely to blame. The hidden persuaders of Englishness were part of it . . . There were other troubles, which may now be over. Anyway, I'm finding it much easier to write.[98]

In London, Sylvia had purchased the book Dr. Beuscher had recommended—*The Art of Loving*, by Erich Fromm. She inscribed it on November 9, and began reading. Sylvia saw herself reflected in Fromm's idea of "idolatrous love," which was particularly influential. She starred and underlined Fromm's words:

If a person has not reached the level where he has a sense of I-ness, rooted in the productive unfolding of his own powers, he tends to "idolize" the loved person. He is alienated from his own powers and projects them into the loved person, who is worshipped as the *summum bonum*, the bearer of all love, all light, all bliss. In this process he deprives himself of all sense of strength, loses himself in the loved one instead of finding himself.[99]

She also underlined passages about sadism, masochism, symbiosis, submission, womanizing, creative partnerships, spousal and maternal dependency, rebirth, and romantic love. Fromm suggested meditative exercises, which Sylvia practiced to calm herself: she should sit with eyes closed, relaxed, let her thoughts go, and "try to have a sense of 'I'; I = myself, as the center of my powers, as the creator of my world." Plath heavily underlined "To have faith requires courage."[100]

By early November the phone at Court Green was working again, and Sylvia was back in touch with friends and family in America.[101] Mrs. Prouty, concerned, phoned as soon as she could. David and Elizabeth Compton visited Sylvia frequently. "How do you deal with somebody who's bereaved?" David had wondered. "I was cautious about being very jolly. I never saw her weeping or anything, but there were low days when it was a good thing that we were able to take the children unobtrusively.... One goes on, doesn't one, puts one foot in front of the other. You have to cope. And she did it pretty well, I think."[102] Clarissa Roche remembered the chill and fog as she alighted from the Devon train with her month-old infant on November 17. Sylvia was waiting for her, holding a huge umbrella that she steadied with both hands. "As I climbed down from the platform, she hugged me and said over and over, 'You've saved my life.'"

Clarissa, a fellow American mother whom Sylvia had known at Smith—also married to a British poet—stayed for four nights. She thought of herself as an "anchor." They spoke of Sylvia's first suicide attempt; Sylvia told Clarissa her "iron will to live" had "saved her." "Death himself knocked her down and the cold concrete of her grave clawed her face, but she won the day and was there—alive, valiant, triumphant. I shall never forget her eloquence or her pride." They spoke, too, about "treading the water of sleepless nights, 'nappies,' near-poverty, spilled porridge, hills of laundry, loneliness, and the cold." Yet they remained "willful about our love for England."[103] Sylvia never spoke to Clarissa about leaving, though she spoke harshly of Ted, calling him "a traitor." She ridiculed the Hugheses—"gross, ill-mannered shopkeepers"—and complained about Ted's lack of manners. Her family, she said, cared deeply about "manners, gentility, respectability."[104] She "romanticized" her father, a "self-made man" who had walked off the boat not knowing any English and ended up at Harvard. She told Clarissa about their closeness—the walks they had taken together and how he had spoken to her as if she were an adult. Sylvia waxed lyrical, too, about her "gypsy grand-mother," probably her maternal, orphaned, Viennese great-grandmother. Sylvia had also told Suzette around this time that she had "gypsy and Jewish blood."[105]

To Clarissa, Sylvia did not seem "heartbroken" over Ted. "Just plain bloody mad. And very very vengeful." Sylvia said Ted had beaten her and caused her miscarriage, and that he had pulled a sink out of a hotel room wall when he was with Assia. All of this was told "in so dramatized a fashion" that Clarissa was skeptical. Sylvia thought that he was seeing other women besides Assia, and suspected that neighbors were gossiping about her, even peering into her windows.

During that visit Sylvia took particular pleasure in deflating literary rep-utations; she told Clarissa that Mrs. Prouty was "a bit of a nit. The general tone was, 'Didn't she realize what a fool she was, having written an abso-lutely terrible book, and trying to compensate for it all those years by giving her money to Smith girls.'" This was not the first time Sylvia had criticized Prouty; Smith friends remembered her occasionally mocking Prouty's "soap opera" novels. Though Sylvia was unquestionably grateful to Prouty, she also chafed against the sense of obligation she felt toward her. Prouty had paid most of Plath's Smith tuition and all of her McLean expenses, and continued to keep Plath afloat with large checks. Sylvia knew she was lucky to have such a generous benefactor, but part of her resented having to accept Prouty's money, for it meant proving herself worthy, over and over. In this way, Syl-via's relationship with Prouty mirrored—though to a lesser extent—her rela-tionship with Aurelia. Plath's resentment helps explain why, in *The Bell Jar,* her portrait of Philomena Guinea, based on Mrs. Prouty, is less sympathetic than Prouty deserved.

Mrs. Prouty was not the only writer Sylvia attacked as she played the cynic for Clarissa. She spoke too of Stephen Spender, "what an ass he was. . . . And she thought Eliot was such a fool for having taken Ted up. She said it wasn't because of Ted's poetry but because he rather fancied him." Sylvia mocked Ted for having played up his Yorkshire accent when they had returned to England, "playing the great country boy. And Eliot fell for it."[106] She felt Ted played to gay writers in London, too, the ones who were always sidling up to her, saying, "Oh, aren't you lucky? He's just like a great cowboy!"[107] She told Clarissa that Alvarez was "her closest friend in London. And that they spent hours and hours talking about suicide. But as far as his knowledge of poetry went, he was absolutely dismissed out the window. She would laugh and laugh and laugh. . . . What fools they all were and how easily she could con them."[108] Shocking as Plath's words sound, this ruthlessness, which Aurelia never forgave or understood, served Plath well in her art.

Clarissa found Sylvia to be a conscientious but detached mother. When Frieda began looking through Clarissa's purse, Sylvia swiftly snatched it away and plucked out a bottle of iron pills that might have harmed the children. She called Frieda and Nicholas her "bunnies" but never hugged them in Clarissa's presence. They were observant and clever, but quiet. Clarissa sensed that Sylvia preferred an orderly, Germanic approach over rambunctious American child-rearing. Elizabeth noticed the same tendency—Sylvia seemed "careful and controlled" with the children, rather than "warm and affectionate." Frieda was not allowed to eat any candy, only raisins, as Sylvia did not want her to "ruin" her teeth.[109] The children were fed, bathed, and put to bed on schedule, but, said Clarissa, "I don't remember any climbing on laps. Certainly the silence I remember." Still, Sylvia spoke of wanting more children, and they joked about a rich Polish army officer Clarissa knew who might be willing to father Sylvia's future brood. "She'd be kept in enormous style." Clarissa was joking, and became alarmed when Sylvia started to take the idea seriously. Sylvia said she was "warm-blooded . . . sexually she was ten-up on Ted."[110] Episodes like this, as well as her paranoia about the villagers watching her, made Clarissa realize that Sylvia needed help, and she tried as best she could to offer it. She speculated that Susan O'Neill-Roe's kindness and hard work had saved Sylvia from suicide that fall.

Clarissa's visit raised Sylvia's spirits; she wrote to Aurelia on November 19 that she was "fantastically busy." A hairdresser began setting her hair once a week in Winkleigh. She spent her evenings playing tarot with Winifred and other local women, and dining with Susan and her parents at their home in nearby Belstone. There she saw the Liberal Party candidate Mark Bonham Carter, who was, Sylvia noted, the son of Lady Violet Bonham Carter—herself the daughter of Prime Minister H. H. Asquith—and the head of Collins publishing house. (Elizabeth said Mark Bonham Carter was devastated after Plath's death. She claimed that Plath had spent time with him in London in 1962–63. Clarissa said Sylvia had told her, during her Devon visit, that she was "leaning on" Mark Bonham Carter.)[111] Sylvia was "riding twice a week now," she wrote Aurelia.[112] "I got off the leading rein on my horse just before I left & have had some heavenly rides under the moors."[113] She was reviewing biographies and children's books for the *New Statesman* and was delighted to see some of her older reviews "take" as blurbs on book jackets.[114] A Norwegian radio station wanted to translate and broadcast *Three Women*, while Peter Davison wrote full of praise for her new poems. He recognized something in them Howard Moss had not. "How good to see a new batch of poems! I find them quite extraordinary, and they strike a new note that I haven't heard in your work before." His "favorite was 'In the Bee Box,'" which he said "fairly hums with fright."[115] Although he sent seven of the poems back, he kept the rest. (*The Atlantic* would publish "The Arrival of the Bee Box" and "Wintering" in April 1963.) Plath told her correspondents she would finish "novel after novel" once she found a nanny.[116]

Her second book of poems was now finished—the last poem to be included was "Death & Co.," written on November 14. She knew they were her strongest yet. She began to negotiate for higher payments from the BBC; when a production company offered just two guineas to record "Mushrooms," Plath balked. She thought it "a tiny sum. Or am I just sounding like an American capitalist."[117] She asked Heinemann to negotiate for five guineas, if possible. Sylvia knew what Ted was paid by the BBC and knew a male poet would have been offered more. She told Aurelia she had "neglected all my own talent, & thank God I have discovered it in time to make something of it!" But, with her shrewd understanding of literary politics, she still tried to capitalize on Hughes's fame. The white-hot rage had died down enough for the two poets to discuss career matters, and Ted advised her to pitch a story about her American childhood to the BBC. When she did so, she referred to Hughes twice in her letter as "my husband."[118]

In the past Sylvia had tried to cozy up to male writers. Now she began reaching out to literary women in London like Doris Lessing, whom she met through Suzette Macedo, and Stevie Smith, whose address Peter Orr had passed on to her. Plath wrote Smith on November 19 that she had been listening to some British Council recordings of her poems and had become "a desperate Smith-addict." She had been trying "for ages" to find Smith's *A Novel on Yellow Paper*—a title she admired given her own fetish for pink-colored paper—but lived far from bookshops in Devon. She asked Smith if she would "come to tea or coffee when I manage to move—to cheer me on a bit. I've wanted to meet you for a long time."[119] Smith replied kindly three days later, offering to send Plath her novel and agreeing that they should meet when Plath arrived in London.[120]

If only she could spend her winters in Yeats's London house and her summers in Devon, she wrote to Ruth Fainlight that November. She had nearly wept on her London trips at the sight of museums and cafés. Convicts had escaped from the Dartmoor prison that month, and she was fearful—she kept "an apple parer ready & the door bolted."[121] In North Tawton she carried around coal buckets and ash cans "like a navvy." Yet she took "terrific pride" in keeping the great stove blazing overnight; Ted, she claimed, had never learned. In Devon she had her bees and her garden and her riding. She invited Ruth to Court Green in April while Alan Sillitoe planned to spend the month in Russia. Ruth began making arrangements, including a visa for her Moroccan nanny and a driver's license for herself.[122]

During the last half of November, the exuberance of "Lady Lazarus" and "Daddy" gave way to quieter, more anxious poems about Assia, Ted, and the children. Plath returned again to the old theme of barrenness. Once, Plath's vilification of barrenness had been a conceptual protest against the idea that an intellectual woman must be bloodless. Now such vilification was less philosophical: Ted had left her for a glamorous, beautiful woman with no children and a history of abortions. Sylvia told others during this time that he was surrounding himself with "barren" women—Assia, Olwyn, Dido Merwin, Susan Alliston. She wrote to Harriet Cooke in Ireland, the wife of the painter Barrie Cooke, whom she had met in London, that the divorce would free her from "the sort of women who live from abortion to abortion & facelift to facelift—not my sort at all."[123]

Assia was clearly the model for "The Fearful," which Plath finished on November 16:

> The thought of a baby—
> Stealer of cells, stealer of beauty—
>
> She would rather be dead than fat,
> Dead and perfect, like Nefertit,
>
> Hearing the fierce mask magnify
> The silver limbo of each eye
>
> Where the child can never swim,
> Where there is only him and him.

If Plath could not have "him," her rival could not have his children. "Childless Woman," finished two weeks later on December 1, is a dramatic monologue in which the unhappy speaker imagines her legacy as "roads bunched to a knot." The childless woman is "Spiderlike": "I spin mirrors, / Loyal to my image." Plath would recall the "dead and perfect" theme again in "The Munich Mannequins," composed in late January 1963: "Perfection is terrible, it cannot have children / Cold as snow breath, it tamps the womb." Deadly perfection, childlessness, and Egyptian imagery would resurface with greater effect in "Edge."

Poetic consolations were few. Motherhood, especially single motherhood, was itself precarious. "Mary's Song" and "Brasilia," written around this time, lament the horror of the modern postwar world that has been forever altered by genocide: "This holocaust I walk in, / O golden child the world will kill and eat." In "Brasilia," Plath conjures a race of "super-people" with "torsos of steel" who threaten. The mother-speaker begs God to protect her child: "leave / This one / Mirror safe, unredeemed // By the dove's annihilation." It seems only the trees outside her window have escaped the burdens of history and motherhood. "Knowing neither abortions nor bitchery, / Truer than women, / They seed so effortlessly!" Plath writes in "Winter Trees." "O mother of leaves and sweetness / Who are these pietàs?" Even this comforting image vanishes at the end of the poem. The doves cry, "easing nothing."

―――――――

AFTER CLARISSA LEFT Court Green, Sylvia foundered. Susan's parents thought she seemed "perfectly happy" as she cooked them a delicious American Thanksgiving dinner, but Sylvia wrote Aurelia on Thanksgiving Day that late November was "absolute hell."[124] Susan was off, her cleaning lady was indisposed, and her backup babysitter sick. A local woman who filled in for Nancy Axworthy during this time remembered Sylvia staying in bed until 11:30 in the morning. "Some days she'd be really miserable. . . . When she used to get strung up with the children she'd throw anything."[125] She struck Elizabeth during this time as very thin and pale, with dark circles under her eyes, and "a darkness about her that was very forbidding." Sylvia seemed distracted as she set out cups of tea at Court Green. "She tried to make the social noises and smile but you weren't really there." Elizabeth had no idea Sylvia had had a previous breakdown, despite the fact that Elizabeth herself opened up to her about her own breakdown after losing a baby. Sylvia never confided anything about her past in America, only that America had "hurt her," and Elizabeth did not probe.[126]

Together they attended a chamber concert in the nearby town of Holsworthy that November. Elizabeth, who was knowledgeable about music, thought the concert would be a welcome distraction for Sylvia. She began to regret the suggestion as they drove. "The tension in her was like a violin string—tighter and tighter," Elizabeth remembered. "She was smoking and smoking, driving fast, on the edge of the seat the whole time. One wanted to make her relax but couldn't get near. There were no tears left." Yet on the way back, even "half-destroyed" with sadness, Sylvia asked Elizabeth to explain the difference between Bach's trumpet, which they had heard at the concert, and the modern trumpet. "You *know* about this," Sylvia said. "Tell me about it." "She wanted to know everything," Elizabeth said.[127]

Sylvia came down with another bad cold that month and could find no time to read *Lord Byron's Wife*, which Karl Miller at the *New Statesman* had sent her to review. The parallels were clear; Plath called it "the most fascinating book" and joked that Miller knew "I'd love to get my hands on it!"[128] By now she had learned that Ted was also seeing Susan Alliston, a secretary he had met at Faber and Faber, who was, coincidentally, the ex-wife of Warren's Harvard roommate Clem Moore ("evidently she wants to meet me, but that is a pleasure she'll have to forgo," Sylvia wrote Aurelia).[129] Sylvia's temporary goodwill toward Ted receded. "I despise him. I think he is a coward & a bastard & want him to have nothing to do with me or the children. He is a gigolo now, vain & despicable. I don't care how much of a poetic genius he is, as a father he is a louse." She admitted to Aurelia that he had been "kind, faithful & loving" during their six years of marriage. But the "strain was too much & it didn't work. He had absolutely no right to have children."[130] A week later, relations had improved. She was going forward with the divorce petition and told her mother, "I think there should be no trouble, as Ted is very cooperative."[131] To Harriet Cooke, too, Sylvia wrote, "Ted & I are friends as much as can be at times like this."[132] Indeed, Hughes was willing to go through with the divorce. "There's no problem . . . so long as I can keep up the cash," he wrote to Olwyn that September.[133]

Plath resumed her fight for Yeats's house, worried that as "an ex-wife" she would be refused. Ted cooperated, but even when they applied as "Mr. and Mrs. Hughes" the landlord wanted more references, since Ted had no regular income. Sylvia listed her mother, "Professor A. S. Plath," as "guarantor and security," and urged Aurelia to "put on a good front for the agents."[134] She offered a year's rent in advance for a five-year lease. She planned to be "rich enough" by then, after a best-selling novel, to buy the entire townhouse and rent out flats. "I have real business sense," she told Aurelia. "I am just short of capital right now."[135] Thanks in part to Mrs. Prouty's recent $500 check, she had already applied to an au pair agency for a German-speaking nanny. But Prouty advised Sylvia not to get carried away by romanticism. She thought Plath's story about Yeats's "message" to her just a coincidence. The Yeats house itself sounded like "'A lovely castle in the air.' But I fear it cannot come true so soon. There are so many obstacles."[136] Prouty had conferred with her lawyer and advised Plath to keep pressure on Hughes to pay alimony and to put Court Green in her name.

In the end, Sylvia did not need her mother as a reference. She simply "had to bluster about being an American," and her lawyer arranged things.[137] She still needed Aurelia's help, however—she asked her to close her two American bank accounts and send the $900 she had stashed away in the U.S.[138] Aurelia sent her own checkbook instead and told her daughter to use whatever money she needed to secure the flat. Sylvia returned the checkbook, refusing the burden of obligation. "You can imagine how silly it is to have something like that around which Ted might see if he comes to visit the children."[139] Aurelia was stung. "Naturally I assumed that you would not leave deposit books lying carelessly about so that they could be noted!" she wrote her daughter in a rare surviving letter. She continued, "the balance of the Lombard account might have served as a comforting backlog—could have been put away with the house deed."[140] In the end, a $700 "investment" from Aunt Dot—a year's rent in advance—secured the flat. Sylvia wept when she received it, and she signed a five-year lease in late November.

The battle of the checkbooks suggests how the relationship between Sylvia and her mother was deteriorating. Aurelia tried her best to support her daughter. When Sylvia called home on December 6, Aurelia wrote, "Bless the telephone—and you for having made use of it to give us the joy of your strong, happy voice. You couldn't have given me a better gift. . . . Your courage, your planning, your writing throughout this time of stress amazes us all and we admire you tremendously, darling!"[141] Such language grated on Sylvia. But when she told Mrs. Prouty she wanted to dedicate her second novel to her, Prouty reminded her of her debt to Aurelia. "She adores you—would die for you, & becomes terribly anxious if many days pass without hearing from you."[142] Such news prompted Sylvia to write to her mother in December, "Everybody—Frank, Dot, Mrs. P. says you worry if I don't write. For goodness sake, remember no news is good news & my work is so constant I barely have a second to fry a steak."[143]

Aurelia's surviving December 1962 letters reveal a desire for control. Sylvia must buy a double bed for the new flat, hook up a baby gate for Nick's safety, and transport the cat in "a closed box (with holes for air) or closed basket; don't attempt to have her loose!" "Wouldn't it be wise to take some of your rugs. . . . Take plenty of Pifcos!"[144] At the zoo, Frieda must be instructed "not to put her fingers or hand into the cages!"[145] Exclamation marks appear in nearly every paragraph of Aurelia's surviving letters, just as they appear in many of Plath's *Ariel* poems.

A troubling passive aggression marked these letters as well. When Sylvia wrote her mother about the prospect of a potential reading in the working-class area of Stevenage, Aurelia told her, on December 4, to choose simple poems.

> When a listener feels a writer has spoken for him—has clarified an emotion or thought—some wonderful sensations may take place within him. He may feel the warmth of "being understood," "being recognized." He feels he "counts," for that which has been his experience has been lifted into an art form. That is why so many of the earlier Frost poems are so loved and will be immortal.[146]

Aurelia's condescending message—that her daughter should write safe, traditional verse—was clear. In a December 8 letter, Aurelia heaped praise on

John Steinbeck and Robert Graves, but then quoted excerpts from Sloan Wilson's *A Sense of Values* about the neurotic tendencies of artists.[147] Many artists, Aurelia wrote, have "severe nervous breakdowns," and their "children do the suffering for them!" Writers were "oversensitive," and success gave them "the opportunity to be immoral." Aurelia warned of the "physical and emotional dangers of success" with a final quote from Wilson's book: "'There is the self-centredness of the artist—almost every writer or artist I ever met was an egomaniac to start with, and success makes them worse. When an egomaniac fails, as everyone has to do once in a while, it seems to him the world has come to an end!'"[148] Aurelia was probably talking about Ted, yet the words could have applied equally to Sylvia. It was the same mixed message Plath had heard since she was a child: excel, but conform.

Such letters help explain why Sylvia chose to stay in England, on her own. Returning to America would have meant, she thought, a terrible regression. She was annoyed that Aurelia hadn't told her Wellesley friends and neighbors about the separation, and that she was still receiving Christmas cards addressed to her and Ted. In late November Sylvia lashed out: "And for goodness sake don't say 'unless you are safe & reasonably happy, I can't live anyway'! One's life should <u>never</u> depend on another's in that way. Why do you identify so with me? That sort of statement only makes one chary of confiding any difficulties in you whatsoever."[149] Three days after her daughter's suicide, Aurelia wrote, "2/14/63 I regret this" in the margin of this letter, next to these sentences. But Sylvia's letter suggests that she alone was responsible for her suicide—not Aurelia, not Ted.

Susan's return in late November righted the foundering ship. Sylvia cooked elaborate dinners and hosted teas for Winifred, Susan's family, and a local literary-minded Irish couple, the Fosters, and their three young children.[150] Sylvia's thumb had healed, thanks to Dr. Horder, though part of its side was gone. She made arrangements to go up to London in early December to buy appliances for the flat and get her skirt hems taken up by a London seamstress. Winifred informed Aurelia that Sylvia was "very cheerful & full of plans for London. . . . she says she feels so free." But Aurelia was worried sick. She had confided to Winifred about her chronic insomnia, due to her anxiety about her daughter.[151]

With Susan in charge of the domestic front, Sylvia turned to her new novel, which she wanted to enter in a contest Aurelia had told her about. The contest deadline was approaching fast, and Plath was determined to meet it: "even if I don't win, which I won't, it will be an incentive."[152] She told Aurelia she planned to finish the novel in early January, once she had a mother's helper in London, and that she would publish it under a pseudonym.

What was left of this novel disappeared after Plath's death, though she left some clues as to its themes. To Mrs. Prouty on November 20, she wrote a detailed outline of what she called "my second novel." (Because she had destroyed the manuscript of her second novel in a bonfire shortly after she learned of Ted's affair with Assia, this was actually her third novel.) It had started out with the title *The Interminable Loaf,* but she had decided to call it *Doubletake,* "meaning that the second look you take at something reveals a deeper, double meaning.... it is semi-autobiographical about a wife whose husband turns out to be a deserter and philanderer although she had thought he was wonderful & perfect."[153] The Hughes figure (the "hero") was meant to be "a painter," as she told Harriet Cooke, "so I'd like to see some of Barrie's stuff." She stressed that it was "a pot-boiler, I fear, due to my need for dough."[154] She told Prouty the book was set in Devon. The scholar Judith Kroll saw some of Plath's rudimentary notes about this novel while researching a book on Plath at Court Green in the 1970s. In these notes, Plath referred to the characters as "'heroine,' 'rival,' 'husband,' and 'rival's husband.'" The rival tells the heroine, "'I shall drive you mad.'" Plath also referred to two current films about a married woman who takes a lover— *Last Year at Marienbad* and *Jules and Jim.*[155]

After Plath's suicide, Hughes found the manuscript of the unfinished novel, which by then she had retitled *Double Exposure,* at her flat. Assia was "shocked" to find herself a character. She and David were, she told Nathaniel Tarn, the "Goof-Hoppers." Nathaniel recorded that David was "detestable & contemptible. A. [Assia] is of course the icy barren woman. In the novel, apart from SP who is full of poems, kicks & kids, there are only saints and miserable sinners. She hopes TH will destroy this."[156] Elizabeth remembered Sylvia telling her that she and her husband, David, appeared in the novel as "plaster saints."[157] Dido Merwin, under the name Camilla, also made an appearance. Olwyn read some of this novel and told Alvarez in 1988 that it was "only a couple of chapters. One of which was simply a blow by blow account of the Wevills May weekend visit, the other, shorter, on a train when she and Ted were going up to London and stoniness had set in. Very slight and less as I recall them than the 150 pp Ted mentioned—around 60 draft pages Id [*sic*] say."[158] The editor Fran McCullough learned from Olwyn that the novel was "wicked ... funny, nasty, precise about Ted & Assia."[159] Ted may indeed have destroyed the novel, as Assia wanted, or perhaps Assia herself destroyed it. He wrote in his introduction to *Johnny Panic and the Bible of Dreams* that it "disappeared somewhere around 1970."[160] In a 1995 *Paris Review* interview, he said he assumed that Aurelia had surreptitiously taken the manuscript on one of her visits to Court Green.[161] It may exist still.

In late November, an American Catholic priest studying at Oxford, Father Michael Carey, began sending Plath his poems. Despite her marital crisis, she read his poems carefully and offered sound advice. She told him to read more of Thomas Wyatt, Gerard Manley Hopkins, T. S. Eliot, Ezra Pound, and Emily Dickinson. "Beware, for Heaven's sake, the fey, the pretty, the 'cute' . . . let the world blow in more roughly. . . . Do read Hopkins. . . . Rhymes, exact rhymes, and especially feminine rhymes tend to 'jingle' too much. . . . Speak <u>straight out</u>. You should give yourself exercises in roughness, not lyrical neatness. Say blue, instead of sapphire, red instead of crimson." In return, she sent him "Mary's Song," which she described as a poem about "The Christ-ness in all martyrs, and written by the mother of a son." She warned him that she was "an atheist." But, "like a certain sort of atheist, my poems are God-obsessed, priest-obsessed. . . . Theology & philosophy fascinate me."[162] Father Carey wrote back that he had blessed her. She thanked him and asked him to bless Yeats's house, too.[163]

Sylvia traveled to London on December 3 to arrange for her new appliances and utilities.[164] She again stayed with the Macedos, and Suzette noticed that she was "calmer" than she had been before. They had dinner together, and "things were easier. She was very determined. She was not going to accept Ted."[165] Plath left them an inscribed copy of *The Colossus*, dated December 3, 1962.

During this trip she had an emotional reunion with Ted. The head of the Poetry Book Society, Eric Walter White, had asked Sylvia and Ted to be his guests at a posh French restaurant, L'Epicure, on Dean Street. In an unpublished poem, Hughes, who was then staying at Dido Merwin's mother's flat at 17 Montague Square, gives a vivid account of that night. He suspected that White wanted to study them "with his gossip's lens," and that Plath wanted a reconciliation.

After the dinner, Ted and Sylvia walked back together to Dido's flat, where Ted became paranoid that Sylvia was looking for clues about his "secret life." Indeed, the living arrangement enraged Sylvia, who suspected that Dido was attracted to Ted. (According to Suzette, this was indeed the case.)[166] Dido had, he wrote, "seized the chance to detest you, /And to hurt you. And I had given her the power. / She had slammed the phone down on your voice / When you had tried to reach me." He "refused" Sylvia the chance to indulge her "suspicion," and so they continued walking outside around Soho Square in the dark winter night. Plath wept copiously: "your front collapsed. / . . . the all-out release / Of a dam-burst. I was appalled."

With my arm round you I tried to calm you.
The support of my arm let you collapse.
I hung on, out of my depth:
In your torrent of grief, I could not check it
Or escape it, or see any way out of it.

. . . .

We went round & round, in your great grief,
In your maelstrom, like debris.
I just concentrated on lasting it out
And keeping your head up. Till I cracked—
And we got into Dido's flat. I thought you might sleep.
But the flood would not stop.
The mountain of pain went on melting . . .

                            . . . Volcanic

Beyond your strength to control it. Futile
Neighbors below banged on their ceiling.

I rolled under it all.
A boulder, irrelevant
While that tidal wave, that eruption
From your childhood, swamped & buried our world.

. . . .

I did not see my chance
To launch an ark. All it needed
Was a little vessel. That was the chance
I was too bewildered to take.
And the next day separated us, barely
Sharing a name, flood-victims, cold-mouthed.[167]

33

Yeats's House

London, December 1962–January 1963

On December 9, Sylvia closed Court Green, bundled up the children, and set out with Susan for London. Movers arranged cheaply by Winifred followed. In a letter to her mother, Sylvia glossed over the move's difficulties, which she described as a madcap "comedy of errors"—misplaced keys, jimmied windows, imperious neighbors. When she finally got inside the flat, there was no electricity, and she had to move furniture by candlelight. But soon enough all "went swimmingly." She installed a gas stove and electricity, and made arrangements for a phone.[1] "I just sit thinking Whew! I have done it, and beaming—shall I write a poem, shall I paint a floor, shall I hug a baby?" Susan helped with the move and stayed an extra day in London so Sylvia could run errands. The local grocers remembered her, as did the diaper service and the laundromat owners. "Well, it was like coming home to a small loving village," she told Aurelia. At night she stood on her small balcony and stared at the full moon "in sheer joy."[2] After the darkness of Devon, she marveled at London's light.

While Ted took the children to the zoo, she swept, scrubbed, and painted. She was proud of herself for taking on "a man's responsibilities as well as a woman's."[3] The well-sized living room with its two floor-to-ceiling street-facing windows took up nearly the entire first floor. The narrow galley kitchen was entered through the living room: moving forward into the kitchen one would have passed, on the right, a refrigerator, then a sink, to come to the oven, set to the right of a large south-facing window.[4] Sylvia painted the living room walls white and installed pine bookcases, rush matting, Hong Kong cane chairs, and a glass-top coffee table. ("I adore planning the furnishing.")[5] She told Aurelia the living room had "a very strong oriental feeling to it."[6] There would be no more hearts and flowers.

Frieda and Nicholas took the largest upstairs bedroom facing the street, while the other street-facing bedroom, barely big enough for a twin bed, would belong to the au pair. Sylvia's bedroom-study faced south with a single large window that overlooked her downstairs neighbor Trevor Thomas's back garden, with its three sycamore trees, and Camden's rooftops.[7] The Macedos had lent her a bed and Suzette brought her to a secondhand shop on Chalk Farm Road, where she purchased some rather battered armchairs. (Sylvia took to the shop's owner—an "intellectual" sandal-and-socks-wearing socialist—and invited him to tea.)[8] She plastered her bedroom walls with white and yellow wallpaper and decorated the rest of the room with "straw mat, black floor borders & gold lampshade—bee colors, & the sun rises over an 18th-century engraving of London each day." She planned to paint the other rooms soon, and sew curtains. Court Green had been a warm red; Yeats's house would be a cool blue. "<u>Blue</u> is my new color, royal, midnight (not aqua!)," she wrote Aurelia. "Ted never liked blue, & I am a really blue-period person now."[9] The new poems, too, would be cooler than the pulsing, blood-red lyrics of *Ariel.* The first published poem she would have read in her London flat was, fittingly, "Event," very clearly about her rift with Hughes, in print in the December 16 *Observer:* "I walk in a ring, / A groove of old faults, deep and bitter. // Love cannot come here." Alvarez could have published "Elm" but chose instead the less powerful but more personal poem.

Plath seemingly told no one the crushing news she had received in a letter dated December 8 from Heinemann: Knopf had rejected *The Bell Jar.* Ever the professional, she replied straightaway to Heinemann, instructing them to send her book to Elizabeth Lawrence, Ted's editor, at Harper & Row in New York.[10] She still hoped her novel would find an American publisher.

She had little time for disappointments, and once again filled her calendar with to-do lists: "paint lounge floor, paint bureau, paint au pair's room & hall, paint downstairs hall; pick up laundry and grey paint; wash hair; call babyminders for Thursday morning."[11] She did not give herself a break until December 20, when she had tea with Catherine Frankfort and saw Ingmar Bergman's *Through a Glass Darkly.* She bought fine new clothes full of blue tones at Dickens and Jones on Regent Street with a $100 Christmas check from Mrs. Prouty, and zipped around London in her Morris. Ted came once a week, usually on Sundays, to take the children to the zoo. She brought them there on her own, too, and to the playgrounds in Primrose Hill. She found an excellent nursery school for Frieda—Dibby's, run by a grandmotherly woman in a nearby basement flat on Regent's Park Road.[12] Frieda was thriving in the company of other children, emerging from the difficult period that had followed her parents' separation. Everything had miraculously fallen into place. "I feel Yeats' spirit blessing me," Sylvia wrote Aurelia.[13]

Sylvia quickly renewed her friendships with Catherine Frankfort and Lorna Secker-Walker, who still lived in Chalcot Square.[14] Lorna and her husband, David, had been offended that Sylvia and Ted hadn't bothered to say good-bye when they left for Devon. But Lorna did not hold a grudge, and besides, she could tell Sylvia "was in bad shape" when she returned."[15] Lorna remembered, "She wasn't the bubbly cheerful person who she'd been before she left London. . . . She was obviously upset, distressed. But she didn't open up about it." Lorna did not even realize, at first, that Sylvia and Ted had separated. She remembered seeing Nick for the first time and saying, "Isn't he like his dad!" "She looked hurt as I said it," and Lorna began to realize that everything had changed.

Sylvia never told Lorna about her history of depression, or about the brilliant poems she had been writing that fall. But she opened up about Ted's affair, directing most of her anger at Assia.[16] She sometimes spoke bitterly of Ted, too, saying that he had changed from the "withdrawn, very shy" man she had known to someone who courted fame and "now liked the gay life. . . . It was she . . . who had pushed him into appearing publicly. She obviously felt that she had made him what he now was, and was now regretting it."[17] She told Lorna, Catherine, and Suzette that Ted ignored Nick on his visits (Ted himself had admitted in letters to others during this time that he favored Frieda). Suzette said, "she grieved for Nicky. . . . she felt Nicky had been deprived." Sylvia "was worried" that Ted's lack of attention affected Nick's health, as he was often sick.[18] "Poor Nicky," Sylvia would often say, looking despondently at him in his playpen.[19] She worried her children would suffer, emotionally and socially, in what was then called a broken home.

But Lorna felt that Sylvia, too, seemed "cut off from her children" at this time. During the first phase of their friendship, "she had obviously adored Frieda" and was very "bound up" with her. Now Sylvia simply "looked exhausted," her sparkle gone.[20] Lorna, like Clarissa, had the sense that Sylvia was simply going through the motions with the children, without much feeling. For the first time, Sylvia spoke honestly to her about the challenges she faced as a mother and a writer. "She said that she felt she couldn't give herself wholly to her work or wholly to the children." Sylvia told Lorna— not boastfully—that she could "write a poem before breakfast," but that it was "so difficult to write a novel because it takes time and I just don't have time."[21] Lorna had put her medical career on hold in order to stay at home with her young daughter, knowing she might never be able to resume that career. But Sylvia, she thought, was different. "I think she was quite a natural sort of mother. But I was slightly surprised at the extent to which she had this other agenda. Clearly, this was all very important to her, where I had just decided at this stage of my life that I was going to devote myself to my children, come what may. I was fortunate in that I did get back into a career, and I had a very satisfactory second career. But it was a chance, and she was not going to take that chance."[22]

Sylvia still socialized with Susan O'Neill-Roe, now attending nursing school in London, and Susan's boyfriend, Corin Hughes-Stanton, a journalist who lived, Sylvia said, "right round the corner."[23] Elizabeth thought that Sylvia also saw more of Mark Bonham Carter in London, while Winifred's eighteen-year-old son Kenneth, a newly minted London policeman, came on at least three occasions to help Sylvia paint floors and furniture.[24] Small professional successes cheered her: she was asked, again, to judge the Cheltenham poetry contest, and *Poetry* accepted "Fever 103°," "Purdah," and "Eavesdropper" just after Christmas. She made plans to return to Court Green in the spring, where she hoped to spend April with Ruth Fainlight. She asked the Fosters to feed her cats for her until her return.

Ted tried to open doors for her. He told the BBC producer Douglas Cleverdon that Sylvia "had written some wonderful new poems," which resulted in an invitation to read her poetry in a twenty-minute sequence, with her own commentary, on the prestigious Third Programme.[25] It was for this occasion that Plath wrote her short introductions to "Ariel," "Daddy," "The Applicant," "Lady Lazarus," "Sheep in Fog," "Fever 103°," "Nick and the Candlestick," "Death & Co.," "Letter in November," "The Bee Meeting," "The Arrival of the Bee Box," and "Wintering," which she sent to Cleverdon in mid-December.[26] He wrote Plath a few days later saying he and George MacBeth were impressed by the poems, but they could not take them all. In January 1963, a BBC features script editor would decide that, though the poems deserved recognition, they were "emotionally overcharged."[27] The program was never produced, but the introductions Plath wrote became an important part of her oeuvre.

Plath showed Alvarez the manuscript of *Ariel*, probably in late November or early December, and he recognized the collection's importance immediately. "A. Alvarez," she wrote home on December 14, "the best poetry critic here thinks my second book, which I've just finished, should win the Pulitzer Prize. Of course it won't, but it's encouraging to have somebody so brilliant think so."[28] Al had become her new sounding board, and she felt, finally, "out of Ted's shadow."[29] But the "brief liaison," as Olwyn had called it, was about to end. Sylvia did not record any visits to Al in her December calendar; on December 17 she wrote "Call Al" in red pencil. The bright, circled words stand out amid domestic errands in black ink. She called him again on Christmas Eve, asking him to come round for dinner and listen to her new poems. Sylvia's call was impulsive; she knew one did not make plans for Christmas Eve on the day itself. Alvarez declined—he was going to V. S. Pritchett's house for dinner—but said he would stop by on the way. Sylvia's journal entry about this evening, as described by Olwyn, suggests she sensed that he was distancing himself now that she had moved closer to him both physically and emotionally.

When she answered the door he was surprised to find her hair loose and long; normally, she wore it up in a braided coronet. The children were already in bed. Her white sitting room seemed chaste and very cold. "I had never seen her so strained," he later wrote. He thought that the mood was due to Christmas, always a difficult season for the depressed. But Sylvia's journal entry suggests that the strain had another source: she sensed this was her last chance with him, and she needed to execute a bravura performance. They drank wine, and she read him "Death & Co." Alvarez found no "weird jollity" in this poem, no sense of triumph as with "Lady Lazarus" and "Daddy." He was deeply disturbed by the poem's ending: "The dead bell, / The dead bell. // Somebody's done for." He thought that she was writing about herself. They argued about the line "The nude / Verdigris of the condor"—he said it was "exaggerated, morbid," though Plath insisted it was an accurate description. "I was only trying, in a futile way, to reduce the tension and take her mind momentarily off her private horrors," he later wrote, "as though that could be done by argument and literary criticism!"[30]

More than twenty-five years later, when Alvarez re-created this sad tableau in his autobiography, he added a more intimate detail:

I listened, and nodded and made the right noises—until I looked at my watch and said, "I've got to go." She said, "Don't, please don't" and began to weep—great uncontrollable sobs that made her hiccup and shake her head. I stroked her hair and patted her back as though she were an abandoned child—"It's going to be OK. We'll meet after Christmas"—but she went on crying and shaking her head. So I went on to my dinner party and never saw her alive again.

I left knowing I had let her down unforgivably. I told myself she was Ted's responsibility and Ted was my friend. But that wasn't the whole story. I wasn't up to her despair and it scared me. My own suicide attempt was two years behind me and I didn't want to go that way again. Anyway, my head was full of Anne.[31]

This scene suggests a breakup, while Alvarez's earlier 1971 memoir had indicated something more casual. "I have never kidded myself that changing from friend to lover would have made a jot of difference to her in the end,"

Alvarez wrote in 1999. But it did make a difference. Although Plath had worried that she might scare him off, her tears, recorded by Alvarez himself, suggest that she had hoped for a deeper commitment.

She stopped visiting his flat, though she made a note in her calendar to tune in to his BBC radio program on January 2. She would send him a letter about her poem "Winter Trees" after it appeared in the January 13 *Observer*. It was the last poem of hers she saw in print. Braving another invitation, she suggested that they bring Frieda, Nicholas, and his son Adam to the zoo together so that she could show him "the nude verdigris of the condor." By then he had fallen in love with Anne. He never replied.

Sylvia and the children spent Christmas Day with the Macedos in Hampstead, where they dined on roast duck and drank cognac. Earlier in December Sylvia had broken down to Suzette—the only time she ever did—and told her she had no friends and no place to go on Christmas.[32] Suzette recalled, "I was so upset by this that I cancelled our arrangements and 'made Xmas' for her and the children, very much last minute shopping in Camden Town." Sylvia had donned her new Jaeger suit, and Frieda and Nick were finely dressed in expensive American clothes. They opened gifts from Helder and Suzette, who remembered the "wonderful candles in the shape of oranges which I lit to Frieda's great amazement and delight."[33] The children both had colds, but the evening was festive. Sylvia had dreaded the prospect of Christmas alone and told Aurelia she "was grateful to have Christmas dinner out with these friends."[34] In her calendar, she wrote "Paint bureau & au pairs [*sic*] room & hall" on Christmas Day, a strategy, perhaps, for getting through the holiday if she found herself alone. Still, she had cause to celebrate: she had received her first copy of *The Bell Jar*, mailed to her on December 12, with its cover of a shadowy young woman under a glass jar. She inscribed it with her Fitzroy Road address and "Christmas 1962." Yet Suzette recalled that Sylvia could not keep her sadness and anger entirely at bay. "Oh, my poor babies," Sylvia said despondently at one point. She spoke bitterly about Assia. "Ted tells me she's like a cold fish in bed," she told Suzette, who remembered that Sylvia was "determined to get her divorce, though we kept telling her, 'You're crazy. It's all too quick.'"[35] Suzette preached "reconciliation, compromise," but Sylvia "said she could not bear anything broken."[36]

The Macedos spent Boxing Day with David and Assia Wevill at their new flat in Highbury, along with Doris Lessing and her son Peter. Assia was still "pretending everything was normal."[37] She asked Suzette if Sylvia had given her anything for Christmas, and Suzette answered, "Oh honey." "Next thing Sylvia was saying, 'How could you be so awful? You apparently told Assia that I gave you nothing but a jar of honey for Christmas,' Suzette recalled, adding, "Ted must have told her that. But Ted was in a terrible state, desperate about the children." He worried mainly about Frieda, who he thought was "regressing."[38] Sylvia spent Boxing Day writing to her mother, Daniel and Helga Huws, and Ruth Fainlight; she had dinner with the Frankforts. Catherine remembered that Sylvia talked "nonstop about home and America" because Catherine's mother-in-law had spent time in the United States. Sylvia had seemed to Catherine "the life and soul of the party . . . gay" that night, but Catherine's perceptive mother-in-law afterward remarked on "what a sad person she was."[39]

Jillian Becker remembered, "Sylvia thought of herself as poor. Insecurity was one of her biggest worries."[40] Suzette reassured Sylvia that, on the contrary, everyone assumed that she had money because she was American. Indeed, with checks arriving regularly from Aurelia, Aunt Dot, Mrs. Prouty, and Ted, who was paying her £22 a week—and with the prospect of regular BBC work on the horizon—money was not a pressing concern for Sylvia.[41] Clarissa Roche was amazed by her setup at Fitzroy Road. "Marvelous heater, a proper cooker and a refrigerator, my God! And she had a car. She really was very very well away for England at the time. But of course not realizing it. As no American could have realized it."[42] Freedom to work, though, was in short supply. Frieda was only in school for three hours each morning, while Nick woke every day with a bang at six a.m. She needed to find an au pair, and soon.

She sounded lonely in her Boxing Day letter to Daniel and Helga. She was not yet ready to give up smoking but had consulted a doctor about weaning herself off the sleeping pills she took nightly and was "now addicted to." She told the Huwses, untruthfully, that the divorce had been Ted's idea and that she had resigned herself to it. Assia, she said, had taught Ted to lie: "she has enjoyed lying & being faithless to all 3 of her husbands & came into my house & wanted all I had & took it. Ted has always seemed so straight to me, brutal if he wanted, but not lying, so that I can hardly believe he thinks it sophisticated & grownup & crafty." Daniel had reassured her that Ted felt much guilt and sadness over his actions and that his guilt made him "very hard & cruel & hurtful." She mentioned the "public humiliation" she faced "being in the same work & Ted being so famous." Sylvia asked the Huwses to be Frieda's new godparents. Later, Daniel would regret his response that as Catholics they could only take on the role symbolically. He felt that it was one more way he had let her down.[43]

AFTER YEARS OF NOSTALGIA for cozy New England winters, Sylvia was grateful for the "fine white snow" that fell on Boxing Day.[44] She marveled at the "Dickensian" scene outside her window and longed to take Frieda sledding on Primrose Hill: "it looks so pretty!" she exclaimed to her mother.[45] But the novelty soon wore thin. She woke each day with surprise, then alarm, as the snow continued to fall. In Devon, she had heard, there were twenty-foot snow drifts and helicopters dropping milk and bread. She congratulated herself on getting out, but London was little better.

That English winter—the Big Freeze—was the coldest of the twentieth century. The temperature stayed below freezing for nearly all of January. Three-foot icicles hung from roof gutters. A fountain in Trafalgar Square froze in mid-drip; double-decker buses were buried in snow. People cycled over the frozen Thames and skied over unplowed streets. Ice locked fishing boats in their ports. Even the fog froze.

Heavy snow in Boston was a seasonal rite; in London, it was a natural disaster. Sylvia wrote Aurelia in early January, "The English, being very English, have of course no snow plows, because this only happens once every five years, or ten. So the streets are great mills of sludge which freezes & melts & freezes. One could cheerfully use a dog sled." Her car was packed in snow, and she decided against shoveling it out until "some of this Arctic is thawed."[46] The worsening weather coincided with the end of her fleeting relationship with Alvarez; the snow began falling two days after their last meeting.

The weather left its mark inside, too. In January, Sylvia's bathtub filled with filthy water; her taps stopped flowing; the ceiling leaked. When she complained, her landlord shrugged and told her the roof was old and not built to withstand snow. He added that the gutter over her bedroom was also faulty. "But where I come from there is snow every winter and the roofs *never* leak," she protested.[47] He returned with a moisture detector and assured her that the ceiling would not buckle, though he warned her that she might not have drinking water for a few days because the pipes had frozen. They tried throwing a bucket of hot water on one of the outside pipes, which only succeeded at angering her downstairs neighbor, Trevor Thomas. Somehow they found a plumber who fixed the kitchen taps, but the bathtub stayed clogged and full of dirty water. The beleaguered family of three had no way to take hot baths—a situation that left them perpetually cold and grubby. Lorna remembered, "To an American, that was serious. To us, it wasn't so serious."[48]

Hot baths, sun, and sleep were Sylvia's home remedies for depression. They eluded her now. She was lucky to have drinking water. (One night she saw an elderly man filling his pitcher from a water tap on a street corner.

"Shocking!" they both cried as they passed each other in the darkness "like sad ships.")[49] The power flickered on and off due to the overloaded city grid, and she began writing, as she told Charles Osborne at *The London Magazine*, "by candlelight with cold fingers, a sinister return to Dickensian conditions thanks to the Electricity Board."[50] Long lines formed at the few shops that had candles, which sold out in minutes.

Linda Gates, an aspiring American actress, arrived in London in February 1964, a year after the Big Freeze. She began dating Alvarez, who had briefly separated from Anne. Linda was appalled by Al's paltry coal heater ("the size of a breadbox") and took to using the toilet at a local department store rather than the freezing, primitive one in his garage. Above all, she remembered the "bitter, bitter cold," and a society inured to life without heat. "We musn't grumble," she heard Britons say over and over. Linda spent her days huddling in a woolly bathrobe in Al's bed trying to stay warm, reading loose sheets of Plath's poems or "depressing" books he recommended like *Jude the Obscure*. She left in April. Her experience increased her admiration for Plath: "she could have fled back to central heating, indoor toilets, men who took you seriously and a secure university appointment to pay the bills."[51]

Plath wrote wryly about her London winter in "Snow Blitz," which she planned to publish in *Punch*.[52] She described the conditions with an amused, if appalled, American sensibility. "The cheer seemed universal. We were all mucking in together, as in the Blitz."[53] Some of her anecdotes sound Pythonesque. Her local pharmacist reported excitedly that he had found a solution to all the snow: a plank to "*push* the snow aside." She joked in "Snow Blitz" that she had been hoping for tranquilizers.

Trevor Thomas, who lived alone in the flat below Sylvia's, remembered a different side of her that winter. Thomas had initially been angry with Plath, as he had been promised the larger flat she eventually secured. He resented the fact that she had been able to put up a year's rent in advance, which meant that he was relegated to the less desirable ground floor (it had been divided into a street-facing bedroom and, behind it, a small sitting room with a fireplace). Thomas later wrote about this time in an unpublished memoir, "Sylvia Plath: Last Encounters." The piece is not entirely reliable—Thomas wrote that Hughes had played bongo drums upstairs after Plath's funeral, a claim he later retracted after Hughes threatened to sue. Many of Thomas's recollections, however, dovetail with Hughes's.[54] Still, she seemed to him frightened and confused that winter, and he summoned up a modicum of pity for the single mother upstairs.

Thomas, born in Wales in 1907, was raised in a mining family and earned a degree in anthropology at Aberystwyth University. He became a specialist in what was then known as "primitive" art—the sort of subject that interested Plath and Hughes—and ascended to the top of his field. He won a Rockefeller Fellowship to study in America and in 1941 was appointed the director of the City of Leicester Museums and Art Gallery, where he built the best German Expressionist collection in Britain. After working in Paris for UNESCO, he was appointed professor of art education and art history at the University of Buffalo in the U.S., where he worked from 1956 to 1960. His career ended after he was arrested for public indecency outside a men's restroom; although Sir Kenneth Clark testified that Thomas would likely succeed him as director of the National Gallery, Thomas eventually pled guilty rather than endure cross-examination about his sexuality. He was let go at the museum, and, after stints in Paris and America, he became the art director of a greeting card company, Gordon Fraser. Later in life, before his death in 1993, Thomas fought for gay rights. Today there is a movement to formally pardon him.[55] Thomas did not include any of this secret history in his memoir. (Nor did Janet Malcolm in *The Silent Woman*, where she characterized him as a strange, narcissistic hoarder.) The man who got to know Sylvia that winter, and the last person to see her alive, had also been cast out of the magic circle.

Thomas found Plath exasperating, but he never turned her away. He had been treated well in America, and he wanted to pay the kindness forward. Sylvia relied on him as the weather worsened. She had few other options. Still, she was a proud woman who rarely opened up to those she did not like or trust. She had two other women friends in her neighborhood on whom she could have leaned; indeed, Catherine helped her with her shopping in mid-January. But she may have sensed in the fifty-six-year-old Thomas a sympathetic listener underneath his brittleness. And she may have guessed the truth of his sexuality, as she had Richard Murphy's.

One day in late January she appeared at his door crying. "I don't know what's happened but all my lights have gone out and my fire's gone off and my children are cold and ill and crying." He told her there had been a power cut. "Oh what's that?" she asked. He explained about the overuse of electric heaters. "Oh, but we don't have power cuts in America," she said. (An *Observer* article corroborates Thomas's memory: on Friday, January 25, and Saturday, January 26, Britain experienced the "worst power crisis" in its history, caused by frozen fog on power lines.)[56] Thomas reassured her that if she cooked with gas her "troubles were over." She didn't seem to realize that she could drink hot tea and warm the children with hot-water bottles until the power came back on. "Oh, you are so wonderful," he remembered her saying.[57] In "Snow Blitz," Plath wrote, "I wrapped my daughter in a blanket with the hot-water bottle and set her over a bowl of warm milk and her favorite puzzle. The baby I dressed in a snowsuit."

There are hints of depression behind the black humor in "Snow Blitz": the joke about needing tranquilizers, the continual disbelief at each new crisis. When the snow began to melt in late January, Plath wrote that the plows finally came. "Where have you been all month?" she asked them. They told her they had been "coming." There were only five. "Dress up warm, lots of tea and bravery. That seemed the answer," she wrote. The entire episode became a metaphor, in "Snow Blitz," for her own worsening battle with depression, her inner "blitz":

> Meanwhile, the pipes stay outside. Where else?
> And what if there *is* another snow blitz?
> And another?[58]

————

CLARISSA AND PAUL ROCHE CAME from Kent to see Sylvia on January 3. There was about a foot of snow on her stoop, and the door was hard to open. Sylvia answered the door in her dressing gown and was so ill she seemed to be mixing up nights and days. The flat, however, was spotless. The beds were made, the children scrubbed, "clean and dressed"—everything pointed to "the astounding orderliness of a real hausfrau." Indeed, the kitchen was so clean Clarissa suspected that Sylvia was not using it. When Sylvia confirmed her suspicions (she had written to the Fosters that she was mainly living on apples, onions, and potatoes she had brought from Court Green), Clarissa cooked her a meal of pork chops and tinned corn, which she "devoured." She went to sleep, then later came down for tea, looking better. She was then, Paul said, "Talkative, laughing, full of interest in everything we were doing. And I thought: this is marvelous, she's in great spirits, there's nothing to worry about." She told Paul, in a "very detached" way—as if she were not speaking about her adulterous husband—that he should ask Ted about BBC work: "Get in touch with Ted; he'll help you; he's very good about things like that."[59]

She spoke again, as she had at Court Green, of her contempt for literary London, even though Clarissa knew that she was "proud to be accepted as a poet by these very people, honored to be published alongside them."[60] Henry Rago at *Poetry* had written in late December, accepting "Fever 103°," "Purdah," and "Eavesdropper," while Tony Dyson wrote in early January asking for more poems for *Critical Quarterly*: "We should like to publish you very much indeed (but you know this)."[61] These affirmations surely lifted Plath's spirits, but not enough. The Roches left that night and invited Sylvia to stay with them in Kent if an au pair did not materialize soon. Sylvia gave Clarissa proofs of *The Bell Jar* and asked her to read them. Clarissa had the sense that

Sylvia had very few friends or visitors, and, indeed, the visit cheered Sylvia enormously. "I shall never forget the dear tea you left me with," she wrote Clarissa. "I really thought I was dying & began having blackouts that [previous] night while the two babies later ran scalding fevers."[62]

Sylvia hid her deepening depression in her letters, which give the impression of a woman in control. She was "in the best of hands" with the "wonderful and understanding" Dr. Horder, who was tending to Nick's wandering eye.[63] "The last 6 months have been a unique hell, but that's finished & I am fine now," she told Marcia Brown Plumer. She had not been in touch with her closest American friend in some time and brought Marcia up to date on her separation from Ted. "I'm in the process of a divorce suit now & will be very glad when <u>that's</u> finished—I somehow never imagined myself as the sort!" The most she could hope for from Ted was £1,000—about $2,800—a year. She would ask him to put Court Green in her name when the time was right, though Hughes wanted her to buy "her half."

> I have been so utterly <u>flattened</u> by having to be a businesswoman, farmer . . . mother, writer & all-round desperado that I'd give anything for a brief week in which somebody, some dear friends, went places, ate, talked, with <u>just me</u>. . . . I feel like a very efficient tool or weapon, used & in demand from moment to moment by the babes. . . . Nights are no good, I'm so flat by then that all I can cope with is music & brandy & water![64]

Meanwhile, Hughes complained to his sister of his financial difficulties. "The Assia saga is doing allright [*sic*]. If I had cash enough, we would be out of this tomorrow. . . . I'm just set on earning enough to leave." Sylvia, he wrote, seemed "much better."[65] He still worried, though, about leaving Frieda, and he sent Olwyn a poem called "Frieda's Early Morning" (eventually revised and retitled "Full Moon and Little Frieda"). It is set in "the dawn twilight" as Frieda sleeps peacefully, "And the roses not stirred."

> Once more everything crawls onto the razor's edge
> From which there is no falling
>
> And massively-golden Jupiter, hanging there in the orchard,
> Seems more like something belonging to us than to the heavens

It seems likely Plath saw this poem at some point, for she echoed Hughes's imagery—roses, a garden, a celestial body, even the word "edge" itself—when she composed "Edge."

Hughes had written to Alvarez the previous autumn, "I shall be out of England as much as I can manage," and that he would try to see him again before he left "for the winter."[66] The letter suggests that Ted knew Assia was still not ready to leave her husband. On January 5, Nathaniel Tarn visited the Wevills at their flat in Highbury. When David left to get cigarettes, Assia began talking about Ted, who was now living in his own small flat in Soho at 110 Cleveland Street. (Sylvia recorded the new address in her address book, in neat, blue ballpoint pen, under "Ted Hughes.") Assia told Nathaniel that Sylvia was "being extremely extravagant & sucking him dry economically." This was an exaggeration, as was Sylvia's claim that Ted was withholding money from her that winter: Sylvia recorded payments in her checkbook from Ted of £50 on December 11 and £75 on January 1.[67] (Assuming that he planned to make comparable payments monthly, the yearly sum would amount to more or less the annual alimony the couple had agreed on.) Assia "raved" about Ted to Nathaniel: "he has everything: charity, energy, love, genius. He is writing enormous quantities of everything." She wanted to leave David but could not "bring herself to." David knew that she was "seeing H. [Hughes] regularly," but the two had simply "stopped talking about it." Nathaniel found Assia filled with "cold calculation"; he could not understand why David "does not kick & go."[68]

Sylvia heard some of this from Suzette, the "postbox." Plath had thought moving to London would increase her sense of independence, but now, with the possibility of a relationship with Alvarez receding, there was only the memory of her husband and the devastating reality of her loneliness. She was closer to Ted in London, and this new proximity meant she heard constant gossip about his new life. Olwyn wrote Alvarez in 1988, "In London most of her intimates seemed to know Assia and David and Ted, so she was doing a lot of propaganda / stirring it, and what not. It meant she never got away from it all and must have caused her much private torment." Underneath her typed words, Olwyn, who once again recalled details from Sylvia's missing journals, scribbled, "it did—this in Journals—as people told her things all the time."[69] Some of the details may have come from Ted himself. Suzette said Sylvia told her Ted tormented her with details of his relationship with Assia during his weekly visits that January, though Helder, who had become much closer to Sylvia that winter over a series of long, philosophical discussions, thought that she had asked Ted about Assia. They "were in this awful game of show-and-tell together," he said.[70]

In early December, Nathaniel wrote that Assia and Ted's affair "was now a matter of common knowledge" "since SP had gone round the whole P.E.N. party telling people about it."[71] David Wevill told the poet Peter Porter that the affair was nobody's business, though admitted that "everyone's very curious, of course."[72] Sylvia confided to her mother that January, "It is very hard for me to think of him living in an expensive flat, being wined & dined, taking his girlfriend to Spain without a care in the world when I have worked so hard all these years & looked so forward to what I saw was to be our good fortune."[73] Despair began to replace rage.

———

SYLVIA DESCRIBED HIKING OVER "treacherous mountains to shop," but she was not holed up indefinitely.[74] Winifred's son Kenneth remembered that the councils had kept central London relatively clear of snow, and in late January the weather began to thaw.[75] The BBC treated Plath to drinks and food; her checkbook shows her shopping for curtains, shelves, a bed, carpets, and other home goods; and she saw plays and movies with Suzette, Catherine, Jillian, and Susan. "Stopped Dead" and "The Applicant" appeared in *The London Magazine* that month, and "Winter Trees" in *The Observer*.

Sylvia continued to seek out other women writers. She wrote again to Stevie Smith, hoping to meet for tea, and she asked Suzette to introduce her to her friend Doris Lessing and *New Yorker* writer Emily Hahn. The Macedos knew Hahn's husband, Charles Boxer, who held a chair in Portuguese at King's College, London. Sylvia gasped when they told her about this connection—"Emily Hahn?!" But Suzette demurred to introduce Sylvia, thinking that Emily was in New York. Sylvia was particularly interested in women writers, Suzette said, "because after the breakup she really said she was going to have a salon, she was going to set herself up, she was going to be independent. . . . Sylvia had this touch of hero-worshipping of writers."[76] In the meantime, Plath made significant strides toward becoming a self-supporting freelance writer in London. With Hughes's help, she lined up BBC commissions, while Alvarez pulled strings to get her on the BBC's prestigious weekly roundtable, *The Critics*. The *Critical Quarterly* solicited more poems and reviews from her in early January and invited her to dinner. *Punch* planned to publish "Snow Blitz" and a short piece about Plath's schoolgirl years in America, "The All-Around Image."

On January 10, Plath ventured over the snow drifts to record her review of Donald Hall's *Penguin Anthology of Contemporary American Poetry* for the BBC.[77] While she must have been disappointed not to be included in Hall's anthology—just as she was left out of Alvarez's—the review gave her the chance to promote the work of her favorite poets. (She had been included, however, in Hall's 1962 anthology, *New Poets of England and America: Second Selection*.)

"A new spirit is at work in American poetry," she began. She spoke of Lowell and the "intimate disarmament" of "Memories of West Street and Lepke." "The shift in tone is already history. . . . The flashing elaborate carapace of *Lord Weary's Castle* dropped for *Life Studies*, walking the tightrope of the psyche naked." This was an elegant restatement of Lowell's famous demarcation between "the cooked" and "the raw." She continued,

> "I myself am hell; / nobody's here—" The inwardness of these images, their plummeting subjectivity, is what Mr. Hall points to as genuinely new to the American scene. The uncanny faculty of melting through the leaves of the wallpaper, through the dark looking-glass into a world one can only call surrealistic and irrational. The analyst's couch has played its role here, I think, that important and purgatorial bit of American literary furniture.

She moved on to W. D. Snodgrass's "Heart's Needle," complimenting his "laconic, wry" verse that showed no "exhibitionism, no thunder and lightning"; she then noted the "claustrophobic flow of nightmare" in Louis Simpson's "There Is." She was naming her influences and promoting her own aesthetic: Simpson's poem sounded like something Plath herself had written—"The mannequins stare at me scornfully," she quotes. "The word 'eros' falls with a hiss of some disease," she said of his poem.

Plath likened this new poetic sensibility to one that was emerging "in modern cinema, by the juxtaposition of images, without editorializing. . . . So much of this poetry is visual." (Indeed, her image of melting through the wallpaper was an allusion to Bergman's *Through a Glass Darkly*.) She discussed Robert Bly's "Sunday in Glastonbury," singling out lines that may have influenced the beginning of "Daddy": "My black shoes stand on the floor. / Like two open graves." She quoted James Merrill, James Wright, and Galway Kinnell, but no women poets. (Only seven of the fifty-one poets in the book were women, but that would not have surprised her.) Nor does she use the word "confessional." Instead she uses "surrealist," twice—a telling indication of how she understood the emerging "confessional" school of poetry with which her name would be forever linked. "There is no sure objective ground," she said of this new poetry. It is "subconscious and archetypal." She ended the review with a line from Kinnell's "Flower Herding on Mount Monadnock": "'And the dimension of depth seizes everything.' That is, I think, what's been happening in a lot of American poetry."

This cerebral, elegant review belied the daily torments of Sylvia's physical and emotional reality. She wrote by candlelight with fingers chilled to the bone and a mind numbed by codeine, praising an editorial selection that did not include her work. Her health, still shaky after her late-summer flu, worsened in January. She had 103° fevers and an upper respiratory infection, while depression and anxiety further curtailed her appetite. She wrote to George MacBeth saying they had all, again, come down with what she called the flu.

In early January, Sylvia began seeing Dr. Horder, who gave her "tonics" to help stimulate her hunger, as she had lost twenty pounds over the summer. He was worried about her lungs and sent her to University College Hospital for a chest X-ray on January 1. She appreciated his solicitude and was relieved that he took her illnesses—both physical and mental—seriously. He estimated that he saw her twenty to thirty times before her death, and never for less than twenty minutes. When she first approached him about treatment, he recalled, "I knew that this was going to be, so to speak, a handful. . . . she'd had a tremendous blow, and I was going to see quite a bit of her. But she wasn't clinically depressed and certainly not suicidal to the best of my knowledge when she returned. Indeed, I remember her being pleased even in the week before her death about a BBC assignment. . . . She wasn't assuming Ted would come back. She was planning a life with the two children."[78]

The children had high fevers, and Frieda developed a worrisome allergy to penicillin. This news, at a time when there were few "second-line" antibiotics, would have heightened Sylvia's anxiety considerably. She herself was so sick that Horder arranged, during the second week of January, "a private day-nurse for 10 days."[79] Otherwise, she told the Roches, "I don't know what I would have done." (The care was not free; Sylvia complained to Aurelia that the nurse's £17 fee had eaten up most of her $50 birthday check.)[80] On January 9, Sylvia wrote the Roches a short letter "from bed where the doctor has put me," thanking Clarissa for her kind notes about *The Bell Jar*. "Your wonderful perceptive letter about the novel—you are the first to read it—came at a most needed moment & I think you see just what I meant it to be. One day when there is a good enough one it shall be dedicated to you both."[81]

Sylvia was so ill she qualified for free housekeeping help from the British Home Health Service. The housekeeper doted on the children, and Sylvia got "a terrific lift from it." She joked that the housekeeper, "Mrs. Vigors (!) . . . had the place gleaming in about 2 hours."[82] She hoped to persuade Mrs. Vigors to come regularly, but she never returned, and Sylvia's mood descended. She wrote her mother on January 16 of "all the heaped snow freezing so the roads are narrow ruts & I have been very gloomy with the long wait for a phone which I <u>hope</u> to get by the end of the month after 2 months wait! which makes one feel cut off, and the lack as yet of an 'au pair.'"[83] She was in the process of hiring a German au pair from Berlin, which Catherine Frankfort had helped facilitate, but nothing was finalized as yet.

Mrs. Prouty continued to send checks and urged Sylvia to spend the money on "the many things burdening you." She offered legal advice, though she could not believe that Ted's kindness was "dead forever." Prouty warned Plath that the plan she had mentioned in a recent letter—to buy 23 Fitzroy Road and rent out its flats—presented too many challenges for a single mother. With all the upkeep and "complaining tenants," Prouty wrote, "I fear there would be little time for your writing."[84] Prouty was probably Plath's only hope for a loan to buy the property. Now that hope was dashed.

Sylvia began socializing with Jillian and Gerry Becker, whom she had met through the Macedos. Suzette had known Jillian Becker (née Friedman) in South Africa, and had introduced her to Sylvia in September 1962. Jillian was an aspiring writer who would go on to become a well-known novelist and journalist. She was wealthy and lived in a large house in nearby Islington with an Irish nanny who, Suzette hoped, might also help Sylvia for she could see that Sylvia was overwhelmed. "She had too much with the kids. She couldn't handle it. . . . I told her, 'You have to use all the means available to you.'" Gerry was a lecturer in English—"a great, big, charming, leonine type," Suzette remembered, whom Sylvia liked very much.[85] Jillian, who was Sylvia's age, admitted that she envied Sylvia's literary success, and that as a Jew, she was slightly wary of her friend's German background. But she was also intrigued by this "intellectual" poet and mother.[86]

That January, Sylvia accompanied Jillian to a film festival at the cinema in Hampstead about once a week—"comedies but they didn't make her laugh," Jillian remembered. Jillian sensed Sylvia was not absorbing the films, and she suggested that they stop going. Sylvia replied, dutifully, "We must see them all." Jillian also took her to a play in the West End; afterward, they sought out a late-night café in Soho, where they "argued about psychoanalysis, she to some extent for and I wholly against it." Sylvia did not discuss her own "problems," but approached psychoanalysis as an intellectual idea.[87]

When Sylvia learned that Jillian was a writer, she tutored her on the proper ways to submit a manuscript. "Amateurism in writing she despised," Jillian remembered.[88] Sometimes they talked about their mothers, "each of us unforgivably," Jillian wrote. "In her case a need to impress her mother had been a driving force. She'd had to present her with success after success." Sylvia was sure that Aurelia saw the breakup of her marriage as "a failure," although she never called it that. Still, Jillian remembered that Aurelia's silent judgment "infuriated" Sylvia. "She hated the shame it would require her to feel. To shut it out she would now deny her mother any part in her life." Sylvia was only too aware of how history was repeating itself. "I'll be a single woman bringing up two children all by myself like my mother," she often said to Jillian and Gerry.[89]

It was at the Beckers', in late January, that Sylvia saw Richard Murphy for the last time. Douglas Cleverdon and his wife, Nest, were there, and they had warned Richard that Sylvia "was in a very tense state." To Richard, she looked "feverish" but "ecstatic" as she spoke of living in Yeats's house. Baby Nick was on her lap, and Frieda was playing nearby. He was relieved that she bore him no ill-will. He would learn of her death on February 14 when he returned to London from Ireland, and would feel guilty for not having provided "the haven she felt she needed in Connemara."[90] A rumor about Plath's supposed advances toward Murphy would begin making the rounds. (Nathaniel Tarn wrote in his diary that he was surprised Edward Lucie-Smith "didn't know about Richard Murphy" and Plath.)[91] Suzette remembered Sylvia speaking generously during this time about three male poets: Richard Murphy, Bill Merwin, and Al Alvarez.[92] A few months later, Richard would be astonished to find Assia and David Wevill at the Pier Bar in Cleggan—come, he presumed, "to find out what had happened in Cleggan to Ted and Sylvia."[93]

———

IN MID-JANUARY, Sylvia became uncharacteristically gloomy about her future, and let down her guard in a letter to Aurelia.

> I just haven't felt to have any <u>identity</u> under the steamroller of decisions & responsibilities of this last half year, with the babies a constant demand.... How I would <u>like</u> to be self-supporting on my writing! But I need <u>time</u>.
>
> I guess I just need somebody to cheer me up by saying I've done all right so far.[94]

The following day, January 17, was Nick's first birthday. Jillian and Suzette had no memory of its being celebrated. This would have been a painful milestone for Sylvia.

Ruth Fainlight thought she understood Sylvia's predicament perfectly, writing from Tangier in early January that she knew no one there and sometimes longed for London. "And yet, thinking about the people whom I call my friends there, the people I used to see, I remember meetings that left me despondent and unsatisfied." Something about London, Ruth wrote, "seemed to be destructive." She felt that she had not had time to settle down in Morocco: "And when I momentarily do sense what being settled down will be like, I usually panic." Ruth had described Sylvia's own complicated feelings about writing, home, and exile. Yet she reassured Sylvia that she looked forward to the April trip to Devon, and plays and movies in London—"and talking and talking and talking."[95] She had arranged a British visa for her nanny, Fatima, and obtained her driving license so that she could drive in Devon. Years later, Fainlight would say of her friendship with Plath that there wasn't enough time.[96]

Aurelia, worried about her daughter's state of mind, asked a favor of Mildred Norton. Perry Norton's wife's cousin, Patricia Goodall, lived in London; would she mind checking in on Sylvia? Patricia obliged, writing to Sylvia of their Wellesley connection and asking if she could "drop in on her" on January 19. Patricia did not want Sylvia to know Mildred had sent her, though Sylvia probably suspected as much, and she played the part. She greeted Patricia, her husband, and her young daughter with a "bright smile and eager American expression." She served tea, and for the next hour, Patricia told Mildred, the three adults "NEVER STOPPED TALKING!" Patricia found the children healthy, in good humor, and well tended, the flat "warm and cheery." Plath spoke of "some success in publishing a book" but "seemed shy about the subject, saying it was being published under an assumed name."[97] Patricia liked Sylvia so much that she invited her to dinner the following week. She hoped a true friendship might form, and asked Mildred not to tell Sylvia the real reason for her visit.

Ted came once a week, Sylvia told friends—"sometimes is nice & sometimes awful."[98] She called him an "apocalyptic Santa Claus" in a letter to Marcia.[99] Although he may have visited more often, his name appears infrequently in Sylvia's calendar between December 10 and January 5 (the last surviving page).[100] His December letter to his brother Gerald in Australia suggests how little he had seen of his wife that winter:

All this business has been terrible—especially for Sylvia, but it was inevitable, and now the storm-centre of it recedes into the distance, I can only be relieved that I've done it. The one factor that nobody but quite close friends can comprehend is Sylvia's particular death-ray quality. In many of the most important ways, she's the most gifted and capable & admirable woman I've ever met—but, finally, impossible for me to live married to. Now we're separated, we're better friends than we've been since we first met. Mainly because we see each other only about once a month, if that. The main grief for me is that a life that had all the circumstances for perfection should have been so intolerable, and that little Frieda loses a father & I lose little Frieda. She's been my playmate for 2 years & become absolutely a necessary piece of my life. . . . I'm feeling a lot better except for dreaming about Frieda every night.[101]

On January 21, Ted wrote to the Merwins, who were abroad, that in London the cold was "freezing people dead." He was trying to get enough money "to leave" Sylvia.[102]

Hughes's journal reveals something of his state of mind that winter. "I am completely responsible for S's fixation on me, I demanded it," he wrote. Now, speaking of Assia, he saw that "only a partial balancing relationship can work & let us live." He vowed

Not to drift helplessly . . . tied to babyish fear of losing her, or making her angry or overthoughtful, or tearful. . . . Because my weakness with women, my difficulty in being rational & disciplined in my dealings with them, my yielding to whatever I may think is their whim is ruining—has probably already ruined my life. And in the end it leads to disaster for them too, meshed in my falsity.

So have I reached a decision? Yes.

My unwillingness to hurt women, my incredible indulgence toward them, is simple reflection of the same attitude toward myself. . . .

My fear of rebuffing & feeling: ends in the utter callousness of my dealings with S.[103]

Ted was now seeing Susan Alliston as well as Assia. Tall, with long, thick bronze hair, Sue resembled Sylvia physically. Hughes later wrote about her "powerful athletic presence," "slate-blue eyes," and extraordinary poetic talent.[104] Like Sylvia, he had thought she was Swedish when he met her in the elevator at Faber and Faber, where she worked as a secretary. She too had literary aspirations; Hughes had read one of her poems in *The Nation* while living in America. He met her after he had separated from Sylvia, at the Lamb pub on Great Conduit Street, around the corner from 18 Rugby Street, where Daniel and Helga still lived. By then Sue had separated from her husband, Clem Moore, Warren's Harvard roommate, whom she had married in December 1959 in Cambridge. (Warren served as the usher.) Sylvia had known Sue for years, and Warren had even visited Sue and Clem during his 1961 visit to England. In late October 1962, when Sylvia was feeling very grim, she told her mother, "Got a <u>darling</u> letter from Clem today, very fond of him, like a second brother, <u>and</u> his mother"—a reference to Sarah-Elizabeth Rodger, the writer on whom she had once modeled her future.[105]

Now Clem's wife was carrying on an affair with her husband. The fact that Ted was conducting a second, simultaneous affair with someone so close to her own family intensified Sylvia's pain and humiliation.

Sue kept a journal during this time, and she ruminated on her relationship with Ted, which began in November 1962. She felt a tremor of excitement when she saw him walk into a party that month, "Somewhat blue-chinned, a little stooped, young, and with some enormous strength extending from him." She knew that he was also seeing Assia, and she tried not to make any claims on him even after they began sleeping together. He made his feelings clear. "Marriage is not for me—nor you, I think," he said to her during one of their early meetings. "Him, well," she mused in her journal, "he's got it in for Anglo-Saxon women, perhaps because too cold. He's now with a non Anglo-Saxon." On January 17, she wrote, "he talks so much, so personally about himself and S[ylvia] and Assia and his plans. He said the exclusivity of the relationship killed something—the keeping always on the same plane, and that she is an absolutist—will not accept a compromise." He spoke to her of his poem "Dark Woman," in which the "blood clot" that killed Percy Key also becomes, symbolically, the woman—Assia—who "brings life to Ted." The other woman in the poem—Sylvia—was "The punctual evening star—the Venus of the piece . . . the polar to 'blood clot' I suppose."[106]

Ted would transform Assia and Sylvia into poetic symbols again in his infamous radio play *Difficulties of a Bridegroom*, in which Sullivan, the hero, runs over a hare while driving up to London to visit his girlfriend. He then has visions of two women: one represents lust, the other chastity. The play was broadcast on the BBC on January 21, and again on February 9, two days before Plath's suicide. For Sylvia, it was a very public—if coded and symbolic—humiliation. The play begins: "Your trouble, Sullivan, you're still suffering from moon-glare. She's attractive, but is she outstanding? You're moon-blind. . . . She somehow reached the secret switch in your brain." Suddenly, Sullivan sees the hare. He grows excited and runs it over. "Speed it up, little experiment, gee up. (Car accelerates.) Forty. Forty five. No, Sullivan, no, O you cruel bastard." Some poachers arrive at the scene, which soon becomes symbolic drama. Wedding bells toll in the background, while a chorus of four maidens describe his bride, the "beautiful maiden" who is a stock Hughesian femme fatale: "Here she comes, her perfumes before her, / A fox in her face, a bat in her hair / And a polecat in her navel."

The seductress seems to possess Sullivan, who promises her "Everything." She demands a flat in Soho, "A red convertible Cadillac. . . . An unlimited allowance for sundries to my taste, wardrobe and so forth. . . . You'll have to get a job, of course." "A job!" Sullivan cries out. He is "seeking the truth" and cares nothing about material things. The woman, known only as "SHE," tells him he should stop dressing in rags and should wear things that express his convictions: "Your tie will be a single adder-skin, with the head and fangs intact, your finger-rings will be the carved eye-sockets of owls." Plath had joyfully replaced and updated Hughes's wardrobe when they first married. Now Hughes was symbolically shedding those clothes, giving in to his instincts, donning the mantle of the hunter.

Yet Sullivan soon realizes that SHE is simply a "Simulacrum," preying on his fears of marriage. He refutes her for his real bride, and SHE vows, "I shall be a maneater and the blood on your head. . . . I shall come after you, how can you leave me?" Now SHE becomes a Platonic vision of perfection, a geometrical abstraction that demands chastity. Plath would have understood. "Danger!" the chorus cries. "Poet!" After SHE instructs him to contemplate her breasts and body and cries, "Convert your genitals to the number one hundred percent," Sullivan is "Burned to black, to white, to ashes, scattered, recovered." He and SHE join together in "the white bed, the deep bed," and the vision ends.

Up in London, Sullivan sells the hare at the butcher shop and meets with his "mistress," who is appalled. He lies to her, saying he killed the hare by accident. "It's evil blood money," she says of the coins he receives for the dead hare. Sullivan responds that if he throws them away, "Somebody picks it up. Then what? The evil goes to them. . . . The thing to do is redeem them." They walk by a vendor, and he buys a rose for her. The play closes on Sullivan's final words. "Let's have a drink."[107] The rose symbolizes the new love that has come from the ashes of his real marriage—the end of Hughes's love for Plath, symbolized by the hare's death, has been "redeemed." The "real" woman at the play's end, likely based on Susan Alliston, is neither a materialistic seductress (Assia) nor a chaste goddess (Sylvia).

Ted explained the meaning of the play in a letter to Olwyn, probably written on February 10, the day before Sylvia's suicide:

> The day after I posted it [the play], I drove up to London, ran over a hare (by pure chance—it's impossible to do deliberately) sold it to a butcher's in Holborn and he gave me 5 bob. I spent it on roses . . . smashed two, and gave 2 to Assia.
>
> Eventually the idea is that Sullivan must first of all recognise and dismiss—by some ordeal or other—the supernatural women which project themselves onto the real woman, and prevent him seeing her as real—as herself. Once he's dealt with his instinct to do this, he can meet that real one. The hare is the tiger is the woman is his blood is all kinds of things. I'm not quite sure. But he has, so to speak, to kill it, master it, or at least

meet it and recognise it, before he can get on with real outside life with a real woman.[108]

At its best, as Sue said, Ted's play was full of "a fin-de-siècle eroticism," so different from "the cool understated kitchen-sink type approach" then fashionable.[109] At its worst, it was self-indulgent and misogynistic, like something Byron would have written, and its symbolism was both arcane and obvious—though Hughes suggested, in his letter to Olwyn, that the play was partly about his own struggle to see women for who they really were, rather than as femme fatales. Ted told Sue, as he had Olwyn, that everything in the play had later happened in real life. "What do you think it might mean?" he asked her. She replied, "Don't worry about it," though she later regretted her dismissal. When they spoke of the play after it first aired on January 21, she gathered that the two women were "metaphors in his mind. Both are destructive possessive and demand too much." Hughes told her both women in the play were "feminine in demanding complete surrender." Sue mused: "If he can evoke so fantastically forcefully and beautifully these two extremes, what could any woman give him?"[110]

Sue wondered whom the hare symbolized. But Sylvia would have understood clearly, as she listened to the play, that the hare's death—the death of their marriage—symbolized Sullivan's rebirth. "Ted always told Sylvia that her shamanic animal was her hare," Elizabeth later said.[111] It was as if Hughes was mocking her portrayal of him as a sadist in her earlier poem "The Rabbit Catcher."

Elizabeth worried that Sylvia was "very low" in London "hearing that, and knowing that all her friends in London would hear that."[112] Daniel Huws thought that the play devastated her. He felt "there was no going back," and that it had been the final humiliation that had pushed Sylvia to suicide. He speculated that Hughes afterward felt so guilty he gave other works the same title to deflect attention from the original.[113] The play remains unpublished. Peter Hall would turn it down for the Arts Theatre in London on the grounds that it was not "a valid piece of theatre," full of "over-blown metaphors," "rhetorical and empty."[114] In a later poem, "The Afterbirth," Hughes wrote of running over the hare on the A30, and his play's effect on Plath: "...it screamed in your ear like a telephone— / ... / Unstoppably, like a burst artery, / The hare in the bowl screamed—"[115]

Alvarez broadcast a positive review of the play on the January 27 edition of *The Critics* on the BBC Home Service. With his intimate knowledge of Sylvia, Ted, and Assia, he understood exactly what Ted was trying to say. ("Love is a threat, the girl is a threat.")[116] Alvarez complimented Hughes's writing as "extraordinarily vivid, imaginative and original," though he averred that the program would have been even better without some of the melodramatic sound effects.[117] Plath listened to *The Critics* regularly—Alvarez had extended an invitation for her to join the program in May 1963. To hear her erstwhile lover praise her husband's play about the symbolic death of their marriage was deeply humiliating. *Difficulties of a Bridegroom* was as cruel, public, and personal as Plath's "Daddy." But Hughes's play would not stand time's test nearly as well as Plath's poem.

Remarkably, on January 23—just two days after the play aired—Sylvia invited Ted to Fitzroy Road for sherry to celebrate the official January 14 release date of *The Bell Jar*. He wrote about the afternoon in an unpublished 1986–87 poetic sequence called "Trial," written during the *Bell Jar* trial in Boston.

> We toasted it. I admired the cover
> The dim, distorted image of a girl
> Dissolving in a Bell Jar. Did I wonder
> "Now dare I read it? Ought I to read it now?"
> The electric bars glared in the wall.
> The matting smelt of tobacco. The glass-topped table
> Bright fresh novelty reminding me
> How you furnished Whitstead before my time.
> Was it then or through the following week
> You showed me the reviews. No pannings. No raves.
> So there it was. The novel had been written,
> And published, and here was the world's response.
> I was relieved to read
> How seriously reviewers addressed it
> Even if they disapproved. And yet, it was clear,
> Nobody had admired a genius
> Out of the ordinary. You were seasoned.
> You hid your reaction, whatever it was
> Under a guarded, ruminative sort
> Of summoning acceptance.[118]

The Bell Jar, which Plath published under the pen name Victoria Lucas, received good reviews in nearly all the prominent British papers; only *The Spectator* was lukewarm. The best reviews came about ten days after the release date. On January 25 the anonymous reviewer for *The Times Literary Supplement* praised Plath's "dry wit" and "convincing" narrative: "Few writers are able to create a different world for you to live in; yet Miss Lucas in *The Bell Jar* has done just this." The reviewer called the novel "a considerable achievement."[119] On the same day, the *New Statesman* called it "clever," and declared it the first "feminine novel . . . in the Salinger mode."[120] Two days later came a solid review in *The Observer*'s "Weekend Review"—the one Plath had been waiting for—by Anthony Burgess, who had just released *A Clockwork Orange* in December: "We've met the situation before, but rarely so mature a fictional approach to it. Where (especially in the asylum scenes) there might have been sensationalism, there is sensitivity and decorum; also, the characterisation is economical but full, and the style is careful without being labored or pretentious."[121] The review was neither celebratory nor damning—it was positive but dull. Worse, *The Bell Jar* was lumped in with five other books in a group review that showcased Julian Mitchell's *As Far As You Can Go* as the best of the lot. The most prescient and perceptive review came from Laurence Lerner (who knew Plath was the author), writing in *The Listener* on January 31. He understood Plath's deeper political message; this was not just a college-girl suicide drama. "I recommend *The Bell Jar* strongly," he wrote. "There are criticisms of American society that the neurotic can make as well as anyone, perhaps better, and Miss Lucas makes them triumphantly." He praised Plath's "triumph" of "language," and closed, "Miss Lucas is tremendously readable, and at the same time has an almost poetic delicacy of perception. This is a brilliant and moving book."[122]

Nearly all the reviews were good, and some, like Lerner's, were excellent. A first-time novelist with a print run of two thousand could hardly ask for a better reception.[123] But Plath's economic future depended on *The Bell Jar*, and the review that had mattered most, in *The Observer*, was not going to make her novel a best seller. Trevor Thomas remembered Sylvia telling him in late January what she had told Aurelia for years: "she wanted to become a famous novelist and make a lot of money."[124] But she learned, in late January, that Harper & Row had turned the book down; *The Bell Jar*—as far as she knew—would not catapult her to fame as *The Ha-Ha* had Jennifer Dawson. *The Ha-Ha*, awarded Britain's prestigious James Tait Black Memorial Prize in 1961, was a first novel about a brilliant female Oxford undergraduate who suffers a breakdown and recuperates in a country-clubbish psychiatric hospital.[125] Plath was reading it the weekend she died—a novelistic doppelgänger to her own double-themed novel.[126] She likely suspected that there was only so much room for novels about college-girl suicides. Hers, it seemed, was a year too late.

Ted and Aurelia both came to believe that reliving the events of *The Bell Jar* pushed Sylvia closer to suicide. Dr. Francis de Marneffe, the psychiatrist who had shared an office with Dr. Beuscher when Plath was at McLean, speculated similarly, wondering "to what extent was Sylvia's suicide connected with the publication of the book and a related sense of remorse, perhaps, of what she had done to other people."[127] Like Plath herself, Hughes searched for the root cause of his wife's depression. Neither could bring themselves to admit that her depression simply *was*. Thinking back to that time, in his "Trial" sequence, Hughes found himself "appalled" by the "malice" of her new poems.

> I'd only heard
> The few you'd let me hear, tantalizing,
> Withholding the rest like a secret.
> I knew that they were going to hurt your mother.
> "Daddy" I'd heard, but how would she bear it?
> Could she bear Medusa? I was right.
> She could not. Did you think of it?
> You declaimed them with a divine malice.
> I was appalled. I was horrified.
> How would you go on living in a world
> Where you'd condemned your parents, publicly,
> Into such everlasting furnaces?

It was "hatred" that had animated the novel as well, Hughes wrote, from beginning to end, "hatred" "most of all / Of your mother—"

> Who bore the hate?
> Not your smile, your platinum
> Veronica Lake bangs. Or your summa.
> A small girl bore it, crouching in a coffin,
>
> That little poltergeist girl, who lived in death
> Curled at the breast of her dead father.
> . . . .
> The buried girl had finally had her say.[128]

34

What Is the Remedy?

London, January–February 1963

The publication of *The Bell Jar* in mid-January should have been a cause for celebration. But for Plath, the victory was hollow. She had hoped for a best seller, fame, and a Primrose Hill townhouse all her own. But there was no windfall. The risk she had taken in fictionalizing her friends and family now hardly seemed worth the potential fallout.

Worse, American publishers were not interested. In early December, Plath learned that Knopf had turned down *The Bell Jar*. In a long, thoughtful letter dated December 28, her Knopf editor, Judith Jones, explained their reasoning.

> Up to the point of her breakdown the attitude of your young girl had seemed a perfectly normal combination of brashness and disgust with the world, but I was not at all prepared as a reader to accept the extent of her illness and the suicide attempt. I had the feeling that you were not letting us in close enough so that we could share in and thereby understand the whole complex of this girl's feelings and attitudes, and as a result the novel never really took hold for me.[1]

Plath instructed Heinemann to send *The Bell Jar* on to Harper & Row, who rejected it in mid-January for similar reasons. The first part, Hughes's Harper editor, Elizabeth Lawrence, wrote, was "arresting," but after Esther's breakdown, "the story for us ceases to be a novel and becomes more a case history. . . . It does not enlarge the reader's knowledge of the girl substantially, or have the necessary dramatic impact. The experience remains a private one." Lawrence continued, "we do not feel that it is truly successful in what it attempts, and there has been so much fiction in recent years dealing with this area of experience that we are doubtful of its chances in the current fiction market."[2] Plath had dared to hope her novel would be a best seller in America, but a few days after January 16, the date of Lawrence's letter, she learned it would not even be published there.

Both publishers were wrong about the book—*The Bell Jar* remains one of the most widely read American novels of the twentieth century. Neither female editor saw how Esther's illness reflected the American body politic. They did not absorb the prescient criticisms of Cold War America, the sympathy for outsiders, or the takedown of traditional femininity. But both, in their rejections, expressed a similar sense of disbelief that would haunt Sylvia's own friends after her suicide. Esther's descent into "madness" did not seem plausible. As the Harper & Row editor pointed out, nothing traumatic had happened to her beyond "a girl's encounter with the big city—universal and individual."[3] In Esther Greenwood, Plath had crafted a heroine based on herself, disguising her illness so well that these editors did not believe her depression's swift severity.

American publication had always mattered a great deal to Plath, and the rejections from Knopf and Harper & Row hit her hard. Just as her rejection from Frank O'Connor's writing class had precipitated her first suicide attempt, these more important and brutal rejections precipitated the second. American publication would have renewed her optimism and self-confidence at a time when she was nearly running on empty. Instead, the rejections depleted her already low reserves of energy and validated her worst self-criticisms.

The Bell Jar's publication, and its American rejection, marked a turning point. Plath's mental health had been precarious after Christmas, but it deteriorated in January. Different stresses contributed to the onslaught. For someone who hated the cold and responded "intensely" to weather, the winter of 1963 was brutal. She was a single mother with two babies living with frozen pipes and intermittent heat and electricity. Since Christmas, she had been ill with a worsening bronchial condition and was not eating properly. She wrote to Hughes's Cambridge friend David Ross asking for help with her "financial affairs," but Ross never replied.[4] Checks from Mrs. Prouty, Aurelia, and Ted kept her afloat that month, but she earned little from her writing. She had just £101 in her Lloyd's Bank checking account on January 1; by January 31, the date of her last surviving check stub, she had only £59.[5] She received more money after this point, for she had £2,147 in her account at the time of her death (equivalent to about $48,000 in 2020 dollars).[6] Some of this money came in late January from Aurelia and Mrs. Prouty; the rest might be explained by a February transfer from her American bank accounts into her British account (Sylvia had instructed Aurelia to empty both of her American accounts and send the total balance to her in late November, when she thought she would need to pay a year's rent on the Yeats flat herself); a substantial maintenance payment from Hughes; and a payment from her publisher, Heinemann. While this money would have assuaged Sylvia's immediate financial anxieties, it was not a vast sum for a single mother in London supporting two children and an au pair. With her hopes for an American publication of *The Bell Jar* dashed, there would be no reliable income stream, no financial independence. Jillian Becker remembered that Sylvia feared having to support her children alone.[7] She had achieved her dream of moving to London and living in Yeats's house but had exposed herself to painful gossip about Ted, Assia, and Sue Alliston. She was becoming an object of pity—a difficult position for a woman with such pride.

Lady Lazarus promises to "eat men like air," yet real life did not provide the freedom of poetry. In her letters, Sylvia put up a brave front about living on her own, but the stigma of divorce and single motherhood was real. Her new life had inspired her to write her best poems yet, but it carried the whiff of shame and failure. To blaze a trail as a woman poet in the early 1960s was isolating and exhausting work. Ted Hughes had made the journey less lonely. Now Plath was on her own in a sexist society where abortion was still illegal and marital rape legal. Alvarez's American girlfriend Linda Gates recalled, "Although Al was very sweet, and tried very hard, it was really a man's world in those days. Women were referred to as 'birds,' and generally sat quietly and listened to the men talk."[8] Paul Roche agreed, calling England then "a man's country."[9] The celebrated biographer and Newnham graduate Claire Tomalin remembered the "shock of adjustment from competitive and high-achieving girl to subjugated wife and mother." One of her most "vivid memories" from the mid-1950s was "crying into a washbasin full of soapy grey baby clothes" while her husband played soccer with friends.[10] These were the years when Hannah Gavron was writing *The Captive Wife*, about the loneliness of housebound mothers in London. Shortly after completing the book, in 1966, Gavron, a young mother herself, gassed herself in a Chalcot Square flat, not far from Plath's.

The feminist Meredith Tax, who spent four years on a Fulbright Fellowship in London during the 1960s, wrote that without a man, a woman during this time was "nowhere, disappeared, teetering on the edge of a void."[11] Her words conjure the interstellar void of Plath's "Edge," with its images of a mother and her children abandoned and alone. In Britain in 1961, just 2 percent of households were run by a single parent—and that figure would remain the same for the next ten years.[12] Being a single mother, Lorna Secker-Walker remembered, was "unusual." So was divorce itself—only 2.1

per 1,000 married people divorced in 1961.[13] Lorna understood why Sylvia would have been anxious about finding another man: "someone at that age—pretty bleak prospects."[14] Plath was thirty.

The novelist Fay Weldon, a friend of Assia's, remembered that in this sexist society, "to be without a man was such a disgraceful thing. It meant you were a total failure, to be alone. To be alone with a child beyond a certain age meant that you had been seen as unfit by men and rejected by them."[15] Hughes suggested, in an unpublished poem, that Plath saw no immediate change on the horizon:

> When you wrote those poems of Ariel
> Had feminism stirred in its crate?
> Surely it had. But not a murmur of it
> Had reached you, or alerted you, or touched
> Your feminine instinct. Not a hint of it.
> Any more than you'd heard a note of the "Beatles"
> Those birds of the muddled dawn—who were already
> 1962—singing unnoticed
> Under a skyline about to be transfigured.[16]

Even Doris Lessing's freethinking heroine in *The Golden Notebook*, Anna Wulf, is not sure she can live without a man. Lessing herself, a former communist who had left two children and a husband behind in Africa in order to pursue an independent writing career in London, might have offered Plath a real-life model of "free" womanhood. She lived with her young son, Peter, in a townhouse on Charrington Street, which she had bought from the proceeds of *The Golden Notebook*. This pivotal novel, which eventually helped Lessing win the Nobel Prize in Literature, addressed madness, single motherhood, writing, male betrayal, literary ambition, politics, and exile—all themes that preoccupied Plath. Lessing inscribed a copy of *The Golden Notebook*, "To Ted and Sylvia, with love from Doris Lessing," on June 14, 1962. In this copy, Plath placed three check marks next to passages about single, artistic, bohemian women who live freely. On page 20, for example, she checked: "Her source of self-respect was that she had not—as she put it—given up and crawled into safety somewhere. Into a safe marriage." On page 46: "We've chosen to live a certain way, knowing the penalties, or if we didn't we know now. . . ."[17] Lessing and her characters lived the free life Plath aspired to. After Plath read the book, Suzette brought her to Lessing's Charrington Street home—this was in December or January—but Lessing spurned her. She was put off by Plath's effusive praise and American gushiness, and thought her "needy and did not want to get involved."[18] Helder

Macedo found Lessing's response especially unfortunate, for when Sylvia got to know someone, "a deux," she dropped the gushiness and became a "precise" and "marvelous" conversationalist, "a probing instrument, concentrated." Helder had asked Sylvia why she "gushed" in groups, and she said "it had to do with her unease as a young woman who couldn't make it socially, didn't know how, and had developed this manner to ingratiate herself."[19] This was why, she said, social events and dinner parties exhausted her. But Lessing knew none of this. She asked Suzette not to bring Sylvia back.

Sylvia's aspiration to live as an independent woman began to collide with the reality of her loneliness, her desire for love, and the stigma she surely felt as a single mother. Her depression worsened after Alvarez ignored her mid-January letter suggesting a date to the zoo, while a flirtatious February letter from John Richardson suggests that she was still looking for male companionship in the weeks before her death. She didn't think she had much choice. Plath told friends she did not want to raise two children on her own as her widowed mother had. She was appalled that, for all her efforts to live a different kind of life, she had ended up in the very same situation as Aurelia, but worse—rejected, unemployed, far away from friends and family.

Plath had always charted her own course as a woman artist, deftly transcending the obstacles put in her way. The imagery of flight that reached its apotheosis in "Ariel" had its roots in her early poem "Aerialist." There, a young woman "parries the lunge and menace" of heavy black bowling balls, swinging pendulums, and roaring trucks as she balances on a high wire in her dream. When she wakes, she is haunted by a sense that "as penalty for her skill," "she must walk in dread"—that "out of spite," the sky will "Fall racketing finale on her luck." Now Plath's luck had run out; the sky had, indeed, fallen. She felt that she could not return to America and Aurelia; nor could she face constant reminders of Ted and Assia in London. Dr. Beuscher was across the ocean and keeping her distance. Sylvia was reading novels about sanatoriums and nervous breakdowns and reliving that experience in her own novel, which had been rejected by American publishers. She probably worried, despite her use of a pseudonym, about the pain the book would cause her American friends and family if they learned of its true author—a reality brought home when she sat at the table of Patricia Goodall, Perry Norton's relation, two nights before she died.

Without the patronage of Hughes or, now, Alvarez, Plath's social capital dissolved. Friends remembered her during this time as gratingly effusive, desperately lonely, a subject of gossip, a burden. Jillian Becker felt that at the very end of Sylvia's life she was "isolated and denigrated."[20] Plath's January and February poems, filled with "translucent calm," as Alvarez said, seemed to absorb this new, unhappy state.[21]

———

ON JANUARY 22, Sylvia wrote her last letter to Olive Prouty. Sad and candid, it offered a brief glimpse of the mental horror she would reveal in her final letter to Ruth Beuscher. Dr. Horder, Sylvia said, had been a "source of great help . . . but I do occasionally miss that wonderful Doctor Ruth Beuscher I had at McLean's who I feel could help me so much now. She did write me a letter or two, very helpful, but it's not the same as those hours of talk." Sylvia hoped her new eighteen-year-old German-speaking au pair, who had moved in that day, would provide her some respite (she could afford the help as Ted was giving her $280 a month, more than the yearly $2,500 required by her lawyer).[22] "I have not been alone with myself for over two months, when I had my dear young nurse in Devon, and this has been the keenest torture, this lack of a centre, a quietness, to brood in and grow from. I suppose, to the writer, it is like communing with God." Prouty had advised her not to resume her novel until she had daily, uninterrupted time to write, and she now looked forward to beginning again. But for once, she told Prouty the truth.

> Frieda makes me so sad. Ted comes once a week to see her, she hangs on him dotingly, then cries "Daddy come soon" for the rest of the week, waking in the night, tearful and obsessed with him. It is like a kind of mirror, utterly innocent, to my own sense of loss. . . . I think my salvation will be to plunge into my work. . . . I must just resolutely write mornings for the next years, through cyclones, water freezeups, children's illnesses & the <u>aloneness</u>. Having been so deeply and spiritually and physically happy with my dear, beautiful husband makes this harder than if I had never known love at all. Now he is famous, beautiful, the whole world wants him and now has him. He has changed so that the old life is impossible—I could never live under the same roof with him again, but I hope for the children's sake that each week he visits I can be brave and merry, without sorrow or accusation, and forge my life anew. . . . I desperately want to make an inner strength in myself, an independence that can face bringing up the children alone & in face of great uncertainties. Do write me again! Your letters are like balm, you understand the writer in me, & that is where I must live.[23]

The letter alarmed Mrs. Prouty, who had always been skeptical of Sylvia's cheerful epistolary front. She replied immediately, sending a check and praising Sylvia's courage and strength. "I know well how you must suffer & suffer & suffer—behind the mask you wear."[24] Mrs. Prouty, Betty Aldrich, the Nortons, Aunt Dot, and Warren all sent letters in late January and early February. To Sylvia, in her depressed state, their love and concern meant more obligation—like the "smiling hooks" of "Tulips."

There was some good news. On January 25, Sylvia met with Philip French, a producer in the Talks Department at the BBC, about appearing as the broadcasting critic on *The Critics* that May. (She would sign a contract to record three programs.) Her behavior seemed normal to French.[25] But Alvarez remembered Karl Miller, literary editor of the *New Statesman*, telling him around this time that Plath did not seem well and that he had turned down "a whole wodge of poems" he found "too extreme."[26] (Miller remembered, "I thought she was going mad . . . and found her poems very disturbing.")[27] Alvarez told Plath about the interaction, reassuring her, without using Miller's name, that "nobody could hear them; they weren't typically English taste."[28] Also on the 25th, she received an enthusiastic acceptance letter from Charles Osborne at *The London Magazine*, who took nine new poems: "Stings," "The Couriers," "Mary's Song," "Cut," "Letter in November," "The Bee Meeting," "An Appearance," "Berck-Plage," and "Years."[29] The turnaround was astonishingly quick: she had sent the poems to Osborne on January 17. Given her recent *New Yorker* rejections, these acceptances were a boon. She was still showing her work to Ted, who was encouraging. Edward Lucie-Smith said that two weeks before Sylvia's suicide, he had coffee with Ted, who told him, "in tones of perfectly detached admiration," "'Oh you should see the poems she's writing now. She's like a woman on fire. They're extraordinary. The best things she's ever done.'"[30]

Alvarez suggested in *The Savage God* that he was the only editor who truly appreciated Plath's work during this time, and, indeed, Osborne later wrote that Plath's poems impressed him "despite themselves."[31] But Plath was not howling in the wilderness. According to her submission list, more than half of her *Ariel* poems—twenty-four of forty—had been accepted by late January 1963 by *The Observer*, *The New Yorker*, *The London Magazine*, *Poetry*, and *The Atlantic*. These were among the world's most prestigious publications for a poet. Although *The New Yorker* had rejected her most recent batch, it still had six poems waiting to go into print: "Elm" (published as "The Elm Speaks"), "Mirror," "Amnesiac," "The Moon and the Yew Tree," "Two Campers in Cloud Country," and "Among the Narcissi." (All would be published posthumously in the August 3, 1963, issue.) But literary validation was no longer enough. She told Dr. Horder her depression was getting worse.

On Sunday, January 27, Sylvia knocked on Trevor Thomas's door around eight p.m. "She stood there with red, swollen eyes, the tears running down her face and with voice shaken by sobs she said: 'I am going to die . . . and who will take care of my children?'" Thomas sat her down in his living room and returned with two glasses of sherry. "Now, tell me what's all this about?" She began crying again. "We were so happy. I don't want to die. There's so much I want to do," she said. He assumed that she had been given a cancer diagnosis. "No, not that," she said. "It's too much. I can't go on." She started a diatribe against Assia, "an evil woman, a scarlet woman, the Jezebel." She said Assia and Ted were on holiday in Spain, spending her money. "Oh! How I hate them!" Then she noticed that Thomas had a copy of *The Observer*, opened to the book review page. She pointed to a poem in the middle of the page—"Full Moon and Little Frieda"—and said it was by her husband, Ted Hughes.[32] Then she pointed to Anthony Burgess's review of *The Bell Jar* on the facing page and revealed that *she* was Victoria Lucas. She grew angry again, talking about how Ted would be "the centre of admiration, free to come and go as he pleases. And here I am, a prisoner in this house, chained to the children. . . . We were so happy, so happy. Oh, if only . . . if only she had never come." She blamed Assia more than Ted, whom she spoke of "in an ambivalent blend of blame, jealousy and wanting him back. She had not entirely given up hope of paradise regained." Plath told Thomas he "reminded her of her father."[33] Thomas's account dovetails with others' stories of Plath at this time. She also raged about Assia and Ted to Jillian the weekend before she died and admitted to others that she felt isolated and burdened by the care of her children. And her plaintive fear of dying echoes similar sentiments in her letters to Dr. Beuscher that fall and winter.

The next day, January 28, Plath mailed Leonie Cohn at the BBC her script, "Ocean 1212-W," with its nostalgia for Winthrop and buried grief for her father.[34] With the decks cleared, Plath turned back to poetry. Her German-speaking au pair had been living with her for a week. But the match was not propitious; Sylvia wrote to Aurelia on February 4 that the girl was "food-fussy & boy-gaga," and to Elizabeth on the same day that she was "trying to knock some notion of maternal responsibility" into her.[35] Still, she had time to write again and did not waste an hour. On January 28 she finished three new poems—"The Munich Mannequins," "Totem," and "Child"—and revised "Sheep in Fog." It was the beginning of another productive period, not unlike the creative outpouring of October. Between January 28 and February 5 Plath wrote eleven poems, some of them her best.

The exuberance of "Ariel" and the campy black humor of "Lady Lazarus" evaporated; their insistent rhythms disappeared. Plath's new register was still, flat. She had returned to the voice of "The Moon and the Yew Tree" and its subject—depression.

"The hills step off into whiteness. / People or stars / Regard me sadly, I disappoint them," she wrote in "Sheep in Fog." She had written an earlier version of the poem, "Fog Sheep," on December 2, 1962. The first draft reveals that the poem had originally been based on the legend of Phaeton and Helios, and that the speaker had crashed after flying too close to the sun (there are two references to "a scrapped chariot").[36] The drafts also suggest that Plath had been influenced by Hughes's poems "Phaetons" and "The Horses." On January 28 she returned to "Fog Sheep," removed the chariot reference, and rewrote the last stanza. She was likely influenced by Theodore Roethke's poem "The Far Field," which had been published in *The Times Literary Supplement* on December 21, 1962.[37] Her dark new ending conjured despair:

> My bones hold a stillness, the far
> Fields melt my heart.
>
> They threaten
> To let me through to a heaven
> Starless and fatherless, a dark water.

Seldom has the existential threat of depression been so memorably aestheticized. Plath described the mood in her BBC introduction: "the speaker's horse is proceeding at a slow, cold walk down a hill of macadam to the stable at the bottom. It is December. It is foggy. In the fog there are sheep."[38] As in "Ariel," the speaker is riding her horse on the moors, but the rhythms and tone of "Sheep in Fog" are somber. The "blue distances" of "Ariel" hold no more promise, nor are they menacing. They simply disappear into the fog, leaving the speaker disoriented. Her horse is now "slow" as dawn surrealistically gives way to night. Indeed, Plath no longer uses enjambment to create the illusion of motion; here the horse's slow walk is emphasized by at least two end-pauses in most stanzas. Desertion and abandonment seem imminent. A line in the poem's second draft hints at its biographical connections: "Now even your kisses stiffen."[39] Plath removed the line, preferring to let the landscape reveal her emotions, just as she had in childhood. The "far fields" do not fill her speaker with promise; instead, they "threaten." She is not blessed by the landscape, as in a Wordsworth poem, or unnerved or emboldened by it, as in a Hughes poem. She is simply emptied. The hills provide no solace. The only striking use of internal assonance and consonance comes in the last line of the poem, where the siren song of the soft vowels in "Starless," "fatherless," "dark," and "water" tempts the speaker ever closer to the abyss.

Plath's poem "Child," too, describes the great distance between wholeness and emptiness, measured not by faraway hills but by the unreachable beauty of a child's eye. The mother wants to fill her child's eyes with "color and ducks," but knows he sees her wringing her hands, and—echoing the last lines of "Sheep in Fog"—"this dark / Ceiling without a star."

"The Munich Mannequins," also finished on January 28, conjures Assia in its first line: "Perfection is terrible, it cannot have children." Naked mannequins in store windows symbolize this terrible state. At the poem's end, Plath mentions "black phones on hooks"—another Assia motif—"Glittering and digesting // Voicelessness. The snow has no voice." "Totem," written on the same day, begins with references to Hughes's radio play *Difficulties of a Bridegroom*; a long journey up to London, butchers' knives, and dead hares— her "totem"—make the subject clear.[40] Plath mentions a "counterfeit snake" modeled, Hughes later said, on the one Assia gave her. Hughes's play had struck a nerve.

The following day, January 29, brought more poems. "Paralytic" is a less successful version of "Tulips," with its desire for nullification (the magnolia "Asks nothing of life"). The speaker is not convalescing but in a permanent state of numbness. Plath also wrote "Gigolo," likely directed at Hughes, that day. Soon after, on February 1, came "Mystic" and "Kindness." The plaintive speaker of "Mystic" asks, "Once one has seen God, what is the remedy?" Hughes would later claim that Plath told him she had seen God during the last two weeks of her life. Yet her poem seems skeptical of religion's consolations:

> Once one has been seized up
>
> Without a part left over,
> Not a toe, not a finger, and used,
> Used utterly, in the sun's conflagrations, the stains
> That lengthen from ancient cathedrals
> What is the remedy?

Plath echoes the "conflagrations" of Yeats's "Easter 1916" where "all is changed, changed utterly" in the wake of rebellion. Here the conflagration is not political, but personal, even philosophical. (It was around this time that Plath was corresponding with Father Michael Carey, advising him to read Yeats.) The poem conjures Saint Augustine's dark night of the soul, though here the soul emerges unscathed as the speaker watches the sun rise and the city come to life. "The children leap in their cots. / The sun blooms, it is a geranium. // The heart has not stopped." The speaker has made it through another night.

"Kindness," like "Totem," also referred to Hughes's *Difficulties of a Bridegroom*. In Plath's poem, Dame Kindness, who seems modeled on Aurelia, offers to soothe the speaker with "sweet" platitudes ("Sugar can cure everything"). Jillian was certain that she herself was the inspiration for the lines "blue and red jewels of her rings" that "smoke / In the windows"—she had such rings, and said that Sylvia had "admired the stained glass" in the kitchen and study of her home in Mountfort Crescent where they often "sat and talked."[41] She wondered if the poem had been about her, for she felt that she had mothered Sylvia during the last months of her life. The poem jumps between Dame Kindness, the "rabbit" of Hughes's radio play, and a Hughes figure who brings the speaker tea. The soothing efforts are no use: "The blood jet is poetry, / There is no stopping it. / You hand me two children, two roses." Plath may have remembered the *Mademoiselle* photographer who gave her a rose to symbolize her poetic ambition. If the husband and mother figures—or, indeed, the culture at large—think they can stanch the "blood jet" of her creativity with feminine bribes of children and roses, they are mistaken. The offerings will not subdue her into silence.

In just two drafts, on February 1, Plath wrote "Words," which grapples with the significance of the poet's legacy. Initially her words are like "Echoes traveling / Off from the center like horses." But slowly, over time, their significance recedes.

> Years later I
> Encounter them on the road—
>
> Words dry and riderless,
> The indefatigable hoof-taps.
> While
> From the bottom of the pool, fixed stars
> Govern a life.

The stars are an ill portent; her own words are unfamiliar. The horse imagery of "Ariel" reappears, but, as in "Sheep in Fog," the energy has halted. In "Ariel," the galloping mare was a symbol of Plath's poetic destiny. Although the ride was risky, the poet managed to hold tight and remain in control. Now the "riderless" words and "fixed stars" suggest defeat, surrender, a dark fate. Plath comes close, here, to saying that the poetic venture has failed her; the sap left in the axe's wake "Wells like tears."

Plath may have looked to Hughes's "Full Moon and Little Frieda," which was published on January 27, 1963, in *The Observer*, when she wrote "Words" on February 1. The pail of milk that Frieda lifts in "Full Moon and Little Frieda" is a "mirror / To tempt a first star to a tremor," an image Plath uses in "Words" to very different effect when she writes, "From the bottom of the pool, fixed stars / Govern a life."[42] The "echoes" of Hughes's poem provide her with an image of fatalism and drowning. Plath's pool image also plays with the reflection between Frieda and the moon at the end of Hughes's poem, when "The moon has stepped back like an artist gazing amazed at a work / That points at him amazed." The image of two artists engaged in an act of mutual admiration might once have existed as an ideal between Plath and Hughes, but now the image served as a bitter reminder that the marriage of true minds had disintegrated while his echoes still rang in her ears.

According to "A Dream," which Hughes later published in *Birthday Letters*, the last lines in "Words" came from him: "Not dreams, I had said, but fixed stars / Govern a life."[43] Plath's words had come full circle. Like the moon and child in "Full Moon and Little Frieda," Hughes stares back at Plath, staring back at him.

Sylvia showed some of these poems to Ted, whom she invited to Fitzroy Road on Sunday, February 3. He was rerecording *Difficulties of a Bridegroom* at the BBC that day, and because of "replays etc" he realized that he would not arrive at her flat at two p.m. as planned. Careful not to upset her, he sent a messenger to tell her he would arrive at three. He wrote in his diary at the time:

> Got there about 3-10. We had meat-loaf. We had the pleasantest most friendly open time since last July. She read me her most recent poems—stronger, calmer. She seemed more whole and in better shape than at any time since she came to London. Yes, we planned. We conspired. When I played with Frieda, she wept. I held them both and she wept. She kept repeating that I would want somebody else and I kept denying it absolutely. For the last few days I have been calling everybody Sylvia. Wanting to turn back but not knowing how to stay out of the old trap. Letting her know that I wanted to take up our old life but that it had to be different. I couldn't be a prisoner, also, the feeling that she was strengthening in her independent life, that she seemed so pleased with, and starting to

write again. And the feeling that my seeing so much of her disabled this effort of hers. The feeling that her centre of gravity was coming back into me. The feeling that I wanted that and encouraged it. She promised to visit me Thursday night. Stayed till about 2 a.m.[44]

The following day, Monday, February 4, Plath wrote "Contusion," a disturbing poem that begins, like "Cut," with bodily injury. Yet the energy of "Cut" is gone. There are no thrills, merely indifference: "Color floods to the spot, dull purple." The bruise inspires a similar series of metaphors, ending with the moment of death when "The heart shuts, / The sea slides back, / The mirrors are sheeted."

"Contusion" suggests the depth of Sylvia's depression, which she half admitted to Aurelia in her last letter of February 4. "I just haven't written anybody because I have been feeling a bit grim—the upheaval over, I am seeing the finality of it all, and being catapulted from the cowlike happiness of maternity into loneliness & grim problems is no fun." Aurelia had again suggested that Sylvia might consider moving back to America, or at least sending Frieda over to give herself a break, but she refused.

I appreciate your desire to see Frieda, but if you can imagine the emotional upset she has been through in losing her father & moving, you will see what an incredible idea it is to take her away by jet to America! I am her one security & to uproot her would be thoughtless & cruel, however sweetly you treated her at the other end. . . . I shall simply have to fight it out on my own over here.

Sylvia's concerns about uprooting Frieda suggest that she was keenly aware of the effect her absence would have on her daughter. That she did, finally, leave her children suggests that her depression worsened swiftly in the next week, and that she became ever more terrified of its consequences. She wrote Aurelia in that same letter, "I am going to start seeing a woman doctor free on the National Health, to whom I've been referred by my very good local doctor which should help me weather this difficult time."[45] She did not use the word "psychiatrist," or "depression," but Aurelia would have understood.

That same day, February 4, Sylvia wrote a happier letter to Marcia, though she broached her depression obliquely: "Everything has blown & bubbled & warped & split—accentuated by the light & heat suddenly going off for hours at unannounced intervals, frozen pipes, people getting drinking water in buckets & such stuff—that I am in a limbo between the old world & the very uncertain & rather grim new." (She used the word "grim" in three letters that day.) She was excited about Marcia and her husband's upcoming visit, as she had been "cut off from my dearest friends & relatives." She voiced, again, her "shock" that her children would grow up without a father, and that if she spent summers at Court Green they would likely not see Ted for half the year. She railed against his new life, full of flings and holidays. "You have no notion how famous he is over here now."[46]

Sylvia's letter to Marcia shows her full of plans less than a week before her suicide. Marcia had offered to help rent Sylvia's properties to Americans, and Sylvia sent her two detailed, paragraph-long advertisements describing the floor plans, rent, and location of Fitzroy Road and Court Green in crisp, efficient prose. She advised Marcia about hotels near her flat in Camden, and she ended her letter by saying, "how very much I need a spring tonic." That day Sylvia settled practicalities with her Devon cleaning lady, Nancy Axworthy, asking her by letter to neuter the cats. "I long to see my home (in Devon) and will be back soon."[47] She also wrote to Elizabeth, telling her she was sending her "a copy of The Bell Jar under separate cover" (though she never did). She was having problems with her au pair and admitted she was "quite grim and hollow feeling about bringing up the babies without a father." Ted came once a week. "I know quite well anything else is impossible, but it is difficult, one keeps wishing for lost Edens." She hoped to return to Devon in June, after she had appeared in May on the BBC program *The Critics*—though she would be "heartbroken" to miss her daffodils. Frieda had settled well into her nursery school, and she was "girding" herself to see a specialist about Nick's eye. "I have squeezed, and I mean squeezed out an article for Punch & one for the Home Service." She was considering renting out Court Green until the summer; she did not wish to, but she needed the extra income. She ended the letter with sincerity and humor: "I have written some more dawn poems, in blood, and hope in a week or so to feel like taking up the novel in which you & David appear briefly as angels, only don't let the news of my pseudonym get around or I'll be sued by everybody in North Tawton!"[48]

Sylvia wrote to Father Michael Carey as well on February 4, telling him she was on the upswing after her "post-flu coma." She felt strong enough again to "cope with sewing curtains & writing dawn poems, and minding babies." Carey had written to her in late January about the "two schools of modern poetry"—those who "wish to be obscure, and those who knife out their thoughts in an almost surgical clarity." He thought that Plath belonged to the latter camp.[49] She replied, "I don't think any good poet wishes to be obscure. I certainly don't; I write, at the present, in blood, or at least with it. Any difficulty arises from compression, or the jaggedness of images thrusting up from one psychic ground root."[50] When Carey had asked her which poet would be the agreed "universal name for the lyrical," Plath answered: Yeats.

By now the "big thaw" had set in, and the snow and ice were starting to melt. The streets were full of dirty slush, and flooding was a problem.[51] Ruth Fainlight wrote Sylvia on February 3 that she would be back in London at their old Pembridge Crescent flat by early March, and that she would spend April with her in Devon. "Everything was packed up," Ruth remembered, "and we'd gone to an awful lot of trouble to get our maid out of Morocco, to come to England."[52] She had no idea the state Sylvia was in. Meanwhile, Sylvia received an invitation from Tony Dyson, dated February 4, to participate in the arts festival at the University College of North Wales in Bangor. On the same day, Susan Alliston wrote to her asking for a meeting. "Do ring me, if ever you feel like it," Sue wrote casually.[53] The invitation—and the naivete it assumed—probably infuriated Sylvia.

On February 4, Sylvia wrote her last letter to Dr. Beuscher—one of six she wrote that day. She had not written to Beuscher since moving to London, and began by telling her about the move and her plans for renting out Court Green. But she quickly moved on to Ted. She feared that she had suffered from what Erich Fromm, in *The Art of Loving*, called "Idolatrous Love": "I lost myself in Ted instead of finding myself." She had made him "both idol & father." Still, her "identity" had been strong enough to make her feel "immense relief" about Ted's departure and the divorce: "now I shall grow out of his shadow, I thought, I shall be _me_." She wanted to take charge of her own life. But she missed her husband. "I had a beautiful, virile, brilliant man & he still is. . . . He has said he is sorry for the lying, and shows concern that we get on our way." She admired him even more now that he was "happy & whole & independent . . . what good friends we could be if I could manage to grow up too." She told Beuscher about Assia ("this ad-agency girl") and said Assia had decided to move back in with David Wevill. Perhaps this news led Sylvia to think that reconciling with Ted was not impossible. Dr. Horder said that he never heard Sylvia express resentment toward Ted during her frequent visits to him that January and February—only toward Assia. "Sylvia still loved Ted and still looked up to him."[54]

Yet she told Dr. Beuscher it was not Ted's departure that so disturbed her, but her depression. The flat tone of this letter differs from the others she had sent to Beuscher—it is the epistolary equivalent of "Edge" rather than "Ariel." "What appals [*sic*] me is the return of my madness, my paralysis, my fear & vision of the worst—cowardly withdrawal, a mental hospital, lobotomies. . . . I know Spain and lovemaking would do me no good now, not until I find myself again. I feel I need a ritual for survival from day to day until I begin to grow out of this death. . . . I keep slipping into this pit of panic

& deepfreeze [*sic*], with my mother's horrible example of fearful anxiety & 'unselfishness' on one side & the beauties of my two little children on the other." She was "living on sleeping pills & nerve tonic." Her new poems were "very good but, I feel written on the edge of madness." People had been kind to her, offering her BBC and magazine commissions, and yet, she wrote,

> I am scared to death I shall just pull up the psychic shroud & give up. A poet, a writer, I am I think very narcissistic & the despair at being 30 & having let myself slide, studied nothing for years, having mastered no body of objective knowledge is on me like a cold, accusing wind. Just now it is torture to me to dress, plan meals, put one foot in front of the other. Ironically my novel about my first breakdown is getting rave reviews over here. I feel a simple act of will would make the world steady & solidify. No-one can save me but myself, but I need help & my doctor is refer- ring me to a woman psychiatrist. . . . I am, for the first time since my marriage, relating to people without Ted, but my own lack of center, of mature identity, is a great torment. I am aware of a cowardice in myself, a wanting to give up. If I could study, read, enjoy people on my own Ted's leaving would be hard, but manageable. But there is this damned, self-induced freeze. I am suddenly in agony, desperate, thinking Yes, let him take over the house, the children, let me just die & be done with it. How can I get out of this ghastly defeatist cycle & grow up. I am only too aware that love and a husband are impossibles to me at this time, I am incapable of being myself & loving myself.

"Now the babies are crying, I must take them out to tea," Plath ended. "With love, Sylvia."[55]

Sylvia's letter to Ruth Beuscher reveals her terror of sinking back into an incapacitating depression. It also shows her skill at obscuring her depression from friends: on the same day she told Dr. Beuscher about her fear of los- ing her mind and her desire to die, she reassured Aurelia about her mental state, discussed rental properties and travel plans with Marcia, wrote to her cleaning lady about neutering cats, told Elizabeth about her new novel, and engaged in literary criticism with a priest. "She was always good at hiding how depressed she was. . . . I could have saved her if I'd been there," Beuscher later claimed.[56] "I permitted myself to be reassured. . . . I spent many years regretting that."[57]

Ted and others thought that Sylvia seemed out of sorts during that first week of February. Jillian remembered that Sylvia left the children with the new au pair during the weekend of February 2–3 and went back to Devon to "collect things."[58] Nancy Axworthy confirmed this "flying visit," saying Sylvia had come down to collect some manuscripts that Saturday and headed home that same day.[59] The car had given her trouble on the trip, and on Monday Sylvia phoned Gerry Becker to ask him if he would take it to a repair shop for her. He obliged, and Jillian, worried, invited her over. Sylvia declined, saying she "felt terrible."[60] Gerry returned the car to her on Tuesday the 5th. When the Beckers did not hear from her on Wednesday, they became concerned. Gerry planned to stop by on Thursday to check on her.

Kenneth Davies, Winifred's son, remembered coming to Fitzroy Road for lunch in early February. He did not "register" a great difference in Sylvia "since the North Tawton days," though things did not seem quite right. When he arrived, he accidentally chained his bicycle to a neighbor's railing. Sylvia opened the window and told him, in a "rather sharp" voice, to move his bike—"so we did not get off to a good start." He entered her "large living room" and noticed "a counter with a number of bar stools. In the middle of the floor was a play pen in which the two children were playing. All three were poorly with colds." They spoke of North Tawton and his new job as a London policeman. She kept the conversation polite and formal. "I can also remember being rather hungry as I had been invited to lunch and none had appeared by four o'clock in the afternoon. Eventually pork and apple sauce arrived and very good it was too."[61] He did not notice anything seriously amiss with Sylvia, but "did pick up that she was not well and put everything down to that . . . she invited me to have lunch again the week after and when I turned up I was told that she had died during the week."[62]

Trevor Thomas described Sylvia during this time as tearful and vulnerable one day, cold and imperious the next. Ted experienced a similar mood shift between his visit on Sunday, February 3, and Monday, February 4, when he and Sylvia spoke by phone.

> On Monday lunchtime she rang. I had to promise to leave England in 2 weeks. I was ruining her life, living in London, she having to hear about me. I asked her who from? She would not say. Very agitated. All the day before just gone. I told her I couldn't leave England. I had no money & nowhere to go. She made me promise. Finally I said I would go but I didn't see how I could. She wanted me never to see her again. She sounded terribly excited. I had talked with Al, the one person who has lent me his opinion, and he thought I was being indulgent, going on . . . that I ought to get out. . . . I promised I would go as soon as I could.[63]

Alvarez seems to have been Hughes's closest friend in London at that point. He may have thought Sylvia and Ted were better off apart, but his own recent involvement with Sylvia complicated his motives.

On Tuesday, February 5, Plath wrote her two last surviving poems, "Edge" and "Balloons." Readers have long expressed amazement that she could have written such dissimilar poems on the same day. One is a cold, expressionist portrait of a dead mother and her dead children, while the other describes Plath's own happy children in her warm, cheerful living room. However, the poems are more connected than they appear. Both feature a mother on her own, trying to protect her children from the world's horrors.

"Balloons" describes the "Guileless and clear" balloons that had been floating around the flat since Christmas, "Delighting / The heart like wishes." But the idyllic tableau breaks apart when the little boy accidentally pops the balloon. His bubble, quite literally, bursts.

> Then sits
> Back, fat jug
> Contemplating a world clear as water.
> A red
> Shred in his little fist.

The rhymes in the last two lines are supposed to disturb: red shreds, fists, breakage, and disappointment are the boy's new realities. This is an initiation. Sweetness and light give way to explosion, diminishment, and violence. Plath cannot protect her children from the wounds they will suffer. The poet's imaginary vision, too, is broken by the child's act, as in "Ariel."

Though surrealist in tone, no other poem in Plath's oeuvre—perhaps in *any* poet's oeuvre—has been as biographically determined as "Edge," which gives the uncanny impression of having been written posthumously. Widely believed to be Plath's last poem, "Edge" has been interpreted literally as a suicide note. Yet the poem is packed with literary and artistic allusions that belie its "confessional" nature. As in "Daddy" and "Lady Lazarus," Plath uses irony to make a devastating political point: only a dead woman is "perfected." Not perfect, *perfected*—like a work of art, an experiment, something controlled, without agency. The short, unadorned couplets, soothing assonances, and stage-lit, interstellar setting of "Edge" challenged perceptions about how poetry was supposed to sound, as well as the realities it could reflect and alter. Rather than a suicide note, "Edge" is self-elegy, and self-absolution.

"Edge" was originally titled "Nuns in Snow," and was written on the back of a draft of "Wintering." Critics have suggested that the snow imagery in that poem carried over to "Edge," though Plath abandoned the idea after two lines ("Here they come / Down there").[64] She changed the title to "The Edge," and then, by the final draft, to "Edge," though the ideas of coldness, celibacy, martyrdom, and purity envisioned in the original title lingered in the new lines.

The poem takes place in that "cold and planetary" space of a Giorgio de Chirico painting, like "The Disquieting Muses" and "The Moon and the Yew Tree." "Down there the dead woman is perfected," Plath wrote in an early draft of the poem, as if viewing the scene from high up, alongside the indifferent moon.[65] After the ascents of "Ariel," "Fever 103°," and "Lady Lazarus," "Edge"—like "Sheep in Fog" and "Words"—seems flat and resigned. Its tonal color is blue, not red. All has stilled.

> The woman is perfected.
> Her dead
>
> Body wears the smile of accomplishment,
> The illusion of a Greek necessity
>
> Flows in the scrolls of her toga,
> Her bare
>
> Feet seem to be saying:
> We have come so far, it is over.

Mothers in Plath's poems cannot protect their children from the world's ravages. In "Edge," there is an end to this anxiety. Plath describes two children "coiled," like Cleopatra's asp, at each empty breast. They are dead like their mother, yet Plath evokes the regeneration of the garden: "She has folded / Them back into her body as petals / Of a rose close when the garden / Stiffens." As Helen Vendler has noted, the gesture is "protective."[66] Jillian thought these lines may have been inspired by a Louis MacNeice poem she quoted to Sylvia shortly before her death. As they sat pensively in her dining room at dusk, looking out at the back garden through the large windows, Jillian recited MacNeice's lines: "The sunlight on the garden / Hardens and grows cold, / We cannot cage the minute / Within its nets of gold." Sylvia told her she had "forgotten about that poem" and was "glad to be reminded of it." She said she appreciated the "rhymes in the middle of the lines."[67] Plath may also have remembered Yaddo's lush rose gardens and Classical statues, as well as its founder Katrina Trask and her four dead children.[68] Yaddo had been a place of regeneration: it was the site of her first poetic breakthrough, her first months of pregnancy, and her first experience of artistic parity with Hughes. It was an artist's Eden, the first and last time she could surrender herself solely to her craft. Yaddo was perpetual spring.

Plath grafted the world of de Chirico onto Yaddo's garden. Many of de Chirico's paintings feature women in Classical dress, with togas and bare feet, reclining horizontally on rectangular slabs amid arched stone buildings, long shadows, and distant trains. In one, the woman is called "Melancholia." In another, she is Ariadne, the Classical heroine who led Theseus out of the labyrinth and saved him from the Minotaur—only to be abandoned by him on the island of Naxos after they eloped. Plath had seen de Chirico's painting *Ariadne* at the Met in New York, which she described in her journal in March 1958: "The statue, recumbent, of Ariadne, deserted, asleep, in the center of empty, mysteriously-shadowed squares. And the long shadows cast by unseen figures—human or of stone it is impossible to tell."[69] She had shown interest in the legend years before, when she wrote "To Ariadne (deserted by Theseus)" in 1949, about her breakup with John Hodges. Aurelia said it marked "the beginning of the appeal of the tragic muse." Plath had then written from the deserted Ariadne's perspective:

> Oh, scream in vain for vengeance now, and beat your hands
> In vain against the dull impassive stone.
> The cold waves break and shatter at your feet;
> The sky is mean—and you bereft, alone.
>
> The white hot rage abates, and then—futility.[70]

The dull stone, mean sky, and loneliness of young Plath's Ariadne seem to foreshadow the deserted woman of "Edge." But Plath had another deserted woman in mind. The asp imagery and the cruelly indifferent moon, "Staring from her hood of bone," invoke Shakespeare's *Antony and Cleopatra*. In the play, Cleopatra puts an asp to her breast to commit suicide; she dies nobly and identifies with the moon. ("My resolution's plac'd, and I have nothing / Of woman in me; now from head to foot / I am marble-constant; now the fleeting moon / No planet is of mine.")[71] Robert Graves had identified Cleopatra as a manifestation of the White Goddess, which would have made her an even more potent female symbol for Plath. D. H. Lawrence's "Prayer," which Plath had marked up in her copy of his *Complete Poems*, was probably also an influence: "O let my ankles be bathed in moonlight, that I may go / sure and moon-shod, cool and bright-footed towards my goal."[72]

By the time Plath wrote "Edge," the desertions endured by Medea, Cleopatra, and Ariadne resonated painfully. She frequently used the word "deserted" in her letters home to describe Hughes's actions. His desertion and, later, Alvarez's were bound up with poetry itself, of a piece with a male lyric tradition that had also "deserted" women. Plath had registered this theme in "The Colossus," where the deserted daughter lives in exile on a remote island, tending the monument of her father. By "Edge," the daughter has become a deserted wife and mother, alone with her children in what Judith Kroll called a "frozen and eternal tableau."[73]

The famous first lines of "Edge" recall poems like "The Fearful," "Barren Woman," and "The Munich Mannequins," where Plath had used the word "perfect" to describe childless women. She may have been thinking, too, about Sara Teasdale's poem "I Shall Not Care," a poem often linked to Teasdale's suicide in 1933.

> When I am dead and over me bright April
> Shakes out her rain-drenched hair,
> Tho' you should lean above me broken-hearted,
> I shall not care.

The speaker declares, "I shall be more silent and cold-hearted / Than you are now."[74]

Plath does not fantasize about revenge in "Edge," which resembles a Classical frieze. Yet it is hard to avoid the conclusion that the poem is a poisoned arrow aimed at Hughes. Plath's speaker now performs the part of the White Goddess, only this time she has no strength left to demolish the myth. As Graves had written, "woman is not a poet: she is either a Muse or she is nothing."[75]

This Goddess is the presiding spirit of "Edge" and has "folded" the speaker back into her own system just as the speaker has folded her dead children back into her body. The images of barrenness and sterility further suggest that Plath imagines her speaker joining the ranks of the Goddess, who is childless. Hughes's abandonment of Plath for a childless woman may have embittered her even more toward the White Goddess myth, and inspired a mocking determination to give Hughes what he "wanted"—a cold, cruel, childless muse to whom he must sacrifice himself. "Edge" also incorporates elements of two Hughes poems published in *The Observer* on January 6, 1963, "Dark Women" (later titled "The Green Wolf") and "New Moon in January." Hughes found manuscript copies of both poems in Plath's flat after her death.[76]

If Plath is talking back to Hughes, who embodied the living male poetic tradition in her own life, she is also talking back to Yeats, in whose shadow she stood, and in whose house she would die. "Edge" bitterly complies with

Yeats's wish for complete womanly surrender in "He wishes his Beloved were Dead," where Yeats writes,

> Were you but lying cold and dead,
> And lights were paling out of the West,
> You would come hither, and bend your head,
> And I would lay my head on your breast;
> And you would murmur tender words,
> Forgiving me, because you were dead:
> Nor would you rise and hasten away,
> Though you have the will of wild birds,
> But know your hair was bound and wound
> About the stars and moon and sun:
> O would, beloved, that you lay
> Under the dock-leaves in the ground,
> While lights were paling one by one.[77]

"Edge" indicts a sexist culture and literary tradition that equated perfect womanhood with passivity and compliancy. In what was probably her last poem, Plath drew on Shakespeare, Greek myth, Graves, de Chirico, Yeats, Teasdale, Lawrence, and Hughes to create art that was utterly new and strange—an alternate poetic tradition for women in the wake of her personal male "desertions" and betrayals. It was as if Plath had finally decided that maternity and poetry, womanhood and ambition, could not be reconciled. "We have come so far, it is over." And yet the poem's savage irony checks its despair. The message of "Edge" is not, as in "The Moon and the Yew Tree," "blackness and silence," but fury.

35

The Dark Ceiling

London, February 1963

On Wednesday, February 6, five days before her death, Sylvia met with the art historian John Richardson, chair of the Library and Arts Committee at the Camden Library and a close friend of Pablo Picasso's. They discussed the 1963 Saint Pancras Arts Festival. The next day, he asked Sylvia to accompany him to a Spike Milligan reading in early March in a flirtatious letter, adding, "Thank you, by the way, for your invitation to drop round on you although I must warn you that I generally take up invitations like that."[1] The letter suggests that Sylvia was hoping to assuage her loneliness and make new professional connections.[2] Leonie Cohn wrote on February 8 from the BBC Talks Department, thanking Plath for her "splendid script," "Ocean 1212-W," and asking, "How soon can you record it?"[3]

On that same Wednesday, February 6, Ted visited Sylvia again at Fitzroy Road. In his diary, he noted a worrisome new tone in her voice:

> On Wednesday I heard from A.[ssia] of S.[ylvia] going the whole story of our marriage and parting to Gerry Becker, and the details of my deterioration etc. and how I had left her in Devon utterly without cash etc. I wrote her a note saying that if she had said this I wanted a reply because I intended to see a solicitor to stop Gerry Becker spreading lies about me. I took it round & confronted her with it. She begged me not to do anything, that she couldn't help what people said. I asked if she had told him that I left her without money etc and she obviously had. That passed, we talked about Yorkshire, just getting out and away from the people. Made plans. She was terribly upset but not more than a thousand times before. She kept asking me if I had faith in her—that seemed new & odd.[4]

Lorna recalled Sylvia visiting her on that last Wednesday or Thursday. She had offered to watch the children while Sylvia shopped for new curtain fabric at Heal's, a posh London store. By this time, Sylvia was already looking for a new au pair—she told Lorna the au pair had left the children alone, and "she felt she had to get rid of her absolutely straight away."[5] Lorna offered to help arrange a new au pair for her through her own German au pair. "I do think she was quite close to finding another," Lorna recalled. Lorna's own au pair said a "friend of hers could come see Sylvia on the Saturday, but then Sylvia wasn't there, she was going to be away for the weekend."[6]

Sylvia was out of sorts when she arrived at Lorna's Chalcot Square flat with the children. Sylvia had said she was looking forward to the outing, but now she could not muster up the energy to leave. She slumped into a chair, wide-eyed and vacant. "She came round, and she just sat, and certainly then she did talk a lot. She said she was writing a novel, and she talked about Alvarez. . . . He was involved in that. And she told me it was going to be under a pseudonym. . . . She was just sort of sitting, staring. And at some point I said to her, 'Do you want to go to Heal's?' and she said, 'Well no, no.' . . . She was staring rather vacantly into space . . . looking kind of not all there." The children both had colds and runny noses. Lorna made tea. "Clearly something was off." But she did not recognize the severity of the situation, for Sylvia had never shared her history of depression.[7] After Sylvia's death, Catherine Frankfort told Lorna that Sylvia had told her she had struggled—and thought she was still struggling—with postpartum depression after Nicholas's birth. Jillian, too, thought Sylvia "was going through a dire post-natal depression . . . which in my experience, personal and by observation, lasts very much longer in many women than popular or medical opinion allows."[8]

When Ted met with Sylvia on Thursday, February 7, she seemed even more confused about where she stood:

> Thursday morning, next morning, she rang, freshly upset, asked to see me. Came to Cleveland St.—for first time. She was back to making me promise to leave immediately, to get right out of England. Had been asked to join the Critics on Sunday, and again kept asking me if I had faith in her to be able to do it. Could not make out if she was trying to call my bluff, with her weeping demand that I leave England immediately—or whether she did need me to go, saw everything in my flat—even that I had a new Shakespeare. We talked again about going to Yorkshire & letting some

weeks or months pass. Then back to me promising I would get out of England. We parted upbeat, about 1-30, but with both still in the air—me to go abroad immediately, or both of us to go to Yorks [Yorkshire].[9]

In his poem "The Inscription," Hughes later re-created this scene. Plath sees his red Oxford Shakespeare, a new version of the same edition she had once ripped apart in February 1961, and opens it "with unbelieving fingers." She reads Assia's inscription and closes it quietly, "Like the running animal that receives / The fatal bullet without a faltering check / In its stride . . ."[10]

In January 1975, Ted recalled this afternoon in a letter to Aurelia.

> The dominant theme towards the end of this is divorce, her steely deter-
> mination to get that divorce. At the time it seemed to me impenetrable.
> So it came as a great shock, on the Thursday before her death, to hear
> that she didn't want a divorce at all—and that I was a complete idiot to
> have ever thought that she did. The whole crazy divorce business was a
> bluff. So what is to be made of that? She mismanaged those last months
> even worse than I did.[11]

Yet Hughes said nothing about Plath disavowing divorce in his 1963 note-book entry. Rather, she seemed to be telling him, in her proud way, that they needed to get back together or never see each other again. She could not remain in limbo. As long as he remained in her orbit, she felt that she would not be able to take control of her life again.

Dr. Horder saw Sylvia often in January, and then every day after Febru-ary 4. Alvarez remembered Dr. Horder as an overworked, humane doctor who suffered from depression himself; he was discharged from the British Army during the Second World War because of it.[12] Lorna remembered that he was "fragile, mental-health wise," and had been in and out of men-tal hospitals voluntarily. "He was a very nice man, a rather intense man."[13] He checked on Sylvia frequently and showed more care and solicitude than her male psychiatrists had in Boston. He was an accomplished pianist and painter, and had a particular sympathy for artists. At this time, most Brit-ish psychiatrists worked in national hospitals and preferred drugs over the more expensive and time-consuming practice of psychotherapy.[14] Because of his own experience with depression, Dr. Horder felt comfortable prescrib-ing antidepressants and prescribed Plath one such drug—either Nardil or Parnate—on February 4.[15] (Through the years, Horder gave interviewers different information, at different times, about the drug's exact name.)

Both Parnate and Nardil are monoamine oxidase (MAO) inhibitors—"uppers" (part of the amphetamine family)—and can cause insomnia. Both were used in cases of severe, treatment-resistant depression. In addition, Sylvia was suffering from a respiratory illness, for which she was taking codeine, then available over the counter. (She wrote a note to herself in her calendar on January 5 to buy codeine.) She was also taking a sleeping pill that contained both a barbiturate and an amphetamine (brand name Drinamyl, no longer manufactured because of its potential for abuse), and another medication for her fevers.[16] Thus, by early February, Plath was taking two amphetamines (the antidepressant and Drinamyl), one opioid (codeine), and one barbiturate (Drinamyl), as well as an unknown medicine for her respiratory illness. The interactions from these drugs alone could have significantly worsened her depression and anxiety; and she had just started taking an antidepressant, which could, in its initial phase, increase anxiety and suicidal thoughts. As if this drug cocktail were not bad enough, the antidepressant could produce serious side effects when combined with phenylpropanolamine, a common ingredient in cold and flu medicine in Britain at the time.[17] It could also produce a hypertensive crisis if taken with certain cheeses, yeasts, and red wine. Hughes later claimed that Plath was allergic to a drug she had been taking at the time of her death, which went by a different name in America.

> Her doctor, excellent and sympathetic, was not to know what her U.S. doctors had learned in 1953: that she must never be given the particular tranquilising drug which he now prescribed. Her peculiarity was to react to this drug with such fits of depression that her life was endangered. She failed to identify the drug, and nobody near her in England knew about such details of her case history. He said the drug, which she was instructed never to take again, intensified feelings of suicidal depression in her.[18]

If Hughes was talking about Plath's antidepressant, he may not have realized that the drug was in fact an "upper" rather than a "downer." Regardless of whether or not Plath was allergic to her antidepressant, it is possible that the drugs she was taking in early February—and their ill-understood interactions—could have significantly worsened her mental health and pushed her closer to suicide. As in the summer of 1953, depression's "cures" likely made her depression worse.

Dr. Horder knew Sylvia was suicidal, and he was aware that in "the first few days" of treatment with an MAO antidepressant, "it's possible to improve the person's energy without improving mood"—thus increasing the risk of suicide. He knew he had to take precautions with her, but, he said, "I was frightened of sending her into a mental hospital." Sylvia had made her terror of shock treatment clear, and he knew sending her to the wrong institution could exacerbate her depression. "There are so few that give a person the privacy that they need and the understanding that they need. . . . There aren't very many such institutions in London and they are difficult to get into." But by late January or early February, he had taken steps to admit her to St. George's Hospital. In his telling, "a letter went astray; a silly failure postponed this."[19]

On Thursday, February 7, Dr. Horder found Sylvia in a grave state. The loss of the au pair and the weeks of loneliness, exhaustion, and isolation ahead had brought her to a breaking point. Dr. Horder told her he wanted her to go into a psychiatric hospital "immediately," but she "would not hear of it."[20] He bought time with a compromise; he suggested that she stay with friends while he searched for a bed in a psychiatric facility. Lorna, who was also a patient of Horder's, thought that he was trying to arrange for Sylvia to go to the Maudsley Hospital, a large psychiatric hospital in south London.

Catherine Frankfort remembered seeing Sylvia during the second half of that week, likely on Thursday. Normally Sylvia "looked after Frieda meticulously," but now Catherine was troubled to see that the "houseproud and clean" Sylvia was "in a strange and undecipherable state. The children's play-pen was filthy, the house chaotic." Sylvia had scheduled a lunch date with her new editor at Heinemann, David Machin, on Monday, February 11, and asked Catherine to babysit. Catherine agreed.[21]

Lorna said that Sylvia phoned her on Thursday or Friday. "Obviously I was concerned about her, as was Catherine. She phoned me to say, 'Look, Lorna, I don't want you to worry about me. I'm *all right*.' She said, 'I'm *fine*, you musn't worry, you must understand I'm fine.' Of course I thought afterwards that she was saying goodbye—this is what I'm going to do and this is what I want to do. . . . She was going to stay with friends over the weekend, she said. I think she had already made up her mind, but who knows. Maybe there were these flashes in and out—she would, she wouldn't." Lorna said she and Catherine were completely unaware of Sylvia's other literary friends— the Macedos, the Beckers, and the Merwins. "She certainly made no attempt to put the friends together."[22] The Macedos and the Beckers, likewise, never heard about Lorna or Catherine.

Sylvia phoned Jillian Becker around four p.m. on Thursday and asked, with some urgency in her voice, if she could come to Islington with the children. ("Can I come at once?") She told Jillian the children had had the measles but were now better.[23] Jillian had a nanny and a large house—the next best thing to a hospital. Jillian told Sylvia to come right over, and she soon arrived at Mountfort Crescent, off Barnsbury Square. According to Jillian, Sylvia told her she felt "terrible" and went upstairs to lie down after a cup of tea.[24] Two hours later, she came downstairs and told Jillian she would "rather not go home."[25] Jillian agreed—it was no trouble, for her two older children were spending the weekend with their father, her first husband, and she had two spare bedrooms. Jillian went back to Sylvia's flat to collect her medication, clothes for the children, and two books—*The Ha-Ha* and Fromm's *The Art of Loving*. She left a note for the milkman to stop delivering milk for one week.[26]

Jillian found the flat clean and tidy; Sylvia had obviously cleaned up after Catherine's visit. (Indeed, Jillian said that Ted "confirmed" to them that Sylvia's flat had been "in perfect order" on Monday, February 11. Plath's manuscripts, he said, were "sorted and tidy and arranged.")[27] In the living room, Jillian picked up a small wooden box, marked "Poor Box," with a slot for coins, displayed on a small shelf. Sylvia told her it had once belonged in Saint Peter's Church in North Tawton. Upstairs, a sign that read, "QUIET! GENIUS AT WORK!" hung on the door of her bedroom study. The desk "was tidy, with very little on it: paper, pens in a jar, and one of the books she'd asked for."[28] Jillian found clothes for Sylvia and Nick but, curiously, very little for Frieda.

Suzette Macedo claimed that Jillian and Sylvia "didn't know each other very well." Suzette accused Jillian of writing her "out of the story" in her memoir about Sylvia's last weekend, *Giving Up*, in an attempt to settle old scores from their South African days.[29] Suzette's own version of Sylvia's last weekend differs from Jillian's. Suzette remembered that Sylvia phoned her on Friday (though it was probably Thursday), saying, "I'm at Jillian's. Why don't you come after work and join us here." When Suzette arrived she found a "strange" scene. The children were upset—they "didn't gel" with the nanny or Jillian's young daughter, Madeleine. Suzette thought they sensed that something was wrong with their mother. Indeed, Suzette found Sylvia "in a terrible state." Plath, sitting in a chair drinking tea, suddenly "went pale." She broke into a sweat and said she had a migraine; she asked if she could go upstairs and lie down in a dark room. (In Jillian's rendering, Sylvia left the room because she was upset by Suzette's presence.)

Suzette tried to give the children a bath, but Frieda became hysterical, saying, "Where's Mummy?" Suzette brought her to Sylvia, and she soon calmed down. "Ill though she was with this terrible headache . . . this blinding headache, she said, '*Hellooo*, my *baaaby*.' I've never forgotten that," Suzette said.[30] Suzette finally gave Frieda a bath, then returned to Sylvia. Suzette remembered that when Jillian invited her to spend the night, Sylvia replied, "I must, without the au pair I cannot cope."[31]

That night Jillian made chicken soup, steak, and potatoes, and brought the food up on a tray to Sylvia, who was staying in her daughter's room. Sylvia ate with relish, as if she were back at Girl Scout camp. Her appetite pleased

Jillian. (Gerry was in bed with a flu, though Jillian thought he may have been avoiding Sylvia's emotional needs.) Sylvia had a long bath, then asked Jillian to stay with her once she was back in bed.[32] She "talked bitterly" about Ted and Assia, and asked Jillian why David had been "so passive" about Assia's adultery. Jillian told her she'd met the Wevills at parties from time to time, and she "couldn't make either of them out." She thought "Assia seemed to have nothing much to say."[33] She found David soft-spoken, "a gentle chap."[34] Sylvia had written to David about Ted and Assia's affair shortly after she had thrown Ted out in July. She told him they "should meet, we must talk."[35] But the meeting never happened. Now Jillian told her that David had punched through a glass-paneled door when Assia told him she was leaving him for Ted. "That was all he did?" Sylvia responded.[36] If this conversation took place the way Jillian remembered, then Sylvia learned, that weekend, that Assia had finally decided to leave her husband for Ted. The news would have shocked Sylvia, who, according to Ted's notebook entries, continued to hope for a reconciliation.

That night Sylvia took what Jillian assumed were her sleeping pills around ten, though they didn't seem to make her tired. She began "rambling" about people Jillian had never met—Dick Norton, Gordon Lameyer, Richard Sassoon—"as if they were mutual friends."[37] She spoke of wanting to take the children someplace warm, perhaps Spain. They needed to be in the sun, by the sea. Jillian assured her that she would take them all to Spain or Italy over the Easter holidays. "Easter—that's a long way off," Sylvia said. Then she spoke about how Ted had taken Assia to Spain. She talked about "that fatal day" when Assia had come to Court Green and destroyed the "ideal life" she and Ted had shared. Sylvia ranted about Assia "teetering in her high-heeled shoes, among the cowpats in the slushy fields," a story Jillian knew was false, as Assia always wore flats. But the image fit; they both thought Assia "vain and shallow." Jillian told Sylvia that Assia had come to one of her parties in the spring or summer of 1962 and asked to listen to a radio program of Plath and Hughes reading their poetry. "Sylvia nodded slowly as I told her this, as if to say *Yes, that figures*."[38]

Sylvia spoke bitterly, too, of Aurelia, Olwyn, Ted, and his family. She was "not terribly coherent," Jillian remembered, and she was skeptical of some of her stories—for instance, that when she held baby Nick in her arms for the first time, Ted "stormed around the house, shouting, 'There is a usurper in the house.'" She also told Jillian that the Hugheses had made her so miserable at the Beacon one Christmas that "she ran out into the snow in her nightdress to get away from them."[39] Sylvia was angry at her father, whom she now conflated with Ted, and at Aurelia, for saying she would end up just like her. She feared that she would never finish her novel, which she told Jillian was about a potter, because she needed "acres of time" to write fiction, and she was "disappointed by the reception of *The Bell Jar*."[40] (When Jillian asked her whether it was "autobiographical," she answered "rather evasively.")[41] She had once showed Jillian a letter she received from *The New Yorker*, rejecting her poems. They had asked her to explain the poems to them. "She was knocked sideways by such a request," Jillian said. "There was this sense of not being appreciated."[42] Yet Sylvia had "no doubt that the poetry was first rate, that she was writing superbly." Sylvia spoke, too, of shock therapy, "a horror to her," Jillian remembered. She finally fell asleep around midnight. "When she was raving, the distance between us was unreachable."[43]

Nick awoke around four a.m. Jillian prepared warm milk and Sylvia fed him. Jillian got him back to sleep. But Sylvia was wide awake again. She could not sleep and wanted to take what she called her "pep" pill because it took "hours" to work. (This was either her antidepressant or a preludin pill; both are part of the amphetamine family.) "This is always the worst time, this hour of the morning," Jillian remembered her saying. Jillian made her tea and gave her the pill, then sat beside Sylvia's bed in a high-backed chair.[44] "She would close her eyes, but suddenly open them, and once half rose, saw that I was still there, and lay down again as if reassured by my presence."[45] Sylvia finally fell asleep between five and six a.m.

On Friday morning Sylvia woke at eight a.m., came downstairs, and said she "felt fine now" as the "pep" pill was working. She ate a hearty breakfast and then called a new au pair with whom she had made some kind of prior, hasty arrangement—perhaps through Lorna's au pair. Sylvia was on the phone for half an hour "trying to persuade this German girl" to come, Jillian remembered, "but the girl apparently protested that she could not."[46] The prospect of managing the children on her own seems to have overwhelmed her, and she called Dr. Horder. Sylvia spoke with him for a long time.

She then passed the phone over to Jillian. Horder asked her how Plath seemed and whether she was taking her pills. He advised Jillian not to coddle her. "She must look after the children. She must feel that she's absolutely necessary." Jillian understood, and she tried to compel Sylvia to care for Frieda and Nick. But she seemed incapable of the most basic motherly duties like feeding, bathing, and changing diapers. "I'd wait for her to pick up a spoon, a sponge or whatever, but she didn't." At one point Sylvia realized that Jillian was in the middle of changing Nick's dirty diaper and said, "Now that's really beyond the call of duty. Let me do it."[47] But it was already done.

Despite some chronological disparities, all the accounts of Plath's last week have one thing in common: she was not herself. She was up and down, "wobbly," as Suzette remembered, tearful, standing for long periods at her window, sitting in a trance in her car.[48] Her moods shifted quickly: she was at turns loving and hostile; she was forgetful; she stopped cooking and seemed suddenly incapable of caring for her children. Lorna remembered her that last week as "phased out.... She looked exhausted, great circles under her eyes. She talked to me then about Ted and how it had gone all horribly wrong, but I didn't know that she'd had post-natal depression after Nicholas, for instance, back in Devon. I didn't know any of that. She didn't talk about it."[49]

To Ted and Trevor Thomas, Sylvia seemed at times drunk, out of it, slurring her words and lapsing back into an American accent. Hughes said that during the last three weeks of her life she kept saying, "I am full of God," and "I keep being picked up by God."[50] She may have been referring to the blessings Father Carey was sending her way in his letters, but the language worried Hughes. Such talk from her—an atheist—was odd. He did not understand what she meant.[51] Dr. Horder found her moods to be "so excessive" that he was sure her depression was biochemical. Jillian was alarmed by how many pills Sylvia took during the nights she stayed and suspected that she may have been taking more than prescribed. Excessive dosage, combined with side effects that would result from mixing an antidepressant, codeine, Drinamyl, and other cold and flu medications, may explain Plath's strange behavior. At the time, both Suzette and Jillian assumed that the pills were to blame, as the normally proud Sylvia was now talking in circles, shutting down, and asking for help. And there was Hughes's recollection that she was taking a "tranquilising drug" at the time of her death, to which she was allergic. The effects of this potent drug cocktail on her emotions and her art can never be fully calculated; antidepressants were in their infancy in the early 1960s, and their interactions with other drugs were not well understood. Plath was not even under the care of a qualified psychiatrist but rather her general practitioner, Dr. Horder, who, while concerned and compassionate, did not possess a specialist's knowledge of psychiatric drugs. As in August 1953, Plath was left to manage a severe depressive crisis almost entirely on her own.

On Friday, February 8, Sylvia left Jillian's at about noon and returned alone to Fitzroy Road, where she had arranged to see Dr. Horder. She told Jillian "she must go, earlier than she'd thought" and would be back late. She asked Jillian if she would watch the children and then drove herself away.[52] Before she left Jillian's, she turned to Frieda, who was standing in the hallway, and said "I *love* you," with strong feeling.[53] The gesture moved Jillian, who had been worried by Sylvia's uncharacteristic lack of attention toward her children. She had barely talked to them or played with them since she arrived, and she had shown no interest in Jillian's daughter.

When Sylvia saw Dr. Horder that Friday, as Eric Walter White later wrote to Jack Sweeney, Horder was "so alarmed by what he found that he told her she must go into a home and he would arrange for a nurse to come to her house the following Monday at 9:00 a.m. to look after the children."[54] White's letter suggests that the nurse was coming to care for the children full-time while Plath admitted herself into a hospital for a short stay—not that the nurse was supposed to help Plath with the children at home. After Plath's death, Dr. Horder would tell the coroner that on that Friday "he became so worried as a result of a long talk with her that he spoke to three psychiatrists, trying to find a hospital bed for her. Two could not provide one, and although the third could, he did not think it would be suitable for her."[55] White's account, which he likely heard from Hughes or someone in Hughes's circle, dovetails with Horder's testimony during the inquest after Plath's death, in which he testified that he had found an opening for her at a hospital on Monday, February 11. ("I couldn't get an admission before Monday, and I thought that would be all right.")[56]

We now know that Dr. Horder was referring to Halliwick Hospital.[57] He spoke with a psychiatrist there about admitting Sylvia on Friday, February 8. Halliwick was, as one history put it, "generously staffed" and "attracted the 'cream' of both staff and patients."[58] It had a reputation of being modern, progressive, and compassionate, and had a new 145-bed unit that was separated from the wards of seriously disturbed patients. But Halliwick was on the grounds of the larger Friern Hospital, built in 1850 and formerly known as the Colney Hatch Lunatic Asylum. The name "Colney Hatch" had as much grim significance for Londoners as "Bedlam" and was notorious for containing six miles of corridors. P. G. Wodehouse and C. S. Lewis had written of its fearsome reputation in their novels. Sylvia was more likely to know about the hospital's dark history rather than its shiny new ward. Dr. Horder was reluctant to "section" Sylvia, but he knew she needed residential care—a few days of voluntary "rest." Sylvia may not have understood the distinction. "She was losing it, and she knew she was," Jillian said. "She was not in possession of her right senses."[59] Thus Sylvia learned on Friday that as early as Monday she would likely be entering a public psychiatric hospital.

This knowledge helps explain why, on Friday, Sylvia mailed a terse, two-sentence letter to Ted—her last letter to him—from Fitzroy Road.[60] It was likely sent in the batch of letters, including her last to Dr. Beuscher, that was postmarked in Primrose Hill at 12:45 p.m. But her letter reached Hughes the same day she sent it. In an undated, unpublished draft of his poem "Last Letter," Hughes hinted that it was a suicide note: "The letter note came Goodbye / My darling love goodbye I am finishing / Everything."[61]

Ted could not later remember how he got to Sylvia's flat, only that he rushed over, that afternoon, full of dread. She came down the stairs slowly and opened the door in an "ordinary" way. He was surprised—as Alvarez had been on Christmas Eve—to see her hair "loose." In the poem she puts on an "Enigmatic smile as he stood there weeping / What does it mean this letter?"[62] Hughes wrote that she led him back up the stairs, where she tore the letter into small pieces and burned it in the ashtray. In a draft of the poem, they spoke of getting back together.

> Her choking throat her plea & his promise
> That they would be under the laburnums in June
> That they would sit again under the laburnums
> All together & this very next week ~~yes this very week~~
> They would go to Scotland ~~yes~~ it was all fixed
> Assured he had gone off assured
> It was all safe assured ~~it was all~~ her ~~counsellers~~ advisers
> Would not defeat them now.[63]

He was "comfortable— / that she would let him get out of the tar-pit." Olwyn remembered Ted telling her that Sylvia had "collapsed on the floor crying" that afternoon. "He knelt down and knew he'd go back."[64] Yet Sylvia might not have taken him back, as he assumed. She told Jillian that "'a reconciliation would make no difference.'" Jillian reflected, "Sylvia was grieving, bereaved." Ted was no longer "pure," her own husband. Sylvia told Jillian her "world had been destroyed (not her marriage, her world)."[65]

Hughes's account of the event, written shortly after Plath's death in 1963, is more circumspect about the last letter's contents. He does not mention any "pleas and promises" of reconciliation.

> Friday about 3-30 a letter came from her. She'd posted it that morning, thinking I'd get it Saturday, probably. It was a farewell love-letter, two sentences. She was going off into the country and intended never to see me again. Very ambiguous. I went straight to Fitzroy Rd. She was there alone, tidying the place up. I was upset & crying, what did she mean, what the hell was going on? She was cool & hostile. Took the note, burned it carefully in the ash-tray & told me to go. Could not get her to talk. She was leaving too. Did not find out for a long time where she went. Becker at funeral did not tell me.[66]

Hughes became convinced that if he had received Plath's letter on Saturday, when he was meant to—and if he had not rushed to her flat to stop her—she would have left London and, perhaps, somehow, survived. In the final version of "Last Letter," he wondered,

One hour later—you would have been gone
Where I could not have traced you.
I would have turned from your locked red door
That nobody would open
Still holding your letter,
A thunderbolt that could not earth itself.
That would have been electric shock treatment
For me.
Repeated over and over, all weekend,
As often as I read it, or thought of it.
... Had you plotted it all?

. . . .

                 ... But what did you say
Over the smoking shards of that letter
So carefully annihilated, so calmly,
That let me release you, and leave you
To blow its ashes off your plan—[67]

Trevor Thomas's account of Plath's last Friday afternoon corresponds with Hughes's. When he came home from work, he said, he saw that the front door of his building was "most unusually wide open." He shut the door. An hour later, when he set out his milk bottles, he saw Sylvia sitting in her car in the snowy street "staring ahead with her hands clasped in her lap." He went to her and asked if she was all right and whether he should call Dr. Horder. "She had a faraway dreamy look, pale and looking ill." She assured him that she was fine. Then she looked straight at him and said, "I'm going away for a long holiday, a long rest." Her children would be staying with friends. "So I won't see you for some time?" he asked. "No," she said.[68] Then she drove away. "A long rest" was a common 1960s euphemism for psychiatric treatment. She had already spoken to—and likely, by late afternoon, seen—Horder, who had made it clear that she needed to be admitted to an inpatient psychiatric facility as soon as possible.

The prospect of a potentially horrific stay in an unknown mental hospital was one that filled Plath with fear. She had already written to Dr. Beuscher on Monday, February 4, of her terror of "mental hospitals" and her desire to end her life. Now she was on the verge of surrendering herself to unknown psychiatrists—likely all men—in a notorious asylum. She likely planned, or began planning, her suicide, on Friday, February 8, as Hughes's draft of "Last Letter" suggests, or perhaps even earlier. She would have had to buy the heavy tape she eventually used to seal off her doors from the gas when the shops were open that Friday or Saturday, as most shops in England were closed on Sundays in 1963.

That Friday, Sylvia returned to the Beckers' by taxi around midnight—she had given the car to Hughes back at Fitzroy Road—in an evening outfit with her hair nicely set. She did not tell Jillian where she had been. She and Sylvia talked for an hour; Sylvia took her "night" pill, then went to bed. Nick woke at five a.m. Jillian picked him up and brought him to Sylvia. Frieda came in and sat on her mother's bed while Sylvia fed Nick. Sylvia put both children back to bed; Jillian, heeding Dr. Horder's instructions, had not offered, and the fact that Sylvia did so herself was "a big deal." Jillian and Sylvia talked "awhile, I gave her her wake-up pill." Sylvia went back to sleep, then awoke around nine a.m.[69]

For years, biographers speculated about where Sylvia went that Friday night. Jillian wondered if she had set off to see the journalist Corin Hughes-Stanton, about whom Sylvia had spoken "mysteriously" several times.[70] Corin was, or had been, dating Susan O'Neill-Roe, though Jillian had the impression that Sylvia was "seeing" him near the end of her life.[71] Sylvia noted in her calendar that she saw Corin on December 22 and December 27. She did not mention Susan in these entries, and the notations—"tea—Corin" and, a week later, "Corin: dinner"—suggest an increasing familiarity.[72] (Corin's father had been a prominent figure in the early-twentieth-century British wood engraving movement and had illustrated several books by D. H. Lawrence. This background surely would have intrigued Plath.) Corin later said he had known Sylvia in late 1962 and early 1963, though he declined to elaborate on what he called "a very private matter."[73]

Jillian also speculated that Sylvia had met up with Ted that Friday night. Anne Stevenson wondered if the appointment was "some ghoulish rendez-vous with Death."[74] A 1963 guestbook reveals a much less dramatic scenario. That night, Sylvia had dinner with the Goodalls, the American friends of the Nortons, now living in London, who had visited her in January. She spent her last dinner party talking, presumably, about America, Wellesley, Aurelia, Mildred, Perry, and Dick.[75]

———

"THE NEXT MORNING she had disappeared," Suzette said. It was Saturday, February 9. "They didn't know where'd she'd gone. Jillian phoned me and said, 'I can't control Frieda, she's crying.' So I went there . . . Frieda was in such a state."[76] Suzette took Frieda on a bus ride to distract her. The child sat in her lap as the bus went past the zoo, which she knew well. The thought of the animals calmed her, but every few minutes she would say, "Where's Mummy?" Suzette told her, "She's gone to the doctor to see about her head-ache." (This was true—Dr. Horder said he saw Sylvia that Saturday.) Suzette got off the bus at one point with Frieda and phoned Jillian, asking if she had heard from Sylvia—she did not want to bring Frieda back until Sylvia had returned. Finally she brought her back at one, as she had to get ready for a two o'clock theater matinee. Suzette later called Jillian from the theater, ask-ing again if Sylvia had returned. Jillian said she had but that she wouldn't say where she had been, only "that it was very, very important." Suzette asked to speak to Sylvia. "Where were you?" she asked. Sylvia said, " 'Something unbelievable has happened.' She gave me to understand it was a decision, and it had to do with Ted." But where did you go? Suzette pressed. "Never mind," Sylvia said. "But it was very important, very important." Suzette offered to return to the Beckers' to mind Frieda, but Sylvia said it was not necessary, that she had "decisions to make."[77] A recently discovered letter from the poet Patric Dickinson provides a clue about where Plath might have gone that day. Dickinson said that one or two days before Plath's suicide, he met with her, at The Running Hare pub, about the American Poetry Night she was producing at the Royal Court Theatre. Yet he may have been referring to his earlier, October 30 appointment with Plath, for he said in his letter that he met Plath only once, and the time and place of the appointment he dated one or two days before her death was exactly that of the October 30 meeting.[78]

Suzette assumed that she had been with Ted. "Assia thought this—that he had said he was going back to her. Because Assia couldn't make up her mind, whether it was David she wanted, Ted she wanted. She wanted them both."[79] Ted, too, vacillated about the future of his marriage. By this time, Assia was pregnant with Hughes's child. Jillian and Suzette both claimed that Sylvia did not know about Assia's pregnancy; she never mentioned anything about it to them. Nor did Sylvia mention Assia's pregnancy to Dr. Beuscher in her February 4 letter, which suggests that she did not then know. Ted was unlikely to have unloaded such news on her that Friday, February 8, if he had landed on her doorstep weeping and desperate with worry that she was suicidal, as he wrote in his journal. Suzette claimed that Assia learned she was pregnant only after Sylvia's death. A letter from Assia to Peter Porter's wife confirms that Assia had an abortion on March 21.[80] Ted helped her recover at Fitzroy Road. Still, Jillian said that Ted told her he had told Sylvia they would be "back together 'by the summer.' " Hughes had said as much in "Last Letter." The phrase troubled Jillian over the years. Why "the sum-mer"? She wondered if Ted had told Sylvia this because he needed time to deal with Assia's pregnancy—to see "that complication through—either to a birth or a termination."[81]

That night the Beckers went out to a dinner party, and a Slade student, an artist, came to keep Sylvia company. They listened to Beethoven and drank wine. When Sylvia asked the student what he painted and he replied, "Abstracts," she said, "What a pity. If I could paint, I would want to paint things. I love the thinginess of things."[82] When the Beckers came home, Gerry went up to bed, and Jillian stayed up talking with Sylvia until two a.m. Then she helped Sylvia settle into bed and gave her the sleeping pill. Nick awoke at four thirty, and they fed him. Sylvia took her "pep" pill and fell back asleep until the morning.[83]

According to Susan Alliston's unpublished journal, Sylvia called Ted at his Cleveland Street flat on Saturday night, then again early on Sunday morning. Sue wrote that Ted "leaned over the telephone, saying 'Yes, yes'— being noncommittal, saying 'Take it easy Sylvie.'" Sylvia did not know that Sue was at Ted's flat, but she was upset about something.

> He came back to bed, turned his back, clasped his head in his arms, "God, God," he said. And said how she seemed drugged or drunk and wanted him to take her away somewhere. "But if I go back, I die," he said. And he starts talking about his family: the uncle forced to marry a cripple out of loyalty & also "2000 on marriage the legacy is," says her mother. The one who hanged himself. How they thought Sylvia like this a bit—grasping, destructive.[84]

In Sue's rendering, Ted's tone is exasperated. He sounds determined to leave Sylvia. He admits that his family thinks her "destructive" and money-grubbing (the "legacy" refers to a £2,000 life insurance policy); he compares his plight to his doomed uncle and hints that he will not stay with a "cripple." The passage throws Hughes's later claims that he and Plath were on the verge of a reconciliation that weekend into question. Yet he would hardly have told Sue, waiting for him in bed, that he was planning to get back together with his wife.

ON SUNDAY MORNING, February 10, as Sylvia was calling Ted, Gerry Becker and Nest Cleverdon took the children to the zoo. Sylvia had not bundled Nick up, which Nest thought odd. (She stopped at her own house on the way to pick up winter clothes.) They returned for a traditional Sunday lunch with wine and all the trimmings. "She helped Nick with his food and seemed, I thought, a little more cheerful, a little less tense," Jillian recalled. After lunch, they "lingered" over coffee, talking. Sylvia ate and drank heartily; then she and the children slept deeply through the afternoon. Red wine, which Jillian implies Sylvia drank that afternoon, can cause dangerous hypertension if taken with Nardil or Parnate. Whether Plath knew this, or experienced symptoms that night (extreme fatigue, headache, confusion, vision problems, and dizziness), is unclear.

When Sylvia woke around four p.m., she had tea with Jillian and Gerry. "She ate and drank and talked, the children played contentedly. Nothing in particular was said or done to change the easy mood we all seemed to share, when Sylvia got up briskly and began gathering things and putting them into carrier bags. She declared she 'must get home tonight.'"[85] She also told Suzette, by phone from the Beckers', that she had to go home because Dr. Horder was sending round a nurse to help her with the children on Monday morning, and she was going to meet her publisher for lunch. "She's coming tomorrow morning, so I have to get home, I have to get the clothes done, I have to get Frieda ready," she said. "I have to go."[86] Suzette said that during this phone call Sylvia was distraught about the fact that the Beckers' Irish nanny had pressed a pound into her hand "for the babies." "Everybody smells the poverty on me," Sylvia said.[87] Sylvia told Gerry the same story that evening.[88] But Jillian thought she sounded upbeat as she said, "I must get back. I have to sort the laundry. And I'm expecting a nurse."[89] "She seemed invigorated, mildly elated, as I'd seldom if ever seen her before."[90]

Sylvia did not tell them that Dr. Horder had found her a bed in a "suitable" hospital and had arranged for her admission on Monday. The nurse was coming not to help her with the children, but to look after them while she was away.[91] Jillian and Gerry tried to persuade her to stay until Monday—Jillian would later ruefully remember that Sylvia had talked about her 1953 suicide attempt several times that weekend—but she quickly packed up and left at around six p.m.[92] It was only later that Jillian realized that Sylvia had forgotten her coat, which remained hanging at the Beckers' with a pair of extra house keys in the pocket. She would wonder if Sylvia had left them intentionally, so that she and Gerry might go after her that night. Or perhaps Sylvia had left the spare set so Jillian would be able to get into the locked house and save the children the next morning.

Gerry drove Sylvia back to Fitzroy Road in his old rattling black taxi. When he stopped at a red light, he heard her weeping in the back seat. He pulled over, got out, and sat in the back on the pull-down seat opposite her. She continued weeping, with her head in her hands. By now the children were crying, too, and he pulled them both onto his lap. He begged Sylvia to come back with him to Islington, but she refused. She grew calmer, "lifted her head and said, 'No, this is nonsense, take no notice. I have to get home.'"

He continued to ask her if she was sure she wanted to go home, and "she answered as often as he asked that she was absolutely sure."[93] He walked her into the flat and helped her get her things upstairs. She put the children to bed and made Gerry some tea. He stayed for two hours. She told him she was looking forward to seeing Marcia at Court Green in the spring, and she invited him and Jillian to visit then, too. She seemed generally "clear-minded and optimistic," though she grew upset when she spoke about Assia and the impossibility of ever reconciling with Ted.[94] Before he left, he told her he would check in on her the next day, and she reassured him that a nurse was coming at seven a.m.[95] He returned to Islington and told Jillian what had happened. He did not think Sylvia "could cope on her own." "I knew he was right," Jillian later wrote, "yet I wasn't entirely sorry she had left. I would not have to go on being nurse to her and her children. My daughters would not have to give up their rooms. I would have no more interrupted nights. And pity tires the heart. For which thoughts I was to endure long remorse."[96]

That evening Dr. Horder came to check on Sylvia, Trevor Thomas remembered, "rather late." He would have almost certainly discussed her looming hospital admission. Around eleven forty-five, Thomas said, she knocked on his door: "there she was, looking very odd indeed as if drugged or doped and faraway, out of this world." (As Sue Alliston noted, Ted, too, had thought that she sounded "drunk" when she called him the day before.) She needed air-mail stamps, as she had run out, and she told him the letters were bound for America and "must go tonight." He remembered that her voice was "slightly slurred and somehow more American." He asked why she had come home early, and she told him, "Oh, we didn't like being away from home. The children were difficult and I wanted to write." Thomas wrote that "she looked so obviously ill I asked if I should phone the doctor. She was quite adamant and she did not want to trouble him."[97] Sylvia's "obvious" signs of illness—which Gerry had not noticed—were likely related not only to depression and her recent flu but also to the drug cocktail she was taking and the interaction of her antidepressant with the red wine she had at Jillian's Sunday lunch.

The most likely recipient of at least one of Sylvia's last letters was her brother, Warren. She would not have wanted Assia, whom she despised, raising Frieda and Nicholas. Warren and Maggie were the obvious choice: she loved and respected her brother, who had bright professional prospects, and Maggie was a warm, "capable" woman she had wanted by her side when she was down with flu that summer. They had no children of their own yet and could devote themselves to hers. He and Maggie would provide a stable, prosperous, German American home where her children would be raised with strong values. Imagining such a future for Frieda and Nicholas may have eased her heartbreak; she may even have assumed, in her deeply depressed state, that they would be better off with Warren and Maggie than with her. Such a letter would also help explain why Warren and Maggie flew over in the immediate aftermath of Sylvia's death and tried to make arrangements to take the children back to America. Aurelia told her friend Richard Larschan in the early 1990s that one of these last letters had been addressed to her, but that Ted told her not to read it in order to spare herself pain. Aurelia did not press him and never read the letter—if, indeed, it ever existed. Richard had his doubts, as Aurelia told him the story when she was in her early eighties and "increasingly demented."[98]

Sylvia wanted to pay Trevor Thomas for stamps then and there with money from her "small purse." Thomas told her not to worry, and she said, "Oh! But I must pay you or I won't be right with my conscience before God, will I?" She asked him what time he went to work in the morning; he told her between eight fifteen and eight thirty a.m. "She wanted to know if I'd be doing that tomorrow morning and when I said 'I hope so, all being well' she said that would be all right then. When I asked why she wanted to know she said: 'Oh nothing, I just wondered, that's all.'" Finally, he told her it was late "and too cold for her to stand there. She had better go to bed. She thanked me and I shut the door."

Ten minutes later he opened the door—the hall light was on—and saw that she was still standing there "with a kind of seraphic expression on her face." "You aren't really well are you?" Thomas said. "I'm sure I should get the doctor." "Oh no," he remembered her saying, "please don't do that. I'm just having a marvelous dream, a most wonderful vision." He invited her in but she refused. It was now twelve thirty in the morning, and he told her he needed to go to bed. When he opened the door again, twenty minutes later, the hall light was still on but she had gone. He assumed that she had gone out to send the letters. "In hindsight I've often wondered if the real purpose of her visit was to find out if I would be around or not when she turned on the gas." He heard her pacing overhead for hours, and he finally fell asleep at about five a.m. He would not wake for twelve hours.

Ted and Sue spent Sunday together, reading each other's poetry and socializing with Tasha Hollis and Ted's old Cambridge friend David Ross at David's flat in Great Ormond Street. They drank wine and discussed poetry. (Ted and Assia often used David's flat when he was out.)[99] Later that night, Ted brought Sue to 18 Rugby Street to avoid "a surprise visitation" from Sylvia. The decision to bring Sue, on the night before Sylvia's suicide, to the house where he and his wife spent their wedding night would haunt him for the rest of his life. "Why did we go there?" he later wrote in "Last Letter."

"Of all places / Why did we go there?" He imagined Sylvia tapping, like Cathy Earnshaw, at his "dark window" in the hours before she died, and calling all night. "Before midnight. After midnight. Again. / Again. Again. And, near dawn, again."[100]

―――――――――

AT ABOUT SEVEN A.M. on Monday, February 11, Sylvia put bread, butter, and two baby bottles of milk in her children's room. She opened their windows, covered them with extra blankets, left the room, and taped around the outside edges of their door.[101] Jillian remembered that Nick always awoke for the morning at six a.m. (Sylvia had recently told Aurelia the same), which suggests that at least one child was awake while she acted. On a small, torn piece of paper, in large block letters, she wrote her last note in separate, angled lines:

PLEASE CALL
DR HORDER
AT
PRI 3804

Her poems had flouted gentility, but she began her last written words with "Please."[102] Across Regent's Park, the Beatles were getting ready to arrive at Abbey Road Studios at ten a.m., where they would record their first album, *Please, Please Me*. The morning of February 11, 1963, was the dawn of the 1960s.

Sylvia Plath laid her last words against the stroller in the flat's entryway. In the kitchen, she stuffed the cracks around the door and window with tea towels and clothes, and taped herself in.[103] She turned on the gas taps, lay down on the floor, and placed her head on a folded cloth atop the oven's drop door. As she died, the sun rose out the large window to her left, flooding the kitchen with light.[104] "The evil times," Hughes later wrote, "were those two or three hours between the effects of one dose wearing off, and the effect of the next dose taking hold, in the early morning. In the last paragraph of her diary, she described her fear of the horror of these hours."[105]

"Ariel" almost anticipates Plath's last morning: the speaker longs to flee the "child's cry" as, "suicidal," she contemplates apotheosis. In a 1998 letter, Hughes called the poem "a prophecy of suicide."[106] But, like "Lady Lazarus" and "Edge," "Ariel" uses suicide metaphorically—as spectacle—to elucidate the risks, rewards, and limits of female ambition. Those poems do not offer an explanation for their author's actual suicide. "Child," with its intimate revelation of depression's dark heart, does. It comes closest to being the note Plath never left.

> Your clear eye is the one absolutely beautiful thing.
> I want to fill it with color and ducks,
> The zoo of the new
>
> Whose names you meditate—
> April snowdrop, Indian pipe,
> Little
>
> Stalk without wrinkle,
> Pool in which images
> Should be grand and classical
>
> Not this troublous
> Wringing of hands, this dark
> Ceiling without a star.

Plath dedicated *Ariel* to her children. Full of grand and classical images, it sat neatly arranged in a black binder on her bedroom desk. Hughes would find it later that day next to manuscript copies of some of his own poems— "Out," "The Road to Easington," "The Green Wolf," "New Moon in January," two Lorca translations—and a stack of nineteen other poems Plath intended for her third collection.[107] Of her mother's greatest work, Frieda Hughes wrote, "The art was not to fall."[108]

Your Wife Is Dead

As Plath prepared to die, Hughes lay in the arms of Sue Alliston at 18 Rugby Street. He drove her to work on Monday morning and then retreated back to the still, snowed-in quiet of his Cleveland Street flat. In "Last Letter," he re-created the scene that morning before Dr. Horder delivered the four words that changed his life:

> I lit my fire. I had got out my papers.
> And I had started to write when the telephone
> Jerked awake, in a jabbering alarm,
> Remembering everything. It recovered in my hand.
> Then a voice like a selected weapon
> Or a measured injection,
> Coolly delivered its four words
> Deep into my ear: "Your wife is dead."[1]

For years, Hughes and Alvarez would speculate that Plath had been playing a game of Russian roulette, hoping the nurse would find her still alive and so achieve another rebirth. Winifred Davies thought the same, that "she was trying to frighten Ted. . . . she was too fond of the children to have made up her mind to do it if she didn't think she would be rescued before it was too late."[2] But the information now available suggests that Sylvia was not thinking of herself: she was thinking of her children. She knew that either Trevor Thomas or the visiting nurse would smell the gas between eight thirty and nine a.m. She calculated the shortest time she would need the gas on in order to minimize its effect on her children, trapped in their room upstairs. She thought that the deadly coal gas would rise—but instead it sank into Thomas's flat below, knocking him out until five p.m. that day. Indeed, he nearly died. Dr. Horder never believed the gambling theory. He was one of the first to arrive at Fitzroy Road that morning, and he would never forget the care Sylvia had taken to seal off the kitchen.[3]

When the visiting nurse, Myra Norris, came round to Fitzroy Road that morning, no one answered the buzzer. She walked to a nearby phone booth and called Dr. Horder to make sure she had the right address. Reassured that she was in the right place, she returned a few minutes after eleven a.m. and saw some builders who, according to the police report, "were working on repairs on the premises." (When Jillian heard about this, she thought with bitter irony that they were finally fixing Sylvia's heat.)[4] The builders had a key to the house and let her in. The nurse immediately smelled gas, ran upstairs, and found Sylvia, still in her "night clothes," lying on the floor with her head on a cloth on the oven door.[5] One of the builders, Charles Langridge, told the police, "The nurse came running out to me crying the woman had gassed herself." They rushed back into the flat, turned off the gas, threw open the windows, and ran upstairs to the cold, crying children, who were, Langridge said, "alright."[6] Together they moved Sylvia into the living room, where the nurse tried artificial respiration. Langridge found Plath's note on the stroller "in the next room," and rushed outside to call both Dr. Horder and an ambulance from a public phone booth. According to the London police report, Horder arrived at eleven thirty and a London County Council ambulance came five minutes later—the nurse was still trying to revive Plath—and brought her to University College Hospital. She was pronounced dead on arrival at 11:45 a.m.[7]

A twenty-four-year-old policeman, John Jones, arrived at the flat at 11:45, and later interviewed Dr. Horder at his office at 114 Regent's Park Road.[8] Horder told him, "She has been under me for treatment for mental depression but had seemed much brighter these last few days. I arranged for the nurse to attend to help her with the children and was very surprised when I found she'd done this."[9] (Horder could not have been that surprised, as he was arranging Plath's admission to a psychiatric ward on the Friday before her death.) Constable Jones then interviewed Dr. Hill, the pathologist who attended to Plath at University College Hospital. Hill told Jones, "She has been dead for about four hours. The body was cold when it arrived."[10] Horder estimated that she had turned on the gas between six thirty and seven.[11] The pathologist thought she had died around seven thirty.

Though Plath had been suffering from fevers and an upper respiratory infection, the autopsy showed that all of her organs were healthy when she died. There were no tumors or indicators of pregnancy. The level of carboxyhaemoglobin—a measure of carbon monoxide poisoning—in her blood was 76.5 percent, well over the 50–60 percent in most victims. There was so much carbon monoxide in her body that her blood, and her flanks, had turned pink. The autopsy stated that there were recent bruises on her forehead and the occipital region on the back of her head, which suggest that she had banged her head, perhaps several times, while losing consciousness.[12] This may have been the result of random spasms, or she may have tried to get up, too late. Both children probably would have been awake and crying by seven a.m.

Dr. Horder first called Jillian, who called Suzette, who called Assia for Ted's number. Suzette then rushed to 23 Fitzroy Road to care for the children. Catherine was one of the first to know. She had earlier promised Sylvia she would babysit that day while she had lunch with her new Heinemann editor, David Machin. When she arrived at Sylvia's flat, she encountered Ted, who pushed past her, "charging up the stairs like Rochester . . . he roared in, looking absolutely distraught." Dr. Horder walked Catherine, in shock herself, over to his car. "We sat there thinking wretchedly how all this had happened, despite our joint efforts. It really hurt him so much and he felt, I think, responsible."[13] Lorna vividly remembered opening the door to find Catherine on her step, crying, telling her, "'Sylvia's killed herself.' The tears."[14]

Ted formally identified his wife's body at University College Hospital, then went round to the Macedos' flat in Hampstead. Suzette remembered him in a very shaken state, quietly telling Helder as he leaned against their wooden chest, "Listen, it was her or me."[15] Hughes would repeat this astonishing phrase to others in the days after Plath's death. Had he, too, contemplated suicide? Was the relationship so dysfunctional that he felt only one of them would survive it? His words suggest he may have been close to breakdown himself.[16]

When Sue heard the news of Sylvia's suicide that afternoon from her ex-husband, Clem Moore, she sent Ted a telegram—"Sorry sorry sorry if I can do anything."[17] That week, she and David Ross visited Ted at Fitzroy Road. "So we drove to the flat," David said, "and there was Ted, and he had the final Sylvia poems, which he proceeded to read to me. And I was absolutely startled with those poems—they were extraordinary and sent shivers up and down my spine that night." David remembered that Ted was alone and that the children were probably sleeping upstairs. Ted had already read the poems in the *Ariel* typescript that afternoon, but David "had the impression he hadn't seen them before" her death. "We were both so startled with these poems." Ted told David that night he planned to "auction" them to publishers.[18]

Jillian and Gerry Becker came to Fitzroy Road on that night of the 11th. Ted talked to Gerry about the children, Jillian remembered, but he asked them no questions about Sylvia. Later that week, however, Ted called Jillian several times in the middle of the night. "What had she said? What had she done?" he demanded. Jillian had the sense that he was not really listening to her answers. Sometimes he became "hostile," accusing her of telling people his children should be raised by Warren and Maggie Plath. "I barely had time to deny it before he'd gone on to something else. . . . And even if he'd been willing to hear me speak, what could I (what could anyone) have said to save him from the furies of his own darkest hours?"[19]

On February 12, Ted sent a telegram to Aurelia's sister Dot, saying simply, "Sylvia died yesterday." He may have thought such devastating news was best delivered by a family member, or he may have felt too guilty to speak to Aurelia. Dot was left to shatter Aurelia's world. Warren and Maggie flew over while Aurelia, lost in grief, remained in Wellesley. She assumed that Sylvia had died of pneumonia until Warren told her, in his February 17th letter from Halifax, the "hard news" that she had died from "carbon monoxide poisoning from the gas stove."[20] He had wanted to defer this news until he returned home, but he feared it would reach her by other sources before then. Later that year, Aurelia visited Jillian. The two women spent many hours walking along the banks of the Thames. "She was a sad, quiet woman who was absolutely devastated."[21]

Ted wrote to Olwyn telling her what had happened. He blamed himself. "She asked me for help, as she so often has. I was the only person who could have helped her, and the only person so jaded by her states & demands that I could not recognize when she really needed it."[22] To Daniel Huws, he wrote bluntly, "No doubt where the blame lies."[23] When Elizabeth Compton came to Fitzroy Road, he told her, "It doesn't fall to many men to murder a genius."[24] Warren wrote Aurelia that when he saw Ted in London shortly after Sylvia's death, "he looked as though he would have been relieved had I struck him or spit in his face."[25] Luke Myers arrived on February 13. Ted told him he thought Sylvia had "intended to be rescued. Shortly before her death, they had agreed to meet within several days. Ted believed that they would have been reunited in two weeks."[26] At night, Hughes lay sleepless and tormented as he listened to the wolves howling in Regent's Park Zoo.

Immediately after Sylvia's suicide, he "felt it had happened a month ago." A month later, he wrote the Merwins, he felt it had "happened yesterday." If only he'd given Sylvia as much "care, thought" as he devoted to some small task, he "could have helped her to live for a lifetime." "But I depended on a resilience in her that I was too blind to see wasn't there." He told the Merwins he was afflicted with the "physical sensation of having been broken to pieces," running "full tilt into a brick wall."[27] In a letter to the Comptons later that summer, he wrote that he understood why the public wanted to see him suffer as "the man who dies of remorse . . . married to a memory, a curator of the shrine." This, he said, would be "justice." He, too, hinted bleakly at suicide:

> When somebody who has shared life with you as much as Sylvia shared it with me, dies, then life somehow dies, the gold standard of it is somehow converted into death, & it is a minute by minute effort to find any sense in life, or any value. I never understood Sylvia's wish to be with her father, as it appeared in her poems, and I never imagined I'd come under the same law. I'm aware that all this has somehow perverted my social sense, or what vestige of it I had. I'm aware of doing things that appal [*sic*] other people, but for which I have only worse alternatives. This is made more complicated by the tricky situation of the children—if it weren't for them the answer would be the simplest.[28]

ON THE MORNING OF FEBRUARY 15, Al Alvarez and the Australian painter Charles Blackman accompanied Ted Hughes to the funeral home at Mornington Crescent. Hughes would later realize that the date fell on the Roman festival of Lupercalia that had inspired his second book—an uncanny coincidence. Alvarez remembered that the room smelled of rotting apples, something unclean. Plath looked gray, ashen, in her coffin, a "ludicrous ruff" at her neck. "It seemed impossible that she was dead," Alvarez wrote.[29]

The inquest on February 15 at the Saint Pancras Coroner's Court was swift and efficient. Dr. Horder had "arranged for Mrs. Hughes, who was suffering from depression, to see a psychiatrist in the week prior to her death. But the letter was delivered to the wrong address." In "recent weeks" Plath had told Dr. Horder of her history with depression and "nervous troubles." He told the court that he had become "so worried as a result of a long talk with her" on Friday, February 8 that he had spoken with three psychiatrists in an attempt to find a hospital bed for her immediately. Only one could provide a bed, but he did not think it "suitable." He spoke to Plath again later that day; she "seemed better" and had decided to spend the weekend with friends. It was then that he arranged for a nurse to come on Monday morning "to help her during what he regarded as a critical time."[30] The coroner, Dr. McEwan, blamed Horder, who said, "I couldn't get an admission before Monday, and I thought that would be all right. I thought she'd be quite safe until then. . . . We all underestimated her."[31]

Hughes, with Alvarez there for support, testified that his wife had previously been suicidal and "had lately had mysterious temperatures and nervous trouble."[32] Alvarez observed the "drab, damp" room, the "muttered evidence, long silences," the nurse, Myra Norris, in tears.[33] Hughes pointed out a man in a dark suit to Alvarez and called him, bitterly, Plath's "boyfriend."[34] This man may have been Corin Hughes-Stanton.

The verdict was recorded: "Carbon monoxide poisoning while suffering from depression. Did kill herself."[35] Later, Horder thought Plath had reached a perilous point where she was roused from lethargy by the antidepressants he had recently prescribed but not yet feeling their relief, which was expected to take ten to twenty days. He came to believe that Plath had "inherited a chemical imbalance that causes some kinds of depression" from her paternal relatives.[36] (Aurelia likely told him that three women in Otto's family, including his mother, had suffered from the disease.)[37]

Lorna remembered that Horder, indeed, blamed himself: "He certainly was clearly very upset, felt he hadn't . . . what had he not done? . . . Maybe in retrospect John Horder thought he should have sectioned her. It's a difficult thing for a doctor to decide, because you're going to be held somewhere against your will . . . this strikes them as being terrible. If people can do it voluntarily, that is infinitely preferable. She was an attractive woman, Sylvia, clearly, and clearly John Horder would have found her attractive. I'm not saying anything more than that. But I'm sure he would have done his best not to upset her . . . but he would have done that for anybody, really, to be fair to him. But at the same time, maybe slightly against his own better judgment, he didn't have her sectioned."[38]

Warren assumed that he and his wife Margaret would bring the children back to America. "Ted does seem genuinely shocked and grieved—also more than a bit guilty, and I hope I can turn this to advantage where the children are concerned," Warren wrote to Aurelia on February 17. "At least it means that the children should be reasonably looked out for until we, God willing, are able to get them & bring them home."[39] Margaret also wrote to Aurelia, assuring her that the children were well-tended by Ted's aunt Hilda and the Macedos. She already felt a searing love for them and vowed to bring them home. If Ted could not be moved to give up custody by "friendly persuasion," Warren wrote Aurelia, they were prepared to dig in for a long legal battle. He had already broached the plan with a British solicitor and told his mother, "We will move forward." Yet three days later he was less sure. "As for Ted, he admits that a life with nannies & such would not be best for the children and that they need some sort of stable existence, but he needs some time to make up his mind to let us take them. . . . There is every evidence that Ted <u>deeply feels the loss of Sylvia</u>, and this somewhat complicates the whole problem of him making a decision about his children."[40] Ted was still wavering on February 25, telling Warren that their "offer might be the final solution to how to take care of Frieda & Nick, but only after he had 'given it a good try.' I have pretty much given up reacting to his sudden changes of attitude any more, preferring to stick to working quietly behind the scenes."[41]

In the end, Ted could not part with Frieda and Nicholas. Warren and Maggie stayed at Fitzroy Road while they were in London, and Ted called Jillian to complain about them—she remembered him telling her, angrily, that Maggie had left Alka-Seltzer out in the bathroom and Frieda could have eaten it. Jillian felt, in his devastated state, that he could not cope with the children.[42] He also wrote angrily to the Merwins of Warren and Maggie's visit. "The Plaths came over to salvage some sort of sustenance for Mrs. Plath's future—feed Nick & Frieda to her. I think it's time to say that."[43]

The funeral services were held in Yorkshire, at two different locations, on February 18. The brief wake, with closed casket, was in a chapel of a funeral home in Hebden Bridge; the funeral was at Saint Thomas the Apostle church in Heptonstall village. Elizabeth and Jillian were upset when they learned that Sylvia was to be buried in the Calder Valley, for she had told them she wanted to be buried in the graveyard next to Court Green. Aurelia and Warren, Jillian remembered, were also upset about the decision.[44] Ted had looked into burying Sylvia in Devon, but the reverend at Saint Peter's Church in North Tawton told him the graveyard was closed. The cemetery in Heptonstall, filled with the graves of Farrars, offered an immediate and practical choice. Plath was still his wife.

But there was another reason he made Heptonstall Plath's final resting place. The hilltop village, positioned at the very top of the valley, was bathed in light all year round and possessed a mythical beauty. All his life, Ted had dreamed of moving up the Calder Valley, into the high country. Heptonstall was the center of what he imagined to be the ancient Celtic kingdom of Elmet, an escape from the modern-day turmoil and pollution below. The air was clearer in Heptonstall, and the long views stunning. This was the center of Hughes's symbolic geography, his still point of the turning world. And he remembered, too, Sylvia's deep love of the moors—the only landscape that rivaled, for her, the sea.

Warren wrote Aurelia that the funeral services were "much better as an experience than we had dared to hope, and I think even Sylvia would have found it simple and beautiful." The chapel in Hebden Bridge was "light and cheerful inside—almost like a tiny chapel in a New England church. Wood, not stone on the inside—simple, with not too many flowers." The wake was small: Ted; Ted's father; his uncle Walt and his wife; cousin Vicky and her husband; Jillian and Gerry Becker; and Warren and Maggie. (Edith's painful arthritis kept her from attending both services.) The cortège then moved up the steep hill to Heptonstall for the funeral service at Saint Thomas the Apostle, where a few more mourners from the village joined them. Jillian thought that the absence of nearly all who knew Sylvia in England—the Macedos, the Roches, the Comptons, Al Alvarez, Susan O'Neill-Roe, Winifred Davies, neighbors from Primrose Hill and North Tawton—testified to how alone and isolated Sylvia had become in her last weeks. Lorna said there was a more practical reason so few attended: Yorkshire was simply too far to travel, at short notice, in the dead of winter. The funeral had been hastily arranged, and many friends may not have known about it. But the lack of mourners also suggested the heavy stigma suicide still carried. Nathaniel Tarn heard that one of Sylvia's old "boyfriends" had kept her suicide out of the London papers the week after her death.[45] Suicide was still a "dirty little secret," Alvarez wrote, "something shameful to be avoided and tidied away, unmentionable and faintly salacious."[46]

Before the funeral, Jillian remembered having tea and sandwiches at the Beacon. Edith asked her how Sylvia had seemed in the days before she died. "We all loved her, you know," Edith said. Billy Hughes stayed quiet.

The service in Heptonstall was, Warren wrote, "brief" and traditional.[47] For a moment, a shaft of sunlight came through a yellow stained-glass window and brightened the church's dim, chill interior. Then the small party followed the coffin to the newer graveyard across the lane, with its view of the surrounding moors. The priest completed the funeral rites, and the group left Ted alone at the grave, which Jillian described as "a yellow trench in the snow."[48] The gravestone would read SYLVIA PLATH HUGHES 1932–1963, above a quotation Hughes had chosen from a Buddhist text, *The Monkey*, which he had often used to comfort her when she was feeling low: "Even amidst the fierce flames, the golden lotus can be planted." In the years to come, Hughes would bury his parents a few meters away.

The funeral party then retreated to what Warren called "a high tea (which none of us had much of) down in Hebden Bridge."[49] Ted sat at the end of a long table, next to the Beckers. Gerry procured a bottle of whiskey, and he and Ted drank in silence. Steak and kidney pies were served. Tea was poured. Suddenly Ted said, "Everybody hated her." Jillian protested that she had not hated Sylvia. "It was either her or me," he said, as if in a trance. He said this phrase several times that day—the same words he had said to the Macedos soon after Plath's death. And then, later, "She made me professional." Still later, "I *told* her everything was going to be all right. I said that by summer we'd all be back together at Court Green." Jillian was skeptical, but she held her tongue. He then asked Jillian if she had read *The Bell Jar*, and if she knew that Sylvia had tried to kill herself before they met. "It was in her, you see," he said. "But I told her that if she wrote about it profoundly enough, she would conquer it." Jillian asked whether he thought Sylvia had written profoundly enough. "No," he said.[50]

———————

ON MARCH 15, Ted wrote to Aurelia for the first time since Sylvia's death:

> I shall never get over the shock and I don't particularly want to. . . .
> The particular conditions of our marriage, the marriage of two people
> so openly under the control of deep psychic abnormalities as both of
> us were, meant that we finally reduced each other to a state where our
> actions and normal states of mind were like madness. My attempt to cor-
> rect that marriage is madness from start to finish. The way she reacted to
> my actions also has all the appearance of a kind of madness—her insis-
> tence on a divorce, the one thing in this world she did not want, the
> proud hostility and hatred, the malevolent acts, that she showed to me,
> when all she wanted to say simply was that if I didn't go back to her she
> could not live. . . .
>
> We were utterly blind, we were both desperate, stupid, and proud—
> and the pride made us oblique, she especially so. I know Sylvia was so
> made that she had to mete out terrible punishment to the people she
> most loved, but everybody is a little like that, and it needed only intel-
> ligence on my part to deal with it. . . .
>
> I don't ever want to be forgiven. I don't mean that I shall become
> a public shrine of mourning and remorse, I would sooner become the
> opposite. But if there is an eternity, I am damned in it. Sylvia was one of
> the greatest truest spirits alive, and in her last months she became a great
> poet, and no other woman poet except for Emily Dickinson can begin to
> be compared with her, and certainly no living American.[51]

Privately, Hughes searched for meaning in his notebook:

> Sylvia's presence, that now seems more impossible than Eden, was my
> daily life only 8 weeks ago, & for 7 years before that, daily daily hourly
> nightly real unalterably real & saturating everything. Now not a trace. . . .
>
> If the presence, or goodwill, of one certain person can so completely
> modify the meaning of life & the move & every action & thought, what
> hope is there of making a stable dwelling-place in the Universe, or in
> the world at large, or in a society. The balance so precariously held. No
> wonder you hang on to anchors. . . .

If a guilty man confesses remorse enough, he is told, then his wife will be restored from the house of the dead. He confesses: is heard, recorded: evidence taken. He writes. More is needed. Again. And again. Hope mounting. Finally out comes one of the genuine masters of the underworld: your wife is dead, she never came back. Why are you making such a fool of yourself. . . .

When somebody you love has died it seems natural & the inevitable way to give up & die too: they have called life's bluff. They have not so much escaped into death, as let death into all the veins & arteries of intimate existence. I see why life was a precarious balloon for Sylvia—she must have suffered this dead-weight all along.[52]

For years, Hughes maintained that he and Plath were on the verge of a reconciliation that last weekend. In March 1963 he wrote to Aurelia,

I had come to the point where I'd decided we could repair our marriage now. She had agreed to stop the divorce. I had that weekend cancelled all my appointments for the next fortnight. I was going to ask her to come away with me on the Monday, on holiday, to the coast, some place we had not been. Think of how it must be for me too.[53]

He wrote his trusted friend Keith Sagar in 1998, "accidents accelerated that last week to free fall 32 ft per sec. we [sic] ran out of time—by days, I think. So I shall always believe."[54] In the appalling aftermath of Plath's death, Hughes may have believed this. But he had brought Sue Alliston to Rugby Street to avoid Plath's phone calls on the night she died, and on March 27, 1963, he wrote to Assia begging her to leave David. "If my feelings about you had been moveable at all, this last 6 weeks would have moved them, but it hasn't, it's just shown me how final they are."[55]

———

ON FEBRUARY 16, Nathaniel Tarn visited David and Assia Wevill at their flat. When David went out for cigarettes, Assia spoke "mildly as if unconcerned" about the details of Sylvia's death. Tarn recorded details of the visit in his diary:

[Sylvia] was depressed—a letter announcing a meeting with a psychiatrist did not reach her. Everyone is blaming himself. The doctor because he gave her pep pills which ran out. Hughes is crushed, D.[avid] also though he didn't like her. A.[ssia] says that the children are not asking for her, the little girl is glad her daddy's back (!!!) "All the women" are blaming Assia—on the night she acted, P.[lath] had talked to a group [of women], including a journalist &, somehow, Suzette Macedo . . . & had told terrible stories. A.[ssia] has been seeing H.[ughes] & the kids every day.

Assia told him Sylvia had been writing "the most incredible poems for weeks."[56]

Ted moved into Sylvia's flat at Fitzroy Road, whose rent had been paid through December 1963. He noticed her wineglasses, which had been "rubbed and polished." In his notebook he wrote,

> Then the stove. Eerie. Gathered an evil something or other . . . distinct and heavy memories. A.[ssia] felt uneasy. I do too but something in me likes that we stay. We smoke. Frieda plays with her silver flask & bog cotton. Frieda vies with A.[ssia], becomes very possessive, won't leave me an inch. I carry her on my shoulder. I love her too much probably, she's a compensation for too much & her love flatters me & comforts me too, how would I feel if she lost interest.[57]

Assia was still living with David but saw Ted regularly. She helped him with the children, reluctantly. Suzette helped too, along with a series of temporary nannies, Olwyn, and Ted's aunt Hilda. Lorna remembered that she and Catherine "were very troubled" by Assia's presence at Fitzroy Road. In April, they attended a birthday party for Frieda, organized by Ted, with their children. The Sillitoes and Dido Merwin were also there. "So there was this party up in that sitting room up on the first floor. And little Frieda looking really very sort of lost, and the little boy . . . oh, very sad. And Ted . . . he wasn't, poor man, himself in very good shape. He had organized the party but you could see his heart wasn't really in it." Assia arrived late "dressed looking as if she was going to Ascot, a pale yellow dress with a jacket. I mean, not at all someone going to a children's party. I can see her now sitting there looking amazing . . . she was beautiful, but . . . poor Ted."[58]

Elizabeth, too, encountered a sad scene at 23 Fitzroy Road not long after Sylvia's death. "I went up to see the children after she died, and Ted came in and he was talking to me in the kitchen, and he gave me *The Bell Jar*. He said, 'This is yours.' I hadn't known [Plath had dedicated the novel to her and David]. He said, 'I feel like a murderer.' And I said, 'You're not a murderer, you didn't murder anybody.' The children were being looked after by a nanny, and my daughter came with me, my oldest daughter, Meg, she had long brown hair, and when Nick saw her he climbed on her and held her hair . . . awful, awful. Ted said, 'I hear the wolves howling and it seems appropriate.' "[59]

After this visit, Elizabeth wrote to Aurelia, "He loves those children, & is taking great care of them. He looks so sad & bent down. . . . And yet I can't blame Ted. He is such a kind & gentle man."[60] Elizabeth continued to see Ted often in North Tawton in the years that followed. "Never was Sylvia mentioned. Never, by anyone." One night while they were sitting and drinking by her fire, Ted told her, "You've got to be aware that if you're creative, you have a demon, and that that demon can destroy people who come close to you."[61]

Ruth Fainlight remembered that when Ted and Assia came around to her flat a few days after she returned from Morocco that February, "they both had this shocked look—like north Italian fifteenth-century Adam and Eve expelled. . . . And of course she was the demon woman, the murderer, everything. That was my preconception. She was extraordinary looking, really beautiful, but she always had this pained, vulnerable quality about her—already."[62]

Ted continued to change his mind about whether he would stay in London, go back to Court Green, or raise the children in Yorkshire. Before Sylvia's death, he had been planning long trips abroad—Germany, Italy, "North Africa, then East, to Egypt & Arabia, up through Syria to Turkey, then East through India & to Japan, then to South America."[63] Now his life was in chaos. To Olwyn he wrote that spring, "But simply to work, as everybody else does, for a few hours a day, I seem to have to push my head like a ship's prow through a sea of yellings, cries, anxious letters, . . . & the incessant querying voices of the unsolved Nanny, the unsolved Home, the unsolved Plaths et al."[64] He had inherited a mother's responsibilities, and a mother's lack of freedom, at exactly the moment he had been plotting his escape. But he loved his children too much to abandon them, and he fretted over their future. When he and Frieda were alone together, they entered, he said, into a "conspiracy of mourning."[65] The nannies he hired were too harsh, Hilda was too puritanical, Assia not maternal enough. At one point he wrote to his old teacher in Mexborough, Pauline Mayne, asking her to leave her family to help him raise his children. She declined.[66] Elizabeth offered to raise Nick in Devon, but he said things would have to "be a great deal more difficult" before he gave up his son—though he later tried to convince the Comptons to move to Yorkshire to help him raise Frieda and Nicholas, an offer they declined.[67] David recalled, "He wanted to go up to Yorkshire and take us and start up a new life there. And I took a train journey up to Mytholmroyd, and came back again very quickly. Yorkshire! This black man came from this black county! There's black rock under the soil and all the houses are built out of the black dust. Oh God, I could not see myself raising Ted and Sylvia's children in Mytholmroyd, sending my children to the school."[68]

Aurelia visited both her daughter's grave and her grandchildren in Yorkshire (they were staying with Hilda) in June 1963. Ted had written to her in May urging her not to smother the children with her misplaced love for Sylvia, nor to "make a battlefield of their loyalties." He told her he had heard rumors that her visit was "an investigation," and he expressed anger about questions Warren had put to him when he was in England for Sylvia's funeral. He dreaded, he wrote, "the effects of that tense, watchful anxiety" that had made his wife's life "so much more difficult than it need have been . . . a more or less constant state of terror that something might go wrong, then panic when it does, even if it's only missing a train." But the letter was an apology, too.

> Please, Aurelia, do not make the mistake of thinking that the way I caused Sylvia to suffer was any indication of my real feelings for her, which are simply unaltered. . . . my love for her simply underwent temporary imprisonment by something which can only be described as madness, as much an attempt to free myself from the strangling quality of our closeness as by an outer cause. My love for her simply continues, I look on her as my wife and the only one I shall ever marry, and these two children are ours.[69]

That June, Aurelia did not reproach him, and she doted on the children. But Ted found the visit "a strain."[70] She asked him, again, to allow Warren and Maggie to raise the children in their large home in an affluent suburb of New York City. Again, he refused.[71] They kept in close touch over the next few years, tied together by loss and the children. They were wary of each other, yet also mutually protective. They had both loved Sylvia, both imperfectly.

When Aurelia next came to England, she was distraught about *The Bell Jar*. Hughes re-created the scene in an unpublished poem.

> In a restaurant in Hammersmith,
> . . . "How could she?
> The only good thing in the whole business
> Is that Mrs Prouty is dead & beyond
> Reading about Philomena Guinea.
> I cannot understand. I cannot. I cannot
> Understand." A lunch of stricken tears.

> Faceless, nameless hardly knowable
> Horror emerged, behind both our faces,
> ... "Why? Why? Why?
> What did I do wrong?"
> And then
> The only drug, the only mouthful that eased:
> "That psychiatrist reinvented her.
> She was shattered & that woman took
> All the bits and glued them back together
> Into a girl
> That simply wasn't my daughter.
> The person who wrote that book was not my daughter."
>
> Bitterness, pure. Helplessness. Bitterness.
> ... from that day
> Sealed my resolve never to let The Bell Jar
> Be published in America.
> She begged "never."
> And I swore: "Never." I saw
> It was enough for her, more than enough
> To deal with in secret ...
> ....
> All her pains & years of the winner's prizes
> Converted to blazing shame, by her daughter.
> As Herself sentenced for her daughter's death
> By her daughter's voice, crying from the grave.[72]

Mindful of the financial cushion the novel would provide for Frieda and Nicholas, Ted published *The Bell Jar* in America in 1971 when he realized that, because of a copyright loophole, it would come out there anyway.[73] Aurelia never forgave him.

———

AFTER SYLVIA'S DEATH, Assia had a row with Suzette, who, Assia claimed, had been "dining out on the story."[74] They would soon make up, and they pondered creating an authors' agency together—Hughes's idea—"Macedo, Hughes, & Gutmann."[75] Meanwhile, Nathaniel Tarn continued taking notes. "Hosts of women appear to have tried to work out their guilt by offering help with the children," he wrote. "A.[ssia] says she put her foot down and brought in a nanny. Things are coming back to normal." Hughes wanted to get away—"lunatic plans as usual including China"—but felt he should stay for the sake of the children. Assia told Nathaniel that Ted "wants to get her [Plath's] poems out as quickly as possible." As for Alvarez, Tarn noted his "hangdog adoration of T. H." and that "S. P. appears to have made passes at him."[76]

In early March, Assia again wavered to Nathaniel about whether to leave David. "She has taken no decision, has no one to talk to & is lost in a maze of reasons for not deciding." There were reasons, she told Tarn, not to stay with Hughes: "1) voracious sexual appetite, 2) superstitious about remarriage 3) black moods 4) lack of contact & sharing his work 5) Puritanism." She and David were no longer sleeping together, and she was pregnant with Ted's child. She probably told Hughes about the pregnancy. Yet, Tarn wrote, "the question of her pregnancy is as far as possible from an over-riding consideration. The woman for all her scheming is really fantastically naive."[77] Assia had become, he wrote, "the tragic muse!"[78] He felt that if David did not leave her, "it will cost him his life."[79] As for Assia, "she will lose herself in the Hughes mystery."[80]

In the weeks after Sylvia's suicide, Assia accompanied Ted to Heptonstall and the Beacon, where she had a massive row with his family. Billy Hughes—a Great War survivor—could not stomach Assia's German heritage and upper-class accent. Edith was scandalized by Assia's three marriages. "A [Assia] loses her temper, touchy," Hughes wrote in his notebook.

> Then a dog-fight, coming and going. Hilda high & weeping, calling A a hor [*sic*] and that kind of woman. . . . Pa & his reason: A being with me after S's death, the root of the scandal, quite correct. Hilda's irrational suspicion and antagonism against Assia . . . moral defendent of the family name, etc. . . . But how loyal she's [Assia] been and still seems to be—even against that lot. But it's easy for her to take [an] absolute stand against Hilda—for me not so.[81]

The tension between Assia and Ted's family later reached a breaking point when all were living under the same roof at Court Green in 1966.

In April 1963, Assia and David Wevill, like Sylvia and Ted before them, traveled to Ireland and stayed with Richard Murphy in Cleggan. They hoped that the trip would ease some of the tension in their marriage, but it had the opposite effect, just as it had for Plath and Hughes. The Wevills agreed to a six-month trial separation, and David left for Spain in early May. Assia moved out of the Highbury flat she had shared with her husband and into 23 Fitzroy Road. She and Ted would live there together until early fall, when he took the children to live at Court Green. When Assia and Ted stayed with

Nathaniel Tarn and his wife, Pat, on August 5–6, 1963, Assia confessed to Pat, to whom she had grown close, that she missed David terribly and that he was the only man she would ever love. "Ted is very kind but she can't stand the children," Tarn recorded. "The little girl."[82] Yet Assia's coolness may have been a pose, for in her diary she wrote of the immense pleasure she took in Nick and Frieda.[83]

In early October, Ted returned to Devon with the children. He wrote Assia from Court Green, "It's completely different down here—so strange to be here without the electrical cloud. The peace is bewildering—I spend a lot of time just standing about."[84] "The electrical cloud" was clearly tied to Plath and the tense atmosphere both had endured in the second half of 1962. Ted told Assia he was going to "try to write myself out of it." Frieda, now three and a half, had started packing her things a few days ahead of time, making sure everything she brought "would be right for Court Green." After a long car ride (both children were "angels"), they stepped out into the dark yard. Ted wrote in his notebook,

> She asked if this was it—then went into the house, quite mystified, look-
> ing about. I was wondering what she would remember. She obviously
> knew her way about, but still didn't seem to remember anything in
> particular. I can't decide whether she just took everything for granted
> as the same, or in fact simply didn't remember. But she obviously does
> remember—since she knows all the people straight off. What strange
> things must have been going on in her head though, those first few days.
> That world was so utterly different than this.[85]

WHEN DAVID WEVILL RETURNED from Spain in late October 1963, he moved into 23 Fitzroy Road with Assia, who was still seeing Ted. David and Assia would move to Belsize Park Gardens in April 1964, hoping to rekindle the marriage, to little avail.

Literary London treated Assia as a pariah after Sylvia's death; David wrote to Nathaniel Tarn in 1969 that Assia was "blamed and never forgiven."[86] Fay Weldon remembered that at literary parties, "people would turn their backs when she came into the room because they blamed her so much." Assia told Fay that Ted called her "'the dark force. You are the dark destructive force that destroyed Sylvia.' To think that she was unmoved by this, or unhaunted by this is impossible."[87] Assia was haunted, too, by Sylvia's ghost, and the knowledge that Ted still loved his dead wife. "Maybe I'll end up writing the biography of Plath," Assia told Nathaniel. She read Sylvia's journal and was surprised that the marriage was "much closer than Ted ever made out." She told Nathaniel, "Ted often misses her [Sylvia] terribly. Also caught in every sort of guilt. 'Of course there are some good days.' "[88]

Linda Gates, Alvarez's American girlfriend, remembered Assia and Ted coming round to Al's flat for dinner in 1964. Ted and Al would talk, leaving Linda with Assia. Assia never mentioned Sylvia, but Linda knew many in Al's circle blamed her for Sylvia's suicide. Linda had attended dinner parties with Al that winter at the homes of Kingsley Amis, Edna O'Brien, and John Mortimer, where everybody drank neat whiskey. The literary scene was cliquey, and she had no real friends of her own. Assia thought that this lone American might be a sympathetic ally. "Assia wanted to be my best friend," Linda remembered. She thought Assia dramatic and passionate—"She lived for love." Assia taught Linda Israeli folk songs on the guitar and spoke of her interest in literature and art. Linda found Assia "very beautiful, very troubled." Assia once told her that she should put belladonna in her eyes, like a Renaissance woman, to make her pupils dilate "orgasmically." Linda found Ted, who didn't speak much to the women, "dark, Celtic, brooding and intense." "He never smiled," she said, but recited poetry and ballads beautifully. "What a man. You could drink his blood." Assia "smoldered a lot. So did Ted."[89]

In autumn 1964, Hughes returned to Yorkshire and hiked the path to Wuthering Heights.[90] It brought him peace at a time of "wasted weeks; steady hell . . . utter emptiness."[91] He dreamed of seeing and loving Sylvia again: "ecstatic joy of her & me. Love, complete reality."[92] But there were nightmares, too. Around the second anniversary of her suicide, he had a "terrible grief dream about Sylvia, long and unending. In a house, large stone, on the moor's edge—the garden was also a cemetary [*sic*]."[93]

Assia was all too aware of how small she stood in Sylvia's shadow. In her 1963 journal she wrote,

> she had a million times the talent, 1,000 times the will, 100 times the greed and passion that I have. I should never have looked into Pandora's box, and now that I have I am forced to wear her love-widow's sacking, without any of her compensations. What, in 5 years' time, will he reproach me for? What sort of woman am I? How much time have I been given? How much time has run out?[94]

When she read Plath's new novel and 1962–63 journals, she told Suzette she was "so distressed by the cruelties and malice" that Plath had "written about her." Suzette said that Assia told Ted to destroy the journals and that Ted had "reassured" her that he would.[95] (He later claimed that he destroyed only the last journal, which covered the weeks preceding her suicide.) According to Assia's close friend Mira Hamermesh, Assia came to believe that Sylvia's suicide had been her fault: "She never, never thought otherwise."[96] Assia would feel Sylvia's "repugnant live presence" at Court Green, but she also admired her "splendid brilliance."[97]

Assia continued to miss David terribly. "What insanity, what methodically crazy compulsion drove me to sentence him to being alone, and myself to this nightmare maze of miserable, censorious, middle-aged furies, and Sylvia, my predecessor, between our heads at night," she wrote in her diary.[98] "Only David can claim me morally. . . . Reality is David, my own income. T[ed] is a long night of nightmares." She dreaded the thought of moving to Yorkshire with Ted ("the North terrifies me") and raising his children. She seemed to understand that a bleak future awaited if she stayed with Ted, yet she could not summon the will to leave him. After a row at the Beacon in spring 1963, Ted kissed her as she leaned over the table to feed Frieda. "I then flared up with enormous love," she wrote in her diary.[99]

Elizabeth Compton, who was looking after Court Green in Ted's absence, remembered Assia's first visit to the house. She came with Hughes, who was there to collect some rugs. After lunch, Assia said to Ted, "Ask her to show me around." According to Elizabeth, "Ted looked down at his place and said, 'Would you mind?' He knew damn well I'd mind. So I went with her to the sitting room and the playroom, then we went up the stairs past the door of her writing room, and she said, 'Don't you feel a traitor?' and I said, 'I certainly do, and I'm not going a step further.' And I went downstairs to where Ted was crying, actually. He was rolling up a rug and tying a string round it, and Assia came into the room and she said, 'Do you think Ted and I can be happy?' And I said, 'Never, never. Look at him, look at the state he's in.' And she had hysterics, she cried, and then he just bundled everything into the car and drove off. It was awful business."[100]

David Compton's memory of the day is similar. Ted, he recalled, was "in a state. . . . I don't know if they'd been snipping at each other all the way down in the car. Anyway, they were basket cases. He had come to pick up something, and he ended up going around that house tearing the curtains off the walls and stuffing them in the car while Assia had Elizabeth in the garden, 'Am I doing the right thing?' and 'What would you do?' And poor Ted. It must have been so dreadful, there was Sylvia's life there, and he just set about breaking it. He knew what those curtains were. . . . It was a very, very sad and too deeply felt occasion, and the only view of them we ever had—of Assia—and it wasn't a happy one. She was a very dramatic-looking woman. At that time she was tortured, feeling bad. She came down with him I suppose hoping to help, maybe, but it didn't work."[101] Elizabeth remembered

Ted weeping in the garden like Heathcliff as he dug up Sylvia's strawberry plants to take back to London.[102]

In March 1965, Assia gave birth in London to a little girl, Alexandra, whom she called Shura. Though she was still living with David, she listed Ted as the father on the birth certificate. Assia delighted in her daughter, and she left David for good in February 1966 when she, Ted, Frieda, Nick, and Shura moved to a cottage named Doonreagan in the west of Ireland, not far from Richard Murphy. The move was supposed to have been permanent—a new start—but in May 1966, Assia returned to Court Green with Ted to help care for his ailing parents.

As the years passed, Ted promised Assia that they would buy a home of their own together, but he never followed through. Still, Assia could not give him up—not even when she was living at Court Green with his parents, who sometimes refused to speak to her. Hughes was "One of God's best creatures," "the beautiful Anatomical Man," she wrote in her journal.[103] There seemed to be no way to live a life of dignity with Ted, and no way to live a fulfilled life without him. She sensed he favored Frieda and Nicholas over Shura, as if he never quite believed she was his. Assia took to spending days in bed in her nightgown or bathrobe as her depression deepened.

Alarmed, Hughes drew up a list of daily domestic duties for Assia; she was to wake at eight o'clock every morning and get dressed right away, cook new recipes each week, play with the children, and teach them German. He hoped the "orders" would rouse her from her depressive stupor—he likely knew of Assia's previous suicide attempts—but to Assia the list was just another reminder that she was not Sylvia, neither a model hausfrau nor a great poet. Jillian remembered,

> Sylvia's death "decided" her relationship with Ted as it had not been really decided before.... With Sylvia's death came (again) Romantic Inevitability—the black destiny to be lived out. She received, and bore, the responsibility for Sylvia's suicide. Ted was tragic; she was evil.... She accepted it—penance and identity all in one.... She was miserable in Devon.... Olwyn went after her as she'd gone after Sylvia only Assia had nothing to fight back with—no intelligence, no sense of entitlement.... He would neither be with Assia nor release her.[104]

According to Ted's friend Keith Sagar, Ted had told Assia he couldn't marry her until his mother passed away. Edith had "so loved Sylvia," and marriage to Assia would upset her too much.[105] Edith's health was very fragile by the mid-1960s, and Assia returned to London alone with Shura in 1967. That year Ted and Assia tried to repair their relationship, to little avail. By then, Ted had begun seeing two other local women in Devon, Brenda Hedden and Carol Orchard.

Ruth Fainlight had become close to Assia in the years since Sylvia's suicide—closer even than she had been to Sylvia—and invited Assia to Christmas in 1968 when she and Shura had nowhere to go. "Everything was awful for her. She said afterward she was going to kill herself at Christmas, but because I had invited her and was so nice, she didn't do it for a few months. Of course I didn't know that. . . . I felt so sorry for Assia. When I met her she was the demon woman, but I didn't sustain that. Then I got to know her, and I liked her. She moved me. She moved me very much."[106] Assia had translated, with Ted, some of the Israeli poet Yehuda Amichai's poems. Ruth knew Amichai well, and she remembered how impressed he had been by Assia's translations, which Assia and Ted read over the BBC. But the collaboration's success was not enough to hold the couple together.

The novelist William Trevor saw Assia a month before her suicide. By this time she was living with Shura in Clapham Common. "She'd had enough of poets," Trevor wrote.

> For the first time she called herself a displaced person, tumbled about by circumstances, and war; for the first time she confessed she had created the woman she seemed to be, teaching herself an upper-class English voice and making the most of her looks, using them as a stepping stone whenever the chance offered. She spoke of her Russian blood, of childhood in Israel, and then being shipped away to Canada and the first of her marriages. The hours she talked that night near Waterloo Station were like hours spent in a cinema. . . . she turned up the collar of a smart tweed coat and for a single instant seemed weary, as though she'd talked too long and said too much. Defeat, suddenly there, distorted her features, dragging at the corners of her mouth.
>
> "Actually I'm afraid," she murmured, before she smiled again and went away.[107]

———

IN MARCH 1969, Assia and Ted journeyed north. He read his poems at a Manchester television studio, and Assia hoped that in the following days they would find a house for themselves and the three children. But after the reading, they had a painful conversation in the pub. Hughes admitted that he could not commit to her. In her diary on March 20, Assia wrote, "'It's

Sylvia—it's because of her'—I can't answer that. No more than if it were a court sentence." Assia felt she must "die, soon. But execute yourself and your little self efficiently. But I can't believe it—any more than I could believe hearing of my own death."[108] The following day Hughes called on his parents, who had moved back to Heptonstall in the fall of 1968. He visited his mother, now in the hospital, and then returned to the Beacon to spend the night with his father. He left Assia in Haworth, where she procured a bottle of sleeping pills. The village's literary associations were painful for her: this was Brontë country, where Ted and Sylvia had played Cathy and Heathcliff on their moorland walks to Wuthering Heights. Jillian said that Assia "told people Sylvia was beckoning her."[109]

Despite their troubles of the day before, Ted picked Assia up the next day, and they looked at some houses in the area. While she fantasized about living together as a family, he found each residence unsuitable. He said good-bye to her in Manchester as she boarded a train back to London, alone. Assia's au pair remembered her looking downcast upon her return; "Mr. Hughes," the au pair said, "didn't want her anymore."[110]

The following day, March 23, 1969, Assia called Ted at Court Green shortly after receiving papers finalizing her divorce from David. She told Ted they were "just like a bad habit" and that they had "better separate for good." He had failed to give her the "hope" she needed that their relationship could work.[111] That night, Assia gassed herself and four-year-old Shura, whom she sedated with sleeping pills, in her London kitchen. Ruth Fainlight, by then one of Assia's closest friends, said, "She just didn't understand the possibility of living without a man. She wasn't equipped to."[112]

Ted arranged her funeral and cremation. "Our life together was so complicated with old ghosts, and dozens of near-separations over the years, but we belonged together so completely and so deeply," he wrote Assia's sister after her suicide.[113] He struggled with guilt and grief. "If I'd put a ring on her finger, she'd still be alive," he told Richard Murphy.[114] Nathaniel Tarn, who had watched the "Greek tragedy" unfold and had half foreseen the consequences, was appalled that no one said Kaddish for her.

Edith Hughes died shortly after Assia's suicide. Hughes would always believe that the shock killed her. David Compton remembered Hughes saying around this time, "Everything I touch dies."[115]

In 1970, Ted married Carol Orchard, who helped raise Frieda and Nicholas. The children eventually went to boarding school. Frieda became a poet and painter; Nicholas a professor in the School of Fisheries and Ocean Science at the University of Alaska. But Nicholas suffered, like his mother, from debilitating depressions. In March 2009, Nicholas Hughes hanged himself in Fairbanks, Alaska. "We say that every suicide in a family makes another one more likely," Dr. de Marneffe, who had known Sylvia at McLean, later said of Nicholas. "His mother was a model one."[116]

Hughes was all too aware of this dangerous familial inheritance. He worried about the trauma and the repercussions of Alvarez's intimate portrait of Plath's last days in *The Savage God*: "you somehow didn't remember how history tries to repeat itself even without human help, it didn't occur to you that her children are left with an even more dangerous situation than hers & with all her vulnerabilities."[117]

———

THOSE WHO SAW SYLVIA during her final months—and even those who did not—would spend years racked with guilt, wondering what more they could have done. Olive Prouty felt that she had done all she could, but it was not enough. "I am so, so sorry," she wrote Aurelia in August 1963, "that you should bear it all again—her suffering and despair. You are the one who is paying the price." In the weeks immediately after Plath's suicide, Prouty blamed Hughes. "She wasn't sunk in deep despair when she found the apartment—furnished it—took the children there. It was after Ted came back into her life again—or tried to—that the blackness returned.—And when illness sapped her strength." Prouty wrote of the group of poems published in *The New Yorker* in August 1963, "what a murderer it makes him out to be—and what a poet it makes her out to be."[118]

Ruth Fainlight learned of Plath's death in *The Observer*, in an article written by Alvarez, a week before she was to return to England from Morocco. "I was absolutely devastated," she said.[119] In a later poem, she wrote, "That poetic meeting never happened, yet / I dream about it. What more to say? Everyone / knows the story's ending."[120]

Elizabeth Compton also learned of Plath's death from Alvarez's *Observer* article. "I was absolutely appalled. . . . I had no idea she was so desperate. . . . I rang up Alvarez and I said, 'This is dreadful. Is it really true?' And he was crying and said, 'What a waste, what a waste.' "[121] Elizabeth then told her husband, David, who recalled, "I was unsurprised. . . . Just the level of intensity with which everything happened in her life—suicide was somehow an essential part of it. What else had she left?"[122]

Sylvia's old Smith friend Ellie Friedman was staying in Oxford in February 1963 and was excited to reunite with Sylvia, who had given her the phone number at Court Green. She called, but "the phone just rang and rang." When she learned what had happened, she remembered the dark confidences Sylvia had shared with her nearly a decade before about her horror of electroshock therapy: "Her terror was that it would happen again. And it might happen again, *but* she had a safety. *If* it happens, she said, 'I will kill myself. I would not hesitate.' If that's where she got to, there was nothing to save her from being committed again and having to go through electroshock therapy. . . . There is no choice. It is like the last stage of a cancer of a mind. You don't know what you're doing. You've been made crazy by the drugs. . . . I don't think the world as we know it knows what mental illness is. They understand panic attacks, they understand anxiety, they understand stress. This is a whole different thing. This is somebody walking off a cliff and falling and smashing their brain. And it happened before to her and it happened again to her. No. She cannot live through it."[123]

Marcia Brown Plumer was devastated, but she was not shocked. "Many people become depressed when they're physically ill. They haven't the energy to cope with ordinary life which, in Sylvia's case, was not ordinary. Having seen her feeling despairing and sunk, just stricken as an ordinarily charming, buoyant, creative, busy eighteen-year-old, and just totally undone by a cold, I then translated that sort of thing into her [later] reaction."[124] Another of Sylvia's Smith friends, Janet Salter Rosenberg, felt differently. "I was furious. I had never been so angry at hearing about somebody's death. Obviously she was very sick. But she'd been there before, and she had survived."[125]

Brian Cox, who had published Plath's work in the *Critical Quarterly*, was teaching a tutorial at the University of Hull when he received the call from Tony Dyson. "I found it almost unbelievable. I was too overcome to continue with the tutorial and asked the students to leave. I sat in my room, very still, too conscious of the silence. I kept thinking of Judge Brack's absurd remark after Hedda Gabler shot herself: 'People don't do such things.' "[126]

Anthony Thwaite, Louis MacNeice, and some other men were having a drink at a pub near the BBC's Broadcasting House when Douglas Cleverdon walked in, "enormously shaken," and told them about Plath's death. One of the men at the table made an appalling remark ("women poets, what do you expect?"). MacNeice "rounded on the man" and told him to shut up. Thwaite felt "colossal shock" that this "quick," "capable, social" person he had grown to know through her BBC work had committed suicide.[127] Edward Lucie-Smith took a harder view. "Sylvia's suicide more than most suicides was a calculated act of revenge. . . . it was in the end effective."[128] Richard Murphy, too, felt her suicide was "an unforgiving blow aimed through herself at Ted."[129]

On March 4, 1963, Aurelia wrote a letter to *The Observer* thanking Sylvia's friends and neighbors for their help. She ended, "Those who systematically and deliberately destroyed her know who they are."[130] Aurelia never sent the letter. By the time she published *Letters Home*, Aurelia ascribed her daughter's suicide to "some darker day than usual." Lorna Secker-Walker agreed: "One must think of her suicide as a moment of madness, and not really relevant to her life, in a sense. Not what her life was about, really."[131]

Aurelia ended an early draft of *Letters Home* with three lines from "Elm" that seemed to predict her own torment:

> I am inhabited by a cry.
> Nightly it flaps out
> Looking, with its hooks, for something to love.

Nearly a year after Sylvia's death, Aurelia told her friend Miriam Baggett, "There are not many who realized the rare treasure I had in my relationship with Sylvia and, therefore, few have any conception of the depth and scope of the loss."[132] Two years later, she spoke more candidly about her grief. She was facing her first spring in five years without seeing Frieda and Nick, and Warren lived three hours away in Westchester County, New York, where he worked at IBM. She had nursed her father through his final years, as he lost his mind to dementia, and had not told him about Sylvia's death. At times she had wished for him to comfort her, but by then, "he was the child, clinging to my hand; and in holding it, I did, at least, feel his love."[133] Now she was on her own in the house where she had once lived with her parents and children, and the solitude was becoming hard to bear. She could function well enough at Boston University when she was teaching others. As she wrote to Miriam,

> When I am alone . . . it is so difficult for me to organize my tasks, to accomplish anything, to concentrate. I often just dissolve into violent weeping, feeling the past crowding in upon me with the accumulated tragedies of the years. Oh, I lecture myself, chiding myself—my health is good; I have my sight; I am blessed having Warren reasonably free of being drafted for this war that just seems senseless to me. I hear his voice weekly over the phone.
>
> It just happens that all my friends here have either husbands still and/or children and grandchildren about them. I feel at times like the Ancient Mariner, walking among fulfilled people with an invisible, but very weighty, albatross about my neck!

Three months later, she told Miriam life had become a "nightmare" as she dealt with Ted and *The Bell Jar:* "this guilt-ridden man, publishing what should never have seen the light of day, to 'establish a fund for the children' and, of course, may thereby damage them irreparably. . . . It is taking all my faith, all my strength to work on seeing 'Life steadily and to see it whole.' "[134]

Aurelia confided to Miriam, too, about her anxiety regarding the children, especially Nick. "Frieda could talk and question: Nick could not—nor can sufficiently yet, and he is a bewildered frustrated child." She worried that Olwyn, with no children of her own and rather "bohemian," was the wrong person to raise them. Aurelia's siblings urged her not to spend her hard-earned savings on transatlantic trips, but she was desperate to stay in her grandchildren's lives. "Somehow I must manage to go over again. They must gradually come to understand that their mother's people exist, that they love them, and that we would always be ready to make a home for them with us." Thoughts of Frieda and Nick kept her alive, she said. Earlier in life, over a fifteen-year period, she had faced the prospect of dying when she suffered internal hemorrhages, but Robert Browning's poem "Prospice" had seen her through. Her experience, as she described it, sounds close to Plath's in "Tulips": "it was always 'one fight more' for the sake of my children. I kept their faces before me, struggling against that temptation to let myself go with the ebbing tide. In other ways, it is still 'one fight more,' the reason not defined, even within me, but the dim sense that maybe, *maybe* those two little ones across the sea might need me."

Privately, Aurelia blamed Sylvia's death on Ted, whose letters to her at Indiana University are full of her angry marginalia. But later she softened her stance and shifted blame to Dr. Beuscher, whom Ted would also come to blame. Aurelia was angry at her daughter, too. In the margin of Judith Kroll's book on Plath's poetry, which Kroll sent to her in the mid-seventies, Aurelia noted that she had always tried to foster her daughter's independence—not so that Sylvia could be free of her, but so that she could free herself from Sylvia. Near a discussion of Plath's poem "Medusa," Aurelia scribbled, "And I worked constantly to free her & encouraged every act of independence! I worked to be free of her & at least live *my* life—not to be drawn into the complexities & crises of hers. I loved spending time with the children—but wanted freedom which Sylvia refused to grant. *She*, in summer '62 showed me a house where she wished me to retire—in Eng!!" In another section of Kroll's book, Plath's distraught mother wrote, "I sent her to camp, let her go to Smith instead of Wellesley College, rejoiced in her Fulbright!! *I* wanted to be free at last!"[135]

In 1976, Aurelia identified the problems of biographical readings in a public lecture for the Authors' Series Talk of the Wellesley College Club:

Sylvia developed her triple literary dictum, which she told me to keep in mind whenever I read any of her creations.

First: The manipulation of experience

Second: Fusion of characters (creation of composite characters)

Third: Her firm belief that "art was a rearrangement of truth."

She had a fantastic memory . . . and a developing psychic insight that she tried to deny, tossing it off as coincidental awareness, but would connect a fragment of her past experience, perhaps one from very early childhood, with imaginary events or universal themes or historic happenings, often resulting in a bizarre, yet strangely enough, credible combination that fused and came alive.[136]

Her tone was less neutral when she spoke openly to friends about her daughter's writing. She told her friend Richard Larschan, "I had written her a very, very affectionate letter for her 30th birthday, and she wrote that stinking poem. She wrote a complete lie in that terrible 'Medusa.' Why she ever wrote anything so cruel . . ."[137] She felt similarly about "The Disquieting Muses." She once told a biographer that the only Sylvia she knew was the "Sylvia revealed in her own letters."[138] The private self of Plath's journals was unknown to her. To Miriam she wrote in 1966, "There is always in my heart the memory of a healthy, bouncing baby who, when she could first form words, greeted me each morning, standing erect in her crib, shouting, 'Happy Day, Mummy! Happy Day!' "[139]

Aurelia was proud of her daughter's achievements, but she never escaped her legacy. In 1984, ten years before her death, Aurelia moved into North Hill, an upscale retirement home in Newton, Massachusetts. She felt she had trouble making friends because of *The Bell Jar*. Bill and Mildred Norton also lived in North Hill, which made her "uncomfortable."[140] Hughes had predicted that Aurelia would have a difficult time coming to terms with Sylvia's portrayal of her in the novel. In the late eighties, he wrote of the painful dynamic between mother and daughter in his "Trial" sequence:

Surely you were unjust to your mother.

Surely she has never found, or suspected,
One fault in her care, in her anguish
Over protecting you.
Yes, you knew that. Long & surely
You had assessed her sacrifice. Yes.
And you knew you had to protect her.
From the behaviour of the dangerous child

Buried in you. Protect her from the heart
You had given your father.
You knew you had to. But you failed to.[141]

Aurelia wrote to the biographer Paul Alexander in 1983 that her daughter's "loss is a constant pain, one that no critic of her writing has ever seemed to sense fully." Yet, she added, "I find some measure of solace in the thought that her genius, evident in both her poetry and prose, will endure."[142]

Aurelia Plath never lost her faith in humankind's potential for goodness. "And as you and I believe," she wrote Miriam in the depths of grief, "whatever the cost, the awareness, the leaping up of the heart must remain with us."[143]

―――――――

"I THINK WE CAN NOW reconstruct what happened," Eric Walter White wrote to Jack Sweeney shortly after Plath's suicide. "Recently her mental condition started to deteriorate as a result of the break-up of her marriage with Ted. Or the marriage with Ted started to break up as a result of the deterioration of her mental condition. Perhaps she wrote *The Bell Jar* as an explanation for her friends. Perhaps the very act of writing it and reliving those dreaded months of mental breakdown ten years ago helped open the wound."[144] And so it began. How could such a "charming, brilliant woman," as White called her, leave behind her two young children at the height of her career? Friends and family thought there had been a mistake. One speculated that she had been murdered. Aurelia initially told friends and neighbors that Sylvia had died of pneumonia.[145] Anita Helle, Otto Plath's great-niece, would hear from her family, growing up, that "Plath committed suicide because she was exhausted and discouraged from having had the flu too long."[146] Wilbury Crockett initially refused to believe that Sylvia had killed herself.[147] When he came to terms with the truth, he wrote to Aurelia, "Not a day goes by that does not bring the question—'Why?' I grieve more than I can say."[148]

Though Hughes and Alvarez, the two men at the center of the last years of Plath's life, later changed their minds about their initial theory that she wanted to be saved, Alvarez never believed the argument that Plath had "a sick and fragile personality" and was destined to repeat her 1953 suicide attempt. "Edge," he noted, "is not the work of someone who is 'out of her mind'; or governed by rogue 'brain chemistry.'"[149] He and Hughes came to believe that she had tapped too deeply into her creative powers, releasing emotions she was not equipped to handle. "A combination of forces, some chosen deliberately, others chosen for her, had brought her to the point where she was able to write as from her true centre about the forces that really moved her: destructive, volatile, demanding, a world apart from everything she had been trained to admire," Alvarez wrote.[150] For both men, Plath was defeated not by depression but by quasi-literary forces. Her grief for her unmourned father "came flooding out," said Alvarez, and conquered her.[151] Hughes, in his writings, portrayed his wife's suicidal drive as a dark, subconscious force that engulfed her as she dove deeper and deeper into the mausoleum of her grief for Otto. Both understood Plath's death in Romantic, Freudian terms: a "genius" artist overcome by her demons, lost on her courageous journey to the center of the Minotaur's lair.

Privately, Hughes was less sure. In the days immediately after, he blamed himself. He told Olwyn in the spring of 1963 that he had stifled his behavior with Sylvia to such an extent that his resentment exploded in a "stupid act of will" that was "the ruin of Sylvia."[152] Yet he soon blamed others, especially Sylvia's "acquaintances" like Suzette and Jillian, who "drove her over" and "disturbed" her mind with "gossip."[153] He told Jillian and Gerry Becker they "should have kept her another day or two" at their house.[154]

Later, he began to consider more seriously the role mental illness had played. "Everybody seems sympathetic," he told Olwyn in February 1963. "Sylvia didn't exactly conceal her temperament."[155] Roughly two months after her suicide, he wrote in his notebook:

How much did depression—from Health, exhaustion, etc,—instead of foreboding, promote the final disaster: crystallizing into pronouncements absolute in character. . . . How much did superstition set the stage?

How powerfully previous examples compelled the course of the disaster: Her obsession with P. Geagh's wife.[156]

How general ideas, general notions—especially psycholog. ones, Jung etc, governed my actions: like edicts. The individuation idea; my ideas concerning her dependence & its effect on me.

How much was she my test—which I failed. How much was I hers.

How absolute her pride was. How absolute my inability to imagine she might be deceiving me in her pride. Her forcing the divorce—that was deceiving herself.

Horror of the person who has seen what we are ashamed of & tried to hide.[157]

Hughes never forgave Ruth Beuscher for persuading Plath to seek a divorce in September 1962. After Plath's death, he found a marked-up copy of Erich Fromm's *The Art of Loving* in her flat. Near her inscription of "November 9, 1962," on the frontispiece, either he or Assia wrote "Sept. 1963" and listed the pages Plath had aggressively underlined.[158] These passages were about sadism, masochism, and womanizing, and all seemed to accuse Hughes. He later learned that Dr. Beuscher had recommended the book to Sylvia. Dr. Beuscher, for her part, recklessly revealed Plath's early medical records to at least two biographers in the 1970s.

By the mid-1980s, Hughes would tell Anne Stevenson that "the key factor" in Plath's suicide was the antidepressant, which, Aurelia had told him, had been tried on Sylvia after her first suicide attempt and that "it induced such an extreme suicidal reaction, in the gap between doses," that she had been instructed by Sylvia's doctors "never to allow it to be given to S[ylvia] under any circumstances."[159] This explanation was a far cry from his earlier psychoanalytical approaches. "It's too facile to regard her death as some inevitable culmination of her inspiration," he wrote Stevenson in 1986. "Her death was the remotest fluke, an unbelievably freakish sequence of unlucky coincidences."[160] He tried as best he could to salvage light from darkness. In a tattered notebook in the British Library lies an early draft of his poem "Remission" (then called "Delivering Frieda"), in which he asked,

> Why did you abandon it? Did her birth
> Give you freedom to die? Did her existence
> Shed you so utterly? Did you smuggle
> Every good thing of yourself, every joyful
> And happy thing of yourself, out with her—?
>
> Her body is the symmetry
>
> Of your dying & death.
>
> She has grown. In her you have grown.
> Again different. But the flare of your fingers
> Has come back, your joyful beseeching hope
> That the good things will happen, has come back—[161]

SYLVIA'S FIRST WORDS on awakening from her suicide attempt in 1953 offered an explanation for her act. "It was my last act of love," she said. She claimed that she had wanted to spare her family from the burdens and humiliations of her disease, and protect herself from a life locked away in the dark bowels of a charity hospital. The second time, the desire to spare her children, and herself, from the ravages of depression was more urgent. She knew Dr. Horder would be admitting her to a psychiatric hospital and this time there would be no limousine to McLean, and no sympathetic young woman psychiatrist like Ruth Beuscher. Sylvia could not afford an expensive private hospital, and she was too proud to ask Mrs. Prouty for help again. She knew Aurelia would bankrupt herself trying to arrange private care. In her February 4 letter to Dr. Beuscher, she claimed that her feelings of animosity toward Ted had receded. It was depression, and its "cures," which terrified her: "What appals [sic] me is the return of my madness, my paralysis, my fear & vision of the worst—cowardly withdrawal, a mental hospital, lobotomies."[162]

In America, free psychiatric care meant substandard care: the dreaded state hospital of her nightmares. Sylvia would have feared "Dickensian" psychiatric treatment in England even more than she had in America, which had a comparatively more progressive approach toward mental illness in the 1960s. She liked and trusted Dr. Horder, but he was not a psychiatrist. Alvarez remembered that Plath had been reluctant to schedule a consultation with a proper psychiatrist, as Horder had advised. "Having been bitten once by American psychiatry, she hesitated for some time before writing for an appointment. But her depression did not lift, and eventually the letter was sent."[163] When she finally did agree to see a psychiatrist, she asked Horder to find her a woman. This was, presumably, the initial psychiatrist he had tried to contact at St. George's Hospital. But the female psychiatrist's letter never arrived at Fitzroy Road. The possibility of admittance to a mental hospital would have likely meant that an unknown, male doctor would be making treatment decisions for her—treatment that might include electroshock.

Alvarez, in his memoir, hints at what Plath herself suggested many times—that her disastrous round of shock treatment at Valley Head may have left her with post-traumatic stress disorder. Aurelia alluded to this condition in a letter to a biographer, writing that Sylvia's "obsessive return to the period of emotional confusion and the horror of that first shock treatment" frightened her: "I so longed for her to free herself from these memories."[164] Hughes later wrote to a correspondent that the "mismanaged" shock treatment "goes straight to the fundamental catastrophe—as she herself understood it." The experience had "pervaded everything she was & did."[165] Plath's terror of depression was one of the cruelest symptoms of depression itself. It is likely no accident that she killed herself on the very day she was supposed to be admitted to a psychiatric hospital—"a home," as Eric Walter White put it—where she had every reason to assume she would lose control of her autonomy.[166] Alvarez recognized the appeal of suicide in such a terrifying context. "Some kind of minimal freedom—the freedom to die in one's own way and in one's own time—has been salvaged from the wreck of all those unwanted necessities."[167]

————

SYLVIA PLATH SOUGHT ALWAYS the light of the mind. That light was her lodestar in the face of depression, when all went "cold and planetary."[168] She tried to feed this clarion flame with literature, art, philosophy, drama, travel, love—anything to prevent its extinguishment. Plath told friends that it was the final dimming of that light, the threat of exile from her own person, that had led her to attempt suicide in 1953. "When you're crazy, that's all you ever are," she told Ellie Friedman in 1954.[169] Plath's last letter to Dr. Beuscher reveals that she thought she was on the verge of another breakdown that would leave her permanently incapacitated. The prospect of losing her sanity seems to have made her consider suicide sometime in late January, when she burst into Trevor Thomas's flat in tears and told him that she did not want to die.

But there may have been a stronger impetus for Plath's final act—stronger, even, than depression: maternal love. In "Delivering Frieda," an early draft of Hughes's poem "Remission," he wrote,

> That last poem you ~~wrote~~ designed, modelling your death,
> You planned to take <include> her with you. You wrote
> "She is taking them with her."
> Poetic justice crossed it out cancelled poetic frenzy.
> You went on alone. Now erase delete
> That line utterly. Reabsorb
> Into unbeing every letter of it—
> Let your last sea-cold kiss evaporate
> From the salt affliction.[170]

Hughes was talking about the first draft of "Edge," where Plath had written, and then crossed out, "She is taking them with her." But he was also referring to something else. According to Ted and Olwyn, who both read Sylvia's last journal, Sylvia had contemplated taking her children "with her" when she committed suicide.[171] This was one of the reasons Hughes claimed to have burned part of Plath's last journal.[172]

Thoughts of harming one's children are symptomatic of severe postpartum depression, known as postpartum psychosis, which in 20 percent of cases can last "beyond the first year after delivery."[173] Mothers with a history of depression are at much greater risk of developing postpartum depression, as Dr. Beuscher had warned Sylvia in the late 1950s. Plath had a history of such psychosis; she had fantasized about killing her mother during her first breakdown, and had told her friend Catherine Frankfort that she thought she was suffering from postpartum depression in the winter of 1962–63.[174] "I am terrified by this dark thing / That sleeps in me," Plath wrote in "Elm." "All day I feel its soft, feathery turnings, its malignity." She may have used what she thought were her last remnants of lucidity and free will to protect her children from herself. For Sylvia Plath knew what happened when the light went out. She had tapped that bottom. She had been there.

A Poet's Epitaph

What can I tell you
Of the life after death?
Of how the year old boy cries all the time,
And cries as the spoon is pushed into his mouth
With disembodied hand
Of how the three year old girl is pale
With the wound she cannot
Touch or see or feel[1]

—Ted Hughes

W hen Sylvia Plath disappeared in August 1953, more than 250 newspaper articles covered the search for the missing Smith beauty. After her death in February 1963, there was just one brief news mention of her "tragic" suicide in the *Saint Pancras Chronicle*, buried deep amid articles about shoplifters and road improvements.[2] The article described the "30-year-old authoress Mrs. Sylvia Plath Hughes, wife of one of Britain's best known modern poets, Ted Hughes." Gas poisoning was a common way for women to kill themselves in mid-century London.[3] The death of a thirty-year-old mother did not merit much attention.

Al Alvarez changed that. On February 17 he published an anguished essay on Plath, titled "A Poet's Epitaph," in *The Observer*. Below a photograph of Plath holding her infant daughter were four astonishing poems: "Edge," "The Fearful," "Kindness," and "Contusion."[4] Alvarez wrote that Plath "died suddenly" at age thirty and that the four poems were all written within a few days of her death. The photo of the young mother seemed to move readers as much as the poems themselves. On the day the article appeared, Nathaniel Tarn wrote in his diary, "A shock, not because of the poems which have moved into Hughes's latest style, but because of P's face. Is it lovely? Yes almost, though perhaps not in detail. It is v. young & fresh & untortured."[5]

With a few poignant and persuasive sentences, Alvarez set the terms of Plath's posthumous reputation: "In the last few months she had been writing continuously almost as though possessed." He called her a "genius" and claimed that her recent poetry "represents a totally new breakthrough in modern verse, and establishes her, I think, as the most gifted woman poet of our time. . . . The loss to literature is inestimable." Although Hughes would later publish and promote Plath's poetry, he was too shell-shocked in the days after Plath's suicide to speak publicly about her death. As her estranged husband, his involvement with her poetic legacy would be complicated and controversial. Alvarez's slate was clean—or so it seemed. He, too, of course, was haunted by guilt. He would later ponder his own role in Plath's suicide, wondering "if all our rash chatter about art and risk and courage, and the way we turned rashness and despair into a literary principle, hadn't egged her on."[6] Privately, he may have wondered if his romantic rejection of Plath had also played a part. But in those early days and weeks, it was Alvarez who rescued Plath from obscurity and who staked his reputation on hers. He would broadcast *The Poetry of Sylvia Plath* on the BBC in July 1963 and discuss her again on the BBC's prestigious Third Programme the following year, whetting readers' appetites for more.[7] Alvarez's *Observer* article helped create the conditions by which Plath achieved one of her deepest ambitions—a mass audience, best-sellerdom. The public became fascinated by the doomed genius. Who was this "fresh" "untortured" young mother staring back at them? What had gone wrong?

In early March 1963, the controller of the BBC Third Programme sent an internal memo to Douglas Cleverdon—who had taken Plath's children to the zoo the day before she died—suggesting that they tone down their coverage of Sylvia Plath: it was not as if T. S. Eliot had died.[8] But momentum was building, and negotiations proceeded quickly. In mid-March, David Machin asked Hughes about publishing another collection of Plath's poetry. Heinemann also wanted to print four thousand more copies of *The Bell Jar* as a Book Club selection; a second Heinemann edition of the novel, under the name Victoria Lucas, was published in 1964 (though Hughes gave Heinemann permission to drop the pseudonym in March 1963).[9] The pseudonym was finally dropped in 1966 when Faber and Faber republished the novel under Plath's real name. Because Plath had died intestate, Hughes was her literary executor—a source of great bitterness to Aurelia.

Hughes began sending out Plath's work, or what remained of it. He hinted that "so-called friends" had stolen many of Plath's manuscripts in the weeks following her suicide.[10] He may have destroyed her last novel, as Assia had wished, as well as her journals from 1960 to 62, though in 1981 Hughes told Alvarez that the journals had "walked, not too long ago."[11] Hughes himself gave mixed messages: he said publicly that he had destroyed Plath's final 1963 journal to protect her children, though he later hinted to the critic Jacqueline Rose that it might still exist.

He was a better steward of Plath's late poems, which began to appear in print in 1963. After Alvarez's article, editors who had turned down Plath's recent work began to reconsider. In April, Peter Davison published "The Arrival of the Bee Box" and "Wintering" in *The Atlantic*, while *The London Magazine* published the seven poems they had accepted before Plath's death. In August, more major poems trickled into publication: "Fever 103°," "Purdah," and "Eavesdropper" in *Poetry;* seven, including "Elm" ("The Elm Speaks") and "The Moon and the Yew Tree," in *The New Yorker*. In October a slew of new poems appeared in *Encounter* and *The Review*, including "Lady Lazarus," "Daddy," and "Ariel."[12] Hughes began negotiations with Faber and Faber in the fall of 1963 to publish *Ariel*. Plath had discussed the cover with Hughes before her death, telling him she wanted a red background with large black print. She had "played with" the idea of having the emblem of a Mongolian horseman riding into a sunrise, or of a rose, on the cover. (She told Hughes she had a distant Mongolian ancestor.)[13] Plath's legacy was now largely in the hands of Alvarez and Hughes, two of the most influential literary men in England. Only T. S. Eliot could have done more for her.

Plath's new poems stunned and confused readers. When Donald Hall demurred in a 1963 review that some of them were too "shocking," Hughes defended Plath. "What a feat! For a change, and at last, somebody's written in blood. Whatever you say about them, you know they're what every poet wishes he or she could do. . . . When poems hit so hard, surely you ought to find reasons for their impact, not argue yourself out of your bruises."[14] Hughes wrote similarly to Keith Sagar about *Ariel* in 1981: "You suggest you find much of it a language of disintegration. I see it as footwork & dexterity—the honest (nakedness) to meet the matter on its own terms, & the brave will to master it—which she did."[15]

The poems achieved exactly what both Plath and Hughes had worked for during the years of their marriage, and Hughes could not help but regard them with a certain propriety. In a letter to his old English teacher John Fisher, he wrote, "Nobody writes like that or ever has done. If any of it is thanks to me, as it may be a little bit, then some of it is thanks to you."[16] In October 1963, Robert Lowell wrote to Elizabeth Bishop—the two were then America's most influential poets—of the poems' force:

Have you read the posthumous poems by Sylvia Plath? A terrifying and stunning group has come out in the last *Encounter*. You probably know the story of her suicide. The poems are all about it. They seem as good to me as Emily Dickinson at the moment. Of course they are as extreme as one can bear, rather more so, but whatever wrecked her life somehow gave an edge, freedom and even control, to her poetry. There's a lot of surrealism which relieves the heat of direct memory, touches me, and I'm pretty sure touches your quiet and humor. She is far better certainly than Sexton or Seidel, and almost makes one feel at first reading that almost all other poetry is about nothing. Still, it's searingly extreme, a triumph by a hair, that one almost wished had never come about.[17]

Lowell had picked up on something essential in Plath's work—its "surrealism"—but the word that would most often be used to describe these new poems was "confessional." In death Plath would be repatriated. Critics, including Alvarez, would link her with fellow American "confessionals" like Lowell and Sexton, rather than the British husband with whom she had shared her life and work for six years. Alvarez's admiration for Plath only increased with time. When Hughes sent him Plath's *Collected Poems* in 1981, he wrote back, "It's a wonderful book & confirms what I've always believed: she's a major poet—by any standards of any age."[18] Alvarez came to feel that Plath's poetry had stood the test of time much better than Hughes's.[19]

In 1965, Hughes published *Ariel* with Faber and Faber. While he largely preserved the original order of Plath's poems, he removed "The Rabbit Catcher," "Thalidomide," "Barren Woman," "A Secret," "The Jailer," "The Detective," "Magi," "Lesbos," "The Other," "Stopped Dead," "Purdah," and "Amnesiac." Most of these poems were personally damaging to him and Assia—though he did not cut "Daddy." He also added thirteen poems that Plath had written, though not included in *Ariel*, in 1962–63, among them "Sheep in Fog," "Balloons," "Kindness," "Words," and "Edge." Plath had ended *Ariel* with the hopeful poem "Wintering," whose last word is "spring." The last three poems Hughes chose for the first published edition of *Ariel*—"Contusion," "Edge," and "Words"—suggested, instead, depression and suicide. Because Hughes had omitted many of the fiery, taunting poems aimed squarely at him (Plath told Mrs. Prouty, for instance, that "Amnesiac" was about Ted: "The little toy wife— / Erased, sigh, sigh"), the tone of Hughes's *Ariel* was bleaker than Plath's original manuscript. Feminist critics such as Marjorie Perloff took note, and the decision would come to haunt him.

Ariel sold fifteen thousand copies in ten months. (The loose poems Plath had left on her desk, presumably the beginnings of a third book of poetry, would eventually be collected in her 1981 *Collected Poems*.) There was no mention of Plath's suicide in the short biography that appeared on the book jacket. The 1966 U.S. Harper & Row edition, however, included a melodramatic introduction by Robert Lowell, who characterized Plath as Medea hurtling toward her own destruction, "playing Russian roulette with six cartridges in the cylinder."[20] M. L. Rosenthal, the critic who coined the term "confessional poetry," published a review of *Ariel* titled "Poets of the Dangerous Way," in which he suggested that the extremities of the age were enough to kill a "sensitive" poet who was "brave enough to face it directly."[21] George Steiner wrote a now-famous review, "Dying Is an Art," in which he wondered whether Plath had the right to appropriate the Holocaust in poems like "Daddy" and "Lady Lazarus." A 1966 *Time* magazine article, "The Blood Jet Is Poetry," sealed the myth. "Daddy" appeared alongside an article about "a pretty young mother of two children . . . found in a London flat with her head in the oven and the gas jets wide open."[22] Sylvia Plath was soon a household name, and *Ariel* would go on to sell hundreds of thousands of copies.

Alvarez had planted the seeds of this myth in his *Observer* article with loaded phrases like "peculiar genius" and "possessed." He would later characterize Plath as a "priestess emptied out by the rites of her cult."[23] In the 1970s, the British poet James Fenton pushed back against Alvarez's "extremist" aesthetic:

> He tells you, in the somberest notes,
>   If poets want to get their oats
> The first step is to slit their throats,
>   The way to divide
> The sheep of poetry from the goats
>   Is suicide.[24]

Other poets and critics, including even Rosenthal, began to deride this "extremism" in literary essays and reviews. But the public perception of Plath as witchy death-goddess had been born and would not soon die.

In 1971, *The Bell Jar* was published in America by Harper & Row under Plath's real name. To date, the novel has sold almost four million copies; about 100,000 copies are sold each year in the U.S. It has become an American classic. In the 1970s, the women's movement began to embrace Plath, whose poems and prose started to appear in *McCall's*, *Ms.*, *Cosmopolitan*, and *Redbook* as well as *The New Yorker*. Hughes felt that the movement had misunderstood Plath when they made her their "Patron Saint" and that she was being used as a pawn to suit political goals she would not have supported.[25] Plath was, he said, "'Laurentian,' not 'women's lib.'"[26] Gravesian muse, warrior saint, or avenging angel, Plath had become a cipher for competing visions of the woman artist. "The notion that she, S., can ever be anything but a mythological figure, adaptable to everybody's metaphysics, has long passed," wrote Hughes to Ruth Fainlight and Alan Sillitoe in the 1980s.[27]

Throughout the 1970s and '80s, Ted and Olwyn made life difficult for hopeful Plath biographers. Hughes detested the biographical genre. "But how can people who boast of their integrity have the effrontery to draw conclusions about the lives of people they never met—how can they float those assured statements on such an absolute lack of any sense of the truth!" he wrote the Sillitoes.[28] His opinion hardly mattered to the protesters who began showing up at his readings. After the feminist poet Robin Morgan accused him in verse of Plath's murder, he stopped going to America, which he called in a 1989 letter to Bill Merwin "enemy country," and leaned on a circle of close, protective friends that included Daniel Huws, Luke Myers, Ruth Fainlight, Alan Sillitoe, the Macedos, Bill and Dido Merwin, Susan Schaefer, Seamus Heaney, and Doris Lessing.[29]

In 1976, Aurelia released *Letters Home*, a selection of Sylvia's letters to her. Hughes, who held Plath's copyright, had allowed her to do so to offset the indignities of *The Bell Jar*, which he still felt guilty about publishing in America. Plath scholars soon discovered that portions of many letters in which Plath expressed anger or complained of illness had been cut. The book seemed a betrayal, for it gave the impression of a cheerful young woman who had never known depression, much less attempted suicide. This was exactly Aurelia's point—the world knew Sylvia Plath as a dark, cynical depressive "case," and she wanted to show that her daughter was not Esther Greenwood.

Her efforts backfired, and Aurelia again became the woman who silenced Plath's mercurial voice in death as she had in life. Ted later blamed himself for allowing Aurelia to reinvent "Sylvia as the ideal & angelic daughter" at the expense of her "diabolical side." He had conspired to create this image in his "long defence of Aurelia's feelings" as well as his children's "image of their mother." In doing so, he wrote Luke Myers, he had unwittingly "promoted the cult which interpreted my continued silence in the blazing martyr-light shed by Sylvia's consecrated image. In which light I could only appear as a demon, the villain, the cause of all Sylvia's pains."[30]

Aurelia maintained that Ted had pressured her to make the cuts.[31] She wrote to Miriam Baggett in 1974 that she submitted a full, uncensored one-thousand-page manuscript to the publishers. Although she knew it would be cut down substantially, she expressed frustration with the final product.

"There are many cuts over which I sorrow, but I keep telling myself that I must remember I could have been forbidden to do the job at all." She complained too of the endless hair-splitting over the identities of Sylvia's friends and associates, and the editor's constant fear of libel lawsuits. "The *next* book I write," she told Miriam, "will be free of all censorship."[32] In fact, Aurelia, Ted, and the book's editor, Frances McCullough, were collectively responsible for the cuts, but Aurelia bore the blame for the book's shortcomings. When Ted allowed Sylvia's abridged journals to be published in 1982, Aurelia again felt betrayed, this time for different reasons: "the entire contents of THE JOURNALS were a terrible shock to me," she wrote to Ted's wife Carol. "She kept one part of her 'double' experience completely private."[33]

Ted felt increasingly haunted by Sylvia's ghost, anxious about her growing fame and its effect on her children: "instead of letting go of the past and living for the future, you find your past in front of you. A monument, sitting on your head."[34] In 1969, he began writing secret poems to and about his dead wife. Some of them were intimate memories—picking daffodils, walks through Grantchester. Others blamed people and places for Sylvia's death: Otto, Assia, Ruth Beuscher, Court Green itself. Still others registered Hughes's discomfort with his own fixed place in Plath's glare. "So here we sit in your mausoleum / While they swing their cameras across / So here we act you / Our lives displaced by your death."[35]

After Assia's suicide, he began to admit that he, too, struggled with, as he put it, "depressions." "It has occurred to me that I am at bottom the gloomy one," he wrote his brother Gerald in 1969. "People who live with me contract the gloom from me, but they don't have the supports that I have to defend themselves from it."[36] His archived notebooks contain unpublished poems of self-admonishment:

> Heart anchors in yesterday, maybe has sunk.
> Why am I compelled to this same
> Crime over and over like a ghost
> Trying to expiate?
> I have no eternity to wear out—
> Just a few years.
>
> Why can I not say: it was a mistake.
> Before God, it was a mistake.
> Yes, it cost a life. It was a mistake.
> It cost two lives—three. It was a mistake.
> Why go on slavishly leaving her

Leaving my happiness, which she is, she is.
Leaving her over and over. Going back
And leaving her weeping again, over and over.

It feels like bewilderment and it is.
It moves me like a puppet, and I am.
In this I have lost freedom.
I have lost power to dream, I am my dream.[37]

When Jane Anderson sued the Sylvia Plath estate for libel in 1982—
Anderson objected to the portrayal of Joan Gilling, based on herself, as a
lesbian in the 1979 film adaptation of *The Bell Jar*—Hughes was deposed
in Boston.[38] The barrage of legal questions on the nature of fiction versus
autobiography brought back memories of Plath writing *The Bell Jar* in 1961.
These memories prompted poems, some of which Hughes wrote during the
trial itself in Boston in 1987 and which he collected in a long sequence called
"Trial." The poems were full of ruminations about the psychological pressures he believed Plath tried to tame as she wrote her novel.

Publishing poems about his dead wife had once seemed "unthinkable"
to him—"so raw, so vulnerable, so unprocessed."[39] The Oxford don Craig
Raine initially dissuaded Hughes from publishing one of them, and Hughes
responded that he might as well "burn the whole lot."[40] Raine convinced
him not to burn them in 1997, and Hughes finally published many of these
poems (though not those in the "Trial" sequence) as *Birthday Letters* in 1998,
a few months before his death from cancer. By then, he had been poet laureate for fourteen years, and become friendly with Prince Charles; he was
appointed a member of the Order of Merit by Queen Elizabeth II in 1998.
He had all the recognition Sylvia had ever hoped for him, but it was not until
he published *Birthday Letters* that he began to feel unburdened by Sylvia's
and Assia's suicides. "My high-minded principal [*sic*] was simply wrong—for
my own psychological & physical health," he wrote Keith Sagar in 1998. "It
was stupid."[41] He felt a great sense of relief and wished that he had published
the book sooner. "If only I could have got it off my back thirty years ago!" he
told the poetry critic Michael Schmidt. "But then I was full of high-minded
reasons not to. Getting sick made it all clear, finally."[42] As he wrote to his son
Nicholas in 1998, since Plath's suicide he had been "living on the wrong side
of the glass door.

That thickening thickening glass window between me and that real self
of mine which was trapped in the unmanageable experience of what had
happened with her and me. And so—because I could never break up the

log-jam . . . never open the giant plate glass door of it, <u>that real self of mine could never get on with its life</u>, could never join me and help me get on with my life.

Publishing the poems helped him, he wrote, experience "a freedom of imagination I've not felt since 1962."[43] Many critics remonstrated with Hughes for eliding his own role in Plath's suicide. Yet the book was wildly successful, and became one of the best-selling poetry collections of all time. "God knows what sort of book it is," Hughes wrote Sagar, "but at least none of it is faked."[44]

————

IN HER FIRST DRAFT of "Edge," Plath wrote, "Now nothing can happen / We stiffen in the air like beacons / At the road's end."[45] These lines suggest the end of an exhausting, anticlimactic quest. On the day she wrote them Plath may have felt that she had come to "the road's end" in her life and in her work. Yet the surreal grandeur of "Edge"—indeed all of *Ariel* and the 1963 poems—opened up new aesthetic possibilities that would change the direction of modern poetry. Plath's posthumously published *Collected Poems*, gathered and edited by Hughes, won the Pulitzer Prize in 1982.

With each passing decade, Sylvia Plath's work seems more astonishing, and its achievements harder earned. As Hughes wrote, "every word is *Baraka*: the flame and the rose folded together. Poets have often spoken about this ideal possibility, but where else, outside these poems, has it actually occurred?"[46] The old comparisons to Medea and Electra no longer hold. If she must be a myth, let her be Ariadne, laying down the threads, leading us out from the center of the labyrinth. Let us not desert her.

Acknowledgments

I am grateful to the following people for sharing their memories of Sylvia Plath, Ted Hughes, Aurelia Plath, Olwyn Hughes, Dr. Ruth Beuscher, and others: Peter Aldrich, Paul Alexander, the late Al Alvarez, Anne Alvarez, Robert Bagg, Jonathan Bate, Jillian Becker, Terry Bragg, Stuart Burne, Janet Burroway, Margaret Affleck Clark, Don Colburn, David Compton, Ruth Crossley, Dr. Francis de Marneffe, Harriett Destler, Ruth Fainlight, Michael Frayn, Linda Gates, Ruth Freeman Geissler, Vivette and Jon Glover, Jean Gooder, Isabel Murray Henderson, Elizabeth Hinchcliffe, the late Philip Hobsbaum, Daniel Huws, Frank Irish, Robert Jocelyn, Elinor Friedman Klein, Karen Kukil, Richard Larschan, Lynne Lawner, Christopher Levenson, Suzette and Helder Macedo, Carol LeVarn McCabe, Phil McCurdy, Marcia Momtchiloff, Richard Murphy, Kenneth Neville-Davies, Dr. Perry Norton, Judith Raymo, the late Wilfrid Riley, Howard Rogovin, Janet Salter Rosenberg, Jon Rosenthal, Neva Nelson, Grace Schulman, Dr. Lorna Secker-Walker, Norman Shapiro, the late Elizabeth Compton Sigmund, May Collacott Target, Claire Tomalin, Betsy Powley Wallingford, David Wevill, Louise Giesey White, Guy Wilbor, Nick Wilding, Mel Woody, and Laurie Totten Woolschlager. Linda Johnson kindly showed me around Sylvia Plath's former home at 23 Fitzroy Road, London, and let me photograph the view from Plath's bedroom study window.

Thank you to those who provided literary support, advice, and camaraderie along the way: Kai Bird, Adam Plunkett, Aidan Levy, Cynthia Carr, Lindsey Whalen, Abigail Santamaria, Ruth Franklin, David Nasaw, Gary Giddins, and Thad Ziolkowski at the Leon Levy Center for Biography, Graduate Center, City University of New York; Hermione Lee and Kate Kennedy at the Oxford Centre for Life-Writing, Wolfson College, Oxford; Anne Thomson at Newnham College, Cambridge; Louisa Carroll at University College Dublin; Ann Bolotin at the Lilly Library, Indiana University; Carrie Hintz, Kathy Shoemaker, and Emily Banks at the Rose Library, Emory University; Fran Baker at the John Rylands

Library, University of Manchester; Helen Melody—who really went above and beyond—at the British Library; Mark Wormald, Terry Gifford, Neil Roberts, and Carrie Smith at the Ted Hughes Society; Lesley Johnson, Nick Wilding, the late Mark Hinchcliffe, Julia Hinchcliffe, Jeni Wetton, and Charlotte Wetton at the Elmet Trust; Gloria Biamonte, Laura D'Angelo, Travis Norsen, and Catherine O'Callaghan at Marlboro College; Jonathan Santlofer at Yaddo; Eli Trautwein, Sandeep Shuvakimur, and Keri Walsh in Chappaqua/Mount Kisco. Thank you to others who have shared my love of Plath's work and provided support in both formal and informal ways over the years: Janet Badia, Tracy Brain, Sarah Corbett, Gail Crowther, Mary Dearborn, Julie Goodspeed-Chadwick, Julie Irigaray, Tim Kendall, Amanda Golden, Teresa Griffiths, Langdon Hammer, Eric Laursen, Elizabeth Lowry, Kathleen Ossip, and Michael Parker. Isobel Hurst put me up in London many times, and joined me on my Plath-related travels in the UK. Special thanks are due to the members of the English and Creative Writing Department at the University of Huddersfield—especially Steve Ely, James Underwood, and Jessica Malay. I feel very lucky to work with such talented, passionate, and good-humored colleagues. For many years of encouragement and support: Grainne Coen, Bridget Steinkrauss, Krista Kubick, Amy Schneider, Lauren Ouziel, Daria Zawadzki, Alexa Carver, Joanna D'Afflitti, Cary Donaldson, Roslyn Clarke, Zahr Said, Tina Benipayo, Christian Kirschke, Leah Clark, Mark Clark, and the rest of the Clark and Valentino clans.

I owe an enormous amount of gratitude to Peter Steinberg. Throughout the research and writing of this book, Peter has been unfailingly generous with his time and knowledge. Peter answered many of my questions, pointed me to sources, and commented—in less than four weeks—upon a sixteen-hundred-page draft of my manuscript. Peter's knowledge of Sylvia Plath and his dedication to her legacy is a legend in its own right. I also owe so much to Karen Kukil, who, for fifteen years, has been a great source of support and information for me in all things Plath. Karen put me in touch with sources, helped me navigate Plath's vast archival holdings at Smith, and never tired of answering my questions. I am greatly indebted to these fine scholars who have each done so much to promote and disseminate Sylvia Plath's work.

I could not have found a more perceptive, sympathetic, and meticulous editor than Deborah Garrison at Knopf, who understood the need for an in-depth critical biography of Sylvia Plath, and who gave me the time and space to write one. At Knopf, thank you to Todd Portnowitz for his help with production and permissions, Amy Stackhouse for copyediting the manuscript, Victoria Pearson for production editorial work, Cassandra Pappas for text design, John Gall for designing the cover, and Josefine Kalls and Jessica Purcell for organizing publicity. In London, thank you to my editor Robin Robertson at Jonathan Cape, and the Andrew Nurnberg Agency for handling foreign rights and translation.

I am grateful to have such a committed agent in Jacques de Spoelberch, who guided me through each stage of this book with great care and solicitude, and shared his own memories of literary life in Boston in the 1950s.

Thank you to the Sylvia Plath and Ted Hughes estates for permission to scan all of Plath's and Hughes's archival material without any conditions attached. Reading a biography of one's parents or husband is surely a difficult task, and I am grateful to both estates for their professionalism throughout the writing of this book. I am also grateful to the Aurelia Plath estate.

This book has benefited from the support of several institutions: in 2017–18, I received a National Endowment for the Humanities Public Scholar Fellowship; in 2016–17, I received a Biography Fellowship at the Leon Levy Center for Biography, City University of New York; in 2017, I was a visiting professor at the University of Huddersfield; in 2016, I was a U.S. Visiting Fellow at the Eccles Centre for American Studies, British Library, and a visiting scholar at the Oxford Centre for Life-Writing at Wolfson College, Oxford. I am grateful for all these awards and affiliations, which were a crucial source of financial and moral support. I would also like to recognize the Women Writing Women's Lives Seminar at the City University of New York, the Elmet Trust in Yorkshire, and the Ted Hughes Network at the University of Huddersfield for helping to promote this biography while it was a work in progress.

This book is partly dedicated to the memory of the poet, scholar, and biographer Jon Stallworthy. Jon supervised my doctoral dissertation at Oxford, and continued to support my work in so many ways until his death in 2014. Jon was generous and gracious and wickedly funny. He took me seriously, and set the bar high. He cheered this book on in its very early stages, and gave me the confidence to believe I could undertake such a long and demanding project—and controversial subject. He is deeply missed.

My greatest thanks go to my husband, Nathan Holcomb, and my children, Isabel and Liam. Isabel was three when I began writing this book in 2011; Liam was born two years later. Writing a biography of an iconic poet while working in academia and raising two small children posed its challenges. This book would have been much harder to write without the help of my mother, Cheryl Valentino Clark, who held down the fort during my trips to England; the wonderful preschool teachers at the Montessori Children's Room in Armonk, New York; and my children's indefatigable pediatrician, Dr. Deborah Mollo. It really does take a village. Nathan has indulged my obsessive interest in postwar poetry since our Oxford days. He has been, and always will be, my first reader.

Notes on Sources

Abbreviations

AP   Aurelia Plath

BJ   Sylvia Plath, *The Bell Jar* (London: Heinemann, 1963; New York: Harper Perennial, 2006)

BL   The British Library, London

CPTH   *Collected Poems of Ted Hughes*, Paul Keegan, ed. (New York: Farrar, Straus and Giroux, 2003)

Diary   Sylvia Plath's unpublished adolescent diary, archived at the Lilly Library, Indiana University, Plath MSS II, Box 7, Folders 1–4

DN   Dick Norton

EBC   Edward Butscher Collection of Papers on Sylvia Plath, Smith College

EF   Elaine Feinstein

EFP   Elaine Feinstein Papers, 4/4, John Rylands Library, University of Manchester, UK

Emory   Stuart A. Rose Library, Manuscript, Archives, and Rare Book Library, Emory University, Atlanta

HC   Heather Clark

HM   Hinchcliffe Manuscript: an unfinished, unpublished Plath biography provisionally titled "The Descent of Ariel: The Death of Sylvia Plath" by Elizabeth Hinchcliffe, mid-1970s, Box 6, Folders 10–12, Frances McCullough Papers 1915–1994, Hornbake Library, University of Maryland, College Park

HRC   Harry Ransom Center, University of Texas at Austin

J   *The Unabridged Journals of Sylvia Plath, 1950–1962*, Karen Kukil, ed. (London: Faber and Faber, 2000)

JP   Sylvia Plath, *Johnny Panic and the Bible of Dreams* (London: Faber and Faber, 1977; 1979). Introduction by Ted Hughes.

L1   *The Letters of Sylvia Plath, Vol. 1: 1940–1956*, Peter K. Steinberg and Karen Kukil, eds. (New York: HarperCollins, 2017)

L2   *The Letters of Sylvia Plath, Vol. 2: 1956–1963*, Peter K. Steinberg and Karen Kukil, eds. (New York: HarperCollins, 2018)

    LH   *Letters Home*, Aurelia Plath, ed. (London: Faber and Faber, 1976; 1999)

  LHMS   Department of Literary and Historical Manuscripts, Morgan Library

   Lilly   Lilly Library, Indiana University, Bloomington, Indiana. All material quoted
           from the Lilly Library comes from Plath MSS II unless otherwise noted.

    LTH   *Letters of Ted Hughes*, Christopher Reid, ed. (London: Faber and Faber, 2007)

 Morgan   Morgan Library and Museum, New York City, N.Y.

   NYPL   Berg Collection, New York Public Library, New York City, N.Y.

    OHP   Olive Higgins Prouty

   Smith   Mortimer Rare Book Room, Smith College, Northampton, Mass.

     SP   Sylvia Plath

    SPC   Sylvia Plath Collection, Smith College

 Stanford Special Collections and University Archives, Stanford University

     TH   Ted Hughes

    UCD   University College Dublin, Ireland

     WP   Warren Plath

In the interests of concision, I have not listed the page numbers of Plath's quoted published poems in the endnotes when the title of the poem is presented in the main text. All published Plath poems quoted in this biography are easily found in Sylvia Plath's *Collected Poems* (London: Faber and Faber, 1981).

Full citations of published sources are provided in that source's first endnote; thereafter, I use a short-form citation. Full initial citations are given in each chapter in which a published source is quoted. The endnotes provide a full bibliography of all sources used in this book.

All unpublished sources are listed in the endnotes. All material with the citation "Lilly" comes from Plath MSS II unless otherwise noted. For all Smith College and Lilly Library archive citations, and most Emory citations, I list the box number followed by the folder number in which the material is located. (For example, "10.1" means Box 10, Folder 1.) Archival citations from the British Library, Harvard, Stanford, Dartmouth, University College Dublin, and other archives are listed according to their individual reference systems. For reasons of space, I have not listed box and folder numbers for all unpublished correspondence in Plath MSS II, Lilly Library, which is organized alphabetically in Boxes 1–6, or Plath's unpublished adolescent diaries, which are organized chronologically in Plath MSS II, Lilly Library, Box 7, Folders 1–4. The Finding Aids for the Sylvia Plath Papers at the Lilly Library and Smith College, and the Ted Hughes Papers (as well as the papers of many of Hughes's contemporaries) at Emory University and the British Library, are available online.

The use of maiden and married names for Plath's female contemporaries is based on chronology. I have used Plath's contemporaries' maiden names in the text when discussing their actions before they were married. When citing correspondence, I use contemporaries' names as they appeared at the time of writing. When quoting recent interviews or emails, I signal this later perspective by using both their maiden and married names in the text and endnotes. Endnotes make the dates of letters and interviews clear.

I have reproduced Plath's words exactly as she wrote them, and use "[*sic*]" to note her spelling errors and her deliberate use of lowercase letters. All ellipses in quotations are the author's unless otherwise noted in the endnotes.

The names of interviewees, plus the month, year, and location of each interview are listed in the endnotes.

Notes

PROLOGUE

1. SP to AP, 7 Nov. 1962. *L2*, 898.
2. Henry James, *Selected Fiction*, Leon Edel, ed. (New York: Dutton & Co., 1953), 482–535. The copy of this book I consulted contains mark-ups and annotations that Plath's former student, Harriet Destler, made in Plath's Smith College Freshman English class.
3. SP to Gordon Lameyer, 28 July 1955. *L1*, 943.
4. SP, 1957–58 Smith College Teaching Notes. 13.9–11, Lilly.
5. HC interview with Elinor Friedman Klein, Oct. 2015, South Salem, N.Y.
6. *J*, 360.
7. Adlai Stevenson, Smith College Commencement Address, 6 June 1955. Commencement Speech files, Class of 1955 records, Smith College Archives. Stevenson's full speech is available online at http://www.equityalliancemn.org.
8. Stephanie Coontz, *A Strange Stirring: The Feminine Mystique and American Women at the Dawn of the 1960s* (New York: Perseus, 2011), 9; Jessica Mann, *The Fifties Mystique* (London: Quartet, 2012), 131.
9. Mann, *The Fifties Mystique*, 197.
10. SP to Gordon Lameyer, 6 Nov. 1954. *L1*, 832.
11. Hermione Lee, *Biography: A Very Short Introduction* (Oxford: Oxford University Press, 2009), 128–29.
12. Maggie Nelson, *The Art of Cruelty: A Reckoning* (New York: W. W. Norton, 2012), 141.
13. Ibid., 260.
14. William H. Pritchard, "An Interesting Minor Poet?," *New Republic* (30 Dec. 1981): 32–35; 33. Pritchard was quoting from a list of "24 Sylvia Plath jokes" he had read in a college newspaper.
15. Claire Dederer, "What Do We Do with the Art of Monstrous Men?" *Paris Review* (20 Nov. 2017).
16. Helen Dudar, "The Virginia Woolf Cult," *Saturday Review* (Feb. 1982): 33–35; 33.
17. "The Blood Jet Is Poetry," review of *Ariel*, *Time* (10 June 1966): 118–20. 118.
18. Webster Schott, "The Cult of Plath," *Washington Post Book World* (1 Oct. 1972), 3.
19. See, for example, critical books on Plath by Jacqueline Rose, Susan Van Dyne, Lynda Bundtzen, Judith Kroll, Tracy Brain, Tim Kendall, Steven Axelrod, and Christina Britzolakis.
20. Andrew Wilson, *Mad Girl's Love Song: Sylvia Plath and Life Before Ted* (New York: Scribner, 2013), 13–14; 80.
21. The article, an interview with Mary Rafferty Haroun and Janet Wagner Rafferty, is from the 1 November 2003 issue.

22. SP to Mel Woody, 5 July 1954. *L1*, 781.
23. HC interview with Phil McCurdy, May 2016, Ogunquit, Maine.
24. HC interview with Elinor Friedman Klein, Oct. 2015, South Salem, N.Y.
25. Anne Stevenson, *Bitter Fame: A Life of Sylvia Plath* (London: Penguin, 1989), 298.
26. Kathleen Spivack, *With Robert Lowell and His Circle* (Boston: Northeastern University Press, 2012), 25.
27. HC interview with Elinor Friedman Klein, Oct. 2015, South Salem, N.Y.
28. SP to Dr. Ruth Beuscher, 4 Feb. 1963. *L2*, 967.
29. *J*, 495.
30. Elizabeth Hardwick, "On Sylvia Plath," *New York Review of Books* (12 Aug. 1971), 3–5.
31. TH to Anne Stevenson, autumn 1986. *LTH*, 517.
32. *The Collected Poems of Langston Hughes*, Arnold Rampersad, ed. (New York: Vintage, 1994), 426.
33. SP to Marcia Brown Plumer, 9 Apr. 1957. *L2*, 110.
34. Jane Baltzell Kopp email to HC, 9 Oct. 2016.
35. See Heather Clark, *The Grief of Influence: Sylvia Plath and Ted Hughes* (Oxford: Oxford University Press, 2011), for a comprehensive overview of Plath and Hughes's literary partnership.
36. See Owen Leeming, *Two of a Kind: Poets in Partnership*. Interview with Sylvia Plath and Ted Hughes. BBC Third Programme, London. Recorded 18 Jan. 1961; broadcast 31 Jan. 1961. National Sound Archives, BL. *The Spoken Word: Sylvia Plath*. British Library/National Sound Archives/BBC Audio Compilation (2010).
37. SP to Anne Sexton, 21 Aug. 1962. *L2*, 812; SP to Brian Cox, 17 June 1961. *L2*, 625.
38. Barrie Cooke to Jack Sweeney, 20 Oct. 1962. LA52/69, Jack and Máire Sweeney Papers, UCD.
39. TH to Anne-Lorraine Bujon, 16 Dec. 1992. *LTH*, 627.
40. TH interview with Drue Heinz, "The Art of Poetry, LXXI," *Paris Review* 134 (1995), in *The Paris Review Interviews*, vol. 3 (London: Picador, 2008), 56–92; 76.
41. SP to TH, 6 Oct. 1956. *L1*, 1281.
42. HC interview with Ruth Fainlight, May 2016, London.
43. In a 16 Oct. 1981 letter to Al Alvarez, Hughes said Plath's "60–62" journals "walked, not too long ago." Add MS 88593, BL.
44. TH to AP, 12 Jan. 1975. 16.3, MSS 644, Emory. Ruth Fainlight agreed with Ted. No women's libber, she said, "would want to be the perfect wife." In this respect, Fainlight felt Plath was "terribly oppressed by the masculine principle." Harriet Rosenstein interview with Ruth Fainlight and Alan Sillitoe, 1970. 1.25, MSS 1489, Emory.
45. Harriet Rosenstein interview with Dr. Ruth Beuscher, 1970. 1.6, MSS 1489, Emory.
46. Anon., "Olwyn Hughes: Grande Dame, Under Siege," *Camden Scallywag* (May 1992): 24–25.
47. Harriet Rosenstein interview with Edward Lucie-Smith, 1970. 2.17, MSS 1489, Emory.
48. SP to Dr. Ruth Beuscher, 22 Sept. 1962. *L2*, 830.
49. SP, "Conversation Among the Ruins," *Collected Poems* (London: Faber and Faber, 1981), 21.
50. *CPTH*, 1078.
51. TH to Anne Stevenson, autumn 1986. *LTH*, 520–21.
52. TH to Lucas Myers, 14 Feb. 1987. *LTH*, 537–38.
53. Ibid., 536.
54. A. Alvarez, *The Savage God: A Study of Suicide* (London: Weidenfeld & Nicolson, 1971; New York: W. W. Norton, 1990), 30.
55. TH to SP, 4 Oct. 1956. *LTH*, 56.
56. EF interview with Suzette Macedo, Oct. 1999. EFP.
57. Elizabeth Sigmund, "Sylvia in Devon: 1962," *Sylvia Plath: The Woman and the Work*, Edward Butscher, ed. (New York: Dodd, Mead and Co., 1977), 102.
58. SP to AP, 19 Apr. 1956. *L1*, 1166.
59. *J*, 412.

60. *CPTH*, 1111.
61. HC interview with Ruth Fainlight, May 2016, London.
62. SP to AP, 11 Feb. 1960. *L2*, 414.
63. W. B. Yeats, *Collected Poems*, Richard Finneran, ed. (New York: Macmillan, 1989), 204–205.

1. THE BEEKEEPER'S DAUGHTER

1. Eda Sagarra, *A Social History of Germany 1648–1914* (Piscataway, N.J.: Transaction Publishers, 2002), 313–18.
2. SP to Hans-Joachim Neupert, 30 May 1950. *L1*, 163.
3. Ibid., 10 Oct. 1949. *L1*, 153.
4. Ibid., 30 May 1950. *L1*, 163.
5. *J*, 453–54.
6. *J*, 166; 209; 215; 306; 319; 407; 475.
7. *J*, 641.
8. HC interview with Perry Norton, Oct. 2012, Auburndale, Mass.
9. One family member claimed that it derived from "von Plath," and, before that, the French "Platheau." Letter from June Helle to Theodore Plath's great-niece Martha Mae Gullickson, 30 Mar. 1984, posted in the Helle family public member page, http://www.ancestry.com. All of the ship passenger registers I consulted listed the Plath family as "Plath."
10. HC conversation with Anita Helle, 27 Oct. 2012, Bloomington, Ind. Helle is Otto Plath's great-niece.
11. On the Federal Census Record for Berkeley, California, 1920, Otto lists Polish as his mother tongue; on the 1930 Federal Census Record for Boston, Massachusetts, he lists German.
12. "Community of Budsin, Kreis Kolmar," http://www.birchy.com. This is a genealogy website for those looking for Posen ancestors.
13. Mathilde (b. 1853–54), Emilie (b. 1858), Augusta (b. 1859), Emil (b. 1860), and Mary (b. 186?). Two more children, whose names and births are unrecorded, probably died young.
14. June Helle to Martha Mae Gullickson, 30 Mar. 1984.
15. Johann emigrated on the *Fulda* from Bremen, Germany, in 1885, and Caroline on the *Gellert*, from Hamburg, Germany, in 1890. Both arrived in New York. John accompanied a seventy-eight-year-old woman, Mrs. J. Plath.
16. June Helle to Martha Mae Gullickson, 30 Mar. 1984.
17. In the 1910 Federal Census Record for Lincoln, Wisconsin, both John and Caroline answered no to questions regarding their literacy and ability to speak English.
18. Marjorie Shong (Fall Creek town clerk) to Harriet Rosenstein, 22 Feb. 1977. 3.6, MSS 1489, Emory.
19. June Helle to Martha Mae Gullickson, 30 Mar. 1984.
20. Ernestine's parents were Michael Kottke and Anna Christina Witt. Marriage database, "The Poznan Project," http://www.poznan-project.psnc.pl.
21. *LH*, 13.
22. This is according to the children's ages as listed on the *Lake Ontario* passenger list in December 1901.
23. June Helle to Martha Mae Gullickson, 30 Mar. 1984.
24. The ship's passenger log lists Ernestine's final destination as "Husband, Emil Plath, Blacksmith, Maza, N.D." Ernestine's occupation is listed as "wife." Emil, however, was her husband's brother. Perhaps Ernestine felt that she needed to list a more established member of the Plath family as her contact, since Theodore may still have been unemployed at this point.
25. Otto lists his father's address on his 1903 high school registration card as Maza, North Dakota.
26. AP, Biographical Jottings About Sylvia Plath ("Illness"). 30.57, SPC, Smith.

27. AP to Elizabeth Compton Sigmund, 18 May 1976. Add MS 88612, BL.
28. Anita Helle, "'Family Matters': An Afterword on the Biography of Sylvia Plath," *Northwest Review* 26 (1988): 148–60. 155.
29. AP, Biographical Jottings About Sylvia Plath ("Illness"). 30.57, SPC, Smith.
30. Oregon State Hospital, Salem, Oregon, medical and court commitment records for Ernestine Plath, b. 1853, d. 28 Sept. 1919. The journalist Amy Standen discovered that Ernestine Plath was one of several thousand former patients at the hospital whose cremains were unclaimed in 2018. Ernestine's records are publicly available at the Oregon State Archives.
31. Helle, "'Family Matters,'" 155–56.
32. HC conversation with Anita Helle, 27 Oct. 2012, Bloomington, Ind.
33. *LH*, 9. He arrived in America on the *Auguste Victoria* in Aug. 1900.
34. Paul Eggert to Harriet Rosenstein, 24 Jan. 1975. 3.4, MSS 1489, Emory.
35. Northwestern College Minutes, 12 May–21 Sept. 1905; 21 Sept. 1905.
36. There were no biology courses offered during Otto's time at the college, only chemistry and physics.
37. Course catalog, College of Northwestern University, 1905–1906.
38. *LH*, 9.
39. Ibid.
40. FBI File on Otto E. Plath, by Armin Nix, #5006 B, 22 Oct. 1918; Carl Lawrenz (President, Wisconsin Lutheran Seminary) to Harriet Rosenstein, 15 Aug. 1974. 3.4, MSS 1489, Emory.
41. *LH*, 10.
42. *BJ*, 166.
43. Aurelia Plath told this to Richard Larschan. HC interview with Richard Larschan, May 2017, Manhattan. Membership records for the organization from the 1920s and '30s no longer exist.
44. Max Gaebler, "Sylvia Plath Remembered," *Wisconsin Academy Review* 46.2 (Spring 2000): 28–32.
45. 1912 University of Washington Yearbook, 176.
46. Otto Plath, "Washington Irving's Einfluss auf Wilhelm Hauff: Eine Quellenstudie." Thesis Submitted for MA in Literature Degree, University of Washington, 1912.
47. In 1929, Otto told Aurelia that he and Lydia only lived together for one year after marrying. Otto's draft registration card, which he filled out on 12 Sept. 1918, while living in Berkeley, California, helps corroborate this statement; he lists his closest living relative as Mrs. Otto Emil Plath, Deaconess Hospital (where she worked as a nurse), in Chicago.
48. FBI File on Otto E. Plath, by Armin Nix, #5006 B, 22 Oct. 1918.
49. "Comings and Goings," *Reno Evening Gazette* (16 Sept. 1914), 8.
50. FBI File on Otto E. Plath, by Armin Nix, #5006 B, 22 Oct. 1918.
51. "German Profs. to Leave U. for War," *Oakland Tribune* (4 Aug. 1914), 16.
52. Marjorie Shong (Fall Creek town clerk) to Harriet Rosenstein, 22 Feb. 1977. 3.6, MSS 1489, Emory.
53. 1920 Federal Census, Berkeley, Calif.
54. Theodore Plath (listed as Theodore Platt) was buried in 1st Addition, Block 265, Lot 1, of the Mountain View Cemetery in Oregon City, Oregon.
55. FBI File on Otto E. Plath, by Armin Nix, #5006 B, 10 Oct. 1918.
56. Ibid., 25 Oct. 1918.
57. Ibid., 22 Oct. 1918. All following quotes from the FBI file are from this date.
58. Otto Emil Plath, Declaration of Intention for US Citizenship, No. 469, 22 June 1921.
59. Otto Emil Plath, Certificate of Naturalization, #2307371, 12 Apr. 1926.
60. Full text of this speech is available at the American Presidency Project, http://www.presidency.ucsb.edu/ws/?pid=65400.
61. George Fulton to Edward Butscher, 20 Nov. 1972. 1.22, EBC, Smith.
62. Thomas Clohesy to AP, 4 Sept. 1966. 29.9, SPC, Smith.

63. AP to Helen Vendler, 5 Jan. 1976. 29.47, SPC, Smith.
64. Andrew Wilson, *Mad Girl's Love Song: Sylvia Plath and Life Before Ted* (New York: Scribner, 2013), 31.
65. HC interview with Richard Larschan, May 2017, Manhattan.
66. Dr. W. M. Wheeler dominated the biology department at the time.
67. Albert Mangelsdorf to Harriet Rosenstein, 22 July 1974. 3.7, MSS 1489, Emory.
68. HM, 7. Hinchcliffe interviewed these men during the 1970s while researching a biography of Plath, which she never published. A copy of the unfinished manuscript is in the Frances McCullough Papers, University of Maryland, and the Al Alvarez Papers, BL.
69. Ibid.
70. HM, 8.
71. HM, 11.
72. Laurence H. Snyder to Harriet Rosenstein, 25 July 1974. 3.7, MSS 1489, Emory.
73. HM, 2.
74. HM, 9–10.
75. Video footage of Aurelia Plath, Nov. 1986, in *Poets of New England: Sylvia Plath and the Myth of the Monstrous Mother*. University of Massachusetts, Amherst, AIMS Video Services, 2001. Courtesy of Richard Larschan.
76. Harriet Rosenstein interview with Leland H. Taylor, 1974–75. 3.7, MSS 1489, Emory.
77. Harriet Rosenstein interview with Frank L. Carpenter, 1974. 3.7, MSS 1489, Emory.
78. George Salt to Harriet Rosenstein, 8 Sept. 1974. 3.7, MSS 1489, Emory.
79. Leland Taylor to Harriet Rosenstein, 23 July 1974. 3.7, MSS 1489, Emory. The other characteristics listed were noted often in interviews and letters from Otto's Bussey housemates. 3.7, MSS 1489, Emory.
80. Philip J. Darlington to Harriet Rosenstein, 14 Aug. 1974. 3.7, MSS 1489, Emory.
81. Leland Taylor to Harriet Rosenstein, 3 Aug. 1974; Clyde Keeler to Harriet Rosenstein, 22 July 1974; George Salt to Harriet Rosenstein, 8 Sept. 1974; W. Ralph Singleton to Harriet Rosenstein, 25 July 1974. 3.7, MSS 1489, Emory.
82. Leland Taylor to Harriet Rosenstein, 22 July 1974. 3.7, MSS 1489, Emory.
83. W. Ralph Singleton to Harriet Rosenstein, 25 July 1974. 3.7, MSS 1489, Emory.
84. Clyde Keeler to Harriet Rosenstein, 1 Aug. 1974. 3.7, MSS 1489, Emory.
85. Laurence H. Snyder to Harriet Rosenstein, 25 July 1974. 3.7, MSS 1489, Emory.
86. Albert Edward Wiggam, "Let's Explore Your Mind," *San Antonio Express* (20 July 1934), 7; "Observations: Bee Sting Poison," *Republican Courier* (9 Apr. 1934), 4.
87. George Fulton to Edward Butscher, 20 Nov. 1972. 1.22, EBC, Smith.
88. Ibid.
89. Harriet Rosenstein interview with Norman Bailey, 1975. 3.7, MSS 1489, Emory.
90. Otto E. Plath, *Bumblebees and Their Ways* (New York: Macmillan, 1934), 1–2.
91. HM, 34.
92. O. E. Plath, *Bumblebees*, 112.
93. Edward Butscher, *Sylvia Plath: Method and Madness* (New York: Seabury Press, 1976), 3; 10.
94. *LH*, 32.
95. HC interview with Betsy Powley Wallingford, Feb. 2013, Sudbury, Mass.
96. HC phone interview with Phil McCurdy, 6 Dec. 2014; HC interviews with Rosenberg and Klein.
97. HC interview with Perry Norton, Oct. 2012, Auburndale, Mass.
98. WP to Edward Butscher, 31 Aug. 1975. 4.120, EBC, Smith.
99. 1901 Census Record, Westgate-on-Sea, Kent, England.
100. *Vancouver* Ship Passenger List (sailing from Naples, Italy, on 18 May, arriving in Boston on 1 June 1902).
101. The sisters sailed to New York on the *Pennsylvania*.
102. Massachusetts state naturalization papers for Francis Schober, Certificate #103097. His address is listed as 95 Gainsboro Street, Boston, in 1909.

103. None of Plath's Grünwald relatives were listed as "Hebrew" on any of the ships' passenger lists or other official documents.

104. SP, "New Poems," typed 13 Dec. 1962 for Douglas Cleverdon. 6.16, SPC, Smith.

105. Harriet Rosenstein interview with AP, 1970. 3.3, MSS 1489, Emory.

106. *LH*, 4.

107. In the 1910, 1920, and 1930 Federal Census Reports for Boston and Winthrop, Aurelia Greenwood Schober always lists her occupation as housewife, while Frank Schober lists his as "waiter," "head waiter," or "manager" of hotels. He makes no mention in the census reports of his accounting, though Aurelia states that he worked as an accountant before the late 1930s in her introduction to *Letters Home*.

108. *LH*, 3–4.

109. *LH*, 5.

110. Linda Heller, "Aurelia Plath: A Lasting Commitment," *Bostonia*, the Boston University Alumnae Magazine (Spring 1976): 36.

111. AP to Frieda Hughes, Sept. 1974, Cruickshank Archive. Wilson, *Mad Girl's Love Song*, 20.

112. *LH*, 5.

113. "Miss Schober to Give B.U. Class Valedictory." Unidentified newspaper clipping. 30.50, SPC, Smith.

114. AP, "Chronology." 30.55, SPC, Smith.

115. *LH*, 6–8.

116. *LH*, 10.

117. Ibid.

118. See Claudia Goldin, "Marriage Bars: Discrimination Against Married Women Workers, 1920's to 1950's." National Bureau of Economic Research, Working Paper Series. Working Paper No. 2747. October 1988, http://www.nber.org/papers/w2747, p. 5.

119. *LH*, 13.

120. Ruth Freeman Geissler to HC, 30 Nov. 2012.

121. *LH*, 6.

122. AP to Frieda Hughes, 21 Apr. 1978. Cruickshank Archive. Wilson, *Mad Girl's Love Song*, 21.

123. *LH*, 13.

124. *LH*, 12–13.

125. Dr. Ruth Beuscher interview with AP, 15 Sept. 1953. 3.10, MSS 1489, Emory.

126. Clyde Keeler to Harriet Rosenstein, 1 Aug. 1974. 3.7, MSS 1489, Emory.

127. HC phone interview with Jillian Becker, 18 Apr. 2017.

128. 8.2, Lilly.

2. DO NOT MOURN

1. T. H. Watkins, *The Great Depression: America in the 1930s* (Boston and New York: Little, Brown, 1993), 13.

2. "There probably had never been so many eruptions of public unrest in such a short period of time over so wide a spectrum of geography and population in the nation's history as those that punctuated the months between the winter of 1930 and the winter of 1933 . . . all of them dutifully and sometimes luridly chronicled in the daily press." Ibid., 81.

3. Ibid., 56.

4. Ibid.

5. *LH*, 10.

6. *LH*, 12.

7. She was delivered by Drs. J. J. Abrams and Edwin Smith. AP, "Chronology." 30.55, SPC, Smith.

8. AP to Judith Kroll, 1 Dec. 1978. 29.26, SPC, Smith.

9. Otto and Aurelia, with their literary backgrounds, probably also had had Shakespeare in mind when they chose the name Sylvia, which features prominently in *Two Gentlemen of Verona*: "Then to Silvia let us sing, / That Silvia is excelling; / She excels each

mortal thing / Upon the dull earth dwelling. / To her let us garlands bring." This passage was later made into a popular song, "Who Is Silvia?" by Franz Schubert, which Otto and Aurelia would have known.

10. Helen Vendler later wrote a moving letter to Aurelia about how her own struggles as a female academic had mirrored Plath's. Helen Vendler to AP, 24 Nov. 1975. 29.47, SPC, Smith.
11. *LH*, 37.
12. AP, draft introduction, *LH*. 30.66a/b, SPC, Smith.
13. Ibid.
14. Ibid.
15. Ibid.
16. 14.4, Lilly.
17. Plath slept with it every night, and by 1935 all that was left of the toy were the ears. AP, Baby Book, 14.4, Lilly.
18. Ibid.
19. *LH*, 13.
20. *JP*, 119–23.
21. *LH*, 16.
22. Video footage of Aurelia Plath, Nov. 1986, in *Poets of New England: Sylvia Plath and the Myth of the Monstrous Mother*. University of Massachusetts, Amherst, AIMS Video Services, 2001. Courtesy of Richard Larschan.
23. *LH*, 16.
24. Harriet Rosenstein interview with Perry and Shirley Norton, 1971–74. 2.27, MSS 1489, Emory.
25. Video, *Poets of New England: Sylvia Plath and the Myth of the Monstrous Mother*.
26. AP, "Chronology." 30.55, SPC, Smith.
27. AP, draft introduction, *LH* ("Otto E. Plath"). 30.66a/b, SPC, Smith.
28. Ibid.
29. HM, 27.
30. She and Otto put down $1,000 toward the $10,000 three-bedroom, seven-room, 1,940-square-foot house. AP, "Chronology." 30.55, SPC, Smith.
31. SP, "Ocean 1212-W." *JP*, 119.
32. AP, "Chronology." 30.55, SPC, Smith.
33. *LH*, 18.
34. SP, high school scrapbook. 10.O3, Lilly.
35. *JP*, 253; 255.
36. *JP*, 117; 121–22.
37. Ruth Freeman Geissler email to Peter K. Steinberg, 29 Jan. 2015 and 27 Oct. 2017. Shared with Geissler's permission.
38. AP, draft introduction, *LH*. 30.66a/b, SPC, Smith.
39. *JP*, 124.
40. AP, draft introduction, *LH*. 30.66a/b, SPC, Smith.
41. Ibid.
42. *LH*, 5.
43. *JP*, 118.
44. SP, "Autograph transcript of 40 juvenile poems." 127550, LHMS, Morgan.
45. SP, high school scrapbook. 10.O3, Lilly.
46. See Rosenstein's Freeman and Sterling files, MSS 1489, Emory.
47. Max D. Gaebler, "Sylvia Plath Remembered," delivered to the Madison Literary Club on 14 Mar. 1983. 2.22, Houghton Mifflin Collection, Smith.
48. *LH*, 19–22.
49. *LH*, 18.
50. Ibid.
51. AP, draft introduction, *LH*, 16. 30.66a/b, SPC, Smith.
52. AP to SP, "Tuesday morning," 1938. Lilly.
53. AP to SP, "Tuesday morning," 1938; AP to SP, 1938. Lilly.
54. AP to SP, 1938. Lilly.

55. AP to SP, 8 Apr. 1939. Lilly.
56. AP to SP, 9 Apr. 1939. Lilly.
57. SP to Otto Plath, 19 Feb. 1940. *L1*, 3–4.
58. SP to Otto Plath, June 1940. Lilly.
59. SP, "Autograph transcript of 40 juvenile poems." 127550, LHMS, Morgan Library.
60. Andrew Wilson, *Mad Girl's Love Song: Sylvia Plath and Life Before Ted* (New York: Scribner, 2013), 89; 3.
61. Harriet Rosenstein, notes on Fran McCullough interview, 1973–74. 2.20, MSS 1489, Emory.
62. *LH*, 23.
63. *JP*, 263–64.
64. Even when Sylvia was a toddler, Aurelia had soothed her with an early version of the song: "I remember that she was sitting in her high chair the first time she heard a clap of thumber [*sic*]. She leaned forward, both hands grasping the tray, and looked at my face intently. I laughed and sang out, 'Boom-boom-boom!' She relaxed, leaning against the back of her chair, now pounding on the tray, calling out laughingly, 'Boom-boom-boom!'" Draft introduction, *LH*. 30.66a/b, SPC, Smith.
65. *LH*, 18.
66. Harriet Rosenstein interview with Fran McCullough, 1973–75. 2.20, MSS 1489, Emory.
67. *LH*, 23.
68. Ibid.
69. Death certificate of Otto Plath, 5 Nov. 1940. Commonwealth of Massachusetts Division of Vital Statistics.
70. Paul Alexander, *Rough Magic: A Biography of Sylvia Plath* (New York: Da Capo Press, 1999), 32. Alexander cites no source for this remark, which likely came from Aurelia Plath.
71. *LH*, 23.
72. Harriet Rosenstein interview with Richard Sassoon, 1974–76. 4.6, MSS 1489, Emory.
73. *LH*, 25.
74. Irving Johnson, "In Memoriam Otto Plath," *Bostonia* 14 (Oct.–July 1940), 23.
75. *BJ*, 167.
76. *LH*, 25–28.
77. Ora Mae Orton to Edward Butscher, 26 Sept. 1973. 2.57, EBC, Smith.
78. Linda Heller, draft of "Aurelia Plath: A Lasting Commitment." Interview with AP, 1976. 30.54, SPC, Smith.
79. *LH*, 24.
80. HM, 34.
81. *JP*, 124.
82. HC interview with Betsy Powley Wallingford, Feb. 2013, Sudbury, Mass.
83. Ibid.
84. HC interview with Janet Salter Rosenberg, Sept. 2015, Dobbs Ferry, N.Y.
85. 10.130, SPC, Smith.
86. Children who lost a parent before age thirteen, firstborn children, and boys who lost mothers (factors that apply to both Plath and her son, Nicholas, who also committed suicide) were particularly vulnerable. Mai-Britt Guldin et al., "Incidence of Suicide Among Persons Who Had a Parent Who Died During Their Childhood: A Population-Based Cohort Study," *JAMA Psychiatry* 72.12 (2015): 1227–34.
87. See also K. M. Abel et al., "Severe Bereavement Stress During the Prenatal and Childhood Periods and Risk of Psychosis Later in Life: A Population-Based Cohort Study," *BMJ* (2014): 348; f7679; and Holly C. Wilcox et al., "Psychiatric Morbidity, Violent Crime, and Suicide Among Children and Adolescents Exposed to Parental Death," *Journal of the American Academy of Child and Adolescent Psychiatry* 49.5 (May 2010): 514–23.
88. Wilcox et al., "Psychiatric Morbidity."
89. Max D. Gaebler, "Sylvia Plath Remembered," delivered to the Madison Literary Club on 14 Mar. 1983. 2.22, Houghton Mifflin Collection, Smith.

90. Elizabeth Sigmund and Gail Crowther, *Sylvia Plath in Devon: A Year's Turning* (Croydon, UK: Fonthill, 2014), 20.
91. HC interview with Janet Salter Rosenberg, Sept. 2015, Dobbs Ferry, N.Y.
92. HC interview with Suzette and Helder Macedo, May 2016, London.
93. TH, "Trial," section 20. Add MS 88993/1/1, BL.

3. THE SHADOW

1. Harriet Rosenstein interview with William Sterling, 1971.4.14, MSS 1489, Emory.
2. *LH*, 28.
3. SP, draft, "Superman and Paula Brown's New Snowsuit." 7.18, Lilly.
4. *JP*, 162.
5. *JP*, 336–37.
6. *JP*, 337–38. Gordon Lameyer's German father, who was sent to such a camp, was also a model. Plath wrote to Gordon in 1959 asking for details of his father's internment.
7. *J*, 475.
8. Harriet Rosenstein interview with David Freeman, 1974. 1.29, MSS 1489, Emory.
9. HC interview with Betsy Powley Wallingford, Feb. 2013, Sudbury, Mass.
10. Her starting salary was $1,800 a year, but she lost her state pension. *LH*, 28–29.
11. *LH*, 29.
12. WP to Edward Butscher, 31 Aug. 1975.4.120, EBC, Smith.
13. SP, high school scrapbook. 10.O3, Lilly.
14. Andrew Wilson, *Mad Girl's Love Song: Sylvia Plath and Life Before Ted* (New York: Scribner, 2013), 39. Linda Wagner-Martin writes in her biography that Plath was not capable of simply "enjoying an activity" unless she could justify it "in terms of possible payment or publication." *Sylvia Plath: A Biography* (New York: Simon & Schuster, 1987), 38.
15. SP, "Poem," *Boston Herald* (10 Aug. 1941), B-8.
16. SP, "Autograph transcript of 40 juvenile poems." 127550, LHMS, Morgan.
17. Plath received recognition again a year later in Aug. 1942 when, at age nine, she won a "Funny Faces" children's art contest (and $1) sponsored by the *Boston Herald*. Her portrait of an older, chubby society lady in a feathered hat was published alongside the other winners. "Funny Faces," *Boston Herald* (2 Aug. 1942), B-10.
18. SP, 1944 notebook. 19.26, SPC, Smith. Though the notebook cover is dated 1944, several pieces inside post-date this year.
19. SP to AP, 20 Mar. 1943. *L1*, 6.
20. SP, "Autograph transcript of 40 juvenile poems." 127550, LHMS, Morgan.
21. SP to AP, Jan. 1943. *L1*, 5.
22. SP to AP, 29 June 1943. *L1*, 9.
23. "Girls Camp Past Is Recalled as Weetamoe Condos Enter the Market," *Ossipee Lake Report* 5.3 (July–Sept. 2006): 1–2.
24. SP to AP, 6 July 1943. *L1*, 11.
25. Ibid.
26. HC interview with Betsy Powley Wallingford, Feb. 2013, Sudbury, Mass.
27. SP, diary, 17 Jan. 1945. All subsequent "diary" citations are from Plath's unpublished 1940s diaries, held in Box 7, Lilly.
28. SP to AP, 20 July 1943. *L1*, 15.
29. SP to AP, 31 July 1943. *L1*, 18.
30. Diary, 5 Jan. 1944.
31. Diary, 22 Jan. 1944.
32. Diary, 10 May 1944.
33. Diary, 27 Dec. 1943.
34. Diary, 1 Jan. 1944.
35. Diary, 8 Oct. 1944.
36. Anne Stevenson, *Bitter Fame: A Life of Sylvia Plath* (London: Penguin, 1989), 4.
37. Perry Norton to HC, 7 Sept. 2012.

38. David Norton would eventually become friendly with Plath's son, Nicholas, at the University of Alaska, where they both worked.
39. HC interview with Perry Norton, Oct. 2012, Auburndale, Mass.
40. William Norton to Edward Butscher, 15 Dec. 1973. 2.55, EBC, Smith.
41. HC interview with Perry Norton, Oct. 2012, Auburndale, Mass.
42. HC conversation with Don Colburn, Jan. 2017, Yaddo, Saratoga Springs, N.Y.
43. HC interview with Perry Norton, Oct. 2012, Auburndale, Mass.
44. HC interview with Betsy Powley Wallingford, Feb. 2013, Sudbury, Mass.
45. Diary, 15 Feb. 1946.
46. Diary, 20 Feb. 1946.
47. "A Great Poet's Wellesley High Classmates Pay Her Tribute," *Wellesley Townsman* (5 Oct. 2000).
48. Diary, 2 & 3 Feb. 1946.
49. *BJ*, 98.
50. Diary, 11 Apr. 1946.
51. Diary, 21 Apr. & 20 May 1946.
52. Diary, 31 Mar. & 23 Jan. 1945.
53. "A Great Poet's," *Wellesley Townsman* (5 Oct. 2000).
54. Ibid.
55. SP to Ann Davidow, c. 12 Jan. 1951. *L1*, 260.
56. Diary, 20 Jan. 1944.
57. Diary, 3 Jan. 1944.
58. Diary, 27 Jan. 1944.
59. Dorothy Humphrey to Edward Butscher, 4 Jan. 1973. 1.31, EBC, Smith.
60. Among the thirty books she listed for the certificate were Carroll's *Alice's Adventures in Wonderland* and *Through the Looking Glass*, Twain's *Tom Sawyer*, Montgomery's *Anne of Green Gables*, the *Iliad* and the *Odyssey*, Alcott's *Eight Cousins*, and Graham's *The Wind in the Willows*. She also listed many other books in her diary that do not appear on the reading certificates—notably *Jane Eyre*, which she read in April after seeing the film version (which she loved so much she watched it twice on the same day), *The Swiss Family Robinson*, and *Gone with the Wind*.
61. SP, "Autograph transcript of 40 juvenile poems." 127550, LHMS, Morgan.
62. Diary, 19 Apr. 1944.
63. Diary, 10 Mar. 1944.
64. Diary, 18 June 1945.
65. Diary, 8 Feb. 1944.
66. Diary, 22 Mar. 1944.
67. Diary, 1 Mar. 1944.
68. Diary, 12 Sept. & 25 Oct. 1944.
69. Diary, 18 Feb. 1944.
70. Diary, 24 Apr. 1944.
71. Diary, 10 Feb. & 16 Mar. 1944.
72. SP, "Autograph transcript of 40 juvenile poems." 127550, LHMS, Morgan.
73. Her homeroom teacher was Miss Brogatti, though her two favorites were her English teacher, Miss Raguse, and her social studies teacher, Miss Chadwick.
74. Diary, 19 Mar. 1944.
75. Diary, 28 Feb. 1944.
76. Diary, 28 Sept. 1945.
77. Diary, 2 Oct. 1945.
78. Diary, 27 Aug. 1945. See Elaine Showalter, *The Female Malady: Women, Madness and Female Culture 1830–1980* (New York: Penguin, 1987).
79. Diary, 13 Dec. 1945.
80. SP, "Autograph transcript of 40 juvenile poems." 127550, LHMS, Morgan.
81. Diary, 14 Nov. 1944.
82. Diary, 23 Apr. 1945.
83. Diary, 24 Dec. 1944.

84. Diary, 28 Dec. 1944.
85. SP to Dr. Ruth Beuscher, 22 Sept. 1962. *L2*, 831.
86. Harriet Rosenstein interview with Pat O'Neil Pratson, 1972. 3.12, MSS 1489, Emory.
87. Harriet Rosenstein interview with Marcia Brown Stern, 1972. 4.16, MSS 1489, Emory.
88. HC interview with Perry Norton, Oct. 2012, Auburndale, Mass.; Ruth Freeman Geissler to HC, 30 Nov. 2012.
89. HC interview with Louise Giesey White, Aug. 2014, Jamestown, R.I.; *J*, 53.
90. HC interview with Phil McCurdy, May 2016, Ogunquit, Maine.
91. HC interview with Louise Giesey White, Aug. 2014, Jamestown, R.I.
92. HC interview with Betsy Powley Wallingford, Feb. 2013, Sudbury, Mass.
93. Diary, 26 June 1945.
94. AP to Paul Alexander, Apr. 1983. Courtesy of Richard Larschan.
95. Diary, 7 Oct. 1944.
96. Mildred Norton to AP, 25 Apr. [c. 1944]. 29.32, SPC, Smith.
97. Diary, 2 Jan. 1945.
98. Diary, 20 Apr. 1945.
99. Diary, 30 Nov. 1946.
100. 21.8, SPC, Smith.
101. 8.14, Lilly.
102. SP to AP, Apr. 1946, Lilly.
103. Diary, 18 Jan. 1945.
104. Diary, 10 Jan. 1945.
105. Diary, 6 Mar. 1945.
106. SP, "Autograph transcript of 40 juvenile poems." 127550, LHMS, Morgan.
107. Diary, 14 Jan. 1945.
108. Diary, 20 Jan. 1945.
109. Diary, 25 Apr. 1945.
110. Diary, 30 Mar. 1945.
111. Diary, 16–18 Apr. 1945.
112. Diary, 11 & 15 Apr. 1945.
113. SP, "Autograph transcript of 40 juvenile poems." 127550, LHMS, Morgan. "The Wind" also dates from 1945.
114. SP, "Autograph transcript of 40 juvenile poems." 127550, LHMS, Morgan.
115. Diary, 12 Feb. 1945.
116. Diary, 5 Apr. 1945.
117. Diary, 26 May 1945.
118. Diary, 14 June 1945.
119. Diary, 21 June 1945.
120. Diary, 20 June 1945.
121. Diary, 22 June 1945.
122. Diary, 1 July 1945. Sylvia referred to her cabin as a "tent."
123. Diary, 7 July 1945.
124. Diary, 5 July & 2 July 1945. *L1*, 22; 24.
125. SP to Aurelia and Frank Schober, 13 July 1945. *L1*, 28.
126. Diary, 30 July 1945.
127. Diary, 6 Aug. 1945.
128. Diary, 3 Aug. 1945.
129. Diary, 10 Oct. 1947.
130. Diary, 18 & 19 May 1946.
131. SP, "The Mummy's Tomb," 17 May 1946. 8.15, Lilly.
132. "A May Morning," for example, recalls a spring oriole sighting, "Morning in the Agora" concerns ancient Greek women at a market, and the *Stardust* novella is full of fairy-tale motifs.
133. SP, "Victory," 15 Nov. 1946. 8.19, Lilly.
134. Diary, 8 Aug. 1945.
135. Diary, 10 Aug. 1945.

136. Diary, 15 Aug. 1945.
137. Diary, 20 Aug. 1945.
138. Diary, 21 Aug. 1945.
139. Diary, 27 Aug. & 5 Sept. 1945.
140. AP, "To My Sylvia." Loose item in SP's 1947 diary. 7, Lilly. Dated 27 Oct. 1945.
141. Diary, 15 Oct. 1945.
142. Diary, 12 Oct. 1945.
143. Diary, 7 Nov. 1945.
144. Diary, 28 Nov. 1945.
145. Diary, 4 Sept. 1945.
146. Diary, 25 Nov. 1945.
147. Diary, 26 Nov. 1945.
148. Diary, 18 Dec. 1945.
149. Diary, 11 Oct. 1945.
150. SP, 1944 Notebook. 19.26, SPC, Smith. This poem post-dates 1944.
151. Diary, 31 Dec. 1945.
152. Ibid.
153. "Sylvia's scrapbook" (1940s poetry scrapbook). 8.6, Lilly.

4. MY THOUGHTS TO SHINING FAME ASPIRE

1. Diary, 30 Apr. 1946. All subsequent "diary" citations are from Plath's unpublished 1940s diaries, held in Box 7, Lilly.
2. Diary, 7 June 1946.
3. SP, "Autograph transcript of 40 juvenile poems." 127550, LHMS, Morgan.
4. Diary, 16 Jan. 1946; *L1*, 42–43.
5. 8.6, Lilly.
6. Several biographers (Butscher, Wagner-Martin, Alexander) have asserted that Plath was extremely close—even romantically involved with—Phil McCurdy during this time. However, Plath does not mention McCurdy once in her 1940s diaries, suggesting that he did not play a formative role in her adolescence. McCurdy, who was born in 1935, noted in our interview that he was two grade levels behind Plath, and that they did not date in high school. Warren Plath has also disputed McCurdy's presence in Plath's life in the 1940s, stating that his "sister and he had at most slight contact during the years he was in junior high school and she was in high school." (WP to Edward Butscher, 31 Aug. 1975. EBC, Smith.) He and Plath did become close in the 1950s.
7. Diary, 11 Mar. 1946.
8. Diary, 22 Mar. 1946.
9. Diary, 10 Apr. 1946.
10. Diary, 8 Apr. 1946.
11. Diary, 5 Mar. 1946.
12. Diary, 8 Mar. 1946.
13. Diary, 27 & 28 May 1946.
14. Diary, 3 June 1946.
15. SP, 1944 notebook. 19.26, SPC, Smith. Though the notebook cover is dated 1944, several pieces inside post-date this year.
16. Diary, 15 & 31 Jan. 1946.
17. Diary, 7 May 1946.
18. Diary, 30 Mar. 1946.
19. Diary, 11 May 1946.
20. "Sylvia's scrapbook" (1940s poetry scrapbook). 8.6, Lilly.
21. Diary, 26 Jan. 1945 & 13 June 1946.
22. Diary, 20 June 1946.
23. Diary, 23, 24, 25 June 1946. Plath refers to this novella as both *Stardust* and *Star-Dust* in these diary entries, though by early 1947 she refers to it regularly in her diary as *Stardust*.
24. Diary, 14 July 1946.

25. Diary, 28 July 1946.
26. Diary, 31 July 1946.
27. Diary, 2 Aug. 1946.
28. Diary, 18 Aug. 1946.
29. Diary, 4 & 19 Aug. 1946.
30. Diary, 25 Aug. 1946.
31. Diary, 26 Aug. 1946.
32. Diary, 17 Oct. 1946.
33. Diary, 30 Aug. 1946.
34. Diary, 7 Sept. 1946.
35. Diary, 3 Aug. 1946.
36. Helen Lawson to Edward Butscher, 27 Nov. 1972. EBC, 1.41, Smith.
37. Diary, 8 Sept. 1946.
38. Diary, 14 Sept. 1946.
39. Diary, 30 Sept. & 6 Oct. 1946.
40. Diary, 21 Oct. 1946.
41. Diary, 1 Nov. 1946.
42. Diary, 31 Oct. 1946.
43. Diary, 5 Nov. 1946.
44. Ibid.
45. Diary, 10 Nov. 1946.
46. *J*, 151.
47. Diary, 13 May 1947. Plath's award certificates for these competitions are held at Lilly.
48. AP's annotation in SP's diary, 22 Nov. 1946.
49. Diary, 31 Jan. 1947.
50. Diary, 26 & 13 Nov. 1946.
51. SP, "From the Memoirs of a Babysitter," 2 Dec. 1946. 8.12, Lilly.
52. Diary, 1 Nov. 1947.
53. Diary, 16 Apr. 1947.
54. Diary, 7 May 1947.
55. Diary, 28 Dec. 1946.
56. Ibid.
57. Diary, 30 Dec. 1946.
58. Diary, 5 Jan. 1947.
59. SP, high school scrapbook. 10.O3, Lilly.
60. Diary, 22 Jan. 1947.
61. Diary, 24 Jan. 1947.
62. Diary, 23 Mar. 1947.
63. Diary, 12 May 1947; diary, 23 Nov. 1946.
64. Diary, 3 Feb. 1947.
65. Diary, 8 Mar. 1947.
66. Diary, 12 Mar. 1947.
67. Diary, 9 Aug. 1947.
68. Diary, 31 Jan. 1947.
69. Diary, 11 Feb. 1947.
70. Diary, 22 Feb. 1947.
71. Diary, 29 July 1947.
72. Diary, 16 Aug. 1947.
73. Diary, 20 Feb. 1947.
74. Diary, 21 Feb. 1947.
75. Diary, 28 July 1947.
76. Diary, 25 May 1947.
77. Ibid.
78. "Sylvia's scrapbook" (1940s poetry scrapbook). 8.6, Lilly.
79. Diary, 16 May 1947.
80. Diary, 18 Apr. 1947.

81. Diary, 30 May 1947.
82. Ibid.
83. 7.12, Lilly.
84. Plath biographer Paul Alexander, for example, says the poem "represents an early window into Plath's potentially extreme emotional states." He also pointed to the narrator's "solipsism" and the poem's "peculiar sentiments." *Rough Magic: A Biography of Sylvia Plath* (New York: Da Capo Press, 1999), 52.
85. Anne Stevenson, *Bitter Fame: A Life of Sylvia Plath* (London: Penguin, 1989), 2.
86. Diary, 11 June 1947.
87. Ibid.
88. Diary, 3 Apr. & 26 Aug. 1947.
89. Diary, 18 June 1947.
90. Diary, 30 June 1947.
91. SP to AP, 1–3 July 1947. *L1*, 94.
92. SP, high school scrapbook. 10.O3, Lilly.
93. Diary, 9 July 1947.
94. Diary, 6 July 1947.
95. Diary, 12 July 1947.
96. Ibid.
97. Diary, 16 Aug. 1947.
98. Diary, 25 July 1947.
99. AP, "For the Authors' Series Talk—Wellesley College Club," 16 Mar. 1976. 30.58, SPC, Smith.
100. Diary, 25 July 1947.
101. Diary, 27 July 1947.
102. Diary, 12 July 1947.
103. Diary, 21 Aug. 1947.
104. Diary, 1 Sept. 1947.
105. Diary, 19 Sept. 1947.
106. SP, high school scrapbook. 10.O3, Lilly.
107. HC interview with Betsy Powley Wallingford, Feb. 2013, Sudbury, Mass.; Ruth Freeman Geissler to HC, 30 Nov. 2012.
108. HC interview with Perry Norton, Oct. 2012, Auburndale, Mass.
109. HC interview with Betsy Powley Wallingford, Feb. 2013, Sudbury, Mass.
110. Stevenson, *Bitter Fame*, 14; Andrew Wilson, *Mad Girl's Love Song: Sylvia Plath and Life Before Ted* (New York: Scribner, 2013), 51.
111. Dr. Ruth Beuscher interview with AP, 15 Sept. 1953. 3.10, MSS 1489, Emory.
112. Diary, 27 Sept. 1947.
113. Diary, 3 Oct. 1947.
114. Diary, 7 Nov. & 22 Dec. 1947.
115. SP to AP, 9 Sept. 1947. *L1*, 108.
116. Diary, 9 & 25 Jan. 1948.
117. Diary, 1 Feb. & 25 Jan. 1948.
118. Diary, 18 Mar. 1948.
119. Diary, 14 Mar. 1948.
120. HC interview with Perry Norton, Oct. 2012, Auburndale, Mass.
121. Dr. Ruth Beuscher interview with AP, 15 Sept. 1953. 3.10, MSS 1489, Emory.
122. Diary, 1 Oct. 1947.
123. Diary, 11 Oct. 1947.
124. Diary, 13 Nov. 1947.
125. Diary, 30 Oct. 1947.
126. Diary, 13 Dec. 1947.
127. Diary, 31 Dec. 1947.
128. SP, "Party Girl." MS notes for short story. Filed under "Star Island." 15.29, SPC, Smith.
129. Diary, 14 Dec. 1947.
130. Ibid.

5. THE VOICE WITHIN

1. Douglas T. Miller and Marion Nowak, *The Fifties: The Way We Really Were* (New York: Doubleday, 1977), 38.
2. Ibid., 44.
3. Plath called Tommy Duggin "atomic" in her diary and wrote that she "dropped a hint, as gentle as an A-bomb that I wasn't busy Thursday A.M." to a boy she wanted to date.
4. Miller and Nowak, *The Fifties*, 62–63.
5. Ibid., 63.
6. SP, "The United States and the World," Mar. 1946. 20.5, SPC, Smith.
7. SP, "A War to End All Wars," Feb. 1946. 20.3, SPC, Smith.
8. The pen-pal program was organized by the US government as part of a broader post-war reconciliation effort, and administered through local schools.
9. SP to Hans-Joachim Neupert, 14 June 1948. *L1*, 110; SP to Hans-Joachim Neupert, 20 Dec. 1948. *L1*, 137.
10. Ibid., 10 Oct. 1949. *L1*, 152.
11. Ibid., 24 Sept. 1948. *L1*, 135.
12. Ibid., 13 Apr. 1947. *L1*, 87–88.
13. SP, high school scrapbook. 10.03, Lilly.
14. SP to Hans-Joachim Neupert, 12 Aug. 1950. *L1*, 168–69.
15. Ibid., 24 Dec. 1950. *L1*, 250–51.
16. Ibid., 12 Aug. 1950. *L1*, 168.
17. Ibid., 24 Dec. 1950. *L1*, 251.
18. Ibid., 24 Aug. 1949. *L1*, 151–52. SP's ellipses.
19. SP, "Witchcraft in America," English 21 (part of Hawthorne paper), 1947–48. 10.1, Lilly.
20. SP and Perry Norton, "Youth's Plea for World Peace," *Christian Science Monitor* (16 Mar. 1950), 19.
21. HC interview with Perry Norton, Oct. 2012, Auburndale, Mass.
22. 8.5, Lilly. The poem was published as "April: 1949" in *The Bradford* on 28 Mar. 1949.
23. *J*, 470.
24. SP's copy of *Emerson: The Basic Writings of America's Sage*, Eduard C. Lindeman, ed. (New York: Pelican 1947), 50. 825 P696L, SPC, Smith.
25. Ibid., 163.
26. Up until the 1950s, Nietzsche was viewed in the United States as a "prophet of the Third Reich," labeled "half a Nazi" in a 1941 study by the Harvard historian Crane Brinton. See Peter Gay, "Introduction," *Basic Writings of Nietzsche*, Walter Kaufmann, trans. (New York: Modern Library/Random House, 2000), xi. It was not until Walter Kaufmann's *Nietzsche: Philosopher, Psychologist, Antichrist* (1950) that the academy began to reassess Nietzsche.
27. The class was History 38b, with Mrs. Koffka.
28. HC interview with Mel Woody, Sept. 2018, Lyme, Conn.
29. SP to Mel Woody, 26 Jan. 1955. *L1*, 871.
30. HC interview with Phil McCurdy, May 2016, Ogunquit, Maine.
31. HC interviews with Perry Norton (2012), Phil McCurdy (2016), and Louise Giesey White (2014).
32. HC interview with Phil McCurdy, May 2016, Ogunquit, Maine.
33. HC interview with Perry Norton, Oct. 2012, Auburndale, Mass.
34. Frank Irish email to HC, 9 Dec. 2012.
35. HC interview with Louise Giesey White, Aug. 2014, Jamestown, R.I.
36. Harriet Rosenstein interview with Pat O'Neil Pratson, 1972. 3.12, MSS 1489, Emory.
37. Anne-Marie Smolski, "Wellesley High School Library Rededicated to Wilbury Crockett," *Wellesley Townsman* (17 May 2012).
38. Harold Kolb Jr., "Mr. Crockett," *Virginia Quarterly* 78.2 (Spring 2002): 312–23, 317.
39. SP to AP, 9 Sept. 1947. *L1*, 108.
40. Diary, 10 Oct. 1947.
41. Harriet Rosenstein interview with AP, 1970. 3.3, MSS 1489, Emory.

42. Harriet Rosenstein interview with Pat O'Neil Pratson, 1972. 3.12, MSS 1489, Emory.
43. HC interview with Louise Giesey White, Aug. 2014, Jamestown, R.I.
44. Kolb, "Mr. Crockett," 312.
45. HC interview with Perry Norton, Oct. 2012, Auburndale, Mass.
46. Kolb, "Mr. Crockett," 312.
47. HC interview with Louise Giesey White, Aug. 2014, Jamestown, R.I.
48. Harriet Rosenstein interview with Pat O'Neil Pratson, 1972. 3.12, MSS 1489, Emory.
49. HC interview with Phil McCurdy, May 2016, Ogunquit, Maine.
50. Bob Tremblay, "Wilbury Crockett Revisited," *Wellesley Townsman* (20 Aug. 1981).
51. Beth Hinchliffe, "Sylvia Plath's Wellesley Years," 21 Feb. 2013, http://www.wicked local.com/wellesley; Beth Hinchliffe, "Sylvia Plath—Legacy Lives in the Wake of Tragedy," *Wellesley Townsman* (2 Apr. 1981).
52. Harriet Rosenstein interview with Wilbury Crockett, 1971. 1.19, MSS 1489, Emory.
53. SP to Hans-Joachim Neupert, 26 Nov. 1949. *L1*, 158.
54. Kolb, "Mr. Crockett," 318.
55. SP to Eddie Cohen, 6 Aug. 1950. *L1*, 164.
56. AP, "Biographical Jottings about Sylvia Plath." 30.57, SPC, Smith.
57. SP to AP, 4 Dec. 1956. *L2*, 27.
58. SP, untitled assignment for Crockett, English 21, 1947–48. 10.1, Lilly.
59. SP, "The Atomic Threat," *Bradford* (26 Apr. 1948), 1.
60. 8.3, Lilly.
61. SP, "*Romeo and Juliet*," English 31, 1948–49. 10.1, Lilly.
62. SP, "*The Scarlet Letter:* Book Review," English 21, 1947–48. 10.1, Lilly.
63. SP, "Reports on Three Short Stories," English 21, 1947–48. 10.1, Lilly.
64. Ibid.
65. SP, "*Mrs. Dalloway*," English 31, 1948–49. 10.1, Lilly.
66. *J*, 495.
67. Assignment on Schweitzer, Mormonism, and *The Snake Pit* for Crockett, English 41. 10.1, Lilly.
68. 10.1, Lilly.
69. Ibid.
70. All of Plath's high school poems quoted in this chapter are in Boxes 7 and 8, Lilly.
71. SP, "T. S. Eliot." 10.1, Lilly.
72. SP to Hans-Joachim Neupert, 10 Oct. 1949. *L1*, 157.
73. *The Collected Poems of W. B. Yeats*, Richard J. Finneran, ed. (New York: Macmillan, 1989), 125.

6. SUMMER WILL NOT COME AGAIN

1. SP to AP, 2 July 1948. *L1*, 113.
2. SP to AP, 3 July 1948. *L1*, 114.
3. SP to AP, 5 July 1948. *L1*, 116; SP to AP, 2 July 1948. *L1*, 113.
4. SP to AP, 13 July 1948. *L1*, 121.
5. SP to AP, 11 & 12 July 1948. *L1*, 120.
6. SP to AP, 17 July 1948. *L1*, 125–26.
7. SP to AP, 20 July (#1) 1948. *L1*, 128.
8. SP to AP, 20 July (#2) 1948. *L1*, 128.
9. SP to AP, 21 July 1948. *L1*, 130.
10. SP, high school scrapbook. 10.O3, Lilly.
11. Harriet Rosenstein interview with AP, 1970. 3.3, MSS 1489, Emory.
12. SP, high school scrapbook, 10.O3, Lilly.
13. The story appeared in *Seventeen* (Jan. 1953): 64–65; 92–94. It was later published in *JP*, 137–47.
14. HC interview with Louise Giesey White, Aug. 2014, Jamestown, R.I.
15. Harriet Rosenstein interview with Pat O'Neil Pratson, 1972. 3.12, MSS 1489, Emory.
16. SP to Eddie Cohen, 6 Aug. 1950. *L1*, 164–65.

17. All stories quoted in this chapter are arranged alphabetically in Box 8, Folders 10–19, Lilly.
18. Harriet Rosenstein interview with AP, 1970. 3.3, MSS 1489, Emory.
19. Harriet Rosenstein interview with Pat O'Neil Pratson, 1972. 3.12, MSS 1489, Emory.
20. SP, high school scrapbook. 10.O3, Lilly.
21. Ibid.
22. *Bradford* (7 June 1949). 10.O2, Lilly.
23. Beth Hinchliffe, "Sylvia Plath's Wellesley Years," 21 Feb. 2013, http://www.wicked local.com/wellesley.
24. SP to Hans-Joachim Neupert, 24 Aug. 1949. *L1*, 151.
25. Diary, 19 June 1949.
26. "Far Horizons," Star Island newsletter (1 July 1949). 10.O3, Lilly.
27. SP to Hans-Joachim Neupert, 4 July 1949. *L1*, 148.
28. Diary, 27 June 1949.
29. Diary, 5 July 1949.
30. Diary, 8 & 22 July 1949.
31. Diary, 22 July 1949.
32. Diary, 12 July 1949.
33. Diary, 16 July 1949.
34. Diary, 22 July 1949.
35. Diary, 2 Aug. 1949.
36. Diary, 3 Aug. 1949.
37. Diary, Aug. 1949, undated entries.
38. *Seventeen* (Aug. 1950): 191; 275–76.
39. 8.4, Lilly.
40. *J*, 163.
41. Diary, Aug. 1949, undated entries.
42. Ibid.
43. Ibid.
44. Ibid.
45. Ibid.
46. SP, high school scrapbook. 10.O3, Lilly.
47. Diary, 13 Nov. 1949. SP's ellipsis.
48. Ibid.
49. Diary, 24 Nov. 1949.
50. Ibid.
51. William H. Young and Nancy K. Young, *The 1950s* (Westport, Conn.: Greenwood Press, 2004), 31.
52. Diary, 24 Nov. 1949. She probably agreed with an article in one of the *Bradford* editions she published in Mar. 1950 that argued going steady in high school was "a mistake" that posed "serious risk." W. G. Stergios, "Going Steady II," *Bradford* (24 Mar. 1950). 10.O2, Lilly.
53. 7.7, Lilly.
54. "When I'm a Parent," *Seventeen* (Nov. 1949): 77.
55. SP to Hans-Joachim Neupert, 24 Aug. 1949. *L1*, 150.
56. HC interview with Betsy Powley Wallingford, Feb. 2013, Sudbury, Mass.
57. HC interview with Richard Larschan, May 2017, Manhattan.
58. AP, handwritten notes on letter from Mary Mensel to SP, 3 Jan. 1950, to scholarship applicants. Lilly.
59. SP to Hans-Joachim Neupert, 26 Nov. 1949. *L1*, 158.
60. Ibid., 20 Feb. 1950. *L1*, 161.
61. 7.13, Lilly.
62. SP, "*Kristin Lavransdatter*," English 41, 1949–50. 10.1, Lilly.
63. Reference of Samuel M. Graves, principal of Gamaliel Bradford High School, Vocational Office, Smith College Archives.
64. From *The Boston Globe*, she won prizes for the Best News Story, Best Poem, and Best Write-Up of Editors' Convention (1950).

65. Wilbury Crockett to John F. Malley, 25 Feb. 1952, "Elks Notebook." 12.6, Lilly. Reference of Samuel M. Graves, Vocational Office, Smith College Archives.
66. Elizabeth Aldrich to Mary Mensel, 3 Feb. 1950, Vocational Office, Smith College Archives.
67. SP, "Family Reunion," *Bradford* (29 Apr. 1950). 10.O2, Lilly.
68. AP, notes on "fact versus fiction" in SP's poems, n.d. Courtesy of Richard Larschan.
69. Diary, 27 Nov. 1949.
70. SP to Hans-Joachim Neupert, 2 Jan. 1950. *L1*, 159.
71. Diary, 13 Nov. 1949.
72. Diary, Aug. 1949, undated entries.
73. Diary, 13 Nov. 1949.
74. SP, high school scrapbook. 10.O3, Lilly.
75. "'The Admirable Crichton' Senior Play Success," *Wellesley Townsman* (20 Apr. 1950). The play was performed on April 14, 1950. 10.O2, Lilly.
76. "Bewitched, Bothered, and Bewildered," *Bradford* (4 Mar. 1950). 10.O2, Lilly. There is no byline, but Plath and Irish likely wrote the piece.
77. "So Long for a While," *Bradford* (4 June 1950). 10.O2, Lilly.
78. AP to Judith Kroll, 1 Dec. 1978. 29.26, SPC, Smith.
79. SP, high school scrapbook. 10.O3, Lilly.
80. Ibid.
81. SP, 1949–50 report card for English 41, US History 31, College Biology, French 3, and Painting 3. 9.12, Lilly.
82. SP, "Elks Notebook." 12.6, Lilly.
83. HC interview with Louise Giesey White, Aug. 2014, Jamestown, R.I.
84. SP's copy of *The Wellesleyan* (1950 yearbook). 10.4, Lilly.
85. 10.1, Lilly.
86. SP, "Character Notebook" (notes for *Falcon Yard*), written on the back of TH's *Bardo Thodol*, 116.1, MSS 644, Emory.

7. THE WHITE QUEEN

1. *J*, 9–10.
2. *J*, 9.
3. *J*, 22–23.
4. *J*, 8.
5. Plath wrote two short pieces about this summer, "The International Flavor" and "Rewards of a New England Summer."
6. SP to Eddie Cohen, 6 Aug. 1950. *L1*, 164.
7. Ted Hughes would also spend a summer harvesting crops alongside German prisoners of war. Ruled blue school notebook, 1–2. Add MS 88918/1/55, BL.
8. HC telephone interview with Phil McCurdy, 6 Dec. 2014.
9. SP to Eddie Cohen, 11 Aug. 1950. *L1*, 167.
10. Ibid.
11. *J*, 10–11.
12. SP, "The Latvian." 8.14, Lilly.
13. *J*, 13.
14. *J*, 16; 20.
15. *J*, 18; 21.
16. *J*, 16–17.
17. SP to Eddie Cohen, 6 Aug. 1950, *L1*, 164; *J*, 38.
18. *J*, 16.
19. Eddie Cohen to SP, 3 Aug. 1950. Lilly.
20. SP to Eddie Cohen, 6 Aug. 1950. *L1*, 165.
21. Eddie Cohen to SP, 8 Aug. 1950. Lilly.
22. Eddie Cohen to SP, 29 Sept. 1950. Lilly.
23. SP to Eddie Cohen, 11 Aug. 1950. *L1*, 165–66.

24. Eddie Cohen to SP, 8 Aug. 1950. Lilly.
25. SP to Eddie Cohen, 11 Aug. 1950. *L1*, 165.
26. Eddie Cohen to SP, 28 Sept. 1950. Lilly.
27. SP to Eddie Cohen, 11 Aug. 1950. *L1*, 167.
28. Ibid., *L1*, 165.
29. Eddie Cohen to SP, 8 Dec. 1950. Lilly.
30. Eddie Cohen to SP, 25 Aug. 1950. Lilly.
31. Eddie Cohen to SP, 5 Oct. 1950. Lilly.
32. Eddie Cohen to SP, 24 Oct. 1950. Lilly.
33. Eddie Cohen to SP, 15 Sept. 1950. Lilly.
34. Ibid. Eddie quotes SP's words in this letter.
35. Ibid.
36. Eddie Cohen to SP, 2 Sept. 1950. Lilly.
37. Eddie Cohen to SP, c. autumn 1950; 7 Nov. 1950. Lilly.
38. SP to Eddie Cohen, c. 11 Sept. 1950. *L1*, 172 (copy re-sent to SP from Eddie Cohen at SP's request, 14 May 1951).
39. Eddie Cohen to SP, 15 & 21 Sept. 1950. Lilly.
40. SP to Hans-Joachim Neupert, 12 Aug. 1950. *L1*, 168.
41. SP to Eddie Cohen, c. 11 Sept. 1950. *L1*, 171.
42. SP to Eddie Cohen, 6 Aug. 1950. *L1*, 164.
43. Eddie Cohen to SP, n.d. (early Sept. 1950). Lilly.
44. SP to Eddie Cohen, c. 11 Sept. 1950. *L1*, 172.
45. Eddie Cohen to SP, 19 Aug. 1950. Lilly.
46. Eddie Cohen to SP, 5 Oct. 1950. Lilly. Eddie quotes SP's words in this letter.
47. *J*, 22.
48. *J*, 17.
49. HC interview with Louise Giesey White, Aug. 2014, Jamestown, R.I. Another Smith friend, Janet Salter Rosenberg, remembered that while the faculty were very liberal, the student body was "80 percent Republican." Interview, Sept. 2015, Dobbs Ferry, N.Y.
50. Nancy Hunter Steiner, *A Closer Look at Ariel: A Memory of Sylvia Plath* (New York: Harper's Magazine Press, 1973), 35–36.
51. SP to Marcia Brown, 12 June 1951. *L1*, 337.
52. SP to AP, 18 Apr. 1951. *L1*, 306.
53. Steiner, *A Closer Look*, 77.
54. Adlai Stevenson, Commencement Address, 6 June 1955. Commencement Speech files, Class of 1955 records, Smith College Archives.
55. Steiner, *A Closer Look*, 81.
56. HC interview with Louise Giesey White, Aug. 2014, Jamestown, R.I.
57. Margaret Shook, "Sylvia Plath: The Poet and the College," *Smith College Alumnae Quarterly* 63.3 (April 1972): 4–9; 7.
58. HC interview with Elinor Friedman Klein, Oct. 2015, South Salem, N.Y.
59. SP to Ann Davidow, 20 May 1951. *L1*, 327–28.
60. SP to AP, 24 Sept. 1950. *L1*, 172.
61. SP to AP, 25 Sept. 1950. *L1*, 174.
62. SP to AP, 24 Sept. 1950. *L1*, 172.
63. SP to AP, 26 Sept. 1950. *L1*, 174.
64. Ibid.
65. SP to AP, 30 Sept. 1950. *L1*, 181.
66. SP to AP, 26 Sept. 1950. *L1*, 175.
67. SP to AP, 27 Sept. 1950. *L1*, 178.
68. SP to AP, 26 Sept. 1950. *L1*, 174. SP's ellipses.
69. Ibid., *L1*, 176–77.
70. Harriet Rosenstein interview with Peter and Jane Davison, 1973. 1.22, MSS 1489, Emory.
71. HC interview with Janet Salter Rosenberg, Sept. 2015, Dobbs Ferry, N.Y.

72. SP to AP, 26 Sept. 1950. *L1*, 177.
73. Margaret Shook, "Sylvia Plath: The Poet and the College," *Smith College Alumnae Quarterly* 63.3 (April 1972): 4–9; 7.
74. SP to AP, 27 Sept. 1950. *L1*, 178.
75. SP to AP, 30 Sept. 1950. *L1*, 181.
76. Ibid., *L1*, 182.
77. SP to AP, 1 Oct. 1950. *L1*, 184.
78. SP to AP, 2 Oct. 1950. *L1*, 185.
79. SP to AP, 30 Sept. 1950. *L1*, 182.
80. SP to AP, 3 Oct. 1950. *L1*, 186.
81. SP to AP, 2 Oct. 1950. *L1*, 185.
82. SP to AP, 4 Oct. 1950. *L1*, 187.
83. SP to AP, 8 Oct. 1950. *L1*, 190–91.
84. SP to AP, 9 Oct. 1950. *L1*, 192–93.
85. SP to AP, 10 Oct. (#1 & #2) 1950. *L1*, 194–96.
86. SP to AP, 12 Oct. 1950. *L1*, 196.
87. *J*, 26–27.
88. *J*, 24.
89. This was a common theme in the recollections of Plath's Smith peers in the Harriet Rosenstein archive, MSS 1489, Emory.
90. *J*, 25.
91. *J*, 32.
92. 8.4, Lilly (c. Sept. 1950–June 1952).
93. Janet Burroway, *Embalming Mom: Essays in Life* (Iowa City: University of Iowa Press, 2002), 20.
94. HC interview with Elinor Friedman Klein, Oct. 2015, South Salem, N.Y.
95. *J*, 559.
96. *J*, 23.
97. *J*, 44.
98. The poem was written on 14 Nov. 1954.
99. *J*, 31.
100. *J*, 36.
101. *J*, 45.
102. SP to AP, 23 Oct. 1950. *L1*, 203.
103. Harriet Rosenstein interview with Constance Taylor Blackwell, 20 Apr. 1974. 1.9, MSS 1489, Emory.
104. SP to AP, 20 Oct. 1950. *L1*, 201.
105. SP to AP, 23 Oct. 1950. *L1*, 204–205.
106. SP to AP, 24 Oct. 1950. *L1*, 205.
107. SP to AP, 25 Oct. 1950. *L1*, 206.
108. SP to AP, 18 Oct. 1950. *L1*, 199.
109. *J*, 35.
110. SP to AP, 27 Oct. 1950. *L1*, 208.
111. SP to AP, 31 Oct. 1950. *L1*, 211.
112. SP to AP, 30 Oct. 1950. *L1*, 210–11.
113. SP to AP, 31 Oct. 1950. *L1*, 213.
114. HC interview with Louise Giesey White, Aug. 2014, Jamestown, R.I.
115. SP to AP, 31 Oct. 1950. *L1*, 212.
116. SP to AP, 9 Nov. 1950 (#1). *L1*, 218.
117. Eddie Cohen to SP, 5 Nov. 1950. Lilly.
118. Ibid.
119. SP to AP, 7 Nov. 1950. *L1*, 218.
120. SP to AP, 11 Nov. 1950. *L1*, 221.
121. SP to AP, 13 Nov. 1950. *L1*, 222.
122. SP to AP, 3 Nov. 1950. *L1*, 215.
123. SP to AP, 10 Nov. 1950. *L1*, 220.
124. HC phone interview with Guy Wilbor, 10 July 2014.

125. SP to AP, 19 Nov. 1950. *L1*, 227.
126. SP to AP, 17 Nov. 1950. *L1*, 226.
127. *J*, 33.
128. *J*, 30.
129. SP to AP, 26 Nov. 1950. *L1*, 229.
130. SP to AP, 28 Nov. 1950. *L1*, 229.
131. SP to AP, 26 Nov. 1950. *L1*, 228.
132. *J*, 30.
133. SP to AP, 29 Nov. 1950. *L1*, 231.
134. *J*, 31–32.
135. *J*, 32–33.
136. SP to AP, 1 Dec. 1950. *L1*, 236.
137. SP to AP, 10 Dec. 1950. *L1*, 244.
138. SP to AP, 3 Dec. 1950. *L1*, 237–38.
139. HC phone interview with Guy Wilbor, 10 July 2014.
140. SP to AP, 15 Dec. 1950. *L1*, 250.
141. SP to Ann Davidow, 7 Jan. 1951. *L1*, 255–66.
142. Ibid., 255. Last ellipsis is SP's.
143. SP, "Tea with Olive Higgins Prouty" (19 July 1955). 9.2, Lilly.
144. SP to AP, 13 Jan. 1951. *L1*, 260–61. SP's ellipsis.
145. Ibid., *L1*, 261.
146. SP to Ann Davidow, c. 12 Jan. 1951. *L1*, 259.
147. Ibid., 20 May 1951. *L1*, 328.
148. *J*, 33.
149. *J*, 43.
150. *J*, 35.
151. SP, "Den of Lions." 8.11, Lilly. The story was published in *Seventeen* in May 1951.
152. SP to AP, 13 Jan. 1951. *L1*, 262.
153. Ibid., *L1*, 261.
154. *J*, 22.
155. SP to AP, 10 Jan. 1951. *L1*, 257.
156. SP to AP, 18 Jan. 1951. *L1*, 265.
157. SP to AP, 21 Jan. 1951. *L1*, 267.
158. Harriet Rosenstein interview with Marcia Brown Stern, 1972–73. 4.16, MSS 1489, Emory.
159. Harriet Rosenstein interview with Peter and Jane Davison, 1973. 1.22, MSS 1489, Emory.
160. Harriet Rosenstein interview with Marcia Brown Stern, 1972–73. 4.16, MSS 1489, Emory.
161. Ibid. See also Rosenstein's interview with Enid Epstein Mark, MSS 1489, Emory.
162. SP to AP, 6 Mar. 1951. *L1*, 294.
163. SP to AP, 20 Feb. 1951. *L1*, 285; SP to Ann Davidow, 14 Feb. 1951. *L1*, 279.
164. HC interview with Louise Giesey White, Aug. 2014, Jamestown, R.I.
165. Harriet Rosenstein interview with Marcia Brown Stern, 1972–73. 4. 16, MSS 1489, Emory.
166. SP to AP, 31 Jan. 1951. *L1*, 269.
167. SP to AP, 3 Mar. 1951. *L1*, 289.
168. SP to AP, 10 Mar. 1951. *L1*, 296.
169. SP to AP, 8 Feb. 1951. *L1*, 276.
170. SP to AP, 1 Mar. 1951. *L1*, 289.
171. SP to AP, 5 Mar. 1951. *L1*, 293.
172. SP to Ann Davidow, 3 Feb. 1951. *L1*, 271.
173. SP to AP, 21 Jan. 1951 (#1 & #2). *L1*, 267.
174. SP to AP, 11 Feb. 1951. *L1*, 278.
175. SP to AP, 22 Feb. 1951. *L1*, 286.
176. Ibid., *L1*, 287.
177. SP to AP, 20 Feb. 1951. *L1*, 284.

178. Ibid., *L1*, 285.
179. SP to Ann Davidow, 5 Mar. 1951. *L1*, 292.
180. SP to AP, 19 Feb. 1951. *L1*, 283.
181. SP to AP, 20 Feb. 1951. *L1*, 285; SP to Ann Davidow, 5 Mar. 1951. *L1*, 291.
182. SP to Ann Davidow, 5 Mar. 1951. *L1*, 291.
183. SP to AP, 5 Mar. 1951. *L1*, 293.
184. DN to SP, 1 Mar. 1951. Lilly.
185. Ibid.
186. SP to AP, 9 Mar. 1951. *L1*, 295.
187. SP to Ann Davidow, 15–16 Mar. 1951. *L1*, 298. First ellipsis is SP's.
188. SP and DN to AP, 10 Mar. 1951. Lilly.
189. DN to SP, 3 Apr. 1951. Lilly.
190. SP to AP, 15 May 1951. *L1*, 322.
191. SP to AP, 10 Mar. 1951. *L1*, 296.
192. SP to Ann Davidow, 9 May 1951. *L1*, 318.
193. Eddie Cohen to SP, 19 Mar. 1951. Lilly.
194. SP to AP, 8 Apr. 1951. *L1*, 302.
195. SP to AP, 10 Apr. 1951. *L1*, 302.
196. SP to AP, 18 Apr. 1951. *L1*, 305.
197. SP to AP, 21 Apr. 1951. *L1*, 308.
198. SP to AP, 27 Apr. 1951. *L1*, 310.
199. SP to AP, 15 May 1951. *L1*, 321–22.
200. SP to AP, 18 Apr. 1951. *L1*, 305.
201. Eddie Cohen to SP, 3 May 1951. Lilly.
202. *J*, 38.
203. SP, "Den of Lions." 8.11, Lilly. Plath's marginalia is undated.
204. Eddie Cohen to SP, 3 May 1951. Lilly.
205. DN to SP, 19 May 1951. Lilly.
206. DN to SP, 3 May 1951. Lilly.
207. Eddie Cohen to SP, 6 May 1951. Lilly. Eddie quotes SP in this letter.
208. SP to AP, 8 May 1951. *L1*, 315–16.
209. SP to Marcia Brown, 6 June 1951. *L1*, 333.
210. Ibid., *L1*, 332.
211. HC interview with Phil McCurdy, May 2016, Ogunquit, Maine.
212. SP to Marcia Brown, 6 June 1951. *L1*, 334.
213. *J*, 52.
214. SP to Marcia Brown, 12 June 1951. *L1*, 335.
215. Ibid., *L1*, 336.

8. LOVE IS A PARALLAX

1. SP to Marcia Brown, 29 May 1951. *L1*, 329–30.
2. SP, "Somebody and We," 15 Nov. 1951. 10.8, Lilly.
3. SP to Marcia Brown, 20 June 1951. *L1*, 341.
4. SP to Ann Davidow, 26 June 1951. *L1*, 347.
5. SP, "Somebody and We." 10.8, Lilly.
6. SP to Ann Davidow, 26 June 1951. *L1*, 349.
7. SP, "Somebody and We." 10.8, Lilly.
8. Reference for SP from Mrs. Mayo, Vocational Office, Smith College Archives.
9. Andrew Wilson, *Mad Girl's Love Song: Sylvia Plath and Life Before Ted* (New York: Scribner, 2013), 137.
10. SP, "Somebody and We." 10.8, Lilly.
11. SP to Marcia Brown, 20 June 1951. *L1*, 340.
12. SP to Ann Davidow, 26 June 1951. *L1*, 349.
13. Ibid., *L1*, 348.
14. SP to Marcia Brown, 20 June 1951. *L1*, 340.
15. SP, "As a Babysitter Sees It," *Christian Science Monitor* (6 Nov. 1951), 19.

16. SP to AP, 6 July 1951. *L1*, 355.
17. SP to AP, 4 Aug. 1951. *L1*, 361.
18. SP to AP, 19 June 1951. *L1*, 339.
19. SP to Ann Davidow, 6 July 1951. *L1*, 352.
20. SP to AP, 19 June 1951. *L1*, 338–39.
21. *J*, 69.
22. *J*, 76–77.
23. SP to Mel Woody, 22 June 1951. *L1*, 345.
24. *J*, 78.
25. *J*, 90.
26. *J*, 85.
27. SP, "Somebody and We." 10.8, Lilly.
28. Ibid.
29. SP to Mel Woody, 22 June 1951. *L1*, 346.
30. Anitas Helle makes this connection in "Electroshock Therapy and Plath's Convulsive Poetics" in *Sylvia Plath in Context*, Tracy Brain, ed. (Cambridge: Cambridge University Press, 2019), 264–74; 267.
31. SP, "I Am An American." 7.12, Lilly. Part of this poem appears in SP to Mel Woody, 22 June 1951. *L1*, 346.
32. Harriet Rosenstein interview with Marcia Brown Stern, 1972. 4.16, MSS 1489, Emory.
33. Anne Harrington, *Mind Fixers: Psychiatry's Troubled Search for the Biology of Mental Illness* (New York: Norton, 2019), 93–94.
34. *J*, 64–65.
35. Harriet Rosenstein interview with Marcia Brown Stern, 1972. 4.16, MSS 1489, Emory.
36. The translation he read to her was by Jesse Lamont, published by Fine Editions Press, 1945. Mel was adamant that this episode occurred in 1951, during Sylvia and Marcia's nannying summer, and not during the summer of 1953 as previous biographers have reported. He said this was the only time (1951) he ever went to the beach with both women. He was in Ohio during the whole summer of 1953.
37. HC interview with Mel Woody, 17 Sept. 2018, Lyme, Conn.
38. SP to Marcia Brown, 21 June 1951. *L1*, 345.
39. SP to AP, 20 Aug. 1951. *L1*, 365.
40. SP to AP, 23 Aug. 1951. *L1*, 366. SP's ellipsis.
41. *J*, 93; *J*, 91.
42. *J*, 71.
43. *J*, 77.
44. *J*, 88. SP's ellipsis.
45. Eddie Cohen to SP, 16 Sept. 1951. Lilly.
46. SP to Marcia Brown, 11 Sept. 1951. *L1*, 368.
47. Ibid.
48. Ibid., *L1*, 369.
49. SP to Ann Davidow, 12 Sept. 1951. *L1*, 371.
50. Ibid., *L1*, 371–72.
51. SP to AP, 26 Nov. 1951. *L1*, 400.
52. SP to Ann Davidow, 12 Sept. 1951. *L1*, 372.
53. SP to Marcia Brown, 11 Sept. 1951. *L1*, 369.
54. Eddie Cohen to SP, 16 Sept. 1951. Lilly.
55. Conversation with Don Colburn (Dick Norton's brother-in-law), Jan. 2017, Yaddo, Saratoga Springs, N.Y.
56. SP to Marcia Brown, 11 Sept. 1951. *L1*, 369–70.
57. *J*, 306.
58. SP to AP, 27 Sept. 1951. *L1*, 374.
59. Ibid., *L1*, 373.
60. DN to SP, 3 Oct. 1951. Lilly.
61. SP to AP, 21 Oct. 1951. *L1*, 389.
62. SP to AP, 8 Oct. 1951. *L1*, 375–81.
63. SP to AP, 14 Oct. 1951. *L1*, 384.

64. DN to SP, 14 Oct. 1951. Lilly.
65. Eddie Cohen to SP, 26 Oct. 1951. Lilly.
66. Ibid.
67. SP to AP, 20 Oct. 1951 (#2). *L1*, 388.
68. SP to AP, 20 Oct. 1951 (#1). *L1*, 387.
69. SP to AP, 21 Oct. 1951. *L1*, 388.
70. DN to SP, 29 Oct. 1951. Lilly.
71. DN to SP, 17 Nov. 1951. Lilly.
72. SP to AP, 9 Dec. 1951. *L1*, 405.
73. SP to AP, 2 Nov. 1951. *L1*, 392.
74. SP to AP, 29 Oct. 1951. *L1*, 392.
75. Ibid., *L1*, 391.
76. SP, Smith scrapbook. 10.O8, Lilly.
77. SP to AP, 29 Oct. 1951. *L1*, 392.
78. SP to AP, 2 Dec. 1951. *L1*, 401.
79. SP to AP, 5 Dec. 1951. *L1*, 402.
80. SP to AP, 2 Dec. 1951. *L1*, 401.
81. SP to AP, 5 Dec. 1951. *L1*, 401–402.
82. SP to Ann Davidow, 18 Feb. 1952. *L1*, 416.
83. Harriet Rosenstein interview with William Sterling, 1972. 4.14, MSS 1489, Emory.
84. SP to Ann Davidow, 18 Feb. 1952. *L1*, 416–17.
85. Eddie Cohen to SP, 26 Oct. 1951. Lilly.
86. SP, Smith scrapbook. 10.O8, Lilly.
87. Wilson, *Mad Girl's Love Song*, 151.
88. SP to Ann Davidow, 18 Feb. 1952. *L1*, 415.
89. DN to SP, 13 Jan. 1952. Lilly.
90. DN to AP, 21 Jan. 1952. Lilly.
91. SP to Ann Davidow, 18 Feb. 1952. *L1*, 418.
92. SP to AP, 23 Jan. & 8 Feb. 1952. *L1*, 410; 412.
93. SP to AP, 23 Jan. 1952. *L1*, 410.
94. SP to Ann Davidow, 18 Feb. 1952. *L1*, 418.
95. SP to AP, 6 Feb. 1952. *L1*, 412.
96. Eddie Cohen to SP, 13 Feb. 1952. Lilly.
97. DN to SP, 16 Jan. 1952. Lilly.
98. SP to AP, 9–11 Feb. 1952. *L1*, 413.
99. SP to Ann Davidow, 18 Feb. 1952. *L1*, 416.
100. DN to SP, 13–15 Feb. 1952. Lilly.
101. DN to SP, 25 Feb. 1952. Lilly.
102. SP to AP, 25 Feb. 1952. *L1*, 421.
103. SP to Ann Davidow, 21 Mar. 1952. *L1*, 431.
104. *J*, 101–102.
105. DN to SP, 13–15 Apr. 1952. Lilly.
106. SP to AP, 16 Mar. 1952. *L1*, 427.
107. DN to SP, 24 Apr. 1952. Lilly.
108. DN to SP, 5 May 1952. Lilly.
109. DN to SP, 13–15 Apr. 1952. Lilly.
110. *J*, 102.
111. *J*, 105.
112. *J*, 106–107.
113. SP to Ann Davidow, 21 Mar. 1952. *L1*, 432.
114. SP to AP, 4 Mar. 1952. *L1*, 424.
115. SP to AP, 30 Apr. 1952. *L1*, 440.
116. SP, Smith scrapbook. 10.O8, Lilly.
117. HC phone interview with Guy Wilbor, 10 July 2014.
118. SP to AP, 30 Apr. 1952. *L1*, 439.
119. The story has not survived in completion.
120. SP to AP, 6 Mar. 1952. *L1*, 425. Plath's article, which is unattributed but which she

references in the same letter to Aurelia, is "'Heresy Hunts' Menace Liberty: Struik Claims," *Springfield Union* (4 Mar. 1952), 2.

121. Peter Steinberg believes that Plath wrote two unattributed articles about Nash's visit, "Ogden Nash's Rhyming Knack Makes Up for His Talent Lack," *Springfield Union* (1 May 1952), 30; and "Ogden Nash Is Speaker," *Daily Hampshire Gazette* (2 May 1953), 6.
122. SP to AP, 11 May 1952. *L1*, 443.
123. HC interview with Janet Salter Rosenberg, Sept. 2015, Dobbs Ferry, N.Y.
124. SP to AP, 9 Apr. 1952. *L1*, 436.
125. Eddie Cohen to SP, 11 May 1952. Lilly.
126. Evelyn Page to Harriet Rosenstein, c. 7 Feb. 1972. 3.1, MSS 1489, Emory.
127. 10.8, Lilly. The class was divided into three units: Judaism, Catholicism, and Protestantism. In addition to her academic assignments, Plath was required to visit a synagogue and attend a Mass.
128. 10.8, Lilly.
129. Ibid.
130. *JP*, 148–59.
131. 8.18, Lilly.
132. *JP*, 153.
133. DN to SP, 21 Apr. 1952. Lilly.
134. SP to AP, 11 May 1952. *L1*, 443.
135. Ibid., *L1*, 444.
136. DN to SP, 13 May 1952. Lilly.
137. Eddie Cohen to SP, 11 May 1952. Lilly.
138. SP to Ann Davidow, 21 Mar. 1952. *L1*, 431.
139. Ibid.
140. SP to Marcia Brown, 8 July 1952. *L1*, 464.
141. SP to AP, 12 June 1952. *L1*, 448.
142. SP to AP, 10 June 1952. *L1*, 446.
143. SP to AP, 12 June 1952. *L1*, 449.
144. Ibid., *L1*, 450.
145. Ibid., *L1*, 449.
146. SP to AP, 21 June 1952. *L1*, 456–57.
147. SP to AP, 12 June 1952. *L1*, 450.
148. SP to AP, 10 June 1952. *L1*, 447.
149. SP to AP, 12 June 1952. *L1*, 447.
150. SP to AP, 14–15 June 1952. *L1*, 452.
151. Ibid., *L1*, 451.
152. Ibid., *L1*, 451–52.
153. SP to AP, 16 June 1952. *L1*, 453.
154. Ibid., *L1*, 454.
155. SP to AP, 21 June 1952. *L1*, 456.
156. SP to AP, 18 June 1952. *L1*, 455.
157. Paul Alexander and Anne Stevenson both mistakenly identified Phil Brawner as Phil McCurdy in their biographies.
158. SP to Marcia Brown, 8 July 1952. *L1*, 464.
159. Harold Strauss to SP, 26 June 1952. Lilly.
160. SP to Marcia Brown, 8 July 1952. *L1*, 465.
161. Ibid., *L1*, 466.
162. *J*, 118.
163. Ibid. Elizabeth Bowen had used a similar phrase in her novel *The Hotel*, but Plath had probably not read it yet.
164. Ibid.
165. SP to Marcia Brown, 16 & 8 July 1952. *L1*, 470; 466.
166. SP to Marcia Brown, 23–24 July 1952. *L1*, 473.
167. Ibid., *L1*, 472.
168. SP to Marcia Brown, 16 July 1952. *L1*, 469.

169. *J*, 144.
170. *J*, 119.
171. SP to Marcia Brown, 23–24 July 1952. *L1*, 471.
172. Ibid., *L1*, 473.
173. SP to AP, 26 July 1952. *L1*, 478.
174. Ibid.
175. Harriet Rosenstein interview with Margaret Cantor, 1972. 1.16, MSS 1489, Emory.
176. SP to AP, 26 July 1952. *L1*, 478.
177. SP to AP, 4 Aug. 1952. *L1*, 487.
178. SP to AP, 10 Aug. 1952. *L1*, 488.
179. SP to AP, 15 Aug. 1952. *L1*, 492.
180. *J*, 145.
181. SP to WP, 24 July 1952. *L1*, 475.
182. SP to AP, 26 July 1952. *L1*, 478.
183. SP to AP, 2 Aug. 1952. *L1*, 481.
184. Ibid., *L1*, 482.
185. Art would eventually found the influential law firm Kramer, Levin; his brother, the playwright Larry Kramer, would write *The Normal Heart*.
186. SP to AP, 2 Aug. 1952. *L1*, 482.
187. SP to WP, 10 Aug. 1952. *L1*, 489.
188. SP to AP, 2 Aug. 1952. *L1*, 482.
189. SP to AP, 19–21 Aug. 1952. *L1*, 494.
190. Ibid., *L1*, 495.
191. SP to AP, 24 Aug. 1952. *L1*, 498.
192. SP to AP, 15 Aug. 1952. *L1*, 492–93.
193. SP to AP, 19–21 Aug. 1952. *L1*, 495.
194. *J*, 125.
195. Ibid.
196. SP to AP, 2 Aug. 1952. *L1*, 480–81.
197. SP to Margaret Cantor, 30 Sept. 1961. *L2*, 655.
198. SP to AP, 24 Aug. 1952. *L1*, 500.
199. SP to AP, 19–21 Aug. 1952. *L1*, 494.
200. SP to AP, 15 Aug. 1952. *L1*, 491.
201. SP to AP, 28 Aug. 1952. *L1*, 501.

9. THE NINTH KINGDOM

1. Mary Ellen Chase to SP, 16 Sept. 1952. Lilly.
2. OHP to SP, 14 Sept. 1952. Lilly.
3. SP to WP, 28 Sept. 1952. *L1*, 507.
4. SP to AP, 25 Sept. 1952. *L1*, 504.
5. SP to AP, 10 Oct. 1952. *L1*, 511.
6. HC interview with Janet Salter Rosenberg, Sept. 2015, Dobbs Ferry, N.Y.
7. SP to WP, 28 Sept. 1952. *L1*, 507.
8. SP to AP, 10 Oct. 1952. *L1*, 512.
9. HC interview with Janet Salter Rosenberg, Sept. 2015, Dobbs Ferry, N.Y.
10. Nancy Hunter Steiner, *A Closer Look at Ariel: A Memory of Sylvia Plath* (New York: Harper's Magazine Press, 1973), 37.
11. SP to AP, 25 Sept. 1952. *L1*, 505.
12. *J*, 147.
13. *J*, 148.
14. SP to AP, 5 Oct. 1952. *L1*, 510. These papers included the *Springfield Daily News*, *Springfield Union*, *Daily Hampshire Gazette*, and *Springfield Sunday Republican*. Peter Steinberg located fifty-five articles by Plath, most "printed primarily without a byline." She wrote thirty-five for the *Daily Hampshire Gazette*. Her most frequent topic was religion. See Crowther and Steinberg, *These Ghostly Archives*, 76–78.

15. SP to AP, 15 Oct. 1952. *L1*, 514.
16. SP to AP, 5 Oct. 1952. *L1*, 509–10.
17. SP to AP, 15 Oct. 1952. *L1*, 513.
18. SP to AP, 5 Oct. 1952. *L1*, 510.
19. SP to AP, 28 Feb.–1 Mar. 1953. *L1*, 572.
20. Perry Norton to SP, 10 Oct. 1952. Lilly.
21. Perry Norton to SP, 14 Oct. 1952. Lilly.
22. *J*, 147; 143.
23. DN to SP, 15 Oct. 1952. Lilly.
24. DN to SP, 20 Oct. 1952. Lilly.
25. SP to AP, 24 Oct. 1952. *L1*, 515.
26. SP to AP, 27 Oct. 1952. *L1*, 518.
27. SP to AP, 2 Nov. 1952. *L1*, 520.
28. SP to WP, 6 Nov. 1952. *L1*, 523.
29. SP to AP, 2 Nov. 1952. *L1*, 520.
30. DN to SP, 30 Oct. 1952. Lilly.
31. DN to SP, 23 Oct. 1952. Lilly.
32. DN to SP, 5 Dec. 1952. Lilly. Dick quotes SP in this letter.
33. DN to SP, 1 Nov. 1952. Lilly.
34. DN to SP, 8 Nov. 1952. Lilly.
35. DN to SP, 25 Nov. 1952. Lilly.
36. SP to AP, 6 Nov. 1952. *L1*, 520.
37. Ibid.
38. SP to WP, 6 Nov. 1952. *L1*, 523.
39. SP to AP, 17 Nov. 1952. *L1*, 525.
40. SP to AP, 6 Nov. 1952. *L1*, 521; *J*, 141.
41. Enid Epstein Mark to Harriet Rosenstein, 14 Nov. 1971. 2.19, MSS 1489, Emory.
42. *J*, 149.
43. *J*, 149–50.
44. *J*, 151.
45. *J*, 153.
46. "Exeter Academy Pupil a Suicide," *New York Times* (20 Nov. 1952); Harriet Rosenstein interview with Pat O'Neil Pratson, 1972, 3.12, MSS1489, Emory; Dr. Ruth Beuscher interview with AP, 15 Sept. 1953, 3.10, MSS 1489, Emory.
47. SP to AP, 19 Nov. 1952. *L1*, 526–28.
48. Eddie Cohen to SP, 2 Jan. 1953. Lilly.
49. SP, n.d. (autumn) 1952. Lilly.
50. Harriet Rosenstein interview with Alison Prentice Smith, 1971–72. 3.13, MSS 1489, Emory.
51. Dr. Ruth Beuscher interview with AP, 15 Sept. 1953. 3.10, MSS 1489, Emory.
52. *J*, 154.
53. SP, *Mary Ventura and the Ninth Kingdom* (London: Faber and Faber, 2019). The published version is based on a revised copy of the story, which Aurelia typed for Plath and sent to *Mademoiselle* in Jan. 1953 and is now in the possession of Judith Raymo.
54. Later, in 1955, Plath considered entering a revised version of "Mary Ventura and the Ninth Kingdom" in a contest sponsored by a religious organization, the Christophers. She finished her revisions in Dec. 1954, a little over a year after her Aug. 1953 suicide attempt. In the new version, Mary (now Marcia) makes her decision to board the train on her own; Plath cut Mary's parents out of the story altogether. In a page-long introduction, she disguised it as a religious allegory about finding Christ: "This is the story of a teen-age girl who passes through the temptation of the material world, grows aware of her own idealism and power to help others, and discovers the City of God." But Plath was an atheist, and she eventually decided not to enter the story. SP, "Teen-agers Can Shape the Future." 8.15, Lilly.
55. SP, "Dialogue," 19 Jan. 1953, for English 347a. 8.11, Lilly.
56. SP, "Manzi Notebook." 10.4–8, Lilly.

57. An abbreviated list of the pre-twentieth-century British authors Plath studied suggests both the depth and the scope of her literary education: Chaucer, Shakespeare, Spenser, Sidney, Marlowe, Jonson, Dryden, Milton, Bunyan, Donne, Swift, Defoe, Fielding, Sterne, Gibbon, Burke, Boswell, Pope, Goldsmith, Cowper, Blake, Burns, Scott, Austen, Wordsworth, Byron, Shelley, Keats, Thackeray, Dickens, Eliot, Hardy, Carlyle, Arnold, Mill, Tennyson, Browning, Rossetti, Swinburne, and Hopkins. Twentieth-century authors included Yeats, Eliot, Auden, Stevens, Forster, Lawrence, Woolf, Joyce, Conrad, Wells, Richards, James, Dreiser, O'Neill, Cather, and Frost. In her notes for her creative writing class, she refers to Proust, Sartre, Flaubert, de Maupassant, Frazer, Shaw, Wolfe, O'Connor, Stafford, Salinger, Hawthorne, and Poe. During her senior year she studied American and Russian literature, and added even more heavyweights to this roster. (Lilly.)

58. SP, "Modern Poetry Notebook." 12.1–3, Lilly.

59. George Gibian to Harriet Rosenstein, 18 Oct. 1971. 1.30, MSS 1489, Emory.

60. SP, "The Dualism of Thomas Mann," 17 Jan. 1951, for English 11. 10.7, Lilly.

61. SP, "Modern Tragedy in the Classic Tradition," Mar. 1951, for English 11. 10.8, Lilly.

62. SP, "The Imagery in *Patterns*," 18 Apr. 1951, for English 11. 10.8, Lilly.

63. *BJ*, 111.

64. SP, "Fish in Unruffled Lakes." 10.8, Lilly.

65. Ibid.

66. SP, "Edith Sitwell and the Development of Her Poetry," 25 Mar. 1953, for Modern Poetry unit. 10.7, Lilly.

67. See Marsha Bryant, "Queen Bees: Edith Sitwell, Sylvia Plath & Cross-Atlantic Affiliations," *Feminist Modernist Studies*, published online 5 June 2019, for more about Sitwell's influence on Plath.

68. SP's ellipses.

69. SP, "The Age of Anxiety and the Escape from Freedom," May 1954, for History 38b. 10.7, Lilly.

70. SP, "The Devil's Advocate," 24 Mar. 1954, for Russian 35b with Mr. Gibian. 10.7, Lilly.

71. TH, *Winter Pollen: Occasional Prose*, William Scammell, ed. (New York: Picador, 1995), 255.

72. SP, "Notes on *Zarathustra*'s Prologue." 8.1, Lilly.

73. *LH*, 40. In her journal, Plath wrote, "I will be a little god in my small way" (22); "Frustrated? Yes. Why? Because it is impossible for me to be God—or the universal woman-and-man" (45).

74. *J*, 106.

75. *J*, 98.

76. *J*, 98–99.

77. *J*, 100.

78. Friedrich Nietzsche, *Thus Spoke Zarathustra* in *The Portable Nietzsche*, Walter Kaufmann, trans. (New York: Vintage, 1974), 139. Although critics have focused on the Biblical allusions in "Ariel," Plath's identification with "God's lioness" in that poem may also allude to Nietzsche's philosophy of autonomy.

79. *J*, 149.

80. DN to SP, 5 Dec. 1952. Lilly.

81. DN to SP, 11 Dec. 1952. Lilly.

82. SP to AP, 2 Dec. 1952. *L1*, 529.

83. SP to WP, 4 Dec. 1952. *L1*, 531.

84. Harriett Destler, one of Plath's Smith students, also dated Myron Lotz and remembered him as tall and "very, very smart." HC phone interview, 23 Sept. 2015.

85. SP to AP, 2 Feb. 1953. *L1*, 556.

86. Ibid., *L1*, 557.

87. SP to WP, 4 Dec. 1952. *L1*, 531.

88. Ibid.

89. DN to SP, 11 Dec. 1952. Lilly.

90. SP to AP, 15 Dec. 1952. *L1*, 536.

91. Ibid., *L1*, 536–37.
92. She stayed with Dick's friend Bill Lynn, a doctor and aspiring author who had become Dick's main outlet for literary conversation. Dick wrote to her that January, "Bill remarked your interest in the crudities of life, swearing, fornication, and all." (14 Jan. 1953. Lilly.)
93. DN to SP, 30 Dec. 1952. Lilly.
94. *JP*, 176.
95. SP, "The Christmas Heart." 8.11, Lilly.
96. SP to Myron Lotz. 9 Jan. 1953. *L1*, 543–44.
97. SP to AP, 28–29 Dec. 1952. *L1*, 538.
98. DN to SP, 30 Dec. 1952. Lilly.
99. SP to AP, 9 Jan. 1953. *L1*, 542.
100. SP to AP, 8 Jan. 1953. *L1*, 539–40.
101. SP to AP, 9 Jan. 1953. *L1*, 542.
102. *J*, 157.
103. Ibid.
104. SP to AP, 25 Jan. 1953. *L1*, 555.
105. *J*, 158.
106. Eddie Cohen to SP, n.d. (late Jan.) 1953. Lilly.
107. SP to AP, 4 Feb. 1953. *L1*, 558–59.
108. DN to SP, 16 Jan. 1953. Lilly.
109. *J*, 155.
110. DN to SP, 27 Jan. 1953. Lilly.
111. Ibid.
112. Ibid.
113. *J*, 153.
114. DN to SP, 27 Jan. 1953. Lilly.
115. SP to AP, 4 Feb. 1953. *L1*, 558.
116. SP to AP, 5 Feb. 1953. *L1*, 559. SP's ellipses.
117. DN to SP, 21 Jan. 1953. Lilly.
118. DN to SP, 26 Jan. 1953. Lilly.
119. *J*, 156.
120. SP to AP, 18 Jan. 1953. *L1*, 551–52.
121. SP to AP, 5 Feb. 1953. *L1*, 559–60.
122. SP to AP, 6 Feb. 1953. *L1*, 562.
123. SP to AP, 5 Feb. 1953. *L1*, 560.
124. *J*, 168.
125. Harriet Rosenstein interview with Marcia Brown Stern, 1972. 4.16, MSS 1489, Emory.
126. SP to AP, 21 Feb. 1953. *L1*, 567.
127. Ibid.
128. SP to AP, 28 Feb.–1 Mar. 1953. *L1*, 575.
129. SP to AP, 21 Feb. 1953. *L1*, 567.
130. SP, "Mad Girl's Love Song," 21 Feb. 1953. 7.13, Lilly; *Mademoiselle* (Aug. 1953), 358.
131. SP, "Doomsday," 21 Feb. 1953, for English 347b. 7.10, Lilly.
132. SP, "To Eva Descending the Stair." 8.4, Lilly.
133. Helen Hennessy to AP, 11 Sept. 1954. Lilly. Helen confided to Aurelia about her career plans to get a graduate degree in English, writing, "I don't know if that will work out."
134. SP to AP, 28 Feb. 1953. *L1*, 573.
135. SP to AP, 25 Feb. 1953. *L1*, 570–71.
136. SP to AP, 28 Feb. 1953. *L1*, 573.
137. SP to AP, 25 Feb. 1953. *L1*, 570–71.
138. AP to DN, 15 Mar. 1953. Lilly.
139. DN to AP, 21 Mar. 1953. Lilly.
140. SP to AP, 28 Feb.–1 Mar. 1953. *L1*, 572.
141. SP to AP, 17 Mar. 1953. *L1*, 588.

142. SP to AP, 25 Feb. 1953. *L1*, 571.
143. William Norton to DN, Feb. 1953. Lilly.
144. SP to AP, 28 Feb. 1953. *L1*, 575; HC phone interview with Harriett Destler, 3 Sept. 2015.
145. SP to WP, 21 Mar. 1953. *L1*, 591.
146. Ibid., *L1*, 589.
147. SP to AP, 28 Apr. 1953. *L1*, 605.
148. *J*, 539–40.
149. SP to AP, 11 Apr. 1953. *L1*, 592.
150. SP to AP, 30 Apr.–1 May 1953. *L1*, 607.
151. SP to AP, 28 Apr. 1953. *L1*, 604.
152. HC interview with Janet Salter Rosenberg, Sept. 2015, Dobbs Ferry, N.Y.
153. Harriet Rosenstein interview with Peter and Jane Davison, 1973. 1.22, MSS 1489, Emory.
154. *J*, 180.
155. SP to AP, 28 Apr. 1953. *L1*, 604.
156. Enid Epstein Mark to Harriet Rosenstein, 14 Nov. 1971. 2.19, MSS 1489, Emory.
157. Harriet Rosenstein interview with Susan Weller Burch, 1974. 1.14, MSS 1489, Emory.
158. SP to AP, 25 Apr. 1953. *L1*, 603.
159. SP to AP, 28 Apr. 1953. *L1*, 605.
160. SP to AP, 5 May 1953. *L1*, 610–11.
161. HC interview with Janet Salter Rosenberg, Sept. 2015, Dobbs Ferry, N.Y.
162. Mildred Norton to SP, 7 May 1953. Lilly.
163. SP to AP, 12 May 1953. *L1*, 616.
164. SP to WP, 13 May 1953. *L1*, 621.
165. SP to AP, 13 May 1953. *L1*, 617. SP's ellipsis.
166. SP to WP, 13 May 1953. *L1*, 620–21.
167. SP to AP, 13 May 1953. *L1*, 618–19.
168. SP to AP, 15 May 1953. *L1*, 625.
169. Ibid., *L1*, 625–26.
170. SP to WP, 13 May 1953. *L1*, 621–22.
171. SP to WP, 21 May 1953. *L1*, 629; *J*, 184–85.
172. HC interview with Janet Salter Rosenberg, Sept. 2015, Dobbs Ferry, N.Y.
173. DN to SP, 27 May 1953. Lilly.
174. SP, "Edge," *Collected Poems* (Faber and Faber, 1981), 272.

10. MY MIND WILL SPLIT OPEN

1. *BJ*, 111.
2. Harriet Rosenstein interview with Marcia Brown Stern, 1972–73. 4.16, MSS 1489, Emory.
3. SP, "Progress Report on <u>The Bell Jar</u>," 1 May 1962. 5.47, SPC, Smith.
4. "A short, short history of MADEMOISELLE." 12.7, Lilly.
5. Janet Burroway, *Embalming Mom: Essays in Life* (Iowa City: University of Iowa Press, 2002), 3.
6. Laurie Glazer Levy, "Outside the Bell Jar," *Sylvia Plath: The Woman and the Work*, Edward Butscher, ed. (New York: Dodd, Mead and Co., 1977), 44.
7. Harriet Rosenstein interview with Peter and Jane Davison, 1973. 1.22, MSS 1489, Emory.
8. Mary Cantwell, *Manhattan, When I Was Young* (New York: Penguin, 1995), 74; 20.
9. Nancy Hunter Steiner, *A Closer Look at Ariel: A Memory of Sylvia Plath* (New York: Harper's Magazine Press, 1973), 44.
10. *BJ*, 99.
11. Elizabeth Winder, *Pain, Parties, Work: Sylvia Plath in New York, Summer 1953* (New York: HarperCollins, 2013), 31.
12. *Mademoiselle* Memo, Geri Trotta to All Guest Editors, c. May 1953. 12.7, Lilly.

13. "Your Job as Mademoiselle's Guest Editor," c. May/June 1953. 12.7, Lilly.
14. *Mademoiselle* Memo, Geri Trotta to All Guest Editors, c. May 1953. 12.7, Lilly.
15. *Mademoiselle* Memo from Natalie Stack to All Guest Editors, 1 June 1953. 12.7, Lilly.
16. SP to AP, 3 June 1953. *L1*, 630.
17. Michael Callahan, "Sorority on E. 63rd St.," *Vanity Fair* (Apr. 2010).
18. SP to AP, 3 June 1953. *L1*, 630.
19. Winder, *Pain, Parties, Work*, 11.
20. SP to AP, 3 June 1953. *L1*, 631.
21. HC phone interview with Laurie Totten Woolschlager, 27 Oct. 2014. When Laurie asked Plath that day what she would like to come back as after her death, Plath answered, "A seagull."
22. Neva Nelson email to HC, 6 Nov. 2014. Elizabeth Winder writes that the group talked about their virginity (or lack thereof) during that first meeting in Grace MacLeod's room, but Neva Nelson said that particular discussion occurred much later, on 25 June, also in Grace MacLeod's room. On that night, the girls threw Grace a small birthday party, and the discussion turned more "personal" after cake and champagne. (Neva still has the handwritten party invitation.) Ms. Nelson asked that I not use her married name.
23. Winder, *Pain, Parties, Work*, 13.
24. Neva Nelson email to HC, 10 Nov. 2014.
25. Winder, *Pain, Parties, Work*, 39–40.
26. Neva Nelson email to HC, 10 Nov. 2014.
27. Ibid.
28. Ibid., 11 Nov. 2014.
29. Ibid., 10 Nov. 1014.
30. Laurie Glazer Levy, "None of Us Understood," *Chicago Tribune* (12 Oct. 2003), 18.
31. Diane Johnson, "Being Green," *Vogue* (Sept. 2003): 200; 208; 216.
32. "Jobiographies," *Mademoiselle* (Aug. 1953): 252.
33. *BJ*, 100–101.
34. SP to AP, 3 June 1953. *L1*, 631.
35. *BJ*, 26.
36. SP to AP, 3 June 1953. *L1*, 631.
37. Ibid., *L1*, 632.
38. Ibid., *L1*, 633.
39. Levy, "Outside the Bell Jar," 44.
40. SP, "Mlle's last word on college, '53," *Mademoiselle* (Aug. 1953): 139.
41. Margaret Shook, "Sylvia Plath: The Poet and the College," *Smith Alumnae Quarterly* 63.3 (April 1972): 4–9; 7.
42. SP to AP, 13 June 1953. *L1*, 637.
43. SP to AP, 8 June 1953. *L1*, 634.
44. DN to SP, 4 June 1953. Lilly. DN quotes SP's words in this letter.
45. SP to AP, 13 June 1953. *L1*, 637.
46. Winder, *Pain, Parties, Work*, 85.
47. "Mademoiselle's Editors and Departments and What They Do," 28 May 1953. 12.7, Lilly.
48. HC phone interview with Laurie Totten Woolschlager, 27 Oct. 2014.
49. *J*, 187.
50. Cantwell, *Manhattan*, 14.
51. SP to AP, 3 June 1953. *L1*, 632.
52. HC phone interview with Laurie Totten Woolschlager, 27 Oct. 2014.
53. HC phone interview with Margaret Affleck Clark, 27 Oct. 2014.
54. Winder, *Pain, Parties, Work*, 89.
55. HC phone interview with Laurie Totten Woolschlager, 27 Oct. 2014.
56. Cyrilly Abels reference for SP, 15 Nov. 1954, Vocational Office Records, Smith College Archives.
57. Winder, *Pain, Parties, Work*, 88.

58. Postwar European Photography Exhibit, 1953. Museum of Modern Art Digital Archive.
59. Photographs of a mannequin standing against a bombed-out background and a black telephone with its long cord hanging recall "The Munich Mannequins," for example.
60. Winder, *Pain, Parties, Work*, 108.
61. SP to WP, 21 June 1953. *L1*, 643.
62. Elizabeth Bowen to SP, 9 June 1953. Lilly.
63. *Mademoiselle* Memo, Jane Mayberry to All Guest Editors, c. May 1953. 12.7, Lilly.
64. SP to AP, 13 June 1953. *L1*, 636; SP to AP, 8 June 1953. *L1*, 634.
65. SP to AP, 8 June 1953. *L1*, 634.
66. DN to SP, 10 June 1953. Lilly.
67. SP to AP, 13 June 1953. *L1*, 636.
68. Ibid., *L1*, 635.
69. Ibid., *L1*, 636.
70. Ibid., *L1*, 635.
71. SP to AP, 13 June 1953. *L1*, 635.
72. *BJ*, 207.
73. SP to AP, 13 June 1953. *L1*, 636.
74. Ibid., *L1*, 638.
75. Ibid., *L1*, 637.
76. HC phone interview with Laurie Totten Woolschlager, 27 Oct. 2014.
77. Ibid.
78. SP to AP, 13 June 1953. *L1*, 637.
79. HC interview with Mel Woody, Sept. 2018, Lyme, Conn.
80. Ibid.
81. *BJ*, 9.
82. *BJ*, 17.
83. HC phone interview with Laurie Totten Woolschlager, 27 Oct. 2014.
84. *BJ*, 23.
85. Winder, *Pain, Parties, Work*, 246.
86. Ibid., 136.
87. Levy, "Outside the Bell Jar," 46.
88. Ibid., 47.
89. SP to WP, 21 June 1953. *L1*, 642.
90. Winder, *Pain, Parties, Work*, 139.
91. *BJ*, 48.
92. *J*, 149.
93. Ibid.
94. SP to WP, 21 June 1953. *L1*, 643.
95. HC phone interview with Laurie Totten Woolschlager, 27 Oct. 2014.
96. *BJ*, 78.
97. *BJ*, 74.
98. Andrew Wilson, *Mad Girl's Love Song: Sylvia Plath and Life Before Ted* (New York: Scribner, 2013), 207.
99. SP to WP, 21 June 1953. *L1*, 642.
100. *BJ*, 1.
101. Robert D. McFadden. "David Greenglass, the Brother Who Doomed Ethel Rosenberg, Dies at 92," *New York Times* (14 Oct. 2014).
102. *The Rosenberg Letters: A Complete Edition of the Prison Correspondence of Julius and Ethel Rosenberg*, Michael Meeropol, ed. (New York and London: Garland, 1994), xxxi.
103. Neva Nelson email to HC, 26 Oct. 2014. Paul Alexander erroneously attributes this story to Janet Wagner Rafferty in his biography of Plath, *Rough Magic*.
104. HC phone interview with Laurie Totten Woolschlager, 27 Oct. 2014.
105. Winder, *Pain, Parties, Work*, 148.
106. HC interview with Laurie Totten Woolschlager, 27 Oct. 2014.
107. Winder, *Pain, Parties, Work*, 148.
108. HC phone interview with Margaret Affleck Clark, 27 Oct. 2014.

109. *J*, 541.
110. *BJ*, 99.
111. *J*, 541–42. SP's ellipsis.
112. Elaine Showalter, *The Female Malady: Women, Madness and English Culture 1830–1980* (London: Virago, 1987), 218.
113. SP, 20 June 1953, Jan.–Aug. 1953 calendar. 7.5, Lilly.
114. Wilson makes this claim in *Mad Girl's Love Song*. The reference to the "East side apt." in Plath's calendar may refer to a pre-party as presumably one of the men would have driven Plath and Janet to Queens.
115. SP to WP, 21 June 1953. *L1*, 642; *J*, 187.
116. Winder, *Pain, Parties, Work*, 178.
117. Wilson, *Mad Girl's Love Song*, 209.
118. Neva Nelson email to HC, 18 Nov. 2014.
119. Ibid. Neva writes, "And, that Sat. after the St. Regis ball, I had a date with my escort, John Appleton (the textbook publisher), and we scouted out the White Horse Tavern half expecting to see Sylvia there, too. But I learned from her later that she'd spent the night sitting outside his hotel room trying to get to see him. (Whether she really spent the whole night there is probably questionable)."
120. *Voices and Visions*, PBS documentary, "Sylvia Plath," South Carolina Educational Television and New York Center for Visual History Production, 1988.
121. SP to WP, 21 June 1953. *L1*, 641–43. SP's ellipsis.
122. Neva Nelson email to HC, 9 Nov. 2014.
123. Carol LeVarn McCabe email to HC, 4 Dec. 2017.
124. Ibid., 6 Dec. 2017.
125. Winder, *Pain, Parties, Work*, 200.
126. Neva Nelson email to HC, 9 Nov. 2014. Ann Burnside Love and Janet Wagner Rafferty also remembered hearing about Plath's escapade.
127. Winder, *Pain, Parties, Work*, 200.
128. Ibid., 192.

11. THE HANGING MAN

1. *J*, 187.
2. *LH*, 123.
3. HM, 33.
4. Ibid.
5. *J*, 544–45.
6. *J*, 544.
7. *J*, 543.
8. SP to Director of Graduate Schools, Columbia University, 3 July 1953. *L1*, 644.
9. *J*, 185.
10. Draft copy, "Letters from Sylvia." 27.66.1, SPC, Smith.
11. *J*, 187.
12. AP to Marcia Brown, 23 July 1953. 2.90, EBC, Smith.
13. SP to Gordon Lameyer, 23 July 1953. *L1*, 646.
14. DN to SP, 7 July 1953. Lilly.
15. DN to SP, 8 July 1953. Lilly.
16. *J*, 543.
17. *BJ*, 122.
18. *LH*, 124.
19. AP, undated handwritten notes on back of letter from Dr. Nancy Andreasen, 30 Aug. 1973. 29.1.2, SPC, Smith.
20. SP, "James Joyce Notebook." 10.10, Lilly.
21. Nora Johnson, *Coast to Coast: A Family Romance* (New York: Simon & Schuster, 2004), 157. Quoted in Amanda Golden, *Annotating Modernism* (New York: Routledge, 2020), 35.
22. *BJ*, 124.

23. *BJ*, 126.
24. SP to Gordon Lameyer, 23 July 1953. *L1*, 646.
25. DN to SP, c. 21 & 30 July 1953. Lilly.
26. James Joyce, *A Portrait of the Artist as a Young Man* (New York: Penguin Classics, 1992), 220.
27. Ibid., 268; SP, "James Joyce Notebook." 10.10, Lilly.
28. Joyce, *Portrait*, 269.
29. *BJ*, 72; 83.
30. *LH*, 123.
31. Andrew Wilson, *Mad Girl's Love Song: Sylvia Plath and Life Before Ted* (New York: Scribner, 2013), 211.
32. Harriet Rosenstein interview with Pat O'Neil Pratson, 1972. 3.12, MSS 1489, Emory.
33. Harriet Rosenstein interview with Marcia Brown Stern, 1972. 4.16, MSS 1489, Emory.
34. *LH*, 123.
35. *J*, 187.
36. Gail Crowther and Peter K. Steinberg, *These Ghostly Archives: The Unearthing of Sylvia Plath* (Croydon, UK: Fonthill, 2017), 71.
37. *Voices and Visions*, PBS documentary, "Sylvia Plath," South Carolina Educational Television and New York Center for Visual History Production, 1988.
38. W. H. Mikesell, ed., *Modern Abnormal Psychology* (New York: Philosophical Library, 1950); Catalog, Sotheby's Fine Books and Manuscripts Sale 4833Y, 6 Apr. 1982, at York Avenue Galleries.
39. *LH*, 124.
40. Plath's Jan.–Aug. 1953 calendar reveals that the appointment with Dr. Racioppi was at nine a.m. on 15 July. 7.5, Lilly.
41. SP, 16 July, Jan.–Aug. 1953 calendar. 7.5, Lilly.
42. *BJ*, 161.
43. SP to Gordon Lameyer, 23 July 1953. *L1*, 645.
44. Dr. Ruth Beuscher interview with AP, 15 Sept. 1953. 3.10, MSS 1489, Emory. Dr. Thornton died in Massachusetts in 1976. Dr. Francis de Marneffe, director emeritus of McLean Hospital, has no recollection of Dr. Thornton.
45. *LH*, 124.
46. *BJ*, 129–31.
47. Harriet Rosenstein interview with AP, 1970. 3.10, MSS 1489, Emory.
48. HC interview with Dr. Francis de Marneffe, Dec. 2014, Westwood, Mass.
49. *LH*, 124.
50. Alex Beam, interview with Dr. Ruth Barnhouse (formerly Beuscher), 9 Aug. 1997, Nantucket, Mass. 24.10, SPC, Smith.
51. Luke Ferreter, "'Just Like the Sort of Drug a Man Would Invent': *The Bell Jar* and the Feminist Critique of Women's Health Care," *Plath Profiles* 1 (2008): 136–58. 143.
52. Ibid., 143.
53. Ibid., 145.
54. Golda M. Edinburg, "Home, Hospital, Home Again," *Boston Sunday Globe* (17 May 1964), 4.
55. Ali Haggett, *Desperate Housewives: Neuroses and the Domestic Environment, 1945–1970* (London: Routledge, 2012), 115.
56. HC interview with Dr. Francis de Marneffe, Dec. 2014, Westwood, Mass.
57. S. B. Sutton, *Crossroads in Psychiatry: A History of the McLean Hospital* (Washington, D.C.: American Psychiatric Press, 1986), 229.
58. Ibid., 227; HC interview with Dr. Francis de Marneffe, Dec. 2014, Westwood, Mass.
59. Sutton, *Crossroads*, 229.
60. SP, handwritten notes on fictional and real aspects in a later draft of *The Bell Jar*, and requests for changes, fall 1961 (probably preparation for her response to James Michie's concerns about libel). SP's "Venus in the Seventh" on verso. 4.25, SPC, Smith.
61. *BJ*, 143.
62. Elaine Showalter, *The Female Malady: Women, Madness and English Culture, 1830–1980* (London and New York: Penguin, 1985), 210.

63. Mary Jane Ward, *The Snake Pit* (New York: Random House, 1946), 43.
64. Harriet Rosenstein interview with Margaret Cantor, 1972. 1.16, MSS 1489, Emory.
65. In her Jan.–Aug. 1953 calendar, Plath wrote, "ShockT" on 29 and 31 July. 7.5, Lilly.
66. Dr. Ruth Beuscher interview with AP, 15 Sept. 1953. 3.10, MSS 1489, Emory.
67. SP to Eddie Cohen, 28 Dec. 1953. *L1*, 655.
68. Ibid., *L1*, 655–66.
69. SP, "Progress Report on The Bell Jar," 1 May 1962. 5.47, SPC, Smith.
70. OHP to Dr. Thornton, 26 Sept. 1953. Quoted in Paul Alexander, *Rough Magic: A Biography of Sylvia Plath* (New York: Da Capo Press, 1999), 130.
71. Dr. Thornton to OHP, 29 Sept. 1953. Quoted in ibid.
72. OHP to AP, 24 Sept. 1953. Lilly.
73. HC interview with Elinor Friedman Klein, Oct. 2015, South Salem, N.Y.
74. Wilson, *Mad Girl's Love Song*, 214–15.
75. HC phone interview with Peter Aldrich, 4 Nov. 2014.
76. Ibid.
77. In *The Bell Jar*, Dodo Conway is an amalgam of Betty, who had nine children, and Plath's neighbor Dorinda "Do" Cruikshank. HC interview with Richard Larschan, May 2017, Manhattan.
78. HC phone interview with Peter Aldrich, 4 Nov. 2014.
79. SP to Myron Lotz, 18 Aug. 1953. *L1*, 648. Plath's ellipsis.
80. Harriet Rosenstein interview with Marcia Brown Stern, 1972. 4.15, MSS 1489, Emory.
81. Dr. Ruth Beuscher interview with AP, 15 Sept. 1953. 3.10, MSS 1489, Emory.
82. Other biographers have mistakenly identified this man as Mel Woody. Mel was in Ohio that summer. Mel Woody email to HC, 19 Sept. 2018.
83. Gordon Lameyer, *Dear Sylvia* (unpublished memoir). Lameyer MSS, Lilly.
84. SP to Eddie Cohen, 28 Dec. 1953. *L1*, 656.
85. Dr. Ruth Beuscher interview with AP, 15 Sept. 1953. 3.10, MSS 1489, Emory.
86. *LH*, 125.
87. SP to Eddie Cohen, 28 Dec. 1953. *L1*, 656.
88. 24 Aug. 1953, Wellesley police records, procured and shared by Peter Steinberg.
89. *LH*, 125.
90. "Wellesley Woods Searched: Police, Boy Scouts Hunt Missing Smith Student," *Boston Evening Globe* (25 Aug. 1953).
91. "Sleeping Pills Missing with Wellesley Girl," *Boston Herald* (26 Aug. 1953).
92. 25 Aug. 1953, Wellesley police records.
93. Harriet Rosenstein interview with Pat O'Neil Pratson, 1972. 3.12, MSS 1489, Emory.
94. "Day-Long Search Fails to Find Smith Student," *Boston Daily Globe* (26 Aug. 1953).
95. "Smith Student Found Alive in Cellar," *Boston Evening Globe* (26 Aug. 1953).
96. HC conversation with Don Colburn, 12 Jan. 2017, Yaddo, Saratoga Springs, N.Y.
97. HC interview with Louise Giesey White, Aug. 2014, Jamestown, R.I., and HC interview with Betsy Powley Wallingford, Feb. 2013, Sudbury, Mass. The quote comes from Louise, but Betsy also remembered Pat spending her days at the house while Sylvia was missing.
98. Max D. Gaebler, "Sylvia Plath Remembered," delivered to the Madison Literary Society on 14 Mar. 1983. 2.22, Houghton Mifflin Collection, Smith.
99. Harriet Rosenstein interview with Pat O'Neil Pratson, 1972. 3.12, MSS 1489, Emory.
100. This number is as of Nov. 2019. See Peter K. Steinberg, "They Had to Call and Call: The Search for Sylvia Plath," *Plath Profiles* 3 (Summer 2010): 107–32. Also, see Steinberg's website at www.sylviaplath.info.fsa.html for the most up-to-date list.
101. This information comes from Warren Plath. See ibid., 108.
102. "Day-Long Search Fails to Find Smith Student."
103. HC interview with Judith Raymo, Apr. 2016, Manhattan.
104. "Sleeping Pills Missing with Wellesley Girl."
105. Harriet Rosenstein interview with Pat O'Neil Pratson, 1972. 3.12, MSS 1489, Emory.
106. 26 Aug. 1953, Wellesley police records.
107. HC phone interview with Richard Larschan, 17 Apr. 2017.
108. HC interview with Elinor Friedman Klein, Oct. 2015, South Salem, N.Y.

109. *LH*, 125.
110. SP to Eddie Cohen, 28 Dec. 1953. *L1*, 656.
111. *LH*, 125–26.
112. AP to OHP, 29 Aug. 1953. Lilly.
113. Ibid.
114. OHP to SP, 22 Aug. 1953; OHP to AP, 26 Aug. 1953. Lilly.
115. AP to OHP, 29 Aug. 1953. Lilly.
116. Ibid.
117. HC interview with Dr. Francis de Marneffe, Dec. 2014, Westwood, Mass.
118. Benjamin Wright to AP, 29 Sept. 1953. Lilly.
119. AP to OHP, 29 Aug. 1953. Lilly.
120. Ibid.
121. OHP to AP, 2 Sept. 1953. Lilly.
122. Ibid.
123. AP to OHP, 29 Aug. 1953. Lilly.
124. Elizabeth Drew to SP, c. 28 Aug. 1953. Lilly.
125. Evelyn Page to SP, 29 (#1) Aug. 1953. Lilly.
126. Robert Gorham Davis to AP, 27 Aug. 1953. Lilly.
127. Gordon Lameyer to AP, 27 Aug. 1953. Lilly.
128. SP to Gordon Lameyer, 31 Aug. 1953. *L1*, 649–50. The second ellipsis is SP's.
129. DN to SP, 2 Sept. 1953. Lilly.
130. SP to Gordon Lameyer, 7 Sept. 1953. *L1*, 651. SP's ellipses.
131. Gordon Lameyer to SP, 14 Oct. 1953. Lilly.
132. Gordon Lameyer to SP, 19 Sept. 1953. Lilly.
133. Dr. Ruth Beuscher interview with AP, 15 Sept. 1953. 3.10, MSS 1489, Emory.
134. *BJ*, 209.
135. OHP to AP, 24 Sept. 1953. Lilly.
136. OHP to Dr. William Terhune, 22 Oct. 1953. Lilly.
137. AP to Paul Alexander, n.d. Courtesy of Richard Larschan.
138. OHP to AP, 2 Sept. 1953. Lilly.

12. WAKING IN THE BLUE

1. SP to Eddie Cohen, 28 Dec. 1953. *L1*, 656–57.
2. S. B. Sutton, *Crossroads in Psychiatry: A History of the McLean Hospital* (Washington, D.C.: American Psychiatric Press, 1986), 256.
3. HC interview with Dr. Francis de Marneffe, Dec. 2014, Westwood, Mass.
4. Alex Beam, *Gracefully Insane: Life and Death Inside American's Premier Mental Hospital* (New York: PublicAffairs Press, 2001), 21.
5. The original hospital was founded in 1811 and situated on a grand eighteen-acre estate in Charlestown, Massachusetts.
6. Beam, *Gracefully Insane*, 49.
7. HC interview with Terry Bragg, McLean archivist and director of staff and professional affairs, Aug. 2014, McLean Hospital, Belmont, Mass. Bragg spoke extensively about McLean's history and gave me a tour of the grounds.
8. Dr. Francis de Marneffe, "McLean Hospital," *American Journal of Psychiatry* 154.1 (Jan. 1997): 109.
9. HC interview with Terry Bragg, Aug. 2014, McLean Hospital, Belmont, Mass.
10. Women's Belknap, where Plath eventually stayed when her condition improved, was located directly next to the central administration building.
11. Dr. Franklin Wood, "A Brief History of the McLean Hospital." 1953 McLean Hospital Annual Report, McLean Hospital Archives.
12. HC interview with Terry Bragg, Aug. 2014, McLean Hospital, Belmont, Mass.
13. 1953 McLean Hospital Annual Report, McLean Hospital Archives.
14. *BJ*, 187.
15. Robert Lowell, *Collected Poems*, Frank Bidart and David Gewanter, eds. (New York: Farrar, Straus and Giroux, 2003), 183–84.

16. Sutton, *Crossroads*, 257.
17. Ibid.
18. HC interview with Terry Bragg, Aug. 2014, McLean Hospital, Belmont, Mass.
19. Sutton, *Crossroads*, 257.
20. HC interview with Terry Bragg, Aug. 2014, McLean Hospital, Belmont, Mass.
21. Dr. Franklin Wood, "Report of the Director of the McLean Hospital." 1953 McLean Hospital Annual Report, McLean Hospital Archives.
22. *BJ*, 209.
23. Dr. Francis de Marneffe, deposition (1987 *Bell Jar* trial). Jane Anderson v. AVCO Embassy Pictures Corp. et al., in the United States District Court, District of Massachusetts, Civil Action no. 82-0752-K. Jane V. Anderson Papers, Series IV, Smith.
24. Ibid.
25. Beam, *Gracefully Insane*, 127.
26. Alex Beam interview with Dr. Ruth Barnhouse (formerly Beuscher), 9 Aug. 1997, Nantucket, Mass. 24.10, SPC, Smith.
27. Dr. Paul M. Howard, "Report of the Clinical Service." 1953 McLean Hospital Annual Report, McLean Hospital Archives.
28. Electroshock treatment began at McLean in 1940–41. HC interview with Terry Bragg, Aug. 2014, McLean Hospital, Belmont, Mass.
29. Dr. Mark Altschule, "Report of the Director of Internal Medicine and of Research in Clinical Physiology." 1953 McLean Hospital Annual Report, McLean Hospital Archives.
30. Sutton, *Crossroads*, 228.
31. Alex Beam interview with Dr. Ruth Barnhouse, 9 Aug. 1997, Nantucket, Mass. 24.10, SPC, Smith.
32. Beam, *Gracefully Insane*, 78.
33. Ibid., 75.
34. HC interview with Dr. Francis de Marneffe, Dec. 2014, Westwood, Mass.
35. Dr. Paul M. Howard, "Report of the Clinical Service." 1953 McLean Hospital Annual Report, McLean Hospital Archives.
36. Ibid. Patients were deemed well when they regained the "ability to have warm relationships, the desire to be effective, the talent for making compromises and sublimations, the ability to reason and act, the willingness to endure anxiety and discomfort, capacity for self-perspective and a sense of humor."
37. "I'm not an analyst myself," she once said. "It would be very hard for me to be an analyst." Alex Beam, interview with Dr. Ruth Barnhouse, 9 Aug. 1997, Nantucket, Mass. 24.10, SPC, Smith. Dr. Barnhouse (formerly Beuscher) told Beam she was turned down at the Boston Psychoanalytic Institute, though she eventually took a two-year extension course there. She did not provide dates. Karen Maroda, "Sylvia and Ruth," *Salon* (29 Nov. 2004); HC interview with Dr. Francis de Marneffe, Dec. 2014, Westwood, Mass.
38. *BJ*, 224.
39. Dr. Ruth Barnhouse to Linda Wagner-Martin, 22 Oct. 1985. Ruth Tiffany Barnhouse Papers, Smith.
40. Alex Beam interview with Dr. Ruth Barnhouse, 9 Aug. 1997, Nantucket, Mass. 24.10, SPC, Smith.
41. Paul Alexander, *Rough Magic: A Biography of Sylvia Plath* (New York: Da Capo Press, 1999), 130.
42. *J*, 491–92.
43. Maroda, "Sylvia and Ruth."
44. Ibid.
45. HC interview with Dr. Francis de Marneffe, Dec. 2014, Westwood, Mass.
46. Harriet Rosenstein interview with Dr. Ruth Beuscher, 1970. 1.6, MSS 1489, Emory.
47. Dr. Ruth Barnhouse to Harriet Rosenstein, 22 May 1990. Ruth Tiffany Barnhouse Papers, Smith.
48. Beuscher later asked Rosenstein to return the letters and the tape, but she refused.
49. Harriet Rosenstein interview with Dr. Ruth Beuscher, 1970. 1.6, MSS 1489, Emory.

50. Dr. Francis de Marneffe, personal notes on Alex Beam's *Gracefully Insane* (n.d., circa 2001) and HC interview, Dec. 2014.
51. SP to Dr. Ruth Beuscher, 4 Feb. 1963. *L2*, 968.
52. Dr. Ruth Beuscher, notes on SP, fall 1953. 3.10, MSS 1489, Emory.
53. SP, notes on *The Bell Jar*, 1961. 4.1, SPC, Smith.
54. Dr. de Marneffe did not know who made the recommendation for treatment, but he noted that if it had been Dr. Beuscher, the recommendation would have been discussed by the senior doctors before it was approved. HC interview, Dec. 2014, Westwood, Mass.
55. Dr. Max Fink, "Primary Sources: Insulin Coma Therapy," *A Brilliant Madness, American Masters*, PBS documentary. Dr. de Marneffe said that in the 1950s McLean tended to prescribe sub-coma insulin for patients diagnosed as schizophrenic. HC interview with Dr. Francis de Marneffe, Dec. 2014, Westwood, Mass.
56. Dr. Ruth Beuscher, notes on SP, fall 1953. 3.10, MSS 1489, Emory.
57. Dr. Ruth Beuscher, notes on SP, fall 1953. 3.10, MSS 1489, Emory.
58. OHP to Dr. Ruth Beuscher, 14 Oct. 1953. Lilly.
59. OHP to Dr. William Terhune, 22 Oct. 1953. Lilly.
60. William James, *The Varieties of Religious Experience: A Study in Human Nature* (New York: Modern Library, 1929). Held in SP's library, 825 P696L, SPC, Smith.
61. OHP to AP, 22 Oct. 1953. Lilly.
62. Ibid.
63. OHP to AP, 26 Oct. 1953. Lilly.
64. OHP to Dr. William Terhune, 2 Nov. 1953. Lilly.
65. OHP to AP, 22 Oct. 1953. Lilly.
66. Harriet Rosenstein interview with Wilbury Crockett, 1971. 1.19, MSS 1489, Emory.
67. *BJ*, 202–203.
68. AP to Judith Kroll, 1 Dec. 1978. 29.26, SPC, Smith.
69. Ibid.
70. AP to Alan Simpson, 4 Jan. 1976. 29.43, SPC, Smith.
71. AP to Judith Kroll, 1 Dec. 1978. 29.26, SPC, Smith.
72. Ibid.
73. Ibid.
74. Dr. Ruth Beuscher, notes on SP, fall 1953. 3.10, MSS 1489, Emory.
75. OHP to Dr. William Terhune, 2 Nov. 1953. Lilly.
76. AP, handwritten notes on back of envelope from OHP, 3 Nov. 1953. Lilly.
77. Beam, *Gracefully Insane*, 154; Andrew Wilson, *Mad Girl's Love Song: Sylvia Plath and Life Before Ted* (New York: Scribner, 2013), 226.
78. HC interview with Dr. Francis de Marneffe, Dec. 2014, Westwood, Mass.
79. OHP to AP, 27 Nov. 1953. Lilly.
80. OHP to AP, handwritten marginalia on OHP's letter to Dr. Erich Lindemann, 21 Nov. 1953. Lilly.
81. OHP to Dr. William Terhune, 2 Nov. 1953. Lilly.
82. HC interview with Dr. Francis de Marneffe, Dec. 2014, Westwood, Mass.
83. OHP to AP, 22 Nov. & 27 Nov. 1953. Lilly.
84. Dr. Ruth Beuscher, notes on SP, fall 1953. 3.10, MSS 1489, Emory.
85. OHP to Dr. Franklin Wood, 23 Oct. 1953; quoted in Alexander, *Rough Magic*, 133.
86. Dr. Franklin Wood to OHP, 25 Oct. 1953; quoted in Alexander, *Rough Magic*, 133.
87. Dr. Ruth Beuscher, notes on SP, fall 1953. 3.10, MSS 1489, Emory; HC interview with Terry Bragg, 14 Aug. 2014, McLean Hospital, Belmont, Mass.
88. Dr. Ruth Beuscher, notes on SP, fall 1953. 3.10, MSS 1489, Emory.
89. OHP to AP, 18 Nov. 1953. Lilly.
90. OHP to Dr. Erich Lindemann, 15 Dec. 1953. Lilly.
91. OHP to Dr. William Terhune, 14 Dec. 1953. Lilly.
92. Ibid.
93. Ibid.
94. AP to OHP, 9 Dec. 1953. Lilly.

95. Dr. Ruth Beuscher to Linda Wagner-Martin, 22 Oct. 1985. Ruth Tiffany Barnhouse Papers, Smith.
96. Ibid.
97. Dr. Ruth Beuscher, notes on SP, fall 1953. 3.10, MSS 1489, Emory.
98. Alexander, *Rough Magic*, 134.
99. Alex Beam, interview with Dr. Ruth Barnhouse, 9 Aug. 1997, Nantucket, Mass. 24.10, SPC, Smith.
100. Harriet Rosenstein interview with Dr. Ruth Beuscher, 1970. 1.6, MSS 1489, Emory.
101. Alex Beam interview with Dr. Ruth Barnhouse, 9 Aug. 1997, Nantucket, Mass. 24.10. SPC, Smith.
102. HC interview with Dr. Francis de Marneffe, Dec. 2014, Westwood, Mass.
103. Ibid.
104. *BJ*, 189.
105. *BJ*, 205.
106. *BJ*, 215–16.
107. Alexander, *Rough Magic*, 134.
108. Ibid., 132.
109. Dr. Ruth Beuscher, notes on SP, fall 1953. 3.10, MSS 1489, Emory.
110. SP to AP, 17 Dec. 1953. *L1*, 651.
111. Dr. Ruth Beuscher, notes on SP, fall 1953. 3.10, MSS 1489, Emory.
112. HC phone interview with Jillian Becker, 18 Apr. 2017.
113. TH to Rosemarie Rowley, 4 Dec. 1997. Add MS 88918/35/28 BL. See Rosemarie Rowley, "Electro-Convulsive Treatment in Sylvia Plath's Life and Work," *Thumbscrew* 10 (Spring 1998), for further discussion about Plath and ECT. Ted Hughes called this article "one of the most important things I've read about S. P." in his 4 Dec. 1997 letter to Rowley.
114. SP to Eddie Cohen, 28 Dec. 1953. *L1*, 657.
115. SP to Dr. Ruth Beuscher, 4 Feb. 1963. *L1*, 967.
116. *J*, 455.
117. Beam, *Gracefully Insane*, 155.
118. Alexander, *Rough Magic*, 134.
119. HC interview with Dr. Francis de Marneffe, Dec. 2014, Westwood, Mass.
120. Dr. Jane Anderson, deposition (1987 *Bell Jar* trial). Jane Anderson v. AVCO Embassy Pictures Corp. et al., in the United States District Court, District of Massachusetts, Civil Action no. 82-0752-K. Jane V. Anderson Papers, Series IV, Smith.
121. Ibid.
122. Ibid.
123. Ibid.
124. HC interview with Dr. Francis de Marneffe, Dec. 2014, Westwood, Mass. In his deposition (1987 *Bell Jar* trial), de Marneffe said, "I think Jane felt that Sylvia was in a sense taking a shortcut to getting out of McLean." Jane Anderson v. AVCO Embassy Pictures Corp. et al., in the United States District Court, District of Massachusetts, Civil Action no. 82-0752-K. Jane V. Anderson Papers, Series IV, Smith.
125. Dr. Francis de Marneffe, deposition (1987 *Bell Jar* trial). Jane Anderson v. AVCO Embassy Pictures Corp. et al., in the United States District Court, District of Massachusetts, Civil Action no. 82-0752-K. Jane V. Anderson Papers, Series IV, Smith.
126. Ibid.
127. *BJ*, 216.
128. SP to Eddie Cohen, 28 Dec. 1953. *L1*, 657.
129. Gordon Lameyer to SP, 22 Nov. 1953. Lilly.
130. SP to Eddie Cohen, 28 Dec. 1953. *L1*, 657.
131. SP to Gordon Lameyer, 25 Dec. 1953. *L1*, 653.
132. SP to Eddie Cohen, 28 Dec. 1953. *L1*, 654–58.
133. Karen Kukil confirms that Dr. Ruth Beuscher told her she had prescribed Plath a diaphragm. Kukil added that, according to birth-control laws in 1954, a second doc-

tor would have had to sign the prescription. Conversation with Karen Kukil, 20 Nov. 2015, at the Mortimer Rare Book Room, Smith College.

134. *BJ*, 223.
135. No letters from him during this time appear in the Plath archives.
136. SP to Eddie Cohen, 28 Dec. 1953. *L1*, 658.
137. See Butscher, Alexander, and Wilson.
138. HC phone interview with Phil McCurdy, 6 Dec. 2014. In 1975, McCurdy wrote to Butscher, "'Physically exploring' would probably be more apt than 'screwing' which suggests more sophistication than we both possessed. She seemed to have a firm, yet sweet and gentle, grasp of what should take place, but my ardor matched hers only intellectually—not, sad to say, romantically or physically." Philip McCurdy to Edward Butscher, 11 Feb. 1975. 1.47, EBC, Smith.
139. HC interview with Phil McCurdy, May 2016, Ogunquit, Maine.
140. SP to Gordon Lameyer, 25 Dec. 1953. *L1*, 652. SP's ellipsis.
141. Dr. Ruth Beuscher, notes on SP, fall 1953. 3.10, MSS 1489, Emory.
142. Ibid.
143. Harriet Rosenstein interview with Dr. Ruth Beuscher, 1970. 1.6, MSS 1489, Emory.
144. Ibid.
145. Anne Harrington, *Mind Fixers: Psychiatry's Troubled Search for the Biology of Mental Illness* (New York: W. W. Norton, 2019), 144.
146. AP, notes on "Sylvia's Copyright." 30.57, SPC, Smith.
147. Harriet Rosenstein interview with Dr. Ruth Beuscher, 1970. 1.6, MSS 1489, Emory.
148. Dr. Ruth Beuscher, notes on SP, fall 1953. 3.10, MSS 1489, Emory.
149. HC interview with Janet Salter Rosenberg, Sept. 2015, Dobbs Ferry, N.Y.
150. Ora Mae Orton to Edward Butscher, 26 Sept. 1973. 2.57, EBC, Smith.
151. *LH*, 5.
152. TH, "Trial," section 14. Add MS 88993/1/1, BL.
153. *BJ*, 202.
154. HC phone interview with Peter Aldrich, 4 Nov. 2014.
155. SP to Marion Freeman, 16 Jan. 1954. *L1*, 664.
156. Alexander, *Rough Magic*, 134.
157. HC interview with Dr. Francis de Marneffe, Dec. 2014, Westwood, Mass.
158. SP, Smith scrapbook. 10.08, Lilly.
159. *BJ*, 244.
160. SP, "James Joyce Notebook." 10.10, Lilly.

13. THE LADY OR THE TIGER

1. SP to Gordon Lameyer, 6 Feb. 1954. *L1*, 677; SP to Jane Anderson, 25 Feb. 1954. *L1*, 693–94.
2. Cyrilly Abels had sent her the tear sheets from Thomas's *Under Milk Wood*, which was published in *Mademoiselle* in Feb. 1954, and Plath proudly quoted the entire introduction to Gordon in a letter. (It was "just too rhythmic and musically vowelish to cut short." SP to Gordon Lameyer, 25 Jan. 1954. *L1*, 672.)
3. SP to Gordon Lameyer, 25 Jan. 1954. *L1*, 669.
4. SP to Gordon Lameyer, 10 Jan. 1954. *L1*, 661–62.
5. SP to Enid Epstein, 18 Jan. 1954. *L1*, 665.
6. SP to Gordon Lameyer, 6 Feb. 1954. *L1*, 677.
7. SP to Jane Anderson, 25 Feb. 1954. *L1*, 694.
8. SP to Phil McCurdy, 7 May 1954. *L1*, 749.
9. Nancy Hunter Steiner, *A Closer Look at Ariel: A Memory of Sylvia Plath* (New York: Harper Magazine Press, 1973), 39–40.
10. SP to Jane Anderson, 25 Feb. 1954. *L1*, 697.
11. Ibid., *L1*, 695.
12. Enid Epstein Mark to Harriet Rosenstein, 14 Nov. 1971. 2.19, MSS 1489, Emory.
13. Ibid.
14. HC interview with Janet Salter Rosenberg, Sept. 2015, Dobbs Ferry, N.Y.

15. SP to Jane Anderson, 25 Feb. 1954. *L1*, 695.
16. HC interview with Louise Giesey White, Aug. 2014, Jamestown, R.I.
17. Harriet Rosenstein interview with Pat O'Neil Pratson, 1972. 3.12, MSS 11489, Emory.
18. SP to Jane Anderson, 25 Feb. 1954. *L1*, 694–95.
19. Harriet Rosenstein interview with Constance Taylor Blackwell, 20 Apr. 1974. 1.9 MSS 1489, Emory.
20. HC interview with Janet Salter Rosenberg, Sept. 2015, Dobbs Ferry, N.Y.
21. SP to Gordon Lameyer, 21 Feb. 1954. *L1*, 692.
22. SP to Gordon Lameyer, 16 Mar. 1954. *L1*, 706.
23. Harriet Rosenstein interview with Jane and Peter Davison, 1972–75. 1.22, MSS1489, Emory.
24. Claiborne Phillips Handleman to Harriet Rosenstein, 27 Jan. 1972. 2.1, MSS 1489, Emory.
25. Ibid.
26. Steiner, *A Closer Look*, 44.
27. Ibid., 45.
28. SP to AP, 3 Feb. 1955. *L1*, 887; SP to AP, 2 Feb. 1955, *L1*, 881.
29. Harriet Rosenstein interview with Susan Weller Burch, 1974. 1.13, MSS 1489, Emory.
30. SP to Gordon Lameyer, 6 Feb. 1954. *L1*, 680–81. All but the first ellipsis are SP's.
31. SP to AP, 8 Feb. 1954. *L1*, 684.
32. SP to AP, 5 Mar. 1954. *L1*, 703.
33. HC interview with Mel Woody, Sept. 2018, Lyme, Conn.
34. SP to Jane Anderson, 25 Feb. 1954. *L1*, 696.
35. SP to AP, 25 Apr. 1954. *L1*, 736.
36. SP to Jane Anderson, 25 Feb. 1954. *L1*, 696.
37. SP to AP, 5 Mar. 1954. *L1*, 702; SP to Jane Anderson, 25 Feb. 1954. *L1*, 697.
38. HC interview with Janet Salter Rosenberg, Sept. 2015, Dobbs Ferry, N.Y. Jane Truslow had emerged "shattered" from her experience with Dr. Booth, Janet said, and took a year's leave.
39. SP to AP, 8 Feb. 1954. *L1*, 685.
40. SP to Gordon Lameyer, 16 Mar. 1954. *L1*, 705.
41. SP to Gordon Lameyer, 21 Feb. 1954. *L1*, 691.
42. The lecture took place on 3 Mar. 1954.
43. SP to Gordon Lameyer, 16 Mar. 1954. *L1*, 706.
44. Feb. 1959, *J*, 470.
45. SP to AP, 18 May 1954. *L1*, 754.
46. SP, Smith scrapbook. 12.O8, Lilly; SP to Gordon Lameyer, 21 Feb. 1954. *L1*, 692.
47. SP, Smith scrapbook. 12.O8, Lilly.
48. SP to Gordon Lameyer, 6 Apr. 1954. *L1*, 715. HC interview with Dr. Francis de Marneffe, Dec. 2014, Westwood, Mass.
49. SP to Gordon Lameyer, 6 Apr. 1954. *L1*, 715.
50. Ibid., *L1*, 715–16.
51. The apartment was at Lexington Avenue and 123rd Street.
52. SP to Gordon Lameyer, 6 Apr. 1954. *L1*, 716–17. SP's ellipsis.
53. HC interview with Janet Salter Rosenberg, Sept. 2015, Dobbs Ferry, N.Y.
54. SP, Smith scrapbook. 12.O8, Lilly.
55. HC interview with Janet Salter Rosenberg, Sept. 2015, Dobbs Ferry, N.Y.
56. Ibid.
57. SP to Gordon Lameyer, 6 Apr. 1954. *L1*, 719.
58. SP to AP, 14 Apr. 1954. *L1*, 725.
59. HC interview with Janet Salter Rosenberg, Sept. 2015, Dobbs Ferry, N.Y.
60. Harriet Rosenstein interview with Jane and Peter Davison, 1972-75. 1.22, MSS 1489, Emory.
61. Harriet Rosenstein interview with Claiborne Phillips Handleman, 1971–74. 2.1, MSS 1489, Emory. Claiborne noted that their friendship ended that spring after she borrowed Sylvia's bike to ride across campus and accidentally returned the wrong bike to Lawrence House. Sylvia became unreasonably angry at her and approached her "in a

rage ... her face was all red and she was trembling," demanding she return her bike. They quickly found the bike, but to Claiborne, it seemed the bike mattered more to Sylvia than their friendship. "It makes me feel very sad now we couldn't talk it out."

62. Harriet Rosenstein interview with Alison V. Smith, 1971. 4.11, MSS 1489, Emory.
63. SP to Gordon Lameyer, 6 Apr. 1954. *L1*, 720.
64. SP to Mel Woody 24 Mar. 1954. *L1*, 713. SP's ellipses.
65. HC interview with Mel Woody, Sept. 2018, Lyme, Conn.
66. SP to Phil McCurdy, 14 Apr. 1954. *L1*, 726–27.
67. SP to Phil McCurdy, 28 Apr. 1954. *L1*, 738. SP's ellipses.
68. SP to AP, 19 Apr. 1954. *L1*, 732.
69. SP to Phil McCurdy, 26 Apr. 1954. *L1*, 737.
70. SP to AP, 19 Apr. 1954. *L1*, 733.
71. HC interview with Mel Woody, Sept. 2018, Lyme, Conn.
72. Claiborne Phillips Handleman to Harriet Rosenstein, 27 Jan. 1972. 2.1, MSS 1489, Emory.
73. *J*, 432.
74. SP to AP, 19 Apr. 1954. *L1*, 732–33. Plath's Cambridge friend Jane Baltzell Kopp remembered her always calling him Sassoon rather than Richard. HC phone interview with Jane Baltzell Kopp, 4 Nov. 2015.
75. Sassoon would later cut Mel and Dick Wertz out of his life after Plath's death. "Dick had said that he was still trying to process what had happened with Sylvia." HC interview with Mel Woody, Sept. 2018, Lyme, Conn.
76. Richard Sassoon to SP, c. late Apr. 1954. Lilly.
77. Richard Sassoon to SP, c. 20 Apr. 1954. Lilly.
78. Richard Sassoon to SP, c. late Apr. & 5 May 1954. Lilly.
79. Ibid.
80. Richard Sassoon to SP, c. 23 Apr. 1954. Lilly.
81. SP, back of envelope, 23 Apr. 1954, sent by Richard Sassoon. Lilly.
82. SP to AP, 25 Apr. 1954. *L1*, 736.
83. Harriet Rosenstein interview with Richard Sassoon, 1974–76. 4.6, MSS 1489, Emory.
84. SP to AP, 16 Apr. 1954. *L1*, 730.
85. SP to AP, 19 Apr. 1954. *L1*, 733.
86. Eddie Cohen to SP, 28 Apr. 1954. Lilly.
87. Eddie Cohen to SP, 6 May 1954. Lilly.
88. Richard Sassoon to SP, c. late Apr. 1954. Lilly.
89. Richard Sassoon to SP, 3 May 1954. Lilly.
90. Ibid.
91. *J*, 191–92. Excerpt from a letter Plath wrote to Sassoon, 22 Nov. 1955. Last ellipsis is SP's.
92. SP to Phil McCurdy, 26 Apr. 1954. *L1*, 737.
93. SP to AP, 25 Jan. 1956. *L1*, 1090–91.
94. Harriet Rosenstein interview with Jane and Peter Davison, 1973.1.22, MSS 1489, Emory.
95. Harriet Rosenstein interview with Constance Taylor Blackwell, 20 Apr. 1974. 1.9, MSS 1489, Emory.
96. SP to AP, 14 Apr. 1954. *L1*, 725.
97. SP to AP, 16 Apr. 1954. *L1*, 729.
98. Mary Mensel to OHP, 3 Sept. 1954. Lilly.
99. Mary Mensel to OHP, 29 Apr. 1954. Lilly; AP's marginalia on same letter.
100. SP to Gordon Lameyer, 6 Apr. 1954. *L1*, 722–23. SP's ellipses.
101. OHP to SP, 9 May 1954. Lilly.
102. OHP to AP, 9 May 1954. Lilly.
103. *LH*, 134.
104. SP to Gordon Lameyer, 11 June 1954. *L1*, 762.
105. SP to Gordon Lameyer, 22 June 1954. *L1*, 764.
106. Richard Sassoon to SP, 11 May 1954. Lilly.
107. SP to AP, 7 May 1954. *L1*, 747.

108. Mel Woody to SP, c. 28 Apr. 1954. Lilly.
109. Ibid.; SP to Mel Woody, 5 May 1954. *L1*, 745–46.
110. SP to Mel Woody, 7 May 1954. *L1*, 748.
111. Harriet Rosenstein interview with Jane and Peter Davison, 1973.1.22, MSS 1489, Emory.
112. HC interview with Mel Woody, Sept. 2018, Lyme, Conn.
113. Ibid.
114. SP, Smith scrapbook. 12.O8, Lilly.
115. Richard Sassoon to SP, 11 May 1954. Lilly.
116. SP to Phil McCurdy, 13 May 1954. *L1*, 752.
117. Ibid., *L1*, 751–52.
118. SP, Smith scrapbook. 12.O8, Lilly.
119. Ibid.
120. Ibid.
121. *LH*, 138.
122. Alan Campbell to SP, 1 June 1954. Plath pasted the letter in her Smith scrapbook. 12.O8, Lilly.
123. SP to Gordon Lameyer, 20 Sept. 1954. *L1*, 801.
124. SP to Mel Woody, 5 July 1954. *L1*, 782.
125. Steiner, *A Closer Look*, 49.
126. Norman Shapiro email to HC, 13 Jan. 2019.
127. Steiner, *A Closer Look*, 49.
128. Plath told Gordon the appointments began on 12 June 1954, and that she would "continue" them all summer. She hoped that Gordon would meet Dr. Beuscher someday and told him she enjoyed "analyzing and philosophizing" with her. SP to Gordon Lameyer, 12 June 1954. *L1*, 763.
129. Harriet Rosenstein interview with Marcia Brown Stern, 1972.4.16, MSS 1489, Emory.
130. SP to Phil McCurdy, 16 Feb. 1954. *L1*, 688.
131. SP to Gordon Lameyer, 22 June 1954. *L1*, 765.
132. Ibid., *L1*, 765–66.
133. Plath wrote the first draft of the story in one day, on 1 Jan. 1955.
134. *JP*, 40.
135. SP to AP, 5 Feb. 1955. *L1*, 888.
136. SP, Smith scrapbook. 12.O8, Lilly.
137. SP to Gordon Lameyer, 3 July 1954. *L1*, 775–76.
138. SP to Gordon Lameyer, 11 June 1954. *L1*, 761.
139. SP to Gordon Lameyer, 23 June 1954. *L1*, 768.
140. Ibid., *L1*, 770–71. SP's ellipses are unbracketed.
141. Gordon Lameyer to SP, 13 July 1954. Lilly.
142. SP to Mel Woody, 5 July 1954. *L1*, 781. SP's ellipses are unbracketed.
143. HC interview with Mel Woody, Sept. 2018, Lyme, Conn.
144. SP to Gordon Lameyer, 11 Aug. 1954. *L1*, 796–97.
145. Steiner, *A Closer Look*, 57.
146. Ibid., 55–56.
147. Nancy Hunter claimed, in her memoir of that summer, that Plath first met Edwin in early Aug. This date is incorrect.
148. Steiner, *A Closer Look*, 58.
149. SP, notes on *The Bell Jar*, spring 1961. 4.1, SPC, Smith. Edwin even shared Otto's pacifist politics—he had been a conscientious objector during World War II and was housed at a camp for COs in New Hampshire.
150. Harriet Rosenstein interview with Nancy Hunter Steiner, 1971. 4.13, MSS 1489, Emory.
151. All of Nancy's quoted recollections come from *A Closer Look*. According to Plath's 1954 calendar, the bar was at 32 Church Street, now the site of the Border Café.
152. SP, 1954–55 calendar. 7.6, Lilly.
153. SP to Gordon Lameyer, 19 July 1954. *L1*, 783.
154. Harriet Rosenstein interview with Nancy Hunter Steiner, 1971. 4.13, MSS 1489, Emory.

155. Richard Wilbur, "Cottage Street, 1953," *Sylvia Plath: The Woman and the Work*, Edward Butscher, ed. (New York: Dodd, Mead and Co., 1977), 30–31.
156. Steiner, *A Closer Look*, 56.
157. *Words in Air: The Complete Correspondence Between Elizabeth Bishop and Robert Lowell*, Thomas Travisano and Saskia Hamilton, eds. (New York: Farrar, Straus and Giroux, 2010), 737–38.
158. *BJ*, 228.
159. Nancy said she came home from class at eleven a.m. and found a note from Plath saying she and Edwin had gone to the beach. Yet Plath wrote in her calendar that she attended her German and English classes that day, took a midterm exam, and studied at Lamont Library.
160. Harriet Rosenstein interview with Nancy Hunter Steiner, 1971. 4.13, MSS 1489, Emory.
161. Steiner, *A Closer Look*, 65.
162. SP, 1954–55 calendar. 7.6, Lilly.
163. TH, deposition (1987 *Bell Jar* trial). Jane Anderson v. AVCO Embassy Pictures Corp. et al., in the United States District Court, District of Massachusetts, Civil Action no. 82-0752-K. Jane V. Anderson Papers, Series IV, Smith.
164. *J*, 438. There are also two notes on Plath's *Bell Jar* outline reading, "Edwin / looses [*sic*] virginity" and "Edwin loss of virginity." SP, notes on *The Bell Jar*, spring 1961. 4.1, SPC, Smith.
165. In Aug. she mentioned him in her Smith scrapbook as part of a group of memorable men she had dated that summer, though in less favorable terms: "dinner farewell at Meadows with Ira: daiquiris in the rain—goodbye also to intriguing, inscrutable Lou, wierd [*sic*] Edwin, and a blazing feminine existence in the heart of my haven Harvard." SP, Smith scrapbook. 12.O8, Lilly.
166. Steiner, *A Closer Look*, 71.
167. SP, 9 Nov. 1954, 1954–55 calendar. 7.6, Lilly.
168. Edwin Autowicz to Fran McCullough, 25 Mar. 1975. 6.5, Hornbake Library, Francis McCullough Papers, University of Maryland.
169. SP, Smith scrapbook. 12.O8, Lilly.
170. Steiner, *A Closer Look*, 73.
171. SP, Smith scrapbook. 12.O8, Lilly.
172. The conversation, according to Plath's calendar, probably took place on Sunday, 1 Aug. Gordon Lameyer, *Dear Sylvia*. Lameyer MSS, Lilly.
173. SP to Gordon Lameyer, 5 Aug. 1954. *L1*, 789.
174. Gordon Lameyer, *Dear Sylvia*. Lameyer MSS, Lilly.
175. SP to Gordon Lameyer, 5 Aug. 1954. *L1*, 791.
176. SP to Gordon Lameyer, 7 Aug. 1954. *L1*, 792.
177. Gordon Lameyer to SP, 9 Aug. 1954. Lilly.
178. SP to Gordon Lameyer, 7 Aug. 1954. *L1*, 793.
179. SP to Gordon Lameyer, 4 Aug. 1954. *L1*, 785.
180. SP, Smith scrapbook. 12.O8, Lilly.
181. SP, 25 Aug. 1954, 1954–55 calendar. 7.6, Lilly.
182. SP, 22 Aug. 1954, 1954–55 calendar. 7.6, Lilly.
183. SP, 24 Aug. 1954, 1954–55 calendar. 7.6, Lilly.
184. SP, 27 Aug. 1954, 1954–55 calendar. 7.6, Lilly.
185. SP, 4 Sept. 1954, 1954–55 calendar. 7.6, Lilly.
186. SP to Enid Epstein, 26 Jan. 1955. *L1*, 867.
187. SP to Gordon Lameyer, 5 Aug. 1954. *L1*, 789. SP's ellipsis.

14. O ICARUS

1. SP, Smith scrapbook. 12.O8, Lilly.
2. She contemplated applying to the MFA program at Iowa but decided against it. Paul Engle to SP, c. 1955. Lilly.

3. SP to Mel Woody, 26 Jan. 1955. *L1*, 874.

4. SP to AP, 27 Sept. 1954. *L1*, 809.

5. Gibian wrote that Plath was "the outstanding student in my experience at Smith College," while Drew wrote, "I have never had a more brilliant and a more charming student." References for SP, 1954–55. Vocational Office Files, Smith College Archives.

6. Mary Ellen Chase, reference for SP, 14 Dec. 1954. Vocational Office Files, Smith College Archives.

7. Alfred Kazin, reference for SP, 6 Jan. 1955. Vocational Office Files, Smith College Archives.

8. SP to AP, 27 Sept. 1954. *L1*, 809.

9. SP to Mel Woody, 17 Dec. 1954. *L1*, 852; SP to AP, 27 Sept. 1954. *L1*, 809.

10. Dr. Ruth Beuscher, reference for SP, 1954–55. Vocational Office Files, Smith College Archives.

11. Mrs. Estella Kelsey, reference for SP 1954–55. Vocational Office Files, Smith College Archives.

12. SP to AP, 27 Sept. 1954. *L1*, 809; SP to AP, 12 Oct. 1954. *L1*, 822.

13. SP to AP, 12 Oct. 1954. *L1*, 822.

14. SP to Gordon Lameyer, 24 Sept. 1954. *L1*, 806.

15. SP to AP, 21 Sept. 1954. *L1*, 804.

16. SP to Gordon Lameyer, 24 Sept. 1954. *L1*, 807. SP's ellipses.

17. SP to AP, 14 Oct. 1954. *L1*, 823–24. SP's ellipses.

18. SP to AP, 24 Oct. 1954. *L1*, 826.

19. SP to Gordon Lameyer, 10 Oct. 1954. *L1*, 818.

20. SP, "The Neilson Professor," *Smith Alumnae Quarterly* 46 (Fall 1954): 12.

21. Preface to *The Commentary Reader: Two Decades of Articles and Stories*, Norman Podhoretz, ed. (New York: Atheneum, 1966), with an introduction by Kazin, p. vii.

22. SP to AP, 24 Oct. 1954. *L1*, 826–28.

23. SP to Gordon Lameyer, 4 Nov. 1954. *L1*, 830.

24. SP to Mel Woody, 17 Dec. 1954. *L1*, 852.

25. SP to Gordon Lameyer, 4 Nov. 1954. *L1*, 831.

26. HC interview with Elinor Friedman Klein, Oct. 2015, South Salem, N.Y.

27. Harriet Rosenstein interview with Elinor Friedman Klein, 1971–72. 2. 10, MSS 1489, Emory.

28. HC interview with Elinor Friedman Klein, Oct. 2015, South Salem, N.Y.

29. Ibid., Dec. 2017, South Salem, N.Y.

30. Harriet Rosenstein interview with Elinor Friedman Klein, 1971–72. 2. 10, MSS 1489, Emory.

31. SP to AP, 12 Oct. 1954. *L1*, 821.

32. Harriet Rosenstein interview with Marcia Brown Stern, 1972. 4.15, MSS 1489, Emory.

33. Harriet Rosenstein interview with Pat O'Neil Pratson, 1972. 3.12, MSS 1489, Emory.

34. George Gibian to Harriet Rosenstein, 18 Oct. 1971. 1.30, MSS 1489, Emory.

35. SP to AP, 14 Oct. 1954. *L1*, 823.

36. SP to Gordon Lameyer, 5 Oct. 1954. *L1*, 815. SP's ellipsis.

37. SP to Gordon Lameyer, 10 Oct. & 20 Sept. 1954. *L1*, 815; 802.

38. SP to AP, 4 Oct. 1954. *L1*, 812.

39. OHP to AP, 2 Oct. 1954. Lilly.

40. Ibid.

41. OHP to SP, 16 Oct. 1954. Lilly.

42. OHP to SP, 10 Dec. 1954. Lilly.

43. SP to AP, 12 Oct. 1954. *L1*, 820. First ellipsis in quoted letter is SP's.

44. Gordon Lameyer to SP, n.d. (fall 1954). Lilly.

45. SP to AP, 2 Nov. 1954. *L1*, 830.

46. SP to Mel Woody, 26 Jan. 1955. *L1*, 872.

47. Richard Sassoon to SP, n.d. (late Dec. 1954). Lilly.

48. Richard Sassoon to SP, n.d. (fall 1954). Lilly.

49. Richard Sassoon to SP, c. fall 1954. Lilly.

50. SP to Mel Woody, 17 Dec. 1954. *L1*, 851. SP's ellipsis.
51. Richard Sassoon to SP, c. fall 1954. Lilly.
52. Ibid.
53. Richard Sassoon to SP, Nov./Dec. 1954. Lilly.
54. Richard Sassoon to SP, c. fall 1954. Lilly.
55. Ibid.
56. Richard Sassoon to SP, c. 1954–55. Lilly.
57. SP to Gordon Lameyer, 22 Nov. 1954. *L1*, 837.
58. SP, 27 Sept. 1954, 1954–55 calendar. 7.6, Lilly.
59. SP, 28 Sept. 1954, 1954–55 calendar. 7.6, Lilly.
60. Gordon Lameyer to SP, 29 Nov. & 2 Dec. 1954. Lilly.
61. SP to Gordon Lameyer, 9 Dec. 1954. *L1*, 846.
62. SP to Gordon Lameyer, 6 Nov. 1954. *L1*, 832.
63. SP to AP, 13 Nov. 1954. *L1*, 835.
64. OHP to SP, 30 Dec. 1954. Lilly.
65. SP to AP, 6 Dec. 1954. *L1*, 843.
66. SP to Gordon Lameyer, 9 Jan. 1955. *L1*, 858.
67. HC interview with Janet Salter Rosenberg, Sept. 2015, Dobbs Ferry, N.Y.
68. SP to Gordon Lameyer, 9 Jan. 1955. *L1*, 858.
69. SP to AP, 13 Dec. 1954. *L1*, 848. In undated letters that fall, Sassoon writes about the trip, and about buying Plath her first escargots.
70. SP, Smith scrapbook. 12.O8, Lilly.
71. SP to Jon Rosenthal, 13 Dec. 1954. *L1*, 850.
72. HC interview with Jon Rosenthal, Nov. 2014, Amherst, Mass.
73. SP to Jon Rosenthal, 2 Dec. 1954. *L1*, 841.
74. SP to Jon Rosenthal, 13 Dec. 1954. *L1*, 849–50.
75. SP, 21 Dec. 1954, 1954–55 calendar. 7.6, Lilly.
76. SP, 22 Dec. 1954, 1954–55 calendar. 7.6, Lilly.
77. HC interview with Jon Rosenthal, Nov. 2014, Amherst, Mass.
78. Harriet Rosenstein, 1974 notes on interview with Jon Rosenthal. Corrected copy provided by Jon Rosenthal.
79. HC interview with Jon Rosenthal, Nov. 2014, Amherst, Mass.
80. SP, 26 Dec. 1954, 1954–55 calendar. 7.6, Lilly.
81. SP to Enid Epstein, 26 Jan. 1955. *L1*, 866.
82. 8.17, Lilly.
83. SP to Mel Woody, 26 Jan. 1955. *L1*, 871.
84. She would write another version of the story in England.
85. *JP*, 268; 270; 272; 273.
86. SP to AP, 29 Jan. 1955. *L1*, 880.
87. *JP*, 274.
88. SP to AP, 15 & 29 Jan. 1955. *L1*, 863; 880.
89. SP to AP, 29 Jan. 1955. *L1*, 880.
90. SP to Gordon Lameyer, 9 Jan. 1955. *L1*, 859. The poems were: "Ballade Banale," "Item: Stolen, One Suitcase," "Morning in the Hospital Solarium," "New England Winter Without Snow," and "Harlequin Love Song."
91. SP to AP, 15 Jan. 1955. *L1*, 861.
92. George Gibian to Harriet Rosenstein, 18 Oct. 1971, and interview with Harriet Rosenstein, 1971. 1.30, MSS 1489, Emory.
93. SP, "The Magic Mirror: A Study of the Double in Two of Dostoevsky's Novels." Smith College senior thesis in English. 11.1, Lilly. 7.
94. Ibid., 5.
95. Ibid., 15–16.
96. *J*, 150.
97. SP, "The Magic Mirror," 10; 13.
98. Ibid., 51.
99. Ibid., 44.

100. SP to Gordon Lameyer, 26 Jan. 1955. *L1*, 869.
101. SP to AP, 29 Jan. 1955. *L1*, 878.
102. SP, 22 Jan. 1955, 1954–55 calendar. 7.6, Lilly.
103. SP to Gordon Lameyer, 10 Feb. 1955. *L1*, 894; SP to Gordon Lameyer, 26 Jan. 1955. *L1*, 869.
104. SP to Mel Woody, 26 Jan. 1955. *L1*, 872.
105. SP to AP, 27 Jan. 1955. *L1*, 874.
106. SP, 27 Jan. 1955, 1954–55 calendar. 7.6, Lilly.
107. SP to Gordon Lameyer, 10 Feb. 1955. *L1*, 894.
108. SP to AP, 5 Feb. 1955. *L1*, 888.
109. SP to AP, 29 Jan. 1955. *L1*, 879.
110. 8.12, Lilly.
111. SP to AP, 29 Jan. 1955. *L1*, 879.
112. Plath wrote in her calendar that she wrote and then typed up the story on 27 Jan.
113. SP to AP, 24 Mar. 1955. *L1*, 905.
114. SP to Gordon Lameyer, 26 Jan. 1955. *L1*, 870.
115. SP, 24 Jan. 1954, 1954–55 calendar. 7.6, Lilly; SP to Mel Woody, 26 Jan. 1955. *L1*, 873.
116. SP to Mel Woody, 26 Jan. 1955. *L1*, 873–74.
117. SP to AP, 2 Feb. 1955. *L1*, 882.
118. SP to Gordon Lameyer, 10 Feb. 1955. *L1*, 895.
119. They were "Rondeau Doublé," "Temper of Time," "Winter Words," "Apparel for April," "Dirge" (retitled "Lament"), "Elegy," "The Dream," "Prologue to Spring," and "Epitaph in Three Parts."
120. SP, Smith scrapbook. 12.O8, Lilly.
121. SP to AP, 2 Feb. 1955. *L1*, 882.
122. OHP to AP, 28 Dec. 1955. Lilly.
123. 7.7, Lilly.
124. *Seventeen* (March 1953), 9.
125. SP to Gordon Lameyer, 10 Feb. 1955. *L1*, 894.
126. SP to AP, 10 Feb. 1955. *L1*, 890–93.
127. Richard Sassoon to SP, c. Feb. Mar., May & Apr. 1955. Lilly. Sassoon promises not to spank Plath but "to beat" her if she ever angers him "greatly." 14 Feb. 1955. Lilly. (Date supplied from content and postmark.)
128. Richard Sassoon to SP, 20 Apr. 1955. Lilly.
129. SP to AP, 16 Apr. 1955. *L1*, 908–909.
130. "Notes from Judges," 21 Apr. 1955. Lilly.
131. SP to AP, 23 Apr. 1955. *L1*, 913.
132. Edward Weeks to SP, 18 Apr. 1955. Lilly.
133. SP to Gordon Lameyer, 26 Apr. 1955. *L1*, 920.
134. SP to AP, 21 Apr. 1955. *L1*, 912.
135. SP to AP, 21 May 1955. *L1*, 929.
136. SP to AP, 25 Apr. 1955. *L1*, 918.
137. SP to Gordon Lameyer, 26 Apr. 1955. *L1*, 919.
138. SP to AP, 21 May 1955. *L1*, 929.
139. SP, Smith scrapbook. 12.O8, Lilly.
140. Nancy Hunter Steiner, *A Closer Look at Ariel: A Memory of Sylvia Plath* (New York: Harper Magazine Press, 1973), 81.
141. *LH*, 176; Harriet Rosenstein interview with Peter and Jane Davison, 1973. 1.22, MSS 1489, Emory.
142. SP, Smith scrapbook. 12.O8, Lilly.
143. SP to Lynn Lawner, 8 June 1955. *L1*, 932.
144. SP to AP, 29 Jan. 1955. *L1*, 880.
145. OHP to AP, 26 June 1955. Lilly.
146. SP to WP, 6 July 1955. *L1*, 936.
147. She wrote in her June–October 1955 calendar that she finished the story on 8 Aug.
148. 8.16, Lilly.

149. *Lyric* took "Apotheosis" and "Second Winter," which appeared in the Winter 1956 issue. The *New Orleans Poetry Journal* took "Lament."
150. The stories were "Superman and Paula Brown's New Snowsuit," "The Day Mr. Prescott Died," and "Tongues of Stone."
151. SP to Gordon Lameyer, 28 July 1955. *L1*, 942.
152. Lucinda Baker, "No Literary Slump for Lucinda," *The Writer's Year Book* 26 (Cincinnati: F. & W. Publishing, 1955), 11–15. Plath annotated the article.
153. SP to AP, 12 Aug. 1955. *L1*, 955.
154. Peter Davison, *The Fading Smile: Poets in Boston from Robert Lowell to Sylvia Plath* (New York: W. W. Norton, 1994), 40.
155. HC interview with Phil McCurdy, May 2016, Ogunquit, Maine.
156. Henry Volkening to SP, 25 Aug. 1955. Lilly.
157. Richard Sassoon to SP, 10 June 1955. Lilly.
158. Richard Sassoon to SP, 4 June 1955. Lilly.
159. SP to WP, 28 July 1955. *L1*, 945.
160. Richard Sassoon to SP, 5 & 8 July 1955. Lilly.
161. Richard Sassoon to SP, 9 Aug. 1955. Lilly.
162. *J*, 432.
163. Richard Sassoon to SP, 9 Aug. 1955. Lilly.
164. Richard Sassoon to Harriet Rosenstein, c. 1974–76. 4.6, MSS 1489, Emory.
165. Richard Sassoon to SP, 18 July 1955. Lilly.
166. Richard Sassoon to SP, 19 July 1955. Lilly.
167. Richard Sassoon to SP, 9 Aug. 1955. Lilly.
168. Richard Sassoon to SP, 9 Aug. 1955. Lilly.
169. Harriet Rosenstein interview with Peter and Jane Davison, 1972–75. 1.22, MSS 1489, Emory.
170. Ibid.
171. Davison, *Fading Smile*, 40.
172. Harriet Rosenstein interview with Peter and Jane Davison, 1972–75. 1.22, MSS 1489, Emory.
173. SP to Gordon Lameyer, 3 Aug. 1955. *L1*, 947.
174. SP to Gordon Lameyer, 24 Aug. 1955. *L1*, 956.
175. Ibid., *L1*, 957.
176. Ibid., *L1*, 955–56.
177. Ibid., *L1*, 957.
178. SP to AP, 30 Aug. 1955. *L1*, 959.
179. SP to Gordon Lameyer, 28 July 1955. *L1*, 942–43.
180. 7.11, Lilly.
181. OHP to SP, 14 Aug. 1955. Lilly.
182. SP to WP, 28 July 1955. *L1*, 944.
183. Ibid.
184. SP to Gordon Lameyer, 11 Aug. 1955. *L1*, 952–53.

15. CHANNEL CROSSING

1. SP to AP, 9 Mar. 1956. *L1*, 1134.
2. Lucas Myers, "Ah, Youth . . . Ted Hughes and Sylvia Plath at Cambridge and After," *Grand Street* 8.4 (Summer 1989): 86–103; 95.
3. SP to Elinor Friedman, 28 Sept. 1955. *L1*, 965.
4. "Remember, this was in 1955, and our cohort consisted mostly of unsophisticated people from conservative backgrounds and aspirations from all forty-eight states. Needless to say, it was noticed with interest." Margaret Bolsterli to Peter K. Steinberg, 20 Jan. 2016. Email shared with HC with Bolsterli's permission.
5. SP to AP, 25 Sept. (#1 & #2) 1955. *L1*, 960; 963.
6. SP to AP, 25 Sept. (#2) 1955. *L1*, 964.
7. SP to Elinor Friedman, 28 Sept. 1955. *L1*, 965.
8. Ibid.

9. SP to AP, 25 Sept. (#1) 1955. *L1*, 961.
10. SP to AP, 25 Sept. (#2) 1955. *L1*, 963.
11. SP to AP, 2 Oct. (#2) 1955. *L1*, 969.
12. SP to AP, 25 Sept. (#1 & #2) 1955. *L1*, 959–62.
13. SP to AP, 2 Oct. (#1) 1955. *L1*, 966.
14. SP to Marcia and Mike Plumer, 14 Dec. *L1*, 1056.
15. SP to AP, 9 Oct. (#1) 1955. *L1*, 975.
16. SP to AP, 9 Oct. (#2) 1955. *L1*, 977.
17. SP to AP, 14 Oct. 1955. *L1*, 981.
18. SP to Marcia Brown Plumer, 14 Dec. 1955. *L1*, 1056.
19. SP to AP, 2 Feb. 1956. *L1*, 1095.
20. Jane Baltzell Kopp remembered that the "appalling" winter of 1955–56 was said to be the coldest in ninety-five years. The gas heaters provided inadequate warmth. "It astounded me that with my head only four inches away from the radiants, it was still so cold in the room that my breath made vapor." See Jane Baltzell Kopp in *Memories of Whitstead*. Privately printed by Rhoda Dorsey, 2007. 20.29, SPC, Smith.
21. See Dina Dincauze's memoir in ibid.
22. HC interview with Jean Gooder, July 2017, Cambridge, UK.
23. SP to AP, 2 Oct. (#1) 1955. *L1*, 966.
24. SP to AP, 9 Oct. (#2) 1955. *L1*, 977.
25. SP to AP, 14 Oct. (#1) 1955. *L1*, 980.
26. Ibid.
27. SP to Jon Rosenthal, 14 Dec. 1955. *L1*, 1054.
28. Jane Baltzell Kopp and Bert Wyatt-Brown among them.
29. SP to Elinor Friedman, 27 Oct. 1955. *L1*, 996.
30. SP to AP, 14 Oct. (#1) 1955. *L1*, 981.
31. SP to AP, 24 Oct. 1955. *L1*, 992.
32. Isabel Murray Henderson email to HC, 1 Nov. 2017.
33. SP to AP, 25 Sept. (#2) 1955. *L1*, 963.
34. SP to AP, 2 Oct. (#2) 1955. *L1*, 968–70.
35. Among those were Jean Pollard (South African), Jane Baltzell (an American Marshall scholar), Clodagh Elizabeth O'Dowd (South African), Isabel Murray (Scottish), Lois Marshall (American Fulbright scholar), Elizabeth Kimber (American), and Margaret Roberts (South African), who took her on a tour of town on the back of her Vespa.
36. SP to AP, 2 Oct. (#2) 1955. *L1*, 968–69.
37. HC phone interview with Jane Baltzell Kopp, 3 Nov. 2015.
38. Jean Gooder email to HC, 7 July 2017.
39. SP to AP, 22 Nov. 1955. *L1*, 1016.
40. *J*, 209.
41. HC interview with Jean Gooder, July 2017, Cambridge, UK.
42. SP to AP, 22 Nov. 1955. *L1*, 1016–17.
43. May Collacott Targett email to HC, 13 Nov. 2017.
44. SP to AP, 17 Jan. 1956. *L1*, 1084.
45. *J*, 224.
46. Dr. Marynia Farnham and Ferdinand Lundberg, *Modern Woman: The Lost Sex* (New York: Harper & Brothers, 1977). First edition published in 1947. Quoted in Amy Westervelt, *Forget Having It All: How America Messed Up Motherhood—and How to Fix It* (New York: Seal Press, 2018), 129–30. Westervelt also notes that J. Edgar Hoover published work in the mid-1940s linking rising juvenile delinquency rates with working mothers (128).
47. Jeremy Gavron, *A Woman on the Edge of Time* (New York: The Experiment, 2016), 61. Shortly after Gavron's death, her PhD thesis was published as *The Captive Wife*, a landmark book in the emerging field of women's studies.
48. SP to TH, 3 Oct. 1956. *L1*, 1266.
49. SP to AP, 25 Feb. 1956. *L1*, 1115.
50. Isabel Murray Henderson email to HC, 1 Nov. 2017.
51. SP, "Cambridge Letter," *Isis* (16 May 1956): 9.

52. *The Poet Speaks: Interviews with Contemporary Poets*, Peter Orr, ed. (New York: Barnes & Noble, 1966). Includes interview with SP conducted on 30 Oct. 1962 in London.

53. HC interview with Jean Gooder, July 2017, Cambridge, UK.

54. SP to AP, 2 Oct. (#2) 1955. *L1*, 970.

55. Harriet Rosenstein interview with Evelyn Evans, 1973. 1.14, MSS 1489, Emory.

56. SP to AP, 5 Oct. 1955. *L1*, 972.

57. SP to AP, 24 Oct. 1955. *L1*, 993.

58. SP to AP, 9 Oct. (#2) 1955. *L1*, 977.

59. SP to AP, 7 Nov. 1955. *L1*, 1003.

60. Christopher Levenson, *Not One of the Boys*, unpublished memoir provided to HC by Levenson.

61. Jane Baltzell Kopp, "'Gone, Very Gone Youth': Sylvia Plath at Cambridge, 1955–1957," *Sylvia Plath: The Woman and the Work*, Edward Butscher, ed. (New York: Dodd, Mead and Co., 1977), 62–63.

62. Philipa Forder Goold in *Memories of Whitstead*, 30. Privately printed by Rhoda Dorsey, 2007. 20.29, SPC, Smith; Goold to Harriet Rosenstein, 2 Apr. 1974. 1.14, MSS 1489, Emory.

63. Students Plath later taught at Smith would remember her voice as British-inflected, while her 1958 recording with Lee Anderson reveals a hybrid British-Boston accent. HC phone interview with Jane Baltzell Kopp, 4 Nov. 2015.

64. Michael Boddy email to EF, Apr. 2001. EFP.

65. SP to AP, 2 Oct. (#2) 1955. *L1*, 969.

66. SP to AP, 14 Nov. (#1) 1955. *L1*, 1005.

67. SP to AP, 9 Oct. (#2) 1955. *L1*, 976.

68. Otto Plath was similarly driven to master new subjects. Jane Baltzell Kopp did not recall Plath ever mentioning Otto, and recalled her discussing Aurelia only occasionally. "There was no way to guess the intensity of the influence." HC phone interview, 4 Nov. 2015.

69. SP to AP, 14 Nov. (#1) 1955. *L1*, 1006.

70. SP to OHP, 13 Dec. 1955. *L1*, 1050–51.

71. OHP to SP, 25 Oct. 1955. Lilly.

72. SP to AP, 14 Dec. 1955. *L1*, 1053.

73. SP to AP, 29 Oct. 1955. *L1*, 998–99.

74. SP to OHP, 13 Dec. 1955. *L1*, 1046.

75. Mary Ellen Chase to SP, 8 Nov. 1955. Lilly.

76. Plath listed her lectures' specific days and times in her Michaelmas term schedule in her 1955–56 Heffer's calendar, now at Lilly.

77. SP to AP, 9 Oct. (#1) 1955. *L1*, 976.

78. SP to Gordon Lameyer, 18 Oct. 1955. *L1*, 989.

79. HC interview with Jean Gooder, July 2017, Cambridge, UK.

80. Christopher Levenson, *Not One of the Boys*.

81. Ibid.

82. SP to AP, 24 (#1) Feb. 1956. *L1*, 1113.

83. HC phone interview with Jane Baltzell Kopp, 4 Nov. 2015.

84. Christopher Levenson email to HC, 18 Oct. 2017.

85. Christopher Levenson email to HC, 21 Oct. 2017.

86. SP to Elinor Friedman, 27 Oct. 1955. *L1*, 994.

87. Harriet Rosenstein interview with Mallory Wober, 1973. 4.23, MSS 1489, Emory.

88. SP, 3 Dec. 1955, 1955–56 calendar. 7.6, Lilly.

89. SP to Elinor Friedman, 12 Dec. 1955. *L1*, 1040.

90. SP to AP, 21 Nov. 1955. *L1*, 1014.

91. SP to AP, 14 Oct. (#2) 1955. *L1*, 982.

92. SP to AP, 21 Nov. 1955. *L1*, 1014.

93. SP to AP, 26 Nov. 1955. *L1*, 1027.

94. SP to OHP, 13 Dec. 1955. *L1*, 1049.

95. Harriet Rosenstein interview with Mallory Wober, 1973. 4.23, MSS 1489, Emory.

96. SP to Elinor Friedman, 12 Dec. 1955. *L1*, 1040.

97. SP to Richard Sassoon, 22 Nov. 1955. *L1*, 1018.
98. SP to AP, 10 Dec. 1955. *L1*, 1033.
99. SP to AP, 14 Nov. (#2) 1955. *L1*, 1009.
100. Harriet Rosenstein interview with Richard Wertz, 1970. 4.20, MSS 1489, Emory.
101. Harriet Rosenstein interview with Mallory Wober, 1973. 4.23, MSS 1489, Emory.
102. SP to Mallory Wober, 19 Dec. 1955. *L1*, 1062.
103. SP to AP, 29 Oct. 1955. *L1*, 998.
104. SP to AP, 7 Nov. 1955. *L1*, 1002.
105. SP to AP, 25 Jan. 1956. *L1*, 1091.
106. SP to AP, 21 Nov. 1955. *L1*, 1012.
107. SP to AP, 29 Jan. 1956. *L1*, 1093.
108. HC phone interview with Jane Baltzell Kopp, 4 Nov. 2015.
109. SP to Jon Rosenthal, 14 Dec. 1955. *L1*, 1055–56.
110. SP to AP, 14 Oct. (#2) 1955. *L1*, 982.
111. SP to Elinor Friedman, 27 Oct. 1955. *L1*, 994.
112. Jane Baltzell Kopp email to Wyatt-Brown, 21 Mar. 2003. Quoted in Bertram Wyatt-Brown, "Neither Priest nor Poet," *Shapers of Southern History: Autobiographical Reflections*, John B. Boles, ed. (Athens: University of Georgia Press, 2004), 62–90. 90.
113. HC phone interview with Jane Baltzell Kopp, 4 Nov. 2015.
114. Harriet Rosenstein interview with Jane Baltzell Kopp, 1974–75. 2.11, MSS 1489, Emory.
115. Harriet Rosenstein interview with Iko and Felicity Meshoulam, 1973. 2.22, MSS 1489, Emory.
116. HC interview with Jean Gooder, July 2017, Cambridge, UK.
117. Harriet Rosenstein interview with Iko and Felicity Meshoulam, 1973. 2.22, MSS 1489, Emory.
118. Ibid.
119. Isabel Murray Henderson email to HC, 1 Nov. 2017.
120. Byatt attended Newnham from 1954 to 1957; Drabble from 1957 to 1960.
121. Mira Stout, "What Possessed A. S. Byatt?," *New York Times* (26 May 1991).
122. SP to AP, 16 Jan. 1956. *L1*, 1081.
123. HC phone interview with Jane Baltzell Kopp, 4 Nov. 2015.
124. *J*, 201.
125. HC interview with Elinor Friedman Klein, Oct. 2015, South Salem, N.Y.
126. John Creaser, "Sylvia Plath in Bartholomew Fair," blog, *The Cambridge Edition of the Works of Ben Jonson Online*, http://universitypublishingonline.org/cambridge/benjonson/blog/sylvia-plath-in-bartholomew-fair/.
127. Ibid.
128. SP to OHP, 13 Dec. 1955. *L1*, 1048.
129. SP to AP, 17 Jan. 1956. *L1*, 1083.
130. SP to AP, 25 Jan. 1956. *L1*, 1089–90.
131. Harriet Rosenstein interview with Dick Wertz, 1970. 4.20, MSS 1489, Emory; SP to Elinor Friedman, 12 Dec. 1955. *L1*, 1040.
132. Plath told Aurelia the hotel was in the "Oriental & Greek quarter." (30 Dec. 1955. *L1*, 1068). Nat LaMar had booked it for her.
133. SP to Mallory Wober, 23 Dec. 1955. *L1*, 1063.
134. HC phone interview with Jane Baltzell Kopp, 4 Nov. 2015.
135. Harriet Rosenstein interview with Elinor Friedman Klein, 1971–72. 2.10, MSS 1489, Emory.
136. SP to Elinor Friedman, 10 Feb. 1956. *L1*, 1104.
137. Ibid.
138. SP to AP, 30 Dec. 1955. *L1*, 1069.
139. Ibid.
140. SP to Mallory Wober, 29 Dec. 1955. *L1*, 1064.
141. SP to AP, 30 Dec. 1955. *L1*, 1069.
142. SP to AP, 14 Dec. 1955. *L1*, 1053.
143. SP to AP, 29 Jan. 1956. *L1*, 1093.

144. Ibid.
145. SP to AP, 14 Dec. 1955. *L1*, 1052.
146. SP to WP, 11 Dec. 1955. *L1*, 1038.
147. *J*, 549.
148. SP to Mallory Wober, 1 Jan. 1956. *L1*, 1072.
149. SP to Elinor Friedman, 10 Feb. 1956. *L1*, 1105.
150. OHP to AP, 16 Jan. 1956. Lilly.
151. SP to AP, 7 Jan. 1956. *L1*, 1074.
152. SP, 6 Jan. 1956, 1955–56 calendar. 7.6, Lilly.
153. Andrew Wilson, *Mad Girls' Love Song: Sylvia Plath and Life Before Ted* (New York: Scribner, 2013), 300.
154. Richard Sassoon, "In the Year of Love and unto Death, the Fourth—an Elegy on the Muse," *Northwest Review* 5.1 (Winter 1962): 110–11. Wilson was the first biographer to discuss this story.
155. Ibid., 116–17.
156. Ibid., 108–109. Sassoon's ellipses.
157. Plath began "The Matisse Chapel" on 17 Jan. and revised the story until she had twenty-five pages that satisfied her. She sent it to *The New Yorker*, but it was rejected without comment that February.
158. 13.4, Lilly.
159. SP, 8 Jan. 1956, 1955–56 calendar. 7.6, Lilly.
160. SP to AP, 10 Jan. 1956. *L1*, 1077.
161. SP to Elinor Friedman, 6–8 Mar. 1956. *L1*, 1131.
162. SP to Richard Sassoon, 6 Mar. 1956. *L1*, 1126.
163. SP to AP, 25 Jan. 1956. *L1*, 1090.
164. SP to AP, 29 Jan. 1956. *L1*, 1092.
165. SP to AP, 17 Jan. 1956. *L1*, 1083.
166. SP, 27 & 29 Jan. 1956, 1955–56 calendar. 7.6 Lilly.
167. SP to AP, 2 Feb. 1956. *L1*, 1095.
168. SP to AP, 6 Feb. 1956. *L1*, 1098.
169. SP, 7 Feb. 1956, 1955–56 calendar. 7.6, Lilly.
170. SP to Mallory Wober, 7 Feb. 1956. *L1*, 1100.
171. Harriet Rosenstein interview with Iko and Felicity Meshoulam, 1973. 2.22, MSS 1489, Emory.
172. Harriet Rosenstein interview with Mallory Wober, 1973. 4.23, MSS 1489, Emory.
173. SP to Jane Anderson, 21 Mar. 1956. *L1*, 1150.
174. *J*, 197–98.
175. HC interview with Philip Hobsbaum, 2001, Glasgow, Scotland.
176. Ibid.
177. Christopher Levenson email to HC, 18 Sept. 2017.
178. She wrote in her 1955–56 Heffer's calendar that she finished the novel on 16 Jan.
179. SP to AP, 6 Feb. 1956. *L1*, 1100.
180. *J*, 198–99.
181. SP to AP, 18 Feb. 1956. *L1*, 1108.
182. *J*, 204.
183. SP, 14 Feb. 1956, 1955–56 calendar. 7.6, Lilly.
184. SP to AP, 10 Feb. 1956. *L1*, 1102.
185. SP, "Leaves from a Cambridge Notebook," *Christian Science Monitor* (5 Mar. 1956), 17. Part II appeared on 6 Mar. 1956, p. 15. Plath's drawing was captioned "Cambridge: A vista of gables and chimney pots."
186. SP, 15–20 Feb. 1956, 1955–56 calendar. 7.6, Lilly.
187. SP, 21–22 Feb. 1956, 1955–56 calendar. 7.6, Lilly.
188. SP, 24 Feb. 1956, 1955–56 calendar, 7.6, Lilly.
189. SP to AP, 24 Feb. 1956. *L1*, 1114.
190. See Jane Baltzell Kopp in *Memories of Whitstead*. Privately printed by Rhoda Dorsey, 2007. 20.29, SPC, Smith.

191. SP to Elinor Friedman, 6–8 Mar. 1956. *L1*, 1131.
192. Ibid., *L1*, 1131–32.

16. MAD PASSIONATE ABANDON

1. Hughes published "The Jaguar" and "The Casualty" in *Chequer*, Nov. 1954, and "Fall-grief's Girl-Friends," "Whenever I Am Got Under My Gravestone" (later retitled "Soliloquy of a Misanthrope"), "If I Should Touch Her She Would Shriek and Weeping" (later retitled "Secretary"), and "When Two Men Meet for the First Time in All" (later retitled "Law in the Country of the Cats") in the *Saint Botolph's Review*. Three of his poems also appeared in *Poetry from Cambridge 1952–54*, edited by Karl Miller.
2. TH, "Law in the Country of the Cats," *Saint Botolph's Review* (1956): 17.
3. David Bradley, Obituary (Ted Hughes), *Pembroke College Gazette*, 73 (Sept. 1999): 21–30.
4. "We always called him Luke." HC interview with Daniel Huws, May 2016, London.
5. Weissbort, Ross, and Minton had been classmates at St. Paul's School in London, and McCaughey had been to Campbell's College in Belfast. Bertram Wyatt-Brown, "Ted, Sylvia, and St. Botolph's: A Cambridge Recollection," *Southern Review* 40.2 (Spring 2004): 352–69; 357.
6. Elaine Feinstein, *Ted Hughes: The Life of a Poet* (London: Weidenfeld & Nicolson, 2001), 31.
7. Christopher Levenson, *Not One of the Boys*, unpublished memoir provided to HC by Levenson.
8. EF interview with Peter Redgrove, Sept. 1999. EFP.
9. TH to Keith Sagar, 10 Oct. 1998. *Poet and Critic: The Letters of Ted Hughes & Keith Sagar*, Keith Sagar, ed. (London: British Library, 2012), 282.
10. HC conversation with Nick Wilding, June 2017, Hebden Bridge, UK.
11. I am grateful to Nick Wilding for showing me "mucky" photographs of Aspinall Street and the surrounding area in the 1930s.
12. As told to Nick Wilding by the late Donald Crossley. HC conversation with Nick Wilding, June 2017, Mytholmroyd, UK.
13. EF interview with Donald Crossley, 2001. EFP.
14. Ruth Crossley email to HC, 22 June 2017.
15. Michael Parker, interview with Wilfrid Riley, 22 July 1977, Heptonstall, UK. Courtesy of Michael Parker.
16. Gerald Hughes, *Ted & I: A Brother's Memoir* (New York: St. Martin's Press, 2012), 61; 64.
17. *CPTH*, 463.
18. Hughes, *Ted & I*, 48.
19. Michael Parker, interview with Wilfrid Riley, 22 July 1977, Heptonstall, UK. Courtesy of Michael Parker.
20. Ibid.
21. Hughes, *Ted & I*, 64; 61.
22. Ibid., 46.
23. Ibid., 54.
24. The teacher's name was Miss McLeod. Keith Sagar, *The Laughter of Foxes: A Study of Ted Hughes* (Liverpool: Liverpool University Press, 2000), 43.
25. Steve Ely has suggested that the money was lent to the Hughes family by wealthier Farrar relatives. Conversation with Steve Ely, 12 Sept. 2015, Mexborough, UK.
26. Steve Ely, *Made in Mexborough: Ted Hughes's South Yorkshire* (Basingstoke: Palgrave Macmillan, 2015), 33–34; 53.
27. Edna Wholey Chilton, "Reminiscence: Ted & Crookhill," 30 July 2000. 1.1, MSS 870, Emory.
28. Ely, *Ted Hughes's South Yorkshire*, 126–27; 131.
29. Ibid., 129.

30. TH to Robert Graves, 20 July 1967. *LTH*, 273.

31. TH to Anne-Lorraine Bujon, 16 Dec. 1992. *LTH*, 625.

32. Ekbert Faas, *Ted Hughes: The Unaccommodated Universe* (Santa Barbara: Black Sparrow Press, 1980), 203.

33. D. H. Lawrence, *Selected Poetry*, Keith Sagar, ed. (London: Penguin, 1972; 1986), 198.

34. Ely, *Ted Hughes's South Yorkshire*, 112–13.

35. Hughes, *Ted & I*, 71.

36. TH to Terry Gifford, 16 Jan. 1994. *LTH*, 658.

37. Feinstein, *Ted Hughes*, 16.

38. See Mark Wormald, "Irishwards: Ted Hughes, Freedom and Flow," *Ted Hughes Society Journal* 6.2 (2017): 58–77.

39. Hughes, *Ted & I*, 70.

40. Ely, *Ted Hughes's South Yorkshire*, 137.

41. See James Underwood, "Mayday on Holderness: Ted Hughes, National Service, and East Yorkshire," *Ted Hughes Society Journal* 6.2 (2017): 86–98.

42. Ibid., 89.

43. Quoted in ibid., 94.

44. TH, autobiographical typescript. Add MS 88918/7/2, BL, as quoted in Underwood, "Mayday," 92.

45. Underwood, "Mayday," 93.

46. TH to Olwyn Hughes, Feb. 1952. *LTH*, 12.

47. "The Little Boys and the Seasons," "The Jaguar," and "The Court-Tumbler and Satirist" appeared in the university anthology *Poetry from Cambridge 1952–54*, Karl Miller, ed. (London: Fortune Press, 1954).

48. HC interview with Daniel Huws, May 2016, London.

49. Brian Cox, "Ted Hughes (1930–1998): A Personal Retrospect," *Hudson Review* 52.1 (Spring 1999): 29–43; 32.

50. HC interview with Jean Gooder, July 2017, Cambridge, UK.

51. Christopher Levenson email to HC, 18 Sept. 2017.

52. Daniel Huws, "Conversation with Hughes's Contemporaries." Transcript of a recording made at the International Ted Hughes Conference, Pembroke College, Cambridge University, 17 Sept. 2010, http://www.ann.skea.com/CambridgeRecording.htm. Terence McCaughey remembered that he met Ted Hughes at Heffer's bookshop in 1951. They were supervised together by M. J. C. Hodgart, an authority on Irish ballads and James Joyce.

53. Jonathan Bate, *Ted Hughes: The Unauthorised Life* (New York: HarperCollins 2015), 546.

54. EF interview with Brian Cox, Oct. 1999. EFP.

55. HC interview with Suzette and Helder Macedo, May 2016, London.

56. Daniel Huws, *Memories of Ted Hughes 1952–1963* (Nottingham: Richard Hollis/Five Leaves, 2010), 39.

57. Bradley, Obituary (Ted Hughes), 21–30.

58. TH to Terence McCaughey, 17 Nov. 1997. Add MS 88616, BL.

59. Nathaniel Minton, *A Memoir of Ted Hughes* (London: Westmoreland Press, 2015), 11.

60. Lucas Myers, *An Essential Self: Ted Hughes and Sylvia Plath* (Nottingham: Richard Hollis/Five Leaves, 2011), 14.

61. TH to SP, 2 Oct. 1956. Lilly.

62. One friend, John Honey, corroborated Hughes's story to Elaine Feinstein. Feinstein, *Ted Hughes*, 29.

63. TH to SP, 2 Oct. 1956. Lilly.

64. Ibid.

65. Daniel Huws, "Conversation with Hughes's Contemporaries." Transcript of a recording made at the International Ted Hughes Conference, Pembroke College, Cambridge University, 17 Sept. 2010, http://www.ann.skea.com/CambridgeRecording.htm.

66. Harriet Rosenstein interview with Iko and Felicity Meshoulam, 1973. 2.22, MSS 1489, Emory.

67. Ibid.

68. Myers, *An Essential Self*, 17–18. Myers, who had been introduced to the group when he published his poetry in *Chequer* in 1954, recalled that Bloom found Hughes's poetry "violent."

69. Levenson, *Not One of the Boys*.

70. TH, *Winter Pollen: Occasional Prose*, William Scammell, ed. (New York: Picador, 1995), 9.

71. *CPTH*, 21.

72. TH to Keith Sagar, 16 July 1979. Sagar, *Poet and Critic*, 75–76.

73. SP to AP, 9 Mar. 1956. *L1*, 1136.

74. TH, "The ear-witness account of a poetry-reading in Throttle College, before the small poets grew up into infinitesimal critics." ENGL 1/155, Cambridge University Library.

75. Feinstein, *Ted Hughes*, 35.

76. TH to Terence McCaughey, spring 1956. Add MS 88616, BL.

77. Philip Hobsbaum, "Ted Hughes at Cambridge," *Dark Horse* 8 (Autumn 1999): 6–12. 10.

78. W. P. Cummane to unnamed Commonwealth Migration Officer, Melbourne, 20 Feb. 1956. There are five official letters detailing Hughes's Australian immigration plans and deferment in the Christopher Reid Papers at the University of Huddersfield.

79. Mrs. Hitchcock was the widow of the former Queen's College rector, who died during World War II. Her son Robin would marry Plath's biographer Anne Stevenson.

80. Wyatt-Brown, "Ted, Sylvia, and St. Botolph's," 353.

81. Hobsbaum, "Ted Hughes at Cambridge," 9.

82. HC interview with Daniel Huws, May 2016, London.

83. Ibid.

84. HC interview with Jean Gooder, July 2017, Cambridge, UK. Luke Myers told the story in his memoir; Michael Boddy captured one of the swans, which they then cooked.

85. Harriet Rosenstein interview with Iko and Felicity Meshoulam, 1973. 2.22, MSS 1489, Emory.

86. Michael Boddy email to EF, 21 Feb. 2001. EFP.

87. Michael Boddy email to EF, 5 Feb. 2001. EFP.

88. Ibid.

89. EF interview with Peter Redgrove, Sept. 1999. EFP.

90. Michael Boddy email to EF, 22 Mar. 2001. EFP.

91. Daniel Huws, "Conversation with Hughes's Contemporaries." Transcript of a recording made at the International Ted Hughes Conference, Pembroke College, Cambridge University, 17 Sept. 2010, http://www.ann.skea.com/CambridgeRecording.htm.

92. HC interview with Jean Gooder, July 2017, Cambridge, UK.

93. Levenson, *Not One of the Boys*.

94. EF interview with Peter Redgrove, Sept. 1999. EFP.

95. Levenson, *Not One of the Boys*.

96. Bertram Wyatt-Brown, "Neither Priest nor Poet: A Search for Vocation," *Shapers of Southern History: Autobiographical Reflections*, John B. Boles, ed. (Athens: University of Georgia Press, 2004), 62–90. 78.

97. Wyatt-Brown, "Ted, Sylvia, and St. Botolph's," 361.

98. Lucas Myers, *Crow Steered Bergs Appeared: A Memoir of Ted Hughes and Sylvia Plath* (Sewanee, Tenn.: Proctor's Hall Press, 2001), 7.

99. TH interview with Ekbert Faas in *Ted Hughes: The Unaccommodated Universe* (Santa Barbara: Black Sparrow Press, 1980), 201.

100. Wyatt-Brown, "Ted, Sylvia, and St. Botolph's," 360.

101. TH to Olwyn Hughes, early 1956. *LTH*, 34.

102. TH to Keith Sagar, 30 Aug. 1979. *LTH*, 426. "High Table" refers to the long, elevated table at the back of Oxford and Cambridge college dining halls where dons and college officials are seated and served.

103. TH to Nick Gammage, 7 Apr. 1995. *LTH*, 679.

104. Wyatt-Brown, "Neither Priest nor Poet," 79.
105. Robert Graves, *The White Goddess: A Historical Grammar of Poetic Myth*, 2nd ed. (New York: Farrar, Straus and Giroux, 1948; 1975), 17.
106. Ibid., 447–48.
107. Ibid., 446.
108. In her journal, Plath talks about looking to Graves's book for potential names for their unborn children (*J*, 377).
109. Diane Middlebrook, *Her Husband, Plath and Hughes: A Marriage* (New York: Viking, 2003), 31.
110. HC interview with Daniel Huws, May 2016, London.
111. *J*, 289.
112. See Heather Clark, *The Grief of Influence: Sylvia Plath and Ted Hughes* (Oxford: Oxford University Press, 2011), for a detailed discussion of Plath's ironic use of Graves.
113. SP, "'Three Caryatids Without a Portico' by Hugo Robus: A Study in Sculptural Dimensions," *Chequer* 9 (Winter 1956): 3. The issue also contained two poems by Christopher Levenson and a story by Bill Carr.
114. Wyatt-Brown, "Neither Priest nor Poet," 79.
115. *CPTH*, 1047.
116. Ibid., 1045.
117. Myers, *Crow Steered*, 25; Lucas Myers, "Ah, Youth . . . Ted Hughes and Sylvia Plath at Cambridge and After," *Grand Street* 8.4 (Summer 1989): 86–103. 92.
118. *CPTH*, 1060.
119. Wyatt-Brown, "Neither Priest nor Poet," 79.
120. Harriet Rosenstein interview with Michael Frayn, 1973. 1.28, MSS 1489, Emory.
121. Ibid.
122. HC conversation with Michael Frayn and Claire Tomalin, 24 Sept. 2018, Manhattan.
123. HC phone interview with Jane Baltzell Kopp, 4 Nov. 2015.
124. HC interview with Daniel Huws, May 2016, London.
125. He had heard about Plath even before he went to Cambridge—a friend of his had married a Smithie, Amy Gardner, who knew Plath and told him to look her up.
126. Wyatt-Brown, "Ted, Sylvia, and St. Botolph's," 361.
127. Michael Boddy email to EF, Apr. 2001. EFP.
128. Wyatt-Brown, "Neither Priest nor Poet," 79.
129. Wyatt-Brown, "Reuben Davis, Sylvia Plath, and Other American Writers," *An Emotional History of the United States*, Peter N. Stearns and Jan Lewis, eds. (New York: NYU Press, 1998), 458. Wyatt-Brown said "she was particularly struck" by these two poems when they spoke for the second time that day.
130. *CPTH*, 29.
131. *CPTH*, 25.
132. Christopher Levenson to Harriet Rosenstein, 14 Apr. 1974. 2.15, MSS 1489, Emory.
133. *J*, 207–208.
134. SP to AP, 25 Feb. 1956. *L1*, 1115.
135. Ibid., *L1*, 1115–16.
136. *Broadsheet* 4 (1 Feb. 1956): 1–3. Original copy sent to HC by Daniel Huws. Huws pointed out to me that Ted Hughes had excoriated the previous issue of *Chequer* in the 8 June 1955 issue of *Broadsheet* under the pseudonym "Jonathan Dyce."
137. SP to AP, 2 Feb. 1956. *L1*, 1096.
138. Wyatt-Brown, "Neither Priest nor Poet," 81.
139. SP to AP, 3 Mar. 1956. *L1*, 1120.
140. Wyatt-Brown, "Neither Priest nor Poet," 81.
141. EF interview with David Ross, Oct. 1999. EFP.
142. Harriet Rosenstein interview with Iko and Felicity Meshoulam, 1973. 2.22, MSS 1489, Emory.
143. HC interview with Jean Gooder, July 2017, Cambridge, UK.
144. Wyatt-Brown, "Neither Priest nor Poet," 82–83. In Wyatt-Brown's article, Jane quotes a letter to her parents dated 2 Mar. 1956.
145. TH to Terence McCaughey, spring 1956. Add MS 88616, BL. Hughes did not men-

tion Plath in the letter, and told McCaughey he might live in Dublin if he could get by cheaply. He wanted to "write and publish," he said, "but I get no leasure [*sic*] in London. My life in London is in fact no life. Automatism in a stunned half-wake."

146. Wyatt-Brown, "Neither Priest nor Poet," 83.
147. Ibid., 82.
148. *J*, 210.
149. Harriet Rosenstein interview with Jane Baltzell Kopp, 1974–75. 2.11, MSS 1489, Emory.
150. Jane Baltzell Kopp, "'Gone, Very Gone Youth': Sylvia Plath at Cambridge, 1955–57," *Sylvia Plath: The Woman and the Work*, Edward Butscher, ed. (New York: Dodd, Mead and Co., 1977), 73. In this article Baltzell misremembers the location of the party as the Saint Botolph's rectory rather than Falcon Yard.
151. HC phone interview with Jane Baltzell Kopp, 4 Nov. 2015.
152. HC interview with Jean Gooder, July 2017, Cambridge, UK.
153. *J*, 211.
154. Huws, *Memories of Ted Hughes*, 34.
155. Myers, *An Essential Self*, 27.
156. Ibid., 16.
157. HC interview with Jean Gooder, July 2017, Cambridge, UK. To protect her privacy, I have not used Shirley's surname.
158. *CPTH*, 1052.
159. Daniel Huws, "Conversation with Hughes's Contemporaries." Transcript of a recording made at the International Ted Hughes Conference, Pembroke College, Cambridge University, 17 Sept. 2010, http://www.ann.skea.com/CambridgeRecording .htm.
160. Bate, *Ted Hughes*, 98.
161. Levenson, *Not One of the Boys*.
162. HC phone interview with Jane Baltzell Kopp, 4 Nov. 2015.
163. Yehuda Koren and Eliat Negev, *A Lover of Unreason: Assia Wevill, Sylvia Plath's Rival and Ted Hughes's Doomed Love* (New York: Carroll and Graf, 2007), 68.
164. *J*, 211.
165. TH, draft of "St Botolph's." Add MS 88918/1/6, BL.
166. *J*, 211–12.
167. TH, draft of "St Botolph's." Add MS 88918/1/6, BL.
168. HC interview with Jean Gooder, July 2017, Cambridge, UK.
169. *J*, 211–12.
170. Luke remembered seeing the Russian's "complete works" on Hughes's Yorkshire bookshelf at the Beacon. Myers, *An Essential Self*, 21.
171. TH, *Winter Pollen: Occasional Prose*, William Scammell, ed. (New York: Picador, 1995), 255.
172. See TH's 1992 letter to Anne-Lorraine Bujon (*LTH*, 621–37) for an extended discussion of these literary influences.
173. TH, "Notes on the Chronological Order of Sylvia Plath's Poems," *TriQuarterly* 7 (Fall 1966): 81–88. 81.
174. *J*, 567; 570.
175. SP to AP, 3 Mar. 1956. *L1*, 1120.
176. *CPTH*, 1052.
177. TH interview with Drue Heinz, "The Art of Poetry, LXXI," *Paris Review* 134 (1995), in *The Paris Review Interviews*, vol. 3 (London: Picador, 2008), 56–92; 76.
178. HC interview with Elinor Friedman Klein, Dec. 2017, South Salem, N.Y.
179. SP, 25 Feb. 1956, 1955–56 calendar. 7.6, Lilly.
180. *CPTH*, 1051–52.
181. *J*, 213; 210.
182. Huws, *Memories of Ted Hughes*, 34.
183. *J*, 213–14.
184. *JP*, 315.
185. *J*, 214.

186. Wyatt-Brown, "Neither Priest nor Poet," 83.
187. Levenson, *Not One of the Boys.*
188. TH, draft of "St Botolph's." Add MS 88918/1/6, BL.

17. PURSUIT

1. SP, 26 Feb. 1956, 1955–56 calendar. 7.6, Lilly.
2. *JP*, 321.
3. SP to AP, 3 Mar. 1956. *L1*, 1120.
4. *J*, 214.
5. SP to AP, 9 Mar. 1956. *L1*, 1133–34.
6. Harriet Rosenstein interview with Kay Burton, 1973. 1.14, MSS 1489, Emory.
7. SP to AP, 9 Mar. 1956. *L1*, 1133–34. The Yeats quote is from his play *The Resurrection* (1931).
8. *J*, 225.
9. SP to Richard Sassoon, 6 Mar. 1956. *L1*, 1129.
10. Harriet Rosenstein interview with Iko and Felicity Meshoulam, 1973. 2.22, MSS 1489, Emory.
11. SP to AP, 6 Mar. 1956. *L1*, 1124.
12. Ibid.
13. *J*, 229–30.
14. SP, 9 Mar. 1956, 1955–56 calendar. 7.6, Lilly.
15. *J*, 233; 235.
16. SP to AP, 10 May 1956. *L1*, 1193.
17. Harriet Rosenstein interview with Jane Baltzell Kopp, 1974–75. 2.11, MSS 1489, Emory.
18. SP to AP, 18 Mar. 1956. *L1*, 1142–43.
19. See SP's 1955–56 calendar. 7.6, Lilly.
20. SP, 13 Mar. 1956, 1955–56 calendar. 7.6, Lilly.
21. SP to WP, 18 June 1956. *L1*, 1208.
22. Jim Downer, "Afterword," *Timmy the Tug,* by Jim Downer and Ted Hughes (New York: Thames and Hudson, 2010).
23. Michael Boddy email to EF, 15 Mar. 2001. EFP.
24. SP, 23 Mar. 1956, 1955–56 calendar. 7.6, Lilly.
25. TH, draft of "18 Rugby Street." Add MS 88918/1/6, BL.
26. *CPTH*, 1057–58. In the poem, Hughes misremembered the date as 13 Apr., "your father's birthday." This was the day Plath flew back to London from Rome.
27. Michael Boddy email to EF, 15 Mar. 2001. EFP.
28. SP, 23–24 Mar. 1956, 1955–56 calendar. 7.6, Lilly.
29. *J*, 552.
30. Jonathan Bate, *Ted Hughes: The Unauthorised Life* (New York: HarperCollins, 2015), 109.
31. Michael Boddy email to EF, 15 Mar. 2001. EFP.
32. *CPTH*, 1058.
33. Emmet Larkin, a graduate student at the London School of Economics. Plath had arranged for him to give her and his friend Janet Drake a ride to Paris.
34. *J*, 552.
35. *J*, 570.
36. *J*, 554.
37. *J*, 553.
38. Ibid.
39. *J*, 559.
40. *J*, 566.
41. *J*, 569.
42. TH to SP, 31 Mar. 1956. *LTH*, 37.
43. SP to AP, 5 Apr. 1956. *L1*, 1158.
44. Richard Sassoon, "The Diagram," *Chicago Review* 17.4 (1965): 111.

45. SP to AP, 17 Apr. 1956. *L1*, 1160.
46. *J*, 565.
47. Ibid.
48. Plath owned both a Royal (likely left behind in Wellesley) and a Smith-Corona around this time. She sold the Smith-Corona in 1957.
49. SP, 6 Apr. 1956, 1955–56 calendar. 7.6, Lilly.
50. SP to AP, 17 Apr. 1956. *L1*, 1160.
51. Gordon Lameyer to SP, 1 May 1957. Lilly.
52. SP, 9 Apr. 1956, 1955–56 calendar. 7.6, Lilly; SP to AP, 17 Apr. 1956. *L1*, 1160.
53. SP, 10 Apr. 1956, 1955–56 calendar. 7.6, Lilly.
54. SP to AP, 17 Apr. 1956. *L1*, 1160.
55. Gordon Lameyer to SP, 1 May 1957. Lilly.
56. SP, 13 Apr. 1956, 1955–56 calendar. 7.6, Lilly.
57. TH to SP, c. 9 Apr. 1956. Lilly.
58. SP to AP, 17 Apr. 1956. *L1*, 1161.
59. SP, 13–14 Apr. 1956, 1955–56 calendar. 7.6, Lilly.
60. SP, 14 Apr. 1956, 1955–56 calendar. 7.6, Lilly.
61. SP, "Venus in the Seventh." 140.11, MSS 644, Emory. I found this fragment, misfiled, at Emory in 2007.
62. SP's ellipses.
63. SP, 15 Apr. 1956, 1955–56 calendar. 7.6, Lilly.
64. Ibid.
65. SP, 17 Apr. 1956, 1955–56 calendar. 7.6, Lilly.
66. SP, 18 Apr. 1956, 1955–56 calendar. 7.6, Lilly.
67. SP to AP, 17 April 1956. *L1*, 1161.
68. SP to Richard Sassoon, 6 Mar. 1956. *L1*, 1127.
69. Ibid.
70. SP to Richard Sassoon, 18 Apr. 1956. *L1*, 1164.
71. SP, 21 Apr. 1956, 1955–56 calendar. 7.6, Lilly.
72. The first four poems' variant original titles in Plath's calendar were, respectively, "Metamorphosis," "Poem for Pan: Under Crunch of My Man's Boot," "Through Fen and Farmland Walking," and "Mad Queen's Song."
73. SP to AP, 29 Apr. 1956. *L1*, 1181.
74. SP to WP, 23 Apr. 1956. *L1*, 1173–74.
75. Ibid., *L1*, 1174–75.
76. SP to AP, 10 May 1956. *L1*, 1194.
77. SP to WP, 23 Apr. 1956. *L1*, 1174; SP, 19 Apr. 1956, 1955–56 calendar. 7.6, Lilly.
78. SP, 1 May 1956, 1955–56 calendar. 7.6, Lilly.
79. SP to AP, 29 Apr. 1956. *L1*, 1179.
80. Ibid., *L1*, 1181.
81. SP, 23 Apr. 1956, 1955–56 calendar. 7.6, Lilly.
82. SP to AP, 3 May 1956. *L1*, 1185.
83. SP to AP, 4 May 1956. *L1*, 1187.
84. SP to AP, 26 May 1956. *L1*, 1201.
85. SP to AP, 29 Apr. 1956. *L1*, 1181.
86. *CPTH*, 1061. Hughes later told Plath the same story in 1962, which Plath relayed to Dr. Beuscher.
87. SP, 28 Apr. 1956, 1955–56 calendar. 7.6, Lilly.
88. SP, 29 Apr. 1956, 1955–56 calendar. 7.6, Lilly.
89. Ibid.
90. SP to AP, 6 May 1956. *L1*, 1189.
91. SP, 5 May 1956, 1955–56 calendar. 7.6, Lilly. Dr. Beuscher said she destroyed all of Plath's pre-1960 letters.
92. SP, 10 May 1956, 1955–56 calendar. 7.6, Lilly.
93. Luke Myers to EF, 25 Nov. 2001. EFP.
94. SP to AP, 3 May 1956. *L1*, 1184.
95. SP to AP, 4 May 1956. *L1*, 1188.

96. SP to AP, 9 May 1956. *L1*, 1192.
97. SP to AP, 18 May 1956. *L1*, 1196.
98. SP to AP, 10 May 1956. *L1*, 1194.
99. HC interview with Elinor Friedman Klein, Oct. 2015, South Salem, N.Y.
100. Jane Baltzell Kopp remembered a member of the Saint Botolph circle remarking, "I never, never thought that Ted would marry an *American* girl." "'Gone, Very Gone Youth': Sylvia Plath at Cambridge, 1955–1957," *Sylvia Plath: The Woman and the Work*, Edward Butscher, ed. (New York: Dodd, Mead and Co., 1977), 76.
101. Daniel Huws, *Memories of Ted Hughes, 1952–1963* (Nottingham: Richard Hollis/Five Leaves, 2010), 35.
102. EF interview with David Ross, Oct. 1999. EFP.
103. TH to Olwyn Hughes, summer 1956. 1.4, MSS 980, Emory.
104. SP to AP, 9 May 1956. *L1*, 1193.
105. SP to AP, 28 May 1956. *L1*, 1204.
106. SP, 11 May 1956, 1955–56 calendar. 7.6, Lilly.
107. SP to AP, 18 May 1956. *L1*, 1196.
108. Elizabeth Sigmund, "Sylvia in Devon: 1962," *Sylvia Plath: The Woman and the Work*, Edward Butscher, ed. (New York: Dodd, Mead and Co., 1977), 104.
109. SP, 11 May 1956, 1955–56 calendar. 7.6, Lilly.
110. SP, 14 May 1956, 1955–56 calendar. 7.6, Lilly.
111. Philipa Forder Goold in *Memories of Whitstead*, 30. Privately printed by Rhoda Dorsey, 2007. 20.29, SPC, Smith.
112. Harriet Rosenstein interview with Jane Baltzell Kopp, 1974–75. 2.11, MSS 1489, Emory.
113. SP, 24 May 1956, 1955–56 calendar. 7.6, Lilly.
114. SP, 12 May 1956, 1955–56 calendar. 7.6, Lilly.
115. SP to AP, 3 May 1956. *L1*, 1184.
116. SP to WP, 23 Apr. 1956. *L1*, 1173.
117. SP to AP, 26 Apr. 1956. *L1*, 1177.
118. Dorothea Krook, "Recollections of Sylvia Plath," *Sylvia Plath: The Woman and the Work*, Edward Butscher, ed. (New York: Dodd, Mead and Co., 1977), 50.
119. Ibid., 55.
120. SP to AP, 29 Apr. 1956. *L1*, 1179.
121. The dates of composition come from Plath's 1955–56 calendar.
122. SP to WP, 23 Apr. 1956. *L1*, 1173.
123. SP to AP, 26 Apr. 1956. *L1*, 1176. Plath was mentioned in the article "'Varsity' Goes to Meet B & K and Has Vodka and Caviar," which appeared on 28 Apr. 1956. She wrote up her own article about the evening, "B. and K. at the Claridge," which was rejected by *The New Yorker* but eventually published in the *Smith Alumnae Quarterly* in Nov. 1956.
124. SP to AP, 26 May 1956. *L1*, 1198; SP, "Sylvia Plath Tours the Stores and Forecasts May Week Fashions," *Varsity* (26 May 1956): 6–7.
125. SP, "An American in Paris," *Varsity* (21 Apr. 1956): 6–7.
126. Lucas Myers, *Crow Steered Bergs Appeared: A Memoir of Ted Hughes and Sylvia Plath* (Sewanee, Tenn.: Proctor's Hall Press, 2001), 52.
127. Michael Boddy email to EF, Apr. 2001. EFP.
128. SP to AP, 29 Apr. 1956. *L1*, 1178.
129. SP to AP, 26 Apr. 1956. *L1*, 1177.
130. SP, 19 May 1956, 1955–56 calendar. 7.6, Lilly.
131. SP to AP, 28 May 1956. *L1*, 1205–206.
132. SP to AP, 10 May 1956. *L1*, 1195.
133. SP to AP, 18 May 1956. *L1*, 1195.
134. SP to AP, 19 Apr. 1956. *L1*, 1165; SP to AP, 4 May 1956. *L1*, 1187.
135. SP to WP, 23 Apr. 1956. *L1*, 1175.
136. SP to AP, 26 Apr. 1956. *L1*, 1176.
137. SP to AP, 23 Apr. 1956. *L1*, 1171–72.
138. OHP to SP, 3 June 1956. Lilly.

139. SP to Gordon Lameyer, 12 Dec. 1955. *L1*, 1043.
140. SP to AP, 19 Apr. 1956. *L1*, 1165–66.
141. Middlebrook, *Her Husband*, 42.
142. Claire Tomalin, "Everything but the Truth," *Independent* (8 Oct. 1994).
143. D. H. Lawrence, *Women in Love* (1920; New York: Bantam, 1996), 164. Plath even felt that Lawrence had intuited her feelings for suicide in *Sons and Lovers*. In her edition of the novel, now held at Smith, she wrote "cf. July 1953" next to a passage about Paul Morel's depression.
144. *J*, 105–107. Plath was clearly moved by the scene in *Women in Love* where Birkin tells Ursula that love is "not meeting and mingling" but "an equilibrium, a pure balance of two single beings:—as the stars balance each other" (160); and, later, "He wanted a further conjunction, where man had being and woman had being, two pure beings, each constituting the freedom of the other, balancing each other like two poles of one force, like two angels, or two demons" (219).
145. SP to AP, 19 Apr. 1956. *L1*, 1166.
146. SP to AP, 26 May 1956. *L1*, 1201.
147. SP to AP, 19 Apr. 1956. *L1*, 1166.
148. Tomalin, "Everything but the Truth."
149. Jane Anderson, deposition (1987 *Bell Jar* trial). Jane Anderson v. AVCO Embassy Pictures Corp. et al., in the United States District Court, District of Massachusetts, Civil Action no. 82-0752-K. Jane V. Anderson Papers, Series IV, Smith.
150. *J*, 567.
151. SP to WP, 18 June 1956. *L1*, 1208.
152. Elaine Feinstein, *Ted Hughes: The Life of a Poet* (London: Weidenfeld & Nicolson, 2001), 60.
153. SP, 13 June 1956, 1955–56 calendar. 7.6, Lilly.
154. HC interview with Richard Larschan, May 2017, Manhattan. Larschan says Aurelia told him the suit was her own, not her daughter's.
155. *CPTH*, 1064.
156. *CPTH*, 1065.
157. SP to AP, 20 Apr. 1957. *L2*, 115.
158. See, for example, SP to William and Edith Hughes, 27 Feb. 1957. *L2*, 77.
159. TH to Gerald and Joan Hughes. 24 Feb. 1957. 1.2, MSS 854, Emory. This sentence does not appear in the published excerpt in *LTH*.
160. *J*, 308.
161. TH to Gerald and Joan Hughes, 24 Feb. 1957. *LTH*, 96.
162. SP, "Suffering Angel," review of *Lord Byron's Wife*, *New Statesman* (7 Dec. 1962): 828–29.
163. *CPTH*, 1064.
164. HC interview with Betsy Powley Wallingford, Feb. 2013, Sudbury, Mass.; HC interview with Richard Larschan, Feb. 2019, Manhattan.
165. HC interview with Elizabeth Compton Sigmund, May 2016, Cornwall, UK.

18. LIKE FURY

1. SP to AP, 8 July 1956. *L1*, 1216.
2. *J*, 249.
3. SP to AP, 8 July 1956. *L1*, 1216; *J*, 252.
4. Ibid., *L1*, 1216.
5. Plath had hoped to meet up with Ellie Friedman in London before she left, but the reunion did not happen. They had made vague plans to travel together to Spain and Morocco that summer.
6. SP to Marcia Brown Plumer, 15 Dec. 1956. *L2*, 37.
7. *CPTH*, 1065–66.
8. SP, 30 June 1956, 1955–56 calendar. 7.6, Lilly.
9. Richard Sassoon to SP, c. June 1956. Lilly.
10. See Woody and Wertz files, MSS 1489, Emory.

11. SP to AP, 4 July 1956. *L1*, 1210–11.
12. SP, 7 July 1956, 1955–56 calendar. 7.6, Lilly.
13. SP to AP, 7 July 1956. *L1*, 1214–15.
14. Ibid., *L1*, 1212.
15. SP to AP, 14 July 1956. *L1*, 1221.
16. A fragment of the story survives at Emory.
17. SP to AP, 14 July 1956. *L1*, 1217.
18. Ibid., *L1*, 1219.
19. They planned to leave on 29 Sept.
20. SP to AP, 7 July 1956. *L1*, 1216.
21. SP to AP, 10 Aug. 1956. *L1*, 1237.
22. *J*, 242.
23. SP to AP, 25 July 1956. *L1*, 1229.
24. SP to WP, 14 July 1956. *L1*, 1225.
25. SP to AP, 14 & 25 July 1956. *L1*, 1219; 1228.
26. *CPTH*, 1068.
27. The Spanish writer Federico García Lorca popularized the concept in a series of lectures in the 1930s.
28. SP to AP, 25 July 1956. *L1*, 1227.
29. *J*, 248.
30. SP to AP, 20–25 Aug. 1956. *L1*, 1239.
31. SP to AP, 2 Aug. 1956. *L1*, 1235.
32. Ibid., *L1*, 1234.
33. *J*, 259.
34. SP, 3 & 9 Aug. 1956, 1955–56 calendar. 7.6, Lilly.
35. SP, 23 July 1956, 1955–56 calendar. 7.6, Lilly.
36. *J*, 250–51.
37. TH to Edith and William Hughes, summer 1956. *LTH*, 45.
38. TH, draft of "Moonwalk." Add MS 88918/1/2–8, BL.
39. SP, 27 July & 9 Aug. 1956, 1955–56 calendar. 7.6, Lilly.
40. SP, 9 Aug. 1956, 1955–56 calendar. 7.6, Lilly.
41. SP, 31 July 1956, 1955–56 calendar. 7.6, Lilly.
42. *J*, 249.
43. SP to AP, 2 Aug. 1956. *L1*, 1234.
44. *CPTH*, 1072–73.
45. SP to AP, 2 Aug. 1956. *L1*, 1234.
46. SP to AP, 20–25 Aug. 1956. *L1*, 1240.
47. WP to AP, 26 Aug. 1956. Lilly.
48. SP to AP, 20–25 Aug. 1956. *L1*, 1240–41.
49. TH to AP, c. late Aug. 1956. Lilly.
50. I am grateful to Nick Wilding for showing me an old advertisement for William Hughes's Hebden Bridge shop during my June 2017 stay in Mytholmroyd.
51. I am grateful to Steve Ely and Ruth Crossley for pointing out the class ramifications of a move "up" the valley during my summer as a visiting professor at the Ted Hughes Network, University of Huddersfield, 2017.
52. HC interview with Elinor Friedman Klein, Oct. 2015, South Salem, N.Y.
53. Conversation with Stuart Burne, 19 June 2017, Heptonstall, UK.
54. Harriet Rosenstein interview with Elinor Friedman Klein, 1971–72. 2.10, MSS 1489, Emory.
55. SP to AP, 2 Sept. 1956. *L1*, 1241.
56. She originally titled the poem "November Graveyard, Haworth," though the striking Heptonstall cemetery in the center of the village was surely an influence.
57. SP to AP, 2 Sept. 1956. *L1*, 1242.
58. SP to AP, 21 Sept. 1956. *L1*, 1248.
59. Gerald Hughes, *Ted & I: A Brother's Memoir* (New York: St. Martin's Press, 2014), 156–57.
60. SP to AP, 11 Sept. 1956. *L1*, 1244.

61. Ibid.
62. *J*, 589.
63. SP to AP, 2 Sept. 1956. *L1*, 1243.
64. Edward Weeks to SP, 27 Aug. 1956. Lilly.
65. SP, 4–6 Sept. 1956, 1955–56 calendar. 7.6, Lilly.
66. SP, "Afternoon in Hardcastle Crags" (incomplete MS). 139.2, MSS 644, Emory.
67. Plath sent the poem to Peter Davison at *The Atlantic* on 28 Sept. 1956, along with "Epitaph for Fire and Flower." It is possible that Plath wrote the poem before September ("Epitaph" was written in Aug. 1956) but probably not before she met Hughes.
68. SP to AP, 24 Feb. 1957. *L2*, 72.
69. SP to AP, 11 Sept. 1956. *L1*, 1245.
70. TH, notebook 5. Add MS 88918/1/6, BL.
71. Ibid.
72. Heptonstall locals remembered that Plath and Hughes rented the cottage next door to the Beacon on one of their visits. Conversation with Nick Wilding, June 2017.
73. Michael Parker, interview with Wilfrid Riley, 22 July 1977, Heptonstall. Courtesy of Michael Parker.
74. OHP to SP, 12 Sept. 1956. Lilly.
75. Elinor Friedman Klein, "A Friend Recalls Sylvia Plath," *Glamour* (Nov. 1966): 184. Aurelia and Warren thought this article was the most accurate published after Plath's death. Aurelia wrote to Ellie thanking her profusely.
76. HC interview with Elinor Friedman Klein, Oct. 2015, South Salem, N.Y.
77. Harriet Rosenstein interview with Elinor Friedman Klein, 1971–72. 2.10, MSS 1489, Emory.
78. Klein, "A Friend Recalls," 184.
79. HC interview with Elinor Friedman Klein, Oct. 2015, South Salem, N.Y.
80. SP, 22 Sept. 1956, 1955–56 calendar. 7.6, Lilly.
81. SP, 21 Sept. 1956, 1955–56 calendar. 7.6, Lilly.
82. SP, 18 Sept. 1956, 1955–56 calendar. 7.6, Lilly.
83. SP to AP, 2 Oct. 1956. *L1*, 1261. They listened to Beethoven's *Grosse Fuge*, the *Emperor Concerto*, and the Fourth and Seventh Symphonies.
84. Peter Redgrove had given a recording of Hughes reading "Gawain and the Green Knight," which he had recorded at a party, to a BBC producer, Donald Carne-Ross.
85. SP, 26 Sept. 1956, 1955–56 calendar. 7.6, Lilly.
86. SP to AP, 28 Sept. 1956. *L1*, 1250.
87. SP to AP, 2 Oct. 1956. *L1*, 1259. The poems would appear in the Jan. 1957 issue. Only Ruth Stone would have as many poems in the same issue.
88. SP to TH, 1 Oct. 1956. *L1*, 1257.
89. TH to SP, 4 Oct. 1956. *LTH*, 56.
90. TH to SP, 9 or 10 Oct. 1956. *LTH*, 67.
91. Ibid., 70.
92. SP, 2 Oct. 1956, 1955–56 calendar. 7.6, Lilly.
93. SP to TH, 3 Oct. 1956. *L1*, 1267.
94. SP to TH, 7–8 Oct. 1956. *L1*, 1286.
95. SP, 16 Oct. 1956, 1955–56 calendar. 7.6, Lilly.
96. Harriet Rosenstein interview with Jane Baltzell Kopp, 1974–75. 2.11, MSS 1489, Emory.
97. SP to TH, 18 Oct. 1956. *L1*, 1308.
98. SP to TH, 9 Oct. 1956. *L1*, 1291.
99. SP to TH, 10 Oct. 1956. *L1*, 1298.
100. SP to TH, 3 Oct. 1956. *L1*, 1265.
101. Ibid., *L1*, 1268.
102. SP to TH, 5 Oct. 1956. *L1*, 1273.
103. Ibid., *L1*, 1274.
104. SP to TH, 5 & 6 Oct. 1956. *L1*, 1274; 1280.
105. TH to SP, 6 Oct. 1956. *LTH*, 63–64.
106. TH to SP, 1 & 2 Oct. 1956. *LTH*, 51.

107. TH to SP, 3 Oct. 1956. *LTH*, 55.
108. Ibid., *LTH*, 52.
109. Ibid., *LTH*, 53.
110. TH to SP, 1 & 2 Oct. 1956. *LTH*, 51.
111. TH to SP, 5 Oct. 1956, Lilly. This plot was omitted from the published letter in *LTH*.
112. TH to SP, 8 Oct. 1956, Lilly. This plot was omitted from the published letter in *LTH*.
113. TH to SP, 3 Oct. 1956. *LTH*, 53–55.
114. TH to SP, 5 Oct. 1956. *LTH*, 58.
115. SP to TH, 6 Oct. 1956. *L1*, 1280.
116. SP to TH, 7–8 Oct. 1956. *L1*, 1285.
117. SP to TH, 1 Oct. 1956. *L1*, 1256.
118. SP to TH, 5 Oct. 1956. *L1*, 1276.
119. SP to TH, 6 Oct. 1956. *L1*, 1279.
120. SP to TH, 20 Oct. 1956. *L1*, 1316.
121. Ibid.
122. SP to TH, 6 Oct. 1956. *L1*, 1279.
123. Ibid., *L1*, 1281.
124. SP to TH, 10 Oct. 1956. *L1*, 1298.
125. SP to TH, 6 Oct. 1956. *L1*, 1280.
126. Ibid., *L1*, 1281.
127. Ibid., *L1*, 1281–82.
128. TH to SP, 9 or 10 Oct. 1956. *LTH*, 65.
129. Ibid., *LTH*, 66.
130. Ibid., *LTH*, 68; 69–70.
131. TH to SP, 23 Oct. 1956. Lilly.
132. TH to SP, 22 Oct. 1956. *LTH*, 82.
133. TH to Gerald and Joan Hughes, 7 Sept. 1956. *LTH*, 46–47.
134. TH to Olwyn Hughes, Aug. 1956. *LTH*, 46.
135. TH to SP, 9 Oct. 1956. Lilly.
136. Ibid.
137. TH to SP, 19 Oct. 1956. Lilly.
138. Christopher Levenson email to HC, 18 Sept. 2017.
139. SP to TH, 7–8 Oct. 1956. *L1*, 1286.
140. TH to SP, 9 Oct. 1956. Lilly.
141. SP to TH, 7–8 Oct. 1956. *L1*, 1288.
142. TH to SP, 22 Oct. 1956. Lilly.
143. SP to Jane Anderson, 25 Feb. 1954. *L1*, 696.
144. SP to TH, 7–8 Oct. 1956. *L1*, 1288; TH to SP, 10 Oct. 1956. Lilly. Tracy Brain has pointed out that the story is indebted to Virginia Woolf's "The Legacy" in *The Other Sylvia Plath* (London: Longman, 2001), 145.
145. *JP*, 49.
146. Ibid., 48.
147. Ibid., 53.
148. In *Poetry in the Making*, Hughes instructs, "Imagine what you are writing about. See it and live it. Do not think it up laboriously, as if you were working out mental arithmetic. Just look at it, touch it, smell it, listen to it, turn yourself into it." Quoted in Keith Sagar, *The Laughter of Foxes: A Study of Ted Hughes* (Liverpool: Liverpool University Press, 2000), 58.
149. TH to Olwyn Hughes, 1957. 1.5, MSS 980, Emory.
150. SP to TH, 9 Oct. 1956. *L1*, 1292.
151. SP to TH, 20 Oct. 1956. *L1*, 1314.
152. SP to TH, 7–8 Oct. 1956. *L1*, 1284.
153. TH to SP, 9 Oct. 1956. Lilly.
154. SP to AP, 8 Oct. 1956. *L1*, 1288.
155. SP, 12 Oct. 1956, Oct. 1956–July 1957 calendar. 7.6, Lilly.
156. Gail Crowther and Peter K. Steinberg, *These Ghostly Archives: The Unearthing of Sylvia Plath* (Croydon, UK: Fonthill, 2017), 69.

157. SP to AP, 8 Oct. 1956. *L1*, 1289.
158. Ibid.
159. SP to AP, 2 Oct. 1956. *L1*, 1261.
160. SP, 21 Oct. 1956, Oct. 1956–July 1957 calendar. 7.6, Lilly.
161. SP, 27 Oct. 1956, Oct. 1956–July 1957 calendar. 7.6, Lilly.
162. TH to SP, 1 & 2 Oct. 1956. *LTH*, 51.
163. SP, 22 & 26 Oct. 1956, 1955–56 calendar. 7.6, Lilly.
164. SP to TH, 22 Oct. 1956. *L1*, 1325–26.
165. SP to TH, 20 Oct. 1956. *L1*, 1317.
166. SP to TH, 21 Oct. 1956. *L1*,1320.
167. Isabel Murray Henderson email to HC, 1 Nov. 2017.
168. SP, 23 Oct. 1956, Oct. 1956–July 1957 calendar. 7.6, Lilly.
169. TH to SP, 23 Oct. 1956. Lilly.
170. TH to SP, 23 Oct. 1956. *LTH*, 83.
171. Ibid., 85.
172. SP, 23 Oct. 1956, Oct. 1956–July 1957 calendar. 7.6, Lilly.
173. Ibid.
174. SP to William and Edith Hughes, 12 Nov. 1956. *L2*, 12.
175. Harriet Rosenstein interview with Irene Morris, 1974–75. 2.24, MSS 1489, Emory.
176. SP to William and Edith Hughes, 12 Nov. 1956. *L2*, 12.
177. SP to AP, 13 Nov. 1956. *L2*, 14.
178. SP to AP, 23 Oct. 1956. *L1*, 1328.

19. ITCHED AND KINDLED

1. TH to AP and WP, 31 Oct. 1956. Lilly.
2. Ibid.
3. SP to AP, 28 Oct. 1956. *L2*, 4.
4. SP to AP, 23 Oct. 1956. *L1*, 1327.
5. SP, 26 Oct. 1956, Oct. 1956–July 1957 calendar. 7.6, Lilly.
6. Harriet Rosenstein interview with Susan Weller Burch, 1974. 1.13, MSS 1489, Emory.
7. *CPTH*, 1078–79.
8. TH to Olwyn Hughes, May 1956, 1.4, MSS 980, Emory.
9. SP to AP, 21 Nov. 1956. *L2*, 19.
10. SP, 18 Nov. 1956, Oct. 1956–July 1957 calendar. 7.6, Lilly.
11. SP, 27 & 29 Oct. 1956, Oct. 1956–July 1957 calendar. 7.6, Lilly.
12. SP, 31 Oct. 1956, Oct. 1956–July 1957 calendar. 7.6, Lilly.
13. SP, 19 Nov. 1956, Oct. 1956–July 1957 calendar. 7.6, Lilly.
14. *CPTH*, 19.
15. In her heavily annotated copy of William James's *Varieties of Religious Experience*, now held at SPC, Smith, Plath wrote, "cf Black Rook" next to a passage on p. 47 that begins, "This enchantment, coming as a gift . . ."
16. Tim Kendall, *Sylvia Plath: A Critical Study* (London: Faber and Faber, 2001), 27.
17. Gail Crowther and Peter K. Steinberg, *These Ghostly Archives: The Unearthing of Sylvia Plath* (Croydon, UK: Fonthill, 2017), 44.
18. TH to AP and WP, 31 Oct. 1956. Lilly.
19. SP to TH, 19 Oct. 1956. *L1*, 1312.
20. Ibid., *L1*, 1313. Hughes wrote to Plath on 20–22 Oct. that Peter Redgrove had also mentioned the competition to him.
21. She sent it out on November 20.
22. SP, 30 Nov. 1956, Oct. 1956–July 1957 calendar. 7.6, Lilly.
23. SP to AP, 1 Nov. 1956. *L2*, 8.
24. SP to WP, 20 Dec. 1956. *L2*, 43.
25. *CPTH*, 1073–74.
26. Ibid.; SP to AP, 1 Nov. 1956. *L2*, 8.
27. SP to AP, 13 Nov. 1956. *L2*, 15.
28. *Memories of Whitstead*. Privately printed by Rhoda Dorsey, 2007. 20.29, SPC, Smith.

29. SP to AP, 6 Nov. 1956. *L2*, 9.
30. SP to AP, 13 Nov. 1956. *L2*, 14.
31. SP to AP, 19 Jan. 1957. *L2*, 56.
32. SP to Marcia Brown Plumer, 15 Dec. 1956. *L2*, 36.
33. SP to AP, 20 Dec. 1956. *L2*, 41.
34. SP to Marcia Brown Plumer, 15 Dec. 1956. *L2*, 34; 38.
35. Ibid., *L2*, 35; 38.
36. *CPTH*, 1075.
37. SP to AP, 13 Nov. 1956. *L2*, 14.
38. TH to AP and WP, Dec. 1956. *LTH*, 90. Di Beddow interviewed three of Hughes's former students, who all remembered him fondly. Conversation with Di Beddow, 15 June 2017, Huddersfield, UK.
39. SP to AP, 2 Jan. 1957. *L2*, 46.
40. SP to Luke Myers, 7 Mar. 1957. *L2*, 85.
41. SP to AP, 19 Jan. 1957. *L2*, 56.
42. SP to AP, 2 Jan. 1957. *L2*, 49.
43. Ibid., *L2*, 47.
44. SP to AP, 14 Jan. 1957. *L2*, 53.
45. SP to AP, 16 Feb. 1957. *L2*, 69; SP to WP, 20 Dec. 1956. *L2*, 43.
46. TH to AP and WP, Dec. 1956. *LTH*, 90.
47. *CPTH*, 1075.
48. OHP to AP, 1 Dec. 1956. Lilly.
49. OHP to AP, 18 Dec. 1956. Lilly.
50. TH to AP and WP, 21 Jan. 1957. *LTH*, 92.
51. SP to AP, 9 Jan. 1957. She was working on "The Laundromat Affair" and a "college girl story about someone like Nancy Hunter" called "The Fabulous Roommate." *L2*, 51.
52. SP to AP, 19 Jan. 1957. *L2*, 57.
53. SP to AP, 28 Jan. 1957. *L2*, 58.
54. SP to AP, 29 Jan. 1957. *L2*, 61.
55. SP to AP, 16 Feb. 1957. *L2*, 70.
56. Jane remembered a letter from Plath to her that mentioned applying for the same Smith job, but she does not remember applying herself. Phone interview with HC, 4 Nov. 2015.
57. Jane Baltzell Kopp, "Gone, Very Gone Youth: Sylvia Plath at Cambridge, 1955–57," *Sylvia Plath: The Woman and the Work*, Edward Butscher, ed. (New York: Dodd, Mead and Co.), 79.
58. HC phone interview with Jane Baltzell Kopp, 4 Nov. 2015.
59. Kopp, "Gone, Very Gone Youth," 79.
60. HC phone interview with Jane Baltzell Kopp, 4 Nov. 2015.
61. SP to AP, 9 Jan. 1957. *L2*, 51.
62. The poems were "Epitaph for Fire and Flower," "On the Difficulty of Conjuring Up a Dryad," "Miss Drake Proceeds to Supper," and "November Graveyard," in *Chequer* 11 (Winter 1956–57); SP to AP, 7 Mar. 1957. *L2*, 83.
63. SP to AP, 3 Feb. 1957. *L2*, 63.
64. Ibid., *L2*, 64.
65. TH to AP, 21 Jan. 1957. *LTH*, 92.
66. SP to AP, 3 Feb. 1957. *L2*, 64.
67. SP to AP, 15 Mar. 1957. *L2*, 91.
68. SP to AP, 19 Mar. 1957. *L2*, 98.
69. SP to AP, 8 Feb. (#1) 1957. *L2*, 66.
70. SP to AP, 26 Mar. 1957. *L2*, 100.
71. SP to WP, 23 Apr. 1957. *L2*, 119–20.
72. SP to Richard Sassoon, 18 Apr. 1956. *L1*, 1164.
73. OHP to SP, 29 Mar. 1957. Lilly.
74. SP to AP, 24 Feb. 1957. *L2*, 71.

75. SP to Lucas Myers, 7 Mar. 1957. *L2*, 86.
76. SP to AP, 24 Feb. 1957. *L2*, 73.
77. TH, "Notes on Published Works," Mar. 1992. 115.24, MSS 644, Emory; SP to AP, 24 May 1957. *L2*, 141.
78. TH to SP, 16 Oct. 1956. Lilly. Hughes wrote, "I'm sorry to steal your own material" in reference to a plot line involving a couple at a party in Cambridge.
79. TH, "Notes on Published Works," Mar. 1992. 115.24, MSS 644, Emory.
80. SP to AP, 16 Oct. 1956, *L1*, 1299; TH to SP, 17 Oct. 1956. Lilly.
81. Christopher Levenson, *Not One of the Boys*, unpublished memoir provided to HC by Levenson.
82. *CPTH*, 36.
83. The English edition came out on 13 Sept. 1957, the American edition on 18 Sept. 1957.
84. Peter Davison, *The Fading Smile: Poets in Boston from Robert Lowell to Sylvia Plath* (New York: W. W. Norton, 1996), 165.
85. Edwin Muir, review of *The Hawk in the Rain*, *New Statesman* (28 Sept. 1957).
86. W. S. Merwin, review of *The Hawk in the Rain*, *New York Times Book Review* (6 Oct. 1957).
87. Robin Skelton, "Current Verses," *Manchester Guardian* (4 Oct. 1957); Al Alvarez, "Tough Young Poet," *Observer* (6 Oct. 1957).
88. John Press, "A Poet Arrives," *Sunday Times* (3 Nov. 1957).
89. A. E. Dyson, "Ted Hughes," *Critical Quarterly* 1.3 (1959): 219–26. 220.
90. TH, *Winter Pollen: Occasional Prose*, William Scammell, ed. (New York: Picador, 1995), 266.
91. TH, unidentified fragment regarding *Crow*. 115.24, MSS 644, Emory.
92. Jacqueline Rose, *The Haunting of Sylvia Plath* (London: Virago, 1991), 156.
93. SP to AP, 24 Feb. 1957. *L2*, 73–74.
94. SP to AP, 19 Mar. 1957. *L2*, 97.
95. SP to AP, 24 Feb. 1957. *L2*, 72.
96. *J*, 269.
97. *J*, 272.
98. *J*, 269; SP to AP, 24 Feb. 1957. *L2*, 73.
99. SP to AP, 24 Feb. 1957. *L2*, 73.
100. *J*, 269.
101. Harriet Rosenstein interview with Susan Weller Burch, 1974. 1.13, MSS 1489, Emory.
102. OHP to SP, 29 Mar. 1957. Lilly.
103. SP to AP, 7 Mar. 1957. *L2*, 84.
104. George Gibian to Harriet Rosenstein, 18 Oct. 1971. 1.30, MSS 1489, Emory.
105. Mary Ellen Chase to Robert Gorham Davis, 3 Feb. 1957; "Faculty—Sylvia Plath Hughes." Box 42, Smith College Archives.
106. SP to AP, 12 Mar. 1957. *L2*, 87.
107. Ibid.
108. SP to Marcia Brown Plumer, 9 Apr. 1957. *L2*, 110–11.
109. SP to AP, 12 Mar. 1957. *L2*, 88.
110. SP to AP, 15 Mar. 1957. *L2*, 93.
111. SP to AP, 26 Mar. 1957. *L2*, 100.
112. Ibid.
113. *J*, 273.
114. *J*, 275.
115. *J*, 268.
116. *J*, 275.
117. SP to AP, 26 Mar. 1957. *L2*, 101.
118. *J*, 269.
119. *J*, 276.
120. In this paper she cited passages from *Lady Chatterley's Lover*, *Fantasia of the Unconscious*, *The Plumed Serpent*, *The Man Who Died*, and *The Woman Who Rode Away*.

121. SP, "D. H. Lawrence: The Tree of Knowledge Versus the Tree of Life," 18 Feb. 1957. 13.4, Lilly.

122. Ibid.

123. SP, "Damn Braces. Bless Relaxes. Blake and Lawrence: A Brief Comparison and Contrast," 14 Mar. 1957. 13.4, Lilly. In this paper, she called Lawrence a prophet "who deplores the short work the scientists and rationalists have made of the luminous mysteries of the universe: of the sun and moon."

124. SP, 1957–58 Smith College Teaching Notes. 13.9–11, Lilly.

125. *J*, 337–38.

126. TH to Anne-Lorraine Bujon, 16 Dec. 1992. *LTH*, 627.

127. TH to AP, 12 Jan. 1975. 16.3, MSS 644, Emory.

128. The Plath poems accepted were "Sow," "The Snowman on the Moor," "Ella Mason and Her Eleven Cats," and "On the Difficulty of Conjuring Up a Dryad."

129. SP to AP, 1 Apr. 1957. *L2*, 102.

130. TH to AP, 15 Apr. 1957. Lilly.

131. SP to AP, 1 Apr. 1957. *L2*, 102.

132. TH to Olwyn Hughes, c. spring 1957. Add 88948/1/1, BL.

133. SP to AP, 1 Apr. 1957. *L2*, 102.

134. TH to Olwyn Hughes, c. spring 1957. Add 88948/1/1, BL.

135. TH to Gerald Hughes and family, May 1957. *LTH*, 97.

136. SP to AP, 10 May 1957. *L2*, 132. The original letter, held at Emory, is from Charles Montieth to TH, 9 May 1957.

137. SP to AP, 10 May 1957. *L2*, 133.

138. Ibid.

139. SP to AP, 15 Mar. 1957. *L2*, 92.

140. SP to AP, 18 Mar. 1957. *L2*, 94.

141. TH to Olwyn Hughes, winter 1957. 1.5, MSS 980, Emory.

142. TH, "Ted Hughes Writes," *Poetry Book Society Bulletin* (15 Sept. 1957), 1.

143. SP to AP, 18 Mar. 1957. *L2*, 94.

144. SP to AP, 28 Apr. 1957. *L2*, 121.

145. SP to Gerald and Joan Hughes, 1 May 1957. *L2*, 124.

146. SP to AP, 7 May 1957. *L2*, 127.

147. SP to Marcia Brown Plumer, 15 Dec. 1956. *L2*, 37.

148. Plath's Cambridge English Tripos Part II exam schedule, May 1957: 27 May, 9–12: "French and Italian Set Books and Unseen Translations"; 27 May, 1:30–4:30: "Essay"; 28 May, 9–12:30: "Criticism and Composition"; 28 May, 1:30–4:30: "English Moralists"; 29 May, 1:30–4:30: "Tragedy"; 31 May, 9–12: "Chaucer." There is a complete copy of this version of *Two Lovers and a Beachcomber* in the Alvarez Papers, Add MS 88589, BL. It differs slightly from the manuscript of the same title that Plath entered in the Yale Younger Poets competition in February 1957.

149. SP to AP, 29 May 1957. *L2*, 145.

150. SP to Jane Baltzell, 18 Feb. 1958. *L2*, 217.

151. SP to AP, 8 June 1957. *L2*, 146.

152. See Anon., "Cambridge Opinions," *Cambridge Review* 78 (28 May 1957): 585–86; 607; 609 and *L2*, 146.

153. SP to AP, 8 June 1957. *L2*, 146.

154. Olwyn Hughes, "Notes on Correspondence [with Ted Hughes]," n.d. 1.1, MSS 980, Emory. Hughes was so impressed by Douglas that he delivered a short program on the BBC about him in 1962, and then, at Faber and Faber's request, edited and introduced a collection of Douglas's poetry.

155. TH to Olwyn Hughes, 20–23 June 1957. *LTH*, 99.

156. The poet and critic Anne Stevenson, who would eventually write a biography of Plath, suggested that Ted and Olwyn were baffled not so much by Plath's temper but by her American assumptions. "Perhaps one reason I agreed to write *Bitter Fame* had to do with Sylvia's Americanness. I felt I knew her in a way Ted didn't. So when Olwyn Hughes began bitching about Sylvia, telling me how absurd she was and how she

expected Ted to do this and expected Ted to do that and completely ruled the household, I said, 'That's just the way Americans *are*.'" Anne Stevenson interview with Cynthia Harvey, *Cortland Review* (14 Nov. 2000).

157. SP to AP, 17 June 1957. *L2*, 149.

20. IN MIDAS' COUNTRY

1. TH to Olwyn Hughes, 20–23 June 1957. *LTH*, 101–102.
2. *J*, 609; 611.
3. Moro was an Amherst alumnus who had met Hughes while earning a master's degree in comparative literature at Cambridge. Lynne Lawner would shortly be heading to Newnham College on a Henry Fellowship.
4. Robert Bagg email to HC, 28 Apr. 2017.
5. HC interview with Elinor Friedman Klein, Oct. 2015, South Salem, N.Y.
6. TH to Olwyn Hughes, 23 June 1957. 1.5, MSS 980, Emory.
7. SP to Lynne Lawner, 1 July 1957. *L2*, 153.
8. Robert Bagg email to HC, 28 Apr. 2017. TH wrote his parents about the telegram. TH to Edith and William Hughes, 29 June 1957. 1.16, MSS 980, Emory.
9. Robert Bagg email to HC, 28 Apr. 2017.
10. SP to Lynne Lawner, 1 July 1957. *L2*, 153.
11. Robert Bagg email to HC, 25 & 26 Apr. 2017.
12. Keightley would later become a renowned professor of Chinese history and a MacArthur Fellow.
13. Robert Bagg email to HC, 28 Apr. 2017.
14. Harriet Rosenstein interview with Perry and Shirley Norton, 1974. 2.27, MSS 1489, Emory.
15. Harriet Rosenstein interview with Wilbury Crockett, 1971. 1.19, MSS 1489, Emory.
16. TH to Edith and William Hughes, 29 June 1957. 1.16, MSS 980, Emory.
17. Ibid.
18. TH to Edith and William Hughes, summer 1957. 1.16, MSS 980, Emory.
19. Robert Bagg email to HC, 28 Apr. 2017.
20. Harriet Rosenstein interview with Karen Goodall, 1974. 1.31, MSS 1489, Emory.
21. SP to Elinor Friedman, 12 July 1957. *L2*, 155.
22. TH to Edith and William Hughes, 29 June 1957. 1.16, MSS 980, Emory.
23. SP to Marcia Brown Plumer, 21 July 1957. *L2*, 164.
24. SP to Elinor Friedman, 12 July 1957. *L2*, 156–57.
25. The colony was on McKoy Road in Eastham.
26. TH to Olwyn Hughes, July 1957. Add MS 88948/1/1, BL.
27. The poems were "The Snowman on the Moor," "On the Difficulty of Conjuring Up a Dryad," "Sow," and "Ella Mason and Her Eleven Cats," in *Poetry* 90 (July 1957): 229–36.
28. *J*, 283.
29. Ibid.
30. SP to Marcia Brown Plumer, 21 July 1957. *L2*, 162.
31. *J*, 285.
32. SP to AP, 18 July 1957. *L2*, 158.
33. "The Laundromat Affair," "The Day of the Twenty-Four Cakes," a Kafka-inspired story called "The Eye-Beam," and "The Trouble-Making Mother." Only "The Laundromat Affair" survives, in partial manuscript form, at Emory.
34. *J*, 287–88.
35. *J*, 289.
36. *J*, 290–91; 289; 291.
37. AP to SP, 21 July 1957. *L2*, 161.
38. *J*, 289; 286.
39. TH to Gerald Hughes and family, 27 Aug. 1957. *LTH*, 109.
40. *J*, 288.

41. Ibid.
42. SP to AP, 6 Aug. 1957. *L2*, 169.
43. Plath and Hughes's friend Al Alvarez wrote in *The Savage God* that he doubted Plath's belief in occult practices.
44. *J*, 287.
45. In her copy of William James's *Varieties of Religious Experience*, Plath wrote, "cf: Sibyl in Dialogue Over a Ouija Board" on p. 37. SPC, Smith.
46. SP, "Character Notebook," notes on *Falcon Yard*. Written on back of TH's *Bardo Thodol*, 116.1, MSS 644, Emory.
47. For example, "Bawdry Embraced," "The Drowned Woman," "The Hag," "Billet-Doux," "A Modest Proposal," "Macaw and Little Miss," "The Martyrdom of Bishop Farrar," "Witches," and "Cleopatra to the Asp."
48. Robert Graves, *The White Goddess: A Historical Grammar of Poetic Myth*. 2nd ed. (New York: Farrar, Straus and Giroux, 1948; 1975), 456.
49. SP to AP, c. 30 July 1957. *L2*, 166.
50. *J*, 293.
51. *J*, 294.
52. TH to Gerald and Joan Hughes, 27 Aug. 1957. *LTH*, 107.
53. TH to Olwyn Hughes, Aug. 1957. 1.5, MSS 980, Emory.
54. *J*, 295.
55. *J*, 294.
56. *J*, 295.
57. *J*, 296; 293.
58. *J*, 296–97.
59. The incident in the poem occurred on a later trip to Cape Cod, in Aug. 1958. TH to Olwyn Hughes, Sept. 1958. Add MS 88948/1/1, BL.
60. *CPTH*, 1084–85.
61. TH to Olwyn Hughes, n.d., c. 1957. 1.5, MSS 980, Emory.
62. TH to Olwyn Hughes, 22 Aug. 1957. *LTH*, 106.
63. TH to Olwyn Hughes, 12 Sept. 1957. 1.5, MSS 980, Emory.
64. TH to Olwyn Hughes, 22 Aug. 1957. *LTH*, 106.
65. Ibid., 107.
66. TH to Edith and William Hughes, summer 1957. 1.16, MSS 980, Emory.
67. TH to Daniel Weissbort, 1957. 1.1, MSS 894, Emory.
68. TH to Olwyn Hughes, 1960. 1.9, MSS 980, Emory.
69. TH to Daniel Weissbort, 21 Mar. 1959. *LTH*, 140.
70. TH to Olwyn Hughes, Nov. 1959. Add MS 88948/1/1, BL.
71. TH to Gerald and Joan Hughes, late June 1957. *LTH*, 103.
72. TH to Olwyn Hughes, 22 Aug. 1957. *LTH*, 107.
73. SP to AP, 23 Sept. 1957. *L2*, 174.
74. Her afternoon classes would meet on Wednesdays, Thursdays, and Fridays, her morning classes on Thursdays, Fridays, and Saturdays.
75. SP to AP, 23 Sept. 1957. *L2*, 175–76.
76. SP to WP, 5 Nov. 1957. *L2*, 184.
77. *J*, 618.
78. *J*, 620.
79. *CPTH*, 1085–86.
80. SP to Marcia Brown Plumer, 21 July 1957. *L2*, 164.
81. The James chapters were "The Religion of Healthy-Mindedness" and "The Sick Soul." The other Hawthorne stories were "The Birthmark," "Ethan Brand," "Lady Eleanore's Mantle," and "Young Goodman Brown."
82. Webster's *The Duchess of Malfi*; Tourneur's *The Revenger's Tragedy*; Aristotle's *Poetics*; Sophocles' *Oedipus Rex* and *Antigone*; Ibsen's *Ghosts*, *Romersholm*, and *The Master Builder*; Strindberg's *Miss Julie*, *A Dream Play*, and *Ghost Sonata*.
83. Plath taught Hopkins's "Pied Beauty," "Spring," "Hurrahing in Harvest," "Inversnaid," "God's Grandeur," "What I Do Is Me," "The Caged Skylark," and "The Windhover," among others. She spent four days teaching the following Yeats poems: "Nineteen

Hundred and Nineteen," "The Second Coming," "Leda and the Swan," "Sailing to Byzantium," "Among School Children," "An Irish Airman Foresees His Death," "Crazy Jane on God," and "A Friend Whose Work Has Come to Nothing." She planned to spend five classes on Eliot, four on "The Waste Land," and one on "The Love Song of J. Alfred Prufrock," "Journey of the Magi," and (possibly) "The Hollow Men." She taught Dylan Thomas's "The Hand That Signed the Paper Felled a City," "The Force Through Which the Green Fuse Drives the Flower," "The Hunchback in the Park," "Twenty-Four Years," "In Memory of Ann Jones," "Fern Hill," "Do Not Go Gentle into That Good Night," and "Over Sir John's Hill." From Auden: "In Memory of W. B. Yeats," "Law, Say the Gardeners, Is the Sun," "Musée des Beaux Arts," "Look, Stranger," "As I Walked Out One Evening," and "Fish in the Unruffled Lakes." SP, 1957–58 Smith College Teaching Notes. 13.9–11, Lilly. Harriet Parsons Destler provided me with a photocopy of the Untermeyer anthology she used in Plath's class, which included her notes and highlights.

84. "Sylvia Plath: Uncensored, *The Unabridged Journals of Sylvia Plath*," WBUR, *The Connection*, hosted by Christopher Lydon. 15 Dec. 2000. Guests: Karen Kukil and Lynda Bundtzen. One of the program's callers had been a student in Plath's class.
85. Plath also taught with a copy of Elizabeth Drew's packet *Poetic Patterns: A Note on Versification*.
86. SP, 1957–58 Smith College Teaching Notes. 13.9–11, Lilly.
87. Ibid.
88. See Amanda Golden's *Annotating Modernism: Marginalia and Pedagogy from Virginia Woolf to the Confessional Poets* (Routledge, 2020), for a fuller account of Plath's engagement with mid-century modernism during her teaching year.
89. Quoted in ibid., 66. SP's annotation on p. 106 of SP's copy of *Axel's Castle* by Edmund Wilson (New York: Charles Scribner's Sons, 1950). SPC, Smith.
90. *J*, 337.
91. SP to WP, 5 Nov. 1957. *L2*, 184.
92. Ibid., *L2*, 187–88.
93. Class of 1961 Notes, *Smith Alumnae Quarterly* (Feb. 1979), 53.
94. Ellen Bartlett Nodelman (with Amanda Golden), "Recollections of Mrs. Hughes's Student," *Plath Profiles* 5, Supplement (Fall 2012): 125–39. 128.
95. HC phone interview with Harriett Destler, 23 Sept. 2015.
96. Ibid. Both Destler and Nodelman used the word "cold" when describing SP's "personal presentation."
97. "Sylvia Plath: Uncensored, *The Unabridged Journals of Sylvia Plath*."
98. Nodelman, "Recollections," 130.
99. Plath annotated this passage in her copy of Edmund Wilson's *Axel's Castle* with two exclamation points in the left-hand margin. SPC, Smith.
100. Class of 1961 Notes, 53.
101. SP to Dorothea Krook, 25 Sept. 1958. *L2*, 279.
102. "Smith Freshman Takes Own Life" and "Hughes Depicts Cambridge Scene," *Sophian* (7 Nov. 1957).
103. Nodelman, "Recollections," 128.
104. Ibid., 132.
105. HC phone interview with Harriett Destler, 23 Sept. 2015.
106. Harriet Rosenstein interview with Paul Roche, 1973. 3.14, MSS 1489, Emory.
107. SP to William and Edith Hughes, 5 Nov. 1957. *L2*, 190.
108. *J*, 623.
109. TH to Olwyn Hughes, fall 1957. *LTH*, 113.
110. SP to WP, 5 Nov. 1957. *L2*, 189.
111. SP to WP, 28 Nov. 1957. *L2*, 192.
112. Anne Stevenson, *Bitter Fame: A Life of Sylvia Plath* (London: Penguin, 1990), 117.
113. SP to WP, 28 Nov. 1957. *L2*, 193.
114. TH to Olwyn Hughes, c. early Dec. 1957. Add MS 88948/1/1, BL.
115. Harriet Rosenstein interview with W. S. Merwin, 1974. 2.21, MSS 1489, Emory.
116. Stevenson, *Bitter Fame*, 117.

117. SP to WP, 28 Nov. 1957. *L2*, 192–93.
118. Ibid.
119. *J*, 348.
120. TH to Olwyn Hughes, c. early Dec. 1957. Add MS 88948/1/1, BL.
121. TH to Olwyn Hughes, 1958. 1.6, MSS 980, Emory.
122. SP to WP, 6 Jan. 1958. *L2*, 202.
123. *J*, 307–308.
124. Ibid.
125. SP to AP, 8 Dec. 1957. *L2*, 198.
126. SP to Olwyn Hughes, 9 Feb. 1958. *L2*, 211.
127. SP to Dorothea Krook, 25 Sept. 1958. *L2*, 280.
128. *J*, 325.
129. SP to Olwyn Hughes, 9 Feb. 1958. *L2*, 211.
130. *J*, 346.
131. Harriet Rosenstein interview with Paul Roche, 1973. 3.14, MSS 1489, Emory.
132. Harriet Rosenstein interview with Clarissa Roche, 1973. 3.14, MSS 1489, Emory.
133. *J*, 342.
134. *J*, 365.
135. SP to Olwyn Hughes, 9 Feb. 1958. *L2*, 212.
136. *J*, 361.
137. The poems (Plath's "The Times Are Tidy" and Hughes's "Pennines in April") would eventually be published, in Jan. 1959, along with an article about the couple's working relationship. *J*, 338.
138. *J*, 377.
139. *J*, 372.
140. *J*, 310.
141. *J*, 318.
142. *J*, 328.
143. *J*, 332.
144. *J*, 315.
145. *J*, 366; 320; 328–29.
146. TH to Lucas Myers, Oct. 1957. *LTH*, 110.
147. TH to Lucas Myers, early 1958. *LTH*, 118.
148. EF interview with Clarissa Roche, Nov. 1999. EFP.
149. George Gibian to Harriet Rosenstein, 18 Oct. 1971. 1.30, MSS 1489, Emory.
150. Harriet Rosenstein interview with Marcia Brown Stern, 1972. 4.16, MSS 1489, Emory.
151. TH to Lucas Myers, early 1958. *LTH*, 118.
152. Ibid., *LTH*, 120.
153. SP to WP, 6 Jan. 1958. *L2*, 203. Schendler's claim comes from a letter from Howard Hirt to Paula Rotholz, n.d., 14 Feb. 1.28, EBC, Smith. Hughes taught on Tuesday, Thursday, and Saturday.
154. SP to Gerald and Joan Hughes, 4 Mar. 1958. *L2*, 220.
155. SP to WP, 11 June 1958. *L2*, 240.
156. *J*, 344.
157. TH to Olwyn Hughes, winter 1958. Add MS 88948/1/1, BL.
158. TH to Lucas Myers, early 1958. *LTH*, 118.
159. TH to Olwyn Hughes, winter 1958. Add MS 88948/1/1, BL.
160. TH to Olwyn Hughes, late Mar. 1958. *LTH*, 122.
161. TH to Olwyn Hughes, May 1958. 1.6, MSS 980, Emory.
162. SP to AP, 22 Mar. 1958. *L2*, 222.
163. *J*, 356.
164. SP to AP, 22 Mar. 1958. *L2*, 223.
165. *J*, 360.
166. SP, introduction to "The Disquieting Muses" on *The Living Poet*, BBC program recorded 26 Oct. 1960; broadcast 20 Nov. 1960. *Sylvia Plath: The Spoken Word* (London: British Library, 2010). Audio CD. The poem was written 22–28 Mar. 1958.

167. Video footage of Aurelia Plath, Nov. 1986, in *Poets of New England: Sylvia Plath and the Myth of the Monstrous Mother*. University of Massachusetts, Amherst, AIMS Video Services, 2001. Courtesy of Richard Larschan.
168. AP, "For the Authors' Series Talk—Wellesley College Club," 16 Mar. 1976. 30.58, SPC, Smith.
169. *J*, 347.
170. *J*, 346.
171. TH to Gerald Hughes, May 1958. 1.2, MSS 854, Emory.
172. *J*, 346.
173. TH to Daniel Weissbort, early 1958. *LTH*, 116.
174. SP and TH to Lucas Myers, 18 Dec. 1957. 1.3, MSS 865, Emory.
175. Graves, *White Goddess*, 449.
176. TH to Daniel Huws, 3 Dec. 1959. *LTH*, 153.
177. *J*, 367–68.
178. SP to WP, 22 Apr. 1958. *L2*, 229.
179. *J*, 368. Aurelia wrote her undated annotations in the margin of SP to Warren Plath, 22 Apr. 1958. *L2*, 229. Phil McCurdy, who sat next to Aurelia at the reading, confirmed this to me.
180. *J*, 368.
181. *J*, 369.
182. Plath would meet Sweeney and Rich again at the Glascock Poetry Contest at Mount Holyoke on 18 Apr. (Both were judges.)
183. Reading by Sylvia Plath, poetry and comments, recorded live with Lee Anderson for the Library of Congress, Springfield, Mass., 18 Apr. 1958. Audio cassette. 23.1, SPC, Smith.
184. TH to Gerald and Joan Hughes, May 1958. 1.2, MSS 854, Emory.
185. *J*, 371–72.
186. SP to WP, 11 June 1958. *L2*, 238.
187. Ibid., *L2*, 239.
188. *J*, 355.
189. *J*, 413–14.
190. *J*, 356.
191. *J*, 373.
192. *J*, 316.
193. *J*, 363.
194. Ibid.
195. *J*, 357.
196. Harriet Rosenstein interview with Paul Roche, 1973. 3.14, MSS 1489, Emory.
197. Harriet Rosenstein interview with Leonard Baskin, 1971. 1.7, MSS 1489, Emory.
198. *J*, 374–75.
199. *J*, 382.
200. *J*, 381.
201. Ibid.
202. HC interview with Betsy Powley Wallingford, Feb. 2013, Sudbury, Mass.
203. *J*, 379.
204. SP to WP, 11 June 1958. *L2*, 243–44.
205. TH to Olwyn Hughes, May–June 1958. Add MS 88948/1/1, BL.
206. *J*, 381.
207. *J*, 385–86.
208. *J*, 386.
209. SP to WP, 11 June 1958. *L2*, 238.
210. *J*, 390–91.
211. *J*, 392.
212. *J*, 389.
213. *J*, 392.
214. *J*, 401.
215. *J*, 400.

216. *J*, 403.
217. Ibid.
218. Ibid.
219. SP to WP, 9 July 1958. *L2*, 262.
220. *J*, 403.

21. LIFE STUDIES

1. HC interview with Janet Salter Rosenberg, Sept. 2015, Dobbs Ferry, N.Y.
2. Harriet Rosenstein interview with Aurelia Plath, 1970. 3.3, MSS 1489, Emory.
3. Harriet Rosenstein interview with Charles Hill, n.d. (early 1970s). 1.30, MSS 1489, Emory.
4. *J*, 423.
5. Ibid.
6. SP to WP, 11 June 1958. *L2*, 240.
7. *The Pocket Book of Modern Verse: English and American Poetry of the Last Hundred Years, from Walt Whitman to Dylan Thomas* (New York: Washington Square Press, 1958). The anthology included Hughes's "The Martyrdom of Bishop Farrar," "The Hag," and "The Thought-Fox."
8. SP to WP, 11 June 1958. *L2*, 242.
9. SP to AP, 10 June 1958. *L2*, 237.
10. Ibid., *L2*, 236.
11. SP to WP, 11 June 1958. *L2*, 241.
12. TH to Olwyn Hughes, June 1958. *LTH*, 124.
13. See *L2*, 237, for a list of the poems she read.
14. SP to WP, 9 July 1958. *L2*, 262.
15. TH to AP, early July 1958. *LTH*, 127–28. He may have been referring to "Whiteness I Remember" and "Fable of the Rhododendron Stealers."
16. Plath probably wrote "Mussel Hunter at Rock Harbor" in early June 1958, for she included it in an 11 June 1958 letter to Warren. Hughes's "Relic" was written by April 1958.
17. *CPTH*, 78.
18. SP to WP, 11 June 1958. *L2*, 243.
19. SP to WP, 25 June 1958. *L2*, 252.
20. SP to WP, 11 June 1958. *L2*, 238.
21. Plath later changed the title to "Night Walk" and, still later, to "Hardcastle Crags."
22. SP to WP, 25 June 1958. *L2*, 252.
23. SP to AP, 25 June 1958. *L2*, 249.
24. SP to WP, 9 July 1958. *L2*, 261.
25. SP to AP, 1 Aug. 1958. *L2*, 267.
26. SP to Peter Davison, 7 Sept. 1958. *L2*, 275.
27. *J*, 394–95.
28. SP to AP, 13 Aug. 1958. *L2*, 270. Plath read Rachel Carson's *The Sea Around Us*, while Hughes read her *Under the Sea Wind*.
29. OHP to AP, 30 July 1958. Lilly.
30. *J*, 422.
31. SP to AP, 5 July 1958. *L2*, 259.
32. Ibid., *L2*, 259–60.
33. *J*, 409.
34. *J*, 406.
35. Moore inscribed the date 16 Apr. 1955. Plath's copy of this book is at SPC, Smith.
36. *J*, 406.
37. Marianne Moore to SP, 13 July 1958. 17.35, SPC, Smith.
38. Marianne Moore to Judith Jones, 7 Apr. 1962. Alfred A. Knopf Papers, 359.10, HRC.
39. Marianne Moore to Henry Allen Moe, Nov. 1961. Rosenbach Museum and Library, Philadelphia, PA.
40. *CPTH*, 1091.

41. SP to AP, 19 July 1958. *L2*, 266.
42. *J*, 395.
43. *J*, 400–405.
44. *J*, 401.
45. *J*, 404.
46. *J*, 409.
47. *J*, 410.
48. *J*, 411.
49. SP to AP, 1 Aug. 1958. *L2*, 267.
50. TH to Gerald and Joan Hughes, Christmas 1958. 1.2, MSS 854, Emory.
51. SP to Olwyn Hughes, 30 June 1958. *L2*, 255.
52. *J*, 411.
53. *J*, 412.
54. *J*, 413. The magazine's other acceptance, eventually titled "Hardcastle Crags" in *The Colossus*, appeared in *The New Yorker* on 11 Oct. 1958.
55. *J*, 409.
56. *J*, 415.
57. *J*, 416.
58. SP to WP, 25 June 1958. *L2*, 253.
59. SP to Dorothea Krook, 25 Sept. 1958. *L2*, 281.
60. SP to Lynne Lawner, 4 Sept. 1958. *L2*, 273.
61. SP to Elinor Friedman, 3 Sept. 1958. *L2*, 271.
62. SP to Dorothea Krook, 25 Sept. 1958. *L2*, 280.
63. TH to Olwyn Hughes, summer 1959. Add MS 88948/1/2, BL.
64. SP to Dorothea Krook, 25 Sept. 1958. *L2*, 281.
65. *J*, 421.
66. TH to William Scammell, 28 Apr. 1998. Add MS 88918/137, BL.
67. *J*, 420; 423; 445.
68. SP to Elinor Friedman, 3 Sept. 1958. *L2*, 272.
69. *J*, 423.
70. *J*, 421.
71. *J*, 420–21.
72. *J*, 423.
73. *J*, 422.
74. SP to Elinor Friedman, 26 Oct. 1958. *L2*, 283.
75. SP to Dorothea Krook, 25 Sept. 1958. *L2*, 282.
76. T. S. Eliot to TH, 30 Oct. 1958. Series 6, OP 12, MSS 644, Emory.
77. SP to Lynne Lawner, 4 Sept. 1958. *L2*, 274.
78. SP to Alice Norma Davis, 24 Sept. 1958. *L2*, 278.
79. *J*, 424.
80. SP to Elinor Friedman, 26 Oct. 1958. *L2*, 283.
81. *J*, 424.
82. *J*, 441.
83. Andrew Lytle to SP, 27 Nov. 1961. *Sewanee Review* Records, UA20.01, University Archives, Jesse Ball DuPont Library, Sewanee University.
84. SP, Notes on *Falcon Yard*, "Character Notebook." 116.1, on back of TH's *Bardo Thodol*, MSS 644, Emory.
85. *J*, 429.
86. *J*, 431–32.
87. *J*, 429–32.
88. *J*, 448.
89. Plath biographer Anne Stevenson also questioned Dr. Beuscher's tactics. "In Boston, Beuscher gave Sylvia 'permission to hate' her mother—rather extreme, don't you think, to give an impressionable girl permission to 'hate' her mother, even though this particular mother, by doing right may actually have perpetrated wrong? A more mature psychiatrist would have realized that the hatred of a mother and the love of the father aren't so simple as the Electra complex formula would have them be. Sylvia

clearly took everything Ruth Beuscher told her to heart." Anne Stevenson, interview with Cynthia Harvey, *Cortland Review* 14 (Nov. 2000).

90. *J*, 451.
91. *J*, 444–45.
92. *J*, 454.
93. Ibid.
94. *J*, 437.
95. *J*, 451.
96. Corinne Robins, "Four Young Poets," *Mademoiselle* (Jan. 1959): 32–35.
97. *J*, 434.
98. *J*, 445.
99. Gordon Lameyer to SP, 21 May 1959. Lilly.
100. *J*, 452.
101. *J*, 459.
102. Anne Sexton, *Anne Sexton: A Self-Portrait in Letters*, Linda Gray Sexton and Lois Ames, eds. (Boston: Houghton Mifflin, 1977; 1991), 56.
103. Sexton, *Letters*, 64.
104. Harriet Rosenstein interview with Stephen Fassett, 1971. 1.26, MSS 1489, Emory.
105. *J*, 465.
106. Stanley Kunitz to Edward Butscher, 17 Aug. 1973. 1.38, EBC, Smith.
107. TH to Olwyn Hughes, late Oct./early Nov. 1958. 1.6, MSS 980, Emory.
108. Peter Davison to Judith Flanders, 9 Nov. 1987. 1.7, Houghton Mifflin Papers, Smith.
109. Linda Wagner-Martin, *Sylvia Plath: A Biography* (New York: Simon & Schuster, 1987), 156.
110. Adrienne Rich to Jack Sweeney, 20 Feb. 1959. LA52/287, Jack and Máire Sweeney Papers, UCD.
111. Wagner-Martin, *Sylvia Plath*, 156.
112. Harriet Rosenstein interview with Ruth Whitman, 1970. 4.22, MSS 1489, Emory.
113. Diane Middlebrook, *Anne Sexton* (Boston: Houghton Mifflin, 1991), 111.
114. Ibid.
115. *J*, 466.
116. *J*, 469.
117. *J*, 471.
118. Adrienne Rich to Jack Sweeney, 20 Feb. 1959. LA52/287, Jack and Máire Sweeney Papers, UCD.
119. Peter Davison, *The Fading Smile: Poets in Boston from Robert Frost to Robert Lowell to Sylvia Plath* (New York: Knopf, 1994), 11.
120. Adrienne Rich, *Essential Essays: Culture, Politics, and the Art of Poetry*, Sandra M. Gilbert, ed. (New York: W. W. Norton, 2018), 9.
121. Quoted in Davison, *The Fading Smile*, 2.
122. Ibid., 3.
123. *Words in Air: The Complete Correspondence Between Robert Lowell and Elizabeth Bishop*, Thomas Travisano and Saskia Hamilton, eds. (New York: Farrar, Straus and Giroux, 2010), 295.
124. Lowell read "Waking in the Blue," about his time at McLean, out loud at his Boston University seminar, which Plath took. "Skunk Hour" was published in *Partisan Review* in Jan. 1958, along with "Man and Wife" and "Memories of West Street and Lepke." More poems would see publication in Jan. 1959.
125. HC interview with Daniel Huws, May 2016, London.
126. Robert Lowell, *Collected Poems*, Frank Bidart and David Gewanter, eds. (New York: Farrar, Straus and Giroux, 2003), 191–92. Lowell's ellipsis.
127. Ibid., 184; 186.
128. TH to Lucas Myers, spring 1958. 1.4, MSS 865, Emory.
129. Hughes told Olwyn that Lowell was "very apprehensive as to how it will be received and talks continually—or too often—about how it won't be liked, how it oughtn't to get any prizes since he has lots of money and is already established, and so on." TH to Olwyn Hughes, Apr. 1959. 1.8, MSS 980, Emory.

130. TH to Olwyn Hughes, Jan./Feb. 1959. Add MS 88948/1/1, BL.
131. TH to William and Edith Hughes, n.d., early 1959. *LTH*, 139.
132. TH to Lucas Myers, spring 1958. 1.4, MSS 865, Emory.
133. In 1976, for example, Hughes wrote to Daniel Weissbort that Lowell's work was "totally ersatz, it is all stage performance, even the careless, slovenly, loose shuffling off of imperfect approximations, on his way to closer sincerities." *LTH*, 372.
134. TH to Olwyn Hughes, Jan./Feb. 1959. Add MS 88948/1/1, BL.
135. A. Alvarez, "Tough Young Poet," *Observer* (6 Oct. 1957), 12.
136. Kathleen Spivack, *With Robert Lowell and His Circle: Sylvia Plath, Anne Sexton, Elizabeth Bishop, Stanley Kunitz, and Others* (Boston: Northeastern University Press, 2012), 71.
137. Travisano and Hamilton, eds., *Words in Air*, 333.
138. Spivack, *With Robert Lowell*, 57.
139. Ibid., 119; 122.
140. Travisano and Hamilton, eds., *Words in Air*, 702.
141. Spivack, *With Robert Lowell*, 63.
142. Andrew Jamison and Ron Eyerman, *Seeds of the Sixties* (Berkeley and Los Angeles: University of California Press, 1994), 158.
143. Rachel Donadio, "1958: The War of the Intellectuals," *New York Times* (11 May 2008).
144. A. Alvarez, "The Bohemian and the Beat," *Observer* (23 Nov. 1958), A16.
145. Norman Podhoretz, "The Know-Nothing Bohemians," *Partisan Review* 25 (Spring 1958): 305–11.
146. SP to Brian Cox, 17 June 1961. *L2*, 625.
147. Jamison and Eyerman, *Seeds of the Sixties*, 152.
148. *J*, 455.
149. *J*, 458.
150. Eddie Cohen to SP, 2 Nov. 1958. Lilly.
151. Harriet Rosenstein interview with Marcia Brown Stern, 1972.4.16, MSS 1489, Emory.
152. *J*, 466.
153. *J*, 463.
154. *J*, 469.
155. *J*, 469–70.
156. *J*, 471.
157. TH to William Scammell, 28 Apr. 1998. Add MS 88918/137, BL.
158. *J*, 470.
159. SP to Gerald and Joan Hughes, 24 May 1959. *L2*, 321.
160. TH to Olwyn Hughes, early 1959. 1.8, MSS 980, Emory.
161. *J*, 467.
162. The class is rumored to have met in Room 222, but the English department's administrator, who worked at BU from 1948 to 2008, confirmed that Lowell was assigned to "random, generic classrooms in the CAS building" when he taught. See Caleb Daniloff, "Icons Among Us: Room 222," *BU Today* (1 Dec. 2009). Sexton had been attending the class since it began in the fall of 1958 at the suggestion of W. D. Snodgrass, whom she had met at the Antioch Writers Conference.
163. *J*, 471.
164. See Plath's 1962 interview with Peter Orr in *The Poet Speaks: Interviews with Contemporary Poets*, Peter Orr, ed. (New York: Barnes & Noble, 1966), 168.
165. Spivack, *With Robert Lowell*, 26.
166. Ibid., 50; 47.
167. Ibid., 33.
168. Ibid., 25.
169. Ibid., 35–36.
170. Middlebrook, *Anne Sexton*, 107.
171. SP to Lynne Lawner, 11 Mar. 1959. *L2*, 303.
172. Maxine Kumin, "How It Was: Maxine Kumin on Anne Sexton," foreword, *Complete Poems of Anne Sexton* (New York: Mariner Books, 1981), xxiv.
173. Travisano and Hamilton, eds., *Words in Air*, 327.
174. TH to Al Alvarez, Jan. 1962. Add MS 88593/1, BL.

175. Middlebrook, *Anne Sexton*, 340.
176. Ibid., 339.
177. SP to Lynne Lawner, 11 Mar. 1959. *L2*, 303.
178. *J*, 475.
179. *J*, 477.
180. SP to Lynne Lawner, 11 Mar. 1959. *L2*, 303.
181. Sexton, *Letters*, 70–71.
182. SP to Lynne Lawner, 11 Mar. 1959. *L2*, 305.
183. Spivack, *With Robert Lowell*, 28.
184. Sexton, *Complete Poems*, 4.
185. Orr, *The Poet Speaks*, 168.
186. Spivack, *With Robert Lowell*, 29.
187. SP to Lynne Lawner, 11 Mar. 1959. *L2*, 305.
188. *J*, 470.
189. *J*, 473.
190. *J*, 474.
191. Ibid.
192. *J*, 475–76.
193. TH, "Notes on the Chronological Order of Sylvia Plath's Poems," *TriQuarterly* (Fall 1966): 81–88. 84.
194. Sexton's poems of motherhood, such as "The Double Image" and "The Fortress," would influence Plath's "Magi," "Parliament Hill Fields," and "Morning Song." Sexton also used the "bell jar" metaphor in her poem "For John, Who Begs Me Not to Enquire Further" ("I tapped my own head; / it was glass, an inverted bowl"), though Plath had already encountered the image in *Generation of Vipers*. Sexton's poem itself was a response to John Holmes's advice to her to stop writing about personal, traumatic experiences.
195. Anne Sexton, "The Barfly Ought to Sing," *TriQuarterly* 7 (Fall 1966): 92.
196. Sexton, *Letters*, 73.
197. *J*, 483.
198. Sexton, *Complete Poems*, 128.
199. Sexton, "The Barfly Ought to Sing," 92.
200. Spivack, *With Robert Lowell*, 36–37.
201. TH to Olwyn Hughes, summer 1958. 1.6, MSS 980, Emory.
202. TH to Lucas Myers, 19 May 1959. *LTH*, 145.
203. TH to Olwyn Hughes, Apr. 1959. 1.8, MSS 980, Emory.
204. TH to Keith Sagar, 18–19 July, 1998. *Poet and Critic: The Letters of Ted Hughes and Keith Sagar* (London: British Library, 2012), 269.
205. TH to Daniel Weissbort, 21 Mar. 1959. *LTH*, 140.
206. TH to Daniel Huws, 3 Dec. 1959. *LTH*, 152.
207. TH to Robert Lowell, 29 Dec. 1966. *LTH*, 265.

22. THE DEVELOPMENT OF PERSONALITY

1. TH to Olwyn Hughes, Apr. 1959. *LTH*, 141–42.
2. TH to Olwyn Hughes, Apr./May 1959. Add MS 88948/1/1, BL.
3. TH to Olwyn Hughes, Jan./Feb. 1959. Add MS 88948/1/1, BL.
4. TH to Olwyn Hughes, Aug. 1959. Add MS 88948/1/1, BL.
5. TH, notebook entry, 12 Apr. 1959. Add MS 88918/129/2, BL.
6. *J*, 477.
7. *J*, 477–78.
8. *J*, 477.
9. *J*, 494.
10. *J*, 480.
11. *JP*, 340–52.
12. *J*, 495.
13. Ibid.

14. *J*, 484.
15. *J*, 485.
16. *J*, 487.
17. *J*, 491–92.
18. *J*, 487.
19. Ibid.
20. *J*, 492–94.
21. *J*, 492.
22. *J*, 492–93; SP to Ann Davidow, 12 June 1959. *L2*, 328.
23. Stanley Burnshaw to Robert Frost, 23 June 1959. 1178.2.24, Dartmouth.
24. Stanley Burnshaw to Robert Frost, 9 July 1959. 1178.2.24, Dartmouth.
25. *J*, 495. Patricia Blake, "I Was Afraid to Be a Woman" and Eugene D. Fleming, "Psychiatry and Beauty" were both published in *Cosmopolitan*, June 1959. Luke Ferretter has discussed these articles' significance in *Sylvia Plath's Fiction: A Critical Study*, pp. 43–47.
26. SP to Ann Davidow, 12 June 1959. *L2*, 328.
27. *J*, 500–501.
28. *J*, 500.
29. See David Trinidad, "On the Road with Sylvia and Ted: Plath and Hughes's 1959 Road Trip Across America," *Plath Profiles* 4 (Summer 2011): 168–92.
30. "She started with us that morning / We set off to roam ~~through~~ across America." TH, draft of "Delivering Frieda." Add MS 88918/1/2-8, BL.
31. SP to AP, 9 July 1959. *L2*, 332.
32. SP to AP, 12 July 1959. *L2*, 336.
33. Ibid., *L2*, 335.
34. SP to AP, 14 July 1959. *L2*, 338.
35. Karen Kukil and Stephen Ennis, *No Other Appetite: Sylvia Plath, Ted Hughes, and the Blood Jet of Poetry* (New York: Grolier Club, 2005), 31.
36. *CPTH*, 1095–98.
37. SP to AP, 18 July 1959. *L2*, 340.
38. SP to AP and WP, 28 July 1959. *L2*, 346.
39. *CPTH*, 1104.
40. Ibid., 1101. Although Hughes depicted Plath as six weeks pregnant in his poem "Grand Canyon," set later that summer, this was probably a point made in hindsight. Only a blood test could confirm a pregnancy in 1959, and Plath did not see a doctor until she returned to Wellesley.
41. TH and SP to AP and WP, 28 July 1959. Lilly.
42. SP to AP, 26 July 1959. *L2*, 343.
43. SP to AP, 2 Aug. 1959. *L2*, 349.
44. SP to AP, 26 July 1959. *L2*, 344.
45. TH to Edith and William Hughes, late July 1959. 1.18, MSS 980, Emory.
46. Frieda Heinrichs to AP, 13 Aug. 1959. Lilly.
47. Ibid.
48. SP to AP, 2 Aug. 1959. *L2*, 350.
49. SP to AP and WP, 3 Aug. 1959. *L2*, 351.
50. Frieda Heinrichs to AP, 13 Aug. 1959. Lilly.
51. SP to AP and WP, 3 Aug. 1959. *L2*, 351.
52. SP to AP and WP, 6 Aug. 1959. *L2*, 352.
53. SP to AP and WP, 8 Aug. 1959. *L2*, 353.
54. TH to AP and WP, 14 Aug. 1959. *LTH*, 152.
55. *CPTH*, 1105.
56. *LH*, 352.
57. Pauline Hanson to Edward Butscher, 27 Nov. 1972. 2.87, EBC, Smith.
58. Alfred Kazin to Elizabeth Ames, 3 Feb. 1955. 374.1–9, Yaddo Records, NYPL. Plath's former Smith professor Newton Arvin invited her to Yaddo. Both Plath and Hughes received A grades on their application from John Cheever, and two B grades from their other recommenders.

59. SP to AP and WP, 10 Sept. 1959. *L2*, 356.
60. Ibid.
61. *A Century at Yaddo* (Saratoga Springs: Corporation of Yaddo, 2000), 43.
62. SP to AP and WP, c. 18 Sept. 1959. *L2*, 359.
63. *J*, 501–502.
64. HC phone interview with Howard Rogovin, 21 Jan. 2017. When the mansion closed for the season, they took their meals in the less opulent "garage."
65. SP to Edith and William Hughes, 8 Oct. 1959. *L2*, 363.
66. SP to AP and WP, 10 Sept. 1959. *L2*, 356.
67. Ibid.
68. See *L2*, 357, for a full list of guests who overlapped with Plath and Hughes.
69. SP to AP, 13 Oct. 1959. *L2*, 365.
70. "May Swenson on S.P.," 3 Oct. 1987. Included in Peter Davison to Judith Flanders, 9 Nov. 1987. 1.7, Houghton Mifflin Papers, Smith. Plath's eyes, of course, were brown.
71. HC phone interview with Howard Rogovin, 21 Jan. 2017.
72. Ibid.
73. Howard also painted two portraits of Hughes. He lost track of the portraits when he moved to his aunt's house after his stay at Yaddo.
74. Jeremy Treglown, "Howard's Way," *Times Literary Supplement* (30 Aug. 2013), 13.
75. HC phone interview with Howard Rogovin, 21 Jan. 2017.
76. *J*, 506.
77. *J*, 501.
78. May Swenson was a guest at Yaddo from Nov. 2 to Dec. 3. Plath admired her second book of poetry, *A Cage of Spines* (1958).
79. *J*, 516.
80. Ibid. The poet Grace Schulman stayed at Yaddo in 1973 and remembered finding Roethke's *The Waking* and Radin's *African Folktales* on a bookshelf outside her West House studio. Grace Schulman email to HC, 2 Jan. 2019. See Schulman, "Sylvia Plath and Yaddo," *Ariel Ascending*, Paul Alexander, ed. (New York: HarperCollins, 1984), 165–77.
81. *J*, 502.
82. *J*, 509.
83. *J*, 517.
84. *J*, 510–11.
85. *J*, 509.
86. *J*, 514.
87. The story survived after Plath's death—Olwyn remembered reading it along with Plath's last journal.
88. *J*, 514.
89. C. G. Jung, *The Development of Personality* (New York: Pantheon, 1954), 74. Yaddo Library copy.
90. Ibid., 78–79.
91. SP, notes on Carl Jung, c. fall 1959. 19.23, SPC, Smith.
92. *J*, 514.
93. Jung, *Development*, 78.
94. In the same dream, she was shaving her legs under the table while a Jewish father told her not to bring her "scimitar to table." The next night she dreamed, famously, of Marilyn Monroe "as a kind of fairy godmother. . . . I spoke, almost in tears, of how much she and Arthur Miller meant to us." Monroe gave her a manicure and invited her to visit her at Christmas, "promising a new, flowering life." *J*, 513–14.
95. Jung, *Development*, 173.
96. Ibid., 176.
97. *J*, 515.
98. *J*, 514.
99. *J*, 515.
100. *J*, 517.
101. *J*, 518–19.

102. *J*, 518.
103. "Medallion" would be rejected by *Harper's* and *The Atlantic Monthly* and published in the *Critical Quarterly Poetry Supplement* in 1960. "The Manor Garden" was published in *The Atlantic* in Sept. 1960. *The New Yorker* rejected "Yaddo: The Grand Manor," which was published in *The Christian Science Monitor* on 21 Oct. 1959.
104. *J*, 519.
105. *J*, 525.
106. *J*, 461.
107. *J*, 525.
108. See Helen Vendler, *Coming of Age as a Poet: Milton, Keats, Eliot, Plath* (Cambridge: Harvard University Press, 2003).
109. *J*, 520–21.
110. During my 2017 Yaddo residency, I saw that the old greenhouse had been replaced by a modern artist's studio, though the footprint is the same.
111. *J*, 520.
112. TH, list of poem subjects, annotated by SP, fall 1959. 149.13, MSS 644, Emory.
113. *J*, 521.
114. Ibid.
115. Ibid.
116. Sylvia Plath, *The Living Poet*. BBC Third Programme. Recorded on June 5, 1961; broadcast on July 8, 1961.
117. TH to Olwyn Hughes, n.d., Oct./Nov. 1959. Add MS, 88948/1/1, BL.
118. SP, *Collected Poems*, Ted Hughes, ed. (London: Faber and Faber, 1981), 289.
119. *J*, 521.
120. TH, *Winter Pollen: Occasional Prose*, William Scammell, ed. (New York: Picador, 1995), 184. *The Sewanee Review* would reject the sequence in May 1960.
121. TH, draft of "Delivering Frieda," eventually published as "Remission." Add MS 88918/1/2-8, BL.
122. *The London Magazine* would eventually publish "The Fifty-Ninth Bear," which Plath wrote at Yaddo, in Feb. 1961.
123. *J*, 522.
124. *J*, 524.
125. TH to William Scammell, 28 Apr. 1998. Add MS 88918/137, BL.
126. *J*, 525.
127. *J*, 524.
128. *J*, 528.
129. The stories were "The Beggar," "The Fifty-Ninth Bear," and "The Mummy."
130. *J*, 521.
131. *J*, 529–30.
132. *J*, 528.
133. *CPTH*, 1111.
134. *J*, 530.

23. THE DREAD OF RECOGNITION

1. The ship left New York City on Dec. 9 and arrived in Southampton on Dec. 14.
2. TH to AP, 13 Dec. 1959. Lilly.
3. TH to Stephen and Agatha Fassett, 14 May 1960. 1.1, MS Am 3133, Houghton Library, Harvard.
4. *LTH*, photo 2b (n.p.).
5. SP to AP, 13 Dec. 1959. *L2*, 372.
6. TH to AP, 13 Dec. 1959. Lilly.
7. SP to AP, 17 Dec. 1959. *L2*, 376.
8. Edith Hughes to AP, c. Dec. 1959. Lilly.
9. SP to AP, 17 Dec. 1959. *L2*, 375–76.
10. Olwyn discusses the bathrobe incident at length in Anne Stevenson's *Bitter Fame*. She says Plath had left an old tattered blue bathrobe at the Beacon, whose pattern Edith

had used to make an identical one, in mauve, for Olwyn. When Plath returned to the Beacon in December 1959, she began using the mauve bathrobe, which Olwyn found odd. Given its similarity to her old bathrobe, Plath may have assumed it was hers. Edith Hughes soon resolved the situation by making a new bathrobe for Plath.

11. SP to AP, 26 Dec. 1959. *L2*, 378–79.
12. SP to Joseph and Dorothy Benotti, 27 Dec. 1959. *L2*, 380.
13. Ibid., *L2*, 380.
14. SP to AP, 16 Jan. (#2) 1960. *L2*, 389.
15. TH, 28 Dec. 1959, notebook entry. Add MS 88918/129/2, BL.
16. The pub is still there, just a short walk down the hill from Heptonstall.
17. *CPTH*, 1111–12.
18. SP to AP, 10 Jan. 1960. *L2*, 383.
19. SP to AP, 24 Jan. 1960. *L2*, 396.
20. SP to Dr. Ruth Beuscher, 18 Feb. 1960. *L2*, 421.
21. SP to AP, 16 Jan. (#1) 1960. *L2*, 385.
22. Daniel Huws, *Memories of Ted Hughes 1952–1963* (Nottingham: Richard Hollis/Five Leaves, 2010), 46–47.
23. SP to AP, 10 Jan. 1960. *L2*, 382; 384.
24. SP to Lynne Lawner, 18 Feb. 1960. *L2*, 419.
25. TH to AP and WP, 11 Jan. 1960. Lilly.
26. TH to Stephen and Agatha Fassett, 14 May 1960. 1.1, MS AM 3133, Houghton Library, Harvard; SP to Dr. Ruth Beuscher, 18 Feb. 1960. *L2*, 421.
27. TH to Stephen and Agatha Fassett, 14 May 1960. 1.1, MS Am 3133, Houghton Library, Harvard.
28. SP to AP, 10 Jan. 1960. *L2*, 383.
29. SP to AP, 16 Jan. (#2) 1960. *L2*, 388; SP to AP, 10 Jan. 1960. *L2*, 383.
30. SP to Marcia Brown Plumer, 8 Feb. (#2) 1960. *L2*, 412.
31. Plath's copy is at SPC, Smith. Grantly Dick-Read, *Childbirth Without Fear: The Principles and Practice of Natural Childbirth.* (London: Heinemann Medical Books Ltd., 1959), 59.
32. Ibid., 30.
33. Ibid., 11.
34. SP to Dr. Ruth Beuscher, 18 Feb. 1960. *L2*, 422.
35. AP to Miriam Baggett, 6 Feb. 1960. 29.2, SPC, Smith.
36. TH to AP, 11 Jan. 1960. Lilly.
37. SP to Olwyn Hughes, 8 Feb. 1960. *L2*, 413.
38. SP to Marcia Brown Plumer, 8 Feb. (#1) 1960. *L2*, 409.
39. SP to AP, 16 Jan. (#1) 1960. *L2*, 386.
40. SP to Lynne Lawner, 18 Feb. 1960. *L2*, 419; SP to Marcia Brown Plumer, 8 Feb. (#1) 1960. *L2*, 410.
41. TH to Olwyn Hughes, Feb. 1960. Add MS 88948/1/2, BL.
42. SP to Lynne Lawner, 18 Feb. 1960. *L2*, 420.
43. TH to AP, 11 Jan. 1960. Lilly.
44. SP to Marcia Brown Plumer, 8 Feb. (#2) 1960. *L2*, 413.
45. SP to AP, 16 Jan. (#1) 1960. *L2*, 384.
46. SP to AP, 19–22 Jan. 1960. *L2*, 393.
47. The other winner was Alan Brownjohn. The poem appeared in "Poetry 1960: An Appetiser," *Critical Quarterly* Poetry Supplement 1 (1960): 20.
48. EF interview with Brian Cox, Oct. 1999. EFP.
49. SP to AP, 16 Jan. (#1) 1960. *L2*, 385.
50. SP to AP and WP, 2 Feb. 1960. *L2*, 402.
51. SP to AP and WP, 7–8 Feb. (#1) 1960. *L2*, 406.
52. SP to AP and WP, 2 Feb. 1960. *L2*, 403. Vivette and Jonathan Glover, who now own the building, remembered Mrs. Morton fondly. They said Plath's description of her flat was wonderfully accurate. HC interview with the Glovers, June 2017, London.
53. TH to Olwyn Hughes, Oct. 1960. Add MS 88948/1/2, BL.

54. TH to Anne Stevenson, autumn 1986. *LTH*, 521.
55. Harriet Rosenstein interview with W. S. Merwin, 1974. 2.21, MSS 1489, Emory.
56. James Michie to SP, 5 Feb. 1960. 17.49, SPC, Smith.
57. TH to Olwyn Hughes, mid-Feb. 1960. Add MS 88948/1/2, BL.
58. SP to AP, 11 Feb. 1960. *L2*, 414–15.
59. Ibid., *L2*, 415.
60. TH to Olwyn Hughes, mid-Feb. 1960. Add MS 88948/1/2, BL.
61. SP to AP, 25–26 Feb. 1960. *L2*, 428.
62. TH, notebook entry, c. Mar. 1960. Add MS 88918/129/2.
63. SP to AP, 25–26 Feb. 1960. *L2*, 428.
64. Catalog, Bonham's auction, 21 Mar. 2018, p. 23.
65. SP to AP, 25–26 Feb. 1960. *L2*, 429.
66. Harriet Rosenstein interview with W. S. Merwin, 1974. 2.11, MSS 1489, Emory.
67. SP to AP, 25–26 Feb. 1960. *L2*, 429–30.
68. SP to Marcia Brown Plumer, 1 Apr. 1960. *L2*, 448.
69. SP to AP, 17 Mar. 1960. *L2*, 438.
70. Anne Stevenson, *Bitter Fame: A Life of Sylvia Plath* (London: Penguin, 1989; 1998), 185.
71. HC interview with Daniel Huws, May 2016, London.
72. Huws, *Memories of Ted Hughes*, 49.
73. SP to AP, 10 Mar. 1960. *L2*, 433.
74. SP to Olwyn Hughes, 2 Apr. 1960. *L2*, 449.
75. SP to AP, 17 Mar. 1960. *L2*, 437.
76. SP to AP, 26–28 Mar. 1060. *L2*, 444. SP's ellipsis.
77. "Poet from the Pennines," *Daily Telegraph* (14 Apr. 1960).
78. Pendennis, "Frogs and Springboks: Ted 'n' Thom," *Observer* (27 Mar. 1960), 9.
79. SP to AP, 26–28 Mar. 1960. *L2*, 444. SP's ellipsis.
80. SP to AP, 24 Mar. 1960. *L2*, 441.
81. TH to Olwyn Hughes, late Mar. 1960. Add MS 88948/1/2, BL.
82. SP to AP, 24 Mar. 1960. *L2*, 440.
83. SP to AP, 26–28 Mar. 1960. *L2*, 443.
84. SP to AP and WP, 31 Mar.–1 Apr. 1960. *L2*, 444–45.
85. TH, notebook entry, 29 Mar. 1960. Add MS 88918/129/2, BL.
86. SP to Dr. Ruth Beuscher, 2 Apr. 1960. *L2*, 450.
87. SP to AP and WP, 31 Mar.–1 Apr. 1960. *L2*, 446.
88. SP to Olwyn Hughes, 2 Apr. 1960. *L2*, 449.
89. SP to Marcia Brown Plumer, 1 Apr. 1960. *L2*, 448; SP to AP and WP, 31 Mar.–1 Apr. 1960. *L2*, 446.
90. SP to AP and WP, 31 Mar.–1 Apr. 1960. *L2*, 446.
91. SP to Lynne Lawner, 30 Sept. 1960. *L2*, 520.
92. TH to Olwyn Hughes, n.d., mid-Feb. 1960. Add MS 88948/1/2, BL.
93. SP to Marcia Brown Plumer, 1 Apr. 1960. *L2*, 448.
94. SP to Dr. Ruth Beuscher, 2 Apr. 1960. *L2*, 451.
95. SP to Lynne Lawner, 30 Sept. 1960. *L2*, 519–20.
96. SP to Dr. Ruth Beuscher, 2 Apr. 1960. *L2*, 451.
97. SP to Gerald and Joan Hughes, 7 Apr. 1960. *L2*, 457.
98. SP and TH to AP, 7 Apr. 1960. *L2*, 455–56.
99. Ibid., *L2*, 455.
100. Ibid., *L2*, 456.
101. SP and TH to AP, 4 Apr. 1960. *L2*, 453.
102. SP and TH to AP, 4 Apr. 1960. Lilly. This portion of this letter is unpublished.
103. SP and TH to AP, 7 Apr. 1960. Lilly. This portion of this letter is unpublished.
104. SP to AP and WP, 31 Mar.–1 Apr. 1960. *L2*, 445.
105. SP to AP, 15 Apr. 1960. *L2*, 459.
106. SP to AP, 21 Apr. 1960. *L2*, 461.
107. Ibid., *L2*, 462.

108. SP to AP, 19 July 1960. *L2*, 496.
109. SP to AP, 25–26 Feb. 1960. *L2*, 429.
110. Stevenson, *Bitter Fame*, 192.
111. EF interview with Peter Redgrove, Sept. 1999. EFP.
112. SP to AP, 15 Apr. 1960. *L2*, 459–60.
113. TH and SP to Olwyn Hughes, c. 16 May 1960. *L2*, 473.
114. SP to AP, 28 Sept. 1960. *L2*, 515.
115. Janet published her first short story in *Seventeen*, and her first poem in *The Atlantic* in 1957.
116. Janet Burroway, *Embalming Mom: Essays in Life* (Iowa City: University of Iowa Press, 2002), 12.
117. SP to Janet Burroway, 3 May 1960. *L2*, 467.
118. Burroway, *Embalming Mom*, 13.
119. Ibid., 15.
120. Janet Burroway to A. C. H. Smith, May 1960, quoted in A. C. H. Smith, *WordSmith: A Memoir* (Bristol, UK: Redcliffe Press, 2012), 86.
121. Janet Burroway to her parents, 10 May 1960. Courtesy of Janet Burroway.
122. Burroway, *Embalming Mom*, 16.
123. Janet Burroway email to HC, 30 Oct. 2015.
124. SP to Lynne Lawner, 30 Sept. 1960. *L2*, 521.
125. Janet Burroway email to HC, 20 Oct. 2015.
126. Burroway, *Embalming Mom*, 17.
127. Ibid., 7.
128. Will Wooten, *The Alvarez Generation: Thom Gunn, Geoffrey Hill, Ted Hughes, Sylvia Plath and Peter Porter* (Liverpool: Liverpool University Press, 2015), 3.
129. Hall would produce poetry pamphlets, published by the Oxford-based Fantasy Press, by Al Alvarez, Geoffrey Hill, Adrienne Rich, Anthony Thwaite, and Thom Gunn in 1953.
130. HC interview with Al Alvarez, May 2016, London. Plath was, Alvarez thought, as good as Keats and Yeats. "Ted was very brilliant in the beginning, but I think he just went off. But Sylvia just went on getting better."
131. A. Alvarez, "Poetry Chronicle," *Partisan Review* 25.4 (1958): 603–609. 604.
132. A. Alvarez, "English Poetry Today," *Commentary* 32.3 (Sept. 1961): 217–223. 221–22.
133. A. Alvarez, *Where Did It All Go Right?* (London: Richard Cohen Books, 1999), 178.
134. Ibid., 183.
135. HC interview with Al Alvarez, May 2016, London.
136. See A. Alvarez, "Something New in Verse," *Observer* (12 Apr. 1959).
137. HC interview with Al Alvarez, May 2016, London.
138. Group poets like Edward Lucie-Smith and Peter Porter would write to *The Spectator* that May, "Mr. Lowell has burst out of the prison of an impressive but highly artificial style and has achieved a kind of fresh, immediate language which appears too rarely in current verse." Edward Lucie-Smith and Peter Porter, letter to *The Spectator*, no. 7829 (15 May 1959): 702.
139. *Words in Air: The Complete Correspondence Between Elizabeth Bishop and Robert Lowell*, Thomas Travisano and Saskia Hamilton, eds. (New York: Farrar, Straus and Giroux, 2008), 299.
140. Lowell told Elizabeth Bishop to call on Alvarez, "my friend," when she was traveling to England in 1964. Ibid., 527.
141. HC interview with Al Alvarez, May 2016, London.
142. Edward Lucie-Smith, "Foreword," *A Group Anthology*, Edward Lucie-Smith and Philip Hobsbaum, eds. (London and New York: Oxford University Press, 1963), v–ix. v.
143. Alvarez, *Where Did It All Go Right?*, 188.
144. A. Alvarez, "An Outstanding Young Poet," *Observer* (27 Mar. 1960), 22.
145. A. Alvarez, "Books of the Year," *Observer* (18 Dec. 1960), 22.
146. Alvarez, *Where Did It All Go Right?*, 198.
147. Ibid., 201.

148. A. Alvarez, *The Savage God: A Study of Suicide* (London: Weidenfeld & Nicolson, 1971; New York: W. W. Norton, 1990), 22; 25.
149. SP to AP, 5 May 1960. *L2*, 468.
150. Ibid., *L2*, 469.
151. TH to John Fisher and family, 31 July 1960. *LTH*, 167.
152. TH to Olwyn Hughes, spring 1960. 1.9, MSS 980, Emory.
153. SP to AP, 5 May 1960. *L2*, 469. Second ellipsis is SP's.
154. TH to Olwyn Hughes, summer 1960. *LTH*, 166.
155. TH to Lucas Myers, early 1960. *LTH*, 157. The "sad circle" comprised other contemporary poets such as George Barker and John Heath-Stubbs.
156. SP to AP, 11 May 1960. *L2*, 472.
157. SP to AP, 21 May 1960. *L2*, 476.
158. Harriet Rosenstein interview with Jane and Peter Davison, 1973. 1.22, MSS 1489, Emory.
159. SP to AP, 5 May 1960. *L2*, 468.
160. SP to AP, 30 May 1960. *L2*, 477–78.
161. Edith Hughes to AP, 11 June 1960. Lilly.
162. SP to AP, 11 June 1960. *L2*, 482.
163. SP to AP, 9 July 1960. *L2*, 494.
164. Ibid., *L2*, 493. In a 9 July letter, Sylvia told Aurelia that Ted had "scrapped" his earlier play, *The House of Taurus*, which had an "antiquated social message."
165. SP to AP, 9 July 1960. *L2*, 494.
166. They included an explanation of an anthology of animal poems, a talk about his poem "Otter," readings of a poem about Frieda, and "The Rain Horse."
167. Throughout this time Plath sent checks (which she received for acceptances) home for her mother to deposit in their Wellesley bank account.
168. SP to AP, 21 May 1960. *L2*, 476.
169. SP to AP, 30 June 1960. Lilly.
170. SP to AP, 24 June 1960. *L2*, 484.
171. Ibid.
172. SP to Bill and Dido Merwin, 24 June 1960. *L2*, 486.
173. SP to Dr. Ruth Beuscher, 7 Nov. 1960. *L2*, 539.
174. HC interview with Ruth Fainlight, May 2016, London.
175. Ibid.
176. TH, notebook entry, 23 June 1960. Add MS 88918/129/2, BL.
177. TH, notebook entry, 7 Jan. 1965. Add MS 88918/129/3, BL.
178. SP to AP, 9 July 1960. *L2*, 492.
179. Philip Day, "A Pride of Poets," *Sunday Times* (26 June 1960). Plath confirmed in her 7 Nov. 1960 letter to Dr. Ruth Beuscher that the quote was hers.
180. SP to AP, 24 June 1960. *L2*, 485.
181. Jessica Mann, *The Fifties Mystique* (London: Perseus, 2012), 176.
182. SP to AP, 16–17 Aug. 1960. *L2*, 503.
183. The editor was probably Thomas Cranfill, who bought Plath's "Flute Notes from a Reedy Pond" and "Witch Burning," and Hughes's "The Caning," "Lines to a Newborn Baby," "Miss Mabrett and the Wet Cellar," "The Captain's Speech," and "The Gibbons." See *L2*, 502, for publication dates.
184. The others were "The Manor Garden," "The Beggars," and "Blue Moles" in *Critical Quarterly* 2 (Summer 1960), and "Metaphors for a Pregnant Woman" in *Partisan Review* (Summer 1960).
185. SP to AP, 16 Aug. 1960. *L2*, 503. Plath likely wrote all three poems in early July. "On Deck" appeared in *The New Yorker* on 22 July 1961; "Two Campers in Cloud Country" appeared in *The New Yorker* on 3 Aug. 1963.
186. K. L. Wisner, B. L. Parry, and C. M. Piontek, "Postpartum Depression," *New England Journal of Medicine* 347.3 (2002): 194–99.
187. HC interview with Lorna Secker-Walker, June 2017, London.
188. SP to AP, 19 July, 16–17 Aug., & 13 Sept. 1960. *L2*, 495; 503; 509.
189. SP to AP, 27 Aug. 1960. *L2*, 505.

190. TH to AP and WP, 22 Aug. 1960. *LTH*, 169. He wanted to buy Plath a three-volume edition of Dickinson's poems for her birthday and told Aurelia he would reimburse her if she sent the book from America. (Plath never mentioned receiving it.)
191. SP to AP, 19 July 1960. *L2*, 495.
192. SP to AP, 9 July 1960. *L2*, 493.
193. SP to AP, 2 Aug. 1960. *L2*, 499.
194. SP to AP, 31 Aug. 1960. *L2*, 508.
195. TH to Olwyn Hughes, Aug. 1960. Add MS 88948/1/2, BL.
196. TH to AP and WP, 22 Aug. 1960. *LTH*, 168–69.
197. TH to Olwyn Hughes, Aug. 1960. Add MS 88948/1/2, BL.
198. SP to AP, 27 Aug. 1960. *L2*, 504–505.
199. SP to AP, 31 Aug. 1960. *L2*, 506.
200. SP to AP, 27 Aug. 1960. *L2*, 504.
201. SP to AP, 31 Aug. 1960. *L2*, 507.
202. SP to AP, 14 Dec. 1960. *L2*, 551.
203. Stanley Kunitz, "The New Books," *Harper's* (Sept. 1960): 96–103; Hughes's photograph appeared in "Signs of an All Too Correct Compassion," *Times Literary Supplement* (9 Sept. 1960), xiii.
204. "Ouija," "Electra on Azalea Path," "Suicide Off Egg Rock," and "Moonrise" appeared in *The Hudson Review* (Autumn 1960); "The Fifteen-Dollar Eagle" in *The Sewanee Review* (Autumn 1960); "Flute Notes from a Reedy Pond" in *Texas Quarterly* (Winter 1960); and "Candles" in *The Listener* (17 Nov. 1960).
205. Probably Charles Monteith, James Michie, and George MacBeth.
206. SP to AP, 28 Sept. 1960. *L2*, 516.
207. SP to AP, 28 Nov. 1960. *L2*, 546–47.
208. SP to Dorothy and Joseph Benotti and Frank Schober, 19 Nov. 1960. *L2*, 544.
209. SP to AP, 19 Nov. 1960. *L2*, 543.
210. SP to AP, 16 Sept. 1960. *L2*, 512.
211. TH to Olwyn Hughes, late Oct. 1960. Add MS 88948/1/2, BL.
212. Lucas Myers, "The Tranquilized Fifties," *Sewanee Review* (Jan.–Mar. 1962): 212–13; 216.
213. SP to Lynne Lawner, 30 Sept. 1960. *L2*, 519.
214. Plath told Mrs. Prouty she dedicated "Candles" to her.
215. Hughes mocked the Three Wise Men on the Christmas card they sent to Ann and Leo Goodman that year, writing of their "prim public relations smiles" "adapted . . . to American tastes." SP and TH to Ann and Leo Goodman, 17 Dec. 1960. *L2*, 552.
216. SP to AP, 26 Oct. 1960. *L2*, 531.
217. SP to AP, 28 Sept. 1960. *L2*, 516.
218. SP to Ann Davidow-Goodman, 9 Oct. 1960. *L2*, 524.
219. Plath mss, 1958–61, Lilly. The poem is typed on the back of SP's "Wuthering Heights." It was rejected by *The New Yorker* and *The Atlantic* in 1960.
220. TH to Olwyn Hughes, from Dordogne, summer 1961. 1.9, MSS 980, Emory.
221. The show, *John Betjeman as the Book Man*, aired on 20 Nov. 1960.
222. SP to Dr. Ruth Beuscher, 7 Nov. 1960. *L2*, 538.
223. SP to AP and WP, 24 Dec. 1960. *L2*, 555.
224. SP to Lynne Lawner, 30 Sept. 1960. *L2*, 521.
225. TH to AP and WP, early Dec. 1960. *LTH*, 171.
226. Roy Fuller, review of *The Colossus*, *The London Magazine* (Mar. 1961): 69–70.
227. Richard Howard, review of *The Colossus*, *Poetry* (Mar. 1963): 412–13. See Peter Steinberg's online bibliography at http://www.sylviaplath.info/worksreviews.html#the colossus for a full list of Plath's reviews.
228. See SP to AP and WP, 24 Dec. 1960. *L2*, 555.
229. SP to AP and WP, 19 Nov. 1960. *L2*, 541.
230. TH to David Machin, 4 Mar. 1964. 1.23, MSS 980, Emory. Hughes complained to Machin, James Michie's successor at Heinemann, that when the book had been published in 1960, friends told him it "'wasn't in the shops.'" In late 1963, Hughes told

Machin, "I asked five of my friends to try and buy me a copy. They could not find <u>one</u>, even in the main London bookshops."

231. SP to AP and WP, 19 Nov. 1960. *L2*, 541.
232. SP to AP, 28 Oct. 1960. *L2*, 534.
233. TH to Olwyn Hughes, late Oct. 1960. Add MS 88948/1/2, BL.
234. SP to Olwyn Hughes, 27 Oct. 1960. *L2*, 533. Plath added her note at the end of Hughes's letter to Olwyn.
235. SP to AP, 26 Oct. 1960. *L2*, 531.
236. *J*, 596–99.
237. Alvarez, Geoffrey Hill, David Wevill, George MacBeth, and Peter Redgrove would all divorce. Wooten, *Alvarez Generation*, 66.
238. SP to Dr. Ruth Beuscher, 7 Nov. 1962. *L2*, 539.
239. *J*, 596–99.
240. TH to AP and WP, Dec. 1960. *LTH*, 172.
241. SP to Olwyn Hughes, 28 Nov. 1960. *L2*, 549; SP to AP and WP, 24 Dec. 1960. *L2*, 554.
242. SP to AP, 14 Dec. 1960. *L2*, 551.
243. TH and SP to Olwyn Hughes, 28 Nov. 1960. Add MS 88948/1/2, BL.
244. TH and SP to Olwyn Hughes, 28 Nov. 1960. *L2*, 549. Hughes's portion of the letter is not transcribed in *L2*.
245. Plath's reading of "A Winter Ship" and seven lines from "The Colossus" were also included in the program. Plath liked her poem "A Winter Ship" enough to have it privately printed on thick, expensive paper, and included in her Christmas cards that year.
246. A. Alvarez, "The Poet and the Poetess," *Observer* (18 Dec. 1960), 21.
247. Harriet Rosenstein interview with Richard Murphy, 1974. 2.25, MSS 1489, Emory.
248. SP to AP and WP, 24 Dec. 1960. *L2*, 555.
249. A. Alvarez, "Books of the Year," *Observer* (18 Dec. 1960), 22.
250. SP to AP and WP, 24 Dec. 1960. *L2*, 555.

24. NOBODY CAN TELL WHAT I LACK

1. SP to AP and WP, 14 Dec. 1960. *L2*, 551.
2. SP and TH to Philip Booth, c. 17 Dec. 1960. *L2*, 553.
3. SP to Dr. Ruth Beuscher, 4 Jan. 1961. *L2*, 562. Evidence in Hughes's notebook journal from the period suggests the row occurred on Dec. 30.
4. SP to AP, 1 Jan. 1961. *L2*, 558.
5. SP to Dr. Ruth Beuscher, 4 Jan. 1961. *L2*, 563–65. Second ellipsis in quoted letter is SP's.
6. Ibid., *L2*, 567.
7. Ibid., *L2*, 565–67.
8. The first two quotes come from Olwyn Hughes to Clarissa Roche, 24 Mar. 1986, William Sigmund Papers, Smith; the third quote comes from Olwyn Hughes to Harriet Rosenstein, 21 June 1976, 2.6, MSS 1489, Emory; the fourth comes from Anon., "Olwyn Hughes: Grande Dame, Under Siege," *Camden Scallywag* (May 1992), 24–25.
9. Jonathan Bate, "Olwyn Hughes obituary," *Guardian* (5 Jan. 2016).
10. See SP to Olwyn Hughes, 20 Nov. 1961, for example. *L2*, 688–90.
11. Olwyn Hughes to Harriet Rosenstein, 21 June 1976. 2.6. MSS 1489, Emory.
12. SP to AP, 10 Jan. 1961. *L2*, 568.
13. TH, notebook entry, 3 Jan. 1961. Add MS 88918/128/1, BL.
14. TH to Olwyn Hughes, 10 Jan. 1961. Add MS 88948/1/2, BL.
15. TH to Lucas Myers, Jan. 1961. *LTH*, 178–79.
16. SP to AP, 10 Jan. 1961. *L2*, 568.
17. Plath had by this time published several poems in the magazine, which Cox and Dyson founded in 1959.
18. SP to AP, 27 Jan. 1961. *L2*, 571.
19. SP to AP, 10 Jan. 1961. *L2*, 569.

20. M. L. Rosenthal, "Poetry as Confession," *The Nation* (19 Sept. 1959).
21. Harriet Rosenstein interview with M. L. Rosenthal, 1971–73. 4.5, MSS 1489, Emory.
22. SP to AP, 10 Jan. 1961. *L2*, 569.
23. SP to AP, 2 Feb. 1961. *L2*, 574.
24. Ibid., *L2*, 575. Hughes had also been offered a six-week summer job teaching at Clark University in Worcester, Mass.
25. See SP to Elizabeth Kray, 26 Apr. 1961. *L2*, 612.
26. The recording, which I have transcribed from the original, is held at the National Sound Archive, BL, and is available on *The Spoken Word: Sylvia Plath*. British Library/National Sound Archives/BBC Audio Compilation (2010).
27. Quoted in Peter K. Steinberg and Gail Crowther, "These Ghostly Archives," *Plath Profiles* 2 (Summer 2009): 183–208. 196.
28. George MacBeth to Anthony Thwaite, n.d., July 1960. BBC Written Archives. Plath had sent him poems on 9 July 1960; he replied on 23 July 1960. Quoted in ibid.
29. TH to William Scammell, 28 Apr. 1998. Add MS 88918/137, BL.
30. TH interview with Drue Heinz, "The Art of Poetry, LXXI," *Paris Review* 134 (1995), in *Paris Review Interviews*, vol. 3 (London: Picador, 2008), 56–92. 76.
31. SP and TH to Philip and Margaret Booth, 29 Mar. 1961. *L2*, 596.
32. SP to Anne Sexton, 5 Feb. 1961. *L2*, 575–76. "Elegy in the Classroom," which famously described Lowell as "gracefully insane," a "boily creature" with "fat blind eyes," could have been another Sexton influence on "Daddy," which locates Otto, likewise transformed into a "ghastly" "brute," before a blackboard.
33. SP to AP, 27 Jan. 1961. *L2*, 572.
34. SP to AP, 6 Feb. 1961. *L2*, 577.
35. The series, *Listening and Writing*, was broadcast in ten talks between October 1961 and May 1964. Nine of the talks would eventually be published in *Poetry in the Making*, which Jonathan Bate called "a classroom *vade mecum* for a generation and indeed one of Hughes's bestselling books." *Ted Hughes: The Unauthorised Life* (New York: Harper-Collins, 2015), 37.
36. Frances McCullough, notes on visit with Ted and Carol Hughes, Devon, c. 7 July 1974. 6.35, Francis McCullough Papers, Hornbake Library, University of Maryland.
37. Bate, *Ted Hughes*, 37.
38. Ibid.
39. National Sound Archive, BL.
40. SP to Bill and Dido Merwin, 24 June 1960. *L2*, 486.
41. SP to Dr. Ruth Beuscher, 22 Sept. 1962. *L2*, 830.
42. SP to AP, 6 Feb. 1961, *L2*, 577.
43. AP to WP, 17 July 1962. Lilly.
44. Harriet Rosenstein interview with Paul Roche, 1973. 3.14, MSS 1489, Emory.
45. Susan Fromberg Schaeffer, *Poison* (New York: W. W. Norton, 2006), 174.
46. Olwyn Hughes to Neil Schaeffer, 7 Sept. 2006. 33.15, Susan Fromberg Schaeffer Papers, Boston University.
47. Olwyn Hughes to Neil Schaeffer, 6 July 2006. 33.16, Susan Fromberg Schaeffer Papers, Boston University.
48. Ibid.; Olwyn Hughes to Neil Schaeffer, 7 Sept. 2006. 33.15, Susan Fromberg Schaeffer Papers, Boston University.
49. This source wishes to remain anonymous. HC interview, 2016.
50. *CPTH*, 1120. The drafts of "The Minotaur" are in Add MS 88918/1/2-8, BL.
51. Frances McCullough, notes on visit with Ted and Carol Hughes, Devon, c. 7 July 1974. 6.35 Frances McCullough Papers, Hornbake Library, University of Maryland.
52. *CPTH*, 1120.
53. Frieda Hughes, "Foreword." *L2*, xxi.
54. SP to Dr. Ruth Beuscher, 11 July 1962. *L2*, 792.
55. HC interview with Suzette Macedo, May 2016, London.
56. Hughes misdates the composition to 1960 in *JP*.
57. *JP*, 185–98.
58. SP to AP, 25 Oct. 1962. *L2*, 888.

59. Luke Ferreter, *Sylvia Plath's Fiction: A Critical Study* (Edinburgh: Edinburgh University Press), 157.
60. HC interview with Ruth Fainlight, May 2016, London.
61. *The Spoken Word: Sylvia Plath*. British Library/National Sound Archives/BBC Audio Compilation (2010).
62. SP to AP, 2 Feb. 1961. *L2*, 574.
63. SP to Bill and Dido Merwin, 7 Mar. 1961. *L2*, 588.
64. SP to AP, 26 Feb. 1961. *L2*, 581.
65. SP to Bill and Dido Merwin, 7 Mar. 1961. *L2*, 588.
66. SP to AP, 1 Mar. 1961. *L2*, 588; SP to Bill and Dido Merwin, 7 Mar. 1961. *L2*, 583.
67. SP to Bill and Dido Merwin, 7 Mar 1961. *L2*, 584.
68. *J*, 602.
69. Howard Moss to SP, 24 Feb. 1961. 17.38, SPC, Smith. The contract also included a cost-of-living adjustment that amounted to "an additional 35% per year." The 25 percent bonus would be "a <u>minimum</u> of $1.90 a line."
70. SP to Bill and Dido Merwin, 7 Mar. 1961. *L2*, 588.
71. "They happen to be two of my best friends and if I didn't think very highly of them indeed I wouldn't be meddling this way. The point is that they're in financial straits (I assume you know they're married, of course you must) and if you had considered, by any chance, offering either of them a first reading contract I know they could use the hundred dollars." Bill Merwin to Howard Moss, 19 Feb. 1961. *New Yorker* Records, NYPL.
72. SP to AP, 6 Mar. 1961. *L2*, 584–85.
73. *J*, 601.
74. *J*, 603.
75. *J*, 604–605.
76. *J*, 601.
77. *J*, 605.
78. SP to AP, 17 Mar. 1961. *L2*, 590–91.
79. TH to AP and WP, 22 Apr. 1961. *LTH*, 182.
80. SP to AP, 17 Mar. 1961. *L2*, 590.
81. *J*, 604.
82. *J*, 599.
83. *J*, 602.
84. *J*, 606.
85. TH to AP and WP, 22 Apr. 1961. *LTH*, 182.
86. See note in *LTH*, 183.
87. Anne Stevenson, *Bitter Fame: A Life of Sylvia Plath* (London: Penguin, 1989; 1998), 210.
88. Bate, *Ted Hughes*, 172.
89. AP to OHP, 18 Apr. 1962. Lilly.

25. THE MOMENT OF THE FULCRUM

1. SP and TH to Philip and Margaret Booth, 29 Mar. 1961. *L2*, 595.
2. SP to AP, 17 Mar. 1961. *L2*, 590.
3. SP to AP, 27 Mar. 1961. *L2*, 592.
4. SP to Philip and Margaret Booth, 29 Mar. 1961. *L2*, 595.
5. SP to AP, 5 Apr. 1961. *L2*, 600.
6. SP to Dorothy Benotti, 29 Mar. 1961. *L2*, 597.
7. SP to AP, 5 Apr. 1961. *L2*, 599. Steinberg and Kukil write in a footnote that there is a contract at the BBC Written Archives Centre for the program dated 4 Apr. 1961, with Plath's name crossed out, and that no known recording exists.
8. "Last Lines," "Sugar Loaf," "Gog," "Wino," "Flanders, 1960," and "Toll of Air Raids" appeared on p. 31.
9. The show, *Wednesday Magazine*, directed by Richard Francis, was broadcast on BBC Television on 19 Apr. 1961.

10. SP to AP, 22 Apr. 1961. *L2*, 609.
11. SP to Dr. Ruth Beuscher, 7 Nov. 1960. *L2*, 538–39.
12. SP to AP, 22 Apr. 1961. *L2*, 609–10.
13. TH to AP and WP, 22 Apr. 1961. *LTH*, 183. Plath wrote to Aurelia about the commission in a letter on 5 Apr. 1961.
14. SP to AP, 5 Apr. 1961. *L2*, 600.
15. Peter Davison to SP and TH, 4 Dec. 1961. 59.23, MS 644, Emory.
16. TH to AP and WP, 22 Apr. 1961. *LTH*, 183.
17. James Michie to SP, Mar. 1961. 17.34, SPC, Smith.
18. SP and TH to Philip and Margaret Booth, 29 Mar. 1961. *L2*, 596.
19. SP to Judith Jones, 5 Apr. 1961. *L2*, 601–602.
20. TH, "Sylvia Plath and Her Journals," *Winter Pollen: Occasional Prose*, William Scammell, ed. (London: Picador, 1994), 183–84.
21. Judith Jones to SP, 29 Mar. 1961. 17.20, SPC, Smith. In addition to "Who," "Maenad," "The Beast," and "Witch Burning," Plath had wanted to omit "Point Shirley," but Jones convinced her to keep it in. Jones recommended removing "The Ghost's Leave-taking," but Plath negotiated to keep it and remove "Black Rook in Rainy Weather" instead. (Roy Fuller had singled out "The Ghost's Leavetaking" as exemplary in his *London Magazine* review of *The Colossus*.) The following poems, which appeared in the Heinemann edition, were excluded from the Knopf edition: "Metaphors," "Black Rook in Rainy Weather," "Maudlin," "Ouija," "Two Sisters of Persephone," "Who," "Dark House," "Maenad," "The Beast," and "Witch Burning."
22. Judith Jones to SP, 29 Mar. 1961. 17.20, SPC, Smith.
23. Jones mentioned the Lamont Poetry Prize in particular. Judith Jones to SP, 28 Apr. 1961. 17.20, SPC, Smith.
24. SP to Theodore Roethke, 13 Apr. 1961. *L2*, 602–603.
25. She also asked John Lehmann at *The London Magazine* for a reference.
26. SP to AP, 1 May 1961. *L2*, 615.
27. SP to Ann Davidow-Goodman, 27 Apr. 1961. *L2*, 614–15.
28. In his deposition in the *Bell Jar* lawsuit Hughes claimed, "She wrote her novel in March, between February or so. She began early in 1961, and she wrote it then, I suppose, two to four months. . . . She had her appendix out so she entered the hospital for a week or two weeks in the middle of writing THE BELL JAR. That was in late March 1961." Hughes misremembered the dates of Plath's hospital stay and may have misremembered the composition dates of *The Bell Jar*. TH, deposition (1987 *Bell Jar* trial). Jane Anderson v. AVCO Embassy Pictures Corp. et al., in the United States District Court, District of Massachusetts, Civil Action no. 82-0752-K. Jane V. Anderson Papers, Series IV, Smith.
29. Ibid.
30. TH, "Trial," section 23. Add MS 88993/1/1, BL.
31. A. Alvarez, "Beyond the Gentility Principle," *Observer* (19 Feb. 1961), 28.
32. *J*, 316.
33. SP to AP, 14 Apr. 1961. *L2*, 605; SP to AP, 22 Apr. 1961. *L2*, 608.
34. HC interview with Lorna Secker-Walker, June 2017, London.
35. Harriet Rosenstein interview with Catherine Frankfort, 1970. 1.27, MSS 1489, Emory.
36. HC interview with Lorna Secker-Walker, June 2017, London.
37. SP to AP, 14 Apr. 1961. *L2*, 606.
38. TH to AP and WP, 22 Apr. 1961. *LTH*, 183.
39. TH to Daniel and Helga Huws, July 1961. *LTH*, 184.
40. SP to AP, 8 May 1961. *L2*, 619.
41. SP to AP and WP, 6 June 1961. *L2*, 622–24. Hughes won £100.
42. Ruth Fainlight, "Jane and Sylvia," *Crossroads* (Spring 2004): 8–19. 9.
43. HC interview with Ruth Fainlight, May 2016, London.
44. Ibid.
45. See Katy Evans Bush, "The Poet Realized: An Interview with Ruth Fainlight," *Contemporary Poetry Review*, http://www.cprw.com/Bush/fainlight.htm.
46. HC interview with Ruth Fainlight, May 2016, London.

47. Fainlight, "Jane and Sylvia," 12.
48. HC interview with Ruth Fainlight, May 2016, London.
49. Fainlight, "Jane and Sylvia," 9.
50. Ibid., 12.
51. HC interview with Suzette and Helder Macedo, May 2016, London.
52. Ibid.
53. Ibid.
54. EF interview with Suzette Macedo, Oct. 1999. EFP.
55. HC interview with Suzette and Helder Macedo, May 2016, London.
56. Conversation with Michael Frayn, 24 Sept. 2018, Manhattan.
57. J. D. Salinger's *The Catcher in the Rye*, Shirley Jackson's *The Bird's Nest*, and A. E. Ellis's *The Rack*, which Hughes remembered Plath reading in early 1960, were also influences.
58. Erich Fromm, *The Sane Society* (1955; New York: Holt, 1990), 19; 18; 6.
59. Suzette Macedo email to HC, 20 May 2016.
60. HC interview with Ruth Fainlight, May 2016, London.
61. Ibid.
62. HC interview with Suzette and Helder Macedo, May 2016, London.
63. Most of the images were taken from the 6 June 1960 issue of *Life*, some from the 4 June and 7 May issues of *The New Yorker*.
64. Robin Peel, *Writing Back: Sylvia Plath and Cold War Politics* (Vancouver: Fairleigh Dickinson Press, 2002), 59. See *Writing Back* for an extended discussion of this collage.
65. *BJ*, 80.
66. For example, David Holbrook, quoted in Peel, *Writing Back*, 55.
67. There are three incomplete drafts of the novel in Box 4, SPC, Smith. The draft in Folder 2 is forty-three pages; the draft in Folder 3 is eighty-nine pages; the draft in Folder 4 is seventeen pages. The later draft is in Folders 5–24.
68. SP to Brian Cox, 17 June 1961. *L2*, 625.
69. See Peter K. Steinberg, "'What's Been Happening in a Lot of American Poetry': Sylvia Plath as Editor and Reviewer," in Gail Crowther and Peter K. Steinberg, *These Ghostly Archives: The Unearthing of Sylvia Plath* (Croydon, UK: Fonthill, 2017), 126–43, for a detailed exploration of this assignment.
70. They wrote of the "notable American emphasis" in their *Critical Quarterly Supplement* in 1964. Fran Baker, presentation on Plath and *Critical Quarterly*, Manchester University, "Archival Afterlives" conference, 28 June 2017.
71. "Private Ground" and "I Am Vertical" appeared in *Critical Quarterly* 3 (Summer 1961). "Zoo Keeper's Wife," "You're," "Small Hours" ("Barren Woman"), "Parliament Hill Fields," "Whitsun," and "Leaving Early" appeared in *The London Magazine* (Aug. 1961).
72. Plath said he was uninvited, yet she wrote to him on 26 Apr. 1961, "Ted and I await your arrival—at any time of the day or night and for one meal or a dozen—with great joy." *L2*, 613.
73. SP to AP, 28 May 1961. *L2*, 621.
74. Harriet Rosenstein interview with Leonard Baskin, 1971. 1.7, MSS 1489, Emory.
75. Leonard Baskin to TH, 28 June 1961. *LTH*, 186–87.
76. TH to Leonard Baskin, Aug. 1961. *LTH*, 186–87.
77. SP to AP, 16 Apr. 1962. *L2*, 758.
78. SP to Leonard Baskin, 16 Apr. 1962. *L2*, 760.
79. SP to AP, 6 June 1961. *L2*, 623.
80. Harriet Rosenstein interview with Anthony Thwaite, 1973. 4.17, MSS 1489, Emory.
81. Sylvia Plath, *The Living Poet*. BBC Third Programme. Recorded on 5 June 1961; broadcast on 8 July 1961. *The Spoken Word: Sylvia Plath*, British Library/National Sound Archives/BBC Audio Compilation (2010).
82. SP to WP, 27 June 1961. *L2*, 627.
83. SP and TH to Bill and Dido Merwin, 30 July 1961. *L2*, 632.
84. SP to WP, 27 June 1961. *L2*, 628.
85. SP to AP, 6 & 10 July 1961. *L2*, 630–31.
86. Anne Stevenson, *Bitter Fame: A Life of Sylvia Plath* (London: Penguin, 1989; 1998), 339.

87. Her brother-in-law had been put to death during the Spanish Civil War.
88. SP to AP, 10 July 1961. *L2*, 631.
89. Frances McCullough, notes on visit with Ted and Carol Hughes, Devon, c. 7 July 1974. 6.35, Francis McCullough Papers, Hornbake Library, University of Maryland.
90. TH to Daniel and Helga Huws, July 1961. *LTH*, 184.
91. TH and SP to Bill and Dido Merwin, 30 July 1961. *L2*, 632. Hughes's portion of the letter is not transcribed. Original held at the Morgan Library.
92. "Live Poetry Reading at the Mermaid Theatre, London," Recorded on 17 July 1961. *The Spoken Word: Sylvia Plath*. British Library/National Sound Archives/BBC Audio Compilation (2010).
93. Jack Sweeney to Stephen and Agatha Fassett, 27 July 1961. 1.1, MS Am 3133, Houghton Library, Harvard.
94. SP to Jack Sweeney, 22 Aug. 1961. *L2*, 638.
95. Stevenson, *Bitter Fame*, 348.
96. TH to Daniel and Helga Huws. *LTH*, 184.
97. Steve Ely, *Ted Hughes's South Yorkshire: Made in Mexborough* (Basingstoke: Palgrave Macmillan, 2015), 143; Edith Hughes to AP, 30 Aug. 1961. Lilly. In this letter, Edith quotes from an article about Hughes's speech in the local newspaper.
98. Edith Hughes to AP, 30 Aug. 1961. Lilly. Ely, *Ted Hughes's South Yorkshire*, 143.
99. Ely, *Ted Hughes's South Yorkshire*, 143.
100. Ibid.
101. AP to WP and Margaret Wetzel, 21 July 1961. Lilly. AP's ellipsis.
102. Clarissa Roche, "Sylvia Plath: Vignettes from England," *Sylvia Plath: The Woman and the Work*, Edward Butscher, ed. (New York: Dodd, Mead and Co., 1977), 83.
103. TH to Anne Stevenson, autumn 1986. *LTH*, 519.
104. SP to Margaret Cantor, 30 Sept. 1961. *L2*, 654.
105. AP to WP, 30 July 1961. Lilly.
106. Sir Arundell, skeptical that a bank would take on two freelance writers, took their mortgage, which came to about half the price (about $4,500 after their down payment of $5,880).
107. AP to WP, 30 July 1961. Lilly.
108. Owen Leeming, *Two of a Kind: Poets in Partnership*. Interview with Sylvia Plath and Ted Hughes. BBC Third Programme, London. Recorded 18 Jan. 1961; broadcast 31 Jan. 1961. National Sound Archives, BL. *The Spoken Word: Sylvia Plath*. British Library/National Sound Archives/BBC Audio Compilation (2010).
109. SP to AP and WP, 25 Aug. 1961. *L2*, 640.
110. Elizabeth Sigmund and Gail Crowther, *Sylvia Plath in Devon: A Year's Turning* (Croydon, UK: Fonthill, 2014), 50.
111. SP to Jack Sweeney, 22 Aug. 1961. *L2*, 639.
112. SP to AP, 13 Aug. 1961. *L2*, 635.
113. In the end, the Maugham committee allowed him to keep the prize money.
114. *J*, 438.
115. SP to AP and WP, 13 Aug. 1961. *L2*, 636.
116. TH to Al Alvarez, late 1961. *LTH*, 190.
117. EF interview with Ruth Fainlight, Feb. 2000. EFP.
118. HC interview with Suzette Macedo, May 2016, London.
119. Harriet Rosenstein interview with Suzette and Helder Macedo, 1973. 2.18, MSS 1489, Emory.
120. Harriet Rosenstein interview with Anthony Thwaite, 1973. 4.17, MSS 1489, Emory.
121. SP to AP, 25 Aug. 1961. *L2*, 641.
122. TH to Olwyn Hughes, 26 Aug. 1961. 1.9, MSS 980, Emory.

26. THE LATE, GRIM HEART OF AUTUMN

1. TH to Olwyn Hughes, 26 Aug. 1961. 1.9, MSS 980, Emory.
2. SP to Helga Huws, 30 Oct. 1961. *L2*, 675.
3. SP to AP, 4 Sept. 1961. *L2*, 644.

4. Ibid., *L2*, 643–44.
5. TH, notebook entry, 11 Sept. 1961. Add MS 88918/128/1, BL.
6. SP to Howard Moss, 11 Sept. 1961. *L2*, 645.
7. SP to AP, 15 Sept. 1961. *L2*, 648. The plank is now at Smith.
8. Harriet Rosenstein interview with Nancy Axworthy, 1.5, MSS 1489, Emory.
9. SP to AP, 15 Sept. 1961. *L2*, 649. Later, Aurelia would highlight this passage, presumably suggesting that it was not the life her daughter wanted. She also underlined another seemingly offending passage in the next letter about Plath mowing the lawn. Plath told Marcia she paid Nancy a little over $2 for her week's work. SP to Marcia Brown Plumer, 7 Dec. 1961. *L2*, 693.
10. TH, "Notes on the Chronological Order of Sylvia Plath's Poems," *TriQuarterly* 7 (Fall 1966): 81–88. 86.
11. *JP*, 110–11.
12. *CPTH*, 1143–44.
13. SP to Margaret Cantor, 30 Sept. 1961. *L2*, 654.
14. SP to AP, 26–30 Oct. 1961. *L2*, 672.
15. SP to Peter Davison, 30 Sept. 1961. *L2*, 656.
16. See Peter K. Steinberg's blog post, "Sylvia Plath Collections: William Heinemann Ltd. Archives," 11 Feb. 2014, https://sylviaplathinfo.blogspot.com/2014/02/sylvia -plath-collections-william.html. The Plath contractual papers in the Heinemann collection are closed to researchers, but Steinberg was allowed limited access to this material when he was editing Plath's letters.
17. Peter K. Steinberg and Gail Crowther report the contents of the new proposed poetry collection, which appear on a torn piece of paper in Plath's Smith archive: "Magi," "Small Hours," "Morning Song," "Face Lift," "Parliament Hill Fields," "A Life," "Candles," "Sleep in the Mojave Desert," "The Hanging Man," "You're," "Tulips," "Widow," "Insomniac," and "The Rival." She added "The Surgeon at 2 a.m." and "The Moon and the Yew Tree." Gail Crowther and Peter K. Steinberg, *These Ghostly Archives: The Unearthing of Sylvia Plath* (Croydon, UK: Fonthill, 2017), 35–36.
18. Harriet Rosenstein interview with Suzette Macedo, 1972. 2.18, MSS 1489, Emory.
19. HC interview with Suzette and Helder Macedo, May 2016, London.
20. SP to Ruth Fainlight, 11 Sept. 1961. *L2*, 647.
21. SP to Helga Huws, 30 Oct. 1961. *L2*, 673–75.
22. SP to Judith Jones, 12 Dec. 1961. *L2*, 702.
23. SP to Howard Moss, 18 Dec. 1961. *L2*, 706.
24. SP to Kathleen and Marvin Kane, 22 June 1962. *L2*, 788.
25. Olwyn Hughes to Clarissa Roche, 25 Sept. 1987. William Sigmund Papers, Smith.
26. SP to AP, 13 Oct. 1961. *L2*, 666.
27. Sylvia Crawford had three daughters. SP to Helga Huws, 30 Oct. 1961. *L2*, 674.
28. SP to AP, 29 Dec. (#2) 1961. *L2*, 709.
29. SP to Helga Huws, 30 Oct. 1961. *L2*, 674.
30. SP to Marcia Brown Plumer, 7 Dec. 1961. *L2*, 693–94.
31. SP to Helga Huws, 30 Oct. 1961. *L2*, 674.
32. SP to Ruth Fainlight, 11 Sept. 1961. *L2*, 647.
33. Kenneth Neville-Davies email to HC, 24 Oct. 2016.
34. SP to Helga Huws, 30 Oct. 1961. *L2*, 674.
35. SP to AP, 22 Oct. 1961. *L2*, 669.
36. SP to Marcia Brown Plumer, 7 Dec. 1961. *L2*, 694.
37. SP to AP, 22 Oct. 1961. *L2*, 669.
38. SP to AP, 5 Nov. 1961. *L2*, 678.
39. One review usually comprised about ten books.
40. AP to SP, 26–30 Oct. 1961. *L2*, 672.
41. SP to AP, 5 Nov. 1961. *L2*, 677.
42. SP to Ruth Fainlight, 6 Oct. 1961. *L2*, 659.
43. See SP to AP, 5 Nov. 1961. *L2*, 676–78. Her poem had won the Guinness Poetry Competition first prize at the Cheltenham Festival of Art and Literature. The judges for this prize were Elizabeth Jennings, Laurie Lee, and Anthony Thwaite.

44. Plath sold 130 pages for $280.
45. SP to AP, 5 Nov. 1961. *L2*, 676.
46. SP to AP, 9 Nov. 1961. *L2*, 681.
47. Ibid., *L2*, 680–81.
48. SP to Gerald and Joan Hughes, 6 Dec. 1961. *L2*, 690.
49. SP to AP, 9 Nov. 1961. *L2*, 680.
50. Ruth Hill to SP, 6 Nov. 1961. 5.46, SPC, Smith.
51. SP to AP, 20 Nov. 1961. *L2*, 687.
52. SP to AP, 5 Nov. 1961. *L2*, 677.
53. SP to AP, 9 Nov. 1961. *L2*, 681.
54. SP to Marion Freeman, 26 Oct. 1961. *L2*, 670.
55. SP to AP, 7 Dec. 1961. *L2*, 698.
56. SP to AP, 22 Oct. 1961. *L2*, 668.
57. 15.20, SPC, Smith.
58. Helena Annan to SP, 19 Jan. 1962. 17.37, SPC, Smith.
59. TH to AP and WP, early Dec. 1960. *LTH*, 172.
60. Harriet Rosenstein interview with William Sterling, 1972. 4.14, MSS 1489, Emory.
61. SP to James Michie, 14 Nov. 1961. *L2*, 683–85.
62. SP to AP, 29 Dec. 1961. *L2*, 706.
63. SP to AP, 7 Dec. 1961. *L2*, 697.
64. Ibid., *L2*, 696–99.
65. SP to AP, 26–30 Oct. 1961. *L2*, 672.
66. See G. S. Fraser, "American Poetry," *Times Literary Supplement* (8 Dec. 1961), 881.
67. TH to Theodore Roethke, early Dec. 1961. Roethke Papers, 8.4, University of Washington.
68. This doll's crib is now held at SPC, Smith.
69. SP to AP, 29 Dec. (#1) 1961. *L2*, 706–708.
70. SP to AP, 29 Dec. (#2) 1961. *L2*, 710.

27. MOTHERS

1. SP to AP, 18–20 Jan. 1962. *L2*, 713.
2. SP to AP, 12 Jan. 1962. *L2*, 711.
3. *J*, 645.
4. *J*, 646–47.
5. SP to AP, 18–20 Jan. 1962. *L2*, 714.
6. *J*, 647.
7. Hughes was deeply troubled by this passage, and he kept it out of Plath's abridged journals when they were published.
8. TH to Esther and Leonard Baskin, late Jan. 1962. *LTH*, 194.
9. *J*, 647.
10. SP to AP, 18–20 Jan. 1962. *L2*, 714.
11. TH to Esther and Leonard Baskin, late Jan. 1962. *LTH*, 194.
12. SP, "Fever" sequence. 9.96, SPC, Smith.
13. *J*, 648.
14. SP to AP, 24–27 Jan. 1962. *L2*, 717.
15. SP to Dorothy Benotti, 31 Jan. 1962. *L2*, 722.
16. SP to AP, 7 Feb. 1962. *L2*, 727.
17. SP to AP, 13 Feb. 1962. *L2*, 729.
18. SP to Dr. Ruth Beuscher, 27 Mar. 1962. *L2*, 748.
19. SP to AP, 13 Feb. 1962. *L2*, 730.
20. Ibid., *L2*, 729.
21. SP to Mary Louise Vincent Black, 30 Jan. 1962. *L2*, 718.
22. SP to AP, 31 Jan. 1962. *L2*, 720.
23. SP to AP, 18–20 Jan. 1962. *L2*, 715.
24. AP to Miriam Baggett, 15 May 1962. 29.2, SPC, Smith.
25. SP to AP, 4 Mar. 1962. *L2*, 735.

26. HC interview with David Compton, May 2016, Bowdoinham, Maine.
27. Harriet Rosenstein interview with David Compton, 1973. 1.18, MSS 1489, Emory.
28. SP to AP, 7 Feb. 1962. *L2*, 728.
29. SP to Olive Eaton, 1 Feb. 1962. *L2*, 725.
30. SP to AP, 13 Feb. 1962. *L2*, 730.
31. SP to AP, 4 Mar. 1962. *L2*, 734.
32. SP to AP, 13 Feb. 1962. *L2*, 731.
33. SP to AP, 24 Feb. 1962. *L2*, 731.
34. SP to AP, 12 Mar. 1962. *L2*, 739.
35. SP to AP, 24 Feb. 1962. *L2*, 733.
36. SP to AP, 7 Feb. 1962. *L2*, 728.
37. SP to Ann Davidow-Goodman and Leo Goodman, 28 Mar. 1962. *L2*, 749.
38. SP to Paul and Clarissa Roche, 12 Mar. 1962. *L2*, 740–41.
39. SP to Helga Huws, 29 Mar. 1962. *L2*, 752.
40. SP to AP, 27 Mar. 1962. *L2*, 746.
41. SP to Dr. Ruth Beuscher, 27 Mar. 1962. *L2*, 748.
42. Dr. Ruth Beuscher to SP, 17 Sept. 1962. 17.24, SPC, Smith.
43. *J*, 655; 662.
44. *J*, 633.
45. EF interview with Elizabeth Compton Sigmund, Sept. 1999. EFP.
46. HC interview with David Compton, May 2016, Bowdoinham, Maine.
47. Harriet Rosenstein interview with Winifred Davies, 8 Aug. 1970. Courtesy of Kenneth Neville-Davies.
48. Kenneth Neville-Davies email to Peter K. Steinberg, 5 Feb. 2016. Quoted with permission of Steinberg and Neville-Davies. Mrs. Hamilton, Plath's neighbor, was Winifred Davies's maternal aunt, who had helped get her the job of midwife in North Tawton. The Davieses were even distantly related to Elizabeth Compton.
49. HC interview with David Compton, May 2016, Bowdoinham, Maine.
50. *J*, 636.
51. *J*, 634.
52. Clarissa Roche, "Sylvia Plath: Vignettes from England," *Sylvia Plath: The Woman and the Work*, Edward Butscher, ed. (New York: Dodd, Mead and Co., 1977), 88–89.
53. *J*, 644.
54. *J*, 631.
55. *J*, 637.
56. *J*, 664; 631.
57. *JP*, 108.
58. TH, draft of "Error." Add MS 88918/1/2-8, BL.
59. SP to Ruth Fainlight, 4 Mar. 1962. *L2*, 737.
60. *JP*, 108.
61. *J*, 651.
62. *J*, 635.
63. *J*, 631–32.
64. *J*, 634.
65. *J*, 635; Anne Stevenson, interview notes with Nicola Tyrer, 14 Oct. 1987. 2.24, Houghton Mifflin Papers, Smith.
66. *J*, 635.
67. Harriet Rosenstein interview with Winifred Davies, 8 Aug. 1970. Courtesy of Kenneth Neville-Davies.
68. SP to AP, 7 Feb. 1962. *L2*, 728.
69. *J*, 632.
70. *J*, 638; 642.
71. *J*, 641.
72. Anne Stevenson, *Bitter Fame: A Life of Sylvia Plath* (London: Penguin, 1989; 1998), 240.
73. *J*, 641.
74. Anne Stevenson, interview notes with Nicola Tyrer, 14 Oct. 1987. 2.24, Houghton Mifflin Papers, Smith.

75. HC interview with David Compton, May 2016, Bowdoinham, Maine.
76. SP, 1962 Letts Royal Office Tablet Diary. 19.2, SPC, Smith.
77. Stevenson, *Bitter Fame*, 241.
78. TH to Olwyn Hughes, summer 1962. Add MS 88948/1/2, BL.
79. SP to AP, 12 Mar. 1962. *L2*, 739.
80. The poems in *Poetry* were "Stars Over the Dordogne," "Face Lift, "Widow," "Heavy Woman," and "Love Letter."
81. SP to AP, 4 Mar. 1962. *L2*, 735.
82. Robin Peel, *Writing Back: Sylvia Plath and Cold War Politics* (Teaneck, N.J.: Fairleigh Dickinson University Press, 2002), 127.
83. *JP*, 92.
84. Archival evidence suggests that Ted Hughes misdated this poem when he included it in the late-1960 section of Plath's *Collected Poems*. It is written on the backs of pages of the third draft of *The Bell Jar*. Hughes wrote in Plath's *Collected Poems* that "Waking in Winter" and "New Year on Dartmoor" were salvaged from a tangle of manuscripts and must be considered unfinished. See Peel, pp. 125–26.
85. All drafts are held at SPC, Smith.
86. SP, "Fever." 9.96, SPC, Smith.
87. SP to AP, 7 June 1962. *L2*, 777. The play was rebroadcast on 13 Sept. 1962.
88. Plath mentioned attending a twelve-week series of Ingmar Bergman films in a 26 Feb. 1961 letter to Aurelia. She later told Aurelia in a 7 June 1962 letter that *Three Women* was "inspired by a Bergman film." *L2*, 777.
89. Stevenson, *Bitter Fame*, 234.
90. In Jan. 1958, Plath wrote that "abortion" was something she had "known," like "suicide," something she should draw on in her writing. She was probably talking about a Smith friend, whose abortion she mentioned in her journal. *J*, 307; 404.
91. The proofs of *The Bell Jar* are dated 1962, and we know Plath made some changes to them before the novel was released on 14 Jan 1963. See Peter K. Steinberg, "Textual Variations in *The Bell Jar* Publications," *Plath Profiles* 5 (2012): 134–39. Plath's May and August 1962 progress reports to the Saxton foundation are held at SPC, Smith. Steinberg notes that Plath likely submitted two other reports in February and November 1962. As she worked on these reports and the proofs, Plath was revisiting the themes of the novel throughout 1962.
92. Anne Sexton would publish "The Abortion" in 1962's *All My Pretty Ones*, yet that poem is full of self-blame.
93. *J*, 374.
94. Sexton would use a similar image to describe a newborn baby in "For God While Sleeping," from *All My Pretty Ones*, but the reference also suggests Hughes's poem "Death of a Pig," an unsentimental piece about butchery.
95. SP to AP, 27 Mar. 1962. *L2*, 744.
96. SP to AP, 24 Feb. 1962. *L2*, 731.
97. SP to AP, 13 Feb. 1962. *L2*, 730.
98. SP to AP, 24 Feb. 1962. *L2*, 732.
99. SP to AP, 12 Mar. 1962. *L2*, 739.
100. SP to George MacBeth, 4 Apr. 1962. *L2*, 754.
101. SP to AP, 12 Mar. 1962. *L2*, 739.
102. Ibid., *L2*, 738.
103. SP to Marvin Kane, 23 Mar. 1962. *L2*, 743.
104. "What Made You Stay?," BBC Home Service broadcast. Recorded on 14 Apr. 1962; broadcast on 7 Sept. 1962. *The Spoken Word: Sylvia Plath*. British Library/National Sound Archives/BBC Audio Compilation (2010).
105. *J*, 668.
106. SP to Joan and Gerald Hughes, 9 May 1962. *L2*, 772.
107. SP to Helga Huws, 29 Mar. 1962. *L2*, 753.
108. SP to AP, 8 Apr. 1962. *L2*, 755.
109. According to Ted Hughes, the elm tree Plath wrote about was knocked down dur-

ing a 1992 storm. Gail Crowther and Peter K. Steinberg, *These Ghostly Archives: The Unearthing of Sylvia Plath* (Croydon, UK: Fonthill, 2017), 56.

110. This image was originally a reflection of the speaker's own face in the windowpane in several earlier drafts, held at SPC, Smith. ("In it am reflected, your face / Hung white & blank in my branches"; "my gilded image at the dawn hour.")

111. SP to Howard Moss, 31 Aug. 1962. *L2*, 815. *The New Yorker* would initially reject it in late June but accept it in September.

112. SP to Ruth Fainlight and Alan Sillitoe, 16 Apr. 1962. *L2*, 762.

113. SP, draft 3b of "Elm." 9.81, SPC, Smith.

114. Fainlight was intrigued by these connections, which she had never considered, when I pointed them out to her in 2016.

115. SP, draft 2b of "Elm." 9.81, SPC, Smith. The line "as a woman with no children" has been excised in the draft and replaced with "like a childless woman."

116. *J*, 668.

117. HC interview with Elizabeth Compton Sigmund, May 2016, Cornwall.

118. Harriet Rosenstein interview with David Compton, 1973. 1.18, MSS 1489, Emory.

119. Elizabeth Sigmund and Gail Crowther, *Sylvia Plath in Devon: A Year's Turning* (Croydon, UK: Fonthill, 2014), 19.

120. Harriet Rosenstein interview with Elizabeth Compton Sigmund, 1973. 4.10, MSS 1489, Emory.

121. Justine Picardie, "The Toxic Avenger," *Independent* (30 Sept. 1995).

122. HC interview with Elizabeth Compton Sigmund, May 2016, Cornwall.

123. Sigmund and Crowther, *Sylvia Plath in Devon*, 19.

124. Plath would send them a handmade quilt from Mytholmroyd for their wedding present.

125. Harriet Rosenstein interview with Elizabeth Compton Sigmund, 1973. 4.10, MSS 1489, Emory.

126. Harriet Rosenstein interview with David Compton, 1973. 1.18, MSS 1489, Emory.

127. HC interview with David Compton, May 2016, Bowdoinham, Maine.

128. Ibid.

129. SP to AP, 25 Apr. 1962. *L2*, 764–66.

130. SP to AP, 21 Apr. 1962. *L2*, 763.

131. SP to AP, 25 Apr. 1962. *L2*, 765.

132. Ibid.

133. *J*, 670–71.

134. Harriet Rosenstein interview with Ruth Fainlight and Alan Sillitoe, 1970. 1.25, MSS 1489, Emory.

135. HC interview with Ruth Fainlight, May 2016, London.

136. Ruth Fainlight, "Jane and Sylvia," *Crossroads* (Spring 2004): 8–19. 14.

137. HC interview with Ruth Fainlight, May 2016, London.

138. Ibid.

139. Fainlight, "Jane and Sylvia," 14.

140. TH, notebook entry. Add MS 88918/128/1, BL.

141. HC interview with David Compton, May 2016, Bowdoinham, Maine.

142. TH to AP and WP, 1 May 1962. *LTH*, 196–97.

143. Sylvia Plath, "Oblongs," *New Statesman* (18 May 1962), 724; review of Peter Hughes, *The Emperor's Oblong Pancake;* Tomi Ungerer, *The Three Robbers;* Wanda Gág, *The Funny Thing;* Benjamin Spock, *Dr. Spock Talks with Mothers;* Elizabeth and Gerald Rose, *The Big River;* and Joan Cass and William Stobbs, *The Cat Show.*

144. SP to AP, 4 May 1962. *L2*, 769.

145. TH to AP and WP, 1 May 1962. *LTH*, 196–97.

146. SP to Judith Jones, 5 May 1962. *L2*, 770.

147. TH to AP, 14 May 1962. Lilly.

148. It was not reviewed in *The New York Times*, *The Washington Post*, the *Chicago Tribune*, or *The Boston Globe*.

149. *J*, 643.

150. SP to AP, 4 May 1962. *L2*, 769.

28. ERROR

1. *CPTH*, 1122.
2. TH to Ben Sonnenberg, 10 Oct. 1961. 1.1, MSS 924, Emory.
3. TH, draft of "Error." Add MS 88918/1/2-8, BL.
4. Ibid.
5. TH, notebook entry, 11 Oct. 1961, p. 50. Add MS 88918/129/2, BL.
6. TH to Olwyn Hughes, summer 1962. Add MS 88948/1/2, BL. Ted's remark echoes almost exactly what Assia told Nathaniel Tarn in July.
7. D. H. Lawrence, *Selected Poetry*, Keith Sagar, ed. (London: Penguin, 1972; 1986), 67.
8. TH to Olwyn Hughes, late summer 1962. *LTH*, 204.
9. TH to Anne Stevenson, autumn 1986. *LTH*, 519; 518.
10. TH, notebook entry, 29 Mar. 1960. Add MS 88918/129/2, BL.
11. *CPTH*, 1124.
12. Harriet Rosenstein interview with Winifred Davies, 1970. Courtesy of Kenneth Neville-Davies.
13. Hughes and Thom Gunn were coeditors, and they intended to include Nemerov, Bowers, Stafford, and Simpson. Hughes asked Alvarez for more suggestions. See *LTH*, 191.
14. TH to Nicholas Hughes, n.d., 1986. *LTH*, 512.
15. See HC, *The Grief of Influence: Sylvia Plath and Ted Hughes* (Oxford: Oxford University Press, 2011), 52.
16. TH interview with Drue Heinz, "The Art of Poetry, LXXI," *Paris Review* 134 (1995), in *The Paris Review Interviews, III* (London: Picador, 2008), 56–92. 76.
17. Gerald Hughes, *Ted & I: A Brother's Memoir* (New York: St. Martin's Press, 2012), 165–66.
18. HC interview with Suzette Macedo, May 2016, London.
19. Susan Alliston, *Poems and Journals 1960–1969* (Nottingham: Richard Hollis/Five Leaves, 2010), 87.
20. Richard Murphy, *The Kick: A Memoir* (London: Granta, 2002), 229.
21. Yehuda Koren and Eliat Negev, *Lover of Unreason: Assia Wevill, Sylvia Plath's Rival and Ted Hughes's Doomed Love* (New York: Carroll and Graf, 2007), 136.
22. HC interview with Suzette and Helder Macedo, May 2016, London.
23. Jillian Becker to Harriet Rosenstein, 21 Mar. 1974. Provided to HC by Jillian Becker.
24. EF interview with Mira Hamermesh, July 1999. EFP.
25. Koren and Negev, *Lover of Unreason*, 12.
26. Ibid., 18.
27. Ibid., 58.
28. William Trevor, *Excursions in the Real World* (London: Penguin, 1993), 116.
29. Koren and Negev, *Lover of Unreason*, 41.
30. Ibid., 53.
31. HC interview with Suzette and Helder Macedo, May 2016, London. Suzette told me it was their mutual friend, Marisa Martinelli, who had gotten Assia into advertising. Assia had been Martinelli's secretary at another agency. Martinelli was struck by Assia's intelligence, and she wrote her a recommendation letter that paved the way for her to work as a copywriter.
32. David Wevill said that Hughes and Plath "weren't involved with the Group during the time I attended the meetings," although archival evidence shows that Hughes contributed poems to Group meetings even in his absence. David Wevill email to HC, 13 Apr. 2016.
33. Koren and Negev, *Lover of Unreason*, 68.
34. Ibid., 69.
35. Ibid., 66.
36. Ibid., 85.
37. Ibid., 79.
38. Ibid., 74.
39. HC interview with Suzette and Helder Macedo, May 2016, London.

40. Assia Lipsey to Michael and Pat Mendelson, 21 May 1960. M1132, Nathaniel Tarn Papers, Stanford.
41. Koren and Negev, *Lover of Unreason*, 79.
42. David Wevill email to HC, 13 Apr. 2016.
43. The Plath poems included "All the Dead Dears," "Black Rook in Rainy Weather," "Miss Drake Proceeds to Supper," and "Epitaph for Fire and Flower." The Hughes poems included were "Thrushes," "The Good Life," "The Historian," "Dick Straightup," and "Crow Hill." David Wevill had four poems, Lucas Myers three. Plath's undergraduate college was listed incorrectly as Brown. *Poetry from Cambridge 1958*, Christopher Levenson, ed. (London: Fortune Press, 1958).
44. Trevor, *Excursions*, 117.
45. Koren and Negev, *Lover of Unreason*, 82.
46. SP to AP, 14 May 1962. *L2*, 773.
47. Koren and Negev, *Lover of Unreason*, 86.
48. HC interview with Suzette and Helder Macedo, May 2016, London.
49. Koren and Negev, *Lover of Unreason*, 88.
50. Anne Stevenson, *Bitter Fame: A Life of Sylvia Plath* (London: Penguin, 1989; 1998), 243.
51. Koren and Negev, *Lover of Unreason*, 45.
52. Julia Matcham to Elizabeth Compton Sigmund, 17 Jan. 1987. William Sigmund Papers, Smith.
53. Nathaniel Tarn, 3 Apr. 1964, diary notes. M1132, Nathaniel Tarn Papers, Stanford.
54. Jillian Becker to Harriet Rosenstein, 5 Mar. 1974. Courtesy of Jillian Becker.
55. My account of this weekend relies on David Wevill's firsthand account in Yehuda Koren and Eilat Negev's biography of Assia Wevill, *Lover of Unreason* (2006), pp. 87–90. Koren and Negev are the only biographers to whom Wevill has spoken extensively about Assia.
56. *CPTH*, 1146.
57. Jonathan Bate, *Ted Hughes: The Unauthorised Life* (New York: HarperCollins, 2015), 186–87.
58. *J*, 301.
59. HC interview with Suzette and Helder Macedo, May 2016, London.
60. EF interview with Suzette and Helder Macedo, Oct. 1999. EFP.
61. *CPTH*, 1145. Hughes has been much criticized for lacing this poem with lines that demonize Assia ("slightly filthy with erotic mystery," "gaze of a demon," etc.), and for indulging in gratuitous Holocaust imagery.
62. *CPTH*, 1145.
63. This detail was provided to Koren and Negev by David Wevill, as well as by Suzette Macedo to Anne Stevenson. Suzette said Assia told her the story herself.
64. Koren and Negev, *Lover of Unreason*, 87.
65. Stevenson, *Bitter Fame*, 242–43.
66. Koren and Negev, *Lover of Unreason*, 87.
67. Ibid., 90.
68. HC interview with Suzette and Helder Macedo, May 2016, London.
69. Harriet Rosenstein interview with Suzette Macedo, 1973. 2.18, MSS 1489, Emory.
70. HC interview with Suzette and Helder Macedo, May 2016, London.
71. Harriet Rosenstein interview with Suzette Macedo, 1973. 2.18, MSS 1489, Emory.
72. HC interview with Suzette and Helder Macedo, May 2016, London.
73. SP to Dr. Ruth Beuscher, 11 July 1962. *L2*, 791.
74. Koren and Negev, *Lover of Unreason*, 90.
75. HC interview with Suzette and Helder Macedo, May 2016, London.
76. Nathaniel Tarn, 19 July 1962, diary notes. M1132, Nathaniel Tarn Papers, Stanford.
77. TH, draft of "The Minotaur, 2." Add MS 88918/1/2–8, BL.
78. TH to Bill and Dido Merwin, 24 May 1962. *LTH*, 199.
79. TH to Olwyn Hughes, late summer 1962. *LTH*, 203–204.
80. TH to Bill and Dido Merwin, 24 May 1962. *LTH*, 199. He mentioned the play to Luke Myers on 2 July, calling it "a semi-dramatic sort of up-to-date Bawdry Embraced."

81. Assia Wevill to SP, 22 May 1962. Add MS 88612, BL.
82. SP to AP, 7 June 1962. *L2*, 777.
83. A. Alvarez, *The Savage God: A Study of Suicide* (London: Weidenfeld & Nicolson, 1971; New York: W. W. Norton, 1990), 28.
84. HC interview with Al and Anne Alvarez, May 2016, London. Al and Anne remembered her as "very beautiful" but a "femme fatale." "We saw a lot of them after" Plath's death, Anne remembered. She and Assia would occasionally go out for drinks; she remembered Assia trying to weaken her confidence when she began her psychotherapy training. "She had a way of undermining whatever you were."
85. David Wevill email to HC, 29 Sept. 2016.
86. Nathaniel Tarn, 22 June 1963, diary notes. M1132, Nathaniel Tarn Papers, Stanford.
87. Ibid., 3 Apr. 1964.
88. Bate, *Ted Hughes*, 190.
89. SP to AP, 7 June 1962. *L2*, 776.
90. SP to Joan and Gerald Hughes, 10 June 1962. *L2*, 780.
91. SP to AP, 7 June 1962. *L2*, 776.
92. *Three Women: A Poem for Three Voices* was broadcast on the BBC's Third Programme on 19 Aug. 1962 and rebroadcast on 13 Sept. 1962. Plath recorded her talk, "Sylvia Plath Speaks on a Poet's View of Novel Writing," for *The World of Books* on 26 June 1962 (broadcast 7 July 1962, on the BBC Home Service; rebroadcast on 13 July 1962). This talk was later published in *JP* as "A Comparison."
93. Eric Walter White to TH, 19 Aug. 1962. 116.9, MSS 644, Emory.
94. SP to AP, 7 June 1962. *L2*, 778.
95. SP to Alfred Fisher, 11 June 1962. *L2*, 781.
96. SP to Gerald and Joan Hughes, 10 June 1962. *L2*, 780.
97. *J*, 656.
98. SP to Marvin and Kathy Kane, 9 June 1962. *L2*, 778.
99. SP to Olwyn Hughes, 18 June 1962. *L2*, 786.
100. HC interview with David Compton, May 2016, Bowdoinham, Maine.
101. SP to Olwyn Hughes, 18 June 1962. *L2*, 786.
102. Ibid., *L2*, 785.
103. SP to AP, 15 June 1962. *L2*, 784.
104. SP to Olwyn Hughes, 18 June 1962. *L2*, 786.
105. SP to Dr. Ruth Beuscher, 11 July 1962. *L2*, 791; 794.
106. TH, notebook entry, June 1962. Add MS 88918/129/2, BL.
107. Ibid.

29. I FEEL ALL I FEEL

1. SP to Olwyn Hughes, 18 June 1962. *L2*, 786.
2. Harriet Rosenstein interview with Winifred Davies, 8 Aug. 1970. Courtesy of Kenneth Neville-Davies.
3. AP to WP, 17 July 1962. Lilly.
4. SP to Marvin and Kathy Kane, 30 June 1962. *L2*, 789.
5. HC interview with Suzette Macedo, May 2016, London.
6. Nathaniel Tarn, 19 July 1962, diary notes. M1132, Nathaniel Tarn Papers, Stanford.
7. William Trevor, *Excursions in the Real World* (London: Penguin, 1993), 118.
8. Ibid., 117.
9. Ibid.
10. Jonathan Bate notes that *Capriccio*, which contained "Chlorophyl," was published in very limited quantities and was the one Trevor "is most unlikely to have known." *Ted Hughes: The Unauthorised Life* (New York: HarperCollins, 2015), 188.
11. HC interview with Elizabeth Compton Sigmund, May 2016, Cornwall.
12. *J*, 670.
13. *J*, 672.
14. *J*, 673.
15. *J*, 671.

16. Anne Stevenson, *Bitter Fame: A Life of Sylvia Plath* (London: Penguin, 1989), 249.
17. Gail Crowther and Peter K. Steinberg, *These Ghostly Archives: The Unearthing of Sylvia Plath* (Croydon, UK: Fonthill, 2017), 33.
18. SP to Dr. Ruth Beuscher, 11 July 1962. *L2*, 791.
19. TH to Gerald Hughes, 2 July 1962. 1.3, MS 854, Emory.
20. Harriet Rosenstein interview with Winifred Davies, 1970. Courtesy of Kenneth Neville-Davies.
21. The poem was first titled "Mannequin"; its penultimate title was "The Other One." 12.188, SPC, Smith.
22. 12.188, SPC, Smith.
23. HC interview with Elizabeth Compton Sigmund, May 2016, Cornwall.
24. Harriet Rosenstein interview with Elizabeth Compton Sigmund, 1973. 4.10, MSS 1489, Emory.
25. Elizabeth Sigmund and Gail Crowther, *Sylvia Plath in Devon: A Year's Turning* (Croydon, UK: Fonthill, 2012), 75.
26. AP, 1962 travel diary. 6.39, Hornbake Library, Frances McCullough Papers, University of Maryland.
27. Ibid.
28. SP to Dr. Ruth Beuscher, 11 July 1962. *L2*, 791–92.
29. AP, 1962 travel diary. 6.39, Hornbake Library, Frances McCullough Papers, University of Maryland.
30. EF interview with Keith Sagar, Jan. 2000. EFP.
31. EF interview with Elizabeth Compton Sigmund, Sept. 1999. EFP.
32. HC interview with Suzette and Helder Macedo, May 2016, London.
33. Ibid.
34. Video footage of Aurelia Plath, Nov. 1986, in *Poets of New England: Sylvia Plath and the Myth of the Monstrous Mother.* University of Massachusetts, Amherst, AIMS Video Services. Courtesy of Richard Larschan. 2001.
35. AP, 1962 travel diary. 6.39, Hornbake Library, Frances McCullough Papers, University of Maryland.
36. EF interview with Suzette Macedo, Oct. 1999. EFP.
37. TH to Elizabeth and David Compton, summer 1963. Add MS 88612, BL.
38. AP, 1962 travel diary. Frances McCullough Papers, University of Maryland.
39. Elizabeth Sigmund, "I Realized Sylvia Knew About Assia's Pregnancy," *Guardian* (22 Apr. 1999). G2, 4.
40. SP to Marvin and Kathy Kane, 15 July 1962. *L2*, 795.
41. HC interview with David Compton, May 2016, Bowdoinham, Maine.
42. SP to Dr. Ruth Beuscher, 11 July, 1962. *L2*, 790–95.
43. Harriet Rosenstein interview with Elizabeth Compton Sigmund, 1973. 4.10, MSS 1489, Emory.
44. Harriet Rosenstein interview with David Compton, 1973. 1.18, MSS 1489, Emory.
45. HC interview with David Compton, May 2016, Bowdoinham, Maine; Harriet Rosenstein interview with Elizabeth Compton Sigmund, 1973. 4.10, MSS 1489, Emory.
46. HC interview with Elizabeth Compton Sigmund, May 2016, London.
47. Harriet Rosenstein interview with Winifred Davies, 8 Aug. 1970. Courtesy of Kenneth Neville-Davies.
48. SP to Clarissa Roche, 11 July 1962. *L2*, 789–90.
49. EF interview with Suzette Macedo, Oct. 1999. EFP.
50. Ibid.
51. Harriet Rosenstein interview with Edward Lucie-Smith, 1970. 2.17, MSS 1489, Emory.
52. Harriet Rosenstein interview with Helder Macedo, 1973. 2.18, MSS 1489, Emory.
53. HC interview with Suzette Macedo, May 2016, London.
54. AP, 1962 travel diary. Courtesy of Richard Larschan.
55. Ibid.
56. TH to Olwyn Hughes, summer 1962. Add MS 88948/1/2, BL.
57. Ibid.

58. Nathaniel Tarn, 19 July 1962, diary notes. M1132, Nathaniel Tarn Papers, Stanford.
59. Bate, *Ted Hughes*, 190.
60. Ibid.
61. EF interview with Suzette Macedo, Oct. 1999. EFP.
62. Jillian Becker, *Giving Up: The Last Days of Sylvia Plath* (New York: St. Martin's, 2002), 35.
63. Nathaniel Tarn, 19 July 1962, diary notes. M1132, Nathaniel Tarn Papers, Stanford.
64. A. Alvarez, *The Savage God: A Study of Suicide* (London: Weidenfeld & Nicolson, 1971; New York: W. W. Norton, 1990), 29.
65. Ibid., 33–34.
66. Suzette Macedo to Harriet Rosenstein, c. 1973. 2.18, MSS 1489, Emory.
67. Nathaniel Tarn, 28 July 1962, diary notes. M1132, Nathaniel Tarn Papers, Stanford.
68. The poems published in the column, from top to bottom, were Plath's "Finisterre," Keith Barnes's "The Madman," Hughes's "Mountains," David Wevill's "Clean Break," D. J. Enright's "Virtue of a Vice," and David Wagner's "Watching." "New Poems," *Observer* (5 Aug. 1962), 14.
69. AP to WP, 17 July 1962. Lilly.
70. Harriet Rosenstein interview with Winifred Davies, 8 Aug. 1970. Courtesy of Kenneth Neville-Davies.
71. Ibid.
72. Stevenson, *Bitter Fame*, 252.
73. Brian Cox, "Ted Hughes (1930–1998): A Personal Retrospect," *Hudson Review* 52.1 (Spring 1999): 29–43. 36.
74. SP to Dr. Ruth Beuscher, 20 July 1962. *L2*, 797.
75. SP to Dr. Ruth Beuscher, 30 July 1962. *L2*, 803.
76. SP to Dr. Ruth Beuscher, 20 July 1962. *L2*, 797–98.
77. Ibid., *L2*, 798.
78. Ibid., *L2*, 799.
79. SP to Dr. Ruth Beuscher, 30 July 1962. *L2*, 803.
80. Ibid., *L2*, 804.
81. Ibid., *L2*, 804–805.
82. Ibid., *L2*, 805–806.
83. Ibid., *L2*, 805.
84. Ibid., *L2*, 807.
85. Ibid., *L2*, 806–807.
86. SP to Al Alvarez, 21 July 1962. *L2*, 800.
87. The anthology was published by Penguin in April.
88. Al Alvarez to SP, 24 July 1962. 17.21, SPC, Smith.
89. Plath had won this contest in 1962. The other judges were George Hartley and John Press.
90. SP to Richard Murphy, 21 July 1962. *L2*, 801.
91. HC interview with Elizabeth Compton Sigmund, May 2016, Cornwall.
92. Harriet Rosenstein interview with Winifred Davies, 8 Aug. 1970. Courtesy of Kenneth Neville-Davies.
93. Clarissa Roche, "Sylvia Plath: Vignettes from England," *Sylvia Plath: The Woman and the Work*, Edward Butscher, ed. (New York: Dodd, Mead and Co., 1977), 89.
94. SP to AP, 27 Aug. 1962. *L2*, 814.
95. LH, 458.

30. BUT NOT THE END

1. *JP*, 11.
2. Harriet Rosenstein interview with Al Alvarez, 1970. 1.2, MSS 1489, Emory.
3. SP to AP, 17 Aug. 1962. *L2*, 810.
4. Harriet Rosenstein interview with Marvin Kane, 1973–74. 2.8, MSS 1489, Emory.
5. OHP to AP, 25 Aug. 1962. Lilly.

6. SP to Dr. Ruth Beuscher, 22 Sept. 1962. *L2*, 828.
7. Ibid.
8. SP to OHP, 29 Sept. 1962. *L2*, 842.
9. SP to Richard Murphy, 17 Aug. 1962. *L2*, 811.
10. Peter Davison to Judith Flanders, 22 Oct. 1987. 1.7, Houghton Mifflin Papers, Smith.
11. Peter Davison to Judith Flanders, 28 Oct. 1987. 1.7, Houghton Mifflin Papers, Smith.
12. Andrew Wilson, *Mad Girl's Love Song* (New York: Scribner, 2013), 310.
13. Peter Davison to Judith Flanders, 22 Oct. 1987. 1.7, Houghton Mifflin Papers, Smith. Davison recalls in this letter that Brinnin learned Plath had crashed the car before their arrival.
14. TH to Anne Stevenson, autumn 1986. *LTH*, 519.
15. SP to AP, 27 Aug. 1962. *L2*, 813–14.
16. Ibid.
17. Harriet Rosenstein interview with Elizabeth Compton Sigmund, 1973. 4.10, MSS 1489, Emory.
18. Harriet Rosenstein interview with Suzette Macedo, 1973. 2.18, MSS 1489, Emory.
19. Ibid.
20. Harriet Rosenstein interview with Clarissa Roche, 1973. 3.14, MSS 1489, Emory.
21. Harriet Rosenstein interview with David Compton, 1973. 1.18, MSS 1489, Emory.
22. Ibid.
23. Elizabeth and David also found "morbid" newspaper clippings Plath had tacked onto her study wall. One was about a woman who had received a face-lift, another about a railway accident, and a third about a son who kept his dead mother's body in his bedroom and tried to bring her back to life with electric shocks. Harriet Rosenstein interview with Elizabeth Compton Sigmund, 1973. 4.10, MSS 1489, Emory.
24. SP to George MacBeth, 15 Aug. 1962. *L2*, 809.
25. SP to AP, 27 Aug. 1962. *L2*, 813.
26. SP to Ruth Fainlight, 8 Sept. 1962. *L2*, 822.
27. SP to AP, 27 Aug. 1962. *L2*, 813.
28. The lesson took place at Lower Corscombe Farm, Corscombe Lane, on 27 Aug. Her riding teacher was Miss P. B. Redwood. *L2*, 813.
29. SP to AP, 27 Aug. 1962. *L2*, 813–15.
30. Plath and Hughes's surviving British checkbook stubs for 1962 run from 30 June to 5 Sept. Withdrawals in Hughes's handwriting, or labeled "Ted"—usually for £10, £15, or £20—are recorded on 2 July, 9 July, 18 July, 21 July, 10 Aug., 15 Aug., 18 Aug., 27 Aug., and 31 Aug., though the mid-August withdrawal would have paid for their train fare to London to stay with Mrs. Prouty. Between 30 June and 22 Aug., the amount of money in their checking account floated between £75 and £193. SP and TH, Lloyd's Bank checkbook stubs, Jan. 1960–Jan. 1963. SPC, 19.5, Smith.
31. If Hughes outlived the term, the policy would be paid out as a pension in future years. SP and TH, Lloyd's Bank checkbook stubs, Jan. 1960–Jan. 1963. SPC, 19.5, Smith.
32. SP to AP, 17 Aug. 1962. *L2*, 810.
33. SP to Anne Sexton, 21 Aug. 1962. *L2*, 812.
34. TH and SP to Eric and Edith White, 3 Sept. 1962. *L2*, 816. Hughes's section is not transcribed. Original letter is held at McMaster University.
35. SP to Elizabeth Compton, 8 Sept. 1962. *L2*, 820.
36. Judith Jones to SP, 30 Aug. 1962. Alfred A. Knopf Papers, 362.2, HRC.
37. Marianne Moore to Judith Jones, 7 Apr. 1962. Alfred A. Knopf Papers, 359.10, HRC.
38. SP to Judith Jones, 5 Sept. 1962. *L2*, 818.
39. SP to William and Edith Hughes, 27 Feb. 1957. *L2*, 77.
40. SP to Dr. Ruth Beuscher, 4 Sept. 1962. *L2*, 816; 818.
41. Ibid., *L2*, 816–17.
42. SP to Dr. Ruth Beuscher, 22 Sept. 1962. *L2*, 830.
43. Ibid., *L2*, 827–32.
44. HC interview with Elizabeth Compton Sigmund, May 2016, Cornwall.
45. SP to Elizabeth Compton, 8 Sept. 1962. *L2*, 820.

46. Richard Murphy, *The Kick: A Memoir* (London: Granta Books, 2002), 223.
47. Mark Wormald email to HC, 23 June 2017. Mark asked Richard Murphy questions on my behalf during a Skype interview on 23 June 2017.
48. Harriet Rosenstein interview with Richard Murphy, 1974. 2.25, MSS 1489, Emory.
49. Murphy, *The Kick*, 223.
50. Harriet Rosenstein interview with Richard Murphy, 1974. 2.25, MSS 1489, Emory.
51. TH to Olwyn Hughes, Sept. 1962. *LTH*, 208. Richard Murphy's father was the last British mayor of Colombo, Sri Lanka. Murphy himself had attended Oxford.
52. Harriet Rosenstein interview with Richard Murphy, 1974. 2.25, MSS 1489, Emory.
53. Ibid.
54. Murphy, *The Kick*, 225.
55. Anne Stevenson, *Bitter Fame: A Life of Sylvia Plath* (London: Penguin, 1990), 351.
56. Murphy, *The Kick*, 224–26.
57. HC interview with Elizabeth Compton Sigmund, May 2016, Cornwall.
58. HC conversation with Robert Jocelyn, earl of Roden, 10 Sept. 2015, Sheffield, UK.
59. Jack Sweeney had known Cooke when he had studied at Harvard before moving to Ireland in 1954. Sweeney facilitated an introduction between the Hugheses and Cooke, who was a great admirer of Hughes's poetry. Barrie told Mark Wormald that he and his wife, Harriet, had met the Hugheses in London in 1960. (Mark Wormald email to HC, 17 June 2017.) In May 1961, Cooke wrote to Sweeney that Plath and Hughes had written to say they were "definitely" coming to Ireland that summer. Cooke and Hughes were contemplating collaborating on a book of poems and drawings and had agreed to put out a joint Christmas card in 1962. The correspondence between Cooke and Sweeney is held in the Jack and Máire Sweeney Papers, UCD.
60. Barrie Cooke, "With Ted Hughes," *The Epic Poise: A Celebration of Ted Hughes*, Nick Gammage, ed. (London: Faber and Faber, 1999), 214.
61. For more details about this trip and Hughes's relationship with Ireland, see Mark Wormald, "Irishwards: Ted Hughes, Freedom and Flow," *Ted Hughes Society Journal* 6.2 (2017): 58–77.
62. Barrie Cooke to Jack Sweeney, c. mid-Oct. 1962. LA52/69, Jack and Máire Sweeney Papers, UCD.
63. TH to Nicholas Hughes, 20 Feb. 1998. *LTH*, 710.
64. Barrie Cooke to Jack Sweeney, 25 Apr. 1969. LA52/69, Jack and Máire Sweeney Papers, UCD.
65. Harriet Rosenstein interview with Richard Murphy, 1974. 2. 25, MSS 1489, Emory.
66. Murphy, *The Kick*, 227.
67. SP to Richard Murphy, 21 Sept. 1962. *L2*, 825–26.
68. SP to AP, 23 Sept. 1962. *L2*, 833. The nanny, Sheena Cartwright, lived in South Devon.
69. Harriet Rosenstein interview with Anthony Thwaite, 1973. 4.17, MSS 1489, Emory; Murphy, *The Kick*, 266.
70. SP to Kathy Kane, 21 Sept. 1962. *L2*, 825.
71. SP to AP, 24 Sept. 1962. *L2*, 836.
72. Harriet Rosenstein interview with Suzette Macedo, 1973. 2.18, MSS 1489, Emory.
73. Dr. Beuscher replied that Plath's "previous distress letter" had not reached her "at once," as she had been away on a month's vacation.
74. Dr. Ruth Beuscher to SP, 17 Sept. 1962. 17.24 SPC, Smith.
75. Though Dr. Francis de Marneffe told me that he thought there had been phone calls between the two, Plath makes no mention of a phone call in any of her letters to Dr. Beuscher. Beuscher's later claim to a biographer (HM) that she told Plath to get help in England does not appear in her surviving letters.
76. SP to Dr. Ruth Beuscher, 22 Sept. 1962. *L2*, 829–30.
77. Ibid., 828.
78. SP, 21 Sept. 1962. Letts Royal Office Tablet Diary. 19.2, SPC, Smith.
79. SP to AP, 23 Sept. 1962. *L2*, 833.
80. SP to Dr. Ruth Beuscher, 22 Sept. 1962. *L2*, 831–32.
81. Winifred Davies to AP, 22 Sept. 1962. Lilly.
82. Harriet Rosenstein interview with Nancy Axworthy, 1973. 1.5, MSS 1489, Emory.

83. TH to Olwyn Hughes, late summer 1962. *LTH*, 203–206.
84. TH to Olwyn Hughes, Sept. 1962. *LTH*, 208.
85. TH to Olwyn Hughes, late summer 1962. *LTH*, 203.
86. TH to Olwyn Hughes, May–June 1958. Add MS 88948/1/1, BL.
87. Harriet Rosenstein interview with Suzette Macedo, 1973. 2.18, MSS 1489, Emory.
88. SP to AP, 26 Sept. 1962. *L2*, 837.
89. Ibid.
90. Suzette Macedo to Harriet Rosenstein, c. 1973. 2.18, MSS 1489, Emory.
91. Anne Stevenson mistakenly dates Plath's first visit to Alvarez as 29–30 Oct. *Bitter Fame*, 273–74.
92. Alvarez lived then at 74A Fellows Road, London NW3. The description of his flat comes from Linda Gates, "Sylvia Plath and I," *Plath Profiles* 5 (2012): 106–108.
93. A. Alvarez, *The Savage God: A Study of Suicide* (London: Weidenfeld & Nicolson, 1971; New York: W. W. Norton, 1990), 29–30.
94. A. Alvarez, "Poetry of Loneliness," *Observer* (14 June 1964), 26. See also A. Alvarez, "Poetry in Extremis," *Observer* (14 Mar. 1965), 26. Plath and Sexton were not included in the first 1962 edition. They were added in the revised 1966 edition.
95. SP's copy of *The New Poetry* (1962). Bonham's catalog for Plath and Hughes auction, 21 Mar. 2018.
96. Alvarez, *Savage God*, 40.
97. HC interview with Daniel Huws, May 2016, London.
98. As recounted in Dennis O'Driscoll, *Stepping Stones: Interviews with Seamus Heaney* (Farrar, Straus and Giroux); Michael Longley, in response to a question from HC about the significance of Alvarez's anthology in Northern Ireland in the early '60s. "Room to Rhyme: Poetry in Crisis 1968–1998" conference, Belfast, Northern Ireland, May 2018.
99. TH to Olwyn Hughes, June 1962. *LTH*, 200.
100. Book 1 featured Lawrence Durrell, Elizabeth Jennings, and R. S. Thomas; Book 2 featured Kingsley Amis, Dom Moraes, and Peter Porter. Will Wooten, *The Alvarez Generation* (Liverpool: Liverpool University Press, 2015), 87.
101. Wooten, *Alvarez Generation*, 67. Harold Rosenberg, *The Tradition of the New* (New York: Horizon Press, 1959), 26.
102. *The New Poetry*, A. Alvarez, ed. (London: Penguin, 1962; 1966), 29.
103. Ibid., 25; 27.
104. Ibid., 26.
105. Peter Porter, "Ted Hughes and Sylvia Plath: A Bystander's Recollection," *Best Australian Essays 2001*, Peter Craven, ed. (Melbourne: Black Inc., 2001), 396–412, 399.
106. Philip Hobsbaum, review of Ted Hughes's *Wodwo*. BBC Third Programme, 14 July 1967.
107. Wooten, *Alvarez Generation*, 23–24.
108. Ibid., 25.
109. While he had been present for the first meeting in Oct. 1955 in Hobsbaum's Edgware Road flat, his departure from England in 1957 meant that he missed two years of meetings. Yet Hughes sent Hobsbaum poems for discussion even when he did not attend meetings. Wooten, *Alvarez Generation*, 23.
110. HC interview with Al Alvarez, May 2016, London.
111. *Poetry from Cambridge 1958*, Christopher Levenson, ed. (London: Fortune Press, 1958). The other woman, with one poem to Plath's four, was Sheila Hardy, also from Newnham.
112. Wooten, *Alvarez Generation*, 81.
113. Philip Larkin's lack of poems in the anthology was due to his high permissions fees rather than Alvarez's "editorial stance." Wooten, *Alvarez Generation*, 78.
114. HC interview with Al Alvarez, May 2016, London.
115. A. Alvarez, *Where Did It All Go Right?* (London: Richard Cohen Books, 1999), 242.
116. Broadcasts on this subject aired in 1962 and 1963; he would publish these features in a book in 1965.
117. A. Alvarez, *Under Pressure: The Writer in Society: Eastern Europe and the U.S.A.* (London: Penguin, 1965), 27.

118. Alvarez, *Where Did It All Go Right?*, 212.
119. She also references "Russia, Poland and Germany" in "The Swarm"; Poland and Germany in "Daddy"; "the cicatrix of Poland, burnt-out / Germany" in "Mary's Song"; and in "Getting There," "It is Russia I have to get across, it is some war or other."
120. There was Peter Porter's "Annotations of Auschwitz" and "Soliloquy at Potsdam"; George MacBeth's "The Disciple," narrated by a Nazi officer, as well as "The Dream" and "The Crucifix"; Anthony Hecht's "More Light! More Light!"; Geoffrey Hill's "Two Formal Elegies: For the Jews in Europe," "Of Commerce and Society," which speaks of Auschwitz, and "Ovid in the Third Reich."
121. Edward Butscher, *Sylvia Plath: Method and Madness* (New York: Seabury Press, 1976), 335.
122. Wooten, *Alvarez Generation*, 114.
123. A. Alvarez, "The Muse in Chains," *Observer* (14 Oct. 1962), 25.
124. Robin Peel, *Writing Back: Sylvia Plath and Cold War Politics* (Vancouver: Fairleigh Dickinson Press, 2002), 127.
125. HC interview with Al Alvarez, May 2016, London.
126. Alvarez has written about his revision suggestions in *The Savage God*.
127. Judging from Plath's 1962 calendar (19.2, SPC, Smith) and letters, the dates for her visits were 24–26 Sept., 29–31 Oct., 5–7 Nov., and 3–6 Dec.
128. SP, 26 Sept. 1962. 1962 Letts Royal Office Tablet Diary. 19.2, SPC, Smith.
129. SP to AP, 26 Sept. 1962. *L2*, 838.
130. SP to AP, 23 Sept. 1962. *L2*, 834.
131. SP to AP, 24 Sept. 1962. *L2*, 835–36.
132. SP to AP, 29 Sept. 1962. *L2*, 839.
133. Ibid., *L2*, 840.
134. SP to Kathy Kane, 29 Sept. 1962. *L2*, 841.
135. SP to Dr. Ruth Beuscher, 29 Sept. 1962. *L2*, 843–45.
136. Dr. Ruth Beuscher to Linda Wagner-Martin, 3 Dec. 1985. Ruth Tiffany Barnhouse Papers, Smith.
137. HM, 40.
138. Dr. Ruth Beuscher to Linda Wagner-Martin, 3 Dec. 1985. Ruth Tiffany Barnhouse Papers, Smith.
139. HM, 40.
140. SP to OHP, 29 Sept. 1962. *L2*, 842–43.
141. Dr. Ruth Beuscher to SP, 26 Sept. 1962. 17.24, SPC, Smith.
142. SP to Dr. Ruth Beuscher, 29–30 Sept. 1962. *L2*, 845. Plath wrote a postscript to this 29 Sept. letter on 30 Sept. when she received Beuscher's reply. The letter is dated 29 Sept. in *L2*.
143. SP to AP, 9 Oct. 1962. *L2*, 847–48. Plath wrote to Beuscher on 9 Oct., "I found he went after Ted with a knife at Waterloo Station & tried to commit suicide after." *L2*, 851.
144. SP to AP, 9 Oct. 1962. *L2*, 847–48.

31. THE PROBLEM OF HIM

1. SP to Richard Murphy, 7 Oct. 1962. *L2*, 846.
2. According to Ted Hughes's dates in SP's *Collected Poems*, Plath wrote twelve poems in 1960, and twenty-two in 1961.
3. Plath had read Dante at Smith, and Jane Baltzell Kopp told me Plath had translated Dante at Cambridge.
4. TH, "Trial," section 16. Add MS 88993/1/1, BL.
5. SP, "New Poems" (typed 13 Dec. 1962 for Douglas Cleverdon at the BBC for a program of new poems). 6.16 SPC, Smith.
6. Hughes told this to Keith Sagar and William Scammell. See HC, *The Grief of Influence*, for fuller discussion about the influences of these poems on Plath's work.
7. Howard Moss to SP, 26 Sept. 1962. *New Yorker* Papers, NYPL.
8. Otto E. Plath, *Bumblebees and Their Ways* (New York: Macmillan, 1934), 36; 51.
9. SP, "New Poems." Al Alvarez Papers, Add MS 88589/8, BL.

10. Ibid.
11. TH to William Scammell, 29 Apr. 1998. Add MS 88918/137, BL.
12. SP, "New Poems." Al Alvarez Papers, Add MS 88589/8, BL.
13. The week of Oct. 7–13 is missing from Plath's 1962 Letts Royal Office Tablet Diary (19.2, SPC, Smith).
14. SP, "New Poems." Al Alvarez Papers, Add MS 88589/8, BL.
15. SP to Dr. Ruth Beuscher, 9 Oct. 1962. *L2*, 851.
16. SP to Dr. Ruth Beuscher, 22 Sept. 1962. *L2*, 832.
17. SP to Dr. Ruth Beuscher, 9 Oct. 1962. *L2*, 853.
18. SP to AP, 9 Oct. 1962. *L2*, 847–50.
19. Nathaniel Tarn, Oct. 1962, diary notes. M1132, Nathaniel Tarn Papers, Stanford.
20. Yehuda Koren and Eliat Negev, *Lover of Unreason: Assia Wevill, Sylvia Plath's Rival and Ted Hughes's Doomed Love* (New York: Carroll and Graf, 2007), 111.
21. Nathaniel Tarn, 1 Oct. 1962, diary notes. M1132, Nathaniel Tarn Papers, Stanford. David and Assia Wevill were still attending the Group together; on 5 Oct. Tarn noted his annoyance that the Wevills had not reacted to or discussed his poems that evening.
22. SP to Howard Moss, 10 Oct. 1962. *L2*, 854.
23. SP, "New Poems." 6.16, SPC, Smith.
24. She handwrote her first draft on the back of Hughes's play *The Calm* and then wrote two more typewritten drafts on the back of Hughes's review of the socialist playwright Arnold Wesker. The fifth typewritten draft is on clean paper. The drafts are at 8.61, SPC, Smith.
25. SP, "New Poems." 6.16, SPC, Smith.
26. Justine Picardie, "The Toxic Avenger," *Independent* (30 Sept. 1995).
27. Maggie Nelson, *The Art of Cruelty: A Reckoning* (New York: Norton, 2011), 246.
28. George Steiner, *Language and Silence: Essays on Language, Literature, and the Inhuman.* 2nd ed. (New Haven: Yale University Press, 1970; 1998), 301.
29. TH, "Notes on the Chronological Order of Sylvia Plath's Poems," *TriQuarterly* 7 (Fall 1966): 81–88. 84.
30. SP, draft of "Daddy." 8.61, SPC, Smith.
31. See Heather Cam, "'Daddy': Sylvia Plath's Debt to Anne Sexton," *American Literature* 59.3 (October 1987): 429–32. "My Friend, My Friend" appeared in *The Antioch Review* 19 (1959): 150, but, as Cam notes, Plath probably saw a version of it in Lowell's seminar.
32. A. Alvarez, "Sylvia Plath," *TriQuarterly* 7 (Fall 1966): 65–74. 71.
33. The article discussed Brueghel's prophetic nature in the context of his paintings *The Triumph of Death* and *The Massacre of the Innocents.*
34. *CPTH*, 165.
35. *CPTH*, 166.
36. Helen Vendler, "An Intractable Metal," *New Yorker* (15 Feb. 1992): 124.
37. SP to AP, 12 Oct. 1962. *L2*, 855.
38. EF interview with Elizabeth Compton Sigmund, Sept. 1999. EFP.
39. SP to AP, 12 Oct. 1962. *L2*, 855–57. The article Plath mentioned was by Elizabeth Jennings, who included Plath among a handful of "Memorable English or American woman poets" that also featured Emily Brontë, Emily Dickinson, Marianne Moore, Edith Sitwell, Anne Ridler, Kathleen Raine, Elizabeth Bishop. Elizabeth Jennings. "Mrs. Browning. By Alethea Hayter," *Listener* (13 Sept. 1962): 400.
40. SP to Warren and Margaret Plath, 12 Oct. 1962. *L2*, 859.
41. Ibid., *L2*, 858.
42. Ibid.
43. Ibid., *L2*, 859.
44. HC interview with Suzette and Helder Macedo, May 2016, London.
45. SP to Warren and Maggie Plath, 12 Oct. 1962. *L2*, 860.
46. SP to AP, 16 Oct. (#1) 1962. *L2*, 861–62.
47. SP to AP, 16 Oct. (#2) 1962. *L2*, 863.
48. SP to AP, 16 Oct. (#1) 1962. *L2*, 862.
49. SP, "Medusa," draft 1, p. 2, composed 16 Oct. 1962. 11.152, SPC, Smith.

50. AP to Judith Kroll, 1 Dec. 1978. 29.26, SPC, Smith.
51. HC interview with Suzette Macedo, May 2016, London.
52. Harriet Rosenstein interview with Suzette Macedo, 1973. 2.18, MSS 1489, Emory.
53. HC interview with Suzette and Helder Macedo, May 2016, London.
54. SP to AP, 16 Oct. (#1) 1962. *L2*, 861.
55. Harriet Rosenstein interview with Marvin Kane, 1973–74. 2.8, MSS 1489, Emory.
56. SP to AP, 16 Oct. (#1) 1962. *L2*, 862.
57. Edith Hughes to AP, 17 Oct. 1962. Lilly.
58. SP to AP, 16 Oct. 1962. *L2*, 860.
59. SP to AP, 18 Oct. 1962. *L2*, 865.
60. Kenneth Neville-Davies revealed this information in an email to Peter Steinberg, 11 Feb. 2016. Cited with permission of Kenneth Neville-Davies.
61. HC interview with Elizabeth Compton Sigmund, May 2016, Cornwall.
62. SP to AP, 16 Oct. (#2) 1962. *L2*, 863.
63. SP to AP, 18 Oct. 1962. *L2*, 865.
64. SP to WP, 18 Oct. 1962. *L2*, 870–71.
65. SP to OHP, 18 Oct. 1962. *L2*, 869. Edith complained to her son Gerald that Sylvia did not let her hold Frieda enough when they visited, and talked about how much it pained her to put the baby down. Edith Hughes to Gerald Hughes, Mar. 1961, quoted in *Ted & I: A Brother's Memoir* (New York: St. Martin's, 2012), 155.
66. SP to OHP, 18 Oct. 1962. *L2*, 868–69.
67. OHP to SP, 27 Nov. 1962. 17.43, SPC, Smith.
68. SP to Clarissa Roche, 20 Oct. 1962. *L2*, 872.
69. There are five drafts of the poem at 9.97, SPC, Smith.
70. SP, "New Poems." 6.16, SPC, Smith.
71. She wrote to Aurelia on 22 Oct. saying that paying for the nanny was "a wise decision for us to make." Lilly.
72. SP to AP, 21 Oct. 1962. *L2*, 873–74.
73. Ibid., *L2*, 875.
74. SP to Dr. Ruth Beuscher, 21 Oct. 1962. *L2*, 879.
75. Ibid., *L2*, 877.
76. Ibid., *L2*, 878.
77. Ibid., *L2*, 877–79.
78. SP to AP, 21 Oct. 1962. *L2*, 875.
79. SP to OHP, 15 Dec. 1962. *L2*, 937.
80. SP to Ruth Fainlight, 22 Oct. 1962. *L2*, 880–82.
81. She did not date them, but their subject and her pen color suggest that she read them also on 22 Oct. Plath's copy of this book is at SPC, Smith.
82. Hughes's edition of Plath's *Collected Poems* gives "Lady Lazarus" a misleading chronology. There, it follows "Cut," "Ariel," and "Purdah." But Plath wrote the first draft of "Lady Lazarus" on 23 Oct., before these other poems. The poem went through six undated handwritten drafts, on the back of chapter 3 of *The Bell Jar*, then four more additional typewritten drafts (on the back of chapter 2 of *The Bell Jar*, drafts of "The Bald Madonnas," and "Totem") dated 23 Oct. She removed one word on 29 Oct. and then made some additional changes in her December *Ariel* typescript. The drafts of the poem are at SPC, Smith.
83. SP, "New Poems." 6.16, SPC, Smith.
84. *CPTH*, 11.
85. Jillian Becker to Harriet Rosenstein, 24 Feb. 1974. Provided by Jillian Becker. See HC, *The Grief of Influence*, for a detailed discussion of the ways in which Plath responded ironically to the White Goddess identification.
86. Paul Giles, *Virtual Americas: Transnational Fictions and the Transatlantic Imaginary* (Durham, NC: Duke University Press, 2004), 222. See also Robin Peel, *Writing Back: Sylvia Plath and Cold War Politics* (Vancouver: Fairleigh Dickinson Press, 2002) for more on this topic.
87. SP to AP, 23 Oct. 1962. *L2*, 882–83.

88. SP to OHP, 25 Oct. 1962. *L2*, 891.
89. Winifred Davies to AP, 3 Nov. 1962. Lilly.
90. SP to OHP, 25 Oct. 1962. *L2*, 891.
91. Harriet Rosenstein interview with Susan O'Neill-Roe Booth, 1973. 1.11, MSS 1489, Emory.
92. Critics have noted that "Dirty girl" suggests menstruation.
93. Harriet Rosenstein interview with Susan O'Neill-Roe Booth, 1973. 1.11, MSS 1489, Emory.
94. HC interview with Suzette and Helder Macedo, May 2016, London.
95. SP to AP, 23 Oct. 1962. *L2*, 884.
96. SP to Clarissa Roche, 25 Oct. 1962. *L2*, 889.
97. SP to AP, 25 Oct. 1962. *L2*, 887–88.
98. Ibid.
99. OHP to AP, 27 Oct. 1962. Lilly.
100. OHP to AP, 3 Nov. 1962. Lilly.
101. Fifty years after its composition, the critic Dan Chiasson wrote, "There is nothing else like this in English; it is, I think, a perfect poem, perfect in its excesses and stray blasphemies . . . which make Plath Plath—that is to say, dangerous, heedless, a menace, and irresistible." "Sylvia Plath's Joy," *New Yorker* (12 Feb. 2013).
102. Robert Lowell, *Collected Poems* (New York: Farrar, Straus and Giroux, 2003), 191.
103. SP, "New Poems." 6.16, SPC, Smith.
104. TH, "Poetry in the Making: Capturing Animals," *Winter Pollen: Occasional Prose* (New York: Picador, 1995), 15.
105. *CPTH*, 21.
106. *J*, 521.
107. *CPTH*, 21.
108. *BJ*, 72.
109. W. B. Yeats, *Collected Poems*, Richard Finneran, ed. (New York: Macmillan, 1989), 194.
110. The drafts of "Ariel" are at 6.15, SPC, Smith.
111. SP, "New Poems." 6.16, SPC, Smith.
112. Giles, *Virtual Americas*, 221–22.
113. Eavan Boland, *A Journey with Two Maps: Becoming a Woman Poet* (New York: Norton, 2011), 158.
114. Ibid., 75.

32. CASTLES IN AIR

1. Plath probably showed Hughes the bee poems before he left Court Green on 11 Oct. 1962.
2. Al Alvarez to SP, c. Oct. 1962. 17.21, SPC, Smith.
3. SP to OHP, 25 Oct. 1962. *L2*, 890.
4. SP to Warren and Margaret Plath, 25 Oct. 1962. *L2*, 893.
5. Other readers that day suggest the dominance of the Group: Zulfikar Ghose, John Lehmann, Peter Porter, Peter Redgrove, and Nathaniel Tarn, who would go on to win the Cheltenham Literature Festival Plath was supposed to have judged in 1963.
6. EF interview with Al Alvarez, July 1999. EFP.
7. A. Alvarez, *The Savage God: A Study of Suicide* (London: Weidenfeld & Nicolson, 1971; New York: W. W. Norton, 1990), 39.
8. Ibid., 37; 39–40.
9. Ibid., 33–34.
10. Ibid., 41.
11. HC interview with Al Alvarez, May 2016, London.
12. Alvarez, *Savage God*, 32. The manuscript is in the Al Alvarez Papers, Add MS 88589, BL.
13. Plath decided on *Ariel* after her 3–5 Dec. 1962 visit to London, when she saw Alvarez and showed him the full manuscript.

14. SP to OHP, 2 Nov. 1962. *L2*, 896.
15. *New Poems 1962: A P.E.N. Anthology of Contemporary Poetry*, Lawrence Durrell, ed. (London: Hutchinson, 1962).
16. SP to OHP, 2 Nov. 1962. *L2*, 895.
17. Harriet Rosenstein interview with Edward Lucie-Smith, 1970. 2.17, MSS 1489, Emory.
18. Michael Hamburger, review of *A Lover of Unreason*, *Modern Poetry in Translation*, series 3, no. 7 (2006).
19. HC interview with Daniel Huws, May 2016. London.
20. Daniel Huws, *Memories of Ted Hughes 1952–1963* (Nottingham: Richard Hollis/Five Leaves), 48.
21. SP to OHP, 2 Nov. 1962. *L2*, 895.
22. SP to Eric Walter White, 26 Oct. 1962. *L2*, 894.
23. Eric Walter White to Jack Sweeney, 11 Feb. 1963. LA52/348, Jack and Máire Sweeney Papers, UCD.
24. Patric Dickinson to Harriet Rosenstein, 1973. 1.24, MSS 1489, Emory. In this letter, Dickinson likely misremembers their meeting as occurring one or two days before Plath's suicide. He states in his 1973 letter that their meeting in the pub was the first and only time he met Plath. SP recorded the Oct. 30 meeting in her calendar.
25. SP to AP, 23 Oct. 1962. According to Peter Steinberg and Karen Kukil, "The American Poetry night was held on 16 July 1963; presented by Eric Mottram, with assistance from John Hollander and Jonathan Williams. Poets included Robert Lowell, Muriel Rukeyser, and Ronald Johnson; Guy Kingsley Poynter read from *Paterson* by William Carlos Williams." *L2*, 883–84.
26. *The Poet Speaks*, Peter Orr, ed. (London: Routledge and Keegan Paul, 1966), 167–68.
27. Ibid., 169–70.
28. SP to OHP, 2 Nov. 1962. *L2*, 895–96.
29. SP to AP, 7 Nov. 1962. *L2*, 898–99.
30. A. Alvarez, *Where Did It All Go Right?* (London: Richard Cohen, 1999), 313; 323; 319.
31. HC interview with Suzette and Helder Macedo, May 2016, London.
32. Ibid.
33. The dates of this visit come from Plath's 1962 Letts Royal Office Tablet Diary, 19.2, SPC, Smith. The program was produced by George MacBeth. Plath read with Donald Hall, Basil Langton, and John Hall Wheelock.
34. SP to AP, 7 Nov. 1962. *L2*, 898.
35. David Wevill email to HC, 29 Sept. 2016.
36. SP to AP, 7 Nov. 1962. *L2*, 898.
37. HC interview with Suzette and Helder Macedo, May 2016, London.
38. Ibid.
39. EF interview with Suzette Macedo, Oct. 1999. EFP.
40. HC interview with Suzette and Helder Macedo, May 2016, London.
41. Ibid.
42. EF interview with Suzette Macedo, Oct. 1999. EFP.
43. Harriet Rosenstein interview with Suzette Macedo, 1973. 2.18, MSS 1489, Emory.
44. HC interview with Suzette and Helder Macedo, May 2016, London.
45. Harriet Rosenstein interview with Suzette Macedo, 1973. 2.18, MSS 1489, Emory.
46. EF interview with Suzette Macedo, Oct. 1999. EFP.
47. Suzette Macedo to Harriet Rosenstein, c. 1973. 2.18, MSS 1489, Emory.
48. HC interview with Suzette and Helder Macedo, May 2016, London. Hughes published the poem without the dedication in Plath's 1981 *Collected Poems*, though Frieda Hughes restored it in her later edition of *Ariel*.
49. SP to AP, 7 Nov. 1962. *L2*, 898–99.
50. Harriet Rosenstein interview with Helder Macedo, 1973. 2.18, MSS 1489, Emory.
51. Jillian Becker to Harriet Rosenstein, 19 Feb. 1974. 1.8, MSS 1489, Emory.
52. SP to AP, 19 Nov. 1962. *L2*, 905.
53. Plath's copy of *The Collected Plays of W. B. Yeats* (New York: Macmillan, 1953) is at SPC, Smith. The quote she underlined is on p. 347.

54. Alvarez, *Savage God*, 43.
55. Anne Stevenson, interview notes with Suzette Macedo, 10 June 1987. 2.24, Houghton Mifflin Papers, Smith.
56. Alvarez, *Savage God*, 32.
57. See William Wooten, "'That Alchemical Power': The Literary Relationship of A. Alvarez and Sylvia Plath," *Cambridge Quarterly* (Sept. 2010): 217–36. 224.
58. Alvarez, *Savage God*, 32–33.
59. Wooten, "That Alchemical Power," 227.
60. Alvarez, *Savage God*, 36–37.
61. SP to AP, 7 Nov. 1962. *L2*, 897–99.
62. HC interview with Suzette and Helder Macedo, May 2016, London.
63. Harriet Rosenstein interview with Helder Macedo, 1973. 2.18, MSS 1489, Emory.
64. SP, "New Poems." Alvarez papers, Add MS 88589/8, BL.
65. Ronald Hayman, *The Death and Life of Sylvia Plath* (New York: Birch Lane Press, 1991), 189. The dedication appears in an early typescript. 10.135, SPC, Smith.
66. Carl Rollyson, *American Isis: The Life and Art of Sylvia Plath* (New York: St. Martin's Press, 2013), 219.
67. Alvarez, *Where Did It All Go Right?*, 315.
68. John Gale, "Thalidomide Baby Fund Launched," *Observer* (21 Oct. 1962), 3; Dr. Abraham Marcus, "New Tests Show Drug Danger," *Observer* (14 Oct. 1962), 12.
69. Mark Wormald email to HC, 16 Nov. 2017.
70. HC interview with Daniel Huws, May 2016, London. Huws remained close to Luke Myers well into the late 1990s, as correspondence in the British Library shows.
71. Luke Myers to EF, 25 Feb. 2001. EFP.
72. HC interview with Daniel Huws, May 2016, London.
73. HC interview with Elizabeth Compton Sigmund, May 2016, Cornwall.
74. HC interview with Al Alvarez, May 2016, London.
75. Al Alvarez to Harriet Rosenstein, 20 June 1974. 1.2, MSS 1489, Emory.
76. Will Wooten is the only scholar to have done significant research on Plath and Alvarez.
77. Hughes never sent the letter. 55.52, MSS 644, Emory.
78. TH to Al Alvarez, n.d., mid-to-late Nov. 1971. Add MS 88593/1, BL. This was Hughes's second letter to Alvarez on the matter.
79. HC interview with Daniel Huws, May 2016, London.
80. TH to Al Alvarez, Nov. 1971. *LTH*, 322; 325.
81. TH to Al Alvarez, mid-to-late Nov. 1971. Add MS 88593/1, BL.
82. TH to Al Alvarez, Nov. 1971. *LTH*, 324.
83. Al Alvarez to Harriet Rosenstein, 20 June 1974. 1.2, MSS 1489, Emory.
84. Al Alvarez to TH, 15 Nov. 1971. Add MS 88593/1, BL.
85. "Sylvia Plath" (letters from Ted Hughes and Al Alvarez), *Observer* (7 Nov. 1971).
86. TH to Al Alvarez, 22 Oct. 1977. Add MS 88593/1, BL.
87. Al Alvarez, "Ted, Sylvia and Me," *Guardian* (4 Jan. 2004): Review 1–2.
88. Add MS 88918/1/2-8, BL.
89. HC interview with Suzette and Helder Macedo, May 2016, London.
90. Olwyn Hughes to Al Alvarez, 24 Oct. 1972. Add MS 88603, BL.
91. Al Alvarez to Olwyn Hughes, 25 Oct. 1972. Add MS 88603, BL.
92. Olwyn Hughes to Al Alvarez, c. Oct. 1972. Add MS 88603, BL.
93. This letter is not in the British Library, but Alvarez's response indicates its content.
94. Al Alvarez to Olwyn Hughes, 10 June 1988. Add MS 88603, BL.
95. Olwyn Hughes to Al Alvarez, 9 June 1988. (The letter was written in response to Alvarez's 10 June 1988 letter. Assuming Alvarez's date is correct, it is misdated.) Add MS 88603, BL.
96. EF, draft of *Ted Hughes: The Life of a Poet*, p. 191. EFP.
97. SP to Bill Merwin, 8 Nov. 1962. *L2*, 901.
98. TH to Bill Merwin, late fall 1962. 1.22, MSS 866, Emory.
99. Plath's copy of *The Art of Loving* is held as part of the Ted Hughes archive at Emory. These highlighted passages appear on pages 99, 112, and 126.
100. In her 4 Feb. 1963 letter, Plath told Beuscher she practiced these exercises. *L2*, 968.

101. In a letter to Olive Prouty dated 2 Nov., Plath wrote, "My phone is in: the number is NORTH TAWTON 447." *L2*, 895.
102. HC interview with David Compton, May 2016, Bowdoinham, Maine.
103. Clarissa Roche, "Sylvia Plath: Vignettes from England," *Sylvia Plath: The Woman and the Work*, Edward Butscher, ed. (New York: Dodd, Mead and Co., 1977), 83; 84.
104. Harriet Rosenstein interview with Clarissa Roche, 1973. 3.14, MSS 1489, Emory.
105. Suzette Macedo to Harriet Rosenstein, c. 1973. 2.18, MSS 1489, Emory.
106. Harriet Rosenstein interview with Clarissa Roche, 1973. 3.14, MSS 1489, Emory.
107. Harriet Rosenstein interview with Elizabeth Compton Sigmund, 1973. 4.10, MSS 1489, Emory.
108. Harriet Rosenstein interview with Clarissa Roche, 1973. 3.14, MSS 1489, Emory.
109. Harriet Rosenstein interview with Elizabeth Compton Sigmund, 1973. 4.10, MSS 1489, Emory.
110. Harriet Rosenstein interview with Clarissa Roche, 1973. 3.14, MSS 1489, Emory.
111. HC interview with Elizabeth Compton Sigmund, May 2016, Cornwall; Harriet Rosenstein interview with Clarissa Roche, 1973. 3.14, MSS 1489, Emory.
112. SP to AP, 19 Nov. 1962. *L2*, 906.
113. SP to Dorothy Benotti, 14 Dec. 1962. *L2*, 930–31.
114. SP to OHP, 20 Nov. 1962. *L2*, 912.
115. Peter Davison to SP, 20 Nov. 1962. 17.22.1, SPC, Smith.
116. SP to AP, 19 Nov. 1962. *L2*, 904.
117. SP to W. Roger Smith, 19 Nov. 1962. *L2*, 908.
118. SP to Leonie Cohn, 20 Nov. 1962. *L2*, 909.
119. SP to Stevie Smith, 19 Nov. 1962. *L2*, 907–908.
120. Stevie Smith to SP, 22 Nov. 1962. 17.46, SPC, Smith.
121. SP to Ruth Fainlight, 20 Nov. 1962. *L2*, 915.
122. HC interview with Ruth Fainlight, May 2016, London.
123. SP to Harriet Cooke, 29 Nov. 1962. *L2*, 925. The Cookes had visited the Hugheses in London in 1960, and SP had corresponded with Harriet about her plan to live in Ireland.
124. SP to AP, 22 Nov. 1962. *L2*, 918.
125. Harriet Rosenstein interview with Bessie Stoneman, 1970. (Filed under John Avery.) 1.4, MSS 1489, Emory.
126. Harriet Rosenstein interview with Elizabeth Compton Sigmund, 1975. 4.10, MSS 1489, Emory.
127. Ibid.
128. SP to AP, 29 Nov. 1962. *L2*, 923.
129. SP to AP, 22 Nov. 1962. *L2*, 920. Susan would write to Plath a week before her suicide that she had wanted to meet her "for at least three years, but circumstances were against." Susan Alliston Moore to SP, 4 Feb. 1963. SPC, Smith.
130. SP to AP, 22 Nov. 1962. *L2*, 919–20.
131. SP to AP, 29 Nov. 1962. *L2*, 923.
132. SP to Harriet Cooke, 29 Nov. 1962. *L2*, 925.
133. TH to Olwyn Hughes, Sept. 1962. *LTH*, 208.
134. SP to AP, 22 Nov. 1962. *L2*, 919.
135. SP to AP, 7 Nov. 1962. *L2*, 898.
136. OHP to SP, 27 Nov. 1962. 17.43, SPC, Smith.
137. SP to Daniel and Helga Huws, 26 Dec. 1962. *L2*, 944.
138. In the 1970s, Aurelia would redact all references to this plan in black ink, worried that she had been involved in a minor tax evasion.
139. SP to AP, 29 Nov. 1962. *L2*, 922.
140. AP to SP, 4 Dec. 1962. 17.41, SPC, Smith.
141. AP to SP, 8 Dec. 1962. 17.41, SPC, Smith.
142. OHP to SP, 27 Nov. 1962. 17.43, SPC, Smith. Plath had already informed Aurelia she would dedicate her second book of poems to Prouty if it were ever published in America.
143. SP to AP, 14 Dec. 1962. *L2*, 928–29.

144. AP to SP, 4 Dec. 1962. 17.41, SPC, Smith.
145. AP to SP, 8 Dec. 1962. 17.41, SPC, Smith.
146. AP to SP, 4 Dec. 1962. 17.41, SPC, Smith.
147. AP to SP, 8 Dec. 1962. 17.41, SPC, Smith. Aurelia writes, "Did you know that Robert Graves was considered for the Nobel prize this year—wish he had received it!!!"
148. Ibid.
149. SP to AP, 29 Nov. 1962. *L2*, 922.
150. According to her 1962 Letts Royal Office Tablet Diary (19.2, SPC. Smith), Plath had tea with Gilbert and Marian Foster on 30 Sept., 25 Nov., and 2 Dec. Gilbert wrote poetry and earned a first-class BA in history at Trinity College Dublin as a mature student.
151. Winifred Davies to AP, 5 Dec. 1962. Lilly.
152. SP to AP, 29 Nov. 1962. *L2*, 922.
153. SP to OHP, 20 Nov. 1962. *L2*, 913.
154. SP to Harriet Cooke, 29 Nov. 1962. *L2*, 924–25.
155. Judith Kroll, *Chapters in a Mythology: The Poetry of Sylvia Plath* (New York: Harper & Row, 1976; Gloucestershire: Sutton, 2007), 69; 236.
156. Nathaniel Tarn, 12 Mar. 1963, diary notes. M1132, Nathaniel Tarn Papers, Stanford.
157. HC interview with Elizabeth Compton Sigmund, May 2016, Cornwall.
158. Olwyn Hughes to Al Alvarez, 9 June 1988. This is misdated; it was probably 10 June. Add MS 88603, BL.
159. Harriet Rosenstein, notes on Fran McCullough interview, 1973–75. 2.20, MSS 1489, Emory.
160. *JP*, 11.
161. TH interview with Drue Heinz, "The Art of Poetry, LXXI," *Paris Review* 134 (1995), in *The Paris Review Interviews, III* (London: Picador, 2008), 56–92.
162. SP to Michael Carey, 21 Nov. 1962. *L2*, 917.
163. SP to Michael Carey, 29 Nov. 1962. *L2*, 926.
164. Plath says the trip lasted five days, although her 1962 Letts Royal Office Tablet Diary (19.2, SPC, Smith) suggests that it was only three.
165. HC interview with Suzette and Helder Macedo, May 2016, London.
166. Ibid. Hughes later wrote in his November 1979 journal about kissing Dido after she declared her attraction to him. Jonathan Bate, *Ted Hughes*, 401.
167. TH, "Soho Square." Add MS 88918/1/6, BL.

33. YEATS'S HOUSE

1. Plath used Douglas Cleverdon's name as a reference for applying for a "priority phone" for her freelance work. SP to Douglas Cleverdon, 16 Dec. 1962. *L2*, 938.
2. SP to AP, 14 Dec. 1962. *L2*, 927–29.
3. SP to Dorothy Benotti, 14 Dec. 1962. *L2*, 931.
4. I am grateful to Linda Johnson for showing me around 23 Fitzroy Road on 6 July 2017 and for explaining the floors' former layout. The elegant townhouse has been beautifully renovated, but the footprint of Plath's top floor, with its three bedrooms, is much as it was in 1962.
5. SP to AP, 14 Dec. 1962. *L2*, 929.
6. SP to AP, 26 Dec. 1962. *L2*, 941.
7. Linda Johnson told me there were three large sycamore trees in the back garden that dated from Plath's time. They have since been cut down.
8. Suzette Macedo to Harriet Rosenstein, c. 1973. 2.18, MSS 1489, Emory.
9. SP to AP, 21 Dec. 1962. *L2*, 941.
10. Elizabeth Alexander to SP, 8 Dec. 1962; SP to Elizabeth Alexander, 10 Dec. 1962. 17.49, SPC, Smith.
11. SP, 18 Dec. 1962. 1962 Letts Royal Office Tablet Diary. 19.2, SPC, Smith.
12. HC interview with Lorna Secker-Walker, June 2017, London.
13. SP to AP, 14 Dec. 1962. *L2*, 928.
14. Catherine lived at 18 Chalcot Crescent and Lorna at 5 Chalcot Square. Lorna Secker-

Walker would eventually become a professor of medicine at the Royal Free Hospital. According to Plath's 1962 Letts Royal Office Tablet Diary (19.2, SPC, Smith), she had tea with Catherine on 20 Dec. and tea with Lorna on 23 Dec.

15. Harriet Rosenstein interview with Lorna and David Secker-Walker, 1970. 4.7, MSS 1489, Emory.
16. HC interview with Lorna Secker-Walker, June 2017, London.
17. Harriet Rosenstein interview with Lorna and David Secker-Walker, 1970. 4.7, MSS 1489, Emory.
18. Harriet Rosenstein interview with Suzette Macedo, 1973. 2.18, MSS 1489, Emory.
19. Harriet Rosenstein interview with Lorna and David Secker-Walker, 1970. 4.7, MSS 1489, Emory.
20. Ibid.
21. Ibid.
22. HC interview with Lorna Secker-Walker, June 2017, London.
23. SP to AP, 29 Nov. 1962. *L2*, 923.
24. Kenneth Neville-Davies (who went by the name Garnett as a young man) remembers that he came on the evening of 23 Dec.; Plath also notes that he came on 30 and 31 Dec.
25. Douglas Cleverdon to SP, 11 & 20 Dec. 1962. SPC, 17.25, Smith.
26. SP, "New Poems," 13 Dec. 1962. 1.16, SPC, Smith. Plath's commentary and copies of "Letter in November," "The Bee Meeting," "The Arrival of the Bee Box," and "Wintering" are in the Al Alvarez Papers at the British Library.
27. Dorothy Barker, internal memo, 18 Jan. 1963. BBC Written Archives. Quoted in Peter K. Steinberg and Gail Crowther, "These Ghostly Archives," *Plath Profiles* 2 (Summer 2009): 183–207. 196.
28. SP to AP, 14 Dec. 1962. *L2*, 928.
29. SP to AP, 21 Dec. 1962. *L2*, 940.
30. A. Alvarez, *The Savage God: A Study of Suicide* (London: Weidenfeld & Nicolson, 1971; New York: W. W. Norton, 1990), 46–48.
31. A. Alvarez, *Where Did It All Go Right?* (London: Richard Cohen Books, 1999), 208–209.
32. Ted said he invited her to the Beacon with the children, but she declined. HC interview with Suzette Macedo, May 2016, London.
33. Suzette Macedo email to HC, 30 Sept. 2016.
34. SP to AP, 26 Dec. 1962. *L2*, 943.
35. EF interview with Suzette Macedo, Oct. 1999. EFP.
36. Suzette Macedo to Harriet Rosenstein, c. 1973. 2.18, MSS 1489, Emory.
37. Anne Stevenson interview with Suzette Macedo, 10 June 1987. 2.24, Houghton Mifflin Papers, Smith.
38. EF interview with Suzette Macedo, Oct. 1999. EFP.
39. Harriet Rosenstein interview with Catherine Frankfort, 1970–71. 1.27, MSS 1489, Emory.
40. Jillian Becker to Harriet Rosenstein, 17 Apr. 1976. Provided to HC by Jillian Becker.
41. Clarissa Roche, who was impressed by Plath's "smart" kitchen and "gadgetry," remembered that "even for an American she was living reasonably well" in Yeats's flat. She felt it "a gross exaggeration to assume she was oppressed by poverty the last weeks of her life." "Sylvia Plath: Vignettes from England," *Sylvia Plath: The Woman and the Work*, Edward Butscher, ed. (New York: Dodd, Mead and Co., 1977), 92.
42. Harriet Rosenstein interview with Clarissa Roche, 1973. 3.14, MSS 1489, Emory.
43. HC interview with Daniel Huws, May 2016, London.
44. SP to Daniel and Helga Huws, 26 Dec. 1962. *L2*, 944.
45. SP to AP, 2 Jan. 1963. *L2*, 948.
46. Ibid., *L2*, 948–49.
47. *JP*, 127.
48. HC interview with Lorna Secker-Walker, June 2017, London.
49. *JP*, 131.
50. SP to Charles Osborne, 9 Jan. 1963. *L2*, 955.
51. Linda Gates, "Sylvia Plath and I," *Plath Profiles* 5 (Fall 2012): 106–108, 108.

52. It would not be published until it appeared in *JP*.
53. *JP*, 131.
54. Trevor Thomas, "Sylvia Plath: Last Encounters," 1989. 1.6, MSS 1318, Emory. According to Linda Johnson, there was also a separate basement flat at the time, which Thomas would not have had access to. She had once rented the basement flat herself, and assumed there was a third tenant in the building in 1962, though neither Plath nor Thomas mentioned another tenant. HC interview with Linda Johnson, current occupant of 23 Fitzroy Road, July 2017, London.
55. See Christopher Bissell and Avi Boukli, "How the Last Man to See Sylvia Plath Alive Was Punished for His Quiet Homosexuality," 21 February 2017, www.theconversation .com.
56. "Frozen Fog Was Cause of 'Worst Power Crisis,'" *Observer* (27 Jan. 1963), 3.
57. Trevor Thomas, "Sylvia Plath: Last Encounters." 1.6, MSS 1318, Emory.
58. *JP*, 133.
59. Harriet Rosenstein interview with Paul Roche, 1973. 3.14, MSS 1489, Emory.
60. Roche, "Sylvia Plath: Vignettes from England," 92–93.
61. Henry Rago to SP, 27 Dec. 1962. 17.42, SPC. Smith; Tony Dyson to SP, 8 Jan. 1963. 17.27, SPC, Smith.
62. SP to Paul and Clarissa Roche, c. 9 Jan. 1963. *L2*, 956.
63. SP to AP, 2 Jan. 1963. *L2*, 949.
64. SP to Marcia Brown Plumer, 2 Jan. 1963. *L2*, 951–52.
65. TH to Olwyn Hughes, Dec. 1962. 1.10, MSS 980, Emory.
66. TH to Al Alvarez, n.d., fall 1962. Add MS 88593/1, BL.
67. SP, Lloyd's Bank checkbook stubs, Jan. 1960–Jan. 1963. 19.5, SPC, Smith.
68. Nathaniel Tarn, 5 Jan. 1963, diary notes. M1132, Nathaniel Tarn Papers, Stanford.
69. Olwyn Hughes to Al Alvarez, 9 June 1988. This is misdated; it was probably 10 June. Add MS 88603, BL.
70. Harriet Rosenstein interview with Suzette and Helder Macedo, 1973. 2.18, MSS 1489, Emory.
71. Nathaniel Tarn, 7 Dec. 1962, diary notes. M1132, Nathaniel Tarn Papers, Stanford.
72. Assia told Nathaniel she was sending David's manuscript to Donald Hall in America and "hoping for the best." Meanwhile, Penguin had offered to publish it. Nathaniel Tarn, 7 Dec. 1962, diary notes. M1132, Nathaniel Tarn Papers, Stanford.
73. SP to AP, 16 Jan. 1963. *L2*, 958.
74. SP to OHP, 22 Jan. 1963. *L2*, 960.
75. "'Tortoise' Thaw Is Creeping On," *Observer* (27 Jan. 1963), 1.
76. HC interview with Suzette and Helder Macedo, May 2016, London.
77. "New Comment," recorded with George MacBeth. Recorded and broadcast 10 Jan. 1963.
78. Harriet Rosenstein interview with Dr. John Horder, 1970–71. 2.2, MSS 1489, Emory.
79. SP to Paul and Clarissa Roche, c. 9 Jan. 1963. *L2*, 956.
80. SP to AP, 16 Jan. 1963. *L2*, 957.
81. SP to Paul and Clarissa Roche, c. 9 Jan. 1963. *L2*, 956.
82. SP to AP, 16 Jan. 1963. *L2*, 959.
83. Ibid., *L2*, 957.
84. OHP to SP, 25 Jan. 1963. 17.43, SPC, Smith.
85. HC interview with Suzette and Helder Macedo, May 2016, London.
86. Suzette Macedo told me she believes that Plath was never as close to the Beckers as Jillian later implied, while Jillian has suggested that the friendship between Suzette and Plath had cooled by early February. HC interview with Suzette Macedo, May 2016, London.
87. Jillian Becker, *Giving Up: The Last Days of Sylvia Plath* (New York: St. Martin's Press, 2003), 27–28.
88. Jillian Becker to Harriet Rosenstein, 18 July 1974. Provided by Jillian Becker.
89. Becker, *Giving Up*, 30.
90. Richard Murphy, *The Kick: A Memoir* (London: Granta Books, 2002), 229–30.
91. Nathaniel Tarn, 3 Apr. 1964, diary notes. M1132, Nathaniel Tarn Papers, Stanford.

92. Anne Stevenson interview with Suzette Macedo, 10 June 1987. 2.24, Houghton Mifflin Papers, Smith.
93. Murphy, *The Kick*, 229.
94. SP to AP, 16 Jan. 1963. *L2*, 958.
95. Ruth Fainlight to SP, 12 Jan. 1963. 17.28, SPC, Smith. Fainlight mentions in this letter that she and Alan Sillitoe had nearly bought the property at 30 Fitzroy Road when Plath and Hughes were living in Chalcot Square. "I've often regretted it—now especially."
96. HC interview with Ruth Fainlight, May 2016, London.
97. *LH*, 496–97.
98. SP to AP, 16 Jan. 1963. *L2*, 958.
99. SP to Marcia Brown Plumer, 4 Feb. 1963. *L2*, 965.
100. Plath wrote that he came by to take the children to the zoo on 12 and 27 Dec. and 3 Jan., and that he came at seven p.m. on 5 Jan.
101. TH to Gerald Hughes, c. Dec. 1962. *LTH*, 209–10.
102. TH to Bill and Dido Merwin, 21 Jan. 1963. 1.23, MSS 866, Emory.
103. TH, notebook entry, c. 1962–63. Add MS 88918/129/3, BL.
104. TH, "Introduction" in Susan Alliston, *Susan Alliston: Poems and Journals 1960–1969* (Nottingham: Richard Hollis/Five Leaves), 13.
105. SP to AP, 18 Oct. 1962. *L2*, 865.
106. Alliston, *Poems and Journals*, 82–83.
107. TH, "Difficulties of a Bridegroom." 122.7, MSS 644, Emory.
108. TH to Olwyn Hughes, 10 Feb. 1963. *LTH*, 212–13.
109. Alliston, *Poems and Journals*, 86.
110. Ibid., 84; 86.
111. HC phone interview with Elizabeth Compton Sigmund, 27 May 2016.
112. Ibid.
113. HC interview with Daniel Huws, May 2016, London.
114. Peter Hall to TH, 27 Sept. 1965. *LTH*, 251.
115. *CPTH*, 1128.
116. Al Alvarez, 27 Jan. 1963 broadcast of *The Critics*. BBC Home Service. Add MS 88562/2, BL.
117. Suzette and Helder Macedo also recalled the ridiculous maiden-chorus, which they imitated during our interview.
118. TH, "Trial," section 15. Add MS 88993/1/1, BL.
119. Anon., "Under the Skin," *Times Literary Supplement* (25 Jan. 1963), 53.
120. Robert Taubman, "Anti-heroes," *New Statesman* (25 Jan. 1963), 127–28.
121. Anthony Burgess, "Transatlantic Englishmen: New Novels," *Observer* (27 Jan. 1963), 22.
122. Laurence Lerner, "New Novels," *Listener* (31 Jan. 1963): 215.
123. The novel was also reviewed in Jan. and Feb. 1963 in the *Sunday Telegraph*, *Time & Tide*, *The Guardian*, *Sphere*, the *Glasgow Herald*, the *Scotsman*, *Evening Times* (Glasgow), *Derbyshire Times*, *Express & Star*, *The Times of London*, *The Spectator*, the *Oxford Mail*, and the *Birmingham Post*. See Peter K. Steinberg's comprehensive list of Plath reviews at http://www.sylviaplath.info for specific dates.
124. Trevor Thomas, "Sylvia Plath: Last Encounters." 1.6, MSS 1318, Emory.
125. *The Ha-Ha* was published on 18 Oct. 1961, two months after Plath finished *The Bell Jar*.
126. This is according to Jillian Becker. Hughes, however, remembered that she was "halfway through *The Rack*," about a group of tuberculosis patients in a sanatorium, when she died. TH to AP, Jan. 1975. 5.18, MSS 644, Emory. According to Hughes, Plath had already read *The Rack* in early 1960. She may have been rereading it, or he may have confused it with Dawson's *The Ha-Ha*.
127. Dr. Francis de Marneffe, deposition (1987 *Bell Jar* trial). Jane Anderson v. AVCO Embassy Pictures Corp. et al., in the United States District Court, District of Massachusetts, Civil Action no. 82-0752-K. Jane V. Anderson Papers, Series IV, Smith.
128. TH, "Trial," sections 16, 13, and 14. Add MS 88993/1/1, BL.

34. WHAT IS THE REMEDY?

1. Judith Jones to SP, 28 Dec. 1962. 17.20 SPC, Smith.
2. Elizabeth Lawrence to SP, 16 Jan. 1963. 17.31, SPC, Smith.
3. Ibid.
4. EF interview with David Ross, Oct. 1999. EFP.
5. SP, Lloyd's Bank checkbook stubs, Jan. 1960–Jan. 1963. 19.5, SPC, Smith.
6. See footnote 2 in *L2*, 919. Mrs. Prouty sent Plath a check in her 25 Jan. letter. After Plath's death, Aurelia wrote angrily of the "$3000 from us you kept" in the margin of Hughes's May 13, 1963 letter to her (Lilly).
7. HC phone interview with Jillian Becker, 18 Apr. 2017.
8. Linda Gates, "Sylvia Plath and I," *Plath Profiles* 5 (Fall 2012): 106–108. 107.
9. Harriet Rosenstein interview with Paul Roche, 1973. 3.14, MSS 1489, Emory.
10. Claire Tomalin, "Everything but the Truth," *Independent* (8 Oct. 1994).
11. Jeremy Gavron, *A Woman on the Edge of Time* (New York: The Experiment, 2016), 246.
12. This figure comes from the UK Office for National Statistics. Quoted in Julie Goodspeed-Chadwick, *Reclaiming Assia Wevill: Sylvia Plath, Ted Hughes, and the Literary Imagination* (Baton Rouge: Louisiana State University Press, 2019), 108–109.
13. Jane Lewis, *Women in Britain Since 1945* (Oxford: Blackwell, 1992), 45.
14. HC interview with Lorna Secker-Walker, June 2017, London.
15. EF interview with Fay Weldon, June 1999. EFP.
16. TH, "Trial," section 34. Add MS 88993/1/1, BL.
17. Plath and Hughes's copy of *The Golden Notebook* is at the Morgan Library in Manhattan.
18. Suzette Macedo email to HC, 30 Sept. 2016. In 1964, Lessing would buy a cottage, Tor Down, twenty minutes away from Court Green. She and Suzette often visited Ted, Assia, and Olwyn at Court Green. Olwyn at one point lived in Lessing's basement flat at Mornington Crescent.
19. Harriet Rosenstein interview with Helder Macedo, 1973. 2. 18, MSS 1489, Emory.
20. HC phone interview with Jillian Becker, 18 Apr. 2017.
21. A. Alvarez, *The Savage God: A Study of Suicide* (London: Weidenfeld & Nicolson, 1971; New York: W. W. Norton, 1990), 52.
22. OHP to SP, 25 Jan. 1963. 17.43, SPC, Smith.
23. SP to OHP, 22 Jan. 1963. *L2*, 960–62. Plath referred to her au pair as a "German girl."
24. OHP to SP, 25 Jan. 1963. 17.43, SPC, Smith.
25. Philip French to SP, 1 Feb. 1963. BBC Written Archives. French sent her a contract to record on 2, 9, and 16 May, which Plath signed and returned. See Peter K. Steinberg's 18 Feb. 2016 blog post, "After Sylvia Plath," on http://www.sylviaplath.info.
26. EF interview with Al Alvarez, July 1999. EFP.
27. EF interview with Karl Miller, n.d., c. 1999–2000. EFP.
28. EF interview with Al Alvarez, July 1999. EFP. Plath had sent Miller several poems on 9 Nov. 1962.
29. Peter K. Steinberg and Karen Kukil note that according to Plath's submissions list, she submitted "An Appearance," "The Bee Meeting," "Years," "The Fearful," "Mary's Song," "Stings," "Letter in November," "The Couriers," "The Night Dances," "Gulliver," "Cut," and "Berck-Plage" on 17 Jan. 1963. *L2*, 955.
30. Harriet Rosenstein interview with Edward Lucie-Smith, 1970. 2.17, MSS 1489, Emory.
31. Charles Osborne, *Giving It Away: Memoirs of an Uncivil Servant* (London: Secker & Warburg, 1986), 291. Quoted in William Wooten, "'That Alchemical Power': The Literary Relationship of A. Alvarez and Sylvia Plath," *Cambridge Quarterly* (Sept. 2010): 217–36. 220.
32. TH, "Full Moon and Little Frieda," *Observer* (27 Jan. 1963), 23.
33. "Sylvia Plath: Last Encounters," unpublished memoir, privately printed, 1989. 1.6, MSS 1318, Emory.
34. SP to Leonie Cohn, 28 Jan. 1963. *L2*, 962. Cohn accepted the piece but would request changes in a letter to Plath dated 8 Feb. 1963, saying the piece was rather "verbless."

Leonie Cohn to SP, 8 Feb. 1963. 17.25, SPC, Smith. It was read by June Tobin on the BBC in Aug. 1963.

35. SP to AP, 4 Feb. 963. *L2*, 964. SP to Elizabeth Compton, 4 Feb. 1963. 4.10, MSS 1489, Emory.

36. SP, draft of "Sheep in Fog." 12.222, SPC, Smith.

37. Peter K. Steinberg suggests Roethke's influence in his 29 Oct. 2013 blog post, "Sylvia Plath Collections: Theodore Roethke Papers," http://www.sylviaplath.info.

38. SP, "New Poems," 13 Dec. 1962. 1.16, SPC, Smith.

39. SP, draft of "Sheep in Fog." 12.222, SPC, Smith.

40. In a 1998 letter to William Scammell, Hughes said the poem also referred to his uncollected poem "Lines for a Newborn Baby." He mentioned that Plath's reference to the hare may have been based on a dinner of jugged hare that he prepared for friends, including Alvarez, who had told her about it. TH to William Scammell, 29 Apr. 1998. Add MS 88918/137, BL.

41. Jillian Becker to Harriet Rosenstein, 16 July 1974. Provided by Jillian Becker.

42. *CPTH*, 182.

43. *CPTH*, 1119. Steven Axelrod maintains that the image came from a passage in *King Lear* that Plath had underlined in her edition of the play: "It is the stars / The stars above us, govern our conditions" (4.4.34–37). *Sylvia Plath: The Wound and the Cure of Words* (Baltimore: Johns Hopkins University Press, 1990), 75.

44. TH, notebook entry, Feb. 1963. (The entry begins "Last Sunday 3 Feb"). Add MS 88918/129/2, BL.

45. SP to AP, 4 Feb. 1963. *L2*, 964.

46. SP to Marcia Brown Plumer, 4 Feb. 1963. *L2*, 964–65.

47. This letter has not survived. It is quoted in HM, 43.

48. SP to Elizabeth Compton, 4 Feb. 1963. 4.10, MSS 1489, Emory.

49. Michael Carey to SP, 28 Jan. 1963. 17.26, SPC, Smith.

50. SP to Michael Carey, 4 Feb. 1963. *L2*, 966.

51. "Big Thaw Brings Biggest Stoppage," *Observer* (10 Feb. 1963).

52. HC interview with Ruth Fainlight, May 2016, London.

53. Susan Alliston Moore to SP, 4 Feb. 1963. 17.36, SPC, Smith.

54. Dr. John Horder to Harriet Rosenstein, 1970–71. 2.2, MSS 1489, Emory.

55. SP to Dr. Ruth Beuscher, 4 Feb. 1963. *L2*, 967–69.

56. HM, 40.

57. Dr. Ruth Barnhouse to Linda Wagner-Martin, 3 Dec. 1985. Ruth Tiffany Barnhouse Papers, Smith.

58. Anne Stevenson interview with Jillian Becker, 10 July 1987. 2.24, Houghton Mifflin Papers, Smith.

59. Harriet Rosenstein interview with Nancy Axworthy, 1973. 1.5, MSS 1489, Emory.

60. Anne Stevenson interview with Jillian Becker, 10 July 1987. 2.24, Houghton Mifflin Papers, Smith.

61. Kenneth Neville-Davies email to HC, 21 Oct. 2016.

62. Kenneth Neville-Davies email to Peter Steinberg, 8 Feb. 2016. Quoted with permission.

63. TH, notebook entry, Feb. 1963. Add MS 88918/129/2, BL.

64. SP, draft of "Edge." 8.77, SPC, Smith.

65. Ibid.

66. Helen Vendler, *Coming of Age as a Poet: Hilton, Keats, Eliot, Plath* (Cambridge; Harvard University Press, 2003), 146.

67. Jillian Becker, *Giving Up: The Last Days of Sylvia Plath* (New York: St. Martin's Press, 2002), 36–37.

68. Trask appeared as a Classical heroine dressed in a toga on a medal prominently displayed in the Yaddo mansion. See also *Eye Rhymes: Sylvia Plath's Art of the Visual*, Kathleen Connors and Sally Bayley, eds. (Oxford: Oxford University Press, 2007), 134.

69. *J*, 359.

70. *LH*, 36.

71. Shakespeare, *Antony and Cleopatra*, V.ii.238–41. Quoted in Judith Kroll, *Chapters in a Mythology: The Poetry of Sylvia Plath* (New York: Harper & Row, 1976; Gloucestershire: Sutton, 2007), 153.
72. D. H. Lawrence, *The Complete Poems* (London: Heinemann, 1957). SP's library, 825P696L, Smith.
73. Kroll, *Chapters in a Mythology*, 151.
74. Sara Teasdale, *The Collected Poems of Sara Teasdale* (Digireads.com Publishing, 2012), 85.
75. Robert Graves, *The White Goddess: A Historical Grammar of Poetic Myth*, 2nd ed. (New York: Farrar, Straus and Giroux, 1948; 1975), 446.
76. See HC, *The Grief of Influence*, for more details about these poems' influence on "Edge."
77. W. B. Yeats, *Collected Poems*, Richard Finneran, ed. (New York: Macmillan, 1989), 72–73.

35. THE DARK CEILING

1. John Richardson to SP, 7 Feb. 1963. 17.45, SPC, Smith. I am grateful to Gail Crowther for confirming Richardson's presence in London in 1963.
2. See Robin Peel, *Writing Back: Sylvia Plath and Cold War Politics* (Vancouver: Fairleigh Dickinson Press, 2002), 250, for a detailed account of the events recorded in this letter.
3. Leonie Cohn to SP, 8 Feb. 1963. 17.25, SPC, Smith. Plath probably received this letter if it was posted on the eighth; her own letter to Hughes, also mailed on the eighth, had arrived on the same day she posted it.
4. TH, notebook entry, Feb. 1963. Add MS 88918/129/2, BL.
5. Harriet Rosenstein interview with Lorna and David Secker-Walker, 1970. 4.7, MSS 1489, Emory.
6. HC interview with Lorna Secker-Walker, June 2017, London.
7. Ibid.
8. Jillian Becker to Harriet Rosenstein, 28 May 1974. 1.8, MSS 1489, Emory.
9. TH, notebook entry, Feb. 1963. Add MS 88918/129/2, BL.
10. *CPTH*, 1154–55.
11. TH to AP, 12 Jan. 1975. 16.3, MSS 644, Emory.
12. Dan Carrier, "Obituary: Dr John Horder, 'father of modern general practice' who excelled as a pianist and artist," *Camden New Journal* (14 June 2012). Dr. Horder went on to become the first British doctor to be "appointed as a consultant to the World Health Organization."
13. HC interview with Lorna Secker-Walker, June 2017, London.
14. Ali Haggett, *Desperate Housewives: Neuroses and the Domestic Environment, 1945–1970* (London: Pickering & Chatto, 2012), 102. Such practice was typical of the time in Britain, where there existed, according to Haggett, "a more informal and unofficial practice of supportive therapy that took place during regular surgery consultations."
15. Dr. John Horder told Elizabeth Hinchcliffe he "specifically" prescribed Plath Parnate. Elizabeth Hinchcliffe email to HC, 5 Jan. 2017. He told Harriet Rosenstein, however, that he prescribed Plath Nardil.
16. HM, 46; SP, 5 Jan. 1963. 1962–63 Letts Royal Office Tablet Diary. 19.2, SPC, Smith.
17. Haggett, *Desperate Housewives*, 98–99.
18. TH, draft introduction to "Sylvia Plath and Her Journals," *Grand Street* 1.3 (Spring 1982): 86–99. 143.3, MSS 644, Emory. Hughes did not include this passage in the published version.
19. Harriet Rosenstein interview with Dr. John Horder, 1970–71. 2.2, MSS 1489, Emory.
20. HM, 45. Hinchcliffe interviewed Dr. Horder for her biography in the 1970s.
21. Harriet Rosenstein interview with Catherine Frankfort, 1970–71. 1.27, MSS 1489, Emory.
22. HC interview with Lorna Secker-Walker, June 2017, London.
23. Harriet Rosenstein interview with Jillian Becker, 1973. 1.8, MSS 1489, Emory.
24. Jillian Becker email to HC, 19 Apr. 2017.

25. Jillian Becker, *Giving Up: The Last Days of Sylvia Plath* (New York: St. Martin's Press, 2002), 3.
26. Jillian Becker, "Chronology," c. 1974. 1.8, MSS 1489, Emory.
27. Jillian Becker to Harriet Rosenstein, 5 Mar. 1974. 1.8, MSS 1489, Emory.
28. Becker, *Giving Up*, 5–6.
29. HC interview with Suzette and Helder Macedo, May 2016, London. Jillian barely mentions Suzette's presence in *Giving Up*, except to call her "quite an artist with gossip," p. 8.
30. HC interview with Suzette and Helder Macedo, May 2016, London.
31. Anne Stevenson interview with Suzette Macedo, 10 June 1987. 2.24, Houghton Mifflin Papers, Smith.
32. Jillian Becker, "Chronology," c. 1974. 1.8, MSS 1489, Emory.
33. Becker, *Giving Up*, 8.
34. HC phone interview with Jillian Becker, 18 Apr. 2017.
35. Anne Stevenson interview with Suzette Macedo, 10 June 1987. 2.24, Houghton Mifflin Papers, Smith.
36. Becker, *Giving Up*, 9.
37. Jillian Becker, "Sylvia Plath: Jillian Becker on the Poet's Last Days," BBC News, *Magazine*, 10 Feb. 2013, http://www.bbc.com/news/magazine-21336933.
38. Becker, *Giving Up*, 10–11. The program was probably *The Poet's Voice*, broadcast on 24 Aug. 1962.
39. HC phone interview with Jillian Becker, 18 Apr. 2017.
40. Harriet Rosenstein interview with Jillian Becker, 1973. 1.8, MSS 1489, Emory. Anne Stevenson interview with Jillian Becker, 10 July 1987. 2.24, Houghton Mifflin Papers, Smith, and HC phone interview with Jillian Becker, 18 Apr. 2017.
41. Jillian Becker to Harriet Rosenstein, 17 Apr. 1976. Provided to HC by Jillian Becker.
42. HC phone interview with Jillian Becker, 18 Apr. 2017.
43. Ibid.
44. Jillian Becker, "Chronology," c. 1974. 1.8, MSS 1489, Emory.
45. Becker, "Sylvia Plath: Jillian Becker on the Poet's Last Days."
46. Jillian Becker to Harriet Rosenstein, 19 Feb. 1974. 1.8, MSS 1489, Emory.
47. Becker, *Giving Up*, 14.
48. HC interview with Suzette and Helder Macedo, May 2016, London.
49. HC interview with Lorna Secker-Walker, June 2017, London.
50. The quotes come from Ted Hughes's notes, which he showed to the scholar Judith Kroll when she visited Court Green in 1974. Judith Kroll, *Chapters in a Mythology: The Poetry of Sylvia Plath* (New York: Harper & Row, 1976; Gloucestershire: Sutton Publishing, 2007), xxxi.
51. Ibid.
52. Jillian Becker, "Chronology," c. 1974. 1.8, MSS 1489, Emory.
53. Becker, "Sylvia Plath: Jillian Becker on the Poet's Last Days."
54. Eric Walter White to Jack Sweeney, 22 Feb. 1963. LA 52/348, Jack and Máire Sweeney Papers, UCD.
55. Anon., "Tragic Death of Young Authoress," *St. Pancras Chronicle* (22 Feb. 1963), AA 33.
56. HM, 49; 54. Elizabeth Hinchcliffe quoted Dr. Horder from the inquest, which is no longer available.
57. Harriet Rosenstein interview with Dr. John Horder, 1970–71. 2.2, MSS 1489, Emory.
58. "Friern Hospital," www.asylum projects.org.
59. HC phone interview with Jillian Becker, 18 Apr. 2017.
60. The postmark on the Feb. 4 letter Plath mailed to Dr. Beuscher on Friday, 8 Feb., from the Fitzroy Road post office area (NW 1) reveals that Plath mailed her letter to Beuscher at 12:45 p.m. She probably mailed her letter to Hughes at the same time.
61. TH, draft of "Last Letter." Add MS 88918/1/2–8, BL.
62. Ibid.
63. Ibid.
64. Anne Stevenson interview with Suzette Macedo and Olwyn Hughes, 10 June 1987. 2.24, Houghton Mifflin Papers, Smith.

65. Anne Stevenson interview with Jillian Becker, 10 July 1987. 2.24, Houghton Mifflin Papers, Smith.
66. TH, notebook entry, Feb. 1963. Add MS 88918/129/2, BL.
67. TH, "Last Letter," *New Statesman* (7 Oct. 2010).
68. Trevor Thomas, "Sylvia Plath: Last Encounters," unpublished memoir, privately printed, 1989. 1.6, MSS 1318, Emory.
69. Jillian Becker, "Chronology," c. 1974. 1.8, MSS 1489, Emory.
70. Anne Stevenson interview with Jillian Becker, 10 July 1987. 2.24, Houghton Mifflin Papers, Smith.
71. Judith Flanders to Corin Hughes-Stanton, 13 Oct. 1987, forwarded with handwritten note to Peter Davison. 1.7, Houghton Mifflin Papers, Smith.
72. SP, Letts Royal Office Tablet Diary, 19.2, SPC, Smith.
73. Anne Stevenson interview with Jillian Becker, 10 July 1987. 2.24, Houghton Mifflin Papers, Smith; Judith Flanders to Corin Hughes-Stanton, 13 Oct. 1987. 1.7, Houghton Mifflin Papers, Smith.
74. Anne Stevenson, *Bitter Fame: A Life of Sylvia Plath* (London: Penguin, 1989), 295.
75. Visitor's book belonging to Patricia Ehle Goodall, 1958–1963. Plath's entry is dated 8 Feb. 1963. 42.6, SPC, Smith.
76. Jillian does not mention the story of the bus ride in *Giving Up*, but she told Harriet Rosenstein, in a 17 Apr. 1974 letter, that "Suzette took the child out" on what she remembered as Friday, 8 Feb. That was the day Jillian remembers Plath speaking about her mysterious appointment—not Saturday, 9 Feb., as Suzette remembers. However, Suzette held a full-time job at a local library and would not have been able to take Frieda for a long bus ride, nor enjoy a theater matinee, on a weekday. Jillian says in her 1974 "Chronology" that Sylvia spent all day Saturday at home with her, but provides no details at all about what they did or spoke about. She wrote nothing about that Saturday—indeed she seemed to skip the day entirely—in *Giving Up*.
77. HC interview with Suzette and Helder Macedo, May 2016, London. In *Giving Up*, Jillian misremembered the night Plath saw the Goodalls as Saturday, rather than Friday.
78. Patric Dickinson to Harriet Rosenstein, 1973. 1.24, MSS 1489, Emory.
79. HC interview with Suzette and Helder Macedo, May 2016, London.
80. Yehuda Koren and Eilat Negev, *Lover of Unreason: Assia Wevill, Sylvia Plath's Rival and Ted Hughes's Doomed Love* (New York: Carroll & Graf, 2007), 119–20.
81. Jillian Becker to Elizabeth Compton Sigmund, 27 Mar. 2002. William Sigmund Papers, Smith.
82. Jillian Becker, "Chronology," c. 1974. 1.8, MSS 1489, Emory, and Stevenson, *Bitter Fame*, 295.
83. Jillian Becker, "Chronology," c. 1974. 1.8, MSS 1489, Emory.
84. Jonathan Bate, *Ted Hughes: The Unauthorised Life* (New York: HarperCollins, 2015), 211.
85. Becker, *Giving Up*, 15–16.
86. HC interview with Suzette and Helder Macedo, May 2016, London. Nathaniel Tarn's notes at Stanford confirm that Plath had spoken to Suzette Macedo on that Sunday.
87. HC interview with Suzette and Helder Macedo, May 2016, London.
88. Jillian Becker to Harriet Rosenstein, 17 Apr. 1974. 1.8, MSS 1489, Emory.
89. Becker, "Sylvia Plath: Jillian Becker on the Poet's Last Days."
90. Becker, *Giving Up*, 17.
91. HM, 49. Elizabeth Hinchcliffe interviewed Dr. Horder in the 1970s.
92. Anne Stevenson interview with Jillian Becker, 10 July 1987. 2.24, Houghton Mifflin Papers, Smith.
93. Becker, *Giving Up*, 21.
94. "Plath—Hughes: One of Us Had to Die," unpublished memoir by Gerry Becker, quoted in Ronald Hayman, *The Death and Life of Sylvia Plath* (New York: Birch Lane Press, 1991), 12. Jillian Becker told Harriet Rosenstein that Gerry stayed with Plath in the flat for "an hour or so" after he dropped her off. 1.8, MSS 1489, Emory.
95. Jillian Becker email to HC, 30 Apr. 2017.

96. Becker, "Sylvia Plath: Jillian Becker on the Poet's Last Days."
97. Thomas, "Sylvia Plath: Last Encounters," 1989. 1.6 MSS 1318, Emory.
98. Richard Larschan email to HC, 28 Nov. 2018.
99. EF interview with David Ross, Oct. 1999. EFP.
100. TH, "Last Letter." Daniel Huws told me Susan's flat was above the one where Plath and Hughes spent their wedding night.
101. According to Plath's autopsy report, she died between seven and eight a.m. SP, University College Hospital autopsy report, 11 Feb. 1963, signed by Dr. Peter M. Sutton, overseen by Dr. Wigglesworth. Warren wrote Aurelia in his 17 Feb. 1963 letter to Aurelia (at Lilly) that the children were "each left with a bottle."
102. The pen seems to have run out as she was writing "Horder," so she stopped writing mid-note to find a new pen. There is a photocopy of Plath's suicide note in HM (no page number). She may have put the first pen down to look up Horder's phone number, then picked up a different one.
103. Dr. Horder told various sources over the years about how Plath had taped and stuffed the cracks in the doors of her flat. See, for example, Plath biographies by Linda Wagner-Martin and Paul Alexander, and Jane Feinmann, "Rhyme, Reason and Depression" (interview with Dr. John Horder), *Guardian* (16 Feb. 1993).
104. The sun rose at 7:23 a.m. on 11 Feb. 1963.
105. TH, draft of introduction to SP's abridged journals. 143.3, MSS 644, Emory.
106. TH to Keith Sagar, 18–19 July 1998. *Poet and Critic: The Letters of Ted Hughes and Keith Sagar*, Keith Sagar, ed. (London: British Library, 2012), 272.
107. Hughes felt that she had written angry "responses" to his poems in her own late work. TH to William Scammell, 29 Apr. 1998. Add MS 88918/137, BL. The letter goes into some depth on the topic of mutual influence between himself and Plath.
108. Frieda Hughes, "Foreword," *Ariel: The Restored Edition* (New York: HarperCollins, 2004), xx.

EPILOGUE: YOUR WIFE IS DEAD

1. TH, "Last Letter," *New Statesman* (11 Oct. 2010).
2. Notes, Harriet Rosenstein interview with Winifred Davies, 1970, provided by Kenneth Neville-Davies.
3. Jane Feinmann, "Rhyme, Reason and Depression" (interview with Dr. John Horder), *Guardian* (16 Feb. 1993).
4. HC phone interview with Jillian Becker, 18 Apr. 2017.
5. This account is drawn from Metropolitan Police Statement of Witness, No. 992, 14 Feb. 1963, given by John Jones; Anon., "Tragic Death of Young Authoress," *St. Pancras Chronicle* (22 Feb. 1963), AA 33; and Elizabeth Hinchcliffe's unpublished biography. Hinchcliffe interviewed the coroner and Dr. Horder in the early 1970s.
6. Metropolitan Police Statement of Witness, No. 992, 14 Feb. 1963, given by John Jones. Provided to HC by Jillian Becker.
7. Several previous Plath biographies have stated that Myra Norris came to Plath's flat at nine a.m. that morning. This timing does not square with Dr. Horder's arrival time of eleven thirty a.m. Even if Myra Norris had to wait in line to make a phone call at a public phone booth, it is unlikely that she waited nearly two hours. Norris was, as Hinchcliffe reported in her unpublished manuscript, likely over an hour late.
8. Dr. Horder was gone by the time he got to Plath's flat.
9. Interview with Dr. John Horder by Constable John Jones, Police Report from 11 Feb. 1963.
10. Ibid.
11. Jillian Becker to Harriet Rosenstein, n.d., 1970s. Provided by Jillian Becker.
12. SP, University College Hospital autopsy report, 11 Feb. 1963, signed by Dr. Peter M. Sutton, overseen by Dr. Wigglesworth. Copy of report provided to HC by Jillian Becker, who was given a copy by an official of the coroner's court, Mr. Goodchild.
13. Harriet Rosenstein interview with Catherine Frankfort, 1970-71. 1.27, MSS1489, Emory.

14. HC interview with Lorna Secker-Walker, June 2017, London. In *The Death and Life of Sylvia Plath*, Ronald Hayman draws on a letter Frankfort wrote Alvarez in 1981 about her experience on the morning of Plath's suicide. The official police report suggests that some of the information in Frankfort's letter—or Hayman's interpretation of that letter—was inaccurate.
15. Suzette Macedo email to HC, 20 May 2016.
16. HC interview with Suzette and Helder Macedo, May 2016, London.
17. Jonathan Bate, *Ted Hughes: The Unauthorised Life* (New York: HarperCollins, 2015), 211.
18. EF interview with David Ross, Oct. 1999. EFP. Feinstein says this incident happened after Plath's funeral, yet in the original interview transcript Ross dates the visit to the evening of 11 Feb. 1963. Sue Alliston does not mention visiting 23 Fitzroy Road on 11 Feb. in her journal, quoted in Bate, 211–12.
19. Jillian Becker, *Giving Up: The Last Days of Sylvia Plath* (New York: St. Martin's, 2002), 23–24.
20. WP to AP, 17 Feb. 1963. Lilly.
21. HC phone interview with Jillian Becker, 18 Apr. 2017.
22. TH to Olwyn Hughes, Feb. 1963. *LTH*, 213.
23. TH to Daniel Huws, Feb. 1963. *LTH*, 214.
24. Sam Jordison, interview with Elizabeth Compton Sigmund, *Guardian* (18 Jan. 2013).
25. WP to AP, 17 Feb. 1963. Lilly.
26. Lucas Myers to EF, 14 Oct. 2001. EFP.
27. TH to Bill and Dido Merwin, Mar. 1963. Add MS 88918/35/23, BL.
28. TH to David and Elizabeth Compton, late summer 1963. Add MS 88612, BL.
29. A. Alvarez, *The Savage God: A Study of Suicide* (London: Weidenfeld & Nicolson, 1971; New York: W. W. Norton, 1990), 56.
30. Anon., "Tragic Death of Young Authoress."
31. HM, 54. Hinchcliffe interviewed Horder and quoted from a copy of the inquest, which is no longer available.
32. Anon., "Tragic Death of Young Authoress."
33. Alvarez, *Savage God*, 56.
34. Ronald Hayman's interview with Al Alvarez, Nov. 1990, is the source for this information in Hayman's *The Death and Life of Sylvia Plath* (New York: Birch Press, 1991), 15.
35. Copy of official "Inquisition," 15 Feb. 1963, provided to HC by Jillian Becker.
36. Feinmann, "Rhyme, Reason and Depression."
37. AP to Paul Alexander, Apr. 1983. Courtesy of Richard Larschan.
38. HC interview with Lorna Secker-Walker, June 2017, London.
39. WP to AP, 17 Feb. 1963. Lilly.
40. WP to AP, 20 Feb. 1963. Lilly.
41. WP to AP, 25 Feb. 1963. Lilly.
42. HC phone interview with Jillian Becker, 18 Apr. 2017.
43. TH to Bill and Dido Merwin, Mar. 1963. Add MS 88918/35/23, BL.
44. Anne Stevenson, interview notes with Jillian Becker, 10 July 1987. 2.24, Houghton Mifflin Papers, Smith.
45. Nathaniel Tarn, 12 Mar. 1963, diary notes. M1132, Nathaniel Tarn Papers, Stanford.
46. Alvarez, *Savage God*, 99.
47. WP to AP, 20 Feb. 1963. Lilly.
48. Becker, *Giving Up*, 42.
49. WP to AP, 20 Feb. 1963. Lilly. Jillian Becker writes, in her 2002 memoir, *Giving Up*, that the funeral reception took place in a private room above a village club in Heptonstall, up the street from the church. Warren's letter, however, provides more accurate contemporary evidence of its location. Jillian does not mention the first service in Hebden Bridge, which Warren describes in detail to Aurelia. After the funeral, Ted drove to Halifax, where Warren and Margaret were staying with a family friend, John Spalding. There, Ted discussed the matter of Frieda and Nicholas with Warren.
50. Becker, *Giving Up*, 44; 46–47.
51. TH to AP, 15 Mar. 1963. *LTH*, 215–16.

52. TH, notebook entry, spring 1963. Add MS 88918/129/3, BL.
53. TH to AP, 15 Mar. 1963. *LTH*, 215.
54. TH to Keith Sagar, 18–19 July 1998. *Poet and Critic: Letters of Ted Hughes and Keith Sagar*, Keith Sagar, ed. (London: British Library, 2012), 272.
55. TH to Assia Wevill, 27 Mar. 1963. *LTH*, 217.
56. Nathaniel Tarn, 16 Feb. 1963, diary notes. M1132, Nathaniel Tarn Papers, Stanford.
57. TH, notebook entry, spring 1963. Add MS 88918/129/3, BL.
58. HC interview with Lorna Secker-Walker, June 2017, London.
59. HC interview with Elizabeth Compton Sigmund, May 2016, Cornwall.
60. Elizabeth Compton to AP, 27 Mar. 1963. Lilly.
61. EF interview with Elizabeth Compton Sigmund, Sept. 1999. EFP.
62. HC interview with Ruth Fainlight, May 2016, London.
63. TH to Olwyn Hughes, spring 1963. Add MS 88948/1/2, BL.
64. Ibid.
65. TH to Elizabeth and David Compton, summer 1963. Add MS 88612, BL.
66. HC conversation with Pauline Mayne's daughters, May 2015, Sheffield, UK, 2015.
67. TH to Elizabeth and David Compton, c. 23 July 1963. Add MS 88612, BL.
68. HC interview with David Compton, May 2016, Bowdoinham, Maine.
69. TH to AP, 13 May 1963. *LTH*, 218–19.
70. TH to Elizabeth and David Compton, c. 23 July 1963. Add MS 88612, BL.
71. Assia recorded the details of this exchange in her diary. Yehuda Koren and Eilat Negev, *Lover of Unreason: Assia Wevill, Sylvia Plath's Rival and Ted Hughes's Doomed Love* (New York: Carroll and Graf, 2006), 130.
72. TH, "Trial," sections 25–26. Add MS 88993/1/1, BL.
73. Hughes asserted copyright by publishing the book in the U.S., thereby ensuring that Frieda and Nicholas would earn the proceeds from both the UK and U.S. publications.
74. Nathaniel Tarn, 12 Mar. 1963, diary notes. M1132, Nathaniel Tarn Papers, Stanford.
75. TH to Olwyn Hughes, fall 1963. Add MS 88948/1/2, BL.
76. Nathaniel Tarn, 12 Mar. 1963, diary notes. M1132, Nathaniel Tarn Papers, Stanford.
77. Ibid.
78. Nathaniel Tarn, 16 Feb. 1963, diary notes. M1132, Nathaniel Tarn Papers, Stanford.
79. Nathaniel Tarn, 28 Feb. 1963, diary notes. M1132, Nathaniel Tarn Papers, Stanford.
80. Nathaniel Tarn, 16 Feb. 1963, diary notes. M1132, Nathaniel Tarn Papers, Stanford.
81. TH, notebook entry, c. 1963. Add MS 88918/128/1, BL.
82. Nathaniel Tarn, 6 Aug. 1963, diary notes. M1132, Nathaniel Tarn Papers, Stanford. Ted and Assia spent the following week in Alvarez's flat.
83. Koren and Negev quote extensively from Assia's diary in *Lover of Unreason*.
84. TH to Assia Wevill, 3 Oct. 1963. 1.6, MSS 1058, Emory.
85. TH, notebook entry, autumn 1963. Add MS 88918/128/1, BL.
86. David Wevill to Nathaniel Tarn, 2 Apr. 1969. M1132, Nathaniel Tarn Papers, Stanford.
87. Elaine Feinstein, *Ted Hughes: The Life of a Poet* (London: Weidenfeld & Nicolson, 2001), 166.
88. Nathaniel Tarn, 22 June 1963, diary notes. M1132, Nathaniel Tarn Papers, Stanford.
89. HC telephone interview with Linda Gates, 13 Dec. 2016.
90. TH, notebook entry, 9 Oct. 1964. Add MS 88918/128/1, BL.
91. TH, notebook entry, 2 Nov. 1964. Add MS 88918/128/1, BL.
92. TH, notebook entry, 15 Sept. 1964. Add MS 88918/128/1, BL.
93. TH, notebook entry, winter 1965. Add MS 88918/128/1, BL.
94. Koren and Negev, *Lover of Unreason*, 126.
95. EF interview with Suzette Macedo, Oct. 1999. EFP.
96. EF interview with Mira Hamermesh, July 1999. EFP.
97. Assia Wevill, journal, Nov. 1966. 1.77, MSS 1058, Emory.
98. Koren and Negev, *Lover of Unreason*, 122.
99. Ibid., 128–29.
100. HC interview with Elizabeth Compton Sigmund, May 2016, Cornwall.
101. HC interview with David Compton, May 2016, Bowdoinham, Maine.

102. Harriet Rosenstein interview with Elizabeth Compton Sigmund, 1973. 4.10, MSS 1489, Emory.
103. Assia Wevill, journal, Nov. 1966. 1.77, MSS 1058, Emory.
104. Jillian Becker to Harriet Rosenstein, 21 Mar. 1974. Provided to HC by Jillian Becker.
105. EF interview with Keith Sagar, Jan. 2000. EFP.
106. HC interview with Ruth Fainlight, May 2016, London.
107. William Trevor, *Excursions in the Real World* (London: Penguin, 1993), 121.
108. Assia's journal is quoted in Koren and Negev, *Lover of Unreason*, 200.
109. Jillian Becker to Harriet Rosenstein, 21 Mar. 1974. Provided to HC by Jillian Becker.
110. This was the statement the au pair gave to the police in 1969. Quoted in Koren and Negev, *Lover of Unreason*, 201.
111. TH to Celia Chaikin, 14 Apr. 1969. *LTH*, 290.
112. EF interview with Ruth Fainlight, Feb. 2000. EFP.
113. TH to Celia Chaikin, 14 Apr. 1969. *LTH*, 290.
114. Richard Murphy, *The Kick: A Memoir* (London: Granta Books, 2000), 279.
115. HC interview with David Compton, May 2016, Bowdoinham, Maine.
116. HC interview with Dr. Francis de Marneffe, Dec. 2014, Westwood, Mass.
117. TH to Al Alvarez, Nov. 1971. *LTH*, 323.
118. OHP to AP, 6 Aug. 1963. Lilly.
119. HC interview with Ruth Fainlight, May 2016, London.
120. Ruth Fainlight, "1963—World Events," *Jubilee Lines*, Carol Ann Duffy, ed. (London: Faber and Faber, 2012).
121. HC interview with Elizabeth Compton Sigmund, May 2016, Cornwall.
122. HC interview with David Compton, May 2016, Bowdoinham, Maine.
123. HC interview with Elinor Friedman Klein, Oct. 2015, South Salem, N.Y.
124. Harriet Rosenstein interview with Marcia Brown Stern, 1972. 4.16, MSS 1489, Emory.
125. HC interview with Janet Salter Rosenberg, Sept. 2015, Dobbs Ferry, N.Y.
126. Brian Cox, "Ted Hughes (1930–1998): A Personal Retrospect," *Hudson Review* 52.1 (Spring 1999): 29–43. 37.
127. Harriet Rosenstein interview with Anthony Thwaite, 1971. 4.17, MSS 1489, Emory.
128. Harriet Rosenstein interview with Edward Lucie-Smith, 1970. 2.17, MSS 1489, Emory.
129. Harriet Rosenstein interview with Richard Murphy, 1974. 2.25, MSS 1489, Emory.
130. AP to *The Observer*, 4 Mar. 1963 (unsent). Lilly.
131. HC interview with Lorna Secker-Walker, June 2017, London.
132. AP to Miriam Baggett, 27 Jan. 1964. 29.2 SPC, Smith.
133. AP to Miriam Baggett, 19 Apr. 1966. 29.2, SPC, Smith.
134. AP to Miriam Baggett, 7 July 1966. 29.2, SPC, Smith.
135. AP's copy of Judith Kroll's *Chapters in a Mythology* is at SPC, Smith.
136. AP, "For the Authors' Series Talk—Wellesley College Club," 16 Mar. 1976. 30.58, SPC, Smith.
137. Video footage of Aurelia Plath, Nov. 1986, in *Poets of New England: Sylvia Plath and the Myth of the Monstrous Mother*. University of Massachusetts, Amherst, AIMS Video Services. Courtesy of Richard Larschan. 2001.
138. AP to Paul Alexander, Apr. 1983. Courtesy of Richard Larschan.
139. AP to Miriam Baggett, 4 Dec. 1966. 29.2, SPC, Smith.
140. Video footage of Aurelia Plath, Nov. 1986.
141. TH, "Trial," section 19. Add MS 88993/1/1, BL.
142. AP to Paul Alexander, Apr. 1983. Courtesy of Richard Larschan.
143. AP to Miriam Baggett, 4 Dec. 1966. 29.2, SPC, Smith.
144. Eric Walter White to Jack Sweeney, 22 Feb. 1963. LA 52/348, Jack and Máire Sweeney Papers, UCD.
145. Harriet Rosenstein interview with Wilbury Crockett, 1971. 1.19, MSS 1489, Emory.
146. Anita Helle, "'Family Matters': An Afterword on the Biography of Sylvia Plath," *Northwest Review* 26 (1988): 148–60. 154–55.
147. HC interview with Phil McCurdy, May 2016, Ogunquit, Maine.

148. Wilbury Crockett to AP, 27 Mar. 1963. Lilly.
149. Al Alvarez, *Risky Business: People, Pastimes, Poker and Books* (London: Bloomsbury, 2007), 217; 219.
150. Alvarez, *Savage God*, 40.
151. Ibid., 36.
152. TH to Olwyn Hughes, spring 1963. Add MS 88948/1/2, BL.
153. TH to Olwyn Hughes, Feb. 1963. Add MS 88948/1/2, BL.
154. HC telephone interview with Jillian Becker, 17 Apr. 2017.
155. TH to Olwyn Hughes, Feb. 1963. Add MS 88948/1/2, BL.
156. Elizabeth Anscombe (1919–2001), Catholic moral philosopher and student of Wittgenstein, also a Newnham alumna who taught at Cambridge. Anscombe translated and edited Wittgenstein's work and is considered to be one of the greatest women philosophers of the twentieth century. She was married to the British philosopher Peter Geach and was a mother of seven. Plath did not mention Anscombe in any of her surviving writings, though she may have been inspired by Anscombe's ability to balance both a large family and a demanding career. Peter Steinberg speculates, however, that Hughes is talking about Plath's Smith friend Jane Truslow, the wife of Peter Davison, whom Plath referred to in a letter, mockingly, as "Peter Geekie" (SP to Elinor Friedman, 9 Apr. 1957. *L2*, 109). Truslow had also lived in Lawrence House and had shock therapy. Steinberg believes that Hughes may have misspelled Davison's nickname in this journal entry. (Peter Steinberg email to HC, May 2018.)
157. TH, notebook entry, spring 1963. Add MS 88918/129/3, BL.
158. The book is now held in TH and SP's library at Emory.
159. TH to Anne Stevenson, autumn 1986. *LTH*, 523–24.
160. Ibid., 523.
161. The first six lines of this draft are excised in TH's hand. Add MS 88918/1/2–8, BL.
162. SP to Dr. Ruth Beuscher, 4 Feb. 1963. *L2*, 967.
163. Alvarez, *Savage God*, 49.
164. AP to Paul Alexander, Apr. 1983. Courtesy of Richard Larschan.
165. TH to Rosemarie Rowley, 4 Dec. 1997. Add MS 88918/35/28, BL. See Rosemarie Rowley, "Electro-Convulsive Treatment in Sylvia Plath's Life and Work," *Thumbscrew* 10 (Spring 1998): 87-99, for further discussion about Plath and ECT. Ted Hughes called this article "one of the most important things I've read about S. P." in his 4 Dec. 1997 letter to Rowley.
166. Eric Walter White to Jack Sweeney, 22 Feb. 1963. LA 52/348, Jack and Máire Sweeney Papers, UCD.
167. Alvarez, *Savage God*, 107.
168. SP, "The Moon and the Yew Tree," *Collected Poems* (London: Faber and Faber, 1981), 172.
169. HC interview with Elinor Friedman Klein, Oct. 2015, South Salem, N.Y.
170. TH, "Delivering Frieda," eventually revised and included in *Birthday Letters* as "Remission." Add MS 88918/1/2–8, BL.
171. Bate, *Ted Hughes*, 515; Jonathan Bate email to HC, 13 June 2016. Olwyn Hughes told Bate she had read a passage in Plath's last journal about "taking the children's lives too" when she died. She told Bate Hughes had also wanted to destroy the journal to "protect the children from the spectacle of reading about their mother humiliating herself with other men"—by which she meant Richard Murphy, Al Alvarez, and, allegedly, W. S. Merwin. Olwyn claimed that Plath had made advances at Merwin in Jan. 1963, though Merwin was in America at this time.
172. In a 1998 letter to Keith Sagar, Hughes wrote, "Heard rumours recently that SP's journals from 1959 to 1963 (end of 62) were 'seen,' in the sixties. They must have existed, for sure, because I burned one covering the last couple of months—and at that point (early 63), that must have been a continuation of journals right up to it. Strange business—trail's gone cold at the moment." Sagar, *Poet and Critic*, 262–63.
173. Donna E. Stewart and Simone Vigod, "Postpartum Depression," *New England Journal of Medicine* (2016): 375; 2177–86.

174. According to the *Diagnostic Statistical Manual-V* of the American Psychiatric Association, "The risk of postpartum episodes with psychotic features is particularly increased for women with prior postpartum mood episodes but is also elevated for those with a prior history of depressive or bipolar disorder (especially bipolar 1 disorder) and those with a family history of bipolar disorders." American Psychiatric Publishing, 2013.

POSTSCRIPT: A POET'S EPITAPH

1. TH, draft of "Life after Death." Add MS88918/2–8, BL.
2. Anon., "Tragic Death of Young Authoress," *St. Pancras Chronicle* (22 Feb. 1963), AA 33. A full obituary ran in the *Wellesley Townsman* on 21 Feb. *The Boston Globe*, the *Boston Herald*, and *The Boston Traveler* ran brief death notices on 27 and 28 Feb. None of them mentioned Plath's profession as a writer.
3. The suicide rate would drop dramatically when the city switched from coal gas to less lethal natural gas.
4. Plath had sent him some of the poems herself, though "Edge" must have come from Hughes.
5. Nathaniel Tarn, diary notes, 17 Feb. 1963. M1132, Nathaniel Tarn Papers, Stanford.
6. A. Alvarez, *Where Did It All Go Right?* (London: Richard Cohen, 1999), 209–10.
7. The programs were broadcast on 10 July 1963 and 18 Feb. 1964, respectively.
8. P. H. Newby to Douglas Cleverdon, 6 Mar. 1963. BBC Written Archives. See Peter K. Steinberg and Gail Crowther, "These Ghostly Archives," *Plath Profiles* 2 (Summer 2009): 183–208. 197.
9. David Machin to TH, 15 Mar. 1963. 17.49, SPC, Smith.
10. TH to Joan Hughes, 1963. 1.3, MSS 854, 1963, Emory.
11. TH to Al Alvarez, 15 Oct. 1981. Add MS 88593, BL.
12. See Peter K. Steinberg's website, http://www.sylviaplath.info, for Plath's complete periodical bibliography.
13. TH to Charles Monteith, 7 Apr. 1964. *LTH*, 233.
14. TH to Donald Hall, late 1963. *LTH*, 225–26.
15. TH to Keith Sagar, 23 May 1981. *Poet and Critic: The Letters of Ted Hughes & Keith Sagar*, Keith Sagar, ed. (London: British Library, 2012), 108.
16. Quoted in Jonathan Bate, *Ted Hughes: The Unauthorised Life* (New York: HarperCollins, 2015), 238.
17. Robert Lowell to Elizabeth Bishop, 27 Oct. 1963. *Words in Air: The Complete Correspondence Between Elizabeth Bishop and Robert Lowell*, Thomas Travisano and Saskia Hamilton, eds. (New York: Farrar, Straus and Giroux, 2008), 513.
18. Al Alvarez to TH, 23 Oct. 1981. Add MS 88593, BL. In this letter, Alvarez told Hughes he shouldn't have destroyed Plath's last journals, just hidden them until "everyone who could be hurt is dead & gone."
19. HC interview with Al Alvarez, May 2016, London.
20. Robert Lowell, "Foreword," in Sylvia Plath, *Ariel* (New York: Harper & Row, 1966), viii.
21. M. L. Rosenthal, "Poets of the Dangerous Way," *Spectator* (Mar. 1965), 367.
22. Anon., "The Blood Jet Is Poetry," *Time* (10 June 1966), 118–20.
23. A. Alvarez, *The Savage God: A Study of Suicide* (London: Weidenfeld & Nicolson, 1971; New York: W. W. Norton, 1990), 46.
24. Will Wooten notes that the stanza "gained a large audience through being quoted" in *The Penguin Book of Contemporary British Poetry*, Blake Morrison and Andrew Motion, eds. (Harmondsworth: Penguin, 1982), 13. Will Wooten, *The Alvarez Generation* (Liverpool: Liverpool University Press, 2015), 156.
25. TH to Keith Sagar, 18–19 July 1998. Sagar, *Poet and Critic*, 270.
26. TH to AP, 12 Jan. 1975. 16.3, MSS 644, Emory.
27. TH to Ruth Fainlight and Alan Sillitoe, c. 1980s. Add MS 88918/35/28, BL.
28. Ibid.
29. TH to Bill Merwin, 9 June 1988. *LTH*, 545.
30. TH to Lucas Myers, 14 Feb. 1987. *LTH*, 536–37.

31. AP, "Points to Bring Out in Talks and Interviews." Aurelia wrote, "I have been bombarded by accusations of deliberate exclusion of pertinent material in my editing of my daughter's letters. My original manuscript contained 1,018 typed pages, which had to be sent to my late daughter's husband for his approval and cutting. . . . What excisions I made were in cases of repetition, domestic details, requests for library materials to which I had access and the like which would hold little or no interest for the reader." Courtesy of Richard Larschan.
32. AP to Miriam Baggett, 13 Nov. 1974. 29.2, SPC, Smith.
33. AP to Carol Hughes, 5 July 1982. 143.1a, MSS 644, Emory.
34. This quote comes from Koren and Negev's interview with Hughes in 1996. Yehuda Koren and Eilat Negev, *Lover of Unreason: Assia Wevill, Sylvia Plath's Rival and Ted Hughes's Doomed Love* (New York: Carroll and Graf, 2006), 227.
35. Add MS 88918/1/2-8, BL.
36. TH to Gerald and Joan Hughes, May 1969. 1.3, MSS 854, Emory.
37. TH, notebook 11. 57.10, MSS 644, Emory.
38. The Plath estate eventually settled with Anderson for $150,000. Bate, *Ted Hughes*, 438.
39. TH to Keith Sagar, 18–19 July 1998. Sagar, *Poet and Critic*, 271.
40. TH to Craig Raine, 5 Apr. 1997. Add MS 88918/35/25, BL.
41. TH to Keith Sagar, 18–19 July 1998. Sagar, *Poet and Critic*, 271.
42. TH to Michael Schmidt, 2 Mar. 1998. Add MS 88918/35/28, BL.
43. TH to Nicholas Hughes, 20 Feb. 1998. *LTH*, 712–13.
44. TH to Keith Sagar, 18–19 July 1998. Sagar, *Poet and Critic*, 270–71.
45. SP, draft of "Edge." 8.77, SPC, Smith.
46. TH, "Notes on the Chronological Order of Sylvia Plath's Poems," *TriQuarterly* 7 (Fall 1966): 81–88. 84.

Index

Plath, Warren (brother) *(continued)*
Hughes and, 457, 477, 900–903, 909
visits in Cape Cod and, 499
visits in England, 544, 664
wedding of Plath and, 448
later years of, 920
Otto and, 39
Paris and, 457
Peter Aldrich and, 272
Plath at Smith and, 307, 338, 344, 348,
360
Plath on, 142
Plath's children and, 598, 900, 902–3, 909
Plath suicide attempt of 1953 and, 257, 272,
274–76
Pollock suicide and, 210
wedding of, 679, 694, 789
Plato, 365, 441, 442, 575
Allegory of the Cave, 56, 91
Plumer, Marcia Brown, 327–28, 371, 439, 441,
449, 478–79, 488, 499, 507, 517, 520, 524,
542, 550, 588–90, 593, 597–98, 614, 666,
669, 690, 839, 846, 866–67, 869, 892, 919
"Babysitters" and, 666
"Dialogue" and, 213–14
Harvard Summer School and, 260–61
Mel Woody and, 175, 177, 249, 325
nanny in Swampscott with Plath, 171–81
Plath at *Mademoiselle* and, 238–39
Plath's depression of 1953 and, 260–61, 264–65,
272–73, 309–10
roommate of Plath at Smith, 68, 151, 161–64,
167–70, 181–88, 197–99, 205, 208, 210,
225, 228
Wylie and, 303
Plumer, Mike, 273, 327, 520, 524, 542, 866–67
Plymouth Rock, 179
Podhoretz, Norman, 549
Poe, Edgar Allan, 81, 91, 110, 341, 378
Poetry at the Mermaid Festival, 657–58
Poetry Book Society, 605, 714, 826
Hawk in Rain as top choice, 492, 497, 499
Hughes as judge for, 667
Poetry from Cambridge (Levenson), 708, 757
Poetry magazine, xxvi, 436–37, 448, 464, 474, 479,
481, 490, 499, 511, 532, 574, 617, 686,
689–90, 831, 838, 860, 931
Plath awarded Bess Hokin Prize, 511
Poetry of Sylvia Plath, The (BBC broadcast), 930
"Poet's Epitaph, A" (Alvarez), 929–30
"Poets of the Dangerous Way" (Rosenthal), 933
Poet Speaks series (British Council)
Plath interview and, 801
Poets' Theatre (Boston), 544, 642
Poet's Voice, The (BBC program), 491, 619, 799
Plath records for, 736
Pointe du Raz, France, 656
Point Shirley (Winthrop), 23, 36, 40, 52, 551,
568
"Poison" (Lawrence), 786
Poison (Schaeffer), 631–33
Poisoned Womb, The (Elkington), 537
Poland, 4, 6, 59, 758, 768
Polish Corridor, 4
Pollard, Charlie, 714

Pollard, John, 97, 128
Pollock, George, suicide of, 210
Pollock, Jackson
Convergence, 756
Poor Little Rich Girl, The (Gates), 83
Popa, Vasko, 486
Pope, Alexander, 378
Porter, Katherine Anne, 239, 548, 572
Porter, Peter, 706, 730, 758, 840–41, 889
Portrait of a Lady (James), 326
Portrait of the Artist as a Young Man, A (Joyce),
227–28, 508, 528
"Ariel" and, 263–64
Bell Jar and, xxiii, 263, 306, 509
Posen Province, 4, 6
Possessed, The (Dostoevsky), 314
Possum Walked Backwards (BBC program), 657
Pound, Ezra, 110, 113, 186, 545, 546, 554, 826
Powley, Betsy. *See* Wallingford, Betsy Powley
Powley, Mark, 64
Powley family, 83, 93
Prager, Robert, lynching of, 14
Pratson, Pat O'Neil, 61, 67–68, 105–6, 120–21,
126, 136, 148, 150, 155, 163, 181, 264, 272,
274–76, 309–10, 439, 441, 530
"Prayer" (Lawrence), 873
"Prayer for My Daughter, A" (Yeats), 575
"Preludes" (Eliot), 112, 142
Prentice, Alison, 212
"Presentiment" (Dickinson), 136–37
Press, John, 477, 485
Press Board, Plath as member of, 184–85, 187,
191, 205, 206, 236
Pride and Prejudice (Austen), 82
Primrose Hill, London, 589, 596, 641, 652
"Princess, The" (Lawrence), 507
Princeton University, 182, 184, 186, 208, 603
Pritchett, V. S., 832
"Prospice" (Browning), 921
"Protestantism in an Age of Uncertainty"
(Greene), 227
Proust, Marcel, 302
Prouty, Olive Higgins, 222, 245, 360, 416, 624,
762, 782–83, 786, 789, 798, 800, 802,
859–60
advice to Plath, on Cambridge, 376, 366
Aurelia and, 324, 344, 356, 361, 389, 480, 640,
792, 823, 918
Bell Jar and, 909
Beuscher, Dr., and, 302–3, 344
birth of Frieda Hughes and, 599
correspondence with Plath, 324, 347, 379–81,
386, 388–89, 644, 737, 782–84, 786, 789,
798, 800, 802, 822, 825, 859–60, 932
encourages Plath's writing, 488
financial aid to Plath, 926
after breakup, 792, 778, 803, 817, 829, 834,
844, 822, 855–56, 860
after suicide attempt of 1953, 270, 296,
305
during marriage, 590, 607, 613, 618
home of, 660
Hughes's Harvard reading and, 520
Plath on, 364
Plath's criticism of, 817

Illustration Credits

Page 7

SP and friends, 1949: Courtesy of Lilly Library

SP's graduation portrait, 1950: Helle Collection, courtesy of Smith College Special
    Collections

SP at Star Island, 1949: Courtesy of Lilly Library, © Estate of AP

SP on graduation day, 1950: Courtesy of Lilly Library, © Estate of AP

Page 8

Paradise Pond, Smith College: © HC

OHP, 1964: Mortimer Rare Book Collection, courtesy of Smith College Special
    Collections

SP and Marcia Brown, 1951: Mortimer Rare Book Collection, courtesy of Smith College
    Special Collections

SP and Haven House friends, 1951: Mortimer Rare Book Collection, courtesy of Smith
    College Special Collections

INSERT II

Page 1

SP and DN at Yale junior prom, 1951: Courtesy of Lilly Library

SP and the Mayo children, 1951: Mortimer Rare Book Collection, courtesy of Smith
    College Special Collections, © Estate of Marcia Brown Stern

SP sunbathing in Marblehead, 1951: Mortimer Rare Book Collection, courtesy of Smith
    College Special Collections, © Estate of Marcia Brown Stern

Page 2

The Mayo mansion: Courtesy of Lilly Library, © Estate of SP

SP with bicycle, 1951: Mortimer Rare Book Collection, courtesy of Smith College Special
    Collections, © Estate of Marcia Brown Stern

SP with Perry Norton, 1953: Courtesy of Lilly Library

SP with Myron Lotz, 1953: Courtesy of Lilly Library

Page 3

SP interviewing Elizabeth Bowen, 1953: Mortimer Rare Book Collection, courtesy of
    Smith College Special Collections, © Black Star

SP at St. Regis Hotel dance, 1953: Mortimer Rare Book Collection, courtesy of Smith
    College Special Collections, © Black Star

Page 4

McLean Hospital: © HC

Dr. Ruth Beuscher and family, late 1950s: Courtesy of British Library

SP, studio portrait, 1954: Courtesy of Lilly Library, photo by Eric Stahlberg

SP, AP, and WP, Christmas 1953: Courtesy of Lilly Library

Page 5

SP in Chatham, 1954: Courtesy of Lilly Library and Elizabeth Lameyer Gilmore, photo by
    Gordon Lameyer

SP and Gordon Lameyer, Chatham, 1954: Courtesy of Lilly Library and Elizabeth
    Lameyer Gilmore

SP with flower, c. 1954–55: Courtesy of Lilly Library and Elizabeth Lameyer Gilmore,
    photo by Gordon Lameyer

Page 6

SP's Smith College room, 1955 (two photos): Courtesy of Lilly Library, © Estate of SP

SP and Marianne Moore, 1955: Mortimer Rare Book Collection, courtesy of Smith
   College Special Collections
WP, SP, 1955: Courtesy of Lilly Library, © Estate of AP

Page 7

Newnham College, Cambridge, UK: © HC
Whitstead, Cambridge, UK: © HC
"May Week Fashions": Courtesy of Rose Library, Emory University

Page 8

SP in Venice, 1956: Courtesy of Lilly Library and Elizabeth Lameyer Gilmore, photo by
   Gordon Lameyer
SP in Paris, 1956: Courtesy of Lilly Library and Elizabeth Lameyer Gilmore, photo by
   Gordon Lameyer
TH, 1960: Courtesy of Rose Library, Emory University, photo by Hans Beacham

INSERT III

Page 1

18 Rugby Street: © HC
Saint George the Martyr: © HC
TH and SP in Paris, 1956: Courtesy of Lilly Library, © WP

Page 2

TH and SP in Yorkshire, 1956: Mortimer Rare Book Collection, courtesy of Smith College
   Special Collections, photo by Harry Ogden
Moorland around Haworth: © HC
The Beacon, Heptonstall, West Yorkshire: © HC

Page 3

SP writing in Heptonstall, West Yorkshire, 1956: Mortimer Rare Book Collection, courtesy
   of Smith College Special Collections, © Elinor Friedman Klein
Heptonstall village center: © HC
Top Withens: © HC
Hilltop view of Heptonstall: © HC

Page 4

TH and SP, Cambridge, UK, 1957: Courtesy of Lilly Library, © Peter Lofts Photography
   / Ramsey and Muspratt, Cambridge, UK
TH, Wellesley, 1957: Courtesy of Lilly Library, © Estate of SP
SP in New York Harbor (two photos): Mortimer Rare Book Collection, courtesy of Smith
   College Special Collections, © Estate of TH

Page 5

TH and SP, New York City, 1959: Courtesy of Lilly Library, photo by Oscar Williams
SP reading *The New Yorker*, 1958: Mortimer Rare Book Collection, courtesy of Smith
   College Special Collections, © Estate of TH
TH and SP in their Boston apartment, 1958 (two photos): Courtesy of Rose Library,
   Emory University, © Black Star

Page 6

SP in Jackson Lake, Wyoming, 1959: Mortimer Rare Book Collection, courtesy of Smith
   College Special Collections, © Estate of TH
TH in North Dakota, 1959: Mortimer Rare Book Collection, courtesy of Smith College
   Special Collections, © Estate of SP

Page 7

TH at picnic table, Wisconsin, 1959: Mortimer Rare Book Collection, courtesy of Smith College Special Collections, © Estate of SP

SP and TH under umbrella, 1959: Courtesy of Rose Library, Emory University

SP feeding a deer, 1959: Mortimer Rare Book Collection, courtesy of Smith College Special Collections, © Estate of TH

SP rowing at Yellowstone, 1959: Mortimer Rare Book Collection, courtesy of Smith College Special Collections, © Estate of TH

Page 8

Yaddo (four photos): © HC

INSERT IV

Page 1

TH and SP in Concord, Massachusetts, 1959: Mortimer Rare Book Collection, courtesy of Smith College Special Collections, © Estate of Marcia Brown Stern

3 Chalcot Square: © HC

SP and TH with baby Frieda, 1960: Mortimer Rare Book Collection, courtesy of Smith, © Smith College Special Collections, photo by Ann Davidow Hayes

SP with Frieda, 1961: Helle Collection, courtesy of Smith College Special Collections, © Estate of TH

Page 2

"A Pride of Poets": Courtesy of Rose Library, Emory University, photo by Philip Day

SP's photos of TH with the Eliots, 1960–61: Courtesy of Rose Library, Emory University, © Estate of SP

Page 3

Court Green, North Tawton, Devon: © HC

North Tawton village center: © HC

Devon countryside: © HC

SP and Frieda, 1962: Courtesy of Lilly Library, © Sue Booth

Page 4

SP and her children, 1962: Courtesy of Rose Library, Emory University, © Siv Arb

23 Fitzroy Road, London: © HC

View from SP's window at 23 Fitzroy Road: © HC

SP's grave: © HC

Page 5

All four photos of Assia Wevill and others: Courtesy of Rose Library, Emory University

Pages 6–8

Art by SP (five photos): Courtesy of Lilly Library, © Estate of SP

A NOTE ABOUT THE AUTHOR

HEATHER CLARK earned her bachelor's degree in English literature from Harvard University and her doctorate in English from Oxford University. Her recent awards include a National Endowment for the Humanities Public Scholar Fellowship; a Leon Levy Biography Fellowship at the Graduate Center, City University of New York; a Visiting U.S. Fellowship at the Eccles Centre for American Studies, British Library; and a Yaddo residency. A former visiting scholar at the Oxford Centre for Life-Writing, she is the author of two award-winning books on postwar poetry, *The Grief of Influence: Sylvia Plath and Ted Hughes* and *The Ulster Renaissance: Poetry in Belfast 1962–1972*. Her work has appeared in publications including the *Harvard Review*, *The Times Literary Supplement*, *PN Review*, and *Thumbscrew*. A native Cape Codder, she divides her time between Chappaqua, New York, and Yorkshire, England, where she is professor of contemporary poetry and director of the Centre for International Contemporary Poetry at the University of Huddersfield.

A NOTE ON THE TYPE

This book was set in Janson, a typeface long thought to have been made by the Dutchman Anton Janson, who was a practicing typefounder in Leipzig during the years 1668–1687. However, it has been conclusively demonstrated that these types are actually the work of Nicholas Kis (1650–1702), a Hungarian, who most probably learned his trade from the master Dutch typefounder Dirk Voskens. The type is an excellent example of the influential and sturdy Dutch types that prevailed in England up to the time William Caslon (1692–1766) developed his own incomparable designs from them.

Composed by North Market Street Graphics,
Lancaster, Pennsylvania

Printed by LSC Communications,
Crawfordsville, Indiana

Designed by Cassandra J. Pappas